EMPLOYMENT DISCRIMINATION STATUTES AT A GLANCE

APPLICABLE TO EMPLOYMENT	APPLICABLE TO NON-EMPLOYMENT ACTIVITIES	AVAILABLE REMEDIES	SOURCE OF ATTORNEYS' FEES
Yes	Yes	—Against individual government official defendants sued in their individual capacities, including state officials (*Hafer v. Melo*). Prospective relief and full, uncapped compensatory damages for actual injuries (*Carey v. Piphus*), as well as punitive damages when defendant acts with evil motive or reckless indifference (*Smith v. Wade*) —Against government entity defendants: same, except no punitives (*City of Newport v. Fact Concerts, Inc.*) —Against state officials sued in their official capacities: prospective relief only (*Will v. Michigan Dep't of Police*)	42 U.S.C. § 1988(b). Experts' fees includable. § 1988(c)
Yes	Yes, but contract rights only	Same as § 1983 above	Same as above
Yes	Yes, but contract rights only	Same § 1983 as above	Same as above
Not if Title VII available (*Great Am. Fedl S & L Ass'n v. Novotny*)	Yes	Same § 1983 as above	Same as above
Only to employment and including claims of unequal pay for equal work covered by equal pay act and certain other intentionally discriminatory gender-based compensation practices, unless differentiation authorized by an equal pay act affirmative defense. (*County of Washington v. Gunther*)	No	—For any violation, injunctive relief, including reinstatement or hire orders; back pay running from no earlier than two years before EEOC charge filed; and front pay, to the extent equitable—§ 706(g), 42 U.S.C. § 2000e–5. —For intentional violations, compensatory and if appropriate punitive damages also available, capped at a combined total, per plaintiff, of $50,000 to $300,000 depending on employer size. 42 U.S.C. §§ 1981(a)(1), (b) —Where employer carries "same-decision" burden, plaintiff limited to injunctive relief and attorneys' fees. § 706(g)(2)(B), 42 U.S.C. § 2000e–5(g)(2)(B). —Where "after-acquired evidence" shows employer would have terminated plaintiff under uniformly applied work rules, liability limited to back pay ending at date evidence discovered, attorneys' fees, and possibly compensatory and punitive damages. (*McKennon v. Nashville Banner*) (case under ADEA)	Title VII, § 706(k), 42 U.S.C. § 2000e–5(k). Experts' fees includable. 42 U.S.C. § 1988(c)
Yes	No	Hire, back pay, variable civil penalties. 8 U.S.C. § 1324b(g)	8 U.S.C. § 1324b(h), (j)(4)
Only to employment	No	—Prospective relief including reinstatement or hire orders, back wages and front pay; for "willful" violations, an equal additional amount of "liquidated" damages. 29 U.S.C. §§ 216 & 217 —No express textual counterpart to Title VII § 706(g)(2)(B) (the "same-decision" limitation on liability) —*McKennon v. Nashville Banner*, discussed under Title VII above, was decided under ADEA	29 U.S.C. § 216(b)
Only to employment	No	Same as ADEA	29 U.S.C. § 216(b)
Yes, except perhaps if Title VII available (circuits split) see § 9.10	Yes	Prospective relief and, at least for intentional violations, full uncapped compensatory and, if appropriate, punitive damages. (*Franklin v. Gwinnett County Pub. Schs.*)	42 U.S.C. § 1988(b)
No, unless providing employment is a primary objective of the federal funding. 42 U.S.C. § 2000–d	Yes	Prospective relief and, at least for intentional violations, full uncapped compensatory and, if appropriate, punitive damages. *See Guardians Ass'n v. Civil Serv. Comm.* and *cf. Franklin v. Gwinnett County Pub. Schs.*	42 U.S.C. § 1988(b)

The Hornbook

Dr. Johnson described the hornbook as "the first book of children, covered with horn to keep it unsoiled." Pardon's New General English Dictionary (1758) defined it as "A leaf of written or printed paper pasted on a board, and covered with horn, for children to learn their letters by, and to prevent their being torn and daubed."

It was used throughout Europe and America between the late 1400s and the middle 1700s.

Shaped like an old-fashioned butter paddle, the first hornbooks were made of wood. The paper lesson the child was to learn was fastened to the wooden paddle and covered with a piece of horn. The transparent strip of horn was made by soaking a cow's horn in hot water and peeling it away at the thickness of a piece of celluloid. The horn was necessary to protect the lesson from the damp and perhaps grubby hands of the child. Hornbooks commonly contained the alphabet, the vowels, and the Lord's Prayer. Later hornbooks were made of various materials: brass, copper, silver, ivory, bronze, leather, and stone.

As the art of printing advanced, the hornbook was supplanted by the primer in the book form we know today. Subsequently West Publishing Company developed its "Hornbook Series", a series of scholarly and well-respected one volume treatises on particular areas of law. Today they are widely used by law students, lawyers and judges.

CIVIL RIGHTS
AND
EMPLOYMENT
DISCRIMINATION
LAW

By

Harold S. Lewis, Jr.
Walter F. George Professor of Law
Mercer University

HORNBOOK SERIES®

WEST PUBLISHING CO.
ST. PAUL, MINN., 1997

Hornbook Series, *Westlaw*, the West Publishing Co. Logo, and the key symbol appearing on the front cover are registered trademarks of West Publishing Co. Registered in the U.S. Patent and Trademark Office.

COPYRIGHT © 1997 By WEST PUBLISHING CO.
610 Opperman Drive
P.O. Box 64526
St. Paul, MN 55164–0526
1–800–328–9352

 TEXT IS PRINTED ON 10% POST CONSUMER RECYCLED PAPER

To Hessie and Mamie, civil rights pioneers of the New South, for inspiring this project; Harold and Marianne, for outfitting; Dale and Debra, for retooling; Leslie and Carmen, for encouragement in seeing it through; and Katherine and Ethan, for carrying on.

*

Preface

This work treats the fundamentals of litigating actions under the historic and contemporary federal statutes that provide protection for civil rights and against employment discrimination. It is intended, first, to offer guidance, structure, judicial authority and critical commentary for law students coming fresh to these intricate and fascinating fields. For more seasoned students, the text selectively ventures analysis of more challenging points of doctrine and synthesis of the overlapping statutory tools. A very high proportion of the cited cases, particularly those concerning employment discrimination, were decided in the past several years, and in particular after the Civil Rights Act of 1991.

To serve the needs of law students, the book tracks the coverage of the most important materials surveyed in the principal civil rights and employment discrimination casebooks. For civil rights, the base texts include Abernathy's *Civil Rights and Constitutional Litigation* (2d ed. West 1992); Eisenberg's *Civil Rights Legislation* (3d ed. Michie 1991); and Low and Jeffries' *Civil Rights Actions* (2d ed. Foundation 1994). For employment discrimination, the coverage roughly tracks Zimmer, Sullivan, Richards and Calloway's *Cases and Materials on Employment Discrimination* (3d ed. Little, Brown 1994); Smith, Craver and Clark's *Employment Discrimination Law: Cases and Materials* (4th ed. Michie 1994); Friedman and Strickler's *The Law of Employment Discrimination: Cases and Materials* (3d ed. Foundation Press 1993); and Player, Shoben and Lieberwitz's *Employment Discrimination Law: Cases and Materials* (West 1990). Professor Player's hornbook *Employment Discrimination Law* (West 1988) is another most useful one-volume summary in that field.

Sorting out the legislation that warrants inclusion in the contemporary category of "employment discrimination" legislation has proven relatively easy. It is by now customary for employment discrimination casebooks to cover the Equal Pay Act of 1963, Title VII of the Civil Rights Act of 1964, as amended, and the Age Discrimination in Employment Act of 1968. The "civil rights" category, by contrast, is more amorphous, really a patchwork of protections. These include judicially revivified Reconstruction-era legislation—the famous "Section 1983" is the centerpiece—as buttressed by several special-purpose statutes of the past thirty years, including Title VI of the 1964 Civil Rights Act, the Civil Rights Attorney's Fees Act of 1976, and Title IX of the Education Amendments of 1972. Deciding which of these statutes to examine, and how deeply, has entailed some arbitrary choices. The choices were dictated by the likely frequency that the law student would encounter the legislation and its overall significance to law study.

This book proceeds from an assumption that guides most contemporary law school courses: the procedural, remedial and technical features of lawsuits asserting civil rights and employment discrimination claims have shaped the content of the resulting judicial decisions at least as much as substantive decisional doctrine. Thus the text often touches on the basic elements of a civil lawsuit: prerequisites to suit; jurisdictional and quasi-jurisdictional limitations; class actions and other party joinder problems; the elements of statutory claims and defenses, including immunities; pleading, discovery, and dispositive pre-trial motions; jury trial and available species of relief; appeal; and the effect of judgments on subsequent state or federal proceedings.

In the employment discrimination realm, substantive developments receive extensive treatment, a virtual necessity in light of the Civil Rights Act of 1991. By contrast, in the pure "civil rights" sphere—that is, the Reconstruction-era legislation that forms the historic heart and numeric core of today's civil rights litigation—emphasis is placed on the distinctive requirements and procedural and remedial features of the statutes themselves. Within the compass of a hornbook one could not begin to do justice to the substance of civil rights, for that would entail a review of the tens of thousands of decisions that elaborate the meaning of countless constitutional and statutory provisions. This self-imposed limitation explains why a book devoted in significant part to a subject styled "civil rights" omits mention of most of the seminal constitutional decisions that have declared those rights, including even *Brown v. Bd of Education!*

Occasionally, however, I've indulged an excursion into constitutional law where the development discussed has particular significance for the scope of a Reconstruction-era statute. These include, in the case of Section 1983, the *Parratt-Zinermon* line of cases limiting the scope of procedural due process where the defendant's alleged conduct is "random and unauthorized"; the *Paul v. Davis-Siegert v. Gilley* sequence that restrictively redefines the "liberty" protected by due process; and the limited responsibility of government agents under the due process clause to prevent the infliction of injury by private third parties, as recently enunciated by the Supreme Court in the much bemoaned *DeShaney* decision. And once in a while constitutional doctrine is discussed because it illuminates by contrast a requirement of a civil rights statute. The Supreme Court's Eighth Amendment jurisprudence on prisoners' conditions of confinement, for example, sketches a "deliberate indifference" standard that has a meaning distinctly different from the "deliberate indifference" the Court has required before a government entity may be held accountable under Section 1983 for any constitutional violation that results from the inaction or omission of the entity's agents.

Acknowledgements

The two principal tasks in hornbook preparation are excavation and explication. The author's job is to sift among the assorted materials of the fields surveyed, dig out the foundations and principal building blocks, and assemble them into a comprehensible, if not entirely harmonious, whole. For faulty design or construction the author is solely responsible. For any successes, he is deeply indebted to a diverse and dedicated team.

The author gratefully acknowledges the support of the Walter F. George Foundation and the faculty, staff, and students of Mercer Law School; Mercer's Dean Larry Dessem and its former and current Deans, Philip D. Shelton and Richard W. Creswell; and Fordham Law School and its Dean John D. Feerick, where this project began. I'm also indebted to Mercer's law library Director, Patricia Cervenka, and its staff, particularly Suzanne Cassidy, for providing timely and able assistance throughout.

This work could not have been completed without the flexibility and patience of Tom Berreman of West Publishing Company or the unflappable indefatigability of Patsy Crammer of Mercer Law School. Annette Maxwell persisted admirably in the face of technology to bring the project to fruition.

Thanks are due also to Mercer Law School alumni Cheryl Long, for her work on the text of the attorneys' fees material, and Ed Stebell, for his contributions to the text of the sections on the Eleventh Amendment and "Parratt" doctrine. David Segal, a Fordham alumnus, and Mercer alumna Lori Reese contributed to the text on the modern disability discrimination statutes. Fordham's Sharon Brodt provided research assistance on procedure, as did Mercer's Chris Balch concerning Sections 1985 and the federal criminal civil rights statutes. Gail Marks, Mercer Class of 1995, provided research assistance concerning the tax treatment of settlements and judgments. Deron Hicks supplied substantial textual material and research assistance on the preclusion and "gap-filling" issues discussed in the Procedure chapter.

Textual contributions were also made by students in Mercer's Civil Rights Class in 1994. Josh Archer surveyed the relationship between Fourteenth Amendment "state action" and the Section 1983 requirement of conduct "under color of" state law. Mujeeb Shah-Khan pursued the procedural intricacies among civil rights pleading, summary judgment practice, and bifurcation of claims against individual and entity defendants. Todd Brooks explored the availability of parallel Section 1983 and Title VII claims for the same alleged conduct in the employment setting. Robert Weber studied the fiendishly difficult opinions in *Wyatt v. Cole* that denied the modern version of qualified immunity to certain "private" Section 1983 defendants. Adam Foodman filled in gaps in the Voting Rights chapter in the wake of the North Carolina "snake district" case, *Shaw v. Reno*. And Kimberly Moore, Mercer Class of 1995, updated and edited text in a number of chapters on employment discrimination.

A special thanks to faculty colleagues who took the time to read and comment on draft-material within their respective areas of specialty: Ted Blumoff, Darryl Brown, David Oedel, Leandra Lederman, Gus Lehouck, Bruce Posnak, and Ivan Rutledge.

I'm especially indebted to Jennifer Scolliard, Mercer Class of 1997, and Stephen J. Tyde, Jr. and Mark Powell of the Class of 1996. Mr. Powell drafted text on housing discrimination, continuing violations, and other selected areas. In addition, he performed yeoman service filling in research gaps, especially on damages, and suggesting changes to structural organization. He also did extensive cite checking, always timely and with good cheer. Ms. Scolliard and Mr. Tyde completed that work, making their own significant editorial and technical contributions.

I am also grateful to the University of Pennsylvania Law Review and Fred B. Rothman & Co. and Theodore Y. Blumoff for permission to reprint and adapt text from "Reshaping Section 1983's Asymmetry," 140 U.Pa.L.Rev.755 (1992), which the author co-wrote with Professor Blumoff", as well as to the St. Louis University Law Review for the same permission respecting the author's article "The Civil Rights Act of 1991 and the Continued Dominance of the Disparate Treatment Conception of Equality," 11 St. Louis U. Pub.L.Rev. 1 (1992). That article was based on a version written before the enactment of the 1991 Civil Rights Act entitled "Piecemeal Temporizing With Employment Discrimination Law: What The Civil Rights Act of 1991 Will Not Resolve" and published in the *Proceedings of New York University's 44th Annual National Conference on Labor* (Little, Brown & Co. 1991). Its reprinting as adapted is with the kind permission of the Institute of Labor Relations at New York University.

WESTLAW® Overview

Civil Rights and Employment Discrimination Law offers a detailed and comprehensive treatment of legal principles and issues relating to federal civil rights. To supplement the information contained in this book, you can access WESTLAW, a computer-assisted legal research service of West Publishing. WESTLAW contains a broad library of legal research resources, including case law, statutes, expert commentary, current developments and various other types of information.

Learning how to use these materials effectively will enhance your legal research. To help you coordinate your book and WESTLAW research, this volume contains an appendix listing WESTLAW databases, search techniques and sample problems.

THE PUBLISHER

*

Summary of Contents

*

Table of Contents

E. THE PRACTICAL CONSEQUENCES OF ASYMMETRICAL
PRIMA FACIE CASES AND DEFENSES IN
INDIVIDUAL AND ENTITY ACTIONS:
OF *PAUL* AND *PARRATT* ;
ZINERMON AND *SIEGERT*

F. SECTION 1983 AS A REMEDY FOR FEDERAL
STATUTORY VIOLATIONS

**CHAPTER THREE. TITLE VII OF THE 1964 CIVIL
RIGHTS ACT: COVERAGE, PROHIBITED GROUNDS OF
DISCRIMINATION, SPECIALLY TREATED PRACTICES,
AND DEFENSES**

A. COVERAGE

B. CONSTITUTIONAL PROBLEMS SURROUNDING REGULA-
TION OF RELIGIOUS DISCRIMINATION

C. THE BASIC SUBSTANTIVE PROHIBITIONS

C. SYSTEMIC DISPARATE TREATMENT

D. THE RELIEF STAGE OF THE BIFURCATED SYSTEMIC DISPARATE TREATMENT ACTION

E. HOW THE INDIVIDUAL AND SYSTEMIC DISPARATE TREATMENT CASES INTERRELATE

F. NEUTRAL PRACTICES WITH DISPROPORTIONATE ADVERSE IMPACT

CHAPTER FIVE. TITLE VII ADMINISTRATIVE PREREQUISITES, PROCEDURES AND REMEDIES

A. ADMINISTRATIVE PREREQUISITES AND PROCEDURES

B. TITLE VII REMEDIES

C. TITLE VII AND ADEA REMEDIES COMPARED

C. VOTE DILUTION CAUSES OF ACTIONS

D. SECTION 5—PRECLEARANCE OF VOTING LAW CHANGES IN HISTORICALLY DISCRIMINATORY JURISDICTIONS

E. CONSTITUTIONAL LIMITS ON DILUTIVE OR SEGREGATIVE ELECTORAL DISTRICTING

F. PROBLEMS PRECIPITATED BY SHAW, AND A POTENTIAL AVOIDANCE

CHAPTER ELEVEN. DISCRIMINATION IN PROPERTY AND HOUSING

A. INTRODUCTION

B. GROUNDS

C. COVERED DEFENDANTS

D. PROHIBITED PRACTICES

F. STATE COURT JURISDICTION

G. STANDING

H. GAP–FILLING FROM STATE LAW UNDER SECTION 1988: SURVIVORSHIP AND LIMITATIONS

I. PLEADING

J. CLASS ACTIONS

K. CLAIM AND ISSUE PRECLUSION IN ACTIONS UNDER TITLE VII AND THE RECONSTRUCTION CIVIL RIGHTS ACTS

CIVIL RIGHTS AND EMPLOYMENT DISCRIMINATION LAW

*

Chapter One

OVERVIEW OF THE RECONSTRUCTION ERA CIVIL RIGHTS LEGISLATION

Analysis

A.   THE CIVIL RIGHTS ACTS OF 1866, 1870, AND 1871

§ 1.1   In General

The Civil Rights Acts of 1866, 1870, and 1871 are generally referred to as the Reconstruction Civil Rights Acts, and they were originally intended to enforce the 13th and 14th Amendments in the post-Civil War era. The most frequently invoked provisions are codified at 42 U.S.C.A. §§ 1981, 1983, and 1985(3). These acts remained dormant for

1

many years but were resurrected in the 1960's.[1]

What is now § 1981 was first enacted in 1866 under authority of the 13th Amendment, and re-enacted in 1870, two years after ratification of the 14th Amendment. This history has spawned doctrinal schisms and jurisprudential inconsistencies. On one hand, the Supreme Court has relied on the 13th Amendment origins of § 1981 (and § 1982, its legislative companion that bars discrimination in the acquiring, holding and disposing of property) to apply these statutes to purely private defendants, at least with respect to transactions held open to the public.[2] On the other, the court has relied on the 14th Amendment origins of § 1981 to limit its reach to violations that reflect race discrimination that is intentional in character.[3] And while the Court has insisted that it is the intent of the enacting Congress that controls the breadth of the §§ 1981 and 1982 definitions of "race,"[4] its reliance on the 13th Amendment origins of these statutes seemingly caused it to depart from the norms of that Congress by holding the statutes to bar purely private discrimination, subject only to possible First Amendment limitations related to freedom of association.[5]

Section 1985(3), like § 1983 and in contrast to §§ 1981 and 1982, creates no rights of its own but simply provides damages and perhaps injunctive relief for the conspiratorial deprivation of certain rights independently secured by the federal Constitution and, perhaps, other federal statutes. But when the conspiracy is among purely private actors, very few rights are protected against such deprivation, and § 1985(3) offers no protection unless the conspirators, public or private, act with a specific racial animus or motive that goes beyond the intent requirement of §§ 1981 or 1982.[6]

Library References:

C.J.S. Civil Rights §§ 2–5, 7–9 et seq.
West's Key No. Digests, Civil Rights ⊙101 et seq.

§ 1.2   Section 1981

Section 1981 secures equal contracting rights without regard to race. It affords "all persons" in the United States "the same right ... to make and enforce contracts ... and to the full and equal benefit of all laws ...

§ 1.1

1. *See Jones v. Alfred H. Mayer Co.*, 392 U.S. 409, 88 S.Ct. 2186, 20 L.Ed.2d 1189 (1968).

2. *Jones v. Alfred H. Mayer Co., supra* (§ 1982); *Runyon v. McCrary*, 427 U.S. 160, 96 S.Ct. 2586, 49 L.Ed.2d 415 (1976) and *Patterson v. McLean Credit Union*, 491 U.S. 164, 109 S.Ct. 2363, 105 L.Ed.2d 132 (1989) (§ 1981).

3. *General Building Contractors Ass'n v. Pennsylvania*, 458 U.S. 375, 102 S.Ct. 3141, 73 L.Ed.2d 835 (1982).

4. *McDonald v. Santa Fe Trail Transp. Co.*, 427 U.S. 273, 96 S.Ct. 2574, 49 L.Ed.2d 493 (1976) and *St. Francis College v. Al-Khazraji*, 481 U.S. 604, 107 S.Ct. 2022, 95 L.Ed.2d 582 (1987) (§ 1981) and *Shaare Tefila Congregation v. Cobb*, 481 U.S. 615, 107 S.Ct. 2019, 95 L.Ed.2d 594 (1987) (§ 1982).

5. *See, e.g., Runyon*, 427 U.S. at 186, 96 S.Ct. at 2602 (Powell, J., concurring).

6. *See Bray v. Alexandria Women's Health Clinic*, 506 U.S. 263, 113 S.Ct. 753, 122 L.Ed.2d 34 (1993).

as is enjoyed by white citizens. . . ." By its terms § 1981 reaches a host of contracting relationships—with private schools, to name just one—not reached by Title VII. And § 1981, unlike Title VII, has no minimum-employee numerical threshold for employer liability. Section 1981 has also been interpreted to provide a civil damages remedy for racial discrimination arising from contracts of employment, even though Congress has comprehensively addressed employment discrimination much more recently in Title VII.[1] Moreover, the Court has held, *Runyon v. McCrary*[2], and reaffirmed, *Patterson v. McLean Credit Union*,[3] that § 1981, long assumed to reach only state action, also reaches purely private conduct.

The Supreme Court has construed the language that secures to all the same contracting rights as "white citizens" to refer only to the racial (as opposed to, say, gender-based or religious) character of the prohibited discrimination, rather than to limit the class of appropriate plaintiffs to non-whites. Accordingly, while the lower courts are in agreement that the statute does not prohibit discrimination because of gender, it is also settled that whites as well as blacks may assert contract denial claims under § 1981 on the basis of race.[4]

The Supreme Court has construed § 1981's ban on "race" discrimination to include also discrimination on the basis of ancestry. The Court has understood ancestry, in turn, to mean membership in an "ethnically and physiognomically distinctive sub-grouping."[5] This somewhat vague formulation has generated predictable confusion among the lower federal courts. We do know that § 1981 "ancestry" does not mean national origin, religion, or alienage status as such.[6] On the other hand, these latter characteristics are often statistically correlated with an individual's descendence from a particular ancestry. For example, in one recent case, a hiring supervisor disparaged the plaintiff's Israeli background and in particular his prior sales experience in Israel, saying "Israel doesn't count." The appellate court ruled that the jury was entitled to treat these comments not just as discrimination on the basis of national origin—actionable under Title VII—but also as discrimination based on the plaintiff's Israeli ancestry, and thus "race" within the meaning of § 1981.[7] It reasoned that the Israeli population was composed primarily of members of a particular ancestry and therefore the jury might have concluded that by disparaging Israel the defendant was

§ 1.2

1. *See Johnson v. Railway Express Agency*, 421 U.S. 454, 95 S.Ct. 1716, 44 L.Ed.2d 295, (1975); *McDonald v. Santa Fe Trail Transportation Co.*, 427 U.S. 273, 96 S.Ct. 2574, 49 L.Ed.2d 493 (1976).

2. 427 U.S. 160, 96 S.Ct. 2586, 49 L.Ed.2d 415 (1976).

3. 491 U.S. 164, 109 S.Ct. 2363, 105 L.Ed.2d 132 (1989).

4. *McDonald, supra* note 1.

5. *St. Francis College v. Al–Khazraji*, 481 U.S. 604, 107 S.Ct. 2022, 95 L.Ed.2d 582 (1987) and *Shaare Tefila Congregation v. Cobb*, 481 U.S. 615, 107 S.Ct. 2019, 95 L.Ed.2d 594 (1987) (protection against ancestry, as opposed to religious, discrimination available to, respectively, Arabs and Jews).

6. *See id.*

7. *Sinai v. New England Telephone and Telegraph Co.*, 3 F.3d 471 (1st Cir.1993).

really, or also, discriminating against plaintiff because of his "race"—in the nineteenth century sense approved by the Supreme Court.

Although § 1981, like Title VII, does not prohibit discrimination on the basis of alienage *per se*, a limited protection from employment discrimination on the basis of non-citizenship status is now provided by the Immigration Reform and Control Act of 1986, discussed in the Employment Discrimination Chapter below. But aliens, like other "persons within the jurisdiction of the United States," may complain of race or ancestry and possibly citizenship[8] discrimination under § 1981, or of race, gender, religious, or national origin, but not ancestry or citizenship discrimination under Title VII.[9] None of the Reconstruction Civil Rights Acts reaches gender or religious discrimination as such, although discrimination on those grounds might violate Equal Protection and accordingly would be redressable under § 1983.

The federal judiciary began to place significant limitations on the utility of § 1981 in *General Building Contractors Assn. v. Pennsylvania*.[10] There the Supreme Court held that a showing of disparate impact does not suffice to prove a § 1981 employment violation, which requires instead a direct or inferential demonstration of discriminatory intent. Consistent with this ruling, the Court in *Patterson* approved for use in § 1981 actions the Title VII intentional disparate treatment mode of proof first outlined in *McDonnell Douglas Corp. v. Green*.[11] Yet at times one encounters some suggestion in the cases that the showing of intent required in § 1981 cases by *General Building Contractors* in practice demands somewhat more "direct" evidence of discrimination than would usually be required under Title VII.[12] And it remains uncertain whether, in § 1981 "mixed motive" situations, the courts will hew to the

8. *Contrast Duane v. GEICO*, 37 F.3d 1036 (4th Cir.1994), *cert. granted* ___ U.S. ___, 115 S.Ct. 1251, 131 L.Ed.2d 132 (1995) (Section 1981 prohibits private defendant alienage discrimination against a lawfully admitted, permanent resident alien) *and Bhandari v. First National Bank of Commerce*, 829 F.2d 1343 (5th Cir.1987) (*en banc*), *vacated on other grounds*, 492 U.S. 901, 109 S.Ct. 3207, 106 L.Ed.2d 558 (1989) (Section 1981 does not prohibit private alienage discrimination). The Fifth Circuit's position was based largely on its unwillingness to "extend" to discrimination based on alienage the application of § 1981's race discrimination ban to private defendants, which the Supreme Court had upheld in *Runyon v. McCrary*, 427 U.S. 160, 96 S.Ct. 2586, 49 L.Ed.2d 415 (1976). The Court's reaffirmation of *Runyon* in *Patterson v. McLean Credit Union*, 491 U.S. 164, 109 S.Ct. 2363, 105 L.Ed.2d 132 (1989) may have eroded the continuing vitality of *Bhandari*. The Fourth Circuit in *Duane* stressed that even undocumented aliens are among the "persons" granted rights by § 1981.

9. *Espinoza v. Farah Mfg. Co.*, 414 U.S. 86, 94 S.Ct. 334, 38 L.Ed.2d 287 (1973)

(Title VII); *Bhandari v. First National Bank of Commerce*, 829 F.2d 1343 (5th Cir. 1987) (*en banc*), *vacated on other grounds by* 492 U.S. 901, 109 S.Ct. 3207, 106 L.Ed.2d 558 (1989) (§ 1981).

10. 458 U.S. 375, 102 S.Ct. 3141, 73 L.Ed.2d 835 (1982).

11. 411 U.S. 792, 93 S.Ct. 1817, 36 L.Ed.2d 668 (1973). *Patterson*, 491 U.S. at 186, 109 S.Ct. at 2377.

12. *See Durham v. Xerox Corp.*, 18 F.3d 836 (10th Cir.1994), *cert. denied*, ___ U.S. ___, 115 S.Ct. 80, 130 L.Ed.2d 33 (1994). Compare the standards the Tenth Circuit applied in *Durham* in upholding district court's grant of summary judgment to the employer on the § 1981 claim with the lower court decisions after *St. Mary's* that deem it inappropriate to grant the defendant summary judgment when the plaintiff produces sufficient prima facie evidence of race discrimination under Title VII. *See* Chapter 4 concerning *St. Mary's* and its progeny.

approach mandated for constitutional violations proved through § 1983;[13] to the somewhat different one mandated by the 1991 Civil Rights Act for post-November 21, 1991 employment practices that violate Title VII;[14] or to the rules laid down by the Supreme Court in *Price Waterhouse v. Hopkins* that the 1991 Act modified and which governed Title VII violations before its effective date.[15] The uncertainty is fueled by the fact that the 1991 Act, which in other respects expressly and materially modifies § 1981, refers only to Title VII in the provisions that modify *Price Waterhouse*.[16]

Section 1981 has also been read more narrowly than Title VII with respect to the ability of plaintiffs to assert the rights of third parties. The problem has recently arisen in connection with suits by "testers" to challenge discriminatory referrals by employment agencies. Testers have been defined as persons of the opposite race "equipped with fake credentials intended to be comparable...." who apply for employment to an agency or employer without an intention to accept an offer if one is forthcoming.[17] The typical ensuing claim is that the employment agency, on grounds of race, failed to refer the African–American (or female) tester but did refer the other (white or male) tester. Title VII provides that any "person claiming to be aggrieved" by an unlawful employment practice may, after exhausting administrative remedies, sue such an agency in court.[18] Consequently, testers may be able to state a Title VII claim despite their own lack of a bona fide interest in employment.[19]

By contrast, the text of § 1981 suggests that only a person deprived of what is otherwise a legal right to make or enforce a contract has standing. Reasoning that testers could not have enforced an employment contract offer because of the material misrepresentations of fact they made to the defendant employment agency about their intentions to secure employment, a panel of the District of Columbia Circuit has recently held that tester plaintiffs cannot state a claim for damages under § 1981: "the loss of the opportunity to enter into a *void* contract—i.e., a contract that *neither* party can enforce—is not an injury cognizable under § 1981, for a void contract is a legal nullity."[20]

---

13. *See Mt. Healthy v. Doyle*, 429 U.S. 274, 97 S.Ct. 568, 50 L.Ed.2d 471 (1977) discussed in Chapter 2.

14. *See* Chapter 4.

15. *Id.*

16. For a discussion of the liability and remedy differences that depend on whether the original *Price Waterhouse* approach or its legislative codification prevails, *see* § 4.5.

17. *See Fair Employment Council of Greater Washington, Inc. v. BMC Marketing Corporation*, 28 F.3d 1268 (D.C.Cir.1994).

18. 42 U.S.C.A. §§ 2000e–5(b), (c), (f)(1).

19. *Fair Employment Council of Greater Washington, supra*; *but see* n.1 of that decision, which reserves decision on the question whether the lack of a bona fide interest in employment defeats standing.

20. *Fair Employment Council of Greater Washington, supra. But cf. Watts v. Boyd Properties*, 758 F.2d 1482 (11th Cir.1985) and *Meyers v. Pennypack Woods Home Ownership Ass'n*, 559 F.2d 894 (3d Cir. 1977), *overruled on other grounds by Goodman v. Lukens Steel Co.*, 777 F.2d 113 (3d Cir.1985), *affirmed*, 482 U.S. 656, 107 S.Ct. 2617, 96 L.Ed.2d 572 (1987) (according fair-housing testers standing to sue under §§ 1982 and 1981, respectively, although not squarely addressing question whether the testers had suffered legal injury within the meaning of those statutes).

This standing problem, however, should be distinguished from the question of how broadly a violation of the plaintiff's own rights under § 1981 may be defined in relation to discriminatory actions immediately directed against another. Here the courts have shown considerable flexibility, permitting the assertion of § 1981 claims where intimate or associational rights of the plaintiff are allegedly invaded by a defendant whose conduct was aimed at third parties.[21] A related, but distinct question is whether the defendant must be the party with whom the plaintiff contracts or seeks to contract. Courts have answered this question in the negative, holding § 1981 violated by a racially motivated interference with a plaintiff's right to enter into contracts with non-whites[22] and by third parties' attempts to punish the plaintiff for making such contracts.[23]

Recent additional restrictions on the use of § 1981 in actions against government defendants, and a short-lived restriction on the availability of § 1981 to attack post-hire conditions of employment, are described below.

The Supreme Court has directed the lower federal courts to borrow analogous state statutes of limitations in actions under § 1981, and has held that pursuing Title VII administrative procedures does not toll the § 1981 statute of limitations.[24] The Court has since clarified that in actions under any of the Reconstruction Civil Rights Acts, the forum state's "personal injury" statute of limitations should apply;[25] and the particular period the court should borrow is the state's general or residual statute on personal injury claims rather than, for example, a statute geared specifically to intentional torts.[26] A more detailed discussion of the selection and application of statutes of limitations under the Reconstruction Civil Rights Act may be found in the Chapter on Procedure.

Title 42 U.S.C.A. § 1977A(a)(1), added by § 102 of the Civil Rights Act of 1991, provides that damages under Title VII are recoverable only if the complainant "cannot recover" under § 1981. But the EEOC,

---

21. *See, e.g., Alizadeh v. Safeway Stores, Inc.*, 802 F.2d 111, 114 (5th Cir.1986) and *Parr v. Woodmen of the World Life Ins. Co.*, 791 F.2d 888, 890 (11th Cir.1986) (upholding § 1981 claims where defendant employer allegedly fired (*Alizadeh*) or refused to hire (*Parr*) the plaintiff because of a spouse's race); *Fiedler v. Marumsco Christian School*, 631 F.2d 1144, 1149 (4th Cir. 1980) (Section 1981 claim stated on claim by white students that private school expelled them because they had associated with blacks).

22. *See, e.g., Des Vergnes v. Seekonk Water District*, 601 F.2d 9 (1st Cir.1979).

23. *See, e.g., Winston v. Lear–Siegler, Inc.*, 558 F.2d 1266, 1270 (6th Cir.1977); *DeMatteis v. Eastman Kodak Co.*, 511 F.2d 306, 312, *modified*, 520 F.2d 409 (2d Cir. 1975); *cf. Sullivan v. Little Hunting Park*, 396 U.S. 229, 237, 90 S.Ct. 400, 404, 24 L.Ed.2d 386 (1969) (same result under § 1982).

24. *Johnson, supra* note 1.

25. *See Wilson v. Garcia*, 471 U.S. 261, 105 S.Ct. 1938, 85 L.Ed.2d 254 (1985) (§ 1983); *Goodman v. Lukens Steel Co.*, 482 U.S. 656, 107 S.Ct. 2617, 96 L.Ed.2d 572, (1987) (§ 1981).

26. *Owens v. Okure*, 488 U.S. 235, 109 S.Ct. 573, 102 L.Ed.2d 594 (1989).

relying on the Sponsors' Interpretive Memorandum,[27] has interpreted that language to bar only double recovery for the same injury, not parallel proceedings under the two statutes. Putative plaintiffs with intentional race discrimination claims against employers large enough to be covered by and not exempt from Title VII can therefore apparently choose whether to proceed under Title VII or § 1981 or both.

That choice will be heavily influenced by the availability of unlimited compensatory and punitive damages under § 1981, free of Title VII's variable caps, and by the immediate access to court under § 1981, free of the Title VII state and federal administrative prerequisite requirements with their rather early filing deadlines. Some such claimants, however, who, despite the availability of attorneys' fees, are unable to attract counsel might nevertheless prefer the Title VII route, because by statute the EEOC is expected to assist with investigation and conciliation. And under the Internal Revenue Service's interpretation that all portions of Title VII disparate treatment monetary awards or settlements, like settlements and awards under § 1981, are excludable from income,[28] the plaintiff may opt for Title VII without regard to tax considerations.

In practice, however, § 1981 will usually look more attractive. Procedurally and remedially, the Reconstruction Civil Rights Acts, § 1981 in particular, may hold several attractions over Title VII. For one, no administrative exhaustion is required.[29] Second, the applicable limitation periods borrowed from state law are normally longer than the usual 180–day or 270–day Title VII deadline for filing charges with federal or state agencies. Third, although jury trials are now available under either statute with respect to claims of intentional discrimination, the nineteenth-century statutes offer compensatory and punitive damages unlimited in amount; while, even after the Civil Rights Act of 1991, Title VII plaintiffs who prove intentional discrimination are subject to caps on those damages that vary with the number of employees working for the defendant employer. In one respect, Title VII lines up precisely with § 1983 and § 1981: punitive damages are not available against a defendant government entity.[30]

But what if the § 1981 defendant is able to prove something akin to what the Supreme Court's *Mt. Healthy v. Doyle*[31] decision encourages § 1983 defendants to prove: that the challenged employment action

27. 137 Cong. Rec. S15484 (Oct. 30, 1991).

28. *See* Employment Discrimination Chapter.

29. *See Patsy v. Board of Regents of the State of Florida*, 457 U.S. 496, 102 S.Ct. 2557, 73 L.Ed.2d 172 (1982) (§ 1983).

30. Section 1981(b)(1) authorizes punitive damages when intentional Title VII discrimination is proved (and other, traditional requirements for punitive damages are satisfied) except against "a government, government agency, or political subdivi-sion." The Supreme Court has held punitive damages generally unavailable in § 1983 actions against government in *City of Newport v. Fact Concerts, Inc.*, 453 U.S. 247, 101 S.Ct. 2748, 69 L.Ed.2d 616 (1981), discussed in Chapter 2. And lower courts have extended the *City of Newport* ruling to actions under § 1981. *See Walters v. City of Atlanta*, 803 F.2d 1135 (11th Cir.1986) and cases there cited.

31. 429 U.S. 274, 97 S.Ct. 568, 50 L.Ed.2d 471 (1977).

would have been taken for lawful reasons independent of the racial component of the employer's overall motivation? The effect of this showing under § 1983 appears to be (except with respect to procedural due process violations) that no federal law violation is established and the defendant may not be mulcted in damages.[32] Under Title VII, as amended in 1991, however, the defendant who makes this "same-decision" showing is relieved only of retroactive, monetary relief; she is still considered to have violated the law and is therefore subject to prospective relief and attorneys' fees.[33] The 1991 amendments to Title VII did not, however, make the same amendment to § 1981 or the ADEA, although it amended those statutes in other respects. Consequently, the post *Mt. Healthy*, pre–1991 regime governing § 1981 defendants who carry the showing is therefore likely to prevail in most circuits.[34] And under that regime the § 1981 defendant is likely to escape without liability, whereas the Title VII plaintiff will establish a violation and thereby have an opportunity to receive declaratory and injunctive relief and, in turn, attorney's fees as a "prevailing party."[35]

A potential plaintiff with an intentional race discrimination claim actionable under both statutes may prefer Title VII if she cannot afford counsel and believes that state or federal agency administrative processing of her charge will induce her employer to settle. In addition, it remains possible, to an as yet uncertain extent, for a plaintiff who cannot prove intentional discrimination and would therefore fail under § 1981, to succeed under Title VII by establishing that an employer's neutral practice had a disproportionate adverse impact on her group and that the employer cannot justify the practice as a matter of job relatedness and business necessity.

In actions against state and local government employers, there is some doubt whether § 1981 is available on its own terms, or whether the plaintiff must also surmount the additional proof requirements and defenses available of § 1983. If the latter, then Title VII once again would become a more attractive option.[36]

32. *See* discussion of *Mt. Healthy* in Chapter 2 concerning § 1983.

33. *See* Chapter 4 on Title VII proof modes and discussion of the *Price Waterhouse* decision in Chapter 2.

34. The Eighth Circuit, purporting to distinguish § 1981 from Section 1983 in this respect, upheld a jury award of damages for a violation of Section 1981 even though the defendant had carried the showing described (for § 1983 cases) by *Mt. Healthy. Edwards v. Jewish Hospital*, 855 F.2d 1345 (8th Cir.1988). The court asserted that § 1981 aims to deter as well as compensate, while § 1983 has only a compensation rationale. Some support may have been drawn for the proposition that § 1983 seeks only to compensate from the Supreme Court's decisions in *Mt. Healthy* and *Carey v. Piphus*, 435 U.S. 247, 98 S.Ct. 1042, 55 L.Ed.2d 252 (1978). But well before *Edwards* was decided the Court had made clear that § 1983 has a distinct deterrent rationale, and that punitive damages are sometimes necessary to fulfill it. *Smith v. Wade*, 461 U.S. 30, 103 S.Ct. 1625, 75 L.Ed.2d 632 (1983).

35. *See* Chapter 12 on Attorneys' Fees under § 706(k) of Title VII and 42 U.S.C.A. § 1988 with respect to actions under all of the Reconstruction Civil Rights Acts.

36. Title VII would appear to be the *only* remedy for race discrimination in federal employment, which has been held outside the reach of § 1981. *Williams v. Glickman*, 936 F.Supp. 1 (D.D.C.1996).

In its 1988 Term, the Court held that discriminatory conduct directed against an employee after her initial hiring falls outside the right granted by § 1981 to "make" a contract free from racial discrimination.[37] The 1991 legislation overturns this decision and thereby restores 42 U.S.C.A. § 1981 as a forceful supplementary vehicle for redressing race or ancestry discrimination in contracting, although only when the defendant's conduct is shown, by direct or indirect evidence, to be *intentional*.[38] The legislation provides that the right to "make" a contract extends beyond initial formation to include "performance, modification and termination" and thus reaches not only dismissal but also ongoing terms and conditions of employment.[39]

Section 1981 contains no threshold numerical requirement for employer coverage. In the course of considering the amendments, Congress observed that § 1981 constitutes the only protection against race or ancestry discrimination for those millions of applicants or employees whose employers are too small to be covered by Title VII. Despite this understanding, the amendments make no attempt to protect those applicants or employees against the other forms of discrimination prohibited by Title VII, that is, sex, religion, or national origin, or against race discrimination resulting solely from the effects of a neutral practice.[40] Indeed, by capping Title VII damages, while leaving uncapped the compensatory and punitive damages recoverable under § 1981, Congress rather pointedly expresses greater concern with intentional race discrimination than with unintentional discrimination or intentional discrimination based on Title VII's other prohibited grounds.

Courts commonly permit the showing of intent requisite under the Reconstruction Acts to be made inferentially, that is, through the *McDonnell Douglas/Burdine/St. Mary's* formula of shifting evidentiary burdens that is paradigmatic under Title VII.[41] Nevertheless, there are rumblings of discontent with the dominant view that treats such inferen-

37. *Patterson v. McLean Credit Union,* 491 U.S. 164, 109 S.Ct. 2363, 105 L.Ed.2d 132 (1989).

38. *See General Bldg. Contractors Ass'n. v. Pennsylvania,* 458 U.S. 375, 102 S.Ct. 3141, 73 L.Ed.2d 835 (1982).

39. Section 101(b) (amending 42 U.S.C.A. § 1981 (1988)).

40. It is well settled that § 1981 affords no protection against discrimination based on gender. *See McDonald v. Santa Fe Trail Transportation Co.,* 427 U.S. 273, 96 S.Ct. 2574, 49 L.Ed.2d 493 (1976). *See also Runyon v. McCrary,* 427 U.S. 160, 96 S.Ct. 2586, 49 L.Ed.2d 415 (1976) (applying § 1981 to purely private conduct and affirmed in that respect by *Patterson v. McLean Credit Union,* 491 U.S. 164, 109 S.Ct. 2363, 105 L.Ed.2d 132 (1989)). While it is also clear that § 1981 does prohibit discrimination based on ancestry (ethnic or physiognomic characteristic), *St. Francis College v. Al–Khazraji,* 481 U.S. 604, 107 S.Ct. 2022, 95 L.Ed.2d 582 (1987); *Shaare Tefila Congregation v. Cobb,* 481 U.S. 615, 107 S.Ct. 2019, 95 L.Ed.2d 594 (1987), those opinions also suggest that it provides no protection against religious discrimination as such. The circuits are split on whether § 1981 reaches private sector discrimination because of alienage. *Duane v. GEICO,* 37 F.3d 1036 (4th Cir.1994) (holding yes), *cert. granted* ___ U.S. ___, 115 S.Ct. 1251, 131 L.Ed.2d 132 (1995); *Bhandari v. First National Bank of Commerce,* 829 F.2d 1343 (5th Cir.1987) (*en banc*), *vacated on other grounds,* 492 U.S. 901, 109 S.Ct. 3207, 106 L.Ed.2d 558 (1989) (holding no).

41. *See, e.g., Patterson v. McLean Credit Union,* 491 U.S. 164, 109 S.Ct. 2363, 105 L.Ed.2d 132 (1989); *Barbour v. Merrill,* 48 F.3d 1270 (D.C.Cir.1995), *cert. dismissed,* ___ U.S. ___, 116 S.Ct. 1037, 134 L.Ed.2d 113 (1996).

tial evidence as an adequate foundation not only for liability but also for punitive damages.[42]

Library References:

> C.J.S. Civil Rights § 43.
> West's Key No. Digests, Civil Rights ⬌118.

§ 1.3   Section 1982

This statute, enacted pursuant to Congress' Thirteenth Amendment authority, traces from the earliest Reconstruction era and secures to all citizens the right, enforceable against private as well as public defendants, to "inherit, purchase, lease, sell, hold and convey real and personal property." Beginning in the 1940's § 1982 was used mostly to challenge racially restrictive covenants in housing subdivisions. Today it also serves to fill the gaps in coverage and supplement the potential remedies of the Fair Housing Act of 1968, as amended. Section 1982 is discussed in more detail in the Fair Housing Chapter.

§ 1.4   Section 1983

Section 1983 authorizes actions at law or suits in equity against any "person" for the deprivation of rights, privileges or immunities secured by the federal Constitution or laws, so long as the defendant acted "under color of" state law, custom or usage.

For most employment discrimination claimants, § 1983 is of less utility than § 1981, for four principal reasons. First, § 1983 provides remedies for deprivations only of rights independently secured by the U.S. Constitution or federal statutes. Second, even those deprivations are actionable only if imposed "under color of" state law. Third, while the Supreme Court has held that municipalities and other local governments are "persons," and hence appropriate defendants, for purposes of § 1983,[1] it simultaneously concluded that municipalities are not subject to liability merely vicariously, for example through *respondeat superior*.[2] Instead, the Court has repeatedly insisted that local government entities are responsible only for official policies or the acts of those employees with "policy making authority," and determining this is a question of law to be decided by reference to local laws, customs, and usages.[3] Fourth, the § 1983 liability of individual government employees has

---

42. On the general Reconstruction Act standard for punitive damages, see *Smith v. Wade,* 461 U.S. 30, 103 S.Ct. 1625, 75 L.Ed.2d 632 (1983), discussed in Chapter 2. For the recent rumblings, see the petition for writ of certiorari in *Barbour v. Merrill,* 48 F.3d 1270 (D.C.Cir.1995), *cert. dismissed,* ___ U.S. ___, 116 S.Ct. 1037, 134 L.Ed.2d 113 (1996).

§ 1.4

1. *Monell v. Department of Social Services of City of New York,* 436 U.S. 658, 98 S.Ct. 2018, 56 L.Ed.2d 611 (1978).

2. *Id.*

3. *Pembaur v. Cincinnati,* 475 U.S. 469, 106 S.Ct. 1292, 89 L.Ed.2d 452 (1986) (plurality opinion); *St. Louis v. Praprotnik,* 485 U.S. 112, 108 S.Ct. 915, 99 L.Ed.2d 107 (1988) (plurality opinion); and *Jett v. Dallas Independent School District,* 491 U.S. 701, 109 S.Ct. 2702, 105 L.Ed.2d 598 (1989) (5–member majority opinion).

been sharply circumscribed by a series of Supreme Court rulings elaborating absolute immunity for legislative, judicial and prosecutorial conduct and an increasingly expansive brand of qualified immunity for the discretionary acts of officials performing executive or administrative functions.[4]

A comprehensive discussion of the prima facie proof elements, defenses, remedies, and related procedural intricacies of § 1983 may be found in the "Section 1983" and "Procedures" Chapters.

Library References:

> C.J.S. Civil Rights §§ 22, 25–26, 30–34, 37, 41–42, 45, 67 et seq.
> West's Key No. Digests, Civil Rights ⊕110 et seq.

§ 1.5   Section 1985(3)

a. *The "Deprivation" Clause*

Section 1985(3) is a purely remedial statute that, like § 1983 but unlike § 1981, creates no substantive rights itself.[1] Its first clause, by far the most frequently litigated, provides a federal cause of action for damages[2] for the redress of conspiracies that have the purpose and result of "depriving either directly or indirectly, any person or class of persons of the equal protection of the laws, or of equal privileges and immunities under the laws...."[3] A plaintiff under this "deprivation" clause must allege and prove (1) the elements of a conspiracy that (2) deprived the plaintiff of rights rather vaguely described with reference to unspecified "laws" providing for "equal protection" or "equal privileges and immunities." The conspiracy elements are standard, requiring principally an agreement by two or more distinct persons or entities[4] to engage in conduct that resulted in the deprivation of the requisite rights, plus some overt act in furtherance of that agreement. The protected "rights" question has proven more difficult. Section 1985(3) undoubtedly applies to conspiracies aimed at infringing certain fundamental constitutional rights. But the Court has struggled with elucidating which federal constitutional provisions secure the kind of "equal" rights § 1983 protects. It was forced to come to grips with that question when

---

4. *See generally Forrester v. White*, 484 U.S. 219, 108 S.Ct. 538, 98 L.Ed.2d 555 (1988) (absolute judicial immunity); *Burns v. Reed*, 500 U.S. 478, 111 S.Ct. 1934, 114 L.Ed.2d 547 (1991) (absolute prosecutorial immunity); and *Harlow v. Fitzgerald*, 457 U.S. 800, 102 S.Ct. 2727, 73 L.Ed.2d 396 (1982) and *Anderson v. Creighton*, 483 U.S. 635, 107 S.Ct. 3034, 97 L.Ed.2d 523 (1987) (easing the standards and procedures for defending on the ground of qualified immunity).

§ 1.5

1. *Great Am. Fed. S & L Ass'n v. Novotny*, 442 U.S. 366, 372, 99 S.Ct. 2345, 2349, 60 L.Ed.2d 957 (1979).

2. The Supreme Court has not decided if § 1985(3) supports a prayer for injunctive relief. *Bray v. Alexandria Women's Health Clinic*, 506 U.S. 263, 283 n. 16, 113 S.Ct. 753, 767 n. 16, 122 L.Ed.2d 34 (1993).

3. 42 U.S.C.A. § 1985(3) (1988).

4. In general, § 1985(3) is not violated by discussions, agreements, or actions taken between two or more individuals who serve the same corporate or other entity. *Wright v. Illinois Dept. of Children & Family Services*, 40 F.3d 1492 (7th Cir.1994); *Johnson v. Hills & Dales General Hospital*, 40 F.3d 837 (6th Cir.1994).

it considered whether the deprivation clause reaches only conspiracies involving government actors or also those where private defendants act alone.

Paving the way for damage actions against purely private actors, the Court in *Griffin v. Breckenridge*[5] held that state action is a required element only if the particular right plaintiff invokes is itself dependent on state action. (Virtually all rights protected by the U.S. Constitution do depend on state action.) Thus, for example, *United Brotherhood of Carpenters and Joiners v. Scott*[6] later held that because the First Amendment prohibits infringements only by government, a § 1985(3) claim against union members for conspiracy to deprive plaintiffs of rights to free speech and association failed for lack of evidence of state involvement.[7]

In holding in *Grifffin* that § 1985(3) could reach certain purely private conspiracies, the Court expressed concern (much as it did when it stretched § 1983 in *Monell* to reach government entity defendants) that the deprivation clause might become a "general federal tort law."[8] To avoid the resulting "constitutional shoals," the Court crafted a distinct element of the claim, one not apparent from statutory text: (3) there must be a class-based motivation behind the defendants' conspiracy to deprive the plaintiff of those equal rights.[9] Specifically, the Court extracted from the textually covered *"equal"* protection, privileges and immunities a requirement that the plaintiff must show "some racial, or perhaps otherwise class-based, invidiously discriminatory animus behind the conspirators' action."[10] Although the Court devised this new requirement to counter the problems it anticipated in applying the deprivation clause to purely private conspiracies, it fastened the requirement on the "equal protection" and "equal privileges" language that must be met to state a claim concerning *any* conspiracy, public or private. The "animus" requirement has accordingly been read as applicable to claims against conspiracies under color of state law as well as those against purely private conspiracies.[11]

By contrast, in a decision that brings the public-private constitutional "rights" question of *Griffin* full circle, the Court has described *Carpenters* as holding that § 1985(3) reaches only those private conspiracies that are aimed at constitutional rights "protected against private, *as well as* official, encroachment."[12] As the Court there observed, § 1985(3) accordingly redresses against private conspiratorial invasion only the Thirteenth Amendment right to be free from involuntary

5. 403 U.S. 88, 99, 91 S.Ct. 1790, 1797, 29 L.Ed.2d 338 (1971).

6. 463 U.S. 825, 103 S.Ct. 3352, 77 L.Ed.2d 1049 (1983).

7. *Carpenters*, at 832, 103 S.Ct. at 3358.

8. 403 U.S. at 102, 91 S.Ct. at 1798.

9. *Id.* at 88, 91 S.Ct. at 1791.

10. *Id.* at 102, 91 S.Ct. at 1798.

11. *Aulson v. Blanchard*, 83 F.3d 1 (1st Cir.1996).

12. *Bray v. Alexandria Women's Health Clinic*, 506 U.S. 263, 278, 113 S.Ct. 753, 764, 122 L.Ed.2d 34 (1993) (emphasis supplied)(quoting *United Brotherhood of Carpenters and Joiners v. Scott*, 463 U.S. 825, 833, 103 S.Ct. 3352, 3358, 77 L.Ed.2d 1049 (1983)).

servitude and a limited right to interstate travel—the lone constitutional provisions heretofore recognized as affording affirmative rights against private as well as public invasion.

The contours of the requisite class-based motivation or animus have not been fully drawn, but there are now some definite demarcations. Conspiracies directed against groups defined by race or racial advocacy are most clearly within the ambit of § 1985(3).[13] As under § 1981, however, the kind of "race" qualifying for protection is not always apparent. For example a circuit court has ruled that a target religious group containing both Jewish and non-Jewish members could not constitute a racial class of § 1985(3) purposes because of its racial diversity.[14] In *Griffin* the Court intimated with its "perhaps" language that certain non-racial but group-based motivations might also sustain a 1985(3) claim. But it held that conspiratorial conduct "motivated by economic or commercial animus" is outside the statute's reach.[15]

It remains uncertain whether gender-based motivation qualifies as an actionable animus, even after the Court's recent decision in *Bray v. Alexandria Women's Health Clinic*.[16] In *Bray*, a women's clinic that provided pregnancy and abortion services alleged that defendant pro-life protesters, all acting without government encouragement or support, conspired to deny women the right to travel in interstate commerce to receive those services. The alleged overt act in furtherance of this conspiracy was the attempt to block the entrance to the clinic, and the conspiracy was said to have been motivated by an invidiously discriminatory class-based animus—a desire to deny women the equal protection of the laws.

The Court did not decide whether gender-based animus is actionable, because it found the "deprivation" claim to fail for two independent reasons. For one, the Court found no actionable right. The right to abortion did not qualify because it is protected only against official and not also private encroachment. The right to interstate travel did not qualify either; it protected interstate travelers only against discriminatory treatment vis-a-vis local intrastate abortion seekers, and there was no such disparity in *Bray*.

By analogy to the construction of § 1985(3)'s criminal counterpart,[17] the Court has also insisted, in *United States v. Guest*,[18] that to be actionable under § 1985(3) a conspiracy must have the specific purpose,

---

13. *Griffin*, 403 U.S. at 102, 91 S.Ct. at 1798.

14. *Jews for Jesus, Inc. v. Jewish Community Relations Council of New York, Inc.*, 968 F.2d 286 (2d Cir.1992).

15. *Carpenters*, 463 U.S. at 834, 103 S.Ct. at 3359 ("antinonunion" motivation). While there is no consensus whether conduct motivated by purely political animus is actionable, it has been held that the target class is cognizable "only when it is com-

prised of a distinctive and identifiable group" whose members could be ascertained "by means of objective criteria." *Aulson v. Blanchard*, 83 F.3d 1 (1st Cir. 1996).

16. 506 U.S. 263, 113 S.Ct. 753, 122 L.Ed.2d 34 (1993).

17. 18 U.S.C.A. § 241.

18. 383 U.S. 745, 86 S.Ct. 1170, 16 L.Ed.2d 239 (1966).

and not merely the effect, of interfering with a protected right. The defendants' conduct must be "aimed at" that right.[19]

In two major respects, then, the Court has sharply circumscribed the scope and utility of § 1985(3)'s "deprivation" clause. First, although the statute's "equal rights" language was written only three years after the Fourteenth Amendment was ratified, *Griffin*'s extratextual gloss on the protected "class" and the related required "animus," confirmed in *Carpenters*, denies protection on many of the grounds embraced by the Fourteenth Amendment. In his separate opinion in *Bray*, for example, Justice Souter argues that certain class categories clearly eligible for heightened scrutiny under the Equal Protection Clause as analogous to race should probably also be covered by § 1985(3)—he lists national origin, alienage, gender, and illegitimacy. But he adds that under the majority's restrictive view of animus, § 1985(3) probably does not provide protection for all these legislative classifications, even though the Clause itself, at least to some degree, clearly does.

Second, the Court has severely curtailed the rights which, when violated, can serve as the springboard to a deprivation clause claim. It began in *Griffin* by expanding, within the racial animus sphere, the rights protected by § 1985(3) beyond those protected by the Fourteenth Amendment—that is, it swept purely private conspiracies within the reach of the statute so that the statute, unlike the Amendment, does not always hinge on state action. Yet the Court ended up in *Carpenters* and *Bray* by *limiting* the statute's ambit of protection in the private realm to the constitutional rights, currently numbered at just two, protected against private interference.

It might appear that joint public-private alleged conspirators who, motivated by racial animus, interfere on racial grounds with First Amendment rights cannot be reached by § 1985(3), because First Amendment rights are not protected against private invasion. But a closer look at *Bray* suggests that the "private rights" limitation applies only to conspiracies by defendants acting *purely* privately. The facts at bar as well as the textual setting of this requirement within the *Bray* opinion[20] support this conclusion.[21]

Still, Section 1985(3)'s deprivation clause, as a source of protection for constitutional rights, is sorely wounded. As long as the protected

19. *Bray,* 506 U.S. at 274, 113 S.Ct. at 762 (quoting *Carpenters,* 463 U.S. at 833, 103 S.Ct. at 3358).

20. The part of the opinion that elaborates the requirement that the right violated be protected against private, and not just official encroachment begins with a paragraph that describes the requirement as pertaining to a § 1985(3) *"private* conspiracy." 506 U.S. at 274, 113 S.Ct. at 762 (emphasis added).

21. *Tilton v. Richardson,* 6 F.3d 683, 686–687 (10th Cir.1993), *cert. denied,* 510 U.S. 1093, 114 S.Ct. 925, 127 L.Ed.2d 218

(1994) (repeatedly stating that the *Carpenters/Bray* "rights" limitations applies only to "private" conspiracies). Similarly, in *Trautz v. Weisman,* 819 F.Supp. 282, 290 (S.D.N.Y.1993), the court implied that the "private rights" requirement applied only to private conspiracies. But the racial *animus* requirement applies to conspiracies under color of state law as well as those that are purely private. *See Aulson v. Blanchard,* 83 F.3d 1 (1st Cir.1996)(class-based discriminatory animus requirement applies to purely public actor conspiracy).

target "class" extends little beyond race or the advocacy of racial views, the clause will be seldom needed when the conspirators include state actors: it is rarely popular or prudent today for government officials to conspire on such grounds. And the clause is largely disabled as applied to the potentially far more numerous category of purely private conspiracies. *Bray* insists that such conspiracies are actionable only when aimed at the two constitutional rights that affirmatively prohibit private as well as public abridgements, but conspiracies to enslave or to infringe the right to interstate travel do not abound.

The Court has left open whether conspiratorial deprivation of equal rights protected by federal or state *statutes* might also trigger § 1985(3) liability.[22] But if, as appears to be the case, the recently refined "animus" requirement (in contrast to the "private rights" requirement)[23] applies to all § 1985(3) deprivation clause conspiracies, public or private, there would appear to be relatively little scope for actions based on violations of federal or state statutes.

Although it has not decided whether violations of federal equal rights statutes may serve as the predicate for § 1985(3) liability, the Court has set one firm outer limit. Section 1985(3) is ousted if the particular federal statute on which plaintiff relies has its own elaborate remedial and procedural scheme.[24] The Court in *Novotny* held that § 1985(3) is unavailable as an alternative remedy for employment discrimination prohibited by Title VII, expressing the fear that it might be used to bypass the detailed state and local administrative procedures, conciliation mechanisms and judicial remedies that Congress specified in the modern statute. In *Carpenters* the Court found it unnecessary to decide whether rights guaranteed by state law are protected under § 1985(3), because it concluded in any event that the plaintiff had failed to demonstrate the requisite class-based animus to support the claim.[25]

There is divergent opinion among the federal circuit courts as to whether a public official sued under § 1985(3) may claim a variant of the qualified immunity defense that is available to an individual defendant under § 1983. A decision denying that defense reasoned that the § 1985(3) requirement of intentional, race-based animus protects against imposition of liability for actions taken in good faith; the additional protection of qualified immunity is not necessary, in other words, to assure that a public official will vigorously discharge the duties of his office.[26] A decision upholding the defense asserts that despite the ultimate protection on the merits that the animus element affords public officials sued under § 1985(3), the same basic rationale warranting qualified immunity under § 1983 obtains: the necessity to defend such

---

22. *Carpenters v. Scott, supra*, 463 U.S. at 829, 103 S.Ct. at 3356.

23. *See* text accompanying footnote 20, *supra*.

24. *Great American Fed. S & L Ass'n v. Novotny*, 442 U.S. 366, 99 S.Ct. 2345, 60 L.Ed.2d 957 (1979).

25. 463 U.S. at 833, 103 S.Ct. at 3358.

26. *Burrell v. Board of Trustees of Georgia Military College*, 970 F.2d 785, 793–794 (11th Cir.1992), *cert. denied* 507 U.S. 1018, 113 S.Ct. 1814, 123 L.Ed.2d 445 (1993).

actions will discourage persons from holding public office, divert public officials' energies from official business, and chill them in the exercise of their duties.[27]

b. The "Hindrance" Clause

Section 1985(3) has a second clause that punishes conspiracies for the purpose of "preventing or hindering the constituted authorities of any State or Territory from giving or securing ... the equal protection of the laws...." Liability under this "hindrance" clause requires at a minimum a conspiracy of sufficient force to overwhelm the capacity of government to administer law evenhandedly. Five members of the Court in *Bray* concluded that a hindrance claim was not properly presented for review. Nevertheless, they suggested that both the private-rights and animus requirements that the Court had elaborated for "deprivation" claims would apply to hindrance claims as well.

The dissenters, by contrast, argued that the hindrance clause is available where overwhelming conspiratorial force disables duly constituted authorities from affording equal protection, even when private defendants target a right dependent on state action and even when they are not animated by race or like class characteristic. Some of the dissenters relied on, and the majority distinguished, the Court's approach to the first clause of § 1985(2), which provides a cause of action against conspirators who seek to intimidate or injure federal court parties or witnesses. The Court had held the *Griffin* animus requirement inapplicable to actions under that clause in *Kush v. Rutledge*.[28] The *Bray* majority noted that the first clause of § 1985(2)—unlike the second clause of that subsection (affording a cause of action against conspirators seeking to obstruct justice within a State or Territory), and unlike both the deprivation and hindrance clauses of § 1985(3)—did not contain the equal protection limitation on protected rights from which the Court had derived the *Griffin* requirement of race-based animus.

But with the resignation of Justice White, lower courts are left in a quandary about applying the deprivation clause restrictions to the hindrance clause. With his vote excluded, the justices split 4–4 on those questions in the extended dictum on the subject in *Bray*. A court of appeals has drawn the following composite picture of the views of the four dissenters on the hindrance clause, as expressed in three dissenting opinions: (1) The conspirators' purpose must be to hinder law enforcement authorities from providing normal police protection to a (2) protected class of persons that may include a class of women, where (3) the class is attempting to exercise any constitutional right (not limited to rights protected against private interference) and (4) the defendants harbor a class-based animus which, however, unlike the animus required for the deprivation clause as construed in *Bray*, is inferable from defendants' activities aimed at conduct engaged in exclusively by members of the plaintiff class. The court of appeals accepted the dissent's

27. *Bisbee v. Bey*, 39 F.3d 1096 (10th Cir.1994).

28. 460 U.S. 719, 103 S.Ct. 1483, 75 L.Ed.2d 413 (1983).

composite as adequate to state a hindrance clause claim. It reasoned that the main impetus for the "rights" and "animus" requirements that the Court has read into the deprivation clause—avoiding the federalization of state tort law—is absent in the context of the hindrance clause, because the foundation of the latter is an allegation that the defendants conspired to interfere with state law enforcement. Further, the textual handle for those requirements—the equal protection language of the deprivation clause—is missing from the hindrance clause. The court concluded that the hindrance clause is violated by a conspiracy to hinder state law enforcement officials from securing to plaintiffs their constitutional right to an abortion.[29]

Library References:

C.J.S. Conspiracy § 10(2); Racketeer Influenced and Corrupt Organizations § 12.

West's Key No. Digests, Conspiracy ⚓7.5.

§ 1.6 Section 1986: Negligent Failure to Prevent a Section 1985 Conspiracy

42 U.S.C.A. § 1986 creates a claim against any person who, "having knowledge that any of the wrongs conspired to be done, and mentioned in § 1985 of this title, are about to be committed, and having power to prevent or aid in preventing the commission of the same, neglects or refuses so to do...." The defendant "shall be liable to the party injured ... for all damages caused by such wrongful act, which such person by reasonable diligence could have prevented...." The elements of the claim include a violation of § 1985; a defendant's actual knowledge of a conspiracy under that section; the defendant's neglect or refusal to prevent it, despite the power to prevent or aid in its prevention; and damages caused by such a wrongful act.[1]

The "power to prevent" element virtually assures that § 1986 defendants will be limited to law enforcement authorities and other public officials. The actual knowledge requirement, however, has been relaxed far below the standard the Supreme Court has set for Eighth Amendment violations by prison officials[2]; indeed that requirement has been held met by "rumors" of a § 1985(3) conspiracy sufficiently alarming to local officials that they took some precautionary measures to

---

29. *National Abortions Federation v. Operation Rescue,* 8 F.3d 680 (9th Cir. 1993). *See also Libertad v. Welch,* 53 F.3d 428 (1st Cir.1995) (upholding hindrance clause claim even if infringed constitutional right is enforceable only against official misconduct, provided conspiracy's purpose is to impede state officials in securing equal protection).

§ 1.6

1. *Clark v. Clabaugh,* 20 F.3d 1290 (3d Cir.1994).

2. *See* discussion of *Farmer v. Brennan,* 511 U.S. 825, 114 S.Ct. 1970, 128 L.Ed.2d 811 (1994), in Chapter 2 (no constitutional violation merely because prison official "should have known" of conditions constituting cruel and unusual punishment, absent actual knowledge thereof).

prevent it.[3] And the "neglects or refuses" language has been read to mean that liability does not depend on a showing that the defendant shares the kind of racially discriminatory animus prerequisite to liability for the underlying § 1985(3) conspiracy.[4]

Library References:

> C.J.S. Civil Rights §§ 225–228.
> West's Key No. Digests, Civil Rights ⊚192.

§ 1.7 The Partial Legislative Overruling of Recent Supreme Court Restrictions on the Use of Section 1981, and the Resulting Relationship Between Section 1981 as Amended and Section 1983

Although *Patterson* reaffirmed the *Runyon* ruling that extended § 1981's application to the private sector, it also sharply restricted the scope of § 1981 claims. The Court recognized that § 1981 protects the right to "enforce" contracts; an employer is therefore prohibited from discriminating on the basis of race or national origin so as to impede the enforcement of contract rights. But five justices also ruled that the statutory prohibition on racial or ethnic discrimination in the "making" of private employment contracts does not extend to conduct occurring after the employment relation is established. Thus the Court held employer racial "harassment," fostering or tolerating a discriminatory work environment, outside the ambit of the statute.

It is somewhat unclear whether *Patterson* precluded a claim of discriminatory discharge, for two reasons. First, discharge arguably goes to the very existence of a contract and not just the way it is performed. Second, after discharge the relationship sought to be preserved by Title VII is at an end anyway and so there is no good reason to construe § 1981 narrowly in order to avoid interference with Title VII conciliation. Nevertheless, federal circuit courts after *Patterson* generally held discharge to be outside the reach of § 1981.[1]

The Civil Rights Act of 1991 overrules the *Patterson* limitation on the scope of the right to "make and enforce" contracts, although perhaps only prospectively. Section 101 of the Civil Rights Act of 1991 adds to § 1981 the following new subsection:

> (b) For purposes of this section, the term "make and enforce contracts" includes the making, performance, modification, and

---

3. *Id.*

4. *Id.*

§ 1.7

1. *See Taggart v. Jefferson County Child Support Enforcement Unit*, 935 F.2d 947 (8th Cir.1991); *McKnight v. General Motors Corp.*, 908 F.2d 104 (7th Cir.1990), *cert. denied*, 499 U.S. 919, 111 S.Ct. 1306, 113 L.Ed.2d 241 (1991); *Courtney v. Canyon Television & Appliance Rental, Inc.*,

899 F.2d 845 (9th Cir.1990); *Lavender v. V & B Transmissions & Auto Repair*, 897 F.2d 805 (5th Cir.1990); *Carroll v. General Accident Ins. Co.*, 891 F.2d 1174 (5th Cir. 1990). *But see Hicks v. Brown Group, Inc.*, 902 F.2d 630 (8th Cir.1990) (distinguishing *Patterson* to uphold discharge claim) *vacated by*, 499 U.S. 914, 111 S.Ct. 1299, 113 L.Ed.2d 234 (1991).

termination of contracts, and the enjoyment of all benefits, privileges, terms, and conditions of the contractual relationship.

The sweeping text of this addition appears to equate the sphere in which contract discrimination is forbidden by § 1981 with the wide ambit of the terms and conditions of employment protected under Title VII. In particular, it is now clear that claims of race-based harassment and discharge are once again actionable under § 1981.

A lower court has expanded this result to preclude federal employment claims under §§ 1983 and 1985(3) as well as 1981 when Title VII is available and the employee relies on common facts in setting out each of the claims.[2]

More recently, in *Jett v. Dallas Independent School District*,[3] the Court reigned in § 1981 as an independent, free-standing source of redress in actions against local and state governments as well. But the Court held in *Jett* that municipalities are liable under § 1981 only if they would be liable under the more stringent standards of § 1983.

The Court had held in *Will v. Michigan Dep't of State Police*[4] that states *eo nominee* are *not* liable under *§ 1983*, in either state or federal court; instead the federal law violations of states were held redressable under that statute only indirectly, through actions against individual state officials for prospective relief.[5]

B. *JETT, WILL,* AND THE CIVIL RIGHTS ACT OF 1991: THE PROOF REQUIREMENTS OF SECTION 1981 IN ACTIONS AGAINST STATE OR LOCAL GOVERNMENTS

Library References:

C.J.S. Civil Rights §§ 143–144, 146, 148–149.
West's Key No. Digests, Civil Rights ⚷146.

§ 1.8 In General

With its decisions in *Will v. Michigan Department of State Police*,[1] and *Jett v. Dallas Independent School Dist.*,[2] the Supreme Court imposed significant restrictions on plaintiffs alleging intentional race discrimination and seeking redress against state and local governments under,

2. *Rowe v. Sullivan*, 967 F.2d 186 (5th Cir.1992). *But cf. La Compania Ocho, Inc. v. U.S. Forest Service*, 874 F.Supp. 1242, 1250–51 (D.N.M.1995) (§ 1981 is available to assert nonemployment discrimination claims against the Federal government, despite negative textual inference of new Section 1981(c)).

3. 491 U.S. 701, 109 S.Ct. 2702, 105 L.Ed.2d 598 (1989).

4. 491 U.S. 58, 109 S.Ct. 2304, 105 L.Ed.2d 45 (1989).

5. For more details on *Jett* and *Will* and the suggestion that they have been legislatively overruled by § 101(c) of the Civil Rights Act of 1991, see *infra* §§ 1.9–1.10.

§ 1.8

1. 491 U.S. 58, 109 S.Ct. 2304, 105 L.Ed.2d 45 (1989).

2. 491 U.S. 701, 109 S.Ct. 2702, 105 L.Ed.2d 598 (1989).

respectively, 42 U.S.C.A. § 1983 and 42 U.S.C.A. § 1981. The Civil Rights Act of 1991 casts some doubt on the continued vitality of *Jett*. How the federal courts interpret the 1991 Act as applied to *Jett* will determine whether and to what degree such a plaintiff can pursue remedies against government under §§ 1981, or only under § 1983.

§ 1.9   Claims Arising From Acts of Discrimination in Employment on or Before Nov. 21, 1991

The Supreme Court has held that the Civil Rights Act of 1991 does not apply retroactively. It prohibits acts of employment discrimination that occur after its enactment on November 21, 1991.[1] As a result, our analysis begins with the interplay of §§ 1981 and 1983 after *Will* and *Jett*, but before Nov. 21, 1991, and without regard to the 1991 Civil Rights Act.

In *Will v. Michigan Department of State Police*,[2] the Supreme Court held that "neither a state or its officials acting in their official capacities are 'persons' under Section 1983."[3] Hence, the Court concluded that under § 1983 states are not suable at all in their own name and state officials sued in their official capacities are subject only to prospective relief.[4]

In that same term, the Court also decided *Jett v. Dallas Independent School Dist.*[5] In *Jett*, the Court severely limited the applicability of § 1981. The Court stated,

> We think the history of the 1866 Act and the 1871 Act ... indicates that Congress intended that the explicit remedial provisions of Section 1983 be controlling in the context of damages actions brought against state actors alleging violation of the rights declared in Section 1981.[6]

Consequently, "the express 'action at law' provided by Section *1983* ... provides the exclusive federal damages *remedy* for the violation of the *rights* guaranteed by Section 1981 when the claim is pressed against a state actor."[7] The Court explained the effect of this holding:

> [T]o prevail on his [Section 1981] claim for damages against the school district, [plaintiff] must show that the violation of his 'right to make contracts' protected by Section 1981 was caused by a custom or policy within the meaning of Monell and subsequent [Section 1983] cases.[8]

§ 1.9

1. *Landgraf v. USI Film Products*, 511 U.S. 244, 114 S.Ct. 1483, 128 L.Ed.2d 229 (1994); *Rivers v. Roadway Express*, 511 U.S. 298, 114 S.Ct. 1510, 128 L.Ed.2d 274 (1994).

2. 491 U.S. 58, 109 S.Ct. 2304, 105 L.Ed.2d 45, (1989).

3. *Id.* at 71, 109 S.Ct. at 2312.

4. *Id.* at 63, 109 S.Ct. at 2308.

5. 491 U.S. 701, 109 S.Ct. 2702, 105 L.Ed.2d 598 (1989).

6. *Id.* at 731, 109 S.Ct. at 2720.

7. *Id.* at 735, 109 S.Ct. at 2723 (emphasis added).

8. *Id.* at 735–736, 109 S.Ct. at 2723.

The language of the *Jett* opinion broadly applies the § 1983 limitations to any § 1981 claim against a "state actor." A plaintiff seeking redress for deprivations of the rights guaranteed by § 1981 must therefore also satisfy the additional prima facie proof element of § 1983—a showing of official policy or custom.

Accordingly, after *Will* and *Jett* but before the 1991 Act, an employee with a claim of intentional discrimination faced several potential roadblocks to redress under §§ 1981 and 1983. The Supreme Court, in *Brown v. GSA*,[9] had held Title VII to preempt § 1981 claims against *federal* employers. Under *Jett*, the plaintiff clearly couldn't win a suit under § 1981 against a *municipality* or *local* government unless he could show a policy or custom as required by § 1983. Because of *Will*, she couldn't sue the *state* as such, under § 1983. And perhaps her § 1981 claim against a *state* would falter as well. After all, the language of *Jett* apparently required the plaintiff to meet all § 1983 requirements in order to perfect a § 1981 claim against a state actor, and under *Will* a state was no longer a § 1983 "person."

On the other hand, under the logic of *Jett*, a plaintiff possibly *could* recover against a state under § 1981. The Court in *Jett* was primarily concerned with preventing a plaintiff from using § 1981 as an "end-around" § 1983's requirements for bringing suit against a state or local governmental actor. But, since the Court had just held in *Will* that states could *not* be sued under § 1983, § 1981 claims against states could no longer be viewed as circumventing § 1983 requirements. That is, allowing a plaintiff to proceed against a state under the less rigorous standards of § 1981 would not have been circumventing the stricter standards of § 1983, since states were no longer suable under § 1983 at all. On this reasoning, a plaintiff could still sue a state under § 1981 without meeting the "policy" hurdle of § 1983.

The Civil Rights Act of 1991 added a new paragraph to § 1981. In § 101(c) of the 1991 Act, Congress provided:

> (c) The rights protected by this section are protected against impairment by nongovernmental discrimination *and impairment under color of state law*.[10]

The crucial inquiry raised by this text is whether Congress intended to overrule *Jett*.

§ 1.10 Claims Arising From Intentional Race Discrimination in Employment After the Effective Date of the 1991 Act

The early reported cases that addressed the issue held or implied

---

9. 425 U.S. 820, 96 S.Ct. 1961, 48 L.Ed.2d 402 (1976).

10. Pub.L. 102–166, § 101 (1991) (codified at 42 U.S.C.A. § 1981(c)) (emphasis added).

that § 101(c) of the 1991 Act overrules *Jett*.[1]

Nevertheless, at least as strong a case can be made that the 1991 Act did not overrule *Jett*. For example, the Act nowhere expressly addresses the *Jett* holding, e.g., by authorizing the § 1981 claim against a state or local government employee to proceed without regard to the limitations of § 1983. Further, the simple statement in new § 1981(c) that § 1981 protects against "impairment under color of state law" does not contradict the holding in *Jett*. In fact, the whole premise of *Jett* was that a plaintiff suing a state or local government employer was not limited to a claim under § 1983 but could assert a claim, albeit a peculiarly limited one, under § 1981 as well. *Jett* only demanded that the plaintiff bringing a § 1981 claim against a government entity satisfy the requirements of § 1983 for entity liability. Viewed this way, the language of new § 1981(c) arguably codifies, rather than overrules, *Jett*.

These conclusions are fortified by the way a Supreme Court that takes a "plain-text" approach to statutory interpretation is likely to view subsection (c). Even if the Court resorts to legislative history it would find only a congressional determination to codify *Runyon*. There is no stated intention to overrule *Jett*, despite the express stated intention found elsewhere in the 1991 legislation to overrule other specifically named Supreme Court decisions. Although most of the recent decisions do not articulate these reasons, several have assumed or concluded that *Jett* enjoys continuing vitality notwithstanding § 1981(c).[2]

Some recent decisions have suggested an intermediate position. These courts treat § 1981(c) as overruling what they take to be the *Jett* holding that § 1981 violations can be remedied only under § 1983. Thus § 1981 stands on its own as the source of a right and a remedy. Nevertheless, these courts also observe that nothing about the 1991 amendment implies that local governments should be liable vicariously under § 1981, any more than they are under § 1983. Rather, "municipal liability for public officials' violations of sec. 1981" must be determined by reference to the principles applicable "under sec. 1983 using the *Monell* analysis." [3]

§ 1.10

1. *See Morris v. Kansas Dept. of Revenue,* 849 F.Supp. 1421, 1426 (D.Kan.1994); *Arnett v. Davis County Sch. Dist.,* 1993 WL 434053 at 5 & n. 8 (D.Utah 1993); *Vakharia v. Swedish Covenant Hosp.,* 824 F.Supp. 769, 785 & n. 1 (N.D.Ill.1993); *Ford v. City of Rockford,* 1992 WL 309603 at 2 (N.D.Ill. 1992).

2. *Dennis v. County of Fairfax,* 55 F.3d 151, 156 n. 1 (4th Cir.1995); *Williams v. Little Rock Mun. Water Works,* 21 F.3d 218 (8th Cir.1994); *Cotterell v. New York City Transit Police Dep't,* 1995 WL 604700 (E.D.N.Y.1995).

3. *Philippeaux v. North Central Bronx Hosp.,* 871 F.Supp. 640, 655 (S.D.N.Y.1994). *See also Gallardo v. Board of County Comm'rs,* 857 F.Supp. 783, 786 (D.Kan. 1994). This reasoning has now been endorsed by a circuit court opinion. *Federation of African American Contractors v. Oakland, Calif.,* 96 F.3d 1204 (9th Cir. 1996). For a discussion of vicarious governmental entity liability under § 1983 as elaborated in *Monell v. Department of Social Servs. of City of New York,* 436 U.S. 658, 98 S.Ct. 2018, 56 L.Ed.2d 611 (1978), see Chapter 2.

§ 1.11   The Practical Significance of the *Jett*-Related Language in the Civil Rights Act of 1991

As discussed above, Title VII, where applicable, displaces preexisting discrimination remedies relating to federal employment, *Brown*, and to conspiracies affecting employment, *Novotny*.[1] As a result, unless Congress acts to overrule *Will* or to clarify that it intended to overrule *Jett*, only plaintiffs challenging the conduct of municipal or other local, as opposed to state or federal, governments may now be able to take advantage of the immediate court access and generous remedies afforded by the Reconstruction Civil Rights Acts; and even those plaintiffs may have to meet the formidable new requirements of § 1983. Yet when a *private* defendant intentionally refuses, because of race or ancestry, to execute or perform an employment contract, the unsuccessful applicant will still clearly have a claim under § 1981, in accordance with new paragraph (c); and after the overruling of *Patterson* by new paragraph (b), that claim will once again secure the right to make and enforce contracts without discrimination across the entire spectrum of the contractual relationship, including terms and conditions of employment after hire. The ironic residue is that § 1981 claims against government defendants are less clearly (in the case of states) or less often (in the case of the federal government) actionable, and may (in the case of local governments) succeed only on stricter terms, than claims against private sector defendants—this despite that fact that, until *Runyon* was decided in 1976, private defendants were not thought subject to suit under § 1981 at all!

§ 1.11

1. Title VII does not displace § 1983, however, in cases where they both apply. *See* "The Combined Use of Section 1983 and Title VII."

Chapter Two

SECTION 1983

Analysis

A. INTRODUCTION

A.   INTRODUCTION

Library References:

     C.J.S. Civil Rights §§ 2–5, 7–9, 11–13, 18, 44.
     West's Key No. Digests, Civil Rights ☞101 et seq.

§ 2.1   In General

Section 42 U.S.C.A. § 1983 (1988) is easily the most important of the Reconstruction Civil Rights Acts, as measured both by the importance of its primarily constitutional workload and by the sheer number of federal cases brought under its auspices. The statute was originally passed as § 1 of the Ku Klux Klan Act of April 20, 1871,[1] and titled "An Act to enforce the Provisions of the Fourteenth Amendment to the Constitution of the United States, and for other Purposes." It provides as follows:

> Every person who, under color of any statute, ordinance, regulation, custom, or usage, of any State or Territory or the District of Columbia, subjects, or causes to be subjected, any citizen of the United States or other person within the jurisdiction thereof to the

§ 2.1

1. Ch. 22, § 1, 17 Stat. 13 (1871).

deprivation of any rights, privileges, or immunities secured by the Constitution and laws, shall be liable to the party injured in an action at law, suit in equity, or other proper proceeding for redress.[2]

Section 1983 therefore creates a claim for legal or equitable relief against (1) every "person" who (2) "under color of" state legislation, custom, or usage (3) "subjects, or causes [another] to be subjected" (4) to the deprivation of rights secured by the federal "Constitution and laws."

Section 1983 as interpreted today takes a strikingly asymmetrical shape. The statute's text simply provides for the liability of defendants who "cause [a plaintiff] to be subjected" to the loss of a federally secured right. In adumbrating this causation requirement, however, the Supreme Court places an additional obstacle in the path of a plaintiff who sues a government entity. An entity's liability is restricted to conduct of its agents that implements entity "policy," defined as "a deliberate choice to follow a course of action ... from among various alternatives." [3] In the typical case, the agent who inflicts the injury does not act pursuant to a formal ordinance or written administrative directive; yet the liability of his entity demands a showing that an official with "final" discretionary authority under positive state law specifically authorized or ratified the agent's injury-producing act.[4] Alternatively, if injury results from an agent's omission, policy may be found in the entity's "deliberate indifference" to a frequently recurring circumstance.[5] Still, if the plaintiff can satisfy any of these formidable policy hurdles, she recovers from an entity defendant even if the federal right violated had not been judicially recognized before the incident that caused the harm.[6] The case against the entity can therefore still serve as a staging ground for dialogue about the creation of new constitutional protections.

By contrast, the prima facie case against a government official is far less exacting. Whenever an individual agent causes a recognized constitutional harm, she is prima facie liable even if the entity approved her conduct and she had a blameless state of mind.[7] Nevertheless, the Court, prompted by concerns about litigation floodgates, federalism, and

---

2. 42 U.S.C.A. § 1983 (1988).

3. *Pembaur v. City of Cincinnati*, 475 U.S. 469, 483, 106 S.Ct. 1292, 1300, 89 L.Ed.2d 452 (1986) (plurality opinion).

4. *See City of St. Louis v. Praprotnik*, 485 U.S. 112, 127, 108 S.Ct. 915, 926, 99 L.Ed.2d 107 (1988) (plurality opinion). *Praprotnik* commanded a majority of the Court in *Jett v. Dallas Independent School Dist.*, 491 U.S. 701, 737–38, 109 S.Ct. 2702, 2724, 105 L.Ed.2d 598 (1989). Alternatively, the policy element may be met by evidence that the agent's act was consistent with a settled entity custom. *See Monell v. Dep't of Social Servs.*, 436 U.S. 658, 690–91, 98 S.Ct. 2018, 2035–2036, 56 L.Ed.2d 611 (1978).

5. *See City of Canton v. Harris*, 489 U.S. 378, 388, 109 S.Ct. 1197, 1205, 103 L.Ed.2d 412 (1989).

6. *See* Sections D and E *infra* this chapter.

7. *Monroe* is still good law on this point. *See Daniels v. Williams*, 474 U.S. 327, 330–331, 106 S.Ct. 662, 664–665, 88 L.Ed.2d 662 (1986) (overruling *Parratt v. Taylor*, 451 U.S. 527, 101 S.Ct. 1908, 68 L.Ed.2d 420 (1981), to the extent that *Parratt* held that negligence was sufficient to state a claim for a state-caused "deprivation," but otherwise leaving undisturbed the conclusion that § 1983 contains no independent state-of-mind requirement).

judicial interference with discretionary government decisions,[8] has crafted an expansive affirmative defense that more than offsets the laxity of
the prima facie requirements. Executive or administrative government
agents, including those whose positions make them most likely to inflict
injury on ordinary citizens, escape liability for damages by grace of
qualified immunity unless the right violated was previously recognized
by judicial precedent of unmistakable application and clarity.[9]

§ 2.2 "Absolute" Immunities

Certain legislative, judicial, and prosecutorial functions cut so close
to the core of representative democracy or the justice system that the
common law has created "absolute" immunity to protect these officials'
freedom of action. "Absolute," as we shall see, does not necessarily free
all these officials from all liability; injunctive relief may still lie, and in
that case the immunity will not free the official from the necessity of
defending her conduct in court. Rather, "absolute" refers to the fact
that within the immunized sphere, such conduct will not give rise to
damages (or, in the case of legislators, any liability) even if motivated by
personal gain, retribution or bias and even if undertaken as part of a
conspiracy.[1] As with the qualified immunity of officials performing
executive or administrative functions, defendants asserting absolute
immunity enjoy the procedural protection of an immediate interlocutory
appeal from the denial of a motion asserting the immunity.[2] This is
necessary so that the person who claims the immunity shall not have to
"answer for his conduct in a civil damages action." [3]

Thus, with respect to their primary functions, individual judges and
prosecutors are accorded an even broader form of immunity from damages than executive or administrative officials. They, and other officials
who exercise judicial or prosecutorial functions,[4] are accorded "absolute"

8. Beginning in 1976, the Court began
to take seriously its concern that absent
significant restraints § 1983 would become
"a font of tort law." *Paul v. Davis,* 424
U.S. 693, 701, 96 S.Ct. 1155, 1160, 47
L.Ed.2d 405 (1976); *see also* Theodore Eisenberg & Stewart Schwab, *The Reality of
Constitutional Tort Litigation,* 72 Cornell L.
Rev. 641, 646–47 (1987) (arguing that the
Court's efforts to curb procedural due process litigation are rooted in a desire to stem
a flood of litigation). Eisenberg and
Schwab conclude, however, that the growth
in civil rights litigation has not been as
explosive as commonly assumed. *See id.* at
693–95, 96 S.Ct. at 1157–1158. *Paul* also
evinces the fear that § 1983 litigation will
become a mechanism for federal trenching
on state prerogatives. *See Paul, supra,* at
700–01, 96 S.Ct. at 1160–1161; *see also
infra* text accompanying notes 7–13, § 2.25
(discussing *Paul*).

9. *See Anderson v. Creighton,* 483 U.S.
635, 646 n. 6, 107 S.Ct. 3034, 3042 n. 6, 97

L.Ed.2d 523 (1987); *Harlow v. Fitzgerald,*
457 U.S. 800, 817–819, 102 S.Ct. 2727,
2738–2739, 73 L.Ed.2d 396 (1982).

§ 2.2

1. *See, e.g., Tenney v. Brandhove,* 341
U.S. 367, 377, 71 S.Ct. 783, 788, 95 L.Ed.
1019 (1951); *Wood v. Strickland,* 420 U.S.
308, 317, 95 S.Ct. 992, 998, 43 L.Ed.2d 214
(1975).

2. *Nixon v. Fitzgerald,* 457 U.S. 731,
742, 102 S.Ct. 2690, 2697, 73 L.Ed.2d 349
(1982).

3. *Mitchell v. Forsyth,* 472 U.S. 511,
525, 105 S.Ct. 2806, 2814, 86 L.Ed.2d 411
(1985).

4. *Supreme Court of Va. v. Consumers
Union,* 446 U.S. 719, 100 S.Ct. 1967, 64
L.Ed.2d 641 (1980).

immunity with respect to all truly "judicial" or "prosecutorial" conduct. The burden of proof in establishing eligibility for absolute immunity lies with the individual asserting it.[5] Eligibility for the immunity depends on a functional characterization of the challenged conduct.[6] This means not only that persons other than judges or prosecutors are entitled to a "quasi" version of absolute immunity to the extent that they undertake functions that a court agrees are "judicial" or "prosecutorial" in character [7]; it also means that judges and prosecutors do not receive absolute immunity with respect to their administrative, executive, investigative or other functions not deemed "judicial" or "prosecutorial."[8]

The absolute immunity of a judge extends to any conduct that may be considered a "judicial act" performed in the exercise of an arguably judicial function. The immunity insulates the judge from damages liability not only for erroneous or malicious conduct, but also for acting "in excess of his authority," even where his "commission of grave procedural errors" denied a party fundamental fairness.[9] Only when the judge acts in the "clear absence of all jurisdiction" does she forfeit the immunity. The Court has recently cited with approval an example

5. *Hafer v. Melo,* 502 U.S. 21, 27, 112 S.Ct. 358, 363, 116 L.Ed.2d 301 (1991) (citing *Burns v. Reed,* 500 U.S. 478, 111 S.Ct. 1934, 114 L.Ed.2d 547 (1991)).

6. *See Forrester v. White,* 484 U.S. 219, 227–29, 108 S.Ct. 538, 544–545, 98 L.Ed.2d 555 (1988).

7. *See, e.g., Mays v. Sudderth,* 97 F.3d 107 (5th Cir.1996)(sheriff absolutely immune for arrest and detention pursuant to facially valid court order despite any knowledge of absence of probable cause for the order); *Wilson v. Kelkhoff,* 86 F.3d 1438 (7th Cir.1996) (members of prisoner review board functioning in quasi-judicial capacity in connection with revocation hearing granted absolute immunity even for procedural activities preliminary to their actual decisionmaking); *Anton v. Getty,* 78 F.3d 393 (8th Cir.1996) (functions of parole officers whose recommendations formed basis of decision to deny release on parole warrant absolute immunity); *Davis v. Bayless,* 70 F.3d 367 (5th Cir.1995) (granting derivative absolute judicial immunity to court-appointed receiver); *Hulsey v. Owens,* 63 F.3d 354 (5th Cir.1995) (parole board officials eligible for absolute immunity respecting essentially judicial decisions made in course of parole revocation hearing); *Bush v. Rauch,* 38 F.3d 842 (6th Cir.1994) (probate court administrator eligible for quasi-judicial absolute immunity in connection with preparation of an assessment of a juvenile pursuant to order of a judicial referee); *White v. Armontrout,* 29 F.3d 357 (8th Cir. 1994) (extradition officer performed duties of a quasi-judicial nature in administering

extradition requests and issuing rendition warrants, and therefore entitled to absolute immunity with respect to those activities). *But see Cleavinger v. Saxner,* 474 U.S. 193, 206, 106 S.Ct. 496, 503, 88 L.Ed.2d 507 (1985) (members of a prison disciplinary committee entitled only to qualified immunity even though they informally adjudicate. The Court observed that the committee members are prison employees rather than professional hearing officers and often make credibility determinations between inmates and fellow employees, "a relationship hardly ... conducive to a truly adjudicatory performance." *Id.* at 203–04, 106 S.Ct. at 502.) *See also Tulloch v. Coughlin,* 50 F.3d 114 (2d Cir.1995) (prison disciplinary officer eligible only for qualified immunity where hearing informal and thus not classically "adjudicative").

8. *Supreme Court of Va. v. Consumers Union,* 446 U.S. 719, 100 S.Ct. 1967, 64 L.Ed.2d 641 (1980). A judge who ordered the handcuffing of a courthouse sandwich seller for purveying "putrid" coffee enjoyed no immunity from damages liability since the conduct fell outside any aspect of the process of judging. *Zarcone v. Perry,* 572 F.2d 52 (2d Cir.1978).

9. *Stump v. Sparkman,* 435 U.S. 349, 98 S.Ct. 1099, 55 L.Ed.2d 331 (1978) (judge immune from liability for having approved a parent's petition seeking the sterilization of a child without affording the child's constitutionally required minimum rights of representation and hearing). *See Brandley v. Keeshan,* 64 F.3d 196 (5th Cir.1995).

intended to distinguish immunized judicial acts—those that are merely "in excess of" authority—and unprotected conduct undertaken without even colorable jurisdiction. Falling in the former category would be a criminal court judge's conviction of a defendant for a non-existent crime; falling in the latter would be the trying of a criminal case by a probate judge.[10] Egregiousness of error, in other words, does not suffice to forfeit the immunity.[11] That requires an act not even arguably falling within the formal description of the bounds of office.

As recent decisions of the Supreme Court attest, the functional characterization process for prosecutors proceeds case by case.[12] Witnesses, too, enjoy absolute immunity from liability for their testimony in

---

10. *Id.* (quoting *Bradley v. Fisher,* 80 U.S. (13 Wall.) 335, 351, 20 L.Ed. 646 (1872)). Similarly, a municipal judge who lacked the authority to issue an arrest warrant in an effort to enforce a judgment of conviction issued by a circuit court was found to have acted only in excess of jurisdiction, not in its complete absence. *Duty v. City of Springdale, Ark.,* 42 F.3d 460 (8th Cir.1994). This "no colorable claim of jurisdiction" theory has recently been applied to deny absolute prosecutorial immunity. *Doe v. Phillips,* 81 F.3d 1204 (2d Cir.1996) (prosecutor's demand that criminal suspect swear to her innocence on a bible in a church held manifestly outside prosecutorial realm).

11. *Stump v. Sparkman,* 435 U.S. 349, 357, 98 S.Ct. 1099, 1105, 55 L.Ed.2d 331 (1978) (citing *Bradley, supra*). *But see Archie v. Lanier,* 95 F.3d 438 (6th Cir.1996) (stalking or sexually assaulting cannot constitute "judicial acts" eligible for absolute immunity even if directed at courthouse personnel or a litigant).

12. *See Burns v. Reed, supra* note 5, 500 U.S. at 492–498, 111 S.Ct. at 1942–45 (holding that the prosecutor's advice to police that they could interview a suspect under hypnosis relates to the prosecutor's investigative role and is not sufficiently connected to the judicial process to warrant absolute immunity); *Buckley v. Fitzsimmons,* 509 U.S. 259, 113 S.Ct. 2606, 125 L.Ed.2d 209 (1993) (prosecutor cannot claim absolute immunity concerning his alleged fabrication of evidence during preliminary criminal investigation or his allegedly false statements at press conference announcing indictment, since neither function concerned his role as an advocate; these "investigative" activities were more analogous to police work and accordingly eligible at most only for qualified immunity).

But in *Burns* the prosecutor was held absolutely immune with respect to his initiating proceedings to obtain a search warrant and advocating positions to secure that warrant during a probable cause hearing. On the other hand, a prosecutor was eligible only for qualified, not absolute immunity for work supporting an arrest warrant— a function considered investigatory instead of advocative. *Fletcher v. Kalina,* 93 F.3d 653 (9th Cir.1996). Another prosecutor received only qualified immunity with respect to his investigation of a child's sexual abuse charges and his advice to police that probable cause existed to arrest the parent. These acts were treated as investigatory, and hence ineligible for the defense, rather than as immunized advocacy. *Hill v. City of New York,* 45 F.3d 653 (2d Cir.1995). *See also Moore v. Valder,* 65 F.3d 189 (D.C.Cir. 1995) ("advocatory" decisions to prosecute and allegedly manipulate evidence absolutely immune; "investigatory" acts of allegedly intimidating and coercing witnesses and leaking grand jury testimony to third parties warrant only qualified immunity). *Ross Yordy Constr. Co. v. Naylor,* 55 F.3d 285 (7th Cir.1995) (decisions to abandon prosecution triggers absolute immunity). And a state prosecutor who countermanded a judge's direction that a court reporter prepare a criminal trial transcript for use in a habeas proceeding was similarly held unprotected by absolute immunity, the challenged conduct being regarded as far removed from the core prosecutorial functions of bringing charges and presenting evidence. *Gagan v. Norton,* 35 F.3d 1473 (10th Cir.1994), *cert. denied,* ___ U.S. ___, 115 S.Ct. 1175, 130 L.Ed.2d 1128 (1995). Similarly, state district attorneys who allegedly delayed a prisoner's retransfer to Federal custody for several weeks *after* the formal conclusion of state criminal proceedings could claim only qualified, not absolute immunity. *Pinaud v. County of Suffolk,* 52 F.3d 1139 (2d Cir.1995).

adversarial hearings, even when the testimony is allegedly perjured.[13] Of course conduct ineligible for absolute immunity may nevertheless warrant qualified immunity.[14]

Legislators enjoy the broadest generally available immunity of all: an absolute immunity not only from damages but also from declaratory and injunctive relief.[15] As with the absolute immunity of judges and prosecutors, this immunity shields only the "legislative functions" of legislators [16] or, occasionally, others.[17] The Supreme Court has extended this immunity to state [18] and regional [19] legislative functions, and the circuits seem agreed that county, city, and other local legislators are eligible as well.[20] But the circuits have had difficulty applying the

13. *Moore v. McDonald*, 30 F.3d 616 (5th Cir.1994).

14. This is vividly illustrated by the decision of the Seventh Circuit on remand from *Burns v. Reed*, discussed in note 12, *supra.* Although the Supreme Court had denied absolute immunity, the Seventh Circuit granted a prosecutor qualified immunity for asking a suspect to submit to hypnosis because courts were then divided about the admissibility of confessions from hypnotized suspects. *Burns v. Reed*, 44 F.3d 524 (7th Cir.1995). The circuits have continued to extend absolute immunity to prosecutors' acts integrally related to the decision whether to initiate prosecution and thereafter in pursuing it, conferring only qualified immunity, however, to advice or conduct part and parcel of preliminary investigation. *Ross Yordy Constr. Co. v. Naylor*, 55 F.3d 285 (7th Cir.), *cert. denied,* ___ U.S. ___, 116 S.Ct. 338, 133 L.Ed.2d 236 (1995); *Hill v. City of New York*, 45 F.3d 653 (2d Cir.1995). The Second Circuit has recently pioneered what will probably prove a rare, alternative circumstance that forfeits absolute immunity. It held that conduct otherwise "prosecutorial" in function is not eligible for absolute immunity if manifestly beyond the outer bounds of a prosecutor's authority or jurisdiction, by analogy to *Stump v. Sparkman*, 435 U.S. 349, 98 S.Ct. 1099, 55 L.Ed.2d 331 (1978), discussed *supra* note 9. *Doe v. Phillips*, 81 F.3d 1204 (2d Cir.1996) (prosecutor compelled suspect to swear to her innocence on a bible in church as a condition of dismissal of charges against her).

15. *See Supreme Court of Va. v. Consumers Union, Inc., supra* note 4, at 730–34, 100 S.Ct. at 1973–1976.

16. *See Hafer v. Melo, supra* note 5, at 27–31, 112 S.Ct. at 363–64; *Burns v. Reed, supra* note 5; *Harlow v. Fitzgerald, supra* § 2.1, note 9, at 807, 102 S.Ct. at 2732. *Cf. Tower v. Glover*, 467 U.S. 914, 920, 104 S.Ct. 2820, 2824, 81 L.Ed.2d 758 (1984): "The Court has recognized absolute § 1983 immunity for legislators acting with their legislative roles...." (citations omitted).

But legislators' political party functions are "administrative" in nature and accordingly not eligible for absolute immunity. *Chateaubriand v. Gaspard*, 97 F.3d 1218 (9th Cir.1996).

17. *Supreme Court of Va. v. Consumers Union, Inc., supra* note 4, at 731, 100 S.Ct. at 1974 (judges enjoy legislative immunity with respect to their role in promulgating rules of conduct for lawyers); *Romero–Barcelo v. Hernandez–Agosto*, 75 F.3d 23 (1st Cir.1996) (legislative committee counsel entitled to absolute immunity concerning conduct during committee hearings); *Redwood Village Partnership v. Graham*, 26 F.3d 839 (8th Cir.) (state agency employees enjoy legislative immunity with respect to promulgation of health care rules), *cert. denied* ___ U.S. ___, 115 S.Ct. 423, 130 L.Ed.2d 337 (1994).

18. *Tenney v. Brandhove*, 341 U.S. 367, 71 S.Ct. 783, 95 L.Ed. 1019 (1951). *See Billingsley v. St. Louis County*, 70 F.3d 61 (8th Cir.1995) (council member receives only qualified immunity in connection with termination of qualified employee); *Roberson v. Mullins*, 29 F.3d 132 (4th Cir.1994) (no absolute legislative immunity respecting county board members' discharge of employee).

19. *Lake Country Estates, Inc. v. Tahoe Regional Planning Agency*, 440 U.S. 391, 99 S.Ct. 1171, 59 L.Ed.2d 401 (1979).

20. *See e.g., Trevino By and Through Cruz v. Gates*, 23 F.3d 1480 (9th Cir.), *cert. denied,* ___ U.S. ___, 115 S.Ct. 327, 130 L.Ed.2d 286 (1994); *Executive 100, Inc. v. Martin County*, 922 F.2d 1536, 1539 (11th Cir.), *cert. denied*, 502 U.S. 810, 112 S.Ct. 55, 116 L.Ed.2d 32 (1991); *Cutting v. Muzzey*, 724 F.2d 259 (1st Cir.1984); *Kuzinich*

required functional analysis of "legislative" acts. For example, at least one circuit appears to hold that legislators perform legislative functions whenever the form of their conduct replicates the traditional way in which legislative bodies act: "voting, debate and reacting to public opinion are manifestly in furtherance of legislative duties." [21] Others look more searchingly at the substance of the particular challenged act, distinguishing "legislative" decisions that implicate policy and have general application from merely "ad hoc," "administrative" or "enforcement" decisions that target one or a few citizens or apply policy previously promulgated. [22] Ancillary, preliminary tasks necessary to the exercise of legislative functions have also served to confer immunity on legislative officials [23]; and that immunity may extend derivatively to subordinate officials whose work is related to the legislative task. [24]

This problem has proved particularly vexing with respect to the land-use decisions of local governments and zoning boards. Several circuit courts characterize zoning or building permit decisions as mere executive enforcement activity that warrants only qualified, not absolute immunity whenever the local legislature or board (1) violates its own procedures [25] or applicable zoning ordinance provisions; [26] (2) enforces existing zoning rules in a way that relates specifically to particular individuals or has an impact that singles them out for different treatment; [27] or (3) makes even traditional "legislative" decisions of general

v. Santa Clara County, 689 F.2d 1345, 1349 (9th Cir.1982); Hernandez v. City of Lafayette, 643 F.2d 1188, 1193 (5th Cir.1981), cert. denied, 455 U.S. 907, 102 S.Ct. 1251, 71 L.Ed.2d 444 (1982); Gorman Towers, Inc. v. Bogoslavsky, 626 F.2d 607 (8th Cir. 1980).

21. DeSisto College, Inc. v. Line, 888 F.2d 755, 765 (11th Cir.1989), cert. denied, 495 U.S. 952, 110 S.Ct. 2219, 109 L.Ed.2d 544 (1990) (quoted in Brown v. Crawford County, 960 F.2d 1002, 1011 (11th Cir. 1992)). However in Smith v. Lomax, 45 F.3d 402 (11th Cir.1995), the same court treated a county governing body's decision to replace its clerk, allegedly for racial reasons, as "administrative" rather than legislative. The court rejected the argument that this personnel issue acquired a protected, legislative character merely because the decision was reached as the result of a formal vote by the legislative body.

22. See, e.g., Trevino By and Through Cruz, supra note 20 (council members who voted to pay a punitive damages award pursuant to statutory authority perform an administrative, not a legislative function, and hence are ineligible for absolute immunity); Haskell v. Washington Township, 864 F.2d 1266 (6th Cir.1988); Cinevision Corp. v. City of Burbank, 745 F.2d 560, 580 (9th Cir.1984), cert. denied, 471 U.S. 1054, 105 S.Ct. 2115, 85 L.Ed.2d 480 (1985); Cut-

ting v. Muzzey, supra note 20; Scott v. Greenville County, 716 F.2d 1409 (4th Cir. 1983).

23. National Ass'n of Social Workers v. Harwood, 69 F.3d 622 (1st Cir.1995) (state representatives absolutely immune concerning rule excluding certain lobbyists from vicinity of legislative deliberations); Ellis v. Coffee County Bd. of Registrars, 981 F.2d 1185 (11th Cir.1993) (county commissioners performed legislative function in investigating the eligibility vel non of listed electors, because they needed that information to perform the concededly legislative function of delineating precinct lines).

24. Id. (conferring legislative immunity on county attorney who served as legal advisor to legislators performing legislative function, because the efficient operation of contemporary government necessitates adjuncts performing responsibilities traditionally executed by the legislators).

25. Donivan v. Dallastown Borough, 835 F.2d 486, 488–89 (3d Cir.1987), cert. denied sub nom. McKinsey v. Donivan, 485 U.S. 1035, 108 S.Ct. 1596, 99 L.Ed.2d 910 (1988).

26. Scott v. Greenville County, supra note 22.

27. Bateson v. Geisse, 857 F.2d 1300, 1304 (9th Cir.1988) (no absolute immunity

application in bad faith, corruptly, or in furtherance of personal rather than public interests.[28] The Eleventh Circuit, however, held in *Brown v. Crawford County, Ga.*[29] that any kind of zoning or land use decision, including action that voids a prior approval of a development plan, is "normally ... a legislative function,"[30] despite its acknowledgement that an act can properly be characterized as legislative only when it has "a policymaking function and general application."[31]

The key to the Eleventh Circuit's approach appears to be its heavy reliance on the form of the local government's decision: a vote.[32] But other circuits have concluded that the fact that the decision is in the form of a legislative body's vote does not necessarily make that decision "legislative" for purposes of absolute immunity.[33] Certainly absolute immunity is not available merely because the action taken was within the scope of the legislators' authority and involved the exercise of a necessary governmental function.[34] The Eleventh Circuit's refusal to look at the motivations of the defendants[35] seems consistent with the traditional purposes of any absolute immunity.[36] To do so would require preliminary fact-based proceedings the burden of which would defeat the objective of relieving the official from the rigors of litigation. But the Court's refusal in *Brown* to examine the exceptional and perhaps unique impact of a building permit moratorium on a single citizen or the alleged irregularity of the county's proceedings gives excessive force to its presumption that a vote signifies a "legislative" act.[37] A recent decision of another circuit seems to point the other way. Although county council members were absolutely immune with respect to a commercial rezoning that the court considered legislative in character, they were

for denying building permits because those do not apply to the general community or involve formulation of public policy); *Cutting v. Muzzey, supra* note 20 (plaintiff's subdivision approval conditioned on his completing a road); *Scott, supra* note 22 (county council placed moratorium on building permit in response to citizens' protests over plaintiff's planned multi-family dwellings).

28. *Haskell, supra* note 22. *See also Scott, supra* note 22, at 1423 (court concurred with plaintiff's allegation that council treated his application with a "lack of impartiality" and a "departure from established practice and applicable law.")

29. 960 F.2d 1002 (11th Cir.1992).

30. *Brown, supra* note 21, at 1012 (citing *Baytree of Inverrary Realty Partners v. City of Lauderhill*, 873 F.2d 1407, 1409 (11th Cir.1989)).

31. *Brown, supra* note 21, at 1011 (citing *Crymes v. DeKalb County*, 923 F.2d 1482, 1485 (11th Cir.1991)).

32. *Brown, supra* note 21, at 1011, 1012.

33. *Cinevision, supra* note 22, at 580. The Eleventh Circuit, outside the zoning context, has subsequently disclaimed that the mere fact that a county government's decision is reached as the result of a vote renders that decision "legislative" in character for purposes of absolute immunity. *Smith v. Lomax,* 45 F.3d 402 (11th Cir. 1995).

34. *Hafer v. Melo, supra* note 5, 502 U.S. at 27, 112 S.Ct. at 363.

35. "Even if Brown could prove conspiracy or bad faith, an unworthy purpose does not preclude absolute immunity to legislators acting in their legislative capacity." *Brown, supra* note 21, at 1012.

36. *See, e.g., Tenney, supra* note 18, at 377, 71 S.Ct. at 788; *see Wood v. Strickland*, 420 U.S. 308, 317, 95 S.Ct. 992, 998, 43 L.Ed.2d 214 (1975) (discussion of absolute immunity in a decision raising the issue of qualified immunity).

37. In appraising this criticism of the opinion in *Brown*, the reader should understand that the author was co-counsel on appeal for the unsuccessful developer plaintiff.

accorded only qualified immunity with respect to enactment of an ordinance that voided a previously approved plan of development.[38]

Apart from absolute legislative immunity, the other immunities, qualified or absolute, ordinarily insulate only against damages.[39] Relatively few plaintiffs who sue individual government officials will attain full or even meaningful relief from prospective remedies alone. And the attempt to secure injunctive or declaratory relief is likely to encounter special standing, abstention, or comity-driven obstacles to federal intervention that may preclude litigation in federal court.[40]

One consequence of this broad immunity for government agents is a distinctly diluted role for claims against individual defendants. In contrast to actions against government entities, there is little potential for dynamic lawmaking in § 1983 actions against individuals.

The Court's wide blanket of qualified immunity for individual defendants has a second serious consequence. The vicious official who intends to harm a citizen may be absolved of any § 1983 liability. This happens either if the right the plaintiff asserts is not judicially recognized to the requisite degree of specificity, or if, despite the settled nature of the right, the factfinder concludes that the defendant could not reasonably have realized that her contemplated conduct would violate it.

§ 2.3 *Monroe* as the Basis for Modern Section 1983 Actions

Judicial dynamism has produced the asymmetric shape of § 1983 actions against individuals and entities. In the past thirty years, in particular, there have been bursts of expansion, followed by equally striking contractions.

By its terms, § 1983 liability attaches to "[e]very person" who causes the loss of rights secured by the Constitution and laws of the United States. Thus an individual state actor is unexceptionally within

---

38. *Acierno v. Cloutier,* ___ F.3d ___, 1994 WL 319783 (3d Cir.), *rehearing granted en banc and vacated on other grounds,* 40 F.3d 597 (3d Cir.1994).

39. *See Pulliam v. Allen,* 466 U.S. 522, 541–44, 104 S.Ct. 1970, 1980–1983, 80 L.Ed.2d 565 (1984) (holding that judges, absolutely immune from damages, are subject to injunctive relief and attorneys' fees); *cf. McCullough v. Horton,* 69 F.3d 918 (8th Cir.1995) (absolute immunity of court clerk does not extend to equitable relief).

40. *See, e.g., City of Los Angeles v. Lyons,* 461 U.S. 95, 111, 103 S.Ct. 1660, 1670, 75 L.Ed.2d 675 (1983) (holding that an individual had no standing to request injunctive relief from police use of chokeholds because he was not in immediate danger of sustaining another direct injury); *Rizzo v. Goode,* 423 U.S. 362, 371–73, 96 S.Ct. 598, 604–605, 46 L.Ed.2d 561 (1976)

(stating that individuals had no standing to request an injunction compelling the police to adopt new procedures where their alleged injury was too speculative to satisfy Article III's "case or controversy" requirement); *Younger v. Harris,* 401 U.S. 37, 49, 54, 91 S.Ct. 746, 753, 755, 27 L.Ed.2d 669 (1971) (holding that federal court in § 1983 action may not enjoin pending state criminal proceeding in which the federal issue could be raised as a defense, and should dismiss); *Railroad Comm'n of Tex. v. Pullman Co.,* 312 U.S. 496, 501, 61 S.Ct. 643, 645, 85 L.Ed. 971 (1941) (holding that federal court § 1983 action for injunction against state-sanctioned conduct should be stayed to enable a state tribunal to interpret unsettled state law if a narrowing interpretation might obviate the need to decide a federal question).

the statute's reach. It is not altogether surprising, therefore, that the Court in *Monroe v. Pape*[1] would carve out an expansive prima facie case in actions against such defendants. *Monroe* marks the modern reemergence of § 1983 from 90 years of relative slumber. It is also the progenitor of the subsequent torrent of § 1983 litigation and as such the ultimate source of the Court's reactive retrenchment.

The invasion of the Monroes' home by Chicago's finest in violation of the Fourth Amendment and the laws of Illinois furnished the occasion for the Court to construe the § 1983 requirement that the defendant inflict the injury "under color of" state law. The Court linked the "under color of" requirement to the long-settled interpretation of state action under the Fourteenth Amendment,[2] which § 1983 was passed to enforce.[3] Justice Douglas' opinion for the Court concluded that § 1983 reaches federally unlawful conduct carried out by individual defendants under the badge of or clothed in state authority, irrespective of state approval.[4] The Court so decided despite indications that state law could provide relief at least as complete as federal law and absent any allegation that the state had discriminatorily denied such relief on other occasions.[5] The special nature of the violation also had implications for remedy and forum. "It is no answer," Justice Douglas wrote, "that the State has a law which if enforced would give relief. The federal remedy is supplementary to the state remedy, and the latter need not be first sought and refused before the federal one is invoked."[6]

§ 2.3

1. 365 U.S. 167, 81 S.Ct. 473, 5 L.Ed.2d 492 (1961), *overruled on a different issue by Monell v. Department of Social Servs.*, 436 U.S. 658, 98 S.Ct. 2018, 56 L.Ed.2d 611 (1978).

2. *See Home Tel. & Tel. Co. v. City of Los Angeles*, 227 U.S. 278, 287–94, 33 S.Ct. 312, 315–317, 57 L.Ed. 510 (1913). The municipal defendant argued in *Home Tel.* that a claim alleging it had imposed confiscatory telephone rates in violation of due process failed for want of state action because no state court had yet sustained the rate under the state's own due process clause. Only when a state court so ruled, defendant's counsel urged, would state authorization occur, and only then would there be the state action requisite for a Fourteenth Amendment violation. *See id.* at 282, 33 S.Ct. at 313; *see also The Civil Rights Cases*, 109 U.S. 3, 3 S.Ct. 18, 27 L.Ed. 835 (1883) (restricting the reach of the Fourteenth Amendment to acts under state authority). The Court held to the contrary that the Fourteenth Amendment could be violated either when the state in its sovereign capacity commits acts that conflict with the amendment, or simply when "state powers [are] abused by those who possessed them." *Home Tel., supra* at 288, 33 S.Ct. at 315. It is now settled that

Fourteenth Amendment constructions of "state action" are authoritative of § 1983's "under color of" language as well. *See Lugar v. Edmondson Oil Co.*, 457 U.S. 922, 935, 102 S.Ct. 2744, 2752, 73 L.Ed.2d 482 (1982). *See* fuller discussion of the Constitution's "state action" and statutory "under color of" requirements *infra* Part B.

3. *See Monroe, supra* note 1, at 171, 81 S.Ct. at 475 (holding that the purpose of the statute is, as its title states, "to enforce the Provisions of the Fourteenth Amendment").

4. *See id.* at 183–85, 81 S.Ct. at 482–483.

5. Justice Frankfurter pointed out that Illinois decisions had found similar police intrusions unlawful and that the complaint lacked concrete allegations of Illinois's unwillingness to enforce those decisions. *See id.* at 224–25 & nn.33–34 (Frankfurter, J., dissenting in part).

6. *Id.* at 183, 81 S.Ct. at 482. The Court found support for its decision in two opinions that had examined the criminal counterpart to § 1983. *See Screws v. United States*, 325 U.S. 91, 108, 65 S.Ct. 1031, 1038, 89 L.Ed. 1495 (1945); *United States v. Classic*, 313 U.S. 299, 326–27 & n. 10, 61 S.Ct. 1031, 1043 & n. 10, 85 L.Ed. 1368

The apparent availability of a remedy under Illinois law, however, casts doubt on whether any of the purposes of § 1983 identified by the majority supports the *Monroe* result. Justice Douglas wrote that the legislation had "three main aims": to override certain state laws; to provide a federal remedy not provided by state law; and to provide such a remedy "where the state remedy, though adequate in theory, was not available in practice."[7] None of these purposes would have been advanced by upholding the legal sufficiency of Monroe's claim.

The better rationale appears in Justice Harlan's concurrence, drawn from the "flavor of the legislative history." He wrote that Congress sought to provide a supplementary remedy because "deprivation of a constitutional right is significantly different from and more serious than a violation of a state right and therefore deserves a different remedy even though the same act may constitute both a state tort and the deprivation of a constitutional right."[8]

B. CONDUCT "UNDER COLOR OF STATE LAW" VERSUS CONSTITUTIONAL "STATE ACTION"

§ 2.4 In General

42 U.S.C.A. § 1983 provides in material part:

The district courts shall have original jurisdiction of any civil action authorized by law to be commenced by any person: To redress the deprivation, *under color of any State law*, statute, ordinance, regulation, custom or usage, of any *right*, privilege or immunity *secured by the Constitution* of the United States or by any Act of Congress providing for equal rights of citizens or of all persons within the jurisdiction of the United States (emphasis added).

Section 1983 requires, independent of the "under color of" requirement, a predicate violation of a federal statute or a constitutional violation.[1] In turn, most § 1983 claims are predicated on violations of the federal constitution, rather than statutory rights; and almost all constitutional violations (save Thirteenth Amendment freedom from involuntary servitude[2] and the right to interstate travel,[3] both of which are enforceable

---

(1941). In both cases, individuals were held criminally liable for conduct that violated not only federal law, but state law as well.

7. *Monroe, supra* note 1, at 173–74, 81 S.Ct. at 477.

8. *Id.* at 196, 81 S.Ct. at 488 (Harlan, J., concurring).

§ 2.4

1. *Siegert v. Gilley,* 500 U.S. 226, 232–233, 111 S.Ct. 1789, 1793–1794, 114 L.Ed.2d 277 (1991).

2. *Bray v. Alexandria Women's Health Clinic,* 506 U.S. 263, 278, 113 S.Ct. 753, 764, 122 L.Ed.2d 34 (1993) (*citing United States v. Kozminski,* 487 U.S. 931, 942, 108 S.Ct. 2751, 2759, 101 L.Ed.2d 788 (1988)).

3. *Id.* (*citing United States v. Guest,* 383 U.S. 745, 759 n. 17, 86 S.Ct. 1170, 1179 n. 17, 16 L.Ed.2d 239 (1966)).

against purely private actors) depend on Fourteenth Amendment "state action." The plaintiff must therefore usually prove not only that the defendant's conduct is "under color of state law" but also that it represents Fourteenth Amendment "state action." [4] Are these requirements identical, or merely substantially overlapping?

Library References:

> C.J.S. Civil Rights §§ 19, 248.
> West's Key No. Digests, Civil Rights ☞196.

§ 2.5 "Under Color of State Law" and "State Action" Compared

The Fourteenth Amendment of the United States Constitution provides:

> All persons born or naturalized in the United States, and subject to the jurisdiction thereof, are citizens of the United States and of the State wherein they reside. *No State* shall make or enforce any law which shall abridge the privileges or immunities of citizens of the United states; nor shall any State deprive any person of life, liberty, or property, without due process of law; nor deny to any person within its jurisdiction the equal protection of the laws (emphasis added).

This text and the Amendment's primary focus on halting state-sanctioned suppression of newly-freed slaves during Reconstruction has long been read to mean that the Fourteenth Amendment reaches only action fairly attributable to government rather than purely private conduct.[1]

When the defendant is a state, county or municipality itself, there is little doubt about state action. Similarly, federal courts, usually relying on the state's statutory and administrative characterizations, have held a wide variety of boards, authorities, and other public or quasi-public entities to be Fourteenth Amendment state actors.[2] But ultimately the characterization is a matter for federal law,[3] so state law, while often persuasive, is not controlling.[4] Thus a federal court has held that a hospital authority is a Fourteenth Amendment state actor subject to

---

4. *See Burch v. Apalachee Community Mental Health Servs., Inc.,* 840 F.2d 797, 802–803 (11th Cir.1988), *affirmed sub nom. Zinermon v. Burch,* 494 U.S. 113, 110 S.Ct. 975, 108 L.Ed.2d 100 (1990).

§ 2.5

1. *The Civil Rights Cases,* 109 U.S. 3, 3 S.Ct. 18, 27 L.Ed. 835 (1883). But "state action" is not required for violations of the Thirteenth Amendment. *Id.* at 20–21, 3 S.Ct. at 28–29.

2. *See, e.g., Krynicky v. University of Pittsburgh,* 742 F.2d 94 (3d Cir.1984), *cert. denied,* 471 U.S. 1015, 105 S.Ct. 2018, 85 L.Ed.2d 300 (1985); *Braden v. University of Pittsburgh,* 552 F.2d 948 (3d Cir.1977).

This question is closely related to questions concerning the status of subordinate entities as organs of a state for purposes of Eleventh Amendment immunity from damages claims in federal courts. *See* the Procedure chapter for more detail concerning the factors used in characterizing these entities.

3. *See Miller–Davis Co. v. Illinois State Toll Highway Auth.,* 567 F.2d 323, 330 (7th Cir.1977).

4. *Tuveson v. Florida Governor's Council on Indian Affairs,* 734 F.2d 730, 732 (11th Cir.1984).

§ 1983 despite a state supreme court decision denying the authority sovereign immunity under state law because it was not "an agency or department of the state."[5] But the decision by a private physician to admit a patient to a private hospital does not become state action even when the authority to admit derives from the state's involuntary commitment statute.[6]

Beginning with *Home Telephone & Telegraph Co. v. City of Los Angeles*,[7] the Supreme Court made plain that Fourteenth Amendment "state action" can be found even when its immediate agent acts in violation of state law—that is, when the defendant acts contrary to state policy.[8] Much later, in *Shelley v. Kraemer*,[9] the Court held that "state action" under the Fourteenth Amendment may (in limited circumstances) exist in cases where a *private* individual enlists the "coercive power" of the State to further private actions.

The Court has similarly defined the § 1983 "under color of state law" requirement. Construing a criminal counterpart to § 1983, the Supreme Court held that a person acts "under color" of state law when he exercises power "possessed by virtue of state law and made possible only because the wrongdoer is clothed with the authority of state law."[10] Then, in *Monroe v. Pape*[11], the Court exponentially expanded the class of potential defendants liable under § 1983. *Monroe* established, and it is now settled,[12] that even the defendant who abuses the power or position he receives from the state is acting "under color of" state law.

Moreover, the statutory authority to punish state agents' unconstitutional conduct even when that conduct transgresses the state's own rules or policies is itself constitutional: "There can be no doubt . . . that Congress has the power to enforce provisions of the Fourteenth Amendment against those who carry a badge of authority of a State and represent it in some capacity. . . ."[13] Combined with *Shelley*, *Monroe* led to an almost immediate dramatic increase in the number of § 1983 cases on the federal docket.

Since *Monroe*, the Court has further clarified, in *United States v. Price*[14] and *Lugar v. Edmondson Oil Co.*,[15] that if the plaintiff can show

5. *Burgess v. Marchwinski*, No. 93–95–3 (M.D.Ga.1994). The state supreme court decision did acknowledge, however, that the authority was "an instrumentality" of state government, obviously a critical factor in the federal law evaluation of state actor status.

6. *Ellison v. Garbarino*, 48 F.3d 192 (6th Cir.1995).

7. 227 U.S. 278, 33 S.Ct. 312, 57 L.Ed. 510 (1913).

8. *Id.* at 287–294, 33 S.Ct. at 315–317.

9. 334 U.S. 1, 68 S.Ct. 836, 92 L.Ed. 1161 (1948).

10. *United States v. Classic*, 313 U.S. 299, 61 S.Ct. 1031, 85 L.Ed. 1368 (1941)

construing § 20 of the Criminal Code, now 18 U.S.C.A. § 242 (as amended, 1988).

11. 365 U.S. 167, 81 S.Ct. 473, 5 L.Ed.2d 492 (1961), *overruled on a different issue by Monell v. Department of Social Servs.*, 436 U.S. 658, 98 S.Ct. 2018, 56 L.Ed.2d 611 (1978).

12. *West v. Atkins*, 487 U.S. 42, 108 S.Ct. 2250, 101 L.Ed.2d 40 (1988).

13. *Monroe*, 365 U.S. at 171, 81 S.Ct. at 475.

14. 383 U.S. 787, 86 S.Ct. 1152, 16 L.Ed.2d 267 (1966).

15. 457 U.S. 922, 102 S.Ct. 2744, 73 L.Ed.2d 482 (1982).

Fourteenth Amendment "state action," she will at the same time satisfy the "under color of" requirement of § 1983. But the reverse is not necessarily true, as the following discussion illustrates.

Library References:

C.J.S. Civil Rights §§ 19, 248.
West's Key No. Digests, Civil Rights ⬿196.

§ 2.6 When Is There Fourteenth Amendment "State Action" With Regard to Private Party Defendants

When the conduct of a private party causes a violation of a plaintiff's constitutional rights, the plaintiff must be able to show "state action" to recover under the Fourteenth Amendment. The typical state action issue is presented when "a private party has taken the decisive step" that caused the plaintiff's harm "and the question is whether the state was sufficiently involved to treat that decisive conduct as state action." [1] From the modern cases at least [2] three Fourteenth Amendment "state action" tests may be distilled.[3]

a. The Public Function Test

First, the plaintiff might be able to show that the private entity, in connection with the allegedly unconstitutional conduct, carried out an "exclusive" "public function." The "public function" test is quite narrow and rarely satisfied. It applies only where a private actor undertakes a function "traditionally the exclusive prerogative of the state." [4] The handful of cases that have met the test involve such activities as conducting an election,[5] running a company-operated town,[6] and providing fire protection or operating a municipal park.[7] Operating

---

§ 2.6

1. *National Collegiate Athletic Ass'n v. Tarkanian*, 488 U.S. 179, 192, 109 S.Ct. 454, 462, 102 L.Ed.2d 469 (1988).

2. Another circuit divides one of the tests, nexus/joint participant, into two separate tests, but does not refer separately to a government compulsion test. *See, e.g., McKeesport Hosp. v. Accreditation Council for Graduate Medical Educ.*, 24 F.3d 519 (3d Cir.1994). Conceivably a court might separately distinguish as many as five alternative tests for state action: governmental function, governmental compulsion, joint participant, nexus, and delegation.

3. *See, e.g., National Broadcasting Co., Inc. v. Communications Workers of America, AFL–CIO*, 860 F.2d 1022, 1026 (11th Cir.1988) (identifying the public function, state compulsion, and nexus/joint action tests).

4. *See Jackson v. Metropolitan Edison Company*, 419 U.S. 345, 353, 95 S.Ct. 449,

455, 42 L.Ed.2d 477 (1974). It has been argued that a more recent reference to this test eliminated the requirement of exclusivity; *and McKeesport Hosp. v. Accreditation Council for Graduate Medical Educ., supra* note 2 (Becker, J., concurring in judgment) (quoting *Edmonson v. Leesville Concrete Co.*, 500 U.S. 614, 640, 111 S.Ct. 2077, 2093, 114 L.Ed.2d 660 (1991)).

5. *Nixon v. Condon*, 286 U.S. 73, 52 S.Ct. 484, 76 L.Ed. 984 (1932); *Terry v. Adams*, 345 U.S. 461, 73 S.Ct. 809, 97 L.Ed. 1152 (1953).

6. *Marsh v. Alabama*, 326 U.S. 501, 66 S.Ct. 276, 90 L.Ed. 265 (1946).

7. *Mark v. Borough of Hatboro*, 51 F.3d 1137 (3d Cir.1995) (volunteer fire company that received government funds); *Evans v. Newton*, 382 U.S. 296, 86 S.Ct. 486, 15 L.Ed.2d 373 (1966) (private estate ran public park).

a private hospital does not fall within this test even if defendants involuntarily admit mentally disturbed patients pursuant to a state statute.[8] Nor does providing private security services for city-owned property or holding an annual festival on public property, even pursuant to a city's permit.[9] District courts are split as to whether a private party that operates correctional facilities under contract is performing an exclusive public function, although the decisions according these operators qualified immunity apparently assume state action.[10]

b. *The State Compulsion Test*

This test, also rarely met, subjects the private actor to liability if the government has coerced the allegedly unconstitutional conduct, or at least provided overwhelming encouragement tantamount to coercion. This test was recently found not satisfied by the relationship between a state board of medicine and the private accreditation council with which it conducted joint inspections of a hospital's graduate residency program. Although Pennsylvania statutes contemplated that the state Board would rely on the accrediting judgments of the accreditation council, the relationship was defined in regulations as one of "comity"[11], and since the Board did not dictate or influence the council's accreditation judgments, no state action was found.[12] Even when a private party acts under regulatory pressure[13] or to resolve litigation asserting noncompli-

---

8. *Rockwell v. Cape Cod Hosp.*, 26 F.3d 254 (1st Cir.1994); *Harvey v. Harvey*, 949 F.2d 1127 (11th Cir.1992).

9. *Wade v. Byles*, 83 F.3d 902 (7th Cir. 1996) (private security guard at city housing authority not performing traditionally exclusive public function); *United Auto Workers, Local No. 5285 v. Gaston Festivals, Inc.*, 43 F.3d 902 (4th Cir.1995) (festival case). The court in *Gaston* pointed out that fairs and festivals have been traditionally carried out mostly by private organizations, and that even the ordinary operation of a park for recreation purposes has been held by the Supreme Court not to represent an exclusively public function. *Gaston*, citing *Flagg Brothers, Inc. v. Brooks*, 436 U.S. 149, 98 S.Ct. 1729, 56 L.Ed.2d 185 (1978). Only when a city is shown to retain actual involvement in the daily operations of a park that it transferred to private hands would there be "state action," resting more on a joint participation rather than an exclusive public function rationale. *See Evans v. Newton*, 382 U.S. 296, 86 S.Ct. 486, 15 L.Ed.2d 373 (1966). Merely permitting a festival committee to adopt and enforce its own rules during a festival does not make a municipality liable for the policies or actions of that committee. *Reinhart v. City of Brookings*, 84 F.3d 1071 (8th Cir. 1996).

10. *Compare Blumel v. Mylander*, 919 F.Supp. 423 (M.D.Fla.1996) *and Citrano v.*

Allen Correctional Ctr., 891 F.Supp. 312 (W.D.La.1995) *and Smith v. United States*, 850 F.Supp. 984 (M.D.Fla.1994) *and Tinnen v. Corrections Corp. of Am.*, 1993 WL 738121 (W.D.Tenn.1993) (finding state action) *with Lloyd v. Corrections Corp. of Am.*, 855 F.Supp. 221 (W.D.Tenn.1994) (finding no state action). One peculiar opinion implicitly determined that operating a correctional institution is an exclusive public function but nevertheless denied the private corporate defendant qualified immunity. The court reasoned that the defendant did not warrant that protection because its motivation was to protect profits rather than serve the public good. *Manis v. Corrections Corp. of Am.*, 859 F.Supp. 302 (M.D.Tenn.1994). To the same effect is *McKnight v. Rees*, 88 F.3d 417 (6th Cir.), *cert. granted* ___ U.S. ___, ___ S.Ct. ___, ___ L.Ed.2d ___, 1996 WL 514475 (1996).

11. *San Francisco Arts and Athletics, Inc. v. United States Olympic Comm.*, 483 U.S. 522, 546, 107 S.Ct. 2971, 2986, 97 L.Ed.2d 427 (1987) (citing *Blum v. Yaretsky*, 457 U.S. 991, 102 S.Ct. 2777, 73 L.Ed.2d 534 (1982)).

12. *McKeesport Hosp.*, *supra* note 2, at 30, 32 (Becker, J., concurring in judgment).

13. *Cf. Mathis v. Pacific Gas and Elec. Co.*, 75 F.3d 498 (9th Cir.1996) (pressure from federal administrative agency).

ance with state law,[14] its conduct typically falls short of state action unless it is "dictated" or "compelled" by the government.

c. The "Nexus"/"Joint Action"/"Symbiotic Relationship"/ "Intertwined" Test

This most commonly satisfied test for Fourteenth Amendment "state action" applies when "the state has so far insinuated itself into a position of interdependence" with a private party as to become a "joint participant in the enterprise." It covers a wide variety of public-private interconnections that range from the state providing the means for or accepting the benefits of the private defendant's actions, substantially financing or regulating (but not compelling) the private party's unconstitutional conduct, or simply delegating to the private party significant state power.

1. State Provides the Means

The cases involving state-provided means begin with *Shelley v. Kraemer*[15]. In *Shelley*, the Supreme Court expounded on the modern conception of Fourteenth Amendment "state action":

> [T]he principle has become firmly embedded in our constitutional law that the action inhibited by the first section of the Fourteenth Amendment is only such action as may fairly be said to be that of the States. That Amendment erects no shield against merely private conduct, however discriminatory or wrongful.[16]

Although the covenant at issue (one that prevented residents of a Missouri neighborhood from selling property to black citizens)[17] would have clearly violated the Fourteenth Amendment's Equal Protection Clause if enacted by the Missouri legislature, it was lawful as an agreement created and involving only private citizens, at least until enforcement was sought.

Some of the private parties who created the restrictive covenant did not voluntarily abide by it. When a resident attempted to sell property to a black citizen, other residents asked the courts of Missouri to block the transaction. The State of Missouri became involved through its court system.[18]

Private defendants may be liable as state actors when the state makes "available to such individuals the full coercive power of government...."[19] The Court found a "nexus" between Missouri and the private defendants because Missouri provided the private defendants with the state's coercive judicial power.[20]

14. *Logan v. Bennington College Corp.,* 72 F.3d 1017 (2d Cir.1995).

15. 334 U.S. 1, 68 S.Ct. 836, 92 L.Ed. 1161 (1948).

16. *Id.* at 13, 68 S.Ct. at 842.

17. *Id.* at 4, 68 S.Ct. at 838.

18. *Id.* at 14, 68 S.Ct. at 842.

19. *Id.* at 19, 68 S.Ct. at 845.

20. *Id.* at 20, 68 S.Ct. at 845.

The Court has since found a "nexus" in several cases where the private defendant uses state judicial mechanisms to cause a constitutional injury to the plaintiff.[21]

2. State Acceptance of Benefits From Private Party

Sometimes the state action requirement is satisfied by evidence that the State knowingly accepted the benefits of unconstitutional behavior.[22] In *Burton*, a restaurant that practiced racial discrimination leased space from the state parking authority in a publicly owned building. The Court held that the State was a joint participant in the restaurant.[23] Lower courts wrestling with similar lease arrangements have sometimes distinguished *Burton* on the ground that the government there benefited as lessor not just from the restaurant's proceeds but specifically from the allegedly unconstitutional race discrimination targeted by plaintiff's claim, which boosted the restaurant's profits. Lease terms are another key factor, with the courts looking to whether the government lessor retains control over the particular conduct or activity alleged to be unconstitutional.[24]

The "benefits" route to showing joint action is rarely successful because the plaintiff has to show that the state "so far insinuated itself into a position of interdependence with the [private defendant] that it was a joint participant in the enterprise"[25]—and one that controlled either all facets of management or at a minimum the assertedly unconstitutional conduct in question. Put otherwise, the closeness of the relationship required to subject the private defendant to liability is captured in the phrase "symbiotic relationship."[26]

On occasion it appears that an arm of the state actually participates with the private party in the challenged action. State action may certainly be found if the private party acted in concert with state

---

21. *See Sniadach v. Family Finance Corp.,* 395 U.S. 337, 338, 89 S.Ct. 1820, 1821, 23 L.Ed.2d 349 (1969) (state action assumed where finance company instituted garnishment action against plaintiff pursuant to Wisconsin state statute); *Mitchell v. W.T. Grant Co.,* 416 U.S. 600, 94 S.Ct. 1895, 40 L.Ed.2d 406 (1974) (involving Louisiana sequestration procedure instituted by a private lien holder). *See also North Georgia Finishing, Inc. v. Di–Chem, Inc.,* 419 U.S. 601, 95 S.Ct. 719, 42 L.Ed.2d 751 (1975); *Connecticut v. Doehr,* 501 U.S. 1, 111 S.Ct. 2105, 115 L.Ed.2d 1 (1991). *Contra Rockwell v. Cape Cod Hosp.,* 26 F.3d 254 (1st Cir.1994) (private hospital officials who involuntarily admitted mentally disturbed patients pursuant to authority conferred by a state statute held not to be acting "under color of" state law within the meaning of § 1983); *Gene Thompson Lumber Co. v. Davis Parmer Lumber Co.,* 984 F.2d 401 (11th Cir.1993) (state action does not exist where civil rights defendant invoked state law, but affirmatively misled state into exercising coercive power).

22. *See Burton v. Wilmington Parking Authority,* 365 U.S. 715, 81 S.Ct. 856, 6 L.Ed.2d 45 (1961).

23. *Id.* at 725, 81 S.Ct. at 862.

24. *Willis v. University Health Servs., Inc.,* 993 F.2d 837, 840–41 (11th Cir.), *cert. denied,* 510 U.S. 976, 114 S.Ct. 468, 126 L.Ed.2d 420 (1993); *NBC v. Communications Workers of America, supra* note 3, at 1027–28; *Greco v. Orange Memorial Hosp.,* 513 F.2d 873 (5th Cir.), *cert. denied,* 423 U.S. 1000, 96 S.Ct. 433, 46 L.Ed.2d 376 (1975).

25. *Jackson, supra* note 4, at 357–58, 95 S.Ct. at 457–58.

26. *Willis, supra* note 24, at 840.

officials.[27]

3. Extensive State Regulation

Plaintiffs have had less success convincing courts that Fourteenth Amendment "state action" inevitably follows from extensive state regulation of a private defendant. The defendant in *Jackson v. Metropolitan Edison Company*[28] was a privately owned and operated Pennsylvania corporation, the Metropolitan Edison Company, that delivered electricity to Pennsylvania residents, including the plaintiff, Ms. Jackson. The Pennsylvania Public Utility Commission issued a certificate of public convenience to the corporation empowering it to sell electricity to the service area in which Ms. Jackson lived. The certificate subjected the company to extensive public regulation by the Commission. The company filed a general tariff with the Commission that gave the company the right to discontinue service to any customer after reasonable notice of nonpayment of bills.[29]

Jackson received electricity from the company, but the Metropolitan Edison Company terminated her service because she failed to pay her electric bill. She filed suit against Metropolitan under § 1983 alleging deprivation of her property in violation of the Fourteenth Amendment's guarantee of due process of law.[30]

The Court observed that the utility was privately owned and operated although subject to extensive state regulation. "[T]he mere fact that a business is subject to state regulation does not by itself convert its action into that of the State for purposes of the Fourteenth Amendment."[31] Even "extensive and detailed" regulation is not necessarily enough.

The Court considered another extensively regulated private defendant in *Blum v. Yaretsky*.[32] Medicaid patients brought a class action suit against their nursing home after its utilization review committee decided that the plaintiff group should be transferred to a home with a lower level of care.[33] The plaintiffs alleged a violation of the Due Process Clause of the Fourteenth Amendment based on the review committee's failure to give adequate notice of the decision to move them and denial of a hearing to challenge the decision. Before addressing the merits of the due process claim, the Court turned to the issue whether the private nursing home's decision was "state action."[34]

The Court noted, as it had in *Jackson*, that New York's extensive regulation of the nursing home was not enough to transmute the actions

---

27. *See, e.g., Edmonson v. Leesville Concrete Co.*, 500 U.S. 614, 111 S.Ct. 2077, 114 L.Ed.2d 660 (1991), *and Adickes v. S.H. Kress & Co.*, 398 U.S. 144, 90 S.Ct. 1598, 26 L.Ed.2d 142 (1970).

28. 419 U.S. 345, 95 S.Ct. 449, 42 L.Ed.2d 477 (1974).

29. *Id.* at 346, 95 S.Ct. at 451.

30. *Id.* at 347, 95 S.Ct. at 451.

31. *Id.* at 350, 95 S.Ct. at 453.

32. 457 U.S. 991, 102 S.Ct. 2777, 73 L.Ed.2d 534 (1982).

33. *Id.*

34. *Id.* at 993–999, 1002, 102 S.Ct. at 2780–2783, 2785.

of the home into "state action." [35]   The Court explained that

> [t]he purpose of [the nexus] requirement is to assure that constitutional standards are invoked only when it can be said that the State is responsible for the specific conduct of which the plaintiff complains. The importance of this assurance is evident when, as in this case, the complaining party seeks to hold the State liable for the actions of private parties.[36]

Citing *Jackson*, the *Blum* Court repeated that government "acquiescence" in the private defendant's conduct is not enough. Rather, a State may be held liable only "when it has exercised coercive power or has provided such significant encouragement" [37] to the private decisionmaker that it is fair to call the action "that of the State." [38]

4. *Extensive Regulation and Funding*

In *Rendell–Baker v. Kohn*[39], the Court explained that regulation and funding without state compulsion of the defendant's particular injury-inflicting conduct do not suffice for Fourteenth Amendment "state action." *Rendell–Baker* involved a § 1983 suit brought by a former vocational counselor and former teachers against their employer, a privately operated school for maladjusted high school students in Massachusetts. The plaintiffs alleged that the school had discharged them in violation of their First, Fifth and Fourteenth Amendment rights. The question for the Court was whether the decision of the private high school could be attributed to Massachusetts.

The school, although "privately" operated, received funds from both state and federal agencies that accounted for at least 90% of the school's operating budget. None of the school's fifty students paid tuition. Additionally, Massachusetts generally regulated the school's functions, including "personnel matters." [40]   Nevertheless, the Court found no Fourteenth Amendment "state action" because even "extreme regulation" by the state was insufficient. "Acts of . . . private contractors do not become acts of the government by reason of their significant or even total engagement in performing public contracts." [41]   The Court found "the decisions to discharge the petitioners were not compelled or even influenced by any state regulation." [42]   The Court also rejected the plaintiff's argument that the school's fiscal relationship with the State was sufficiently close to deem its functions melded with those of the State.[43]

---

35. *Id.* at 1004, 102 S.Ct. at 2785.

36. *Id.*

37. *Id.*

38. *Id.*

39. 457 U.S. 830, 102 S.Ct. 2764, 73 L.Ed.2d 418 (1982).

40. *Id.* at 831–835, 102 S.Ct. at 2766–2768.

41. *Id.* at 841, 102 S.Ct. at 2771.

42. *Id.* See also *George v. Pacific–CSC Work Furlough*, 91 F.3d 1227 (9th Cir.1996) (insufficient nexus between county and defendant private employer's decision to fire an employee where contract under which private employer operated correctional facility for county permitted county to regulate employer's employees in some respects but not in respect of decisions to terminate).

43. *Id.*

5. State Delegation of Governmental Authority

This route to state action is closely related to and sometimes analyzed as the "traditional governmental function" approach discussed above. It has also recently been argued that a delegation to private hands of state authority may meet the nexus or joint participant tests even if the function in question is not a traditional or exclusive state function.[44] That is one way to understand cases that have held hospital authorities to be state actors even though running a hospital is not considered a traditional governmental function.[45] On the other hand, a state medical board that retained all formal authority to make final decisions concerning the accreditation of hospital programs but deemed its function fulfilled by following the decisions of a private accrediting council was held not to have made a delegation of this kind even though it adopted wholesale or indeed "rubber stamped" the council's conclusions. The state board "remains the state actor" because it "remains ultimately responsible for approving medical training facilities. . . ."[46]

Library References:

C.J.S. Constitutional Law §§ 955–963.
West's Key No. Digests, Constitutional Law ⚏254.

§ 2.7   Corporate Chartering as "State Action"

The Supreme Court held that the actions of a private defendant were not attributable to the federal government under the Fifth Amendment in *San Francisco Arts & Athletics, Inc. v. United States Olympic Committee.*[1]

The plaintiff group was an organization based in San Francisco that sponsored the "Gay Olympic Games." The United States Olympic Committee (USOC) has the right to prohibit the use of the word "Olympic" and the use of Olympic symbols for commercial or promotional uses under § 110 of the Amateur Sports Act.[2] The USOC exercised this power and ordered the plaintiff organization to stop using the word "Olympic" in association with their event. The San Francisco Arts & Athletics (SFAA) group brought suit alleging among other claims, that the USOC enforced its rights under § 110 in a discriminatory manner in violation of the Fifth Amendment.[3] The question before the Court was

---

44. *McKeesport Hosp.*, *supra* note 2, at 33 (Becker, J. concurring in judgment).

45. *See Stern v. Tarrant County Hosp. Dist.*, 755 F.2d 430, 433 (5th Cir.), *vacated on other grounds*, 778 F.2d 1052 (5th Cir. 1985), *cert. denied*, 476 U.S. 1108, 106 S.Ct. 1957, 90 L.Ed.2d 365 (1986) (cited by Becker, J., concurring in judgement in *McKeesport Hosp.*, *supra* note 2).

46. *McKeesport Hosp.*, *supra* note 2, at 18.

§ 2.7

1. 483 U.S. 522, 107 S.Ct. 2971, 97 L.Ed.2d 427 (1987).

2. 92 Stat. 3048, 36 U.S.C.A. § 380.

3. "This Court's approach to Fifth Amendment equal protection claims has been … precisely the same as to equal protection claims under the Fourteenth Amendment." *Weinberger v. Wiesenfeld*, 420 U.S. 636, 638 n. 2, 95 S.Ct. 1225, 1228 n. 2, 43 L.Ed.2d 514 (1975).

whether the USOC was a Fifth Amendment state actor because Congress had granted the Committee its corporate status.[4]

That Congress granted the USOC corporate status did not suffice for "state action"; all corporations act under charters granted by some government, the Court explained.[5] Nor did congressional grant of the power to organize amateur sports transform USOC into a state actor: "neither the conduct nor the coordination of amateur sports has been a traditional governmental function."[6] Most important, Congress did not "significantly encourage" the particular challenged decision of the USOC, and therefore the action of the private entity could not be attributed to the government.[7]

Library References:

> C.J.S. Constitutional Law §§ 955–963.
> West's Key No. Digests, Constitutional Law ☞254.

§ 2.8   Public Defendants and the § 1983 "Under Color of State Law" Requirement

A related, but distinct, requirement of any § 1983 action is a showing that the defendant acted "under color of state law." *Monroe v. Pape*[1], as observed above, held that state officials act "under color" of state law if they are clothed with the trappings of state authority regardless of whether state law approves or disapproves the particular conduct that triggers the federal constitutional or statutory claim.[2] The Court so held by analogy to its decision in *Home Telephone* more than five decades earlier that conduct by a person generally authorized to act under state law is "state action" for purposes of the Fourteenth Amendment, even if the particular conduct at issue was not state authorized.[3] After *Monroe*, any act carried out by an individual clothed with the authority of the state is similarly actionable under § 1983, even if the state affirmatively forbade the specific acts of the individual defendant.[4]

After *Monroe*, the courthouse doors may be open in four situations. (1) Most clearly, a state official acting within the scope of her authority and *commensurately* with affirmative state authorization may be sued under § 1983 for conduct allegedly violating the federal constitution or laws. (2) *Monroe* added that an official acting within the scope of her employment, but whose actions are affirmatively *contrary* to the rules of the state, also acts "under color of state law." (3) *A fortiori* the official acting within the scope of her authority and whose challenged conduct is

---

4. 483 U.S. at 524–529, 107 S.Ct. at 2975–2977.

5. *Id.* at 543–44, 107 S.Ct. at 2985.

6. *Id.* at 545, 107 S.Ct. at 2985.

7. *Id.* at 546–547, 107 S.Ct. at 2986–2987.

§ 2.8

1. 365 U.S. 167, 81 S.Ct. 473, 5 L.Ed.2d 492 (1961), *overruled on a different issue by*

Monell v. Department of Social Servs., 436 U.S. 658, 98 S.Ct. 2018, 56 L.Ed.2d 611 (1978).

2. *Id.* at 183–186, 81 S.Ct. at 482–484.

3. *See Home Tel. & Tel. Co. v. City of L.A.*, 227 U.S. at 287–94, 33 S.Ct. at 315–17.

4. 365 U.S. at 183, 81 S.Ct. at 482.

simply unaddressed by any state policy acts "under color of state law," too. But some decisions have placed a caveat on, or perhaps only defined, these three "scope of authority" situations by insisting that the agent's conduct in question be at least arguably connected to her assigned work. Thus acts committed by a police officer even while on duty and in uniform are not under color of state law unless they are in some way "related to the performance of police duties." [5]

(4) What of the fourth situation, where a state official's conduct is entirely outside the scope of her employment, but she carries the badges or emblems of state authority when she comes into contact with the plaintiff? Several circuits have indicated that there are situations when the state official, although clearly outside the scope of employment, nevertheless acts "under color of state law" for the purposes of § 1983. In *Davis v. Murphy*,[6] two Milwaukee police officers were sued for shouting racial epithets and provoking a fight with five black citizens who were driving in a car behind the officers. The defendants identified themselves as police officers and were carrying their guns and badges. Milwaukee Police Department regulations stated that officers were "to be always subject to duty." [7] The Seventh Circuit found that the officers were acting "under color of state law" even though acting outside the scope of their employment.[8]

Clearly, however, some off-duty conduct of state agents is not under color of state law. The Second Circuit recently so held in the case of an off-duty policeman who used his own weapon to shoot a guest in his own home. The Court observed that in using the weapon the defendant, intoxicated, was not invoking the authority of his department.[9] That same conclusion was reached when one of the defendant officers was the brother-in-law of the alleged victim of an assault.[10] And some statuses are even more "off" than off-duty. A police officer shot the plaintiff's father after the officer had been stripped of his authority to perform any police duties because of a pending psychological examination. The

---

5. *Gibson v. City of Chicago*, 910 F.2d 1510, 1516 (7th Cir.1990) (quoting *Briscoe v. LaHue*, 663 F.2d 713, 721, n. 4 (7th Cir.1981) (quoting *Johnson v. Hackett*, 284 F.Supp. 933, 937 (E.D.Pa.1968)), *affirmed*, 460 U.S. 325, 103 S.Ct. 1108, 75 L.Ed.2d 96 (1983)). *See Martinez v. Colon*, 54 F.3d 980 (1st Cir.) (on-duty harassment of fellow officer a purely personal pursuit and hence not actionable although carried out with service revolver), *cert. denied*, ___ U.S. ___, 116 S.Ct. 515, 133 L.Ed.2d 423 (1995). *See also Jojola v. Chavez*, 55 F.3d 488 (10th Cir. 1995) (school custodian who molested student not exercising state authority). *But see Seltzer–Bey v. Delo*, 66 F.3d 961 (8th Cir.1995) (corrections officer's sexual assault of inmate under color of state law even though defendant's motivation was self-gratification).

6. 559 F.2d 1098 (7th Cir.1977).

7. *Id.* at 1100–1101.

8. *See also Traver v. Meshriy*, 627 F.2d 934, 937–38 (9th Cir.1980) (off duty police officer who detained bank customer could be sued under § 1983, even though the officer was working outside the scope of his employment); *Pickrel v. City of Springfield*, 45 F.3d 1115 (7th Cir.1995)(off-duty police officer working at fast food restaurant as a private security guard acted under color of state law by wearing uniform, displaying badge and charging patron with resisting a peace officer, all in proximity to his parked squad car).

9. *Pitchell v. Callan*, 13 F.3d 545 (2d Cir.1994).

10. *Barna v. City of Perth Amboy*, 42 F.3d 809 (3d Cir.1994).

Seventh Circuit held that while a state official may misuse powers he has the authority to use, if the official has no powers, then no powers exist to misuse.[11] Apparent authority, for this court, is no substitute for a manifest lack of actual authority.

In sum, the decisions in the "off-duty" cases sprawl untidily across three loose categories. There is the "actual authority" approach, which rules out the possibility that an off-duty official is acting "under color of state law" if there is some crisp indicator that in fact he lacked authority to act despite having cloaked himself in a mantle of authority.[12] In the limited setting of off-duty officials, this approach echoes the more general position, repudiated by *Monroe v. Pape,* that conduct is "under color of" state law only when it enjoys state authorization and approval. Second, there is the "indicia of authority" approach, far friendlier to a finding that the defendant has acted "under color of" state law. This approach answers the question affirmatively if the defendant displays sufficient trappings of state authority to lead a reasonable third-party observer to believe that the defendant is acting with government authorization.[13] And there is understandably scant authority for a third approach, which turns resolution of the question on the victim's or the defendant's own subjective perception that the defendant was acting under color of state law, even when there is no objective reason to believe that he was.[14]

Library References:

> C.J.S. Civil Rights §§ 19, 248.
> West's Key No. Digests, Civil Rights ☞196.

§ 2.9 Private Defendants and the "Under Color of State Law" Requirement

a. *Lugar v. Edmondson Oil Co.*[1]

In *Edmondson,* the Court analyzed the interplay between the Fourteenth Amendment requirement of "state action," needed to establish most constitutional claims brought under § 1983, and the statute's own requirement of action "under color of state law."

A debtor brought an action under § 1983 against a corporate creditor and its president alleging that, in attaching his property pursuant to the law of Virginia, the defendants acted jointly with the state to deprive

---

11. *Gibson v. City of Chicago, supra* note 5, at 1517.

12. *See, e.g., Barna; Searcy v. City of Dayton,* 38 F.3d 282 (6th Cir.1994); *Pitchell supra* note 9; and *Gibson.*

13. *See, e.g., Pickrel, supra* note 8; *Gentry v. Lee's Summit,* 10 F.3d 1340 (8th Cir.1993); *Revene v. Charles County Commissioners,* 882 F.2d 870 (4th Cir.1989); *Lusby v. T.G. & Y.,* 749 F.2d 1423 (10th Cir.1984).

14. *See, e.g., Layne v. Sampley,* 627 F.2d 12 (6th Cir.1980); *Keller v. District of Columbia,* 809 F.Supp. 432 (E.D.Va.1993); *Manning v. Jones,* 696 F.Supp. 1231 (S.D.Ind.1988).

§ 2.9

1. 457 U.S. 922, 102 S.Ct. 2744, 73 L.Ed.2d 482 (1982).

him of his right to due process under the Fourteenth Amendment.[2] In overruling the Court of Appeals, the Court stated that "[w]hether they are identical or not, the state-action and the under-color-of-state-law requirements are obviously related. Indeed, until recently this Court did not distinguish between the two at all."[3]

The first question was whether the creditor's invocation of the state's prejudgment attachment procedure represented "state action" for purposes of the Fourteenth Amendment. The Court cited the *Sniadach* and *North Georgia Finishing* cases as authority for the finding that the present attachment procedure involves "state action" that satisfies the Fourteenth Amendment requirement. "[T]he Court has consistently held that constitutional requirements of due process apply to garnishment and prejudgment attachment procedures whenever officers of the State act jointly with a creditor in securing the property in dispute."[4]

The Court then considered whether the creditor's actions were also "under color of state law" within the meaning of § 1983. The Court stated that:

> If a defendant debtor in state-court collection proceedings can successfully challenge, on federal due process grounds, the plaintiff creditor's resort to the procedures authorized by state statute, it is difficult to understand why that same behavior by the state-court plaintiff should not provide a [federal or state court] cause of action under Section 1983. If the creditor-plaintiff violates the debtor-defendant's due process rights by seizing his property in accordance with statutory procedures, there is little or no reason to deny to the latter a cause of action under the federal statute, Section 1983, designed to provide judicial redress for just such constitutional violations.[5]

The Court made clear that "[i]f the challenged conduct of respondents constitutes [Fourteenth Amendment] state action ... then that conduct was also action under color of state law and will support a suit under Section 1983."[6] However, the reverse is not necessarily true:

> First, although we hold that conduct satisfying the state-action requirement of the Fourteenth Amendment satisfies the statutory requirement of action under color of state law, *it does not follow that all conduct that satisfies the under-color-of-state-law requirement would satisfy the Fourteenth Amendment requirement of state action.* If action under color of state law means nothing more than that the individual act "with knowledge of and pursuant to that statute"[7] then clearly under *Flagg Brothers* that would not, in itself, satisfy the state-action requirement of the Fourteenth Amendment. Sec-

---

2. *Id.* at 924–925, 102 S.Ct. at 2747.

3. *Id.* at 928, 102 S.Ct. at 2749. *See also United States v. Price*, 383 U.S. 787, 86 S.Ct. 1152, 16 L.Ed.2d 267 (1966).

4. 457 U.S. at 932–33, 95 S.Ct. at 2751–52.

5. *Id.* at 934, 102 S.Ct. at 2752.

6. *Id.* at 935, 102 S.Ct. at 2752.

7. *Id.* at 935 n.18, 102 S.Ct. at 2752 n.18 (citing *Adickes v. S. H. Kress & Co.*, 398 U.S. 144, 162 n. 23, 90 S.Ct. 1598, 1611 n. 23, 26 L.Ed.2d 142 (1970)).

ond, although we hold in this case that the under-color-of-state-law requirement does not add anything not already included within the state-action requirement of the Fourteenth Amendment, § 1983 is applicable to other constitutional provisions and statutory provisions that contain no state-action requirement. Where such a federal right is at issue, the statutory concept of action under color of state law would be a distinct element of the case not satisfied implicitly by a finding of a violation of the particular right.[8]

In *Burrell v. Board of Trustees of Georgia Military College*[9], the Eleventh Circuit repeated that the § 1983 "under color of state law" requirement does not necessarily satisfy the Fourteenth Amendment's "state action" requirement. The Eleventh Circuit stated that although misuse of state power may amount to conduct "under color of state law" for purposes of § 1983, the plaintiff must independently show Fourteenth Amendment "state action" by showing that the defendant's challenged actions were taken with the power granted by the state.[10] In other words, the defendant may have worn the state's clothing but not used the state's "night stick" to inflict the plaintiff's injury. Thus while private persons undoubtedly act "under color of" state law when they conspire with government officials to deprive the plaintiff of federally protected rights,[11] the violation may not reflect the required "state action" if implemented through purely private means. The *Edmondson* and *Burrell* opinions illustrate why in most § 1983 actions the plaintiff must first make sure that the defendant's action can be characterized as "state action" under the Fourteenth Amendment. If so, the path has been paved for proving a predicate violation of federal constitutional law; at the same time, the plaintiff will be assured that the defendant's conduct is also "under color of" state law. Similarly, recent decisions in the circuits reflect that § 1983 actions are far more commonly dismissed for failing to meet the Fourteenth Amendment "state action" requirement than for failing to satisfy the "under color of state law" requirement of § 1983.[12]

8. *Id.* at 935 n.18, 102 S.Ct. at 2752 n.18 (emphasis added). However, the Supreme Court has recently indicated that only two constitutional rights—freedom from involuntary servitude under the Thirteenth Amendment and a limited right to interstate travel—are affirmatively protected against any invasion, even by a private actor. *See Bray v. Alexandria Women's Health Clinic,* 506 U.S. 263, 113 S.Ct. 753, 122 L.Ed.2d 34 (1993), discussed in section 1.5, *supra.*

9. 970 F.2d 785 (11th Cir.1992), *cert. denied,* 507 U.S. 1018, 113 S.Ct. 1814, 123 L.Ed.2d 445 (1993). The author was co-counsel for the governmental defendants in *Burrell.*

10. *Id.* at 790, n.12.

11. *See, e.g., Adickes v. S.H. Kress & Co.,* 398 U.S. 144, 90 S.Ct. 1598, 26 L.Ed.2d

142 (1970); *Davis v. Union National Bank,* 46 F.3d 24 (7th Cir.1994); *Burrell v. Board of Trustees of Georgia Military College,* 970 F.2d 785 (11th Cir.1992), *cert. denied,* 507 U.S. 1018, 113 S.Ct. 1814, 123 L.Ed.2d 445 (1993).

12. *Roche v. John Hancock Mut. Life Ins. Co.,* 81 F.3d 249 (1st Cir.1996) (where police exercised independent judgment in applying for arrest warrant, employer who investigated threatening phone calls and forwarded information to police not state actor in connection with employee's arrest); *Willis v. University Health Servs.,* 993 F.2d 837 (11th Cir.) (hospital not state actor under "public function," "joint action/symbiotic relationship," or "nexus/state compulsion" tests), *cert. denied,* 510 U.S. 976, 114 S.Ct. 468, 126 L.Ed.2d 420 (1993); *Comiskey v. JFTJ Corp.,* 989 F.2d 1007 (8th

Library References:

> C.J.S. Civil Rights § 250.
> West's Key No. Digests, Civil Rights ⊗198(3.1).

C. THE CASE AGAINST INDIVIDUAL DEFENDANTS AND THEIR QUALIFIED IMMUNITY

§ 2.10 In General

The case against an individual agent appears to be surprisingly straightforward. But the Court has constructed the comprehensive affirmative defense of immunity that, if applicable, more than offsets the loose prima facie requirements. These two characteristics stand in antithesis from the stringent prima facie case and non-existing immunity intrinsic to the case against an entity. If the plaintiff establishes liability in an individual defendant, he is eligible for compensatory damages and, in a proper case, punitive damages.

§ 2.11 The Prima Facie Case

The prima facie case against the defendant sued in her individual capacity remains, somewhat remarkably, judicially unembellished. The plaintiff's evidence simply tracks the statute in a straight forward fashion. He must first allege that the defendant is a "person" as that term is used in the text of the statute.[1] Second, there must have been a deprivation of some right of the plaintiff that is protected under the Constitution[2] or by federal law.[3] Third, the private defendant must have acted "under color of" state law in effecting the deprivation. Finally, the plaintiff must show that the deprivation caused some harm remediable by injunction or damages.[4] And *Monroe*, of course, dramati-

---

Cir.1993) (bar not state actor, despite state's regulatory involvement, where state neither created nor enforced alleged discriminatory policy of offering female, but not male patrons free drinks); cf. *Edwards v. Wallace Community College,* 49 F.3d 1517 (11th Cir.1995) (because defendant co-employees lacked supervisory authority over plaintiff they did not act pursuant to power possessed by virtue of state authority and thus were not acting "under color of" state law even though they allegedly harassed plaintiff on the job during working hours); *Hiser v. City of Bowling Green,* 42 F.3d 382 (6th Cir.1994) (city not acting "under color of" state law when police informant stole check from and killed his apartment mate, because these acts fell outside scope of informant's work for police).

§ 2.11

1. 42 U.S.C.A. § 1983 (1988). Although this requirement is a significant hurdle in suits against local entities and states, it will always be met in regard to private persons.

2. Rather than, say, an ancillary sub-constitutional evidentiary protection, like the rights protected by *Miranda v. Arizona,* 384 U.S. 436, 86 S.Ct. 1602, 16 L.Ed.2d 694 (1966). *Neighbour v. Covert,* 68 F.3d 1508 (2d Cir.1995) (violations of *Miranda* rights not actionable under § 1983).

3. Not state law. *See Podgurski v. Suffolk County,* ___ F.3d ___ (2d Cir.1995) (boundary dispute against county not actionable as federal law violation), *cert. denied,* 116 S.Ct. 711, 133 L.Ed.2d 666 (1996) (mem.).

4. Qualified immunity, as it now stands, insulates defendants from monetary damages only. An injunction may still be issued constraining the defendant in some way, and thus § 1988 would still provide for an award of attorney fees, despite a finding of qualified immunity. *See* § 2.12 n. 2,

cally widened the field for individual liability by making it immaterial whether the defendant acted pursuant or contrary to local government authorization.[5]

Library References:

> C.J.S. Civil Rights §§ 307, 308.
> West's Key No. Digests, Civil Rights ⟐242(1).

§ 2.12 A Brief History [1] of Individual Defendant Immunity

Not long after *Monroe*'s expansive statement of individual liability, the Court began to embrace a doctrine of qualified immunity from damages [2] calculated to counter its generous prima facie case. The early history of immunity reflects the Court's effort to apply a transplanted common law doctrine to the particular circumstances of § 1983 defendants. This approach found support in the language of 42 U.S.C.A. § 1988, which counsels courts to fill § 1983 cracks with spackle from state common law.[3] The Court's early grapplings with qualified immunity for individual defendants—*Tenney v. Brandhove*,[4] *Pierson v. Ray*,[5] *Imbler v. Pachtman*,[6] and *Scheuer v. Rhodes*[7]—were obedient to this task

infra. Plaintiffs' attorneys are thus not wholly without inducement for accepting cases where a grant of qualified immunity is likely.

A fifth element, i.e., that a policy or practice be shown, is only applicable in § 1983 actions against entity defendants.

5. 365 U.S. at 183–85, 81 S.Ct. at 482–83. *See* § 2.3, *supra.*

§ 2.12

1. A comprehensive history of § 1983 immunities is well beyond the scope of this work. As a starting point, *see* Peter H. Schuck, *Suing Government: Citizen Remedies for Official Wrongs* 89–93, 203–05 (1983). A brief survey of the history of judicial immunity is contained in Peter H. Schuck, *The Civil Liability of Judges in the United States*, 37 Am. J. Comp. L. 655, 662–65 (1989).

2. The defense does not shield the officials who claim it from liability for equitable remedies, including reinstatement. *See, e.g., Pace v. Moriarty*, 83 F.3d 261 (8th Cir.1996). But the "damages" from which individual defendants are exempt when qualified immunity attaches may include costs, attorneys' fees and related expenses even in suits seeking only injunctive or other equitable relief. *D'Aguanno v. Gallagher*, 50 F.3d 877 (11th Cir.1995).

3. Section 1988 directs in part that state common law, to the extent that it is not inconsistent with federal law, shall apply "in all cases [for the protection of civil rights] where [federal laws] are not adapted to the object, or are deficient in the provisions necessary to furnish suitable remedies." *Id.* Some of the interpretive difficulties with this provision are explored by Jack M. Beermann, *A Critical Approach to Section 1983 with Special Attention to Sources of Law*, 42 Stan.L.Rev. 51, 58–75 (1989). He also concludes that the common law to which § 1988 directs the courts is not the common law the courts have followed. *See id.* at 61–63. Section 1988 is examined in more detail in the Procedure Chapter below.

4. 341 U.S. 367, 379, 71 S.Ct. 783, 789, 95 L.Ed. 1019 (1951) (creating absolute immunity for state legislators' activity).

5. 386 U.S. 547, 554, 557, 87 S.Ct. 1213, 1218, 1219, 18 L.Ed.2d 288 (1967) (establishing a "qualified" defense of "good faith and probable cause" for police officers and absolute immunity for judicial officers).

6. 424 U.S. 409, 427, 96 S.Ct. 984, 993, 47 L.Ed.2d 128 (1976) (declaring absolute immunity for prosecutorial activity).

7. 416 U.S. 232, 238–49, 94 S.Ct. 1683, 1687–93, 40 L.Ed.2d 90 (1974) (containing Chief Justice Burger's full explanation of the "reasonable grounds" and "good-faith belief" version of qualified immunity for executive officers); *see also* Jerry L. Mashaw, *Civil Liability of Government Officers: Property Rights and Official Accountability*, 42 Law & Contemp. Probs. 8, 14–21 (1978) (providing a useful overview of executive immunity and its rationales).

of infusing a general statutory liability standard with common law learning.[8]

In *Scheuer*, for example, the Court relied on two customary rationales for executive immunity: a "fairness" concern stemming from the injustice of holding an official liable for discretionary acts in the absence of bad faith, and the fear of deterring and interfering with the functions of state government ("federalism").[9] Objective "reasonableness" and subjective "good faith" elements of qualified immunity were to be measured by the totality of the circumstances confronting the official at the time of the challenged conduct, considered in light of the scope of the officer's discretion.[10] A year later, however, in *Wood v. Strickland*,[11] the Court departed from this traditional approach, the first step on a march to the avowedly policy-based test it would announce in *Harlow v. Fitzgerald*[12] and *Anderson v. Creighton*—the test that still prevails.[13]

Wood[14] introduced a new variable into the qualified immunity calculus by specifying that the "objective" prong of immunity identified in

8. *See* Mashaw, *supra* note 7, at 14–16 (arguing that executive immunity, as distinguished from sovereign and probably judicial immunity, is a relatively recent development).

9. *See Scheuer v. Rhodes*, 416 U.S. 232, 240, 94 S.Ct. 1683, 1688, 40 L.Ed.2d 90 (1974). *See supra* § 2.2, at 240. In a rare category of cases where the executive or administrative official's challenged conduct is mandated by state or federal law, a key reason for immunity disappears and the defense will not lie. *See McCullough v. Horton*, 69 F.3d 918 (8th Cir.1995) (state court clerk could not claim immunity for failing to provide transcript to inmate as required by court order).

10. *See id.* at 247–48, 94 S.Ct. at 1692. While the Court did not purport to premise its search for the existence of immunities on § 1988, it clearly did rest its finding on common law understandings. *See id.* at 238–48 & n.4, 94 S.Ct. at 1687–93 & n.4. Moreover, the Court's result was consistent with contemporary common law understanding. *See Restatement (Second) of Torts* § 895D (1979).

11. 420 U.S. 308, 95 S.Ct. 992, 43 L.Ed.2d 214 (1975), *overruled by Harlow v. Fitzgerald*, 457 U.S. 800, 102 S.Ct. 2727, 73 L.Ed.2d 396 (1982).

12. 457 U.S. 800, 818, 102 S.Ct. 2727, 2738, 73 L.Ed.2d 396 (1982) (holding that discovery should not be permitted until the court answers the threshold question "whether [the] law was clearly established at the time an action occurred").

13. 483 U.S. 635, 639–41, 107 S.Ct. 3034, 3038–40, 97 L.Ed.2d 523 (1987) (applying the qualified immunity doctrine to

the execution of a search warrant, and holding that *Harlow* eliminated an inquiry into the subjective intent of the official and that the trial court should test the "objective legal reasonableness" of the challenged conduct against "clearly established" law). This departure from the immunity formula received from the common law rested "solely on the basis of policy considerations such as whether liability would have an undue chilling effect on decisionmaking." Larry Kramer & Alan O. Sykes, *Municipal Liability Under § 1983: A Legal and Economic Analysis,* 1987 Sup.Ct.Rev. 249, 266 (1987). *But cf.* John C. Jeffries, *Compensation for Constitutional Torts: Reflections on the Significance of Fault,* 88 Mich. L. Rev. 82, 86 n.22 (1989) (suggesting that there may be some vitality left in the subjective prong if plaintiff "makes concrete and detailed allegations fairly suggestive of official bad faith"). The Court of Appeals for the District of Columbia recognizes such a remnant of the subjective test. It permits the plaintiff to defeat immunity by pleading malice with specificity and offering noncircumstantial proof of that state of mind. *See Siegert v. Gilley*, 895 F.2d 797, 800–02 (D.C.Cir.1990) (finding that "the invalidating motivation [must be] pleaded with the offer of noncircumstantial proof required to satisfy our heightened pleading standard"), *affirmed on other grounds,* 500 U.S. 226, 111 S.Ct. 1789, 114 L.Ed.2d 277 (1991). *But see* text accompanying note 24, *infra.*

14. The case arose when school board members expelled several high school students, arguably without sufficient procedural safeguards. Although acknowledging that under existing precedent some process

Scheuer required the defendant to demonstrate the reasonableness of her conduct in relation to the content of "settled, indisputable law." Immunity attached only if defendants proved two conditions: (1) that the challenged act was objectively reasonable in light of settled law *and* (2) that the conduct was motivated by subjective good faith.[15]

Justices Powell and Rehnquist, two of the four dissenters from this part of the opinion, would later take leading roles in forging more generous immunities. They referred to the majority's description of the objective branch as a "harsh standard, requiring [defendants to have] knowledge of what is characterized as 'settled, indisputable law' [and accordingly leaving] little substance to the doctrine of qualified immunity."[16] That standard, they argued, would impose damage liability even if the administrator, acting in good faith, was ignorant of the law. Under such conditions, liability would rest on "an unwarranted assumption as to what school officials know or can know about the law and constitutional rights."[17] The problem, Justice Powell predicted, was that "[t]hese officials [would] now act at the peril of some judge or jury subsequently finding that a good-faith belief as to the applicable law was mistaken."[18]

was required before school children could be expelled, *see* 420 U.S. at 323 n.15, 95 S.Ct. at 1001, n.15, the Court did not reach the procedural due process question because it had not been decided by the Court of Appeals. *See id.* at 323, 95 S.Ct. at 1001. Thus, the cause was remanded. *Cf. id.* at 327, 95 S.Ct. at 1003 (Powell, J., concurring in part and dissenting in part) (noting that a second school board hearing may have cured defects at a prior hearing). On this point there was unanimity. *See id.*

The more difficult issue was whether the school board members were entitled to some form of immunity. Justice White treated the general question of immunity for school administrators as one of first impression. He began by noting the split in the lower courts concerning the proper standard for the context, *see id.* at 315 & n.7, 95 S.Ct. at 997 & n.7. He then surveyed *Tenney v. Brandhove*; *Pierson v. Ray*; and *Scheuer v. Rhodes*, resolving the issue in favor of qualified, good faith immunity for school board members from liability for damages in § 1983 actions, *see id.* at 316–322.

15. *See id.* at 321–22, 95 S.Ct. at 1000–1001.

16. *Id.* at 329, 95 S.Ct. at 1004 (Powell, J., concurring in part and dissenting in part).

17. *Id.*

18. *Id.* Justice Powell rightly doubted that school officials would have knowledge of any but the most settled constitutional law. As a predictor of the future develop-

ment of the immunity defense, however, he proved wrong in two respects.

First, it was uncertain in 1975 that doctrinal "settledness" or the reasonableness of the official's conduct would be questions for a jury. Not until *Harlow* and *Anderson*, respectively, were these questions addressed, and they were held generally to be questions for the Court. Second, as Justice Powell later realized, requiring the defendant to have knowledge of "settled, indisputable law" before subjecting her to liability in practice imposes a litigation hardship on the plaintiff rather than the defendant.

Proving that law is indisputably settled appears to be a formidable task. In *Wood* itself, for example, the district court had made a specific finding, unchallenged on appeal, that the officials bore no ill will toward the students. *See Wood*, 420 U.S. at 314, 95 S.Ct. at 997. Accordingly, defendants surmounted the subjective prong of the new test. The debate centered on the objective prong of the test and whether it was fair to charge the defendants with knowledge of the local status of the right to process before expulsion, or with knowledge of what constituted "settledness." The right to process as a necessary procedural incident to a ten-day *suspension* from public school had been decided in *Goss v. Lopez*, 419 U.S. 565, 95 S.Ct. 729, 42 L.Ed.2d 725 (1975), earlier in the same term. In arguing against the majority's "standard of required knowledge" in *Wood*, Justice Powell questioned whether school administrators

His prediction proved ironic in *Harlow*[19] when those same dissenters, now joining a majority, *confined* the inquiry to the factor they had

could be expected to know that *Goss* was settled law. *See Wood*, 420 U.S. at 329, 95 S.Ct. at 1004 (Powell, J., concurring in part and dissenting in part).

Justice Powell's doubt, in the specific context, is problematic for a number of reasons. First, the *Wood* majority did not purport to decide whether the law was "settled," but simply remanded. Because it was not then clear whether the "settledness" issue raised a legal or factual question, the dissent's concern was somewhat premature. Second, despite Powell's claim that "most lawyers would have thought, prior to [*Goss*], that the law to the *contrary* was settled, indisputable and unquestioned," *id.*, the majority noted that the courts of appeals had uniformly held that process was due before dismissal from public school. *See id.* at 323 n.15, 95 S.Ct. at 1002 n.15. Perhaps more important, in *Goss* itself the Court listed ten lower court cases that had required process before expulsion and dozens of others requiring process before dismissals. *See Goss*, 419 U.S. at 576–78 n.8, 95 S.Ct. at 737–38 n.8. Included within that list were district and appellate court decisions from the Eighth Circuit, which decided *Wood*.

Moreover, Justice Powell's lament was somewhat disingenuous. He dissented in *Goss*, but he went to great lengths in that opinion to distinguish the need for procedural safeguards that would accompany an expulsion—the situation in *Wood*—from the absence of need in the context of a relatively short suspension—the context of *Goss*. *See id.* at 585, 589, 590, 591, 595, 95 S.Ct. at 741, 743, 744, 745, 746 (Powell, J., dissenting) (distinguishing between relatively "routine" forms of discipline and more severe forms of school dismissals and punishment). He specifically noted that both historically and under the laws of the state where *Goss* arose, a hearing was required for the "incomparably more serious matter" of expulsion. *Id.* at 585 n.2, 95 S.Ct. at 741 n.2; *see also id.* at 595 & n.14, 95 S.Ct. at 746 & n.14 (suggesting that the Court should not and need not interfere with traditional disciplinary schemes used in public schools, which included no hearing for "routine" suspensions). Finally, he agreed with the majority's suggestion that any " 'fair-minded school principal' " would impose upon himself some minimum procedural safeguards prior to expulsion. *Id.* at 596 n.15, 95 S.Ct. at 747 n.15 (quoting majority opinion). In short, there was clear legal and historical precedent for the major-

ity's position; it was "indisputably settled" in this context, and there was no "harshness" involved.

19. *Harlow, supra,* note 12, and its successor, *Anderson v. Creighton, supra* note 13, were not under § 1983 but actions against federal agents that arose directly under the Constitution. The Court first recognized an implied private right of action against individual federal agents for Constitutional violations in *Bivens v. Six Unknown Named Agents of Fed. Bureau of Narcotics*, 403 U.S. 388, 91 S.Ct. 1999, 29 L.Ed.2d 619 (1971) (permitting damages action against federal narcotics agents for arrest and search violative of 4th Amendment). *See also Davis v. Passman*, 442 U.S. 228, 99 S.Ct. 2264, 60 L.Ed.2d 846 (1979) (permitting employment discrimination claim against member of Congress under the equal protection component of the 5th amendment's due process clause). The principal rationale for implying a *"Bivens "* claim rests on the imperative of providing redress for constitutional violations committed by federal agents even absent a Congressionally granted remedy. Nevertheless, the Court has refused to imply such a claim where the alleged constitutional violation occurred in the course of government action subject to an elaborate remedial scheme that did not afford damages against the offending agent. *Schweiker v. Chilicky*, 487 U.S. 412, 108 S.Ct. 2460, 101 L.Ed.2d 370 (1988) (claim asserting due process violations in the denial of Social Security disability benefits); *Mata v. Federal Bureau of Investigation,* 71 F.3d 513 (5th Cir.1995), *cert. denied,* ___ U.S. ___, 116 S.Ct. 1877, 135 L.Ed.2d 173 (1996) (Title VII provides exclusive claim and remedy for federal sector employment discrimination, thus ousting implied claim under *Bivens*). And in *United States v. Stanley,* 483 U.S. 669, 107 S.Ct. 3054, 97 L.Ed.2d 550 (1987), the Court denied relief under the Constitution precisely because the Federal Tort Claims Act gave none. In effect this approach gives Congress the last word on the appropriate measure of compensation for Constitutional violations. *See generally* Bandes, "Reinventing *Bivens*! The Self–Executing Constitution" 68 S.Cal.L.Rev. 289 (1995).

The Court has held that § 1983 and *Bivens* immunities are interchangeable. *See, e.g., Harlow,* 457 U.S. at 818 n.30, 102 S.Ct. at 2738 n.30; *Butz v. Economou,* 438 U.S. 478, 496–504, 98 S.Ct. 2894, 2905–2910, 57 L.Ed.2d 895 (1978). In *Butz,* this inter-

once found illegitimate, the state of constitutional precedent on the eve of the challenged conduct.[20] The new majority discarded the subjective prong and in the process effected a dramatic expansion of the affirmative defense. By declaring the new immunity forfeitable solely by reference to the state of the law, the Court turned its back on the common law tradition that tied immunity to lack of culpability and, in turn, the absence of a need to deter. Instead, *Harlow's* majority justified abandoning the good faith requirement largely as a response to the practical litigation burdens encountered by government officials accused of federal law violations when they attempted to establish their immunity.[21]

The new majority must have realized on reflection that, from the defendant's perspective, the troublesome aspect of common law qualified immunity was the subjective prong, which entailed "broad-ranging discovery and the deposing of numerous persons, including an official's professional colleagues. Inquiries of this kind can be peculiarly disruptive of effective government." [22] To avoid such disruptions, the Court simply jettisoned the subjective standard, relying entirely on an inquiry into the official defendant's "presumptive knowledge of and respect for

---

changeability worked to narrow the federal officials' immunity from the absolute immunity they were then afforded against ordinary, nonconstitutional torts under *Barr v. Matteo*, 360 U.S. 564, 79 S.Ct. 1335, 3 L.Ed.2d 1434 (1959), to the modest version of common law qualified immunity then prevalent under § 1983. *See* Laura Oren, *Immunity and Accountability in Civil Rights Litigation: Who Should Pay?*, 50 U.Pitt.L.Rev. 935, 970–72 (1989). Only a few years later, however, in *Harlow*, the Court relied on the interchangeability notion to extend the generous qualified immunity the Court subsequently had granted federal officials in *Bivens* actions to defendants under § 1983. One commentator has written that the linkage between doctrine developed in § 1983 and *Bivens* actions may be threatened by the Court's recent indications (see § 2.2 *supra*) that the common law as understood in 1871 is the paramount guidepost for fashioning § 1983 rules of liability, remedy and immunity, a principle that does not pertain to the judge-made cause of action declared in *Bivens*. See Steinglass, *Section 1983 Litigation In State Courts* (Clark Boardman) § 2.5(c), p. 2–47 and § 5.2(b), p. 5–7 (12/94).

More recently, the Court has unanimously declined to extend the *Bivens* principle to claims against federal government agencies, as distinct from their agents. *Federal Deposit Insurance Corporation v. Meyer*, 510 U.S. 471, 114 S.Ct. 996, 127 L.Ed.2d 308 (1994). Noting that the *Bivens* remedy is an effective deterrent against the commission of constitutional violations by federal

agents, the Court reasoned that affording a parallel claim against their employing entity would undermine that deterrence. The Court also expressed particular concern that affording a remedy against the agency would allow the plaintiff to circumvent the individual agent's official qualified immunity. These conclusions are curious given the Court's equation of the purposes and scope of § 1983 and *Bivens* immunity. If affording a remedy against the employing entity under § 1983, as the Court did in *Monell*, does not unduly undermine the desired deterrence of the agent or unwisely circumvent the agent's qualified immunity, why should the result be different in the *Bivens* setting?

20. *See Harlow, supra* note 12, at 818, 102 S.Ct. at 2738 (holding that objective reasonableness of an official's conduct is to be "measured by reference to clearly established law ... at the time an action occurred").

21. *See id.* at 806, 814–19, 102 S.Ct. at 2732, 2736–39. The new test was foreshadowed by the Court's decision in *Procunier v. Navarette*, 434 U.S. 555, 564 & n. 11, 98 S.Ct. 855, 861 & n. 11, 55 L.Ed.2d 24 (1978) (requiring a closeness between precedent and the right asserted). *See also* Oren, *supra* note 19, at 980–81 & n.195 (discussing *Procunier* and the fine distinctions that could make a precedent inadequate to establish an asserted right).

22. *Harlow, supra* note 12, at 817, 102 S.Ct. at 2738 (footnotes omitted).

'basic, unquestioned constitutional rights.' " [23]   Arguably, even if plaintiff produces evidence of defendant's malicious state of mind, the immunity would not be defeated.[24] If, *as a matter of law*, the official could not have known about the existence of the right allegedly infringed, he escaped accountability. "Democracy in the jury box" [25] was abandoned. Concomitantly, the individual defendant action lost its utility as a medium for expounding new constitutional rights, because only rights well settled by earlier decisions would be actionable.

Anderson extended *Harlow's* immunity standard to a lower-level official and expanded it in substance by conferring immunity unless the alleged federal law violation was established in a highly "particularized" way. Under this formulation, a right is clearly established only if it was announced in circumstances so closely analogous that a reasonable official in the defendant's position should realize the applicability of the settled precedent. Further, the officer does not forfeit the immunity merely because it was clearly settled that his conduct was in violation of state (or, in a *Bivens* action, federal) law; rather, it must be settled that the *federal right plaintiff relies on* was then definitively declared by an authoritative decision closely on point.[26]

Deciding on the degree of particularity by which prior decisions must condemn the defendant's currently challenged conduct is often a litigation-breeding enterprise. For example, in *Mendoza v. Block,*[27] a Ninth Circuit panel considered it clearly established that police officers' excessive force in making an arrest violates the Fourth Amendment rights of the arrestee, adding that this conclusion holds in "any arrest situation where force is used, whether it involves physical restraint, use of a baton, use of a gun, or use of a dog. We do not believe that a more particularized expression of the law is necessary for law enforcement officials using police dogs to understand that under some circumstances the use of such a 'weapon' might become unlawful." But a subsequent panel of the same circuit later limited the quoted statement to "the proposition that some uses of dogs will in particular instances violate clearly established law . . . ." The panel went on to hold that at the time defendant police officers acted, it was not "clearly established that it was

---

23. *Id.* at 815, 102 S.Ct. at 2736 (quoting *Wood,* 420 U.S. at 322, 95 S.Ct. at 1001).

24. *See Foy v. Holston,* 94 F.3d 1528 (11th Cir.1996). One passage in *Malley v. Briggs,* 475 U.S. 335, 106 S.Ct. 1092, 89 L.Ed.2d 271 (1986) seems to render the defendant's state of mind irrelevant: "Under the *Harlow* standard, . . . an allegation of malice is not sufficient to defeat immunity if the defendant acted in an objectively reasonable manner." Yet in the same opinion Justice White wrote: "As the qualified immunity defense has evolved, it provides ample protection to all but the plainly incompetent *or* those who *knowingly violate*

the law." (emphasis supplied). *See* note 13, *supra.*

25. The phrase is borrowed from Aviam Soifer, *Moral Ambition, Formalism, and the "Free World" of DeShaney,* 57 Geo. Wash. L. Rev. 1513, 1528 (1989).

26. *See, e.g., Russell v. Selsky,* 35 F.3d 55 (2d Cir.1994) (prison regulation prohibited defendant from serving as both review officer and hearing officer in disciplinary proceeding, but court conferred immunity on defendant who did so because clear precedent did not then accord inmates a due process right to fair hearing).

27. 27 F.3d 1357, 1361–62 (9th Cir. 1994).

unlawful to use police dogs to search for and apprehend concealed suspects by biting and seizing them."[28]

Anderson, an FBI agent, participated in an illegal search of the Creightons' home in an effort to find Mrs. Creighton's brother, a bank robbery suspect. The agents, pleading qualified immunity, admitted knowing that warrantless searches generally violated the Fourth Amendment but asserted that they could not have realized the illegality of their conduct on the facts in question.[29] Justice Scalia, speaking for the majority, ruled that an officer could not be said to have unreasonably disregarded "clearly established" law unless authoritative constitutional precedent closely on point existed at the time of the alleged violation.[30] This standard subtly alters the *Harlow* settledness requirement. Whereas *Harlow* stripped the official of immunity whenever a court determined by an objective test that he should have been aware of the law declaring the plaintiff's right,[31] *Anderson* does not unless the Court finds in addition that the official should reasonably understand that "what he is doing violates that right." [32]

28. *Chew v. Gates,* 27 F.3d 1432, 1448–1449 (9th Cir.1994), *cert. denied,* ___ U.S. ___, 115 S.Ct. 1097, 130 L.Ed.2d 1065 (1995). The panel relied on the fact that the only reported decision passing on the constitutionality of using dogs to apprehend fleeing or concealed suspects by biting and seizing them had upheld the practice, even though the Ninth Circuit judges "seriously doubt[ed] whether we would ever have reached a similar result." *Id.* at 1447. In Fourth Amendment excessive force cases, the right is well settled in the abstract but its violation almost always turns on disputed facts. Rather than dismiss such cases on the ground that the violation, as alleged, is not clearly established, courts tend to defer ruling on the ultimate "objective reasonableness" prong of the qualified immunity defense until the facts are settled at trial. *See Clash v. Beatty,* 77 F.3d 1045 (7th Cir.1996).

29. *See Anderson, supra* note 13, at 638–41, 107 S.Ct. at 3038–3040. The Fourth Amendment setting brings to mind the Court's refusal to apply "new rules" of law in most federal habeas cases, further stifling the development of constitutional law in the realm of criminal procedure. *See Teague v. Lane,* 489 U.S. 288, 330, 109 S.Ct. 1060, 1086, 103 L.Ed.2d 334 (1989) (Brennan, J., dissenting) (objecting to the plurality's "formidable new barrier to relief" in cases in which "a federal habeas petitioner's claim, if successful, would result in the announcement of a new rule of law"); Rudovsky, *supra* § 2.3, note 5, note 48, at 56 ("[T]he court has placed significant limits on the power of a federal habeas corpus court to articulate new constitution-

al law."). Professor Arkin believes that the potential of *Teague* to restrict the development of new rules may be overstated, principally because the majority of such claims already faced one or more of the procedural bars to habeas that the Court had erected in earlier decisions. *See* Marc M. Arkin, *The Prisoner's Dilemma: Life In the Lower Federal Courts After Teague v. Lane,* 69 N.C. L. Rev. 371, 392 & n.166 (1991). Professor Rudovsky argues further that another potential arena for the development of criminal constitutional law, suppression hearings, has been largely closed off because the unlawful police conduct does not eventuate in arrest and prosecution or because of the operation of the good faith exception to the exclusionary rule. *See* David Rudovsky, *The Qualified Immunity Doctrine in the Supreme Court: Judicial Activism and the Restriction of Constitutional Rights,* 138 U.Pa.L.Rev. 23, 55–56 (1989) (citing *United States v. Leon,* 468 U.S. 897, 104 S.Ct. 3405, 82 L.Ed.2d 677 (1984)).

30. *See Anderson,* 483 U.S. at 641, 107 S.Ct. at 3039.

31. Government officials "are shielded from liability for civil damages insofar as their conduct does not violate clearly established statutory or constitutional rights of which a reasonable person would have known." *Harlow,* 457 U.S. at 818, 102 S.Ct. at 2738.

32. *Anderson,* 483 U.S. at 640, 107 S.Ct. at 3039. Thus the immunity is not forfeited unless it is "apparent" that "an official action" is unlawful when measured against pre-existing law. *See id.*

The Court justified this more lenient version of *Harlow* immunity as necessary to ward off the disruptiveness attendant upon litigation. *Harlow*, the Court eventually realized, would not sufficiently enable individual defendants to escape discovery unless the trial court applied the new doctrine with reference to a narrowly drawn conception of analogous precedent.[33] Chief Justice Burger's common law approach in *Scheuer*—the scope of the qualified immunity available to executive officers should vary with the "scope of discretion and responsibilities of the office and all the circumstances as they reasonably appeared ... at the time and in light of all the circumstances"[34]—was overridden by the desire of the emerging Rehnquist Court to relieve public officials of the burden of litigation.

The resolution of the "settledness" question, which the Court advertises as part of an objective test, in fact turns on an early,[35] subjective[36]

---

33. *See id.* at 638–41, 107 S.Ct. at 3038–40; *see also Mitchell v. Forsyth*, 472 U.S. 511, 526, 105 S.Ct. 2806, 2815, 86 L.Ed.2d 411 (1985) (authorizing immediate appeals from denials of qualified immunity and stating that *Harlow* is designed to enable defendants who meet its minimum requirements to be dismissed from the action "before the commencement of discovery").

34. *Scheuer v. Rhodes*, 416 U.S. 232, 247–48, 94 S.Ct. 1683, 1692, 40 L.Ed.2d 90 (1974). *See also* Gary S. Gildin, *Immunizing Intentional Violations of Constitutional Rights Through Judicial Legislation: The Extension of Harlow v. Fitzgerald To Section 1983 Actions*, 38 Emory L.J. 369, 374–79 (1989) (describing the traditional common law approach to qualified immunity and criticizing the *Harlow* Court's departure from it because "[a]fter *Harlow*, even if a federal officer intended to harm the plaintiff, he is immune [from damages] if the constitutional interest in issue was not clearly established at the time of the violation"). This assertion may be slightly overstated. *See supra* note 24 and accompanying text.

35. Recent decisions reflect the federal courts' renewed determination to afford defendants an early resolution of that defense. *See Siegert v. Gilley*, 500 U.S. 226, 231, 111 S.Ct. 1789, 1793, 114 L.Ed.2d 277 (1991) (holding on immediate "collateral order" appeal that "whether the constitutional right asserted is 'clearly established' at the time the defendant acted" should be decided before plaintiff is permitted to conduct discovery of the underlying claim); *Gaines v. Davis*, 928 F.2d 705, 707 (5th Cir.1991) (holding on immediate "collateral order" appeal that district court's order was overly broad because it failed to limit the scope of depositions to the issue of qualified immunity). The lower courts have been moving to this position, treating the issue of quali-

fied immunity as a threshold issue to be resolved in the early stages of a case. *See, e.g., Finnegan v. Fountain*, 915 F.2d 817, 820 (2d Cir.1990) (stating that the application of qualified immunity is a question of law for the court and not the jury to decide); *Bennett v. Parker*, 898 F.2d 1530, 1534 (11th Cir.1990), *cert. denied*, 498 U.S. 1103, 111 S.Ct. 1003, 112 L.Ed.2d 1085 (1991) (stating that, when "faced with a motion for summary judgment based on a defense of qualified immunity, the district courts should first focus on whether the plaintiff has established a constitutional violation before determining whether material issues of fact are present"); *Krause v. Bennett*, 887 F.2d 362, 369 (2d Cir.1989) (holding that when qualified immunity can be shown as a matter of law, defendants motion for judgment notwithstanding the verdict should be granted); *Eng v. Coughlin*, 858 F.2d 889, 895 (2d Cir.1988) (remanding case to district court to rule on claims of qualified immunity that were not considered when ruling on motion for summary judgment). *See also Tatro v. Kervin*, 41 F.3d 9 (1st Cir.1994) (jury instructions could not insist that § 1983 plaintiff had to prove that an arrest was "clearly" lacking probable cause or "clearly" effected with excessive force, for that would constitute a disguised, belated assertion of the qualified immunity defense that should have been determined at the outset of the action by the court as a matter of law). But if plaintiff alleges a clearly established federal law violation, discovery may proceed on the fact question whether a reasonable person in defendant's position should have realized that her conduct would violate that law. *See Largent v. Dallas*, 44 F.3d 1004 (5th Cir.) (unpublished), *cert. denied*, __ U.S. __, 115 S.Ct. 2002, 131 L.Ed.2d 1003 (1995).

36. See note 36 on page 59.

characterization by trial and appellate judges. Indeed, when *Harlow/Anderson* immunity is timely pleaded and moved on, the § 1983 plaintiff must prove in response almost exactly what the government must prove in a *criminal* civil rights prosecution: the deprivation of a "federal right made definite by decision or other rule of law." [37] The court in *Elder v. Holloway*[38] held among other things that a federal circuit court of appeals might refer to its "own and other relevant precedents," not just to decisions of the Supreme Court, in determining whether the law allegedly violated was "clearly established" at the time defendant acted. But *Elder* did not present the question whether these "other relevant precedents" include district court decisions from the same or other circuits, or only decisions by other federal courts of appeals.

Moreover, as applied by the *Anderson* majority, the category of "settled" law may shrink significantly for want of sufficiently similar prior cases.[39] At the extreme advocated by *Anderson's* dissenters, on the

36. The initial characterization process is termed "subjective" for the following reason. The FBI agent who committed the alleged violation in *Anderson* knew that the provision in question, the Fourth Amendment, demanded a warrant. *See Anderson*, 483 U.S. at 641, 107 S.Ct. at 3039. The right was not clearly established, however, because the Court concluded that a question remained as to whether a reasonable police officer, despite the lack of probable cause, could have believed probable cause existed. *See id.* This determination, in turn, required the trial court to make an appraisal of existing precedent on the eve of the alleged injury to determine its "closeness" to the circumstances the defendant confronted. *See id.* at 646 n.6. The last step in the trial or reviewing court's determination, like the initial decision made by the police, is inherently subjective; it requires appraisal of the similarity between the conduct under scrutiny and the conduct described in prior constitutional cases.

37. *Screws v. United States*, 325 U.S. 91, 103, 65 S.Ct. 1031, 1036, 89 L.Ed. 1495 (1945) (construing 18 U.S.C.A. § 52 (codified as amended at 18 U.S.C.A. § 242 (1988)), the criminal counterpart to § 1983, as requiring proof of scienter, but noting that "bad purpose or evil intent alone may not be sufficient"). The "requisite bad purpose" of *Screws* has been held satisfied if the evidence shows that the criminal defendant had the purpose to deprive the citizen of the "interests protected" by the violated federal right, even absent any consciousness of the unlawfulness of his conduct. *See United States v. Ehrlichman*, 546 F.2d 910, 921 (D.C.Cir.1976),

cert. denied, 429 U.S. 1120, 97 S.Ct. 1155, 51 L.Ed.2d 570 (1977). The § 1983 plaintiff, therefore, must demonstrate little less against an individual immunity-claiming government official than the government must show in a criminal prosecution for a violation of the same rights.

38. 510 U.S. 510, 114 S.Ct. 1019, 127 L.Ed.2d 344 (1994). One circuit applies this standard by insisting that there be a decision of the Supreme Court or its own circuit on point, "or the clearly established weight of authority from other courts must have found the law to be as the plaintiff maintains." *Seamons v. Snow*, 84 F.3d 1226, 1238 (10th Cir.1996) (quoting *Medina v. City and County of Denver*, 960 F.2d 1493, 1498 (10th Cir.1992).

39. The lower courts differ on just how closely the facts of the instant case must correspond to those of a previously decided circuit or Supreme Court decision for the immunity to attach. At one extreme is the presumption that the immunity prevails unless prior decisions "truly compel the conclusion that the defendant's actions violated federal law," *Lassiter v. Alabama A&M University*, 28 F.3d 1146, 1149 (11th Cir.1994), by reference to law "developed in such a concrete and factually defined context [as] to make it obvious to every reasonable person" that defendant's conduct would have been unlawful. *Beauregard v. Olson*, 84 F.3d 1402, 1404 (11th Cir.1996). Yet other courts, citing *Anderson* itself, observe that the precise conduct at issue need not have been held unlawful by a previous case. *See, e.g., Ayeni v. Mottola*, 35 F.3d 680, 686 (2d Cir.1994), *cert. denied*, ___ U.S. ___, 115 S.Ct. 1689, 131 L.Ed.2d 554

other hand, a right is clearly established if it fits within a broad generic description of any federal Constitutional or statutory right. The upshot is that the settledness concept, as viewed by the several justices in *Anderson*, is zero-sum, scarcely ever satisfied or so easily satisfied as to be meaningless. A majority adopted the strict view and as a consequence qualified immunity is now routinely invoked and very frequently upheld.[40]

In practical litigation terms, the plaintiff must now surmount two distinct barriers to state a sufficient § 1983 claim whenever the individual defendant timely pleads the defense of qualified immunity. First, aided by the Supreme Court's reaffirmation of liberal pleading standards with respect to elements of the prima facie civil rights case,[41] but limited by the Court's recent restrictions on alleging particular constitutional claims,[42] the plaintiff must state a claim currently deemed legally sufficient. The defendant must raise the qualified immunity defense affirmatively, or risk waiving it in accordance with Federal Rule of Civil Procedure 8(c).[43] Second, the plaintiff will bear the burden of responding to the defendant's affirmative defense of qualified immunity by satisfying the court, well before trial and usually even before discovery, that the claim in question was well settled in law at the time the defendant acted. Only if plaintiff succeeds on these two questions of law will the defendant be required to engage in discovery and ultimately establish that, on the facts as she faced them at the time, a reasonable official in her position would not have known that what she did would cross the boundaries of that clearly settled law. Where the underlying constitutional violation requires evidence of improper motivation, it has been held that circumstantial as well as direct evidence of the prohibited state of mind will suffice to withstand summary judgment on the ground of qualified immunity.[44]

(1995). Still another, echoing the Supreme Court's language, writes that the "plaintiff need not show that the specific action at issue has previously been held unlawful," only that the unlawfulness be "apparent" in light of preexisting law. *Hilliard v. City and County of Denver,* 930 F.2d 1516, 1518 (10th Cir.), *cert. denied,* 502 U.S. 1013, 112 S.Ct. 656, 116 L.Ed.2d 748 (1991).

40. *See, e.g., Johnson v. Moore,* 948 F.2d 517, 520 (9th Cir.1991) (holding qualified immunity applies when the right alleged to have been violated is not sufficiently clear to the state official concerned); *Johnson v. Boreani,* 946 F.2d 67, 71 (8th Cir.1991) (concluding that, under the facts, summary judgment is appropriate and necessary to achieve purposes of qualified immunity defense established in *Anderson*); *Vaughan v. Ricketts,* 859 F.2d 736, 739 (9th Cir.1988) (entitling defendant to summary judgment and granting him qualified immunity if he can establish that it was reasonable to believe his act comported with the Constitu-

tion), *cert. denied,* 490 U.S. 1012, 109 S.Ct. 1655, 104 L.Ed.2d 169 (1989).

41. *See* the discussion of *Leatherman v. Tarrant County Narcotics Intelligence and Coordination Unit,* 507 U.S. 163, 113 S.Ct. 1160, 122 L.Ed.2d 517 (1993), in Chapter 13 on Procedure (reaffirming a liberal pleading standard for testing the legal sufficiency of allegations about the "failure to train" variant on "custom" in an entity action).

42. *See* §§ 2.19 and 2.25, *infra.*

43. *Gomez v. Toledo,* 446 U.S. 635, 100 S.Ct. 1920, 64 L.Ed.2d 572 (1980); *Moore v. Morgan,* 922 F.2d 1553 (11th Cir.1991) (defendant has the burden of pleading qualified immunity because it is an affirmative defense that avoids liability even assuming plaintiff establishes all the prima facie elements of a § 1983 claim).

44. *Tompkins v. Vickers,* 26 F.3d 603 (5th Cir.1994).

Siegert v. Gilley[45] appears to direct the trial court to turn first to the question of legal sufficiency. Most circuits with reported decisions on the question as of submission of this manuscript have construed *Siegert* to require district courts (or the circuit courts on an appeal from the denial of qualified immunity) to determine whether the plaintiff has alleged a cognizable federal law violation under current law before considering the twin "clearly established law" and "objective reasonableness" elements of the qualified immunity defense.[46] These courts accordingly turn to the question whether the defendant's alleged conduct violated clearly established law as of the time of the events in question only if and after they have determined that the plaintiff's allegations state a *currently* cognizable claim.

Only one reported federal appellate decision since *Siegert* has expressed a view that the court hearing a summary judgment motion based on qualified immunity "is concerned *only* with the law at the time of the defendant's actions"—that is, with whether the law was *then* "clearly established."[47] Putting aside the questionable soundness of this construction of *Siegert,* in context this discussion was needless.[48] There is virtue, however, in the debate, for it suggests a more flexible, third way

45. 500 U.S. 226, 111 S.Ct. 1789, 114 L.Ed.2d 277 (1991). *Siegert* is also discussed in Chapter 13.

46. *See, e.g., Wilson v. Formigoni,* 42 F.3d 1060, 1064 (7th Cir.1994); *LeRoy v. Illinois Racing Board,* 39 F.3d 711, 713 (7th Cir.1994); *Boyd v. Knox,* 47 F.3d 966, 968 (8th Cir.1995); *Brown v. Nix,* 33 F.3d 951, 953–55 (8th Cir.1994); *Buckley v. Fitzsimmons,* 20 F.3d 789, 792 (7th Cir.1994); *Calhoun v. New York State Division of Parole Officers,* 999 F.2d 647 (2d Cir.1993); *Hinton v. City of Elwood,* 997 F.2d 774 (10th Cir.1993); *Foulks v. Cole County,* 991 F.2d 454, 456 (8th Cir.1993); *Grady v. El Paso Community College,* 979 F.2d 1111, 1113, 1114 (5th Cir.1992); *Silver v. Franklin Township Board of Zoning Appeals,* 966 F.2d 1031, 1034–36 (6th Cir.1992); *Hunter v. District of Columbia,* 943 F.2d 69, 76 (D.C.Cir.1991). These courts view the "current cognizability" question as equivalent to the question raised by a motion to dismiss for failure to state a claim under Federal Rule of Civil Procedure 12(b)(6). Some understand the *Siegert* marching orders to require them to decide the current cognizability question as antecedent to the two-part "clearly established law" and "objective reasonableness" inquiries that compose the affirmative defense of qualified immunity under *Harlow* and *Creighton.* Others expand the qualified immunity defense to include three parts, with the issue of current legal cognizability preceding the determination whether the law was clearly established at the time the defendant acted,

which in turn precedes the fact-based question of the defendant's objective reasonableness. However phrased, these decisions require determining whether the plaintiff's allegations state a claim as of the time the motion is decided before addressing whether the asserted federal law violation *was* clearly established at the time of the alleged wrongful acts.

47. *DiMeglio v. Haines,* 45 F.3d 790 (4th Cir.1995) (emphasis supplied). This panel opinion denigrates the timing distinction made by the Supreme Court in *Siegert* as a "tautology" that merely makes "the self-evident point that a plaintiff has not alleged the violation of a right clearly established at the time of the conduct, if he has not alleged the violation of a right that exist[s] when the motion is decided." *Id.* at 11.

48. The court starts by explaining for thirteen pages why the eight other circuits had misread *Siegert* to require a preliminary inquiry into whether the plaintiff's predicate claim is currently cognizable, instead of immediately and only asking whether defendant's conduct was actionable at the time it occurred. In the next three pages, however, the panel observes four times that the claim before it was not clearly recognized *either* when defendant acted *or* currently. Thus the extended discussion setting forth the panel's unique interpretation of *Siegert* appears to have made no difference to resolution of the legal sufficiency of the complaint at hand.

of reading *Siegert:* on summary judgment the trial court might have discretion to turn first to the current *or* the past legal settledness of the asserted federal right, depending upon which question is easier to resolve or entails less burden for the court. And at least one circuit takes this approach, turning to the "clearly established" issue first where doing so will avoid the additional analysis and needless precedent-setting involved in determining constitutional questions of first impression.[49]

If, for example, there appears to be a close or difficult question whether the allegation states a currently cognizable claim, it probably makes sense, as the Fourth Circuit panel opinion would dictate, for the court to address the *Harlow–Creighton* "clearly settled" inquiry at the outset. If, on the other hand, the right allegedly violated seems to have been clearly established at the time of the events in question but has subsequently been limited or overruled by a restrictive constitutional interpretation issued before the motion is decided, the court should be able to turn to the "current cognizability" question presented by an ordinary motion to dismiss for failure to state a claim upon which relief may be granted. Certainly *Siegert* does not imply that the defendant who elects to assert the qualified immunity defense by moving for summary judgment waives the lesser-included question of current legal sufficiency that he might have raised separately under Federal Rule of Civil Procedure 12(b)(6).

Thus under the *Siegert* approach, the plaintiff's damages claim may fail in either of two ways. If the law has moved in a pro-defense direction after the events in question, *current* legal insufficiency may alone lead to dismissal, either on a motion to dismiss for failure to state a claim or on summary judgment.[50] And the plaintiff also loses where a court recognizes the claimed right as of the time of decision but concludes that the right *was* not well established, by the Supreme Court or in the relevant circuit, when the alleged injury was inflicted.[51] Of course

---

49. *See Spivey v. Elliott,* 41 F.3d 1497, 1499 (11th Cir.1995). A subsequent Eleventh Circuit panel described *Spivey* as showing that "we have not considered the *Siegert* approach mandatory...." *Cottrell v. Caldwell,* 85 F.3d 1480, 1490 (11th Cir. 1996). But in *Cottrell* the court did follow the *Siegert* direction to decide the current legal cognizability of the claim first.

50. *Cottrell v. Caldwell,* 85 F.3d 1480, 1490–1491 (11th Cir.1996). See, e.g., *Burrell v. Board of Trustees of Ga. Military College,* 970 F.2d 785 (11th Cir.1992), *cert. denied,* 507 U.S. 1018, 113 S.Ct. 1814, 123 L.Ed.2d 445 (1993) (facts, viewed through evolving summary judgment standards, were insufficient to show alleged conspiracy between defendant public officials and the private employer that inflicted plaintiff's actual injury, and therefore claim failed to meet § 1983's "under color of" requirement or the state action requirement of the

First Amendment). See also *Wooten v. Campbell,* 49 F.3d 696, 699 (11th Cir.), *cert. denied,* ___ U.S. ___, 116 S.Ct. 379, 133 L.Ed.2d 302 (1995).

51. *Friedman v. South,* 92 F.3d 989 (9th Cir.1996) (an inmate's right to kosher food not clearly established when dependent upon retroactive application of Religious Freedom Restoration Act); *Beauregard v. Olson,* 84 F.3d 1402 (11th Cir.1996) (even assuming tax collector's deputized employees had ministerial rather than sensitive political duties so that their termination for political reasons violated First Amendment, that right not established at the time); *Hogan v. Carter,* 85 F.3d 1113 (4th Cir.1996) (administering psychotropic medication to prison inmate before conducting predeprivation hearing not violative of a right that was clearly established when the prison physician acted); *Suissa v. Fulton County,* 74 F.3d 266 (11th Cir.1996) (supervisor's attempt to impinge on deputy's free speech concerning contents of grievance report did not amount to clearly established prohibition on retaliation for exercising First Amendment rights); *Anderson v. Romero,* 72 F.3d 518 (7th Cir.1995) (inmate's right to confidentiality of HIV-positive status not clearly established); *Sparks v. Stutler,* 71 F.3d 259 (7th Cir.1995) (when inmate had catheter forcibly inserted into urinary tract, his right to be free from such procedure not clearly established); *St. Hilaire v. City of Laconia,* 71 F.3d 20 (1st Cir.1995) (no clearly established duty to announce identity and purpose before use of deadly force); *Haney v. City of Cumming,* 69 F.3d 1098 (11th Cir.1995) (as non-physicians, county investigator and prison guard violated no clearly established right to psychiatric or medical need of suicidal prisoner); *Price v. Sasser,* 65 F.3d 342 (4th Cir.1995) (at time of assault, sheriff had no clearly established duty to protect inmate from other inmates); *Gunaca v. Texas,* 65 F.3d 467 (5th Cir.1995) (despite settled right of certain public officials to be free from political retaliation, no Supreme Court or Fifth Circuit decision had applied that right to the employment of a district attorney's investigator). *See, e.g., Trigalet v. Young,* 54 F.3d 645 (10th Cir.1995) (police liability for injury inflicted by third party suspect during chase was clearly established by circuit law only *after* events in question). *Singer v. Maine,* 49 F.3d 837 (1st Cir.1995) (predicate violation of employee's Fifth Amendment right against self incrimination not clearly established when she refused to answer questions during investigation); *Hale v. Townley,* 45 F.3d 914 (5th Cir.1995) (constitutional prohibition on retaliating against an individual for filing and winning a lawsuit not sufficiently clearly established to pin damages liability on a police officer who rammed his fist into the testicles of a night club operator with such retaliatory intent); *Rodgers v. Jabe,* 43 F.3d 1082 (6th Cir.1995) (when prison officials limited inmates' outdoor exercise, the amount of exercise to which prisoners were entitled had not been clearly established according to the law of the circuit); *Cummins v. Campbell,* 44 F.3d 847 (10th Cir. 1994) (university officials who apparently prima facie violated students' First Amendment rights by delaying approval for the showing of a film celebrating Christ entitled to qualified immunity because the law then did not preclude the countervailing argument that even the university's indirect sponsorship of the film might be viewed as excessive entanglement with religion). *See, e.g., Kernats v. O'Sullivan,* 35 F.3d 1171 (7th Cir.1994) (police officer's ejection of tenant, although an abuse of power, was not a clearly unlawful Fourth Amendment

"seizure" at time it took place); *Foster v. Lake Jackson,* 28 F.3d 425 (5th Cir.1994) (constitutional right of access to the courts had been held violated, when defendants acted, to right to file suit, so alleged right to proceed in litigation free of discovery abuse after filing was not then clearly established); *Chew v. Gates,* 27 F.3d 1432, 1446– 1449 (9th Cir.1994), *cert. denied,* ___ U.S. ___, 115 S.Ct. 1097, 130 L.Ed.2d 1065 (1995) (when police officers acted it was not clearly established that unleashing police dogs on concealed suspects by biting and seizing them constituted deadly force or that any such force was unreasonable); *Prue v. City of Syracuse,* 26 F.3d 14 (2d Cir.1994) (although policeman's right to a pretermination hearing was established when he was denied reinstatement, it was not then established that his particular property interest was sufficient to trigger the protections of due process); *Harper v. Harris County,* 21 F.3d 597 (5th Cir.1994) (law at time of arrest required arrestee claiming excessive force to prove injury, so defense upheld even though significant injury is not a current requirement); *Doe v. Bennett,* 2 F.3d 1412 (5th Cir.1993), *cert. denied,* ___ U.S. ___, 114 S.Ct. 1189, 127 L.Ed.2d 539 (1994) (social worker who allegedly violated father's liberty interest in care and custody of his children did not violate a right sufficiently particularized at the time of her behavior that she would have understood that her conduct—including procuring false evidence, withholding other evidence, and making misrepresentations to judges and prosecutor—violated that right); *Wu v. Thomas,* 996 F.2d 271 (11th Cir.1993), *cert. denied,* ___ U.S. ___, 114 S.Ct. 1543, 128 L.Ed.2d 195 (1994) (in § 1983 claim based on violation of the 1964 Civil Rights Act, university officials qualifiedly immune because it was not clearly established when they acted that their retaliation against an employee for filing civil rights complaint violated Title VII when it took the form of creating a hostile environment rather than exacting a monetary or other tangible reprisal); *Woodward v. City of Worland,* 977 F.2d 1392 (10th Cir.1992), *cert. denied sub nom. Woodard v. Seghetti,* 509 U.S. 923, 113 S.Ct. 3038, 125 L.Ed.2d 724 (1993) (qualified immunity sustained because it was unclear, under law of the circuit at the time police officers and supervisors acted, that sexual harassment violated Equal Protection Clause); *Mouille v. City of Live Oak,* 977 F.2d 924 (5th Cir. 1992) (qualified immunity to be assessed under circuit authority in effect at time of alleged injury that established a substantive due process test for excessive force that was more congenial to defendant than the

what is clearly established may have changed, before the defendant acted, to the plaintiff's advantage too.[52] But the more the right in question is highly dependent on varying facts or subject to balancing—examples are alleged violations of procedural due process or the Fourth or First Amendments—the greater the likelihood that the qualified immunity defense will succeed. In these cases, in other words, it is less likely that a particular set of pleaded facts will correspond as closely as *Anderson v. Creighton* demands to the facts of an authoritative decided case.[53] Nevertheless, the defendant's summary judgment motion may be

stricter, Fourth Amendment standard subsequently announced by Supreme Court), *cert. denied sub nom. Liberda v. City of Live Oak*, 508 U.S. 951, 113 S.Ct. 2443, 124 L.Ed.2d 660 (1993).

52. *See Duckworth v. Ford*, 995 F.2d 858 (8th Cir.1993) (retaliation against public employee for opposing defendant official's successful candidacy was a clearly established First Amendment violation by the time defendant acted, although it may not have been one previously); *cf. Valencia v. Wiggins*, 981 F.2d 1440 (5th Cir.), *cert. denied* , 509 U.S. 905, 113 S.Ct. 2998, 125 L.Ed.2d 691 (1993) (defendant inflicted injuries on pretrial detainee wantonly and sufficiently severely to disqualify defendant from claiming immunity under both Fourteenth Amendment standard currently applicable to excessive force claim and even under the test in effect in circuit at the time of events in question).

53. *See, e.g., Waters v. Churchill*, 511 U.S. 661, 114 S.Ct. 1878, 128 L.Ed.2d 686 (1994) (to be protected, speech of public employee must be of public concern and her interest not outweighed by injury to employer's efficiency interest as employer assessed that injury based on facts about the plaintiff's conduct that it reasonably believed to be true); *Veneklase v. Fargo, N.D.*, 78 F.3d 1264 (8th Cir.1996) (no clearly established right to picket on a route fronting several individual residences where facts of prior Supreme Court decision protected picketing in front of a particular residence); *Beauregard v. Olson*, 84 F.3d 1402 (11th Cir.1996), *supra*, note 51; *Baxter by Baxter v. Vigo County School Corp.*, 26 F.3d 728 (7th Cir.1994); *Dartland v. Metropolitan Dade County*, 866 F.2d 1321, 1323 (11th Cir.1989) (absence of "bright line" determining when public employer may punish employee's speech leads to conclusion that any right violated was not clearly established); *Compare Sims v. Metropolitan Dade County*, 972 F.2d 1230 (11th Cir.1992) (courts should use their own knowledge of the law to determine settledness, not just cases cited by plaintiffs); *cf. Harden v. Adams*, 760 F.2d 1158 (11th Cir.), *cert. de-*

nied sub nom. Grimmer v. Harden, 474 U.S. 1007, 106 S.Ct. 530, 88 L.Ed.2d 462 (1985) (expressing reluctance to resolve complex First Amendment issues on summary judgment). It is true that before *Churchill* some circuits showed substantial solicitude to plaintiffs in overcoming the qualified immunity barrier to First Amendment claims. *See, e.g., Marshall v. Allen*, 984 F.2d 787 (7th Cir.1993); *Buzek v. County of Saunders*, 972 F.2d 992 (8th Cir.1992); *Patrick v. Miller*, 953 F.2d 1240 (10th Cir.1992); *Thompson v. City of Starkville*, 901 F.2d 456 (5th Cir.1990); *Dube v. State Univ. of New York*, 900 F.2d 587 (2d Cir.1990), *cert. denied*, 501 U.S. 1211, 111 S.Ct. 2814, 115 L.Ed.2d 986 (1991). Nevertheless, one would predict that after *Churchill* fewer First Amendment cases will even present the "clearly established" legal issue, because more complaints will be dismissed for failure to state a claim upon which relief can be granted under *Seigert*. Further, one might anticipate that after *Churchill* even clearly established legal claims are less likely to surmount the *fact* prong of qualified immunity: it will less often be so in public employment cases that a reasonable defendant in the particular circumstances will be found to have overweighted the employer's efficiency needs as against the free speech interest of the plaintiff. *See Johnson v. Clifton*, 74 F.3d 1087 (11th Cir.1996) (police chief who allegedly retaliated against officers for testifying about him to a grand jury receives qualified immunity because no clearly established law explained to him that their testimony was a matter of public rather than personal concern to the officers); *but see Penrod v. Zavaras*, 94 F.3d 1399 (10th Cir.1996) (prisoner's right not to be retaliated against for petitioning government to redress grievances clearly established); *Cooper v. Smith*, 89 F.3d 761 (11th Cir.1996) (clearly established that a sheriff's disciplining a deputy for cooperating with investigation violated First Amendment); *Hafley v. Lohman*, 90 F.3d 264 (8th Cir.1996) (retaliation against public employee whistleblower for informing her supervi-

denied if there is a triable issue whether he knew or should have known that his conduct would violate clearly established law; he must therefore endure discovery and trial on that issue.[54] Because qualified immunity is an affirmative defense, the reasonableness issue is one on which the defendant risks the persuasion burden at trial. We might therefore expect that summary judgment on this issue would seldom be granted— only when every reasonable jury, from the evidence adduced on the motion, would have to find by a preponderance of the evidence that a hypothetical reasonable officer in the circumstances would not have realized that his conduct would violate settled law.[55] In practice, however, summary judgment is often granted on this second prong of the immunity, even where the defendant has less than overwhelming evidence about the reasonableness, in context, of his challenged action.

Application of summary judgment to the objective reasonableness issue is even more troublesome, and may be conceptually impossible, where the predicate constitutional violation includes its own subjective or "state of mind" element. An example is the wrongful intent that is prerequisite to a violation of the Equal Protection Clause.[56] How, if at all, should the ordinary qualified immunity showing, which requires no evidence by the defendant about his state of mind, be modified to take into account a state-of-mind element in the underlying predicate right? This is particularly vexing because the second prong of the defense refers to the reasonableness of a hypothetical reasonable officer, while the subjective element in the predicate right refers to the state of mind of the defendant himself. The incongruity logically leads to the following, apparently nonsensical formulation of the second-prong, summary judgment question in a case alleging denial of equal protection: "Would a reasonable jury, from the evidence on the motion, have to find by a preponderance of the evidence that a *hypothetical reasonable official* in the defendant's position would not have realized that the *defendant himself* acted with an intent to discriminate because of race or gender?" A jury could hardly determine what an objectively reasonable third party should have realized about the defendant's own subjective state of mind![57] Still less can a court, on summary judgment, predict from the

---

sors about efforts to hide documents from an impending criminal investigation violated clearly established rights); *Newell v. Sauser,* 64 F.3d 1416 (9th Cir.1995) (confiscating legal materials from cell of "jailhouse lawyer" violated clearly established First Amendment right).

54. *Largent v. Dallas,* 44 F.3d 1004 (5th Cir.1995) (unpublished), *cert. denied,* ___ U.S. ___, 115 S.Ct. 2002, 131 L.Ed.2d 1003 (1995).

55. *See Anderson v. Liberty Lobby,* 477 U.S. 242, 106 S.Ct. 2505, 91 L.Ed.2d 202 (1986) (equating the ultimate burden on summary judgment with that prevailing at trial, including the relevant burden of proof).

56. *See, e.g., Village of Arlington Heights v. Metropolitan Housing Development Corp.,* 429 U.S. 252, 97 S.Ct. 555, 50 L.Ed.2d 450 (1977); *Washington v. Davis,* 426 U.S. 229, 96 S.Ct. 2040, 48 L.Ed.2d 597 (1976).

57. Usually the defendant's state of mind is pertinent only if the underlying constitutional violation turns on improper motive. *Grant v. City of Pittsburg,* 98 F.3d 116 (3d Cir.1996). But the same problem may arise even where the underlying predicate right ultimately turns on an officer's objectively reasonable conduct, rather than his state of mind. For example, in *Graham v. Connor,* 490 U.S. 386, 109 S.Ct. 1865, 104 L.Ed.2d 443 (1989), the court held that the

evidence offered on the motion whether a jury determination either way on such a question could be reasonable.

A recent decision imaginatively expands the defense to conduct that *followed* the conduct to which qualified immunity attached—even though it was clearly established that the subsequent conduct, standing alone, was unconstitutional. In a pro-police reverse twist on the fruit of the poisonous tree doctrine, the Second Circuit held state troopers entitled to derivative qualified immunity for falsely arresting the plaintiff homeowner because the arrest resulted from a seizure of stolen property as to which the troopers were qualifiedly immune under the standard *Harlow/Anderson* test.[58]

Another court, arguably illegitimately, extends the clearly established requirement to the *state* law definition of the kind of "property" interests protected against unreasonable. deprivation by Fourteenth Amendment due process.[59] Of course qualified immunity should attach where a federal due process right, whether or not contingent on an interest created by state law, was itself not clearly established by federal decisions when the defendant acted.[60] It is quite another thing, however, to require the plaintiff to point to state law decisions clearly establishing the kind of property or contract rights that the Supreme Court has long held protected against arbitrary deprivation by the federal due process clause. By hypothesis, it is only *federal* rights that the plaintiff need show were clearly established, because Section 1983 redresses the violation of those rights alone. The counterargument, flowing from *Anderson v. Creighton,* is that qualified immunity is designed to enable a reasonable government actor in defendant's situation to know that her

Fourth Amendment, rather than substantive due process, furnished the constitutional yardstick for measuring whether a police officer uses excessive force in making an arrest; and it reaffirmed that the fourth amendment issue turns on the objective reasonableness of the officer's actions, not his "evil intentions." Yet in a footnote the court observed that the finder of fact, "in assessing the credibility of an officer's account of the circumstances that prompted the use of force, a factfinder may consider, ... evidence that the officer may have harbored ill-will toward the citizen." But that means that decision on the qualified immunity defense in such a case, which in *Graham* itself the court agreed was limited to a test of objective reasonableness, will necessarily involve an evaluation of the officer's state of mind in order to conclude whether there has been a violation of the nominally objective predicate right.

58. *Bradway v. Gonzales,* 26 F.3d 313 (2d Cir.1994).

59. *Lassiter v. Alabama A & M University, Bd. of Trustees,* 28 F.3d 1146 (11th Cir.1994) (plaintiff's property right in employment not unambiguously established by words of his employment contract or by Alabama decisions, which only after his firing recognized implied employment rights based on personnel manual). This decision is questionable not only because it requires that a state law component of a clearly established Section 1983 predicate federal right also be clearly established, but because it answers that question in part by reference to contract terms, rather than to U.S. Supreme Court or federal circuit authority. *See Elder v. Holloway,* 510 U.S. 510, 114 S.Ct. 1019, 127 L.Ed.2d 344 (1994) (directing lower courts to assess whether a federal predicate right is clearly established by looking to their "own and other relevant precedents").

60. *Soliday v. Miami County, Ohio,* 55 F.3d 1158 (6th Cir.1995) (at time coroner ordered cremation of deceased arrestee without contacting any relatives, federal decisions had not yet established that Ohio laws conferring rights on decedents' spouses amounted to a constitutionally cognizable "liberty" interest).

contemplated conduct would violate federal law; and where a predicate federal right, like procedural due process, turns on the existence of an underlying state property or liberty interest, the official can confidently conclude that she will violate federal law if she denies notice or hearing only if she also has reason to know that the prospective plaintiff is entitled to notice or hearing by virtue of well developed state law.

Finally, at least one court seems to confer qualified immunity if the predicate constitutional right, whether or not clearly established, is in some sense less than "fundamental." [61] By contrast, somewhat paradoxically, it is often difficult for defendants to prevail on qualified immunity where the right in question—excessive force is the paradigm—is well established in general terms but its violation *always* turns on the particular facts and circumstances. [62]

Library References:

C.J.S. Civil Rights §§ 278, 282.
West's Key No. Digests, Civil Rights ☜211.

§ 2.13 Interlocutory Appeal From Denial of the Motion: Classifying the "Law" and "Fact" Prongs

Ironically, given the justifications for its creation, the new qualified immunity regime has proven difficult to administer. An increasingly complex jurisprudence of appellate jurisdiction consumes much of the same time and funds of officials that the doctrine sought to spare. It is clear that the review on interlocutory appeal of orders denying qualified immunity is de novo.[1] But in a number of contexts, circuit courts are understandably unsure whether to accept jurisdiction over all such appeals, or only those that raise issues of law.[2]

61. *Jarvis v. Wellman,* 52 F.3d 125 (6th Cir.1995).

62. *See, e.g., Clash v. Beatty,* 77 F.3d 1045, 1047 (7th Cir.1996) (finding it sufficient to deny the motion that police may not, without violating the Fourth Amendment, shove, push or otherwise assault nonprovocative, innocent citizens and declining to insist that plaintiff cite a case involving the same kind of shove at issue). *See also Myers v. Oklahoma County Bd. of County Com'rs,* 80 F.3d 421 (10th Cir.), *cert. denied sub nom. Sharp v. Myers,* ___ U.S. ___, 117 S.Ct. 383, ___ L.Ed.2d ___ (1996) (rejecting interlocutory appeal from order denying summary judgment motion in excessive force case).

§ 2.13

1. *Elder v. Holloway,* 510 U.S. 510, 114 S.Ct. 1019, 127 L.Ed.2d 344 (1994).

2. *Compare Krohn v. United States,* 742 F.2d 24, 28 (1st Cir.1984) ("[T]he inhospitality [*Harlow*] evidenced towards groundless suits against officials, would best be effected by making denials of [qualified] immunity immediately appealable....") *and McSurely v. McClellan,* 697 F.2d 309, 316 (D.C.Cir.1982) ("[A]ppellate review of a denial of a motion for summary disposition must be available to ensure that government officials are fully protected against unnecessary trials under qualified immunity on the same basis as for absolute immunity.") *with Peppers v. Coates,* 887 F.2d 1493, 1496–97 (11th Cir.1989) (citing prior Eleventh Circuit authority and stating that the denial of summary judgment on the basis of qualified immunity "is reviewable after final adjudication of the case, and the collateral order doctrine cannot be invoked prematurely to confer immediate jurisdiction upon this court"). *But see Hudgins v. City of Ashburn,* 890 F.2d 396, 402–03 (11th Cir.1989) (describing the "clearly established" test as an issue of law eligible for interlocutory decision). A panel decision of the Eleventh Circuit reviews in detail the contradictory holdings of its prior panels. The panel concluded that immediate appeal

Immediate appeal makes sense only with respect to the qualified immunity issues that may be decided as a matter of law. As the Supreme Court wrote in *Mitchell v. Forsyth*[3], the denial of a claim of qualified immunity is an appealable "final decision" within the meaning of 28 U.S.C.A. § 1291, despite the absence of a final judgment, "to the extent that it turns on an issue of law...."[4] And *Mitchell* quite properly characterizes the qualified immunity question—whether the conduct in question violated clearly established law—as an "essentially legal question."[5] Indeed, "law" seems a fair characterization of both questions encompassed by the "clearly established" inquiry: the issue *Siegert v. Gilley* insists be decided first (whether the plaintiff has stated a claim for violation of what is currently cognizable as a constitutional right) and the issue identified by *Harlow/Anderson* (whether that right was clearly established by closely analogous circuit or Supreme Court decisions at the time the defendant acted).[6]

But what of the remaining, ultimate issue the court must face in ruling on the defense if it concludes that the law *was* clearly established? Even Justice Scalia, who wrote *Creighton*, described as "fact-specific" the objective question whether a reasonable official in the defendant's position could have believed his conduct to be lawful given the information known to him at the time and the requirements of established law.[7] Yet he nevertheless asserts that the ultimate determination of immunity must be decided "as a matter of law."[8] And more recently the Court, in *Hunter v. Bryant*,[9] has admonished the lower federal courts that immunity "ordinarily should be decided by the court long before trial," and should therefore not be "routinely" placed in the hands of the jury (or, in a bench trial, decided by the judge as trier of fact).[10]

The Supreme Court has resolved a circuit dispute over whether the defendant should be granted an immediate appeal when qualified immunity is denied solely on the objective reasonableness issue—that is, after it has been determined or conceded that the right allegedly violated by the individual *was* clearly established. The Court held in *Johnson v. Jones*[11] that no interlocutory appeal lies from an order denying summary judgment based on the qualified immunity defense when it is clear from

is available from the denial of summary judgment on the qualified immunity defense regardless of whether the decision below turns on the "legal" determination that the right at issue is clearly established or on the "factual" determination that a reasonable person in the defendant official's position should have understood that her conduct would violate that right. *See Howell v. Evans*, 922 F.2d 712, 716–18 (11th Cir.), *vacated on grant of rehearing*, 931 F.2d 711 (11th Cir.1991).

3. 472 U.S. 511, 105 S.Ct. 2806, 86 L.Ed.2d 411 (1985).

4. *Id.* at 530, 105 S.Ct. at 2817.

5. *Id.* at 526, 105 S.Ct. at 2816.

6. *Elder v. Holloway*, 510 U.S. 510, 114 S.Ct. 1019, 127 L.Ed.2d 344 (1994) (whether a federal right was clearly established when the defendant acted is a question of law, not "legal facts").

7. *Anderson v. Creighton*, 483 U.S. 635, 641, 107 S.Ct. 3034, 3039, 97 L.Ed.2d 523 (1987).

8. *Id.* at 641, 107 S.Ct. at 3039.

9. 502 U.S. 224, 112 S.Ct. 534, 116 L.Ed.2d 589 (1991).

10. 502 U.S. at 226–230, 112 S.Ct. at 534, 536–537.

11. ___ U.S. ___, 115 S.Ct. 2151, 132 L.Ed.2d 238 (1995).

the record that the decision turned solely on a determination that there was sufficient evidence about a question of fact to warrant a trial.[12] In doing so the Court recognized that appellate courts might still have to grapple with such "evidence sufficiency" questions when they are pendent to other qualified immunity issues that are eligible for interlocutory review—for example, whether the applicable law was "clearly established." For example, a district judge may offer no reason for denying summary judgment after a defendant argues first, that there is no genuine fact issue about the nature of his conduct (a "pure" fact question that is not immediately reviewable) and second, that his proven or admitted conduct is objectively reasonable (a mixed question of law and fact that apparently is immediately reviewable). In such circumstances, the Supreme Court acknowledged, the appellate court may have to "undertake a cumbersome review of the record to determine what facts the district court ... likely assumed" when it found the law "clearly established." [13]

The problem of labeling the qualified immunity issue as "fact" or "law" gains heightened significance from an even more recent decision of the Court, *Behrens v. Pelletier.*[14] *Behrens* arose from a *Bivens* action against a federal official. The Supreme Court explicitly permitted the individual defendant to take successive interlocutory appeals. The Court affirmed the defendant's right to appeal from the denial of summary judgment, after an initial unsuccessful appeal from the denial of a motion to dismiss for failure to state a claim, repeating the *Mitchell v. Forsyth* rationale that the collateral order exception is designed to afford government officials the right not merely to avoid standing trial but also to avoid pre-trial discovery.[15]

On the peculiar facts of *Behrens,* the defendant presented an unusually appealing case for successive appeals. Its contention that it had not violated any clearly established federal rights was never reached by either the district or circuit court on the first interlocutory appeal. But the Supreme Court went out of its way to add that

> "even in a case proceeding in a more normal fashion[,] resolution of the immunity question may 'require more than one judiciously timed appeal' because the legally relevant factors bearing upon the *Harlow* question will be different on summary judgment than on an earlier motion to dismiss. At that earlier stage, it is the defendant's conduct as alleged in the complaint that is scrutinized for 'objective reasonableness.' On summary judgment, however, the plaintiff can no longer rest on the pleadings ... and the Court looks to all of the evidence before it...." [16]

12. *See Rambo v. Daley,* 68 F.3d 203 (7th Cir.1995); *Winfield v. Bass,* 67 F.3d 529 (4th Cir.1995) (applying *Johnson* by denying interlocutory appeals on pure evidence sufficiency issues).

13. *Johnson v. Jones,* ___ U.S. ___, 115 S.Ct. at 2159.

14. ___ U.S. ___, 116 S.Ct. 834, 133 L.Ed.2d 773 (1996).

15. *Id.* at ___, 116 S.Ct. at 839.

16. *Id.* at ___, 116 S.Ct. at 840.

The quoted statement is confusing if read to suggest, contrary to the apparent meaning of *Johnson v. Jones,* that the *Mitchell* interlocutory appeal lies from summary judgment denials that turn solely on the sufficiency of the evidence. It is probably better read to mean that when summary judgment turns on the objective legal reasonableness of the official's conduct, that mixed question of law and fact is distinct from a "clearly established law" issue previously decided against the official on motion to dismiss, and as such may be eligible for a successive interlocutory appeal.

The Court in *Behrens* did recognize that there might be "abuse" in successive pre-trial assertions of immunity. But it expressed confidence that the courts of appeals would exercise their supervisory powers to reject frivolous claims, for example by the use of summary procedures.[17] At a minimum, the Court must have had in mind that, under *Johnson v. Jones,* a successive appeal should be summarily dismissed to the extent it turns solely on the trial court's resolution of the facts (that principle should apply on *any* interlocutory appeal, initial or successive). But would it also be abusive for the defendant to make a second qualified immunity motion on a pure "law" ground distinct from a law ground raised by the initial motion? For example, suppose the defendant makes a motion to dismiss for failure to state a claim based on the qualified immunity issue that *Siegert v. Gilley* instructs trial courts to consider first: whether the plaintiff's allegations state a *currently* cognizable violation of federal law. Suppose further that this motion is denied, and the denial is affirmed on interlocutory appeal. Would it be "abusive" for the defendant then to make a second motion based on the ultimate qualified immunity question posed by *Harlow* and *Creighton*—whether the rights in question were "clearly established" by authoritative Supreme Court or circuit precedent at the time the defendant acted? Or would it be "abusive" for the defendant to take a second interlocutory appeal if this second motion is denied? The argument that it would is that the defendant could have presented both "law" grounds at the time of the initial pretrial motion, either to dismiss or for summary judgment.

More fundamentally, *Behrens* sheds some light on how to characterize the *ultimate* qualified immunity question—whether a reasonable person in defendant's position should have realized that her contemplated comment would violate clearly established law. Is that a question of "fact" ineligible for interlocutory review under *Johnson,* or a question sufficiently infused with "law" to be eligible for interlocutory review either initially or, under *Behrens,* after a second unsuccessful motion? The Court writes that "*Johnson* permits petitioner to claim on appeal that all of the conduct which the District Court deems sufficiently supported for purposes of summary judgment met the *Harlow* standard of 'objective legal reasonableness'."[18] The implication is that if the defendant below relied in moving for summary judgment on the ultimate "legal" issue of objective legal reasonableness, a denial of the motion is

17. *Id.* at ___, 116 S.Ct. at 840–41.   18. *Id.* at ___, 116 S.Ct. at 842.

eligible for interlocutory review even if premised on disputed facts about the defendant's conduct. That "legal" issue remains: whether, given the circumstances confronting the defendant (determined most favorably to the plaintiff resisting the motion), a reasonable person in defendant's position should have realized that his act or omission would violate established, closely analogous precedent.[19] So *Behrens* reads *Johnson* narrowly, to preclude interlocutory appeal only when, as will seldom be the case, the summary judgment evidentiary dispute is *limited* to the question of what actually happened in real life. Despite *Johnson,* then, the appellate court's interlocutory jurisdiction is intact "where the denial [of qualified immunity] is based even in part on a disputed issue of law." [20]

Behrens decides another frequently recurring issue at the fringes of qualified immunity: whether to grant immediate review where the defendant also faces a § 1983 claim for equitable relief, or any other claim not barred by the immunity doctrine. In that situation the defendant will have to go to trial—and suffer the demands of discovery— to resist injunctive relief even if the immunity defense to the damages claim is sustained on interlocutory appeal. Confirming the predominant opinion of the circuit courts, *Behrens* holds that the individual defendant may proceed with an otherwise available interlocutory appeal even though he will almost certainly face trial on other claims as to which no qualified immunity lies.[21] The Court considered this conclusion necessary to implement the qualified immunity objective of relieving the individual defendant from the burdens of discovery and trial, not just from litigation as an entirety. Were it to hold otherwise, the Court observed, the plaintiff could unilaterally subvert the government official's interlocutory appeal by seeking injunctive relief in addition to damages on a § 1983 claim, or by asserting one or more non-immune claims in the same action.

Indeed, when both damages and prospective relief are sought, perhaps the defendant should sometimes be entitled to an interlocutory appeal under the *Mitchell* rationale even when his summary judgment motion is *granted.* Suppose the defendant had sought qualified immunity on the broad ground, which *Siegert* directs lower courts to decide first, that the plaintiff's allegations are *currently* legally deficient. If the motion prevails on that ground, defendant will avoid liability altogether. By contrast, if his motion succeeds only on the "law" prong identified by *Harlow* and *Creighton* (namely that the violation was not clearly established by closely analogous precedent *when the defendant acted*), the defendant is absolved only of damages liability and will still face trial with respect to the prospective relief. The considerations underlying

---

19. *See Beauregard v. Olson,* 84 F.3d 1402, 1403–04 (11th Cir.1996); *Heidemann v. Rother,* 84 F.3d 1021, 1026–1028 (8th Cir.1996).

20. *Cottrell v. Caldwell,* 85 F.3d 1480, 1485 (11th Cir.1996).

21. It will be remembered that qualified immunity protects only individual defendants, not government entities, and that it shields individual defendants only from damages, not injunctive or other prospective relief. See supra § 2.11 n. 4 and § 2.12 n. 2.

Mitchell—that the qualified immunity defense is intended as an immunity *from suit*—would suggest in this situation that an immediate appeal should lie even though the defendant has prevailed on a narrower ground. A plaintiff, by contrast, cannot secure interlocutory relief from an order granting qualified immunity to fewer than all defendants; the collateral order exception to the final decision rule, as exemplified by *Mitchell,* does not apply here because the plaintiff is said to be able to obtain effective review of such an order on appeal after a final judgment.[22]

Pendent Jurisdiction On Qualified Immunity Appeal

A related difficulty is presented when, on an individual defendant's interlocutory appeal from the denial of qualified immunity, a co-defendant invokes the circuit court's appellate jurisdiction to consider a different defense. The Supreme Court has recently held, in *Swint v. Chambers,*[23] that the exceptional interlocutory jurisdiction conferred on a federal circuit court by *Mitchell v. Forsyth* to review the denial of qualified immunity does not carry with it "pendent" or "supplemental" appellate jurisdiction to review at the same time an order denying an entity co-defendant's motion asserting that its agent was not carrying out official "policy."

The court expressed doubts about its own power to expand interlocutory appellate review by judicial decision. But noting its earlier decisions that had flirted with pendent appellate jurisdiction, the Court concluded that it "need not definitively or preemptively settle here whether or when it may be proper for a court of appeals with jurisdiction over one ruling to review, conjunctively, *related* rulings that are not themselves independently appealable."[24] Even were the Court to approve pendent appellate jurisdiction as a general proposition, the parties in *Swint* did not contend (nor could they plausibly have contended) that the decision denying the county's motion based on deficiencies in the "policy" element "was inextricably intertwined with that court's decision to deny the individual defendants' qualified immunity motions, or that review of the former decision was necessary to ensure meaningful review of the latter."[25] Similarly an individual defendant's statute of limitations defense would not be "related" to her defense of qualified immunity. On the other hand, suppose the ruling below denying an individual defendant's qualified immunity motion focused on the issue that *Siegert v. Gilley* directed trial courts to determine at the threshold, namely, the current legal sufficiency of the alleged federal constitutional or statutory violation. The identical issue, if resolved favorably to the

---

22. *LaTrieste Restaurant and Cabaret,* 96 F.3d 598 (2d Cir.1996); *Winfrey v. School Bd. of Dade County,* 59 F.3d 155 (11th Cir.1995).

23. ___ U.S. ___, 115 S.Ct. 1203, 131 L.Ed.2d 60 (1995).

24. *Id.* at ___, 115 S.Ct. at 1205 (emphasis supplied).

25. *Id.*

individual defendant, would also dispose of the liability of a co-defendant entity who employed her.[26]

Relatedness, in short, is not necessarily absent where a different party seeks to join an individual defendant's appeal from a qualified immunity denial;[27] and it is not necessarily present when the would-be pendent issue is raised by the same individual defendant who is entitled to appeal under the *Mitchell* "collateral order" doctrine. Moreover, the parties' own view that pendent appellate jurisdiction serves judicial economy will not substitute for the required relatedness. All parties in *Swint*—even the plaintiffs who in the trial court had defeated the county's motion based on "policy"—sought immediate review of that decision, to no avail.

Finally, it should be remembered that even if the Supreme Court, either by rule or decision, ultimately approves the doctrine of pendent appellate jurisdiction in the qualified immunity context, the relatedness requirement, while necessary, should not suffice. Notwithstanding an appellate court's power to assume pendent jurisdiction over an issue that overlaps with the immunity question, the exercise of that power, under standard "pendent" or "supplemental" jurisdiction doctrine, remains discretionary.[28] *Id.* The discretionary factors take into account not only judicial economy but "injudicious intermeddling, and justice in the disposition...."[29]

§ 2.14 Private Party Qualified Immunity

Prior to 1970, it was assumed that private actors were not subject to liability under § 1983 because of their inability to act "under color of" state law. *Adickes v. S.H. Kress & Co.*[1] removed this absolute impediment to suit against private persons by finding that such persons could be liable under § 1983 for "wilfully conspiring" with a state actor to deprive the plaintiff of rights protected by § 1983.

The inquiry into whether a private defendant had acted under color of state law was reformulated more expansively in *Lugar v. Edmondson Oil Co.*[2] The Court there held that a private defendant acts "under color of" if, whether or not he has conspired with a state agent, his actions are "fairly attributable" to the state.[3] This "fair attribution" test consists of two elements: (1) "the deprivation must be caused by the exercise of some right or privilege created by the State or by a rule of

---

26. See discussion of *Heller v. City of Los Angeles* in Chapter 13 on Procedure.

27. *See Hill v. Dekalb Regional Youth Detention Center,* 40 F.3d 1176, 1183–84 (11th Cir.1994) (qualified immunity raised by co-defendant).

28. *See, e.g.,* 28 U.S.C.A. § 1367(c).

29. *O'Bar v. Pinion,* 953 F.2d 74, 80 (4th Cir.1991), applied recently in *DiMeglio v. Haines,* 45 F.3d 790 (4th Cir.1995).

§ 2.14

1. 398 U.S. 144, 152, 90 S.Ct. 1598, 1605, 26 L.Ed.2d 142 (1970).

2. 457 U.S. 922, 102 S.Ct. 2744, 73 L.Ed.2d 482 (1982).

3. 457 U.S. at 937, 102 S.Ct. at 2754. Note that this inquiry into whether a private defendant acts "under color of" state law is distinct from whether "state action" exists for purposes of the Fourteenth Amendment.

conduct imposed by the State or by a person for whom the State is responsible," and (2) the private defendant must have "acted together with or ... obtained significant aid from state officials" or engaged in conduct "otherwise chargeable to the State." [4] The defendants in *Lugar* were found to fall within the test simply because they invoked unconstitutional prejudgment property seizure devices. While the Court was thus willing to bring certain private conduct within the boundaries of § 1983 protections, it refrained from addressing whether private defendants who act concertedly with public officials are entitled to the same immunity from suit as public officials or whether in actions against private defendants plaintiffs would be required "to carry additional burdens."

The somewhat labyrinthine development of qualified immunity as applied to public officials set the stage for the question left unresolved in *Lugar*—whether private defendants invoking state replevin, attachment, or garnishment statutes are entitled to the same revised, expansive qualified immunity enunciated by *Harlow* and *Creighton* as their public counterparts.[5] The majority in *Wyatt v. Cole*,[6] writing through Justice O'Connor, held they are not. Because the *Wyatt* defendants had been granted this recently enlarged kind of "objectively determined, immediately appealable immunity," the Court refused to analyze whether the defendants could claim the older "common law" defense conferred by *Pierson*. The Court found that one of the key policy reasons favoring the *Harlow* brand of qualified immunity—the need for government officials to make discretionary decisions without undue fear of suit or liability—was absent in *Wyatt*, where a private creditor, acting purely for personal gain, set in motion the state's property-seizure machinery.[7] It remained to be seen, however, on remand, whether the defendants were entitled to an "affirmative defense [like that approved in *Pierson*] based on good faith and/or probable cause" or whether plaintiffs could be required "to carry additional burdens" in actions against private, as distinct from governmental, defendants.[8]

4. *Wyatt v. Cole,* 504 U.S. 158, 161, 112 S.Ct. 1827, 1830, 118 L.Ed.2d 504 (1992) (citing *Carey v. Piphus,* 435 U.S. 247, 253–258, 98 S.Ct. 1042, 1047–1049, 55 L.Ed.2d 252 (1978)).

5. This was the issue as framed in *Wyatt*, and the majority there emphasized that their holding was limited to that precise issue. At least one appellate court *Burrell v. Board of Trustees of Ga. Military College,* 970 F.2d 785, 795 (11th Cir.1992), *cert. denied,* 507 U.S. 1018, 113 S.Ct. 1814, 123 L.Ed.2d 445 (1993), has, however, seized upon the generality of the Court's statement in *Wyatt* concerning what had been left unresolved—"we do not foreclose the possibility that private defendants *faced with § 1983 liability under Lugar* ... could be entitled to an affirmative defense"—by reading *Wyatt* as not limited to attachment

cases. 504 U.S. at 169, 112 S.Ct. at 1834 (emphasis added).

6. 504 U.S. 158, 112 S.Ct. 1827, 118 L.Ed.2d 504 (1992).

7. Specifically, the majority in *Wyatt* found that the type of private defendants to whom they were denying qualified immunity held "no office requiring them to exercise discretion; nor [were] they principally concerned with enhancing the public good." 504 U.S. at 168, 112 S.Ct. at 1833. Denying qualified immunity here, in short, would not "unduly impair[ ]" the public interest. *Id.*

8. 504 U.S. at 169, 112 S.Ct. at 1834. The majority thus implies that defenses for private defendants, acting with personal motives, should be determined under the pre-*Harlow* law of defenses as defined by *Pierson, Wood,* and *Scheuer.*

Although *Wyatt* produced a majority opinion, five justices either dissented or concurred. These opinions must therefore be closely parsed for clues about the future of qualified immunity for private, noncreditor defendants and of lesser defenses for the private creditor defendants. *Wyatt* provides three separate models for defining the defense available to private parties who are sued because of their use of state replevin, garnishment, or attachment statutes. The majority implies that *Pierson* may supply their only applicable defense;[9] on this view, these defendants would bear the significant compound objective and subjective burdens announced by *Pierson*, *Wood*, and *Scheuer*.

Justice Kennedy, joined by Justice Scalia, concurred in the majority opinion, but wrote separately to elaborate on the defense available to the private defendants on remand. His baseline was formed by the common law torts of malicious prosecution and abuse of process, which he found most closely analogous to the case of a creditor misusing state prejudgment seizure laws. At common law, a defendant was liable for these torts if plaintiff could prove that defendant (a) possessed a generalized, subjectively malicious intent for filing suit, and (b) lacked probable cause for initiating suit. Lack of probable cause, in turn, could be shown in one of two ways: by demonstrating either that defendant's belief in the existence of probable cause was held in subjective bad faith (a mental element distinct from the malice that prompted filing of suit) or that defendant acted objectively unreasonably. Justice Kennedy found that at common law a private defendant could be liable if he in fact knew of the suit's invalidity, notwithstanding his objectively reasonable reliance on a state statute. Specifically, in Kennedy's view, a private defendant whose actions were objectively reasonable nevertheless remained liable if the plaintiff could prove that the defendant acted with (a) a subjectively malicious intent in bringing suit, and (b) more specifically, a subjective

---

9. Justice O'Connor stated that *Pierson* was "of no avail" to the defendants in this case because what they had received below was a grant of *Harlow*-type immunity, thus acknowledging the difference between these two defenses, 504 U.S. at 165, 112 S.Ct. at 1832. However, Justice O'Connor did label *Pierson* as the proper model for determining the availability of a "good-faith defense." *Id.* The majority left open whether the defendants in this case would be entitled to an "*affirmative* defense based on good faith and/or probable cause." *Id.* at 168, 112 S.Ct. at 1834 (emphasis supplied). As is the case with any true affirmative defense, *Pierson*, *Wood*, and *Scheuer* placed the burden of establishing the defense on the defendant. *Id.*

Justice O'Connor's opinion also allows for the possibility that lower courts will apply *Pierson* to private defendants in contexts other than in cases like *Wyatt*, where a private party invoked state prejudgment property seizure mechanisms. At least one court of appeals has read the majority opinion in *Wyatt* as not being restricted to private defendants utilizing state replevin, garnishment, or attachment statutes. *Burrell v. Board of Trustees of Ga. Military College, supra* note 5, at 795 ("Instead of restricting its holding to attachment cases, the Court merely left open 'the possibility that private defendants faced with [section] 1983 liability under *Lugar* ... could be entitled to an affirmative defense....' "). Although this observation was pure dictum, the Eleventh Circuit did express serious doubt that privately acting private defendants of any kind would be able to assert qualified immunity in the wake of *Wyatt*. 970 F.2d at 795; *see infra* notes 15–18 and accompanying text for a discussion of *Burrell*.

bad faith belief about the existence of probable cause.[10]

Thus under Justice Kennedy's faithful transplantation of the "historical" common law, the plaintiff shouldered two burdens in establishing the prima facie case. These burdens compose a mirror image of the objective "probable cause" and "subjective good faith" prongs of the § 1983 version of the "common law" compound *defense* announced during the 1960s and 1970s in *Pierson, Wood,* and *Scheuer.*[11] But his probable cause showing could be made disjunctively, and only the objective portion of the probable cause question was deemed a question of law.

Chief Justice Rehnquist, in a dissent joined by Justices Souter and Thomas, took issue with the majority, arguing that the contemporary *Harlow* version of § 1983 qualified immunity should have been granted on the record before the Court. The Chief Justice reached this conclusion by virtually equating the "historical" common law defense that the majority left open for consideration on remand with the modern *Harlow* version of qualified immunity. Under the Chief Justice's reading of the common law, as under Justice Kennedy's, a defendant would be liable if *plaintiff* made a conjunctive showing of subjective malice and lack of probable cause.[12] However, viewing the historical inquiry into probable cause through the anachronistic lens of *Harlow*, decided more than a century later, the Chief Justice found that it *"principally "* focused on objective reasonableness;[13] lack of probable cause should therefore no longer be demonstrable through defendant's subjectively held bad faith belief in its existence. The Chief Justice's rule allows a private defendant who acted with a subjective bad faith belief in the existence of probable cause to be exonerated, as a matter of law, so long as his actions were objectively reasonable. Justice Kennedy, by contrast, would allow the probable cause question to be either a question of law or a question of fact, depending upon whether plaintiff chooses the "objective" or "subjective" mode of proof. The plaintiff, in other words, might still get to the jury.

Several circuits have addressed the other issue left unresolved by *Wyatt*—whether qualified immunity might be an available to private defendants in non-creditor cases. Most broadly, the Ninth Circuit has asserted that after *Wyatt* "the law is settled that private parties are not entitled to qualified immunity in actions brought pursuant to 42 U.S.C. § 1983."[14] In *Burrell v. Board of Trustees of Georgia Military College,* the Eleventh Circuit Court of Appeals expressed grave reservations

---

10. *Wyatt,* at 172, 112 S.Ct. at 1836 (Kennedy, J., concurring).

11. Indeed, under Justice Kennedy's analytic, future determinations regarding the parameters of defenses and immunities in § 1983 actions would be made according to immunity/defense law as it existed prior to *Wood, Scheuer,* and *Pierson.* Although he concurs with the result, Justice Kennedy's

method in this regard is at odds with the majority's.

12. *Id.* at 176 n.1, 112 S.Ct. at 1838 n.1 (Rehnquist, C.J., dissenting).

13. *Id.* at 178, 112 S.Ct. at 1839 (Rehnquist, C.J., dissenting) (emphasis supplied).

14. *Penman v. Korper,* 977 F.2d 590 (9th Cir.1992).

about "the current vitality of [some] court [sic] of appeals decisions allowing [privately acting] private defendants to assert qualified immunity in non-attachment cases." [15] The court described the decisions granting qualified immunity to private non-creditor defendants as limited to situations where the private defendants had functioned as public actors—either pursuant to a government imposed contractual duty or in the public interest.[16] In contrast, qualified immunity had been (and, the court thought, should continue to be) denied to all private defendants, creditors or not, when they were acting purely in furtherance of their private interests.[17] But the Eleventh Circuit also intimated that qualified immunity might be available to private defendants in a mixed motive case—where the private defendant's acts in concert with public officials are not "solely" for the purpose of depriving plaintiff of rights protected by § 1983.[18]

15. 970 F.2d 785, 795 (11th Cir.1992), *cert. denied,* 507 U.S. 1018, 113 S.Ct. 1814, 123 L.Ed.2d 445 (1993). The court felt no compunction to address the effect *Wyatt* had on cases granting qualified immunity in the non-attachment context, however, since those cases were all distinguishable from the case before the court. *Id.*

16. Although the facts of the cases granting qualified immunity to private defendants were not entirely commensurate, they shared the common thread that the private defendant in each was under some government-imposed obligation to act or acted in furtherance of the public interest.

The court in *Burrell* analyzed three immunity-granting cases. In *DeVargas v. Mason & Hanger–Silas Mason Co.,* 844 F.2d 714 (10th Cir.1988), the Tenth Circuit granted qualified immunity to private persons who are sued on the basis of actions taken pursuant to a government contract to perform a governmental function. *Frazier v. Bailey,* 957 F.2d 920 (1st Cir.1992), specified that the duties to be performed under the government contract by the private party must be such that the private actor is deemed the functional equivalent of a government employee. In the non-contract context, *Rodriques v. Furtado,* 950 F.2d 805 (1st Cir.1991), found a physician under court order to be entitled to qualified immunity because she was cloaked with "the responsibilities of a public official [acting] in the public interest." Thus to fall within the rationale of these decisions, the private defendant must demonstrate that she was acting pursuant to a government contract or that her primary motivation was the public welfare.

17. The actions taken by the private defendants in the immunity-denying cases cited in *Burrell* may best be described as personally, as opposed to publicly, motivat-

ed. The defendants who acted in concert with government actors in these cases to evict a plaintiff, *Howerton v. Gabica,* 708 F.2d 380 (9th Cir.1983), indict a plaintiff for perjury, *Felix de Santana v. Velez,* 956 F.2d 16 (1st Cir.), *cert. denied,* 506 U.S. 817, 113 S.Ct. 59, 121 L.Ed.2d 28 (1992), or, as plaintiff's sibling or guardian, sterilize a plaintiff against her will, *Downs v. Sawtelle,* 574 F.2d 1 (1st Cir.), *cert. denied,* 439 U.S. 910, 99 S.Ct. 278, 58 L.Ed.2d 255 (1978), were considered to have acted on the basis of personal motives.

But then what motivations would fit the "governmental purpose" category? Courts are willing to grant qualified immunity where a private defendant's actions are motivated by a concern for the public welfare. *See Wyatt,* 504 U.S. at 167, 112 S.Ct. at 1833 ("principally concerned with enhancing the public good"), and *Rodriques,* 950 F.2d at 815 (acting "in the public interest"). Many actions that arguably fit the description of "personally motivated" may also be characterized as an attempt to enhance the public good. For example, the defendant-spendthrift guardian in *Downs* might have argued that his attempt to exercise dominion over the plaintiff was motivated by a duty to the public at large. The success of such an argument will, however, depend on the latitude allowed defendants in asserting that their actions in fact served the public welfare. *See generally Sherman v. Four County Counseling Center,* 987 F.2d 397, 406 (7th Cir.1993) (referring to the detrimental impact on the public welfare by denying qualified immunity to private hospitals that accept state mental patients for treatment).

18. The Eleventh Circuit stated that "private defendants cannot claim the protection of qualified immunity" where they

Applying the distinction drawn in *Burrell*, the Seventh Circuit in *Sherman v. Four County Counseling Center*[19] found that the defendant, a private hospital, had acted pursuant to a court order and in accordance with procedures mandated by state law. Moreover, plaintiff had failed to allege that defendant had acted with improper motive or to further its own pecuniary interest, and defendant's exercise of discretion had been in discharge of government imposed duties. These facts placed the case, the Seventh Circuit thought, within the category identified by *Burrell* as warranting qualified immunity.[20] The court in *Sherman* therefore proceeded to apply *Harlow's* defendant-friendly tests in determining whether a grant of qualified immunity was appropriate.

Together, *Burrell* and *Sherman* seem to stand for the proposition that a non-creditor private defendant may be eligible for modern qualified immunity *a la Harlow* if its conduct is to some degree dictated by public norms or designed to serve a public end.[21] The future of qualified immunity for private defendants will apparently turn on how courts delineate the requisite governmental functional equivalence and public purpose. The ever increasing government inclination to privatize, and the public's desire to achieve efficiency in government, suggest that courts expressing policy-based concerns similar to the rationale of *Harlow* will be increasingly receptive to assertions of "private qualified immunity" by government contractors.[22] Indeed, without a grant of qualified immunity, or contractual indemnity in lieu, the private sector may be less disposed to accept governmental contracts.

Many other private defendants, even though not under contract with the government, nevertheless act in concert with public officials. Whether these private defendants will receive qualified immunity hinges upon, in *Wyatt's* terms, whether "the public interest will be ... unduly impaired if immunity is denied." [23] *Sherman* puts some flesh on the bare bones of the requisite "public interest." The court there found that the defendant private hospital was fulfilling a public duty when it treated the plaintiff. Extending qualified immunity in this situation would encourage public service, the Court concluded, and thereby benefit

---

are "alleged to have acted in concert with public officials for *the sole purpose* of depriving another of her constitutional rights." 970 F.2d at 796.

19. 987 F.2d 397 (7th Cir.1993).

20. The court rejected plaintiff's argument that the corporate form of this private defendant likened that defendant to a public entity and thus served to deny qualified immunity. That argument has been tentatively accepted elsewhere. *See, e.g., Moore v. Wyoming Medical Ctr.*, 825 F.Supp. 1531, 1542 (D.Wyo.1993).

21. *See, e.g., Warner v. Grand County*, 57 F.3d 962 (10th Cir.1995) (director of a private crisis center who conducted a strip search at a police station at the request of the arresting officer held entitled to quali-

fied immunity because acting as public officer's agent).

22. *See Williams v. O'Leary*, 55 F.3d 320 (7th Cir.1995) (granting qualified immunity to contract physician serving state prison). *Contra, McKnight v. Rees*, 88 F.3d 417 (6th Cir.), *cert. granted* ___ U.S. ___, ___ S.Ct. ___, ___ L.Ed.2d ___, 1996 WL 514475 (1996).

23. 504 U.S. at 167–68, 112 S.Ct. at 1833–34. One court has extended the narrower "good faith" brand of immunity to private actors who, although executing a judicial search and seizure order in a federal civil lawsuit, were acting to further private interests. *Vector Research, Inc. v. Howard & Howard*, 76 F.3d 692 (6th Cir. 1996) (*Bivens* action).

not only individuals, but the community as a whole. Mental patients would be able to remain closer to home and family, rather than being taken away to some distant state-operated facility. If private hospitals refused to accept state mental patients, greater loads would be imposed on an already over-burdened state system. Thus the "public interest in maximizing the number of facilities available for the detention and treatment of the mentally ill" was best served by a grant of qualified immunity to the private defendant.[24]

Library References:

> C.J.S. Civil Rights §§ 278, 282, 315, 316.
> West's Key No. Digests, Civil Rights ☞211, 269.

§ 2.15 Compensatory and Punitive Damages

If the judge or jury finds liability—if the plaintiff establishes all elements of the prima facie case and surmounts the immunity defense—compensatory damages may be awarded in any appropriate amount [1] for actual economic loss (medical expenses or lost income, for example), pain and suffering, humiliation, embarrassment, emotional distress, and, at least in some circuits,[2] harm to reputation. Compensatory damages are not presumed, however, and the plaintiff must plead and prove them.[3] As the following section discusses, nominal damages are appropriate or required for the violation of certain important "absolute" constitutional rights like procedural due process. The plaintiff may often be unable to prove that economic loss was caused by the mere denial of notice or hearing, so the provision of nominal damages, with the consequent possibility of attorneys' fees, is designed to ensure a practical incentive to vindicate that right. But damages that do not compensate for provable harm must remain truly minimal: the Court has rejected the notion of presumed substantial damages for the "inherent value" of the invaded constitutional right.[4]

Punitive damages may also be awarded against § 1983 individual defendants under certain circumstances. Compensatory damages are not a prerequisite for punitives, which may be awarded when plaintiff recovers any relief on the merits—declaratory or injunctive relief, nominal or actual damages.[5] Indeed if ordinary compensatory damages (say

---

24. *Sherman*, 987 F.2d at 406.

§ 2.15

1. *See Memphis Community Sch. Dist. v. Stachura*, 477 U.S. 299, 106 S.Ct. 2537, 91 L.Ed.2d 249 (1986).

2. *See, e.g., Fraternal Order of Police v. Tucker*, 868 F.2d 74 (3d Cir.1989); *Anderson v. Central Point Sch. Dist.*, 746 F.2d 505 (9th Cir.1984); *Marrero v. City of Hialeah*, 625 F.2d 499 (5th Cir.1980), *cert. denied, sub nom. Rashkind v. Marrero*, 450 U.S. 913, 101 S.Ct. 1353, 67 L.Ed.2d 337 (1981).

3. *Carey v. Piphus*, 435 U.S. 247, 98 S.Ct. 1042, 55 L.Ed.2d 252 (1978).

4. *Memphis Community Sch. Dist. v. Stachura*, 477 U.S. 299, 106 S.Ct. 2537, 91 L.Ed.2d 249 (1986). *See Malloy v. Monahan*, 73 F.3d 1012 (10th Cir.1996) (plaintiff's testimony provided an adequate foundation for recovering lost profits from home rehabilitation business).

5. *See, e.g., Smith v. Wade*, 461 U.S. 30, 55 n. 21, 103 S.Ct. 1625, 1639 n. 21, 75 L.Ed.2d 632 (1983); *Davis v. Mason County*, 927 F.2d 1473 (9th Cir.), *cert. denied*, 502 U.S. 899, 112 S.Ct. 275, 116 L.Ed.2d 227 (1991). See § 2.16.

for emotional distress, pain and suffering, out of pocket medical and psychiatric expenses) are awarded, there is authority that punitives must bear a "reasonable relationship" to them.[6] If, on the other hand, the only merits relief is nominal damages, there is no fixed limit on the punitives.[7] A plaintiff with particularly appealing prospects for an outsize punitive award may therefore ironically be somewhat better off if she recovers only nominal damages and not the other, more standard species of compensatory damages—provided of course that the expected punitives are large enough to offset those compensatories.

The central question in imposing punitive damages is determining what level of culpability warrants their imposition: should damages designed to punish an actor be awarded for negligent behavior, or should they be reserved for conduct exhibiting a more culpable state of mind, such as recklessness or purposefulness? The Supreme Court set the currently prevailing standard in *Smith v. Wade*.[8]

Wade was assigned to a reformatory for youthful offenders where the defendant worked as a guard. After other inmates acted violently toward him, he voluntarily checked into the institution's protective custody unit and was placed in a cell with one other inmate. Defendant Smith placed in the cell a third inmate who had been segregated for fighting. Another cell was available in the same area with only one occupant, but Smith made no effort to discover this fact. Further, another inmate had been beaten to death in the same area, while Smith was on duty, only a few weeks earlier. Wade alleged that his cellmates beat and sexually assaulted him and that Smith violated Wade's Eighth Amendment rights because Smith knew or should have known that such an incident was likely. The jury found Smith liable and awarded Wade $5,000 in punitive damages, under instructions allowing punitive damages if the defendant's conduct displayed a "reckless or callous disregard of, or indifference to, the rights or safety of others...."[9] Smith appealed that award.

Before the Supreme Court, Smith argued that the test for a punitive damages award under § 1983 should be one of "actual malicious intent—'ill will, spite, or intent to injure,"[10] particularly because, in the Eighth Amendment context, any lesser standard would permit punitive damages with no greater evidence of culpability than that necessary to establish liability. The Court discussed the historical variations among the standards states had applied in awarding punitive damages under

---

6. *See Edwards v. Jewish Hospital*, 855 F.2d 1345 (8th Cir.1988).

7. *Id.* Federal courts place the burden on the defendant of proving that its precarious financial condition renders a punitive award excessive. *Chavez v. Keat*, 34 Cal. App.4th 1406, 41 Cal.Rptr.2d 72 (1995) (citing federal cases).

8. 461 U.S. 30, 51, 103 S.Ct. 1625, 1637, 75 L.Ed.2d 632 (1983). The Court has not specifically decided whether the early satis-

fiable *Smith* standard permits an award of punitive damages in any case in which intentional discrimination is shown—in every case, that is, in which § 1981 or § 1983 liability is established. *Barbour v. Merrill*, 48 F.3d 1270 (D.C.Cir.1995), *cert. dismissed*, ___ U.S. ___, 116 S.Ct. 1037, 134 L.Ed.2d 113 (1996).

9. *Id.* at 33, 103 S.Ct. at 1628.

10. *Id.* at 37, 103 S.Ct. at 1630.

the common law at the time § 1983 was adopted, concluding that the majority allowed punitive damages without a showing of intent. The most important difference among the states was "over the degree of negligence, recklessness, carelessness, or culpable indifference that should be required—not over whether actual intent was essential." [11]

The district judge had instructed the jury that Smith could be liable for violating the Eighth Amendment only if his conduct evidenced "a callous indifference or a thoughtless disregard" [12] for Wade's rights. Smith argued that the standard for punitive damages should be even higher, because punitive awards are meant to redress "extraordinary misconduct." [13] Otherwise, Smith maintained, prison guards could not avoid punitive damage assessments because the standard for punitive damages was so close to the standard for the underlying constitutional violation. The Court rejected that contention, reasoning that "the need for exceptional clarity in the standard for punitive damages arises only if one assumes that there are substantial numbers of officers who will not be deterred by ..." the threat of personal liability for other damages. [14] The Court held that punitive damages may be awarded when the defendant's conduct evinces a "reckless or callous disregard for the plaintiff's rights, as well as intentional violations of federal law." [15]

Although § 1983 contains no state of mind requirement, many of the predicate constitutional violations do depend on a showing of intent. As a practical matter, therefore, plaintiffs must often prove an intentional violation of a federally protected right in order to establish § 1983 liability. Against this background what did the Court in *Wade* really mean, by its "as well as" language? Did it mean, as its words would suggest, that *in addition* to the showing of intent often required for liability the defendant must have exhibited a callous disregard for federally protected rights, or did it mean simply that punitive damages are appropriate whenever there is evidence of an intentional violation of law? The latter interpretation, although textually problematic, seems to rest on the basically plausible premise that a showing of the state of mind necessary for an intentional violation of federal rights may include a showing of callous disregard for those rights. The First Circuit has adopted that interpretation, construing the quoted clause from *Wade* to mean that a showing of intent sufficient to establish liability also authorizes punitive damages. [16] But the Seventh Circuit has interpreted

11. *Id.* at 40, 103 S.Ct. at 1632.

12. *Id.* at 33, 103 S.Ct. at 1628.

13. *Id.*

14. *Id.* at 50, 103 S.Ct. at 1637. The Court in *Smith* thus takes a step beyond its observation several years earlier in *Carey v. Piphus*, 435 U.S. 247, 256, 98 S.Ct. 1042, 1049, 55 L.Ed.2d 252 (1978) that Congress may not have intended any "deterrent more formidable than that inherent in the award of compensatory damages."

15. *Id.* at 51, 103 S.Ct. at 1637.

16. *See Rowlett v. Anheuser–Busch, Inc.*, 832 F.2d 194, 205 (1st Cir.1987) (Section 1981 case discussing *Smith v. Wade*; "the state of mind necessary to trigger liability [in most § 1983 cases] is at least as culpable as that required to make punitive damages applicable"). There is, however, some emerging doubt whether punitive damages are available where intent is proved only inferentially. *Barbour v. Merrill*, 48 F.3d 1270 (D.C.Cir.1995), *cert. dismissed*, ___ U.S. ___, 116 S.Ct. 1037, 134 L.Ed.2d 113 (1996).

Wade to mean that punitive damages are available only when, in addition to any showing of intent that may be necessary for underlying liability, the defendant demonstrates "a specific intent to violate a knowable right." [17] This, in turn, requires that "the application of the law to the facts at hand" must be "so clear at the time of the act that reasonably competent people would have agreed on its application." [18] In effect, this places on the plaintiff a "clearly established law" requirement for punitive damages against an individual defendant that corresponds to a key element of the qualified immunity defense. But most individual defendants assert that defense routinely. It must therefore be said that when the plaintiff overcomes that defense and demonstrates liability she will likely also be eligible for punitive damages, even in courts that take a stricter view of *Wade.* On the other hand, the significant expansion and relaxation of the qualified immunity defense since *Wade* will make fewer individual defendants subject to *any* damages, including punitives.

Over the past decade, the Supreme Court has several times revisited the issue of alleged violations of the Eighth Amendment in the prisoner context, the very setting that gave rise to the decision in *Wade.*[19] Those decisions may alter the debate over the test for punitive damages in prisoner-plaintiff cases in a direction favorable to defendants. In the most recent decision in this line, *Farmer v. Brennan,*[20] the Court held that a prison official does not violate the Eighth Amendment, even where the risk of substantial harm to inmates was obvious and a reasonable person would have noticed it, if he was not actually aware of the risk. In light of this higher, "subjective recklessness" threshold for the predicate Eighth Amendment liability of prison caretakers, the Supreme Court may now more likely agree with the "plain text," stricter reading of *Wade.* Punitive damages may be available only if the plaintiff shows knowledge or state of mind more acute or focused than that prerequisite for primary liability, because punitive awards are meant to punish aggravated forms of wrongdoing. In *Farmer,* the Court qualified its holding by observing that so long as the defendant knew of the risk posed to prisoners in general by a given practice, he could be liable, even without knowing that the risk in question would befall the particular plaintiff.[21] Perhaps that knowledge may become the "plus" factor required before prison caretakers become subject to punitive damages.

---

17. *Williamson v. Handy Button Machine Co.,* 817 F.2d 1290, 1296 (7th Cir. 1987) (Section 1981 case; citing *Soderbeck v. Burnett County,* 752 F.2d 285, 289–91 (7th Cir.1985)).

18. *Id.*

19. *See* text in § 2.19 *infra* accompanying notes 6–11.

20. 511 U.S. 825, ___, 114 S.Ct. 1970, 1978, 128 L.Ed.2d 811 (1994).

21. *Id.*

§ 2.16 "Mixed Motive" Cases: Are Damages Available if Defendant Carries the "Same–Decision" Showing?

In the famous *Mt. Healthy* decision,[1] the Supreme Court held that once the plaintiff shows that constitutionally protected speech was a "substantial" or "motivating" factor[2] in the adverse action he suffered, a government employer may avoid liability for those damages that flow from an unconstitutional suppression of speech if it can prove "by a preponderance of the evidence that it would have reached the same decision ... even in the absence of the [employee's] protected conduct." There is widespread agreement that where the defendant carries the *Mt. Healthy* showing in these "mixed-motive" cases, the § 1983 plaintiff may not receive *compensatory* damages for injuries caused by the tangible detriment, for example employment discharge, of which she complains. This is because the defendant has in substance defeated causation by showing that those injuries would have been inflicted for independent, lawful reasons.[3]

But that leaves two possibilities for the *"Mount Health-*ied plaintiff" to recover substantial damages. First, she might be eligible for any compensatory damages that she can prove followed from the unconstitutional conduct itself, apart from those related to the imposition of the tangible detriment. Second, she might be entitled to nominal damages. The Supreme Court has indicated that punitive damages (i.e., those otherwise warranted under *Smith v. Wade*) are available *if* the § 1983 plaintiff obtains any relief on the merits, including nominal damages or an injunction or declaratory judgment; actual compensatory damages, in other words, are not a prerequisite.[4] And there is authority for the

§ 2.16

1. *Mt. Healthy City School Dist. Board of Education v. Doyle,* 429 U.S. 274, 97 S.Ct. 568, 50 L.Ed.2d 471 (1977).

2. *Id.* The Court has since interpreted *Mt. Healthy* to mean that the defendant, to avoid or minimize liability, must undertake the required "same-decision" showing whenever the plaintiff has shown that an unconstitutional motive was a "but-for cause" of the adverse action. *Givhan v. Western Line Consolidated School District,* 439 U.S. 410, 417, 99 S.Ct. 693, 697, 58 L.Ed.2d 619 (1979). The Justices subsequently engaged in extended semantic debate on whether a comparable "but-for" showing was required to trigger the defendant's same-decision showing in intentional discrimination cases under Title VII. *Price Waterhouse v. Hopkins,* 490 U.S. 228, 109 S.Ct. 1775, 104 L.Ed.2d 268 (1989).

There is a division in the circuit authority as to whether the "reverse discrimination" plaintiff who demonstrates the unlawfulness of a race-preferential policy under the

Equal Protection Clause enjoys the usual *Mt. Healthy* burden shift to the defendant. *Compare Hopwood v. Texas,* 78 F.3d 932, 956 (5th Cir.1996) (holding yes), *cert. denied,* ___ U.S. ___, 116 S.Ct. 2580, ___ L.Ed.2d ___ (1996) *with Henson v. University of Arkansas,* 519 F.2d 576, 577–78 (8th Cir.1975) (per curiam) (holding no).

3. *Carey v. Piphus,* 435 U.S. 247, 260, 98 S.Ct. 1042, 1050, 55 L.Ed.2d 252 (citing *Mt.Healthy,* 429 U.S. at 285–286, 97 S.Ct. at 575–576). *See* Nahmod, *Civil Rights and Civil Liberties Litigation: The Law of Section 1983* (3d ed. 1991) 281–283.

4. *Smith v. Wade,* 461 U.S. 30, 55 n. 21, 103 S.Ct. 1625, 1639, n. 21, 75 L.Ed.2d 632 (1983). *See also Carey v. Piphus,* 435 U.S. 247, 256 n. 11, 98 S.Ct. 1042, 1049 n. 11, 55 L.Ed.2d 252 (1978) (noting without approval or disapproval decisions that awarded punitive damages for the sole purpose of deterring or punishing constitutional violations). There is authority that the prevailing plaintiff in a Reconstruction Civil Rights Act case is entitled to nominal dam-

proposition that, while punitive damages must bear a proportional relationship to any compensatory damages awarded, they need not be proportional to nominal damages.[5]

These possibilities acquire larger significance because recovery of nominal, punitive damages or both would constitute relief on the merits that would make these plaintiffs "prevailing parties" eligible for an award of attorneys' fees under the Civil Rights Attorney's Fees Awards Act of 1976.[6] And the prospect of a fee recovery would tend to entice counsel to represent potential plaintiffs who were victimized by unconstitutional conduct but whose consequent tangible loss can be independently, lawfully explained by the defendant.

In *Carey v. Piphus*,[7] the Supreme Court held that the plaintiff who proves a violation of the special, "absolute" right to *procedural due process* is eligible to receive certain forms of damages even though the defendant, by prevailing on the *Mt. Healthy* showing, has broken the chain of causation between unconstitutional conduct and loss of job or consequent emotional distress.[8] Specifically, that plaintiff is entitled to nominal damages of no more than $1 and may recover any damages for emotional distress (mental suffering or emotional anguish) that he can prove were caused by the denial of notice or hearing, as distinct from those damages caused by the loss of job or other adverse action taken by the defendant.[9] But that still leaves the question whether the § 1983 plaintiff who can demonstrate that the violation of a right *other* than procedural due process was a "motivating factor" in the adverse action taken against her can obtain *any* damages where the defendant, per *Mt. Healthy*, proves that the plaintiff would have suffered the adverse action in any event.

Scholarly commentary has suggested[10] or argued[11] in the affirmative, reasoning that while the adverse consequence of employment loss

ages whether or not she can prove actual injury, *Hicks v. Brown Group, Inc.*, 902 F.2d 630, 652–54 (8th Cir.1990), but only if the request for nominal damages is timely. For this purpose "timely" means making the request for nominal damages in a request to charge the jury, see *Kerr–Selgas v. American Airlines, Inc.*, 69 F.3d 1205 (1st Cir.1995) and *Cooper Distrib. Co. v. Amana Refrigeration, Inc.*, 63 F.3d 262 (3d Cir. 1995), or even as early as the pretrial order, *Walker v. Anderson Elec. Connectors*, 944 F.2d 841 (11th Cir.1991).

5. *See Edwards v. Jewish Hospital of St. Louis*, 855 F.2d 1345, 1352 (8th Cir.1988) (case under § 1981).

6. Amending 42 U.S.C.A. § 1988. *See Carey v. Piphus*, 435 U.S. 247, 256–57, 98 S.Ct. 1042, 1049, 55 L.Ed.2d 252 nn.11–12 (1978). *See also Farrar v. Hobby*, 506 U.S. 103, 113 S.Ct. 566, 121 L.Ed.2d 494 (1992) (holding that recovery of nominal damages alone makes plaintiff a "prevailing party"

eligible for fees under § 1988, but that the amount of the fee award that is "reasonable" where the nominal damages represent an insignificant portion of the relief originally sought is ordinarily nothing).

7. 435 U.S. 247, 98 S.Ct. 1042, 55 L.Ed.2d 252 (1978).

8. *Id.* at 266, 98 S.Ct. at 1054.

9. Such compensatory damages, however, require proof and may not be presumed to follow upon every denial of procedural due process. *See Carey, supra.*

10. Sullivan, Richards, Zimmer & Calloway, *Cases and Materials on Employment Discrimination* 1097 (Little Brown 3d ed. 1994) (citing *Edwards v. Jewish Hospital*, 855 F.2d 1345 (8th Cir.1988)). *Edwards* supports awarding damages to the mixed-motive plaintiff in an action under *§ 1981*,

11. See note 11 on page 85.

cannot be attributed to unconstitutional conduct when the employer makes the *Mt. Healthy* showing, plaintiffs should forfeit only those elements of damage attributable to that loss.[12] Accordingly, the contention is that while backpay and other compensatory damages attributable to the defendant's challenged action (e.g., discharge) must be denied, compensatory damages resulting from the defendant's reliance on another, unconstitutional motive are available, as are nominal and therefore punitive damages.[13] Where malice is present and plaintiff's counsel therefore anticipates the possibility of recovering punitive as well as nominal damages concerning the unlawful, "motivating" factor, this approach, should it prevail, would provide an incentive to prosecute a § 1983 action notwithstanding the anticipation that defendant can make a successful *Mt. Healthy* showing.[14]

This view derives some support from the language of the *Mount Healthy* opinion, which, however, also may be read to mean that the "same-decision" showing does not merely limit available remedies but defeats liability for a constitutional violation. The Court answered in the negative an issue it defined as follows: whether, despite the defendant's showing, plaintiff's demonstration that First and Fourteenth Amendment violations had figured substantially in the challenged employment decision "would *necessarily* amount to a constitutional violation *justifying remedial action*."[15] If the quoted phrase is truncated after "constitutional violation," it would seem that the Court intended to hold that no violation may be found if the defendant makes the required showing. On the other hand, the "necessarily" qualification leaves the door open for a plaintiff to argue that liability may lie despite a defendant's "same-decision" showing. Likewise "justifying remedial action" may be viewed as a critical modifier of "constitutional violation," suggesting that defendant's showing doesn't defeat the formal finding of

but not § 1983. In fact the *Edwards* opinion specifically distinguishes the statutes, acknowledging that a prior Eighth Circuit panel had concluded in *Hervey v. City of Little Rock*, 787 F.2d 1223 (8th Cir.1986), that the mixed-motive plaintiff *cannot* receive damages in actions under § 1983. The authors nevertheless write that the "more sensible" approach outlined in *Edwards* "may emerge" in cases under § 1983 as well as § 1981.

11. *See* Nahmod, *Civil Rights and Civil Liberties Litigation: The Law of Section 1983* (3d ed. 1994) 281–283 and 1993 Cumulative Supplement, at 95 (arguing that the "proper interpretation of *Mount Healthy*" calls for the defendant who carries the "same-decision" burden to remain liable, but only for the reduced remedies that can fairly be said to have been caused by the constitutional violation).

12. *See, e.g., Merritt v. Mackey*, 932 F.2d 1317 (9th Cir.1991).

13. *Cf. Edwards v. Jewish Hospital*, 855 F.2d 1345 (8th Cir.1988) (awarding nominal and punitive damages and denying compensatory damages after the defendant's "*Mount Healthy*" showing on a § 1981 claim only because plaintiff could showed that emotional distress was caused by his discharge, rather than by the employer's reliance on his race). See also Nahmod, *supra*, 3d ed. at 283 (compensatory damages caused by defendant's reliance on unconstitutional motive recoverable despite defendant's *Mount Healthy* showing).

14. The prospect of punitives is important. A recent Supreme Court decision would usually award $0 in attorney's fees under § 1988 to plaintiffs who recover only nominal damages in actions under § 1983, at least when they had sought more substantial relief. *See* discussion of *Farrar v. Hobby* in Chapter 12 on Attorney's Fees, below.

15. *Mount Healthy*, 429 U.S. at 285, 97 S.Ct. at 575 (emphasis supplied).

a violation but, depending on the circumstances, limits or eliminates remedies. This view is somewhat fortified by the Court's statement in *Mount Healthy* that its specific concern was with the trial court's "conclusion that Doyle is entitled to reinstatement with backpay," [16] and with its insistence on a "test of causation which distinguishes between a result caused by a constitutional violation and one not so caused." [17] The problem for the Court was that *even if* a violation had been shown, there had not yet been proof of a loss attributable to that violation. It remanded for application of the "same-decision" test, but provided no specific direction for further proceedings.

The Court's references to *Mount Healthy* a year later in *Carey* are consistent with that reading. It stressed that § 1983 damages are appropriate only when the defendant's conduct is "found ... to have been violative of ... constitutional rights and to have caused compensable injury." [18] Citing *Mount Healthy*, the Court agreed that the *Carey* defendant's "same-decision" showing meant that the *Carey* plaintiffs' suspensions could not be considered caused by defendant's failure to accord them procedural due process; and in turn damages for those suspensions would represent a "windfall" rather than the required "compensation." [19] But it added that the "interests protected by a *particular* constitutional right may not also be protected by" the ordinary principles of damages derived from the common law of torts [20]; and it recognized that some, but not necessarily all, victims of procedural due process might suffer emotional distress from the denial of process itself. That distress would be compensable, the Court held, even though the distress related to a "justified deprivation"—e.g. a loss of employment that the employer has proven would have come about for independent, lawful reasons—is not.

Can either or both of the *Carey* conclusions—procedural due process denials entitle plaintiffs to $1 in nominal damages and make them eligible for provable compensatory damages caused by the denial itself— be generalized to all constitutional violations that might be vindicated through § 1983? The *nominal* damages holding was restricted quite clearly to the Court's recognition that deprivations of that "absolute" right is of "importance to organized society" and must be "scrupulously observed." [21] The compensatory damages holding, however, was not expressly so limited, for it was premised on general § 1983 principles of damages. Nevertheless, the post-*Mount Healthy* authority outside the procedural due process arena suggests that carrying the "same-decision" burden relieves the defendant of a finding of constitutional violation and accordingly of all monetary remedies. The court of appeals decisions

16. *Id.* at 284, 97 S.Ct. at 574.

17. *Id.* at 286, 97 S.Ct. at 575.

18. 98 S.Ct. at 1047, 435 U.S. at 254 (quoting *Wood v. Strickland*, 420 U.S. 308, 319, 95 S.Ct. 992, 999, 43 L.Ed.2d 214 (1975)) (emphasis supplied in *Wood*).

19. 435 U.S. at 260, 98 S.Ct. at 1050.

20. *Id.* at 258, 98 S.Ct. at 1049.

21. 435 U.S. at 266, 98 S.Ct. at 1054. *Accord, Farrar v. Hobby*, 506 U.S. 103, 113 S.Ct. 566, 121 L.Ed.2d 494 (1992).

have so decided or assumed, and none distinctly to the contrary has been found.

A recent reference by the Court to *Mt. Healthy* fortifies the conclusion that the employer who carries the same-decision burden is probably relieved of all liability, not merely of damages. The Court described *Mt. Healthy* as holding "that if the lawful reason alone would have sufficed to justify the firing, the employee could not prevail in a suit against an employer." The rule, wrote the Court, was prompted by a desire to relieve the employer of the burden of disentangling an independently sufficient lawful motive from an unlawful one where both played a part in the challenged action.[22] In context, the Court distinguished *Mt. Healthy* from situations where it is assumed or proven that the employer's sole motive in imposing an employment detriment is unlawful, but the employer subsequently happens upon evidence that it claims would have then led it to take the same action lawfully. The Court held that in the latter situation, an employer is liable for the economic damage caused by its initial, unlawful conduct only until it discovers the separate, "after-acquired" evidence. Although the question was not directly presented, the Court's clear implication in placing *Mt. Healthy* in the "mixed-motives" rather than the "after-acquired evidence" category was that the employee whose demonstration of discrimination is trumped by the "same-decision" showing cannot prevail at all—in effect, has not demonstrated a constitutional violation.

Library References:

C.J.S. Civil Rights §§ 315, 316.
West's Key No. Digests, Civil Rights ☞269.

D. THE CASE AGAINST ENTITY DEFENDANTS

§ 2.17   In General

The case against an entity defendant fundamentally differs from the case against an individual. The prima facie case against an entity requires, in addition to the elements of the case against an individual, a showing that an entity "policy" caused the injury. This showing is made by demonstrating either established policy or deliberate indifference to a protected right. The entity has no affirmative defense of immunity. And even after the burdensome "policy" hurdle has been cleared, the plaintiff is entitled only to compensatory damages.

§ 2.18   The Origins and Evolution of the "Policy" Requirement

Monroe approved a wide variety of claims against individual defendants for federal law violations their entity principals had not autho-

---

22. *McKennon v. Nashville Banner Publishing Co.,* ___ U.S. ___, ___, 115 S.Ct. 879, 885, 130 L.Ed.2d 852 (1995). *McKennon* has thus been read to assert that the *Mt.* *Healthy* approach defeats liability "outright" in a § 1983 mixed-motive case. *O'Day v. McDonnell Douglas Helicopter Co.,* 79 F.3d 756 (9th Cir.1996).

rized. At the same time, however, it declared that local government entities lie wholly outside the ambit of § 1983. Although from a plain-meaning perspective everything such an entity does is surely "under color of" state law,[1] the Court concluded that it simply was not a "person" civilly liable for that conduct.

This conclusion was premised upon the significance the Court attached to the rejection of an amendment to the original statute, proposed by Senator Sherman, that would have made government entities liable to citizens injured by specific acts of violence committed by private citizens.[2] The federal compulsion to monitor citizen conduct that would have been imposed on state entities under the amendment seemed to offend the prevailing theory of dual sovereignty, which forbade the national government from imposing duties or obligations on officers of the state or state instrumentalities.[3]

Seventeen years later, the Court gave a very different reading to that same history. Justice Brennan's opinion in *Monell v. Department of Social Services*[4] agreed that the 1871 Congress, in rejecting the Sherman Amendment, doubted its " 'constitutional power to impose ... [civil liability] upon county and town organizations.' "[5] But the real vice of the Amendment, according to the revisionist view, was that the duty imposed on state policies was new; it was the federal imposition on the states of a fresh obligation that aroused the ire of the Amendment's victorious opponents. Section 1983, the *Monell* Court observed, imposed no such new obligation on any state or local government. Instead, it merely subjected local government to civil liability for violating federal constitutional obligations already a part of the organic law of the land.[6]

§ 2.18

1. *See Monell v. Department of Social Servs.*, 436 U.S. 658, 707, 98 S.Ct. 2018, 2044, 56 L.Ed.2d 611 (1978) (Powell, J., concurring) ("No conduct of government comes more clearly within the 'under color of' state law language of § 1983.").

2. *See Monroe v. Pape*, 365 U.S. 167, 188–92, 81 S.Ct. 473, 485–86, 5 L.Ed.2d 492 (1961), *overruled in part by Monell*, 436 U.S. 658, 98 S.Ct. 2018, 56 L.Ed.2d 611 (1978).

3. *See id.* at 190, 81 S.Ct. at 485; *see also Monell*, 436 U.S. at 669–83, 98 S.Ct. at 2025–32 (surveying the drafting Congress's debate over potential dual sovereignty limitations on their authority).

4. 436 U.S. 658, 98 S.Ct. 2018, 56 L.Ed.2d 611 (1978).

5. *Id.* at 664, 98 S.Ct. at 2022 (*quoting Monroe*, 365 U.S. at 190, 81 S.Ct. at 485).

6. *See id.* at 669–83, 98 S.Ct. at 2025–32. The *Monell* majority relied on history that illustrated how such preexisting constitutional duties were enforced civilly against municipalities during the reign of dual sov-

ereignty. In effect, then, it drew a distinction between the legislative imposition of new obligations and the judicial declaration of rights discovered in extant text, with only the former offending dual sovereignty. The Court's attempt to reconcile opposition to the Sherman Amendment based on dual sovereignty with its application of § 1983 to local government entities encounters an additional difficulty after passage of § 1983. The statute's framers might well regard expansive constitutional constructions first announced after the statute's enactment, as well as the federal statutory obligations that now may be enforced against local government through § 1983 actions, *see infra* Part F, as fresh obligations offensive to dual sovereignty. Mitigating this difficulty is the fairly rapid waning of dual sovereignty after enactment of § 1983, and the use of § 1983 to impose liability for violations of federal statutory rights is a fairly recent development. *See Maine v. Thiboutot*, 448 U.S. 1, 6–8, 100 S.Ct. 2502, 2505–2506, 65 L.Ed.2d 555 (1980) (defining the "and laws" language of § 1983 to apply to the deprivation of statutory benefits).

This explains why several opponents of the Amendment nevertheless voted to enact § 1983 into law.[7]

Having cleared away the constitutional objection *Monroe* had raised, the *Monell* majority turned to the statutory question: whether the 1871 Congress intended to include local government entities within the definition of "person" suable under § 1983. The Court answered affirmatively, relying principally on the Dictionary Act of 1871, passed only two months before the law that became § 1983. The Dictionary Act provided that " 'in all acts hereafter passed ... the word "person" may extend ... to bodies politic and corporate.' "[8] The majority concluded in summary fashion that corporations, including municipal corporations, were customarily treated identically with natural persons for purposes of constitutional and statutory construction.[9]

The *Monell* retrospective on the 1871 Congress's doubt about its constitutional power to subject local governments to civil liability is not controversial on its merits. Even Justice Rehnquist in dissent acknowledged the probable correctness of the majority's conclusion on that point.[10] What is remarkable is that the Court would return to that issue only seventeen years after *Monroe's* excursion through the same history, and in the same year the Senate was considering overturning the *Monroe* exclusion of municipal governments from the reach of § 1983.[11] The majority itself recognized the awkwardness of the rapid overruling.[12]

Still, it is not surprising that the Court would strain so hard to sweep government entities within § 1983. The extant qualified immunity doctrine, while not yet overwhelmingly tilted in favor of the defendant, was tied to the concept of reasonableness and therefore made recovery against individual officers uncertain. Further, even if the plaintiff prevailed the officer was likely to be judgment-proof, and the practice of indemnification, although widespread, was equally uncertain and uneven. Some governments would not indemnify at all, and others only for conduct comporting with varying definitions of scope of authori-

---

7. *See* Larry Kramer & Alan O. Sykes, *Municipal Liability Under § 1983: A Legal and Economic Analysis,* 1987 Sup.Ct.Rev. 249, 260 (1987).

8. *Monell,* 436 U.S. at 688, 98 S.Ct. at 2034 (*quoting* Act of Feb. 25, 1871, ch. 71, § 2, 16 Stat. 431 (1871)).

9. *See id.* at 688–89, 98 S.Ct. at 2034–35.

10. *See id.* at 723, 98 S.Ct. at 2052 (Rehnquist, J., dissenting) (stating that "it may well be that on the basis of this closer analysis ... a conclusion contrary to ... *Monroe* ... could have been reached ... 17 years ago"); *see also id.* at 722, 98 S.Ct. at 2052 (granting that the Court was "probably correct" in its analysis of the Sherman Amendment debates).

11. *See id.* at 719, 98 S.Ct. at 2050.

12. The majority labored to explain why stare decisis should not preclude it from overruling this portion of *Monroe.* The *Monell* overruling of the *Monroe* entity immunity holding in such a short time span is a striking early instance of the demise of statutory stare decisis, so decisively reaffirmed as late as 1938 in Justice Brandeis's celebrated opinion in *Erie R.R. v. Tompkins,* 304 U.S. 64, 79–80, 58 S.Ct. 817, 823, 82 L.Ed. 1188 (1938). That demise is catalogued, almost defiantly, in the per curiam opinion of the Court that sua sponte called for rebriefing and reargument in *Patterson v. McLean Credit Union,* 485 U.S. 617, 618, 108 S.Ct. 1419, 1420, 99 L.Ed.2d 879 (1988) (citing cases).

ty.[13] Indemnification thus did not assure the satisfaction of judgments in many cases embraced by *Monroe*'s broad "under color of" umbrella.

The Court was also influenced by the fundamental structural consideration that § 1983, itself constitutionally dependent upon state action, was specifically aimed at state-sponsored conduct. If local government officials and low-level employees could be reached precisely because they carried the badge of government authority, is it reasonable to suppose that the 1871 Congress intended to absolve the very governments who handed out the badges? [14]

But *Monell* announced an equally important restriction on the scope of the new liability of entities. Having stretched jurisprudential convention to arrive at a result on the "person" definition that was consonant with constitutional history and pre-*Monroe* precedent, the Court in *Monell* strained every bit as hard to narrow the terms of local government liability.[15] The Court held that local government entities can be liable under § 1983 only if the conduct causing the constitutional violation is carried out "pursuant to official municipal policy of some nature." [16]

How Justice Brennan for the majority derived the "policy" limitation is a source of wonder. He began the journey with the statute's text, noting that the defendant, to be liable, must " 'subject[ ], or cause[a plaintiff] to be subjected' " to the deprivation of federally secured

---

13. The availability of indemnification then, as today, is not entirely clear. The Yale Project, sampling Connecticut district court filings from 1970–77, found that no costs were borne by police officers sued under federal statutes. *See* Project, *Suing the Police in Federal Court*, 88 Yale L. J. 781, 810–11 (1979) (noting that Connecticut required indemnification under Conn. Gen. Stat. § 7–465 (1977)). By the same token, one commentator writes that other municipalities were experiencing difficulty purchasing comprehensive liability insurance for employees and elected officials. *See* Martin J. Jaron, Jr., *The Threat of Personal Liability Under the Federal Civil Rights Act: Does It Interfere with the Performance of State and Local Government?*, 13 Urb. Law. 1 (1981), *reprinted in Section 1983: Sword and Shield* 309, 327–29 (Robert H. Freilich & Richard G. Carlisle eds., 1983); *see also* Schuck, *supra* § 2.22, note 1 at note 85 (discussing self-insurance and the purchase of insurance by states, localities, and public officials). Most observers seem to agree that some form of indemnification was and is available, although the scope varies from jurisdiction to jurisdiction. *See, e.g., id.* at 86 (explaining that "[m]ost states provide some form of indemnification or other protection against adverse judgments or settlements, but some apparently provide it only in narrowly circumscribed

situations" (citation omitted)); Peter W. Low & John C. Jeffries, Jr., *Federal Courts and the Law of Federal–State Relations* (2d ed. 1989) (pointing out that although most government employers choose to protect their employees against damage liability, the availability of such protection often depends on statutes, ordinances, and practices in each jurisdiction).

14. Indeed, Justice Powell noted the "oddness" of imposing liability on the agent but not the principal for whom the agent worked. *See Monell*, 436 U.S. at 705, 98 S.Ct. at 2043 (Powell, J., concurring).

15. *Monell*, 436 U.S. at 714, 98 S.Ct. at 2047 (Stevens, J., concurring in part). The narrowing construction is contained in a separate discussion that one justice termed "merely advisory" and "not necessary to explain the Court's decision." The city's pregnancy leave requirement was adopted "as a matter of official policy," and the majority admitted that "this case unquestionably involve[d] official policy as a moving force of the constitutional violation." 436 U.S. at 694, 98 S.Ct. at 2037. *Monell*, therefore, furnished no occasion to consider the circumstances under which local governments should be liable for *unauthorized* federal law violations.

16. *Id.* at 691, 98 S.Ct. at 2036.

rights.[17] That sparse language, he concluded, "cannot be easily read to impose liability vicariously on governing bodies...." Because Congress provided "that *A's* tort became *B's* liability if *B* 'caused' *A* to subject another to a tort suggests that Congress did not intend Section 1983 liability to attach where such causation was absent."[18] And only some custom or deliberate act labelled "official policy" would show causation by a government entity.

Ascribing such independent, greater-than-boilerplate significance to causation language in a statute remediating constitutional torts is somewhat surprising, since causation is an invariable prerequisite of liability for civil harms. The language Justice Brennan construed is susceptible to equally plausible alternative interpretations. One way an entity may "cause" a person to be subjected to a constitutional injury, for example, is simply to charge its agents to meet specified objectives without taking reasonable steps to prevent them from trampling on federally protected rights. No deliberative act on the part of the employer is required to "cause" deprivations in this fashion. Although this interpretation is perhaps dubious as applied to those predicate violations dependent upon an element of wrongful intent,[19] no textual imperative extends such a limitation to the deprivation of other constitutional or statutory rights, or to the interpretation of § 1983 itself. And it is not apparent why the Court deems an injury to be caused by the entity when its agent acts pursuant to official policy, but not otherwise.[20] Perhaps "subjects, or causes to be subjected" refer not to a government authorization requirement but simply to the differing degrees of proximity between the depriver and the deprived that varying circumstances may present.[21]

---

17. *Id.* at 691–92, 98 S.Ct. at 2036–37 (quoting § 1983).

18. *Id.* at 692, 98 S.Ct. at 2037 (emphasis added).

19. *See, e.g., Personnel Adm'r v. Feeney*, 442 U.S. 256, 279, 99 S.Ct. 2282, 2296, 60 L.Ed.2d 870 (1979) (holding that the "intent" necessary to state a claim for denial of equal protection of the laws requires plaintiff to show that the decision was made "because of, 'not merely in spite of' its adverse effects"); *Estelle v. Gamble*, 429 U.S. 97, 106, 97 S.Ct. 285, 292, 50 L.Ed.2d 251 (1976) (holding that "deliberate indifference" is demanded to state an Eighth Amendment claim for deprivation of medical attention).

20. *See* Kramer & Sykes, *supra* note 7.

21. Virtually the same phrase first appears in § 2 of the Act of April 9, 1866, ch. 31, 14 Stat. 27 (1866) (codified in scattered sections of 42 U.S.C.A.). Section 1 of that Act declared rights to contract and dispose of property free from racial discrimination. Section 2, described by Senator Trumbull, a sponsor, as "the valuable section of the bill so far as protecting the rights of freedmen is concerned," prescribes criminal punishments for any person who, under color of state law, "shall subject or cause to be subjected" any "inhabitant" to the deprivation of § 1 rights. 1 *Statutory History of the United States* 112 (Bernard Schwartz ed., 1970). Senator Trumbull explains that ensuring the freedom of newly freed slaves requires criminal sanctions for "any person who [under color of law] shall deprive another of any right or subject him to any punishment in consequence of his ... race." *Id.* Provided he acts under color of law, therefore, a putative defendant could himself immediately "subject" an inhabitant to the deprivation of a § 1 right, or could accomplish the same end by "causing" another to "subject" the inhabitant to the deprivation. Thus, a deputy sheriff could deny a § 1 right directly or prevail upon a fellow deputy or a private citizen to do so. Significantly, in none of these examples would the initiator-defendant be implementing any "policy" in the sense of a deliberate decision of his entity.

Justice Brennan bolstered his government authorization interpretation by arguing that failure to require official policy behind the challenged conduct would create a federal law of respondeat superior that "would have raised all the constitutional problems" that caused the rejection of the Sherman Amendment.[22] He reasoned that encumbering local governments with civil liability whenever their agents violate constitutional norms would be tantamount to federal imposition of an "obligation to keep the peace, an obligation Congress chose not to impose because it thought imposition of such an obligation unconstitutional."[23]

Many federal constitutional and statutory duties, however, are not tantamount to a "new" obligation to keep the peace. For example, the challenged requirement in *Monell*—that pregnant city employees take unpaid leaves of absence while still medically able to work[24]—violated either equal protection or the then current "irrebuttable presumption" variation of due process.[25] Even if an individual supervisor had imposed this requirement in an ad hoc manner, rather than pursuant to city policy or custom, imposing liability on the city would certainly not have burdened it with an obligation to keep the peace or with any other "new" obligation not already mandated by the Constitution.[26]

---

22. *Monell*, 436 U.S. at 693, 98 S.Ct. at 2037.

23. *Id.* The Court has continued to eschew efforts that would, in effect, obligate local governments or governmental units to keep the peace among civilians. *Cf. DeShaney v. Winnebago County Dep't of Social Servs.*, 489 U.S. 189, 198–203, 109 S.Ct. 998, 1005–1007, 103 L.Ed.2d 249 (1989) (holding that the failure of a county department of social services to provide a minor with adequate protection against his father's violence did not violate that minor's due process rights). *DeShaney* has been read more generally to mean that members of the public have no actionable constitutional claim against government for failing to protect them from harm inflicted by third parties. *See L.W. v. Grubbs*, 974 F.2d 119 (9th Cir.1992), *cert. denied* , 508 U.S. 951, 113 S.Ct. 2442, 124 L.Ed.2d 660 (1993). For a discussion of the "special relationship" and "state-created danger" exceptions to this prevailing general principle of substantive due process doctrine, see text *infra* § 2.19 accompanying notes 46 through 51. An unusual and provocative discussion of the interface between "private action" and the requirement of state action may be found in Laurence H. Tribe, *The Curvature of Constitutional Space: What Lawyers Can Learn From Modern Physics*, 103 Harv. L. Rev. 1, 8–13 (1989) (discussing *DeShaney*). See also Blumoff, "Some Moral Implications of Finding No State Action," 70 Notre Dame L. Rev. 95 (1994)

(viewing the Court's approach in *DeShaney* as abdicating its role to shape public values).

24. *See Monell*, 436 U.S. at 660–61, 98 S.Ct. at 2020–21.

25. *See, e.g., Cleveland Bd. of Educ. v. LaFleur*, 414 U.S. 632, 643–48, 94 S.Ct. 791, 798–800, 39 L.Ed.2d 52 (1974) (stating that a school board's presumption that a woman five or more months pregnant is physically unfit to teach in a classroom is an "irrebuttable presumption" and thus suspect under the Due Process Clause); *Stanley v. Illinois*, 405 U.S. 645, 654, 92 S.Ct. 1208, 1214, 31 L.Ed.2d 551 (1972) (ruling that an Illinois statute containing an irrebuttable presumption that unmarried fathers are incompetent to raise their children violated the Due Process Clause).

26. The obligation of state officials to obey the Constitution was not a "new" one offensive to the dual sovereignty conception of the Sherman Amendment opponents, who recognized as much in enacting § 1983. *See supra* text accompanying notes 5–7. In principle, vicarious municipal liability for the constitutional torts of a municipality's agents simply holds the municipality to the same preexisting constitutional standards incumbent on state officers. The distinction that the individual state officer need only answer for his own behavior, while the municipality must answer for that of its employee, is irrelevant to the "new obligation" objection that ani-

Why would the Court blithely take away, with its "policy" requirement, so much of what it had labored mightily to give by overruling the restrictive *Monroe* definition of "person"? Despite authoring *Monell*'s majority opinion, Justice Brennan's subsequent enthusiasm for the dictum is doubtful. Seeking to contain his Frankenstein, he later described the "policy" requirement as intended merely to distinguish the municipality's acts from those of its employees.[27] Eventually he would take sharp issue with decisions that found policy only in positive local legislation or in a pattern so regular it amounted to "custom."[28] Only two years after *Monell*, in the course of rejecting entity immunity, he endorsed the very "loss-spreading" principle that *Monell* had found inadequate to justify subjecting entities to respondeat superior.[29] In short, the policy dictum may simply have been the price that some justices paid for their brethren's agreement to override stare decisis—the volte face from *Monroe*—that made it possible to reach entities at all.

Since first invented in *Monell*, "policy" now embraces not only conduct formally adopted by the entity or enshrined in settled custom but also decisions of a final policy-making official who commits the federal law violation herself or ratifies the unlawful act of a delegate. The "policy" barrier thus echoes dissenting Justice Frankfurter's argument in *Monroe* that an agent's actions must have state authorization to occur "under color of" state law.[30] In fact, "policy" circumscribes the scope of entity liability even more sharply than Justice Frankfurter would have curbed the liability of individual defendants in *Monroe*. Not only do entities, like their agents under Justice Frankfurter's view, escape liability for conduct undertaken without "authority"; under *Monell* and its progeny, the agents' authorized acts cannot be attributed to the entity unless the authorization stems from sources sufficiently high or formal to qualify as an aspect of official policy.

The requirement of a "final" policymaker emerged, again as dictum,

mated opposition to the Sherman Amendment. *See* Kramer & Sykes, *supra* note 7, at 259–60. Indeed respondeat superior was a well-established common law rule at the time. *See City of Oklahoma City v. Tuttle,* 471 U.S. 808, 835–39, 105 S.Ct. 2427, 2442–45, 85 L.Ed.2d 791 (1985) (Stevens, J., dissenting).

27. *See Pembaur v. City of Cincinnati,* 475 U.S. 469, 479–81, 106 S.Ct. 1292, 1298–99, 89 L.Ed.2d 452 (1986).

28. *See City of St. Louis v. Praprotnik,* 485 U.S. 112, 142–47, 108 S.Ct. 915, 934–37, 99 L.Ed.2d 107 (1988) (Brennan, J., concurring); *Tuttle, supra* note 26, at 831–33, 105 S.Ct. at 2440–41 (Brennan, J., concurring in part). The *Monell* opinion provides that the entity may be liable for constitutional violations inflicted through settled practice or "custom" even when governmental officials have not approved

that practice formally, i.e. through "policy." *Compare Sargi v. Kent City Bd. of Educ.,* 70 F.3d 907 (6th Cir.1995) (no violation where driver failed to intervene after child had seizure on school bus); *with Greensboro Professional Fire Fighters Ass'n Local 3157 v. City of Greensboro,* 64 F.3d 962 (4th Cir.1995) (treating custom or practice as an alternative predicate for municipal liability, even absent "policy"); *Navarro v. Block,* 72 F.3d 712 (9th Cir. 1995).

29. *See Owen v. City of Independence,* 445 U.S. 622, 655, 100 S.Ct. 1398, 1417, 63 L.Ed.2d 673 (1980).

30. *See Monroe v. Pape,* 365 U.S. 167, 257, 81 S.Ct. 473, 522, 5 L.Ed.2d 492 (1961) (Frankfurter, J., concurring in part and dissenting in part), *overruled in part by Monell v. Dep't of Social Servs.,* 436 U.S. 658, 98 S.Ct. 2018, 56 L.Ed.2d 611 (1978).

in a plurality opinion in *Pembaur v. City of Cincinnati*.[31] A county prosecutor and subordinate law enforcement officials authorized and executed, respectively, the service of capiases by breaking down the door of a private physician's office. All of the Justices agreed that the conduct that gave rise to the action violated the Constitution only if a Fourth Amendment precedent, *Steagald v. United States*,[32] were to apply retroactively. The plurality allowed the action to proceed against the county because a state statute specifically authorized the county prosecutor to advise the local police on such matters as the lawfulness of entry.[33] It has become conventional for the definition of a "final policymaker" to be dictated by the provisions of state law.[34]

The "final policymaker" requirement appears in response to dissenting Justice Powell's charge in *Pembaur* that the plurality had reopened the door to respondeat superior.[35] Justice Powell argues convincingly that the off-hand, hasty decision of a harried assistant prosecutor (made during a telephone conversation while a horde of municipal police officers, axes poised, awaited his direction) does not amount to policy [36]— at least not if, as the plurality insisted, "policy" requires "a deliberate choice to follow a course of action ... made from among various alternatives." [37] Generally speaking, Justice Powell would have found "policy" only when a legislative body adopts a rule of universal applicability like the pregnancy policy at issue in *Monell*.[38] Justice Brennan, for the *Pembaur* plurality, pushed the liability potential somewhat further, so that even individual decisions may represent the entity's policy, but only if "the decisionmaker possesses final authority to establish policy with respect to the action ordered." [39]

The individual *Pembaur* defendants were absolved by *Harlow's* version of "clearly established" qualified immunity.[40] Because their liability was premised on applying *Steagald* retroactively, the legal question was not resolved at the time the capias was served. These

---

31. 475 U.S. 469, 106 S.Ct. 1292, 89 L.Ed.2d 452 (1986).

32. 451 U.S. 204, 101 S.Ct. 1642, 68 L.Ed.2d 38 (1981).

33. *See Pembaur, supra* note 31, at 484–85, 106 S.Ct. at 1300–01.

34. *See, e.g., Swint v. Wadley*, 5 F.3d 1435 (11th Cir.1993), *cert. granted*, ___ U.S. ___, 114 S.Ct. 2671, 129 L.Ed.2d 808 (1994) (state law defines Alabama county sheriffs as state official for civil liability purposes, so county is not responsible under § 1983 county sheriffs' conduct).

35. *See id.* at 499–502, 106 S.Ct. at 1308–1309 (Powell, J., dissenting). Within two years, Brennan attempted to disown, at least in part, the same requirement of finality. *See City of St. Louis v. Praprotnik*, 485 U.S. 112, 144–46, 108 S.Ct. 915, 935–36, 99 L.Ed.2d 107 (1988) (Brennan, J., concurring).

36. *See Pembaur, supra* note 31, at 501, 106 S.Ct. at 1309 (Powell, J., dissenting).

37. *Id.* at 483, 106 S.Ct. at 1300 (plurality opinion).

38. *See id.* at 499–502, 106 S.Ct. at 1308–1309 (Powell, J., dissenting).

39. *Id.* at 481, 106 S.Ct. at 1299.

40. *See id.* at 475, 106 S.Ct. at 1296 (plurality opinion). Whether the prosecutor, in contrast to the subordinate officers, would have been eligible for absolute immunity per *Imbler v. Pachtman*, 424 U.S. 409, 96 S.Ct. 984, 47 L.Ed.2d 128 (1976), turns on whether his advice concerning the capias service would be classified as intimately related to the prosecutor's role as an advocate for the public in the judicial system. *See supra* § 2.2, note 12.

defendants did not, therefore, act in violation of clearly established law. Thus if Justice Powell's analysis, exonerating the county, had carried the day, *no one* would have been liable to the plaintiff for what the Court agreed was a constitutional violation.

But suppose the precedent on which the individual defendants' liability turned had been decided *before* the *Pembaur* events and was deemed sufficiently clearly established to satisfy *Harlow* and *Anderson*. There could still be no actionable entity policy as defined by Justice Powell, because no positive legislation or government pronouncement gave the prosecutor final authority to make policy about the service on Dr. Pembaur. In such a case, the Court would likely visit liability not upon the entity but upon the police officers alone,[41] even though they had followed standard departmental operating procedure by calling the assistant prosecutor for instructions. The result works at cross-purposes with one of the traditional rationales for individual immunity, fairness to the government agent.

The finality requirement, borne of the floodgates fear, eventually evolved so stringently that it frequently forecloses the accountability of a solvent entity. In *City of St. Louis v. Praprotnik*,[42] the Court tightened the finality qualification by demanding ratification of delegates' decisions and rationales.[43] After reiterating that "the authority to make municipal policy is necessarily the authority to make *final* policy,"[44] the Court explained that the act of an individual that departs from the final policymaker's instructions is not the act of the municipality. Accordingly, when a policymaker delegates policymaking responsibility, entity liability attaches only if "the authorized policymakers approve a subordinate's decision and the basis for it."[45]

This demand, articulated without accompanying justification, creates a prima facie burden of Herculean proportions. First, it promises to have widespread application. Few citizens deal with "final policymakers" on a day-to-day basis; they deal more commonly with subordinates whose decisions require clearance. Second, the injury is seldom related to the "basis" of, or intent behind, the subordinate's policy choice, but more often results from the implementation of an earlier choice.

41. The Court expressed no opinion on the availability of qualified immunity for the *Pembaur* prosecutor. *See* 475 U.S. at 474 n.2, 106 S.Ct. at 1295 n.2. It is now apparent that the prosecutor, if not eligible for absolute immunity with respect to the giving of advice concerning service of the capias would be eligible for qualified immunity under *Harlow. See Burns v. Reed*, 500 U.S. 478, 495, 111 S.Ct. 1934, 1944, 114 L.Ed.2d 547 (1991).

42. 485 U.S. 112, 108 S.Ct. 915, 99 L.Ed.2d 107 (1988).

43. Only a plurality reached this conclusion, but their views commanded a majority in *Jett v. Dallas Independent School District*, 491 U.S. 701, 737–38, 109 S.Ct. 2702, 2724, 105 L.Ed.2d 598 (1989).

44. *Praprotnik, supra* note 35, at 127, 108 S.Ct. at 926 (*citing Pembaur*, 475 U.S. at 481–84, 106 S.Ct. at 1299–1301).

45. *Id.* The Court hastened to distinguish the case where "a particular decision by a subordinate was cast in the form of a policy statement and expressly approved by the supervising policymaker." *Id.* at 130, 108 S.Ct. at 928. One wonders how often that really happens.

The facts of *Praprotnik* illustrate the problem. Plaintiff complained that he was laid off from city employment in violation of the First Amendment because he was a whistle-blower. He was subjected to retaliation, the jury found, for appealing an adverse personnel decision that, in turn, was the result of his public opposition to a controversial decision to purchase an expensive piece of sculpture.[46] A majority of the Court agreed that the supervisor who discharged plaintiff lacked final personnel policymaking authority and therefore absolved the entity.[47] A plurality offered several interrelated reasons for its conclusion: the superior who made the decision to lay off the plaintiff possessed only discretionary implementation authority under the policymaking aegis of the city's civil service commission; the superior's control fell short of full-fledged delegated authority with respect to personnel policy; and, the possibility that an official could make a personnel decision based on a retaliatory motive was at odds with the city charter provision that specified "merit and fitness" as the sole criteria.[48] The Court concluded that the city had "enacted no ordinance designed to retaliate against respondent"[49] and that the only "final" decisions were those of the Civil Service Commission.[50]

The circuits have struggled to identify the characteristics that render an individual official or collective body a "final policymaker" whose actions may be attributed to the entity. Formally they recognize that state law "will always direct a court to some official or body that has responsibility for making law or setting policy in any given area of a local government's business,"[51] and that local officials may implement government policy through their decisions in the field even in the absence of formal legislation. In some cases, local legislation points to the injury-inflictor as a final policymaker. For example, in one early post-*Praprotnik* decision, a municipal court judge was held a final policymaker with respect to the discharge of his court clerk, because it was clear from a personnel manual that the city had absolutely delegated to the judge the authority to make final personnel decisions.[52] Similarly, a city manager was held a final policymaker with respect to employment

46. *See id.* at 150–55, 108 S.Ct. at 938–40 (Stevens, J., dissenting).

47. *See id.* at 131, 108 S.Ct. at 928 (O'Connor, J., plurality opinion); *id.* at 137, 108 S.Ct. at 931 (Brennan, J., concurring in judgment, writing for three Justices).

48. *See id.* at 124–30, 108 S.Ct. at 924–28.

49. *Id.* at 128, 108 S.Ct. at 926.

50. *See id.* at 129, 108 S.Ct. at 927 (*quoting St. Louis City Charter*, art. XVIII, § 2(a)).

51. *Flores v. Cameron County, Texas*, 92 F.3d 258 (5th Cir.1996) (quoting *Proprotnik* and *Pembauer*). In *Brown v. City of Fort Lauderdale*, 923 F.2d 1474 (11th Cir.1991), for example, the court noted a "rich variety of ways in which the power of government is distributed among a host of different officials and official bodies" that may share policymaking authority. It therefore directed the district court to examine not just state law "but also the relevant customs and practices" of the defendant government entity to determine if individual officials were permitted in fact to wield policymaking authority respecting personnel decisions.

52. *Williams v. Butler*, 863 F.2d 1398 (8th Cir.1988) (en banc), *cert. denied*, 492 U.S. 906, 109 S.Ct. 3215, 106 L.Ed.2d 565 (1989).

decisions because the city's charter prohibited the county commissioners from reviewing the manager's decisions.[53]

On the other hand, while sometimes liability is predicated on "the delegation of final policymaking authority from one official to another and the ratification of a subordinate's actions by a final policymaker,"[54] delegation followed by the the delegator's complete inattention to the delegee's decisions has been held to insulate the entity from liability, since it cannot approve the "basis" for decisions of which it has chosen to remain unaware![55] And where a school board retained the authority to review the hiring and firing decisions of a school principal, the school district could not be liable for the principal's decisions because its delegation of authority was not final.[56] Nor was a city liable for sexual discrimination and harassment against female police officers by supervisors ultimately responsible to the police commissioner, where the commissioner had not authorized or acquiesced in their conduct.[57] Of course in these "benign neglect" scenarios plaintiffs may attempt to fasten liability on the entity through the alternative to "policy", namely "custom": "a series of decisions by a subordinate official ... of which the supervisor must have been aware." [58]

Some government entities have benefitted from an apparent extension of *Praprotnik:* an entity escapes liability if legislation recites that the ultimate governing body either retains the authority to prohibit or in fact prohibits the allegedly unlawful conduct. Thus in cases involving alleged discriminatory or retaliatory terminations by a sheriff and police chief who had final, unreviewable authority to make the challenged decisions, the government entities nevertheless avoided liability because local ordinances prohibited the kind of discrimination involved.[59] These decisions reason that as an abstract matter a person who otherwise perfectly fits the description of a "final policymaker" *could not* have been authorized to engage in conduct formally prohibited by the entity's positive law. Another court took the doctrine a step further. A county was not liable for the medical decisions of a jailer with unreviewable final authority because a state statute reserved to the county legislature the authority to enact ordinances and issue regulations regarding medi-

53. *Martinez v. City of Opa–Locka,* 971 F.2d 708 (11th Cir.1992).

54. *Mandel v. Doe,* 888 F.2d 783, 791 (11th Cir.1989).

55. *See Flores v. Cameron County, Texas,* 92 F.3d 258 (5th Cir.1996).

56. *Eugene v. Alief Independent School Dist.,* 65 F.3d 1299 (5th Cir.1995) (citing Texas law); *Jantz v. Muci,* 976 F.2d 623 (10th Cir.1992), *cert. denied,* 508 U.S. 952, 113 S.Ct. 2445, 124 L.Ed.2d 662 (1993).

57. *Hill v. Clifton,* 74 F.3d 1150 (11th Cir.1996) (police chief lacked final policymaking authority to demote officer, and city manager with policymaking authority did not approve chief's allegedly improper reasons for the demotion); *Andrews v. City of Philadelphia,* 895 F.2d 1469 (3d Cir.1990).

58. *Praprotnik,* 485 U.S. at 130, 108 S.Ct. at 927.

59. *Lankford v. City of Hobart,* 73 F.3d 283 (10th Cir.1996) (even assuming police chief accused of sexually harassing employees had final policymaking authority, no municipal liability where city had written policy expressly forbidding sexual harassment); *Auriemma v. Rice,* 957 F.2d 397 (7th Cir.1992); *Crowley v. Prince George's Co.,* 890 F.2d 683 (4th Cir.1989), *cert. denied,* 506 U.S. 833, 113 S.Ct. 101, 121 L.Ed.2d 61 (1992).

cal care, even though it had never, in fact, done so![60] In effect, these doctrines revive, in favor of entity defendants challenging the prima facie showing of "policy," the "under color of state law" argument, rejected in *Monroe,* that there can be no Section 1983 liability where an agent of government acts in violation of local law.

The dominant influence of local law in determining whether an entity may be liable by virtue of the conduct of a "final policymaking official" is illustrated by contrasting Eleventh Circuit decisions respecting the duties of Alabama sheriffs. In *Parker v. Williams*[61], county liability concerning a sheriff's hiring decisions at a county jail was upheld, even though the sheriff was a state employee, because state statutes provided that counties and their sheriffs maintained county jails in partnership. By contrast, in *Swint v. City of Wadley*[62], the county could not be held liable for the sheriff's authorization of a raid on criminal suspects because the state's statutes bestowed law enforcement duties on the sheriffs alone.

Praprotnik's requirements pay excessive respect to federalism and raise a substantial question about fairness to individual defendants. Federalism concerns were actually implicated only tangentially, since imposing liability on the entity would not have intruded on the legitimate exercise of discretionary government authority: prohibiting retaliation for exercising First Amendment rights is not meddlesome interference and requires no wholesale reordering of personnel decisionmaking.[63] From the fairness perspective, *Praprotnik* sacrifices the subordinate who in good faith inadvertently violates a clearly established constitutional right. Liability is possible only for the underling, despite the superior's approval of the injurious decision, so long as the superior does not also approve its "basis."

The Court's insistence on entity "policy," and the finality and ratification refinements in particular, are theoretically and practically suspect. Theoretically, any liability imposed upon government is necessarily vicarious: governments operate only through human agency. Thus the Court's insistence that the "entity" act advertently (either through deliberative policy, or, where the injury is caused by omission, through the somewhat oxymoronic "deliberate indifference" demanded by *City of Canton v. Harris*[64]) is hard to understand. Practically, from

---

60. *Johnson v. Hardin County,* 908 F.2d 1280 (6th Cir.1990).

61. 862 F.2d 1471, 1478–79 (11th Cir. 1989).

62. 5 F.3d 1435, 1450–1451 (11th Cir. 1993), *rev'd on other grounds, sub nom. Swint v. Chambers County Comm'n,* ___ U.S. ___, 115 S.Ct. 1203, 131 L.Ed.2d 60 (1995). *Accord, McMillian v. Johnson,* 88 F.3d 1573 (11th Cir.), *cert. filed sub nom. McMillian v. Monroe Co., Ala.,* ___ U.S. ___, ___ S.Ct. ___, ___ L.Ed.2d ___, 1996 WL 605185 (1996).

63. Today at least it appears settled that retaliation for exercising free speech rights protected by the First Amendment is actionable under § 1983. See *Maynard v. City of San Jose,* 37 F.3d 1396 (9th Cir. 1994).

64. 489 U.S. 378, 392, 109 S.Ct. 1197, 1206, 103 L.Ed.2d 412 (1989) (remanding the question whether a city's failure adequately to train police officers to assess a detainee's need for medical assistance stemmed from "deliberate indifference"). *See* § 2.19 following.

the viewpoints of both the state actor who commits and the person who suffers the violation, the actor's authority appears complete. *Pembaur's* prosecutor and *Praprotnik's* perpetrator both assumed they had authority to do what they did, their relevant subordinates assumed the same, and the victims suffered as a result.

Library References:

> C.J.S. Civil Rights § 272.
> West's Key No. Digests, Civil Rights ☞206(3).

§ 2.19   "Deliberate Indifference": Showing *Monell* "Policy" Where an Entity Unconstitutionally Fails to Train or Otherwise Act

"Deliberate indifference" is the Court's surrogate test for "policy" where the constitutional violation allegedly results from government inaction or omission. In the seminal case *City of Canton v. Harris*,[1] the plaintiff had been detained by the police and manifested symptoms of emotional or mental distress. She asserted that the police failed to provide her medical care or attention and that this failure to act caused her further injury. She claimed that the city's failure to train its personnel to cope with emotional distress violated a constitutional right comparable to the right to medical care enjoyed by a detainee or arrestee who manifests symptoms of physical illness.

The Supreme Court held that in order to show that a failure to train or similar failure to act amounts to advertent "policy" fairly attributable to the entity, a plaintiff must demonstrate that the need for such training was "obvious" from "usual and recurring situations."[2] A government entity therefore usually cannot be liable to a suspect on the basis of a detective's single mistaken identification of her, because an isolated incident does not tend to show the persistent or repeated violation essential to show "custom" or "policy" under *City of Canton*.[3] That kind of obviousness is required to demonstrate that "the inadequacy [of training was] so likely to result in the violation of constitutional rights, that the policymakers ... can reasonably be said to have been deliberately indifferent to the need."[4] Speaking through Justice White, the Court also insisted on a clear causal link between an unconstitutional omission and harm suffered by the plaintiff. For example, if an entity provides appropriate training but the injury is inflicted by an agent who,

§ 2.19

1. 489 U.S. 378, 109 S.Ct. 1197, 103 L.Ed.2d 412 (1989).

2. *Id.* at 391, 109 S.Ct. at 1206.

3. *Campbell v. City of San Antonio*, 43 F.3d 973 (5th Cir.1995); *Church v. City of Huntsville*, 30 F.3d 1332, 1345 (11th Cir. 1994). Nevertheless, summary judgment has been denied upon a determination that a city's practice of using only one jailer amounted to official custom or policy, *Scott v. Moore*, 85 F.3d 230 (5th Cir.1996); and at least one circuit turns over to a jury the question whether local government acquiesced in an alleged custom of tolerating excessive force by police. *Beck v. City of Pittsburgh*, 89 F.3d 966 (3d Cir.1996).

4. *City of Canton*, 489 U.S. at 390, 109 S.Ct. at 1205.

having received that instruction, disregards it, only the agent could be liable.[5]

The Court more recently has shed light on the ways in which "deliberate indifference" for § 1983 purposes may be shown. It has distinguished the *Canton* requirement from the element a prisoner must show to demonstrate that the government's infliction of pain upon him violates the Eighth Amendment's cruel and unusual punishment clause. For Eighth Amendment liability, the prison official must unnecessarily and wantonly inflict injury upon the prisoner either intentionally or with a state of mind characterized at a minimum by "deliberate indifference"[6] to a substantial and serious risk of harm to the inmate.[7] Federal intermediate appellate courts had equated this Eighth Amendment "deliberate indifference" with one or another form of recklessness.[8] In *Farmer v. Brennan*[9] the Supreme Court clarified that the Amendment is violated only if the prison official is "subjectively" reckless in the criminal sense, that is, consciously disregards a substantial risk of serious harm despite his *actual knowledge* of that risk.[10] Specifically distinguishing the "deliberate indifference" concept declared by *Canton*, the Court held that a prison official does not violate the Eighth Amendment, even where the risk of substantial harm to inmates was obvious and a reasonable prison official would have noticed it, if she was not actually aware of that risk.[11]

The Court emphasized that § 1983, unlike the Amendment, contains no state of mind requirement. Rather, "deliberate indifference" was "used in the Canton case [not to define a predicate constitutional violation but] for the quite different purpose of identifying the threshold for holding a city responsible for the constitutional torts committed by its ... agents."[12] Unlike the Eighth Amendment requirement, entity liability for omissions under § 1983 does not depend on actual notice; "constructive notice of the need for preventative action can form the

---

5. *Id.* at 391, 109 S.Ct. at 1206.

6. *See, e.g., Wilson v. Seiter,* 501 U.S. 294, 302–03, 111 S.Ct. 2321, 2326–27, 115 L.Ed.2d 271 (1991).

7. *See Helling v. McKinney,* 509 U.S. 25, 113 S.Ct. 2475, 125 L.Ed.2d 22 (1993).

8. *See, e.g.,* cases cited by the Court in *Farmer v. Brennan,* 511 U.S.825 n. 4, 114 S.Ct. 1970 n. 4, 128 L.Ed.2d 811 (1994).

9. 511 U.S. 825, 114 S.Ct. 1970, 128 L.Ed.2d 811 (1994).

10. *Id.* at ___, 114 S.Ct. at 1978. It is not necessary for the plaintiff to show that the known harm *would* befall any particular inmate, let alone the plaintiff, or to show that it would be inflicted by any particular inmate. And the factfinder may, but need not, conclude that the defendant official knew of the substantial risk from the very fact of its obviousness. Further, the official would not escape liability if, strongly suspecting the existence of such a

risk, she failed to verify the underlying facts. *Id.* at ___, 114 S.Ct. at 1980–82. But if the factfinder concludes that the defendant was in fact unaware of such a substantial risk of harm, she may not be held liable even if the risk was obvious and a reasonable official in the defendant's position would have been aware of it.

11. *Id.* at ___, 114 S.Ct. at 1980. *See also Ruark v. Drury,* 21 F.3d 213 (8th Cir. 1994), *cert. denied* , ___ U.S. ___, 115 S.Ct. 66, 130 L.Ed.2d 23 (1994) (jail officials must not only be aware of risk of substantial harm to inmate but their failure to respond must be prompted by "obduracy" or "wantonness").

12. *Id.* at ___, 114 S.Ct. at 1981 (*quoting Collins v. City of Harker Heights,* 503 U.S. 115, 124, 112 S.Ct. 1061, 1068, 117 L.Ed.2d 261 (1992)).

basis of a showing of deliberate indifference." [13] Thus as far as § 1983 is concerned, the entity faces liability when it either knows *or should know* of a recurring situation within its bailiwick that threatens a constitutional deprivation and fails to take appropriate responsive measures.[14] The § 1983 plaintiff bears the burden of demonstrating the entity agent's actual knowledge only when, as with Eighth Amendment claims, a violation of the particular predicate right depends upon the defendant's acting with that state of mind.

Justice O'Connor, writing for three Justices in *Canton,* seemed to perceive that there are two issues, one factual and one legal, necessarily embedded in the element of obviousness. The factual issue is whether the situation confronting the entity was sufficiently recurrent that a constitutional harm resulting from inaction was apparent. But knowledge or reasonably imputable knowledge that a failure to act would obviously violate a constitutional right may also assume that the right in question had been previously determined, a distinct legal question. Justice O'Connor concluded that this legal component "ha[d] not and could not" be met in *City of Canton.*[15] After all, she argued, the Court had "not yet addressed the precise nature of the obligations that ... Due Process ... places upon the police to seek medical care for pretrial detainees who have been *physically* injured." [16] A fortiori, she seemed to argue, there was no clear legal obligation with respect to the duty to prevent emotional or mental harms. There were, consequently, "no clear constitutional guideposts for the municipalities." [17] Absent such guideposts, the need for training could not, as a matter of simple logic, be obvious.

The majority did not confront the issue directly, noting only that "we must assume that [plaintiff's] constitutional right ... was denied by city employees-whatever the nature of that right might be." [18] We are thus left to speculate whether the majority, in remanding, was authorizing the court of appeals on remand to recognize a new constitutional duty on the part of municipalities to provide adequate training for the treatment of mentally disabled pretrial detainees. The majority's failure to dispel Justice O'Connor's suspicions on this point permits the infer-

---

13. *Reynolds v. Borough of Avalon,* 799 F.Supp. 442, 446 (D.N.J.1992) (*citing Canton*).

14. *See Simmons v. City of Philadelphia,* 947 F.2d 1042, 1061 n. 14 (3d Cir. 1991), *cert. denied,* 503 U.S. 985, 112 S.Ct. 1671, 118 L.Ed.2d 391 (1992). Examples include a government's failure to inform police officers about the constitutional limitations on the use of deadly force, *see City of Canton,* 489 U.S. at 390 n.10, 109 S.Ct. at 1205 n.10, or a failure to institute a policy against, or procedures to report sexual harassment, or to advise employees of their rights and obligations under such a policy. *Reynolds, supra* note 13, at 446.

These omissions could rise to the level of § 1983 "deliberate indifference" even if the policymakers lacked actual knowledge about prior incidents, provided the circumstances had recurred frequently enough to make the need for action obvious. *City of Canton,* 489 U.S. at 390 n.10, 109 S.Ct. at 1205 n.10.

15. *Id.* at 394, 109 S.Ct. at 1207 (O'Connor, J., concurring in part and dissenting in part).

16. *Id.* at 397, 109 S.Ct. at 1209.

17. *Id.*

18. *Id.* at 389 n.8, 109 S.Ct. at 1205 n.8.

ence that the city would face potential liability for what was at best a dimly sketched right.

Some support for this conclusion may be drawn from Justice White's repeated generalized references to the denial of "medical attention" or "care," shorn of Justice O'Connor's distinction between care for physical and psychiatric conditions.[19] Liability would then be fastened on a municipality for a violation of rights that, at the very least, does not meet the highly particularized version of the "clearly established" requirement adumbrated in *Anderson v. Creighton*,[20] for the liability of individual defendants.[21]

Of course neither the disposition nor the discussion in *City of Canton* compels this interpretation. The Court did not purport to highlight the contours of the right.[22] It was apparently open on remand for the city to argue that there was no or little circuit authority supporting a right of pretrial detainees to psychiatric care and, even if there was, that it was not sufficiently settled when they acted that failure to furnish such care would "obviously" violate that constitutional right. The Court's "whatever the nature of the right" statement can be read to suggest that it was simply dealing with the § 1983 issue (whether the *Monell* "policy" requirement could ever be satisfied by entity omission) and that it did not undertake to decide whether the particular predicate right alleged was constitutionally cognizable.

Accordingly, should a reconstituted Court (Justices Souter, Thomas, Ginsburg and Breyer having replaced Justices Brennan, Marshall, White, and Blackmun) address the issue squarely, it may agree with Justice O'Connor that the § 1983 predicate right must to some degree be settled before an entity may be held liable on the basis of an agent's omission. If so, the entity in such cases would enjoy a prima facie escape from liability that in substance mirrors the immunity from damages enjoyed by individual officials via an affirmative defense.[23] An implicit settledness requirement, even if it is less stringent than the clearly established law necessary to overcome the qualified immunity defense of individual defendants, would lessen the significance of the Court's refusal in *Owen v. City of Independence*[24] to accord entities a formal immunity. Indeed, if the predicate right is unsettled enough to prevent the plaintiff from satisfying the "obviousness" facet of "deliberate indifference," the entity in an omission case may be somewhat better off than the individual defendant; it would be spared liability not only from damages but also from injunctive or declaratory relief and therefore from attorney's fees incident thereto.[25]

19. *See id.* at 381–82, 389 n.8, 109 S.Ct. at 1201, 1205 n.8.

20. 483 U.S. 635, 107 S.Ct. 3034, 97 L.Ed.2d 523 (1987).

21. *See supra* § 2.12.

22. *See City of Canton*, 489 U.S. at 389 n.8, 109 S.Ct. at 1205 n.8.

23. *See supra* § 2.12.

24. 445 U.S. 622, 100 S.Ct. 1398, 63 L.Ed.2d 673 (1980).

25. The Court in *Supreme Court of Va. v. Consumers Union, Inc.*, 446 U.S. 719, 100 S.Ct. 1967, 64 L.Ed.2d 641 (1980), authorized attorney's fees even where only injunctive relief was obtained.

Subsequent decisions have pointed up some of the ambiguities implicit in the *Canton* standard for the liability of government entities based on the omissions of their agents. Despite some occasional loose language to the contrary,[26] the circuits seem to be in accord that under *Canton* entity liability may be predicated either on actual or constructive notice of the risks posed by a failure to act. Indeed the word "obvious" itself implies that the conclusion that the "entity" reasonably should have drawn (about a risk of constitutional injury if action is not taken) is based on events or data that fall short of giving certain knowledge. But what is it that the entity must know, or reasonably should have known, before the entity can be liable? Is it that a failure to take action is likely, or "substantially certain," to result in a violation of constitutional rights?[27] Or is it knowledge that the wrong decision by the entity's employee will frequently result in the deprivation of a citizen's constitutional rights?[28] And while the facts giving rise to *Canton* itself, and most of its progeny, involve a pattern or history of prior, similar constitutional violations,[29] from time to time entity liability is grounded on a single failure to act, i.e., on a unique, previously unencountered situation, where that failure would result in a constitutional violation deemed obvious because the facts are flagrant or the law violation well settled.[30]

Owen v. City of Independence,[31] in the course of denying any sort of across-the-board, generally available Section 1983 immunity to local government entities, suggests another rationale, not mentioned in the *City of Canton* opinion, for treating "omissions" claims more skeptically than those alleging affirmatively unlawful conduct. In *Owen*, Justice Brennan for the majority labored mightily to minimize the scope of the common law tort immunity that extended to "discretionary" (but not "ministerial") government functions. He explained that the immunity excused the local government entity from "acting in one manner or another," but "once any particular decision was made, the city was fully liable for injuries incurred in the [tortious] execution of its judgment." Yet if this was so, what would be the consequences of carrying forward that common law immunity to Section 1983? Might it not be plausibly

---

26. *See Mateyko v. Felix,* 924 F.2d 824 (9th Cir.1990) (finding no municipal liability absent evidence that a city had actual knowledge that failing to provide a lengthier, more detailed training program on tazer guns would create an unjustifiable risk to the citizenry).

27. *See Popham v. City of Talladega,* 742 F.Supp. 1504, (N.D.Ala.1989), *affirmed,* 908 F.2d 1561 (11th Cir.1990).

28. *See Walker v. City of New York,* 974 F.2d 293 (2d Cir.1992).

29. *See, e.g., Young v. City of Augusta,* 59 F.3d 1160 (11th Cir.1995); *Walker, supra; Dorman v. District of Columbia,* 888 F.2d 159 (D.C.Cir.1989).

30. *See Atchinson v. District of Columbia,* 73 F.3d 418 (D.C.Cir.1996) (improper training claim legally sufficient although based on single episode of officer shooting plaintiff in broad daylight after ordering him to freeze); *Brown v. Bryan County,* 67 F.3d 1174 (5th Cir.1995), *cert. granted sub nom. Board of County Com'rs of Bryan County, Oklahoma v. Brown,* __ U.S. __, 116 S.Ct. 1540, 134 L.Ed.2d 645 (1996); *Oviatt v. Pearce,* 954 F.2d 1470 (9th Cir. 1992). This phenomenon is also at work in the closely related setting of the liability of supervisors, discussed in Section 2.23, *infra.*

31. 445 U.S. 622, 100 S.Ct. 1398, 63 L.Ed.2d 673 (1980).

maintained, for example, that while local government has a duty to execute in a constitutional manner those functions it ventures to undertake, the constitution cannot prescribe what those functions are? Put otherwise, isn't it constitutional for the entity to fail to act at all? Had that argument been presented and prevailed in *City of Canton,* the Court might have extended the common law's version of "good faith" immunity to local government defendants in any Section 1983 action predicated on the entity's federally unlawful failure to act. And because such an immunity defense is rooted in Section 1983 itself, not tied to a particular predicate right, it might even avail the government defendant in circumstances where a failure to act is prima facie unlawful under the Constitution.[32]

Thus while the prima facie elements of "policy" that *City of Canton* imposes on the plaintiff in a failure-to-act case are undoubtedly formidable, many plaintiffs would fare still worse if the court had transported to Section 1983 the common law's good-faith defense for discretionary functions.

A recent decision well illustrates how a plaintiff may alternatively attempt to show "policy" either by proving *Praprotnik*-type approval by a final policymaker or by framing the case in *Canton* terms as involving a deliberately indifferent failure to act. In *Chew v. Gates,*[33] a city defendant attempted to avoid liability for a police practice of using dogs to bite, maul, and thereby apprehend concealed suspects, arguing that such a "policy was attributable only to the officers responsible for training the canine units." The Court rejected this argument, however, citing *Praprotnik* for the proposition that a government entity "cannot escape liability for the consequences of established and ongoing departmental policy ... simply by permitting such basic policy decisions to be made by lower level officials who are not ordinarily considered policymakers."[34] The court added that "even if we were to accept the city's argument that no jury could find that departmental canine policy was officially sanctioned, municipal liability could be found under the 'deliberate indifference' formulation of *Monell* liability." Citing *City of Canton,* the panel explained that the entity's failure to adopt a departmental policy governing police use of animals that were shown to have bitten suspects more than 40% of the time those animals were used reflected "deliberate indifference" to constitutional rights.[35]

The careful reader will have observed that the opinion in *Chew* refers to a jury function in deciding "deliberate indifference," whereas the Supreme Court has insisted that determining the other variants of policy—legislation, a governing body's official pronouncement, and a "final policymaking official"—is a question of law for the court. The

---

32. A failure to act may become actionable, for example, as a violation of due process under the "custody" and "special relationship" exceptions to the general rule of *DeShaney* that government is not obliged to offer protection against harm inflicted by private third parties. See *infra* this Section.

33. 27 F.3d 1432 (9th Cir.1994).

34. *Id.* at 1445.

35. *Id.*

criticism in Justice O'Connor's *City of Canton* opinion of Justice White's allusions to juries in the majority's opinion provides support for the conclusion that the majority did contemplate that juries would decide at least the fact-laden issues of whether the need for entity action was "so obvious" that failure to act would amount to deliberate indifference, and of whether a failure to train was the cause of the plaintiff's particular harm. Nevertheless, a separate procedural development makes it less than inevitable that juries will get to decide these questions even when the plaintiff chooses the "omissions" over the "final policymaker" approach to establishing entity liability. Under the Supreme Court's recent solicitous treatment of summary judgment, entities can still achieve dismissal before trial by convincing the judge that no reasonable jury could find each of the distinct, demanding elements of deliberate indifference by a preponderance of the evidence.[36]

In any event liability of the government itself now lingers only in the relatively rare situations where the entity broadcasts the unconstitutionality of its practice in a formal pronouncement,[37] acts pursuant to its legislative body [38] or positive state legislation,[39] manifestly endorses subordinates' discrete decisions through delegation or ratification at the highest administrative level,[40] or inflicts the federal injury through an omission characterized by "deliberate indifference." [41] Further, in all but the last situation, the question will be one of state law to be decided before trial by the court.[42] All of these paths to "policy," and hence to an actionable prima facie claim, are strewn with obstacles not presented by respondeat superior.[43]

Further, recent restrictions on the substantive reach of due process contribute to the decreasing utility of the Reconstruction Statutes in actions complaining about the ordinary, daily employment decisions of government employers. Citing its concern that the Due Process Clause not become a font of tort law, the Supreme Court held in *Collins v. City of Harker Heights, Texas*[44] that Due Process, far from assuring relief against mistaken or demonstrably erroneous personnel decisions, does not even guarantee municipal (or, presumably, state or county) govern-

36. *See Anderson v. Liberty Lobby, Inc.*, 477 U.S. 242, 252, 106 S.Ct. 2505, 2512, 91 L.Ed.2d 202 (1986) (noting in a First Amendment action that, in ruling on summary judgment under Federal Rule of Civil Procedure 56, a trial judge should consider "whether a reasonable factfinder could conclude ... the plaintiff had shown actual malice with convincing clarity"). These ramifications of *Canton* are discussed in more detail in the chapter on Procedure.

37. *See Monell v. Department of Social Servs.*, 436 U.S. 658, 98 S.Ct. 2018, 56 L.Ed.2d 611 (1978).

38. *See Owen v. City of Independence*, 445 U.S. 622, 100 S.Ct. 1398, 63 L.Ed.2d 673 (1980).

39. *See Pembaur v. City of Cincinnati*, 475 U.S. 469, 106 S.Ct. 1292, 89 L.Ed.2d 452 (1986).

40. *See City of St. Louis v. Praprotnik*, 485 U.S. 112, 108 S.Ct. 915, 99 L.Ed.2d 107 (1988).

41. *See City of Canton v. Harris*, 489 U.S. 378, 109 S.Ct. 1197, 103 L.Ed.2d 412 (1989).

42. *See* discussion of *Canton*, above.

43. *See* Kramer & Sykes, *supra* § 2.3 note 2, at 254.

44. 503 U.S. 115, 112 S.Ct. 1061, 117 L.Ed.2d 261 (1992).

ment employees "a workplace that is free of unreasonable risks of harm." [45]

The case was brought by the widow of a city employee who died of asphyxia after entering a manhole over a sewer line in the course of his employment duties. The complaint alleged that the city was on notice from a prior incident of the general risks of entering its sewer lines and that it had a custom and policy of failing to train about those dangers. But there was no allegation that plaintiff's decedent's supervisor inflicted any deliberate harm or, in the Court's words, that he "knew or should have known that there was a significant risk" that the decedent would be injured when the supervisor directed him to enter the sewer.

The Court accepted for purposes of the motion to dismiss that the complaint alleged deliberate indifference arising from the city's failure to train sufficiently to satisfy the *City of Canton* variant on *Monell's* custom or policy prerequisite to § 1983 liability. Further, the Court rejected two blanket bars on the use of § 1983 that had been erected by the court of appeals below: plaintiff was not per se precluded from proceeding either because the injury was inflicted against a government employee or because she failed to allege an "abuse of governmental power separate and apart from . . . proof of a constitutional violation."

Nevertheless, the Court found no predicate Due Process violation and hence no violation of § 1983. It acknowledged that in certain unusual situations—it referred to the retaliation for political speech at issue in *Praprotnik*, the gender discrimination asserted in *Monell*, and arbitrary conduct that shocks the conscience—government employees could state First Amendment, Equal Protection, or Due Process claims. But it wrote that the Due Process Clause has principally been applied to deliberate decisions by governmental officials. The Court implied that a government employee who voluntarily accepted an offer of employment and hence is not in custody could state a due process claim with respect to the regular duties of that employment only by alleging conduct evincing some level of culpability greater than mere negligence. The Court distinguished conditions of custody or confinement that implicate liberty and trigger some minimal substantive due process standards of care for arrestees because the state has placed them in peril, increased their risk of harm, or acted to render them more vulnerable to danger. [46]

---

45. More recently the Court has reemphasized this point by recognizing that the government has a freer hand in regulating its employees' speech than those of ordinary citizens because of the enhanced efficiency concern it has as employer and not simply as sovereign. *Waters v. Churchill*, 511 U.S. 661, 114 S.Ct. 1878, 128 L.Ed.2d 686 (1994).

46. *Citing Revere v. Massachusetts General Hosp.*, 463 U.S. 239, 103 S.Ct. 2979, 77 L.Ed.2d 605 (1983); pretrial detainees, *Bell v. Wolfish*, 441 U.S. 520, 99 S.Ct. 1861, 60 L.Ed.2d 447 (1979); convicts, *Turner v. Safley*, 482 U.S. 78, 107 S.Ct. 2254, 96 L.Ed.2d 64 (1987); and mental patients, *Youngberg v. Romeo*, 457 U.S. 307, 102 S.Ct. 2452, 73 L.Ed.2d 28 (1982); *but cf. Albright v. Oliver*, 510 U.S. 266, 114 S.Ct. 807, 127 L.Ed.2d 114 (1994) (criminal defendant apparently still in custody has no substantive due process right to be free from baseless initiation of prosecution because his injury was potentially redressable under an amendment, the Fourth, more explicitly addressed to the type of government conduct at issue) (plurality opinion).

In brief, the government employer and employee do not stand in the kind of "special relationship" characterized by official physical restraint or custody that on occasion has warranted an exception to the general rule that the state has no constitutional duty to protect persons from negligence or third-person private violence.[47]

Despite *Collins*, it appears that a government employee may state a Due Process claim against her employing entity where the government has engaged in affirmative conduct that places the plaintiff in especial danger. In *L.W. v. Grubbs*,[48] a registered nurse employed by a state correctional institution alleged that she was directed to work alone in a clinic with a particular inmate who "was a violent sex offender who had failed all treatment programs at the institution."[49] Purporting to distinguish *Collins* on this point, the Ninth Circuit observed that the government defendants thereby "took affirmative steps to place her at significant risk, and that they knew of the risks." The court noted instances where this "danger creation" exception to the government's general exemption from liability for third-party acts[50] warranted uphold-

---

47. Courts have found such a relationship where state agencies have removed children from their home and assumed guardianship, then exposed them knowingly or recklessly to placements posing serious risks of physical harm. *See Camp v. Gregory,* 67 F.3d 1286 (7th Cir.1995), *cert. denied,* ___ U.S. ___, 116 S.Ct. 2498, 135 L.Ed.2d 190 (1996). But for the most part, this "special relationship" exception has not extended a duty of care enforceable under due process beyond involuntarily committed mental patients and incarcerated prisoners. *See, e.g., J.O. v. Alton Community Unit Sch. Dist. 11,* 909 F.2d 267, 272 (7th Cir.1990), *cert. denied ,* 506 U.S. 1087, 113 S.Ct. 1066, 122 L.Ed.2d 371 (1993). For example, the relationship between a student and his school district usually falls outside the "special relationship" exception, for want of the physical custody element stressed by the Supreme Court in *DeShaney. See, e.g., Sargi v. Kent City Bd. of Educ.,* 70 F.3d 907 (6th Cir.1995) (no violation where driver failed to intervene after child had seizure on school bus); *Walton v. Alexander,* 44 F.3d 1297 (5th Cir.1995) (en banc) ("special relationship" exception unavailable to student who voluntarily enrolled in residential special education program, defeating student's right to protection from sexual molestation by fellow student at a school for the deaf); *Johnson v. Dallas Independent School District,* 38 F.3d 198 (5th Cir.1994); *Leffall v. Dallas Independent School District,* 28 F.3d 521 (5th Cir.1994); *Graham v. Independent Sch. Dist. No. I–89,* 22 F.3d 991 (10th Cir.1994) (no § 1983 liability of school for independent conduct of its students); *D.R. by L.R. v. Middle Bucks Area Vocational Tech. School,* 972 F.2d 1364 (3d Cir.1992), *cert. denied,* 506 U.S. 1079, 113 S.Ct. 1045, 122 L.Ed.2d 354 (1993); *J.O. v. Alton Community Unit Sch. Dist. 11,* 909 F.2d 267 (7th Cir.1990), *cert. denied ,* 506 U.S. 1087, 113 S.Ct. 1066, 122 L.Ed.2d 371 (1993). *Cf. Spivey v. Elliott,* 41 F.3d 1497 (11th Cir.1995) (no "clearly established" constitutional right of student at a residential school for the hearing impaired to protection from a classmate's sexual assault). Given the tilt of these decisions, it is not surprising that an appellate court recently ruled that university officials enjoyed qualified immunity from liability for failing to protect a student from another student's threats, because it was not "clearly established" that they had a federal duty to protect him. *Alexander v. University of North Florida,* 39 F.3d 290 (11th Cir.1994). But protection of students from gender based harassment by fellow students may lie under Title IX of the Education Amendments of 1972. *See Seamons v. Snow,* 84 F.3d 1226, 1232 n. 7 (10th Cir.1996) (noting but not reaching the issue); *Davis v. Monroe County Bd. of Educ.,* 74 F.3d 1186 (11th Cir.), *vacated,* 91 F.3d 1418 (1996).

48. 974 F.2d 119 (9th Cir.1992), *cert. denied ,* 508 U.S. 951, 113 S.Ct. 2442, 124 L.Ed.2d 660 (1993).

49. *Id.* at 120.

50. *DeShaney v. Winnebago County Dep't of Social Servs.,* 489 U.S. 189, 109 S.Ct. 998, 103 L.Ed.2d 249 (1989). *See* note 32, *supra,* and accompanying text. The danger-creation exception has been summarized as follows: "If the state puts a man in a position of danger from private

ing a due process claim on behalf of persons other than governmental employees,[51] and concluded that *Collins* did not preclude use of this exception by the plaintiff because of her employee status.

But an argument could be made in such situations that even if there is a predicate due process violation, liability would in any event exceed the permissible scope of Section 1983. In *Monell*, Justice Brennan, writing for the majority, distinguished between the kinds of obligations that, consistent with the "dual sovereignty" theory prevailing in 1871 when the statute was enacted, could and could not constitutionally be imposed on local government entities by means of liability under Section 1983. Congress, he concluded, acted with the understanding that it could constitutionally enforce obligations already incumbent on local government by virtue of the constitution—for instance, to refrain from conducting unlawful searches and seizures, inflicting excessive force, or trampling first amendment freedoms. But Congress also believed that it could not, without unduly intruding on state sovereignty, saddle local government with fresh, affirmative obligations, like the duty to protect citizens from violence at the hands of other citizens that the rejected Sherman Amendment would indirectly have created. Yet in substance it is obligations of the latter sort that are sought to be enforced by *"DeShaney"* claims—those that would hold schools responsible for student-on-student violence or, more generally, would attribute the acts or omissions of third parties to local government entities. Section 1983 claims based on such rights might therefore ultimately be held subject to a good-faith immunity, even if cognizable constitutionally. This possibility is enhanced by a resurgence of dual sovereignty rhetoric in the opinions of the Court.[52]

Of course there are many other constitutional rights that were first declared, or applied as against the states, since 1871, and their enforcement through Section 1983 has therefore effectively imposed "new" constitutional obligations on local government. Indeed the same could be said of virtually all federal statutory rights enforced through Section

persons and then fails to protect him, it will not be heard to say that is role was merely passive...." *Bowers v. DeVito*, 686 F.2d 616 (7th Cir.1982).

51. *Cornelius v. Town of Highland Lake*, 880 F.2d 348 (11th Cir.1989), *cert. denied sub nom. Spears v. Cornelius*, 494 U.S. 1066, 110 S.Ct. 1784, 108 L.Ed.2d 785 (1990); *Wood v. Ostrander*, 879 F.2d 583 (9th Cir.1989), *cert. denied* , 498 U.S. 938, 111 S.Ct. 341, 112 L.Ed.2d 305 (1990). *But see Leffall v. Dallas Indep. Sch. District*, 28 F.3d 521 (5th Cir.1994) (even a negligent failure to provide adequate security at a school dance would not fit within the state-created danger exception, because a substantive due process claim also requires showing that defendants' acted with a culpable state of mind akin to "deliberate in-

difference"). It remains clear that an ordinary citizen cannot state a due process claim against local government simply because its police fail to rescue her from the criminal depredations of another private actor unless there is a special relationship or the government created the peril in which she found herself. *Gazette v. City of Pontiac*, 41 F.3d 1061 (6th Cir.1994) (plaintiff's due process rights not violated where she was abducted by employee of private car wash).

52. *See, e.g., New York v. United States*, 505 U.S. 144, 112 S.Ct. 2408, 120 L.Ed.2d 120 (1992); *Gregory v. Ashcroft*, 501 U.S. 452, 111 S.Ct. 2395, 115 L.Ed.2d 410 (1991).

1983, the vast majority of which originated after 1871. Viewed this way, the third-party liability situations are merely a small subset of a huge number of "new" federal rights. And Section 1983 judgments have routinely vindicated these new rights, notwithstanding the *Monell* majority's conclusion that the 1871 Congress would have doubted its power to enforce them against local government.

Too, governmental employees frequently advance § 1983 claims alleging that race, sex, age or alienage discrimination on the job violates equal protection.[53] But these claims are also rather restricted. Presumably because of the purposeful discrimination requirement inherent in the Equal Protection Clause itself, courts entertaining employment discrimination claims under § 1983 have eschewed Title VII's somewhat more easily proven "neutral practice/disproportionate adverse impact" theory in favor of the elements, defenses, allocation and order of proof developed in Title VII cases asserting intentional, individual disparate treatment.[54] In general, when § 1983 is used as a parallel remedy for employment discrimination—that is, when the defendant government entity has acted under "color of state law" and has injured the plaintiff through the application of "policy"—courts have equated the protection afforded by the two statutes and hence accepted for § 1983 purposes the same proof modes that establish intentional discrimination under Title VII.[55] A recent decision accordingly holds harassment on the basis of national origin actionable on the same terms under § 1983 as under Title VII.[56] But reliance on § 1983 as a separate remedy for violation of Title VII also submits the plaintiff to the additional requirements of § 1983: the policy element against entity employers, and the qualified immunity defense to claims against individual superiors.[57]

53. Governmental employees also bring § 1981 claims alleging racial discrimination in the right to make and enforce contracts. The Supreme Court has required use of Title VII's intentional discrimination proof mode in these actions (against private as well as public employers), *Patterson v. McLean Credit Union,* 491 U.S. 164, 186, 109 S.Ct. 2363, 2377, 105 L.Ed.2d 132 (1989), because the Court has construed § 1981 itself to be violated only upon proof of intentional discrimination. *General Bldg. Contractors Ass'n, Inc. v. Pennsylvania,* 458 U.S. 375, 102 S.Ct. 3141, 73 L.Ed.2d 835 (1982).

54. *See St. Mary's Honor Center v. Hicks,* 509 U.S. 502 n. 1, 113 S.Ct. 2742 n. 1, 125 L.Ed.2d 407 (1993).

55. *See Wu v. Thomas,* 863 F.2d 1543, 1549 n. 9 (11th Cir.1989); *Alexander v.*

Chicago Park Dist., 773 F.2d 850, 856 (7th Cir.1985), *cert. denied* 475 U.S. 1095, 106 S.Ct. 1492, 89 L.Ed.2d 894 (1986); *Carrion v. Yeshiva Univ.,* 535 F.2d 722, 729 (2d Cir.1976). The relationship between Title VII and § 1983 is discussed in more detail in a separate chapter. In sharp contrast, the availability of Title VII displaces rather than supplements relief under 42 U.S.C.A. § 1985(3) and, for federal employees, under § 1981. *See* Overview Chapter on the Reconstruction Civil Rights Acts, at 21.

56. *Boutros v. Canton Regional Transit Authority,* 997 F.2d 198 (6th Cir.1993).

57. *See Wu v. Thomas,* 996 F.2d 271 (11th Cir.1993) (upholding qualified immunity defense to liability or conduct arguably but not *clearly* violating Title VII), *cert. denied* , ___ U.S. ___, 114 S.Ct. 1543, 128 L.Ed.2d 195 (1994).

§ 2.20 No Affirmative Defense of Immunity for Entity Defendants

Despite the limits on government employee suits against their entities, and the increasingly difficult "policy" barrier facing all § 1983 plaintiffs who sue government entities, the Court has held that entity defendants enjoy no affirmative defense comparable to the immunity enjoyed by defendant individuals. In *Owen v. City of Independence*,[1] the Court denied municipalities a good faith immunity from suit under § 1983, discounting the likelihood that entity liability would chill the vigorous execution of government function. The majority questioned whether "the hazard of municipal loss will deter a public officer from the conscientious exercise of his duties."[2] Denying entities immunity appears to recognize the protection they enjoy from the restrictions that *Monell* places upon the prima facie claim; seldom will an isolated entity act meet the rigors of "policy."[3] (The Court has protected public funds to some degree by precluding punitive damages even when an entity action lies.[4])

Owen denied the municipality only the *qualified* or "good faith" immunity enjoyed by its agents for executive or administrative acts; it did not explicitly address whether an entity could derivatively claim *absolute* immunity when called to account for the legislative or judicial functions of its agents. The concept of absolute immunity for entities is somewhat peculiar on its face because, at least in the context of legislative acts, it seeks immunity for prototypical, officially authorized government policies—the kind of conduct for which *Monell* subjected entities to liability in the first place. Until recently, the circuit courts uniformly acknowledged this incongruity, rejecting assertions of absolute legislative immunity by local government entities and individual legislators sued in their official capacity.[5] Further, in *Lake Country Estates, Inc. v. Tahoe*

---

§ 2.20

1. 445 U.S. 622, 100 S.Ct. 1398, 63 L.Ed.2d 673 (1980).

2. *Id.* at 656, 100 S.Ct. at 1418.

3. *Compare Pembaur, supra* § 2.18, note 31, at 484–85, 106 S.Ct. at 1300–01 (noting that the assistant prosecutor's advice to deputies to break down door to serve capiases constituted policy in violation of Fourth Amendment when state law specifically sanctioned the advice-giving function) *and City of Newport v. Fact Concerts, Inc.,* 453 U.S. 247, 253, 101 S.Ct. 2748, 2752, 69 L.Ed.2d 616 (1981) (recognizing that a vote by the City Council itself to cancel contract, based on content of group's music, violated First Amendment) *with Praprotnik, supra* § 2.18, note 42, at 123, 108 S.Ct. at 924

(holding that a plaintiff's allegation that he was fired because he was a whistle-blower did not constitute policy if, inter alia, city employee who discharged plaintiff did not have final policy-making authority).

4. *See infra* § 2.21 following.

5. *See Reed v. Shorewood,* 704 F.2d 943, 953 (7th Cir.1983) (municipality denied the absolute legislative immunity of its policymakers); *W.D.D. Inc. v. Thornbury Township,* 839 F.2d 151, 154 n. 3 (3d Cir.), *cert. denied,* 488 U.S. 892, 109 S.Ct. 228, 102 L.Ed.2d 218 (1988) (*vacated on other grounds,* 850 F.2d 170 (3d Cir.1988)); *Goldberg v. Town of Rocky Hill,* 973 F.2d 70 (2d Cir.1992).

Regional Planning Agency,[6] the Supreme Court, in extending legislative immunity to regional legislators, did not confer it on the agency they served. And in *Spallone v. United States*,[7] the Supreme Court, presented with claims of absolute immunity by local legislators, noted without criticism the lower courts' decisions finding liability on the part of the legislators' entity, the city.

But two recent pronouncements by circuit court judges at least suggest that an entity may claim the absolute immunity of its individual legislators.[8] This development would appear to be stillborn in light of the latest observations on the subject by the Supreme Court in *Leatherman v. Tarrant County Narcotics Intelligence and Coordination Unit*,[9] where the Court rejected the Fifth Circuit's heightened pleading rule for § 1983 actions against municipalities.[10] Writing for a unanimous Court, Chief Justice Rehnquist dismissed the argument that the standard, more relaxed, requirements of notice pleading would improperly subject local government to expensive and time consuming discovery, thereby "eviscerating their immunity from suit...." That argument, he wrote, "wrongly equates freedom from liability [which the municipality would enjoy if the plaintiff cannot show the 'policy' required by *Monell* and its progeny] with immunity from suit...." *Monell* and *Owen*, he continued, "make it quite clear that, unlike various government officials, municipalities do not enjoy immunity from suit—*either absolute or qualified*—under § 1983."

Library References:

C.J.S. Civil Rights §§ 279, 280.
West's Key No. Digests, Civil Rights ⚷214.

§ 2.21 Punitive Damages Not Available

The menu of damages available to a plaintiff suing an individual and to a plaintiff suing an entity lays bare another asymmetry between the two cases. The case against an individual offers both compensatory and punitive damages, but, barring scarcely imaginable circumstances, the case against an entity defendant offers only compensatory damages.[1] In *City of Newport v. Fact Concerts, Inc.*,[2] the Court held that municipalities are ordinarily immune from punitive damages under § 1983. This is true even though establishing a violation by a municipality in effect

6. 440 U.S. 391, 99 S.Ct. 1171, 59 L.Ed.2d 401 (1979).

7. 493 U.S. 265, 110 S.Ct. 625, 107 L.Ed.2d 644 (1990).

8. *Hollyday v. Rainey*, 964 F.2d 1441, 1443 (4th Cir.), *cert. denied* , 506 U.S. 1014, 113 S.Ct. 636, 121 L.Ed.2d 567 (1992) (opinion of Judge Hall); *Brown v. Crawford County*, 960 F.2d 1002, 1012 n. 17 (11th Cir.1992).

9. 507 U.S. 163, 113 S.Ct. 1160, 122 L.Ed.2d 517 (1993).

10. *See* discussion of *Leatherman* in the "Procedure" Chapter below.

§ 2.21

1. *See Memphis Community Sch. Dist. v. Stachura*, 477 U.S. 299, 106 S.Ct. 2537, 91 L.Ed.2d 249 (1986) (authorizing compensatory damages).

2. 453 U.S. 247, 271, 101 S.Ct. 2748, 2762, 69 L.Ed.2d 616 (1981).

requires proof of intentional discrimination—via established "policy" [3] or "deliberate indifference." [4]

The city of Newport, R.I., licensed plaintiff Fact Concerts, Inc. to present a jazz concert near the city. Shortly before the date of the concert, Fact Concerts hired a band city council members believed to be a rock and roll band. Although Fact Concerts explained that the band was in fact a jazz band, the council did not investigate that assertion, instead focusing on the fact that the band might attract a rowdy crowd. The facts indicate that the council was actually more concerned with the idea of avoiding rock and roll music than with the claimed public safety issues. [5] The potential revocation received considerable attention in the media, and although the band performed and the concert took place without incident, fewer than half the available tickets were sold. Fact Concerts brought suit against the city and its officials, alleging a violation of First Amendment rights and due process under color of state law, seeking both compensatory and punitive damages.

The Court noted two primary remedial goals of § 1983; deterring misconduct and compensating the injured. [6] Further, it observed that punitive damages are designed specifically to punish wrongdoers as well as prevent future misconduct. [7] In light of these objectives, the Court concluded that punitive damages are not "sensibly" assessed against a government entity. [8] First, a municipality cannot act on its own, and a judgment assessing punitive damages against it would actually punish the taxpayers, rather than the wrongdoer. [9] Second, the Court reasoned that compensatory damages adequately deter § 1983 violations because (1) an official would not be deterred by the threat of damages assessed against his employer, (2) compensatory damages are just as likely as punitives to induce the public to vote a law-violating official out of office, and (3) large punitive damages are likely to endanger the financial integrity of governmental entities. [10]

Despite its concern to protect blameless taxpayers, the *Newport* Court did not foreclose completely the possibility of visiting punitive damages on entities in cases where its taxpayers could fairly be considered directly responsible for "an outrageous abuse of constitutional rights." [11] But such a case is scarcely imaginable. After one decision that rejected the possible exception, *Webster v. City of Houston*, [12] com-

---

3. *St. Louis v. Praprotnik*, 485 U.S. 112, 108 S.Ct. 915, 99 L.Ed.2d 107 (1988). *See supra* § 2.18.

4. *City of Canton v. Harris*, 489 U.S. 378, 109 S.Ct. 1197, 103 L.Ed.2d 412 (1989). *See supra* § 2.19.

5. *See* 453 U.S. at 250 n.3, 101 S.Ct. at 2751 n.3 (Council members concerned with attracting "long-haired hangers-on").

6. *Id.* at 266–67, 101 S.Ct. at 2759–60.

7. *Id.* at 268, 101 S.Ct. at 2760.

8. *Id.* at 267, 101 S.Ct. at 2760.

9. *Id.*

10. *Id.* at 268–70, 101 S.Ct. at 2760–61.

11. *Id.* at 267 n.29, 101 S.Ct. at 2760 n.29.

12. 689 F.2d 1220 (5th Cir.1982), *rehearing granted*, 711 F.2d 35 (5th Cir. 1983).

mentators asked, "If the[se] facts [. . .] do not attain the necessary level of outrageousness, what facts would?" [13]

In *Webster*, seventeen-year-old Randy Webster stole a van from a dealership, and three police officers gave chase. Randy eventually lost control of the van. The police removed him from the vehicle, subdued him, and *then* shot and killed him. Afterwards, they planted a weapon in his hand. At trial, the long-standing police department "policy" allowing the use of "throw down" weapons to cover-up police misconduct was revealed. The jury found that the City of Houston and the officers violated Randy Webster's constitutional rights and assessed punitive damages of $1 million against the officers and $200,000 against the city.

The Court of Appeals, relying on *City of Newport*, reversed the verdict as to punitive damages against the city. The majority noted that "the plight of Randy Webster, however reprehensible, however tragic, does not rise to the level of outrageous conduct" contemplated by *Newport*[14] because the Congress that drafted the original 1871 version of § 1983 lived in a time of terrible violence, too.

Circuit Judge Goldberg disagreed with the majority on this point. He argued that *Webster* fit the exception imagined by the *Newport* court. While the entire costs of the city's discrimination reached the *Newport* court in the form of lost revenue, the entire costs of the widely accepted "throw down weapon" policy revealed in *Webster* did not reach the court. "It is only by threat of punitive damages that we can arouse policymakers from their dozing to eradicate policies such as this." [15] Goldberg's comments received considerable attention but have had little impact. Despite the escape hatch left by the Supreme Court in *City of Newport*, municipalities—local and state governments and their agencies—have remained immune from punitive damages. No reported case has been discovered that has found the kind of outrageous taxpayer-directed discrimination *Newport* requires for the imposition of punitive damages on entities.

Library References:
> C.J.S. Civil Rights §§ 315, 316.
> West's Key No. Digests, Civil Rights ☞269.

§ 2.22 A Hybrid: Suits Against State Officers in Their Official and Individual Capacities

Sharply to be distinguished from § 1983 claims against a state, and from "official-capacity" actions against an individual state officer, are "personal-capacity" suits intended to establish the officer's individual liability.

---

13. *See* Low & Jeffries, *Civil Rights Actions,* 2d ed. (Foundation 1994) at 299 n. 2.

14. 689 F.2d at 1229.

15. *Id.* at 1238.

Will v. Michigan Dep't of State Police[1] teaches that the state itself is not a "person" liable under Section 1983; and neither, at least with respect to damages, is a state officer sued in his official capacity, since to that extent he is functionally only a stand-in for the state. But does the logic of *Will* also preclude damages from state officers named in their *personal* capacities for conduct undertaken in their official capacities? That is, since any defendant must have acted "under color of" state law to be liable under Section 1983, does this mean that the individual defendant has necessarily also acted "officially" and as such acquires the state's own immunity from Section 1983 liability?

The Supreme Court rejected this argument in *Hafer v. Melo*,[2] holding state officials named in their personal capacities fully responsible in damages for federal law violations, even though their injury-inflicting conduct took place under color of state law. The Court explained that "officers sued in their personal capacity come to court as individuals," even when the conduct for which they are sought to be held accountable was undertaken in their official capacities.[3] In a reverse spin on the argument rejected in *Monroe v. Pape*,[4] Hafer asserted alternatively that she could only be personally liable for those acts that were outside her authority or inessential to the performance of her official functions; essential, authorized conduct should be attributable to the state and therefore beyond the ambit of Section 1983. The Court rejected this position, too, observing that the statute typically reaches state executive and administrative conduct that violates federal law, subject only to qualified immunity, even when that conduct is official and necessary.

Hafer thus clarifies that a plaintiff may recover damages under Section 1983 against an individual state official sued in her *personal* capacity even though, per *Will,* the state itself is not suable in its own name. Of course in such personal-capacity actions, as in similar suits against city or county officials, the plaintiff need not show that the officer defendant acted pursuant to governmental policy or custom; on the other hand, such defendants, unlike those sued in an official capacity, may invoke the defense of qualified immunity.[5] At the same time, *Hafer* reaffirms that the Section 1983 plaintiff may still recover prospective relief (of a kind not forbidden by the Eleventh Amendment)[6] from a state official named as a defendant in her *official* capacity—in suits for prospective relief, in other words, the official-capacity defendant *is* a

§ 2.22

1. 491 U.S. 58, 109 S.Ct. 2304, 105 L.Ed.2d 45 (1989). See *infra* this section and § 2.26 for fuller discussion of *Will.*

2. 502 U.S. 21, 112 S.Ct. 358, 116 L.Ed.2d 301 (1991).

3. *Id.* at 26, 112 S.Ct. at 362.

4. There the individual defendants argued that they could only be acting "under color of" state law if their conduct *were* authorized and approved by their employing entities. See Section 2.3, above.

5. *Hafer,* 502 U.S. at 25, 112 S.Ct. at 361.

6. In general, the Eleventh Amendment would forbid even prospective relief to the extent that the costs of future state compliance with federal law would include compensation to victims for past federal law violations. See discussion of *Edelman v. Jordan,* 415 U.S. 651, 94 S.Ct. 1347, 39 L.Ed.2d 662 (1974), and *Milliken v. Bradley (II),* 433 U.S. 267, 97 S.Ct. 2749, 53 L.Ed.2d 745 (1977), in Chapter 13, § 13.7.

"person." [7] Indeed because *Will* found the state not suable *eo nominee* under Section 1983, naming the state agent in her official capacity is the *only* route to injunctive or declaratory relief against federally unlawful state conduct.

When the plaintiff takes pains in drafting the complaint to indicate that he intends to sue the public official in her individual capacity, therefore, the official remains a full-fledged § 1983 "person" subject to all appropriate relief, including damages.[8] We thus have a variegated meaning for the word "person," depending on whether a state official is sued in her official or her individual capacities; and under the *Will* decision we also have a dual definition even within the category of official-capacity defendant: she is a § 1983 "person," and hence suable, only to the extent that the relief sought against her is the kind the Eleventh Amendment would permit against a state—that is, prospective relief.

The remaining question, then, is whether, where the plaintiff seeks prospective relief for a federal law violation against a *local* governmental entity, there is any utility in the common practice of joining the government agent as a companion "official capacity" defendant. If in fact the agent is deemed to serve a city, county or other local government or government agency that is truly distinct from the state, naming that agent in her official capacity appears to be a redundancy with no operative litigation significance: for both Eleventh Amendment and Section 1983 purposes, naming the official capacity defendant is simply another way of naming the entity itself,[9] and the local entity is suable directly as a "person." But on occasion there is room for genuine doubt about the entity's status as a "local" or "state" instrumentality. Although such determinations are ultimately a matter of federal law, they are sometimes highly unpredictable. The federal characterization borrows heavily from a welter of potentially applicable state law provisions governing the organic relationship between the state and its subsidiaries, the allocation of functions between them, program funding, and financial responsibility.[10] Given this uncertainty, if there is any chance that the target government entity may be adjudged a tentacle of the state, the plaintiff's lawyer in search of prospective relief may find that the apparent redundancy of adding an official-capacity defendant agent

---

7. *Will v. Michigan Dept. of State Police,* 491 U.S. 58, 71 n. 10, 109 S.Ct. 2304, 2312 n. 10, 105 L.Ed.2d 45 (1989). By analogy to the jurisprudence that had grown up under the Eleventh Amendment, the Court wrote that "official-capacity actions for prospective relief are not treated as actions against the State."

8. *See Hafer v. Melo,* 502 U.S. 21, 112 S.Ct. 358, 116 L.Ed.2d 301 (1991). Failure to specify in the caption that the individual defendant is being sued in an individual

capacity forfeits the plaintiff's right to damages. *Colvin v. McDougall,* 62 F.3d 1316 (11th Cir.1995).

9. *See, e.g., Hafer,* discussing *Kentucky v. Graham,* 473 U.S. 159, 105 S.Ct. 3099, 87 L.Ed.2d 114 (1985).

10. *See* Chapter 13, § 13.7, concerning the use of state law to characterize defendants as "the state" *vel non* for Eleventh Amendment purposes.

represents salvation. Under *Hafer* and *Will,* the presence of the official-capacity defendant would preserve the possibility of obtaining prospective relief, and in turn attorney's fees,[11] although not damages.

Library References:

> C.J.S. Civil Rights §§ 274, 276.
> West's Key No. Digests, Civil Rights ⊕207(1).

§ 2.23 Personal Liability of Supervisors Compared

The preceding sections have explored the prerequisites for liability of government entities and the alternative of suit against an entity official in her official capacity where the entity cannot be sued directly. The prima facie cases against both are identical, and neither enjoys any general immunity. Indeed where it is *necessary* to sue the official in her official capacity (as in the case of a state official whose entity cannot be reached directly under Section 1983), the actions differ only in the sphere of damages. An entity suable under the statute would be exposed to compensatory (though not punitive) damages, but its official sued officially is subject only to prospective relief and attorney's fees.

It is often advantageous, however, for the victim of a federal law violation to join a higher-ranking official as a defendant in her *personal* capacity, even when a claim does lie against the official's entity. The supervisor, manager, or high-ranking policymaking official may be liable under some circumstances where the entity would not be; and if adjudged liable, she may in appropriate cases have to respond in punitive damages, unavailable against the entity itself. In the discussion that follows, the word "supervisor" will denote such a superior official, sued in an "individual" or "personal" capacity for damages.

A plaintiff may seek to hold the supervisor defendant personally liable in a wide range of situations. A police chief, for example, might personally accompany subordinate officers who conduct a raid on the plaintiff's establishment. By so participating, she is probably subjecting herself to prima facie liability on the same terms as those pertaining to her subordinate officers. Alternatively, the plaintiff might seek to hold the supervisor responsible even absent such participation. For example, the chief might have pre-approved the raid despite information from which she knew or should have known that the raid might violate federal rights. Or she may have failed adequately to train or supervise the subordinate officers conducting the raid, a failure the plaintiff may try to causally link to a deprivation of federal rights. Finally the chief, even if she had no knowledge that the raid in question was going to occur, may have promulgated a departmental policy that permitted or encouraged

---

11. Fees to the prevailing party under the Civil Rights Attorney's Fees Awards Act of 1976, which was codified as the last sentence in 42 U.S.C.A. § 1988, would be available, notwithstanding the Eleventh Amendment, even if the Section 1983 action were heard in federal court. *Hutto v. Fin-*

an unconstitutional raid.[1]

In the first, "participation" variant, there is no reason to differentiate the standards under which the chief should be liable from those applicable to the subordinates. In the terms of Section 1983, each is a "person" who through personal involvement has "subject[ed]" the plaintiff to a deprivation of federal rights. In all the latter situations, however, the chief's conduct may only be reached by the immediately following, disjunctive phrase of the statute: she is then a "person" who has "cause[d the plaintiff] to be subjected" to the federal law violation. In outlining the terms of an entity's liability in *Monell*, the Supreme Court addressed this language in a way that also seems peculiarly appropriate to these "non-participation" situations involving a supervisor:

> Indeed, the fact that Congress did specifically provide that A's [that is, the subordinate's] tort became B's [that is, the supervisor's] liability if B 'caused' A to subject another [that is, the plaintiff] to a tort suggests that Congress did not intend § 1983 liability to attach where such causation was absent.[2]

To observe that supervisors may be liable under the "caused to be subjected" branch of the statute, however, does not supply the precise elements of such liability. Outside the direct participation situation, after all, the supervisor and the subordinate are differently situated, for only the subordinate has inflicted the ultimate injury on the plaintiff on the sense of the traditional tort concept of proximate cause. Yet the supervisor, like the subordinate, is an individual defendant sued in her personal capacity, who therefore may assert the defense of qualified immunity. On the other hand, it is that same humanness of the supervisor that sets her apart from the entity she serves. The supervisor can therefore be liable where the entity sometimes cannot, for "causing" the subordinate to inflict an injury or by failing to take precautions (or taking the wrong precautions) against a risk of constitutional harm that should have been apparent from a pattern of prior similar events. And perhaps because the supervisor, unlike her entity, can fall back on the generous qualified immunity defense, there is rough justice in holding her prima facie responsible for failing to avoid harm even in the unprecedented situations in which *City of Canton* always absolves the entity. There are thus two key distinguishing characteristics of supervisory liability in non-participation contexts: the supervisor faces civil liability because of constitutional injury inflicted by a subordinate, yet sometimes is in a better position to know about and prevent the injury than her employing entity.

ney, 437 U.S. 678, 98 S.Ct. 2565, 57 L.Ed.2d 522 (1978).

§ 2.23

1. The author is indebted to Michael Rafter, Mercer University Class of 1995, for suggesting these variations, which he elaborated from the facts of *Swint v. Wadley,* 5 F.3d 1435 (11th Cir.1993), *modified on rehearing,* 11 F.3d 1030 (11th Cir.1994), *cert. denied,* ___ U.S. ___, 115 S.Ct. 1312, 131 L.Ed.2d 194 (1995).

2. *Monell v. Department of Social Services of City of New York,* 436 U.S. 658, 98 S.Ct. 2018, 56 L.Ed.2d 611 (1978).

This odd situation of the "man in the middle" gives rise to incongruous possibilities. It would seem reasonable to assert, for example, in line with the conventional wisdom that Section 1983 simply provides remedies for violations declared elsewhere in federal law, that the supervisor may only be liable when she has violated all the elements of the same predicate right infringed by her subordinate. As we have seen, however, some predicate rights—notably those protected by Equal Protection and the Eighth Amendment—are violated only when the defendant is shown to have acted with a highly culpable state of mind.[3] In the failure to train or failure to supervise variations, the plaintiff will often be unable to prove that the supervisor failed to act with any such culpable state of mind. Yet in some such cases—those where a pattern of recurring situations should have made the risk of constitutional injury created by a failure to train or supervise "obvious"—the supervisor's *entity* would be liable under the standard of *City of Canton*. The supervisor might then escape liability for which both his subordinate and entity might be responsible.[4]

An alternative approach overcomes this incongruity but generates others. The "causation interpretation" holds that a defendant (e.g., a supervisor) who acts or fails to act under color of state law in such a way as to require, encourage, or permit another (e.g., a subordinate), also acting under color of state law, to violate the plaintiff's federally guaranteed rights, has herself violated Section 1983. It is of course prerequisite that the *subordinate* committed all the elements composing the predicate violation, including any requisite state of mind; but it is sufficient for the liability of the *supervisor* that she violated some separate duty, deriving from Section 1983, federal common law, or even state law, to prevent the subordinate from inflicting injury.[5] Under this interpretation, a defendant supervisor whose failure to forestall a subordinate from infringing a federal right is merely negligent or reckless might be liable even though she did not possess the more culpable state of mind that the subordinate must have had in order to violate that right.

This interpretation solves the incongruity of absolving a supervisor from liability for an intent-based predicate violation by the subordinate even where the entity would be liable under the standard of *City of Canton*. But if the requisite state of mind for supervisory liability is mere negligence, the supervisor under this approach might be liable in

3. The requisite scienter is described in Equal Protection decisions as involving an "intent" to discriminate. In most Eighth Amendment situations involving prisoners, it takes the form of "deliberate indifference" defined as a failure to prevent substantial bodily harm despite actual knowledge of the particular risk that will produce it. *See* note 15, *infra.*

4. Professor Nahmod has favored this "Fourteenth Amendment" interpretation of Section 1983 that imposes liability only on defendants who can be found to have violated each of the elements of a predicate constitutional or statutory standard, including any requisite scienter. See Nahmod, "Constitutional Accountability in Section 1983 Litigation," 68 Iowa L.Rev. 1 (1982).

5. *Id.* An approach like this is endorsed by Professor Brown, in "Accountability in Government and Section 1983," 25 U.Mich. Journal L.Ref. 53 (1991).

cases where the entity, under *City of Canton,* is not. And even if the prerequisite mental state for supervisory liability is brought into line with the kind of "deliberate indifference" described in *Canton,* this approach violates the understanding that Section 1983 itself (as distinguished from some of the predicate rights for which it provides a remedy) has no uniform state of mind requirement. Even if, for example, as is the case with most First and Fourth Amendment violations, the plaintiff need not prove any scienter on the part of the *subordinate,* the supervisor could be liable only upon proof of a reckless state of mind mandated by Section 1983 itself. Further, as is true of the entity's own liability under *Canton,* the ultimate source of the supervisor's duty is Section 1983, contrary to the convention that the statute creates no rights or duties of its own.

The courts have had little difficulty with two small pieces of this puzzle. First, in the situation where the supervisor actively participates in the subordinate's violation, the supervisor is liable on the same terms as the subordinate for "subjecting" the plaintiff to a federal law deprivation.[6] Second, where the plaintiff seeks to hold the supervisor liable by reference to the conduct of a subordinate, the supervisor is not liable unless the subordinate has in fact breached a constitutional obligation, with whatever required scienter the predicate violation entails.[7]

Confusion abounds, however, concerning the terms of supervisor liability in non-participation cases. For the most part, the courts have opted for the "causation" approach. The decisions that take this tack rely heavily both on the causation language of Section 1983 and the analogy from precedent furnished by *City of Canton.* The "deliberate indifference" that these courts prescribe for supervisory liability is equated with the *Canton* standard for entity liability. This means that ordinarily the plaintiff cannot prevail, when seeking to hold the supervisor liable for an omission, by pointing only to one or even several isolated prior incidents posing a risk of constitutional harm. Instead, plaintiff must show continued supervisor inaction despite documented widespread occurrences.[8]

---

6. *See, e.g., Tilson v. Forrest City Police Department,* 28 F.3d 802 (8th Cir.1994), *cert. denied,* __ U.S. __, 115 S.Ct. 1315, 131 L.Ed.2d 196 (1995); *Anderson v. Branen,* 17 F.3d 552 (2d Cir.1994) (supervisor held to same reasonableness standard as his subordinate officer); *Sample v. Diecks,* 885 F.2d 1099 (3d Cir.1989).

7. *See Hinkle v. City of Clarksburg,* 81 F.3d 416 (4th Cir.1996); *Scott v. Henrich,* 39 F.3d 912 (9th Cir.1994), *cert. denied,* __ U.S. __, 115 S.Ct. 2612, 132 L.Ed.2d 855 (1995); *Thompson v. Boggs,* 33 F.3d 847 (7th Cir.1994), *cert. denied,* __ U.S. __, 115 S.Ct. 1692, 131 L.Ed.2d 556 (1995); *Spears v. City of Louisville,* 27 F.3d 567 (6th Cir.1994); *Danese v. Asman,* 875 F.2d 1239 (6th Cir.1989). *See also Tilson v.*

Forrest City Police Department, 28 F.3d 802 (8th Cir.1994), *cert. denied,* __ U.S. __, 115 S.Ct. 1315, 131 L.Ed.2d 196 (1995) (police chief could not be liable for failing to promulgate adequate written procedures governing a criminal investigation where his subordinate officers were not shown to have followed unlawful procedures in taking the plaintiff into custody).

8. *See Love v. Haigler,* 47 F.3d 1165 (4th Cir.1995); *Shaw v. Stroud,* 13 F.3d 791 (4th Cir.1994). *Cf. Febus–Rodriguez v. Betancourt–Lebron,* 14 F.3d 87 (1st Cir. 1994) (for supervisor to be liable, subordinate's prior incidents of misconduct must be related to conduct currently challenged). *But cf. Atchinson v. District of Columbia,* 73 F.3d 418 (D.C.Cir.1996) (supervisory liabili-

But the analogy to *Canton* also means that the supervisor need only have constructive rather than actual knowledge of the subordinate's involvement in conduct that threatens a substantial risk of constitutional injury to citizens in the plaintiff's position.[9] Unfortunately, the elements of constructive knowledge are phrased variously in the circuit decisions. There are statements in the cases that the supervisor is liable if she either knew "or reasonably should have known" of the situation in which the subordinate would likely subject the plaintiff to a deprivation of federal rights;[10] or if she failed to take action that is "obviously necessary" to prevent the harm to persons in plaintiff's position.[11] Other courts impose the same prima facie requirement in substance, using different words. For example, several circuits require what they call "reckless" or "callous" indifference, "gross negligence," or "deliberate indifference."[12] The Eleventh Circuit implements that standard by borrowing the phraseology of the qualified immunity defense, transplanting it to the prima facie case against the supervisor.[13] Of course, where the supervisor, with actual knowledge of the peril, nevertheless affirmatively approves the subordinate's conduct that endangers the plaintiff's rights, the supervisor's liability is even clearer.[14]

Still other appellate decisions, however, including even some in the same circuits, articulate a more stringent version of the "causation" approach that limits supervisors' liability to situations where they are personally involved in inflicting the violation or had *actual* knowledge of the conduct of the subordinate who committed the federal law violation. These courts find that "deliberate indifference" in the *City of Canton* sense requires a conscious acceptance of a known and serious risk; the supervisor therefore lacks the scienter required by Section 1983 unless

ty can attach to even isolated misconduct of subordinate if violation sufficiently serious or flagrant).

9. *Id.*

10. *See e.g., Taylor v. Michigan Dep't of Corrections,* 69 F.3d 76 (6th Cir.1995); *Snell v. Tunnell,* 920 F.2d 673 (10th Cir. 1990); *Howard v. Adkison,* 887 F.2d 134 (8th Cir.1989). *See generally Doe v. Taylor Independent School District,* 15 F.3d 443 (5th Cir.1994) (equating individual supervisor's liability with the standard used to assess the liability of a new municipality under *Canton*).

11. *Doe v. Taylor Independent School District, supra.*

12. *Baker v. Putnal,* 75 F.3d 190 (5th Cir.1996); *Hill v. Dekalb Regional Youth Detention Center,* 40 F.3d 1176 (11th Cir. 1994); *Gaudreault v. Municipality of Salem,* 923 F.2d 203 (1st Cir.1990), *cert. denied,* 500 U.S. 956, 111 S.Ct. 2266, 114 L.Ed.2d 718 (1991); *Gutierrez–Rodriguez v. Cartagena,* 882 F.2d 553 (1st Cir.1989); *Howard v. Adkison,* 887 F.2d 134 (8th Cir. 1989); *Meriwether v. Coughlin,* 879 F.2d 1037 (2d Cir.1989). The court in *Gutier-*

rez–Rodriguez observed that there is no significant difference between a "gross negligence amounting to deliberate indifference" and a "reckless and callous indifference" standard.

13. *Greason v. Kemp,* 891 F.2d 829 (11th Cir.1990) (supervisor is liable "when a reasonable person in the supervisor's position would have known that his conduct infringed the constitutional rights of the plaintiff ... and his conduct was causally related to the constitutional violation committed by his subordinate"). *Accord Belcher v. City of Foley,* 30 F.3d 1390, 1397 (11th Cir.1994).

14. *Swint v. Wadley,* 5 F.3d 1435 (11th Cir.1993), *modified on rehearing,* 11 F.3d 1030 (11th Cir.1994), *cert. denied,* ___ U.S. ___, 115 S.Ct. 1312, 131 L.Ed.2d 194 (1995) (sheriff who approved a raid by subordinate officers that violated established law, and did so with knowledge of the defective manner in which an earlier raid had been conducted, potentially liable for improper supervision).

he knowingly acquiesces in unconstitutional behavior.[15] This approach is echoed by language in another opinion that hinged supervisory liability for devising an unconstitutional policy about the use of deadly canine force, or for failing adequately to train or supervise a subordinate in the use of that force, on whether the supervisor "authorized, approved, or acquiesced" in such a policy.[16] Interestingly, however, the court that announced this test also indicated that if such involvement could be shown, those supervisors might be liable even though the subordinate officer who unleashed the force had been found nonliable because he acted reasonably given the procedures established by his superiors.[17] Perhaps it is fair to generalize that courts are more likely to impute constructive knowledge to a supervisor in a "failure to train" case, where recurrent situations make obvious the need for training subordinates in a particular task. By contrast, courts will more likely require the plaintiff to show the supervisor's actual knowledge of subordinate misconduct in cases alleging a failure to supervise or discipline.

The residue of these decisions is that a supervisor may be liable either because of her personal involvement in the constitutional injury inflicted on the plaintiff or because of her "deliberate indifference." But there remains continuing uncertainty whether this "deliberate indifference" demands evidence of a more culpable state of mind than is reflected in a city's simple failure to take precautionary measures in the face of persistent evidence of the need to do so. One structural argument against the higher standard is that the "actual knowledge" test effectively eliminates the individual supervisor's defense of qualified immunity: how could a supervisor show that she reasonably failed to appreciate that inaction would likely violate the plaintiff's settled right where plaintiff has already shown that she knowingly acquiesced in the unconstitutional behavior? On the other hand, even the more lenient version of supervisory "deliberate indifference" alters the qualified immunity defense procedurally: in effect plaintiff has to show the supervisor's unreasonable failure to act as part of the prima facie case. Accord-

---

15. *Baker v. Monroe Township,* 50 F.3d 1186 (3d Cir.1995); *Woodward v. City of Worland,* 977 F.2d 1392 (10th Cir.1992); *Andrews v. City of Philadelphia,* 895 F.2d 1469 (3d Cir.1990). *See Boyd v. Knox,* 47 F.3d 966 (8th Cir.1995) (where the predicate violation involved a prison official's alleged indifference to a prisoner's medical needs, the official must actually know of and disregard a particular, serious potential harm). The *Boyd* standard seems dictated more by the particular Eighth Amendment violation in question than by the panel's view of a general Section 1983 requirement for supervisor liability. The opinion relies on the Supreme Court's recent opinion in *Farmer v. Brennan,* 511 U.S. 82, ___, 114 S.Ct. 1970, 1979, 128 L.Ed.2d 811 (1994), which holds that a prison official must have actual knowledge of a substantial risk of harm before his failure to take steps to

safeguard an inmate violates that Amendment. *See also Rascon v. Hardiman,* 803 F.2d 269 (7th Cir.1986) (supervisor must have knowingly, wilfully, or recklessly caused the alleged deprivation by failing to act).

16. *Chew v. Gates,* 27 F.3d 1432, 1438–1439 (9th Cir.1994), *cert. denied,* ___ U.S. ___, 115 S.Ct. 1097, 130 L.Ed.2d 1065 (1995); *Zuchel v. City and County of Denver,* 997 F.2d 730 (10th Cir.1993); *Davis v. Mason County,* 927 F.2d 1473 (9th Cir.), *cert. denied,* 502 U.S. 899, 112 S.Ct. 275, 116 L.Ed.2d 227 (1991). *See also Neely v. Feinstein,* 50 F.3d 1502 (9th Cir.1995) (supervisor's conscious indifference to risk that aide would sexually abuse psychiatric patient defeats qualified immunity).

17. *Id.*

ingly, the burden of persuading that a *supervisor* unreasonably failed to act falls on the plaintiff, while the same burden, if part of the qualified immunity defense of a *subordinate,* is the defendant's.

E. THE PRACTICAL CONSEQUENCES OF ASYMMETRICAL PRIMA FACIE CASES AND DEFENSES IN INDIVIDUAL AND ENTITY ACTIONS: OF *PAUL* AND *PARRATT, ZINERMON* AND *SIEGERT*

Library References:

> C.J.S. Civil Rights §§ 307, 308.
> West's Key No. Digests, Civil Rights ⊕242(1).

§ 2.24 In General

The divergence of the prima facie elements and defenses in § 1983 actions against individuals and entities may be viewed as responses by the Court to three perceived problems: unfairness to individual defendants, the opening of litigation floodgates, and threats to federalism resulting from intrusive interference with vigorous state administration of public functions. This Section explores the varying techniques the Court has employed to address these issues, the resulting differentiation of the individual and entity cases, and the consequences for dynamic lawmaking. Broadly speaking, the case against an individual includes a somewhat easily established prima facie case countered by an extensive immunity and offers no opportunity for development in constitutional doctrine. On the other hand, although the case against an entity begins with a formidable prima facie case, it is unchecked by a general immunity defense and therefore still holds out the possibility of doctrinal development.

§ 2.25 Individual Defendant Cases

In suits against individual defendants the Court has responded to the swelling of § 1983 litigation after *Monroe,* and the consequent constraints on government decisionmaking, not only by fortifying the qualified immunity defense but also by defining more restrictively certain predicate constitutional violations.

a. Recapping the Prima Facie Case

The plaintiff's prima facie case is judicially unembellished and tracks the language of the statute in a straightforward manner. The plaintiff must allege and persuade the factfinder by a preponderance of the evidence that the defendant, (1) under color of state law, (2) deprived or caused the plaintiff to be deprived (3) of a federally protected right and (4) with resulting harm to the plaintiff. While the plaintiff may encounter difficulty in establishing these elements she need not make the formidable additional showing of "policy" required for the prima facie case against an entity.

b. The Enlargement of Qualified Immunity

As we have seen, the early common law immunity doctrine typified by cases like *Scheuer v. Rhodes*[1] demanded a fact-based inquiry that sought to unfetter discretionary administration of the law. This qualified immunity insulated individual public officials, ineligible for absolute immunity, from liability without fault through the general defense of good faith and probable cause.[2] *Scheuer* identified two bases for this qualified immunity: the injustice of punishing the officer who, in good faith, exercises discretion as a requirement of his job, and the fear that the threat of liability would chill the officer's execution of his duties "with the decisiveness and judgment required by the public good."[3]

Yet in *Harlow v. Fitzgerald*[4] and again in *Anderson v. Creighton*,[5] the Court jettisoned this heavily fact-laden version of common law immunity. It substituted a two-part inquiry that begins and usually ends with a legal question, the settledness of the specific right at issue. More rarely, if the right is deemed well-settled, the test of immunity unfolds into a factual inquiry about the reasonableness of official conduct in light of that highly particularized precedent. These decisions were avowedly designed to enable defendants to obtain early dismissals before extensive (and preferably, before any) discovery. Substantively, they broaden immunity so that it is generally no longer defeasible by evidence of subjective bad faith.[6] What had traditionally been a jury question aimed at determining the justice of excusing the officer in light of all the circumstances she confronted in the course of discretionary decision-making is now usually a question of law for the trial judge.

Although qualified immunity may protect the defendant from monetary damages, the doctrine cannot shield him from injunctive relief. And a grant of an injunction would authorize an award of attorney's fees under § 1988. Thus an attorney may still find incentive to take a case where a grant of qualified immunity is likely.

c. Paring Down the Predicate Constitutional Violations and Restricting Constitutional Development

At the same time, the Court was further closing the floodgates[7] on individual actions by narrowing certain predicate constitutional protections. In *Paul v. Davis*,[8] the Court announced its determination to

---

§ 2.25

1. 416 U.S. 232, 94 S.Ct. 1683, 40 L.Ed.2d 90 (1974).

2. *See supra* § 2.22.

3. 416 U.S. at 240, 94 S.Ct. at 1688.

4. 457 U.S. 800, 102 S.Ct. 2727, 73 L.Ed.2d 396 (1982).

5. 483 U.S. 635, 107 S.Ct. 3034, 97 L.Ed.2d 523 (1987).

6. *See* § 2.12, text accompanying note 24. In at least one circuit, however, specifically pleaded and proven malice may sometimes defeat the immunity. *See supra*

§ 2.12, note 13, re *Siegert v. Gilley*, 895 F.2d 797, 800–02 (D.C.Cir.1990), *affirmed on other grounds*, 500 U.S. 226, 111 S.Ct. 1789, 114 L.Ed.2d 277 (1991).

7. *See* Eisenberg & Schwab, *supra* § 2.1, note 8, at 646–47 (arguing that the *Paul* and *Parratt* lines of authority, discussed below, had their impetus in a desire to control the flood of litigation).

8. 424 U.S. 693, 96 S.Ct. 1155, 47 L.Ed.2d 405 (1976).

prevent the Fourteenth Amendment from becoming "a font of tort law" [9] through the medium of actions under § 1983. Justice Rehnquist, following a course laid out in *Board of Regents of State Colleges v. Roth*,[10] contracted the circumstances under which any process is due to avoid " 'alter[ing] the basic relations between the States and the national government.' " [11]

The plaintiff in *Paul* alleged that police had deprived him of his liberty by posting his name as an "active shoplifter" before any adjudication on the charge. Laboring to avoid finding a predicate liberty interest, the Court distinguished *Wisconsin v. Constantineau*,[12] where the Court had held that "[w]here a person's good name ... is at stake because of what the government is doing to him, notice and an opportunity to be heard are essential." In *Paul*, by contrast, the Court refused to recognize a generalized constitutional liberty interest to be free from state-perpetrated defamation and it found "no specific constitutional guarantee" safeguarding reputation. Moreover, plaintiff could cite no source of a liberty interest in state law.[13]

Concurrently, in the *Parratt*[14] line of cases, the Court sharply curtailed the procedural "deprivations" redressable by due process, thereby affording state actors an escape from federal liability for otherwise actionable conduct. In *Parratt*, prison officials negligently deprived an inmate of his property. The Court, recognizing that property deprivations ordinarily require predeprivation process, held that a postdeprivation state tort law remedy satisfies the obligation to provide process whenever the deprivation is effected by the "random and unauthorized" conduct of government officials. This result obtains, the Court wrote, even if the state remedy is more restrictive and affords lesser relief than

---

9. *Id.* at 701, 96 S.Ct. at 1160.

10. 408 U.S. 564, 569–79, 92 S.Ct. 2701, 2705–10, 33 L.Ed.2d 548 (1972) (holding that untenured teacher had no property right and was not deprived of liberty upon nonrenewal of his contract). The significance of *Roth* in the development of Fourteenth Amendment jurisprudence occupies a central role in Henry P. Monaghan, *Of "Liberty" and "Property,"* 62 Cornell L. Rev. 405, 409 (1977) (concluding that after *Roth*, "life, liberty and property" no longer "embrace the full range of state conduct having serious impact upon individual interests").

11. *Paul*, 424 U.S. at 700, 96 S.Ct. at 1160 (*quoting Screws v. United States*, 325 U.S. 91, 109, 65 S.Ct. 1031, 1039, 89 L.Ed. 1495 (1945) (plurality opinion)). For a blistering critique of *Paul* that remains as convincing today as when it was written, see Monaghan, *supra* note 10. On Justice Rehnquist's federalism concerns see Melvin R. Durchslag, *Federalism and Constitutional Liberties: Varying the Remedy to Save the Right*, 54 N.Y.U.L.Rev. 723, 739–41

(1979). *See generally* Sheldon H. Nahmod, *Due Process, State Remedies, and Section 1983*, 34 Kan. L. Rev. 217, 217–18 (1985) (discussing the several policies that drove the Burger Court's § 1983 jurisprudence).

12. 400 U.S. 433, 91 S.Ct. 507, 27 L.Ed.2d 515 (1971).

13. For a brief time, however, some residual constitutional interest in reputation appeared to survive *Paul*. *See Paul* 424 U.S. at 700, 96 S.Ct. at 1160 *and Owen v. City of Independence*, 445 U.S. 622, 100 S.Ct. 1398, 63 L.Ed.2d 673 (1980). But any such hope was dashed by *Siegert v. Gilley*, 500 U.S. 226, 231, 111 S.Ct. 1789, 1793, 114 L.Ed.2d 277 (1991), which held that the fourteenth amendment provides no redress even when the defamation accompanies permanent termination from government employment.

14. *See Parratt v. Taylor*, 451 U.S. 527, 536–42, 101 S.Ct. 1908, 1913–16, 68 L.Ed.2d 420 (1981), *overruled in part by Daniels v. Williams*, 474 U.S. 327, 106 S.Ct. 662, 88 L.Ed.2d 662 (1986).

§ 1983. It reasoned that the random and unauthorized nature of the deprivation made it impracticable for the state to provide predeprivation process because the state official could not predict precisely when the deprivation would occur.

The *Parratt* doctrine reached its apogee three years later in *Hudson v. Palmer*,[15] where the Court ruled that the rationale of *Parratt* extended to intentional conduct. The Court in *Hudson* could "discern no logical distinction between negligent and intentional deprivations of property insofar as the 'practicality' of affording pre-deprivation process is concerned." The State could no more predict its agents' random and unauthorized intentional conduct than it could anticipate similar negligent conduct. Postdeprivation state tort law remedies, therefore, provided all the process that was due.

Parratt has turned out to have had a shorter reach than was generally thought when it was decided. For one thing, the Court has whittled away at the kinds of conduct that constitute a deprivation of due process; and if there is no "deprivation," the *Parratt* "postdeprivation remedy" exception in "random and unauthorized" situations never comes into play.

For example, it is now clear that the defendant must hold a "more than negligent" state of mind before his conduct can rise to the level of a "deprivation" actionable as a denial of due process. Thus in *Daniels v. Williams*,[16] and *Davidson v. Cannon*,[17] the Court concluded that negligent acts do not provide an adequate predicate for due process violations. In *Davidson*, the Court found no liberty deprivation, and therefore no violation of due process, when prison officials negligently failed to protect an inmate from a beating at the hands of another inmate, despite evidence that the officials had some foreknowledge of the possibility.[18] And in *Daniels*, a companion case that in this respect overruled *Parratt*, the Court explained that some degree of fault greater than "mere lack of care" is prerequisite to an actionable "deprivation of Due Process."[19]

Further, the Court has declared two sorts of limitations on the applicability of *Parratt* as an escape from liability even in the dwindling number of "more than negligent" settings in which the Court still finds due process "deprivations." First, in *Logan v. Zimmerman Brush Co.*,[20] the Court limited *Parratt* to instances of random and unauthorized conduct by government officials, as distinct from established procedures declared by state law. Plaintiff in *Logan* challenged his firing in the proper state administrative agency, but the agency negligently failed to hold a hearing within the time limit mandated by statute. Rejecting *Parratt*'s applicability, the Court stated that "[u]nlike the complainant

---

15. 468 U.S. 517, 104 S.Ct. 3194, 82 L.Ed.2d 393 (1984).

16. 474 U.S. 327, 106 S.Ct. 662, 88 L.Ed.2d 662 (1986).

17. 474 U.S. 344, 106 S.Ct. 668, 88 L.Ed.2d 677 (1986).

18. *See id.* at 347–48, 106 S.Ct. at 670.

19. 474 U.S. at 330–31, 106 S.Ct. at 664–65. *See Trigalet v. Young*, 54 F.3d 645 (10th Cir.1995) (recklessness suffices).

20. 455 U.S. 422, 102 S.Ct. 1148, 71 L.Ed.2d 265 (1982).

in *Parratt*, Logan is challenging not the [commission's] error, but the 'established state procedure' that destroys his entitlement without according him proper procedural safeguards." Because the state system itself rather than the random and unauthorized conduct of state officials destroyed plaintiff's property interest, the Court concluded that predeprivation process was required, despite the existence of an adequate state remedy.

Second, in *Zinermon v. Burch*,[21] the Court limited *Parratt/Hudson*'s "random and unauthorized" exception to cases where it would be impossible or at least extremely difficult for the government officials on the scene to provide process before a deprivation. In *Zinermon*, plaintiff claimed that state officials wilfully and recklessly disregarded his rights to due process by admitting him "voluntarily" to a state mental hospital when the staff knew or should have known that he was incompetent to give the informed consent required by statute. Distinguishing *Parratt* and *Hudson*, the Court determined that defendants' conduct was something other than "random and unauthorized."

The moment of deprivation and the fact that some prospective patients might lack capacity were predictable, the Court wrote. Therefore the state, before taking plaintiff's liberty, could have accorded him a predeprivation hearing that would have guarded against an admission in violation of the statute. Moreover, the Court concluded, the conduct in question could not be considered "unauthorized" in the *Parratt/Hudson* sense, because the State had delegated to the hospital staff the authority to make admissions decisions even if it had not prescribed any particular procedure to determine the competence to consent requisite to a voluntary admission. The Court thus held *Parratt/Hudson* inapplicable when identified government personnel with evident statutory discretion to provide appropriate process can feasibly provide a predeprivation hearing that will reduce the risk of an erroneous deprivation.

The Court in *Zinermon* also assuaged the fear that *Parratt* would excuse violations of substantive due process. It placed *Parratt* squarely within the procedural due process context created by *Mathews v. Eldridge*.[22] *Parratt*, stressed the Court, was simply a special application of the *Mathews* balancing test for determining what procedural safeguards are constitutionally required—an application that tilted the scales against the provision of predeprivation process. In so saying, the Court folded *Parratt* into a line of cases bracketed by *Zinermon* and *Logan*. *Parratt* does not control either when, as in *Logan*, the state formally creates established procedure but as a practical matter makes it unavailable, or when, as in *Zinermon*, the state fails to provide predeprivation process that it readily could have provided. Viewed with the hindsight of *Zinermon*, *Parratt* accordingly leaves unaffected the *Monroe* holding that individual defendants may still be accountable under § 1983 for

21. 494 U.S. 113, 110 S.Ct. 975, 108 L.Ed.2d 100 (1990). *Zinermon* is discussed in more detail *infra* at text accompanying notes 29–35.

22. 424 U.S. 319, 96 S.Ct. 893, 47 L.Ed.2d 18 (1976).

violations of most (clearly established) constitutional rights (other than random and unauthorized procedural due process violations for which state law allows a post-deprivation remedy) even when their conduct is entirely unauthorized by their governing principal.[23]

But *Parratt* does block relief for at least procedural due process claims even when the defendant's conduct reflects the required level of due process culpability the Court now requires (i.e., recklessness or intent) and even when, notwithstanding *Paul/Roth/Siegert*, the complaint in other respects states a cognizable deprivation of liberty or property. As such, *Parratt* still constitutes a separate limitation on the process that is due whenever conduct is random and unauthorized; in such cases, almost any state post-deprivation remedy supplants federal relief. *Parratt* thus stands as a striking counterpoint to Justice Harlan's observation in *Monroe* that Congress apparently contemplated *fuller* relief under § 1983 than the states might afford for the same misconduct.[24]

23. At least four members of the current Court are on record as being uncomfortable with the reach of *Parratt*. Justices Kennedy and Thomas, concurring in the judgment only in *Albright v. Oliver*, 510 U.S. 266, 114 S.Ct. 807, 127 L.Ed.2d 114 (1994), complain that the Court has not given the doctrine its full sway. As they see it, *Parratt* is designed to further the resolve expressed in *Paul* to prevent § 1983 from becoming an open-ended font of tort law. To that end they regard *Parratt* not merely as a limit on the scope of procedural due process but as a prohibition of relief under § 1983—for any due process claim, procedural or substantive—where the state actor's challenged conduct is random and unauthorized and state law provides an adequate postdeprivation remedy. Given Illinois' malicious prosecution civil remedy, and their characterization of the defendant's conduct as random and unauthorized, they would have denied the *Albright* plaintiff any remedy under § 1983 even assuming, contrary to the plurality's holding, that a substantive due process claim was stated.

At the other end of the spectrum, dissenting Justice Stevens (who lamented in his opinion that he was the author, while a judge on the Seventh Circuit Court of Appeals, of a forerunner of *Parratt*) joined by Justice Blackmun, began by describing *Parratt* as "categorically inapplicable" to substantive due process claims, on the authority of *Zinermon*. Issue was clearly joined on this point with Justices Kennedy and Thomas, who had objected that *Zinermon* itself was an evasion of *Parratt* achieved by mischaracterizing the *Zinermon* claim as based on substantive, rather than procedur-

al, due process. Indeed Justices Stevens and Blackmun deem *Parratt* "reconcilable with § 1983" in only a handful of "situations in which no constitutional violation [apparently of procedural due process] occurs." They virtually limit *Parratt* to its facts—a negligent, rather than reckless or intentional loss of property—and in particular find it inapplicable to most deprivations of liberty. In the process, they implicitly call into question the *Parratt* progeny like *Daniels*, *Davidson*, and *Hudson* that denied § 1983 remedies for random and unauthorized government agent conduct, more culpable than negligence, that resulted in deprivations of liberty.

If either of these polar positions commands a majority on the Court, the aggregate effect of *Parratt* on § 1983 would be altered. Should the Kennedy/Thomas view prevail, *Parratt* would become a broad-spectrum limitation on remedies under § 1983 within the entire sphere of due process, even without narrowing the formal scope of due process itself. Should the Stevens/Blackmun view prevail, it would be considerably more clear than it appears today that *Parratt*, far from limiting § 1983 remedies generally, is merely a declaration about the scope of procedural due process that would logically exist in its absence. To them the decision simply affirms that the only process that is due when a government agent acts negligently—by definition, an act the government entity cannot anticipate and for which it accordingly cannot provide process beforehand—is a subsequent state law remedy for damages.

24. *See Monroe v. Pape*, 365 U.S. 167, 196 n. 5, 81 S.Ct. 473, 488 n. 5, 5 L.Ed.2d

As the foregoing discussion reveals, the Court, concerned about calendar congestion, fairness to government officers, and intrusion on state prerogatives, has constricted the scope of due process and equal protection principally in the course of deciding § 1983 suits against individual defendants. True, the pattern is wavy. For example, the Court has, at least formally, eschewed de minimis exceptions to claims based on liberty [25] as well as property.[26] Nevertheless, constitutional claims rooted in the protection of property seemingly stand on a surer footing with the current Court than claims based on liberty. As we have seen, the Court has excluded whole categories of losses from the "liberty" protected by substantive (*Paul*; *Siegert*; *DeShaney*; *Collins*) and procedural (*Parratt*; *Zinermon*) due process. It also excludes any substantive due process claim based on allegations that the Court construes as implicating a more specific Bill of Rights provision—the Fourth Amendment, as in *Albright v. Oliver*, or the Eighth, as in *Graham v. Connor*—apparently regardless of whether the more specific guarantee favors or undermines the plaintiff's case. Yet at the same time the Court has extended the embrace of the Fourth Amendment's unlawful seizure protection to reach invasions of the defendant's property as well as his person.[27]

Still, neither the newly shrunken circumference of these important predicate constitutional rights nor the "clearly established" approach to individual defendant immunity represents a broad-spectrum restriction on the scope of § 1983 itself. Instead, the recent doctrinal accretions simply reduce the plaintiff's chances of success in stating a claim—of procedural due process violations, for example, under the *Parratt* line of cases, or of substantive due process violations, as evidenced by *Roth/Paul/Siegert* and *Albright*, *Collins*, and *Graham*. Similarly, the qualified immunity decisions, *Harlow*, *Creighton v. Anderson*, and *Siegert*, while they doom all constitutional claims against individual defendants when the right asserted was not judicially articulated with clarity at the time of the challenged conduct, do not by themselves increase the

492 (1961) (Harlan, J., concurring), *overruled in part by Monell v. Dep't of Social Servs.*, 436 U.S. 658, 98 S.Ct. 2018, 56 L.Ed.2d 611 (1978). *See Myers v. Klevenhagen,* 97 F.3d 91 (5th Cir.1996) (per curiam) and *Hamlin v. Vandenberg,* 95 F.3d 580 (7th Cir.1996) (*Parratt* precludes procedural due process claims by prisoners because of "adequate" state post-deprivation remedies). There may be some minimal requirements respecting the adequacy of a state's post-deprivation process. For example, a state forfeiture proceeding has been held to be an inadequate remedy for seizure of a vehicle where the state failed to bring that action despite plaintiff's requests over three years.

25. *Albright v. Oliver, supra* note 23.

26. *Connecticut v. Doehr,* 501 U.S. 1, 12, 111 S.Ct. 2105, 2113, 115 L.Ed.2d 1 (1991);

Peralta v. Heights Medical Center, Inc., 485 U.S. 80, 85, 108 S.Ct. 896, 899, 99 L.Ed.2d 75 (1988) (temporary or partial impairments of property trigger procedural due process protection); *Rush v. Savchuk,* 444 U.S. 320, 100 S.Ct. 571, 62 L.Ed.2d 516 (1980) (the slight and speculative jeopardy to an insured's property where he is indemnified and defended by his insurer nevertheless qualifies for the full protections of the personal jurisdiction branch of substantive due process).

27. *Soldal v. Cook County, Ill.*, 506 U.S. 56, 113 S.Ct. 538, 121 L.Ed.2d 450 (1992). This decision has recently been fortified by a court of appeals opinion that liberally conferred standing on such a property claimant under the Fourth Amendment. *See Bonds v. Cox*, 20 F.3d 697 (6th Cir. 1994), discussed in the Procedure chapter.

plaintiff's prima facie burden under § 1983. Nevertheless, the combination of sharply curtailed predicate protections and the greatly expanded qualified immunity defense does as a practical matter significantly disable § 1983 individual-defendant litigation from pushing the frontiers of federally protected rights.[28]

d. Tactics in Individual Defendant Litigation After Zinermon and Siegert

Ironically, it is in a procedural due process case—the least fruitful category of predicate constitutional claim after *Parratt*, *Hudson*, and *Davidson*[29]—that the Court allows room for the individual action to facilitate substantive doctrinal evolution. A close look at this decision, *Zinermon v. Burch*,[30] and its aftermath is necessary to appreciate this possibility.

Burch attempted to have himself "voluntarily" admitted to a state mental hospital at a time he claimed he was disoriented and psychologically incompetent to give informed consent. He alleged that the staff knew or should have known that he was incompetent and, by admitting him nevertheless, wilfully or recklessly disregarded his rights to due process. The Eleventh Circuit reversed the district court's ruling that because the staff's conduct was random and unauthorized Burch had failed to state a claim under *Parratt* and *Hudson*. As framed by the Supreme Court majority, the issue was whether Florida, in delegating to mid-level state hospital employees the voluntary admission decision, owed prospective patients some *pre*-admission process to determine whether consent was in fact informed.[31]

A five-member Supreme Court majority affirmed, distinguishing *Parratt* and *Hudson* on the ground that the defendants' conduct was something other than "random and unauthorized." For one thing, the Court found that because the moment of deprivation and the fact that

---

28. More ominously still, the "clearly established" barrier may affirmatively encourage officials who otherwise would be probable civil defendants to take a chance on constitutionally questionable conduct. Government agents know their decisions are largely free from constitutional scrutiny to the extent that no specific precedent unequivocally prohibits them. *See* David Rudovsky, *The Qualified Immunity in the Supreme Court: Judicial Activism and the Restriction of Constitutional Rights*, 138 U.Pa.L.Rev. 23, 54 (1989). For example, Professor Rudovsky foresees the possibility that *Anderson*'s double bite at reasonableness might reduce the Fourth Amendment's own probable cause requirement into a subconstitutional inquiry into the reasonableness of the officer's belief about the reasonableness of an arrest or search, despite the absence in fact of probable cause. *See id.* at 52–53. This result would freeze the state of constitutional law. *See id.* at 53.

29. *See* subpart c. immediately preceding.

30. 494 U.S. 113, 110 S.Ct. 975, 108 L.Ed.2d 100 (1990).

31. *See id.* at 114–15, 132, 110 S.Ct. at 977–78, 987. Florida had a complex series of procedures for use in determining the propriety of involuntary psychiatric admissions. *See id.* at 121–22, 110 S.Ct. at 981. Those procedures, however, did not cover the case in which a person attempted to admit himself as a voluntary patient when there was reason to doubt his capacity to give informed consent. The statute governing voluntary admissions required "express and informed consent" to be given "voluntarily [and] in writing," but provided no process for determining voluntariness. *Id.* at 122, 110 S.Ct. at 981 (quoting Fla. Stat. §§ 394.465(1)(a), 394.455(22) (1990)).

some prospective patients might lack capacity were predictable, the State, before taking Burch's liberty, could have accorded him a pre-deprivation hearing that would have guarded against an admission in violation of the statute.[32]   Moreover, the conduct could not be considered "unauthorized" in the *Parratt/Hudson* sense because the state had delegated authority to the hospital staff to make admissions decisions, without prescribing any particular procedure to determine the competence to consent requisite to a voluntary admission.[33]

Zinermon thus renders *Parratt* and *Hudson* inapplicable when identified government personnel with evident statutory discretion to provide appropriate process can feasibly provide a pre-deprivation hearing that will reduce the risk of an erroneous deprivation of liberty.[34]   In general, when the moment of deprivation is predictable and accordingly predeprivation process is possible, *Parratt* will not doom a claim of procedural due process.[35]   By declaring new doctrine, *Zinermon* appears to refute

32.   *See id.* at 132–33, 110 S.Ct. at 987. Among the important aspects of the decision was the majority's statement that liberty as well as property interests are subject to the *Parratt/Hudson* doctrine. *See id.* at 131–32, 110 S.Ct. at 986–87.

33.   *See id.* at 137, 110 S.Ct. at 989. Justice Blackmun articulated the distinction somewhat differently and perhaps less clearly. He stated that *Parratt* does not apply because (a) the state could foresee that mental patients might lack capacity, (b) providing pre-deprivation process was not literally impossible in view of the established procedure for determining involuntary admissions, and (c) the conduct was not "unauthorized," since the State had delegated admissions decisions to the hospital staff. *See id.* at 136–37, 110 S.Ct. at 989–90. Points (a) and (c) seem to be reasons that support point (b), rather than independent criteria that distinguish *Parratt* and *Hudson.*

34.   The case has cleared up several questions concerning the reach of the *Parratt* doctrine. It can now be said with confidence that the holdings of *Parratt* and *Hudson* regarding "random and unauthorized" avoidance of liability are limited to procedural due process claims involving situations in which pre-deprivation process is literally impossible. The Court has assuaged the fear, identified by Henry P. Monaghan, *State Law Wrongs, State Law Remedies, and the Fourteenth Amendment,* 86 Colum. L. Rev. 979, 985–86 (1986), that *Parratt* also restricted substantive due process claims. The *Zinermon* condition that the process plaintiff demands must have "value," *see Zinermon,* 494 U.S. at 134, 110 S.Ct. at 988, would not even be an issue if the subject were fundamental, substantive

rights. This conclusion is fortified by the lengths to which the majority and dissent went to place *Parratt* squarely within the procedural due process context created by *Mathews v. Eldridge,* 424 U.S. 319, 96 S.Ct. 893, 47 L.Ed.2d 18 (1976). *See Zinermon,* 494 U.S. at 127–129, 110 S.Ct. at 984–985; *id.* at 147–48, 110 S.Ct. at 994 (O'Connor, J., dissenting). *See generally* Laura Oren, *Signing Into Heaven: Zinermon v. Burch, Federal Rights, and State Remedies Thirty Years After Monroe v. Pape,* 40 Emory L.J. 1, 67 (1991) (concluding that *Parratt* is now a narrow doctrine). But the *Zinermon* end-run of *Parratt* may ultimately be limited to situations where the discretion of the entity's actors to design pre-deprivation procedures is "uncircumscribed" and results from "statutory oversight." *See Easter House v. Felder,* 910 F.2d 1387, 1401 (7th Cir.1990) (*en banc*), *cert. denied* , 498 U.S. 1067, 111 S.Ct. 783, 112 L.Ed.2d 846 (1991). *But cf. Cushing v. City of Chicago,* 3 F.3d 1156, 1165–66 (7th Cir.1993) (distinguishing *Easter House*). And recent rumblings suggest that some justices are eager to extend (or restore) *Parratt* to preclude substantive due process claims. *See Albright v. Oliver,* 510 U.S. 266, 114 S.Ct. 807, 127 L.Ed.2d 114 (1994), discussed *supra* n.23. *See also Cathey v. Guenther,* 47 F.3d 162 (5th Cir.1995) (applying doctrine to destruction of property case).

35.   *See, e.g., Alexander v. Ieyoub,* 62 F.3d 709 (5th Cir.1995); *Armendariz v. Penman,* 31 F.3d 860 (9th Cir.1994), *vacated,* 75 F.3d 1311 (9th Cir.1996); *Gentry v. City of Lee's Summit, Missouri,* 10 F.3d 1340 (8th Cir.1993); *Mertik v. Blalock,* 983 F.2d 1353 (6th Cir.1993); *Ezekwo v. New York City Health & Hosp. Corp.,* 940 F.2d 775 (2d Cir.1991); *Plumer v. State of Mary-*

the argument that the state of constitutional law is frozen in § 1983 damage actions against individual defendants. Even if Burch himself loses on qualified immunity, in any subsequent action the law declared by *Zinermon* will be settled, and local governments put on notice that in the mental health context they must adopt appropriate procedures to determine voluntariness.

It appeared, however, after *Zinermon* that tactically shrewd defense counsel could thwart the law-evolution potential of the individual defendant action. The practical lesson of the case may simply have been that defendants should press for a decision on the affirmative defense of immunity rather than move to dismiss the complaint for legal insufficiency under *Parratt*.[36] For example, had defense counsel in *Zinermon* followed that tack, the *Parratt* question would probably never have arisen: even assuming Burch had a right to the procedural protections he claimed, that right was not clearly settled at the time he was admitted. Damage actions against entities accordingly seemed the only

---

land, 915 F.2d 927 (4th Cir.1990); and *Fields v. Durham,* 909 F.2d 94 (4th Cir. 1990). Of course, rejection of the *Parratt* defense merely indicates that *some* process is due; the due process claim may still fail if for some other reason the court finds that the plaintiff received all the process that was due in the particular circumstances. *See, e.g., Caine v. Hardy,* 943 F.2d 1406, 1412 (5th Cir.1991); *Plumer, supra,* 915 F.2d at 931; *Fields, supra,* 909 F.2d at 97–98. And *Parratt* will also continue to be applied where the court concludes that the moment of deprivation was unpredictable, unauthorized, or unforeseeable. *See Lowe v. Scott,* 959 F.2d 323 (1st Cir.1992). Last, courts have devised an "emergency circumstances" exception that permits application of *Parratt,* despite *Zinermon,* when the circumstances surrounding a particular, predictable deprivation necessitate prompt action by the government actor. *See Harris v. City of Akron,* 20 F.3d 1396 (6th Cir. 1994). The cases are not clear, however, whether *Zinermon* trumps *Parratt* when the moment of deprivation is predictable but the official is not authorized to effect the deprivation.

36. *See Danese v. Asman,* 875 F.2d 1239, 1240 (6th Cir.1989), *cert. denied* , 494 U.S. 1027, 110 S.Ct. 1473, 108 L.Ed.2d 610 (1990). The plaintiff in *Danese* might well have succeeded with a procedural due process claim that could have skirted *Parratt* via *Zinermon* had not the defendant successfully pressed the qualified immunity defense first. *See id.* at 1242–44.

As a purely procedural matter, defendants are entitled to move separately on the defenses of legal insufficiency and qualified immunity, provided both defenses are prop-

erly preserved in the responsive pleading. *See* Fed. R. Civ. P. 12(b), 8(c), 7(b). The former defense attacks the legal adequacy of the plaintiff's claim and is resolved solely by reference to the allegations of the complaint, while the latter asserts an affirmative defense, which, if legally sufficient and factually supported, avoids liability for damages even if the elements of the claim are adequately pleaded and proven. Given the ease of deciding the legal insufficiency issue, and its ripeness at the threshold of a lawsuit, a defendant would ordinarily make that motion first.

Substantively, however, the current version of qualified immunity subsumes the question of legal sufficiency that is normally raised by a motion to dismiss for failure to state a claim. While it remains unclear how settled a right must be to meet the Court's requirements, a determination that a particular right is well settled must mean at a minimum that the right has been recognized by a court of some dignity and does state a legally sufficient claim. Rejection of the qualified immunity defense on its first, legal prong would thus doom a follow-up motion to dismiss for failure to state a claim. By the same token, however, a plaintiff's claim, although adequate to survive a motion to dismiss for legal insufficiency, may not implicate a right that is settled to the degree necessary to avoid the defense of qualified immunity. From an efficiency standpoint it seemed after *Zinermon* that the individual defendant was better advised to move on qualified immunity at the outset, even though the ultimate denial of that motion would spell the defeat of the legal insufficiency defense as well.

sure vehicle for the creation of new constitutional protections, so long as counsel for individual defendants raised the qualified immunity defense initially.[37] This conclusion seemed buttressed by the extreme latitude appellate courts have granted the *Harlow/Anderson* immunity defense—insisting on its resolution before discovery,[38] permitting immediate appeals from the denial of qualified immunity motions,[39] and applying zealously the "clearly established" concept.[40]

But these tactics should now be of little moment after *Siegert v. Gilley*.[41] Plaintiff, a former government psychiatrist, brought a defamation action, presumably under what he perceived to be the residue of *Paul v. Davis*.[42] The Court of Appeals for the District of Columbia assumed, without deciding, that plaintiff stated a claim under *Paul*, but remanded the case with instructions to dismiss because, among other things, the right was not clearly established.[43]

The Supreme Court majority affirmed, but rejected the sequencing of issues implicit in the circuit court's analysis. Concluding that "[a] necessary concomitant to the determination of whether the constitutional right asserted ... is 'clearly established' ... is the determination of whether [there is] ... a constitutional right at all," [44] the Court found no such right, despite *Paul*.[45] This approach, by scrutinizing a component of the defense that is identical to the "rights" element of a § 1983 plaintiff's prima facie claim, has the potential to absolve the defendant from any liability, including prospective relief and attorneys' fees; by contrast, the qualified immunity defense as such relieves the individual

---

37. *See, e.g., P.C. v. McLaughlin*, 913 F.2d 1033, 1039–41 (2d Cir.1990) (determining that the issue of whether officials complied with federally incorporated state statutory requirements for admitting plaintiff to residential school for retarded individuals, and thus with requirements of the Education of the Handicapped Act of 1975, 20 U.S.C.A. §§ 1401, 1415(b)(1)(C), (b)(2) (1988), was pretermitted by a grant of qualified immunity through the application of *Harlow*).

38. *See* § 2.12.

39. *See* § 2.13.

40. *See generally* § 2.12, note 50. *See also Auriemma v. Rice*, 895 F.2d 338, 340, 344 (7th Cir.), *affirmed in part and reversed in part*, 910 F.2d 1449 (7th Cir.1990), *cert. denied*, 501 U.S. 1204, 111 S.Ct. 2796, 115 L.Ed.2d 970 (1991) (holding that police superintendent qualifies for immunity when prior decisions failed to establish clearly that he could not reasonably have relied on race as a factor in reorganizing his department, even though he did not purport to be implementing an affirmative action plan when he promoted black officers and de-

moted only white officers); *Danese v. Asman, supra* note 36, at 1244 (stating that a pretrial detainee's generalized right to medical care does not clearly establish a correlative right to be screened to determine if such care is needed). The divergence of approaches to § 1983 entity and individual actions becomes evident upon comparison of *Danese* and *City of Canton v. Harris*, 489 U.S. 378, 109 S.Ct. 1197, 103 L.Ed.2d 412 (1989). *Danese* provides immunity although the right is arguably clearly established, but in *City of Canton*, an entity action, a majority refused to foreclose an almost identical claim despite its novelty. *See* § 2.19.

41. 500 U.S. 226, 111 S.Ct. 1789, 114 L.Ed.2d 277 (1991).

42. 424 U.S. 693, 96 S.Ct. 1155, 47 L.Ed.2d 405 (1976).

43. *See Siegert v. Gilley*, 895 F.2d 797, 803 (D.C.Cir.1990), *affirmed*, 500 U.S. 226, 111 S.Ct. 1789, 114 L.Ed.2d 277 (1991).

44. *Siegert*, 500 U.S. at 232, 111 S.Ct. at 1793.

45. *See supra* § 2.25, note 13.

defendant from liability for damages alone.[46] In this way the *Siegert* prescription for sequencing these issues promises some government officials even greater freedom from the expense and time demands of litigation than they enjoyed when trial courts turned immediately to the question whether an assumed right was clearly established.[47]

§ 2.26 Entity Defendant Cases

a. *The Prima Facie Element "Policy"*

In actions against entity defendants the Court has for the most part addressed the same problems of fairness, federalism, and floodgates not by eroding selected predicate federal rights or enlarging immunities (as it did in actions against individual defendants), but by heightening the plaintiff's prima facie showing necessary to state any claim under § 1983. In *Monell*, the Court appeared to conclude that it would be unfair to encumber entities with liability on the same terms as it had exposed individual defendants under *Monroe*—that is, liability for any conduct carried out under the emblem of government authority, whether or not authorized in fact or enshrined in official policy. The *Monell* court addressed this concern by generically reducing the scope of the § 1983 prima facie claim against an entity.[1]

The Court's policy-impelled changes on the entity side reflect more than modest tinkering with particular species of claims such as due

---

46. *See Siegert*, at 233, 111 S.Ct. at 1794. The "damages" shielded by qualified immunity may, however, include costs, attorneys' fees, and related expenses, even in purely equitable suits. *D'Aguanno v. Gallagher*, 50 F.3d 877 (11th Cir.1995).

47. *See id.* at 232, 500 U.S. at 1793; *Burrell v. Board of Trustees of Ga. Military College*, 970 F.2d 785 (11th Cir.1992), *cert. denied*, 507 U.S. 1018, 113 S.Ct. 1814, 123 L.Ed.2d 445 (1993). The author participated as co-counsel to the government defendants in *Burrell*. The court of appeals, on interlocutory review of an order denying motions to dismiss and summary judgment based on qualified immunity, never decided whether the particular First Amendment right plaintiff claimed had been clearly established at the time of her termination from private employment. Instead, it found no genuine issue of fact as to a conspiracy between the government defendants and the private defendants who actually effected that termination. Without such a conspiracy there was wanting the "state action" necessary to establish a predicate § 1983 claim under the First Amendment, and the complaint failed to target conduct "under color of" state law.

Burrell thus illustrates the flexibility the *Siegert* sequencing affords individual defendants who assert qualified immunity (as

well as courts desirous of granting them pretrial dismissal). Although the court of appeals repeatedly emphasized that it viewed its interlocutory jurisdiction as limited to the question of qualified immunity, its decision did not turn on an evaluation of the core constitutional right in question or its settledness when the defendants acted. Rather, in substance the court treated the complaint, after the factual development generated by a motion for summary judgment, as failing to state a claim because of a deficiency in the "under color of" element essential to any § 1983 action. And dismissal on that ground proved to be a more comprehensive victory for the defendants than if they had merely been relieved of trial on damages because of qualified immunity. Because the court of appeals had found in essence that no § 1983 claim could be stated, for want of state action or action under color of state law, the trial court dismissed all the § 1983 claims against them in their entirety when the case returned to the district court after the Supreme Court's denial of certiorari.

§ 2.26

1. *See Monell v. Department of Social Servs.*, 436 U.S. 658, 691, 98 S.Ct. 2018, 2036, 56 L.Ed.2d 611 (1978) and its progeny, discussed in detail above in §§ 2.18 and 2.19.

process. Rather, in § 1983 entity litigation the Court has placed whole-sale limitations on the nature of claims assertable against the government. The original architect of these restrictions, Justice Brennan, would only two years later consider it " 'uniquely amiss' " if the government entity, " 'to which all in our society look for the ... setting of worthy norms and goals for social conduct,' " was to enjoy a qualified immunity to backstop the stringent prima facie case set out in *Monell*.[2] In effect, the majority he spoke for in *Owen* found that *Monell* already provided an adequate response to fears about fairness. "Policy" ensures that the government can be held responsible only for conduct unequivocally attributable to its advertent decisions.

b. *The Missing Immunity Defense*

Given the formidable, even forbidding, requirements of *Monell*'s prima facie policy element and its even more rigorous subsequent fortification, it is tempting to conclude that the Court's decision in *Owen* to eschew developing a common law of immunity for entity defendants is largely an empty gesture. Who needs immunity from a case so hard to build? But there is operative and symbolic significance in the Court's refusal to confer on government entity defendants an immunity parallel to the one that it would soon confer unrestrainedly on their agents.

The *Owen* dissenters may have overstated their case by asserting that the majority's rejection of immunity imposes "strict liability" on local government entities.[3] It is clear hyperbole, for example, to suggest that strict liability operates in a "failure to act" case like *City of Canton*, in which entity liability attaches only upon a showing of "deliberate indifference." The *Owen* dissenters were on target, however, when they lamented that denying entities immunity sometimes ends up subjecting them to civil liability for constitutional violations announced for the first time in the instant litigation.

By denying entities an immunity defense parallel to that enjoyed by their agents, *Owen* preserves the possibility that § 1983 entity cases may continue to serve as a crucible for the development of federal constitutional law, provided the plaintiff can thread the prima facie policy needle of *Monell* and its progeny.[4] The dissenters saw this clearly. Inveighing

2. *Owen v. City of Independence*, 445 U.S. 622, 651, 100 S.Ct. 1398, 1415, 63 L.Ed.2d 673 (1980) (*quoting Adickes v. S.H. Kress & Co.*, 398 U.S. 144, 190, 90 S.Ct. 1598, 1620, 26 L.Ed.2d 142 (1970) (Brennan, J., concurring in part and dissenting in part)).

3. *See Owen v. City of Independence*, 445 U.S. 622, 658, 100 S.Ct. 1398, 1419, 63 L.Ed.2d 673 (1980) (Powell, J., dissenting).

4. This statement may be somewhat overbroad. Two situations come to mind in which the entity, like its individual agents, may enjoy additional protection just because the predicate right allegedly violated is not well settled.

First, the entity may enjoy immunity from damages when the decision declaring its liability breaks sharply with past precedent. Second, when the plaintiff asserts that entity "policy" takes the form of an omission, plaintiff is required to demonstrate that it should have been obvious to the entity's agent that failure to act would violate a constitutional right. That, in turn, implies that the right in question must have been somewhat settled before the events at issue in the action. *See supra* § 2.19, text accompanying notes 23–24 (discussing *City of Canton v. Harris*, 489 U.S. 378, 109 S.Ct. 1197, 103 L.Ed.2d 412 (1989)). If the Court comes to recognize

against what they foresaw as "strict liability on municipalities for constitutional violations," they accused the majority of ignoring "the vast weight of common-law precedent as well as the current state law of municipal immunity."[5] The result, according to the dissent, was that the government entity, unlike its agent, would be liable if it "incorrectly—though reasonably and in good faith—forecasts the course of constitutional law."[6]

Justice Brennan, for the majority, responded that by compounding the qualified immunity for individuals with a "good faith" immunity for the entity the Court might completely "freez[e]" constitutional development.[7] Second, he declared that if officials prove unable to forecast some doctrinal development, "it is fairer to allocate any resulting financial loss to the inevitable costs of government borne by all the taxpayers, than to allow its impact to be felt solely by those whose rights, albeit newly recognized, have been violated."[8]

A recent development, however, raises the possibility that the Court might depart from *Owen* and carve out some degree of governmental immunity under Section 1983. A growing number of Justices have expressed support for the proposition that the common law of 1871 should take primacy over judicial declarations of statutory policy in shaping § 1983 doctrine concerning elements of liability, damages, and even immunities.[9] The dissenters in *Owen* took sharp issue with the

this legal requirement explicitly, entities in these omission cases would escape all liability for newly declared rights. They would be better off than similarly situated individual defendants, who are shielded only from damages liability under the "clearly established" version of qualified immunity.

Nevertheless, in other contexts the entity action remains the primary vehicle for creating new constitutional rights. An instructive example of this progenerative potential is glimpsed by comparing *Owen*, an entity action, with *Paul v. Davis*, 424 U.S. 693, 96 S.Ct. 1155, 47 L.Ed.2d 405 (1976), an action against an individual. In *Owen*, the majority strained the record to find that the defamatory statements about the plaintiff police chief were made in the course of his discharge from public employment and thus implicated a liberty interest protected by due process under the decision in *Wisconsin v. Constantineau*, 400 U.S. 433, 91 S.Ct. 507, 27 L.Ed.2d 515 (1971), *see supra* § 2.25, text accompanying note 12, and *Board of Regents of State Colleges v. Roth*, 408 U.S. 564, 92 S.Ct. 2701, 33 L.Ed.2d 548 (1972), *see supra* § 2.25, note 10. *See Owen*, 445 U.S. at 633–34 n.13, 100 S.Ct. at 1406–07 n.13. In *Paul*, by contrast, the Court labored to avoid finding a predicate liberty interest by conjuring up the thinnest imaginable distinctions to distinguish *Constantineau*. *See* Monaghan, *supra* § 2.25,

note 10, at 423–29; David L. Shapiro, *Mr. Justice Rehnquist: A Preliminary View*, 90 Harv. L. Rev. 293, 324–28 (1976). It may not be a coincidence that in *Owen*, unlike *Paul*, the defendant was an entity. *Cf. supra* § 2.25, note 40 (comparing *City of Canton* with *Danese v. Asman*, 875 F.2d 1239 (6th Cir.1989), *cert. denied* , 494 U.S. 1027, 110 S.Ct. 1473, 108 L.Ed.2d 610 (1990)).

5. *Owen*, 445 U.S. at 658, 100 S.Ct. at 1419 (Powell, J., dissenting). Beginning only two years later with *Harlow v. Fitzgerald*, 457 U.S. 800, 102 S.Ct. 2727, 73 L.Ed.2d 396 (1982), the Court superseded the common law approach to individual immunity with its more expansive version driven by concerns for calendar congestion and effective government administration. *See supra* § 2.12.

6. *Owen*, 445 U.S. at 668, 100 S.Ct. at 1424 (Powell, J., dissenting).

7. *See id.* at 651 n.33, 100 S.Ct. at 1415 n.33.

8. *Id.* at 655, 100 S.Ct. at 1417.

9. *See* Section 2.2, *supra*. Nevertheless, lower courts are adhering to *Owen's* flat denial of entity immunity. *Berkley v. Common Council of Charleston, W. Va.*, 63 F.3d 295 (4th Cir.1995) (en banc).

majority's conclusion that there was no municipal immunity at common law. They observed that municipalities were generally not held liable for conduct undertaken in a "governmental" rather than "proprietary" capacity, and stressed that local governments enjoyed a good-faith immunity respecting the manner in which they discharged their "discretionary," as opposed to "ministerial" duties. Should the Court come to accept the *Owen* dissenters' reading of the 19th-century common law, it might feel impelled to exalt that reading over the statutory policies of compensation and deterrence that figured so heavily in the *Owen* decision to deny local government immunity.

c. An Open Door for Constitutional Development

Plaintiffs suing local government entities may proceed to trial even if the particular federal right allegedly invaded by that policy lacked prior judicial recognition—a circumstance that would establish immunity for an individual defendant.[10] Still, even those plaintiffs who can demonstrate that the violation of a constitutional right took place under the aegis of an entity's official policy must allege at the threshold the violation of a constitutional right that the court is *currently* willing to recognize. And in that connection it should be borne in mind that the Court has given increasingly restrictive readings to the liberty component of the Fourteenth Amendment's Due Process Clause.[11]

Entity liability under § 1983 for newly declared constitutional rights, a possibility reaffirmed in dictum by a plurality in *American Trucking Associations, Inc. v. Smith*,[12] was realized in *Owen* itself. The

---

10. With respect to entity omissions, and thus the "deliberate indifference" standard, it may be difficult for the plaintiff to show that the need for entity action was "obvious" in the absence of settled law. *See City of Canton v. Harris*, 489 U.S. 378, 390 n. 10, 109 S.Ct. 1197, 1205 n. 10, 103 L.Ed.2d 412 (1989) (*citing Tennessee v. Garner*, 471 U.S. 1, 105 S.Ct. 1694, 85 L.Ed.2d 1 (1985)); Mark R. Brown, *Correlating Municipal Liability and Official Immunity Under Section 1983*, 1989 U. Ill. L. Rev. 625, 656 (1989).

11. *See, e.g., Farmer v. Brennan*, 511 U.S. 825, 114 S.Ct. 1970, 128 L.Ed.2d 811 (1994) (prison official violates Eighth Amendment by failing to protect inmate health or safety only when defendant is deliberately indifferent in the sense of "subjective recklessness": plaintiff must prove that defendant in fact knew that inmates faced a substantial risk of serious harm and disregarded that risk by failing to take reasonable precautions); *Albright v. Oliver*, 510 U.S. 266, 114 S.Ct. 807, 127 L.Ed.2d 114 (1994) (criminal suspect has no substantive due process right to be free from baseless initiation of prosecution because Fourth Amendment is explicitly addressed to the type of government conduct at issue) (plurality opinion) (*Albright* has since been read "virtually to foreclose" converting a malicious prosecution claim into a § 1983 claim asserting a violation of substantive due process. *Perez–Ruiz v. Crespo–Guillen*, 25 F.3d 40 (1st Cir.1994)); *Collins v. City of Harker Heights*, 503 U.S. 115, 112 S.Ct. 1061, 117 L.Ed.2d 261 (1992) (government employer has no duty enforceable as an aspect of substantive due process to provide safe working environment to its employees); *Siegert v. Gilley*, 500 U.S. 226, 111 S.Ct. 1789, 114 L.Ed.2d 277 (1991) (defamation attributable to federal agency and uttered shortly after employee's termination from the agency's employment implicates no liberty interest protected by due process); *Graham v. Connor*, 490 U.S. 386, 109 S.Ct. 1865, 104 L.Ed.2d 443 (1989) (excessive force claims analyzed under Fourth Amendment rather than due process standards because that amendment was an explicit textual source of protection against the alleged police misconduct at issue).

12. 496 U.S. 167, 183, 110 S.Ct. 2323, 2334, 110 L.Ed.2d 148 (1990) (O'Connor, J., plurality opinion) (rejecting retroactive application of *American Trucking Ass'ns, Inc.*

plaintiff, a former police chief, was discharged under stigmatizing circumstances and denied an opportunity publicly to clear his name. The majority agreed that a due process hearing was required and held that local governments enjoyed no § 1983 immunity.[13] The dissenters argued vehemently that the Court had not previously accorded employees at will a "name clearing" hearing after their discharge. Consequently, no protectable species of property or liberty existed, at least if there was no public disclosure of the reasons for discharge; the majority's denial of immunity thus cleared the way for the Court to declare a theretofore unsettled constitutional right.[14]

This same dynamic was also at work in *Praprotnik*, in which the plaintiff lost not because the entity was relieved of the duty to anticipate developments in constitutional law but because the Court found the alleged retaliatory conduct not fairly attributable to the entity.[15] A suit against individual defendants, by contrast, might have been barred at the threshold because the Court had not unambiguously recognized the right of a public employee to be free from retaliation for using a state-created grievance mechanism.[16] In a case against an individual defendant claiming qualified immunity, the majority would have been constrained to observe that federal law had not clearly established the precise permutations of the First Amendment right against retaliation at issue in *Praprotnik*; *Anderson* would accordingly have suggested qualified immunity.

Finally, *City of Canton* graphically underscores how entities, unlike their officials, may be accountable for merely nascent constitutional violations. Explaining why they would have denied the plaintiff a remand to establish "deliberate indifference," the dissenters, speaking

v. Scheiner, 483 U.S. 266, 107 S.Ct. 2829, 97 L.Ed.2d 226 (1987), against a state as a matter of judicial policy, while adhering to the view that § 1983 confers no general immunity on municipalities). Notwithstanding its apparent endorsement of *Owen*, the *Smith* decision, in tandem with recently decided *Dennis v. Higgins*, 498 U.S. 439, 446–51, 111 S.Ct. 865, 870–73, 112 L.Ed.2d 969 (1991) (allowing suits for violation of the Commerce Clause to proceed under § 1983), contains some potential for stimulating a limited, partial entity immunity.

13. See *Owen, supra* note 43, at 635–38, 100 S.Ct. at 1407–09.

14. See *id.* at 661–64, 100 S.Ct. at 1420–23 (Powell, J., dissenting). The durability of expanded constitutional rights declared in § 1983 actions is another matter. For example, the *Owen* dissenters' position on the predicate "name-clearing" claim now apparently commands a majority of the Court. See *Siegert v. Gilley*, 500 U.S. 226, 231, 111 S.Ct. 1789, 1793, 114 L.Ed.2d 277

(1991) (holding insufficient to state a claim plaintiff's allegation that his former supervisor's defamatory statements violated due process by causing the loss of current and future government employment). But *Siegert*'s negative reprise on the type of liberty interest in reputation that *Owen* recognized does not alter the fact that the § 1983 action against the entity in *Owen* did generate new doctrine at the time.

15. See *Praprotnik*, 485 U.S. at 128–30, 108 S.Ct. at 926–28.

16. In *Mount Healthy City Sch. Dist. Bd. of Educ. v. Doyle*, 429 U.S. 274, 283–84, 97 S.Ct. 568, 574–75, 50 L.Ed.2d 471 (1977), the Court recognized that an untenured teacher could not be dismissed for exercising his First Amendment rights. The plurality in *Praprotnik*, without mentioning *Mount Healthy*, expressed no opinion on "whether the First Amendment forbade the city to retaliate ... for having taken advantage of the [available] grievance mechanism in 1980." *Praprotnik*, 485 U.S. at 127, 108 S.Ct. at 926.

through Justice O'Connor, complained that the predicate right of a
pretrial detainee to medical attention for emotional injury had not been
definitively established. She confronted the majority with what she
deemed to be a legal requirement implicit in the "deliberate indifference" formulation—a reasonably well-settled constitutional right.[17]
Notwithstanding these protests, the majority ordered a remand perhaps
permitting the plaintiff to convince the lower courts that the police
officers had committed a constitutional predicate violation and that the
city could fairly be responsible for it.[18]

§ 2.27   The Residue: A Mixed Picture

No unitary explanation of these divergent developments has proven
entirely satisfactory. Why would the Court start by easing the plaintiff's
prima facie burden against individual defendants, only to end up by
cutting back on key predicate constitutional protections and insulating
many of the remaining federal law violations with a defendant—friendly
form of qualified immunity? Why on the other hand would the Court
erect such a formidable barrier as "policy" to the liability of government
entities?

Professors Low and Jeffries have suggested, for example, that the
latest formulations of *Monell* "policy" in cases such as *Praprotnik* and
City of Canton confer a de facto qualified immunity on entities, and
hence wreak the revenge of the *Owen* dissenters.[1] If this were correct,
the current asymmetry in form would really bring about a symmetry in
substance, with immunity being the bridge between the two types of
actions. The suggestion fails, however, because the *Monell* "policy"
stricture, even as rigidly applied, is still only an effort to identify
liability-conducive conduct that the factfinder can fairly impute to the
entity; it does not categorically preclude novel federal claims. If the
plaintiff demonstrates "policy" or its "deliberate indifference" surrogate,[2] the entity may face liability for unsettled federal constitutional or
statutory violations, despite its agents' reasonable behavior. For individual defendants, either of these characteristics—the unsettled nature
of the predicate right or the objective reasonableness of the state actor's

17. *See City of Canton v. Harris*, 489
U.S. 378, 396–97, 109 S.Ct. 1197, 1208–09,
103 L.Ed.2d 412 (1989) (O'Connor, J., concurring in part and dissenting in part).

18. To a lesser degree the phenomenon
was also at work in *Pembaur*. The new law
on which the liability of all *Pembaur* defendants turned had been declared by *Steagald*. Yet the Supreme Court noted that
three circuits, including the one in which
the defendants' conduct took place, had
reached conclusions contrary to *Steagald* as
of the events in question. *See Pembaur*,
475 U.S. at 486, 106 S.Ct. at 1301 (White,
J., concurring); *id.* at 492–93, 106 S.Ct. at
1305–06 (Powell, J. dissenting); *supra*
§ 2.18, text accompanying notes 31–41.

Since the relevant law had not then been
firmly established, the individual defendants were entitled to exoneration by virtue
of qualified immunity even if *Steagald* were
given retroactive effect. The Court in
Pembaur did expose the entity to liability
on the basis of a retroactive application of
Steagald, subject only to the prima facie
showing of "policy."

§ 2.27

1. *See* Peter W. Low & John C. Jeffries,
Jr., *Civil Rights Actions*, 39 (Foundation
1988) (Supp.1991).

2. *See supra* § 2.19.

conduct—would provide immunity, at least from damages. There is no symmetry in substance.

It has similarly been suspected that the *Parratt* doctrine is the individual defendant's counterpart to the *Monell* requirement of a policy or custom.[3] But, *Parratt* is simply not the comprehensive barrier to claims against individuals that the evolved version of "policy" raises to claims against entities. The circuitous logic of *Parratt*, in which the state provision of remedial process *after* the deprivation of constitutionally protected liberty or property transforms a denial of property without due process into a denial *with* due process,[4] pertains only to constitutional violations that turn on the denial of some sort of process.[5] Indeed, the *Parratt* opinion itself stressed that the reason certain forms of post-deprivation process sanitized apparently unlawful conduct was to prevent the Fourteenth Amendment, and that amendment only, from becoming the dreaded " 'font of tort law.' "[6]

Thus the *Parratt* opinion cited as support *Paul v. Davis*,[7] in which the same fear had driven it to limit the scope of constitutionally protected liberty to deprivations that included the loss of a state-defined right. Justice Rehnquist, also the author of *Parratt*, stated explicitly that the holding did not affect enforcement of interests that have their origin directly in the Bill of Rights. On the authority of *Monroe*, Rehnquist wrote that those interests may be redressed under § 1983 "independently of state law."[8] Consequently, and especially in light of *Zinermon*,[9] it is apparent that *Parratt* leaves unaffected the *Monroe* holding that individual defendants may be liable under § 1983 for violations of constitutional rights other than procedural due process. Potential liability per *Monroe* holds even when the individual defendant's conduct is entirely unauthorized by her governing principal and when her conduct, authorized or not, is random in the sense that it was not dictated or endorsed by the kind of entity policy that *Monell* requires for the liability of an entity.

Nor does expediency fully account for these developments. The Court has, of course, noted and apparently acted upon concerns about calendar congestion. Its responses have ranged from broadening the immunities available to individual defendants, paring down the scope of

---

3. *See* Susan Bandes, *Monell, Parratt, Daniels, and Davidson: Distinguishing a Custom or Policy from a Random, Unauthorized Act*, 72 Iowa L. Rev. 101 (1986).

4. *See* Monaghan, *supra* § 2.25, note 34, at 985–86.

5. *See supra* § 2.25, text accompanying notes 21–35, esp. notes 23, 34 (discussing *Zinermon v. Burch*, 494 U.S. 113, 110 S.Ct. 975, 108 L.Ed.2d 100 (1990), which strongly suggests that Parratt now will be confined to procedural due process claims alone, as a special application of the formulation of *Mathews v. Eldridge*, 424 U.S. 319, 348–49, 96 S.Ct. 893, 909–10, 47 L.Ed.2d 18 (1976)).

6. *Parratt v. Taylor*, 451 U.S. 527, 544, 101 S.Ct. 1908, 1917, 68 L.Ed.2d 420 (1981) (*quoting Paul v. Davis*, 424 U.S. 693, 701, 96 S.Ct. 1155, 1160, 47 L.Ed.2d 405 (1976)), *overruled in part by Daniels v. Williams*, 474 U.S. 327, 106 S.Ct. 662, 88 L.Ed.2d 662 (1986).

7. 424 U.S. 693, 96 S.Ct. 1155, 47 L.Ed.2d 405 (1976).

8. *Id.* at 711 n.5, 96 S.Ct. at 1165 n.5.

9. *See supra* § 2.25, text accompanying notes 29–35.

constitutionally protected "property" and "liberty," restrictively redefining "deprivations," and hinging the obligation to provide process on the subsequent availability of doubtfully efficacious state remedies. And in service of efficiency the Court has employed a common technique to dam the flow of entity and individual litigation: early disposition by the court. On the entity side, it has delegated to trial judges the function of deciding whether an entity's official has final policymaking authority, characterizing this as a question of state law.[10] Similarly, an individual official's assertion of qualified immunity turns initially, and usually ultimately, on the legal question whether plaintiff's claimed right is clearly established as a matter of federal law. In both instances liability is determinable in the first instance by the judge and offers a potentially quick escape from the litigation. Still, if a desire to stanch the dikes has spurred the Court to sap § 1983's strength as a vehicle for vindicating federal constitutional rights, what explains the Court's generally indulgent approach to § 1983 as a remedy for violations of federal *statutory* rights?[11] That story follows.

F. SECTION 1983 AS A REMEDY FOR FEDERAL STATUTORY VIOLATIONS

§ 2.28 In General

In *Maine v. Thiboutot*,[1] the Court, fully cognizant of the enormous resulting potential increase of § 1983 "filings in our already overburdened courts,"[2] nevertheless charted a course conspicuously hospitable to the assertion of these historically tangential claims.

Section 1983 got off to an uncertain start as a remedy for federal statutory violations. In *Pennhurst State School and Hospital v. Halder-*

---

10. This was a major point of contention in *City of St. Louis v. Praprotnik*, 485 U.S. 112, 108 S.Ct. 915, 99 L.Ed.2d 107 (1988). Justice O'Connor, for the plurality, opined that federal courts are "not ... justified in assuming that municipal policymaking authority lies somewhere other than where the applicable [state or local] law purports to put it." *Id.* at 126, 108 S.Ct. at 925. In contrast, Justice Brennan would have treated the issue as a question of fact; he argued unsuccessfully that denominating the issue as one of state law permitted the municipalities to escape liability "for the acts of all but a small minority of actual city policymakers" named in a statute. *Id.* at 132, 108 S.Ct. at 928 (Brennan, J., concurring). Justice O'Connor's position has carried the day. *See Jett v. Dallas Indep. Sch. Dist.*, 491 U.S. 701, 737–38, 109 S.Ct. 2702, 2724, 105 L.Ed.2d 598 (1989) (remanding for a determination whether a school superintendent, who approved an allegedly racially motivated reassignment, had "final policymaking authori-

ty" over employee transfers under state law).

11. This trend is manifest in, for example, *Wilder v. Virginia Hosp. Ass'n*, 496 U.S. 498, 509, 110 S.Ct. 2510, 2517, 110 L.Ed.2d 455 (1990); *Golden State Transit Corp. v. City of Los Angeles*, 493 U.S. 103, 105, 110 S.Ct. 444, 448, 107 L.Ed.2d 420 (1989); *and Wright v. Roanoke Redev. and Hous. Auth.*, 479 U.S. 418, 107 S.Ct. 766, 93 L.Ed.2d 781 (1987). *See* Henry P. Monaghan, *Federal Statutory Review Under Section 1983 and the APA*, 91 Colum.L.Rev. 233, 247 (1991) (concluding that "section 1983's availability turns only on whether federal statutory law creates a 'primary' right, even though the federal law does not otherwise establish a 'remedial' right").

§ 2.28

1. 448 U.S. 1, 100 S.Ct. 2502, 65 L.Ed.2d 555 (1980).

2. *Id.* at 23, 100 S.Ct. at 2514 (Powell, J., dissenting).

man,[3] Justice Rehnquist articulated two related but distinct potential limitations on the use of § 1983 to remedy violations of other federal statutes. The first was a substantive rights restriction, corresponding to the *Paul* or *Parratt* restrictions in due process cases, that inquires whether the particular § 1983 plaintiff has a private right of action to enforce the predicate statute. The second was a more general limitation that would oust § 1983 even when the plaintiff has standing to enforce the underlying federal statutory guarantee if that statute could be read to provide the " 'exclusive remedy for violations of its terms.' " [4] In *Golden State Transit Corp. v. City of Los Angeles*,[5] the Court clarified that the plaintiff has the burden of proving that her claim under Section 1983 involves the violation of a federal right of action, of which she is the beneficiary, as opposed to a mere violation of federal law. By contrast, respecting the second limitation sketched in *Pennhurst,* it is the defendant who bears the burden of demonstrating that Congress, by providing a comprehensive, detailed remedial scheme for enforcement of the predicate statute, has expressly or impliedly foreclosed the possibility of enforcement under Section 1983.

On this second issue, Justice White dissenting in *Pennhurst*, argued that the Court should read *Thiboutot* as erecting the "presumption that a federal statute creating federal rights may be enforced in a Section 1983 action," rebuttable only by an express indication in the underlying statute that Congress considered its stated remedies to be exclusive.[6]

In three recent decisions that presumption has apparently carried the day.[7] The Court has found § 1983 available if the predicate statute provides either no remedy, as in *Golden State Transit Corp.*, or only an administrative remedy, as in *Wilder* and *Wright*, for the kind of violation alleged. Only when the entitlement statute created its own judicial remedy[8] or a "carefully tailored administrative and judicial mechanism" [9] was § 1983 held displaced as a matter of congressional intent.

3. 451 U.S. 1, 101 S.Ct. 1531, 67 L.Ed.2d 694 (1981) (hereinafter *Pennhurst* I).

4. *Id.* at 28, 101 S.Ct. at 1545 (quoting *Thiboutot*, 448 U.S. at 22 n.11, 100 S.Ct. at 2514 n.11 (Powell, J., dissenting)).

The second limitation was applied soon thereafter, but has since waned. Justice Powell found the "exclusive remedy" standard met in *Middlesex County Sewerage Auth. v. National Sea Clammers Ass'n*, 453 U.S. 1, 13, 101 S.Ct. 2615, 2622, 69 L.Ed.2d 435 (1981) (finding that Congress had provided "unusually elaborate [judicial] enforcement provisions" that should oust § 1983).

5. 493 U.S. 103, 106, 110 S.Ct. 444, 448, 107 L.Ed.2d 420 (1989).

6. *Pennhurst* I, 451 U.S. at 51, 101 S.Ct. at 1557 (White, J., dissenting in part); *cf. Bush v. Lucas*, 462 U.S. 367, 390, 103 S.Ct.

2404, 2417, 76 L.Ed.2d 648 (1983) (Marshall, J., concurring in unanimous decision) (precluding *Bivens* recovery for a government employee if Congress provided a comprehensive administrative and judicial remedy that was "substantially as effective as a damages action").

7. *See* text following this section.

8. *See Middlesex County Sewerage Authority v. National Sea Clammers*, 453 U.S. 1, 101 S.Ct. 2615, 69 L.Ed.2d 435 (1981).

9. *Smith v. Robinson*, 468 U.S. 992, 1009, 104 S.Ct. 3457, 3467, 82 L.Ed.2d 746 (1984). *But see* Handicapped Children's Protection Act of 1986, 20 U.S.C.A. § 1415 (1988) (overruling *Smith* and authorizing attorneys' fees pursuant to 42 U.S.C.A. § 1988 in connection with successful constitutional or federal statutory claims even when the same relief, with an express fee authorization, is available under the Edu-

The cases therefore seem to hold that § 1983 is supplanted only when Congress has provided a carefully considered federal [10] *judicial* remedy for the predicate statutory violation.[11]

The first limitation Justice Rehnquist articulated in *Pennhurst*, a narrow definition of the "rights secured by" a predicate federal statute, until recently also garnered little support.[12] After *Golden State*, a § 1983 plaintiff ordinarily will have an enforceable "right" of action for local governmental violations of other federal statutes whenever the statutory provision in question can be said to have been intended to benefit that plaintiff. The § 1983 right of action is defeasible only if the predicate provision reflects a mere "congressional preference" rather than a binding governmental obligation or if the plaintiff's interest is so "vague and amorphous" that the judiciary cannot enforce it.[13]

Only once, since *Pennhurst*, has the Court found a federal statutory mandate too generalized to give rise to a "right" enforceable through

---

cation of the Handicapped Act, 20 U.S.C.A. §§ 1401–1485 (1988)).

10. *Wilder* provided support for a "federal" qualification by rejecting the argument that the availability of state judicial review of Virginia's implementation of the Medicaid amendment was relevant to the availability of relief under § 1983. *See Wilder v. Virginia Hosp. Ass'n, supra* note 11, § 2.27 at 524 n.20, 110 S.Ct. at 2525 n.20.

11. *Compare Seamons v. Snow,* 84 F.3d 1226, 1233 (10th Cir.1996); *Doe v. Petaluma City Sch. Dist.,* 54 F.3d 1447 (9th Cir. 1995) (holding or assuming that Title IX claim gives rise to § 1983 "and laws" claim); and *Lillard v. Shelby County Bd. of Educ.,* 76 F.3d 716 (6th Cir.1996) (Title IX enforcement scheme, even including implied judicial cause of action, insufficiently comprehensive to foreclose § 1983 action based on independent due process rights) *with Pfeiffer by Pfeiffer v. School Bd. for Marion Ctr. Area,* 917 F.2d 779 (3d Cir. 1990) (Title IX administrative enforcement scheme, coupled with implied judicial cause of action, comprehensive enough to foreclose all § 1983 claims) *and Mennone v. Gordon,* 889 F.Supp. 53 (D.Conn.1995) (rejecting use of § 1983 as vehicle for Title IX claim). *But see Hobbs v. Hawkins,* 968 F.2d 471 (5th Cir.1992) (civil rights claim for damages for a violation of right to a free election under Labor Management Relations Act held preempted by a comprehensive administrative enforcement mechanism).

12. In *Wright, supra* note 11, § 2.27, the Court held that low-income tenants had a right, enforceable through § 1983, to sue a housing authority for utility charges that

allegedly exceeded ceilings established by administrative regulations issued under federal housing legislation, where the regulations defined the "reasonable amount" allowed. Justice Kennedy raised the "rights" objection again in *Golden State Transit Corp. v. City of Los Angeles,* 493 U.S. 103, 110 S.Ct. 444, 107 L.Ed.2d 420 (1989), but was joined only by Chief Justice Rehnquist and Justice O'Connor. *See id.* at 114–19, 110 S.Ct. at 452–55 (Kennedy, J., dissenting). The Court permitted a private cab company in *Golden State* to maintain a § 1983 damages action against Los Angeles after the city conditioned renewal of its franchise on the company's reaching agreement with a union on a new labor contract. The Court viewed the company as having an enforceable "right" to a remedy for conduct by the city that the National Labor Relations Act in terms prohibited only as between employers and unions.

The Court continued to reject the "rights" argument in its 1990 term. In *Wilder, supra* note 11, § 2.49, the Court permitted Medicaid providers to sue under § 1983 for reimbursement at rates that federal law demanded be "reasonable and adequate," where the predicate statute and implementing regulations at least identified the "factors to be considered" in determining the required rates. *Suter v. Artist M.,* 503 U.S. 347, 356, 112 S.Ct. 1360, 1366, 118 L.Ed.2d 1 (1992) (citing *Wilder*); *cf. Dennis v. Higgins,* 498 U.S. 439, 111 S.Ct. 865, 112 L.Ed.2d 969 (1991) (giving similar broad meaning to the constitutional "rights" enforceable through § 1983).

13. *Wilder,* 496 U.S. at 509, 110 S.Ct. at 2517 (quoting, respectively, *Pennhurst* and *Golden State*).

§ 1983. In *Suter v. Artist M.*,[14] the Court considered a claim based on alleged violations of a statutory provision that conditioned federal funding for state child welfare, foster care and adoption programs upon a state's submission of a plan approved by the Secretary of Health and Human Services. To be approved the plan had to contain assurances that the state would make "reasonable efforts" to avoid removing children from their homes and reasonable efforts, if they were removed, to reunify their families. The Court observed that, in contrast to the provisions at issue in *Wright* and *Wilder*, neither the statute nor its implementing regulations offered the states concrete guidance about the required "reasonable efforts," other than that they must be described in a plan to be approved by the Secretary. It concluded that the term therefore imposed a mere "generalized duty" unenforceable through an action under § 1983 action or, for the same reason, through a private right of action implied directly under the adoption statute.[15] But whenever Congress does specify the state's duties in a regulatory statute, a plaintiff who is an intended beneficiary of the statute will have a "right" to enforce it against local governments and officials and state officials.[16]

The federal circuit courts seem to have mounted something of a rear-guard action against *Suter,* distinguishing it with regularity. Although these courts have sometimes noted that the court in *Suter* "did not reverse *Golden State, Wilder,* or *Wright,* it also did not follow the two-part paradigm set out in *Golden State.*"[17] Instead, these courts have read *Suter* as simply reemphasizing the point made in *Pennhurst* that conditions imposed on the grant of federal monies under the Congressional spending power "must be imposed unambiguously."[18] In finding that Section 1983 may be used to vindicate other relatively vague, statutory provisions—not all that different from the "reasonable efforts" requirement of the Child Welfare Act that *Suter* held too vague to be enforced under Section 1983—these courts have stressed that in *Wilder* the court authorized the use of Section 1983 to enforce the "reasonable and adequate" reimbursement rates standard in the Boren Amendment to the Medicaid Act. What distinguishes cases like *Wilder* from cases like *Suter,* these courts have concluded, is a detailed specification, either

14. *See supra* note 12.

15. In turn, an authoritative judicial determination that there is no implied private right of action under a particular statute may mean that federal courts will lack subject matter jurisdiction to revisit that issue in a subsequent case, at least for a period of time sufficiently long to respect a later court's conception of stare decisis. *See Bell v. Hood,* 327 U.S. 678, 682, 66 S.Ct. 773, 776, 90 L.Ed. 939 (1946).

16. Because of *Will v. Michigan Dep't of State Police,* 491 U.S. 58, 109 S.Ct. 2304, 105 L.Ed.2d 45 (1989), and the vapors of the Eleventh Amendment, *see supra* §§ 2.22 and 2.26 and *infra* § 13.7, the entitlement suit must take the form of an action against an individual state official yet in substance it is a suit against a state entity charged with a violation in implementing a federal statute or regulation. Thus, there is no "settled law" defense; in any case the settled nature of the right exists a priori in the federal enactment. Additionally, there is no doubt about the existence of state "policy" for purposes of entity liability, because the policy resides in the challenged regulation.

17. *Miller v. Whitburn,* 10 F.3d 1315, 1319 (7th Cir.1993); *Arkansas Medical Society, Inc. v. Reynolds,* 6 F.3d 519, 524 (8th Cir.1993).

18. *Id.* citing *Suter,* 503 U.S. at 356, 112 S.Ct. at 1366.

in the predicate statute alone or in its implementing regulations, of factors that aid judges in determining whether the state has complied with a federal mandate or followed specific directions for executing a generalized state plan.[19]

Thus in *Lampkin v. District of Columbia*,[20] the court held the right to educate homeless children, created by the McKinney Homeless Assistance Act, enforceable through Section 1983. While its description of the contents of the required state plan was no more elaborate than that contained in the adoption statute at issue in *Suter*, "the McKinney Act provides specific directions for the plan's execution," as well as "obligations that are independent of the plan." Similarly, in *Miller v. Whitburn*,[21] a child was permitted to enforce a right to "necessary . . . treatment" under the Medicaid Act because the statute, together with its implementing regulations, specified "in copious detail" those services for which a Medicaid-participating state must provide payment in order to discharge its obligation to make . . . services available to all "qualified individuals." Although the state agency administering the program had substantial discretion to choose how to comply with the federal mandate to pay for necessary treatment, and in particular could exclude "experimental" treatment, federal courts could review under Section 1983 whether the agency's definitions of "experimental" comported with relevant federal definitions of that term.[22] And in *Arkansas Medical Society v. Reynolds*,[23] a Medicaid Act provision requiring a state plan to provide for care and services "to the extent that such care and services are available to the general population in the geographic area" was held sufficiently definite to be enforceable under Section 1983. The court found this "equal access" provision arguably more specific than the language of the Boren Amendment found enforceable in *Wilder*, because its legislative history and implementing regulations in effect defined "general population" to require a comparison of Medicaid recipients' access with that of the insured population, rather than the entire population of the surrounding geographic area.

Why would the Court assiduously nick away at § 1983 jurisdiction in its primary sphere, the vindication of constitutional rights, yet open the doors to an acknowledged potential onslaught of litigation whenever any of a multitude of federal statutes, mostly *not* providing for civil rights, is violated under color of state law? Particularly inexplicable is this embrace of federal statutory claims under § 1983 after the Court had just announced a notably more restrictive approach to implying

---

19. *See also Freestone v. Cowan*, 68 F.3d 1141 (9th Cir.1995) (Social Security Act requirement that states adopt a plan for child support enforcement sufficiently definite to be enforceable). *But see City of Chicago v. Lindley*, 66 F.3d 819 (7th Cir.1995) (Older Americans Act provision that agencies "take into account" geographical and social factors in erecting formula for distributing funds too amorphous to create rights enforceable under § 1983).

20. 27 F.3d 605, 610–612 (D.C.Cir. 1994).

21. 10 F.3d 1315, 1319–1320 (7th Cir. 1993).

22. *Id.* at 1320.

23. 6 F.3d 519 (8th Cir.1993).

judicial rights of action directly under other federal statutes.[24] The Court's open-ended receptiveness to § 1983 statutory claims is even more baffling because this result is not compelled. For example, there is a more than respectable historical argument that the addition in 1874 of the words "and laws" to § 1983 was intended merely to parallel the subject matter jurisdiction conferred by the forerunner of 28 U.S.C.A. § 1343(3), a section limited to claims arising under "any law providing for equal rights."[25] On that reading, the Court might have restricted "and laws" claims to statutes forbidding discrimination, rather than embracing violations of all manner of ordinary federal commerce and welfare laws.

Library References:

C.J.S. Civil Rights §§ 2, 3, 14–17, 21.
West's Key No. Digests, Civil Rights ☜108.1.

24. *See, e.g., Transamerica Mortgage Advisors, Inc. v. Lewis,* 444 U.S. 11, 24, 100 S.Ct. 242, 249, 62 L.Ed.2d 146 (1979) (holding that there is "a limited private remedy under the Investment Advisors Act of 1940" despite no express provision for a private cause of action); *Touche Ross & Co. v. Redington,* 442 U.S. 560, 576–77, 99 S.Ct. 2479, 2489–90, 61 L.Ed.2d 82 (1979) (refusing to find a private cause of action under § 17(a) of the Securities Exchange Act of 1934, 15 U.S.C.A. § 78g(a) (1988), despite having previously found one under § 14(a), 15 U.S.C.A. § 78n(a) (1988)). This curiosity is elaborated by Monaghan, *supra* § 2.25, note 34.

25. *See Maine v. Thiboutot,* 448 U.S. 1, 14–19, 100 S.Ct. 2502, 2509–2512, 65 L.Ed.2d 555 (1980) (Powell, J., dissenting) (reviewing the historical argument); *cf.* John C. Jeffries, Jr., *Damages for Constitutional Violations: The Relation of Risk to Injury in Constitutional Torts,* 75 Va. L. Rev. 1461, 1485 n.60 (1989) (discussing the Supreme Court's efforts to except particular statutes from its general rule that § 1983 provides a private damages action for all federal statutes).

SUMMARY OF THE "AND LAWS" BRANCH OF § 1983

Section 1983 claim can be predicated on violation of *any* federal statute (*Thiboutot*), subject to the following "rights" and "remedies" caveats:

IF	*UNLESS*
Plaintiff shows she is an intended beneficiary of the federal statutory standard and thus has an enforceable *"right"*;	*Defendant shows* that comprehensive *remedies* provided by the predicate statute impliedly preclude a civil claim under Section 1983.
	x *National Sea Clammers*
	x *Smith v. Robinson*
	(predicate statutes provided limited *judicial* remedies)
and	
That right, as elaborated by the statute, its legislative history, and federal implementing regulations, is sufficiently definite for judicial enforcement.	
	√ *Wright v. Roanoke*
	(predicate statute provided only *administrative* remedies)
√ *Wilder*	
x *Suter*	
Post-*Suter* circuit decisions mostly distinguish *Suter*, follow *Wilder*	

√	=	Claim recognized
x	=	Claim rejected

Chapter Three

TITLE VII OF THE 1964 CIVIL RIGHTS ACT: COVERAGE, PRO-HIBITED GROUNDS OF DIS-CRIMINATION, SPECIALLY TREATED PRACTICES, AND DE-FENSES

Analysis

§ 3.1   In General

Title VII of the Civil Rights Act of 1964 is the most broadly based and influential federal statute prohibiting discrimination in employment. Its prohibitions on discrimination based on race, color, sex, religion or national origin extend to all "terms, conditions or privileges" of employment,[1] a phrase the federal courts have construed quite broadly to embrace any benefit actually conferred or burden actually imposed in the workplace, whether or not provided for by contract.[2] The statute therefore protects against discrimination across the full range of employment practices or decisions, embracing such intangible aspects of employment as workplace assignments, environment, and even mentoring opportunities[3] as well as more tangible problems like refusals to hire or promote, unequal pay or discriminatory discharge.

§ 3.1

1. Section 703(a)(1), 42 U.S.C.A. § 2000e–2(a)(1).

2. *See, e.g., Hishon v. King & Spalding,* 467 U.S. 69, 104 S.Ct. 2229, 81 L.Ed.2d 59 (1984) and opinion of Powell, J., concurring (after a specified number of years employed a law firm associate had the right to be considered for partnership without regard to gender because that was the firm's practice, even if such consideration was not specifically promised). From the tenor of the *Hishon* decision, it is extremely doubtful that the relationship among partners is regulable by the employment discrimination statutes. Nevertheless, appellate decisions since *Hishon* appear to assume that a court may order partnership as a remedy for discrimination against an associate or employee respecting the decision to admit to membership as a partner. *See Hopkins v. Price Waterhouse,* 920 F.2d 967 (D.C.Cir.1990); *Ezold v. Wolf, Block, Schorr & Solis–Cohen,* 751 F.Supp. 1175 (E.D.Pa.1990), *reversed* 983 F.2d 509 (3d Cir.1992). Corporate directors who work as officers and continue to perform work typical of employees are not sufficiently like "partners" to forfeit protection. *EEOC v. Johnson & Higgins, Inc.,* 91 F.3d 1529 (2d Cir.1996) (case under ADEA). Despite the generally broad interpretation courts have accorded the phrase "terms and conditions" of employment, under both Title VII and ADEA, occasionally a decision will express a de minimis exception, as in the case of a lateral transfer, *Williams v. Bristol-Myers Squibb Co.,* 85 F.3d 270, 70 FEP 1639 (7th Cir.1996), or even undeservedly lower performance ratings. *Rabinovitz v. Pena,* 89 F.3d 482 (7th Cir.1996); *Smart v. Ball State University,* 89 F.3d 437 (7th Cir.1996).

3. *Jensvold v. Shalala,* 829 F.Supp. 131 (D.Md.1993) (gender discrimination in affording plaintiff less adequate mentoring than male employees actionable).

This broad sweep distinguishes Title VII from statutes, like EPA, that prohibit employment discrimination solely with respect to one term or condition of employment, such as compensation. Further, the Title VII prohibitions on race, color, sex, religious and national origin discrimination set it apart from single-focus statutes that ban only sex discrimination (EPA and Title IX); age discrimination (the Age Discrimination in Employment Act of 1967, or "ADEA"); race, ancestry and possibly national origin discrimination (42 U.S.C.A. §§ 1981 and 1985(3) and Title VI);[4] or handicap discrimination (the Rehabilitation Act of 1973 as expanded and partially supplanted by the Americans with Disabilities Act of 1990, or "ADA").

Title VII was amended by the Civil Rights Act of 1991. The principal stated purposes of the Act were to "provide appropriate remedies for intentional discrimination and unlawful harassment in the workplace:" to "confirm statutory authority and provide statutory guidelines for the adjudication of disparate impact suits under Title VII....;" and to "respond to recent decisions of the Supreme Court by expanding the scope of relevant civil rights statutes...."[5].

This chapter gives a broad overview of Title VII as amended by the Civil Rights Act of 1991. Specifically, this chapter addresses which employees and employers are within the scope of Title VII. The chapter also considers what actions fall within the boundaries of Title VII. The following chapter, Chapter VI, discusses the modes of proving a Title VII claim. Chapter VII then looks at administrative prerequisites and procedures as well as Title VII remedies.

Library References:

> C.J.S. Civil Rights §§ 143, 144, 146, 157, 160 et seq.
> West's Key No. Digests, Civil Rights ☞141 et seq.

A. COVERAGE

Library References:

> C.J.S. Civil Rights §§ 148, 149, 185–187.
> West's Key No. Digests, Civil Rights ☞143, 169.

§ 3.2   Protection for Individuals

Title VII's principal operative provisions defining unlawful employment practices, contained in § 703, extend protection to any "individual," whether or not an employee. This is somewhat curious because the statute contains a separate, if singularly unilluminating definition of "employee": "any individual employed by an employer." Relying on

---

4. As explained in more detail in the Chapters discussing the two cited Reconstruction Act statutes, their protection extends somewhat beyond our current conception of race as such. Generally speaking, the § 1981 prohibition extends as well to ancestry, although perhaps not to national origin; the § 1985(3) prohibition includes protection for those discriminated against on the basis of racial advocacy even if they do not suffer race discrimination per se.

5. Civil Rights Act of 1991, Pub.L. 102–166, §§ 3(1), (3), and (4), 105 Stat. 1071.

the broad protection afforded by § 703 to "any individual," courts have had no difficulty according plaintiff status and standing on former employees as well as applicants. Further, they have sometimes even recognized claims on behalf of persons who fall outside any common-law understanding of the employee-employer relationship, provided the circumstances satisfy an "economic realities" test that protects those in a position to suffer the kind of discrimination Title VII was designed to prevent. Occasionally, however, a court will rely on the "employee" definition to deny protection to persons who do not satisfy the common law's test for employee status, the "totality of the working relationship." [1]

By contrast, the § 704 protection against retaliation for opposing unlawful employment practices or participating in proceedings to protest them extends to "employees or applicants for employment." [2] The circuits are divided over whether this language denies protection to former employees who complain of otherwise actionable retaliation against them—bad references, for example—that occurred after the employment relation was severed. Most afford protection so long as the conduct complained of relates to or arises out of the employment relationship.[3]

§ 3.3 Employers Governed by Title VII/ADEA

Title VII applies to employers, employment agencies, apprenticeship programs and labor organizations whose activities affect interstate commerce. There are very few categorical exclusions from the definition of

§ 3.2

1. *See, e.g., Daniels v. Browner,* 63 F.3d 906 (9th Cir.1995) (ADEA did not explicitly waive federal agency's sovereign immunity with respect to plaintiff whose work for agency was under cooperative agreement with private non-profit organization authorized by separate legislation designed to promote community service activities; hence plaintiff not "employee"); *Wilde v. County of Kandiyohi,* 15 F.3d 103 (8th Cir. 1994). The EEOC, for example, takes the position that "employee" status should be denied to prison inmates who perform mandatory, on-site labor. A recent appellate decision suggests that voluntary prison labor not conforming to the characteristics outlined by EEOC may confer "employee" status on an inmate. *Moyo v. Gomez,* 32 F.3d 1382 (9th Cir.1994), *cert. denied,* ___ U.S. ___, 115 S.Ct. 732, 130 L.Ed.2d 635 (1995).

2. See, e.g., *Moyo v. Gomez,* 32 F.3d 1382 (9th Cir.1994), *cert. denied,* ___ U.S. ___, 115 S.Ct. 732, 130 L.Ed.2d 635 (1995) (prison guard stated retaliation claim for protesting prison's practice of denying black

inmates showers after job shifts on same terms as white inmates).

3. *Contrast Veprinsky v. Fluor Daniel, Inc.,* 87 F.3d 881 (7th Cir.1996); *Charlton v. Paramus Board of Education,* 25 F.3d 194 (3d Cir.1994); *Sherman v. Burke Contracting, Inc.,* 891 F.2d 1527 (11th Cir.), *cert. denied,* 498 U.S. 943, 111 S.Ct. 353, 112 L.Ed.2d 317 (1990); *Bailey v. USX Corp.,* 850 F.2d 1506 (11th Cir.1988); *Pantchenko v. C.B. Dolge Co.,* 581 F.2d 1052 (2d Cir.1978); and *Rutherford v. American Bank of Commerce,* 565 F.2d 1162 (10th Cir.1977) ("employee" includes former employee) *EEOC v. Metzger,* 824 F.Supp. 1 (D.D.C.1993), *with Robinson v. Shell Oil Co.,* 70 F.3d 325 (4th Cir.1995) (en banc), *cert. granted,* ___ U.S. ___, 116 S.Ct. 1541, 134 L.Ed.2d 645 (1996); *Polsby v. Chase,* 970 F.2d 1360 (4th Cir.1992) *vacated sub nom. Polsby v. Shalala,* 507 U.S. 1048, 113 S.Ct. 1940, 123 L.Ed.2d 646 (1993), and *Reed v. Shepard,* 939 F.2d 484 (7th Cir.1991) (Congressional specification of "applicants" but not "former employees" in addition to "employees" impliedly precludes coverage of former employees except with respect to their re-application for employment).

"employer" in either Title VII or ADEA. They include private membership clubs exempt from taxation under the Internal Revenue Code and Indian tribes.[1] By far the most significant exclusion is numerical: an employer is covered by Title VII only if it has 15 or more employees, and by ADEA only if it has 20 or more employees, for each working day in 20 or more calendar weeks in the current or prior calendar year. Courts have wrestled with whether to pierce the corporate veil so as to subject a parent corporation to potential liability for the conduct of a subsidiary;[2] whether to consider part-time employees;[3] whether to consider all of an employer's employees when the alleged unlawful employment practice is confined to a discrete operating location;[4] whether to impose liability on a successor employer after a sale of the business or bankruptcy;[5] whether a government-appointed receiver is a Title VII "employer" of employees of a failed financial institution[6]; and whether an employment agency or union meets the statutory "employer" definition even when it has fewer than 15 employees.[7] These and other coverage questions, like

§ 3.3

1. *See generally* Section 701(b), 42 U.S.C.A. § 2000e–5(g) (Title VII) and 29 U.S.C.A. § 626(b), incorporating 29 U.S.C.A. § 216(b) (ADEA). As long as a club is "private" in the sense of being owned and run by a restricted membership, not advertising publicly to solicit members, and limiting use of facilities to members and their guests, the exemption applies even if the club is of large size and even though no exemption is needed to protect the members' constitutional associational rights. *EEOC v. The Chicago Club*, 86 F.3d 1423 (7th Cir.1996).

2. *Cook v. Arrowsmith Shelburne, Inc.*, 69 F.3d 1235 (2d Cir.1995) (sustaining claim against parent that controlled labor relations of wholly owned subsidiary); *Armbruster v. Quinn*, 711 F.2d 1332 (6th Cir. 1983) (where evidence of interrelationship between subsidiary and corporate parent is sufficient, the two entities are jointly responsible for acts of subsidiary).

3. *Compare EEOC v. Metropolitan Educational Enterprises*, 60 F.3d 1225 (7th Cir. 1995), *cert. granted sub nom. Walters v. Metropolitan Educ. Enters.*, ___ U.S. ___, 116 S.Ct. 1260, 134 L.Ed.2d 209 (1996); *EEOC v. Garden & Assocs.*, 956 F.2d 842, 843 (8th Cir.1992); *Zimmerman v. North Am. Signal Co.*, 704 F.2d 347, 354 (7th Cir.1983) (employees must actually report to work each day of the work week to be counted) *with Vera–Lozano v. International Broadcasting*, 50 F.3d 67 (1st Cir.1995); *Thurber v. Jack Reilly's, Inc.*, 717 F.2d 633, 634 (1st Cir.1983) (employees are counted if they are on the payroll, regardless of how often they work), *cert. denied*, 466 U.S. 904, 104 S.Ct. 1678, 80 L.Ed.2d 153 (1984). *See*

the EEOC's "Policy Guide on Whether Part–Time Employees May Be Counted to Satisfy Number Required for Title VII and ADEA Coverage," 8 FEP Manual (BNA) 405:6857 (April 20, 1990).

4. *Owens v. Rush*, 636 F.2d 283 (10th Cir.1980) (sheriff's department named as defendant in Title VII action employed less than 15 people was considered an "employer" for Title VII purposes because the county employed more than 15 people).

5. *See, e.g., Rojas v. TK Communications, Inc.*, 87 F.3d 745 (5th Cir.1996) (declining to impose liability on corporation that met the standard indicia of successor because predecessor continued as viable entity and plaintiff sought only monetary relief, not reinstatement); *EEOC v. G–K–G, Inc.*, 39 F.3d 740 (7th Cir.1994) (affirming general rule that a mere purchaser of corporate assets does not acquire the seller's liability for unlawful employment practices unless, as was the case there, the successor receives notice of the claim before the sale and maintains "substantial continuity" of operations).

6. *See Nowlin v. Resolution Trust Corp.*, 33 F.3d 498 (5th Cir.1994) (holding that the appropriate standard is the "hybrid test," which considers all relevant factors including the right to control terms of the plaintiffs' employment, rather than the "borrowed servant" doctrine from common law tort).

7. *See Greenlees v. Eidenmuller Enterprises*, 32 F.3d 197 (5th Cir.1994) and *Kern v. City of Rochester*, 93 F.3d 38 (2d Cir. 1996) (rejecting this interpretation in the case of employment agencies and unions,

the status of nonprofit organizations as employers and the liability of companies for the employment practices of subcontractors, are capably discussed in detail in several standard works.[8]

States, their political subdivisions, and agencies of each are also employers under both statutes.[9] The constitutionality of applying Title VII to state defendants, and their amenability to suit in federal court is settled. Even before *Garcia v. San Antonio Metropolitan Transit Authority*,[10] determined that the Tenth Amendment does not supersede Congress' Commerce Clause authority to regulate the wages and hours of state employees, the Supreme Court had held in *Fitzpatrick v. Bitzer*,[11] that Title VII's grounding in § 5 of the Fourteenth Amendment empowered Congress to override the Eleventh Amendment barrier to state liability in federal court.

The federal government and its agencies are not defined "employers,"[12] but special provisions in each statute[13] mandate that personnel actions affecting most federal employees be made free from discrimination based on any of the grounds those statutes address.

Both Title VII and ADEA define a covered "employer" to include any "agent" of an employer.[14] At a minimum, this definition makes the employer as an entity liable for the acts of subordinates by means of respondeat superior. The circuits that have confronted the issue have usually concluded, however, that a supervisor is not such an "agent"

respectively, contrary to the view of the EEOC). Unions may be liable as labor organizations representing employees in collective bargaining without regard to the number of employees represented, but are liable in their capacity as "employer" only if they satisfy the "employer" definition, including the requirement of at least 15 employees. *Yerdon v. Henry*, 91 F.3d 370 (2d Cir.1996).

8. *EEOC v. Association of Community Organizations*, 67 FEP 508, 1995 WL 107075 (E.D.La.1995) (organization is covered "employer" because of its involvement in and relationship to commerce despite nonprofit status); *cf. Fitzgerald v. Mountain States Tel. & Tel. Co.*, 68 F.3d 1257 (10th Cir.1995) (absent ratification or approval of subcontractor's alleged discriminatory misconduct contracting company not liable under § 1981). *See generally*, Player, *Employment Discrimination Law* (West 1990).

9. Title VII § 701(b) and (a), 42 U.S.C.A. § 2000e(b), (a); ADEA § 11(b)(2), 29 U.S.C.A. § 630(b)(2). But the state must employ the plaintiff directly; thus it is not liable for aiding and abetting a local school district's mandatory retirement of a plaintiff teacher, either because it failed to repeal legislation preempted by ADEA or on a theory that the state was the plaintiff's de

facto employer as ultimate regulator of the local school district. *EEOC v. Illinois*, 69 F.3d 167 (7th Cir.1995).

10. 469 U.S. 528, 105 S.Ct. 1005, 83 L.Ed.2d 1016 (1985).

11. 427 U.S. 445, 96 S.Ct. 2666, 49 L.Ed.2d 614 (1976).

12. Title VII § 701(b), 42 U.S.C.A. § 2000e(b), and ADEA § 11(b)(2), 29 U.S.C.A. § 630(b)(2).

13. Title VII § 717, 42 U.S.C.A. § 2000e–16 and ADEA § 15, 29 U.S.C.A. § 633a. But while § 7.17(a) bans discrimination respecting "all personnel activities" against civilian employees in military departments, the federal security clearance process has been held beyond Title VII scrutiny. *Brazil v. United States Department of the Navy*, 66 F.3d 193 (9th Cir. 1995), *cert. denied*, ___ U.S. ___, 116 S.Ct. 1317, 134 L.Ed.2d 470 (1996). Similarly, a civilian employee of the National Guard who was denied a military promotion was held to have failed to state a Title VII claim. *Mier v. Owens*, 57 F.3d 747 (9th Cir.1995). *Accord, Randall v. United States*, 95 F.3d 339 (4th Cir.1996) (statute applies only to civilian members of military departments).

14. 42 U.S.C.A. § 2000e(b) (Title VII); 29 U.S.C.A. § 630(b)(ADEA).

who can be subjected to personal liability.[15] The argument favoring individual liability is arguably slightly stronger now that the 1991 Civil Rights Act affords, in cases of intentional discrimination, elements of relief (namely compensatory and punitive damages) satisfiable by individual defendants.[16] Nevertheless, the provisions of that Act that add damages liability do not refer to individual liability. Further, the retention of a fifteen-employee threshold for employer liability suggests the continuing Congressional reluctance to impose liability on small entities, and therefore presumably also individual employees.[17] Where supervisory employees are held subject to Title VII their liability has been limited to conduct deemed to have been undertaken in their official capacities [18] and where they exercised independent authority or were unmistakably acting as "agent" of the employer.[19] Two recent Fourth Circuit cases neatly illustrate how a court may read the term "agent" broadly for purposes of imposing liability on the employer [20] yet exclude from its reach the personal liability of an employer officer.[21]

a. American Corporations' Employees Working Abroad and "Foreign" Employers' Personnel Stationed in U.S. and Overseas: Of National Origin, Alienage and Ancestry Discrimination Under Title VII/ADEA, IRCA, and 42 U.S.C.A. § 1981

Discrimination on any ground against an *alien* (for this purpose, someone who has not yet attained full American citizenship) working

---

15. *Compare Ball v. Renner*, 54 F.3d 664 (10th Cir.1995) and *Paroline v. Unisys Corp.*, 879 F.2d 100, 104 (4th Cir.1989), *vacated in part*, 900 F.2d 27 (4th Cir.1990) (holding affirmatively) with *Haynes v. Williams*, 88 F.3d 898 (10th Cir.1996) (no individual liability under Title VII as amended in 1991); *Stults v. Conoco, Inc.*, 76 F.3d 651 (5th Cir.1996) (no ADEA liability of supervisors); *Williams v. Banning*, 72 F.3d 552 (7th Cir.1995); *Tomka v. Seiler Corp.*, 66 F.3d 1295 (2d Cir.1995); *Gary v. Long*, 59 F.3d 1391 (D.C.Cir.), *cert. denied*, ___ U.S. ___, 116 S.Ct. 569, 133 L.Ed.2d 493 (1995); *Greenlaw v. Garrett*, 59 F.3d 994 (9th Cir.1995); *Smith v. Lomax*, 45 F.3d 402 (11th Cir.1995); *Birkbeck v. Marvel Lighting Corp.*, 30 F.3d 507 (4th Cir.), *cert. denied*, ___ U.S. ___, 115 S.Ct. 666, 130 L.Ed.2d 600 (1994) (under ADEA); *Grant v. Lone Star Co.*, 21 F.3d 649 (5th Cir.1994), *cert. denied*, ___ U.S. ___, 115 S.Ct. 574, 130 L.Ed.2d 491 (1994); *Smith v. St. Bernards Regional Medical Ctr.*, 19 F.3d 1254 (8th Cir.1994); *Sauers v. Salt Lake County*, 1 F.3d 1122, 1125 (10th Cir.1993); *Miller v. Maxwell's International, Inc.*, 991 F.2d 583, 587–88 (9th Cir.1993), *cert. denied*, ___ U.S. ___, 114 S.Ct. 1049, 127 L.Ed.2d 372 (1994); *Busby v. City of Orlando*, 931 F.2d 764, 772 (11th Cir.1991); *Harvey v. Blake*, 913 F.2d 226, 227–28 (5th Cir.1990); *York v. Tennessee Crushed Stone Ass'n.*, 684 F.2d 360, 362 (6th Cir.1982) (holding negatively). *Cf.*

Jones v. Continental Corp., 789 F.2d 1225 (6th Cir.1986) (dictum stating that individuals are liable for Title VII violations as "agents"). *See also U.S. EEOC v. AIC Sec. Investigations Ltd.*, 55 F.3d 1276 (7th Cir. 1995) (sole shareholder not employer under ADA).

16. *U.S. E.E.O.C. v. AIC Security Investigations, Ltd.*, 823 F.Supp. 571 (N.D.Ill. 1993).

17. *Miller v. Maxwell's International, Inc.*, *supra*; *Stefanski v. R.A. Zehetner & Associates, Inc.*, 855 F.Supp. 1030 (E.D.Wis. 1994).

18. *See Harvey v. Blake*, 913 F.2d 226, 227–28 (5th Cir.1990), *limiting Hamilton v. Rodgers*, 791 F.2d 439, 442–43 (5th Cir. 1986); *Stefanski v. R.A. Zehetner, supra.*

19. *Dirschel v. Speck*, 1994 WL 330262 (S.D.N.Y.1994).

20. *E.E.O.C. v. Watergate at Landmark Condominium*, 24 F.3d 635 (4th Cir.), *cert. denied*, ___ U.S. ___, 115 S.Ct. 185, 130 L.Ed.2d 119 (1994) (resident owners of condominium treated as employer "agents" for purposes of imposing ADEA liability on condominium).

21. *Birkbeck v. Marvel Lighting Corp.*, 30 F.3d 507 (4th Cir.1994) (vice president of employer not a proper ADEA defendant).

outside the United States for either an American or non-U.S. company is not prohibited by either Title VII or ADEA. This results from an exemption to Title VII [22] and a restriction in the ADEA's definition of "employee." [23] Somewhat more difficult questions concern the statutory protection available to nonalien employees of American companies stationed overseas and to the American- and overseas-based employees of foreign enterprises.

Unlike the ADEA, which was amended in 1984 to apply to the overseas work of American corporations and American-controlled foreign corporations,[24] Title VII until recently had no language specifically extending its application to work performed for the more than 2000 U.S. firms operating more than 21,000 foreign subsidiaries abroad.[25] These include U.S. citizens who work overseas for an American employer on a long-term basis, those who maintain their American residency during temporary assignments overseas, and American-based employees who routinely travel outside U.S. territorial limits in the course of their employment. If given a choice, the plaintiff would usually find it more advantageous to litigate in the United States under U.S. employment discrimination law than to litigate overseas under foreign law, as the foreign tribunals customarily place far greater limits on discovery (particularly depositions) and relief (especially injunctions directing reinstatement and punitive damages). The Supreme Court, reviving a nineteenth-century presumption against extraterritorial application of American statutes absent express statutory direction, limited Title VII's scope to unlawful employment practices arising in connection with work performed in the United States.[26] The Civil Rights Act of 1991 overturns that decision by defining most covered employees [27] to include U.S. citizens "with respect to employment in a foreign country." [28]

This protection for U.S. citizens is now coextensive with that earlier provided by the ADEA. It subjects to Title VII jurisdiction not only U.S. corporations but also those foreign corporations "controlled" by American employers,[29] and it appears to provide dual defendants in this

22. Section 702, 42 U.S.C.A. § 2000e–1.

23. ADEA § 11(f), 29 U.S.C.A. § 630(f). *See Denty v. SmithKline Beecham Corp.,* 907 F.Supp. 879 (E.D.Pa.1995) (British-controlled employer not subject to ADEA respecting American citizen's application for positions with non-U.S. work sites).

24. ADEA § 4(h), 29 U.S.C.A. § 623(h).

25. See 1 World Trade Academy Press, Directory of American Firms Operating in Foreign Countries (10th ed. 1984).

26. *EEOC v. Arabian American Oil Co.,* 499 U.S. 244, 111 S.Ct. 1227, 113 L.Ed.2d 274 (1991).

27. The 1991 amendment does not appear to extend to federal employees covered under § 717 of Title VII. Thus if the presumption against extraterritorial application of federal statutes announced in *EEOC*

v. Arabian American Oil Co., 499 U.S. 244, 111 S.Ct. 1227, 113 L.Ed.2d 274 (1991) survives the 1991 Act, federal employees may be unprotected with respect to their work overseas. *See* Street, "U.S. Corporations on Foreign Soil," *NBA Magazine,* p. 8 (May 1991).

28. Section 701(f), 42 U.S.C.A. § 2000e(f).

29. This follows indirectly from § 702(c)(2), 42 U.S.C.A. § 2000e–1(c)(2), which provides that the "title shall *not* apply with respect to the foreign operations of an employer that is a foreign person *not* controlled by an American employer." Section 702(c)(3) identifies four factors critical to the determination of "control" of the foreign enterprise by the American company: interrelationship of operations, com-

situation by presuming that unlawful employment practices of the controlled foreign affiliate are engaged in by the controlling (American) employer as well.[30] But it exempts conduct that would cause any employer to violate the national law of the foreign workplace.[31] This exemption is not triggered simply because the type of discrimination in question (e.g., gender or religious) is permitted by foreign law; rather, that law must affirmatively prohibit the particular employer conduct (e.g., hiring a woman as a driver in Saudi Arabia) that compliance with Title VII would otherwise require the employer to permit. But the foreign "law" that would be violated if ADEA were respected may include a collective bargaining agreement with a foreign labor union.[32]

Truly foreign corporations—those not "controlled" by a U.S. business—are not subject to Title VII with respect to work *outside* the United States. U.S. citizens working abroad meet the amended § 701 definition of "employee," and firms chartered in other nations are not excluded from the definition of "employer." To relieve foreign corporations of liability with respect to foreign work, therefore, Congress in 1991 had to specifically provide that the basic prohibitions of the Title do not apply "with respect to the foreign operations of an employer that is a foreign person." [33]

If the employer is not shielded by a treaty authorizing discrimination in the selection of executives on the basis of citizenship,[34] the more than half a million American-based employees of foreign corporations [35] may rely on Title VII and ADEA. But those statutes may not afford them protection against some of the more common forms of discrimination they may encounter. In the first place, although Title VII prohibits national origin discrimination, it does not reach discrimination based on alienage status (i.e. noncitizenship), which is dealt with by the Immigration Reform and Control Act of 1986 ("IRCA") or ancestry (i.e., ethnic or physiognomic characteristic transcending national borders, e.g., against Arabs or Jews), covered by § 1981. Title VII therefore will not avail a plaintiff whose employer, whether U.S or foreign, excludes applicants solely because they lack U.S. citizenship or belong to a distinct cultural subgroup. Further, although Title VII and IRCA prohibit discrimination

mon management, centralized control of labor relations, and common ownership or financial control. This unweighted, multifactor approach obviously leaves undecided the status of firms that were "American" in origin, as measured by locus of operations and number of employees, but then became predominantly transnational. It also sheds little light on the relative importance of such factors as principal place of business and residency or citizenship of directors or shareholders.

30. Section 702(c)(1), 42 U.S.C.A. § 2000e–1(c)(1).

31. Section 702(b), 42 U.S.C.A. § 2000e–1(b).

32. *Mahoney v. RFE/RL, Inc.,* 47 F.3d 447 (D.C.Cir.), *cert. denied,* __ U.S. __, 116 S.Ct. 181, 133 L.Ed.2d 120 (1995).

33. Sections 702(c)(2), 42 U.S.C.A. § 2000e–1(c)(2). The foreign corporation's *United States* operations are not exempted. *See EEOC v. Kloster Cruise Ltd.,* 888 F.Supp. 147 (S.D.Fla.1995) (ADEA).

34. Such treaties are discussed below at text accompanying notes 49 through 55.

35. See Street "Extraterritoriality, Conflict of Laws and Anti–Discrimination Laws," Presentation by Lairold M. Street, EEOC Office of Legal Counsel, at Association of American Law Schools Annual Meeting, January 6, 1995.

on the basis of national origin [36], evidence that the plaintiff's compatriots are as well as or better represented in such an employer's workforce than others can defeat a claim that a U.S. citizenship requirement is in fact a smokescreen for intentional discrimination based on national origin.[37] It may be, however, that a neutral practice has the effect of discriminating on the basis of national origin; and if that is the case, a plaintiff excluded as a result of that practice may be able to state a prima facie national origin claim notwithstanding the fair or favorable treatment of her group.[38]

Since 1988, limited protection against discrimination in hiring because of alienage, i.e. citizenship status, is separately provided to lawfully admitted aliens, and a few others, by IRCA.[39] But unlike the IRCA protection against national origin, which extends to "any individual," the protection against alienage discrimination applies only to a rather narrowly defined "protected individual" who is well on the way to achieving full U.S. citizenship or have been granted refugee or asylum status.[40] Correlatively, IRCA imposes fines and imprisonment on employers who knowingly hire or employ undocumented persons or fail to check their authorization to work—in other words, it requires employers to discriminate against those aliens.[41]

The fact that an alien is not lawfully admitted within the meaning of IRCA does not deprive him of capacity to sue and receive remedies under Title VII for the kinds of discrimination that are prohibited by that statute.[42] This follows not only from the fact that Title VII defines "employees" broadly as "individuals" employed by an employer but also from a negative implication of its alien exemption clause, which precludes application of the statute to the employment of aliens *outside* the

---

36. Title VII protection on this basis applies only with respect to an "employer" defined by that statute, that is, one with 15 or more employees in 20 or more calendar weeks in the current or preceding year. By contrast, IRCA § 102's prohibition of national origin discrimination against any individual, 8 U.S.C.A. § 1324b(a)(1)(A) (1986), applies to employers with as few as four employees. 8 U.S.C.A. § 1324b(a)(2)(A).

37. *See Espinoza v. Farah Mfg. Co.*, 414 U.S. 86, 94 S.Ct. 334, 38 L.Ed.2d 287 (1973). Compare the discussion of § 1981 in the Overview Chapter on the Reconstruction Civil Rights Acts, above (Section 1981 reaches ancestry but not national origin and perhaps not alienage discrimination).

38. *See Connecticut v. Teal*, 457 U.S. 440, 102 S.Ct. 2525, 73 L.Ed.2d 130 (1982), discussed in Chapter 4. *But see Muzquiz v. W.A. Foote Memorial Hosp., Inc.*, 70 F.3d 422 (6th Cir.1995) (practice with assumed disproportionate impact on physicians trained in Mexico not tantamount to na-

tional origin discrimination against Mexicans or Mexican Americans).

39. Section 102, 8 U.S.C.A. § 1324a (1988 & Supp. IV 1992).

40. Sections 102(a)(1)(B) and 103, 8 U.S.C.A. § 1324b(a)(3) (1986).

41. Section 101, 8 U.S.C.A. § 1324a. It does not provide penalties against the undocumented workers themselves for accepting U.S. employment. Only the fraudulent presentation of employment verification documents is criminalized. 8 U.S.C.A. § 1324c (Supp. IV 1992).

42. *See Egbuna v. Time–Life Libraries, Inc.*, 95 F.3d 353 (4th Cir.1996); *EEOC v. Hacienda Hotel*, 881 F.2d 1504 (9th Cir. 1989) (decided under pre-IRCA law); *EEOC v. Tortilleria "La Mejor"*, 758 F.Supp. 585 (E.D.Cal.1991) (decided after IRCA, and relying on legislative history to the effect that IRCA was not intended to limit the powers of state or federal labor standards agencies, including specifically the EEOC).

United States.[43] The problem is that alien victims of the kinds of discrimination Title VII bans will often as a practical matter be ineligible for important Title VII remedies. If reinstatement would require the employer to violate IRCA, the mixed-motive or after-acquired evidence doctrines [44] would probably preclude a reinstatement order. A worker's undocumented status may also effect her eligibility for or the appropriate amount of back or front pay, since she may be "unavailable" for work after termination—either literally (e.g., out of the country) or legally, because of IRCA.[45]

As observed above,[46] discrimination against aliens in general is not, absent adverse impact, treated as discrimination on the basis of any particular national origin, and is therefore not condemned by Title VII. There is sauce for the gander, however, even though the goose gets none: discrimination *against* U.S. citizens, in favor of citizens of a particular nation, does amount to prohibited national origin discrimination under Title VII [47] as well as IRCA.[48] The rationale may be that only in the latter situation can it be said with some confidence that the discrimination relates to a particular national origin—putting aside the dubious assumption that U.S. citizenship corresponds to any particular national origin. Title VII protection from this "anti-American" discrimination based on national origin is limited, however, by treaty exemptions designed to give foreign companies operating in the United States a free hand in selecting their own citizens for executive positions.

The U.S.-Japanese Treaty of Friendship, Commerce and Navigation, for example, authorizes "companies of either party," such as a Japanese-chartered employer, "to engage, within the territories of the other Party ... executive personnel ... of their choice." A U.S.-chartered American subsidiary of a foreign corporation will ordinarily not be deemed a company of the signatory entitled to this exemption.[49] But in a case where the foreign parent admitted [50] that it dictated the American

---

43. The Supreme Court relied on that implication in finding Title VII protection for aliens against discrimination based on national origin. *Espinoza v. Farah Manufacturing Co.*, 414 U.S. 86, 95, 94 S.Ct. 334, 340, 38 L.Ed.2d 287 (1973). On the other hand, that implication was not sufficient in the Court's opinion to overcome the ordinary presumption against extraterritorial application of U.S. statutes. *See EEOC v. Arabian American Oil Co.*, 499 U.S. 244, 111 S.Ct. 1227, 113 L.Ed.2d 274 (1991), *supra* note 27. The Civil Rights Act of 1991 overturns *Arabian American*'s result by the addition to § 701(f), defining "employee," of a sentence that includes citizens, but not aliens, "with respect to employment in a foreign country." 42 U.S.C.A. § 2000e(f).

44. *See* Chapter 4.

45. *See generally* Ontiveros, "To Help Those Most in Need: Undocumented Workers' Rights and Remedies Under Title VII," 20 N.Y.U. Rev. of Law & Social Change 607, 631–638 (1993–94).

46. *See Espinoza, supra* note 43.

47. *MacNamara v. Korean Air Lines*, 863 F.2d 1135 (3d Cir.1988), *cert. denied*, 493 U.S. 944, 110 S.Ct. 349, 107 L.Ed.2d 337 (1989).

48. *See* Zimmer, Sullivan, Richards and Calloway, Cases and Material on Employment Discrimination 695 (Little Brown, 3d ed. 1994) (asserting that "plain language" of IRCA forbids such discrimination).

49. *Sumitomo Shoji America, Inc. v. Avagliano*, 457 U.S. 176, 102 S.Ct. 2374, 72 L.Ed.2d 765 (1982).

50. Such an admission may be rare, because a parent company may justifiably fear that in other proceedings the admission that the subsidiary is not independent

subsidiary's discriminatory discharges of executives, the subsidiary was allowed to assert the parent's treaty rights.[51] These treaties have in other respects been construed narrowly, though, so as to permit only discrimination based on citizenship and not, for example, based on race, sex or age.[52] Nevertheless, they have been read to permit citizenship discrimination even when it has a statistical adverse impact on the basis of national origin. This happens, for example, where the executives preferred by the treaty hail from a homogeneous ethnic population, so that all or virtually all those preferred by virtue of their citizenship also share the same national origin.[53] Thus while companies of signatory countries are, despite these treaties, subject to liability, in their executive hiring and firing, for *intentional* discrimination based on national origin (but not citizenship), they cannot be liable for a citizenship-preference practice that merely has a disproportionate adverse impact on a particular national origin.[54] Courts have reached this result in order to avoid indirect nullification of the guest company's treaty right to discriminate in favor of its own country's citizens.[55]

The schematic that follows summarizes the complex set of relationships among the Title VII, IRCA and § 1981 protections for alien and citizen plaintiffs, against foreign or domestic employers, respecting work in the United States or abroad, on grounds of national origin, citizenship, and ancestry:

would forfeit the foreign parent corporation's usual limited liability protection under state corporation law. That is, it might then become liable for the debts of its dominated subsidiary.

51. *Fortino v. Quasar Company*, 950 F.2d 389 (7th Cir.1991). *Accord, Papaila v. Uniden America Corp.*, 51 F.3d 54 (5th Cir. 1995).

52. *MacNamara, supra* note 51; *cf. Spiess v. C. Itoh & Co.*, 643 F.2d 353, 362–363 (5th Cir.1981), *vacated by* , 457 U.S. 1128, 102 S.Ct. 2951, 73 L.Ed.2d 1344 (1982).

53. *See Fortino* and *MacNamara, supra* notes 51 and 52 (Japanese and Korean executives, respectively).

54. *MacNamara, supra* note 52.

55. *Fortino, supra* note 51.

Coverage Under Title VII/ADA, ADEA, IRCA and Section 1981 of U.S. and Foreign Employers, in Suits By Alien and Citizen Plaintiffs, Respecting Work in U.S. and Abroad

	Ground Protected	U.S. Def't or U.S.-Controlled Corp.	Foreign Def't Not Controlled by U.S. Corp.	In U.S.	Work Abroad
I. TITLE VII, ADA and ADEA **A. Citizen Plaintiff**	Title VII: Race, Sex, Religion, National Origin ADA: Disability ADEA: Age	Potentially Prohibited if 15+ Employees; (ADEA 20+ Employees)	↑	Prohibited by ADA, ADEA and Title VII, absent treaty exemption allowing de facto national origin discrimination in hiring executives	Prohibited, unless foreign law bans conduct that Title VII, ADEA, or ADA requires. Title VII § 702(b); ADA § 102(c)(1); ADEA § 630(f)
	Title VII: Race, Sex, Religion, National Origin ADA: Disability ADEA: Age		Title VII/ADA: Potentially Prohibited if 15+ Employees (ADEA: If 20+ Employees)	Prohibited by ADA, ADEA and Title VII, absent treaty exemption allowing de facto national origin discrimination in hiring executives	No coverage: Title VII § 702(c)(2); ADA § 702(c)(2)(B); ADEA § 623(h)(2)
B. Legal or Illegal Alien Plaintiff	Title VII: Race, Sex, Religion, National Origin ADA: Disability ADEA: Age	Potentially Prohibited if 15+ Employees; (ADEA: 20+)		Prohibited by ADA, ADEA and Title VII, absent treaty exemption allowing de facto national origin discrimination in hiring executives	No coverage: See Title VII, § 701(f) and 702(a); ADA § 101(4); ADEA § 630(f)
	Title VII: Race, Sex, Religion, National Origin ADA: Disability ADEA: Age		Title VII/ADA: Potentially Prohibited if 15+ Employees ADEA: No coverage: § 623(h)(2)	Prohibited by ADA and Title VII, absent treaty exemption allowing de facto national origin discrimination in hiring executives	No coverage: Title VII, § 702(c)(2). See Title VII § 701(f). ADA § 102(c)(2)(B), see § 101(4)
II. IRCA **A. Any Individual Plaintiff**	National Origin	Prohibited if 4+ Employees			Presumably not, based on presumption against extraterritorial application in EEOC v. Arabian American Oil Co., 499 U.S. 244 (1991).
B. "Protected Person" Plaintiff	Alienage	Prohibited if 4+ Employees			
III. SECTION 1981 Any Plaintiff	Intentional Race and Ancestry and Maybe Alienage but not Gender, Religion, or National Origin	Prohibited, no employee minimum			

b. *Religious Employers: Coverage, Exemptions, Defenses*

Religious organizations are also viewed as Title VII "employers," and as such may be subject to a specially defined duty not to discriminate on that ground.[56] But they are specifically permitted to make certain employment decisions on the basis of religion. A welter of related and somewhat overlapping statutory and constitutional provisions afford different kinds of covered employers exemptions from or exceptions to liability for religious discrimination. In addition, the special prohibition on religious discrimination—subsuming the ordinary imperative not to discriminate and a duty to make "reasonable accommodation" to an employee's religious beliefs and practices—is subject to the general affirmative defense that permits an employer to discriminate under circumstances where the exclusion is a "bona fide occupational qualification." The nature of the two-part prima facie prohibition on religious discrimination is discussed in § 5.23 below. The exemptions, exceptions and BFOQ defense for religious and other employers will be treated here. The following schematic depicts the relationships among the statutory and constitutional exemptions, the prima facie case, and the BFOQ defense.

OVERVIEW: DISCRIMINATION BECAUSE OF RELIGION

Statutory Exemptions and Constitutional Overrides

—The § 702 exemption, strictly limited to pervasively religious institutions like churches, missions and seminaries (*Kamehameha*), declares Title VII inapplicable with respect to the employment "of individuals of a particular religion" in any of its activities, for any position. [It does not exempt from regulation for sex, race, national origin (or age) discrimination.] Section 702 upheld as against the objection that it unconstitutionally "establishes" the institutions it protects, at least with respect to their nonprofitmaking activities. *Corporation of Presiding Bishop v. Amos,* 483 U.S. 327, 107 S.Ct. 2862, 97 L.Ed.2d 273 (1987).

—§ 703(e)(2) excludes from the definition of "unlawful employment practice" the hiring of employees of a particular religion by educational institutions insufficiently religious to qualify for the § 702 exemption but that are (a) substantially owned, supported, controlled or managed by a particular religion or (b) direct their curriculum "toward the propagation of" a particular religion. [Again, race, sex, national origin (and age) discrimination are still prohibited.] *Kamehameha*

—If the ground alleged is sex, race, national origin, or age—where, that is, the foregoing statutory exemptions will not avail the employer—it may invoke a Free Exercise or Establishment Clause (excessive government entanglement) override of Title VII or ADEA regulation. These may succeed where the position (e.g., minister) or duties (e.g., teacher of theology) in question lie close to the religious core of the

---

56. *See* § 3.12, below, discussing the way in which the definition of "religion" in § 701(j) expands the duty not to discrimi-nate on the basis of religion as set forth in § 703.

institution, or perhaps where the reason for discharge relates to malperformance of subsidiary religious duties. See *McClure* (Free Exercise Clause) and *Southwestern Baptist Theological Seminary* (Establishment Clause) line of cases.

Prima Facie Prohibitions

—If no statutory or constitutional exemption applies, turn to the prima facie case: Section 703(a)(1), amplified by the 701(j) definition of "religion":

A. Has employer drawn a distinction because of "religion" (See Posner, J. concurring in *Pime*) (discrimination based on non-membership in Jesuit order not because of "religion") or imposed a neutral practice with adverse impact on a particular religion or persons outside a favored faith?

B. Even if employer has made no hostile discrimination, has it breached the 701(j) duty to accommodate:

1. "Reasonable accommodation" need not fully meet needs of employee's religious belief or practice without cost to employee, and employer need not accept the particular accommodation proposed by employee (*Philbrook*); and

2. A reasonable accommodation works "undue hardship" and is thus not required if it requires employer to incur more than de minimis cost (*Trans World Airlines, Inc. v. Hardison*).

So diluted, § 701(j) does not violate Establishment Clause—*Protos*

BFOQ Defense

In a refusal to hire case, if statutory exemptions and constitutional overrides fail and plaintiff establishes prima facie religious discrimination, employer has BFOQ defense of § 703(e)(1). As restrictively construed by *Johnson Controls*, employer must show that its religious exclusion relates to the "essence" of its business and that all or substantially all persons of the excluded faiths could not fulfill the requirements of the job in question. *Kamehameha*; *cf. Pime* (pre-*Johnson Controls*)

Religious Freedom Restoration Act

It is unclear if this statute, 103 P.L. No. 141, 42 U.S.C.A. § 2000bb–2 et seq. (1993), which applies to "all Federal and State law," affects only government employment or, through Title VII and ADEA regulation, private employment as well. Section 3 provides that "government" may "substantially burden a person's exercise of religion" only in furtherance of "a compelling governmental interest" and if it uses "the least restrictive means" of furthering that interest.

§ 3.4 "Purely" Religious Organizations

In general, the more thoroughly "religious" the employer, the more widely it is insulated from liability with respect to terms and conditions of employment and even wholly sectarian activities. This discussion will identify those employers in descending degree of religiosity, and hence insulation.

First, any pervasively "religious" employer—paradigmatically a church, mission, seminary or one of their branches or subunits—is exempt by virtue of § 702(a)[1] from liability for religious discrimination. This section exempts a "religious corporation, association, educational institution, or society" from Title VII "with respect to the employment of individuals of a particular religion to perform work connected with the carrying on" of any of the institution's "activities." But the exemption has been widely interpreted not to ban discrimination based on race, gender, or national origin,[2] with important exceptions.[3]

For the most part, only churches or institutions owned or partly owned by them have qualified for the § 702 exemption.[4] The determination whether an organization, including an educational institution, is eligible for its sweeping protection hinges on whether "the corporation's purpose and character are primarily religious." That question, in turn, is answered on a case-by-case basis, with the court weighing "[a]ll significant religious and secular characteristics."[5] A nondenominational school that was established under a will requiring all trustees and teachers to be Protestants and that began classes with daily prayer but whose purpose, curriculum, and activities had evolved over the years from primarily religious to predominantly secular and most of whose students were not Protestant was held to reflect "a primarily secular rather than a primarily religious orientation" and hence held ineligible for the exemption.[6]

The § 702 exemption extends to any of the religious employer's activities, secular or sectarian, and applies regardless of the particular term and condition of employment involved. A 1972 amendment to

---

§ 3.4

1. 42 U.S.C.A. § 2000e–1(a).

2. *See Martin v. United Way of Erie County*, 829 F.2d 445, 449 (3d Cir.1987); *Rayburn v. General Conference of Seventh-day Adventists*, 772 F.2d 1164, 1170–71 (4th Cir.1985), *cert. denied*, 478 U.S. 1020, 106 S.Ct. 3333, 92 L.Ed.2d 739 (1986); *EEOC v. Pacific Press Publishing Association*, 676 F.2d 1272 (9th Cir.1982); *McClure v. Salvation Army*, 460 F.2d 553 (5th Cir.), *cert. denied*, 409 U.S. 896, 93 S.Ct. 132, 34 L.Ed.2d 153 (1972). *Cf. DeMarco v. Holy Cross High School*, 4 F.3d 166, 173 (2d Cir.1993) (discussing § 702 of Title VII in ADEA case).

3. The religious employer may be exempt from liability even for discriminating on these others grounds if discrimination on any such ground is a tenet of its religion. In that event, what appears at first blush to be race or gender discrimination ultimately is viewed as discrimination because of religion; in that event, the employer may be entitled to the statutory exemption or the

practice may simply not be regulable at all because of the religion clauses of the First Amendment. See § 3.7, *infra; cf. Geary v. Visitation of Blessed Virgin Mary*, 7 F.3d 324, 328 (3d Cir.1993) (ADEA claim against Catholic school not barred by First Amendment where no claim that Catholic doctrine mandated age discrimination). Alternatively, if the discrimination is alleged with respect to the terms and conditions of employment of clergy, any Title VII regulation, including investigation by EEOC, may conflict with the demands of the First Amendment. *See* text accompanying note 2, § 3.7 *infra* and cases cited in that note.

4. *EEOC v. Kamehameha Schools/Bishop Estate*, 990 F.2d 458, 461 n. 7 (9th Cir.), *cert. denied*, 510 U.S. 963, 114 S.Ct. 439, 126 L.Ed.2d 372 (1993), and cases cited therein.

5. *Id.* at 460.

6. *Id.* at 461.

§ 702 deleted the word "religious" that had appeared before "activities" in the original 1964 legislation, and so the exemption has since been understood to shield a covered institution from liability for religious discrimination even with respect to its secular activities, provided those are non-profitmaking.[7] It has nevertheless withstood challenge as an unconstitutional establishment of religion.[8] The Court in *Amos* reasoned that § 702, by lifting what would otherwise be government regulation of religion, merely permits the religious organization to advance its own religion and does not result in the government itself advancing a particular religion.

The distinctions among the grounds on which Title VII bans discrimination, the § 702 exemption, and a separate, nonstatutory overriding defense based on the First Amendment are pointed up by a recent case in which a parochial school's married librarian was terminated for being pregnant by someone other than her husband. Even though the employer decision to fire the plaintiff was driven by its religious beliefs, it appeared that the discrimination was on the ground of pregnancy and therefore, in Title VII terms, because of sex rather than religion. Accordingly, the court ruled that the § 702 defense was not available. But if it turned out that the real reason for termination was her adultery rather than her pregnancy, the ground of discrimination would be sex-neutral and therefore not prohibited by Title VII.[9] (Then there would be no Title VII violation even if the adultery ground were not tantamount to religious discrimination—that is, even if the defendant could not avail itself of the § 702 exemption from liability for discrimination because of religion.) Moreover, the court added that ultimately the First Amendment might halt the action in any event if the proceedings, or a judgment of liability, were determined to interfere unduly with the church school's free exercise of religion.

An overlapping defense based on the religion clauses of the First Amendment is available to truly "religious" institutions, educational or not, where litigation raises the spectre of excessive government monitoring of religious decisionmaking or matters of doctrine. Where a university's canon law department was governed by the Vatican, for instance, the claim of a faculty member in that department who alleged sexually discriminatory tenure denial was rejected, wholly apart from § 702(a), because the court decided it lacked competence to review competing opinions about materially religious subjects in published articles. Both the Free Exercise and Establishment Clauses would be violated by scrutiny under Title VII that would "impair a religious institution's

---

7. *See generally EEOC v. Fremont Christian School*, 781 F.2d 1362, 1366 (9th Cir.1986); *Rayburn v. General Conference of Seventh–day Adventists*, 772 F.2d 1164, 1169 (4th Cir.1985), *cert. denied*, 478 U.S. 1020, 106 S.Ct. 3333, 92 L.Ed.2d 739 (1986); *EEOC v. Pacific Press Publishing Association*, 676 F.2d 1272 (9th Cir.1982); *EEOC v. Mississippi College*, 626 F.2d 477, 485 (5th Cir.1980), *cert. denied*, 453 U.S. 912, 101 S.Ct. 3143, 69 L.Ed.2d 994 (1981).

8. *Corporation of Presiding Bishop v. Amos*, 483 U.S. 327, 107 S.Ct. 2862, 97 L.Ed.2d 273 (1987).

9. *Vigars v. Valley Christian Center*, 805 F.Supp. 802 (N.D.Cal.1992).

choice of those who teach its doctrine and participate in church governance." [10]

§ 3.5 Religiously Affiliated Educational Institutions

Because relatively few organizations are sufficiently religious to qualify for the broad exemption from Title VII afforded by § 702, Congress added a limited exception from liability designed to benefit religiously affiliated schools.

Under § 703(e)(2) of Title VII,[1] an *educational* institution not qualifying as sufficiently religious to be exempt under § 702(a) but which is substantially supported or directed by a particular religion, or has a religiously oriented curriculum, may "hire and employ" persons of the particular religion with which it is affiliated. Section 702(a), it will be remembered, provides that Title VII "shall not apply" to the "purely" religious institutions it protects. By contrast, § 703(e)(2) more modestly states that it is not an "unlawful employment practice" for an "educational institution or institution of learning to hire and employ employees of a particular religion" if that employer is "in whole or in substantial part, owned, supported, controlled, or managed by a particular religion"[2] (hereinafter, the "structure clause") or maintains a curriculum "directed toward the propagation of a particular religion" (the "curriculum clause").[3]

It is only somewhat easier for a religiously affiliated educational institution to qualify for the more limited § 703(e)(2) hiring immunity than for a religious organization or school to qualify for the broader exemption under § 702. One court, for example, declined to decide whether the defendant university qualified for the § 703(e)(2) exemption even though it had a long history as a Jesuit institution, until 1970 had only Jesuit trustees, still required that more than one-third of the trustees and the President be Jesuit, and enrolled students of predominantly Catholic background.[4] It further appears that to qualify under the curriculum clause it is not enough that a school require religious education courses, schedule prayers and services, and employ Protestant teachers for principally secular subjects. "Courses *about* religion and a general effort to teach good values do not constitute a curriculum that propagates religion, especially in view of the Schools' express disclaimer of any effort to convert their non-Protestant students."[5]

The courts have consistently held that the § 703(e)(2) exception to the definition of an unlawful employment practice by a religiously affiliated school, like the § 702 exemption from Title VII for a religious

10. *EEOC v. Catholic University of America*, 856 F.Supp. 1 (D.D.C.1994).

§ 3.5

1. 42 U.S.C.A. § 2000e–2(e)(2).

2. *See Pime v. Loyola University*, 803 F.2d 351 (7th Cir.1986).

3. *See EEOC v. Kamehameha Schools/Bishop Estate*, 990 F.2d 458, 464–

65 (9th Cir.), *cert. denied*, 510 U.S. 963, 114 S.Ct. 439, 126 L.Ed.2d 372 (1993).

4. *Pime v. Loyola University*, 803 F.2d 351 (7th Cir.1986).

5. *EEOC v. Kamehameha Schools/Bishop Trust, supra*, 990 F.2d at 465.

organization, does not shield the defendant from Title VII liability when the institution discriminates against an employee or applicant (say one who seeks a secular job like science teacher or custodian of a seminary or university) on some basis *other* than religion—sex, race, national origin, or retaliation.[6]

ADEA has no express exemption for religious or religiously affiliated institutions. But because ADEA's substantive prohibitions are derived *in haec verba* from Title VII,[7] courts have crafted an immunity from age discrimination liability of the same scope, and with the same limitations, for religious organizations that meet the § 702 (or, apparently, § 703(e)(2)) requirements.[8]

§ 3.6 All Employers: the "BFOQ" Affirmative Defense

Under § 703(e)(1),[1] *any* employer, even one wholly sectarian, may "hire and employ" (a labor organization may "admit or employ" in apprenticeship or retraining programs) on the basis of religion where religion is a "bona fide occupational qualification ['BFOQ'] reasonably necessary to the normal operation" of the enterprise. The principal discussion of the BFOQ defense, as it applies to express gender and national origin discrimination, is set forth in Chapter VI immediately following. The discussion here will be confined to its role in defending against express discrimination based on religion.

Section 703(e)(1) has the same textual limitation to hiring as does Section 703(e)(2). Accordingly, the BFOQ affirmative defense protects employers from liability only for certain religiously discriminatory hiring decisions; it does not excuse discrimination concerning subsequent terms and conditions of employment like compensation, promotion, discipline, harassment or discharge.[2]

Moreover, the Supreme Court's decision in *U.A.W. v. Johnson Controls*[3] confirms the narrowness of the BFOQ exception—in any context, i.e., gender or national origin as well as religion. The bare language of § 703(e)(1) would appear satisfied if an employer can show that a refusal to hire based on religion, sex, or national origin is reasonably necessary to the normal operation of the defendant's overall "enterprise." As a textual matter, that is, the employer need not show that the exclusion on those grounds is conducive to the sound performance of the particular

6. *EEOC v. Fremont Christian School,* supra § 3.4, note 7; *Martin v. United Way of Erie County,* 829 F.2d 445 (3d Cir.1987) (dictum); *EEOC v. Southwestern Baptist Theological Seminary,* 651 F.2d 277 (5th Cir.1981), *cert. denied,* 456 U.S. 905, 102 S.Ct. 1749, 72 L.Ed.2d 161 (1982); *EEOC v. Mississippi College, supra.*

7. *See Lorillard v. Pons,* 434 U.S. 575, 584, 98 S.Ct. 866, 872, 55 L.Ed.2d 40 (1978).

8. *See DeMarco v. Holy Cross High School,* 4 F.3d 166, 173 (2d Cir.1993);

Geary v. Visitation of the Blessed Virgin Mary Parish School, 7 F.3d 324, 331 (3d Cir.1993); *Martin, supra* note 6 (dictum).

§ 3.6

1. 42 U.S.C.A. § 2000e–2(e)(1) (which also applies to discrimination based on sex or national origin, but not race).

2. *See EEOC v. Fremont Christian School,* 781 F.2d at 1367.

3. 499 U.S. 187, 111 S.Ct. 1196, 113 L.Ed.2d 158 (1991).

plaintiff's job, only that it will further general business goals. Nor does the text of the BFOQ defense suggest that the discriminatory job qualification must relate to the heart of employer's business, only to its "normal operation." Yet the Court has concluded that to prevent the exception from virtually eliminating an applicant's protection against these forms of express discrimination, the employer must show that its discriminatory rule bears a "high correlation" to the plaintiff's ability to perform the job in question *and* relates to the "essence" or "central mission" of the employer's business.[4] Relying on *Johnson Controls*, an appellate court has recently denied the BFOQ defense to schools that insisted on hiring Protestant teachers to maintain a Protestant "presence" assertedly important to their general educational operations. First, the court defined the real mission of the schools as providing native Hawaiians "a solid education in traditional secular subjects" and "moral guidance" useful for developing a "system of values," rather than educating the students "from the Protestant point of view." It could find no correlation in the record between the employer's insistence on "nominally Protestant" teachers and the provision of superior instruction or moral guidance. And it concluded that even assuming maintenance of a Protestant "presence" went to the essence of the schools' business, the 100% presence mandated by the employer's Protestant-only hiring rule exceeded the requirements of its mission and actual daily operations.[5]

B. CONSTITUTIONAL PROBLEMS SURROUNDING REGULATION OF RELIGIOUS DISCRIMINATION

Library References:

> C.J.S. Civil Rights §§ 159, 165.
> West's Key No. Digests, Civil Rights ⊕151.

§ 3.7 In General

Subjecting a religiously based institution to Title VII regulation (and hence to the administrative scrutiny of EEOC and indirect regulation by

---

4. 499 U.S. at 201, 111 S.Ct. at 1205 (quoting *Dothard v. Rawlinson*, 433 U.S. 321, 333, 335, 97 S.Ct. 2720, 2728, 2729, 53 L.Ed.2d 786 (1977) and *Western Air Lines, Inc. v. Criswell*, 472 U.S. 400, 413, 105 S.Ct. 2743, 2751, 86 L.Ed.2d 321 (1985)).

5. *EEOC v. Kamehameha Schools/Bishop Estate*, 990 F.2d at 465–466. In reaching the last conclusion, the court distinguished *Pime v. Loyola Univ. of Chicago*, 803 F.2d 351 (7th Cir.1986). In *Pime* the Seventh Circuit upheld a university's BFOQ defense to a Jesuit hiring preference on the ground that the discriminatory qualification served to maintain a small minority Jesuit presence on the faculty. But the

Ninth Circuit, observing that *Pime* was decided before *Johnson Controls*, also suggested that apart from whether the schools in the case before it needed an exclusively Protestant faculty "presence" to meet their overall business needs, the defendants' religious requirement was infirm because it did not relate to the plaintiff's capacity to perform the duties of a substitute French teacher. Under *Johnson Controls*, in other words, the employer claiming a BFOQ must show a strong correlation between its discriminatory rule and the plaintiff's ability to do the job in question as well as a link to the business as a whole.

the courts) for discrimination on grounds other than religion has survived most challenges based on the Free Exercise Clause. The critical inquiry under that clause concerns the impact of statutory regulation on the institution's exercise of its sincerely held religious beliefs. Because of the statutory exemptions, the statutory regulation will not extend to employment practices motivated or compelled by the religious beliefs of the employer or its affiliated church. Accordingly, although defense of an employment discrimination charge may have substantial adverse impact on a church or other religious institution, the administrative proceeding or action should have slight or no impact on the religious practices or beliefs of its adherents. Any such incidental impact has been held outweighed by the government's "compelling" interest in ending employment discrimination.[1]

Where, however, the challenged employment practice relates to a staff member who occupies the functional status of clergy within the employer's denominational structure or belief system, courts have construed Title VII and the ADEA not to reach the practice in order to avoid transgressing the free exercise rights of the religious organization or its members.[2] On occasion, a lower court has permitted a discrimination claim to move forward when the plaintiff occupies a sensitive position but one that lies somewhat less close to the core of the religious enterprise.[3] But all regulation has been barred as burdening a religious school's right to free exercise when pursuit of the claim would entail government intrusion into the sponsoring church's choice of a teacher of theology.[4] The opinion, terming the plaintiff a "ministerial" employee with "pervasive" religious duties, distinguished cases in which the federal employment discrimination regulation concerned lay teachers of secular subjects.

The distinct question remains whether judicial regulation under Title VII or ADEA that is not challenged, or survives a challenge, under §§ 702 or 703(e)(2) violates the Establishment Clause by fostering "an excessive government entanglement with religion."[5] In *N.L.R.B. v.*

---

§ 3.7

1. *See, e.g., EEOC v. Fremont Christian School supra* § 3.5, note 6, *EEOC v. Pacific Press Publ. Association supra* § 3.4, note 7, and *Mississippi College, supra* § 3.5, note 6.

2. *EEOC v. Catholic Univ. of Am.,* 83 F.3d 455 (D.C.Cir.1996) (plaintiff faculty member a nun who acted as functional equivalent of a minister); *Young v. Northern Illinois Conference of United Methodist Church,* 21 F.3d 184 (7th Cir.1994), *cert. denied,* ___ U.S. ___, 115 S.Ct. 320, 130 L.Ed.2d 281 (1994); *Rayburn v. General Conference of Seventh–day Adventists,* 772 F.2d 1164, 1170–71 (4th Cir.1985), *cert. denied,* 478 U.S. 1020, 106 S.Ct. 3333, 92 L.Ed.2d 739 (1986); *EEOC v. Southwestern*

Baptist Theological Seminary, supra § 3.5, note 6; *EEOC v. Mississippi College, supra* § 3.5, note 6; *McClure, supra* § 3.4, note 2; (Title VII cases): *Scharon v. St. Luke's Episcopal Presbyterian Hosp.,* 929 F.2d 360, 363 (8th Cir.1991); *Minker v. Baltimore Annual Conference of United Methodist Church,* 894 F.2d 1354, 1356–58 (D.C.Cir. 1990) (ADEA cases).

3. *Elbaz v. Congregation Beth Judea, Inc.,* 812 F.Supp. 802, (N.D.Ill.1992).

4. *Powell v. Stafford,* 859 F.Supp. 1343 (D.Colo.1994) (case under ADEA).

5. *See Lemon v. Kurtzman,* 403 U.S. 602, 612–613, 91 S.Ct. 2105, 2111–2112, 29 L.Ed.2d 745 (1971).

Catholic Bishop of Chicago,[6] where lay faculty sought to unionize under the protection of federal law, the Supreme Court construed the National Labor Relations Act as not affording jurisdiction over religiously associated organizations absent an affirmative, clearly expressed contrary intention of Congress. Yet it later intimated in dictum that the First Amendment does leave room for some degree of state intrusion into religious schools' employment practices.[7] We know for sure, then, only that subjecting a religiously affiliated organization to the full regulatory umbrella of the national laws governing employee self-organization and collective bargaining falls on the prohibited side of the line.

Lower courts have muddled through this quagmire by generally extending protection against employment discrimination to those teaching staff and supporting personnel of schools and seminaries who have no religious duties or whose religious duties, if any, are "easily isolated and defined" rather than pervasive.[8] *Catholic Bishop* has been distinguished on the ground that regulation of the labor relations of parochial schools by the National Labor Relations Board under the National Labor Relations Act is far more comprehensive and ongoing than the "limited inquiry required in anti-discrimination disputes."[9] But where a terminated Catholic school teacher brought Title VII charges alleging *religious* discrimination, the religion clauses were held too implicated to permit determination by secular courts.[10] At least one appellate opinion permitting an age discrimination action to go forward notwithstanding the entanglement objection[11] has nevertheless expressed concern that government could become an arbiter of the truth or validity of religious beliefs when a court determines whether a religious employer's stated

---

6. 440 U.S. 490, 99 S.Ct. 1313, 59 L.Ed.2d 533 (1979).

7. *Ohio Civil Rights Comm'n v. Dayton Christian Schools, Inc.*, 477 U.S. 619, 106 S.Ct. 2718, 91 L.Ed.2d 512 (1986).

8. *See Weissman v. Congregation Shaare Emeth*, 38 F.3d 1038 (8th Cir.1994) (rejecting excessive entanglement defense to ADEA action brought by administrator of synagogue whose duties were principally or entirely non-sectarian, absent specific allegation that he was terminated for reasons related to arguably religious duties or for other religious reasons); *Geary v. Visitation of the Blessed Virgin Mary Parish School*, 7 F.3d 324 (3d Cir.1993) (allowing ADEA claim to proceed by terminated lay teacher in church-operated elementary school, distinguishing cases where religious discrimination was alleged, where plaintiff had religious duties, or clergy were involved); *DeMarco v. Holy Cross High School*, 4 F.3d 166 (2d Cir.1993) (holding that the *Catholic Bishop* presumption against coverage does not bar the ADEA claim of a math teacher in a religious

school even though the faculty were also expected to serve as spiritual exemplars); *EEOC v. Fremont Christian School*, 781 F.2d 1362 (9th Cir.1986); *EEOC v. Mississippi College*, 626 F.2d 477 (5th Cir.1980) (largely secular schools) *cert. denied*, 453 U.S. 912, 101 S.Ct. 3143, 69 L.Ed.2d 994 (1981); *EEOC v. Southwestern Baptist Theological Seminary*, 651 F.2d 277 (5th Cir.1981) (sectarian school), *cert. denied*, 456 U.S. 905, 102 S.Ct. 1749, 72 L.Ed.2d 161 (1982).

9. *DeMarco, supra* note 8; *Soriano v. Xavier Univ. Corp.*, 687 F.Supp. 1188, 1189 (S.D.Ohio 1988). *See also Geary, supra* note 8 (permitting ADEA action by lay employee of church-operated elementary school but noting the school's light burden of showing that a religious reason actually motivated the challenged employment action).

10. *Little v. Wuerl*, 929 F.2d 944 (3d Cir.1991).

11. *DeMarco, supra* note 8.

justification for an employment action is "implausible" [12] or "false." [13] The Second Circuit sought to alleviate this problem by declaring that the factfinder will be required "to presume that an asserted religious motive is plausible in the sense that it is reasonably or validly held." [14] Thus while the factfinder may determine whether an employer took adverse action against the plaintiff because of a failure to fulfill religious duties, a lawful reason, or because of age, an unlawful one, the court may not question the validity or necessity of the duties themselves. [15] These cases suggest that employer counsel for such religious or religiously affiliated institutions would be well advised, whenever consistent with the facts, to plead specifically that the duties at issue in an adverse disciplinary action are religious or that the action was taken for religious reasons. [16]

As we shall see, [17] the substance of the employer's Title VII duty not to discriminate because of religion—particularly the "reasonable accommodation" feature of that duty—has been distinctly diluted by judicial interpretation, perhaps to ensure that the statute, so construed, will survive these First Amendment challenges.

C. THE BASIC SUBSTANTIVE PROHIBITIONS

Library References:

C.J.S. Civil Rights §§ 143, 144, 146, 157, 160 et seq.
West's Key No. Digests, Civil Rights ⚷141 et seq.

§ 3.8 In General

The deceptively simple substantive prohibitions of Title VII are contained in § 703(a). Section 703(a)(1) declares it an "unlawful employment practice" for a covered employer

> to fail or refuse to hire or to discharge any individual, or otherwise to discriminate against any individual with respect to his compensation, terms, conditions or privileges of employment, because of such individual's race, color, religion, sex, or national origin.

Section 703(a)(2) forbids limiting the employment "opportunities" of an applicant or incumbent employee on any of the same grounds. The

---

12. *See Hazen Paper Co. v. Biggins*, 507 U.S. 604, 613, 113 S.Ct. 1701, 1708, 123 L.Ed.2d 338 (1993).

13. *See* discussion under "Individual Disparate Treatment," Chapter VI below, concerning *St. Mary's Honor Center v. Hicks*, 509 U.S. 502, 502, 113 S.Ct. 2742, 2744, 125 L.Ed.2d 407 (1993).

14. *DeMarco, supra* note 8, at 171.

15. *Id.*; *cf. Estate of Thornton v. Caldor, Inc.*, 472 U.S. 703, 105 S.Ct. 2914, 86 L.Ed.2d 557 (1985) (O'Connor, J., concurring) (observing in dictum that a court, in ruling on a plaintiff's claimed entitlement to accommodation under § 701(j) of Title

VII, discussed in § 3.12 below, need only ascertain whether the belief is religious and sincerely held, and may not inquire into its verity).

16. *See, e.g., Weissman v. Congregation Shaare Emeth*, 38 F.3d 1038 (8th Cir.1994) (allegation that employer dissatisfied with plaintiff's job performance insufficient to trigger entanglement concern absent specific allegation that plaintiff's performance was deficient respecting any religious duties or that he was terminated for other religious reasons).

17. *See* § 3.12, *infra* this chapter.

controversies addressed by the case law have centered on two inter-twined issues. First, what employer conduct or classifications corre-spond to the forbidden kinds of discrimination—what, in other words, constitutes discrimination on the grounds of "race, color, religion, sex or national origin"? As we shall see, the answers to these questions are not always self-evident. Discrimination based on alienage status, for example, is not tantamount to the prohibited discrimination based on national origin, even though a non-U.S. citizen would not have that status unless she or a forbearer recently arrived here from another nation. Whites may sue for race discrimination, as may blacks, based on the racial animus directed against them by other blacks.

The second pervasive issue concerns the nature and degree of the nexus that must exist between prohibited employer conduct and harm to a plaintiff's employment status. When, in other words, is adverse action taken by the employer "because of" prohibited discrimination? For example, the Supreme Court has treated as prohibited gender discrimi-nation certain forms of employer speech and action characterized by sex stereotyping; but it has simultaneously demanded evidence that the employer actually relied on the stereotype as a factor in the challenged employment decision before that decision could constitute an unlawful employment practice under Title VII.[1]

The Seventh Circuit, for example, has held that an interviewer's questions about child-bearing and child-rearing plans, asked only of women, did not violate Title VII where the interviewer was apparently reassured by the plaintiff's answers and she could not otherwise show that her rejection was attributable to the employer's stereotypical be-liefs.[2] In this respect Title VII contrasts with some state and local antidiscrimination laws, as well as the Americans With Disabilities Act, which treat such questions as per se violations. The same court has also ruled that the plaintiff must show a nexus between a supervisor's occasional or sporadic slurs related to an employee's protected character-istic and a subsequent adverse employment action. Thus a supervisor's repeated directive that a Korean–American "learn to speak English" constituted circumstantial evidence of prohibited national-origin based animus but did not suffice to establish unlawful discrimination absent evidence that the employer ultimately relied on the impermissible crite-rion in discharging the employee.[3]

---

§ 3.8

1. *Price Waterhouse v. Hopkins*, 490 U.S. 228, 109 S.Ct. 1775, 104 L.Ed.2d 268 (1989). *See, e.g., Panis v. Mission Hills Bank N.A.*, 60 F.3d 1486 (10th Cir.1995) (plaintiff failed to offer facts warranting trial on whether bank relied on gender-based stereotype by terminating her on "customer confidence" grounds after her husband was indicted for scheming to de-fraud another bank's customers).

2. *Bruno v. Crown Point, Ind.*, 950 F.2d 355 (7th Cir.1991), *cert. denied*, 505 U.S. 1207, 112 S.Ct. 2998, 120 L.Ed.2d 874 (1992).

3. *Hong v. Children's Memorial Hospi-tal*, 993 F.2d 1257 (7th Cir.1993), *cert. de-nied*, ___ U.S. ___, 114 S.Ct. 1372, 128 L.Ed.2d 48 (1994).

In a similar vein the Seventh Circuit has declared a per se rule that will almost always insulate employers from liability for word-of-mouth hiring. The court appeared to agree that an employer's virtually complete reliance on word-of-mouth recruiting by a largely Korean workforce resulted in the overwhelming exclusion of persons of other national origins.[4] But as long as the employer had evidence that this method of recruiting was cost efficient, the disparate result was held not to be evidence of intentional discrimination "even if the employer would prefer to employ people drawn predominantly or even entirely from his own ethnic or, here, national-origin community." The court explained that discrimination "is not preference or aversion; it is acting on the preference or aversion."

The courts have answered the statute's definitional silence on this causation or nexus question by developing different evidentiary allocations and burdens that are deemed equivalent to proof that adverse action was imposed "because of" an employer's reliance on a prohibited characteristic. These proof modes are discussed in Chapter VI below.

Because Title VII applies so comprehensively to employment decisions affecting millions of private employees and is therefore invoked and litigated so pervasively, decisions interpreting its conceptual framework of discrimination, and even some of its defenses, have frequently served as interpretive models for other statutes. These include not only the cognate ADEA—constructions of which have also cross-pollinated Title VII[5]—but also the Reconstruction Acts, notably 42 U.S.C.A. §§ 1981 and 1983. For example, courts have transplanted the evolving judicial elaboration of unlawful individual disparate treatment under Title VII to both of these nineteenth century statutes,[6] and even imported into § 1981 the explicit textual Title VII defense for bona fide seniority systems.

D. THE MEANING OF DISCRIMINATION BECAUSE OF "RACE," "COLOR," "NATIONAL ORIGIN," "RELIGION," AND "SEX"

Library References:

C.J.S. Civil Rights §§ 146, 147, 157, 158, 165.
West's Key No. Digests, Civil Rights ⚯142.

§ 3.9 The Meaning of "Race"

For the most part the Supreme Court has defined the concept of "race" in connection with actions under 42 U.S.C.A. § 1981, the 1866

---

4. *EEOC v. Consolidated Service Systems*, 989 F.2d 233 (7th Cir.1993). *See also Foster v. Dalton*, 71 F.3d 52 (1st Cir.1995) (discrimination based on cronyism not prohibited).

5. *See Western Air Lines, Inc. v. Criswell*, 472 U.S. 400, 105 S.Ct. 2743, 86 L.Ed.2d 321 (1985).

6. *See St. Mary's Honor Center v. Hicks*, 509 U.S. 502 n. 1, 113 S.Ct. 2742 n. 1, 125 L.Ed.2d 407 (1993).

statute which secures to all persons the same right to make and enforce contracts, including contracts of employment, as is enjoyed by white citizens.   See discussion in the Chapter entitled "Overview of the Reconstruction–Era Legislation."   In one of those decisions, however, *McDonald v. Santa Fe Trail Transportation Co.*,[1] the Court held that the Title VII prohibition on race discrimination is enforceable by whites as well as blacks.[2]   But some circuits have required in such cases evidence of "background circumstances" tending to prove that the defendant is the "unusual employer who discriminates against the majority." [3]   In a failure to promote situation, the white or male plaintiff can meet this burden by proving that the plaintiff's qualifications were superior to those of the successful minority applicant [4]—a showing the Supreme Court has specifically ruled is not indispensable in the ordinary Title VII case.[5]

The race concept has been viewed broadly under § 1981 as well.   In *St. Francis College v. Al–Khazraji*[6] and *Shaare Tefila Congregation v. Cobb*,[7] the Court held that the § 1981 ban on race discrimination could be enforced by Arabs and Jews, respectively, if they could prove adverse treatment on the basis of their ancestry.   Observing that these holdings in effect mean that whites can maintain a viable § 1981 claim against other whites, one court has concluded that a black plaintiff may maintain a Title VII claim based on alleged race discrimination by a black supervisor.[8]   And the distinct Title VII prohibition on discrimination because of "color" has supported claims by lighter- or darker-skinned blacks based on discrimination by a black employer agent with skin of a different hue.[9]

§ 3.10   Accent or Language Rules as National Origin Discrimination

Discrimination because of national origin presents special difficulties because it is relatively seldom that defendants refer explicitly to the

---

§ 3.9

1. 427 U.S. 273, 96 S.Ct. 2574, 49 L.Ed.2d 493 (1976).

2. Examples of claims of "reverse discrimination" by white or male plaintiffs are discussed in Chapters 4 (concerning race- or gender-based employment decisions made pursuant to an agreement settling a prior charge of discrimination) and 5 (concerning the lawfulness of employment decisions made pursuant to "voluntary" and court-decreed affirmative action programs).

3. *See, e.g., Parker v. Baltimore & Ohio R.R.*, 652 F.2d 1012, 1017 (D.C.Cir.1981); *Notari v. Denver Water Dept.*, 971 F.2d 585 (10th Cir.1992).   Again because of skepticism about anti-white animus under current social conditions, it has sometimes been doubted that the inferential mode of proving intentional discrimination authorized by the *McDonnell Douglas* formula discussed in detail in Chapter 4 is available in cases of reverse discrimination.   *See, e.g., Hill v. Burrell Communications Group, Inc.*, 67 F.3d 665, 668 n. 2 (7th Cir.1995).

4. *Harding v. Gray*, 9 F.3d 150, 154 (D.C.Cir.1993).

5. *Patterson v. McLean Credit Union*, 491 U.S. 164, 109 S.Ct. 2363, 105 L.Ed.2d 132 (1989).

6. 481 U.S. 604, 107 S.Ct. 2022, 95 L.Ed.2d 582 (1987).

7. 481 U.S. 615, 107 S.Ct. 2019, 95 L.Ed.2d 594 (1987).

8. *Hansborough v. City of Elkhart Parks and Recreation Department*, 802 F.Supp. 199 (N.D.Ind.1992).

9. *See Walker v. Secretary of the Treasury*, 713 F.Supp. 403 (N.D.Ga.1989).

particular country of origin of the plaintiff or his ancestors. One example we saw above, an employer rule requiring citizenship as a precondition to hire, is an example. Because citizenship as such is not a forbidden ground of discrimination, the rule might violate Title VII if but only if in operation it has disproportionate adverse impact on persons of an identifiable national origin.[1] Similarly, ethnic slurs more commonly stain an individual's ancestry (e.g., slurs pertaining to Arabs, Jews, or persons hailing from Asia, Africa, Central or South America, Mexico, or Puerto Rico), another basis of discrimination not forbidden by Title VII, than her particular national origin. In addition, employer practices or rules based on language characteristics will usually also be neutral on their face. They therefore could violate Title VII only if applied in ways that are designed to injure or that have disproportionate adverse impact on persons of a particular national origin.

Two language problems of this kind have surfaced in the cases— discrimination based on foreign accent, and "speak-English-only" rules. Several circuit courts have considered discrimination because of accent, where the adverse employer action is typically meted out ad hoc, rather than pursuant to an across-the-board rule. Consequently, the decisions evaluate the evidence in these cases under the theory of individual disparate treatment, rather than disproportionate adverse impact. The leading case, *Fragante v. City and County of Honolulu,*[2] relied on an EEOC Guideline[3] to conclude that proof of discrimination based on foreign accent establishes a prima facie case of discrimination based on national origin. Addressing the employer's disparate treatment defense, the court wrote that an adverse employment decision taken because of accent is lawful only when the accent "interferes materially with job performance."[4] Further, because accent and national origin "are obviously inextricably intertwined in many cases," the Court cautioned that a "searching look" is demanded to ensure that employer assertions about a candidate's poor communications skills are not used as a cover or pretext for national origin discrimination.[5]

The few appellate opinions on the issue treat English-only rules as neutral employer practices that are subject to evaluation on the theory of disproportionate adverse impact because of their potential adverse effect

---

§ 3.10

1. *See* Chapter 4 below on the several Title VII proof modes. Some courts require identifiability of plaintiffs particular country of origin with more specificity than do others. *See Gomez v. Allegheny Health Services,* 71 F.3d 1079 (3d Cir.1995), *cert. denied,* ___ U.S.___, 116 S.Ct. 2524, ___ L.Ed.2d ___ (1996).

2. 888 F.2d 591 (9th Cir.1989), *cert. denied,* 494 U.S. 1081, 110 S.Ct. 1811, 108 L.Ed.2d 942 (1990).

3. See 29 C.F.R. § 1606.1 *et seq.*

4. *Id.* at 596.

5. 888 F.2d at 596 (citing 29 C.F.R. § 1606.6(b)(1)). *Id. Accord, Odima v. Westin Tucson Hotel Co.,* 991 F.2d 595, 600 (9th Cir.1993); *Ang v. Procter & Gamble Co.,* 932 F.2d 540, 550 (6th Cir.1991). *See also Carino v. University of Oklahoma Bd. of Regents,* 750 F.2d 815, 819 (10th Cir. 1984); *Berke v. Ohio Dept. of Public Welfare,* 628 F.2d 980, 981 (6th Cir.1980). *Cf. Stephen v. PGA Sheraton,* 873 F.2d 276 (11th Cir.1989) (race discrimination claim rebutted by credible evidence that plaintiff did not speak or understand English sufficiently to perform assigned duties).

on non-English speakers as well as bilinguals.[6] EEOC's pertinent guideline declares a presumption that a "speak-English-only" rule applied at all times in the workplace discriminates on the basis of national origin. Even if the rule is limited to certain times, the guideline gives it the same prima facie effect and says it must be "justified by business necessity." Moreover, failure to give employees advance notification of the required circumstances and consequences of violation will be considered "evidence of" national origin discrimination.[7]

The part of this guideline that specifies a business necessity defense would appear to be of no current import. Title VII itself, as amended by the Civil Rights Act of 1991, requires the employer, once a prima facie case of disproportionate adverse impact is made, to "demonstrate that the challenged practice is job related for the position in question *and* consistent with business necessity."[8] While there will continue to be great uncertainty about the content of "business necessity" under the new statute, it is clear that neutral practices will now also have to be justified as "job related for the position in question," a requirement absent from the EEOC Guideline. See Chapter 5 for complete discussion of the concepts of "business necessity" and "job related."

The currently significant issue raised by the Guideline is its presumption that an English-only rule has adverse impact in all circumstances, particularly as applied to bilingual employees. This presumption, if accepted, establishes the plaintiff's prima facie case, thereby casting on the employer the burden of justification. The early opinions, *Garcia v. Gloor*[9], *Garcia v. Rush–Presbyterian–St. Luke's Medical Center*[10] and *Jurado v. Eleven–Fifty Corporation*,[11] concluded that employees fluent in both English and Spanish were not adversely impacted by even sweeping English-only rules, because they could readily comply with the employer's directive and thus avoid tangible employment detriment. Later, the Ninth Circuit, relying on the EEOC's Guideline, struck down a rule that forbade Spanish-speaking translators from speaking Spanish except while on break, at lunch, or actually translating.[12] The court found the prima facie case met the EEOC presumption and rejected the proffered employer justifications that the rule was necessary to promote racial harmony and to prevent the workplace from becoming a "Tower of Babel." Specifically disagreeing with the Fifth Circuit in *Garcia v. Gloor*, the court held that the mere fact that the plaintiff was bilingual and could comply with the employer's rule did not shield the rule from liability, because bilinguality "does not eliminate the relationship be-

---

6. *See, e.g., Garcia v. Gloor*, 618 F.2d 264 (5th Cir.1980), *cert. denied,* 449 U.S. 1113, 101 S.Ct. 923, 66 L.Ed.2d 842 (1981).

7. 29 C.F.R. § 1606.7 (1993).

8. 42 U.S.C.A. § 2000e–2(k)(1)(A) (Supp. 1992) (emphasis added).

9. *See supra* note 6.

10. 660 F.2d 1217, 1222 (7th Cir.1981) (upholding employer rule requiring the ability to speak English as not having a disproportionate adverse impact on Latinos and in any event as job related).

11. 813 F.2d 1406 (9th Cir.1987).

12. *Gutierrez v. Municipal Court*, 838 F.2d 1031 (9th Cir.1988), *vacated as moot,* 490 U.S. 1016, 109 S.Ct. 1736, 104 L.Ed.2d 174 (1989).

tween his primary language and the culture that is derived from his national origin.''

More recently, however, the Ninth Circuit has repudiated this approach and rejected the EEOC Guideline. In this highly publicized case, *Garcia v. Spun Steak Co.*,[13] the Supreme Court has denied certiorari despite the urging of the Justice Department. The Ninth Circuit in *Spun Steak* expressly subscribed to the Fifth Circuit's approach in *Garcia v. Gloor*[14] and insisted that adverse impact must be proved and not merely presumed. The Ninth Circuit's most recent general approach is likely to stand as a leading opinion because it represents the view of a circuit with an enormous immigrant population that will feel the brunt of such workplace rules.[15] But the scope of *Spun Steak* as applied to varying employer rules is uncertain. For example, there the court found, with somewhat curious logic,[16] that the employer's English-only rule had no disproportionate adverse impact because the plaintiff, being bilingual, could readily comply without jeopardizing his employment. That rationale would of course not pertain to monolingual Spanish speakers. In any event, the *Spun Steak* policy was justified as a business necessity because it facilitated worker safety on a production line. That defense might not be available where a similar rule is applied to office personnel or to off-duty inter-employee conversations.[17]

Another circuit has held that an English-only rule challenged by Spanish-speaking employees cannot constitute unlawful disparate treatment absent evidence that English speakers were permitted to speak in languages other than English.[18] A related, emerging contention is that a policy of *permitting* employees to speak their native foreign language on the job may violate the right of English speakers to be free from discrimination based on national origin. The argument is said to draw support from the EEOC's national origin guideline which identifies an individual's primary language as an ''essential national origin characteristic.'' A claim to this effect has recently survived an employer's motion for summary judgment.[19] But a claim that an employer practice requiring employees with fluency in Spanish to use that skill on the job unlawfully discriminates failed where non-Hispanics also used Spanish-

---

13. 998 F.2d 1480 (9th Cir.1993), *cert. denied*, ___ U.S. ___, 114 S.Ct. 2726, 129 L.Ed.2d 849 (1994).

14. *See supra* note 6.

15. More recently the Ninth Circuit has declared unconstitutional a state constitutional provision purporting to enshrine English as the state's official language and requiring all government employees to ''act'' in English only. *Yniguez v. Arizonans for Official English*, 69 F.3d 920 (9th Cir. 1995) (en banc), *cert. granted sub nom. Arizonans for Official English v. Arizona*, ___ U.S. ___, 116 S.Ct. 1316, 134 L.Ed.2d 469 (1996).

16. *See Garcia v. Spun Steak Co.*, 13 F.3d 296, 298 (9th Cir.1993) (Reinhardt, J., dissenting from denial of rehearing en banc).

17. Alternatively, a policy that applies only to on-duty conversations may be upheld as having minimal restrictive impact, as in *Jurado, supra.*

18. *Long v. First Union Corp. of Virginia*, 86 F.3d 1151 (4th Cir.1996) (unpublished).

19. *McNeil v. Aguilos*, 831 F.Supp. 1079 (S.D.N.Y.1993).

speaking skills on the job, at least in the absence of a pattern of systematic disparate treatment.[20]

§ 3.11 Discrimination Based on Sex

Whereas the problem with national origin discrimination is that it is often not relied on expressly, the definitional problem with many permutations of sex discrimination frequently is that sex, while an explicit part of an employer's decision or rule, is not the sole factor. For example, the employer's rule in *Phillips v. Martin Marietta Corp.*,[1] disqualified from employment women, though not men, with pre-school-aged children. The rule, then, excluded only women, but not all women; the question was whether this was the kind of express discrimination on the basis of sex that would require the greatest level of employer justification. The Supreme Court, reversing the court of appeals, held that the employer's ground of discrimination impermissibly created "one hiring policy for women and another for men." It was no defense that the policy could be conceptualized as distinguishing between candidates on a compound "sex-plus" ground not forbidden by Title VII—with the plus factor here being the early stages of motherhood. In reaching this conclusion, the Court noted that Congress had rejected proposed amendments to the statute that would have forbidden only discrimination that is "solely" on one of the prohibited grounds. The *Martin Marietta* logic also makes it unlawful gender discrimination to reject applicants or fail to promote employees who are married women, but not married men.[2]

Since only women become pregnant, it might seem that a distinction on the basis of pregnancy would be tantamount to express or facial discrimination because of gender. That result might clearly have been expected after *Martin Marietta*, which seemingly would have considered it irrelevant that pregnancy discrimination also draws a distinction on the basis of the "plus" characteristic of pregnancy. The Supreme Court held otherwise, however, in *General Electric Co. v. Gilbert*,[3] when it concluded that a pregnancy exclusion from an otherwise comprehensive disability insurance plan did not discriminate against women because it distinguished on a "gender-neutral" basis between pregnant women and non-pregnant persons. Congress legislatively overruled this result in the Pregnancy Discrimination Act of 1978, discussed in § 5.31 below.

Relying on the *Gilbert* reasoning, employers also contended that pension plan provisions requiring greater contributions by female employees, or awarding them lesser retirement benefits despite their equal

---

20. *Morales v. Human Rights Division,* 878 F.Supp. 653 (S.D.N.Y.1995); *see Cota v. Tucson Police Dept.,* 783 F.Supp. 458, 473–74 (D.Ariz.1992).

§ 3.11

1. 400 U.S. 542, 91 S.Ct. 496, 27 L.Ed.2d 613 (1971).

2. *Sprogis v. United Air Lines, Inc.,* 444 F.2d 1194 (7th Cir.1971). *But cf. Fisher v.*

Vassar College, 70 F.3d 1420 (2d Cir.1995) (holding not sex specific and therefore not actionable under Title VII a policy that favored those without children and those capable of raising them without a significant career interruption over employees who require lengthy child-rearing leaves).

3. 429 U.S. 125, 97 S.Ct. 401, 50 L.Ed.2d 343 (1976).

contributions, are geared to the neutral factor of greater average female longevity rather than to gender. The Supreme Court, however, found gender an inadequate proxy for greater female longevity, noting that a significant part of the differential might be explainable by other factors, such as the heavier incidence of smoking among men. In any event, again stressing Title VII's focus on the individual, the Court expressed concern that even an accurate generalization about greater female longevity obscures the fact that many women will live less long than many men, and each such woman is entitled to benefits calculated without regard to gender-based averages. Accordingly, the Court has invalidated plans that require women to make greater contributions or that award them lesser benefits.[4] These decisions have revolutionized the employer-sponsored pension industry, forcing many insurers to offer plans featuring gender-neutral annuity assumptions.

Lower courts have long held, with substantial unanimity, that discrimination because of one's sexual orientation or behaviors does not amount to gender discrimination prohibited by Title VII.[5] These courts have relied heavily on the repeated failure in Congress of bills that would have prohibited sexual orientation discrimination. For these courts, unless an antihomosexual policy is disparately enforced in favor of or against members of a particular gender, the employer rule is simply not on the basis of gender. Efforts to circumvent this barrier, either by proceeding on a disparate impact theory or by asserting that a campaign of anti-homosexual hostility amounted to unlawful environmental harassment based on gender, have also failed.[6] For example, an anti-homosexual practice, neutral on its face and neutrally applied, may nevertheless result in disproportionately greater exclusion of male homosexuals (as will be the case, if, for example, they are more readily identifiable) and might therefore be said to discriminate because of gender. But since the impetus for the discrimination is anti-homosexual rather than anti-male animus, recognizing the impact theory would amount to an end-run around the Congressional purpose not to forbid discrimination based on sexual orientation.[7] In a relatively small num-

4. *See, respectively, Los Angeles Department of Water & Power v. Manhart*, 435 U.S. 702, 98 S.Ct. 1370, 55 L.Ed.2d 657 (1978); *Arizona Governing Committee v. Norris*, 463 U.S. 1073, 103 S.Ct. 3492, 77 L.Ed.2d 1236 (1983).

5. *See Garcia v. Elf Atochem North America*, 28 F.3d 446 (5th Cir.1994) (alternative holding); *Dillon v. Frank*, 952 F.2d 403 (6th Cir.1992); *Williamson v. A.G. Edwards and Sons, Inc.*, 876 F.2d 69 (8th Cir.1989), *cert. denied*, 493 U.S. 1089, 110 S.Ct. 1158, 107 L.Ed.2d 1061 (1990); *De-Cintio v. Westchester County Medical Ctr.*, 807 F.2d 304 (2d Cir.1986), *cert. denied*, 484 U.S. 825, 108 S.Ct. 89, 98 L.Ed.2d 50 (1987); *Ulane v. Eastern Airlines, Inc.*, 742 F.2d 1081 (7th Cir.1984), *cert. denied*, 471 U.S. 1017, 105 S.Ct. 2023, 85 L.Ed.2d 304

(1985); *DeSantis v. Pacific Tel. & Tel. Co.*, 608 F.2d 327 (9th Cir.1979); *Smith v. Liberty Mut. Ins. Co.*, 569 F.2d 325 (5th Cir. 1978). *See also Hopkins v. Baltimore Gas & Electric Co.*, 871 F.Supp. 822 (D.Md.1994); *Vandeventer v. Wabash Nat'l Corp.*, 867 F.Supp. 790 (N.D.Ind.1994); *Goluszek v. Smith*, 697 F.Supp. 1452 (N.D.Ill.1988). *But see Joyner v. AAA Cooper Transportation*, 597 F.Supp. 537 (M.D.Ala.1983), *affirmed without opinion*, 749 F.2d 732 (11th Cir. 1984); *Wright v. Methodist Youth Services, Inc.*, 511 F.Supp. 307 (N.D.Ill.1981).

6. *See, respectively, DeSantis, supra* note 5, and *Dillon, supra* note 5.

7. *See, e.g.*, the majority's response in *DeSantis v. Pacific Tel. & Tel. Co.*, 608 F.2d 327 (9th Cir.1979) to the partial dissenting opinion of Judge Sneed.

ber of jurisdictions, however, state and local laws provide protection from this type of employment discrimination.

Similarly, rules prohibiting the employment of spouses in the same office, department or plant of one company have been viewed as neutral on their face, actionable only if they are disparately enforced against members of a particular gender or if they have the statistical effect of disproportionately adversely impacting wives or husbands.[8] A no-dating rule is likewise neutral on its face and could violate Title VII only if disparately enforced or disproportionately impacting.[9]

Grooming and dress code regulations that on their face pertain only to one gender—men must have short hair, for example—have nevertheless been judicially assessed as neutral rather than as a form of express disparate treatment. The leading case, *Willingham v. Macon Telegraph Publishing Co.*,[10] offered a variety of reasons in support of this conclusion, none of which withstands hard scrutiny. For example, the court wrote that men could readily comply with a short-hair rule because it related to a "mutable" characteristic, and the statute was concerned only with assuring that employment opportunities not be denied on the basis of "immutable" characteristics like race or sex. This view has been otherwise expressed as asserting that the "primary thrust"[11] of Title VII is to ban employer reliance on sex stereotypes that pose "distinct employment disadvantages for one sex."[12] Yet religion, also prohibited by Title VII, is clearly mutable. And although gender, too, is within limits mutable (through the agency of transsexual surgery), the court certainly did not suggest that any other gender-based rules were outside the scope of the statute.

Perhaps recognizing the frailty of this distinction, the court fell back on the assertion that hair length did not relate to a "fundamental right." But Title VII is designed precisely to go beyond the minimal fundamental rights that enjoy constitutional protection; it does so by assuring that employment status is not disadvantaged by any distinction based on race, sex, religion or national origin.[13] Neither the text nor history of

---

8. *See Yuhas v. Libbey–Owens–Ford*, 562 F.2d 496 (7th Cir.1977), *cert. denied*, 435 U.S. 934, 98 S.Ct. 1510, 55 L.Ed.2d 531 (1978) (holding that such a disparate adverse impact was justifiable because the no-spouse rule plausibly improved the work environment). *Cf. Scott v. Dynasty Transportation Inc.*, 1994 WL 160545 (E.D.La. 1994), where the court rejected a retaliation claim resulting from the plaintiff's protest of his wife's discharge on the ground that discrimination because of "familial relations" is not a Title VII unlawful employment practice. This ruling evidently overlooked the fact that retaliation claims under § 704 lie regardless of whether the underlying employer conduct against which the retaliation plaintiff protested is itself a violation of the statute. See discussion of Retaliation, *infra*.

9. *See Sarsha v. Sears, Roebuck & Co.*, 3 F.3d 1035 (7th Cir.1993).

10. 507 F.2d 1084 (5th Cir.1975) (en banc).

11. *Craft v. Metromedia, Inc.*, 766 F.2d 1205 (8th Cir.1985), *cert. denied*, 475 U.S. 1058, 106 S.Ct. 1285, 89 L.Ed.2d 592 (1986).

12. *Knott v. Missouri Pacific Railroad*, 527 F.2d 1249, 1251 (8th Cir.1975).

13. Of course it must be acknowledged that in the realm of voluntary employer affirmative action, white and male employees seem to enjoy *less* protection from reverse discrimination under Title VII than they do under the Constitution. Compare the *Weber* and *Johnson* decisions with *Wy-*

the statute supports the distinction that conduct or behavior protected by the statute must be deemed "fundamental" from any other legal perspective.

The same approach has disadvantaged women with respect to regulations governing attire and grooming. Even when the employer's rule specifically imposes more demanding clothing and coiffure requirements on one gender than the other, the tendency has been for the courts to assert that the employer has one omnibus grooming regime that naturally has distinctive variations to account for gender differences. In a variation on this theme, courts will observe that the employer has *some* grooming standard for each gender and will treat that standard as the common, neutral employer practice. The fact that the employer imposes different, or more stringent, or differentially applied dress or grooming requirements on its employees of different genders is usually just ignored or minimized.[14] Plaintiffs have also been compelled to litigate no-beard rules within the framework of disproportionate adverse impact rather than disparate treatment.[15] The consequence of these decisions is that employers are far more easily able to justify such rules as a matter of business necessity or job relatedness than they would be if the rules were classified as discriminating facially on the basis of gender.

The general judicial rejection of women's gender discrimination complaints about harsher grooming or clothing requirements represents an exception to the Supreme Court's general recognition that employer practices driven by sex stereotyping unlawfully discriminate because of gender.[16] A recent Third Circuit decision illustrates the continuing vitality of the concept in other contexts.[17] A female employee was ostracized by co-workers and received an adverse evaluation because of rumors that she was having an affair with her male supervisor; those rumors were fueled by the fact that the supervisor repeatedly borrowed money from her in private. The court held that she could proceed to trial with a claim of sexual harassment. A reasonable jury, the court explained, could conclude that she suffered the adverse effects of the rumors because she was a woman, even though the supervisor's practice of borrowing money would have been gender neutral had he borrowed from a man. In the court's view, the harm or "sting" of the practice

---

gant and *Croson* in the section on affirmative action in Chapter 5, § 5.15.

14. *Craft v. Metromedia, Inc.*, 766 F.2d 1205 (8th Cir.1985), *cert. denied*, 475 U.S. 1058, 106 S.Ct. 1285, 89 L.Ed.2d 592 (1986); *Carroll v. Talman Federal Savings & Loan Association*, 604 F.2d 1028 (7th Cir.1979), *cert. denied*, 445 U.S. 929, 100 S.Ct. 1316, 63 L.Ed.2d 762 (1980); *Barker v. Taft Broadcasting Co.*, 549 F.2d 400 (6th Cir.1977); *Earwood v. Continental Southeastern Lines, Inc.*, 539 F.2d 1349 (4th Cir. 1976); *Fagan v. National Cash Register Co.*, 481 F.2d 1115 (D.C.Cir.1973). Similarly, the Court in *Willingham, supra* note 10, accepted as an alternative ground that the

employer maintained "[some, albeit different] grooming standards for female employees; thus in this respect each sex is treated equally." 507 F.2d at 1091–1092.

15. *See, e.g., Bradley v. Pizzaco of Nebraska, Inc.*, 7 F.3d 795 (8th Cir.1993); *Fitzpatrick v. City of Atlanta*, 2 F.3d 1112 (11th Cir.1993).

16. *Price Waterhouse v. Hopkins*, 490 U.S. 228, 109 S.Ct. 1775, 104 L.Ed.2d 268 (1989).

17. *Spain v. Equal Employment Opportunity Commission*, 26 F.3d 439 (3d Cir. 1994).

derived from traditional negative stereotypes that linked women's workplace advancement and their sexual behavior. In this way the employer risks liability for creating a sexually hostile work environment absent any showing of sexual misconduct: the supervisor's practice was confined to the clearly gender-neutral act of borrowing money, and the rumors that surrounded that practice were not attributable to the supervisor or the employer! Before the reader concludes, however, that the court went overboard on punishing sex stereotyping, one last point should be made: the defendant employer was the EEOC. Perhaps then this is simply a case of a sometimes overscrupulous enforcer being held to overscrupulous standards.

There are a number of other frequently litigated issues that wrestle with the question when grounds of discrimination that correlate differentially or exclusively with one gender amount to the prohibited discrimination "because of sex." Most of these are specially treated by Title VII or related statutes and will be considered now.

a. *Sexual and Racial Harassment*

Early decisions doubted whether a supervisor's imposition of adverse terms and conditions of employment on a subordinate employee for resisting the superior's sexual advances constituted discrimination "because of sex" even where the superior and subordinate were of different genders. After all, these cases reasoned, the selection of a "target" would usually not be based on the factor of gender alone, except perhaps if the superior targeted *all* subordinate employees of the opposite gender. That is, there would usually be a "plus" factor in the superior employee's calculus, usually the target's relative attractiveness or vulnerability to the superior. More recently, however, the Supreme Court has appeared to assume that, as in *Martin Marietta*, the target's gender need not be the sole motivating factor in the superior's advance in order for the subsequent reprisal to be actionable. The court held in *Meritor Savings Bank, FSB v. Vinson*[18] that it is sufficient if gender is a "but-for" cause of the advance. This of course would be the case in the most commonly charged sexual harassment scenario, an advance by a heterosexual directed toward a person of the opposite gender.

Nevertheless, the requirement that the discrimination be based on and directed against a particular gender, and not merely against sexual behavior attributable to persons of either gender, has some continuing significance in the law governing harassment. It undercuts claims based on anti-homosexual harassment unless the discrimination is limited to homosexuals of one gender, e.g., lesbians, or there is evidence that homosexuality by an employee of a different gender would be tolerated.[19]

---

18. 477 U.S. 57, 106 S.Ct. 2399, 91 L.Ed.2d 49 (1986).

19. *See, e.g., Garcia v. Elf Atochem North America,* 28 F.3d 446 (5th Cir.1994); *Hopkins v. Baltimore Gas & Electric Co.,* 871 F.Supp. 822 (D.Md.1994); *but see*

Barnes v. Costle, 561 F.2d 983 (D.C.Cir. 1977). *Cf. James v. Ranch Mart Hardware, Inc.,* 1994 WL 731517 (D.Kan.1994) (a male-to-female transsexual could state a claim under state law analogous to Title VII by alleging that a female-to-male transsexu-

It apparently also exempts from Title VII scrutiny sexual advances or reprisals made by a bisexual supervisor, who by hypothesis would not be selecting a target because of the target's particular gender.[20] Some courts, however, have distinguished harassment by a bisexual from "equal opportunity harassment" by a heterosexual. In one recent case the defendant's male agent subjected both male and female victims, including both halves of a married couple, to a pattern of sexually abusive remarks.[21] In the court's view, the agent would not have sought to demean the male or female victims "but-for" their respective genders, and accordingly the court viewed as actionable the conduct directed against both genders.[22] A circuit court has subsequently endorsed this reasoning.[23] These decisions rest on the understanding that sometimes a harasser is motivated not by a wish to gratify sexual desires but rather by a desire to subordinate or demean women.[24] By the same token, where a male supervisor's environmentally harassing conduct is in fact directed only against women, it is no defense to conjecture that men might find the supervisor's conduct equally offensive.[25]

These variations are part of a more general emerging issue subsumed in the phrase "same-sex harassment." When a male harasses another male (or a female another female) not because of the harassee's sexual orientation but "because" of the harassee's gender, the Title VII prohibition, as interpreted by *Meritor,* would seem to be violated. As the EEOC's Compliance Manual asserts, "the crucial inquiry is whether the harasser treats . . . members . . . of one sex differently from members of the other sex." [26] A few circuit court opinions, admittedly nondefinitive, accordingly leave the door open to the possibility that same-gender harassment will sometimes state a claim, so long as in each case the harassment is found to be directed against a member of a particular gender (and not against either or both genders) because of that victim's gender.[27]

al would not have faced similar discrimination).

20. *See Vinson v. Taylor,* 760 F.2d 1330, 1333 n. 7 (D.C.Cir.1985) , *affirmed sub nom. Meritor Sav. Bank v. Vinson,* 477 U.S. 57, 106 S.Ct. 2399, 91 L.Ed.2d 49 (1986); *Rabidue v. Osceola Refining Co.,* 805 F.2d 611, 620 (6th Cir.1986), *cert. denied,* 481 U.S. 1041, 107 S.Ct. 1983, 95 L.Ed.2d 823 (1987) (dictum); *Henson v. City of Dundee,* 682 F.2d 897, 902 (11th Cir.1982) (dictum); *Bundy v. Jackson,* 641 F.2d 934, 942 n. 7 (D.C.Cir.1981).

21. *Chiapuzio v. BLT Operating Corp.,* 826 F.Supp. 1334 (D.Wyo.1993).

22. *Id.* at 1337.

23. *Steiner v. Showboat Operating Co.,* 25 F.3d 1459 (9th Cir.1994).

24. *See, e.g., EEOC v. Farmer Brothers Co.,* 31 F.3d 891 (9th Cir.1994) (evidence of this type of harassment relevant to whether discharges of women were made because of their gender). "Reverse harassment" of a male subordinate by a female supervisor may also violate Title VII. *EEOC v. Domino's Pizza, Inc.,* 909 F.Supp. 1529 (M.D.Fla. 1995). An employer is entitled to jury instructions that explain that not all sexually tinged conduct is sexually motivated or directed against members of only one gender. *Gillming v. Simmons Industries,* 91 F.3d 1168 (8th Cir.1996).

25. *Hutchison v. Amateur Electronic Supply, Inc.,* 42 F.3d 1037 (7th Cir.1994).

26. EEOC   Compliance   Manual, § 615.2(b)(3).

27. *See, e.g., Wrightson v. Pizza Hut of America,* 99 F.3d 138 (4th Cir.1996) (same-sex claim lies where male perpetrator is homosexual and advance is at least in part because of victim's male gender); *Baskerville v. Culligan Int'l Co.,* 50 F.3d 428 (7th Cir.1995); *Steiner v. Showboat Operating Co.,* 25 F.3d 1459 (9th Cir.1994).

By contrast, at least one circuit opinion has rejected same-gender harassment liability categorically.[28] The opinion reflects the same transcendent, purposive reasoning that led the courts of appeals, years earlier, to conclude unanimously that discrimination based on a victim's sexual orientation is not banned by the statute: harassment of men by men or women by women is simply too removed from the core variations of gender discrimination that the 1964 Congress had in mind when Section 703(a)'s prohibition on discrimination "because of sex" was enacted.[29]

Even those courts willing to entertain a "same-gender" claim, however, insist on proof that the victim's gender was at least the "but-for" factor in the harassment. That evidentiary minimum is exactly, and only, what the Supreme Court in *Meritor* required in the classic case of opposite gender heterosexual harassment. Thus it would be fatal to a same-sex claim if there is persuasive evidence that the alleged harasser aims similar conduct at members of the opposite gender, or for non-gender reasons targets only certain members of the plaintiff's gender. In practice this "but-for the victim's gender" requirement should usually mean that same-sex heterosexual harassment will not be actionable, while same-sex homosexual harassment will be.

For example, conduct motivated by the harasser's homosexual interest in the harassee (rather than by the harassee's own sexual orientation, which the circuit courts have unanimously held nonactionable) falls on the actionable side of the line. Although such conduct targets only certain members of the victim's gender, it would not occur unless the victim were of a particular gender. Further, assuming the harasser is not bisexual, that conduct would not be aimed at members of the opposite gender. By contrast, same-gender harassment by a heterosexual that is inspired by the particular victim's prudishness, shyness or apparent relative vulnerability to sexually tinged teasing or taunting would generally not be actionable. That conduct selects victim characteristics not possessed by many members of the victim's gender, and it might be aimed at members of the other gender who possessed the same fragile characteristics.[30] One judge has suggested navigating these shoals by erecting a rebuttable presumption that harassment of a person of the opposite gender is "because of" that person's gender, while harassment of a person of the same gender is not.[31]

28. *Garcia v. Elf Atochem North Am.,* 28 F.3d 446 (5th Cir.1994).

29. *Accord Hopkins v. Baltimore Gas and Elec. Co.,* 77 F.3d 745 (4th Cir.1996) (Wilkinson, C.J. and Hamilton, J., concurring).

30. *See Mayo v. Kiwest Corp.,* 94 F.3d 641 (4th Cir.1996); *McWilliams v. Fairfax County Bd. of Supervisors,* 72 F.3d 1191, 1196 (4th Cir.1996). But cf. *Quick v. Donaldson Co.,* 90 F.3d 1372 (8th Cir.1996)

(heterosexual employees' physical grabbing of sexual organs of plaintiff who alleged he was falsely considered homosexual held actionable "because of sex" where record suggested that members of one sex were exposed to adverse treatment not encountered by members of the other.

31. *Hopkins v. Baltimore Gas and Electric Co.,* 77 F.3d 745 (4th Cir.1996) (opinion of Niemeyer, J.).

The same "because of sex" requirement will also usually defeat the typical claim of sexual favoritism, in which a plaintiff denied a job or benefit alleges that another employee was hired or promoted because he or she participated in a consensual romantic relationship with a supervisory or managerial agent of the employer.[32]   In that situation both women and men are disadvantaged for a reason other than, or in addition to, their gender, viz., they were not the object of the agent's sexual interest.[33]   Thus in these settings the "gender-plus" liability avoidance persists, despite the Supreme Court's repudiation of it in *Phillips* and *Meritor*.   If, however, an employee is coerced into sexual participation as a condition of receiving a job benefit, other employees of the same gender could prevail with a variant on the standard sexual harassment theme if they could prove that sexual favors were demanded generally as the "quid pro quo" for advancement.[34]

Ultimately the judicial rationale for relieving employers of liability based on sexual orientation and sexual favoritism discrimination is extratextual.   It rests instead on a judicial perception about the underlying or motivating purposes of Title VII: to free applicants and employees from the imposition of adverse (thus excluding sexual favoritism discrimination) working conditions on the basis of the very few characteristics protected by Title VII (thus excluding sexual orientation discrimination).[35]

The principal remaining litigated issues regarding sexual harassment are not related to the definition of sex discrimination, but instead concern the meaning of the phrase "terms, conditions or privileges of employment" as used in § 703(a)(1).   It is certainly clear that a claim lies when submission to an employer's sexual demands is expressly made the "quid pro quo" of continued employment, pay increases, promotion or other tangible job benefits.[36]   Because only supervisors or managers could credibly affect those benefits, and they are clothed by the employer

---

32. *See Becerna v. Dalton,* 94 F.3d 145 (4th Cir.1996); *Mundy v. Palmetto Ford, Inc.,* 998 F.2d 1010 (4th Cir.1993); *DeCintio v. Westchester County Medical Center,* 821 F.2d 111 (2d Cir.), *cert. denied,* 484 U.S. 965, 108 S.Ct. 455, 98 L.Ed.2d 395 (1987); *Ayers v. AT & T,* 826 F.Supp. 443 (S.D.Fla.1993); *EEOC: Policy Guide on Employer Liability For Sexual Favoritism Under Title VII,* 405 FEP Man. (1/12/90). In *Herman v. Western Financial Corp.,* 254 Kan. 870, 869 P.2d 696 (1994), the claim that failed was that the plaintiff was subjected to additional work burdens because her supervisor was preoccupied by an affair with one of the plaintiff's co-workers. Such a claim could amount to gender discrimination, the court wrote, only if those additional burdens were experienced by women and not men. *But see King v. Palmer,* 778 F.2d 878 (D.C.Cir.1985) (inexplicably, though only implicitly, finding preferential treat-

ment of paramour actionable under Title VII).

33. Sometimes these claims fail on the separate ground that the plaintiff's terms and conditions of employment were not harmed by a supervisor's romantic relationship with a co-worker. *Candelore v. Clark County Sanitation Dist.,* 975 F.2d 588 (9th Cir.1992). In another case, a related claim that the plaintiff was fired because of her *knowledge* of an apparently voluntary supervisor-subordinate relationship, failed as also not asserting discriminating treatment based on gender. *Ellert v. University of Texas,* 52 F.3d 543 (5th Cir.1995).

34. *See, e.g., Dirksen v. City of Springfield,* 842 F.Supp. 1117 (C.D.Ill.1994).

35. *See DeCintio, supra* note 32.

36. *Meritor Savings Bank v. Vinson, supra* note 20.

with at least apparent authority to do so, a finding of quid pro quo harassment by an employer agent results, as with most other violations of Title VII, in automatic respondeat superior liability of the employer.[37]

But the EEOC's Guidelines also define quid pro quo harassment to occur when submission to unwelcome sexual advances or conduct is made, "either explicitly or implicitly" a term of condition of the target's employment; and when submission to or rejection of such conduct is in fact "used as the basis for employment decisions...."[38] Relying on the Guidelines, a recent Ninth Circuit opinion has held that "quid pro quo sexual harassment occurs whenever an individual explicitly or implicitly conditions a job, a job benefit, or the absence of a job detriment, upon an employee's acceptance of sexual conduct."[39] The opinion indicated that in order to determine when submission is made an implicit condition of employment, courts may apply either an objective standard—whether a reasonable person in the plaintiff's position would have believed that he was being subjected to quid pro quo harassment—or a subjective one— whether the alleged harasser in fact intended to condition the plaintiff's employment terms or conditions on compliance. Under either test, the court wrote, the critical evidence may be a "verbal nexus ... between a discussion about job benefits and a request for sexual favors." The court found quid pro quo harassment under each approach where, immediately after the plaintiff's unwilling performance of oral sex on the defendant's supervisor, he granted her request for a leave of absence and where, on another occasion, she performed oral sex on him immediately after they had discussed her leave and attendance record. The court ultimately adopted a per se rule that "a supervisor's intertwining of a request for the performance of sexual favors with a discussion of actual or potential job benefits or detriments in a single conversation constitutes quid pro quo harassment."[40]

What if the employee submits to the superior's sexual demands and accordingly suffers no tangible economic loss? It is implicit in the Ninth Circuit decision just discussed that there is quid pro quo discrimination nevertheless. The Second Circuit expressly reached that conclusion based on a supervisor's mere threat that a subordinate's working conditions would be adversely affected if she refused to acquiesce in his sexual demands. It was enough that the supervisor adjusted noneconomic terms of plaintiff's employment—work independence, hours, etc.—according to the degree to which she responded to his demands. In the terms of the EEOC Guidelines, it could thus be said that the supervisor

37. *Nichols v. Frank*, 42 F.3d 503 (9th Cir.1994) (citing cases); *Pierce v. Commonwealth Life Ins. Co.*, 40 F.3d 796, 803 (6th Cir.1994); 29 CFR § 1604.11(c); EEOC Policy Guidance on Current Issues of Sexual Harassment, 8 FEP (BNA) 405:6681, 6694 (1990).

38. 29 C.F.R. §§ 106.11(a)(1) to (2) (1993).

39. *Nichols v. Frank, supra*, 42 F.3d at 511. *See also Collins v. Baptist Memorial*

Geriatric Center, 937 F.2d 190, 196 (5th Cir.1991), *cert. denied*, 502 U.S. 1072, 112 S.Ct. 968, 117 L.Ed.2d 133 (1992); *Chamberlin v. 101 Realty, Inc.*, 915 F.2d 777, 783 (1st Cir.1990); *Spencer v. General Electric Co.*, 894 F.2d 651, 658 (4th Cir.1990); *Highlander v. K.F.C. National Management Co.*, 805 F.2d 644, 648 (6th Cir.1986).

40. *Nichols v. Frank, supra*, at 513.

based employment decisions on the target's rejection of *or* "submission to" his unwelcome sexual advances.[41]   If it ruled otherwise, the court reasoned, employer agents would simply be encouraged to persist with a course of harassment until a subordinate submits.

But is it actionable if the victim is subjected to worsened working conditions or other "environmental" harassment that affects only intangible aspects of the job?   The Supreme Court has affirmed its traditional broad interpretation of the covered "terms and conditions of employment,"[42] holding that harassment by an authorized employer representative is actionable, even without impact on tangible terms of employment like pay or benefits, if it is sufficiently severe or pervasive to create an "abusive working environment."[43]   Plaintiffs have not demonstrated a hostile work environment, however, when they show no more than an episodic pattern of antipathy based on race, national origin, or sex.[44]   For example, a claim of racial harassment failed where plaintiff pointed to two overtly racial remarks at the beginning of an eight-year period of employment that were followed, after a two-year respite, by what the court characterized as only "general ridicule" that was neither overtly racial and did not single out the plaintiff for abuse.[45]   Moreover, a plaintiff who could prove only that her work environment was made abusive, without being able to show tangible detriment to her employment status such as a denied promotion, diminished compensation, or termination could recover no monetary relief until Title VII was amended by the Civil Rights Act of 1991.[46]   Section 102 of the 1991 Act now authorizes compensatory and, if appropriate, punitive damages for all intentional forms of unlawful discrimination, including harassment, even absent harm to the plaintiff's economic terms of employment.   Title VII claims based on race, color, religion or national origin may also be maintained upon proof of either the "quid pro quo" or "hostile environment" variations of unlawful harassment.[47]

41.   29 CFR § 1604.11 *et seq.*; *Karibian v. Columbia University*, 14 F.3d 773 (2d Cir.), *cert. denied*, ___ U.S. ___, 114 S.Ct. 2693, 129 L.Ed.2d 824 (1994).

42.   *See Hishon v. King & Spalding*, 467 U.S. 69, 104 S.Ct. 2229, 81 L.Ed.2d 59 (1984).

43.   *Meritor*, *supra* note 20.

44.   *See, e.g., Lopez v. S.B. Thomas, Inc.*, 831 F.2d 1184, 1189 (2d Cir.1987).

45.   *Bolden v. PRC, Inc.*, 43 F.3d 545 (10th Cir.1994).   *But see Aman v. Cort Furniture Rental Corp.*, 85 F.3d 1074 (3d Cir.1996) (actionable racially hostile environment can be predicated on the use of facially neutral racial "code words" if circumstances suggest intended racial implications).

46.   *Landgraf v. USI Film Products*, 511 U.S. 244, 114 S.Ct. 1483, 128 L.Ed.2d 229 (1994).   This may explain why Anita Hill did not assert a timely charge of environ-mental sexual harassment against EEOC based on the alleged conduct of her supervisor at the time, EEOC Chair (now U.S. Supreme Court Justice) Clarence Thomas.

47.   *Patterson v. McLean Credit Union*, 491 U.S. 164, 180, 109 S.Ct. 2363, 2374, 105 L.Ed.2d 132 (1989); *Price Waterhouse*, *supra* note 16 at 243 n. 9, 109 S.Ct. at 1787 n. 9.   The EEOC asserts that the same standards it uses to assess claims of environmental sexual harassment—the plaintiff's subjective perception of "unwelcomeness" and an alteration of the conditions of the victim's employment or creation of an abusive working environment, viewed from the perspective of a reasonable person but taking the victim's [usually woman's] perspective into account—should also be used to decide harassment claims based on race, religion or national origin.   Enforcement Guidance on *Harris v. Forklift Systems, Inc.*, March 8, 1994, relying on Justice Ginsburg's concurring opinion in *Harris*.

Nevertheless, a supervisor's or co-worker's sexually aggressive or demeaning conduct that is unaccompanied by the imposition of detrimental tangible terms and conditions of employment is less likely to be undertaken pursuant to the alleged harasser's scope of authority and is therefore less fairly attributable to the employer. More stringent proof standards have accordingly been developed for these "hostile environment" claims.

In general, the federal courts require the "hostile environment" plaintiff to prove that he or she (1) is a member of a protected class; (2) was subjected to verbal, visual or physical conduct that was unwelcome; (3) suffered harassment that was based on one of the grounds prohibited by Title VII, for example, gender or race, as distinct from, say, sexual orientation or physical attractiveness; (4) suffered harassment of sufficient nature and magnitude to have created an intimidating, hostile or offensive work environment by unreasonably interfering with the plaintiff's work performance, creating an abusive work environment, or both; and (5) suffered harassment by the kind of personnel and in circumstances that should fasten liability on the employer under general principles of agency law.[48]

Element (2), whether the plaintiff was subjected to an advance that was "unwelcome," depends at the threshold on determining whether there was in fact an advance.[49] If there was an advance, its welcomeness vel non is determined by a subjective test. Until recently, sufficient evidence of the plaintiff's off-hours conduct and attitudes has sufficed to refute her assertion that workplace harassment was unwelcome. An employer may attempt to overcome a showing that an actionable level of interference was unwelcome with evidence about the plaintiff's past sexual conduct, "fantasies," or failure to object to sexual advances.[50] But recent decisions caution against equating participation in off-duty sex-related activities with acquiescence to sexual advances on the job. For example, evidence that the plaintiff had posed nude for a magazine

48. *See, e.g., Meritor, supra* note 20; *Ellison v. Brady,* 924 F.2d 872 (9th Cir.1991); *Carrero v. New York City Housing Authority,* 890 F.2d 569 (2d Cir.1989); *Hall v. Gus Construction Co.,* 842 F.2d 1010 (8th Cir. 1988); *Hicks v. Gates Rubber Company,* 833 F.2d 1406 (10th Cir.1987); *Rabidue v. Osceola Refining Co.,* 805 F.2d 611 (6th Cir. 1986), *cert. denied,* 481 U.S. 1041, 107 S.Ct. 1983, 95 L.Ed.2d 823 (1987); *Scott v. Sears, Roebuck & Co.,* 798 F.2d 210 (7th Cir.1986); *Henson v. City of Dundee,* 682 F.2d 897 (11th Cir.1982).

49. For trials commencing after December 1, 1994, Federal Rule of Evidence 415 provides that "evidence of that party's commission of another offense or offenses of sexual assault ... is admissible and may be considered as provided in Rule 413 ... of these rules." Such evidence "may be considered for its bearing on any matter to which it is relevant." Rule 413(a). *See* Rule 413(c). *See also* Duane "The New Federal Rules of Evidence on Prior Acts of Accused Sex Offenders: A Poorly Drafted Version of a Very Bad Idea," 157 F.R.D. 95, 115–118 (1994). *But see Frank v. County of Hudson,* 924 F.Supp. 620 (D.N.J.1996) (despite FRE 413 and 415, evidence of alleged harasser's abuse of stepdaughter years before events in question held inadmissible in employment discrimination action alleging his harassment of adult subordinates because probative value found outweighed by potential for prejudice).

50. *Meritor, supra* note 20. A recent decision holds as a matter of law that an advance is not subjectively unwelcome unless the victim perceives its offensiveness contemporaneously, rather than only later after a resignation. *Faragher v. City of Boca Raton,* 76 F.3d 1155 (11th Cir.1996).

did not negate her evidence that she did not welcome the employer's sexual advances in the workplace.[51]   Indeed even a plaintiff's "vulgar and unladylike" language and behavior on the job did not negate her showing that she did not welcome the crude sexual epithets, sexually insulting messages, and offensive demonstrative conduct (including urination and self-exposure) directed at her by her male co-workers.   On this issue it was important to the court that the plaintiff plainly resented their conduct and complained of it repeatedly to her supervisor.[52]

In *Meritor*, the Supreme Court recognized the relevance of a plaintiff's sexually provocative speech or dress to the question of unwelcomeness.   Yet Federal Rule of Evidence 412, as amended effective December 1, 1994, may rule out all but the most important probative evidence of the plaintiff's prior sexual behavior.[53]   Nevertheless, the potential inadmissibility of any such evidence would not necessarily prevent the employer from pursuing these topics in discovery.

By contrast, an objective test is used in assessing element (4). Whether conduct reaches a level of unreasonable interference with the employee's ability to work or creates a sufficiently intimidating work environment "should be evaluated from the objective standpoint of a 'reasonable person.' "[54]   Thus a "normal" level of workplace obscenity, isolated sexual suggestiveness or propositions, and even some single instances of unwelcome touching, may not amount to unreasonable interference.[55]   The circuit courts are still sorting out whether the

51. *Burns v. McGregor Electronic Industries*, 989 F.2d 959 (8th Cir.1993); *Swentek v. USAIR, Inc.*, 830 F.2d 552 (4th Cir.1987) (use of foul language or sexual innuendo in consensual setting does not waive plaintiff's protections against unwelcome on-the-job harassment); *cf. Williams v. District Court*, 866 P.2d 908 (Colo.1993) (information about defamation plaintiff's sexual history discoverable because it may lead to admissible evidence about his reputation relevant to his claim for damages, even if sexual history information not admissible on the issue whether employer failed promptly to investigate sexual harassment allegations against him).

52. *Carr v. Allison Gas Turbine Division*, 32 F.3d 1007 (7th Cir.1994).

53. FRE 412, applicable to trials commencing after December 1, 1994, now provides that in a civil action, "evidence offered to prove the sexual behavior or sexual predisposition of any alleged victim is admissible if ... its probative value *substantially* outweighs the danger of harm to any victim and of unfair prejudice to any party." Fed.R.Evid. 412(b)(2) (emphasis added).   This section also provides that evidence of the alleged victim's "reputation is admissible only if it has been placed in controversy by the alleged victim." That precondition, at least, would seem to be met

whenever a plaintiff alleges sexual harassment, since unwelcomeness is an essential element of that claim.   But the FRE 412 amendment tilts the scales against admissibility in three respects, as compared to standard probative value-prejudicial impact balancing under FRE 403.   First, it reverses the presumptive weighting, by requiring the proponent to justify admissibility rather than requiring the opponent to justify exclusion.   Second, the prerequisites for admissibility are more stringent, because the value of the proffered evidence must "substantially" outweigh the specified dangers.   Third, harm to the victim must be explicitly placed on the exclusion side of the balance, in addition to party prejudice.

54. "EEOC: Policy Guidance on Current Issues of Sexual Harassment," *supra* note 37.

55. *See McKenzie v. Illinois Dept. of Transportation*, 92 F.3d 473 (7th Cir. 1996) (reasonable person could not perceive any unreasonable interference with work environment as a result of three sexually suggestive comments over three-month period); *DeAngelis v. El Paso Mun. Police Officers Ass'n*, 51 F.3d 591 (5th Cir.), *cert. denied,* __ U.S. __, 116 S.Ct. 473, 133 L.Ed.2d 403 (1995) (derogatory references to plaintiff in police asso-

"person" from whose standpoint reasonableness should be assessed is the genderless prototype of torts litigation (the erstwhile "reasonable man") or a reasonable victim, usually, in this context, a woman.[56] The EEOC blurs this division, by advocating a "reasonable person" standard but adding that in applying that standard the factfinder "should consider the victim's perspective and not stereotyped notions of acceptable behavior." [57]

The Supreme Court recently attempted to delineate in somewhat greater detail the contours of the "abusive work environment" sufficient under *Meritor* to render environmental sexual harassment actionable. The lower courts in *Harris v. Forklift Systems, Inc.*[58] had denied recovery because a series of gender-related insults and unwanted sexual innuendos, although offensive to the hypothetical reasonable woman, were not shown to have seriously affected the plaintiff's psychological well-being.[59]

The Court located the required level of injury somewhere "between making actionable any conduct that is merely offensive and requiring the conduct to cause a tangible psychological injury." [60] Justice O'Connor's opinion for the majority reiterates that when the defendant's conduct consists entirely of uttering epithets or sexual innuendo, those must be sufficiently severe or pervasive "to create an objectively hostile or abusive work environment," one that a "reasonable person would find hostile or abusive." In addition, the victim must "subjectively perceive the environment to be abusive"; [61] otherwise there would be no alteration of the conditions of her employment.

But the opinion leaves open at least as many questions as it answers. The Court's invocation of the mantra that the environment the defendant creates must be "abusive" or "hostile" to a "reasonable" person (or woman) sheds little light. Justice O'Connor does little more

---

ciation newsletter too sporadic and infrequent and insufficiently offensive to alter working condition objectively). *Ellison, supra* note 48.

56. *Contrast Rabidue v. Osceola Refining Co.*, 805 F.2d 611 (6th Cir.1986), *cert. denied*, 481 U.S. 1041, 107 S.Ct. 1983, 95 L.Ed.2d 823 (1987) (reasonable person) *with Steiner v. Showboat Operating Co.*, 25 F.3d 1459 (9th Cir.1994); *Burns v. McGregor Electronic Industries*, 989 F.2d 959, 962 n. 3 (8th Cir.1993); *Ellison v. Brady*, 924 F.2d 872 (9th Cir.1991); *Andrews v. City of Philadelphia*, 895 F.2d 1469 (3d Cir.1990); *Yates v. Avco Corp.*, 819 F.2d 630 (6th Cir. 1987); and *Robinson v. Jacksonville Shipyards, Inc.*, 760 F.Supp. 1486 (M.D.Fla. 1991) (reasonable woman).

57. "Policy Guidance on Current Issues of Sexual Harassment," *supra* note 37. The Commission asserts that the Supreme Court also used a reasonable person standard in *Harris v. Forklift Systems, Inc. See*

"Enforcement Guidance on *Harris*," *supra* note 47. But the grant of certiorari did not include that issue, and Justice O'Connor's opinion for a unanimous Court did not focus on it.

58. 510 U.S. 17, 114 S.Ct. 367, 126 L.Ed.2d 295 (1993).

59. The Court thus had no occasion to choose between the viewpoint of the reasonable person or woman, since the lower courts rejected plaintiff's claim even from the reasonable woman's perspective.

60. *Id.* at ___, 114 S.Ct. at 370.

61. *Id.* This requirement has been held to demand that the plaintiff have a present-sense awareness—that is, while she is employed—of the unwelcomeness of the advance, as opposed to, say, a realization only after leaving the defendant's employ that the conduct in question offended her. *Faragher v. City of Boca Raton*, 76 F.3d 1155 (11th Cir.1996).

than identify a number of unweighted, nonexhaustive factors relevant to the "abusive" "hostile" environment question: the nature of the discriminatory conduct, i.e., whether it is merely offensive or also physically threatening or humiliating; the conduct's frequency and severity; and whether it unreasonably interfered with the plaintiff's work performance. None of these is identified as indispensable or even preeminent, and this leads the EEOC to conclude that none is.[62] In the end the Court holds only that psychological harm is just another, nonessential factor relevant to the issue of abusiveness.

Justice Ginsburg, concurring, opines that the inquiry should "center, dominantly, on whether the discriminatory conduct has interfered with the plaintiff's work performance."[63] For her this would mean showing only that the defendant's conduct made it more difficult for the plaintiff to do her job, and not that the plaintiff's productivity actually declined. A recent court of appeals decision appears to hold just that: a supervisor's sexual innuendo and banter was actionable because it was unwelcome and made it more difficult for plaintiff to do her job, even though it was not of sufficient severity to prevent her from timely meeting her work obligations. But as Justice Scalia, also concurring, observes, the *Harris* majority stopped short of holding that interference with the plaintiff's work performance alone signifies the ultimate criterion, alteration of the conditions of employment.

The *Harris* majority did write, quoting *Meritor*, that an "environmental" violation takes place when workplace intimidation, ridicule and insult are "sufficiently severe or pervasive to alter the conditions of the victim's environment *and* create an abusive working environment."[64] The required alteration of the conditions of the victim's work environment may be another way of saying that the defendant's conduct made it more difficult for the plaintiff to do her job. But as the quoted *dual* requirement suggests, there is force in Justice Scalia's point that the majority did not hold, as Justice Ginsburg would apparently have preferred, that a showing that the plaintiff's job has been made more difficult suffices. Adding to the uncertainty are recent decisions holding that although interference with the plaintiff's work performance may suffice to show the required, objectively determinable deterioration in her work environment, it is not essential to that showing. It is enough if the offensive conduct is shown, through the totality of the circumstances, to create an abusive work environment[65] or even just that it

---

62. "Enforcement Guidance on *Harris*," *supra* note 47. Thus, the Guidance asserts, the Court in *Harris* adopted the "totality of the circumstances" approach for the objective "abusive work environment" question as well as the subjective "unwelcomeness" issue, as previously advocated by the agency in its 1990 Policy Guidance "Current Issues of Sexual Harassment." Similarly, because no bright line separates merely vulgar banter (usually lawful) from a consistently hostile or severely abusive environment, the jury's verdict on this question must usually be respected. *Baskerville v. Culligan International Co.*, 50 F.3d 428 (7th Cir.1995).

63. 510 U.S. at ___, 114 S.Ct. at 372.

64. *Harris*, *supra* note 58, at ___, 114 S.Ct. at 370.

65. *King v. Hillen*, 21 F.3d 1572 (Fed. Cir.1994).

adversely affected plaintiff's daily working conditions.[66]

The environmental brand of sexual harassment, then, "is often a cumulative process rather than a onetime event. In its early stages, it may not ... cross the threshold that separates the nonactionable from the actionable ..., or may not cause sufficient distress ..., or may not have gone on long enough to charge the employer with knowledge and a negligent failure to take effective remedial measures." To avoid encouraging premature litigation, therefore, courts will give plaintiffs complaining of environmental sexual harassment the benefit of the "continuing violation" theory, which permits suit on conduct that occurred before the applicable limitations period where that conduct could only have been recognized, within that period, as actionable harassment in light of subsequently occurring events.[67]

Ordinarily the employer will be presumptively liable for otherwise actionable environmental harassment committed by a supervisor or other representative of management simply because the conduct occurred in the course and scope of the harasser's employment,[68] although some courts have limited employer responsibility to situations in which management-level employees knew or should have known of the supervisor's harassment.[69] An employer may even be held liable, on an "apparent authority" rationale, for environmental harassment by the plaintiff's co-workers or other relatively low-level personnel, or even a third party like a customer, but only where employer supervisory or managerial agents learn or should have learned of the conduct.[70] But if an employer

66. *Carr v. Allison Gas Turbine Division*, 32 F.3d 1007 (7th Cir.1994).

67. *Galloway v. General Motors Service Parts Operations*, 78 F.3d 1164 (7th Cir. 1996).

68. See, e.g., *Sauers v. Salt Lake County*, 1 F.3d 1122 (10th Cir.1993) (agency relationship sufficient to impose liability on employer for supervisor's harassment depends only on whether the supervisor possessed authority to control the work environment, whether or not employer knew of his conduct or was negligent in employing or retaining him). *See also Pierce v. Commonwealth Life Insurance Co.*, 40 F.3d 796, 803–804 (6th Cir.1994) (distinguishing the liability of employers for environmental harassment by supervisors from employer liability for environmental harassment by co-workers, which applies only if the employer knew or should have known of the harassment and failed to take immediate corrective action) (Kentucky law).

69. See *EEOC v. Hacienda Hotel*, 881 F.2d 1504, 1515–16 (9th Cir.1989). A former employer was relieved of liability for harassment by the plaintiff's supervisor where plaintiff failed to complain to supervisor's superior and evidence failed to show

that employer had learned of the alleged harassment before plaintiff resigned. *Andrade v. Mayfair Management, Inc.*, 88 F.3d 258 (4th Cir.1996). *Cf., Splunge v. Shoney's, Inc.*, 97 F.3d 488 (11th Cir.1996) (mere constructive knowledge of supervisors' harassment warrants compensation, but not punitive damages).

70. "EEOC Guidelines on Discrimination Because of Sex," 29 C.F.R. § 1604.11(d) (1993). *See Reed v. A.W. Lawrence & Co.*, 95 F.3d 1170 (2d Cir.1996) (employer knowledge of co-employee's behavior enables employer liability). *But see Zimmerman v. Cook County Sheriff's Dept.*, 96 F.3d 1017 (7th Cir.1996) (plaintiff must draw co-worker harassment to employer's attention through specific notice or complaint); *Doe v. R.R. Donnelley & Sons Co.*, 42 F.3d 439 (7th Cir.1994) (co-employee harassment not actually witnessed by plaintiff's supervisor or otherwise brought to employer's attention); *Pierce v. Commonwealth Life Insurance Co.*, 40 F.3d 796, 803 (6th Cir.1994). *See also Sauers v. Salt Lake County*, 1 F.3d 1122, 1125 (10th Cir. 1993); *Levendos v. Stern Entertainment, Inc.*, 909 F.2d 747, 752 (3d Cir.1990); *Vance v. Southern Bell Tel. & Tel. Co.*, 863 F.2d 1503, 1512 (11th Cir.1989) (applying

has promulgated, publicized, and enforced a clear and firm policy against sexual harassment, together with an effective and fair grievance procedure,[71] the EEOC believes that it may avoid liability not only for co-worker but also for supervisory sexual advances or other environmental harassment (unaccompanied by a tangible detriment to terms and conditions of employment) by taking timely and effective corrective action after notice. Because the employer requires such notice before it can take the steps necessary to overcome the plaintiff's showing, it may prove fatal to a victim's case if she does not promptly resort to a specific, well-publicized, legitimate, and established internal complaints procedure.[72] Expert testimony that few victims of sexual harassment complain contemporaneously has persuaded at least one court, however, to excuse some degree of tardiness in complaining.[73] On the other hand, the obligation to take remedial measures that is triggered by employer knowledge, imputed knowledge, or formal complaint requires employer action, and the defense fails if the employer does nothing, even if the harasser voluntarily ceases.[74]

Where there is a complaint to management of non-quid pro quo conduct—either informally, or through an internal grievance procedure, or by a formal charge with EEOC or a state or local antidiscrimination agency—the EEOC enforcement position would allow the employer to avoid liability by taking prompt and appropriate corrective action tailored to the severity of the offense.[75] Circuit decisions after *Harris*

the standards of "co-worker" cases where a low-level supervisor uses no actual or apparent authority to further the harassment); *Menchaca v. Rose Records*, 67 FEP 1334, 1995 WL 151847 (N.D.Ill.1995) (employer liable when manager stood by while regular customer allegedly harassed cashier). In one recent state court case an employer was even held liable for a *subordinate's* environmental harassment of a *supervisor* where the employer, despite knowledge, failed to take prompt remedial measures and indeed punished the supervisor! *Hanlon v. Chambers*, 195 W.Va. 99, 464 S.E.2d 741 (1995).

71. Both EEOC and the Supreme Court have suggested that such a procedure cannot be fair if it requires that the alleged victim lodge the complaint with the alleged harasser. See EEOC Guidelines and *Meritor*. By the same token, however, the employer must enjoy reasonable latitude to conduct a vigorous internal examination without risking additional charges of sexual harassment. Thus one court has held that even a hostile, unprofessional and abusive investigation of sexual harassment charges ultimately determined to be unfounded cannot be the basis of a separate sexual harassment claim by the exonerated suspect. *McDonnell v. Cisneros*, 84 F.3d 256 (7th Cir.1996).

72. *See* "Policy Guidance on Current Issues of Sexual Harassment," *supra* note 37; *Gary v. Long*, 59 F.3d 1391 (D.C.Cir.1995), *cert. denied,* ___ U.S. ___, 116 S.Ct. 569, 133 L.Ed.2d 493 (1995).

73. *Snider v. Consolidation Coal Co.*, 973 F.2d 555 (7th Cir.1992) *cert. denied* , 506 U.S. 1054, 113 S.Ct. 981, 122 L.Ed.2d 134 (1993).

74. *Reed v. A.W. Lawrence & Co.*, 95 F.3d 1170 (2d Cir.1996) (employer liable for co-worker harassment where it had not provided reasonable channels to complain.) *Fuller v. City of Oakland*, 47 F.3d 1522 (9th Cir.1995).

75. *See* "Policy Guidance on Current Issues of Sexual Harassment," *supra* note 37. For indications of the uncertainty surrounding the case-by-case appraisal of "appropriate" corrective action, *compare Spicer v. Commonwealth of Va. Dept. of Corrections*, 66 F.3d 705 (4th Cir.1995) (en banc) (counseling and training of supervisors deemed adequate response to co-worker harassment) *with Jeffries v. Metro–Mark, Inc.*, 45 F.3d 258 (8th Cir.1995) (employer response to co-worker racial harassment adequate where plaintiff reported only two of alleged multiple incidents). *See also Hirras v. National R.R. Passenger Corp.*, 95 F.3d 396 (5th Cir.1996) (investigatory efforts by employer suffice to avoid liability).

endorse this view.[76] They take the position that even if the conduct of the plaintiff's superior (or, a fortiori, co-worker) is sufficiently severe and pervasive to create an abusive or hostile environment and alter plaintiff's conditions of employment, the employing entity is not liable for that misconduct if its corrective measures, once notified of the environmental harassment, are timely and efficacious. Another circuit has relieved the employer of liability for sexual harassment by a supervisor where it found that the supervisor was not wielding "actual" authority, the plaintiff did not subjectively attribute his acts to the company, and she thought she had an available avenue of complaint to the company president.[77] Such decisions heighten the need for a resolution of the question whether supervisors may be held individually liable for Title VII violations as "agents" of the employer. See discussion earlier in this Chapter.

In one recent decision, however, the employer was held potentially liable for environmental harassment by a supervisor despite a lower court finding that it had provided a reasonable procedure for asserting complaints of harassment and had promptly investigated and fairly resolved the charge before it. The Second Circuit read *Meritor* to require lower courts to apply general agency principles to determine employer liability for *any* type of harassment by a supervisor, including the environmental variety. Applying those principles, the court found potential employer liability because the supervisor had been able to force the plaintiff to endure a "prolonged, violent, and demeaning sexual relationship" as a result of the employer's having delegated to him substantial authority to create a discriminatory and abusive work environment. So unlike pure agency or respondeat superior liability, the employer lost only because the particular supervisor used "his actual or apparent authority to further the harassment...." [78] The court's approach holds an employer liable for hostile environment discrimination attributable to the conduct of a supervisor almost as readily as for quid pro quo discrimination, that is even when the employer took prompt appropriate remedial action under available and arguably reasonable complaint procedures.[79]

76. *Waymire v. Harris County,* 86 F.3d 424 (5th Cir.1996) (reprimand considered prompt, adequate remedial action absolving employer of liability for coworker's harassment); *Fleenor v. Hewitt Soap Co.,* 81 F.3d 48 (6th Cir.1996) (employer absolved for coworker's harassment); *Saxton v. American Tel. & Tel. Co.,* 10 F.3d 526 (7th Cir. 1993); *Nash v. Electrospace System, Inc.,* 9 F.3d 401 (5th Cir.1993).

77. *Bouton v. BMW of North America, Inc.,* 29 F.3d 103 (3d Cir.1994).

78. *Karibian v. Columbia University,* 14 F.3d 773, 779–780 (2d Cir.1994). *Cf. Hicks v. Gates Rubber Co.,* 833 F.2d 1406 (10th Cir.1987) (supervisor's environmental harassment attributable to employer only if plaintiff relied on supervisor's apparent authority, supervisor used the agency relationship to further the harassment, or employer was negligent or reckless).

79. *But see Dennis v. County of Fairfax,* 55 F.3d 151 (4th Cir.1995) (employer that takes timely, adequate corrective action relieved of liability despite the nature or severity of the underlying wrongdoing). Perhaps in the end the divergent conclusions in these cases turn on the courts' assessment of whether the employer's corrective action was in fact adequate.

Because sexual harassment by a supervisor partakes of what tort law has termed a "frolic and detour," something outside his assigned duties, it is not surprising that employers have asserted rights to indemnity or contribution with respect to supervisory conduct that has resulted in employer liability. But the Supreme Court has held that no such right is provided by Title VII itself,[80] and there is authority that it is therefore inappropriate for a federal court to look to state law to fill the void.[81] "Reverse discrimination" claims by supervisors disciplined for violating their employer's anti-sexual harassment policy have not to date fared well.[82] The distinct likelihood that supervisor and employer defendants may have adverse interests and legal positions in sexual harassment litigation based on the hostile environment theory [83] also strongly suggests that they should be represented by separate counsel.

On the other hand, unsuccessful sexual harassment charges in litigation have spawned defamation suits by the alleged harasser against accusers and against employers who placed stock in the charges and took unilateral corrective action.

Prior to the Civil Rights Act of 1991, Title VII authorized only equitable remedies, including back pay and injunctive relief, and did not permit awards of compensatory or punitive damages. There was thus little incentive to sue under Title VII for the environmental version of sexual harassment, unaccompanied by the tangible threat or reality of job termination, demotion, or other adverse employment action that would result in a reduction or loss of pay or benefits. Where such cases were brought, the circuit courts divided on whether Title VII afforded any remedy for proven harassment that preceded a lawful discharge.[84] The Civil Rights Act of 1991 expressly authorizes compensatory and, except against government employers, punitive damages, capped in amounts that vary with size of employer, for "intentional" violations of Title VII.[85] Arguably most if not all racial and sexual harassment

80. *Northwest Airlines, Inc. v. Transport Workers Union*, 451 U.S. 77, 101 S.Ct. 1571, 67 L.Ed.2d 750 (1981).

81. *Gilmore v. List & Clark Construction Co.*, 866 F.Supp. 1310 (D.Kan.1994).

82. See, e.g., *Pierce v. Commonwealth Life Insurance Co.*, 40 F.3d 796 (6th Cir. 1994) (disciplined male supervisor's claim that his female subordinate engaged in even more egregious conduct but was not disciplined fails to state claim under Kentucky law because the female employee, who had no duty to enforce the employer's sexual harassment policy, was not "similarly situated").

83. Where the sole basis of employer liability is based on "quid pro quo" discrimination, it is less clear that the interests of separate employer and supervisor defendants are adverse. In that situation both defendants have a single, common escape from liability: preventing the the factfinder from concluding by a preponderance of the evidence that the plaintiff suffered a tangible job detriment or failed to receive a tangible job benefit because she refused to submit to a sexual demand by a representative of management with authority to impose the detriment or withhold the benefit.

84. *Contrast Huddleston v. Roger Dean Chevrolet, Inc.*, 845 F.2d 900 (11th Cir. 1988) (approving nominal damages) with *Swanson v. Elmhurst Chrysler Plymouth, Inc.*, 882 F.2d 1235 (7th Cir.1989) (no nominal damages), *cert. denied*, 493 U.S. 1036, 110 S.Ct. 758, 107 L.Ed.2d 774 (1990).

85. *See* Chapter 5, Section C for a complete discussion of remedies available under Title VII.

violations, would fall within this category, providing renewed impetus for the filing of hostile environment claims.

b. First Amendment Implications of Imposing Liability for Environmentally Harassing Speech

It seems even clearer after Harris that speech alone may violate Title VII. That is to say, there is little question that sexually offensive, demeaning or obscene speech or pictorial displays may alone adversely alter the conditions of the plaintiff's employment.[86] Few courts have addressed the constitutional problems that arise where the supervisor's or co-worker's allegedly harassing "conduct" consists entirely of speech or symbolic speech.[87] When that is so, federal regulation in the form of Title VII procedures and judicial sanctions implicates the First Amendment.[88] The situation is aggravated by the reality that employers have an incentive to overregulate the speech of their employees by taking the "prompt and effective corrective action" that the courts have held will absolve them of liability for the sins of co-workers and sometimes even supervisors.[89]

Two features of emerging harassment law fuel that incentive. First, as the vague *Harris* language underscores, the contours of the violation are vague. Generally courts have found that a plaintiff states a prima facie case under Title VII when the environment is pervasively disrespectful to women or minorities.[90] Similarly, sexual propositions in the workplace can create a hostile environment.[91] The only guidance given employers is that, "verbal conduct of a sexual nature [that] has the purpose or effect of unreasonably interfering with an individual's work performance or creating an intimidating, hostile, or offensive work

---

86. *See, e.g., Robinson v. Jacksonville Shipyards*, 760 F.Supp. 1486 (M.D.Fla. 1991) (liability predicated on displays of pornographic pinups and explicit sexual comments directed towards the plaintiff and other women).

87. Distinguishable from this situation is quid pro quo harassment, where the employment-related threat or benefit that hinges on compliance with a superior's sexual demand may itself be regarded as a form of conduct that violates Title VII, *see NLRB v. Gissel Packing Co.*, 395 U.S. 575, 89 S.Ct. 1918, 23 L.Ed.2d 547 (1969) (decision under National Labor Relations Act). Also less likely to raise First Amendment problems is gender-demeaning or stereotypical speech that the plaintiff cites as evidence that a distinct employment decision— a failure to promote, for instance—was based on a prohibited ground, as in *Price Waterhouse*.

88. *Cf. Baliko v. Stecker*, 275 N.J.Super. 182, 645 A.2d 1218 (App.Div.1994) (under State discrimination law). A district court in Minnesota considered and rejected the argument that Title VII's regulation of

speech infringed on the First Amendment. *Jenson v. Eveleth Taconite Co.*, 824 F.Supp. 847, 884 n. 89 (D.Minn.1993). This court determined that Title VII could proscribe conduct, including expression, occurring in the workplace when the same conduct could not be regulated outside the workplace. *Id.*

89. *See* Kingsley R. Browne, *Title VII as Censorship: Hostile–Environment Harassment and the First Amendment*, 52 Ohio.St. L.J. 481 (1991); *see also,* Jules B. Gerard, *The First Amendment in a Hostile Environment: A Primer on Free Speech and Sexual Harassment*, 68 Notre Dame L. Rev. 1003 (1993).

90. *See State v. Human Rights Commission*, 178 Ill.App.3d 1033, 128 Ill.Dec. 141, 534 N.E.2d 161 (1989); *Lipsett v. University of Puerto Rico*, 864 F.2d 881 (1st Cir.1988); *EEOC v. Murphy Motor Freight Lines, Inc.*, 488 F.Supp. 381 (D.Minn.1980); *Moffett v. Gene B. Glick Co.*, 621 F.Supp. 244 (N.D.Ind.1985).

91. *See Continental Can Co. v. State*, 297 N.W.2d 241 (Minn.1980); *Ellison v. Brady*, 924 F.2d 872 (9th Cir.1991).

environment" is harassment.[92]   Moreover, the existence of a hostile environment is determined by a totality of the circumstances test.   The employer is uncertain as to whether a hostile environment exists until the court makes that determination.

Second, it has now become almost a bromide within employer-defense circles it is settled that an effective policy and procedure against sexual harassment avoids employer liability for harassment by subordinate employees and for environmental harassment by supervisors. Accordingly, when, as will frequently be the case, the employer is in doubt, it has the incentive, in order to avoid the vagaries of liability for uncertain workplace speech and pictorial displays, to overregulate and overpunish.

Library References:

> C.J.S. Civil Rights §§ 172, 173.
> West's Key No. Digests, Civil Rights ⊸158.

§ 3.12   The Special Statutory Concept of "Religion"

Employers not qualifying for immunity from liability for religious discrimination under § 702 or § 703(e)(2), or for the BFOQ defense with respect to religiously-based hiring decisions (see Part A., above) are subject to a special affirmative obligation somewhat distinct from the normal duty not to discriminate.   Section 703(a)(1) forbids an employer from discriminating because of "religion"; and § 701(j), added in 1972, in turn defines "religion" to include "all aspects of religious observance and practice as well as belief, unless an employer demonstrates that he is unable to reasonably accommodate to an employee's . . . religious observance or practice without undue hardship. . . ."

At the threshold, when does an employer rule discriminate because of "religion"?   Circuit courts have assumed that employer rules excluding all but "Protestants" (no particular denomination required)[1] and preferring "Jesuits" (members of a Catholic order)[2] do draw distinctions on that prohibited statutory ground.   In the latter case, the panel rejected the approach suggested by a concurring judge who argued that rejection of the Jewish plaintiff was not on an unlawful ground.   Judge Posner wrote that plaintiff's rejection because he was not a Jesuit was *not* tantamount to a rejection for not being a Catholic, since a non-Jesuit Catholic would also have been denied the job.   Implicitly Posner's position was that adverse distinctions drawn on the basis of being or not being Jesuit are not actionable, while those relating to Catholicism are, even though only Catholics can be Jesuit.   This position could be

---

92. 29 C.F.R. § 1604.11(a).

§ 3.12

1. *EEOC v. Kamehameha, supra* § 3.6, note 5.

2. *Pime v. Loyola University, supra* § 3.6, note 5.

rephrased as an argument that discrimination on the basis of "religion-plus" (being Catholic *plus* being a Jesuit) is not prima facie unlawful while discrimination on the basis of religion alone is. As such, it seems discredited by the Supreme Court's rejection in *Phillips*[3] of the employer's assertion that its rule was not unlawful sex discrimination because it excluded not women alone but only those who shared the "plus" factor of having pre-school-aged children.[4]

On facts that sharpened the distinction between a religion and one of its orders, a later panel of the Seventh Circuit grappled with a Catholic plaintiff's claim that she was denied employment by another university because of sex and the school's Jesuit preference policy. The court rejected her claims, finding that she was denied an academic appointment not because of her gender but because her views did not conform to Catholic doctrine.[5] But if that were so, and if "religion" includes "all aspects of religious ... belief," why was she not held to have been discriminated against on the basis of religion, as she apparently claimed? Did the court perhaps place a sub rosa interpretive gloss on the statute to the effect that a defendant may lawfully discriminate against a Catholic on the basis of non-adherence to Catholic belief?[6]

More typically, the plaintiff complains of a particular employer practice that burdens the practice of his religion. The prima facie case consists of evidence that an employer practice conflicts with the employee's exercise of a sincerely held religious belief, that the employee has put the employer on notice of the conflict, and the employer has nevertheless imposed an employment detriment.[7] But two Supreme Court decisions have greatly eased the resulting employer obligation to reasonably accommodate the religious practice.

In *Ansonia*, the Court suggested that if an employer's schedule conflicts with the plaintiff's religious need to refrain from secular employment on holy days, the employer could ordinarily satisfy its accommodation obligation by offering the employee additional unpaid leave rather than affording additional paid leave. In particular, the employer

---

3. *Phillips v. Martin Marietta Corp.*, 400 U.S. 542, 91 S.Ct. 496, 27 L.Ed.2d 613 (1971), discussed *supra* § 3.11 at text accompanying notes 1 through 3.

4. This discussion is based on textual notes in Zimmer, Sullivan, Richards and Calloway, *Cases and Materials On Employment Discrimination* 647 (3d ed. Little Brown 1994).

5. *Maguire v. Marquette University*, 814 F.2d 1213, 1216–1217 (7th Cir.1987).

6. The authors of a noted casebook wonder further if in fact plaintiff *could* be considered a Catholic if her views conflicted with the established Catholic Church position. *Cases and Materials on Employment Discrimination, supra* note 4, at 649.

7. *See Ansonia Board of Education v. Philbrook*, 479 U.S. 60, 107 S.Ct. 367, 93 L.Ed.2d 305 (1986). It is unclear whether this prima facie showing under Title VII may now be made more easily by governmental employees who challenge employer burdens on the practice of their religion under the Religious Freedom Restoration Act of 1993, 42 U.S.C. § 2000bb et seq. RFRA requires government defendants to demonstrate that such a burden represents the least restrictive means to further a compelling governmental interest. RFRA has survived a recent establishment clause, separation of powers and Tenth Amendment challenge. *Flores v. City of Boerne*, 73 F.3d 1352 (5th Cir.1996).

was not required to accept the plaintiff's proffered fuller accommodation if the employer's own accommodation is "reasonable." The Court wrote that the employer there would violate Title VII only if it overtly discriminated against a religiously-necessitated employee absence if under similar circumstances it would provide paid leave for a non-religious reason. The Court therefore requires little more of an employer to meet this special statutory accretion to the definition of religion than to refrain from the ordinary kinds of disparate treatment or neutral-practice/disproportionate adverse impact.[8] (Contrast the far more substantial duty to accommodate disabilities under the ADA of 1990).

Second, the Court has held that an employer's reasonable accommodation, even as alleviated by *Ansonia*, works "undue hardship" whenever it results "in more than a *de minimis* cost."[9] An accommodation that requires the employer to hire an additional worker in order to permit the plaintiff to observe his religion every Saturday works undue hardship.[10] So do accommodations that permit a religious observer to skip assignments that would have to be picked up by others, or that allow the observer to work less than others, even if he reimburses the employer for the resulting additional costs.[11] Nor will a court likely require the employer to accommodate in a way that requires it to violate a collective bargaining agreement.[12] And when an employee's religious vow commanded her to wear an anti-abortion button that contained a graphic photograph, an employer was held to have adequately accommodated by permitting her to wear the button so long as the photograph was covered.[13] Largely because the duty to accommodate has thus been substantially diluted by judicial construction, § 701(j) has survived challenge under the First Amendment's Establishment Clause.[14]

8. *But cf.* Opuku–Buateng v. State of Calif., 95 F.3d 1461 (9th Cir.1996) (employer did not carry burden of persuading that proposed accommodation of voluntary shift trading would mark undue hardship); EEOC v. United Parcel Service, *94 F.3d 314 (7th Cir.1996) (directing trial court to consider whether permitting employee to wear beard in accordance with dictates of his religion, notwithstanding employer's beard ban for public contact positions, would work an undue hardship).*

9. *Trans World Airlines, Inc. v. Hardison*, 432 U.S. 63, 74 n. 9, 97 S.Ct. 2264, 2272 n. 9, 53 L.Ed.2d 113 (1977). *But see Brown v. Polk Co., Iowa*, 61 F.3d 650 (8th Cir.1995) (the hardship must be "real," not speculative, and employer had only shown that a supervisor's spontaneous prayers and affirmations of Christian belief would potentially polarize staff or make them fearful or uncomfortable), *cert. denied,* __ U.S. __, 116 S.Ct. 1042, 134 L.Ed.2d 189 (1996).

10. *Cooper v. Oak Rubber Co.*, 15 F.3d 1375 (6th Cir.1994).

11. *Lee v. ABF Freight System, Inc.*, 22 F.3d 1019 (10th Cir.1994).

12. *See TWA v. Hardison* and *Lee v. ABF Freight System, Inc., supra* note 11.

There is some circuit conflict concerning whether an employer meets its obligations when it refuses to alter a shift system even where no premium pay or significant efficiency loss would be entailed. *Compare Beadle v. Tampa*, 42 F.3d 633 (11th Cir. 1995), *cert. denied,* __ U.S. __, 115 S.Ct. 2600, 132 L.Ed.2d 846 (1995) (accommodation adequate) *with Brown v. General Motors Corp.*, 601 F.2d 956 (8th Cir.1979) (accommodation insufficient).

13. *Wilson v. U.S. West Communications*, 58 F.3d 1337 (8th Cir.1995).

14. *Protos v. Volkswagen of America, Inc.*, 797 F.2d 129 (3d Cir.), *cert. denied,* 479 U.S. 972, 107 S.Ct. 474, 93 L.Ed.2d 418 (1986). But if Title VII's requirement is violated, so is the Free Exercise Clause. *Brown, supra* n. 9.

Library References:

C.J.S. Civil Rights §§ 159, 165.
West's Key No. Digests, Civil Rights ☞151.

E. PARTICULAR PRACTICES GIVEN SPECIAL STATUTORY TREATMENT

§ 3.13 Wage Discrimination and the Interrelationship With EPA

As discussed below in Chapter VIII, the EPA prohibits only sex-based pay differentials for "equal work," defined to mean jobs involving substantially the same skill, effort, and responsibility. EPA also contains four listed affirmative defenses to a claim of unequal pay for equal work.

The "Bennett Amendment" to Title VII, the last sentence of § 703(h), attempts to harmonize the two statutes' treatment of sex-based wage discrimination. It provides that a successful affirmative defense to an EPA claim does double duty as a defense to liability under Title VII. Lower courts are divided, however, on the converse question, whether EPA liability automatically means Title VII liability as well.[1] See Chapter VII, Section D for a complete discussion of the differences between EPA and Title VII.

On the other hand, intentional sex-based wage discrimination may violate Title VII even if no member of the opposite sex performs "equal work" within the meaning of EPA.[2] But the related "comparable worth" theory has generally been rejected. An employer does not violate Title VII merely by observing market norms that result in its paying more for male-dominated jobs than for female-dominated jobs that have similar value to the employer but would not be considered "equal" under EPA.[3] Nor can the Equal Pay Act be used to assert a claim for equal benefits based on the alleged "comparable worth" of male- and female-dominated jobs when those jobs do not entail the substantially equal skill, effort and responsibility that EPA claims require.[4] See Chapter VIII, Section F for a fuller discussion of the theory of comparable worth.

Even without explicit authorizing text in EPA, the circuit courts have held unlawful employer retaliation against employees for asserting

---

§ 3.13

1. *Compare EEOC v. White and Son Enterprises,* 881 F.2d 1006 (11th Cir.1989) *and Kouba v. Allstate Insurance Co.,* 691 F.2d 873, 875 (9th Cir.1982) (automatic Title VII liability) *with Tidwell v. Fort Howard Corp.,* 989 F.2d 406 (10th Cir.1993) (Equal Pay Act evidence did not show intentional discrimination violative of Title VII) *and Fallon v. Illinois,* 882 F.2d 1206 (7th Cir.1989) (Title VII liability standard is higher, since plaintiff bears burden of persuasion throughout).

2. *County of Washington v. Gunther,* 452 U.S. 161, 101 S.Ct. 2242, 68 L.Ed.2d 751 (1981); *EEOC v. Reichhold Chemicals, Inc.,* 988 F.2d 1564 (11th Cir.1993).

3. *See American Federation of State, County and Municipal Employees v. State of Washington,* 770 F.2d 1401 (9th Cir.1985), *rehearing denied,* 813 F.2d 1034 (9th Cir. 1987).

4. *Beavers v. American Cast Iron Pipe Co.,* 975 F.2d 792 (11th Cir.1992).

an EPA claim or protesting an EPA violation.[5]

Library References:

C.J.S. Civil Rights § 174.
West's Key No. Digests, Civil Rights ☞161.

§ 3.14 Restrictions Relative to Pregnancy and Abortion

The Pregnancy Discrimination Act of 1978, or "PDA," added to Title VII a new § 701(k). This amendment defines the sex discrimination prohibited by § 703 to include distinctions "on the basis of pregnancy, childbirth or related medical conditions...." The PDA, in other words, effectively equates pregnancy discrimination with discrimination "because of sex" within the meaning of § 703. Refusing to hire or firing someone because she is pregnant therefore violates § 703, and such a violation is a form of facial or express gender discrimination, defensible only by establishing a BFOQ. The PDA thus accomplishes the objective that principally motivated its enactment, overturning the Court's conclusion in *General Electric Co. v. Gilbert*[1] that discrimination based on pregnancy is not based on gender.

The PDA does not require an employer to provide leaves or benefits for pregnancy that it does not provide to male employees for "comparable" conditions; as the Court wrote in *California Federal Savings & Loan Ass'n v. Guerra,*[2] the amendment's dominant principle is nondiscrimination, rather than preference. PDA does not even require an employer to provide *any* leaves or benefits for pregnancy if it treats similar disabilities the same.[3] For the same reason, the Act does not require

5. *See, e.g., EEOC v. White and Son Enterprises*, 881 F.2d 1006 (11th Cir.1989).

§ 3.14

1. 429 U.S. 125, 97 S.Ct. 401, 50 L.Ed.2d 343 (1976). *See* discussion of *Gilbert* earlier in this chapter, at text accompanying note 3, § 3.11 supra.

2. 479 U.S. 272, 286–87, 107 S.Ct. 683, 692–93, 93 L.Ed.2d 613 (1987).

3. *Barrash v. Bowen*, 846 F.2d 927 (4th Cir.1988) (per curiam). *See also Hishon v. King & Spalding*, 467 U.S. 69, 75, 104 S.Ct. 2229, 2233, 81 L.Ed.2d 59 (1984) (Title VII only requires equal treatment of employees if and after an employer has decided to provide a benefit). *But see* "EEOC: Policy Guidance On Parental Leave," 405 FEP Man. 6885 (8/27/90) (acknowledging that Title VII does not require an employer to provide a parental or child care leave but cautioning that conditioning such a leave on a facially neutral criterion—for example, authorizing the leave only for working spouses—may constitute an unlawful employment practice if it results in a disproportionate adverse impact on one or another gender). A circuit court has recently

expressly approved use of the neutral practice/disproportionate adverse impact proof mode in a case under PDA. *Garcia v. Woman's Hospital of Texas,* ___ F.3d ___ (5th Cir.1996) (weight lifting requirement). See *Chapter 4 on the required "adverse impact" proof.*

The Supreme Court has also construed the provision of the Federal Unemployment Tax Act that forbids states from denying benefits because of pregnancy not to require a state to treat pregnancy more favorably than other disabilities. In *Wimberly v. Labor & Industrial Relations Comm.*, 479 U.S. 511, 107 S.Ct. 821, 93 L.Ed.2d 909 (1987), the Court upheld a state unemployment compensation statute that deemed all disability leaves unsupported by good cause, with no exception for maternity. It is clear that neither *Guerra* nor *Wimberly* would permit an employer to treat pregnancy disadvantageously relative to other disabilities. But while *Guerra* holds that the PDA does not prohibit preferential employer treatment of pregnancy mandated by state law, at least in the limited sphere of actual physical disability, it does not hold that PDA itself mandates such treatment; and *Wim-*

more indulgence for absence [4] or tardiness [5] occasioned by pregnancy than for absences or tardiness attributable to any other ailment or medical condition.

On the other hand, as *Guerra* held, the Act does not preempt state legislation that preferentially treats pregnant employees by affirmatively requiring employers to offer leave benefits to pregnancy-disabled employees that the employer does not offer to others.[6] The Court has since explained that the state statute in question was not preempted because it "was not inconsistent with the purposes of the . . . [PDA] and did not require an act that was unlawful under Title VII." [7] Similarly, an employer is not forbidden from offering greater health insurance benefits for pregnancy than for other medical conditions as a matter of contract.[8] On the other hand, an employer may not give female parents child care leaves, keyed to childbirth rather than to pregnancy disability, if fathers are denied leave under similar circumstances.[9]

There are some tensions and apparent contradictions in the patchwork of holdings under the PDA. How, for example, could *Guerra* affirm that the PDA enacts a nondiscrimination principle but then sustain state-mandated preferential employer treatment of pregnancy-related disabilities as not inconsistent with PDA's purposes? Why should a woman asserting a PDA violation be relieved of showing that a man received better treatment, if PDA enshrines only a principle of nondiscrimination? [10] If, on the other hand, PDA contemplates preferential handling of pregnancy, why have EEOC and lower courts since limited the permissible preference to periods of actual physical disability, and not to subsequent child-rearing leaves? The answers reside in the awkward construction of PDA's text and the history antedating its enactment.

---

berly makes it clear that in any event no such preferential treatment is not mandated by FUTA.

4. *Bush v. Commonwealth Edison Co.*, 990 F.2d 928, 931 (7th Cir.1993), *cert. denied*, ___ U.S. ___, 114 S.Ct. 1648, 128 L.Ed.2d 367 (1994); *Rush v. McDonald's Corp.*, 966 F.2d 1104, 1107 (7th Cir.1992).

5. *Troupe v. May Department Stores Co.*, 20 F.3d 734 (7th Cir.1994).

6. *California Federal Savings & Loan Association v. Guerra*, 479 U.S. 272, 107 S.Ct. 683, 93 L.Ed.2d 613 (1987).

7. *Johnson Controls*, 499 U.S. at 209, 111 S.Ct. at 1209 (distinguishing the possible tort liability that might be imposed on an employer who obeys *Johnson Controls'* interpretation of the PDA by permitting a fertile employee to work at a job that might endanger the health of her fetus; such tort liability would be preempted because it would "punish employers for *complying* with Title VII's clear command") (citing *Florida Lime & Avocado Growers, Inc. v.*

Paul, 373 U.S. 132, 142–43, 83 S.Ct. 1210, 1217–18, 10 L.Ed.2d 248 (1963)). *See* Grover, "The Employer's Fetal Injury Quandary After *Johnson Controls*," 81 Ky.L.J. 639 (1992–93).

8. *Aubrey v. Aetna Life Ins. Co.*, 886 F.2d 119 (6th Cir.1989).

9. *Schafer v. Board of Public Educ.*, 903 F.2d 243 (3d Cir.1990); *Barnes v. Hewlett–Packard Co.*, 846 F.Supp. 442 (D.Md.1994).

10. Where an employer terminated an employee who, as the result of pregnancy complications, took an amount of sick leave that was within the limitations of the employer's stated leave policy, a circuit court held that she was not required to show that a nonpregnant employee was treated more favorably under similar circumstances. Rather, it was the employer's burden to show the "unusual scenario" that it had discharged others for using their allotted leave. *Byrd v. Lakeshore Hospital*, 30 F.3d 1380 (11th Cir.1994).

The legislative history reflects PDA's principal purposes: not only to overturn the result of *Gilbert*, which dealt with leaves for still-disabled pregnant workers, but also to assure that working women would not be treated adversely respecting pregnancy disability or benefits relative to employees with other disabilities. The two clauses of the first sentence of § 701(k) attempt to implement these purposes, the first clause by addressing *Gilbert*, the second by enshrining a broad principle of nondiscrimination:

> The terms "because of sex" or "on the basis of sex" include, but are not limited to, because of on or on the basis of pregnancy, childbirth, or related medical conditions; and women affected by pregnancy, childbirth, or related medical conditions shall be treated the same for all employment-related purposes ... as other persons not so affected but similar in their ability or inability to work....

The second clause, which the Court has read as merely illustrative of and not exhausting the reach of the first,[11] asserts the standard equal treatment or nondiscrimination principle characteristic of Title VII liability. Women affected by pregnancy-related medical conditions "shall be treated the same" as, but not better than, other employees with similarly disabling conditions. The definition in the first clause, by clarifying that the § 703(a) prohibition on discrimination against an individual "because of sex" includes discrimination based on "medical conditions" related to pregnancy or childbirth, takes care of the holding of *Gilbert*. But considered in isolation that clause may also be read to accord special treatment, at least for pregnancy-related *medical conditions*, since it requires no similarly situated male employee comparator.[12] Hence *Guerra* could plausibly assert, by reference to the second clause, that PDA does not by its own force require covered employers to offer pregnant workers better leaves than those offered others for similarly disabling conditions, and at the same time assert, by reference to the first clause, that PDA's "purposes" are not offended by state laws that mandate (or apparently by voluntary employer policies that offer) preferential treatment of pregnancy during a "period of *actual physical disability*."[13]

By thus conferring somewhat schizoid protection, Congress has left the courts to unravel a number of related interpretive difficulties. Suppose an employer acknowledges that the plaintiff's pregnancy played a part in its decision not to hire her,[14] to place her on involuntary

---

11. *Newport News Shipbuilding & Dry Dock Co. v. EEOC*, 462 U.S. 669, 679 n. 14, 103 S.Ct. 2622, 2629 n. 14, 77 L.Ed.2d 89 (1983). *Accord Guerra*, 479 U.S. at 284, 107 S.Ct. at 691.

12. *See, e.g., Newport News*, 462 U.S. at 684–685, 103 S.Ct. at 2631–2632 (asserting that PDA "has now made clear that, for all Title VII purposes, discrimination based on a woman's pregnancy is, on its face [and

without more], discrimination because of her sex.").

13. 479 U.S. at 290, 107 S.Ct. at 694 (emphasis in original).

14. *See Marafino v. St. Louis County Circuit Court*, 707 F.2d 1005 (8th Cir.1983). *Cf. Boyd v. Harding Academy of Memphis, Inc.*, 88 F.3d 410 (6th Cir.1996) (employer's termination of pregnant teacher held on basis of her extramarital sexual relation-

disability leave,[15] or even to terminate her,[16] but also demonstrates that the adverse action was taken in accordance with a neutral, evenly applied disability rule that would have disqualified similarly disabled men or other women. Here the equal treatment approach has prevailed and liability rejected.

Where, on the other hand, the plaintiff simply produces evidence that the adverse action was based on pregnancy,[17] and the employer fails to offer comparative evidence involving the disabilities of other employees, the first clause of the PDA has supported the per se equation of distinctions based on pregnancy with discrimination "because of sex." [18] In effect this was the path the Supreme Court followed in *International Union, U.A.W. v. Johnson Controls*,[19] where an employer rule denying women jobs in positions where they would encounter special levels of lead was applied only to fertile, not all women. Finally, the permission for employers to accord pregnancy preferential treatment that is inferable from the first clause is sharply circumscribed. *Guerra* is reasonably clear that PDA does not mandate such treatment, and so does not require an employer to afford reasonable accommodation to pregnancy by offering *any* leaves, benefits or relaxed work assignments that it does not offer to employees with other disabilities.[20] And *Guerra* also sug-

---

ship, rather than her pregnancy, and hence not violative of Title VII, even though she was fired only when she became pregnant and not a year earlier when she had miscarried).

15. *EEOC v. Detroit–Macomb Hospital Corp.*, 952 F.2d 403 (6th Cir.1992).

16. *See Morrocco v. Goodwill Indus.*, 1993 WL 268625 (M.D.N.C.1993). The author is indebted to Professors Zimmer and his colleagues for these three examples, set forth at Zimmer, Sullivan, Richards and Calloway's *Cases and Materials On Employment Discrimination* 540 (3d ed. Little Brown 1994).

17. It is not always self-evident if the employer took the challenged action "because" of pregnancy even when pregnancy is the visible trigger for invocation of a broader employer rule. *See, e.g., Fleming v. Ayers & Associates*, 948 F.2d 993 (6th Cir.1991) (discharge of plaintiff because of the high medical costs of caring for her hydrocephalic child held not because of her pregnancy and indeed unrelated to the fact that plaintiff was a woman); *Marafino v. St. Louis County Circuit Court, supra* note 14 (employer demonstrated that its practice was not to hire anyone, including the pregnant plaintiff, who would require a leave soon after starting work). And plaintiff has the burden of showing the employer's knowledge of her pregnant status. *Geraci v. Moody–Tottrup Int'l Inc.*, 82 F.3d 578 (3d Cir.1996).

18. *See, e.g., Byrd v. Lakeshore Hospital, supra,* see note 10 and accompanying text; *Tamimi v. Howard Johnson Co.*, 807 F.2d 1550 (11th Cir.1987) (court found requirement that plaintiff wear makeup attributable to her pregnancy and employer's view that she was "less attractive when pregnant"); *Maddox v. Grandview Care Center*, 780 F.2d 987 (11th Cir.1986) (maternity leave, and none other, limited to three months).

19. 499 U.S. 187, 111 S.Ct. 1196, 113 L.Ed.2d 158 (1991).

20. *See, e.g., Armstrong v. Flowers Hosp., Inc.*, 33 F.3d 1308 (11th Cir.1994) (PDA did not require a hospital to accommodate a pregnant nurse's request that she be reassigned so as not to have to treat a patient with AIDS, because PDA does not require preferential treatment). Similarly, the PDA does not confer immunity on a pregnant employee from the ordinary consequences of employer decisions taken for reasons unrelated to her pregnancy. *Smith v. F.W. Morse & Co.*, 76 F.3d 413 (1st Cir.1996) (plaintiff's position eliminated during her pregnancy because manager concluded position was redundant; fact that this decision coincided with pregnancy and followed manager's questions about the plaintiff's plans to have more children generated inference of discriminatory animus for trier of fact to resolve but did not suffice to establish a per se violation of PDA). *But cf. Quaratino v. Tiffany & Co.*, 71 F.3d 58

gests that voluntary preferential treatment of pregnancy is probably offensive to the overarching Title VII principle of nondiscrimination when it relates to pregnancy-related circumstances other than associated medical conditions. Viewed this way, PDA eases proof of liability for pregnancy-based intentional discrimination, but carves out only a very limited arena for preferential treatment.

Although the legislative history of PDA focused on the health and medical requirements of female employees, a majority of the Court has held that the amendment also prohibits employer-sponsored health insurance provisions that exclude spousal pregnancies and thereby offer male employees inferior total coverage than their female co-workers.[21] PDA also proscribes discriminating against an employee for undergoing an abortion, either by terminating her employment or, apparently, denying her sick leave available for other medical disabilities. But PDA explicitly relieves employers from subsidizing abortions through health insurance benefits, except in cases of "medical complications" or "where the life of the mother would be endangered if the fetus were carried to term."

Courts are still exploring the full reaches of the medical conditions related to pregnancy with respect to which the PDA applies. In *International Union, U.A.W. v. Johnson Controls*,[22] the Supreme Court held prima facie violative of PDA employer policies precluding fertile women from holding certain jobs in which their fetuses would be exposed to workplace environment health risks. Employers justified these rules as necessary to protect employees' fetuses or offspring from health risks, or to protect the employer from tort liability in the event employees' fetuses or children suffered injury that could be traced to the workplace. In effect the Court treated a woman's potential *capacity* to become pregnant as pregnancy itself or one of her [23] "related medical conditions"

(2d Cir.1995) (position-elimination defense may be overcome by evidence that management considered replacing plaintiff well before her leave commenced and interviewed a non-pregnant woman for her job).

21. *Newport News Shipbuilding and Dry Dock Co. v. EEOC*, 462 U.S. 669, 103 S.Ct. 2622, 77 L.Ed.2d 89 (1983). This result is also somewhat strange in view of the text and history of PDA. The first clause, defining "because of sex," works in tandem with the § 703(a) prohibition on discrimination against an individual concerning "his" (or, where appropriate, "her") terms or conditions of employment because of "such individual's" gender. That clause doesn't easily fit the facts of *Newport News*, where the employer deprived male employees of a benefit not by reference to their own gender but because of the pregnant condition, and hence under § 701(k) the gender, of their spouses. The second clause is no more easily adapted to *Newport News*. The "women affected by

pregnancy" there were the plaintiffs' spouses, not employees of the defendant employer. How, then, could they have been treated differently from "other persons not so affected but similar in their ability or inability to work"?

22. 499 U.S. 187, 111 S.Ct. 1196, 113 L.Ed.2d 158 (1991).

23. Where an employer discharged a woman because of the high medical costs of caring for her child, however, no liability was found because, the court reasoned, "related medical conditions" as used in PDA refers to conditions of "pregnant women, not conditions of the resulting offspring." *Fleming v. Ayers & Associates*, 948 F.2d at 996–97. Similarly, the Supreme Court observed in passing in *Newport News* that an employer's exclusion of benefits for the pregnancy-related medical expenses of relatives, as distinct from spouses, would not violate PDA. Denying benefits to those relatives—daughters or mothers, for exam-

that triggers PDA protection. Presumably, then, *Johnson Controls* also provides support for the preexisting lower court decisions that have treated childrearing within the broad concept of "related medical conditions." Citing *Johnson Controls*, a district court has recently swept within PDA's embrace discrimination against a woman who was absent from work because of treatments for infertility. The opinion reasoned that she, too, was discriminated against because of "potential or intended pregnancy"; her inability to become pregnant without medical intervention was akin to the natural ability of fertile women to become pregnant that was protected in *Johnson Controls*.[24] But under the compromise course the courts have steered between the two key clauses of § 701(k), medical or physical conditions on the fore or aft periphery of pregnancy should be handled under the nondiscrimination principle, with voluntary employer preference reserved for the sphere of the plaintiff's own actual physical disability.[25]

While PDA thus does not compel employers covered by Title VII to afford maternity leaves or benefits not provided for other disabilities, the Family & Medical Leave Act of 1993[26] requires employers with 50 or more employees to permit eligible employees, female and male alike, to take up to twelve weeks of unpaid leave per year after the birth or adoption of a child, as well as for serious health emergencies affecting the employee or his close relatives.[27]

Library References:

C.J.S. Civil Rights § 172.
West's Key No. Digests, Civil Rights ⬤162.

§ 3.15   Fetal Vulnerability Rules

Because, as just observed, fetal vulnerability rules are prima facie subject to PDA, they must be treated as a form of express gender discrimination that can survive scrutiny only if they pass muster under the BFOQ defense. That, however, is unlikely under traditional BFOQ standards, since protection of employees' offspring would not normally be essential to the operation of an employer's business. In order to uphold these rules as a matter of public policy or personal morality,

ple—would adversely affect the terms and conditions of female as well as male employees, whereas denial of benefits for the pregnancy-related expenses of spouses adversely affects male employees only.

24. *Pacourek v. Inland Steel Co.,* 858 F.Supp. 1393 (N.D.Ill.1994). And a circuit court has held that PDA protects employees from termination not only for exercising the right to have an abortion, but, by analogous extension from *Johnson Controls,* also for contemplating an abortion. *Turic v. Holland Hospitality, Inc.,* 85 F.3d 1211 (6th Cir.1996).

25. Thus a circuit court has recently rejected the reasoning of *Pacourek, supra,*

holding that a penalty on infertility, unlike potential pregnancy, is not related to sex, at least where the policy is or might be applied to exclude health care benefits to infertile males as well as females. *Krauel v. Iowa Methodist Medical Center,* 95 F.3d 674 (8th Cir.1996).

26. Pub. L. No. 103–3, 29 U.S.C.A. §§ 2601–2654.

27. For details about the eligibility requirements and ancillary protections surrounding the leaves mandated by FMLA, as well as funding provisions, see Malin, "Fathers and Parental Leave," 72 *Tex.L.Rev.* 1047, 1079 *et seq.* (1994).

courts sometimes modified the BFOQ requirements or permitted the policies to be defended as though they were neutral practices.[1] EEOC also took the position that even though the discrimination resulting from fetal protection policies is expressly gender based, employers should not be restricted to the BFOQ defense but should be permitted to justify those policies under the somewhat less stringent standard of "business necessity."[2]

The Supreme Court has since definitively rejected these end-runs around the PDA, ruling that fetal protection policies exclude fertile women from employment opportunities on the basis of gender and are accordingly defensible only as BFOQs. Further, the Court stringently applied the BFOQ defense. In attempting to prove that fertile employees lacked essential job qualifications, employers had sought to justify their exclusion by invoking protection of the fetus. The Court held that the safety of an employee's fetus, as distinct from the safety of plant visitors or customers, is not essential to the operation of the employer's business in the sense meant by the BFOQ defense.[3] Perhaps the broadest significance of *Johnson Controls* is its explication of dual requirements for any BFOQ. Not only must the employer's gender-, religion- or national origin-based exclusion substantially relate to the plaintiff's ability to perform her particular job; it must also go to the "essence" or "central mission" of the employer's business.[4]

Library References:

> C.J.S. Civil Rights § 172.
> West's Key No. Digests, Civil Rights ⇒162.

§ 3.16 Seniority Systems

Two unarguably neutral practices are singled out for special treatment by the text of Title VII. Section 703(h) provides that "notwithstanding any other provision" of Title VII, an employer does not commit an unlawful employment practice by imposing different terms or conditions of employment pursuant to a bona fide seniority or merit system. The employer is immune from liability even if the effect or impact of these systems falls more heavily on the plaintiff's protected group.

§ 3.15

1. *See International Union, UAW v. Johnson Controls*, 886 F.2d 871 (7th Cir. 1989), *reversed by* , 499 U.S. 187, 111 S.Ct. 1196, 113 L.Ed.2d 158 (1991); cf. *Hayes v. Shelby Memorial Hospital*, 726 F.2d 1543 (11th Cir.1984) (invalidating employer policy despite relaxed standards).

2. "EEOC: Policy Statement of Reproductive and Fetal Hazards Under Title VII," (10/7/88). *But cf.* "EEOC: Policy Guide on Supreme Court's *Johnson Controls* Decision," 405 FEP Man. 6941 (6/28/91) (reinstating BFOQ standard after *Johnson Controls*).

3. *International Union, UAW v. Johnson Controls, Inc.*, 499 U.S. 187, 111 S.Ct. 1196, 113 L.Ed.2d 158 (1991).

4. 499 U.S. at 201, 111 S.Ct. at 1204. *Johnson Controls* is discussed in greater detail in connection with the § 703(e)(2) exemption for religious institutions treated above and, especially, the defense of "bona fide occupational qualification" in Chapter 4.

Judicial construction of these provisions, however, has afforded far greater protection for seniority and merit systems than for professionally developed ability tests.

Unless the plaintiff is able to prove that a seniority system was initially adopted or maintained with a specific discriminatory purpose, and is thus not "bona fide," a seniority system cannot be the basis of employer liability.[1] And such a system is lawful even though it was first *adopted* after the enactment of Title VII.[2] Absent proof of discriminatory purpose by the employer and union in adopting or maintaining such a system, § 703(h) insulates a bona fide seniority system from being declared an unlawful employment practice notwithstanding that it perpetuates underlying hiring, assignment or promotion discrimination that took place before or even after the effective date of Title VII.[3] Thus a bona fide system may not be dismantled wholesale by declaratory judgment or injunction. But where other, primary unlawful employment practices are proved—hiring, assignment, or promotion discrimination, for example—courts have the remedial authority in effect to adjust the system's seniority ladder incrementally by awarding retroactive seniority for bidding or other competitive purposes to proven victims of discrimination.[4]

A system will not forfeit its status as bona fide merely because it has the effect of disproportionately "locking in" minority employees to lower paying or less skilled positions—for example, by discouraging them from transferring to better jobs in separate bargaining units where they might forfeit accumulated seniority with the company. The mere impact of the system does not standing alone demonstrate the requisite discriminatory purpose.[5] Factors in assessing a system's bona fides include whether it discourages different protected groups equally from transferring between units; whether, if the seniority units are in separate bargaining units, the bargaining unit structure is rational and conforms to industry practice; whether the system has its "genesis" in prohibited discrimination; and whether subsequent negotiations that have maintained the system were tainted by unlawful motivation.[6]

§ 3.16

1. *International Brotherhood of Teamsters v. United States*, 431 U.S. 324, 97 S.Ct. 1843, 52 L.Ed.2d 396 (1977).

2. *American Tobacco Co. v. Patterson*, 456 U.S. 63, 102 S.Ct. 1534, 71 L.Ed.2d 748 (1982); *United Air Lines, Inc. v. Evans*, 431 U.S. 553, 97 S.Ct. 1885, 52 L.Ed.2d 571 (1977).

3. *Teamsters, supra* note 1.

4. *See* the discussion in Chapter 5 of *Franks v. Bowman Transportation Company*, 424 U.S. 747, 96 S.Ct. 1251, 47 L.Ed.2d 444 (1976), as modified by the remedial portion of the *Teamsters* opinion.

5. *Teamsters, supra* note 1; *James v. Stockham Valves & Fittings*, 559 F.2d 310, 352 (5th Cir.1977), *cert. denied* , 434 U.S. 1034, 98 S.Ct. 767, 54 L.Ed.2d 781 (1978). An apparent exception is represented by *EEOC v. E.I. Du Pont de Nemours & Co.*, 1992 WL 465707 (W.D.Ky.1992), where the court relied heavily on the fact that more than 98% of the higher paying jobs were held by white employees in condemning as non-bona fide a seniority system that had been in operation for fifteen years, including eight years after the effective date of Title VII.

6. *James, supra* note 5 at 352.

The Court has broadly interpreted the kinds of collectively bargained arrangements that qualify as "seniority systems" entitled to the special protection of § 703(h). For example, a requirement that an employee work for a specified time *before* entering the permanent employee seniority ladder has itself been held to constitute part of a protected seniority system.[7] On occasion, however, a plaintiff has succeeded in sidestepping § 703(h) by framing a challenge to an employer decision that is related to but distinct from the functioning of a seniority system.[8]

The seniority system defense is bolstered in procedural ways as well. First, even though the structure and text of § 703(h) appear to create a true affirmative defense, the employer does not have to persuade the court that the system is bona fide. The employer is well advised to plead the defense affirmatively in its answer. But in response to a plaintiff's prima facie evidence that a facially neutral system had disproportionate adverse impact, the employer need only prove that the personnel decision in question was made pursuant to that system.[9] To overcome the defense the *plaintiff* must then prove by jurisprudence that the system is *not* bona fide.[10] Second, the Supreme Court has held that trial court determinations about the adopters' intent—the ultimate issue on the bona fides of a seniority system—are unmixed findings of fact, reversible under Federal Rule of Civil Procedure 52(a) only if "clearly erroneous."[11]

The intensity of the Supreme Court's commitment to insulate seniority systems from injunction was most recently evidenced by a decision, *Lorance v. AT & T Technologies*[12], that the limitations period for a claim attacking the bona fides of a seniority system runs from the date a system is adopted, even if the plaintiff could not then have anticipated harm from the system or for that matter first became employed thereafter. Section 112 of the Civil Rights Act of 1991 overrules *Lorance* by providing statute of limitations accrual dates later than the original adoption of an intentionally discriminatory, collectively bargained seniority system. Where applicable, the limitations period on such a claim will now begin to run only when the plaintiff became subject to the system's challenged provision or, later still, when that provision was first applied

7. *California Brewers Association v. Bryant*, 444 U.S. 598, 100 S.Ct. 814, 63 L.Ed.2d 55 (1980). *But see Mitchell v. Jefferson County Bd. of Education*, 936 F.2d 539 (11th Cir.1991) (salary schedule that called for annual step increase held not part of a seniority system).

8. *See, e.g., Council 31, American Federation of State, County and Municipal Employees v. Ward*, 978 F.2d 373 (7th Cir. 1992) (challenge to employer's decision to lay off employees in a particular office held not to constitute a challenge to the seniority system that governed how those layoffs were implemented).

9. In this respect the seniority system defense is treated procedurally much like the affirmative action plan "defense." See Chapter 5, *infra*.

10. *See Firefighters, Inc. v. Bach*, 611 F.Supp. 166 (D.Colo.1985); Hillman, "*Teamsters, California Brewers and Beyond: Seniority Systems and Allocations of the Burden of Proving Bona Fides*," 54 St. Johns L.Rev. 706 (1980).

11. *Pullman–Standard v. Swint*, 456 U.S. 273, 102 S.Ct. 1781, 72 L.Ed.2d 66 (1982).

12. 490 U.S. 900, 109 S.Ct. 2261, 104 L.Ed.2d 961 (1989).

to the plaintiff.[13] This change aids attacks on seniority systems, but only on those that discriminate intentionally; the legislation leaves undisturbed the Court's holdings that a system's mere adverse effect on a group is immune from Title VII challenge.[14]

Library References:

C.J.S. Civil Rights §§ 166, 169, 390.
West's Key No. Digests, Civil Rights ⊕149.

§ 3.17 Professionally Developed Ability Tests

Section 703(h) also permits employers to act upon the results of a "professionally developed ability test." But in sharp contrast to the great deference shown seniority systems, the judicial protection accorded these tests has been inconsistent. In many cases it has proven even *more* difficult for an employer to defend the adverse impact of a paper-and-pencil test than to avoid liability for other neutral practices. This is because, soon after Title VII became effective, the EEOC issued "guidelines" on employee selection procedures that require employers to conduct highly technical and demanding "validation" studies of ability tests to demonstrate that they reliably pinpoint desired employee traits essential to a particular job. The Supreme Court's deferral to those guidelines in *Albemarle Paper Co. v. Moody*[1] required employers to incur considerable expense in validation efforts before they could safely hinge employment decisions on the results of tests having significant differential adverse impact.

Lower courts have since somewhat eased validation requirements, holding that employers need not slavishly adhere to the difficult and complex EEOC guidelines. Instead employers may defend more generally with evidence that tests are "predictive of or significantly correlated with important elements of work behavior ... relevant to the job ... for which candidates are being evaluated."[2] Nevertheless, even this version of the validation defense places a considerably greater burden on an employer than merely producing evidence that "a challenged practice serves, in a significant way," one of many possible "legitimate employment goals."[3]

By its terms the Civil Rights Act of 1991, in an effort to restore the rigor of the defense, requires employers to justify the adverse impact of a particularly identified neutral practice by demonstrating the practice to

13. Section 112 (amending Title VII § 706(e), 42 U.S.C.A. § 2000e–5(e) (1988)).

14. *Pullman–Standard v. Swint*, 456 U.S. 273, 102 S.Ct. 1781, 72 L.Ed.2d 66 (1982); *California Brewers Ass'n v. Bryant*, 444 U.S. 598, 100 S.Ct. 814, 63 L.Ed.2d 55 (1980); *United Air Lines, Inc. v. Evans*, 431 U.S. 553, 97 S.Ct. 1885, 52 L.Ed.2d 571 (1977); *International Bhd. of Teamsters v. United States*, 431 U.S. 324, 97 S.Ct. 1843, 52 L.Ed.2d 396 (1977).

§ 3.17

1. 422 U.S. 405, 430, 95 S.Ct. 2362, 2378, 45 L.Ed.2d 280 (1975).

2. *Contreras v. City of Los Angeles*, 656 F.2d 1267 (9th Cir.1981), *cert. denied*, 455 U.S. 1021, 102 S.Ct. 1719, 72 L.Ed.2d 140 (1982).

3. *Wards Cove Packing Co. v. Atonio*, 490 U.S. 642, 109 S.Ct. 2115, 104 L.Ed.2d 733 (1989).

be "job related for the position in question and consistent with business necessity...."[4] If the courts should abandon the relaxed scrutiny delineated by *Contreras* and hold professionally developed ability tests either to the new statutory standard or to strict compliance with the EEOC guidelines, employers would once again find it considerably more difficult to justify those tests than § 703(h) apparently intended. The 1991 amendments do not address validation standards in particular, but add a prohibition against the practice known as "race norming." The Act makes it unlawful in selecting, referring, or promoting employees to adjust or use different cutoff scores or otherwise alter test results because of race, color, religion, sex or national origin.

The Civil Rights Act of 1991 specifically forbids employers to use the employment related test in a way that would expand employment opportunities for minorities. Such tests have long been held unlawful when they disproportionately screen out applicants or employees on the basis of race, sex, religion or national origin and the employer cannot justify their use through a job-relatedness or business necessity defense. As a remedy for such violations, courts sometimes ordered employers not to fill vacancies on a rank-order basis but instead to fill them from among candidates with examination scores that fell within specified "bands" or ranges, in order to minimize the differential impact.[5] The new legislation does not directly attack this judicial remedy, and indeed one section specifically reaffirms "court-ordered remedies, affirmative action, or conciliation agreements, that are in accordance with the law."[6] Yet it adds a provision that makes it an unlawful employment practice for an employer itself "to adjust the scores of, use different cutoff scores for, or otherwise alter the results of, employment related tests" on any of the prohibited grounds of discrimination.[7] Apparently, then, it is now specifically unlawful for an employer to do directly what a court may order it to do in order to offset the discriminatory effects of an employment related test.[8]

4. *See* Chapter 4, below.

5. *See, e.g., Bridgeport Guardians, Inc. v. City of Bridgeport*, 933 F.2d 1140 (2d Cir.), *cert. denied*, 502 U.S. 924, 112 S.Ct. 337, 116 L.Ed.2d 277 (1991).

6. Section 116.

7. Section 106 (amending § 703 of Title VII, 42 U.S.C.A. § 2000e–2).

8. In between are cases where an employer adopts banding on its own initiative but does so in order to achieve goals set forth in a consent decree. *See Officers for Justice v. Civil Service Commission of San Francisco*, 979 F.2d 721 (9th Cir.1992) (banding upheld, without regard to § 106 of the 1991 Act, as a measure that did not violate Title VII or the Equal Protection Clause because of the city's past discrimination), *cert. denied*, 507 U.S. 1004, 113 S.Ct. 1645, 123 L.Ed.2d 267 (1993).

If employers can band when ordered to do so by a court, but not on their own, § 106 represents a reverse twist on the respective roles of employers and courts with respect to affirmative action. With certain constraints, an employer is generally free to favor black or female applicants or employees on grounds of race or gender under the terms of a voluntary affirmative action plan adopted despite the absence of any past employer violation of Title VII; put otherwise, the employer can act where the court would be without any authority to order any remedy. *See United Steelworkers of America v. Weber*, 443 U.S. 193, 99 S.Ct. 2721, 61 L.Ed.2d 480 (1979) and *Johnson v. Transportation Agency*, 480 U.S. 616, 107 S.Ct. 1442, 94 L.Ed.2d 615 (1987).

It is possible, however, that although the language of the new ban on race norming or score adjustment defines only an "unlawful

F.   RETALIATION

§ 3.18   In General

To protect employees who seek to vindicate their rights under § 703, a separate provision, § 704(a), broadly prohibits retaliation. Two basic species of conduct are protected: 1) participation in any administrative or judicial investigation, proceeding, or hearing to enforce Title VII rights; and 2) less formal, but good faith opposition to practices that an employee reasonably believes to be prohibited by the Act.

Once conduct is characterized as protected, the prima facie case is straightforward. The plaintiff must produce evidence of (1) her participation in proceedings authorized by Title VII or her opposition to one or more *apparently* prohibited practices (the practice opposed must be one "made an unlawful employment practice by" Title VII, although the plaintiff may prevail even if the employer was not in fact violating the statute) [1]; (2) her employer's awareness of her protected participation or opposition; (3) an adverse term or condition of employment she sustained thereafter; and (4) a causal connection between the adverse employment action and the protected opposition or participation. [2] Evidence that the adverse action was taken shortly after the protected participation or opposition fortifies or perhaps suffices to show the required causal link; the passage of several years between the protected conduct and the act of alleged retaliation may defeat the inference of

---

employment practice" that might be committed by a "respondent," it will ultimately be held to ban such measures as part of a court-ordered remedy. Dole Interpretive Memorandum, *infra* § 4.10, n. 30, concerning "Section 9. Discriminatory Use of Test Scores."

§ 3.18

1. The plaintiff's own activity must be the predicate for protection against retaliation. *See Holt v. JTM Industries, Inc.,* 89 F.3d 1224 (5th Cir.1996)(spouse lacks standing to complain about retaliation he suffered solely in respect of protected activity engaged in by his wife). Yet it is settled that the practice the § 704 plaintiff opposed need not have actually violated Title VII in order for her opposition to it to be protected. *See Jennings v. Tinley Park Community Consolidated School District No. 146,* 864 F.2d 1368 (7th Cir.1988); *Sias v. City Demonstration Agency,* 588 F.2d 692 (9th Cir. 1978). But the requirement that opposition be to a practice "made an unlawful employment practice" by Title VII probably

means that a retaliation claim cannot succeed if it is based on opposition to conduct that generically is not even arguably prohibited by Title VII or took place when the employer was not subject to its regulation. *See Winsey v. Pace College,* 394 F.Supp. 1324 (S.D.N.Y.1975) (opposition claim fails because conduct plaintiff opposed occurred before employer became subject to Title VII and therefore could not have been made unlawful by the statute). *See* Schlei and Grossman, *Employment   Discrimination Law* 543 n. 38, 547 (describing *Winsey* as involving a plaintiff mistake of law rather than fact) (2d ed. 1983). A compromise position is expressed as follows by one court: while the plaintiff need not demonstrate that the conduct she protested was an unlawful employment practice, her belief that the conduct was unlawful must be reasonable. *Berg v. LaCrosse Cooler Co.,* 612 F.2d 1041 (7th Cir.1980). *Accord, Trent v. Valley Elec. Ass'n Inc.,* 41 F.3d 524 (9th Cir.1994).

2. *See, e.g., EEOC v. Crown Zellerbach Corp.,* 720 F.2d 1008, 1012 (9th Cir.1983).

retaliatory motive;[3] but the passage of a substantial period of time does not conclusively refute the possibility of the required causation.[4]

Once plaintiff makes the prima facie showing, the case proceeds similarly to one of individual disparate treatment. The employer must produce evidence of a legitimate nondiscriminatory reason for the challenged employment action. If the employer produces that evidence, the plaintiff bears the ultimate burden of persuasion on the issue of pretext.[5] Section 703(m), the "mixed motives" provision that relieves an employer of retroactive relief when it demonstrates that it would have taken the same action apart from an unlawful ground, includes among such grounds only "race, color, religion, sex, or national origin," with no mention of retaliation.

The "opposition" right has been subject to a number of fact-sensitive qualifications, developed case by case, concerning the lawfulness or reasonableness of the manner and means of opposition. In *McDonnell Douglas Corp. v. Green*, the Supreme Court wrote that employers are not required to "absolve" employees who engage in "unlawful activity against it."[6] Employee protests that constitute both opposition to practices made unlawful by Title VII as well as violations of established, legitimate work rules have posed especially difficult problems. The linchpin is the "reasonableness" of the opposition. When a court adjudges an employee's manner of opposition to have gone beyond what is necessary for effective protest—when, for example, she gratuitously embarrasses a superior—employee discipline will likely be upheld. The court balances the legislative purpose to protect reasonable opposition to arguably discriminatory employer conduct against the ever-present Congressional desire to preserve managerial control.[7] At the same time, however, an employer's unilateral sense of diminished loyalty resulting from the opposition will not by itself be considered a legitimate, nondiscriminatory reason for discipline.[8]

---

3. *Chavez v. Arvada*, 88 F.3d 861 (10th Cir.1996)(ten year interval between filing of charge and nonpromotion excessive, absent evidence tying employer action to the protected activity); *Candelaria v. EG & G Energy Measurements, Inc.*, 33 F.3d 1259 (10th Cir.1994).

4. *Shirley v. Chrysler First, Inc.*, 970 F.2d 39 (5th Cir.1992).

5. *Zanders v. National Railroad Passenger Corp.*, 898 F.2d 1127 (6th Cir.1990).

6. 411 U.S. 792, 803, 93 S.Ct. 1817, 1825, 36 L.Ed.2d 668 (1973). The Court did not actually decide the validity of the plaintiff's claim under § 704, but its language seems to extend to any claim under Title VII. *See also Hochstadt v. Worcester Foundation for Experimental Biology*, 545 F.2d 222, 229–234 (1st Cir.1976) (conduct with the potential to disrupt work excessively held unreasonable and hence unpro-

tected). *But cf. Folkerson v. Circus Circus Enters.* (9th Cir.1995) (unpublished opinion) (even physical violence may constitute protected opposition if proportionate to threat of physical harm directed at plaintiff).

7. *Wrighten v. Metropolitan Hosp., Inc.*, 726 F.2d 1346 (9th Cir.1984); *Hochstadt*, 545 F.2d at 231. *See also O'Day v. McDonnell Douglas Helicopter Co.*, 79 F.3d 756 (9th Cir.1996) (standard under ADEA).

8. *See Jennings v. Tinley Park Community Consolidated School District No. 146*, 864 F.2d 1368 (7th Cir.1988); *EEOC v. Crown Zellerbach Corp.*, 720 F.2d 1008, 1014 (9th Cir.1983) (if the test were mere disloyalty, even reasonable opposition would be unprotected, since all opposition may be considered disloyal).

By contrast, the "participation" protection, designed to assure free access to the administrative and judicial bodies empowered to investigate and adjudicate Title VII violations, is virtually unlimited. Just as an "opposing" plaintiff's underlying informal complaint need not have been in fact well founded [9] under § 703 to support a claim of unlawful retaliation under § 704, so a "participating" plaintiff need not have prevailed in the proceeding initiated by her formal charge or lawsuit. Indeed it has been held that an employer's unilateral view that an employee lied in the EEOC charge documents cannot justify retaliatory action against him.[10] Further, a plaintiff asserting that he was retaliated against for having filed an EEOC charge generally need not file a distinct retaliation charge with EEOC or otherwise exhaust administrative remedies before suing for retaliation in federal court. Such retaliation is actionable even if it occurs after dismissal of the plaintiff's EEOC charge.[11]

Section 704 in terms protects only "employees or applicants," unlike § 703's embrace of "any individual." Most courts that have considered the question have nevertheless concluded that even a former employee may maintain a claim of retaliation, and even for post-employment conduct. The classic example would be negative references or "blacklisting" as where a former employer advises a prospective employer that the plaintiff had filed an EEOC charge against it.[12] But the retaliation against the ex-employee must somehow impair an existing or subsequent prospective employment relationship.[13] Retaliation charges may be based on the manner in which an employer defends a charge or complaint of discrimination.[14] Similarly, despite language in § 704 that appears to limit protection to those who have opposed or participated personally, the Sixth Circuit has recently upheld the legal sufficiency of a

---

9. Although it must have attacked a practice "made unlawful by" the statute. *See* text accompanying note 1.

10. *Pettway v. American Cast Iron Pipe Co.*, 411 F.2d 998 (5th Cir.1969); *EEOC v. Snyder Doors*, 844 F.Supp. 1020 (E.D.Pa. 1994).

11. *Malarkey v. Texaco, Inc.*, 983 F.2d 1204 (2d Cir.1993); *cf. Cornwell v. Robinson*, 23 F.3d 694 (2d Cir.1994) (same principle applied when subsequent charge alleges "harassment"). But the Second Circuit has upheld as an exercise of managerial discretion an employer's decision to refer internal complaints that result in the filing of discrimination charges before administrative agencies or courts to its law department instead of its equal employment opportunity unit. *United States v. N.Y.C. Transit Authority*, 97 F.3d 672 (2d Cir. 1996).

12. *Berry v. Stevinson Chevrolet*, 74 F.3d 980 (10th Cir.1996) (filing criminal charge against former employee constitutes

actionable retaliation); *see, e.g., Charlton v. Paramus Bd. of Educ.*, 25 F.3d 194 (3d Cir.1994), *cert. denied*, ___ U.S. ___, 115 S.Ct. 590, 130 L.Ed.2d 503 (1994); *Bailey v. USX Corp.*, 850 F.2d 1506 (11th Cir.1988); *O'Brien v. Sky Chefs, Inc.*, 670 F.2d 864, 869 (9th Cir.1982), *overruled on other grounds by Atonio v. Wards Cove Packing Co.*, 810 F.2d 1477, 1481–82 (9th Cir.1987) (en banc); *Pantchenko v. C.B. Dolge Co.*, 581 F.2d 1052, 1055 (2d Cir.1978); *Rutherford v. American Bank of Commerce*, 565 F.2d 1162, 1165 (10th Cir.1977); *EEOC v. Metzger*, 824 F.Supp. 1 (D.D.C.1993) (holding retaliation against former employee actionable). *But see Robinson v. Shell Oil Co.*, 70 F.3d 325 (4th Cir.1995) (en banc), *cert. granted*, ___ U.S. ___, 116 S.Ct. 1541, 134 L.Ed.2d 645; *Reed v. Shepard*, 939 F.2d 484 (7th Cir.1991) (holding contra).

13. *Nelson v. Upsala College*, 51 F.3d 383 (3d Cir.1995).

14. *See, e.g., EEOC v. Plumbers Local 189*, 311 F.Supp. 464 (S.D.Ohio 1970) (defense lawyer's questioning held retaliatory).

retaliation claim by an employee whose co-employee protested on his behalf.[15]   In any event the plaintiff may state a claim for retaliation based on his own association with members of racial minorities [16] or because he was required by his employer to discriminate against others.[17]

Library References:

> C.J.S. Employer–Employee Relationship §§ 68, 70, 72, 79.
> West's Key No. Digests, Master and Servant ☜30(6.5).

G.   CONSTRUCTIVE DISCHARGE

Library References:

> C.J.S. Civil Rights §§ 151, 152.
> West's Key No. Digests, Civil Rights ☜145.

§ 3.19   In General

Closely related to but distinguishable from environmental harassment and retaliation is the doctrine of constructive discharge.   In essence, the claim avails an employee whose departure is in form voluntary but who in fact was virtually compelled to quit as the result of discriminatory job terms or harassment extreme in significance, duration or offensiveness.   The consequence of establishing the claim is a broader remedy: the plaintiff who succeeds will be eligible for an order directing reinstatement as well as available monetary relief.

At a minimum the claim requires the standard showing that the plaintiff's involuntary resignation was caused by differential treatment unlawful because based on her race, sex, religion, national origin or age. Evidence that the plaintiff would have resigned for independent personal reasons or work-related reasons unconnected with substantial, aggravated discrimination [1] breaks the causal connection and therefore defeats the constructive discharge claim.[2]   This is akin to the same-decision showing which, under *Price Waterhouse*, sufficed to avoid employer liability altogether and today, under the Civil Rights Act of 1991, still limits available relief.[3]

The element that has generated the most litigation centers on the reasonableness of the employee's decision to quit in relation to particular unlawful employer conduct.   The decisions are uniform that an employee has been constructively discharged when his termination results from

---

15.   *EEOC v. Ohio Edison Co.*, 7 F.3d 541 (6th Cir.1993). *Cf. McDonnell v. Cisneros*, 84 F.3d 256 (7th Cir.1996) (finding actionable the retaliation claim of a manager who had not protested himself but who was punished for having failed to prevent the protests of subordinates).

16.   *Maynard v. City of San Jose*, 37 F.3d 1396 (9th Cir.1994).

17.   *Moyo v. Gomez*, 40 F.3d 982 (9th Cir.1994).

§ 3.19

1.   The conditions must be more than intolerable; they must have resulted from discrimination on an unlawful ground. *Chambers v. American Trans Air, Inc.*, 17 F.3d 998 (7th Cir.), *cert. denied,* ___ U.S. ___, 115 S.Ct. 512, 130 L.Ed.2d 419 (1994).

2.   *See Henson v. Dundee*, 682 F.2d 897 (11th Cir.1982).

3.   *See* Chapter 4, below.

intolerable working conditions that the employer created with the specific intent of forcing the employee to resign. Some circuits consider evidence of subjective intent,[4] or of "aggravating circumstances," [5] indispensable to constructive discharge. More, however, subscribe to an "objective" test, requiring only a finding that the complained of conduct would have the foreseeable result of creating working conditions sufficiently unpleasant or difficult that a reasonable person in the employee's position would feel compelled to resign.[6] Because the employer conduct that gives rise to colorable claims of constructive discharge is usually extreme or persistent, those claims are often joined with companion claims under state law for such torts as outrage or intentional infliction of emotional distress.[7]

Most acts of discrimination are such that a "reasonable" employee should stay on the job; oppose the employer practice informally or by filing a charge; and trust in the efficacy of the separate § 704 protection against retaliation. Classic instances include wage discrimination, nonpromotion, or assignment to less attractive or lucrative (but not intolerably demeaning) positions.[8] At the other end of the spectrum, where the

4. *See Allen v. Bridgestone/Firestone, Inc.,* 81 F.3d 793 (8th Cir.1996); *Martin v. Cavalier Hotel Corp.,* 48 F.3d 1343, 1354 (4th Cir.1995)(permitting that "intent," however, to be shown by evidence demonstrating that the resignation was "the 'reasonable forseeable consequence' of the employer's conduct," 48 F.3d at 1356); *Bristow v. Daily Press, Inc.,* 770 F.2d 1251 (4th Cir.1985), *cert. denied,* 475 U.S. 1082, 106 S.Ct. 1461, 89 L.Ed.2d 718 (1986); *Coe v. Yellow Freight System, Inc.,* 646 F.2d 444 (10th Cir.1981). *Cf. Johnson v. Shalala,* 991 F.2d 126 (4th Cir.1993), *cert. denied,* ___ U.S. ___, 115 S.Ct. 52, 130 L.Ed.2d 12 (1994) (under Rehabilitation Act of 1973). The Tenth Circuit may have changed course with the panel opinion in *Rupp v. Purolator Courier Corp.,* 45 F.3d 440 (10th Cir.1994), which requires only "working conditions so difficult that a reasonable person in the employee's position would feel compelled to resign." *See also Burks v. Oklahoma Publishing Co.,* 81 F.3d 975 (10th Cir.1996).

5. *Dashnaw v. Pena,* 12 F.3d 1112 (D.C.Cir.1994), *cert. denied,* ___ U.S. ___, 115 S.Ct. 417, 130 L.Ed.2d 333 (1994) (case under ADEA holding failure to promote does not amount to required aggravated circumstances).

6. See, e.g., *Rupp v. Purolator Courier Corp.,* 45 F.3d 440 (10th Cir.1994); *Morgan v. Ford,* 6 F.3d 750 (11th Cir.1993), *cert. denied,* ___ U.S. ___, 114 S.Ct. 2708, 129 L.Ed.2d 836 (1994); *Hukkanen v. International Union of Operating Engineers Local No. 101,* 3 F.3d 281 (8th Cir.1993); *Ste-*

phens v. C.I.T. Group/Equipment Financing, Inc., 955 F.2d 1023 (5th Cir.1992) *Schafer v. Board of Public Education,* 903 F.2d 243 (3d Cir.1990); *Brooms v. Regal Tube Co.,* 881 F.2d 412 (7th Cir.1989); *Watson v. Nationwide Insurance Co.,* 823 F.2d 360 (9th Cir.1987); *Bruhwiler v. University of Tenn.,* 859 F.2d 419 (6th Cir.1988); *Calhoun v. Acme Cleveland Corp.,* 798 F.2d 559 (1st Cir.1986); *Wardwell v. School Bd. of Palm Beach County,* 786 F.2d 1554 (11th Cir.1986); *Meyer v. Brown & Root Const. Co.,* 661 F.2d 369 (5th Cir.1981).

In *Hukkanen,* the Court dispensed with an express finding that resignation was a reasonably foreseeable consequence of the defendant's agent's sexual harassment, deeming that finding implicit in the lower court's finding that a reasonable person in plaintiff's position would have felt compelled to quit.

7. *Rupp v. Purolator Courier Corp.,* 45 F.3d 440 (10th Cir.1994), illustrates that the same employer conduct may constitute constructive discharge for Title VII purposes yet not be sufficiently aggravated, indecent or shocking to amount to tortious wrongdoing under state law.

8. *See Bourque v. Powell Electrical Mfg. Co.,* 617 F.2d 61 (5th Cir.1980) (unequal pay); *Cazzola v. Codman & Shurtleff, Inc.,* 751 F.2d 53 (1st Cir.1984) (reassignment); *cf. King v. AC&R Advertising, Inc.,* 1994 WL 88998 (C.D.Cal.1994) (salary reduction, other benefits cuts, and demotion did not amount to constructive discharge under California law.)

prospects of proving constructive discharge are much improved, lie the "aggravating circumstances" sometimes required to meet the objective test of "intolerable" working conditions. These include subjecting the plaintiff to repeated slurs,[9] assigning him especially demeaning work for unlawful discriminatory reasons, or subjecting him to egregious, unrelenting, and unremedied harassment. Sexual harassment in particular has served as a predicate for constructive discharge [10] but is not necessarily sufficiently severe to meet a particular circuit's test.[11] Indeed in one recent decision,[12] an employee who was subjected to shift changes, public berating, and demeaning job assignments for reporting apparent sexual harassment directed against a co-employee established constructive discharge, even though the retaliation lasted only three weeks. On occasion, "objective test" courts have dispensed with the necessity of aggravating circumstances, ruling that a "single non-trivial incident of discrimination" may suffice to make resignation reasonable.[13] Between the polar extremes are situations where the plaintiff is subjected to "unreasonably exacting standards of job performance"; one court recently announced a virtual presumption that an employee with this complaint cannot reasonably resign, or else the courts would be undermining employer insistence on high standards.[14]

The employee must therefore make a critical decision, usually without benefit of counsel, concerning how to respond to varied employer actions. If racial slurs are so offensive or repeated that an employee who quit over them would later be deemed by a court to have acted reasonably, the employee could safely quit or take the lesser measure of remaining on the job and demanding an apology. If he keeps working but his demand leads to his discharge, he might well have a claim for retaliation in violation of § 704.[15] But if he overestimates the seriousness or offensiveness of the employer's discrimination and quits, he may find that his only remedy is backpay from the time of the underlying discrimination until the date of his "voluntary" termination.

9. *But see Ugalde v. W.A. McKenzie Asphalt Co.*, 990 F.2d 239 (5th Cir.1993) (supervisor's ethnic slurs not sufficient to lead a reasonable person in plaintiff's position to resign where employer had agreed to transfer employee to another job).

10. *See, e.g., Hukkanen v. International Union of Operating Engineers Local No. 101, supra* note 6; *Snider v. Consolidation Coal Co.*, 973 F.2d 555 (7th Cir.1992), *cert. denied*, 506 U.S. 1054, 113 S.Ct. 981, 122 L.Ed.2d 134 (1993). The Ninth Circuit recently suggested that a constructive discharge claim could be established entirely on the basis of crude and abusive sexual epithets. *Steiner v. Showboat Operating Co.*, 25 F.3d 1459 (9th Cir.1994).

11. *See Landgraf v. USI Film Products*, 968 F.2d 427 (5th Cir.1992), *affirmed*, 511 U.S. 244, 114 S.Ct. 1483, 128 L.Ed.2d 229 (1994); *Yates v. Avco Corporation*, 819 F.2d 630 (6th Cir.1987).

12. *Rupp v. Purolator Courier Corp.*, 45 F.3d 440 (10th Cir.1994).

13. *Schafer v. Board of Public Educ., supra* note 6 (male resigned after being denied pregnancy leave to care for his child in violation of Title VII as amended by Pregnancy Disability Act).

14. *Clowes v. Allegheny Valley Hospital*, 991 F.2d 1159, 1162 (3d Cir.) (case under ADEA), *cert. denied*, 510 U.S. 964, 114 S.Ct. 441, 126 L.Ed.2d 374 (1993).

15. The example is suggested by Player, *Employment Discrimination Law* (West 1988), at 401 (*citing Walker v. Ford Motor Co.*, 684 F.2d 1355 (11th Cir.1982)).

H. UNION LIABILITY

Library References:

C.J.S. Civil Rights § 154.
West's Key No. Digests, Civil Rights ☞147.

§ 3.20 In General

Labor unions are not excluded from the general definition of "employer," and consequently may be liable for violations of § 703(a) on the same terms as any other employer. In addition, § 703(c) declares distinct unlawful practices applicable to labor organizations alone. One, found in § 703(c)(3), is to "cause or attempt to cause an employer" to discriminate in violation of § 703. Another, declared by § 703(c)(2), is to rely on prohibited grounds in segregating or classifying union members or applicants, or in failing to refer individuals for employment, so as to deprive them of employment opportunities. Finally, wholly apart from any effect on employment opportunities, labor organizations are prohibited by § 703(c)(1) from excluding applicants from membership or otherwise discriminating against them. Construing this last prohibition quite broadly, the Supreme Court has held that a union commits an unlawful employment practice by refusing to file race-bias grievances presented by black members, even when it does so in order to avoid antagonizing the employer and in turn to improve its chances of success on other collective bargaining issues, and even though the percentage of all types of grievances filed on behalf of black members is proportional to their representation in the union.[1]

Unions may also be liable for retaliation under § 704. For example, a union that refused to process race discrimination grievances under a collective bargaining contract whenever the would-be grievant had a charge pending against the union with a state or federal antidiscrimination agency was found to have violated Title VII. Liability attached even though the union processed other grievances as fairly for black as for white members and claimed that its policy was compelled by the employer.[2]

§ 3.20

1. *Goodman v. Lukens Steel Co.*, 482 U.S. 656, 107 S.Ct. 2617, 96 L.Ed.2d 572 (1987).

2. *Johnson v. Palma*, 931 F.2d 203 (2d Cir.1991).

Chapter Four

MODES OF PROOF FOR
A TITLE VII CLAIM

Analysis

---

§ 4.1 In General

The most critical and frequently litigated questions under Title VII concern the theories on which liability may be predicated and the corresponding modes of proof. When, in brief, does a distinction drawn by an employer to regulate terms and conditions of employment discriminate because or on the basis of race, gender, religion or national origin? Broadly speaking, it may be said that there are two generic forms of employer conduct actionable under Title VII. First there are a variety of

217

forms of intentional discrimination or "disparate treatment"; a broad legislative and social consensus supports imposing liability on employers when such conduct can be proved.[1] More controversial is employer liability for "neutral," that is facially nondiscriminatory, work practices that have greater adverse statistical impact on members of the plaintiff's protected group (and therefore, inferentially, on the plaintiff) than on others. The rubric under which liability is imposed in such circumstances is denoted by the terms "disproportionate adverse impact" or "disparate impact." Distinct proof modes have been developed to provide guidance to judges and now juries in determining liability under each of these theories. Each mode presents its own conceptual and practical difficulties, and these in turn have generated a burgeoning body of judicial decisions. It bears emphasis that these categories are not analytically airtight and that particular employer practices, in the hands of capable advocates, may implicate two or more modes of proof.

A. INDIVIDUAL DISPARATE TREATMENT— "DIRECT" EVIDENCE

Library References:

> C.J.S. Civil Rights §§ 161, 162, 394, 395.
> West's Key No. Digests, Civil Rights ☞153, 382.1.

§ 4.2 In General

The most obvious way of showing an unlawful employment practice is to offer "evidence that can be interpreted as an acknowledgement of discriminatory intent by the defendant or its agents...."[1] Examples include epithets or slurs uttered by an authorized agent of the employer, or, even more clearly, an employer policy framed squarely in terms of race, sex, religion, or national origin. When produced, such "direct" evidence will without more ordinarily suffice to show that an adverse employment condition, or limitation on an employment opportunity, was imposed "because of" the plaintiff's protected group characteristic.

Definitional and application problems surrounding "direct" evidence abound. It is even sometimes difficult to determine whether an employer policy may be said to discriminate expressly or facially on the basis of race, color, sex, religion or national origin. In the notorious *Gilbert*[2] decision that prompted Congress to spank the Court by enacting the Pregnancy Discrimination Act of 1978, the Court held that an employer rule that denied disability benefits for pregnancy but no other physical

---

§ 4.1

1. See Blumoff & Lewis, "The Reagan Court and Title VII: A Common–Law Outlook On a Statutory Task," 69 N.C.L. Rev. 1 (1990).

It bears emphasis that these categories are not analytically airtight and that particular employer practices, in the hands of

capable advocates, may implicate two or more modes of proof.

§ 4.2

1. *Troupe v. May Department Stores Company*, 20 F.3d 734 (7th Cir.1994).

2. *General Electric Co. v. Gilbert*, 429 U.S. 125, 97 S.Ct. 401, 50 L.Ed.2d 343 (1976).

conditions did not discriminate "because of gender" within the meaning of § 703. The rule, the Court explained, treated pregnant women differently, relative to benefits, not only from men but also from non-pregnant women. The rule therefore did not draw a distinction on the basis of gender, even though its sting was felt only by women.

By the same reasoning, the practice of excluding fertile women from working in areas where they will encounter sufficient lead exposure to endanger a fetus or potential fetus might be conceived of as not predicated on gender: it, too, treats fertile women differently not only from all men but also from nonfertile women. Yet the Supreme Court, evidently chastened by the legislative overruling of the result in *Gilbert*, viewed such a practice as expressly gender discriminatory, observing that the adverse effects of the practice fell 100% on women.[3] Similarly, an employer or union requirement that a new applicant be related by blood or marriage to an existing employee or union member, while neutral in form, may result in the absolute exclusion of members of a protected group that historically was systematically excluded through intentional discrimination. Such practices have been viewed on occasion as instances of express, egregious discrimination.[4] In other words, practices that are formally neutral may be analyzed as intentional disparate treatment when their adverse impact is not merely substantial but absolute, or put otherwise, when they correlate to a very high degree with exclusion of a group protected by Title VII.[5]

Unsurprisingly, outside the realm of policies that discriminate by their clear terms on the basis of a protected characteristic, cases presenting smoking-gun exemplars of "direct," "express" or "facial" evidence are relative rarities. Three decades after the effective date of Title VII employers are familiar with the requirements and penalties of the statute and consequently more apt to comply or better skilled in disguising noncompliance. In *Price Waterhouse v. Hopkins*,[6] the Supreme Court has, however, treated employers' agents' statements reflecting stereotypical views of women as direct evidence of gender discrimination, even when the views expressed bear somewhat tangentially on the plaintiff's capacity to perform the core elements of the position.

Justice O'Connor's concurring opinion sets out three prerequisites for employer speech to constitute "direct" evidence: the remarks must

---

3. *International Union, UAW v. Johnson Controls, Inc.*, 499 U.S. 187, 111 S.Ct. 1196, 113 L.Ed.2d 158 (1991). The Court also relied for this conclusion on § 701(k) of Title VII, added by the Pregnancy Discrimination Act of 1978, which equates any discrimination concerning pregnancy or, as the Court held in *Johnson Controls*, the *capacity* to become pregnant, with express gender discrimination for purposes of § 703(a).

4. See, e.g., *E.E.O.C. v. Enterprise Association Steamfitters Local No. 638*, 542 F.2d

579 (2d Cir.1976), *cert. denied*, 430 U.S. 911, 97 S.Ct. 1186, 51 L.Ed.2d 588 (1977).

5. *Compare Hazen v. Biggins*, 507 U.S. 604, 113 S.Ct. 1701, 123 L.Ed.2d 338 (1993) (discrimination that correlates to some degree with age is not unlawful disparate treatment under ADEA, discussed *infra* in the Chapter on Age Discrimination.)

6. 490 U.S. 228, 109 S.Ct. 1775, 104 L.Ed.2d 268 (1989) (plurality opinion and opinion of O'Connor, J.).

be by the applicable decision maker, be related to the decision process, and not "stray." [7] The opinions in the case suggest that stereotypical attitudes become "direct" evidence only when extrinsic evidence gives reason to believe that the the decisionmaker who voices them is motivated by a factor made unlawful by Title VII. On that question, there remains considerable uncertainty about how to differentiate those gender- or age-related comments [8] or conduct [9] that amount to "direct" evidence of discrimination and therefore, standing alone, create a prima facie case, from merely "isolated" incidents or "stray" remarks. Even though slurs and stereotypes are sometimes treated as "direct" evidence of discriminatory intent, their real meaning or purpose may be equivocal.[10] The frequent ambiguity of language and intent lends support to Judge Posner's observation that perhaps the "only true direct evidence of intent that will ever be available" consists of outright litigation admissions or policies that discriminate by their own terms on grounds prohibited by the statute.[11]

Even if such comments are accepted as "direct" evidence of discrimination, the plaintiff may also have to prove that the attitudes they reflect played at least a motivating part in the employment decision

7. 490 U.S. at 277, 109 S.Ct. at 1804. The requirement that the speech be by a decision maker will sometimes encounter crosscurrents from the "same actor" doctrine. This rule of evidence favorable to the defendant permits the inference that the employer did not discriminate when the same employer agent hired as well as fired the plaintiff. *Buhrmaster v. Overnite Transp. Co.,* 61 F.3d 461 (6th Cir.1995) (sex discrimination).

8. Compare *Radabaugh v. Zip Feed Mills, Inc.,* 997 F.2d 444 (8th Cir.1993) (corporate documents citing as an advantage that "Top and middle level managers are mostly young, well educated and results oriented" cannot be discounted as "stray" remarks even though the documents did not directly concern the employment decision at issue) *with Hudgens v. Owens-Brockway Glass Container, Inc.,* 1994 WL 81689 (W.D.Tex.1994) (statement by plaintiff's supervisor that "I'm going to have to go outside the department to get the next foreman, because none of the younger men in the department want[s] it" treated as not even probative of age discrimination even though it concerned the promotion in question). *See also Merrick v. Farmers Ins. Group,* 892 F.2d 1434 (9th Cir.1990) (calling the selectee preferred to plaintiff a "bright, knowledgeable young man" only a stray comment); *Smith v. Firestone Tire & Rubber Co.,* 875 F.2d 1325 (7th Cir.1989) (a manager's expression of dislike for plaintiff's "type" too ambiguous to be definitively linked to plaintiff's race).

9. *See Davis v. Chevron U.S.A., Inc.* 14 F.3d 1082 (5th Cir.1994) (testimony that interviewer stared at plaintiff "from neck down" is not direct evidence of gender discrimination).

10. *See Gray v. University of Arkansas,* 883 F.2d 1394 (8th Cir.1989) (doubting that supervisor meant what he said because he was then suffering from mental illness). The author is indebted to Professors Zimmer, Sullivan, Richards and Calloway who have collected several of the foregoing examples in the third edition of their fine casebook, *Cases and Materials on Employment Discrimination* (Little Brown 1994). Expressing doubt whether evidence of supervisory speech reflecting negative stereotypes is in fact "direct" evidence, one court has read *Price Waterhouse* as not requiring direct evidence to set in motion the mixed-motive burden shifting endorsed by that decision. *Tyler v. Bethlehem Steel Corp.,* 958 F.2d 1176 (2d Cir.), *cert. denied,* 506 U.S. 826, 113 S.Ct. 82, 121 L.Ed.2d 46 (1992).

11. *Troupe v. May Department Stores, supra* note 1. Terming the task of distinguishing direct from indirect evidence "hopeless," the Second Circuit has similarly observed: "Even a highly probative statement like 'You're fired, old man' still requires the factfinder to draw the inference that the plaintiff's age had a causal relationship to the decision." *Tyler v. Bethlehem Steel, supra* note 10, at 1185–1187.

under challenge.[12] Discrimination "in the air," that is, must be brought to ground, lest Title VII be used as a mechanism for controlling pure thought or speech.[13] To do so the plaintiff must show first that a discriminatory attitude was to some degree actually relied on by the relevant decisionmaker.[14] In one recent decision,[15] for example, Chief Judge Posner wrote for a panel, "Discrimination is not preference or aversion; it is acting on the preference or aversion." For this reason, he concluded, an employer who would prefer to exclude members of national origin groups other than his own does not violate Title VII even if the employment practice in question (there, word-of-mouth hiring) brings about that result, so long as the practice is motivated only by other reasons, e.g., efficiency.[16] Similarly, a statement attributable to management or even a sign on the employer's premises expressing a disinclination to hire members of a protected group probably does not by itself violate Title VII, although it would violate the fair employment laws of some states and municipalities.[17] Finally, to bring a prejudicial statement to actionable territory the plaintiff must also show that the difference in treatment adversely affected a term or condition of the plaintiff's employment.[18]

12. *See, e.g., Price Waterhouse, supra* note 6 (liability turns on whether the unlawful factor or factors among two or more "mixed" motives played a motivating part in the challenged decision).

13. In some of its evolving variations, "environmental" sexual harassment has the potential of punishing pure speech or expression and hence running afoul of the First Amendment. See the section on sexual harassment in Chapter 3.

14. *See, e.g., Trotter v. Board of Trustees of University of Alabama,* 91 F.3d 1449 (11th Cir.1996); *Bruno v. City of Crown Point,* 950 F.2d 355 (7th Cir.1991), *cert. denied* 505 U.S. 1207, 112 S.Ct. 2998, 120 L.Ed.2d 874 (1992) (remarks reflecting gender discrimination by interviewer not shown to have been a factor in plaintiff's rejection). The decisions differ, however, over such factors as whether a negative stereotype uttered by a decisionmaker has to focus upon the alleged disqualification of plaintiff in particular, or only her group, see *Haynes v. W.C. Caye & Co.,* 52 F.3d 928 (11th Cir.1995)(statement about the incompetence of women in general to do the kind of job in question sufficient); and as to the requisite proximity in time between the decisionmaker's utterance and his imposition of an adverse term and condition of employment. *O'Connor v. Consolidated Coin Caterers Corp.,* 56 F.3d 542, 549 (4th Cir. 1995), *rev'd on other grounds,* __ U.S. __, 116 S.Ct. 1307, 134 L.Ed.2d 433 (1996)(supervisor's statements, two weeks and two

days, respectively, before ADEA plaintiff's discharge, that plaintiff was "too damn old" and that the company needed "young blood," held not tantamount to direct evidence of age discrimination because not immediately connected with termination decision).

15. *EEOC v. Consolidated Service Systems,* 989 F.2d 233, 236 (7th Cir.1993).

16. *Id.* at 236. *See also Chambers v. American Trans Air Inc.,* 17 F.3d 998 (7th Cir.1994) (verbal expressions of bigotry aimed at women insufficient for plaintiff to resist summary judgment absent evidence of how sexism translated into lesser wage increases for her than for similarly situated males).

17. Title VII's only express pure-speech prohibition is found in § 704(b), which bans "any notice or advertisement relating to employment" that indicates a preference or limitation based on one of the prohibited grounds. But certain forms of "environmental" sexual harassment based on employer or co-worker speech alone might be seen as another exception to Judge Posner's general observation. That is precisely why such regulation has raised First Amendment concerns. See Chapter 3.

18. *See Crady v. Liberty National Bank & Trust Co.,* 993 F.2d 132 (7th Cir.1993) (ADEA case finding no violation because transfer did not diminish plaintiff's compensation or responsibilities).

§ 4.3 The "BFOQ" Affirmative Defense

Section 703(e)(1) affords an employer a defense—the only defense—to policies or work rules that expressly or facially discriminate on the basis of gender, religion or national origin. It authorizes the employer to "hire and employ" (and a labor organization or joint labor management committee to "admit or employ" to membership or apprenticeship or retraining programs) on the basis of gender, religion or national origin when any of those characteristics is a "bona fide occupational qualification ['BFOQ'] reasonably necessary to the normal operation" of the enterprise. It does not excuse discrimination in post-hire terms and conditions of employment—compensation, promotion, discipline, harassment or discharge [1]—or any discrimination on the basis of race. ADEA contains a similarly worded BFOQ defense, and the Court has construed the corresponding provisions of the two statutes virtually identically.[2] Perhaps because BFOQ serves as a defense to intentional, facial discrimination, the form most disfavored by the public and the Congress, the federal courts have given the defense very limited sway.

As its text would suggest, BFOQ is a true affirmative defense which the employer therefore has the burden of pleading and proving by a preponderance of the evidence. But the bare language of § 703(e)(1) would appear satisfied if an employer can show that a refusal to hire based on religion, sex, or national origin is reasonably necessary to the normal operation of the defendant's overall "enterprise." The text, that is, would not seem to require the employer to show that its discriminatory exclusion is conducive to the sound performance of the particular plaintiff's job, only that it is necessary to further general business goals. Nor does the text suggest that the discriminatory job qualification must relate to the heart of employer's business, only to its "normal operation." Yet in order to prevent the exception from virtually eliminating an applicant's protection against these forms of express discrimination, the Supreme Court has required the employer to show that its discriminatory rule relates to a trait that goes to the "essence" of the enterprise *and* bears a "high correlation" to the plaintiff's ability to perform her particular job.[3]

The two basic elements of the defense derive from a pair of decisions of the former Fifth Circuit, *Diaz v. Pan American World Airways, Inc.*,[4] and *Weeks v. Southern Bell Telephone & Telegraph Company.*[5] *Diaz* insisted that the job qualification or employee trait for which the employer's practice or policy screens must be closely related to the "essence" of the business. In that case, for example, the psychological reassurance or sexual titillation ostensibly afforded airline passengers by

---

§ 4.3

1. See *EEOC v. Fremont Christian School*, 781 F.2d 1362, 1367 (9th Cir.1986).

2. See, e.g., *Western Air Lines, Inc. v. Criswell*, 472 U.S. 400, 105 S.Ct. 2743, 86 L.Ed.2d 321 (1985).

3. *Criswell, supra* note 2; *Johnson Controls, supra* § 4.2 note 3.

4. 442 F.2d 385 (5th Cir.), *cert. denied*, 404 U.S. 950, 92 S.Ct. 275, 30 L.Ed.2d 267 (1971).

5. 408 F.2d 228 (5th Cir.1969).

a requirement that flight attendants be female could not justify the exclusion of males once the court defined the essence of the business as safe transportation rather than maximum profit. Federal judges have since steadfastly refused to permit employers to define the essence of their business as maximizing profit, because then customer preference—often the embodiment of the very kind of accumulated prejudice or stereotype Title VII seeks to overcome—could be invoked to justify a vast range of absolute exclusions of women, minorities, and adherents of particular religions.[6] Despite the stringency of the *Diaz* "essence of the business" test, it remained uncertain until recently whether the trait for which the discriminatory employment rule selects must also relate to the duties of the particular jobs to which the rule is applied.

Weeks added the second layer. Even if an exclusion of members of a particular protected group is designed to enhance execution of a function critical to the business, the employer's evidence must demonstrate that "all or substantially all" members of the excluded group lack the required trait and would therefore be unable adequately to perform that function. This test is not quite as rigorous as the rule once prevalent in the Ninth Circuit[7] that the BFOQ defense could exclude members of a particular gender only from jobs they were biologically incapable of performing—male wet nurse or female sperm donor, But the *Weeks* test nevertheless defeats most assertions of the defense. By putting employers to their proof, it will doom most BFOQ defenses rooted in the assertion that only members of a particular gender have the strength or endurance required by the job.

Purporting to apply the *Weeks* test, the Supreme Court a decade ago appeared to endorse an alternative, less stringent version of the defense: prove that some, rather than "substantially all," members of the excluded gender, religion or national origin lack the critical ability to perform the trait essential to the business and that it would be highly impracticable to determine by individualized testing which ones could.[8] Casting further doubt on the Court's commitment to the *Weeks* "substantially all" test was an early decision, *Dothard v. Rawlinson*,[9] that upheld the exclusion of women from contact positions as guards in unusually dangerous maximum security prisons in Alabama. The exigent circumstances there that threatened the physical safety of employees and inmates salvaged the BFOQ defense even though Alabama had failed even to offer evidence that substantially all of the women who would seek those jobs would be incapable of maintaining order and safety. The Court merely hypothesized that women guards would be attacked (by sex offender inmates and others deprived of regular heterosexual contact) because they were women, skipping over the fact, stressed by Justice Marshall in dissent, that *all* guards in the Alabama maximum security

---

6. *See Fernandez v. Wynn Oil Co.*, 653 F.2d 1273 (9th Cir.1981).

7. *Rosenfeld v. Southern Pacific*, 519 F.2d 527 (9th Cir.1975).

8. *Western Air Lines v. Criswell*, 472 U.S. 400, 105 S.Ct. 2743, 86 L.Ed.2d 321 (1985).

9. 433 U.S. 321, 97 S.Ct. 2720, 53 L.Ed.2d 786 (1977).

system were targets simply because they were despised authority symbols.

The Supreme Court's decision in *U.A.W. v. Johnson Controls*[10] confirms the narrowness of the BFOQ defense, and appears to have closed to employers the doors it had left ajar in previous decisions. The employer's rule barred all still-fertile women of any age, marital status, or child-bearing inclination from holding a job in which they would likely be exposed to levels of lead that endangered the health of a fetus they might be carrying. First, the Court made clear, as it had in an ADEA case,[11] that in applying the *Diaz* prong of the defense, the trait the employer seeks to ensure with its discriminatory rule must not only be essential to the business as a whole but must also pertain to the particular position in question. It stressed the "occupational" limitation in § 703(e)(1), concluding that the defense fails unless the employer demonstrates objectively that the exclusion is not only "reasonably necessary" to the "normal operation"[12] of the "particular"[13] business but also relates to "job-related skills and aptitudes." The Court rejected the defense because, so far as the record revealed, "Fertile women ... participate in the manufacture of batteries as efficiently as anyone else."[14] In this connection the Court distinguished *Dothard* and *Western Air Lines, Inc. v. Criswell*,[15] writing that third-party safety concerns were allowed to figure into the BFOQ analyses there only because inmate or customer safety "went to the core of the employee's job performance"—something demonstrably not the case with batterymaking.

Johnson Controls appears also to have restricted or eliminated the employer's option to skirt *Weeks* by showing only that some, rather than "substantially all" members of the excluded group lack traits essential to the job and business and that it is "impracticable" to ascertain the ones who do. The employer contended that it had to exclude all fertile women from the jobs in question because it could not feasibly determine which of them would become pregnant and thus endanger their fetuses and, in turn, subject the company to the risk of tort liability. The Supreme Court responded by reaffirming *Weeks*. Even assuming, it

10. 499 U.S. 187, 111 S.Ct. 1196, 113 L.Ed.2d 158 (1991).

11. *Trans World Airlines, Inc. v. Thurston*, 469 U.S. 111, 105 S.Ct. 613, 83 L.Ed.2d 523 (1985).

12. As Justice Marshall had observed in his dissent in *Dothard*, it is doubtful whether the exclusion of women would have been essential to the "normal" operation of Alabama's maximum security prisons, and as such could not be justified by the rampant violence, unconstitutional conditions of confinement, and other exceptional circumstances that then prevailed.

13. The statutory requirement of evidence that the rule is needed to meet the

needs of a "particular" business also helps explain why general definitions of business essence in terms of profit or customer preference have not carried the day.

14. The Court also dismissed as "word play" an argument that the essence of *Johnson Controls'* business was "to make batteries without risk to fetuses." 499 U.S. at 207, 111 S.Ct. at 1208.

15. 472 U.S. 400, 105 S.Ct. 2743, 86 L.Ed.2d 321 (1985) (considering but ultimately rejecting a BFOQ defense based on alleged increased safety concerns related to the deteriorating health of flight engineers retained after age 60).

wrote, that the company had shown sufficient job- and business-related justification for excluding any fertile women, it had not shown that "substantially all of its fertile women employees" presented the risk on which the company relied.[16] When the two requirements, re-refined by *Johnson Controls*, are combined, the defendant faces a formidable task: "An employer must direct its concerns about a woman's ability to perform her job safely and efficiently to those aspects of the woman's job-related activities that fall within the 'essence' of the particular business."[17]

Johnson Controls also squarely rejected arguments to expand the scope of the defense to embrace the employer's economic concerns associated with hiring members of a particular gender, religion, or national origin. The argument was generated by the employer's "fear that hiring fertile women will cost more" as the result of "the spectre of an award of damages" in tort actions that might be brought for prenatal injury or wrongful death. "The extra cost of employing members of one sex ... does not provide an affirmative Title VII defense for a[n express] discriminatory refusal to hire members of that gender."[18] Here it is important to remember, however, that BFOQ is a defense to intentional, disparate treatment discrimination. By contrast, cost savings are in effect available as a defense to claims that an employer's neutral practice disproportionately adversely impacted the plaintiff's group.[19]

Given the stringency of the BFOQ defense, its principal remaining utility may lie in resisting claims of age discrimination, especially in cases where an employee's deteriorating physical capabilities correlate strongly with aging and would impair safe hands-on performance.[20] It is scarcely conceivable, moreover, that the BFOQ defense could ever justify a slur, as opposed to an employer policy. Lower courts have, however, upheld relaxed applications of the defense to accommodate a legitimate business need to assure customer privacy.[21] Moreover, EEOC guidelines

16. The Court found that *Johnson Controls* had fallen short of that showing because so few fertile women become pregnant in any one year and none of the babies born to its pregnant employees had birth defects or abnormalities.

17. *Johnson Controls*, 499 U.S. at 205, 111 S.Ct. at 1206.

18. *International Union, UAW v. Johnson Controls, Inc., supra* note 10 (individual disparate treatment case); see also *City of Los Angeles, Dep't of Water and Power v. Manhart*, 435 U.S. 702, 98 S.Ct. 1370, 55 L.Ed.2d 657 (1978) (systemic disparate treatment case).

19. *See* discussion below of the plaintiff's "less discriminatory alternative" rebuttal to the defendant's job relatedness/business necessity defense in disproportionate adverse impact cases. The statute as amended in 1991 may be construed to carry forward the Supreme Court's observations in the 1988 *Watson* case that a plaintiff's proposed less discriminatory alternative to the defendant's challenged practice must be "equally as effective" as the defendant's neutral practice under challenge, and that cost is a factor in equal effectiveness. *See* § 4.10 text accompanying notes 19–20 and 43–45, *infra*.

20. *See Usery v. Tamiami Trail Tours, Inc.*, 531 F.2d 224 (5th Cir.1976), cited with approval in *Criswell, supra* note 15, at 412, 105 S.Ct. at 2750.

21. *Healey v. Southwood Psychiatric Hosp.*, 78 F.3d 128 (3d Cir.1996) (gender a BFOQ justifying assignment of female hospital employee to night shift to further the privacy interests and therapeutic needs of patients); *Tharp v. Iowa Dep't of Corrections*, 68 F.3d 223 (8th Cir.1995) (rule precluding male employees from working cer-

relax the rules where employers have an interest in the gender-authenticity of such employees as actresses, actors, strippers, and food and drink servers at restaurants or bars where a primary job and business function is the projection of a sexually provocative display.[22] Finally, the Supreme Court has dispensed altogether with the necessity of justifying otherwise permissible "benign," "voluntary" employer affirmative action programs under the BFOQ standards.[23]

B. INDIVIDUAL DISPARATE TREATMENT— INFERENTIAL PROOF

Library References:

> C.J.S. Civil Rights §§ 161–162, 391–392, 425.
> West's Key No. Digests, Civil Rights ⊙153, 377.1.

§ 4.4   In General

Because direct evidence of intent is so uncommon, courts have recognized alternative ways of establishing unlawful discrimination. The Seventh Circuit Court of Appeals recently classified circumstantial evidence into three types which, alone or in reinforcing combination, may suffice to show intentional discrimination forbidden by Title VII. First there is suspicious timing, ambiguous statements, or other "behavior toward or comments directed at other employees in the protected group . . . from which an inference of discriminatory intent might be drawn." Second is evidence, statistical or anecdotal, that persons outside the plaintiff's protected group, otherwise similarly situated to the plaintiff, were better treated with respect to the relevant terms and conditions of employment. This of course is the essence of disparate treatment, but plaintiffs should take care that their "comparator" is in

tain shifts in women's prison unit justified by inmates' privacy interests in having only women conduct body searches), *cert. denied,* ___ U.S. ___, 116 S.Ct. 1420, 134 L.Ed.2d 545 (1996); *Backus v. Baptist Medical Center,* 510 F.Supp. 1191 (E.D.Ark.1981), *vacated as moot,* 671 F.2d 1100 (8th Cir.1982) (essential to hospital's business to safeguard patient concerns about privacy in the assignment of nurses) noted by the Supreme Court in *Johnson Controls,* 499 U.S. at 205, 111 S.Ct. at 1206, *Fesel v. Masonic Home of Delaware, Inc.,* 447 F.Supp. 1346 (D.Del.1978) (nursing home attendants), *affirmed,* 591 F.2d 1334 (3d Cir.1979). *Cf. Hodgson v. Robert Hall Clothes, Inc.,* 473 F.2d 589 (3d Cir.1973), *cert. denied,* 414 U.S. 866, 94 S.Ct. 50, 38 L.Ed.2d 85 (1973) (not challenging assignment of men only as salespersons in men's clothing department in case under EPA). *But see U.S. EEOC v. Sedita,* 755 F.Supp. 808, 810 (N.D.Ill.1991)

(defense to a hiring rule that excluded men rejected for failure of proof that the privacy interests of health club customers were "entitled to protection under the law" and that no less discriminatory alternatives existed), *vacated on reconsideration,* 816 F.Supp. 1291 (1993) (evidence indicated men might invade privacy interests). *But cf. Johnson v. Phelan,* 69 F.3d 144 (7th Cir. 1995) (naked male detainee's due process and Eighth Amendment rights not violated when he was monitored by female guards absent allegation that monitoring was designed to embarrass or humiliate him).

22. *See* 29 C.F.R. § 1604.2 (1979) (actors and actresses).

23. *Johnson v. Transportation Agency,* 480 U.S. 616, 107 S.Ct. 1442, 94 L.Ed.2d 615 (1987). See Chapter 5 on the conditions that make such programs permissible despite their facial reliance on factors prohibited by Title VII.

fact similarly situated from the standpoint of status and conduct.[1]

The third, or "pretext" mode, is perhaps most easily understood as an even more indirect way of showing the second, or "comparative" mode. This method of proving "individual disparate treatment" owes its origin to *McDonnell Douglas Corp. v. Green,*[2] and was later elaborated in several other Supreme Court decisions culminating in *Texas Dept. of Community Affairs v. Burdine,*[3] and, most recently, *St. Mary's Honor Center v. Hicks.*[4] The plaintiff makes a *McDonnell Douglas prima facie* case—and thereby survives a Federal Rule of Civil Procedure 41(b) involuntary dismissal motion, or, in the jury trials authorized by the Civil Rights Act of 1991, a Rule 50(a)(1) motion for judgment as a matter of law at the close of her case in chief—by offering evidence that she (1) belongs to a protected group; (2) applied for or continued to desire the position in question; (3) met minimum uniform qualifications to receive or retain the position; and (4) was rejected. This evidence, the Court has explained, eliminates several of the most common nondiscriminatory reasons for the plaintiff's rejection, nonpromotion, discipline or discharge and thus makes it more likely that the employer's real reason, or one of them, was a status protected by Title VII.

The elements, as the Court in *McDonnell Douglas* noted, are flexibly adapted to the facts of a given case. For example, an employee complaining of promotion denial need not show element (2), that she applied for the higher position, if it was the employer's routine practice to offer promotions to persons with her seniority and position.[5] Moreover, the first of the numbered prima facie elements is *pro forma*—anyone, even a white male, can claim protected group status by contrasting himself in racial, religious, national origin, or gender terms to the group he claims was preferred.[6] The third element, qualifications, has the greatest practical importance, as it eliminates the most common nondiscriminatory reason for rejection where an application has been made. The Court

§ 4.4

1. *See, e.g., Hargett v. National Westminster Bank, USA,* 78 F.3d 836 (2d Cir.1996)(African–American employee could be subjected to harsher discipline than ostensible white comparators because he held position of higher rank and authority and accordingly could be held to higher standard of judgment and behavior); *Ricks v. Riverwood International Corp.,* 38 F.3d 1016 (8th Cir.1994) (plaintiff could be discharged for felony drug conviction even though white coworker not discharged for the felony of armed false imprisonment because drugs were a particular workplace hazard and employer had drug use and testing policy); *Harvey v. Anheuser–Busch, Inc.,* 38 F.3d 968 (8th Cir.1994) (discharge upheld because less severely disciplined employees had not engaged in same offense).

2. 411 U.S. 792, 93 S.Ct. 1817, 36 L.Ed.2d 668 (1973).

3. 450 U.S. 248, 101 S.Ct. 1089, 67 L.Ed.2d 207 (1981).

4. 509 U.S. 502, 113 S.Ct. 2742, 125 L.Ed.2d 407 (1993).

5. *Loyd v. Phillips Bros., Inc.,* 25 F.3d 518 (7th Cir.1994).

6. *See McDonald, supra* § 3.9, note 1. But some circuits are skeptical that *McDonnell Douglas'* inferential mode of proving intentional discrimination should avail white race discrimination claimants, *Hill v. Burrell Communications Group, Inc.,* 67 F.3d 665, 668 n. 2 (7th Cir.1995); or they require special "background circumstances," like the white plaintiff's superior qualifications relative to a selectee, "to support the suspicion that the defendant is the unusual employer who discriminates against the majority." *See Parker v. Baltimore & Ohio R.R.,* 652 F.2d 1012, 1017 (D.C.Cir.1981).

has now declared relatively clearly that this showing refers to minimal or absolute rather than relative or comparative qualifications.[7] A final element, sometimes relaxed or waived by lower courts, is evidence that the employer, after rejecting the plaintiff, continued to seek applicants with her general qualifications or selected a person from outside her protected group.[8] And in rehiring cases, the plaintiff need not show that he was identically situated with others of a different race who were initially terminated[9] or who resigned[10] at the same time; it suffices that the plaintiff's former position was filled by a member of a different race or simply that he was qualified for the new job for which he was rejected.

The Supreme Court has made some seemingly contradictory pronouncements about the quantum of evidence the plaintiff must adduce to survive this prima facie stage of the case. On the one hand, when Title VII claims were entirely equitable and triable only to a judge, the Court wrote that the plaintiff must satisfy the trier of fact that the required elements are established by a preponderance of the evidence produced to that point in the trial.[11] More recently, however, after the Civil Rights Act of 1991 paved the way for jury trials and legal relief in disparate treatment cases, the Court has indicated that the requisite quantum is "infinitely less than what a directed verdict demands."[12] Taken literally, the latter statement suggests that the case should advance to the next stage even if reasonable jurors could not find plaintiff's way by a preponderance of the evidence on one or more of the elements that the plaintiff must ultimately prove.

If the plaintiff establishes the prima facie case, a judicially created presumption declares the resulting inference of discrimination conclusive unless the defendant offers evidence that it had one or more "legitimate, nondiscriminatory reasons" for an employment decision.[13] The preliminary question whether plaintiff established a *prima facie* case loses all significance once defendant presents its proof. Put otherwise, the definition of the prima facie case merely aids the court in determining whether to grant a defendant's motion for judgment as a matter of law

---

7. *Patterson v. McLean Credit Union,* 491 U.S. 164, 109 S.Ct. 2363, 105 L.Ed.2d 132 (1989) (plaintiff need not prove that she was better qualified than the white employee who received the contested promotion). *See also MacDonald v. Eastern Wyoming Mental Health Center,* 941 F.2d 1115 (10th Cir.1991); *Denison v. Swaco Geolograph Co.,* 941 F.2d 1416 (10th Cir. 1991); *Siegel v. Alpha Wire Corp.,* 894 F.2d 50 (3d Cir.), *cert. denied,* 496 U.S. 906, 110 S.Ct. 2588, 110 L.Ed.2d 269 (1990). *Cf. St. Mary's Honor Center v. Hicks,* 509 U.S. 502, 113 S.Ct. 2742, 125 L.Ed.2d 407 (1993) (referring to the "minimal requirements" of plaintiff's prima facie individual disparate treatment case).

8. *See Patterson v. McLean Credit Union, supra* note 7, at 186, 108 S.Ct. at 2377 (adapting Title VII's individual disparate

treatment mode of proof to race discrimination claim under 42 U.S.C.A. § 1981). It should be stressed, however, that the plaintiff's replacement by a member of the same race does not prevent her from establishing prima facie that the initial decision to discharge her was unlawfully race based. *Carson v. Bethlehem Steel Corp.,* 82 F.3d 157 (7th Cir.1996).

9. *Talley v. Bravo Pitino Restaurant, Ltd.,* 61 F.3d 1241 (6th Cir.1995).

10. *Richardson v. Leeds Police Dep't,* 71 F.3d 801 (11th Cir.1995).

11. *Burdine, supra* note 3.

12. *St. Mary's Honor Center v. Hicks, supra* note 4.

13. *McDonnell Douglas, supra* note 2.

under FRCP 50(a) at the close of plaintiff's case (or "directed verdict" as it is still known in most state courts). But once both sides rest, the trier of fact must evaluate all admitted evidence, including but not limited to the plaintiff's *prima facie* evidence, to decide if plaintiff has carried the ultimate burden of demonstrating intentional discrimination.[14] Thus jury instructions in an age discrimination case that in effect permitted the jurors to find that age was a determining factor in the plaintiff's termination if they believed his prima facie evidence that younger employees were treated more favorably during a reduction in force have been held harmfully prejudicial to the employer.[15] A trial judge's ultimate determination about discriminatory intent—whether shown through direct or indirect evidence—is one of fact and may therefore be overturned on appeal only if "clearly erroneous."[16]

Traditionally, most courts have viewed as "legitimate" virtually any reason the employer shows it relied on[17] that can be distinguished from the five group characteristics protected by statute and from the few "proxy" factors that perfectly correspond with one of those groups. This view is evidently driven by deference to the employer's superior knowledge of its own productivity, safety and efficiency requirements.[18] It is fortified by the Court's recent decision in *Hazen Paper Co. v. Biggins*,[19] that factors highly but incompletely correlating with age, e.g., pension status or years of service, are factors other than age not expressly prohibited by the Age Discrimination in Employment Act (even if unlawful under ERISA), rather than unlawful proxies for intentional age discrimination. If a practice or policy, the terms of which are not expressly geared to a prohibited factor, nevertheless has a substantial (but not exclusive)[20] adverse impact on the plaintiff's protected group, that practice will violate Title VII or ADEA, if at all, only on the "neutral practice/disproportionate adverse impact" theory of proof discussed below.

Indeed, at least with the hindsight of *Biggins*, it appears that several circuit decisions that had condemned word-of-mouth hiring as intentionally discriminatory (because it was highly, although not perfectly, correlated with carrying forward past racial or national origin imbalances in the employer's work force) are better justified as resting on

14. *United States Postal Service Bd. of Governors v. Aikens*, 460 U.S. 711, 103 S.Ct. 1478, 75 L.Ed.2d 403 (1983).

15. *Seman v. Coplay Cement Co.*, 26 F.3d 428 (3d Cir.1994).

16. *Anderson v. City of Bessemer*, 470 U.S. 564, 105 S.Ct. 1504, 84 L.Ed.2d 518 (1985); Federal Rule of Civil Procedure 52(a).

17. When an employer did not know about an applicant's poor credit history when it decided not to hire him, its proffered reason that it relied on that history was held not "legitimate." *Turnes v. AmSouth Bank,* 36 F.3d 1057 (11th Cir.1994).

There is also authority, however, that the employer may assert as a defense in court a reason that in fact commanded only minority support on the key employer committee responsible for the adverse employment decision in question. *Bina v. Providence College*, 39 F.3d 21 (1st Cir.1994).

18. *See Furnco Construction Corp. v. Waters*, 438 U.S. 567, 98 S.Ct. 2943, 57 L.Ed.2d 957 (1978).

19. 507 U.S. 604, 113 S.Ct. 1701, 123 L.Ed.2d 338 (1993).

20. *See* discussion at text accompanying notes 3–5, *supra*, § 4.2.

showings that the effects of that neutral practice fell far more harshly on the plaintiffs' protected groups.[21] Of course if the practice is conceptualized as neutral, the employer will be called on only to produce and persuade about the "business necessity/job relatedness" defense that pertains to the neutral practice proof mode; and although the issue is not free from doubt, even after the legislative overhaul of the neutral practice defense by the 1991 Civil Rights Act, the neutral practice defense remains arguably easier to carry than the "bona fide occupational qualification" defense that alone will overcome a plaintiff's showing of express or facial intentional discrimination.

There is one apparent exception to the rule that a reason must not be grounded in one of the five prohibited characteristics to be a "legitimate" one that will rebut the *McDonnell Douglas* prima facie case. When whites or males mount "reverse discrimination" attacks on employment practices, employers will sometimes respond that the decision in question was made pursuant to an agreement settling a minority member or woman's claim of discrimination. There is no doubt here that the employment decision now challenged was taken on the basis of race or gender; but that is precisely what the settlement agreement called for. There is federal circuit court authority that reliance on a settlement in good faith of a claim of discrimination constitutes a legitimate business reason for the discriminatory employment practice that defeats the requisite showing of intent.[22] Further, the employer's agreement to the settlement has been held not to constitute an independent act of unlawful discrimination.[23]

Although the opinion in *McDonnell Douglas* suggested that the employer need only "articulate" a legitimate, nondiscriminatory reason, perhaps simply in an argument or brief, the Court, after a couple of false starts, definitively determined in *Burdine* that the employer's burden, while not onerous, may be discharged only through evidence that clearly explains its proffered reason or reasons.[24] But the Court has insisted that the defendant's burden is one of production only and that the burden of persuading about intentional discrimination resides with the plaintiff throughout. Accordingly, like the presumptions described in

---

21. *Compare EEOC v. Metal Service Co.*, 892 F.2d 341, 350–351 (3d Cir.1990); *Barnett v. W.T. Grant Co.*, 518 F.2d 543, 549 (4th Cir.1975); *Parham v. Southwestern Bell Tel. Co.*, 433 F.2d 421, 426–27 (8th Cir.1970) (word-of-mouth hiring that perpetuated such imbalances viewed as circumstantial evidence of disparate treatment) *with EEOC v. Consolidated Service Systems*, 989 F.2d 233, 235 (7th Cir.1993) (same practice not intentionally discriminatory despite strong tendency to extend the dominance of national origin group in employer's workforce to the exclusion of others).

22. But because the burden of persuasion on the ultimate issue of the employer's motivation remains with the plaintiff throughout, the employer's evidence may be offered entirely through cross-examination of plaintiff's witnesses; an employer may meet it, that is, without calling any witnesses of its own. *Diehl v. Tele–Solutions*, 57 F.3d 482 (6th Cir.1995).

23. *Marcantel v. State of Louisiana*, 37 F.3d 197 (5th Cir.1994); *Carey v. U.S. Postal Service*, 812 F.2d 621 (10th Cir.1987).

24. *Id.* and *EEOC v. McCall Printing Corp.*, 633 F.2d 1232 (6th Cir.1980).

Federal Rule of Evidence 301, the *McDonnell Douglas* presumption of unlawful discriminatory motive that arises from a successful prima facie case disappears and has no further force in the litigation if the employer discharges its relatively modest burden of producing evidence of a legitimate, nondiscriminatory reason for the challenged employment action—the bubble bursts.

A plaintiff can nevertheless prevail on rebuttal. To do so the plaintiff must persuade the court that the defendant's purported legitimate reason is a smokescreen or "pretext" for intentional discrimination. It bears emphasis, however, that the plaintiff does not encounter this burden until after the defendant has produced evidence of one or more specific legitimate nondiscriminatory reasons. Thus in making the prima facie case the plaintiff need only show that she possessed the base, minimum qualifications the employer uniformly required for attaining or retaining a job. She need not do more at that stage of the case—for example, rebut employer assertions that she engaged in misconduct or possessed qualifications equal to or superior to the employee retained or selected in her stead. Such a requirement would in effect prematurely demand that she prove that the employer's reason is pretextual before the employer is called on clearly to identify, through evidence, its legitimate nondiscriminatory reason. That, in turn, would prematurely force the plaintiff to turn to the ultimate issue in the case, intentional discrimination.[25]

Until recently, the Court had written that the plaintiff could make the pretext showing, by the standard preponderance of the evidence quantum, in either of two generic ways: by demonstrating through its own affirmative evidence, including that previously adduced prima facie, that the employer, in reaching its decision, explicitly relied on plaintiff's protected group status, rather than on its proffered legitimate reason; or, less directly, simply by convincing the judge or jury that the proffered reason is an implausible explanation for the challenged decision.[26] The Supreme Court recently held, in *St. Mary's Honor Center*, that the latter showing merely permits but does not mandate a judgment for the plaintiff.[27] In jury-triable intentional discrimination cases authorized by the Civil Rights Act of 1991, therefore, the jury should be charged accordingly.[28] But the Court reaffirmed that evidence of the falsity of the employer's proffered legitimate reason could suffice. Thus the court rejected a "pretext-plus" rule that had evolved in some of the circuit courts which had required plaintiffs to prove discriminatory intent not only by establishing the falsity of the employer's explanation but also

---

25. *See, e.g., Patterson v. McLean Credit Union, supra* note 8; *Davenport v. Riverview Gardens School Dist.*, 30 F.3d 940 (8th Cir.1994).

26. *Burdine, supra* note 3; *Aikens, supra* note 14.

27. *St. Mary's Honor Center, supra* note 4.

28. The Court alluded to the availability of jury trials. It mentioned judgment under Federal Rule of Civil Procedure 50(a)(1), which by its terms applies "during

through affirmative independent evidence.[29]

The *St. Mary's* dissent expressed concern that plaintiffs' discovery and trial burdens will be unjustly magnified and employers more often erroneously exculpated if the fact finder's determination that the employer's reason is unworthy of belief does not compel the conclusion that its false reason is a pretext for prohibited discrimination. The majority, however, was fearful of erroneously inculpating the employer every time an employer witness testifies to a reason for the challenged employment action that is not in fact the employer's real reason, which may happen where the real reason is embarrassing[30] or even illegal[31] but not violative of Title VII. The Court has shown somewhat less understanding about prevarication by plaintiffs who have proven unlawful employment discrimination but after termination are discovered by the former employers to have committed resume fraud. This "after-acquired evidence" defense is discussed below.

Despite some language in the *St. Mary's* majority opinion to the contrary, it appears that convincing evidence of the implausibility of the employer's proffered nondiscriminatory explanation, while not compelling a conclusion that the plaintiff has shown unlawful pretext, should continue to suffice to meet that burden if the factfinder further determines that the disbelieved reason was offered to mask prohibited race, gender, religious or national origin discrimination rather than something else.[32] A recent EEOC Enforcement Guidance explicitly confirms this conclusion.[33]

Post-*St. Mary's* decisions reflect the raft of interpretive problems the Court left in the wake of its contrapuntal opinion. On remand from the Supreme Court in *Biggins*, for example, the First Circuit, obedient to the Court's decision there, did not consider evidence that the company

a trial by jury," and it referred broadly to decisions by the "trier of fact."

29. *See, e.g., Mesnick v. General Electric*, 950 F.2d 816 (1st Cir.1991), *cert. denied*, 504 U.S. 985, 112 S.Ct. 2965, 119 L.Ed.2d 586 (1992); *Galbraith v. Northern Telecom*, 944 F.2d 275 (6th Cir.1991), *cert. denied*, 503 U.S. 945, 112 S.Ct. 1497, 117 L.Ed.2d 637 (1992). Even after *St. Mary's*, however, the plaintiff who does not attempt to discredit the employer's nondiscriminatory explanation may bear the burden of producing affirmative evidence of unlawful motivation going beyond the prima facie case. *Burns v. AAF–McQuay*, 96 F.3d 728 (4th Cir.1996).

30. *See, e.g., Winder v. Wickes Lumber Co.*, 51 F.3d 1051 (11th Cir.1995) (per curiam) (manager falsely asserted that he had terminated African–American plaintiff during force reduction for receiving a less than satisfactory performance evaluation that manager in fact had not read before terminating plaintiff instead of white employee,

but manager's real reason—his personal acquaintance with the white subordinate's work—held not based on discrimination because of race) (unpublished opinion); *Bell v. AT & T*, 946 F.2d 1507 (10th Cir.1991) (false reason apparently offered to hide nepotism); *Shager v. Upjohn Co.*, 913 F.2d 398 (7th Cir.1990).

31. One can imagine an employer that, for reasons of public relations, produces evidence of a false reason where the real reason was that the plaintiff had committed a felony related to employment, *e.g.*, arson on the premises. *Cf. Carter v. Maloney Trucking & Storage, Inc.*, 631 F.2d 40 (5th Cir. 1980) (plaintiff murdered another employee).

32. *See* 509 U.S. at 511 & n. 4, 113 S.Ct. at 2749 & n.4. *Binder v. Long Island Lighting Co.*, 57 F.3d 193 (2d Cir.1995).

33. Enforcement Guidance on *St. Mary's Honor Center v. Hicks*, 509 U.S. 502, 113 S.Ct. 2742, 125 L.Ed.2d 407 (1993).

terminated plaintiff to deprive him of pension vesting as evidence of intentional unlawful age discrimination. Nevertheless, it upheld the verdict for plaintiff principally because it determined that the jury disbelieved the employer's assertion that plaintiff was terminated because of disloyalty.[34] That reason may have been offered only to mask pension discrimination that the Supreme Court had found *not* unlawful under ADEA. But other evidence that only older employees were required to sign confidentiality agreements persuaded the court that the jury could properly assign age discrimination as "the real reason" for the termination.[35] Some circuit opinions are even more direct in reading *St. Mary's* as requiring the plaintiff to "do more than merely prove the articulated reasons false"[36]—that is, offer independent, affirmative evidence that the defendant's agents discriminated against plaintiff at least in part because of her protected group status.[37] While it is submitted that this more demanding approach misreads *St. Mary's* as a blueprint for Title VII cases, it may represent a sensible adaptation of the Supreme Court's opinion to cases under ADEA. This is because, as discussed in Chapter 7 below, *Biggins* now imposes on the age discrimination plaintiff the ultimate burden of demonstrating that age played a "determinative" role in the employer's decision, not, as with race or gender under the amended Title VII, merely a "motivating" factor.

Still other post-*St. Mary's* circuit opinions display understandable uncertainty about how to apply its teachings to motions for summary judgment or directed verdict. Certainly it is clear that judgment for the employer is consistent with *St. Mary's* where the employee fails to offer any kind of "pretext" evidence refuting the employer's evidence of a legitimate, nondiscriminatory reason. Where the employer proffers such a reason, the plaintiff is not entitled to a trial, or to have a case go to the jury, based solely on evidence presented pretrial or during its case in chief that satisfied the minimal elements of the *McDonnell Douglas* prima facie case.[38] This is so even though, under *St. Mary's*, the trier of fact may take the prima facie evidence into account in assessing whether

---

34. *Biggins v. Hazen Paper Co.,* ___ F.3d ___, 1993 WL 406515 (1st Cir.1993), *withdrawn,* 1994 WL 398013 (1st Cir.1994).

35. *See also Anderson v. Baxter Healthcare Corp.,* 13 F.3d 1120 (7th Cir.1994) (observing that *St. Mary's* rejected the "pretext-plus" approach and instead permitted fact finder to infer intentional discrimination on prohibited ground from the prima facie case coupled with its disbelief of employer's proffered reason).

36. *Howard v. BP Oil Co., Inc.,* 32 F.3d 520, 525 (11th Cir.1994).

37. *See, e.g., Jiminez v. Mary Washington College,* 57 F.3d 369 (4th Cir.1995); *Smith v. Stratus Computer, Inc.,* 40 F.3d 11, 16 (1st Cir.1994)(even at summary judgment, requiring evidence of unlawful discrimination in addition to evidence enabling factfinder to disbelieve defendant's proffered legitimate nondiscriminatory reason);

Meeks v. Computer Assoc. Int'l, 15 F.3d 1013, 1019 n. 1 (11th Cir.1994).

38. *Pritchard v. Southern Co. Services,* 92 F.3d 1130 (11th Cir.1996); *Wallis v. J.R. Simplot Company,* 26 F.3d 885 (9th Cir. 1994) (so holding under ADEA as well as Title VII); *Davis v. Chevron U.S.A.,* 14 F.3d 1082 (5th Cir.1994). *See generally Durham v. Xerox Corp.,* 18 F.3d 836 (10th Cir.), *cert. denied,* ___ U.S. ___, 115 S.Ct. 80, 130 L.Ed.2d 33 (1994); *Anderson v. Baxter Healthcare Corp.,* 13 F.3d 1120 (7th Cir. 1994); *Mitchell v. Data Gen. Corp.,* 12 F.3d 1310 (4th Cir.1993); *Geary v. Visitation of the Blessed Virgin Mary,* 7 F.3d 324 (3d Cir.1993); *LeBlanc v. Great Am. Ins. Co.,* 6 F.3d 836 (1st Cir.1993), *cert. denied,* ___ U.S. ___, 114 S.Ct. 1398, 128 L.Ed.2d 72 (1994).

plaintiff has shown the falsity of defendant's asserted legitimate reason or has otherwise proven that the employer's reason was a pretext for discrimination on a prohibited ground.

But what if the plaintiff, in resisting summary judgment or before resting at trial, does offer evidence tending to refute the employer's proffered reason, failing, however, to offer "affirmative" evidence that the employer's real or motivating reason was discrimination on a ground prohibited by Title VII or ADEA? The *St. Mary's* majority observed, if only in passing, that "it is not enough to disbelieve the employer." Citing this language, a number of circuits have required the plaintiff to produce independent evidence of unlawful motivation in order to survive defendant's motion for summary judgment or, before or after verdict, for judgment as a matter of law.[39] One recent opinion of a divided Fifth Circuit panel, for example, labels as "dictum" the statement in *St. Mary's* that a factfinder's disbelief of the ostensibly legitimate reasons advanced by the employer, coupled with plaintiff's prima facie evidence, may "suffice to show intentional discrimination."[40] The opinion appears to rest on the assumption that the standard *McDonnell Douglas* prima facie case is not by itself sufficient evidence of discriminatory animus.[41] Subsequently the Fifth Circuit en banc concluded that although *St. Mary's* may not require independent evidence of discriminatory intent beyond the falsity of the proffered reason, a plaintiff's verdict may be searchingly scrutinized for "substantial evidence" of that falsity.[42]

Other circuits,[43] however, have squarely rejected the argument that the plaintiff must produce affirmative, independent evidence of discrimi-

---

39. *See Hoeppner v. Crotched Mountain Rehabilitation Center,* 31 F.3d 9, 17 (1st Cir.1994); *Manzer v. Diamond Shamrock Chemicals Co.,* 29 F.3d 1078, 1084 (6th Cir.1994); *Wolenski v. Manville Corp.,* 19 F.3d 34 (10th Cir.1994); *LeBlanc v. Great American Ins. Co.* 6 F.3d 836, 841 (1st Cir.1993), *cert. denied,* ___ U.S. ___, 114 S.Ct. 1398, 128 L.Ed.2d 72 (1994); *Bodenheimer v. PPG Industries,* 5 F.3d 955 (5th Cir.1993) (ADEA). *Cf. Hardin v. Hussmann Corp.,* 45 F.3d 262, 264 (8th Cir. 1995) (where employer defends ADEA prima facie case by asserting that plaintiff was terminated as part of a reduction in force, plaintiff must produce "additional" evidence that age played a role).

40. *Rhodes v. Guiberson Oil Tools,* 39 F.3d 537 (5th Cir.1994).

41. Thus the two judges in the majority assert that under the reading of *St. Mary's* offered here, an employer could be found liable on a "trial record ... absolutely devoid of any evidence or testimony that relates to discriminatory actions or animus." 39 F.3d at 545.

42. *Rhodes v. Guiberson Oil Tools,* 82 F.3d 615 (5th Cir.1996) (en banc). The Second Circuit has similarly subjected close examination under the "clearly erroneous" standard of FRCP 52(a) a district judge's factual finding that an employer's proffered reasons were a pretext for sex discrimination. *Fisher v. Vassar College,* 70 F.3d 1420 (2d Cir.1995). In a similar vein, the Eleventh Circuit upheld judgment for defendant as a matter of law because plaintiff's evidence tending to undermine the employer's reasons for terminating her did not suggest any suspicion of mendacity. *Walker v. NationsBank,* 53 F.3d 1548, 1557 (11th Cir.1995). Although the Supreme Court in *St. Mary's* did recognize that a factfinder might disbelieve a reason honestly or dishonestly presented by an employer witness, the opinion did not appear to require categorically that a plaintiff proceeding solely on the basis of the prima facie case and evidence that the employer's reason is unworthy of credence must also cast doubt on the employer's credibility.

43. In the case of the Sixth Circuit, it is a different panel of the same circuit that has applied *St. Mary's* more leniently to the plaintiff.

natory animus in addition to the prima facie evidence coupled with the evidence that the employer's proffered explanation was false. For these courts, evidence raising a genuine question about falsity, coupled with the still surviving (but no longer presumption-raising) prima facie *McDonnell Douglas* proof, is enough to warrant a trial, submit a case to the jury, or support a jury verdict under instructions consistent with *St. Mary's*.[44]

There remains the possibility, of course, that the courts taking the stricter approach have been swayed more by the relative weakness of the plaintiffs' prima facie evidence in particular cases than by the belief that she must produce affirmative evidence of unlawful motive in all cases. This may be only a particular instance of a more general question about the power of the presumption accorded the plaintiff based upon the bare prima facie evidence of inferential disparate treatment. Notwithstand-

---

44. *See Barber v. CSX Distribution Servs.*, 68 F.3d 694 (3d Cir.1995) (summary judgment); *Binder v. Long Island Lighting Co.*, 57 F.3d 193, 200 (2d Cir.1995)(reversing judgment as a matter of law, or "JNOV," in case under ADEA); *Barbour v. Merrill*, 48 F.3d 1270, 1277 (D.C.Cir. 1995)(Rule 50(a) judgment as a matter of law properly denied where plaintiff introduced evidence sufficient for jury to accept the prima facie case and disbelieve the employer's legitimate nondiscriminatory reasons); *Cole v. Ruidoso Mun. Schools*, 43 F.3d 1373 (10th Cir.1994) (summary judgment improper where material issue of fact remained as to whether disbelief of defendant's proffered reason, coupled with plaintiff's prima facie case, showed sex discrimination); *Torre v. Casio, Inc.*, 42 F.3d 825 (3d Cir.1994) (ADEA) and *Fuentes v. Perskie*, 32 F.3d 759 (3d Cir.1994) (ADEA) (to withstand summary judgment plaintiff need only have evidence from which the trier of fact could reasonably believe that an unlawful discriminatory reason was a motivating cause *or* could reasonably disbelieve the reason proffered by the employer); *Gaworski v. ITT Commercial Finance Corp.*, 17 F.3d 1104 (8th Cir.), *cert. denied,* ___ U.S. ___, 115 S.Ct. 355, 130 L.Ed.2d 310 (1994); *Anderson v. Baxter Healthcare Corp.*, 13 F.3d 1120 (7th Cir.1994); *Mitchell v. Data General Corp.*, 12 F.3d 1310 (4th Cir.1993); *Washington v. Garrett*, 10 F.3d 1421 (9th Cir.1993); *Hairston v. Gainesville Sun Publishing Co.*, 9 F.3d 913 (11th Cir.1993); *Kline v. Tennessee Valley Authority*, 1 F.3d 1241 (6th Cir.1993). *See also Ellis v. NCNB Texas National Bank*, 842 F.Supp. 243 (N.D.Tex.1994). *Cf. EEOC v. Ethan Allen, Inc.*, 44 F.3d 116 (2d Cir.1994) (employer's inconsistent explanations of its ostensibly legitimate nondiscriminatory reasons warrants denying summary judgment

in ADEA case). *But cf. Sheridan v. E.I. Du Pont de Nemours and Co.*, 74 F.3d 1439 (3d Cir.1996) (acquiescing in precedent holding evidence of falsity suffices to permit trial on ultimate question of intentional discrimination, but proposing more stringent test of whether a reasonable trier of fact could find discrimination was more likely than not determinative of the challenged employment act).

But at least three circuits have fairly explicitly announced differential standards to govern pretrial versus trial proceedings. These courts have required the lesser showing of mere disbelief of the employer's stated reason to survive summary judgment, but more affirmative and possibly even independent evidence of intentional discrimination at trial when defendant moves before or after judgment for judgment as a matter of law under FRCP 50(a). *See Randle v. Aurora*, 69 F.3d 441, 452 (10th Cir. 1995); *Howard v. BP Oil Co.*, 32 F.3d 520, 525 (11th Cir.1994); *Anderson v. Baxter Healthcare Corp.*, 13 F.3d 1120, 1124 (7th Cir.1994). Such decisions reflect a common sense appreciation that summary judgment is typically decided upon evidence presented only through papers, while at trial plaintiff's live witnesses might have a more effective or fuller opportunity to develop evidence persuasive on the ultimate issue of intentional discrimination. Yet they are somewhat inconsistent with the Supreme Court's equation of the summary judgment and directed verdict standards in *Anderson v. Liberty Lobby, Inc.*, 477 U.S. 242, 106 S.Ct. 2505, 91 L.Ed.2d 202 (1986). And formally the opinions insist that they are applying the same standard on summary judgment as on Rule 50 motions before or after verdict. *See, e.g., Rhodes v. Guiberson Oil Tools*, 75 F.3d 989 n. 4 (5th Cir. 1996) (en banc).

ing *McDonnell Douglas* and *Burdine*, some prima facie evidence may only be strong enough to *threaten* the defendant with an adverse judgment if it fails to produce evidence of a legitimate nondiscriminatory reason but insufficiently strong to *entitle* plaintiff to such a judgment. This could happen "if plaintiff's prima facie case is held to be inadequate in law or fails [by a preponderance of the evidence] to convince the factfinder." [45] In other words, there will always be a question about "the strength of the inference of discrimination based on the prima facie case," [46] and sometimes it may be so slight that the Federal Rule 301 presumption may not be invoked.

If it is correct, despite *St. Mary's*, that the fact finder will continue to be permitted to infer unlawful age discrimination in most cases where the "legitimate nondiscriminatory reason" proffered by the employer is disbelieved, one may imagine a fairly complex, sequential series of decisions to be made by the judge, or instructions to be followed by the jury, in post–1991 Act intentional discrimination actions. First, in rare cases the trial judge must at the close of defendant's case grant the plaintiff judgment as a matter of law under FRCP 50(a)(1). This would happen only if any rational person would have to find by a preponderance the existence of the facts constituting the plaintiff's prima facie case, for example, the defendant failed even to produce evidence recognized as a nondiscriminatory reason for the challenged action.

Second, far more commonly, the judge at the close of all the evidence may, at the employer's request, have to charge the members of the jury that if the plaintiff has persuaded them not to believe the evidence the employer produced about a purported legitimate nondiscriminatory reason, they nevertheless *need not* conclude that the employer relied on that reason as a pretext for unlawful discrimination. Third, the judge may also have to charge, at plaintiff's request, that the jury members *may* find unlawful pretext, and hence the ultimate fact of intentional discrimination, based solely on their disbelief of defendant's proffered legitimate reason, together with the prima facie evidence earlier presented by plaintiff during her case in chief, even absent other more "direct" or "affirmative" evidence of unlawful pretext.

Still, it should be remembered that even after *St. Mary* 's a plaintiff *may* prevail on pretext by buttressing its case about the falsity of the employer's stated reason with more direct or affirmative evidence that the employer relied on a group characteristic prohibited by statute. Alternatively, such evidence may suffice by itself to show intentional discrimination, as it does in the cases of "express" or "facial" discrimination mentioned above—e.g., cases involving slurs by employer agents or explicit employer prohibitions against the hire or placement of members of a particular protected group. Moreover, the Court has placed no

---

45. Zimmer, Sullivan, Richards and Calloway, *Cases and Materials on Employment Discrimination* 150 n.4 and accompanying text (3d ed. Little Brown 1994).

46. *Mardell v. Harleysville Life Insurance Co.,* 31 F.3d 1221 (3d Cir.1994), *petition for cert. filed,* ___ U.S. ___, 115 S.Ct. 1397, 131 L.Ed.2d 286 (1995).

categorical limitations on the types of affirmative evidence that may establish pretext in the *McDonnell Douglas/Burdine/St. Mary's* indirect disparate treatment case. For example, a plaintiff is not required to demonstrate that she was better qualified than a successful applicant, but may alternatively or additionally present evidence, including statistical evidence, that the employer had previously practiced unlawful discrimination against her or her group.[47]

On the other hand, a plaintiff's demonstration in a non-promotion case that he was in fact the most qualified applicant is not necessarily tantamount to a showing that the employer understood or agreed with that assessment and promoted another as a pretext for discrimination. The employer's explanation, in other words, may be wrong but credible and therefore nonpretextual in the sense intended by *St. Mary's*.[48] This result is an example of what EEOC apparently had in mind when it noted, in its recent enforcement guidance, that "[w]hile *Hicks* does not, as a matter of law, require a plaintiff to produce additional evidence of intent to discriminate where the employer's explanation for its actions is found not to be credible, it does, as a practical matter, permit a fact finder to require such affirmative evidence."[49] Similarly, evidence offered by an employer that tends to negate an inference of intentional discrimination has been held to warrant judgment as a matter of law even where the reviewing court acknowledges that a reasonable jury had ample evidence from which to disbelieve the employer's stated legitimate nondiscriminatory reason.[50]

It should be stressed that all these modes of intentional discrimination are designed to ferret out and penalize only employer conduct that adversely differentiates on the basis of one or more[51] of Title VII's prohibited grounds; they are not designed to assure workplace norms or mores that are fair in other respects. Thus any reason for the employer's challenged decision deemed not "because of" race, gender, religion or national origin (or a proxy for one of those grounds) is likely to be viewed as legitimate, even if the trier of fact also considers that reason unfair, unreasonable or unenlightened.[52] The employment discrimina-

---

47. *See McDonnell Douglas*, 411 U.S. at 804–805, 93 S.Ct. at 1825–1826; *Patterson*, 491 U.S. at 185–188, 109 S.Ct. at 2377–2379.

48. *Hughes v. Brown*, 20 F.3d 745 (7th Cir.1994).

49. Enforcement Guidance on *St. Mary's*, *supra*, at n. 6.

50. *Isenbergh v. Knight–Ridder Newspaper Sales, Inc.*, 84 F.3d 1380, 1388 (11th Cir.1996)(case under ADEA).

51. There is authority that a plaintiff complaining about discrimination on a "compound" basis—race and gender, for example, or gender and national origin—must demonstrate that the employer discrimi-

nates on those grounds in combination, not merely on one or the other. *Lam v. University of Hawaii*, 40 F.3d 1551 (9th Cir.1994). This suggests that the plaintiff's counsel in such a case should take care to plead alternative unlawful grounds in the alternative if it is possible to do so consistent with the rules governing ethics in pleading.

52. Consider, for example, Judge Posner's observation in *Troupe, supra* that "Employers can treat pregnant women as badly as they treat similarly affected but nonpregnant employees . . .," so long as the adverse treatment is predicated on a feature of the workplace or of employee behavior that is distinct from pregnancy or gender.

tion statutes do not, in short, require just cause for discipline.[53] On the other hand, the Title VII theory of disparate treatment does punish employer conduct that would otherwise be manifestly just or even legally mandated except for having been tainted, in whole or significant part, by discrimination on one of the prohibited grounds. Where, for example, the white plaintiff was discharged for conduct that apparently constituted felonious theft, the Supreme Court nevertheless found that the employer had violated Title VII because African–American employees who had engaged in the same conduct were subjected to lesser discipline.[54]

§ 4.5   The Problem of "Mixed Motives"

The classic evidentiary structure erected by *McDonnell Douglas* and *Burdine*, while furnishing a workable matrix for inferentially ferreting out intentional discrimination, does not fully come to grips with the complexities of many cases because it assumes that an employer's motivation was grounded *entirely* on a prohibited reason *or* a legitimate one. In fact, employers commonly advance more than one asserted legitimate reason for a challenged employment decision, and courts often conclude that an employer relied on one or more of those reasons as well as a reason condemned by Title VII.

The Supreme Court has recently addressed the reality of "mixed motive." In *Price Waterhouse v. Hopkins*,[1] a Supreme Court plurality concluded that when an employer undertakes a challenged employment decision for more than one reason, and the reason that is unlawful under Title VII is a "motivating," or "substantial motivating" factor in the employer's decision, liability will attach unless the employer can prove by a preponderance of the evidence that it would have reached the same decision for one or more independent, lawful reasons. The justices in the plurality rejected the dissenters' suggestion that an employer should also be freed of liability if the court finds such an independent reason existed at the time of the challenged decision, regardless of whether the employer relied on it. The plurality insisted that the employer, to be relieved of liability, must have *acted* on the basis of a lawful reason, one of which it necessarily had knowledge.

If an employer carries that persuasion burden, the plurality wrote, it should be found not to have committed an unlawful employment practice, despite the evidence of partial unlawful motive.[2] If on the other

---

53. *See Hazen Paper Co. v. Biggins,* 507 U.S. 604, 113 S.Ct. 1701, 123 L.Ed.2d 338 (1993) (case under ADEA). *But see* Blumrosen, "Strangers No More: All Workers Are Entitled To 'Just Cause' Protection Under Title VII," 2 Ind. Rel. L.J. 519 (1978).

54. *McDonald v. Santa Fe Trail, Transportation Co.,* 427 U.S. 273, 96 S.Ct. 2574, 49 L.Ed.2d 493 (1976). The same principle was recently applied in favor of an African–American former state trooper who, unlike his similarly situated white officers, was not reinstated after having been acquitted of felony charges. *Johnson v. Arkansas State Police,* 10 F.3d 547 (8th Cir.1993).

§ 4.5

1. 490 U.S. 228, 109 S.Ct. 1775, 104 L.Ed.2d 268 (1989).

2. *Id.* at 245 n.10, 109 S.Ct. at 1788 n. 10.

hand the employer cannot carry by a preponderance of the evidence the "same-decision" showing, it will be liable. Indeed, even a plaintiff using evidence of indirect disparate treatment who fails its burden of persuading that a lawful reason proffered by the employer at trial is a pretext for prohibited discrimination (see the *McDonnell Douglas/Burdine/St. Mary's Honor Center* mode of proof discussed above) can still prevail under *Price Waterhouse* by showing another employer motive that was both unlawful and a motivating factor in the challenged decision.[3]

A critical fifth vote for saddling the employer with the burden of persuasion on this "same decision" issue was cast by Justice O'Connor. She, however, would have imposed that burden only where the plaintiff proffers "direct evidence" that the discriminatory factor played a substantial role in the employer's decision.[4] Justice White, who wrote the other concurrence, took no position on whether the plaintiff's prima facie evidence must be "direct" to trigger the employer's burden of persuasion, but he agreed that plaintiff's case must be "substantial."[5]

The three dissenting justices would not have compelled the employer to persuade on any issue. They relied primarily on decisions of the Court that had imposed the persuasion burden on the plaintiff through all stages of an "individual disparate treatment" case, in which the plaintiff seeks to prove discrimination inferentially.[6] As a matter of principle, the dissenters wrote, cases where the plaintiff's prima facie evidence may be characterized as "direct" or "substantial" are indistinguishable from those where her showing is inferential. In each situation, the sole statutory question is whether the employer has made an adverse employment decision "because of" a prohibited characteristic, and on that question the plaintiff must produce evidence of, and persuade about, "but-for" causation.[7]

Much has been written about the Price Waterhouse decision.[8] Observers differ on whether affording the employer an escape from liability when it discharges the "same-decision" burden is on balance a development favorable to plaintiffs or defendants.[9]

---

3. *See Stacks v. Southwestern Bell Yellow Pages, Inc.*, 996 F.2d 200 (8th Cir. 1993).

4. 490 U.S. at 276, 109 S.Ct. at 1804 (O'Connor, J., concurring).

5. *Id.* at 259, 109 S.Ct. at 1795 (White, J., concurring).

6. *See Texas Dep't of Community Affairs v. Burdine*, 450 U.S. 248, 101 S.Ct. 1089, 67 L.Ed.2d 207 (1981); *McDonnell Douglas Corp. v. Green*, 411 U.S. 792, 93 S.Ct. 1817, 36 L.Ed.2d 668 (1973).

7. *Price Waterhouse*, 490 U.S. at 280–282, 109 S.Ct. at 1806–1807 (Kennedy, J., dissenting).

8. *See* Blumoff & Lewis, The Reagan Court and Title VII: A Common–Law Outlook On a Statutory Task, 69 N.C.L. Rev. 1

(1990); A. Blumrosen, Society in Transition II: Price Waterhouse and the Individual Employment Discrimination Case, 42 Rutgers L. Rev. 1023 (1990).

9. *Compare* Justice Department Memorandum for the Attorney General, prepared by the Civil Rights Division (February 7, 1991) (arguing that the decision has worked favorably for plaintiffs, since they have prevailed in fifteen (15) of nineteen (19) subsequent reported lower court decisions applying *Price Waterhouse* and that the plurality approach was as or more favorable to plaintiffs than the approach taken by eight of the eleven courts of appeals to address the issue) with Blumoff & Lewis, *supra* note 8, at 56, 66 (observing that *Price Waterhouse* shifts no burden to the employer on the threshold question of unlawful motivation,

In any event the Civil Rights Act of 1991 substantially incorporates and in one respect enhances the plurality's pro-plaintiff perspective in defining the circumstances that impose the "same decision" persuasion burden on the employer. Section 107, embodied in new Title VII Section 703(m), declares that an unlawful employment practice is established when the plaintiff demonstrates that employer reliance on protected group status was a "motivating factor" for "any" employment practice, "even though other factors also motivated the practice." [10]   The language requiring a "motivating" factor, derived from the plurality opinion in *Price Waterhouse*, evolved in the legislative process from the less stringent "contributing." It first surfaced in a Democratic substitute bill passed June 5, 1991 that was designed to allay business and Administration concerns. The resulting linguistic connotation, against the background of existing appellate jurisprudence about mixed motive, suggests that at least this change should marginally improve the litigation prospects of defendant employers.[11] And the "motivating" requirement appears significantly less burdensome than the counterpart demonstration of a "determinative" factor that has evolved in cases under the ADEA.

On the other hand, by omitting any reference to the kind of "direct" or "substantial" evidence of unlawful discrimination that the *Price Waterhouse* concurrers would have required, the Act apparently [12] re-

since the "same decision" phase of the case arises only after the plaintiff, through direct or inferential evidence, has shown such motivation; further observing that the plurality's position had previously been adopted by most federal appellate courts that had addressed the issue). *See also* Blumrosen, Society in Transition II: Price Waterhouse and the Individual Employment Discrimination Case, 42 Rutgers L. Rev. 1023, 1052 (1990). (*Price Waterhouse* affords defendants an additional opportunity to evade liability because the "mixed motive cases presuppose that the plaintiff has [already] persuaded the court that the illicit factor did influence the employment decision.").

10. (Adding Title VII § 703(m), 42 U.S.C.A. § 2000e–2(m) (1988)).

11. *See* Blumoff and Lewis, *supra,* 69 N.C.L.Rev. at 66 (seven federal circuit courts before *Price Waterhouse* required the employer to make the same-decision showing to avoid liability when impermissible motivation played *any* part in the adverse decision or when that motive was either a "substantial" *or* a "motivating" one.) *But see EEOC v. Our Lady of Resurrection Medical Ctr.,* 77 F.3d 145 (7th Cir.1996) (using "determining factor" language in Title VII race case; this is the arguably more stringent standard used in actions under ADEA). *See* Chapter 7, *infra*.

12. That appears to be the dominant conclusion of the lower courts even in cases decided under *Price Waterhouse* itself rather than under the 1991 Act. *See Stacks v. Southwestern Bell Yellow Pages, Inc.,* 996 F.2d 200, 202 n. 1 (8th Cir.1993); *Ostrowski v. Atlantic Mutual Insurance Cos.,* 968 F.2d 171 (2d Cir.1992); *Tyler v. Bethlehem Steel Corp.,* 958 F.2d 1176, 1183–85 (2d Cir.), *cert. denied,* 506 U.S. 826, 113 S.Ct. 82, 121 L.Ed.2d 46 (1992); *but cf. Griffiths v. CIGNA Corp.,* 988 F.2d 457, 470 (3d Cir.), *cert. denied,* 510 U.S. 865, 114 S.Ct. 186, 126 L.Ed.2d 145 (1993) (to trigger the mixed motive burden shifting, the plaintiff must produce "circumstantial evidence" of conduct or comments by decisionmakers that "directly" reflect their discriminatory attitude.) The author is somewhat at a loss to understand what the Third Circuit has in mind here, unless it means that the testimony about the decisionmaker's "directly" discriminatory conduct or comments need not come in the form of an admission by the decisionmaker herself.

More recently, the Third and Fourth Circuits, harkening back to the concurring opinions of Justices O'Connor and White in *Price Waterhouse*, have squarely insisted on *"direct"* plaintiff's evidence that the employer *substantially* relied on an unlawful factor before a plaintiff is entitled to an instruction placing the burden on defendant

quires the employer to bear the same-decision burden regardless of the kind or strength of the plaintiff's prima facie case, so long as she has shown in some fashion that discrimination was a motivating factor. Whether plaintiff's initial proof takes the form of "direct" anecdotal testimony of discriminatory motive, substantial (or for that matter insubstantial) evidence that a decision, practice or policy treats her less favorably by reference to a prohibited characteristic, or simply the more common "inferential" formula,[13] she will now have demonstrated intentional discrimination forbidden by Title VII.

To avoid monetary liability, the employer must then demonstrate "that it would have taken the same action in the absence of the impermissible motivating factor"[14]—even if there is evidence that at the time of the adverse employment action the employer knew that the employee had disobeyed work rules or lied.[15] The Act codifies the *Price Waterhouse* requirement that the required employer "demonstration," once triggered, extends to the burden of persuasion as well as production on this question.[16]

In fact the legislation goes somewhat beyond the *Price Waterhouse* plurality by providing, in new Title VII Section 706(g)(2)(B), that even the defendant who makes the required demonstration is relieved only of monetary liability. If unlawful discrimination was a "motivating" factor in the challenged employment decision, the employer has committed a law violation remediable by prospective relief and attorneys' fees.[17]

to show that it would have reached the same decision independent of such reliance. *Miller v. CIGNA Corporation,* 47 F.3d 586 (3d Cir.1995) (en banc) (case under ADEA); *Fuller v. Phipps,* 67 F.3d 1137, 1142 (4th Cir.1995). This view draws little support from the text of Title VII Section 703(m), added by the 1991 amendments. But that legislation did not amend the ADEA, and indeed the Supreme Court has subsequently written that in ADEA cases the plaintiff's ultimate burden is to show that age played not merely a motivating but a "determinative" role in the challenged employment decision. *See Hazen Paper Co. v. Biggins,* 507 U.S. 604, 113 S.Ct. 1701, 123 L.Ed.2d 338 (1993). Although "determinative" clearly does not mean "sole" factor, *Miller v. CIGNA,* 47 F.3d at 597, or even a "predominant" factor in the sense of one that outweighs all others, it may suggest a "but-for" factor without which the challenged decision would not have been made. In that event a "same-decision" aspect of the case would make no sense, for it would negate what the plaintiff is required to prove; thus ADEA plaintiffs required to prove that age was a "but-for" factor would not be eligible for any "same-decision" instruction placing the reverse burden on the employer. *See Id.* (ADEA plaintiff who proceeds with *McDonnell Douglas* rather

than "direct" evidence of age discrimination has "but-for" burden and therefore gets no *Price Waterhouse* instruction.) Even if "determinative" means only a somewhat weightier factor than a merely motivating one, there may be some horse sense in demanding that the prima facie evidence of the ADEA, as distinguished from the Title VII, plaintiff, be of a more probative nature or magnitude (e.g., "direct" or "substantial" or both) before he is entitled to that instruction.

13. Blumoff & Lewis, *supra* note 8, at 9–10, 58. *Cf.* Blumrosen, *supra* note 9, at 1057–59 (observing that intentional discrimination may consist either of "evil motive" or simply unequal treatment).

14. Section 107(b) (amending Title VII § 706(g), 42 U.S.C.A. § 2000e–5(g) (1972)).

15. *Stacks v. Southwestern Bell Yellow Pages, Inc.,* 27 F.3d 1316 (8th Cir.1994).

16. Section 104 (adding subsection 701(m) to Title VII, 42 U.S.C.A. § 2000e–m).

17. Section 107(b)(3) (adding paragraph (2)(B) to § 706(g) of Title VII, 42 U.S.C.A. § 2000e–5(g)). Although the subject is still one of debate among the circuits, the absence of any reference in the text of Section

Price Waterhouse, reflecting the law prevailing before the effective date of the 1991 Act, illustrates the potential significance of this and another change worked by the Act. The court of appeals there viewed the evidence as showing that all three employer decisionmakers admitted relying on a reason that would constitute retaliation under Title VII § 704. But it also found that they had relied as well on several lawful reasons for not promoting the plaintiff, and that she had failed to persuade that the unlawful reason was "substantial" as well as "motivating." It therefore agreed with the district court that the plaintiff's evidence did not cast on the employer the burden of making the *Price Waterhouse* "same-decision" showing.[18] The new statutory text, by contrast, would have permitted the plaintiff to cast the "same-decision" showing on the defendant upon proof that unlawful discrimination was a "motivating," even if not a "substantial motivating" reason for the challenged action.

Further, let us suppose that the employer could then have shown that when it acted its lawful reasons, independent of the unlawful one, would have led it to decline to promote the plaintiff. Under the 1991 Act, but not *Price Waterhouse,* the employer would nevertheless be adjudged to have committed a Title VII violation for which it could be saddled with injunctive relief and attorneys' fees. Its showing would relieve it only of monetary liability. These liberalizations of the mixed-motive case manifest Congress' resolve to facilitate proof of individual, intentional discrimination on the grounds prohibited by Title VII.[19] In

703(m) to "direct" or "substantial" evidence as a prerequisite to placing the "same-decision" persuasion burden on the defendant suggests that this defense is available regardless of whether plaintiff's prima facie case showing *one* unlawful motivation rests on direct or indirect evidence. *See Kerr–Selgas v. American Airlines, Inc.,* 69 F.3d 1205, 1210 (1st Cir.1995). But a circuit that does require "direct" evidence may encounter difficulty applying that prerequisite, because there is so much uncertainty whether certain kinds of employer speech constitute "direct" evidence of discriminatory intent. See § 4.2 *supra.* It may therefore be tempting for such a court to pretermit the problem by turning immediately to see if the employer has carried the same decision defense, and then limiting plaintiff's relief under Section 706(g)(2)(B) if it answers that question "Yes" but not if it answers that question "No." In light of *St. Mary's* it may not be fair to the defendant to avoid characterizing the prima facie case. This is because if plaintiff's prima facie evidence is in fact the weaker, inferential "indirect" variety authorized by *McDonnell Douglas/Burdine,* and she offers no "affirmative" evidence of unlawful discrimination, *St. Mary's* requires her to persuade the trier of fact not

only that defendant's proffered legitimate reason is false, but also that the defendant acted with unlawful discriminatory intent. The court may well overlook that fundamental liability inquiry, and require the defendant to pay at least attorneys' fees and maybe full monetary relief, if it skips over the details of plaintiff's threshold burden of demonstrating at least one unlawful motivation and proceeds directly to the employer's "same-decision" route to limiting relief.

18. *Price Waterhouse,* 825 F.2d at 471.

19. In *Patterson v. McLean Credit Union,* 491 U.S. 164, 109 S.Ct. 2363, 105 L.Ed.2d 132 (1989), the Supreme Court assimilated the *McDonnell Douglas/Burdine* mode of inferential proof into the trial of claims under § 1981. Nevertheless, the Civil Rights Act of 1991 contains no amendment to § 1981 or the ADEA similar to § 703(m) or § 706(g)(2)(B), even though it does amplify § 1981 remedies and modify ADEA procedures. In mixed-motive situations, therefore, § 1981 may ultimately be construed as subject to the pre-existing *Mt. Healthy* regime, in which there lingers at least an argument that a plaintiff may recover punitive damages even when the employer carries the "same-decision" burden.

doing so, Congress reflects the public's widespread agreement not to tolerate intentional discrimination in the realm of private employment.[20]

Price Waterhouse aggravates the problem of complicated instructions. At some point before instructing the jury, the trial judge must decide if there is sufficient evidence that the challenged employment action was motivated by both lawful and unlawful factors to warrant a *Price Waterhouse* instruction.[21] If so, she will have to issue an intricate, additional set of instructions concerning whether, if the jury finds (using, for example, the complex *McDonnell Douglas* framework) at least one unlawful employer motivation, the employer has persuaded that it would have reached the same decision for independent lawful reasons. This instruction must apparently be given, at the employer's request, even if the employer takes the primary position that the prohibited reason played no part in its challenged action.[22] But the defendant, fearful that the jury might then be more likely to find a forbidden motive, or hopeful that it might believe the "same-decision" burden is on the plaintiff, is often unwilling to ask for a *Price Waterhouse*/Section 703(m) instruction.[23] Presumably the plaintiff might then seek the instruction, on the theory that half a loaf (prospective relief and attorney's fees) is better than none. The plaintiff has been held entitled to the burden-shifting instruction on this "defense" where the evidence could support a finding of unlawful as well as lawful motives.[24]

See Chapter 2 concerning remedies under § 1983. By contrast, in ADEA mixed-motive cases, plaintiffs may remain under the pre–1991 Act *Price Waterhouse* regime, which would foreclose them from receiving even the limited prospective relief available under § 706(g)(2)(B) where the employer makes the kind of showing required by § 703(m). *See* the pertinent discussion of that issue in the chapters that treat those statutes.

20. Blumoff & Lewis, *supra* note 8, at 8–9. A poll-taker recently summarized his conclusions as follows: "If civil rights is defined as quotas, it's a losing hand. If it's defined as protection against discrimination and efforts to promote opportunity, then it will remain a mainstream value in American life." Rights–Bill Backers Issue Call To More Transcendent Battle, N.Y. Times, April 3, 1991, § A, at 18 (quoting Geoffrey Garin).

21. *See Radabaugh v. Zip Feed Mills Inc.,* 997 F.2d 444 (8th Cir.1993) (case under ADEA).

22. *Cf. Gooden v. Neal,* 17 F.3d 925, 929 (7th Cir.1994) (action under 42 U.S.C.A. § 1983, with employer relying on doctrine of *Mt. Healthy City School District v. Doyle,* 429 U.S. 274, 97 S.Ct. 568, 50 L.Ed.2d 471 (1977), the counterpart to *Price Waterhouse* for mixed-motive constitutional cases), *cert. denied,* ___ U.S. ___, 115 S.Ct. 73, 130

L.Ed.2d 28. But a recent circuit decision warns defendant's counsel that special jury interrogatories raising the same-decision defense should be drafted with extreme care when the plaintiff presses multiple grounds of discrimination. In *Kerr–Selgas v. American Airlines, Inc.,* 69 F.3d 1205 (1st Cir. 1995), the jury's special verdicts reflected that it had found both gender discrimination and retaliation to be motivating factors in plaintiff's termination. Yet on each issue the jury also found, in separate responses, that the employer would more likely than not have made the same employment decisions even absent, respectively, gender discrimination and retaliation (the jury also found, concerning a pendent wrongful discharge claim, that the defendant did not have just cause for plaintiff's dismissal). Nevertheless, the court upheld a plaintiff's verdict because the form of the special interrogatories did not exclude the possibility, with respect to the gender claim, that defendant acted from an unlawful *retaliatory* motive. Similarly, the jury might have found that, respecting the retaliation claim, the defendants acted unlawfully based on *gender!*

23. *See Ostrowski v. Atlantic Mutual Insurance Cos.,* 968 F.2d 171, 181 (2d Cir. 1992).

24. *Id.*

Loose language in one decision suggests that plaintiffs must stake out early in the lawsuit whether they are seeking to prove a "pretext" case or a "mixed motive" case. Only in the latter event, this opinion asserts, would the plaintiff be entitled to an instruction allowing it to prevail by demonstrating that the unlawful motive was "significant," "determinative," "substantial," or "motivating." Otherwise, the plaintiff must prove that the adverse employment action was the product of a discriminatory motive alone.[25] This conclusion appears to conflict with the Supreme Court's recognition in *Price Waterhouse* that the full range of questions for the jury may not be apparent until all the evidence is in, as well as its observation that Congress rejected an amendment that would have limited the ban of Title VII to discrimination "solely" on one of its prohibited grounds.[26]

A more fluid approach is reflected in a recent circuit opinion which recognizes that the ordinary *McDonnell–Douglas/St. Mary's* inferential disparate treatment case, together with its *Price Waterhouse*/Section 703(m) overlay, operate on a continuum. This view starts from the premise that, as *Hazen Paper* instructs, "because of" does not mean "solely because of." It means rather that the unlawful factor is a "but-for" or "motivating" (in a Title VII case) or "determinative" (in an ADEA case) cause of the employer's adverse action. *St. Mary's,* then, is significant because it illustrates that the trier of fact need not choose between finding that the alleged discriminatory motive or the employer's proffered nondiscriminatory explanation was the sole cause of the challenged action. Alternatively, the trier may conclude that the employer acted for reasons not advanced by either party—in which case it should not find unlawful discrimination. Or it may conclude that a discriminatory motive and some nondiscriminatory explanation, whether or not it is the one advanced by the employer, both played a role. In that event the trier must decide if the discriminatory component of the overall complex of employer reasons was "motivating," and, if so, whether the employer has demonstrated under Section 706(g)(2)(B) that it "would have taken the same action in the absence of the impermissible motivating factor...." Therefore in most cases the charge to the jury should allow for the possibility that the employer's decision was the product of more than one consideration, and should instruct that at a minimum the plaintiff has the burden of demonstrating that a prohibited consideration had a motivating (Title VII) or determinative (ADEA) influence on the outcome.[27] This analysis is useful because it points up that all the

25. *Griffiths v. CIGNA Corp.*, 988 F.2d 457 (3d Cir.), *cert. denied*, 510 U.S. 865, 114 S.Ct. 186, 126 L.Ed.2d 145 (1993).

26. *See Price Waterhouse*, 490 U.S. at 241 n.7, 109 S.Ct. at 1786 n.7. The Fourth Circuit has explicitly recognized that sorting out whether the evidence supports instructions or verdicts under the *McDonnell Douglas* approach (which assumes a unitary employer motive), the *Price Waterhouse* or § 703(m) approach (which assume mixed

employer motives in ADEA and Title VII cases, respectively), or under both such approaches is an analytical task for the court and factfinder after the evidence is in, not a subject of advance mandatory election by plaintiff's counsel. *Russell v. Microdyne Corp.*, 65 F.3d 1229 (4th Cir.1995).

27. *Miller v. CIGNA Corp.*, 47 F.3d 586 (3d Cir.1995) (en banc) (case under ADEA).

complexities of mixed-motive analysis may but need not arise in the same case that presents all the complexities of inferential evidence analysis, including *St. Mary's.*

We can now see the significance of the addition to Title VII of Sections 703(m) and 706(g)(2)(B), and, in contrast, the significance of their omission from the ADEA. First, thanks to Section 703(m), the plaintiff's ultimate burden in establishing Title VII liability is only to demonstrate that an unlawful ground motivated, rather than determined, the imposition of an employment detriment or denial of an employment benefit. Second, this should mean, where the Title VII plaintiff attempts to meet this burden through the indirect *McDonnell Douglas* formula, that judges ruling on summary judgment and FRCP 50 motions will apply the *St. Mary's* requirements for "pretext" less stringently than in corresponding litigation under ADEA. Third, a Title VII plaintiff who takes the *McDonnell Douglas* path and presents evidence sufficient under *St. Mary's* to survive a Rule 50 motion at the close of all the evidence should be entitled to a Section 703(m) instruction imposing on the employer the burden of demonstrating that it would have reached the same decision independent of the unlawful reason; it is not at all clear that a counterpart ADEA plaintiff who presents only indirect evidence of age discrimination is eligible for such an instruction under *Price Waterhouse.*[28] Fourth, under Section 706(g)(2)(B), the Title VII defendant who carries the "same-decision" showing is nevertheless liable and subject to limited declaratory and injunctive relief and attorneys' fees; the ADEA defendant who carries that showing per *Price Waterhouse* is relieved of liability altogether.

§ 4.6 The Defense or Mitigation of "After–Acquired Evidence"

An emerging line of cases limits or altogether negates an employer's liability for reinstatement and back pay (or for the front pay and capped damages now available under the Civil Rights Act of 1991, see Chapter 5, Section B.) if the employer can produce subsequently discovered evidence of a legitimate nondiscriminatory reason that would have induced it to take the same action had the facts come to light before the adverse action. This "after-acquired evidence" defense presupposes that the employer has committed an unlawful employment practice and that the tardily discovered legitimate reason was not a substantial part of its motivation when it demoted or terminated the plaintiff.[1]

Where there is resume fraud, theft, or other serious misconduct that took place before hire but was discovered only after the employer

---

28. *See Miller v. CIGNA Corporation,* 47 F.3d 586 (3d Cir.1995) (en banc), discussed in Chapter 7 concerning the ADEA.

§ 4.6

1. Only if the employer acted on, and hence knew about the facts underlying its legitimate reason at the time it made the challenged decision may it rely on the *Price Waterhouse* "same-decision" rule, now codified by the 1991 Civil Rights Act, which relieves the employer of all monetary liability.

imposed the adverse term and condition of employment, some courts have found no liability whatsoever. These decisions proceed on the property right theory that the employee would never have held the job to begin with had the employer known of her misconduct at the time of hire. The adverse employment action therefore cannot be considered caused by the employer's discriminatory conduct during the plaintiff's period of employment, because the plaintiff never had a property right to the job. Under this approach the employer cannot be required either to reinstate the plaintiff or provide any financial compensation, because there is no unlawful employment practice.[2] So conceived, the "after-acquired evidence" defense is more complete than the "same-decision" avoidance of *Price Waterhouse*, which, as modified by the Civil Rights Act of 1991, still leaves the "mixed-motives" employer subject to liability for prospective relief (like reinstatement) and attorney's fees.

Courts taking this approach have subsequently extended their complete exclusion of liability to situations where the misconduct (discovered after the challenged employment decision) occurred during rather than before the period of the plaintiff's employment[3]. And one has asserted, at least as an alternative ground of decision, that the bar applies even where the plaintiff's misconduct is nonserious and nonpervasive.[4] But other courts in this camp have held that the defendant in a resume fraud case must show that under its ordinary, neutrally applied policies or practices it would not have hired the plaintiff had it known of the concealed or misrepresented fact[5] or that it would have fired her upon learning of on-the-job misconduct of comparable nature and magnitude.[6] For example, where the misconduct takes place pre-hire, one circuit adopting this general approach allows the defense only if the employer can show that the misrepresentation or omission on an employment application or resume was material to the position applied for and relied on by the employer in reaching the hiring decision.[7]

Initially the Seventh Circuit appeared to agree that after-acquired evidence could be a complete defense to liability, but only if the employer could prove that the misconduct would have been grounds for firing,

---

2. *See, e.g., Welch v. Liberty Machine Works, Inc.,* 23 F.3d 1403 (8th Cir.1994); *Milligan–Jensen v. Michigan Technological University,* 975 F.2d 302 (6th Cir.1992), *cert. granted,* 509 U.S. 903, 113 S.Ct. 2991, 125 L.Ed.2d 686 (1993), *cert. dismissed,* 509 U.S.943, 114 S.Ct. 22, 125 L.Ed.2d 773 (1993); *Washington v. Lake County, Ill.,* 969 F.2d 250 (7th Cir.1992); *Dotson v. U.S. Postal Service,* 977 F.2d 976 (6th Cir.), *cert. denied,* 506 U.S. 892, 113 S.Ct. 263, 121 L.Ed.2d 193 (1992) (same complete denial of relief under Rehabilitation Act); *Summers v. State Farm Mutual Automobile Ins. Co.,* 864 F.2d 700 (10th Cir.1988) (denying all relief to plaintiff whose employer discov-

ered after termination his falsification of company records).

3. *McKennon v. Nashville Banner Publishing Co.,* 9 F.3d 539 (6th Cir.1993), *reversed,* ___ U.S. ___, 115 S.Ct. 879, 130 L.Ed.2d 852 (1995).

4. *O'Driscoll v. Hercules Inc.,* 12 F.3d 176 (10th Cir.), *petition for cert. filed* 62 USLW 3757 (April 1, 1994).

5. *See Washington v. Lake County, Ill., supra,* note 2.

6. *See Kristufek v. Hussmann Foodservice Co.,* 985 F.2d 364 (7th Cir.1993).

7. *Johnson v. Honeywell Info. Systems, Inc.,* 955 F.2d 409 (6th Cir.1992).

rather than merely not hiring, the plaintiff.[8] Subsequently, different panels of the Seventh Circuit [9] have joined other circuits [10] that limit but do not altogether preclude relief against the employer who successfully maintains the after-acquired evidence defense. These courts for the most part stop the accrual of backpay at the time the employer, in the course of responding to the employee's allegations of discrimination, discovers the employee's disqualifying conduct. In a sense, then, these courts afford the employer relief for its discovery of plaintiff misconduct that the employer would not have discovered absent the employer's unlawful actions and ensuing administrative or judicial proceedings.

The Eleventh Circuit has expressly rejected the "rule that an employer may avoid all liability for a discharge based solely on unlawful motives by proving that it would have discharged the plaintiff . . . *if* it had possessed full knowledge of the circumstances existing at the time of the discharge." [11] In the words of the Third Circuit, which has joined the Eleventh on this issue, "after-acquired evidence is inadmissible, because irrelevant, at the *liability* stage of a cause of action brought under Title VII of ADEA." [12] The evidence is irrelevant, in the view of these courts, because by definition it was not available to the employer at the time of the challenged decision, an indispensable prerequisite of the "mixed motive" defense approved by *Price Waterhouse.*[13]

Instead, these courts adjust remedies in an effort to balance the statutory policy of making the victim of discrimination whole against the goal often expressed by the Supreme Court of interfering minimally with the employer's management prerogatives. If the employer can prove that the after-acquired evidence would have led it to discharge the plaintiff, the Eleventh Circuit [14] equitably relieves it of liability for the prospective remedies of reinstatement, front pay, and injunctions. The Third Circuit writes more equivocally that reinstatement will be barred by after-acquired evidence only where that remedy "would be particularly invasive of the employer's 'traditional management prerogatives.' " [15]

8. *Washington v. Lake County, Ill.*, 969 F.2d 250 (7th Cir.1992).

9. *Powers v. Chicago Transit Authority*, 890 F.2d 1355 (7th Cir.1989); *Smith v. General Scanning, Inc.*, 876 F.2d 1315 (7th Cir.1989) (ADEA decision denying reinstatement, awarding back pay, but limiting it to the period before employer discovered resume fraud); *accord, Kristufek v. Hussmann Foodservice Company*, 985 F.2d 364 (7th Cir.1993) (reduced by remittitur).

10. *Proulx v. Citibank*, 862 F.2d 304 (2d Cir.1988); *Smallwood v. United Air Lines*, 728 F.2d 614 (4th Cir.), *cert. denied* , 469 U.S. 832, 105 S.Ct. 120, 83 L.Ed.2d 62 (1984).

11. *Wallace v. Dunn Construction Company, Inc.*, 968 F.2d 1174, 1182 (11th Cir. 1992), *rehearing granted*, 32 F.3d 1489 (11th Cir.1994).

12. *Mardell v. Harleysville Life Insurance Co.*, 31 F.3d 1221, 1238 (3d Cir.1994), *petition for cert. filed* (Oct. 24, 1994) (No. 94–742).

13. *Mardell*, 31 F.3d at 1228.

14. Less definitely, the Third Circuit writes that "where an equitable remedy, such as reinstatement, would be particularly invasive of the employer's 'traditional management prerogatives,' the after-acquired evidence *may* bar that remedy." *Mardell*, 31 F.2d at 1240 (emphasis added).

15. *Mardell*, 31 F.3d at 1240 (quoting *Burdine*, 450 U.S. at 259, 101 S.Ct. at 1096 and *United Steelworkers v. Weber*, 443 U.S. 193, 207, 99 S.Ct. 2721, 2729, 61 L.Ed.2d 480 (1979)).

Further, under the Eleventh and Third Circuit's view of the equities, the employer is ordinarily liable for back pay up until judgment, that is, even for the period after it discovers the plaintiff's misconduct. Only if the employer can prove that it would have discovered the plaintiff's misconduct or pre-hire misrepresentation independent of its discrimination—that is, apart from an employer-initiated search for evidence to inculpate the plaintiff in response to the plaintiff's charges of discrimination—is it relieved of back pay liability, and then only for the period after it would have discovered the misconduct.[16] Otherwise the plaintiff would be in a worse position because of the employer's discrimination, undermining Title VII's make-whole goal of compensation.[17] Moreover, the Eleventh Circuit now denies even this version of the defense unless plaintiff's misconduct is related to the employer's alleged unlawful employment practice and in fact caused the employer injury.[18]

The logic of the Eleventh and Third Circuits—that the employer should not be entirely relieved of liability on the basis of evidence that it would not have searched for or discovered absent its discriminatory discharge of the plaintiff and consequent search for damning evidence—also supports full awards of other retroactive relief, for example compensatory or punitive damages available under the Civil Rights Act of 1991. Further, the Eleventh Circuit ruled that the after-acquired evidence defense would not prevent the plaintiff from recovering declaratory relief or nominal damages. That ruling may be critically important to a plaintiff who cannot produce persuasive evidence of back pay or compensatory or punitive damages: declaratory relief, nominal damages or both would be essential for her to be deemed a "prevailing" party eligible for attorneys' fees.[19]

In sum, the remedial handling of after-acquired evidence in the Eleventh and Third Circuits affords the employer a diluted defense with consequences that are almost a mirror image of those that attend the mixed-motive showing under *Price Waterhouse*. Those circuit courts will usually relieve the employer who succeeds with after-acquired evidence of the key prospective relief of reinstatement, but ordinarily saddle it with full retroactive relief. As codified in the 1991 Civil Rights Act, the doctrine of *Price Waterhouse*, by contrast, relieves the employer who at the time of decision acted with mixed motives from liability for monetary, retrospective remedies but leaves it potentially liable for appropriate prospective relief.

The Supreme Court has now issued a decision under the Age Discrimination in Employment Act that applies the more sweeping form

---

16. *Wallace v. Dunn Construction Company, Inc.*, 968 F.2d at 1182; *Mardell*, 31 F.3d at 1229. The EEOC's General Counsel takes the same approach as the Eleventh Circuit, concluding that after-acquired evidence of misconduct is not a defense to liability but simply halts the accrual of back pay at the date the employer proves it would have terminated the charging party for a lawful, nondiscriminatory reason. Re-vised Litigation Guidance on the Civil Rights Act of 1991 and Related Matters, March 1, 1993.

17. *See Mardell*, 31 F.3d at 1229.

18. *Calloway v. Partners National Health Plans*, 986 F.2d 446 (11th Cir.1993).

19. *See* Attorneys' Fees Chapter, below.

of the after-acquired evidence defense.[20]   The straws in the wind pointed in different directions.   On the one hand, the Court's recent decisions holding nonretroactive key provisions of the 1991 Civil Rights Act [21] suggested a certain willingness to countenance violations for which there is no remedy.   On the other, the new damages remedies the 1991 Act creates for violations of Title VII, like the monetary remedies under ADEA, are legal in nature, which reduce the force of the employer's argument that it is inequitable to order relief to an employee known at the time of judicial decision to have engaged in misconduct.   And the Court also recently ruled that the National Labor Relations Board could grant relief to a fired employee even though he may have lied during Board proceedings.[22]

The Court has recently issued its decision in *McKennon*,[23] steering a middle course similar but not identical to that charted by the Eleventh Circuit.   To capitalize on employee misconduct discovered only after the employer discriminatorily imposed an employment detriment, the employer bears the burden of proving "that the wrongdoing was of such severity that the employee *in fact would* have been *terminated* on those grounds alone if the employer had known of it at the time of the discharge." [24]   It appears from this standard that it is unnecessary for the court to agree that the employee's misconduct is "serious" or "pervasive" as long as the employer can prove that under its established rules, applied without discrimination, it would have discharged the employee had it known of such conduct when it occurred.[25]

20. *McKennon v. Nashville Banner Publishing Co.*, 9 F.3d 539 (6th Cir.1993), *reversed*, ___ U.S. ___, 115 S.Ct. 879, 130 L.Ed.2d 852 (1995).

21. *See Landgraf v. USI Film Products*, 511 U.S. 244, 114 S.Ct. 1483, 128 L.Ed.2d 229 (1994); *Rivers v. Roadway Express, Inc.*, 511 U.S. 298, 114 S.Ct. 1510, 128 L.Ed.2d 274 (1994).

22. *ABF Freight System v. NLRB*, 510 U.S. 317, 114 S.Ct. 835, 127 L.Ed.2d 152 (1994).

23. *McKennon v. Nashville Banner Publishing Co.*, ___ U.S. ___, 115 S.Ct. 879, 130 L.Ed.2d 852 (1995).

24. *Id.* at ___, 115 S.Ct. at 882 (emphases added).   Thus the mere *possibility* that the employer could have terminated the plaintiff under its usual work rules does not suffice to meet the employer's burden. *Shearin v. IBM Corp.*, 1995 WL 133761 (S.D.N.Y.1995).   The employer must show that it would have discharged the plaintiff had it known of the misconduct. *Ricky v. Mapco, Inc.*, 50 F.3d 874, 876 (10th Cir. 1995).   The EEOC, to decide whether the employer would have discharged the plaintiff, first looks to the employer's handling of past comparable incidents.   Failing those, it considers such criteria as whether the mis-

conduct is criminal or "compromised the integrity of the employer's business . . . ." EEOC Enforcement Guidance on After Acquired Evidence, No. 915.002 (12/14/95). And the employer must show that had it known of plaintiff's misconduct at the relevant time, it would, applying general neutral rules, have *fired* her, not merely failed to *hire* her. *Shattuck v. Kinetic Concepts, Inc.*, 49 F.3d 1106 (5th Cir.1995) (post-*McKennon* ADEA case).   Although *McKennon* involved misconduct during employment, one circuit court has clarified that its limitation on liability applies equally to an employee misrepresentation in the application process. *Wallace v. Dunn Constr. Co.*, 62 F.3d 374 (11th Cir.1995) (en banc).   By contrast, *post*-employment misconduct cannot serve as the predicate for the *McKennon* limitation. *Sigmon v. Parker Chapin*, 69 FEP 69 (S.D.N.Y.1995); *Carr v. Woodbury County Juvenile Detention Ctr.*, 905 F.Supp. 619 (N.D.Iowa 1995).

25. *See, e.g. O'Driscoll v. Hercules, Inc.*, 12 F.3d 176 (10th Cir.1994), *vacated* in light of *McKennon*, ___ U.S. ___, 115 S.Ct. 879, 130 L.Ed.2d 852 (1995).   The employer must carry this burden by the normal "preponderance of the evidence" quantum. *O'Day v. McDonnell Douglas Helicopter Co.*, 79 F.3d 756 (9th Cir.1996).

Still, the employer demonstration of such misconduct serves only to limit liability, not as a complete defense. The Supreme Court observed that under ADEA as well as Title VII, remedies serve the twin objectives of deterring violations and compensating past injuries. The plaintiff advances those objectives, the Court wrote, by demonstrating the employer's discrimination. Allowing after-acquired evidence to serve as a complete bar to liability would unjustifiably undermine the statutes' remedial goals. In reaching this conclusion, the Supreme Court specifically distinguished mixed-motive situations; after-acquired evidence does not even figure in the decisional calculus until the factfinder has determined that the employer's sole or motivating basis for the challenged employment decision was unlawful (and that the employer would not have reached the same decision independent of its pure or partial unlawful motivation).[26]

But the Court was equally insistent that the employee's wrongdoing could not simply be disregarded in the formulation of an appropriate remedy. In this connection the Court read ADEA's authorization of legal or equitable relief as a mandate for the trial court to take the employee's wrongdoing into account as a way of recognizing the significant managerial prerogatives that ADEA, like Title VII, preserves to the employer. While acknowledging that the relevant equitable considerations will vary from case to case, the Court nevertheless concluded that "here, and as a general rule in cases of this type, neither reinstatement nor front pay is an appropriate remedy. It would be both inequitable and pointless to order the reinstatement of someone the employer would have terminated, and will terminate, in any event and upon lawful grounds."[27]

The Court considered the "proper measure of backpay" to present "a more difficult problem." Ordinarily, the compensatory objective of ADEA remedies would require a backpay award that would make the employee whole—restore her to the position she would have occupied absent the unlawful discrimination. The justices were unwilling to implement that objective fully in the face of evidence of employee wrongdoing that, had the employer known about it, would have led to her lawful termination. Moreover, parting company to this degree with the approach taken by the Eleventh Circuit, the Court wrote that it could not "require the employer to ignore the information, even if it is acquired during the course of discovery in a suit against the employer and even if the information might have gone undiscovered absent the suit."[28]

Declining to formulate an across-the-board backpay rule, the Court did conclude, however, that the "beginning point" in the trial court's formulation of a "monetary remedy" should be calculation of backpay from the date of the unlawful discharge to the date the new information

---

26. *McKennon,* ___ U.S. ___ at ___, 115 S.Ct. at 885.

27. *Id.* at ___, 115 S.Ct. at 886.

28. *Id.*

was discovered.[29] This reverses the Eleventh Circuit presumption about backpay, which left the employer ordinarily liable for backpay past the discovery date and through the date of judgment. On the other hand, unlike the "mixed-motive" employer who establishes that it would have taken the challenged action at the time even absent reliance on a motivating factor forbidden by Title VII,[30] the employer who carries the persuasion burden on after-acquired evidence will almost surely sustain some monetary liability, even if that liability terminates as of the date of discovery of employee wrongdoing.

In a somewhat vague afterthought the Court added that the trial judge could "consider taking into further account extraordinary equitable circumstances that affect the legitimate interests of either party."[31] Further, because the Court in *McKennon* remanded for further consistent proceedings concerning remedy, the Court had no occasion to consider whether a backpay award in any amount could be doubled to provide the "liquidated" damages that ADEA and EPA authorizes in the case of "willful" violations. Nor did the Court discuss whether the employer who prevails on a showing of after-acquired evidence may thereby avoid the two species of monetary relief provided for Title VII cases by the 1991 Civil Rights Act, but unavailable in cases under ADEA: compensatory and punitive damages.

In principle, the line drawn by the Court for backpay—presumptively available before but not after the date of the employer's discovery of the information that would have led to termination independent of the unlawful employment practice—should apply to ADEA "liquidated" damages and Title VII compensatory and punitive damages as well. As the Court wrote about backpay, an absolute rule barring these remedies "would undermine the ADEA's objective of forcing employers to consider and examine their motivations, and of penalizing them for employment decisions that spring from age discrimination."[32] On this reasoning, only "extraordinary equitable circumstances" would defeat claims under

---

29. *Id.* *See Russell v. Microdyne,* 65 F.3d 1229 (4th Cir.1995). In *Ricky v. Mapco,* 50 F.3d 874 (10th Cir.1995), the court permitted the jury to award back pay not just through the date of the employer's discovery of the plaintiff's misconduct, but through the date it determines the employer would have fired him.

30. *See* Section 107(b) of the 1991 Civil Rights Act, discussed in Section 4.5 *supra.*

31. ___ U.S. at ___, 115 S.Ct. at 886. It is the EEOC's position that one such extraordinary circumstance warranting additional relief is presented whenever the employee misconduct is discovered during an investigation launched by the employer after a formal or informal charge of discrimination is made to discredit a complaining party or discourage other charges or opposi-

tion to unlawful activity. In that case EEOC would extend backpay beyond the date of discovery of employee wrongdoing until the underlying charge is resolved. *See* EEOC Enforcement Guidance on After Acquired Evidence *supra,* note 24. But it is commonplace for employee misconduct to be discovered as the result of an investigation prompted by a charge or complaint of discrimination. This "extraordinary" circumstance threatens to render the ordinary *McKennon* backpay end date a nullity. Instead, discovery after investigation should void the *McKennon* back pay reduction only where the employer acts with subjective retaliatory purpose rather than merely to limit relief.

32. *Id.* at ___, 115 S.Ct. at 886.

Title VII for compensatory damages, punitive damages or both through that date of discovery. Neither type of damages would constrain significant managerial prerogatives or discretion, the sole equitable consideration the Court identified as a reason for restricting plaintiff's recovery.

EEOC and circuit court decisions have since opined that Title VII compensatory and punitive damages and ADEA liquidated damages are available notwithstanding after-acquired evidence.[33] Further, EEOC does not view the *McKennon* concern of protecting the employer's interest in severing the employment relationship as a warrant to place a time limit on compensatory damages for emotional harm. Rather, the after-acquired showing limits only those out-of-pocket losses that are analogous to backpay. Nor does EEOC see in *McKennon* a ban or limitation on punitive damages, provided the plaintiff proves the employer's malice or reckless indifference.[34]

The after-acquired evidence defense has practical potency well beyond its limitation on relief. Defense counsel will routinely pursue discovery on the issue, which should raise the costs to plaintiff and intimidate some serious wrongdoers. And at trial even defendants who fail in their burden of proving misconduct so serious as to warrant discharge may nevertheless succeed in damaging the plaintiff's credibility, with a consequent loss of jury sympathy and potential reduction of compensatory and punitive awards. Plaintiffs may counter these tactics with motions to limit discovery, or with motions *in limine* to exclude misconduct evidence unless the employer makes a threshold showing that under established policies or practices it would have fired employees for the misconduct in question.

Now that the Supreme Court has recognized after-acquired evidence as a factor that lessens relief, trial judges in Title VII jury actions will have to issue still another set of instructions on top of the many already required in even the simplest cases of individual disparate treatment. Presumably these would be the last in the series, following any required instructions on mixed motive. For example, the jury might be charged that if it finds the employer would have made the challenged decision for lawful reasons independent of other, unlawful reasons that the jury finds the employer also took into account, the employer is presumptively liable only for prospective relief and attorney's fees under the Civil Rights Act of 1991's modification of *Price Waterhouse*; but that if the jury also finds after-acquired evidence of employee misconduct sufficiently serious that the employer would have terminated the plaintiff upon discovery, the jury shall relieve the employer from prospective relief as well. The only potential relief remaining in that situation would be a declaratory judgment, an injunction, or nominal damages, and perhaps attorney's

---

33. *Russell v. Microdyne,* 65 F.3d 1229 (4th Cir.1995) (Title VII); *Wallace v. Dunn Constr. Co.,* 62 F.3d 374, 380 (11th Cir. 1995) (en banc) (ADEA); EEOC Enforce-ment Guidance on After Acquired Evidence (December 14, 1995).

34. EEOC Guidance on After Acquired Evidence, *supra* note 24.

fees to the extent of the plaintiff's limited success.[35] The mind-bending possible permutations will surely tax the capacities of the typical jury.

C. SYSTEMIC DISPARATE TREATMENT

Library References:

> C.J.S. Civil Rights §§ 161–162.
> West's Key No. Digests, Civil Rights ⊃153.

§ 4.7 In General

Intentional discriminatory treatment may also be demonstrated in the aggregate. "Systemic disparate treatment" proof depends primarily upon statistical evidence of gross disparities between the actual and expected representation of the plaintiff's group in one or more levels of an employer's workforce. According to the underlying theory, articulated in *International Brotherhood of Teamsters v. United States*,[1] an employer that does not routinely discriminate should over time achieve within its employee complement an incidence of protected group representation not significantly less than the group's representation in an available pool of qualified applicants.[2]

Systemic disparate treatment, the residue of a number of individually discriminatory decisions, is evidenced by a significant workforce underrepresentation of a protected group relative to the incidence one would expect based on its members' interest, availability and qualifications. Unlike the impact case, it is predicated on a showing of intentional discrimination. Further, the systemic treatment case is typically brought by several joined plaintiffs or a plaintiff class, and endeavors to prove that the defendant, as the result of an unspecified variety of policies, practices, and individual decisions by employer agents, discriminated against members of the protected group in general. In the systemic treatment case all members of the protected group denied hire or promotion to the job level during the period when the protected group was found to be grossly underrepresented are presumptively entitled to remedies, regardless of which particular employer policies or decisions by employer agents led to their rejection.[3] By contrast, relief in the "impact" case is limited to those plaintiffs, sometimes as few as one, who suffered an employment detriment as the result of a particular practice

---

35. *McKennon*, decided under ADEA, has been held fully applicable to cases under Title VII. *Wehr v. Ryan's Family Steak Houses*, 49 F.3d 1150 (6th Cir.1995). Fees were recently awarded where a plaintiff recovered only nominal damages after defendant carried the "same decision" showing under Section 706(g)(2)(B), which authorizes such fees expressly in those circumstances. *Sheppard v. Riverview Nursing Center*, 88 F.3d 1332 (4th Cir.1996). For considerations bearing on availability and

calculation of attorney's fees in such pyrrhic victory settings, see Section 12.2 *infra*.

§ 4.7

1. 431 U.S. 324, 97 S.Ct. 1843, 52 L.Ed.2d 396 (1977).

2. *Id.* at 388 n.15, 97 S.Ct. at 1882 n. 15.

3. *Franks v. Bowman Transp. Co.*, 424 U.S. 747, 96 S.Ct. 1251, 47 L.Ed.2d 444 (1976).

shown to have had disproportionate adverse impact on the plaintiff's group.

Occasionally, an employer's policy will on its face draw a distinction on the basis of a prohibited characteristic; a group of plaintiffs suing as a class or joined under Federal Rule 20 could then establish systemic disparate treatment on the basis of the policy alone.[4]

More typically, the plaintiffs will offer statistical evidence in an attempt to show a raw, substantial underrepresentation of their protected group relative to the numbers of their members that might have been expected had the employer hired or promoted randomly. This prima facie statistical case of systemic disparate treatment compares the employer's actual or "observed" number of protected group members hired for or promoted to the job in question against a hypothetical number of protected group members that an employer who hired or promoted randomly might have been "expected" to select. The theoretical underpinning of statistically-premised judicial findings of systemic disparate treatment is that, "absent explanation, it is ordinarily to be expected that nondiscriminatory hiring practices will in time result in a work force more or less representative of the racial and ethnic composition of the" relevant pool.[5] Although anecdotal evidence of instances of individual disparate treatment certainly fortifies the inference of systemic disparate treatment raised by statistical disparities, it has been held that statistical disparities alone may prove intentional discrimination, at least where the disparities are gross.[6]

In undertaking a showing of gross underrepresentation of the protected group the plaintiff must take care to calculate the "expected" number by reference to the relevant pool from which the selection will be made; and that pool must be refined to account for the minimum qualifications, including geographic proximity, requisite for the job in question.[7] *See Hazelwood School District v. United States*, 433 U.S. 299, 97 S.Ct. 2736, 53 L.Ed.2d 768 (1977). In an order that ascends with the complexity of the skill level of the job at issue, this pool may range from general population (*Teamsters*) or workforce (*Hazelwood*) statistics within an actual or feasible recruiting zone,[8] to a nationwide pool of

---

4. *See, e.g., Los Angeles Department of Water & Power v. Manhart*, 435 U.S. 702, 98 S.Ct. 1370, 55 L.Ed.2d 657 (1978); *Arizona Governing Committee v. Norris*, 463 U.S. 1073, 103 S.Ct. 3492, 77 L.Ed.2d 1236 (1983) (policies that, respectively, required greater contributions from female than male employees for the same periodic pension benefits and provided women lesser periodic pension benefits than men for equal amounts contributed).

5. *Teamsters*, 431 U.S. at 339 n.20, 97 S.Ct. at 1856 n.20.

6. *Equal Employment Opportunity Commission v. O & G Spring and Wire Forms Specialty Co.*, 38 F.3d 872 (7th Cir.1994),

cert. denied, ___ U.S. ___, 115 S.Ct. 1270, 131 L.Ed.2d 148 (1995).

7. *See Hazelwood School District v. United States*, 433 U.S. 299, 97 S.Ct. 2736, 53 L.Ed.2d 768 (1977).

8. *See Abron v. Black & Decker Manufacturing Co.*, 439 F.Supp. 1095, 1105 (D.Md.1977) (measuring availability pool from which potential protected group member "expectation" percentage will be drawn as the "appropriate labor force ... encompassed in the area within which the employer can reasonably expect people to commute"), *affirmed in part, vacated in part*, 654 F.2d 951 (4th Cir.1981). A strong indication that an employer can reasonably be

candidates with the key educational or experience credentials. In the case of promotions that the employer has historically made exclusively or primarily from within, the pool would consist of lower-level employees in the employer's own workforce who meet the base requirements for promotion.

Defining the pool from which the expected percentage of minority representation should be calculated is often keenly contested. While protected group representation in a recruiting-zone population or local workforce may suffice where the jobs in question are largely unskilled,[9] or from the percentage of protected group members employed by other area employers for jobs that are moderately skilled,[10] the fair measurement of disparities in highly skilled positions demands refinement not just for availability and interest but, above all, for specialized qualifications.[11] Courts have on occasion dispensed with refined evidence of the characteristics of the pool from which applicants are drawn when the disparities presented are extreme. The classic example is where the protected group in question constitutes what has been termed the "inexorable zero"—no representation at all in the employer's workforce.[12]

Whatever comparison is used, plaintiff must establish a statistically significant "gross" disparity between observed and expected protected group representation. The magnitude of this disparity must be sufficient to show that discrimination was an employer's routine operating procedure such that relief should be granted to the entire underrepresented class. This generally requires expert testimony concerning the statistical technique of binomial distribution and its key measure, standard deviation. The actual and expected numbers of protected group members, together with the total number of persons hired for or promoted to the job during the liability period alleged in the complaint, are fed into the binomial distribution formula, which is designed to gauge the degree to which an "underrepresentation" departs from hypothetical "random" or "chance" hiring or promotion. Statisticians have conventionally ruled out chance as the likely cause of a negative deviation from the norm when the formula shows that the observed number falls more than 1.95 standard deviations below the expected number; this convention holds that there is then less than a 5% chance that the underrepre-

expected to recruit from a particular area is evidence that the defendant itself, see *Abron*, or neighboring employers in the same business, see *Hazelwood*, have in fact hired from that area in the past.

9. *Teamsters*, *supra* note 1.

10. This was the availability pool used in *Hazelwood*, where the position in question was that of public school teacher.

11. *See Hazelwood School District v. United States*, 433 U.S. 299, 97 S.Ct. 2736,

53 L.Ed.2d 768 (1977); *cf. Wards Cove Packing Co. v. Atonio, infra* § 4.10, n. 15.

12. *Teamsters*; *EEOC v. O & G Spring & Wire Forms Specialty Co.*, 38 F.3d 872 (7th Cir.1994), *cert. denied*, __ U.S. __, 115 S.Ct. 1270, 131 L.Ed.2d 148 (1995). *But see Carter v. Ball*, 33 F.3d 450 (4th Cir.1994) (unless protected group's representation is compared with its representation in a labor pool from which qualified applicants are drawn, even an "inexorable zero" is not probative).

sentation is itself the result of chance.[13] Apparently determined to avoid "false positives"—implicating an innocent employer—the Supreme Court has written somewhat vaguely that unlawful discrimination may be suspected as the cause of an underrepresentation only "if the difference between the expected value and the observed number is 'greater than two or three [negative] standard deviations' "[14]—a level at which statisticians would exclude chance as the explanation with overwhelming confidence.

It is because the law requires an underrepresentation of this magnitude that a court may rely solely on statistical evidence to indict an employer for systemic disparate treatment discrimination in violation of § 703(a) without running afoul of a distinct provision of Title VII, § 703(j). Section 703(j) provides that Title VII shall not be

> "interpreted to require any employer to grant preferential treatment ... because of race, color, religion, sex, or national origin ... on account of an imbalance which may exist with respect to the total number or percentage of persons of any race, color, religion, sex or national origin employed by any employer ... in comparison with the total number or percentage of persons of such race, color, religion, sex, or national origin in any community ... or in the available work force in any community...."

The Court in *Teamsters* could plausibly deny that holding an employer liable for systemic treatment discrimination upon proof of a gross statistical underrepresentation was tantamount to a requirement, condemned by § 703(j), "that a work force *mirror* the general population."[15] Many employee complements will fail to mirror the protected group's percentage in a surrounding population or work force without falling short *enough* to violate the "two or three standard deviation" test or therefore to violate § 703(a).

A more sophisticated statistical technique, multiple regression analysis,[16] will usually be required to establish the requisite disparity when variations in the particular term and condition of employment at issue—for example, compensation—are explainable by reference to a large number of factors. The Court has indicated, however, that a plaintiff's

13. *But see* Kingsley Browne, Statistical Proof of Discrimination: Beyond "Damned Lies," 68 *Wash.L.Rev.* 477 (1993) (disputing the assumption that such statistical showings can realistically demonstrate that an "underrepresentation" is the product of chance, and therefore challenging statistically based judicial conclusions that exclude chance as the explanation for workforce disparities).

14. *Hazelwood*, 433 U.S. at 309 n.14, 97 S.Ct. at 2742 n.14 (quoting *Castaneda v. Partida*, 430 U.S. 482, 497 n. 17, 97 S.Ct. 1272, 1281 n. 17, 51 L.Ed.2d 498 (1977)).

15. *Teamsters*, 431 U.S. at 339 n.20, 97 S.Ct. at 1856 n.20 (emphasis added).

16. *See generally* Barbara A. Norris, A Structural Approach to Evaluation of Multiple Regression Analysis as Used to Prove Employment Discrimination: The Plaintiff's Answer to Defense Attacks of "Missing Factors" and "Pre–Act Discrimination," 49 Law & Contemp. Probs. 65 (1986); Thomas J. Campbell, Regression Analysis in Title VII Cases: Minimum Standards, Comparable Worth, and Other Issues Where Law and Statistics Meet, 36 Stan. L. Rev. 1299 (1984); Note, Beyond the Prima Facie Case in Employment Discrimination Law: Statistical Proof and Rebuttal, 89 Harv. L. Rev. 387 (1975).

multiple regression analysis need not eliminate all potential nondiscriminatory explanations of disparity, only the most significant.[17]

Once the plaintiff group adduces express or statistical evidence of systemic disparate treatment, the employer has an opportunity to offer what *Teamsters* termed a nondiscriminatory "explanation" by way of rebuttal. Absent a defense, liability will be deemed established and the case moves to a second, bifurcated remedy phase. The employer's principal defense in these cases is to present evidence that casts doubt on the logical, statistical, or legal probative value of plaintiff's evidence. For example, an employer may avoid the force of evidence of disparity by showing infirmities in the plaintiff-defined pool that exaggerate the availability of qualified members of the protected group [18]; by challenging the validity of the statistical conclusions drawn by plaintiff's expert, including objections to insufficient sample size [19]; or by demonstrating (as will seldom be the case twenty-five years after the effective date of the Act) that a protected group's underrepresentation is attributable largely to then-lawful, even if discriminatory, hiring that took place before the employer became subject to Title VII.[20]

In the alternative, the employer may affirmatively present counter-comparative statistics. A more restrictively refined availability pool, for example, may generate negative disparities of a magnitude (less than two or three standard deviations) that judges will deem insignificant to alter the status quo and impose liability on an employer. Indeed, the employer may refute the existence of any negative disparity by offering data suggesting that it hired or promoted a *greater* number of protected group members than their availability in the employer-advocated pool would predict: in that instance, the standard deviation would be positive. Most powerfully, an employer that has maintained records differentiating its applicants by race, national origin or gender [21] may be able to

17. *Bazemore v. Friday,* 478 U.S. 385, 106 S.Ct. 3000, 92 L.Ed.2d 315 (1986). *But see Smith v. Virginia Commonwealth University,* 84 F.3d 672 (4th Cir.1996) (en banc) (defendant unlawfully relied on multiple regression analysis to justify increase in female faculty members' salaries where analysis left out key performance, productivity, and merit factors that university considered in determining prior pay increases).

18. Thus, where the employment is in the typical American metropolitan area in which minority groups are more heavily concentrated in the urban core, the defendant would usually assert that the entire "Standard Metropolitan Statistical Area" defined by the federal government, rather than the central city alone, is the proper measure of applicant, and hence protected group, availability. See *Hazelwood, supra* note 11.

19. *See Mayor of Philadelphia v. Educational Equality League,* 415 U.S. 605, 620–621, 94 S.Ct. 1323, 1333–1334, 39

L.Ed.2d 630 (1974), cited in *Teamsters,* 431 U.S. at 339 n.20, 97 S.Ct. at 1856 n.20; *Birkbeck v. Marvel Lighting Corp.,* 30 F.3d 507 (4th Cir.1994), *cert. denied* __ U.S. __, 115 S.Ct. 666, 130 L.Ed.2d 600 (1994) (case under ADEA holding sample size of four laid-off employees too small to serve as predicate for a statistically significant conclusion that employer practiced age discrimination).

20. *See Hazelwood, supra* note 11.

21. The EEOC's recordkeeping regulations do not require employers to keep records differentiating applicants by their protected group status, and indeed many state fair employment laws prohibit employers from asking applicants to indicate their race or gender. The regulations only require employers to keep applications for one year. 29 C.F.R. § 1602.14 (1994).

offer "applicant flow" statistics to establish that it hired at least as great a percentage of protected group members as of others.[22] Such evidence tends to show the particular defendant's comparative treatment of actual members of the protected group and others who had the requisite interest to offer themselves for hire or promotion. Applicant flow evidence is therefore generally credited with greater probative value than standard deviation evidence drawn from the number of hires or promotions that might theoretically have been expected based on protected group availability in an appropriately defined pool of persons none of whom may have actually sought employment with the defendant.

In the face of a showing of gross underrepresentation of the protected group, as evidenced by substantially unimpeached standard deviation data, applicant flow data could nevertheless point in favor of the employer. When the employer treated fairly or even favorably a relatively small number of protected group members applied. But why did so few protected group members apply, given their significant representation in the underlying pool? One possibility is a self-selected lack of interest in the particular employment, despite presumptive minimum qualifications and availability.[23] That argument appears to have lesser force when the court views the statistical underrepresentation as overwhelming, and particularly when there are no protected group members in the job in question.[24] Another explanation of underapplication by the protected group is a well-developed, notorious employer reputation for discrimination against the group in question, a reputation so extreme as to render it "futile" for a member of that group to apply. If the plaintiffs can prove that more protected group members would have applied during the period of the alleged discrimination but for the employer's discriminatory practices, they may persuade a court to disregard or discount the employer's applicant flow evidence.[25] An employer unable to impeach or

---

22. *Hazelwood, supra* note 11. The employer demonstrates that conclusion by presenting evidence of simple arithmetic proportions. The percentage of protected group members selected (from among protected group members who applied) is compared with the corresponding percentage of nonprotected group members selected. *See also Anderson v. Douglas & Lomason Co.,* 26 F.3d 1277 (5th Cir.1994), *cert. denied,* ___ U.S. ___, 115 S.Ct. 1099, 130 L.Ed.2d 1066 (1995), (deferring to district court decision to credit employer expert's analysis of applicant flow figures). *But see EEOC v. American National Bank,* 652 F.2d 1176, 1193–97 (4th Cir.1981) (employer's applicant flow figures, to be probative, must correspond to the same time periods and kinds of workers whose availability is reflected in the plaintiff's statistics that the applicant flow data is designed to refute). And of course applicant flow figures may reinforce the *plaintiff's* showing of gross statistical underrepresentation if employer

records show that it hired a signifcantly lower percentage of qualified protected group applicants than of others. *See EEOC v. Olson's Dairy Queens, Inc.,* 989 F.2d 165 (5th Cir.1993).

23. *See EEOC v. Sears, Roebuck & Co.,* 839 F.2d 302 (7th Cir.1988) (upholding women's lesser interest in commissions sales jobs as an explanation that serves to rebut systemic disparate treatment evidence of gender discrimination in hiring, promotion, and compensation).

24. *EEOC v. O & G Spring and Wire Forms Specialty,* 38 F.3d 872 (7th Cir.1994) (rejecting employer argument that blacks had "self-selected" themselves out of the applicant pool for low-skilled jobs held predominantly by Polish- and Spanish-speaking employees, many of whom did not speak English).

25. *Cf. International Brotherhood of Teamsters v. United States,* 431 U.S. 324, 97 S.Ct. 1843, 52 L.Ed.2d 396 (1977) (per-

counter a finding of gross statistical underrepresentation must nevertheless be permitted to attempt to offer some other nondiscriminatory "explanation" for the disparity.[26] A controversial defense accepted by some courts is that, relative to others, the particular protected group lacked interest in or qualifications for the job in question. A highly publicized Seventh Circuit decision so held with respect to women seeking positions as commissioned salespersons.[27] The court seemed to consider it irrelevant whether, assuming the validity of the key fact findings, the relative lack of interest in or qualifications to hold those positions was "inherent" in women or a product of stereotyping long rooted in American history or culture. In particular, the court did not consider it important to examine the "employer's [own] role in shaping the interest of applicants." [28]

An employer may also explain an unimpeached, prima facie gross statistical underrepresentation by offering evidence that one of its own neutral practices had disproportionate adverse impact on the protected group.[29] This puts the employer in the odd position of becoming its own accuser, since such a practice may independently give rise to Title VII liability even without proof of discriminatory intent.[30] In effect, the employer argues that one unlawful employment practice (a facially neutral test or experience requirement that disproportionately affects the protected group) explains another (the significant bottom-line underrepresentation of the protected group in the job level for which the test or experience requirement screens). By undertaking this showing the employer may limit its liability to those members of the protected group who were personally affected by the neutral practice. Better yet, the court may conclude that the neutral practice which accounts for an underrepresentation is itself justified because it is "job related for the position in question and consistent with business necessity" within the meaning of § 703(k)(1)(A)(i), added by § 105(a) of the Civil Rights Act of 1991. Courts before the 1991 Civil Rights Act that have permitted employers to defend a gross underrepresentation by pointing to such a neutral practice have required them to bear the burden of persuasion on the neutral practice justification.[31]

It is unclear whether these decisions will survive a companion amendment to Title VII, also added by § 105(a) of the Civil Rights Act of 1991, that provides: "A demonstration that an employment practice is required by business necessity may not be used as a defense against a

---

mitting individual nonapplicants to obtain relief at the remedy stage of a systemic disparate treatment case if they can make such a showing of futility).

26. *Teamsters, supra,* note 25 at 393 n. 20, 97 S.Ct. at 1884 n. 20.

27. *EEOC v. Sears, Roebuck & Co.,* 839 F.2d 302 (7th Cir.1988).

28. *Id.* (Cudahy, J., concurring in part and dissenting in part).

29. *See, e.g., Griffin v. Carlin,* 755 F.2d 1516 (11th Cir.1985); *Segar v. Smith,* 738 F.2d 1249 (D.C.Cir.1984), *cert. denied sub nom. Meese v. Segar,* 471 U.S. 1115, 105 S.Ct. 2357, 86 L.Ed.2d 258 (1985).

30. *See* Part F immediately following.

31. *Griffin v. Carlin, supra* note 29; *Segar v. Smith, supra* note 29.

claim of intentional discrimination under this title." [32] At a minimum this provision confirms the Court's position in *International Union, UAW v. Johnson Controls, Inc.,*[33] that a facially discriminatory practice may be excused, if at all, only under the stringent BFOQ defense, and not merely by a showing of job relatedness and business necessity. Read broadly, however, the new § 703(k)(2) could also be applied to cases where the prima facie evidence of intentional discrimination consists of gross statistical disparities sufficient to establish systemic disparate treatment of the plaintiff class. If so, the Section would appear to deny the employer the last-chance defense discussed in *Griffin* and *Segar.*[34]

D. THE RELIEF STAGE OF THE BIFURCATED SYSTEMIC DISPARATE TREATMENT ACTION

Library References:

C.J.S. Civil Rights §§ 161–162, 407, 419.
West's Key No. Digests, Civil Rights ⚖153, 391.

§ 4.8 In General

Systemic treatment trials are conducted in distinct liability and remedial phases. First, from evidence of a facially discriminatory policy, from statistics alone, from anecdotal evidence, or some combination of the above, the court determines whether the employer has intentionally discriminated against the plaintiff's protected group. If so, individual members of the plaintiff class who reapply (or, in certain cases, apply for the first time) for a position or promotion at this stage of the action may thus become eligible to receive the full panoply of all otherwise appropriate Title VII remedies: not only declaratory and injunctive relief but reinstatement, back pay, retroactive seniority and, since the violation involves intentional discrimination, the capped compensatory and punitive damages made available by the Civil Rights Act of 1991.

The Supreme Court has substantially eased the individual plaintiff's burden of demonstrating entitlement to relief at the remedy stage of the systemic treatment case. Even if the prima facie case consists only of statistical evidence, that evidence, if believed by the factfinder and not successfully rebutted with a nondiscriminatory explanation, gives rise to a presumption that each plaintiff who unsuccessfully sought hire, promotion, or retention during the established liability period was rejected because of his or her protected group status.[1] So long as the individual applied for the position in question during the established liability period, she need not even produce evidence of her minimum qualifica-

32. Title VII, § 703(k)(2).

33. 499 U.S. 187, 111 S.Ct. 1196, 113 L.Ed.2d 158 (1991).

34. See Part F immediately following for a fuller discussion of the impact case under the 1991 CRA.

§ 4.8

1. *Franks v. Bowman Transportation Co.,* 424 U.S. 747, 772, 96 S.Ct. 1251, 1268, 47 L.Ed.2d 444 (1976), text accompanying note 3, § 4.7, *supra.*

tions. Proof of a broad-based policy of unlawful discrimination, in other words, generates "reasonable grounds to infer that individual hiring decisions were made in pursuit of the discriminatory policy and to require the employer to come forth with evidence dispelling that inference." [2] Although the prima case case does not "conclusively demonstrate that all of the employer's decisions were part of the proven discriminatory pattern and practice," it creates "a greater likelihood that any single decision was a component of the overall pattern." [3] The employer is now a "proven wrongdoer," and must bear the burden of showing nondiscriminatory reasons for rejecting any individual plaintiff.[4]

To rebut the presumption, the employer may avoid liability to individual plaintiffs or plaintiff class members by persuading a court that they were not in fact victims of discrimination. For example, the employer may demonstrate that there were no vacancies in the pertinent position at the time a particular class member applied, that the plaintiff lacked minimum qualifications that the employer insisted upon at the time of the plaintiff's rejection, or that a successful applicant was better qualified.[5] Even class members who did not apply for a position during the proven liability period may sometimes receive individual relief; but they carry the heavy burden of persuading that it was futile for them to apply because of an employer's notorious reputation for egregious discrimination against their protected group and that they would have applied otherwise.[6] It does not suffice for nonapplicants to show only that they are interested in obtaining a job at the time of judgment; discriminatees may be awarded retroactive seniority for the period they would have accrued seniority had the employer not discriminated, so the job available through court order may be far more attractive than it was originally. Further, they, unlike "applicant" plaintiff class members, bear the burden of showing their own minimum qualifications at the time that, but for futility, they prove they would have applied.[7]

E. HOW THE INDIVIDUAL AND SYSTEMIC DISPARATE TREATMENT CASES INTERRELATE

Library References:

C.J.S. Civil Rights §§ 161–162.
West's Key No. Digests, Civil Rights ☞153.

§ 4.9 In General

Given the relative ease of establishing a *prima facie* case of individual disparate treatment under *McDonnell Douglas/Burdine*, and the ex-

---

2. *Teamsters*, 431 U.S. at 359 & n.45, 97 S.Ct. at 1866 & n.45.

3. *Id.*

4. *Id.*

5. *Franks v. Bowman Transportation Co.*, 424 U.S. 747, 773 n. 32, 96 S.Ct. 1251, 1268 n. 32, 47 L.Ed.2d 444 (1976); *Team-*

sters, 431 U.S. at 359 n.45, 97 S.Ct. at 1866 n.45.

6. *Teamsters*, 431 U.S. at 365, 97 S.Ct. at 1870, text accompanying note 25, § 4.7 *supra.*

7. *Id.* at 369 n.53, 97 S.Ct. at 1872 n.53.

pense and difficulty of gathering and analyzing the data necessary to establish a case of systemic disparate treatment, solo plaintiffs usually proceed with "direct" or inferential evidence alone. Nevertheless, there is a complementary relationship between evidence of individual and systemic disparate treatment. A well financed individual plaintiff may fortify the individual disparate treatment case with evidence of statistically discriminatory patterns. Similarly, a plaintiff class may, and as a practical matter is well advised, to bolster a case of systemic discriminatory treatment with anecdotal evidence of discrimination against its individual members. The advocate should bear in mind that statistical systemic treatment evidence merely suggests that the employer routinely discriminated, but by itself does not suggest how. Counsel may fill the gap for skeptical judges by offering "direct" or inferential evidence that individual plaintiffs were discriminatorily treated. In both *Teamsters* and *Hazelwood* the Supreme Court observed that the plaintiffs had breathed life in the statistical evidence by offering evidence of individual disparate treatment.

On the other hand, the failure of a systemic treatment class action— or of the government plaintiff equivalent, a "pattern or practice" action by the U.S. Attorney General under Section 707—does not imply lack of merit to the individual disparate treatment case of any particular member of the plaintiff class.[1] Nor, as we shall see shortly, does that failure negate the employer's potential liability to an individual member of a plaintiff class for harm caused by a neutral employment practice. A given practice may have disproportionately adversely impacted those members of the plaintiff group who encountered it even though the group fared well at the "bottom line" that registers the aggregate of all employer policies, practices and discrete decisions by employer agents.[2]

F. NEUTRAL PRACTICES WITH DISPROPORTIONATE ADVERSE IMPACT

Library References:

> C.J.S. Civil Rights §§ 161–162.
> West's Key No. Digests, Civil Rights ☞153.

§ 4.10 In General

The federal courts have at times struggled to clarify the evidentiary frameworks for proving individual and systemic disparate treatment, but there has been no real question that such intentional conduct constitutes unlawful discrimination. By contrast, neutral employer practices that in

---

§ 4.9

1. *See* discussion of *Cooper v. Federal Reserve Bank of Richmond*, 467 U.S. 867, 104 S.Ct. 2794, 81 L.Ed.2d 718 (1984), in Procedure chapter below.

2. *Connecticut v. Teal*, 457 U.S. 440, 102 S.Ct. 2525, 73 L.Ed.2d 130 (1982).

operation fall with disproportionate adverse impact on the plaintiff's protected group have proven far more troublesome.

Initially a strong judicial consensus emerged that Congress intended to eradicate such practices on much the same terms as intentional acts of discrimination. Writing for a unanimous Court in *Griggs v. Duke Power Co.*,[1] Chief Justice Burger wrote that practices fair in form but discriminatory in effect may violate Title VII even though the employer's motivation in adopting the practice is neutral or benign. The early cases developing this theory considered the lawfulness of "objective" (really, specific or concrete or readily identifiable) employer practices such as educational requirements or standardized aptitude or psychological tests.[2] The classic example is a labor union's requirement that an applicant for membership had to be sponsored by one of the existing members, all of whom were white. When none of the 30 members admitted under this policy during a six-year period were African-Americans or Hispanic, the plaintiff had proven prima facie that this "neutral" practice had a disproportionate adverse impact on members of the protected group.[3]

Occasionally, however, disproportionate adverse impact analysis was applied to a "subjective" employer process such as the unstructured evaluation of black employees by white foremen.[4] The Supreme Court recently approved the use of impact analysis to scrutinize these "subjective" promotion decisions,[5] a decision not addressed and therefore apparently left undisturbed by the Civil Rights Act of 1991. Even a single employer practice—for example, a one-time layoff—may trigger disproportionate adverse impact analysis; the practice need not be a repeated or customary method of operation to be subject to impact scrutiny.[6] Yet even after the 1991 Act, there are decisions ruling out the use of disparate impact proof when, in the court's view, the plaintiff fails to specify a particular aspect of an employer's subjective decisionmaking process that is allegedly responsible for an underrepresentation of the plaintiff class.[7]

§ 4.10

1. 401 U.S. 424, 91 S.Ct. 849, 28 L.Ed.2d 158 (1971).

2. *See Griggs* and *Albemarle Paper Co. v. Moody*, 422 U.S. 405, 95 S.Ct. 2362, 45 L.Ed.2d 280, (1975); height and weight requirements, *Dothard, supra* § 4.3, note 9; or rules prohibiting the employment of drug addicts, *New York City Transit Authority v. Beazer*, 440 U.S. 568, 99 S.Ct. 1355, 59 L.Ed.2d 587 (1979); arrestees, *Gregory v. Litton Systems, Inc.*, 472 F.2d 631 (9th Cir. 1972); convicts, *Green v. Missouri Pacific R.R. Co.*, 523 F.2d 1290 (8th Cir.1975); or debtors whose wages have been frequently garnished, *Wallace v. Debron Corp.*, 494 F.2d 674 (8th Cir.1974).

3. *E.E.O.C. v. Steamship Clerks Union, Local 1066*, 48 F.3d 594 (1st Cir.1995).

4. *Rowe v. General Motors Corp.*, 457 F.2d 348 (5th Cir.1972).

5. *Watson v. Fort Worth Bank and Trust*, 487 U.S. 977, 108 S.Ct. 2777, 101 L.Ed.2d 827 (1988).

6. *Council 31, American Federation of State, County and Municipal Employees v. Ward*, 978 F.2d 373 (7th Cir.1992). *But see EEOC v. Chicago Miniature Lamp Works*, 947 F.2d 292, 304–05 (7th Cir.1991) (word-of-mouth recruiting not an employer "practice" subject to scrutiny under disparate impact theory). *Contra, Thomas v. Washington County School Board*, 915 F.2d 922, 924–26 (4th Cir.1990).

7. *See, e.g., Anderson v. Douglas & Lomason Company*, 26 F.3d 1277 (5th Cir. 1994), *cert. denied*, ___ U.S. ___, 115 S.Ct.

In *Connecticut v. Teal*,[8] the Supreme Court clarified that a single component of an employer's multi-stage selection process may have unlawfully discriminatory adverse impact on the particular protected group members it screens out even if the protected group as a whole fares better than a non-minority group in the overall process. The Court explained that the "principal focus" of Title VII is "the protection of the individual employee," rather than of minority groups. It rooted the disproportionate adverse impact theory in the language of § 703(a)(2): even though a plaintiff is not "discriminated against" in the disparate treatment sense intended by § 703(a)(1), neutral practices may, in the language of § 703(a)(2), "deprive or tend to deprive ... [the] individual of employment opportunities ...." Section 703(a)(2) is accordingly not concerned solely with how the plaintiff's group fares at the statistical "bottom line" of jobs or promotions, but also with "limitations" or "classifications" that deprive individual members of that group of the chance to advance. In sum, a racially balanced workforce—even one that results from affirmative action in favor of the plaintiff's protected group—does not immunize an employer from liability for a specific act of discrimination, whether intentional or neutral.

How to measure whether an employer's neutral practice has a "disproportionate" adverse impact on a protected group is a question that is addressed only vaguely by the Court's cases and remains unresolved by the 1991 Act. Some courts have adopted as a measure of disproportion the "eighty percent rule" from EEOC's Uniform Guidelines on Employee Selection Procedures.[9] These provide that a protected group's selection rate which is less than 80 percent of the rate for the group with the greatest success will be regarded by the Commission for enforcement purposes as evidence of adverse impact.[10]

But the 80% rule has come under increasing attack from academic and court critics alike. It does not take sample size into account and thus may fail to detect statistically significant adverse impact on large samples[11], and its comparison of group pass rates may not measure the magnitude (as opposed to mere statistical significance) of a disparity as

---

1099, 130 L.Ed.2d 1066 (1995) (employer policy requiring individuals to fill out applications at the plant insufficiently specific).

8. 457 U.S. 440, 102 S.Ct. 2525, 73 L.Ed.2d 130 (1982). *Teal* has recently been applied to the interview component of the selection process for a firefighter position. *Thomas v. City of Omaha*, 63 F.3d 763 (8th Cir.1995). *Cf. Cronin v. Aetna Life Insurance Co.*, 46 F.3d 196 (2d Cir.1995) (statistical evidence that overall impact of reduction in force was not age discriminatory does not negate possibility of employer disparate treatment liability for discriminating against the plaintiff in the way in which the RIF was conducted).

9. *See* Blumoff & Lewis, *supra* § 4.5, note 8 at 21–22.

10. 29 C.F.R. § 1607.4. *See Connecticut v. Teal*, 457 U.S. 440, 444 n. 4, 102 S.Ct. 2525, 2528 n. 4, 73 L.Ed.2d 130 (1982).

11. *See* Shoben, "Differential Pass–Fail Rates in Employment Testing: Statistical Proof Under Title VII," 91 Harv.L.Rev. 793 (1978). Professor Shoben proposes instead that courts use an "independent proportions" test to measure disparities between the success and failure of two protected groups with respect to a particular employer practice or a "chi square" test suitable for comparing the success/failure frequencies of more than two groups.

well as other techniques.[12] Justice O'Connor, writing for a plurality in *Watson v. Fort Worth Bank & Trust.*,[13] observed that EEOC's 80% test, while perhaps appropriate as a rough administrative guide for allocating agency prosecutorial resources, was not binding on judges. Insisting that the plaintiff should have to produce evidence that the challenged practice had a "significantly discriminatory impact," Justice O'Connor alluded to the need for a more rigorous and reliable measure of intergroup disparity. Justice O'Connor hinted that a better measure of whether a practice has legally and not just statistically significant adverse impact is the binomial distribution analysis approved by the Court for cases of systemic disparate treatment.[14]

A year later, a majority of the court in *Wards Cove Packing Co. v. Atonio* appeared to agree with this approach when it required a prima facie demonstration that the challenged practice has a "significantly disparate impact" on the protected group.[15] Further, the Court in *Wards Cove* appeared to demand prima facie evidence virtually indistinguishable from the statistical showing it had required for systemic *treatment* cases. These developments leave a lingering question. Why would a plaintiff undertake an impact challenge to a neutral practice—a proof mode the Court devised in *Griggs* precisely as an alternative to proof of intentional discrimination—if she must develop the same data and proffer the same expert statistical testimony that a class must adduce when it undertakes to show across-the-board intentional discrimination?

The seeds of a coming collapse in the Court's commitment to the neutral practice theory were unwittingly planted in *Griggs* itself. The Court wrestled with inventing a judge-made defense to the judge-made *prima facie* case and produced several different verbal formulations of notably different stringency. In later years a Court less enamored of the disparate impact theory would exploit the resulting confusion. If, as *Teal* explained, balanced "bottom line" hiring or deployment of the work force does not serve as a defense to a practice's disproportionate adverse impact, what does? The Court wrote in *Griggs* that an employer could avoid liability if it could show that the challenged requirement "related" to the job in question. But related to what degree? Elsewhere in *Griggs* the Court described the defense, in increasing order of rigor, as requiring evidence that the employer practice be "demonstrably" or "manifestly" related to the job in question or that the practice be a matter of business "necessity".

This last suggestion, that an employer must show a neutral practice to be necessary or essential to its business, rather than just desirable, was inconsistent with an emerging third phase of the "neutral practice"

12. David C. Baldus & James W. L. Cole, *Statistical Proof of Discrimination* (1989).

13. 487 U.S. 977, 108 S.Ct. 2777, 101 L.Ed.2d 827 (1988).

14. *Id.* at 984 note 1 and accompanying text.

15. 490 U.S. 642, 657, 109 S.Ct. 2115, 2125, 104 L.Ed.2d 733 (1989).

case. In *Albemarle Paper Co. v. Moody* [16], the Court explained in dictum that even if an employer (by whatever standard) justifies the adverse effect of its practice by reference to a business reason, the plaintiff may still prevail by demonstrating that the employer could have met its needs with a "less discriminatory alternative." If the plaintiff does show such an alternative, however, it necessarily demonstrates that the employer's chosen practice could not have been a matter of strict necessity. By the same token, if the employer's own, second-stage evidence must show genuine business "necessity," the third stage becomes superfluous: how could a less discriminatory alternative fully meet the employer's needs if the employer's original, chosen practice was essential?

After *Griggs* the Court also waffled on whether the plaintiff or defendant bears the burden of persuading on the justification issue (whatever its content) once a plaintiff carries the day on the prima facie case. The Court more often wrote that the employer defense is an affirmative one on which the employer bears the burden of persuasion [17] but on occasion implied otherwise.[18]

In 1989 the Court resolved both these questions—the nature of the employer defense and the allocation of the burden of persuasion—so as to undermine severely the *Griggs* neutral practice mode of proof. Ironically, this resolution began the year before with *Watson*, the case which extended the application of disproportionate adverse impact analysis to subjective employer practices. A plurality there also wrote that an employer may defend adverse impact merely by producing evidence that its practice is "based on legitimate business reasons." As the dissent complained, this description renders the employer defense to a neutral practice case virtually indistinguishable from the easily established "legitimate non-discrimination reason" defense to a *McDonnell Douglas/Burdine* case of individual disparate treatment.

This position of the *Watson* plurality then commanded a majority in *Wards Cove*, which also apparently extends the holding to cases that challenge the more traditional "objective" neutral practices.[19] A neutral practice that disproportionately adversely affects the plaintiff's protected group could survive Title VII challenge, the Court held, if it simply "serves, in a significant way, the legitimate employment goals of the employer." The practice need not be " 'essential' or 'indispensable' to the employer's business. . . ." The *Wards Cove* opinion is equally explicit that the employer carries only the burden of producing evidence, the burden of persuasion remaining with the plaintiff.

16. 422 U.S. 405, 95 S.Ct. 2362, 45 L.Ed.2d 280 (1975).

17. *See, e.g., Dothard, supra* § 4.3, note 9.

18. *See, e.g., New York City Transit Authority v. Beazer*, 440 U.S. 568, 99 S.Ct. 1355, 59 L.Ed.2d 587 (1979).

19. For a fuller discussion of the *Wards Cove* decision, see Blumoff and Lewis, "The Reagan Court and Title VII: A Common-Law Outlook On a Statutory Task," 69 N.C.L.Rev. 1 (1990). Among other points, the authors assert that most of the restrictions on the disproportionate adverse impact case announced in that decision were unnecessary, because the only issue remaining on appeal concerned plaintiffs' plainly deficient statistical evidence of systemic disparate treatment.

Finally, as though to confirm the *Watson* dissent's lament that the Court was improperly equating the disproportionate adverse impact case with a case of individual disparate treatment, the *Wards Cove* majority wrote that by showing a lesser discriminatory alternative the plaintiff demonstrates that the employer's chosen practice was merely a "pretext" for discrimination. In this way the Court suggests that a method of demonstrating unlawful discrimination which *Griggs* developed precisely for cases where discriminatory intent could *not* be shown still turns, in the end, on employer intent. This approach echoes Justice O'Connor's suggestion in *Watson* the year before that the prima facie impact case may demand statistical evidence of the same reliability and magnitude as the Court had required for cases of systemic disparate treatment.

Removing any doubt about its hostility to the neutral practice case, the Court then cautions the judiciary against too readily accepting a plaintiff's proposed lesser discriminatory alternative. The alternative must be "equally effective" as the employer's chosen practice, and such factors as "cost or other burdens" are "relevant in determining whether they would be equally as effective...." The Court added that if a plaintiff could demonstrate the existence of a less discriminatory alternative so defined, in essence it would be showing that the employer's reliance on its original, challenged practice would be a "pretext" for discrimination. By thus implying that impact proof ultimately shows an employer's state of mind that is prohibited in any event by individual or systemic treatment evidence, the Court leaves us to wonder about the independent utility of the impact case so resoundingly supported by the unanimous decision in *Griggs* less than two decades before.

The Civil Rights Act of 1991 attempted to overrule significant aspects of the *Wards Cove* decision—just how effectively remains to be seen. As we consider the specifics, it is important to keep in mind that *Wards Cove* enfeebled group attacks on neutral practices by altering preexisting understandings about the three major phases of the disparate impact case: (1) plaintiff's prima facie evidence that a particular employment practice caused a specified disproportionate adverse impact on plaintiff's group; (2) the nature and quantum of the employer's defense to disproportionate impact; and (3) the plaintiff's rebuttal that an alternative practice would have largely, rather than perfectly, served the employer's legitimate goals, with lesser adverse impact on the group.

The legislation unequivocally declares that the employer's justification to a prima facie case is an affirmative defense on which the employer must persuade as well as produce evidence. In most other respects, though, the Act reflects Congress' inability to reach a unitary understanding about any of the three previously declared stages of the disproportionate adverse impact case. It fails to clarify the magnitude of the required prima facie case of disproportionate impact; it procedurally complicates the prima facie showing by requiring that the plaintiff ordinarily disentangle the effects of bundled employer practices; it declares that the defense consists of separate elements of job relatedness and business necessity, but offers only a calculatedly ambiguous understanding of what business necessity means; and it carries forward the seemingly unworkable *Wards Cove* innovation that the employer may avoid liability by adopting an alternative practice, perhaps even at the eleventh hour in the middle of a trial. On balance, therefore, the legislation falls well short of restoring the impact case to its pre-*Wards Cove* state.

The central provision, § 703(k)(1)(A), declares that an impact-based unlawful employment practice is proved when:

(i) a complaining party demonstrates that a respondent uses a particular employment practice that causes a disparate impact on the basis of race, color, religion, sex, or national origin and the respondent fails to demonstrate that the challenged practice is job related for the position in question and consistent with business necessity; or

(ii) the complaining party makes the demonstration described in subparagraph (C) with respect to an alternative employment practice and the respondent refuses to adopt such alternative employment practice.

The legislation sheds no light on the required magnitude of prima facie differential impact. In the hands of a Court that has proven resolutely hostile to borderline Title VII evidentiary showings,[20] the legislative void on this question may well be filled by restrictive new mathematical requirements that could be justified on the authority of *Watson* and *Wards Cove*, which in this respect remain untouched.

Wards Cove, again furnishing a majority for a proposition that a plurality had endorsed in *Watson*, also required the plaintiff to isolate the single practice among several that produces an alleged adverse impact.[21] New § 701(k)(1)(B)(i) relieves the plaintiff who is attempting to demonstrate adverse impact under § 703(k)(1)(A)(i) from having to disentangle bundled practices, but only if she can "demonstrate" (again a burden of persuasion as well as production) "that the elements of a respondent's decisionmaking process [a 'process' is apparently a package of 'practices'] are not capable of separation for analysis."[22] Otherwise she must show that "each particular challenged employment practice causes a disparate impact...."[23] These provisions invite satellite litigation over the extent to which the plaintiff has taken advantage of discovery and the employer has forthrightly responded. Employer initiated motions on the issue are more than a remote possibility.[24]

20. *See* Blumoff & Lewis, *supra* § 4.5, note 8; Blumrosen, *supra* § 4.5, note 8.

21. *Wards Cove*, 490 U.S. at 657, 109 S.Ct. at 2125; *see also id.* at 672 (Stevens, J., dissenting).

22. Section 105(a) (adding Title VII § 703(k)(1)(B)(i)).

23. *Id.*

24. Unlike plaintiffs' counsel, who typically depend on recovering attorneys' fees from the defendant, but who can do so under § 701(k) only if their clients prevail, counsel for defendant employers are typically compensated by the hour regardless of the outcome of the litigation.

A related provision, § 703(k)(1)(B)(ii), is apparently intended to apply when the plaintiff has been allowed, by virtue of § 703(*l*), to attack an entire selection process without demonstrating the adverse impact of each particular component practice. Subdivision (ii) relieves the employer of showing the business necessity[25] of any particular practice that *it* can demonstrate does not cause a disparate impact on plaintiff's group. In tandem, subdivisions (i) and (ii) of § 703(k)(1)(B) seem to assume that sometimes the employer will be able to disentangle the effects of bundled practices even after the plaintiff has satisfied the court that, after discovery, she cannot.

The Court's most publicized and excoriated innovation in *Wards Cove* was to relax both the nature and quantum of an employer's defensive evidence required to justify practices shown to have had a disproportionate adverse impact. Eschewing earlier appellate formulations that sometimes required the employer to demonstrate that its practice was essential to the safe and efficient conduct of its business, the Court wrote that the prima facie case is countered if the defendant merely produces some evidence that the challenged practice serves, "in a significant way, the legitimate goals of the employer."[26] An intricate legislative compromise appears in the end to stiffen the easily satisfied *Wards Cove* version of the defense only slightly insofar as it relates to the overall enterprise, yet also to require the employer to show some link between its chosen practice and the needs of the particular job.

Once the plaintiff demonstrates that a specific practice causes a disparate impact (of still unquantified magnitude), the employer must, after the effective date of the 1991 Act, "demonstrate that the challenged practice is job- related for the position in question and consistent with business necessity...."[27] Further, the obligation to "demonstrate" these elements imposes on the employer, as was generally held before *Wards Cove*, the burden of persuasion on this defense.[28] The net result is that the text of the legislatively overhauled impact defense closely resembles the two-pronged *Diaz/Weeks* BFOQ defense to an expressly discriminatory policy after *Johnson Controls*. The employer bears the compound burden of showing that a neutral practice is necessary for the business (probably a less demanding showing than the *Diaz* "essence of the business" requirement) and is keyed to the particular occupation it screens for (although only "related" to that job, a showing considerably less demanding than the required *Weeks* proof that

---

25. For reasons unexplained, the text does not in terms relieve the employer of showing the job-relatedness of such a practice.

26. *Wards Cove*, 490 U.S. at 659 n.9, 109 S.Ct. at 2126 n.9.

27. Section 105(a) (adding Title VII § 703(k)(1)(A)(i), 42 U.S.C.A. § 2000e–2(k)(1)(A)(i))(emphasis added). This compound requirement of a job link and an overall business justification is similar to the defense provided by § 103(a) of the Americans With Disabilities Act of 1990, 42 U.S.C.A. § 12113, for employer screening devices that have adverse impact on disabled individuals. Such practices will not violate that statute if they are "shown to be job-related and consistent with business necessity...."

28. *See supra* text accompanying notes 17–18.

"all or substantially all" protected group members could not perform it). It is true that requiring the employer to link its practice to requirements of the job, and not just to unspecified "legitimate goals" of the business as a whole, seems to place the plaintiff in a somewhat better posture than she was in after *Wards Cove*. But what do job-relatedness and business necessity now mean? Congress tell us in a preliminary provision on legislative purpose, Section 3, that it seeks to codify those concepts as they were defined by *Griggs* and in subsequent Supreme Court disparate impact decisions before *Wards Cove*.[29] In an unusual attempt to control the judicial interpretive process in advance, Congress adds in § 105(b) that only one specified interpretive memorandum may be "relied upon in any way as legislative history in construing or applying ... any provision of this Act that relates to *Wards Cove*— Business necessity/cumulation/alternate business practice." Unfortunately, the referenced memorandum dated October 25, 1991 rather unhelpfully repeats virtually verbatim Section 3's statement that the business necessity and job relatedness concepts in the Act are akin to those developed by the Supreme Court before *Wards Cove*.

Leaving the definition of the defense for decision by a conservative federal bench could result in a formulation markedly less stringent than the consensus approach of the intermediate appellate courts during the years preceding *Wards Cove*.[30] There is even some possibility that the Supreme Court will return to a definition that approximates the lax *Wards Cove* standard: whether the challenged practice serves to some unspecified degree unspecified general business goals. The Court's latitude to do so arises from the opposing directions in which its pre-*Wards Cove* decisions point.

The Court's early post-*Griggs* impact opinions contained language announcing a stringent standard. In *Albemarle Paper Co. v. Moody*,[31] the

---

29. In contrast, predecessor versions of the legislation had "purposes" sections that expressed the intention to overrule the *Wards Cove* business necessity definition. *See, e.g.*, HR 1, Section (o)(2).

30. *See* Blumoff & Lewis, *supra* § 4.5, note 8 at 16–17 (discussing judicial descriptions of the defense that required the employer to show a "demonstrable" or "manifest" relationship between the challenged practice and important elements of the job). *See, e.g., Contreras v. City of Los Angeles*, 656 F.2d 1267 (9th Cir.1981), *cert. denied* , 455 U.S. 1021, 102 S.Ct. 1719, 72 L.Ed.2d 140 (1982). Somewhat surprisingly, considering its purpose to allay employer concerns, the Democratic substitute measure that the House passed on June 5, 1991 appeared to strengthen the required job-related link, describing it as a "substantial and manifest relationship" between the challenged practice and "requirements for effective job performance." That language

has disappeared from the legislation enacted into law.

It should be noted, moreover, that under Senator Dole's interpretive memorandum on the Civil Rights Act of 1991, 137 Cong. Rec. S15472–S15478 (daily ed. October 30, 1991), which President Bush has directed executive branch officials to respect as "authoritative interpretive guidance," President's Statement on Signing the Act, November 21, 1991, DLR No. 226, p. D–1, November 22, 1991, the job-related prong of the defense—"job-related for the position in question"—is, in the Senator's words, "to be read broadly, to include any legitimate business purpose, even those that may not be strictly required for the actual day-to-day activities of an entry level job." Dole Memorandum Section–By–Section Analysis concerning section 8.

31. 422 U.S. 405, 425, 95 S.Ct. 2362, 2375, 45 L.Ed.2d 280 (1975).

Court fastened on the *Griggs* formulation that demanded a "manifest relation" between the neutral practice and requirements of the job in question. In *Dothard v. Rawlinson*,[32] the Court's language was even more exacting. It borrowed the *Griggs* assertion that "the touchstone is business necessity," which it proceeded to equate with a showing that the disparately impacting neutral practice be "necessary to safe and efficient job performance...." Taken literally, almost no practices could be justified under the latter standard, since safety and efficiency are generally tradeoffs; a practice necessary to safety would scarcely ever be necessary to efficiency. But these statements seem the sheerest dictum in each case. In *Albemarle*, the employer's attempted validation of a battery of tests failed to show that they predicted superior job performance for many of the jobs for which the tests were administered; because, by the employer's own reckoning, the tests bore no relation to those jobs, the question whether they had to have a "manifest" relation to them was never presented. And in *Dothard*, the Court observed that the state had not produced any evidence attempting to link height and weight requirements with the strength required for the jobs in question. Once again, therefore, the Court's footnoted mention of a "business necessity" test under which the practice could be justified only if necessary to safety and efficiency went well beyond the needs of the case.

The Court's later post-*Griggs*, pre-*Wards Cove* decisions have used much looser language. The opinion in *Teal* wrote mildly that to defend a test the employer need only show that it measures "skills related to effective performance" of the job in question.[33] No dimension of performance was specified, nor any degree of linkage between the employer's requirement and "effective" performance. In *New York City Transit Authority v. Beazer*,[34] the Court again referred to a "manifest relationship" standard but deemed it met if the employer's general "legitimate employment goals of safety and efficiency" are "significantly served by— even if they do not require" the practice in question.[35] While this statement, too, might be dismissed as dictum—the Court also criticized weaknesses in the plaintiff's prima facie evidence, so there may have been no prima facie showing against which to defend—in context it looks more like an alternative holding. Then in *Watson*, the most immediate *Wards Cove* precursor, a plurality cited *Beazer* in asserting that the

---

32. 433 U.S. 321, 331 n. 14, 97 S.Ct. 2720, 2728 n. 14, 53 L.Ed.2d 786 (1977).

33. 457 U.S. at 451, 102 S.Ct. at 2533.

34. 440 U.S. 568, 99 S.Ct. 1355, 59 L.Ed.2d 587 (1979).

35. *Id.* at 587 n.31, 99 S.Ct. at 1366, n.31. If this analysis is right, and a *Beazer* or *Watson* formulation of business necessity ultimately prevails, that prong of the defense to a disproportionately impacting neutral practice will remain significantly less stringent than the bona fide occupational qualification (BFOQ) defense to a practice, policy or rule that expressly discriminates on the basis of sex, religion, or national origin. *International Union, UAW v. Johnson Controls*, 499 U.S. 187, 111 S.Ct. 1196, 113 L.Ed.2d 158 (1991) (Congress narrowed the BFOQ defense "to qualifications that affect an employee's ability to do the job"). Under the position taken by Senator Dole's interpretive memorandum, see supra note 30, even the job-relatedness prong of the impact defense would not require a strict relationship between the challenged practice and the requirements of the job in question.

employer could meet a manifest relationship standard if its challenged practice "significantly served" "legitimate business purposes."[36]

Set against this chronology, of course, is the simple fact that Congress advertently did *not* permit reference to *Wards Cove* itself, the opinion that manifests in full flower the lax standards for job relatedness and business necessity earlier enunciated by *Beazer* and *Watson*. Further, the purposes section "would be superfluous if Congress did not believe that the Court had changed the concepts of business necessity and job relatedness in *Wards Cove*," and it rejects that change.[37] In addition, because Congress restored the burden of proof concerning the impact defense to the employer, in contrast to the disparate treatment model, it makes "no sense to apply the loose definition of 'business necessity' [which was] derived from [*Wards Cove*'s] analogizing disparate impact to disparate treatment...."[38] Given the vague terms of the Congressional reprise on *Wards Cove*, it is scarcely surprising that commentators have taken diametrically opposed positions about the likely ultimate interpretation of these concepts.[39]

Two recent decisions subsequent to the 1991 Act, in reaching different conclusions about the validity of a no-beard rule, illustrate how application of the new job relatedness and business necessity defense may vary depending upon the requirements of the job. In September 1993 the Eleventh Circuit, on the assumption that the standards of the 1991 Act applied, upheld a fire department's beard ban despite its acknowledged disproportionate adverse impact on black men. The evidence established that black males who shave are far more likely than whites to suffer from the bacterial disorder pseudofolliculitis barbae, or PFB. The court found the practice justified as a matter of business necessity, citing expert testimony that any amount of facial hair could prevent a secure seal between the face and self contained breathing apparatuses, thereby jeopardizing a firefighter's safety.[40] Interestingly, it made no mention of job relatedness, even though the statute now

---

36. 487 U.S. at 998, 108 S.Ct. at 2791. Admittedly, because *Watson* was only a plurality opinion, it may not qualify as one of the opinions of the Supreme "Court" to which Section 3 authorizes judges to refer in fleshing out job relatedness and business necessity.

37. Note, "The Civil Rights Act of 1991: The Business Necessity Standard," 106 Harv.L.Rev. 896, 911, (1993) (noting that Title VII's new definition of the compound defense is identical to the language in the Americans With Disabilities Act, which requires employers to show a "close connection between a challenged practice and an employee's ability to perform the job," and thus declares a standard far more stringent than *Wards Cove*'s "legitimate goals of the employer") (citing 137 Cong. Rec. S13,582 (daily ed. Sept. 24, 1991); comments of Sen. Durenburger on ADA).

38. *Id.* at 913.

39. *Compare* Kingsley Browne, "The Civil Rights Act of 1991: A 'Quota Bill,' A Codification of *Griggs*, a Partial Return to *Wards Cove*, or All of the Above?" 43 *Case Western L.Rev.* 287, 348–63 (1993) (interpreting "business necessity" as used in the legislation to mean no more than "job related," or at most to mean the same thing as the *Wards Cove* standard "serves, in a significant way") *with* Note, "The Civil Rights Act of 1991: The Business Necessity Standard," *supra* note 37.

40. *Fitzpatrick v. City of Atlanta*, 2 F.3d 1112 (11th Cir.1993). The opposite conclusion was reached on a different record in *Kennedy v. District of Columbia*, 654 A.2d 847 (D.C.App.1994) (decision under Washington, D.C. Human Rights Act).

expressly requires the adverse impact to be justified by both business necessity and the requirements of the job in question.

Only a month later, by contrast, the Eighth Circuit struck down Domino's Pizza's no-beard rule as it was enforced against black males suffering from PFB. In general, the court wrote, the company could establish any grooming or dress standards it chose. But when those standards have a disproportionate adverse impact on a group defined by race (though apparently not sex [41]), the justification must rise to the level of a true business necessity. In the court's view, even strong evidence that customers preferred clean-shaven deliverymen would not suffice as a business justification, because the employer had failed to show "that customers would order less pizza in the absence of a strictly enforced no-beard rule." [42]

Even more curious is the Act's treatment of the plaintiff's rebuttal. At first blush the Act appears to ameliorate the obstacles *Wards Cove* had placed in the plaintiff's path when she tries to surmount the employer's defense by proving the existence of a less discriminatory alternative. But then it also appears to give the employer a trump card that lets it escape liability altogether simply by adopting that alternative when all else fails. The rebuttal phase of the impact case is of potentially enormous significance. Employers often succeeded with the business justification defense in the eighteen years between *Griggs* and *Wards Cove*, and the new legislation's compound but dubiously rigorous defensive standard—job-relatedness and business necessity—may prove no more demanding than it was then. It may therefore be predicted that the outcome of many impact cases will ultimately hang on the fate of the plaintiff's rebuttal.

The Act responds to the *Wards Cove* requirement that an alternative practice be "equally effective" by returning to "the law as it existed on June 4, 1989, [the day before the *Wards Cove* decision] with respect to the concept of 'alternative employment practice.' " [43] Of course this still leaves the possibility that the courts will continue to adhere to the *Wards Cove* insistence on equal effectiveness, with its focus on avoiding additional cost to the employer, because that notion had earlier surfaced in the plurality opinion in *Watson*.[44] In any event, even if the Act is construed to allow the plaintiff to rebut with a less effective, somewhat more expensive alternative, it is doubtful that the Court will read it to require an employer to bear as much additional expense as the Ameri-

---

41. *See* discussion of grooming and dress standards in Chapter 3 above.

42. *Bradley v. Pizzaco of Nebraska, Inc.,* 7 F.3d 795 (8th Cir.1993).

43. Section 105(a) (adding subparagraph (k)(1)(C) to § 703 of Title VII, 42 U.S.C.A. § 2000e–2).

44. In this connection it may be significant that courts are free when they try to pour content into the less restrictive alternative concept to look to the whole of "the law" that preceded *Wards Cove*, not just to the decisions of "the Supreme Court" that Congress in Section 3 and the Interpretive Memorandum made the sole source of reference for elucidating the "business necessity" and "job relatedness" standards. Presumably, therefore, judges will be free to borrow the equal effectiveness restriction enunciated by *Watson*, despite the fact that Justice O'Connor there wrote only for a plurality.

cans With Disabilities Act requires employers to bear in making "reasonable accommodations" to individuals with disabilities.[45]

Finally, even if the plaintiff meets whatever new standards the Court may demand for demonstrating a less discriminatory alternative, the rebuttal may ultimately fail because the Act also carries forward another innovation of *Wards Cove* that first surfaced in *Watson*: there will be no law violation unless in addition "the respondent refuses to adopt such alternative employment practice."[46] Section 703(k)(1)(A)(ii) provides that an unlawful employment practice is established if the plaintiff "makes the demonstration described in subparagraph (C) with respect to an alternative employment practice [the subparagraph that returns to the pre-*Wards Cove* law] *and* the respondent refuses to adopt such alternative practice."

When must such a refusal take place to pin liability on the employer under this provision? "Respondent" and "complaining party" rather than "defendant" and "plaintiff" are the words used here, which might suggest that the employer's last chance to trump a showing of violation is during state, local or EEOC proceedings rather than at trial. But the section in which the refusal-to-adopt provision is found prescribes for the entire "title" how to establish an "unlawful employment practice" based on disparate impact. This implies that an employer may defeat the plaintiff's newly relaxed showing of a lesser discriminatory alternative as late as the latter stages of a trial on the merits.[47] That construction is supported by the present-tense verbs in Section 703(k)(1)(A)(ii): the violation is established if the respondent "refuses to adopt" an alternative practice, but that happens only after the complaining party "makes the demonstration" of such a practice. A "demonstration," in turn, probably cannot be made until judicial trial; "demonstrates" is defined by new § 701(m) to refer to satisfying burdens of production and persuasion.

---

45. Section 102(b)(5)(A) of the Americans With Disabilities Act of 1990 [hereinafter ADA], effective as to private employment on July 26, 1992, defines unlawful discrimination to include a failure to make "reasonable accommodations to the known physical or mental limitations of an otherwise qualified individual with a disability ... unless [the employer] ...can demonstrate that the accommodation would impose an undue hardship on the operation of the business...." 42 U.S.C.A. § 12112(b)(5). "Undue hardship," in turn, is defined to mean "an action requiring significant difficulty or expense...." Section 101(10) of ADA, 42 U.S.C.A. § 12111(10). Thus a covered employer must incur all expenses short of those deemed "significant" in order to avoid discriminating in violation of ADA. Even if the Court, in construing the Civil Rights

Act of 1991, rejects the Watson plurality's statement that the plaintiff's less discriminatory alternative must be "equally" as effective, cost considered, as the employer's original chosen practice, it is unlikely to require the employer to bear the full range of additional expense mandated under the ADA's explicit conception of "reasonable accommodation."

46. Section 105(a)(ii) (adding subsection (k)(1)(A)(ii) to § 703 of Title VII, 42 U.S.C.A. § 2000e–2). The *Watson* plurality opinion would appear to be part of the "the law" to which courts may recur when they adumbrate the meaning of the less restrictive alternative concept. *But see supra* note 36.

47. See Blumoff & Lewis, supra § 4.5, note 8, at 43–44.

In any event, whether it refers to agency or court proceedings, § 703(k)(1)(A)(ii) is set in *some* sort of adversary context. This casts doubt on the assertion of one scholar that the 1991 Act imposes on employers an independent duty, arising before any charge is filed, to ascertain whether a less discriminatory alternative exists before they select a neutral employment practice and that they are therefore liable even for practices justified by business necessity "when the risk of . . . a discriminatory result could have been avoided by using a less harmful selection device." [48]

If a conservative Supreme Court holds that a last-minute employer adoption of the plaintiff's proffered alternative avoids all liability (because, in the words of the Act, there would then be no "unlawful employment practice"), the named plaintiffs, who successfully attacked the employer's original practice through all three phases of the impact case, will be deprived of any relief and, in turn, eligibility for attorneys' fees. Although protected group members who work for that employer will enjoy the benefits of the adopted lesser discriminatory practice in futuro, what incentive would prospective plaintiffs have to sue (or prospective plaintiffs' counsel to take the case)? The problem is particularly acute because in the end Congress failed to overturn Supreme Court decisions approving of defendants' procedural maneuvers that avoid or diminish their liability for attorneys' fees to prevailing plaintiffs. [49]

The structure of new § 703(k)(1)(A), added by the 1991 Act, has suggested to commentators [50] that the plaintiff now has two independent paths to proving disproportionate adverse impact. She can prevail under subdivision (i), they contend, by demonstrating the adverse impact of a discrete practice if the defendant "fails to demonstrate" job relatedness and business necessity; or under subdivision (ii) if she "makes the demonstration described in subparagraph (C) [51] with respect to an alternative employment practice and the respondent refuses to adopt such alternative practice." The commentators' reading is supported as a formal matter by the punctuation in subparagraph (k)(1)(A), where a semicolon precedes "or (ii)." But in practice the less restrictive alternative approach of subdivision (ii) may become pertinent only when it

---

48. Oppenheimer, "Negligent Discrimination," 141 Univ. of Penn.L.Rev. 899, 933, 935 (1993).

49. H.R. 1 had proposed overruling those decisions. Section 9, for example, struck statutory text that the Court had construed to allow a defendant's offer of judgment under the Federal Rules of Civil Procedure to relieve it of liability to a prevailing plaintiff for subsequently accruing attorneys' fees. H.R. 1 § 9 (amending Title VII § 706(k) and effectively overruling *Marek v. Chesny,* 473 U.S. 1, 105 S.Ct. 3012, 87 L.Ed.2d 1 (1985)). It also required parties or their counsel to attest, before entry of a consent order or judgment, that a waiver of

statutory attorneys' fees was not compelled as a condition of settlement. *Id.* (effectively overruling *Evans v. Jeff D.,* 475 U.S. 717, 106 S.Ct. 1531, 89 L.Ed.2d 747 (1986)).

50. Zimmer, Sullivan, Richards and Calloway, *Cases on Employment Discrimination* 443–445 (3d ed. Little, Brown 1994); Oppenheimer, "Negligent Discrimination," 141 Univ. of Penn.L.Rev. 899, 935–936 (1993).

51. Subdivision (C) refers to a showing of an "alternative employment practice" that is "in accordance with the law as it existed on June 4, 1989," the day before *Wards Cove* was decided.

always has, that is when a fact finder concludes that the employer prevails rather than "fails" on its defense. How, after all, can a plaintiff show under subdivision (ii) that a proposed alternative practice has *less* adverse impact except by contrast to the adverse impact of the employer's original, challenged practice that the plaintiff had to prove prima facie under subdivision (i)?

Put otherwise, subdivision (ii) does not identify separate real-life employer conduct that gives rise to liability, only a different way of showing the unlawfulness of the employer practice challenged by the complaint.[52] If the subdivisions are thus read together as creating only one, unified multi-stage mode of proof, subdivision (ii) perpetuates the logical conundrum of prior law by predicating employer liability on an alternative practice assumed to be available even when the employer's challenged practice has been shown, at least in theory, a matter of strict business "necessity." Of course the Court could resolve the conundrum by reading its pre-*Wards Cove* cases, referenced by Section 3 and the Interpretive Memorandum, to require something less than strict necessity.

In sum, the Civil Rights Act of 1991 reflects Congressional equivocation about the group protection theory advanced by the disproportionate adverse impact mode of proof. Although it describes a defensive standard likely to be somewhat more rigorous than that declared by *Wards Cove*, it leaves the prima facie case vulnerable not only to ad hoc statistical requirements but also to unrealistic trial court conclusions that discovery devices suffice to enable the plaintiff to disentangle the effects of compound employer practices. More clearly still, the Act fails in the end to restore the pre-*Wards Cove* status of the plaintiff's rebuttal, by affording the employer a last-ditch means of avoiding liability altogether.

---

52. See text accompanying note 20, *supra.*

Chapter Five

TITLE VII ADMINISTRATIVE PREREQUISITES, PROCEDURES AND REMEDIES

Analysis

§ 5.1 In General

Title VII sets out federal and state agency prerequisites to suit. In general, the private sector applicant or employee need only comply with two such prerequisites: (1) timely filing of a charge with the U.S. Equal Employment Opportunity Commission ("EEOC"), either in the first instance or, in the majority of states that have parallel state or local antidiscrimination legislation and agencies, after filing with those agencies; and (2) timely filing of a federal or state court action within 90 days after receipt from EEOC of a "notice of right to sue." Failure to follow the specified procedures and meet the charge-filing and suit-commencement deadlines usually results in dismissal of the administrative charge or ensuing judicial action.

This chapter identifies the agency and court procedures and the relationship between them, discusses the possible retroactivity of particular sections of the Civil Rights Act of 1991, and outlines the remedies available under Title VII as amended by the 1991 Act.

Library References:

> C.J.S. Civil Rights §§ 340 et seq.
> West's Key No. Digests, Civil Rights ⟜331 et seq.

A. ADMINISTRATIVE PREREQUISITES AND PROCEDURES

§ 5.2 In General

Although 1972 amendments gave EEOC the right to seek judicial relief in the first instance, most judicial action takes the form of private suits in federal district court. The path to court is strewn with a series of intricate and time-consuming administrative procedures at the state and federal levels. These requirements are designed to give state or local antidiscrimination agencies and EEOC opportunities to obtain voluntary resolution of discrimination disputes, as well as to promote federal-state comity.

The complainant must first file a written charge with the EEOC,[1] "sufficiently precise to identify the parties and to describe generally the action or practice complained of."[2] In addition, however, the statute requires "deferral" to a state or local agency where local law prohibits

---

§ 5.2

1. Section § 706(b), 42 U.S.C.A. § 2003–5(b).

2. 29 C.F.R. § 1601.12(b)(1992). This EEOC regulation has been construed liberally to require only the bare minimum there specified. *Waiters v. Robert Bosch Corp.*, 683 F.2d 89, 92 (4th Cir.1982). For example, an EEOC intake questionnaire was held tantamount to a formal charge of age discrimination where the interview notes of the agency's intake officer referred to the plaintiff as a "charging party" and the questionnaire itself identified both the plaintiff and the employer as well as the alleged discriminatory conduct. *Downes v. Volkswagen of America, Inc.*, 41 F.3d 1132 (7th Cir.1994). *Contra Diez v. Minnesota*

the unlawful employment practice alleged and establishes an agency with authority to grant or seek relief concerning that practice.[3] In the few states that do not have such fair employment practices legislation and enforcement agencies, or where the local law does not provide its authority jurisdiction over a particular violation, a charge must be filed with EEOC within 180 days of an alleged unlawful employment practice.[4] In the great majority of states that do have such laws and agencies, the charge must be filed with EEOC within the earlier of 300 days of the alleged violation, or 30 days after the charging party receives "notice that the state or local antidiscrimination agency has terminated" proceedings under state or local law.[5] But unless it dismisses a charge earlier, this state or local "deferral" agency must be given 60 days in which to attempt to resolve the dispute before EEOC may proceed.[6] This latter requirement suggests not only that the state filing must precede a filing with EEOC,[7] but also, by subtracting 60 from 300, that the charge must ordinarily be filed with the state or local "deferral" agency within 240 days of the alleged unlawful employment practice.[8] However, a state or local filing later than 240 but still within 300 days of the alleged unlawful practice will be considered timely if the state or local agency terminates its proceedings before day 300.[9] Moreover, the plaintiff gets the benefit of the 300–day period for filing with EEOC, and may use the 240–day "plus" schedule approved by *Mohasco* for filing with the state or local agency, even if the latter filing is untimely under the state or local antidiscrimination law to which the EEOC is deferring.[10]

It will be noted that the foregoing time limitations specified by statute refer to filing directly "with" the state or local agency and then "with" EEOC. In fact, informal administrative agreements between EEOC and many state and local deferral agencies, now sanctioned by case law, have altered these requirement so that a filing with one can constitute a filing with the other, and the EEOC filing may even precede the local one. For example, the state or local administrative filing will

Mining and Manufacturing Co., 88 F.3d 672 (8th Cir.1996).

3. Section 706(c), 42 U.S.C.A. § 2000e–5(c).

4. Section 706(e), 42 U.S.C.A. § 2000e–5(e).

5. Section 706(e), 42 U.S.C.A. § 2000e–5(e).

6. *See generally* § 706 of Title VII.

7. *See Mohasco Corp. v. Silver,* 447 U.S. 807, 100 S.Ct. 2486, 65 L.Ed.2d 532 (1980). One circuit has accordingly held that a federal action may not be stayed pending state agency deferral because prior resort to the state agency is a jurisdictional prerequisite to a timely filing with EEOC and, in turn, to the commencement of an action in feder-

al court. *Citicorp Person-to-Person Financial Corp. v. Brazell,* 658 F.2d 232 (4th Cir.1981). In this respect the Title VII scheme differs from that under ADEA, where the state agency and EEOC filings may be simultaneous. *Oscar Mayer & Co. v. Evans,* 441 U.S. 750, 755, 99 S.Ct. 2066, 2071, 60 L.Ed.2d 609 (1979).

8. The Court so held in *Mohasco.*

9. *See Id.*

10. *EEOC v. Commercial Office Products,* 486 U.S. 107, 108 S.Ct. 1666, 100 L.Ed.2d 96 (1988). *Cf. Ashley v. Boyle's Famous Corned Beef Co.,* 66 F.3d 164 (8th Cir.1995) (en banc) (no laches defense to monetary relief under Title VII for unreasonable delay provided charge filed within 300 days).

be considered adequate even where the complainant has filed a charge only or initially with EEOC, if EEOC itself refers the charge to the local agency and suspends its proceedings for the required 60 days or until local proceedings terminate.[11]   Conversely, a "work sharing" agreement may specify that where the complainant files first with a state or local agency, that agency becomes EEOC's agent for receiving the charge even if it never forwards the charge to EEOC.[12]

Where a state or local agency waives the right to process the charge initially, or to proceed if the charge is filed more than a specified time after the occurrence of the alleged unlawful employment practice, the circuit courts have extended the Supreme Court's approval of work-sharing agreements by holding that the state's waiver is a "termination" of state or local proceedings that authorizes the EEOC to begin its investigation without waiting 60 days.[13]   In such a jurisdiction the complainant need never file with a state or local agency and need file a charge with EEOC only within 300 days of the alleged unlawful employment practice, instead of the 240 days that would govern if there were no work-sharing agreement.   The state or local agency may retain jurisdiction, however, to process the charge thereafter if it chooses.[14]

In brief, although § 706 appears to require that the state or local filing precede the filing of a charge with EEOC, it is apparent from the Court's approval of deferral and work-sharing agreements that in practice EEOC is often the first, and sometimes the only agency to investigate and conciliate charges, even in deferral states.   Nevertheless, where the state or local agency has made a prior determination, the statute directs EEOC to give its findings "substantial weight" in determining whether there is reasonable cause to support the charge.[15]

The 180–day or 300–day charge-filing deadline periods are triggered only when the alleged unlawful employment practice is complete and when the applicant or employee knows or should know of the facts that support a claim under the statute.   For this purpose the date of an alleged unlawful employment practice is usually the date on which the complaining applicant or employee should be aware of the consequences and unlawfulness of employer conduct, not when those consequences become manifest.[16]   This approach can cut both ways: starting the

11. This practice was devised by EEOC regulations, 29 C.F.R. § 1601.13 (1993), and approved by the Supreme Court in *Love v. Pullman*, 404 U.S. 522, 92 S.Ct. 616, 30 L.Ed.2d 679 (1972).

12. *See, e.g., Williams v. Washington Metropolitan Area Transit Authority*, 721 F.2d 1412 (D.C.Cir.1983).

13. *See Ford v. Bernard Fineson Dev. Ctr.*, 81 F.3d 304 (2d Cir.1996); *Griffin v. City of Dallas*, 26 F.3d 610 (5th Cir.1994) (Texas Commission on Human Rights ("TCHR") waiver of right to proceed if

charge filed more than 180 days after alleged Title VII violation held to authorize EEOC, as TCHR's agent, to initiate charges immediately after it received a charge, without waiting 60 days); *Worthington v. Union Pac. R.R.*, 948 F.2d 477 (8th Cir.1991).

14. *EEOC v. Commercial Office Products, supra.*

15. Section   706(b),   42   U.S.C.A. § 2000e–5(b).

16. *Delaware State College v. Ricks*, 449 U.S. 250, 101 S.Ct. 498, 66 L.Ed.2d 431 (1980).

charge-filing clock well before a termination is consummated[17] or stopping the clock from running until, after termination, the employee learns the facts that suggest the termination was unlawful.[18] Pursuing a grievance under a collective bargaining agreement will not toll the time to file a charge with EEOC.[19] But the 180–day and 300–day EEOC charge-filing deadlines, although critical, are not technically jurisdictional. Rather they are procedural preconditions to suit, analogous to statutes of limitations, and thus may be waived, estopped, or equitably tolled.[20]

A recent Third Circuit opinion illustrates both the accrual date definition problem and the doctrine of equitable tolling. A law firm employee asserted a claim of discriminatory dismissal in her EEOC charge, later amending that charge to complain of a subsequent failure to rehire. These claims would have been untimely under the applicable 300–day charge-filing period if they accrued on the date of her dismissal. But the plaintiff claimed in addition that the firm had actively misled her about the reason for termination, misrepresenting that there was insufficient work for her to do when in fact there was. The court held that under the "discovery" rule, which marks the running of a claim when the plaintiff learns of an injury, both claims were barred. Plaintiff knew of the termination when it occurred, making her dismissal claim untimely, and the failure to [re-]hire claim was therefore simply an amendment to an untimely charge. By contrast, if her claim of misrepresentation proved well founded, the court held, the plaintiff could benefit from equitable tolling. Active deception will toll the running of the charge-filing period until the facts that would support a charging party's allegations become apparent or should be apparent to a person having a reasonably prudent regard for her rights.[21]

Tolling does not necessarily require positive misconduct on the part of the employer. Some courts have equitably tolled the 300–day EEOC filing deadline when an unrepresented claimant receives misleading advice about filing from a state deferral agency, even when the advice is

---

17. *See Ricks, supra* note 16 (charge-filing clock began to run when university professor was notified that his contract would come to an end a year later, even though that decision was subject to change through internal grievance proceedings).

18. *See, e.g., E.E.O.C. v. City of Norfolk Police Dept.,* 45 F.3d 80 (4th Cir.1995) (claim that white officers suspended because of pending criminal charges were immediately reinstated when charges dismissed while plaintiff was not accrued only on date plaintiff learned or should have learned of their reinstatement). *Sturniolo v. Sheaffer, Eaton, Inc.,* 15 F.3d 1023 (11th Cir.1994) (180–day period under ADEA did not begin to run until plaintiff knew or

should have known that he had been replaced by a younger person). *But see Hulsey v. Kmart, Inc.,* 43 F.3d 555 (10th Cir. 1994) (claim accrued when plaintiffs learned of their demotions and transfers, rather than at later dates they suspected those actions were taken because of their age).

19. *International Union of Electrical Workers v. Robbins & Myers,* 429 U.S. 229, 97 S.Ct. 441, 50 L.Ed.2d 427 (1976).

20. *Zipes v. Trans World Airlines, Inc.,* 455 U.S. 385, 102 S.Ct. 1127, 71 L.Ed.2d 234 (1982).

21. *Oshiver v. Levin, Fishbein, Sedran & Berman,* 38 F.3d 1380 (3d Cir.1994).

only ambiguous rather than false.[22] But equitable tolling will not save the untimely filing of a claimant who simply waits until others similarly situated complete a successful challenge to the policy affecting them all.[23] Further, there is no general doctrine that allegations of constructive discharge will equitably toll the relevant deadlines.[24]

Library References:

> C.J.S. Civil Rights §§ 342, 345, 360, 362.
> West's Key No. Digests, Civil Rights ⬢341.

§ 5.3 Continuing Violations

The judicially created continuing violations doctrine allows a court to find liability for a discriminatory act that occurred "outside," that is, before the beginning of, the statute of limitations period. Unlike the generous acceptance afforded the doctrine in cases brought under the Equal Pay Act,[1] the courts have sometimes severely restricted the doctrine's application in Title VII cases. With most employment practices challenged under Title VII, courts limit the employer's liability to discriminatory *acts* that occur within the limitations period; adverse *effects* of pre-period discriminatory conduct do not ordinarily revive the statute on that conduct even when those effects are felt within the period. As we shall see, however, the difference between the judicial acceptance of the doctrine in Title VII and EPA cases is perhaps ultimately explained by the differing conduct reached be each. The sole violation under EPA, discrimination in compensation, is by its nature continuing; Title VII, by contrast, reaches in addition a variety of other employer conduct, much of which can be conceived of as one-time or static.

In considering potentially "continuing" violations of Title VII, courts have made it clear that the timing of the specific discriminatory act identified in the complaint is crucial. At least with regard to most employment practices, it is the unlawful employment practice, not its later effects, that triggers the statute. But this apparently simple principle is complicated in circumstances where the plaintiff becomes aware or suffers the consequences of such a one-time act only later. Early commentators wrote that "[w]here the initial invasion is of an 'inherently unknowable' type the period should be postponed until the plaintiff should reasonably learn of the cause of action, whether the

---

22. *See, e.g., Anderson v. Unisys Corp.,* 47 F.3d 302 (8th Cir.1995) (letter from state agency informed claimant that he had one year from the alleged discriminatory act to file an administrative charge with that agency, but also advised that the agency would file the charge with EEOC if the charge alleged federal law violations, with no mention that the EEOC filing deadline was 300 days), *cert. denied,* ___ U.S. ___, 116 S.Ct. 299, 133 L.Ed.2d 205 (1995).

23. *Chakonas v. City of Chicago,* 42 F.3d 1132 (7th Cir.1994). *But cf.* the "single-filing" rule, discussed in Section 5.7, *infra.*

24. *Hulsey v. Kmart, Inc.,* 43 F.3d 555 (10th Cir.1994) (case under ADEA).

§ 5.3

1. *See* § 8.10.

defendant's conduct ceases before or after the manifestation of harm." [2] The Fifth Circuit wrote in a similar vein that the EEOC charge-filing period does not begin to run "until the facts that would support a charge of discrimination under Title VII were apparent or should have been apparent to a person with a reasonably prudent regard for his rights similarly situated to the plaintiff." [3] Another important variable is the special substantive law treatment of bona fide seniority systems. A seniority systems violates Title VII only if the complainant proves intentional discrimination in its adoption or maintenance.[4]

Title VII's provision permitting back pay to accrue as far back as two years (i.e., roughly 730 days) before the filing of a charge with EEOC [5], considered together with its 180–or at most 300–day EEOC charge-filing deadline,[6] may obliquely support the continuing violations theory, by suggesting that Congress "envisioned continuing remediable violations that existed prior to the running of the period." [7] The argument is that unless Congress had continuing violations in mind, it would have limited relief to acts occurring no more than 180 or 300 days before the filing of the EEOC charge.[8] But this textual support is equivocal, because it is also possible to limit the 2–year relief period to cases of fraudulent concealment or estoppel.[9]

The first important Supreme Court case addressing the continuing violations doctrine is *United Air Lines, Inc. v. Evans*.[10] Evans was fired from her job as a flight attendant in 1968 because of an employment practice that required female attendants to be single. She was rehired in 1972 after the policy was terminated, but United refused to credit her

---

2. Developments in the Law, Statutes of Limitations, 63 Harv. L. Rev. 1177, 1207 (1950) (citations omitted).

3. *Reeb v. Economic Opportunity Atlanta, Inc.*, 516 F.2d 924, 931 (5th Cir.1975) (employee learned that she had been terminated on the basis of sex discrimination after the Title VII limitations period had run). *See also Galloway v. General Motors Service Parts Operations*, 78 F.3d 1164 (7th Cir.1996) (applying principle to environmental sexual harassment claims to discourage initiation of formal legal proceedings until harassing conduct is sufficiently continuous or aggravated that a plaintiff should be expected to recognize the conduct as actionable).

4. *See* § 703(h) of Title VII (codified at 42 U.S.C.A. § 2000e–2(h) (1994)), as construed by *International Brotherhood of Teamsters v. United States*, 431 U.S. 324, 97 S.Ct. 1843, 52 L.Ed.2d 396 (1977), *California Brewers Ass'n v. Bryant*, 444 U.S. 598, 100 S.Ct. 814, 63 L.Ed.2d 55 (1980), and *American Tobacco Co. v. Patterson*, 456 U.S. 63, 102 S.Ct. 1534, 71 L.Ed.2d 748 (1982).

5. Section 706(g), 42 U.S.C.A. § 2000e–5(g).

6. Section 706(e)(1), 42 U.S.C.A. § 2000e–5(e)(1).

7. Zimmer, Sullivan, Richards, Calloway, *Cases and Materials On Employment Discrimination* (Little, Brown, 3d ed. 1994) 965.

8. For example, in one recent decision, an appellate court approved the district court's awarding backpay to individuals who had applied to work earlier than two years before the filing of an EEOC charge, on the theory that, absent discriminatory hiring, they might have been employed during that two-year period. The court added, however, that any backpay recovery for those individuals would be limited to the time beginning two years before the filing of the charge. *EEOC v. O & G Spring and Wire Forms Specialty Co.*, 38 F.3d 872 (7th Cir.1994), *cert. denied*, ___ U.S. ___, 115 S.Ct. 1270, 131 L.Ed.2d 148 (1995).

9. Laycock, "Continuing Violations, Disparate Impact in Compensation and Other Title VII Issues," 49 Law & Contemporary Problems 53, 58 (Autumn 1986).

10. 431 U.S. 553, 97 S.Ct. 1885, 52 L.Ed.2d 571 (1977).

with seniority for the time she worked prior to 1968. Evans would have been eligible for greater benefits, including higher pay, had she been credited for the earlier time worked. Her complaint alleged that United discriminated against her, first, by firing her in 1968 and, second, by rehiring her without seniority in 1972. She brought suit under Title VII after Title VII's statute of limitations for filing administrative charges with EEOC and local agencies had run on both claims. She argued, however, that United was guilty of a continuing violation of Title VII because the seniority system gave "present effect to a past act of discrimination." [11]

The Supreme Court affirmed a dismissal of her complaint as time barred. Writing for the majority, Justice Stevens rejected the plaintiff's argument based on the effects created by the seniority system, asserting that the "critical question is whether any present *violation* exists." [12] In short, the Court held that actionable discriminatory conduct must occur within the limitations period. Of the three possible unlawful acts— termination, rehiring without seniority, and application of the current seniority system to her terms and conditions of employment—only the last was within the period. Unfortunately for Evans, the statute had run on the 1968 firing; and the rehire claim could not be saved by a continuing violations theory predicated on the effects of the seniority system because § 703(h) was construed to immunize such systems unless they were adopted with intentionally discriminatory purpose.

Three years later, the court applied the *Evans* principles to an alleged discriminatory discharge. In *Delaware State College v. Ricks,* [13] plaintiff (Ricks) filed a complaint with the EEOC alleging that the college had discriminated against him on the basis of race when it decided to deny him tenure. The district court dismissed the complaint, which was filed April 4, 1975, as untimely. The court concluded that the statute of limitations had begun to run on June 26, 1974, when Ricks was notified of the college's tenure decision, rejecting Rick's argument that it did not run until his contract expired in June of 1975 because the termination was a delayed effect of the discrimination committed against him. Quoting *Evans*, the Court reaffirmed that present effects of past discrimination are insufficient to extend the limitations period. The *Ricks* opinion specifically held that Title VII violations occur when discriminatory decisions are made, not thereafter when their effects are felt. [14] The discrimination occurred in 1974 when the tenure decision was made, and accordingly, the district court's dismissal was upheld.

---

11. *Id.* at 558, 97 S.Ct. at 1889.

12. *Id.* (emphasis added).

13. 449 U.S. 250, 101 S.Ct. 498, 66 L.Ed.2d 431 (1980).

14. *Id.* at 258, 101 S.Ct. at 504 (citing *Abramson v. University of Hawaii,* 594 F.2d 202, 209 (9th Cir.1979)). *See Ashley v.* *Boyle's Famous Corned Beef Co.,* 66 F.3d 164 (8th Cir.1995) (en banc) (applying *Ricks* to hold that claim about initial job assignment, like most hiring or firing claims, cannot benefit from continuing violation theory, but holding contra regarding ongoing pay discrimination practice).

Nine years later, the Court returned to the continuing violations doctrine in *Lorance v. AT & T Technologies, Inc.*[15] In that case, the plaintiffs challenged the company's seniority system on the basis that it discriminated against women. The system in question had been adopted in 1979, but its effects were not felt until 1982. Plaintiffs filed their complaint with the EEOC in 1983. The district court dismissed the complaint as untimely and the Supreme Court affirmed, relying on both *Evans* and *Ricks*. *Lorance* held that a plaintiff may challenge the application of a facially neutral seniority system, adopted with discriminatory intent, only when the system is applied *to her* within the limitations period, although it acknowledged that "a *facially* discriminatory . . . system can be challenged anytime."[16] The Civil Rights Act of 1991 overruled *Lorance* by providing that a violation of Title VII occurs, with respect to a seniority system, not only when the system is adopted, but also when a person is injured by it.[17] Of course the current, Congressional approach does not really revive the continuing violations doctrine in the case of seniority systems; by late dating the occurrence of the unlawful employment practice, Congress made resort to the doctrine unnecessary.[18]

It is clear, however, that some Title VII violations are subject to the continuing violations doctrine. In *Bazemore v. Friday*,[19] plaintiffs challenged a public employer's pay system as racially discriminatory. The employer argued that the statute's charge filing period should run from the dates it adopted and first applied the system. But the Court held that "[e]ach week's pay check that delivers less to a black than to a similarly situated white is a wrong actionable under Title VII."[20] It also concluded that the employer was responsible for discriminatory payments made after Title VII was enacted even though the discrimination had begun before the defendant was subject to the statute.

This decision is distinguishable from *Evans,* where the plaintiff failed to challenge any ongoing discrimination. By contrast, the defendant in *Bazemore* had not "made all . . . [its within-time] employment decisions in a wholly nondiscriminatory way."[21] The Court noted that evidence of past discrimination "might in some circumstances support the inference that such discrimination continued, particularly where

---

15. 490 U.S. 900, 109 S.Ct. 2261, 104 L.Ed.2d 961 (1989).

16. 490 U.S. at 912, 109 S.Ct. at 2269 (emphasis added).

17. Section 706(e)(2).

18. Notwithstanding this provision in the Civil Rights Act, the Court may still apply its reasoning in *Lorance* in other situations. *See, e.g., Newport News Shipbuilding & Dry Dock Co. v. EEOC*, 462 U.S. 669, 686, 103 S.Ct. 2622, 2632, 77 L.Ed.2d 89 (1983) (Rehnquist, J., dissenting) (Pregnan-cy Discrimination Act of 1978 overturned only the holding, not the reasoning of an earlier Court decision). The dissenters in *Newport News* now hold a majority on the Court, and thus this approach to Congressional overruling of the Court's prior construction of Title VII may now find more support.

19. 478 U.S. 385, 106 S.Ct. 3000, 92 L.Ed.2d 315 (1986).

20. *Id.* at 396, 106 S.Ct. at 3006.

21. *Id.* at 379 n.6, 106 S.Ct. at 3006 n.6.

relevant aspects of the [discriminatory] decisionmaking process had undergone little change." [22] The *Lorance* majority later described *Bazemore* as involving an intentional violation that occurred within the relevant Title VII time period.

In grappling with these mixed signals from the Supreme Court, the lower federal courts have described two contrasting idealized types of claims. First is the claim, typified by a case like *Bazemore*, that an employer continuously maintains an unlawful employment practice. In such a case the "continuation of the violation into the present" [23] means that the employee may file her EEOC charge within 300 (or, in the relatively few states that do not have local antidiscrimination laws and "deferral" agencies, 180) days "after the last occurrence of an instance of that practice." [24] Second is the claim, typified by cases like *Ricks* and *Lorance*, "where the employer engaged in a discrete act of discrimination," [25] the effects of which continue. In such a case the "present consequence of a one-time violation" does not extend the period, and so the EEOC charge must be filed within 300 (or 180) days of that discrete act.[26]

Practices falling within the first category, that are considered to continue in and of themselves rather than simply through their effects, include, in addition to the salary discrimination discussed in *Bazemore*, ongoing denials of promotion [27] and racial or sexual harassment. Thus so long as at least one alleged active harassment occurred within the 300-day charge-filing period, courts will admit related evidence, antedating the beginning of that period, that constitutes part of the same general pattern of conduct that altered the plaintiff's conditions of employment or created an abusive work environment. Decisions differ, however, in the degree of nexus they require between the harassing conduct occurring before and that occurring within the charge-filing period.

The decisions reflect that, notwithstanding *Lorance*, most neutral practices with allegedly unlawful discriminatory effects may be challenged as continuing violations. The *Lorance* plaintiffs were out of time to challenge the facially neutral seniority system there as having been originally adopted with discriminatory intent; and it was only the special, substantive insulation that § 703(h) affords bona fide, facially neutral seniority systems that prevented them from attacking the sys-

22. *Id.* at 402, 106 S.Ct. at 3010 (Brennan, J., concurring) (quoting *Hazelwood Sch. Dist. v. United States*, 433 U.S. 299, 309–10, 97 S.Ct. 2736, 2742–43, 53 L.Ed.2d 768 (1977)).

23. *Webb v. Indiana National Bank*, 931 F.2d 434, 438 (7th Cir.1991).

24. *Beavers v. American Cast Iron Pipe Co.*, 975 F.2d 792, 796 (11th Cir.1992).

25. *Id.*

26. *Webb, supra* note 23, 931 F.2d at 438. For other decisions recognizing this distinction, see *EEOC v. Westinghouse Electric Corp.*, 725 F.2d 211, 219 (3d Cir.1983); *Williams v. Owens–Illinois, Inc.*, 665 F.2d 918, 925 n. 3 (9th Cir.1982); and *Association Against Discrimination in Employment, Inc. v. Bridgeport*, 647 F.2d 256, 274 (2d Cir.1981).

27. *Gonzalez v. Firestone Tire & Rubber Co.*, 610 F.2d 241, 249 (5th Cir.1980).

tem's ongoing consequences.[28] Other courts have similarly cabined *Lorance* to the seniority system context.[29]

Despite this general agreement on which kinds of are susceptible to continuing violation treatment, there remain differences in application. It is not always easy to distinguish between an ongoing unlawful practice and "the delayed consequence of a single discriminatory act" that took place long before an EEOC charge is filed.[30] The circuits are split, for example, on when the limitations period begins to run on challenges to hiring lists compiled from discriminatory test results. The Ninth Circuit, reasoning that no one on such a list would be *certain* of a discriminatory impact until the list was no longer in use, concluded that an EEOC complaint was timely if filed within a limitations period marked from the date the hiring list expired.[31] But the Third Circuit, following the *Ricks* holding that the discriminatory decision puts the complainant on notice of *likely* adverse effect, requires that the complaint be filed within a limitations period that runs from the date the hiring list was compiled.[32] And while the First Circuit holds that a challenge to a subjective employment evaluation is not time barred if filed within a limitations period that runs from the date the evaluation resulted in adverse effect,[33] the Seventh Circuit holds that it is an actual denial of training, not a later layoff based on the lack of training, that triggers the statute.[34]

§ 5.4   From EEOC to Action in Federal or State Court

The EEOC investigation ultimately arrives at one of two basic conclusions. After investigation, the Agency may find "reasonable cause" to believe that the Act has been violated, and must then undertake conciliation; or it may find "no reasonable cause" and issue a notice of dismissal.[1] In either event, a complainant is entitled upon demand to receive a "right-to-sue" letter from EEOC no later than 180 days after the effective date of the filing of a charge with the agency.[2] Since EEOC frequently takes years to process charges, the question has

28. *Id.*, (describing the Supreme Court itself in *Lorance* as acknowledging that the allegations of the plaintiffs there "normally would have been sufficient to state a [timely] cause of action for discrimination under the disparate impact theory.")

29. See, e.g., *Webb v. Indiana National Bank, supra* note 23, 931 F.2d at 438; *Hendrix v. Yazoo City*, 911 F.2d 1102, 1104 (5th Cir.1990).

30. See *Beavers v. American Cast Iron Pipe Co., supra* note 24, 975 F.2d at 799.

31. *Bouman v. Block*, 940 F.2d 1211 (9th Cir.1991), *cert. denied*, 502 U.S. 1005, 112 S.Ct. 640, 116 L.Ed.2d 658 (1991).

32. *Bronze Shields, Inc. v. New Jersey Dep't of Civil Serv.*, 667 F.2d 1074 (3d Cir.

1981), *cert. denied*, 458 U.S. 1122, 102 S.Ct. 3510, 73 L.Ed.2d 1384 (1982).

33. *Johnson v. General Electric*, 840 F.2d 132 (1st Cir.1988).

34. *Hamilton v. Komatsu Dresser Indus., Inc.*, 964 F.2d 600 (7th Cir.), *cert. denied*, 506 U.S. 916, 113 S.Ct. 324, 121 L.Ed.2d 244 (1992).

§ 5.4

1. 42 U.S.C.A. § 2000e–5.

2. *Id. McDonnell Douglas Corp. v. Green*, 411 U.S. 792, 93 S.Ct. 1817, 36 L.Ed.2d 668 (1973), holds *inter alia* than an EEOC finding of no reasonable cause does not impair the charging party's ability to proceed against the respondent in court.

arisen how long a prospective Title VII plaintiff may wait beyond 180 days before demanding a right-to-sue letter. Courts have occasionally barred Title VII actions in these circumstances on grounds of laches, when a delay of several years in demanding a suit letter was deemed unreasonable and caused tangible prejudice to the defendant.[3] An appellate court has recently reached the opposite conclusion under ADEA, reasoning that laches cannot be a bar under a federal statute that contains a statute of limitations, as ADEA did until its recent amendment in 1991.[4] And what if EEOC, recognizing that its backlog prevents it from promptly addressing the charge, is willing to issue the right to sue notice *before* the end of its 180–day period of presumptive exclusive jurisdiction? The plaintiff may proceed to court, provided she files within 90 days of receiving the notice.[5]

Title VII affords plaintiffs a liberal federal venue choice among the districts where the alleged unlawful employment practice occurred; where records pertaining to the practice are maintained; or where the plaintiff allegedly would have worked but for the unlawful practice.[6] When the prospective defendant cannot be "found" in any of the above districts, the statute provides as a default the district where it has its principal office.[7] The text also indicates that each of these districts is a suitable place for the action to be transferred under 28 U.S.C.A. §§ 1404 and 1406.[8] It has recently been held that in considering a motion for transfer under Title VII, the court should apply the same considerations of party and witness convenience that ordinarily apply under those sections, rejecting the argument that the special Title VII venue choices are intended to give plaintiff the last word on forum selection.[9]

Although the vast majority of Title VII actions have been brought in federal court, it is settled that state courts have concurrent jurisdiction.[10] The reasons a plaintiff may opt for state over federal court are similar to the choice-influencing considerations pertaining to claims under

---

3. *See, e.g., National Association of Government Employees v. City Public Service Bd. of San Antonio*, 40 F.3d 698 (5th Cir. 1994) (invoking doctrine to bar suit brought nine years after termination of EEOC conciliation efforts, during which period Department of Justice failed to issue plaintiffs right to sue letter or notify them of intent to prosecute and plaintiffs' counsel made no inquiry of either agency as to status of charges. The Fifth Circuit applied the standard elements of common law laches, an unexcused delay by plaintiff in initiating suit that causes the defendant undue prejudice in its ability to defend.

4. *Miller v. Maxwell's International, Inc.*, 991 F.2d 583 (9th Cir.1993).

5. *Sims v. Trus Joist MacMillan*, 22 F.3d 1059 (11th Cir.1994) (EEOC's use of its full 180 days of exclusive jurisdiction is not a prerequisite to the subject matter

jurisdiction of a court). *Bryant v. California Brewers Association*, 585 F.2d 421, 424 (9th Cir.1978). District court decisions are divided on the issue.

6. Title VII § 706(f)(3), 42 U.S.C.A. § 2000e–5(f)(3).

7. *Id.*

8. *See id.*, providing that the "principal office" district shall be considered one in which the action "might have been brought," a designation that makes it a suitable transferee district under the Supreme Court's decision in *Hoffman v. Blaski*, 363 U.S. 335, 80 S.Ct. 1084, 4 L.Ed.2d 1254 (1960).

9. *Ross v. Buckeye Cellulose Corp.*, 980 F.2d 648, 655 (11th Cir.1993).

10. *Yellow Freight v. Donnelly*, 494 U.S. 820, 110 S.Ct. 1566, 108 L.Ed.2d 834 (1990).

§ 1983.[11] For example, a political read of the state court judge, as compared to the counterpart federal judge who is significantly insulated from popular reaction to her decisions by life tenure during good behavior, may attract the plaintiff. So might less congested state court calendars. Differences in evidentiary and procedural rules may also influence decision. And the plaintiff's interest in interim or injunctive relief may be better served by filing in state court.[12]

In any event, a complainant who wishes to sue in either state or federal court must commence an action (by filing a complaint with the court) [13] within 90 days after *receipt* of the EEOC "right-to-sue" letter or notice of dismissal.[14] That deadline is generally strictly enforced, although it, like the administrative charge-filing deadline, is amenable to equitable tolling, estoppel, or waiver.[15] To benefit from tolling, however, the plaintiff may have to show her own due diligence [16]; and if she asserts that she was misled into failing to file within 90 days, she may have to show active deception on the part of the defendant or that she was lulled into inaction in reliance on state or federal agency pending proceedings or advice.[17] Related actions under the Reconstruction Civil Rights Acts may be commenced even before Title VII charges have been administratively processed, but the limitations periods and administrative deadlines of the respective statutes must be satisfied independently.[18]

Because the only two prerequisites for Title VII private party [19] actions are a timely filed EEOC charge (i.e., within 180 or, in a deferral

---

11. These are discussed more fully in Chapter 13 on Procedure.

12. Of course a putative plaintiff with intentional race discrimination claims and a need for immediate injunctive relief will in that respect be better served by proceeding under § 1981 than under Title VII, because no administrative exhaustion is required under the Reconstruction-era statutes.

13. Federal Rule 3, which equates commencement with the timely filing of the complaint, rather than with subsequent service, provides the guide for measuring compliance with the 90–day requirement. *See West v. Conrail*, discussed in the Procedure Chapter.

14. In the case of federal employees, the plaintiff must commence the civil action within 90 days after the administrative complaint is dismissed. *Robbins v. Bentsen*, 41 F.3d 1195 (7th Cir.1994).

15. *See Baldwin County Welcome Center v. Brown*, 466 U.S. 147, 104 S.Ct. 1723, 80 L.Ed.2d 196 (1984). The requirement that a putative plaintiff receive a right-to-sue letter before, rather than after, commencing a civil action is a statutory precondition subject to equitable modification, rather than an inflexible jurisdictional prerequisite; nevertheless, a plaintiff's lack of coop-

eration with EEOC held to disentitle her to such equitable relief. *Forehand v. Florida State Hospital*, 89 F.3d 1562 (11th Cir. 1996).

16. *See South v. Saab Cars USA, Inc.*, 28 F.3d 9 (2d Cir.1994) (mailing complaint to the sheriff, rather than the court, one day before the deadline not sufficient diligence to permit plaintiff to invoke equitable tolling).

17. *See Simons v. Southwest Petro–Chem, Inc.*, 28 F.3d 1029 (10th Cir.1994) (defense counsel's mere acknowledgement that employee would file a second suit after taking a voluntary dismissal without prejudice not sufficiently deceptive to trigger equitable tolling); *Biester v. Midwest Health Servs., Inc.*, 77 F.3d 1264 (10th Cir.1996) (depression of plaintiff, represented by counsel, insufficient to justify tolling).

18. *Johnson v. Railway Express Agency, Inc.*, 421 U.S. 454, 95 S.Ct. 1716, 44 L.Ed.2d 295 (1975). *See* text accompanying note 24, § 1.2.

19. There is authority that federal employees, apparently unlike employees of either private or state or local government employers, must actually *exhaust* their ad-

state, 300 days after the alleged unlawful employment practice) followed by commencement of a judicial action within 90 days after the charging party receives EEOC's notice of right to sue, the right to bring a judicial lawsuit does not turn on EEOC's evaluation of the probable merits of a charge. The judicial action may be commenced even if EEOC concludes that there is no reasonable cause to believe that the employer has violated Title VII,[20] and probably even if it believes that a settlement offer it has procured from the employer affords the charging party full relief.[21] An EEOC determination that there was no reasonable cause to believe that race discrimination allegations were true may be admissible under the public record exception to the hearsay rule in a private action for employment discrimination.[22] Similarly, an EEOC or state agency determination that there is reasonable cause is also admissible.[23] But the agency's determination of "reasonable cause" or "no reasonable cause" will be given only such weight at trial as the federal court believes it deserves. If EEOC certifies to the court that a case initiated by a private party is of "general public importance," it may intervene as of right in the proceeding.[24]

Library References:

C.J.S. Civil Rights §§ 363–367, 379.
West's Key No. Digests, Civil Rights ⚖361.

§ 5.5 Arbitration as Precluding the Civil Lawsuit: The Potential of the Gilmer Decision

Until recently, it was taken as gospel that a putative plaintiff's resort to a grievance or arbitration procedure (prosecuted by her union) would not bar her later judicial action under Title VII, even after an

ministrative remedies, and so may lose the right to sue if they reject what a court later determines to have been an offer of full relief at the agency level. *Francis v. Brown*, 58 F.3d 191 (5th Cir.1995). *Wrenn v. Secretary, Dept. of Veterans Affairs*, 918 F.2d 1073 (2d Cir.1990), *cert. denied*, 499 U.S. 977, 111 S.Ct. 1625, 113 L.Ed.2d 721 (1991). *But see Greenlaw v. Garrett*, 59 F.3d 994 (9th Cir.1995) (pro se federal Title VII plaintiff need not assess if administrative relief is full in order to exhaust remedies).

20. *McDonnell Douglas.*

21. *Long v. Ringling Brothers–Barnum & Bailey Combined Shows Inc.*, 9 F.3d 340 (4th Cir.1993) (reversing a summary judgment entered against plaintiff who had rejected employer's settlement offer during EEOC conciliation, even where trial court viewed settlement as affording maximum relief then available under Title VII); *cf. Wrenn v. Secretary, Dept. of Veterans Affairs*, 918 F.2d 1073 (2d Cir.1990) (holding otherwise where settlement offer made dur-

ing federal employee administrative complaints process under ADEA that the court held claimant had duty to exhaust in good faith).

22. *Barfield v. Orange County*, 911 F.2d 644 (11th Cir.1990).

23. *Heyne v. Caruso*, 69 F.3d 1475 (9th Cir.1995); *Gilchrist v. Jim Slemons Imports*, 803 F.2d 1488, 1500 (9th Cir.1986); *Plummer v. Western Int'l Hotels Co.*, 656 F.2d 502, 504 (9th Cir.1981) (reversible error to exclude EEOC reasonable cause determination because probative value outweighs prejudicial effect); *Heyne, supra* (same conclusion regarding state agency determination of probable cause). *But cf. Gilchrist, supra* (district court should exercise discretion whether to admit EEOC letter of violation, which represents a determination that a violation has occurred).

24. Section 706(f)(1), 42 U.S.C.A. § 2000e–5(f)(1). See Federal Rule of Civil Procedure 24(a)(authorizing intervention as of right when so provided by federal statute).

unfavorable arbitral disposition.[1] That was the message of *Alexander v. Gardner–Denver Co.*,[2] a 1974 decision of the Supreme Court. Today, however, the judicial avenue of redress may be altogether foreclosed to an uncertain number of potential plaintiffs who have agreed to arbitrate claims of employment discrimination. The entering wedge posing this possibility is a 1991 decision by the Supreme Court that arose from an agreement to arbitrate incorporated by securities industry rules into the individual employment contract of a brokerage house employee. In *Gilmer v. Interstate/Johnson Lane Corp.*,[3] the Court ruled that an employee who made such an agreement could be compelled to arbitrate his statutory discrimination claim—there, under the Age Discrimination in Employment Act—by virtue of the Federal Arbitration Act ("FAA"). The Court also strongly implied, although it did not hold, that an adverse arbitration award would bar the plaintiff's subsequent ADEA action (although not a classwide enforcement action by EEOC). In so suggesting the Court distinguished *Gardner–Denver* as a case where the agreement to arbitrate (1) was collectively bargained and (2) submitted to arbitration claims concerning the interpretation and application of the terms of the union contract, rather than claims of statutory employment discrimination. The majority's opinion reflected some sensitivity to the risk that a union's agreement to arbitrate might effectively bargain away the statutory rights of union members.[4] Consistent with this reasoning, post-*Gilmer* decisions have usually continued to apply *Gardner–Denver* when the agreement to arbitrate is contained in a collectively bargained agreement.[5]

§ 5.5

1. *Alexander v. Gardner–Denver Co.*, 415 U.S. 36, 94 S.Ct. 1011, 39 L.Ed.2d 147 (1974). Indeed *Alexander* and subsequent circuit authority permit the grievant who prevails in arbitration to pursue any additional applicable relief available under Title VII in a later judicial action, subject to the traditional ban on duplicative recovery. *Id.* at 51 n. 14, 94 S.Ct. at 1021 n. 14; *Cooper v. Asplundh Tree Expert Co.*, 836 F.2d 1544, 1553–54 (10th Cir.1988).

2. *Id.*

3. 500 U.S. 20, 111 S.Ct. 1647, 114 L.Ed.2d 26 (1991).

4. The Fifth Circuit has since distinguished *Alexander*, and followed *Gilmer*, in ordering the submission of a Title VII sexual harassment claim to arbitration under the authority of the Railway Labor Act ("RLA"). *Hirras v. National R.R. Passenger Corp.*, 10 F.3d 1142 (5th Cir.1994), *cert. granted and judgment vacated*, ___ U.S. ___, 114 S.Ct. 2732, 129 L.Ed.2d 855 (1994). Unlike the general national labor statutes at issue in *Alexander* that allow the employer and union to agree upon the scope of grievance arbitration and give the union wide discretion whether to prosecute an individual grievance within that scope, the RLA mandated the arbitration of so-called "minor disputes" arising from claims "founded upon some incident of the employment relationship ... independent of those covered by the collective bargaining agreement." That circuit treats claims under *state* anti-discrimination law as preempted by § 301 of the Taft–Hartley Act where their resolution turns on interpreting the terms of a collective bargaining agreement. *Reece v. Houston Lighting & Power Co.*, 79 F.3d 485 (5th Cir.1996); *but cf. Ramirez v. Fox Television Station, Inc.*, 998 F.2d 743 (9th Cir.1993) (state law claim not preempted by § 301 where its resolution does not turn on the meaning of collective bargaining agreement). *Cf. Chaulk Services, Inc. v. Massachusetts Commission Against Discrimination*, 70 F.3d 1361 (1st Cir.1995) (state sex discrimination proceedings preempted by earlier filed unfair labor practice charges before National Labor Relations Board where state law claim and unfair labor practice charge brought by union are founded upon identical facts).

5. *See, e.g., Tran v. Tran*, 54 F.3d 115, 117–118 (2d Cir.1995), *cert. denied*, ___ U.S. ___, 116 S.Ct. 1417, 134 L.Ed.2d 542 (1996)

Some federal appellate courts have since incrementally extended *Gilmer* beyond ADEA by compelling arbitration, in the same securities industry setting, of claims asserted under Title VII.[6] These courts have found that *Gilmer* can coexist with *Gardner–Denver* because the latter simply holds that an employee has not waived the right to pursue the Title VII statutory remedy merely by permitting his union to arbitrate a grievance procedure contractually agreed to and controlled by his employer and his union. By contrast, these courts have ruled, the individual employee's acquiescence in the arbitration clause, manifested by her signing the registration application that stock exchanges require of applicants for employment with member firms, evidences a voluntary personal commitment to arbitrate all claims related to that employment.[7] These agreements to arbitrate statutory discrimination claims were therefore deemed enforceable under the FAA when contained in contracts which, like most, touch interstate commerce.

Whether the federal judiciary will in the end enforce individual employees' agreements to arbitrate discrimination claims outside the securities industry setting may depend in part on how broadly the courts interpret an exception to FAA's enforcement powers contained in FAA § 1. That provision excludes from FAA's reach arbitration agreements

(Fair Labor Standards Act claims not waived by collectively bargained agreement to arbitrate); *Bates v. Long Island R.R.*, 997 F.2d 1028 (2d Cir.), *cert. denied*, 510 U.S. 992, 114 S.Ct. 550, 126 L.Ed.2d 452 (1993); *EEOC v. Board of Governors of State Colleges and Universities*, 957 F.2d 424 (7th Cir.), *cert. denied*, 506 U.S. 906, 113 S.Ct. 299, 121 L.Ed.2d 223 (1992) (employee may not be denied access to collectively bargained grievance procedure even though he is simultaneously pursuing a Title VII claim based on same conduct). *But see Austin v. Owens-Brockway Glass Container, Inc.*, 78 F.3d 875 (4th Cir.), *cert. denied*, ___ U.S. ___, 117 S.Ct. 432, ___ L.Ed.2d ___ (1996) (*Gardner-Denver* held effectively overruled by *Gilmer*). On the other hand, the Supreme Court has held that an employer must honor its obligations under a collective bargaining agreement even though that agreement conflicts with its obligations under a Title VII consent decree. *W.R. Grace & Co. v. Local Union 759*, 461 U.S. 757, 103 S.Ct. 2177, 76 L.Ed.2d 298 (1983).

6. *Hurst v. Prudential Securities Inc.*, 21 F.3d 1113 (9th Cir.1994); *Bender v. A.G. Edwards & Sons, Inc.*, 971 F.2d 698 (11th Cir.1992) (sexual harassment claim); *Mago v. Shearson Lehman Hutton Inc.*, 956 F.2d 932 (9th Cir.1992); *Willis v. Dean Witter Reynolds, Inc.*, 948 F.2d 305 (6th Cir.1991); *Alford v. Dean Witter Reynolds, Inc.* 939 F.2d 229 (5th Cir.1991).

7. *See Williams v. Cigna Financial Advisors, Inc.*, 56 F.3d 656 (5th Cir.1995) (ar-

bitration clause held to encompass age discrimination claim, and plaintiff's agreement to arbitrate held knowing and voluntary waiver of right to judicial forum consistent with Older Workers Benefits Protection Act and ADEA.) Two circuit opinions involving alleged agreements by securities industry employees to arbitrate discrimination claims under the rules of the National Association of Securities Dealers ("NASD") have more strictly scrutinized whether the agreement to arbitrate statutory rights was knowing and voluntary. In *Farrand v. Lutheran Brotherhood*, 993 F.2d 1253 (7th Cir. 1993), the Court ruled that the scope of arbitration to which employees agree by agreeing to arbitrate disputes under the rules of the NASD does not include employment disputes because the NASD rules themselves are not specific on that point. More recently, in *Prudential Ins. Co. of America v. Lai*, 42 F.3d 1299 (9th Cir.1994), the Ninth Circuit reached the same conclusion but also rested decision on its own determination that the plaintiffs in that case did not knowingly waive rights to the judicial determination of Title VII claims in forms they signed when employed by Prudential. The Ninth Circuit decision is potentially more far reaching because it requires a discrete, case-by-case inquiry into whether the plaintiffs at bar knowingly and voluntarily waived the right to litigate a statutory employment claim.

in "contracts of employment of seamen, railroad employees, or any other class of workers engaged in foreign or interstate commerce." In *Gilmer* the majority found it unnecessary to construe the quoted language because the agreement to arbitrate was contained not in an employment contract as such but in the rules of the securities industry. Since *Gilmer*, some federal courts have opted for the narrow, "transportation-only" interpretation of § 1, enforcing agreements to arbitrate both Title VII and ADEA claims where those agreements are found in the individual employment contracts of medical and legal professionals [8] and other nontransportation employees.[9] These courts have construed the § 1 exclusionary clause to apply only to employment contracts of seamen, railroad workers, and other classes of workers similarly engaged in moving goods through interstate commerce, or, somewhat more broadly, to agreements to arbitrate reached through collective bargaining.

One circuit court has even applied *Gilmer* to a nontransportation employer at the junction where *Gilmer* clashes with *Gardner-Denver*: when an arbitration clause *is* contained in a collective agreement. *Gardner-Denver* could have been simply distinguished on the ground that the parties' agreement to arbitrate, unlike the one in *Gardner-Denver*, expressly provided for the grievance machinery to cover disputes about statutory rights and not just the terms of the collective agreement. Instead, the court wrote more generally that as long as an agreement to arbitrate is voluntary, it is valid whether contained in "a securities registration application, a simple employment contract, or a collective bargaining agreement." [10]

Another post-*Gilmer* district court, however, has pointed out that even if an antidiscrimination clause in the collective agreement tracks the language of a statutory guarantee, the clause confers a separate right rooted in contract and may be interpreted by an arbitrator to have its own distinctive meaning. In that light the plaintiff's statutory claims asserted in court are not subject to the standard arbitration clause because they do not concern the interpretation or application of the collective agreement. Accordingly, the court hewed to *Gardner–Denver* by holding that the arbitrator's decision did not foreclose the right to sue.[11] Further, in an effort to harmonize *Gilmer* with *Gardner–Denver*, another district court has held *Gilmer* limited to the pre-arbitration question whether a lawsuit may be stayed and the plaintiff ordered to

8. *Crawford v. West Jersey Health Systems*, 847 F.Supp. 1232 (D.N.J.1994); *cf. Williams v. Katten, Muchin & Zavis*, 837 F.Supp. 1430 (N.D.Ill.1993) (discrimination claim was by former law partner, raising a question whether the agreement could even be considered a contract of "employment" within the meaning of § 1).

9. *Rojas v. TK Communications, Inc.*, 87 F.3d 745, 747–748 (5th Cir.1996); *Asplundh Tree Expert Company v. Bates*, 71 F.3d 592, 596–601 (6th Cir.1995); *Hull v. NCR Corp.*, 826 F.Supp. 303 (E.D.Mo.1993);

Williams v. Katten, Muchin & Zavis, 837 F.Supp. 1430 (N.D.Ill.1993); *DiCrisci v. Lyndon Guaranty Bank of New York*, 807 F.Supp. 947 (W.D.N.Y.1992).

10. *Austin v. Owens–Brockway Glass Container, Inc.*, 78 F.3d 875 (4th Cir.1996), *cert. denied*, ___ U.S. ___, 117 S.Ct. 432, ___ L.Ed.2d ___ (1996). *Contra, Block v. Art Iron Inc.*, 866 F.Supp. 380 (N.D.Ind.1994).

11. *Greene v. United Parcel Service*, 864 F.Supp. 48 (N.D.Ill.1994).

submit her claim to arbitration. Under this view *Gardner–Denver* still governs the question whether the post-arbitration award precludes litigation of statutory employment discrimination claims under a doctrine akin to res judicata or claim preclusion; and *Gardner–Denver* holds it does not.[12]

It is therefore possible that, regardless of the ultimate outcome of the § 1 issue, the Supreme Court may reaffirm the holding of *Gardner–Denver* by permitting Title VII or ADEA plaintiffs to pursue their statutory discrimination claims in court after an adverse arbitration award, issued pursuant to the authority of the FAA, determines their rights under a collective bargaining agreement. To reconcile *Gilmer* with the full implications of *Gardner–Denver* the Court might go further still and deny enforceability under the FAA to arbitration promises contained in agreements that are collectively bargained. Even then non-union employers subject to Title VII, the ADEA, and the Americans with Disabilities Act will have an incentive to "negotiate"—more realistically, at least where jobs are scarce, to insert unilaterally—agreements to arbitrate statutory discrimination claims in individual employment contracts. Those agreements would presumably be enforceable, despite *Gardner–Denver*, unless the § 1 exclusion is construed to apply to industries other than those there specifically listed.

Finally, even if the § 1 exclusion of enforceability is construed broadly, or *Gilmer* is construed to require only front-end enforceability of promises to arbitrate, rather than deference to rendered arbitration awards, the decision may spur enforcement under *state* law of promises to arbitrate claims under the federal employment discrimination statutes. *Gilmer* does after all declare that nothing in the history or purposes of ADEA, or presumably Title VII, is hostile to the resolution of discrimination claims by the procedures of modern arbitration. This judicial receptiveness to arbitration contrasts markedly with the hostility the Court showed as recently as *McDonald v. City of West Branch*,[13] and *Barrentine v. Arkansas–Best Freight System*,[14] which held arbitration procedures inadequate to resolve claims under, respectively, § 1983 and the Fair Labor Standards Act. But in recent years the Court has gone out of its way to reverse the ancient judicial hostility to the arbitration of statutory rights, a development that has emboldened federal judges to order the arbitration of employment discrimination claims in the years since *Gilmer*.[15]

---

12. *Hillding v. McDonnell Douglas Helicopter Co.*, 59 FEP Cases 869, 1992 WL 443421 (D.Ariz.1992).

13. 466 U.S. 284, 104 S.Ct. 1799, 80 L.Ed.2d 302 (1984).

14. 450 U.S. 728, 101 S.Ct. 1437, 67 L.Ed.2d 641 (1981).

15. *See, e.g., Mitsubishi Motors Corp. v. Soler Chrysler–Plymouth, Inc.*, 473 U.S. 614, 105 S.Ct. 3346, 87 L.Ed.2d 444 (1985) (action under the Sherman Act); *Shear-*

son/American Express, Inc. v. McMahon, 482 U.S. 220, 107 S.Ct. 2332, 96 L.Ed.2d 185 (1987) (action under the Securities Exchange Act of 1934 and the Racketeer Influenced and Corrupt Organization Act); *Rodriguez De Quijas v. Shearson/American Express, Inc.*, 490 U.S. 477, 109 S.Ct. 1917, 104 L.Ed.2d 526 (1989) (action under Securities Act of 1933 and the Securities and Exchange Act of 1934); *Gilmer v. Interstate/Johnson Lane Corp.*, 500 U.S. 20, 111

Although the Civil Rights Act of 1991 is silent on the *Gilmer* issue, § 118 provides additional impetus for the arbitration of several kinds of statutory discrimination claims. It provides that, "to the extent authorized by law," arbitration and other "alternative" dispute resolution procedures are encouraged "to resolve disputes arising under the Acts or provisions of Federal law amended by this title"—including Title VII, ADEA, § 1981, and ADA. Indeed federal courts have recently relied on § 118 in holding that claims under the ADA and Title VII could not proceed in court where the plaintiff had not first pursued a grievance arbitration remedy. In one of these decisions, a court of appeals extended *Gilmer* to Title VII claims at the urging of a securities industry employer.[16] In another, a circuit court required arbitration under a collective bargaining agreement that specifically required the employer to comply with federal civil rights laws. The court dismissed *Gardner–Denver* as "old law" superseded by *Gilmer* and relied on changes in legal

---

S.Ct. 1647, 114 L.Ed.2d 26 (1991) (action under Age Discrimination in Employment Act). In *Gilmer* the Court expressly repudiated the "mistrust of the arbitral process" reflected in its earlier decisions about the arbitration of statutory claims.

Applying the Supreme Court's directive to resolve all doubts concerning arbitrability in favor of arbitration, *Moses H. Cone Mem. Hosp. v. Mercury Constr. Corp.*, 460 U.S. 1, 23, 103 S.Ct. 927, 941, 74 L.Ed.2d 765 (1983), recent circuit court decisions strain to find Title VII and ADEA claims, respectively, arbitrable under individual employment agreements. *Armijo v. Prudential Ins. Co. of Am.*, 72 F.3d 793 (10th Cir.1995) (Title VII claims); *Matthews v. Rollins Hudig Hall Co.*, 72 F.3d 50 (7th Cir.1995) (ADEA claim). In particular, the circuits, relying on the judicially crafted FAA presumption of arbitrability, have found that general language in individual employment contracts (whereby the parties agree to resolve all contract-related disputes) is adequate to embrace statutory discrimination claims. *See Rojas v. TK Communications, Inc.*, 87 F.3d 745, 749 (5th Cir.1996); *Matthews v. Rollins Hudig Hall Co.*, 72 F.3d 50, 55 (7th Cir.1995); *Asplundh Tree Expert Co. v. Bates*, 71 F.3d 592, 595 (6th Cir.1995).

Interestingly, the courts have not been nearly so ready to infer a knowing, voluntary waiver of the same statutory rights when the employer relies on a complete release of those rights contained in an ad hoc agreement entered into at the time of a termination. *See Fuentes v. United Parcel Service, Inc.*, ___ F.3d ___ (11th Cir.1996); *Beadle v. City of Tampa*, 42 F.3d 633 (11th Cir.), *cert. denied*, ___ U.S. ___, 115 S.Ct. 2600, 132 L.Ed.2d 846 (1995). Perhaps the

difference is that in the arbitration setting the employee is not waiving the statutory right altogether, but "merely" the judicial forum and probably also some of the remedies that Congress provided for its vindication. *See DeGaetano v. Smith Barney, Inc.*, 1996 WL 44226 (S.D.N.Y.1996) (because § 118 of the 1991 Civil Rights Act evinces legislative receptiveness to alternative methods of dispute resolution, arbitration of Title VII claims is not necessarily inconsistent with Congressional intent merely because a particular arbitration agreement precludes certain statutory remedies like punitive damages or attorneys' fees).

16. *Hurst v. Prudential Securities Inc.*, 21 F.3d 1113 (9th Cir.1994). In a subsequent case, however, another panel of the same court rejected the same employer's demand to arbitrate when it found that the waiver by the particular employees in question was not fully knowing. In so holding the court relied on legislative history underlying § 118 to the effect that alternative dispute resolution mechanisms were "intended to supplement, not supplant, the remedies provided by Title VII," HR Rep. No. 40 (I), 102nd Cong. 1st Sess., reprinted in 1991 U.S.C.C.A.N. 549, 635, and that the provision is designed to encourage arbitration only "where the parties knowingly and voluntarily elect to use these methods," 137 Cong. Rec. S. 15472, S. 15478 (Daily Ed. October 30, 1991), statement of Senator Dole. *Prudential Ins. Co. of America v. Lai*, 42 F.3d 1299 (9th Cir.1994). *See also DeGaetano v. Smith Barney*, 1996 WL 44226 (S.D.N.Y.1996) (relying on § 118 as evidence negating any Congressional intent to preclude a waiver of judicial remedies to enforce Title VII).

culture that have increasingly favored arbitration as a means to resolve statutory discrimination claims, including *Gilmer* itself and § 118.[17]

In sum, the Supreme Court may resolve these questions in a number of distinct ways. It might construe § 1 of FAA broadly, so that *Gilmer* would remain as authority for ordering pre-suit arbitration only in the rare situation where the agreement to arbitrate is not contained in a § 1 "contract of employment." At the other extreme, the Court might overrule *Gardner–Denver* by asserting that its numerous recent decisions facilitating arbitration, coupled with § 118, have sapped the vitality of its earlier decisions that denied preclusive effect to arbitration awards in actions under other labor and civil rights statutes.[18]

But there are a number of more moderate possibilities. For all covered enterprises except those in the transportation industries mentioned in § 1, the Court could compromise, as some lower courts already have, by expanding *Gilmer* beyond ADEA to reach Title VII claims, without overruling or limiting *Gardner–Denver*. This could mean that the putative plaintiff who has agreed to arbitrate grievances or disputes related to statutory discrimination prohibitions must first submit to arbitration procedures, but would not be bound by the arbitral award. Or the Court might limit *Gardner–Denver*'s permission to sue after an unfavorable arbitration award to the collective bargaining setting, where the plaintiff is not in control of the grievance and arbitration process and thus can less plausibly be said to have waived a judicial forum. Then all potential plaintiffs outside the transportation industries who have agreed to arbitrate the controversy at hand (or perhaps only those whose agreements to arbitrate specifically encompass claims of *statutory* employment discrimination) would be remitted to pre-suit arbitration per *Gilmer*, but only those whose promises to arbitrate are contained in collectively bargained agreements would escape preclusion from an adverse award.

There are still other possible variations. Suppose the Court, in the spirit of § 118 and the new solicitude for arbitration, departs from the civil rights analogue, overrules *Gardner–Denver* and holds generally that awards resulting from a "quasi-judicial" arbitration process [19] may have preclusive effect on subsequent judicial actions under Title VII and ADEA. Then presumably the plaintiff who prevailed in arbitration could use preclusion offensively in a subsequent federal statutory action, just as a victorious employer could preclude the plaintiff defensively.[20]

---

17. *Austin v. Owens–Brockway Glass Container, Inc.,* 78 F.3d 875 (4th Cir.), *cert. denied,* ___ U.S. ___, 117 S.Ct. 432, ___ L.Ed.2d ___ (1996).

18. See text accompanying notes 13 and 14 *supra.*

19. See also the discussion in the Procedure chapter on University of *Tennessee v. Elliott,* which holds that a prior administrative decision may have preclusive effect in

federal litigation if it is "quasi-judicial" in character.

20. See discussion of preclusion principles in Chapter 13; *cf. Meredith v. Beech Aircraft Corp.,* 18 F.3d 890 (10th Cir.1994) (judgment in favor of plaintiff in prior Title VII action has collateral estoppel or "issue preclusion" effect in second Title VII action brought by different employee against same employer).

Questions would nevertheless remain as to the scope of such preclusion in any individual case.

The Supreme Court has not decided whether *Gardner–Denver* still applies to permit post-arbitration judicial enforcement of Title VII following confirmation of the arbitral award in state court. Some circuits have denied preclusion in this situation, finding that the state court's limited scope of review could not constitute a final judgment on the merits and in any event did not involve the same "claim" as that afforded by Title VII.[21] Another circuit, however, invoked collateral estoppel or "issue preclusion" in a Title VII action after finding that the state court which had confirmed the arbitration award had ruled not just on plaintiffs' collective bargaining rights but also on the merits of their Title VII claims.[22]

Library References:

C.J.S. Arbitration §§ 126–128; Labor Relations §§ 478 et seq.
West's Key No. Digests, Arbitration ☞81; Labor Relations ☞464.

§ 5.6 Suit by EEOC

The EEOC has an option other than issuing a determination of reasonable or no reasonable cause and a notice of right to sue. It may initiate suit in its own name against private[1] employers.[2] Unlike individual plaintiffs, the agency faces no fixed deadlines within which it must file suit, and there is even authority that it may commence an action based on a charge filed by an employee whose own judicial action was dismissed as untimely.[3] Thus only a delay long enough to invoke the defense of laches serves as a check on EEOC's promptness in bringing suit.[4]

But unlike private litigants, who need satisfy *only* charge-filing and action-commencement time requirements in order to sue, EEOC, freed of

---

21. *Ryan v. City of Shawnee*, 13 F.3d 345 (10th Cir.1993); *Kirk v. Board of Educ. of Bremen Community High Sch.*, 811 F.2d 347 (7th Cir.1987); *Bottini v. Sadore Management Corp.*, 764 F.2d 116 (2d Cir.1985). To similar effect is *Aleem v. General Felt Indus. Inc.*, 661 F.2d 135, 137 (9th Cir. 1981).

22. *Rider v. Commonwealth of Pennsylvania*, 850 F.2d 982 (3d Cir.), *cert. denied*, 488 U.S. 993, 109 S.Ct. 556, 102 L.Ed.2d 582 (1988). *Cf. Caldeira v. County of Kauai*, 866 F.2d 1175 (9th Cir.) (precluding § 1983 action in deference to state court confirmation in which plaintiff had opportunity to challenge the merits of the arbitrator's decision), *cert. denied*, 493 U.S. 817, 110 S.Ct. 69, 107 L.Ed.2d 36 (1989).

§ 5.6

1. Suits against a state or local "government, governmental agency, or political subdivision" named in a charge filed with EEOC may be brought by the Attorney General. *See* §§ 706(f)(1) and 707, 42 U.S.C.A. §§ 2000e–5(f)(1) and 2000e–6.

2. *Id.*

3. *See EEOC v. Harris Chernin, Inc.*, 10 F.3d 1286 (7th Cir.1993) (upholding EEOC's right to sue independent of the individual plaintiff's rights, but limiting it to injunctive relief). Indeed it has recently been held that EEOC has authority to sue even when all the protected group members for whom it purports to speak have signed affidavits disclaiming their personal interest in pursuing a claim. *EEOC v. Johnson & Higgins, Inc.*, 91 F.3d 1529 (2d Cir. 1996)(case under ADEA).

4. *See Occidental Life Ins. Co. of California v. EEOC*, 432 U.S. 355, 97 S.Ct. 2447, 53 L.Ed.2d 402 (1977).

those fetters, has other pre-suit responsibilities. It must comply with the statutory requirements of notifying the charged party within 10 days after it receives a charge [5] and attempting during the administrative process to eliminate unlawful employment practices through "conference, conciliation, and persuasion." [6]

If EEOC files suit before one can be commenced by a private charging party, the private party is limited to intervention in EEOC's action and may not file her own.[7] And EEOC may attempt to preserve its suit priority by rescinding a previously issued notice of right to sue before the private action is commenced.[8] If, however, the charging party commences an action under Title VII before EEOC does, EEOC may not commence its own action but may only exercise its statutory right to intervene.[9]

If EEOC wins the race to the courthouse, there is authority suggesting that the charging party, to avoid being bound by an adverse judgment and to preserve a right to appeal a judgment against EEOC, must intervene.[10] It is unclear whether this authority survives *Martin v. Wilks*[11] or is affected by the provision of the 1991 Act that bars challenges to employment practices authorized or commanded by litigated judgments or consent decrees only if the challenger received notice of the proceedings or was adequately represented in them by another party— e.g., EEOC.[12]

Library References:

> C.J.S. Civil Rights §§ 358 et seq.
> West's Key No. Digests, Civil Rights ☜374.

§ 5.7 Plaintiff Joinder and Class Actions; Identity of Defendants

Title VII actions in federal court are limited by statutory requirements concerning parties and allegations. The EEOC charge which forms the predicate for a Title VII action may be filed either "by or on

---

5. 42 U.S.C.A. § 2000e–5(b); *see EEOC v. Burlington Northern, Inc.*, 644 F.2d 717, 720–21 (8th Cir.1981).

6. *Id. See EEOC v. Klingler Elec. Corp.*, 636 F.2d 104 (5th Cir.1981).

7. *See Behlar v. Smith*, 719 F.2d 950 (8th Cir.1983).

8. *Lute v. Singer Co.*, 678 F.2d 844 (9th Cir.1982), *amended, rehearing denied*, 696 F.2d 1266 (9th Cir.1983).

9. *Johnson v. Nekoosa–Edwards Paper Co.*, 558 F.2d 841 (8th Cir.1977); *cf. EEOC v. Huttig Sash & Door Co.*, 511 F.2d 453, 455 (5th Cir.1975) (EEOC limited to intervention if it raises issues pertaining and seeks relief only on behalf of the private

plaintiff). There is authority under the ADEA, however, that EEOC may either intervene *or* commence an independent action even if the complainant has filed first. *EEOC v. G–K–G, Inc.*, 39 F.3d 740 (7th Cir.1994); *EEOC v. Wackenhut Corp.*, 939 F.2d 241 (5th Cir.1991) (authorizing suit by EEOC filed after action by individual plaintiff).

10. *Adams v. Proctor & Gamble Mfg. Co.*, 697 F.2d 582 (4th Cir.1983) (en banc).

11. 490 U.S. 755, 109 S.Ct. 2180, 104 L.Ed.2d 835 (1989).

12. Section 108 (adding subsection 703(n)(1) to Title VII, 42 U.S.C.A. § 2000e–2(n)(1)).

behalf of" a person who is "aggrieved."[1]   Thus named plaintiffs who have filed charges may prosecute the action on behalf of class members in a Federal Rule 23 class action, and those class members need not themselves have filed individual EEOC or state agency charges if the class is certified.[2]   But the Supreme Court, with its 1980 decision in *General Telephone Co. of Southwest v. Falcon*,[3] has strictly applied the Rule 23 requirements for class certification.

Rule 23, applicable also to class actions under the Americans with Disabilities Act and § 1981, has the following four requirements:

(1) a sufficient number of class members that ordinary joinder under Rule 20 would be impracticable;

(2) questions of law or fact common to the class;

(3) claims (or, in a defendant class action, defenses) of the representative parties that are "typical" of those of the class as a whole; and

(4) a likelihood that the representative parties will fairly and adequately protect the interests of the class.

The first two requirements are usually easily met in employment discrimination class actions, which characteristically involve a plaintiff class.   Numerosity is seldom a problem, with classes containing as few as 18 members having been certified.[4]   And so long as the named plaintiffs assert that disparate treatment on a prohibited ground is classwide, or that one or more neutral practices has classwide impact on a protected group, the commonality requirement is also rarely a barrier.   Employment discrimination by its very nature partakes of classwide discrimination.

The third and fourth factors, typicality and representativeness, have proven most difficult to surmount.   For a putative class to comply with Rule 23's requirement that the claims of the named plaintiffs be "typical" of those of the class, *Falcon* insists that in most cases the complement of named plaintiffs in a private Title VII class action include at least one representative who complains not only on the same prohibited ground of discrimination (e.g., race or sex) as the putative class, but also of each particular discriminatory practice the class proposes to attack. In a famous footnote 15, the court recognized an exception that permits certification despite diversity in the practices challenged by the representative plaintiffs and class members where those practices are the product of a common device (e.g. a test) or common decisionmaker applying the

---

§ 5.7

1. Section 706(f)(1). For a discussion of whether testers have standing to file suit under Title VII and related statutes, see the Procedure chapter.

2. *Albemarle Paper Co. v. Moody*, 422 U.S. 405, 95 S.Ct. 2362, 45 L.Ed.2d 280 (1975).

3. 457 U.S. 147, 102 S.Ct. 2364, 72 L.Ed.2d 740 (1982).

4. *Cypress v. Newport News Gen. &*

same subjective criteria.[5] Indeed, defendants have argued that *Falcon* also demands that at least one of the named plaintiffs must have allegedly suffered the same detrimental term or condition of employment—failure to hire, unequal pay or discipline, nonpromotion, on-the-job harassment, discharge—as the members of each class or subclass sought to be represented. Thus, unless the named plaintiff or plaintiffs who originally retained class counsel happen to embody all the characteristics of the putative class members, share all their same grievances and suffer their same injuries, *Falcon* effectively compels class counsel to try to assemble a wider group of named plaintiffs. Then some, but not all of the wider group can individually assert that they, as applicants or employees, were aggrieved by the particular employment practices, and affected in the same terms and conditions of employment, as other members of the class.

Falcon has had at least two distinct consequences. First, by effectively requiring the formation of a large and diverse plaintiff group, it has more sharply put into focus the ethical concerns associated with the solicitation of additional named plaintiffs. The Court has been rather lenient about permitting plaintiff class counsel, directly or through the original clients, to encourage others similarly situated to join the named plaintiff group, particularly when the class action is serving a "private attorney general" function in combatting race discrimination.[6]

Second, defendants have been resourceful in responding to the larger named plaintiff complements that *Falcon* in effect compels. *Falcon* has spurred more elaborate and expensive motion practice about the propriety of class certification and limitations on precertification discovery. Defendants commonly assert, frequently with success,[7] that the resulting diverse named plaintiff group—representing, for example, applicants, employees, and former employees; subordinates and superiors; unsuccessful test takers and victims of discriminatory discipline; women sexually harassed, and those suffering unequal pay; persons discharged, and persons not promoted—is rife with internal conflicts, so that, in Rule 23's terms, the named plaintiffs are not fairly "representative" of the class members whose fate will ride with them if the class is certified. To alleviate such conflicts, plaintiffs or district courts have sometimes proposed that the class be subdivided into "subclasses" that one or more of the named plaintiffs can fairly represent. On occasion, however, the result of forming subclasses is that each is fewer than the approximately 30 or so that the courts have generally required before a plaintiff group is sufficiently numerous to warrant class action certification. In this

Nonsectarian Hospital Ass'n, 375 F.2d 648 (4th Cir.1967).

5. See, e.g., *Carpenter v. Stephen F. Austin State University*, 706 F.2d 608 (5th Cir. 1983) (applying note 15 to certify class of current, past and future employees respecting varied job positions).

6. *Gulf Oil Co. v. Bernard*, 449 U.S. 1033, 101 S.Ct. 607, 66 L.Ed.2d 495 (1980).

7. See, e.g., *Watson v. Fort Worth Bank & Trust*, 798 F.2d 791 (5th Cir.1986), *vacated on other grounds*, 487 U.S. 977, 108 S.Ct. 2777, 101 L.Ed.2d 827 (1988) (application and promotion discrimination); *Briggs v. Anderson*, 796 F.2d 1009 (8th Cir.1986) (current and terminated employees); *Walker v. Jim Dandy Co.*, 747 F.2d 1360 (11th Cir.1984) (employee and applicant classes).

way a defendant's Rule 23 objections snowball: a challenge to typicality generates a challenge to representativeness that in turn generates a challenge to numerosity. By their nature these challenges invite early consideration of the merits of the class members' claims, although the court is formally prohibited from considering those merits in determining whether to certify.[8]

The rejection on the merits of class claims of systemic treatment does not bar the claims of individual class members alleging disparate treatment à la *McDonnell Douglas/Burdine*.[9] Moreover, when a court denies class action certification, the claims of individual class members who have not filed a charge with EEOC or commenced a judicial action may still be timely. This is because the filing of a class action has been held to toll, until the denial of certification, both the 90–day period for filing suit[10] and the applicable deadline (180 or 300 days) for filing a charge with EEOC.[11] Even when a class was decertified because no class representative had standing to assert the claim subsequently brought by individual plaintiffs, those plaintiffs have been allowed to "piggyback" on the timely filed EEOC charges of the class action plaintiffs.[12] But rejection of class claims on the merits has preclusive effect under federal common law in subsequent actions asserting the same pattern claims.[13] And the pendency of a class action in which class status was denied or a class decertified does not toll the charge-filing or action-commencement deadlines for class members who bring a subsequent *class* action— otherwise there would be "endless rounds of litigation ... over the adequacy of successive named plaintiffs to serve as class representatives." [14]

A "single-filing" rule recognized by at least five federal circuits outside the class action context permits plaintiffs who have not filed their own EEOC charge to piggyback on a charge or charges filed by coplaintiffs. The plaintiffs are relieved of filing their own charges if the claims of all parties are based on a common employer practice or practices during the same rough time frame and the filed charge or charges timely and adequately alerted the employer to the alleged illegality of all the practices ultimately challenged in court.[15] It is not a

8. *Eisen v. Carlisle & Jacquelin*, 417 U.S. 156, 177, 94 S.Ct. 2140, 2152, 40 L.Ed.2d 732 (1974).

9. *Cooper v. Federal Reserve Bank of Richmond*, 467 U.S. 867, 104 S.Ct. 2794, 81 L.Ed.2d 718 (1984).

10. *Crown, Cork & Seal Co. v. Parker*, 462 U.S. 345, 103 S.Ct. 2392, 76 L.Ed.2d 628 (1983).

11. *Griffin v. Singletary*, 17 F.3d 356 (11th Cir.1994), *cert. denied sub nom. Florida v. Platt*, ___ U.S. ___, 115 S.Ct. 723, 130 L.Ed.2d 628 (1995).

12. *Id.*

13. *See* Procedure Chapter, below.

14. *Griffin v. Singletary, supra* note 11.

15. *EEOC v. Wilson Metal Casket Co.*, 24 F.3d 836 (6th Cir.1994) (citing cases). *See also Howlett v. Holiday Inns, Inc.*, 49 F.3d 189 (6th Cir.) (allowing age discrimination plaintiff who filed untimely charge with EEOC to invoke the rule even though timely foundation charge did not allege classwide discrimination), *cert. denied.* ___ U.S. ___, 116 S.Ct. 379, 133 L.Ed.2d 302 (1995). *But see Washington v. Brown & Williamson Tobacco Corp.*, 756 F.Supp. 1547 (M.D.Ga.1991), *aff'd*, 959 F.2d 1566 (11th Cir.1992) (no piggybacking by applicant challenging failure to hire where plaintiff who did file charge was current

prerequisite to single filing that the foundation claim allege classwide discrimination.[16] The rule has also been applied to permit the plaintiff who has not filed an EEOC charge to intervene in an action brought by the plaintiff who has,[17] or to join that action as coplaintiff after an unsuccessful attempt at intervention.[18]

Another requirement, that the action be brought "against the respondent named in the charge," [19] has sometimes been construed to authorize jurisdiction over a successor employer [20] or even over a defendant improperly named, or not formally named in the charge at all, if its identity is sufficiently revealed in the substance of the charge or if that employer is closely related to a named respondent.[21] In some circuits the civil action has even been allowed to reach defendants not likely to have received notice of the original EEOC charge if the agency's investigation, reasonably confined to the facts alleged in the charge, would have focused on them.[22]

Library References:

> C.J.S. Civil Rights § 333.
> West's Key No. Digests, Civil Rights ☞364.

§ 5.8 Relation of Federal Lawsuit to EEOC Investigation

Since the EEOC charge is the necessary foundation for a Title VII action, the issues that may be litigated in federal court will be tied to some degree to the contents of the charge. But recognizing that EEOC charges are often drafted by unrepresented employees ill-equipped to craft them with care, courts following the leading case of *Sanchez v. Standard Brands, Inc.*[1] have permitted Title VII plaintiffs to try claims "like or related to allegations contained in the charge and growing out of such allegations during the pendency of the case before the Commission."

The widespread adoption of the *Sanchez* rule puts a premium on defendants' efforts to limit the scope of EEOC proceedings. Generalizations about the meaning of "like or related" are particularly hazardous.

employee who therefore lacked standing to complain about hiring).

16. *Howlett v. Holiday Inns Inc.,* 49 F.3d 189 (6th Cir.1995).

17. *See Wheeler v. American Home Products Corp.,* 582 F.2d 891 (5th Cir. 1977).

18. *Calloway v. Partners National Health Plans,* 986 F.2d 446 (11th Cir.1993).

19. Section 706(f)(1).

20. *See, e.g., EEOC v. MacMillan Bloedel Containers, Inc.,* 503 F.2d 1086 (6th Cir.1974).

21. *See, e.g., Evans v. Sheraton Park Hotel,* 503 F.2d 177 (D.C.Cir.1974) (international union must defend when charge named two of its locals). For the standing

of "testers" to prosecute violations of the employment discrimination laws, see the Procedure chapter below.

22. *See, e.g., Tillman v. Milwaukee,* 715 F.2d 354 (7th Cir.1983); *Tillman v. Boaz,* 548 F.2d 592 (5th Cir.1977).

§ 5.8

1. 431 F.2d 455, 466 (5th Cir.1970); *Cornwell v. Robinson,* 23 F.3d 694 (2d Cir. 1994) (harassment allegations were reasonably related to discrimination charges concerning a previous tour of duty and therefore need not be separately charged before EEOC but may be added by amended complaint in the district court).

But it may be ventured that allegations in a Title VII judicial complaint that add a new *ground* of discrimination (race or sex, for instance) are less likely to be entertained than are allegations that touch on additional *terms or conditions of employment* or implicate other potential plaintiffs in different departments or divisions. Even then, plaintiffs whose administrative charges complained of adverse treatment respecting limited terms and conditions of employment will be permitted to target in court only those other terms and conditions of employment that EEOC could reasonably have been expected to be investigated based on the charge.[2] The Seventh Circuit appears to be moving to an alternative, and apparently stricter, standard: whether the claims in the judicial action are "fairly encompassed" within or "implied" by the charge the plaintiff filed with EEOC. Decisions applying the new standard have precluded allegations by the same plaintiff on the same prohibited ground of discrimination that attack different terms and conditions of employment or implicate different individuals from those targeted by the EEOC charge.[3] At least where the additional practices sought to be challenged in court are plausibly asserted to arise out of the practices cited in the EEOC charge,[4] it would appear that this standard bars the litigation of claims that would be heard under the *Sanchez* "like or related" test.

An especially liberal application of the charge-filing requirement generally permits a plaintiff to press a retaliation claim under § 704, without first filing a separate EEOC charge of retaliation, where that claim grows out of a properly filed predicate charge of discrimination under § 703.[5] But that liberality is extended only when the underlying charge of primary discrimination was itself administratively exhausted and timely.[6] Some circuits have limited the federal court's ancillary

---

2. *See Park v. Howard Univ.*, 71 F.3d 904 (D.C.Cir.1995), *cert. filed* (July 2, 1996) (hostile work environment sex discrimination claim cannot proceed based on EEOC charge limited to sex and national origin discrimination concerning a selection process).

3. *Chambers v. American Trans Air, Inc.*, 17 F.3d 998 (7th Cir.1994) (gender-based pay discrimination alleged in EEOC charge cannot support judicial claim of gender-based promotion denials, even though plaintiff asserted that the promotion denials caused the pay differentials); *Kirk v. FPM Corp.*, 22 F.3d 135 (7th Cir.1994) (race-based failure to promote allegation in EEOC charge cannot support judicial claim of race-based discriminatory denial of educational opportunities, despite plaintiff's assertion that the latter arose from the former). *Cf. Cheek v. Western & Southern Life Ins. Co.*, 31 F.3d 497 (7th Cir.1994) (gender discrimination complaint based on different events and implicating different

individuals not like and related even in the *Sanchez* sense to EEOC charge also alleging discrimination based on gender).

4. This would appear to be the case in *Kirk*, but perhaps not *Chambers*, both cited in the note immediately preceding.

5. *See, e.g., Malarkey v. Texaco, Inc.*, 983 F.2d 1204 (2d Cir.1993). The reverse is not true: a primary discrimination claim may not be tacked onto a claim of retaliation, where only the latter was administratively charged. *Noreuil v. Peabody Coal Co.*, 96 F.3d 254 (7th Cir.1996).

6. *Jones v. Runyon*, 91 F.3d 1398 (10th Cir.1996) (no subject matter jurisdiction under "piggybacking" approach over retaliation charge sought to be heard in conjunction with underlying Title VII claim that itself was not exhausted before EEOC); *Hargett v. Valley Fed. Sav. Bank*, 60 F.3d 754 (11th Cir.1995) (original plaintiff's charge must be timely).

jurisdiction in such cases to charges of alleged retaliation occurring after, and not before, the filing of the underlying charge.[7]

Library References:

C.J.S. Civil Rights § 329.
West's Key No. Digests, Civil Rights ⚷362.

§ 5.9 Employer Recordkeeping Requirements

Pursuant to statutory authority,[1] EEOC has promulgated regulations requiring employers to maintain records pertinent to a wide range of employment decisions. These require employers to retain all personnel records for six months after they are created and, when a charge is filed, to retain all records relevant to that charge "until final disposition of the charge or action."[2] In employment discrimination actions, the employer has custody of virtually all records critical to resolution of the disputed claim; hence in the reported decisions it is the employer that allegedly violated the Title VII recordkeeping requirements.

But judicial enforcement of employer recordkeeping violations has generally been conspicuously lenient. Typically the courts of appeals that have found employers to have destroyed documents in violation of the EEOC regulation give the plaintiff the benefit of a "presumption that the destroyed documents would have bolstered her case."[3] But then they either assume[4] or conclude[5] that the presumption was "overcome"—the evidence for which may simply be an innocent explanation by an authorized employer agent, coupled with his assertion that he had not been instructed to preserve records in accordance with the government regulation. Alternatively, these decisions often find that other employer evidence either supports a proposition that the destroyed records might have negated, or undermines a proposition they might have established, so the recordkeeping violation of Title VII should simply be overlooked.[6] And those courts that impose sanctions have denied substantial sanctions, preferring instead such milder measures as requiring the defendant to bear the costs of record reconstruction; limiting its production of evidence on the matters reflected in the destroyed documents; or invoking the presumption that the records

---

7. *McKenzie v. Illinois Department of Transportation,* 92 F.3d 473 (7th Cir.1996); *Ang v. Procter & Gamble Co.,* 932 F.2d 540 (6th Cir.1991).

§ 5.9

1. Section 709(c), 42 U.S.C.A. § 2000e–8(c).

2. 29 CFR § 1602.14 (1994).

3. *See, e.g., Favors v. Fisher,* 13 F.3d 1235, 1239 (8th Cir.1994); *Hicks v. Gates Rubber Co.,* 833 F.2d 1406, 1419 (10th Cir. 1987); *Capaci v. Katz & Besthoff, Inc.,* 711 F.2d 647, 661 n. 7 (5th Cir.1983), *cert. de-*

nied, 466 U.S. 927, 104 S.Ct. 1709, 80 L.Ed.2d 182 (1984). *Cf. EEOC v. American National Bank,* 652 F.2d 1176, 1195–96 (4th Cir.1981) (employer not relieved of ordinary litigation inferences drawn from its not possessing data merely because EEOC regulations did not affirmatively require retention of that data at relevant time).

4. *Capaci, supra* note 3.

5. *Favors v. Fisher, supra,* 13 F.3d at 1239.

6. *Id.*; see generally the terms of the proposed remand in *Hicks v. Gates Rubber Co., supra* note 3.

would have supported plaintiff's case.[7] Default, it is said, requires bad faith resistance to discovery orders; it is not enough that the violation is technically "willful" because the records were destroyed after defendant's receipt of the EEOC notice of charge that contained an admonition about the employer's recordkeeping obligations under the EEOC regulation.[8] Yet even a court that imposed sanctions after finding "outrageous" and "deliberate, willful and contumacious" violations designed to "make forever unavailable" pertinent records and documents and which in fact prejudiced the plaintiffs [9] drew back from default or dismissal. In that court's view, it would also have to be shown that alternative sanctions would fail adequately to punish and deter. Until such a showing could be made, the court ordered the defendant to pay the plaintiffs twice the amount of all attorneys' fees and costs associated with presenting motions relative to the recordkeeping violations and possible record reconstruction possibilities, together with a fine to be paid into the court. The court observed that these steps would probably not fully compensate plaintiffs for the harm they sustained but that "plaintiffs have not been wholly deprived of the means to attempt their proof." [10]

B. TITLE VII REMEDIES

§ 5.10 Reinstatement and Back Pay

The range of judicial remedial authority is prescribed by § 706(g). This section provides for injunctions and "such affirmative action as may be appropriate," including orders directing reinstatement or hire, back pay, and other equitable relief. It also "limits" a defendant's back pay liability retrospectively to no earlier than two years before the filing of a charge with EEOC. "Limits" is placed in quotation marks because the statute's deadlines for filing a charge with EEOC are only 180 days, in the handful of states that do not have their own local antidiscrimination laws and agencies, or 300 days in the majority of states that do. Thus in effect the 2–year "limit" on back pay authorizes its award *earlier* than the "trigger" date that starts the running of Title VII's administrative charge-filing deadlines.

Prevailing plaintiffs are routinely awarded injunctions against ongoing violations, and, where disparate treatment has been proved,[1] rein-

---

7. *EEOC v. Jacksonville Shipyards, Inc.*, 690 F.Supp. 995, 998–999 (M.D.Fla. 1988).

8. *Id.* at 998.

9. *See, e.g., Capellupo v. FMC Corp.*, 126 F.R.D. 545, 551–52 (D.Minn.1989).

10. *Id.* at 553.

§ 5.10

1. Where the plaintiff has proven only that she was denied employment by virtue of a neutral practice that disproportionately adversely impacted her group, the court has less assurance than in a case of proven disparate treatment that she is otherwise qualified for the position she seeks. In such cases the court may direct the employer to reconsider the plaintiff's application under standards that meet the applicable defense to a neutral practice case. *Young v. Edgcomb Steel Co.*, 499 F.2d 97 (4th Cir.1974).

statement or, if there is no position available at the time of judgment, priority in filling vacancies.[2] As with the systemic disparate treatment case, discussed above,[3] reinstatement may be denied, however, where the discriminatee, although qualified when unlawfully rejected, is no longer qualified for the position in question at the time of judgment.[4] Back pay is also awarded almost as a matter of course. This is because, as the Supreme Court has explained, back pay serves both of the Act's remedial goals: to restore discrimination victims to the approximate status they would have enjoyed absent discrimination (the "make whole" purpose), and to deter employer violations. Accordingly, the Court, while recognizing that federal judges enjoy some discretion to withhold any Title VII remedy in particular circumstances, held in *Albemarle Paper Co. v. Moody*[5] that back pay may be denied only for unusual reasons which, if applied generally, would not impede those remedial objectives. For example, the "neutral practice/disproportionate adverse impact" case dispenses with evidence of discriminatory intent, and a general good faith exception to back pay liability would therefore seriously erode the advantages of that mode of proof. The Court has consequently rejected such an exception.[6] It has also held that the ordinary Eleventh Amendment immunity of states from federal court monetary awards is overridden in Title VII actions because Congress enacted the statute in at least partial reliance on its powers under the Fourteenth Amendment to enforce the Equal Protection Clause.[7]

Back pay is the total compensation the employee has lost from the date of the adverse employment decision through the date of final

2. *Anderson v. Phillips Petroleum Co.,* 861 F.2d 631 (10th Cir.1988). But plaintiffs are not ordinarily entitled to a preliminary injunction because monetary relief after trial will be an adequate remedy at law. *Adam–Mellang v. Apartment Search, Inc.,* 96 F.3d 297 (8th Cir.1996).

3. See the discussion of the remedy stage of a bifurcated systemic disparate treatment action in Chapter 4.

4. *See, e.g., Kamberos v. GTE Automatic Electric, Inc.,* 603 F.2d 598 (7th Cir.1979), *cert. denied,* 454 U.S. 1060, 102 S.Ct. 612, 70 L.Ed.2d 599 (1981).

5. 422 U.S. 405, 95 S.Ct. 2362, 45 L.Ed.2d 280 (1975).

6. *Albemarle.* On occasion, the presumption in favor of back pay has been overcome. In *Los Angeles Dep't of Water and Power v. Manhart,* 435 U.S. 702, 98 S.Ct. 1370, 55 L.Ed.2d 657 (1978), discussed in Chapter 3, the Court held unlawful as express gender discrimination the City's requirement that women contribute greater amounts than men to purchase a pension benefit of the same monthly amount. The Court nevertheless declined to order it to refund excess contributions. It referred to its ruling as a "marked departure from past practice" and expressed concern that the brunt of the requested remedy would fall on innocent third parties—pensioners or current employees participating in the fund. 435 U.S. at 719–721, 98 S.Ct. at 1380–1382.

Presumably, under the reasoning in *Albemarle,* the mere fact that liability may not have been anticipated should not have sufficed to relieve the defendant of retroactive monetary liability, for if good faith were a generally applied defense it would eviscerate the compensatory goal of Title VII remedies. (Among other things, there could never be monetary liability in a neutral practice/disproportionate adverse impact case.) The concern for innocent third parties is also a bit peculiar, since the burden of sizeable monetary awards against private employers is also felt by innocent third parties, their shareholders, yet courts have not hesitated too make such awards against private corporations. Perhaps there lurks here a tacit public-private distinction, an underlying awareness that the ultimate payors in *Manhart* may have been the city's taxpayers. See dissenting opinion of Marshall, J.

7. *Fitzpatrick v. Bitzer,* 427 U.S. 445, 96 S.Ct. 2666, 49 L.Ed.2d 614 (1976).

judgment. The plaintiff must make efforts to mitigate her losses. Back pay awards are reduced by amounts the plaintiff earned, or with reasonable diligence could have earned, since the date of a discharge or failure or refusal to hire (on the other hand, a failure to mitigate does not absolutely forfeit the right to recovery for back pay).[8] One circuit has recently held that self-employment is an acceptable form of mitigation for this purpose.[9] The back pay clock should stop when "the sting" of discriminatory conduct has ended.[10]

Title VII authorizes the award of back pay to a date as early as two years before the filing of the required EEOC charge—as distinct from the later date on which the complaint is filed in a judicial action. In states without their own anti-discrimination laws and agencies, EEOC may immediately assert jurisdiction over a plaintiff's initial charge; and any charging party may demand a notice of right to sue from EEOC after it has exercised that jurisdiction for 180 days. Even in the majority of states, where the charging party must, at least in theory, exhaust administrative remedies before state or local "deferral" agencies, the plaintiff may be able to invoke EEOC's jurisdiction promptly if the state or local agency waives its right to proceed either in the individual case or by a "work-sharing" agreement with EEOC. And at the outside the plaintiff has 300 days from the latest alleged unlawful employment practice to file with EEOC, which then can be compelled to authorize suit 180 days later. Thus as a practical matter most Title VII judicial actions will be commenced well before two years have expired after the filing of the EEOC charge. The two-year back pay accrual rule nevertheless permits back pay for violations that occurred up to two years before that charge was filed. That is to say, back pay may be recovered for "continuing violations" that began before the last event that triggers Title VII's "statute of limitations."[11]

Although, as the next section considers, the 1991 Act adds compensatory and punitive damages as "legal" remedies to the Title VII plaintiff's arsenal, it does not change the "equitable" character of the pre-existing remedies like back pay. Determination of eligibility for back pay, although virtually automatic under the *Albemarle* presumption, is therefore formally for the court, not the jury, as is the critical calculation of the back pay amount.[12] Yet at least one circuit has held

---

8. *Booker v. Taylor Milk Co.,* 64 F.3d 860 (3d Cir.1995).

9. *Smith v. Great American Restaurants, Inc.,* 969 F.2d 430 (7th Cir.1992) (ADEA case).

10. *Syvock v. Milwaukee Boiler Mfg. Co.,* 665 F.2d 149, 160 n. 14 (7th Cir.1981).

11. *See, e.g., Palmer v. Kelly,* 17 F.3d 1490 (D.C.Cir.1994) (plaintiff who retired only 9 days after discriminatory promotion denial, and who was thus arguably eligible only for 9 days of back pay, nevertheless received backpay for the full two years be-

fore he filed with EEOC, when court determined that the employer had continually denied promotions because of race). For a closer look at the intricacies of the "continuing violation" theory, see the Equal Pay Chapter.

12. *Simpson v. Lucky Stores,* 1993 WL 414668 (N.D.Cal.1993). Thus one court has recently suggested a rule of law based on the "lost-chance" concept used in tort cases to calculate back pay where it is less than certain that the plaintiff would have been hired or promoted even absent discrimination—as where two or more candi-

that "the issue of reasonable mitigation is ultimately a question of fact for the jury." [13]

Because each species of Title VII relief before the 1991 Civil Rights Act was considered equitable, jury trials were not until recently available unless a Title VII claim was joined with a claim for legal relief—for instance, a claim under § 1981. Although the Supreme Court strongly suggested that there was no right to jury trial under Title VII, it has never actually ruled on the question.[14] There clearly is a jury trial right under § 1981,[15] and where an action presents claims under both statutes, the right to jury trial under § 1981 may not be estopped by the prior bench trial of an equitable claim. Rather, prior jury determinations of facts reached in deciding the legal, § 1981 claims should be adopted by the trial court when it later determines any equitable claims under Title VII.[16] But a district court has ruled that it is not precluded from granting back pay as a remedy additional to whatever damages remedies may have been awarded by the jury.[17]

The "equity" characterization has also limited the available monetary relief under Title VII (before the 1991 amendments) to an award of back pay, precluding more generous measures such as compensation for emotional distress or punitive damages.[18] The equitable nature of all Title VII awards before the new Act also led some courts to deny nominal damages, viewing them as compensatory in nature.[19] But prejudgment, as well as the standard post-judgment, interest is an ordinary item of compensation integrally related to back pay,[20] routinely awarded in Title VII actions.[21] It may even be an abuse of discretion to

---

dates seek only one available position. The court suggested that the plaintiff be awarded the same percentage of back pay as his percentage chance of being promoted. *Doll v. Brown*, 75 F.3d 1200 (7th Cir.1996) (case under Rehabilitation Act). EEOC Guidelines recognize a "no-injury" defense but require the employer to prove by "clear and convincing" evidence that, despite its discriminatory conduct, the plaintiff suffered no harm as a result. 29 C.F.R. §§ 1614.203, 1614.501(b), (c).

13. *Smith v. Great American Restaurants, Inc.*, 969 F.2d 430, 439 (7th Cir. 1992).

14. *United States v. Burke*, 504 U.S. 229, 112 S.Ct. 1867, 119 L.Ed.2d 34 (1992); *Chauffeurs, Teamsters and Helpers Local No. 391 v. Terry*, 494 U.S. 558, 110 S.Ct. 1339, 108 L.Ed.2d 519 (1990).

15. *Johnson v. Railway Express Agency, Inc.*, 421 U.S. 454, 95 S.Ct. 1716, 44 L.Ed.2d 295 (1975).

16. *Cf. Lytle v. Household Manufacturing, Inc.*, 494 U.S. 545, 110 S.Ct. 1331, 108 L.Ed.2d 504 (1990), esp. n.4.

17. *Hennessy v. Penril Datacomm Networks*, 864 F.Supp. 759 (N.D.Ill.1994), *aff'd in relevant part*, 69 F.3d 1344 (7th Cir. 1995).

18. *See Cumpiano v. Banco Santander Puerto Rico*, 902 F.2d 148 (1st Cir.1990).

19. *See Kerr–Selgas v. American Airlines, Inc.*, 69 F.3d 1205, 1210 n. 6 (1st Cir.1995); *Griffith v. State of Colo., Div. of Youth Services*, 17 F.3d 1323 (10th Cir. 1994); *Walker v. Anderson Electrical Connectors*, 944 F.2d 841 (11th Cir.1991).

20. *Donnelly v. Yellow Freight System, Inc.*, 874 F.2d 402 (7th Cir.1989), *affirmed on other grounds*, 494 U.S. 820, 110 S.Ct. 1566, 108 L.Ed.2d 834 (1990). *Cf. Barbour v. Merrill*, 48 F.3d 1270 (D.C.Cir.1995) (same holding under § 1981), *cert. dismissed*, ___ U.S. ___, 116 S.Ct. 1037, 134 L.Ed.2d 113 (1996).

21. *Loeffler v. Frank*, 486 U.S. 549, 108 S.Ct. 1965, 100 L.Ed.2d 549 (1988) (available even against Federal government, notwithstanding sovereign immunity); *Clarke v. Frank*, 960 F.2d 1146 (2d Cir.1992).

deny it,[22] absent unusual reasons.[23]

Any prevailing party, plaintiff or defendant, is of course eligible for an award of "costs" under Federal Rule of Civil Procedure 54(d). These are limited, however, to items specified by 28 U.S.C.A. § 1920: clerk and marshal fees, fees by court reporters for transcripts "necessarily obtained for use in the case"; printing disbursements and witness fees; specified docket fees; and fees for court-appointed experts and certain interpreters. Most important, "costs" as used in Rule 54(d) do *not* include the prevailing party's attorneys' fees. This is consistent with the ordinary "American rule" which, absent express statutory authorization, calls for each side to pay its own attorneys' fees.[24] Section 701(k) of Title VII is one such statute. It provides that a prevailing party may recover a reasonable attorney's fee as part of "costs." [25] And for purposes of calculating the postjudgment interest allowed by 28 U.S.C.A. § 1961 "on any money judgment in a civil case recovered in a district court," these statutorily shifted attorneys' fees shall be included as part of the judgment.[26]

Section 113 of the Act authorizes the court to include the fees of experts, without a specific cap, as part of the award of attorneys' fees to prevailing Title VII plaintiffs, contrary to the thrust of two recent decisions of the Court.[27] This change facilitates the neutral practice case as well as the case of intentional discrimination. But the Act's authorization of prospective relief, and hence attorneys' fees, despite the defendant's discharge of the "same decision" burden in the intentional "mixed motive" situation,[28] affords greater relative inducement to bring intentional discrimination claims.

Library References:

> C.J.S. Civil Rights §§ 388, 417–418, 422, 425.
> West's Key No. Digests, Civil Rights ⬤➾394, 401.

22. *Sellers v. Delgado Community College*, 839 F.2d 1132 (5th Cir.1988).

23. *Hutchison v. Amateur Electronic Supply, Inc.*, 42 F.3d 1037 (7th Cir.1994); *EEOC v. Delight Wholesale Co.*, 973 F.2d 664 (8th Cir.1992).

24. *Alyeska Pipeline Serv. Co. v. Wilderness Society*, 421 U.S. 240, 95 S.Ct. 1612, 44 L.Ed.2d 141 (1975).

25. See Chapter 12 on Civil Rights Attorney's Fee Act of 1988.

26. *Carter v. Sedgwick County, Kansas*, 36 F.3d 952 (10th Cir.1994).

27. Section 113(b) (amending § 706(k) of Title VII, 42 U.S.C.A. § 2000e–5(k)).

See Crawford Fitting Co. v. J. T. Gibbons, Inc., 482 U.S. 437, 107 S.Ct. 2494, 96 L.Ed.2d 385 (1987) ($30 per day witness fee limit of 28 U.S.C.A. § 1821(b) defines full extent of a federal court's power to shift litigation costs); *West Virginia University Hospitals, Inc. v. Casey*, 499 U.S. 83, 111 S.Ct. 1138, 113 L.Ed.2d 68 (1991) (applying Crawford limits to expert witness fees recoverable under 42 U.S.C.A. § 1988, the counterpart for civil rights actions to the attorneys' fee provision of Title VII § 706(k)).

28. *See* § 4.5.

§ 5.11 Compensatory and Punitive Damages for Title VII and Americans With Disabilities Act Violations After November 20, 1991

Section 102 of the Civil Rights Act of 1991, codified at 42 U.S.C.A. § 1981a, authorizes jury trials and compensatory and punitive damages for claimants alleging intentional discrimination in actions under, among other statutes, Title VII and the Americans With Disabilities Act. These remedies are "in addition to any relief authorized by" § 706(g) of Title VII,[1] and the compensatory portion of an award "shall not include backpay, interest on backpay, or any other type of relief authorized under" § 706(g) of Title VII—in other words, the equitable relief available before the Civil Rights Act of 1991.[2] But compensatory and punitive damages are available only if the "complaining party cannot recover under 42 U.S.C.A. 1981."[3] Citing applicable legislative history, however, the EEOC has interpreted the latter restriction only to bar double recovery under Title VII and § 1981, not to interfere with administrative or judicial processing of claims under either statute prior to judgment.[4]

The Act expressly denies either form of damages to challengers of facially neutral practices. Title VII plaintiffs who prevail only by demonstrating the disproportionate adverse impact of neutral practices,[5] or ADA plaintiffs who demonstrate only a failure to reasonably accommodate by an employer who "demonstrates good faith efforts,"[6] are still limited to the traditional, equitable Title VII remedies of prospective relief and back pay. Perhaps more than any other, these provisions manifest the congressional view that intentional discrimination deserves more serious legal sanctions.

Section 1981a also makes compensatory, but not punitive, damages available to plaintiffs who prosecute intentional discrimination claims successfully against a government agency or subdivision.[7] The EEOC has ruled that the Act permits federal employees to recover compensatory damages (for intentional discrimination) during the federal administrative complaints process as well.[8]

---

§ 5.11

1. Section 102 (adding § 1977A(1) to the Revised Statutes, 42 U.S.C.A. § 1977A(1)), 42 U.S.C.A. § 1981a(a)(1).

2. 42 U.S.C.A. § 1981a(b)(2).

3. *Id.*

4. EEOC Policy Guide on Compensatory and Punitive Damages Under 1991 Civil Rights Act, July 7, 1992. BNA Fair Employment Manual 405:7091, 7092 (1992)(hereinafter, "EEOC Damages Guid-

ance"). *See Bradshaw v. University of Maine,* 870 F.Supp. 406 (D.Me.1994) (plaintiff not required to elect an available claim under § 1981 when allegations also state claim under Title VII for the relief provided by new § 1981a).

5. 42 U.S.C.A. § 1981a(a)(1).

6. 42 U.S.C.A. § 1981a(a)(3).

7. *Compare* § 102(b)(2) with § 102(b)(1).

8. *Jackson v. Runyon,* Appeal No. 01923399 (1992).

Punitive damages are authorized against nongovernmental defendants who are proven to have engaged in an unlawful discriminatory practice "with malice or with reckless indifference to the federally protected rights of an aggrieved individual." [9]   Although the precise standards governing jury awards of punitive damages will require considerable case law explication by analogy to punitive damages in tort, it has already been held that, as under §§ 1981 and 1983,[10] compensatory damages are not a prerequisite to a punitive award.[11]

Section 1981a(b)(3) places dollar caps that vary with employer size on the *sum* of compensatory and punitive damages "for each complaining party." [12]   For this purpose, compensatory damages are defined by § 1981a(b)(2) to include monetary relief for "future pecuniary losses, emotional pain, suffering, inconvenience, mental anguish, loss of enjoyment of life, and other nonpecuniary losses." [13]   These caps are set at $50,000 for businesses that employ between 15 and 100 persons [14]; $100,000 where the employer has between 101 and 200 employees; $200,000 where the employer has between 201 and 500 employees; and $300,000 for all employers with 501 or more employees.[15] Because these damages are "in addition to" traditional Title VII equitable relief, complaining parties' recoveries of back pay, interest on backpay, or any other relief formerly available under Title VII before the 1991 amendment may be recovered in full, without regard to the caps.[16] Moreover, despite the somewhat uncertain status of front pay under the pre–1991

---

9.   42 U.S.C.A. § 1981a(b)(1).

10.   *See Smith v. Wade,* 461 U.S. 30, 55 n. 21, 103 S.Ct. 1625, 1639, 75 L.Ed.2d 632 (1983) and textual discussion of Reconstruction Act damages in Chapter 2.

11.   *Hennessy v. Penril Datacomm Networks, Inc.,* 69 F.3d 1344 (7th Cir.1995). *But cf. Kerr-Selgas v. American Airlines, Inc.,* 69 F.3d 1205 (1st Cir.1995) (punitives unavailable absent either compensatory or nominal damages for employment discrimination claim not under federal law).

12.   A plaintiff's argument for recovering up to the cap separately for compensatory and punitive damages has been rejected; the cap defines the maximum amount available for both kinds of harm defined. *Hogan v. Bangor and Aroostook R.R.,* 61 F.3d 1034 (1st Cir.1995). On the other hand, it seems clear that where there are multiple parties who have joined together under FRCP 20 or 23 to assert common claims, "Each complaining party may receive (to the extent appropriate) up to the cap amount." EEOC Memorandum on Computation of Compensatory and Punitive Damages (April 18, 1995). § 1981a(c)(2) further provides that "the court shall not

inform the jury" about the statutory damages caps. This stricture has been held also to preclude counsel from referring to the caps, for example during closing argument. *Sasaki v. Class,* 92 F.3d 232 (4th Cir.1996).

13.   42 U.S.C.A. § 1981a(b)(2).

14.   Certain entities having fewer than 15 employees are nevertheless subject to Title VII—e.g., labor organizations and employment agencies. *See* EEOC Compliance Manual, Vol. II, Sec. 605. BNA FEP Manual 405:6607. Thus the damages caps, applicable in terms only to employers with 15 or more employees, could be read by negative implication to impose unlimited damages liability on those smaller entities, or, alternatively, to free them from damages liability altogether. EEOC has rejected "both interpretations and concludes that all covered employment agencies and labor organizations with 100 or fewer employees are subject to the $50,000 cap on damages." EEOC Damages Guidance, at 405:7093.

15.   Section 102(b)(3), 42 U.S.C.A. § 1981a(b)(3).

16.   EEOC Damages Guidance, 405:7094.

Act case law,[17] EEOC considers it a type of relief previously authorized by Title VII and hence excluded from the § 1981a(b)(2) definition of compensatory damages and in turn not subject to a cap.[18] In any event, a plaintiff with a state law claim that authorizes unlimited damages may avoid the Title VII and ADA damages caps altogether, and in some circumstances may assert that claim in the same federal court action.[19]

Which components of a compensatory damages award are subject to the caps? EEOC has concluded that the general category of compensatory damages encompasses all of the following species of relief: "past pecuniary loss (out-of-pocket loss), future pecuniary loss,[20] and nonpecuniary loss (emotional harm)." Included within pecuniary losses, past or future, are such "quantifiable" losses caused by discriminatory conduct as moving and job search expenses and psychiatric, physical therapy, and other medical expenses.[21] Nonpecuniary losses include damages for "intangible injuries of emotional harm such as emotional pain, suffering, inconvenience, mental anguish, and loss of enjoyment of life," as well as injury to professional standing, character, reputation, credit standing, or health.[22] Section 1981a(b)(3) throws *future pecuniary*, as well as *all nonpecuniary*, losses into the compensatory-cum-punitive damages pot that is subject to a cap. In other words, past pecuniary losses are uncapped. And in the Commission's view the line that divides past from future pecuniary losses is "the date of the resolution of the damage claim, i.e., conciliation, settlement, or the conclusion of litigation."[23]

In sum, the caps limit "only claims that typically do not lend themselves to precise quantification, i.e., punitive damages, future pecuniary losses, and [all] nonpecuniary losses."[24] And although front pay might be considered a form of nonpecuniary loss because it is so devilishly difficult to measure,[25] it is nevertheless removed from the compensatory-punitive pot capped by subsection (b)(3), EEOC believes,

17. *See* text accompanying notes 13–14, § 5.14, *infra.*

18. EEOC Damages Guidance, at 405:7094.

19. See the section on Supplemental Jurisdiction in Chapter 13 on procedure.

20. *See Fitzgerald v. Mountain States Tel. & Tel. Co.,* 46 F.3d 1034 (10th Cir. 1995), *vacated on rehearing in part,* 60 F.3d 837 (10th Cir.1995) (compensatories extended to plaintiff's loss of future business opportunities with defendant).

21. EEOC Damages Guidance, at 405:7095. *See also Malloy v. Monahan,* 73 F.3d 1012 (10th Cir.1996) (permitting recovery of lost profits in Reconstruction Civil Rights Act case).

22. *Id.* at 405:7096. Traditional authority to the effect that an award for emotional distress might rest on the plaintiff's own testimony, without specific evidence of the economic value of that loss, see, e.g.,

Bolden v. SEPTA, 21 F.3d 29 (3d Cir.1994) (collecting cases) and *H.C. by Hewett v. Jarrard,* 786 F.2d 1080, 1088 (11th Cir.1986); *Stallworth v. Shuler,* 777 F.2d 1431, 1435 (11th Cir.1985); *Marable v. Walker,* 704 F.2d 1219, 1220 (11th Cir.1983), is being tested by recent decisions that insist on corroborating testimony by a spouse, coworkers, friends, relatives and perhaps even treating or other medical experts. *See Price v. City of Charlotte, N.C.,* 1996 WL 495542 (4th Cir.1996); *Patterson v. P.H.P. Healthcare Corp.,* 1996 WL 420169 (5th Cir. 1996); *Fitzgerald v. Mountain States Telephone and Telegraph Co.,* 68 F.3d 1257 (10th Cir.1995).

23. *Id.* at 405:7095.

24. *Id.* at 405:7094.

25. *See* text accompanying notes 16 through 19, § 5.14, *infra.*

since it is excluded at the outset from the subsection (b)(2) definition of compensatory damages.

Standards for the award of punitive damages are likely to be borrowed from the principles applied under the Reconstruction Civil Rights Acts. The "malice ... or reckless indifference" required by § 1981a(b)(1) seems in substance indistinguishable from the standard the Supreme Court announced for punitive damages under § 1983: juries may assess punitive damages "when the defendant's conduct is shown to be motivated by evil motive or intent, or when it involves reckless or callous indifference to the federally protected rights of others." [26]

The key question in deciding the availability and appropriate amount of punitive damages is what mental state in addition to that inherent in any intentional violation of Title VII or ADA is requisite for the award. Malice is readily found when there is proof of ill will accompanying the defendant's conduct.[27] Malice will also normally be found where there is proof of retaliation for opposing at least well founded complaints of unlawful activity.[28] EEOC suggests that the following additional unweighted factors should be taken into account: egregiousness of the conduct, as where it shocks or offends the conscience; the nature, extent and severity of the harm suffered by the complaining party; duration of the discriminatory conduct; whether the respondent engaged in similar conduct in the past; evidence of conspiracy or cover-up; and the employer's response after notice to discriminatory conduct by its agents.[29]

Absent one or more of these probative factors, there is a wide range of circumstances in which the propriety of punitives is uncertain. At one extreme, it seems clear that mere proof of an intentional violation does not warrant a punitive award in a variety of situations analogous to the ADA defendant that is expressly exempt from punitives if it makes a good-faith but ultimately inadequate effort to reasonably accommodate an employee's disability. For example, the employer may have been unaware of a statutory prohibition or reasonably believed that its conduct was not reached by the prohibition or relied plausibly on an affirmative defense that privileged its conduct.[30] At the other extreme, a

26. *Smith v. Wade*, 461 U.S. 30, 56, 103 S.Ct. 1625, 1640, 75 L.Ed.2d 632 (1983).

27. *See, e.g., Soderbeck v. Burnett County*, 752 F.2d 285, 289 (7th Cir.), *cert. denied*, 471 U.S. 1117, 105 S.Ct. 2360, 86 L.Ed.2d 261 (1985).

28. *See., e.g., Hunter v. Allis–Chalmers*, 797 F.2d 1417, 1425 (7th Cir.1986); *Erebia v. Chrysler Plastic Products Corp.*, 772 F.2d 1250, 1260 (6th Cir.1985), *cert. denied*, 475 U.S. 1015, 106 S.Ct. 1197, 89 L.Ed.2d 311 (1986).

29. EEOC Damages Guidance, at 405: 7100–7101. *See Preston v. Income Producing Management, Inc.*, 871 F.Supp. 411

(D.Kan.1994) (employer inaction after sexual harassment complaint, coupled with manager's contribution to harassing environment, warrant punitives).

30. *See, e.g., Hazen Paper Co. v. Biggins*, 507 U.S. 604, 113 S.Ct. 1701, 123 L.Ed.2d 338 (1993) employer not liable even for ADEA liquidated damages if it "incorrectly but in good faith and nonrecklessly believes that the statute permits a particular age-based decision...." *But see Barbour v. Merrill*, 48 F.3d 1270 (D.C.Cir.1995) (evidence establishing intentional civil rights violation under Reconstruction Acts may suffice for punitive award, provided

trial court's instructions were held to authorize punitive damages in a reconstruction act case when, in addition to proof of an intentional wrong, it merely advised the jury that such awards were designed to punish the defendant for "outrageous conduct" and "to deter him and others like him from similar conduct in the future." [31]

Courts have particularly struggled with establishing reasonable limits on the amount of a punitive award. In general, the award should "bear some relation" to the nature of defendant's conduct and the harm it caused; [32] and taking defendant's resources into account, it should "sting" rather than "destroy." [33] But the EEOC takes the position that in general punitive awards under Title VII and ADA should rarely be grossly excessive, because the sum of punitive damages together with future pecuniary losses and all nonpecuniary losses must stay within the caps of § 1981a(b)(3). [34]

Library References:

C.J.S. Civil Rights §§ 416, 418–419, 422, 425.
West's Key No. Digests, Civil Rights ☞400.

§ 5.12 1996 Legislation Treats Virtually All Settlement or Judgment Proceeds in Employment Discrimination and Civil Rights Actions As Includable In Gross Income, Except In Cases of Physical Injury

Plaintiffs are of course more inclined to settle for less if they are persuaded that the proceeds of a settlement will not be taxed. Until August 20, when President Clinton signed the Small Business Job Protection Act of 1996, Section 104(a)(2) of the Internal Revenue Code, 26 U.S.C. § 104(a)(2), excluded from gross income "the amount of any *damages* received (whether by suit or agreement ...) *on account of personal injuries* or sickness...." [1] An elaborate and confusing jurisprudence developed separately under ADEA and Title VII concerning the extent to which various elements of recovery under those statutes could

jury finds that defendant's conduct merits punishment).

31. *Rowlett v. Anheuser–Busch, Inc.,* 832 F.2d 194, 205 (1st Cir.1987).

32. *Rowlett,* 832 F.2d at 207. One circuit, for example, has held that a punitive award may not be given in the maximum amount permitted by an applicable cap unless the violation was egregious. *Hennessy v. Penril Datacomm Networks, Inc.,* 69 F.3d 1344 (7th Cir.1995). *Compare Emmel v. Coca–Cola Bottling Co. of Chicago,* 95 F.3d 627 (7th Cir.1996) (affirming maximum punitive award because defendant intentionally disregarded statutory rights).

33. *Keenan v. City of Philadelphia,* 1991 WL 40355 (E.D.Pa.1991), *order affirmed in*

part, vacated in part 983 F.2d 459 (3d Cir. 1992). EEOC has summarized a number of factors relevant to ascertaining the defendant's financial position for this purpose. EEOC Damages Guidance, at 405:7101– 7102. *See Chavez v. Keat,* 34 Cal.App.4th 1406, 41 Cal.Rptr.2d 72 (1995) (citing federal rule that places burden of producing evidence of defendant's financial condition on defendant).

34. EEOC Damages Guidance, at 405:7101 n.18.

§ 5.12

1. 26 U.S.C.A. § 104(a)(2) (emphasis added).

be excludable under Section 104(a)(2) as "damages" received by a taxpayer plaintiff "on account of personal injuries or sickness." [2]

The "personal injuries or sickness" requirement was acutely raised by employment discrimination, and to a lesser degree civil rights, claims. In most such cases the plaintiff's immediate injuries, while arguably "personal," and commonly resulting in emotional distress that is sometimes medically treated, are nonphysical. In 1995 the Supreme Court held that in the typical, nonphysical situation, neither the back pay nor the liquidated damages recoverable in an action under the Age Discrimination in Employment Act could ordinarily be considered "damages" on account of "personal injuries." [3] That decision rested uncomfortably with the Court's strong suggestion three years earlier that the back pay and emotional distress damages recoverable under Title VII, as amended by the 1991 Civil Rights Acts, would be excludable from the plaintiff's income under Section 104(a)(2). [4] At the same time, it was settled by text added to Section 104 in 1989 that punitive damages, available since November 1991 in Title VII actions, would not be excludable in a case—like most employment discrimination and many civil rights cases—that did "not involv[e] physical injury or physical sickness." (Although the issue was far from settled, the implication was that punitive damages were excludable in cases that did involve physical injury or sickness.)

All this changed with the stroke of President Clinton's pen. Two additions to the text of Section 104(a)(2), underlined for the reader's convenience, tell most of the tale:

> (a).... gross income does not include—

> (2) the amount of any damages (*other than punitive damages*) received (whether by suit or agreement ...) on account of personal *physical* injuries or *physical* sickness;

The rest of the tale is told by an addendum to Section 104(a):

> For purposes of paragraph (2), emotional distress shall not be treated as a physical injury or physical sickness. The preceding sentence shall not apply to an amount of damages not in excess of the amount paid for medical care ... attributable to emotional distress.

The English translation? The most important change from current law, particularly for Title VII cases, is the requirement of *physical* injury as a precondition for exclusion under Section 104(a)(2). In the usual Title VII or ADEA case, where the employer's conduct does not result in

2. The case law and Treasury regulations implementing Section 104(a)(2) still govern the excludability of amounts received under binding written agreements, court decrees, or mediation awards in effect on, or issued on or before, September 13, 1995, or of amounts actually received by the taxpayer (under agreements executed after September 13, 1995) on or before August 20, 1996, the effective date of the amendments. The former law is discussed in detail in Lewis, *Litigating Civil Rights and Employment Discrimination Cases* § 7.27 (West 1996).

3. *Commissioner v. Schleier*, ___ U.S. ___, 115 S.Ct. 2159, 132 L.Ed.2d 294 (1995).

4. *United States v. Burke*, 504 U.S. 229, 112 S.Ct. 1867, 119 L.Ed.2d 34 (1992).

"physical" injury or sickness, no part of any judgment or settlement for back or front pay will be eligible for exclusion under Section 104(a)(2). Second, because the first sentence of the addendum excludes emotional distress from the Section 104(a)(2) definition of "physical" injury or sickness, the part of any settlement or judgment representing recovery for the intangible harms of emotional distress will also be nonexcludable in non-physical cases.[5] Third, however, where a civil rights (or, more rarely, employment discrimination) plaintiff does suffer some actual "physical" injury as the result of the defendant's conduct, he may exclude "any damages" received in respect of those injuries. Accordingly, the pertinent House Committee Report indicates that such a plaintiff may exclude not just the part of a settlement or judgment received on account of lost income, but also the part received on account of emotional distress. Fourth, because of the "(other than punitive damages)" language, punitive damages will now almost never[6] be eligible for exclusion, even when they are awarded in cases of *physical* injury.

The essence of these changes, as applicable to claimants under federal employment discrimination and civil rights laws, may be summarized as follows: (1) At least some "physical" (probably bodily) injury or sickness is necessary for the taxpayer to exclude from gross income *any* settlement or judgment proceeds, except the relatively minor portion representing reimbursement for medical expenses attributable to emotional distress; (2) where the settlement or judgment resolves a claim involving *some* "physical" injury or sickness, the taxpayer may exclude all back pay, front pay, or compensatory damages that are received "on account of" that injury or sickness, including *all* emotional distress damages, not just those that reimburse for medical expenses; but (3), even in cases of actual physical injury or sickness, punitive damages will not be excludable.

The threshold requirement for excludability is whether, assuming the plaintiff obtains the kind of "damages" for "personal injuries" that § 104(a)(2) makes excludable, she receives them "by suit or agreement." A recent appellate decision holds that the receipt by an employee of a

---

5. The second sentence of the addendum offers a tiny consolation to the employment discrimination or civil rights plaintiff who suffers no actual physical injury but incurs medical expenses attributable to emotional distress. That sentence *treats* the portion of any settlement or judgment representing reimbursement for those expenses as a "physical" injury and therefore excludable. (Those who have taken a course in basic income taxation will know that this exclusion for medical expenses should result in better tax treatment than a mere deduction.) But of course the portion of a recovery attributable to nonpecuniary, intangible emotional distress will usually be much greater than the medical expenses for that distress; and intangible emotional distress is defined as something other than

physical injury or sickness, and therefore as nonexcludable, by the first sentence of the addendum. Accordingly, except for medical expense reimbursement, recoveries for emotional distress will be nonexcludable under amended Section 104(a)(2), provided the defendant's conduct did not cause some *actual* physical injury.

6. In certain wrongful death actions resulting from the infliction of physical injury or sickness, punitive damages will continue to be excludable where the applicable state law authorizes *only* punitive awards for wrongful death. 26 U.S.C.A. § 104(c). This exception should have little or no application to employment discrimination or civil rights claims under federal law.

lump sum termination payment that the company increased because of his willingness to waive all claims relating to his employment or termination, including claims related to age discrimination, could not be considered "damages," or therefore the result of a "settlement," so defined. The court reasoned that a "claim must be asserted before it can be settled; plaintiff waived all claims before asserting them...." [7] This ruling is apparently in some tension with Tax Court practice, the waiver procedure approved for ADEA claims by the OWBPA, as well as the expressed preference of § 118 of the 1991 Civil Rights Act for alternative means of dispute resolution.[8] Its lesson to older employees facing a reduction in force would appear to be not to enter into a valid agreement waiving ADEA rights under the terms of OWBPA, but instead to have a lawyer assert a formal charge or claim before settling with the employer. This seems an unnecessary expense and formality, since it is well established that sums paid pursuant to settlement of an ADEA claim, once a claim is asserted, may be excludable under § 104(a)(2).[9]

C. TITLE VII AND ADEA REMEDIES COMPARED

§ 5.13 In General

Before the 1991 legislation, Title VII plaintiffs were limited to actual out of pocket loss in the form of back or front pay. By contrast, plaintiffs under the Age Discrimination in Employment Act of 1967 (ADEA) could also recover, in willful cases, an equal additional amount of liquidated damages.[1] It is true that after the amendments, the recovery by the Title VII intentional discrimination plaintiff of compensatory or punitive damages or both may exceed the liquidated double damages available to the willful violation plaintiff under ADEA; and that ADEA plaintiffs, even after the 1991 amendments, may not recover compensatory or punitive damages.[2] In practice, however, many ADEA plaintiffs will still recover more. Long-tenured older workers typically receive far higher base compensation than most Title VII plaintiffs, and

---

7. *Taggi v. United States*, 35 F.3d 93 (2d Cir.1994).

8. *See* §§ 7.6 to 7.8, *infra*.

9. *Downey v. Commissioner of Internal Revenue*, 33 F.3d 836 (7th Cir.1994); *Bennett v. United States*, 30 Fed.Cl. 396 (1994); *Rickel v. Commissioner of Internal Revenue*, 900 F.2d 655 (3d Cir.1990).

§ 5.13

1. Age Discrimination in Employment Act of 1967, § 7(d), 29 U.S.C.A. § 626(b) (1982), incorporates by reference the remedies authorized under the Fair Labor Standards Act (FLSA), 29 U.S.C.A. §§ 216–17 (1982). The liquidated damages authorized in turn by § 216(b) of FLSA are defined as

an additional amount equal to the amount of unlawfully withheld unpaid minimum wages. The Supreme Court has held that liquidated damages are appropriate when an employer knows that, or recklessly disregards whether, its conduct violates the ADEA. *McLaughlin v. Richland Shoe Co.*, 486 U.S. 128, 108 S.Ct. 1677, 100 L.Ed.2d 115 (1988). See Chapter 7, Section 7.10 for a discussion of ADEA remedies.

2. *Capparell v. National Health Management, Inc.*, 1993 WL 516399 (E.D.Pa. 1993). For more on the effects of the 1991 Act on ADEA, see Eglit, "The Age Discrimination In Employment Act, Title VII, And The Civil Rights Act of 1991: Three Acts And A Dog That Didn't Bark," 39 Wayne L. Rev. 1093 (1993).

ADEA juries have been notoriously willing to deem the circumstances of an older worker's discharge "willful."

ADEA plaintiffs are more likely to maintain their remedial edge with respect to smaller employers. The Title VII cap on the sum of compensatory damages (defined to include all monetary relief for future pecuniary and past and future nonpecuniary losses) and punitive damages is $100,000 where the employer has between 101 and 200 employees; $200,000 where the employer has between 201 and 500 employees; $300,000 for larger employers; but only $50,000 for the 98% of all businesses that employ 100 or fewer persons.[3]

Another surviving advantage for ADEA plaintiffs, at least textually, is the availability of jury trials in any kind of action where legal relief is sought, even where the plaintiff complains only of a facially neutral practice.[4] In reality, however, although the new Act in terms authorizes Title VII jury trials only for claims that authorize compensatory or punitive damages, which in turn means claims of intentional discrimination, most Title VII plaintiffs assert only such claims; they should therefore gain the advantages of jury trial to the same extent as their ADEA counterparts. In view of the Act's provisions easing the proof under Title VII of intentional discrimination in mixed-motive situations, and its incentives to assert intentional claims to obtain compensatory and punitive damages, most Title VII plaintiffs may be expected to assert at least one claim alleging discriminatory intent (and, as discussed in Chapter 7, are more likely to prevail in indirect evidence and mixed-motive cases than their ADEA counterparts). To the extent that facts found by the jury on the intentional discrimination claim may be relevant to a separate neutral practice/adverse impact claim, the jury's findings on the intent claim should bind the trial court in reaching its determination about the neutral practice.[5] Moreover, since relatively few age discrimination claims proceed on the neutral practice theory, and indeed there is a serious question after *Biggins v. Hazen Paper Co.*

---

3. Section 102(b)(3). The 98% estimate comes from the Dole interpretive memorandum, supra note 30, § 4.10. The memorandum does not state if the 98% estimate includes the many employers too small to be covered by Title VII at all, i.e., those employing fewer than 15 employees during at least 20 calendar weeks in the current or preceding calendar year. Title VII § 701(b), 42 U.S.C.A. § 2000e(b).

4. *Lowe v. Commack Union Free School Dist.*, 886 F.2d 1364 (2d Cir.1989), is an example of a neutral practice case under ADEA. Whether the theory survives the Supreme Court's decision in *Hazen Paper Co. v. Biggins*, 507 U.S. 604, 113 S.Ct. 1701, 123 L.Ed.2d 338 (1993), is discussed in Chapter 7.

5. Where mixed legal and equitable claims are intertwined by common questions of fact, the Supreme Court has required that the legal claims be tried first to the jury. When the trial court thereafter determines the equitable claims, it will be bound by the jury's explicit or implicit fact findings on the common questions. This order of trial preserves the seventh amendment rights of the party demanding jury trial on legal claims. See *Lytle v. Household Mfg. Inc.*, 494 U.S. 545, 110 S.Ct. 1331, 108 L.Ed.2d 504 (1990) (applying *Beacon Theatres, Inc. v. Westover*, 359 U.S. 500, 79 S.Ct. 948, 3 L.Ed.2d 988 (1959) to an action presenting intertwined claims under Title VII and 42 U.S.C.A. § 1981).

whether that theory continues to be viable under ADEA,[6] Title VII and ADEA plaintiffs in practice will enjoy the right to demand a jury trial with respect to the vast majority of claims each asserts.

D. RETROACTIVE SENIORITY FOR PROVEN VICTIMS OF DISCRIMINATION—A FIRST LOOK AT THE PROBLEM OF "REVERSE DISCRIMINATION"

§ 5.14　In General

More complex and controversial than the availability of back pay in Title VII actions are awards of retroactive "remedial" seniority to victorious discriminatees who secure orders directing their hire, promotion or reinstatement. These are awards of seniority that enhance the measure of employer-paid compensation or benefits. Because remedial seniority restores discriminatees to their "rightful place"—the rung on the ladder to which they likely would have climbed between the date of discrimination and date of judgment—and produces benefits that are paid by the adjudicated wrongdoer (the employer), it serves both Title VII remedial objectives, deterrence as well as compensation. Accordingly, in *Franks v. Bowman Transportation Co.*,[1] the Supreme Court held that retroactive remedial seniority for those economic purposes is presumptively available on the same terms as back pay. In doing so the Court rejected the argument that § 703(h)—which insulates bona fide seniority systems from being declared unlawful, and therefore protects them from *wholesale* dismantling by injunction—also prohibits the *incremental* adjustment of places on the seniority ladder that results when judges award discriminatees fictional, retroactive seniority as a remedy for an underlying discrimination in hiring, assignment or promotions.

On the other hand, retroactive seniority also serves an alternative or additional purpose: improving the discriminatee's position relative to other employees in competing for scarce job resources like better-paying positions, more favorable hours, or, most critically, protection against demotion or layoff. Unlike seniority for benefits purposes, retroactive "competitive" seniority furthers only the goal of compensation, not employer deterrence. In *Franks*, the Court recognized that such protection is necessary to make a proven victim of discrimination whole; without it, she is vulnerable to layoff, termination or simply poorer job assignments without any of the seniority protection that she would almost surely have earned absent the employer's unlawful conduct.[2] It

---

6. *See* Chapter 7 on the neutral practice/disproportionate adverse impact theory under ADEA.

§ 5.14
1. 424 U.S. 747, 96 S.Ct. 1251, 47 L.Ed.2d 444 (1976).

2. *Franks v. Bowman Transportation Co.*, 424 U.S. 747, 96 S.Ct. 1251, 47 L.Ed.2d 444 (1976).

therefore held, following *Albemarle Paper Co. v. Moody*,[3] that the "competitive" as well as the "benefits" brand of retroactive fictional seniority is presumptively available.

A year later, in *International Brotherhood of Teamsters v. United States*,[4] the Court also agreed that an award of retroactive seniority, because it is essential to redress proven discrimination, is also not a "preference" prohibited by § 703(j).[5] But there, in contrast to the situation in *Franks*, immediate implementation of retroactive seniority for competitive purposes would have visited highly visible harm on incumbent employees already out on layoff: restoring the discriminatees to "their" rung on the seniority ladder would have delayed the incumbents' day of recall. On those facts the Court drew back from authorizing the automatic or immediate implementation of retroactive seniority for competitive purposes. Rather, to decide "when" and "the rate at which" discriminatees may be made whole by such awards, it directed the district courts to exercise their "qualities of mercy and practicality"[6] in balancing several unweighted equities. These include the number of protected group and non-protected group persons interested in the scarce resource, the number of current vacancies, and the economic prospects of the industry.[7] *Teamsters* left undisturbed the *Franks* holding that seniority for benefits purposes should be implemented presumptively, unequivocally and immediately after issuance of a judgment.

Although the Supreme Court has implied that § 706(g) provides limited discretion to "bump" an incumbent employee in order to reinstate a proven victim or "discriminatee," lower courts have displayed great reluctance to do so,[8] even when the order protects the displaced employee's former level of compensation.[9] They have instead sometimes awarded the discriminatee "front pay." Front pay is a discretionary remedy granted by the court as a substitute for reinstatement if reinstatement is impossible, impracticable or inequitable. It may be the only feasible way to make a victim of discrimination whole where there is no available position in which to reinstate her, or where, as in a constructive discharge or other harassment case, reinstatement would be unsuccessful or unproductive because of the workplace hostility that either prompted the claim or resulted from its prosecution.[10]

3. 422 U.S. 405, 95 S.Ct. 2362, 45 L.Ed.2d 280 (1975). See text accompanying notes 5–6, § 5.10, *supra*.

4. 431 U.S. 324, 97 S.Ct. 1843, 52 L.Ed.2d 396 (1977).

5. *Teamsters*, 431 U.S. at 375 n. 61, 97 S.Ct. at 1975 n. 61.

6. *Teamsters*, 431 U.S. at 375, 97 S.Ct. at 1875 (quoting *Hecht Co. v. Bowles*, 321 U.S. 321, 329–330, 64 S.Ct. 587, 591–592, 88 L.Ed. 754 (1944)).

7. *Teamsters*; see also *Franks* (Powell, J., concurring).

8. *See, e.g., Walsdorf v. Board of Commissioners*, 857 F.2d 1047 (5th Cir.1988);

Harper v. General Grocers Co., 590 F.2d 713 (8th Cir.1979).

9. *Patterson v. American Tobacco Co.*, 535 F.2d 257 (4th Cir.), *cert. denied*, 429 U.S. 920, 97 S.Ct. 314, 50 L.Ed.2d 286 (1976).

10. *See, e.g., Robinson v. Southeastern Pennsylvania Transportation Authority*, 982 F.2d 892 (3d Cir.1993) (court declined to reinstate victorious plaintiff who had characterized his supervisors as "South African dogs"); *Ellis v. Ringgold School Dist.*, 832 F.2d 27 (3d Cir.1987), *cert. denied*, 494 U.S. 1005, 110 S.Ct. 1298, 108 L.Ed.2d 475 (1990); *Sanchez v. Philip Morris Inc.*, 774

Squarely endorsed by only one member of the Supreme Court,[11] the lower federal courts have come to presume the front pay award appropriate where reinstatement is infeasible or ill advised.[12]   Most circuit courts, in decisions before the 1991 Act, held front pay available under Title VII.[13]   The principal argument against front pay revolved around the fact that all Title VII remedies were then equitable, and some judges characterized front pay as "legal."[14]   Now that the 1991 Act adds legal remedies to the menu of relief under Title VII, the Supreme Court, in dictum, has noted the availability of front pay with approval.[15]

Front pay leaves the incumbent in place and, beginning as of final judgment, orders the employer to pay the discriminatee an amount equivalent to what he would earn if actually reinstated.[16]   Because of the uncertain duration of the period during which the victim of discrimination would have remained employed after judgment, or at what level and pay, the front pay remedy is fraught with computational difficulties. Given its purpose to restore an injured party to the position she would have occupied absent the employer's unlawful discrimination, determining the appropriateness, duration and amount of front pay is an exercise that entails "predicting the future":

> "[S]uch an exercise involves an attempt to determine the degree to which a plaintiff possesses qualities that would make plaintiff successful in attaining career advancement.   For advancements that come simply with longevity, courts have uniformly assumed that such advancement would occur, in the absence of specific disqualifying information.

> On the other hand, courts will not automatically assume that a person discriminated against possesses characteristics so sterling as

F.Supp. 626 (W.D.Okl.1991), *reversed on other grounds*, 992 F.2d 244 (10th Cir.1993) (front pay preferable to reinstatement where plaintiff would have to work with employees who testified against him). Front pay is a substitute for, not a supplement to, reinstatement; remedies may not be cumulative. *Suggs v. ServiceMaster Educ. Food Management,* 72 F.3d 1228 (6th Cir.1996).

11. *See Franks* (Burger, C.J., concurring).

12. *See, e.g., Carter v. Sedgwick County, Kansas,* 36 F.3d 952 (10th Cir.1994); *Farber v. Massillon Bd. of Education,* 917 F.2d 1391 (6th Cir.1990), *cert. denied,* 498 U.S. 1082, 111 S.Ct. 952, 112 L.Ed.2d 1041 (1991).

13. *Compare Weaver v. Casa Gallardo, Inc.,* 922 F.2d 1515, 1528 (11th Cir.1991) *and Green v. U.S.X. Corp.* 843 F.2d 1511, 1531–32 (3d Cir.1988) *and Pitre v. Western*

Elec. Co., 843 F.2d 1262, 1278–79 (10th Cir.1988) *and Shore v. Federal Express Corp.,* 777 F.2d 1155, 1159 (6th Cir.1985) *and Goss v. Exxon Office Systems Co.,* 747 F.2d 885, 889 (3d Cir.1984) (acknowledging the remedy) *with McKnight v. General Motors Corp.,* 908 F.2d 104, 117 (7th Cir.1990) (expressing doubt whether Title VII authorizes front pay, but asserting that the ADEA does). *See* Belton, *Remedies in Employment Discrimination Law* § 10.3 (John Wiley, 1992) (citing cases).

14. *McKnight v. General Motors Corp., supra,* 908 F.2d at 116–117.

15. *United States v. Burke,* 504 U.S. 229, 238 n. 9, 112 S.Ct. 1867, 1873 n. 9, 119 L.Ed.2d 34 (1992).

16. *See Patterson v. American Tobacco Co.,* 535 F.2d 257 (4th Cir.), *cert. denied ,* 429 U.S. 920, 97 S.Ct. 314, 50 L.Ed.2d 286 (1976).

to receive every advancement not made illegal or logically impossible under the employer's rules."[17]

The award will not necessarily terminate when plaintiff quits subsequent, substitute employment; on the other hand, in recognition of the duty to mitigate, the employer need only pay such a plaintiff the difference between the amount she would have received had she remained employed (or secured substantially equivalent employment) and the amount she could have continued to receive in the *lesser*-paying substitute job that she quit.[18]

It appears that courts also enjoy equitable discretion to reduce the front pay award by amounts received from "collateral sources," a question on which the circuits are split as applied to backpay.[19]

All that can be said with confidence is that purely arbitrary limits on front pay may be overturned as an abuse of the trial court's discretion.[20] On occasion, awards of as long as 25 years have been made when that represents plaintiff's first eligibility for a full pension.[21]

Lower courts have divided over how to allocate front pay issues between judge and jury. The First Circuit, for example, appears to allow juries to determine not only the amount of front pay but the threshold question of its availability.[22] By contrast, the Sixth Circuit insists that the propriety of front pay in any amount is an equitable question for the court that "must ordinarily precede ... submission of the case to the jury."[23] An Eighth Circuit opinion articulates the same position, holding that the jury decides only the appropriate amount.[24] And the dominant view is that in computing an appropriate amount, the jury may rely on lay testimony about future earnings and other compensation, as well as appropriate inflation and discount rates.[25]

---

17. *Griffin v. Michigan Dept. of Corrections,* 5 F.3d 186, 189 (6th Cir.1993).

18. *Shore v. Federal Express Corp.,* 42 F.3d 373 (6th Cir.1994). *See Suggs v. ServiceMaster Educ. Food Management, supra* note 10 (directing district court to specify the duration, amount and end date of award, and to deduct amounts plaintiff could earn during front pay period through reasonable efforts to secure comparable substitute employment).

19. *See Lussier v. Runyon,* 50 F.3d 1103 (1st Cir.1995) (case under Rehabilitation Act of 1973).

20. *See, e.g., Carter v. Sedgwick County, Kansas,* 36 F.3d 952 (10th Cir.1994) (reversing a six-month limit on front pay and directing trial court to fashion a front pay award that would compensate the victim "for the continuing future effects of discrimination until the victim can be made whole.") (quoting its prior decision in *Car-*

ter v. Sedgwick County, 929 F.2d 1501, 1505 (10th Cir.1991)).

21. *Padilla v. Metro-North Commuter Railroad,* 92 F.3d 117 (2d Cir.1996) (over 20 years of front pay in case under ADEA); *Tyler v. Bethlehem Steel,* 958 F.2d 1176 (2d Cir.1992) (17 years of front pay in ADEA case).

22. *Sinai v. New England Telephone & Telegraph Co.,* 3 F.3d 471 (1st Cir.1993).

23. *Roush v. KFC National Management Co.,* 10 F.3d 392 (6th Cir.1993).

24. *Cassino v. Reichhold Chemicals, Inc.,* 817 F.2d 1338 (9th Cir.1987), *cert. denied,* 484 U.S. 1047, 108 S.Ct. 785, 98 L.Ed.2d 870 (1988). The Court also held that the jury must reduce the amount of a front pay award to the extent it finds the plaintiff failed reasonably to mitigate damages.

25. *Id.* at 1345 (citing cases).

E. AFFIRMATIVE ACTION BY "VOLUNTARY" PROGRAMS AND JUDICIAL DECREES

§ 5.15 In General

"Voluntary," "benign" employer affirmative action, and reverse discriminatory remedies imposed by court order or consent decree, raise similar yet legally distinct questions of fairness as between minority and majority group employees. Strictly speaking, employer affirmative action in the form of self-imposed quotas or goals does not really implicate the judiciary's remedial authority under § 706(g) at all. An employer simply institutes racial or gender preferences, without court compulsion, typically to avoid lawsuits by the group benefiting from the preference or to preserve federal contracts that require affirmative action.[1] Rather, such a plan is unlawful, if at all, because it operates to prefer members of defined minority or female groups or classes, rather than individuals proven to have suffered discrimination at the hands of the defendant employer. As a result, these preferences are suspect under § 703 as ordinary unlawful employment practices directed against any majority group members or males who are denied employment opportunities by the plan.[2] The jeopardy would seem considerable because the Court has regularly emphasized that the statute seeks to protect individuals from discrimination on the basis of group characteristics, rather than groups as such.[3]

But the Supreme Court, in a landmark 1979 opinion, *United Steelworkers v. Weber*,[4] that expressly elevated a supposed legislative "spirit" over statutory text, gave qualified approval to "voluntary," "benign" racial preferences. A majority held that the employer there had lawfully taken race into account in preferring black employees as a group for admission to an on-the-job training program—a preference that on its face violated the specific terms of § 703(d). The Court acknowledged that the white race of Brian Weber was the factor that resulted in his denial of the employment benefit, in apparent violation of that section. But it concluded from the spirit animating Title VII's enactment that

---

§ 5.15

1. Thus challenges by white or male plaintiffs to voluntary affirmative action plans have been distinguished from reverse discrimination claims based on the employer's implementation of an agreement settling charges of discrimination already pending before EEOC or in court. In the latter setting, employers almost always prevail with the argument that a settlement in good faith of a charge of discrimination is a legitimate, nondiscriminatory reason for the hiring or promotion decision under

challenge. See *Marcantel v. State of La., Dept. of Transportation*, 37 F.3d 197 (5th Cir.1994), discussed in Chapter 3, above.

2. *See, e.g., Billish v. City of Chicago*, 962 F.2d 1269 (7th Cir.1992); *Baker v. Elmwood Distrib. Inc.*, 940 F.2d 1013 (7th Cir.1991); *United States v. City of Chicago*, 870 F.2d 1256 (7th Cir.1989).

3. *See, e.g., Teal, Manhart.*

4. 443 U.S. 193, 99 S.Ct. 2721, 61 L.Ed.2d 480 (1979).

Congress would not have intended § 703 to apply in the context of the "benign" program at issue. The Court relied instead on a weak negative pregnant from § 703(j), which provides that nothing in Title VII shall "require" employers with work forces racially imbalanced vis-a-vis surrounding local population percentages to grant minorities preferential treatment in order to redress such imbalances. Section 703(j), however, was not at all on point, for Brian Weber was certainly not arguing that the defendants were required to discriminate against him. Rather, he was claiming that § 703(d)—so directly implicated by the training program opportunity in question that, as the dissent observed, it might have been written with him in mind—plainly prohibited that discrimination.

Further, it appeared from the *Weber* opinion that an employer could justifiably adopt race-conscious programs of this type whenever it found a manifest underrepresentation of blacks in a traditionally segregated job category; the employer need not first uncover evidence of its *own* prior discrimination in filling those positions.[5] Finally, the employer plan in *Weber* was approved despite being arguably involuntary: the plan was adopted after the Office of Federal Contract Compliance Programs had threatened the employer with debarment from federal contracts under Executive Order 11246 if it did not increase its skilled minority representation.

Perhaps to ease its misgivings about approving a form of race discrimination that the text of § 703(d) expressly prohibited, the *Weber* majority listed a number of sanitizing factors to circumscribe the scope of lawful "benign" discrimination. It observed that the employer plan before it did not require white employees to be discharged and therefore did not "unnecessarily trammel" their interests; that it did not absolutely bar white employees from the skilled positions, but merely limited their numbers; and that it was a temporary measure, intended not to maintain a racial balance but to eliminate a manifest imbalance in the skilled job categories. The Court satisfied itself on these points again in *Johnson v. Transportation Agency of Santa Clara County,*[6] when it extended the *Weber* principle by upholding an explicit *gender* preference for *promotions,* this time in the face of the apparently plain prohibition of § 703(a). But it has been held that where race is used as a tie-breaker to choose which employee will be subject to *layoff,* the minority preference plan violates Title VII because it is "overly intrusive to the rights of nonminorities."[7] In a highly-publicized reverse-discrimination case, a public school system's desire for racial diversity among its faculty was held not a permissible purpose justifying severe harm to a nonminority employee under Title VII, even on the assumption that Title VII

---

5. The Court confirmed this reading of *Weber* in *Johnson v. Transportation Agency,* 480 U.S. 616, 633 n. 10, 107 S.Ct. 1442 1453 n. 10, 94 L.Ed.2d 615 (1987).

6. 480 U.S. 616, 107 S.Ct. 1442, 94 L.Ed.2d 615 (1987).

7. *United States v. Board of Education of Piscataway,* 832 F.Supp. 836, 850 (D.N.J. 1993), *affirmed,* 91 F.3d 1547 (3d Cir.), *cert. filed* ___ U.S. ___, ___ S.Ct. ___, ___ L.Ed.2d ___, 65 U.S.L.W. 3354 (1996).

would permit more race-conscious preferential treatment under such a program than would the Supreme Court's current race-neutral concept of equal protection.[8] Moreover, even when the sting of an affirmative action program is felt only by an applicant for employment—that is, affects initial hire rather than promotion, layoff, or discharge—a program that absolutely excludes members of one race violates Title VII.[9]

More forthrightly in *Johnson* than in *Weber*, Justice Brennan for the majority acknowledged that the employer need not itself have firm or indeed any evidence of its own prior discrimination against the group that benefits from the program. Instead, it is a sufficient predicate for instituting a race- or gender-based affirmative action program that the beneficiary group is merely underrepresented in a traditionally segregated job category for any reason—societal prejudice, self selection, discrimination by other businesses or unions. Further, "underrepresentation" may be measured in relation to that group's representation in the surrounding labor market, unrefined for interest or qualifications. And the Court even dispensed with the necessity of a specific end date for the program because no specific number of slots were set aside for members of the beneficiary group. But race-conscious affirmative action must have the purpose of remedying the effects of past discrimination against a group that itself was the victim of that discrimination.[10]

Affirmative action plans have fared less well when challenged as violations of equal protection. For example, the Court concluded in *Wygant v. Jackson Board of Education*[11] that a public employer, before instituting such a program, must have "convincing evidence" of its own prior discrimination and must employ means narrowly tailored to rectify that conduct. The collective bargaining agreement in *Wygant* required the layoff of non-minority teachers with greater seniority than minority teachers who were retained, a feature that might also have offended the *Weber* sanitizing factor of "unnecessary trammeling." In any event, the *Wygant* plurality's broader approach commanded a majority of the Court

8. *Id.*

9. That is the position advanced by the Department of Justice in *United States v. Illinois State University,* ___ F.Supp. ___, 1996 WL 640398 (C.D.Ill.1996) (complaint filed March 2, 1995).

10. *Cunico v. Pueblo School District No. 60,* 917 F.2d 431, 437 (10th Cir.1990). A recent circuit decision extends the Supreme Court's *Johnson* rationale by permitting ad hoc gender discrimination against males in the assignment of shifts at a state prison, even absent any formal affirmative action plan. The court reasoned that it could employ the limiting factors of *Weber* and *Johnson* instead of finding the gender discrimination per se unlawful because the discriminating assignments favored women, whom it deemed a specially protected Title VII class. It concluded that the "minimal restriction" on male employment opportunities was justified by legitimate penological and privacy concerns furthered by the gender based assignment policy. *Tharp v. Iowa Dep't of Corrections,* 68 F.3d 223 (8th Cir.1995), *cert. denied,* ___ U.S. ___, 116 S.Ct. 1420, 134 L.Ed.2d 545 (1996). In effect this approach permits an employer to defend express discrimination without having to establish a BFOQ. *But see Smith v. Virginia Commonwealth Univ.,* 84 F.3d 672 (4th Cir.1996) (en banc) (female-preferential salary increases informally instituted in response to salary equity study not necessarily a defense to Title VII and Equal Pay Act reverse discrimination claims by male employees).

11. 476 U.S. 267, 106 S.Ct. 1842, 90 L.Ed.2d 260 (1986).

in *City of Richmond v. J.A. Croson Co.*[12], where the Court struck down a municipal program to set aside a minimum amount of subcontracting work for minority business enterprises. The Court insisted that the Equal Protection Clause is violated whenever government takes race into account unless (1) it has a compelling justification and (2) the means adopted are narrowly tailored to go only so far as that justification requires. A circuit court, taking note of the first of these *Croson* requirements, has observed that a local government will now be hard pressed to justify a race-based set-aside program unless it can offer current statistical evidence demonstrating its own prior discriminatory practices and their ongoing effects.[13]

In public contracting and employment settings, it is not a sufficiently compelling justification for the government to offer a purportedly "benign" preference designed to redress broad societal or historical discrimination against African–Americans; in general, race has been accepted as a lawful factor in doling out benefits only to redress a governmental unit's own prior discrimination, and only as long as and to the extent necessary to remedy the discriminatory injury the government inflicted.[14] No formal, judicial determination of past discrimination by the governmental unit in question is necessary to show the requisite compelling governmental interest.[15] But the evidence of such discrimination must be "strong" or "convincing."[16] For this purpose the plaintiff may use reliable statistical evidence of the kind that establishes a prima facie case of systemic disparate treatment under Title VII—evidence reflecting a gross disparity between, on one hand, the percentage of protected group members one would "expect" to see selected based on their percentage representation in a qualified labor pool, and, on the other, the actual percentage of those persons selected.[17]

There nevertheless lingers even after these decisions authority for the proposition that in the context of public education racial diversity of the student body is a compelling governmental interest distinct from any

---

12. 488 U.S. 469, 109 S.Ct. 706, 102 L.Ed.2d 854 (1989).

13. *Associated General Contractors of Connecticut, Inc. v. New Haven, Connecticut,* 41 F.3d 62 (2d Cir.1994). *See also Alexander v. Estepp,* 95 F.3d 312 (4th Cir. 1996) (striking down county's affirmative action program that set caps on the number of white, male firefighters to be hired because less drastic means were available to counteract alleged prior discriminatory attitudes and because plan benefitted other minorities not shown to have been discriminated against at all). *But see Wittmer v. Peters,* 87 F.3d 916 (7th Cir.1996) (upholding "role model" theory as adequate constitutional justification for preferring African-American correctional officers for promotion based on expert testimony that African-American lieutenants were "needed because the black inmates are believed un-

likely to play the correctional game of brutal drill sergeant and brutalized recruit unless there are some blacks in authority" in quasi-military "boot camp" setting).

14. *See, e.g.,* the dicta to that effect in *City of Richmond v. Croson, supra,* 488 U.S. at 493 (plurality opinion); *Hopwood v. Texas, supra,* 78 F.3d 932, 944 (5th Cir.), *cert. denied, Texas v. Hopwood,* ___ U.S. ___, 116 S.Ct. 2581, 135 L.Ed.2d 1095 (1996).

15. *See Croson; Brunet v. City of Columbus,* 1 F.3d 390, 406 (6th Cir.1993), *cert. denied sub nom. Brunet v. Tucker,* 510 U.S. 1164, 114 S.Ct. 1190, 127 L.Ed.2d 540 (1994).

16. *United Black Firefighters Ass'n v. City of Akron,* 976 F.2d 999 (6th Cir.1992) (relying on *Croson*).

17. *Id.* at 1011.

government interest in providing a remedy for its own prior discrimination.[18]

In a closely watched reverse discrimination challenge to features of the University of Texas Law School's admissions process that gave preferential consideration to racial and ethnic minorities, the Fifth Circuit has squarely rejected that proposition. The law school used an "index" that represented a weighted composite of the undergraduate grade point averages and law school aptitude scores of its applicants. Race or ethnic status functioned as a "plus" factor in admissions because the school maintained separate presumptive index levels for minorities and whites such that some minority candidates would almost certainly be admitted with indices considerably lower than the indices of white candidates who would almost certainly be rejected. Even within a nonpresumptive, discretionary selection range, the files of minority applicants were separately and in practice preferentially reviewed by a minority subcommittee whose decisions were "virtually final." And as a consequence of segregated waiting lists, even minority applicants not initially admitted received preferential treatment.

Unsuccessful white applicants challenged this scheme principally as a violation of equal protection, as well as of Title VI. Relying heavily on recent Supreme Court authority surveyed elsewhere in this section that subjects all governmental racial classifications, whether or not characterized as "benign," to strict scrutiny, the Fifth Circuit ruled these preferential features unconstitutional. It noted at the outset that in *Wygant* the Supreme Court had already rejected as "compelling" justifications the goals of counteracting "societal" discrimination and of increasing minority role models. It then rejected the view advanced by Justice Powell in *Bakke* that attaining a diverse student body is a sufficiently important goal in the context of higher education to warrant the use of race—either per se or as a proxy for other constitutional factors like cultural, economic or educational disadvantage—as one of several factors that a state-run professional school may permissibly consider. The problem for the Fifth Circuit was that even if the reliance on race is restricted to the margins, race is then the factor that ultimately may tip the scales among minimally qualified applicants.

Instead, the Fifth Circuit viewed the residue of modern equal protection jurisprudence as recognizing only one state interest sufficiently compelling to justify even narrowly tailored race-preferential programs: remedying the current effects of past racial discrimination practiced by the particular governmental unit defendant that is taking race into account. Texas' law school, in other words, could not defend on the basis of even strong evidence of past racial discrimination in Texas public education as a whole, or even in Texas higher education; it could rely only on as yet unremedied discrimination formerly practiced by the

---

18. *Regents of Univ. of Cal. v. Bakke,*   (1978) (plurality opinion by Powell, J.).
438 U.S. 265, 98 S.Ct. 2733, 57 L.Ed.2d 750

law school itself. The record did not support such a finding in the view of the Fifth Circuit, still less that the Law School's several admissions preferences were "narrowly tailored" to redress only any lingering effects of its own prior discrimination against the preferentially treated groups. In particular, the court declined to recognize the school's awareness of its prior history of race discrimination or its still subsisting reputation for discrimination among members of the beneficiary groups as the kind of continuing effects of past discrimination that are constitutionally remediable through race-conscious means.[19]

Unlike "voluntary" affirmative action, judgments directing preferential treatment for a minority or gender group, issued after litigated findings of discrimination or upon the parties' consent, squarely test the limits of a court's remedial authority under § 706(g) to "order such affirmative action as may be appropriate." In the case of public employers, these judgments may also deny the disfavored racial or gender groups equal protection. The justices have been deeply divided over the equitable propriety under § 706(g) of consent judgments that afford relief to minority group members who are not themselves proven victims of discrimination. The degree of "trammelling" appears important. An opinion that in dictum declared such relief beyond a court's authority concerned a consent judgment modification that would have required more senior non-minority firefighters to be laid off before their more junior minority counterparts.[20] Yet the Court subsequently upheld a district judge's authority to approve a consent judgment that established firefighters' promotion quotas but did not compel layoffs or terminations.[21]

Although formal, judicial findings of past discrimination are not indispensable to the approval of group-based remedies, the Supreme Court has more often upheld programs that were judicially ordered after litigated findings of persistent, egregious discrimination.[22] One judgment, for example, would have absolutely excluded certain whites from union membership, in turn precluding their employment. But the goal was upheld in part because there was evidence of long-standing intentional discrimination and contumacious defiance of prior judicial orders.[23] Moreover, as the Supreme Court had stressed in *Wygant*, the burdens of a hiring goal are "diffused to a considerable extent among society generally" and do not "impose the same kind of injury" as layoffs or

19. *Hopwood v. Texas,* 78 F.3d 932 (5th Cir.), *cert. denied, Texas v. Hopwood,* ___ U.S. ___, 116 S.Ct. 2581, 135 L.Ed.2d 1095 (1996).

20. *Firefighters Local Union No. 1784 v. Stotts,* 467 U.S. 561, 104 S.Ct. 2576, 81 L.Ed.2d 483 (1984).

21. Local No. 93, *Local No. 93, International Ass'n of Firefighters v. City of Cleveland,* 478 U.S. 501, 106 S.Ct. 3063, 92 L.Ed.2d 405 (1986). *But see Bennett v. Arrington,* 20 F.3d 1525 (11th Cir.1994), *cert. denied,* ___ U.S. ___, 115 S.Ct. 1695,

131 L.Ed.2d 558 (1995) (striking down 50% indefinite-duration promotion quota for fire department lieutenants).

22. *Local 28, Sheet Metal Workers' International Ass'n v. EEOC,* 478 U.S. 421, 106 S.Ct. 3019, 92 L.Ed.2d 344 (1986) (membership goal for defendant union); *United States v. Paradise,* 480 U.S. 149, 107 S.Ct. 1053, 94 L.Ed.2d 203 (1987) (quota promotion plan).

23. *Local 28, Sheet Metal Workers' International Ass'n v. EEOC, supra* note 22.

even promotions. It remains unclear, however, just *why* the animus or stubborn litigiousness of an employer or union justifies a race-based remedy the burden of which is felt principally not by the adjudicated wrongdoer but by an applicant for employment or union membership, even if it "only" costs the remedy's victim a chance at employment or a promotion rather than an existing job.

The strict scrutiny approach to "benign" racial preferences reflected in the Supreme Court's recent equal protection decisions,[24] notably *Wygant* and *Croson*, has since been applied to employment discrimination consent decrees involving government employers.[25] And circuit decisions have held that a preference enjoys no greater protection because it is embodied in a judicial decree than when it is part of an employer's "voluntary" affirmative action plan.[26] It is therefore quite likely, if not logically compelled,[27] that an affirmative action plan or consent decree affecting a state or local government employer [28] may pass

---

24. See text accompanying notes 11 through 12, *supra*.

25. *See, e.g., Aiken v. City of Memphis*, 37 F.3d 1155 (6th Cir.1994); *United Black Firefighters Ass'n v. City of Akron*, 976 F.2d 999 (6th Cir.1992).

26. *See, e.g., United Black Firefighters Ass'n v. Akron*, 976 F.2d 999, 1008 (6th Cir.1992) (citing *Croson*); *In re Birmingham Reverse Discrimination Employment Litigation*, 833 F.2d 1492, 1501 (11th Cir. 1987), *aff'd sub nom. Martin v. Wilks*, 490 U.S. 755, 109 S.Ct. 2180, 104 L.Ed.2d 835 (1989).

27. See text accompanying notes 33, 34, *infra*.

28. The Court upheld a *federal* contracting minority set-aside program similar in relevant respects to the one struck down in *Croson* in reliance on Congress' special enforcement powers under § 5 of the 14th Amendment. *Fullilove v. Klutznick*, 448 U.S. 448, 100 S.Ct. 2758, 65 L.Ed.2d 902 (1980). Expanding on the *Fullilove* doctrine, the Court in *Metro Broadcasting, Inc. v. F.C.C.*, 497 U.S. 547, 110 S.Ct. 2997, 111 L.Ed.2d 445 (1990), held that "benign, race-conscious measures mandated by Congress" do not violate the constitution so long as they are substantially related to important governmental objectives, even though they do not seek to remedy prior discrimination. There the "important governmental objective" was to enhance broadcast programming diversity. *Adarand Constructors, Inc. v. Pena*, ___ U.S. ___, 115 S.Ct. 2097, 132 L.Ed.2d 158 (1995) afforded the four dissenting justices in *Metro Broadcasting* an opportunity to overturn *Fullilove* by insisting that congressional preference programs meet the same "strict scrutiny" equal protection standards that the Court imposes on

state and local governments under *Croson*. The program at issue in *Adarand* provided prime contractors in federal highway construction projects bonuses if they awarded subcontracts to "disadvantaged business enterprises." Implementing regulations established a presumption "that socially and economically disadvantaged individuals include" a number of designated racial and ethnic minorities.

The Court has since decided *Adarand*, holding that "all racial classifications, imposed by whatever federal, state, or local governmental actor, must be analyzed ... under strict scrutiny." Any such classification must therefore be "narrowly tailored" or "necessary" to "further compelling governmental interests." The lead opinion endorses the *Wygant* conclusion that the level of equal protection scrutiny of a racial classification does not change just because it operates to disadvantage a group that historically has not been the target of government discrimination; and it specifically rejects the *Metro Broadcasting* conclusion that racial classifications adopted for ostensibly "benign" purposes by the *federal* government need only satisfy "intermediate" scrutiny—that is, need only "substantially" relate to "important" governmental objectives. Even *Fullilove* was branded "no longer controlling" to the uncertain extent that it departed from strict scrutiny and held federal racial classifications to a less rigorous standard.

The Court remanded for a determination, first, whether the lowbidding nonminority subcontractor plaintiff in fact was denied a subcontract as the result of an irrebuttable racial preference or, for example, as the result of an individualized assessment of

muster under Title VII's *Weber/Johnson* standards as not constituting impermissible reverse discrimination yet run afoul of the Constitution.[29] Now the flow is beginning to run the other way. The new "race-neutral" constitutional guideposts seem to have heightened the circuit courts' scrutiny *under Title VII* of government employer affirmative action and consent decrees; the previously prevailing permissiveness appears to be waning.[30] Indeed the Eleventh Circuit has frankly acknowledged that its "application of the *Johnson* [i.e., Title VII] manifest imbalance test ... is informed by *Croson's* discussion of the necessity [under the Equal Protection Clause] for a government entity to identify with specificity the discrimination it seeks to remedy through race

economic or social disadvantage. If the former, the lower courts were directed to decide if any interests served by the federal subcontractor compensation clauses at issue were "compelling." Finally, the majority cautioned that any racial preference implemented through the application of the federal regulations and purportedly justified by the goal of eliminating the effects of prior discrimination must be narrowly tailored to serve such a compelling interest—at a minimum, that is, the lower court must decide whether the government had considered race-neutral means to increase minority business participation and whether the program of racial preference would last no longer than necessary to eliminate those effects.

What state or governmental interests may suffice as "compelling" after *Adarand* is significantly less clear. Only Justice Scalia, concurring in part, asserts that there is never a compelling interest justifying race discrimination "in order to 'make up' for past racial discrimination in the opposite direction." But the majority's opinion suggests that such a remedial justification will be applied strictly. It observes that the *Wygant* plurality not only rejected the minority role model justification for a government affirmative action program in employment, but in particular required as a predicate convincing evidence of the government employer's own prior race discrimination. Justice Souter, dissenting, explicitly offered Congress' special authority under Section 5 of the 14th Amendment, deferred to by the *Fullilove* plurality, "as the source of an interest of the national government sufficiently important to satisfy ... strict scrutiny." In effect this is an argument that the federal government, though held to the same formal strict scrutiny standard as state and local governments, nevertheless may more easily meet the requirement of a compelling interest for affirmative action. Justice O'Connor for the majority was noncommittal on that point, content to observe "that various

Members of this Court have taken different views of the authority § 5 of the Fourteenth Amendment confers upon Congress to deal with the problem of racial discrimination, and the extent to which courts should defer to Congress' exercise of that authority."

29. *See, e.g., Brunet v. City of Columbus*, 1 F.3d 390 (6th Cir.1993) (upholding constitutional challenge under § 1983 to fire department's consent decree that gave hiring preference to women); *Peightal v. Metropolitan Dade County*, 940 F.2d 1394 (11th Cir.1991).

30. *See, e.g., In re Birmingham Reverse Discrimination Employment Litigation*, 20 F.3d 1525 (11th Cir.1994) *cert. denied*, ___ U.S. ___, 115 S.Ct. 1695, 131 L.Ed.2d 558 (1995); *Ensley Branch v. Seibels*, 31 F.3d 1548 (11th Cir.1994). Justice Scalia, dissenting in *Johnson v. Transportation Agency of Santa Clara County*, 480 U.S. 616, 107 S.Ct. 1442, 94 L.Ed.2d 615 (1987), foreshadowed this approach by proposing that *Weber* be reevaluated in light of the Court's Fourteenth Amendment jurisprudence. This same phenomenon was at work in *United States v. Board of Education of Piscataway*, 832 F.Supp. 836, 844–848 (D.N.J.1993), affirmed 91 F.3d 1547 (3d Cir.), *cert. filed*, ___ U.S. ___, ___ S.Ct. ___, ___ L.Ed.2d ___, 65 U.S.L.W. 3354 (1996), where the court rejected the educational goal of promoting racial diversity among faculty as an adequate justification under Title VII for race-conscious affirmative action. The court's construction of Title VII was heavily influenced by the Supreme Court's recent Fourteenth Amendment decisions that reject general societal discrimination and a "role model" theory as justifications for affirmative action, notwithstanding the indication of *Regents of Univ. of Cal. v. Bakke*, 438 U.S. 265, 98 S.Ct. 2733, 57 L.Ed.2d 750 (1978), that the attainment of a diverse *student* body in an institution of higher education is such a constitutionally permissible goal.

conscious measures." [31]   The recent decisions have been particularly critical of promotion preferences when they are not narrowly tailored to remedy prior discrimination by the government defendant.[32]

These decisions are curious.   First, it is difficult to see why the Title VII test adumbrated in *Johnson* should be "informed" by the requirement of a finding that the particular defendant discriminated against the preferred group, when the Court in *Johnson* expressly rejected the argument that such a finding was essential to justify affirmative action under Title VII.   Second, why equate the recently declared constitutional standard and the longer-standing, distinctly laxer statutory standard?   Perhaps the assumption is that, in the case of a public employer, the statutory permissiveness on affirmative action must give way to the stricter equal protection standard announced in cases like *Wygant* and *Croson*.   But is this necessarily so?   In relation to discrimination *against* minorities and women, Title VII was Congress' attempt to provide protection, first in the private and then in the public sector, that was *not* afforded by the Constitution.   Thus the Supreme Court has traditionally defended the permissive Title VII standards it has devised to facilitate "benign" reverse discrimination against whites and men as consonant with the *statute's* imperative to end discrimination against minorities and women.   It is unclear why that permissive construction of Title VII (however mistaken or misguided it may be) [33] should suddenly fail affirmatively acting state and local government employers when their racial or gender preferences are challenged under Title VII, merely because it is now settled that such conduct would violate the Constitution in settings not reached by Title VII.[34]

---

31.   *In re Birmingham Reverse Discrimination Employment Litigation*, 20 F.3d 1525 (11th Cir.1994).

32.   *Aiken v. City of Memphis*, 37 F.3d 1155 (6th Cir.1994); *In re Birmingham Reverse Discrimination Employment Litigation*, 20 F.3d 1525 (11th Cir.1994); *Black Fire Fighters Association of Dallas v. City of Dallas*, 19 F.3d 992 (5th Cir.1994).   *Aiken* and *Birmingham* do differ, however, in the way they apply the "narrowly tailored" prong.   The Eleventh Circuit, in *Birmingham*, held that an interim 50% minority promotion goal was impermissible as a means of reaching an ultimate goal of 28% minority representation because the 50% goal bore no relation to the minorities' past underrepresentation or therefore to remediable injury.   By contrast, the Sixth Circuit in *Aiken* read the Supreme Court's plurality opinion in *United States v. Paradise*, 480 U.S. 149, 179–180, 107 S.Ct. 1053, 1071, 94 L.Ed.2d 203 (1987) to authorize such interim goals so long as the ultimate percentage goal is tied to the pool of qualified minority applicants.   On that point the Sixth Circuit struck down a city's plan because the ultimate minority promotion goals were keyed

to minority hiring goals which in turn were based on local labor force statistics that were undifferentiated by the requisite qualifications for initial hire.   The Fifth Circuit has recently upheld consent decree provisions calling for police department promotions where the remedial promotions were offered on a one-time-only basis for no longer than five years and where the decree did not call for the discharge of nonminority officers.   *Edwards v. City of Houston*, 37 F.3d 1097 (5th Cir.1994).

33.   I have argued that *Weber* and *Johnson* rely on a weak negative pregnant in § 703(j), a provision not in point, in preference to the apparently plain prohibitions of §§ 703(d) and 703(a), the provisions directly at issue in *Weber* and *Johnson*, respectively.   See text accompanying notes 4 through 5, *supra*.

34.   The majority in *Johnson v. Transportation Agency of Santa Clara County*, 480 U.S. 616, 628 n. 6, 107 S.Ct. 1442, 1450 n. 6, 94 L.Ed.2d 615 (1987), for example, rejected the notion that a public employer's obligations under Title VII were coextensive with its obligations under the Constitution.

Indeed, it is even plausible that the tail, Title VII, can wag the dog, Equal Protection, when a government employer's conduct is challenged *under the Constitution*. Put otherwise, the Court's permissive construction of Title VII as respects "benign" affirmative action might actually trump the Court's own interpretation of the demands of Equal Protection as elaborated in *Wygant*. After all, in authorizing federal courts to award monetary relief against state and local government defendants notwithstanding the Eleventh Amendment, the Supreme Court relied on the fact that Congress' authority to enact Title VII derived from § 5 of the Fourteenth Amendment.[35] Title VII might thus be viewed as a particularized expression of the Fourteenth Amendment's mandate for the employment setting, one that arguably prevails over the more general Fourteenth Amendment understanding that governs in, say, the government contract setting of *Croson*. Although the Court also applied its strict scrutiny approach in *Wygant*, an employment case, the argument advanced here was not squarely presented. The Court considered only a general equal protection challenge to the layoffs; it did not consider whether its prevailing interpretation of Title VII, and hence, through § 5, of the Fourteenth Amendment, should "inform" its more general view of what the Fourteenth Amendment demands. Stated baldly, the argument here asserts that Congress may by statute (as interpreted, in this case, by the Court) authoritatively construe the equal protection clause to permit state and local government employers to engage in the kind of broad, "benign" affirmative action that Title VII encourages and permits—so authoritatively as to foreclose a later determination by the Court (e.g., in *Wygant*) that those same governments are subject to a considerably stricter, race-blind conception of equal protection.

Of course this argument rests at bottom on the assumption that Congress, by the exercise of its § 5 powers, may effectively construe the Fourteenth Amendment *contrary* to a construction placed on it by the Court. It thus raises a stark challenge to the American principle of judicial review enunciated in *Marbury v. Madison*[36] under which the Court ultimately decides what the Constitution commands.[37] Even more

35. *Fitzpatrick v. Bitzer*, 427 U.S. 445, 96 S.Ct. 2666, 49 L.Ed.2d 614 (1976). *But see United Steelworkers of America v. Weber*, 443 U.S. 193, 99 S.Ct. 2721, 61 L.Ed.2d 480 (1979), quoted in *Johnson v. Transportation Agency, Santa Clara County*, 480 U.S. 616, 107 S.Ct. 1442, 94 L.Ed.2d 615 (1987) ("Title VII . . . was enacted pursuant to the commerce power to regulate purely private decisionmaking and was not intended to incorporate and particularize the commands of the Fifth and Fourteenth Amendments.")

36. 5 U.S. (1 Cranch) 137, 2 L.Ed. 60 (1803).

37. *See, e.g.*, R. Bork, Constitutionality of the President's Busing Proposals 10 (1972) (commenting on *Katzenbach v. Morgan*, 384 U.S. 641, 86 S.Ct. 1717, 16 L.Ed.2d 828 (1966)), discussed *infra* note 38. But see Gordon, "The Nature and Uses of Congressional Power Under Section Five of the Fourteenth Amendment to Overcome Decisions of the Supreme Court," 72 Nw. U.L.Rev. 656 (1977) (asserting that Court retains ultimate interpretive primacy where decision turns on "normative" rather than "empirical" matters concerning the assembling of legislative facts). *See also* Nathanson, "Congressional Power to Contradict the Supreme Court's Constitutional Decisions. Accommodation of Rights in Conflict," 27 Wm. & M.L.Rev. 331 (1986).

modest propositions—for example, that Congress through § 5 may add to substantive rights the courts have previously found in the Fourteenth Amendment—are highly controversial in constitutional jurisprudence.[38] The particular challenge posed here is further complicated by two factors. First, and cutting against the argument, the permissive approach to affirmative action taken by the statute, and hence by "Congress," really only emerged from a judicial gloss placed on it by *Weber* and *Johnson*, i.e., by the Court. But second, and cutting somewhat in favor of the contention, that gloss—and hence the § 5 determination of "Congress"—was in place *before* the Court's recent equal protection decisions that insist on strict scrutiny even of "benign" racial discrimination. Further, the Court until recently recognized that Congress may use its § 5 authority to require minority set-asides in federal contracting that would be infirm if adopted by a state or locality[39]; might Congress then not also be empowered through Title VII to permit states and localities to engage in employment affirmative action that would otherwise violate the Court's strict scrutiny interpretation of the Fourteenth Amendment?[40]

38. For example, in *Katzenbach v. Morgan*, 384 U.S. 641, 86 S.Ct. 1717, 16 L.Ed.2d 828 (1966), a majority of the Court, over a dissent that would have limited Congress' § 5 role to providing remedies for conduct elsewhere proscribed by the Amendment, found in § 5 "a positive grant of legislative power authorizing Congress to exercise its discretion in determining whether and what legislation is needed to secure the guarantees of [the Equal Protection Clause of Section 1] of the Fourteenth Amendment." A second rationale in the majority's opinion is still more pertinent to the argument in text. Justice Brennan asserted that Congress through § 5 may authoritatively interpret conduct as violative of the primary Fourteenth Amendment guarantees, notwithstanding a prior holding of the Court to the contrary. *See* Barron, Dienes, McCormack, and Redish, *Constitutional Law: Principles and Policy* 174 (Michie 4th ed. 1992). To an uncertain degree, however, that rationale has been undercut by the Court's decision in *Oregon v. Mitchell*, 400 U.S. 112, 91 S.Ct. 260, 27 L.Ed.2d 272 (1970), which struck down provisions of the 1970 Voting Rights Act that purported to lower the voting age to 18 in state elections.

One reason for the Court's hesitancy to embrace fully a Congressional interpretive power under § 5 (aside from preserving its own institutional prerogatives) is undoubtedly the difficulty of limiting the sphere of Congressional interpretive primacy in light of the renowned, grand vagueness of the § 1 clauses—due process and equal protection—that § 5 permits Congress to imple-ment. *See* Note, "Congressional Power to Enforce Due Process Rights," 80 Colum.L.Rev. 1265 (1980).

It is not much of a stretch to argue, for example, that because § 2 of the Voting Rights Act is also an exercise of Congress' Fourteenth Amendment powers, it can constitutionally authorize precisely the kind of race-based congressional redistricting designed to assure or expand minority representation that the Supreme Court, in *Shaw v. Reno*, 509 U.S. 630, 113 S.Ct. 2816, 125 L.Ed.2d 511 (1993), recently condemned as offensive to a "general," race-neutral understanding of equal protection, at least when the new district shapes are so "bizarre" as to leave no other reasonable conclusion but that the shape was dictated by considerations of race. *See* Chapter 10. (That argument was apparently not made and was not discussed in the *Shaw* opinion.) But could Congress then mandate application of all federal procedural rules in state courts if it thought that necessary to secure due process to litigants? And does § 5 authorize Congress, in an effort to secure the due process right to life, to define life as existing from conception? *See* S. 158 and H.R.900, 97th Cong., 1st Sess. (1981).

39. *Compare Fullilove v. Klutznick*, 448 U.S. 448, 100 S.Ct. 2758, 65 L.Ed.2d 902 (1980) *with Croson. But see Adarand Constructors, Inc. v. Pena, supra* note 28.

40. *See* Note, "City of Richmond v. J.A. Croson Co: A Federal Legislative Answer," 100 *Yale L.J.* 451, 468 (1990) ("The court's determination that a state's race-based program is unconstitutional does not preclude

After *Croson*, the Court, left to its own devices, might be inclined to overrule *Weber* itself, as one justice has urged.[41] Indeed even an affirmative action plan valid under *Weber* might be held unlawful under § 703(m) of Title VII, as amended by the 1991 CRA. That section provides that an unlawful employment practice is "established" when race or gender is shown to be "a motivating factor ... even though other [e.g., benign, compensatory] factors motivated the practice." The preface to § 703(m), though, reads "Except as otherwise provided in this title...."; and part of that title, § 116 of the Civil Rights Act of 1991, provides that its amendments shall not be construed to affect "court-ordered remedies, affirmative action, or conciliation agreements, that are in accordance with the law."

Does this "savings" clause protect only affirmative action plans that are "court-ordered"? It might if that compound adjective were construed to modify "affirmative action" as well as "remedies," for then only "court-ordered," as distinct from voluntary *Weber/Johnson*-type affirmative action would be saved. That would leave the Court free to overturn the rather lenient *Weber/Johnson* standards in place before the CRA of 1991. But how could "court-ordered" modify both "remedies" and "affirmative action" without also modifying "conciliation agreements," the third remedy source in the statutory list? And since conciliation agreements are understood, by their nature, not to be court ordered, then perhaps "court-ordered" modifies only the first item on the list, "remedies." Even non-court-ordered, i.e., "voluntary" affirmative action plans would then be saved, provided they are in accordance with the standards of pre-November 1991 law. EEOC has given § 116 this latter reading.[42] Without even wrestling with the text, which it found "clear" as applied to a court-ordered consent decree, the Ninth Circuit has concluded that § 116 modifies the general prohibition of § 703(m) to uphold the continued validity of an affirmative action plan designed to comply with that decree.[43]

congress from independently sanctioning a similar race-based program under its section 5 enforcement powers."). *But see Adarand Constructors, Inc. v. Pena*, ___ U.S. ___, 115 S.Ct. 41, 129 L.Ed.2d 936 (1994), discussed in footnote 28, *supra*.

41. *Johnson v. Transportation Agency, supra* note 6 (Scalia, J., dissenting). Further support for the suggestion in text may be gleaned from the Court's opinions in *Martin v. Wilks*, 490 U.S. 755, 109 S.Ct. 2180, 104 L.Ed.2d 835 (1989) and *Independent Fed'n of Flight Attendants v. Zipes*, 491 U.S. 754, 109 S.Ct. 2732, 105 L.Ed.2d 639 (1989), discussed in the section that follows.

42. EEOC Enforcement Guidance dated July 7, 1992, Part IV.

43. *Officers for Justice et. al. v. The Civil Service Commission of the City and County of San Francisco*, 979 F.2d 721 (9th Cir.1992). The Sixth Circuit has even upheld an affirmative action program designed to meet the requirements of a conciliation agreement when the employer overshot the target requirements for women apprentices but did so as part of a good faith attempt to comply with the agreement. *Plott v. General Motors Corp.*, 71 F.3d 1190 (6th Cir.1995), *cert. denied,* ___ U.S. ___, 116 S.Ct. 1546, 134 L.Ed.2d 649 (1996).

Library References:

　　C.J.S. Civil Rights §§ 168–169.
　　West's Key No. Digests, Civil Rights ⊸154.

F.　PROCEDURES AND REMEDIES IN AFFIRMATIVE ACTION CHALLENGES

§ 5.16　In General

The Court's early support for "voluntary" affirmative action by Title VII employers, both private[1] and public[2], was expressed in a parallel procedural holding. When a white or male plaintiff challenges an employment practice as a form of intentional discrimination, the employer may assert that the practice was dictated by the provisions of a valid affirmative action plan. The Court might have treated the employer justification as a true affirmative defense, thereby casting on it burdens of both production and persuasion. Instead, it treated the plaintiff's prima facie case as resting essentially on the inferential *McDonnell Douglas* mode of proof, and accordingly held that the employer may justify simply by producing evidence that its challenged decision was made pursuant to an affirmative action plan. It is then the plaintiff's burden to prove either that the decision was not made pursuant to the plan, or that the plan is invalid.[3] The Court has similarly held that when race-based government action is challenged under the Equal Protection Clause, "the ultimate burden remains with the employees to demonstrate the unconstitutionality of an affirmative-action program."[4] Some courts have modified the equal protection burdens by placing on the defendant the burden of producing evidence of the plan's constitutionality, still leaving the plaintiff with the "ultimate burden of proving its unconstitutionality."[5]

But there is less consensus about the remedies appropriately awarded nonminority plaintiffs even when they succeed in demonstrating the unconstitutionality of a voluntary or court-ordered affirmative action plan. Some courts have taken the position, for example, that white plaintiffs who demonstrate that they were denied the right to compete on an equal basis because of their race are entitled to damages to the extent of any demonstrated economic loss or emotional distress, even if they fail to demonstrate that, but for the race-based preference, they

---

§ 5.16

1. *See United Steelworkers v. Weber,* 443 U.S. 193, 99 S.Ct. 2721, 61 L.Ed.2d 480 (1979).

2. *See Johnson v. Transportation Agency of Santa Clara County,* 480 U.S. 616, 107 S.Ct. 1442, 94 L.Ed.2d 615 (1987).

3. *Johnson, supra,* note 2. *Smith v. Virginia Commonwealth Univ.,* 62 F.3d 659 (4th Cir.1995).

4. *Wygant v. Jackson Board of Education,* 476 U.S. 267, 277–78, 106 S.Ct. 1842, 1848–50, 90 L.Ed.2d 260 (1986).

5. *Aiken v. City of Memphis,* 37 F.3d 1155 (6th Cir.1994) (citing *Brunet v. City of Columbus,* 1 F.3d 390, 404–05 (6th Cir. 1993), *cert. denied sub nom. Brunet v. Tucker,* 510 U.S. 1164, 114 S.Ct. 1190, 127 L.Ed.2d 540 (1994)).

would have been selected.[6] Others, by contrast, deem that failure so fundamental as to deprive the plaintiffs of standing to sue at all.[7]

Library References:

>   C.J.S. Civil Rights §§ 168–169.
>   West's Key No. Digests, Civil Rights ⟜154.

6. *See, e.g., Price v. City of Charlotte, N.C.,* 93 F.3d 1241 (4th Cir.1996) (promotion denial in city employment); *Hopwood v. Texas,* 78 F.3d 932 (5th Cir.), *cert. denied, Texas v. Hopwood,* ___ U.S. ___, 116 S.Ct. 2581, 135 L.Ed.2d 1095 (1996) (denial of admission to state's law school).

7. *See, e.g., Grahek v. City of St. Paul, Mn.,* 84 F.3d 296 (8th Cir.1996) (city hiring).

Chapter Six

THE COMBINED USE OF SECTION 1983 AND TITLE VII FOR DISCRIMINATION CLAIMS AGAINST STATE AND LOCAL GOVERNMENT EMPLOYERS

Analysis

---

§ 6.1 Introduction

With the enactment of Title VII of the Civil Rights Act of 1964 and the resurgence of 42 U.S.C.A. § 1983, employment discrimination plaintiffs have been provided several vehicles through which to remedy the injuries they have suffered. The interrelation between them has provided a great deal of controversy. Much of this controversy surrounds the issue of whether Title VII provides the exclusive remedy for employment discrimination, thereby impliedly preempting § 1983. The United States Supreme Court has yet to directly address this issue. Nonetheless, its resolution will have far reaching effects. Specifically, a decision on this issue will determine whether plaintiffs suing "state action" employers will be allowed access to the uncapped compensatory damages under § 1983, as opposed to the capped compensatory damages under Title VII, either by proving a parallel constitutional predicate violation or simply by fitting the Title VII violation under the "and laws" language of § 1983—i.e., showing a federal statutory violation under color of state law.

Library References:

> C.J.S. Civil Rights §§ 226–229, 231–232, 341.
> West's Key No. Digests, Civil Rights ⊙194, 332.

A. TO WHAT EXTENT, IF ANY, DOES A TITLE VII CLAIM PREEMPT A CONSTITUTIONAL OR FEDERAL STATUTORY CLAIM UNDER SECTION 1983?

§ 6.2 In General

There are several sources of possible Title VII/§ 1983 preemption authority even apart from doctrine developed in deciding employment discrimination claims "under color of state law."

One line of cases has focused on the "and laws" language of 42 U.S.C.A. § 1983. In *Maine v. Thiboutot*,[1] the Supreme Court held that the § 1983 remedy "broadly encompasses violations of federal statutory as well as constitutional law." However, in *Pennhurst State Sch. and Hosp. v. Halderman*,[2] the Court limited the availability of the "and laws" language as a source of relief, holding that "§ 1983 would not be available where the 'governing statute provides an exclusive remedy for violations of its terms' "[3] Similarly the court denied plaintiffs' claims under the "and laws" language of § 1983 in *Middlesex County Sewerage Auth. v. National Sea Clammers Ass'n*[4] and *Smith v. Robinson*.[5] In *National Sea Clammers,* the Court, relying on the *Pennhurst* limitation, held that a § 1983 claim was unavailable[6] because the Federal Water Pollution Control Act (FWPCA) and the Marine Protection Research and Sanctuaries Act of 1972 (MPRSA) contained express remedies that demonstrated that Congress intended to foreclose implied private actions as well as supplement any remedy that otherwise would be available under § 1983.[7]

In *Smith,* the Court considered whether the comprehensive remedial structure of the Education of the Handicapped Act (EHA) precluded

---

§ 6.2

1. 448 U.S. 1, 4, 100 S.Ct. 2502, 2504, 65 L.Ed.2d 555 (1980).

2. 451 U.S. 1, 101 S.Ct. 1531, 67 L.Ed.2d 694 (1981).

3. *Id.* at 28, 101 S.Ct. at 1545 (quoting *Thiboutot,* 448 U.S. at 22, 100 S.Ct. at 2513).

4. 453 U.S. 1, 101 S.Ct. 2615, 69 L.Ed.2d 435 (1981).

5. 468 U.S. 992, 104 S.Ct. 3457, 82 L.Ed.2d 746 (1984).

6. 435 U.S. at 19, 101 S.Ct. at 2626.

7. *Id.* at 21, 101 S.Ct. at 2627.

bringing a claim under § 1983.[8] The Court held that "[w]e have little difficulty concluding that Congress intended the EHA to be the exclusive avenue through which a plaintiff may assert an equal protection claim to a publicly financed special education." [9]

In these § 1983 "and laws" cases, the Court seems to focus on whether the federal statute under consideration provides its own comprehensive remedial scheme—and in particular a judicial remedy. The more comprehensive and the more judicial the remedial scheme, the more willing the Court has been to find preemption.[10] Consequently, the comprehensiveness of the federal statute that provides the substantive cause of action likely will play a major role in whether a claim under § 1983 will be precluded. And Title VII is widely viewed as extremely comprehensive in its detailing of state and federal administrative and judicial procedures and remedies.[11]

Another line of cases addresses the preemptive effect of Title VII on Reconstruction-era statutes other than § 1983. *Great American Fed. S. & L. Assn. v. Novotny*,[12] analyzed "[w]hether the rights created by Title VII may be asserted within the remedial framework of Section 1985(3)." In concluding that Title VII preempts § 1985(3), the Court noted,

> [Section] 1985(3) may not be invoked to redress violations of Title VII.... Unimpaired effectiveness can be given to the plan put together by Congress in Title VII only by holding that deprivation of a right created by Title VII cannot be the basis of a cause of action under Section 1985(3).[13]

In *Novotny*, the Court found persuasive the reasoning of *Brown v. General Services Administration*.[14] The Court in *Brown* considered [w]hether § 717 of the Civil Rights Act of 1964 provided the exclusive judicial remedy for a claim of employment discrimination in the federal sector, thereby preempting a claim under § 1981.

> The balance, completeness, and structural integrity of § 717 are inconsistent with the petitioner's contention that the judicial remedy afforded by § 717(c) was designed merely to supplement other putative judicial relief. His view fails, in our estimation, to accord due weight to the fact that unlike these other supposed remedies, § 717 does not contemplate merely judicial relief. Rather, it provides for a careful blend of administrative and judicial enforcement powers.[15]

---

8. 468 U.S. at 1002–1003, 104 S.Ct. at 3463–3464.

9. *Id.* at 1009, 104 S.Ct. at 3467.

10. *See supra* § 2.28.

11. *See, e.g., Rivers v. Roadway Express*, 511 U.S. 298, 114 S.Ct. 1510, 128 L.Ed.2d 274 (1994).

12. 442 U.S. 366, 99 S.Ct. 2345, 60 L.Ed.2d 957 (1979).

13. *Id.* at 378, 99 S.Ct. at 2352.

14. 425 U.S. 820, 96 S.Ct. 1961, 48 L.Ed.2d 402 (1976).

15. *Id.* at 832–33, 96 S.Ct. at 1967–68. *See also Perez v. FBI,* 71 F.3d 513 (5th Cir.), *cert. denied,* ___ U.S. ___, 116 S.Ct. 1877, 135 L.Ed.2d 173 (1996) (extending *Brown* by holding that the exclusive Title VII remedy for federal employment discrimination also ousts constitutional claims under *Bivens v. Six Unknown Named Agents*

The Court concluded that it "would require the suspension of disbelief to ascribe to Congress the design to allow its careful and thorough [Title VII] remedial scheme to be circumvented by artful pleading."[16] Lower courts have held otherwise, however, with respect to employment discrimination claims by state and municipal employees.

Although both *Novotny* and *Brown* relied to a certain extent on the comprehensive nature of the remedy provided in the federal statute under consideration, both cases also focused on additional elements. In *Novotny*, for example, the Court paid particular attention to the fact that § 1985(3) is a purely remedial statute that itself confers no independent rights.[17] *Brown* is in considerable tension with *Johnson v. Railway Express Agency*,[18] decided a year earlier. There the Court approached the preemption issue in terms of congressional intent. In deciding that Title VII does not preempt § 1981 where the claim does not concern federal employment, the Court reiterated the conclusion of *Alexander v. Gardner–Denver Co.*[19] that

> " '[T]he legislative history of Title VII manifests a congressional intent to allow an individual to pursue independently his rights under both Title VII and other applicable state and federal statutes.' "[20] The Court added,

> "Despite Title VII's range and its design as a comprehensive solution for the problem of invidious discrimination in employment the aggrieved individual clearly is not deprived of other remedies he possesses and is not limited to Title VII in his search for relief."[21]

Relying on the legislative history of the Civil Rights Act of 1972 to the effect that Title VII and § 1981 "augment each other and are not mutually exclusive,"[22] the Court concluded that the "remedies available under Title VII and under § 1981, although related, and although directed to most of the same ends, are separate, distinct, and independent."[23]

Several dominant factors may be distilled from these decisions, despite their not entirely consistent results. First, does the later statute provide a comprehensive and precisely tailored remedial structure? Second, is the earlier statute purely remedial, or does it provide substantive rights as well? Third, does the legislative history of the modern statute suggest that Congress intended to repeal the earlier statute?

---

of Federal Bureau of Narcotics, 403 U.S. 388, 91 S.Ct. 1999, 29 L.Ed.2d 619 (1971)).

16. *Id.* at 833, 104 S.Ct. at 1968. *See also Rowe v. Sullivan,* 967 F.2d 186 (5th Cir.1992). *See* § 9.10 on whether Title VII's detailed enforcement scheme forecloses a judicial remedy for the violation of a subsequently enacted civil rights statute, Title IX of the Education Amendments of 1992.

17. 442 U.S. at 376, 99 S.Ct. at 2351.

18. 421 U.S. 454, 95 S.Ct. 1716, 44 L.Ed.2d 295 (1975).

19. 415 U.S. 36, 94 S.Ct. 1011, 39 L.Ed.2d 147 (1974).

20. *Johnson v. Railway Express Agency,* 421 U.S. at 459, 95 S.Ct. at 1720 (quoting *Alexander v. Gardner–Denver Co.,* 415 U.S. 36, 48, 94 S.Ct. 1011, 1020, 39 L.Ed.2d 147 (1974)).

21. *Id.* at 459, 95 S.Ct. at 1720.

22. 421 U.S. at 459, 95 S.Ct. at 1720 (citing H.R. Rep. No. 92–238, p. 19 (1971)).

23. *Id.* at 461, 95 S.Ct. at 1720.

The first two factors suggest that Title VII should preempt § 1983 employment discrimination claims for which both statutes provide a remedy. Not only is Title VII a comprehensive and carefully tailored remedial scheme, but § 1983, like § 1985(3), is a purely remedial statute that declares no substantive rights of its own. On the other hand, because § 1983 was discussed in the debates surrounding the Civil Rights Act of 1964 and the 1972 amendments to the 1964 Act, yet not expressly preempted, the legislative history of Title VII suggests that Congress did not intend to preempt § 1983. Although these factors push in different directions, the decisions of the courts of appeals on the issue are surprisingly uniform.

Library References:

C.J.S. Civil Rights § 341.
West's Key No. Digests, Civil Rights ⚖332.

B. SECTION 1983 CLAIMS GENERALLY NOT PREEMPTED BY TITLE VII WITH RESPECT TO EMPLOYMENT DISCRIMINATION UNDER COLOR OF STATE LAW

§ 6.3 In General

The federal Courts of Appeals are in accord that the mere availability of a Title VII claim does not altogether preempt a § 1983 constitutional claim based on the same circumstances. All but one of these courts,[1] however, also hold that such a plaintiff cannot rest simply on the "and laws" language of § 1983, that is cannot use § 1983 to challenge conduct that violates Title VII but not the constitution.[2] Rather, to proceed under § 1983, these courts require the plaintiff to prove an independent *constitutional* violation, typically of the Fourteenth Amendment, to serve as the predicate for his § 1983 claim. The significance of the distinction is illustrated by a Title VII "neutral practice/disparate impact" claim,

---

§ 6.3

1. *See Wu v. Thomas,* 863 F.2d 1543 (11th Cir.1989) (allowing the plaintiff to state a claim under the "and laws" language of § 1983 by relying solely on a violation of Title VII itself).

2. *Pontarelli v. Stone,* 930 F.2d 104 (1st Cir.1991); *Carrero v. New York City Housing Auth.,* 890 F.2d 569 (2d Cir.1989); *Bradley v. Pittsburgh Bd. of Educ.,* 913 F.2d 1064 (3d Cir.1990); *Keller v. Prince George's County,* 827 F.2d 952, 957 (4th Cir.1987); *Johnston v. Harris County Flood Control Dist.,* 869 F.2d 1565 (5th Cir.1989), *cert. denied,* 493 U.S. 1019, 110 S.Ct. 718, 107 L.Ed.2d 738 (1990); *Day v. Wayne County Bd. of Auditors,* 749 F.2d 1199 (6th Cir.1984); *Alexander v. Chicago Park Dist.,* 773 F.2d 850 (7th Cir.1985), *cert. denied,* 475 U.S. 1095, 106 S.Ct. 1492, 89 L.Ed.2d 894 (1986); *Hicks v. St. Mary's Honor Ctr.,* 970 F.2d 487 (8th Cir.1992), *rev'd on other grounds,* 509 U.S. 502, 113 S.Ct. 2742, 125 L.Ed.2d 407 (1993); *Roberts v. College of the Desert,* 870 F.2d 1411 (9th Cir.1988); *Notari v. Denver Water Dep't,* 971 F.2d 585, 587 (10th Cir.1992). *But cf. Jackson v. City of Atlanta, Texas,* 73 F.3d 60, 63 n. 13 (5th Cir.1996) (insisting that complaint clearly identify a distinct constitutional right allegedly violated before allegations actionable under Title VII may also state claim under Section 1983). *But see Hughes v. Bedsole,* 48 F.3d 1376, 1383 n. 6 (4th Cir.1995) (holding, in reliance on *Novotny* and without citing its own decision in *Keller,* that no § 1983 claim for sex discrimination violating the Fourteenth Amendment lies where a plaintiff could have sued under Title VII).

which may violate Title VII, as amended by the Civil Rights Act of 1991, but fails to show the intentional discrimination requisite for a violation of the Equal Protection Clause.[3]

Library References:

> C.J.S. Civil Rights § 341.
> West's Key No. Digests, Civil Rights ⟐332.

C. WHAT ELEMENTS MUST BE PROVEN UNDER SECTION 1983 AND TITLE VII IN CIRCUITS THAT PERMIT PROOF OF BOTH

§ 6.4 In General

Many courts have concluded that the purposeful discrimination element of a § 1983 claim based on an equal protection violation is the same as a showing of purposeful discrimination under Title VII. The standard formula under Title VII for showing purposeful discrimination inferentially was set out in *McDonnell Douglas Corp. v. Green*,[1] and later reaffirmed in *Texas Dept. of Community Affairs v. Burdine*.[2]

The *McDonnell Douglas* framework "establishe[s] an allocation of the burden of production and an order for the presentation of proof in Title VII discriminatory treatment cases."[3] First, the plaintiff must establish by a preponderance of the evidence a prima facie case of racial discrimination.[4] The plaintiff can satisfy this burden by showing (1) that he belongs to a racial minority, (2) that he applied for and was qualified for a job for which the employer was taking applications, (3) that, despite his qualifications, he was rejected, and (4) that, after his rejection, the job remained open, and the employer continued to take applications from people with plaintiff's same qualifications.[5] Second, if the plaintiff makes out a prima facie case, the defendant has the burden to produce evidence of some non-discriminatory reason for the plaintiff's rejection.[6] Last, if the defendant rebuts by producing that evidence, the plaintiff can prevail nevertheless by proving by a preponderance of the evidence that the defendant's proffered reason was in fact a pretext for discrimination on a ground prohibited by the statute.[7]

In the context of a § 1983 claim, the Supreme Court has assumed that "the McDonnell Douglas framework is fully applicable to racial-

---

3. *Compare* § 105 of the Civil Rights Act of 1991 codifying the Title VII "impact" on "effects" case *with Washington v. Davis*, (only intentional discrimination violates equal protection) 426 U.S. 229, 96 S.Ct. 2040, 48 L.Ed.2d 597 (1976).

§ 6.4

1. 411 U.S. 792, 93 S.Ct. 1817, 36 L.Ed.2d 668 (1973).

2. 450 U.S. 248, 101 S.Ct. 1089, 67 L.Ed.2d 207 (1981).

3. *St. Mary's Honor Center v. Hicks,* 509 U.S. 502, 503, 113 S.Ct. 2742, 2746, 125 L.Ed.2d 407 (1993).

4. *McDonnell Douglas Corp.,* 411 U.S. at 802, 93 S.Ct. at 1824.

5. *Id.* at 802, 93 S.Ct. at 1824.

6. *Id.* at 802, 93 S.Ct. at 1824.

7. *Id.* at 804, 93 S.Ct. at 1825.

discrimination-in-employment claims under 42 U.S.C.A. § 1983." [8] The Eighth Circuit has concluded likewise. In *Richmond v. Board of Regents of the University of Minnesota*,[9] the court observed.

> To meet her burden of showing a prima facie case of discrimination under *Title VII*, section 1981, section *1983*, or the ADEA, Richmond must show: that she belongs to a protected class; that she was qualified for the job from which she was discharged; that she was discharged; and that after her discharge, the employer sought people with her qualifications to fill the job. (emphasis added).[10]

Similarly, in *Boutros v. Canton Regional Transit Authority*,[11] the Sixth Circuit observed that "the required elements of prima facie proof necessary for a plaintiff charging a racially hostile work environment under both Title VII and 42 U.S.C. Section 1983 are the same." In other words, by satisfying the *McDonnell Douglas* formula for showing intentional discrimination under Title VII, or by showing intentional discrimination more directly, a plaintiff also establishes a Fourteenth Amendment violation and therefore is eligible to recover under § 1983.

But this only establishes a predicate violation—the plaintiff still must contend with the distinct additional requirements and defenses of § 1983. Whether, as in most circuits, the plaintiff has to show a separate constitutional predicate violation or, as in the Eleventh, can proceed under § 1983 merely by showing a violation of Title VII, the plaintiff also must show the other elements of a § 1983 prima facie case and contend with its defenses. In particular, the plaintiff must show that the employment discrimination occurred "under color of state law," and, in the case of municipalities and other local governments, that the discrimination occurred as result of an "official policy or custom" or "deliberate indifference." Further, even if the plaintiff makes out his prima facie case, the plaintiff must overcome an individual defendant's assertion of qualified immunity.[12]

Library References:

C.J.S. Civil Rights §§ 143–144, 146, 157, 160.
West's Key No. Digests, Civil Rights ⚷141 et seq.

8. *St. Mary's Honor Center v. Hicks,* 509 U.S. 502, 503–06 n. 1, 113 S.Ct. 2742, 2746–2747 n. 1, 125 L.Ed.2d 407 (1993).

9. 957 F.2d 595, 598 (8th Cir.1992).

10. *Citing McDonnell Douglas Corp.,* 411 U.S. at 802, 93 S.Ct. at 1824.

11. 997 F.2d 198, 202 (6th Cir.1993).

12. *See Wu v. Thomas, supra* § 6.3 note 1.

Chapter Seven

THE AGE DISCRIMINATION IN EMPLOYMENT ACT OF 1967, AS AMENDED ("ADEA")

Analysis

---

§ 7.1 Introduction

There is a paradox about age discrimination. Age of course differs from race, sex, religion and national origin in that it more clearly lies on a continuum, and everyone who lives to be 40 crosses into the federally protected category. The universal vulnerability to age discrimination and consequent identification with its victims generated widespread political support for protection. This support found expression in ADEA remedies that, as originally enacted in 1967, were more generous than those afforded by Title VII as originally enacted in 1964. Indeed, in the 1960's Congress decided to entrust juries with fairly considering claims of age, but not the Title VII grounds of discrimination, and at least in

344

part this is a reflection of the universality of aging.[1] Initially, these factors also appeared to have engendered sympathetic handling of age claims not only by juries but by the federal judiciary as well.

On the other hand, perhaps because of its very universality, age is a ground of discrimination that is subject to less social stigma than those banned by Title VII. There is a greater general willingness to acknowledge that some types of performance decline with advancing age than that work-related capabilities vary by gender, national origin, or race. Age discrimination is therefore seen as a less invidious form of discrimination; protection is needed more from exaggerated than from statistically supportable stereotypes, from "arbitrary"[2] rather than all discrimination.

In recent years, these latter attributes have come to the fore, with consequent alteration of the legislative and legal landscape. Age discrimination protection remains at a 20–employee threshold for employer coverage, while Title VII and the Americans with Disabilities Act apply to employers with only 15 or more employees. As we shall see, when Congress in the Civil Rights Act of 1991 eased the Title VII plaintiff's burden of proving disparate treatment discrimination, especially for the common case where employer motives are mixed, it did not make any comparable amendment to ADEA. Soon thereafter, the Supreme Court declared in *Hazen Paper Co. v. Biggins*[3] that the plaintiff's ultimate burden in an ADEA disparate treatment case is to demonstrate that the employer's reliance on age had a "determinative influence on the outcome," a requirement more onerous than the Title VII plaintiff's burden, after the 1991 amendments, to show that race, sex, religion or national origin was a "motivating factor." Following suit, some federal courts, taking note of the 1991 amendments to Title VII and of *Hazen,* have announced more difficult standards for ADEA than for Title VII plaintiffs trying to prove disparate treatment discrimination inferentially; they have, for example required that the plaintiff suing under ADEA, unlike her Title VII counterpart after 1991, must present prima facie evidence of disparate treatment that is "direct," "substantial" or both before the defendant bears the burden of persuading that it would have reached the same decision in reliance on lawful factors alone. Similarly, the ADEA defendant who carries the "same-decision" burden apparently defeats liability altogether, whereas the 1991 Civil Rights Act subjects the Title VII defendant who carries that burden to potential liability for declaratory relief and attorneys' fees. Still other lower federal courts have explicitly permitted employers to defend ADEA claims by relying on

---

§ 7.1

1. There is also authority to the effect that Congress could not then conceive that all or largely white juries, particularly in the deep South, could fairly entertain claims of discrimination because of race. See (D.Ala.1991). The Civil Rights Act of 1991 does authorize trial by jury for Title VII claims of intentional or disparate treat-ment discrimination accruing after November 21, 1991.

2. Age Discrimination in Employment Act, 29 U.S.C.A. § 621, "Statement of Findings and Purpose."

3. 507 U.S. 604, 113 S.Ct. 1701, 123 L.Ed.2d 338 (1993).

the high cost of employing, and the asserted declining productivity of older workers; the similar Title VII BFOQ defense has been in distinctly bad odor since the *Johnson Controls* decision and new § 703(k)(2) added in 1991. Moreover, shortly after Congress took steps in 1991 to revive the judicially eroded disproportionate adverse impact theory under Title VII, federal judges, again taking their cues from *Hazen,* are looking skeptically at the entire concept of disproportionate adverse impact under ADEA. Finally, while the 1991 amendments gave the Title VII plaintiff virtual parity with the ADEA plaintiff with respect to a right to trial by jury, the ADEA monetary remedies originally authorized in 1970 (back pay and, for willful violations, an equal additional amount of "liquidated" damages) remain unchanged and have arguably been eclipsed by the more generous compensatory and punitive damages now available under Title VII per the 1991 amendments.

The ADEA prohibits age discrimination against employees or job applicants who are 40 years of age or older. It is therefore clear that the plaintiff must be 40 at the time of the alleged unlawful employment practice.[4] In view of the principal purposes underlying its enactment, ADEA has also been held not to prohibit "reverse" age discrimination in *favor* of an older worker.[5] But the fact that age lies along a continuum has created definitional confusion about prohibited discrimination when the plaintiff compares himself to another, younger member of the protected group who allegedly received more favorable treatment than or replaced the plaintiff. The circuits were split as to whether this "comparator" must be under forty. The Supreme Court has just resolved this dispute by rejecting the position that the ADEA plaintiff must show she was replaced by someone younger than forty.[6] Prima facie she need only produce evidence that generates an inference that the employer relied on age in making the challenged decision. The Court added, however, that "such an inference cannot be drawn from the replacement of one worker with another worker *insignificantly younger.*"[7] The opinion nevertheless implies that in rare circumstances a plaintiff may be able to prove an employer's reliance on age even if a replacement is not substantially younger than she.[8]

Indeed, an over-forty plaintiff need not show prima facie that he was replaced at all if younger, otherwise similarly situated employees were retained when plaintiff was let go and assumed plaintiff's duties after employer decided it could not afford a replacement.[9] It has even been

---

4. *See, e.g., Doyle v. Suffolk County,* 786 F.2d 523 (2d Cir.), *cert. denied,* 479 U.S. 825, 107 S.Ct. 98, 93 L.Ed.2d 49 (1986).

5. *See Hamilton v. Caterpillar, Inc.,* 966 F.2d 1226 (7th Cir.1992) (upholding employer provision of early retirement benefits only to workers over 50 with specified years of service). EEOC Interpretive Rules, 29 C.F.R. § 1625.2(b) (1986), contemplate limited preferential treatment of older workers (i.e., vis-a-vis an over–40 plaintiff) with respect to benefits like severance pay.

6. *O'Connor v. Consolidated Coin Caters Corp.,* ___ U.S. ___, 116 S.Ct. 1307, 134 L.Ed.2d 433 (1996).

7. *Id.* at ___, 116 S.Ct. at 1310 (emphasis added).

8. *Id.*

9. *Torre v. Casio, Inc.,* 42 F.3d 825 (3d Cir.1994).

held that a claim lies when the employer, after rejecting the plaintiff, hires, promotes or retains an older employee [10], it would seem that plaintiff's difficult proof problems here are best overcome by evidence that favorable treatment of the older comparator was either an afterthought, unrelated to intentional age discrimination against the plaintiff, or an after-the-fact ploy to mask the unlawful treatment of plaintiff.

A related issue is whether over-forty employees, although clearly within the group protected from discrimination on the ground that they are too old, state a cognizable claim when they complain that they suffered discrimination because they are too young. In a recent case of first impression at the appellate level, the Seventh Circuit rejected an attempt by workers aged 40–50 to assert that a special early retirement program made available only to workers at least 50 years old amounted to unlawful reverse discrimination against the plaintiff class. In effect the court construed the statutory phrase prohibiting discrimination against an employee "because of his age" as a one-way street banning only discrimination *against* an individual who is older. The court relied on what it took to be Congress' desire in enacting ADEA to protect older persons from discrimination rooted in stereotypes that ability and productivity diminish with age. [11]

ADEA was amended in 1986 to remove the then current upper age limitation, 70, for the vast majority of covered employees. Thus, in general, ADEA prohibits mandatory retirement because of age at any age for covered employers. The most important surviving exception authorizes the mandatory retirement at age 65 of a highly compensated person "employed in a bona fide executive or a high policy making position" who has an "immediate, nonforfeitable annual retirement benefit" aggregating $44,000. [12] But to be "entitled" to that nonforfeitable benefit within the meaning of the exemption, and hence denied protection, it may not suffice that the executive is actually receiving in excess of $44,000. Two circuits have divided on whether payments in the requisite amount must be due and owing *at retirement* under the terms of a pension, profit-sharing, savings, or deferred compensation plan, or whether an employer may, on an ad hoc basis, purchase the right to discriminate by inflating the plaintiff's <u>post</u>-retirement income to push it over the $44,000 threshold. [13]

Until recently, other exceptions permitted the mandatory retirement of tenured college- and university-level professors and law enforcement

10. *See Greene v. Safeway Stores, Inc.*, 98 F.3d 554 (10th Cir.1996); *Walther v. Lone Star Gas Co.*, 952 F.2d 119 (5th Cir. 1992).

11. *Hamilton v. Caterpillar, Inc.*, 966 F.2d 1226, 1227 (7th Cir.1992) (citing *Wehrly v. American Motors Sales Corp.*, 678 F.Supp. 1366 (N.D.Ind.1988)).

12. ADEA § 12(c)(1), 29 U.S.C.A. § 631(c)(1).

13. *Compare Passer v. American Chemical Society*, 935 F.2d 322, 328–330 (D.C.Cir.

1991) (arrangement must be fixed before retirement) *with Morrissey v. Boston Five Cents Savings Bank*, 54 F.3d 27 (1st Cir. 1995) (permitting an age-based mandatory retirement under the policymaker exemption by an employer that, after a forced retirement decision, declared "nonforfeitable" just enough of the forfeitable portion of a pension benefit so that the total nonforfeitable benefit exceeded $44,000).

officers and firefighters. They were subject to involuntary retirement at age 70 (professors) or, in the case of public safety officers, younger, at the local governments' discretion. Those exceptions expired December 31, 1993. The President has just signed legislation re-establishing a retirement exemption with respect to the public safety officers,[14] but it does not address the now expired exemption concerning tenured faculty. Additional exceptions respecting federal employees are discussed below.

ADEA covers "employers"[15] who have 20 or more employees for each working day in each of 20 weeks in the current or preceding calendar year[16]; labor unions having 25 members; and employment agencies.[17] As of July 1994, the numerical coverage threshold under the 1990 Americans with Disabilities Act has been coextensive with that under Title VII, namely 15 employees; this will mean that fewer persons will be protected from age than from the other major forms of discrimination, an irony given the usually more stringent prohibition against age discrimination. The Older American Act Amendments of 1984 specifically protect U.S. citizens "employed by an employer in a workplace in a foreign country." At a minimum this covers overseas employees of American corporations.[18] State and local governments were included in the term "employer" by amendments in 1974. Age discrimination claims against these entities are constitutional exercises of Congressional authority under the Commerce Clause.[19] In fact, some lower courts have

---

14. ADEA § 4(j), 29 U.S.C. § 623(j), as reenacted and amended by the Age Discrimination in Employment Amendments of 1996, Pub.L. 104–208, effective September 30, 1996. After approximately four years, however, a state or local government seeking to continue to rely on the retirement exemption must provide individual firefighters or law enforcement officers who have reached that government's mandatory retirement age an annual opportunity to demonstrate their continued physical and mental fitness by passing valid, nondiscriminatory job performance tests that are to be identified by federal regulations. Within certain limits, these amendments also permit state and local governments to establish maximum ages for hiring firefighters and law enforcement officers.

15. As under Title VII, the appellate courts have held that an individual supervisor of the corporate employer is not himself an "employer" liable under ADEA. *See, e.g., Birkbeck v. Marvel Lighting Corp.*, 30 F.3d 507 (4th Cir.), *cert. denied,* ___ U.S. ___, 115 S.Ct. 666, 130 L.Ed.2d 600 (1994).

16. *Hoekel v. Plumbing Planning Corp.*, 20 F.3d 839 (8th Cir.), *cert. denied,* ___ U.S. ___, 115 S.Ct. 448, 130 L.Ed.2d 358 (1994).

17. The scope of the term "employer" under both Title VII and ADEA is discussed at the outset of Chapter 3.

18. See references to ADEA overseas coverage in Chapter 3 concerning Title VII. *But see Brownlee v. Lear Siegler Management Services Corp.*, 15 F.3d 976, 978 (10th Cir.), *cert. denied,* ___ U.S. ___, 114 S.Ct. 2743, 129 L.Ed.2d 862 (1994) (no ADEA violation where employees hired to work in Saudi Arabia under employer's contract with Saudi air force were terminated at Saudi officials' insistence because Saudis considered them too old; age-discriminatory animus of air force cannot be imputed to its "agent," the plaintiffs' employer).

19. *EEOC v. Wyoming*, 460 U.S. 226, 103 S.Ct. 1054, 75 L.Ed.2d 18 (1983). *See also* the discussion of *Garcia*, overruling *National League of Cities*, in connection with the Equal Pay Act, Chapter 8, *infra.* Congress's exercise of Fourteenth Amendment authority in providing express ADEA liability of states has been held to override their Eleventh Amendment immunity when they are sued for damages in federal court as employers, see *Hurd v. Pittsburgh State Univ.*, 29 F.3d 564 (10th Cir.), *cert. denied,* ___ U.S. ___, 115 S.Ct. 321, 130 L.Ed.2d 282 (1994), but not as an employment agency. *Blanciak v. Allegheny Ludlum Corp.*, 77 F.3d 690 (3d Cir.1996).

now held the ADEA to constitute the exclusive remedy for age discrimination in government employment.[20]

But elected officers of state and local government are excluded from the "employee" definitions and thus enjoy no protection under Title VII or ADEA.[21] Moreover, until recently, these definitions also excluded from protection members of such officers' personal staffs, immediate advisors, and other appointees responsible for setting policy, unless they were subject to state or local civil service laws. Reasoning that Congress did not exclude judges from the class of excluded policymaking appointees with the specificity required to overcome the presumption of state sovereignty implicit in the Tenth Amendment, the Supreme Court held that they, like elected judges, were outside the protection of ADEA.[22] The Civil Rights Act of 1991 overturns the result of *Gregory* and more generally protects the other, previously exempt appointees of elected officials by extending to them all "rights" and "protections" of both Title VII and ADEA, together with the "remedies" that would ordinarily be available in actions against state or local government—that is, all but punitive damages.[23] But unlike other state or local government (or private) employees, whose charges are simply investigated and perhaps conciliated by EEOC and who are therefore entitled to a de novo hearing in state or federal court, these newly-covered government appointees are remitted to an adjudicatory hearing before EEOC, subject only to limited judicial review.[24]

Although the Act does not include the federal government within the definition of "employer," a separate provision requires that personnel actions affecting most federal employees 40 or older shall be made "free from any discrimination based on age."[25] Specific provisions in other statutes authorize mandatory separation of federal air traffic controllers and law enforcement officers and firefighters at various specified ages,[26] and it appears that only civilian members of the military departments are covered.[27] EEOC has adjudicatory authority to resolve federal employees' age discrimination complaints. In contrast to federal employee complaints under Title VII, the age discrimination complainant may bypass any process available from his employing agency as well as from EEOC and proceed directly to federal court for a de novo hearing. A complainant making this choice need only give EEOC, within 180 days after the alleged unlawful employment practice, 30 days' notice of its intent to sue.[28] The federal age discrimination complainant who chooses

20. *See Zombro v. Baltimore City Police Department*, 868 F.2d 1364 (4th Cir.), *cert. denied*, 493 U.S. 850, 110 S.Ct. 147, 107 L.Ed.2d 106 (1989).

21. See Title VII § 701(f), 42 U.S.C.A. § 701(f), and ADEA § 11(f), 29 U.S.C.A. § 630(f).

22. *Gregory v. Ashcroft*, 501 U.S. 452, 111 S.Ct. 2395, 115 L.Ed.2d 410 (1991).

23. *See* § 321(a), incorporating § 302(1) (Title VII rights), § 302(2) (ADEA rights),

and § 307(h) (Title VII and ADEA remedies).

24. Section 321(c) and (d).

25. ADEA § 15, 29 U.S.C.A. § 633a.

26. See 5 U.S.C.A. § 8335.

27. *Helm v. California*, 722 F.2d 507 (9th Cir.1983).

28. ADEA § 15(c), (d), 29 U.S.C.A. § 633a(c), (d).

to initiate administrative review of the challenged decision will be deemed to have exhausted those remedies if the employing agency or EEOC has taken no action on a charge within 180 days of its filing. Alternatively, if the agency or EEOC reaches a decision, the complainant has 90 days within which to file a judicial action.[29]

ADEA forbids age discrimination in hiring, firing or classifying employees or job applicants, and in any other "terms, conditions, or privileges of employment."[30] It also bans bias in employment advertisements or referrals. The prima facie theories of liability under ADEA parallel those of Title VII, from which its language was derived. Many cases involve express or direct evidence, such as statements attributed to management agents that the employer needs "new blood" or strives to become "young, lean, and mean." Liability may not be predicated on such statements when they are merely "stray remarks in the workplace," by which courts usually mean that they are uttered by co-employees or low-level supervisors or are divorced from the decisional process affecting the particular plaintiff.[31] But express statements reflecting preference for youth or animus toward age lose their "stray" character and become actionable when announced by top executives or incorporated into official company planning documents [32] or when uttered by a representative of management with decisionmaking authority with respect to the plaintiff.[33] And the fact that such comments were made over a long period of time argues for rather than against their admissibility; while any particular comment may be remote in time from the alleged violation, as a whole the comments may show a pattern of age-based animus.[34] Moreover, age-related remarks that can be linked to managers responsible for overseeing the implementation of a layoff are relevant as tending to show that the layoffs themselves were tainted by unlawful motivation.[35]

The most common mode of proof tracks the individual *"McDonnell Douglas"* disparate treatment case of the kind that also predominates under Title VII.[36] In these cases employers have enjoyed particular

---

29. *See Adler v. Espy*, 35 F.3d 263 (7th Cir.1994).

30. 29 U.S.C.A. § 623(a)(1). Citing the quoted language and relying on the common purposes of ADEA and Title VII, a circuit court has recently held that ADEA also prohibits the creation of an age-hostile environment. *Crawford v. Medina General Hospital,* 96 F.3d 830 (6th Cir.1996).

31. Even a supervisor's comment that the plaintiff was an "old fart" did not demonstrate that the employer's stated reason for not rehiring plaintiff was pretextual absent a nexus between the supervisor's state of mind and the employer's reason for its decision. *Bolton v. Scrivner, Inc.,* 36 F.3d 939 (10th Cir.1994). *See also Thomure v. Phillips Furniture Co.,* 30 F.3d 1020 (8th Cir.1994), *cert. denied,* ___ U.S. ___, 115

S.Ct. 1255, 131 L.Ed.2d 135 (1995) (employer comment that plaintiff might want to consider retirement "stray" when made in response to plaintiff's complaints about deeper wage cuts for older employees).

32. *Radabaugh v. Zip Feed Mills Inc.,* 997 F.2d 444 (8th Cir.1993).

33. *EEOC v. Manville Sales Corp.,* 27 F.3d 1089 (5th Cir.1994), *cert. denied,* ___ U.S. ___, 115 S.Ct. 1252, 131 L.Ed.2d 133 (1995).

34. *Id.*

35. *Armbruster v. Unisys Corp.,* 32 F.3d 768 (3d Cir.1994).

36. *See O'Connor v. Consolidated Coin Caterers Corp.,* ___ U.S. ___, 116 S.Ct. 1307, 134 L.Ed.2d 433 (1996) (accepting parties' assumption and extensive circuit court au-

success when the plaintiff's termination can be shown to have taken place as part of a comprehensive, economically motivated reduction in force. Because such a force reduction is itself a legitimate reason for termination, courts typically require plaintiffs discharged in those circumstances to produce "plus" evidence beyond the prima facie case tending to show that age was a factor in the challenged termination.[37] In recent appellate decisions, one plaintiff carried that burden by offering evidence of two age-related comments by company officials in connection with the transfer of two younger employees into the department from which plaintiff had been downsized.[38] Another succeeded by showing half-hearted efforts to place him in alternative positions for which he was qualified.[39] In the latter case, the company's statistical evidence tending to show that the organization as a whole was not age-discriminatory failed to conclusively negate the inference plaintiff's evidence raised that he individually had been treated unfavorably because of his age. If the plaintiff makes that showing, the employer must then come forward with an age-neutral justification for the discharge of the particular plaintiff—a neutral justification, that is, separate and apart from the fact that termination took place as part of the reduction in force.[40] Indeed in one circuit the "RIFFed" plaintiff enjoys an easier burden than the "single-discharge" plaintiff. She need only show that younger employees receive more favorable treatment during a RIF, and not that their particular replacements were younger.[41] The inference of discriminatory treatment is not drawn so lightly in a single-discharge case where there can be no assumption that the job requirements are fungible, that is unless the single plaintiff's responsibilities are absorbed by others.[42]

The plaintiff must show prima facie that one or more persons younger, and perhaps even subsequently younger than herself (even if forty or older), were retained while she was dismissed despite having met the employer's legitimate performance expectations. Even then, the employer can avoid liability by offering evidence of a legitimate nondis-

thority that the basic *McDonnell Douglas* evidentiary framework applies to ADEA claims); *Roper v. Peabody Coal Co.*, 47 F.3d 925 (7th Cir.1995); *Rinehart v. City of Independence*, 35 F.3d 1263 (8th Cir.1994), *cert. denied,* __ U.S. __, 115 S.Ct. 1822, 131 L.Ed.2d 744 (1995); *Seman v. Coplay Cement Co.*, 26 F.3d 428 (3d Cir.1994); *Roush v. KFC Nat. Mgt. Co.*, 10 F.3d 392 (6th Cir.1993), *cert. denied,* __ U.S. __, 115 S.Ct. 56, 130 L.Ed.2d 15 (1994); *Lindsey v. Prive Corp.*, 987 F.2d 324 (5th Cir. 1993); *Goldstein v. Manhattan Indus., Inc.*, 758 F.2d 1435 (11th Cir.), *cert. denied,* 474 U.S. 1005, 106 S.Ct. 525, 88 L.Ed.2d 457 (1985); *Haskell v. Kaman Corp.*, 743 F.2d 113 (2d Cir.1984); *Cuddy v. Carmen*, 694 F.2d 853 (D.C.Cir.1982); *Douglas v. Anderson*, 656 F.2d 528 (9th Cir.1981); *Loeb v. Textron, Inc.*, 600 F.2d 1003 (1st Cir.1979); *Schwager v. Sun Oil Co. of Pa.*, 591 F.2d 58 (10th Cir.1979). *See* Chapter 4, Section B for a more complete discussion of the disparate treatment claim under Title VII.

37. *See, e.g., Hardin v. Hussmann Corp.*, 45 F.2d 262 (8th Cir.1995). *Healy v. New York Life Ins. Co.*, 860 F.2d 1209 (3d Cir.1988), *cert. denied,* 490 U.S. 1098, 109 S.Ct. 2449, 104 L.Ed.2d 1004 (1989).

38. *Hardin, supra* note 37.

39. *Cronin v. Aetna Life Insurance Co.*, 46 F.3d 196 (2d Cir.1995).

40. *Viola v. Philips Medical Systems of North America & North American Philips Corp.*, 42 F.3d 712 (2d Cir.1994).

41. *Collier v. Budd Co.*, 66 F.3d 886 (7th Cir.1995).

42. *Gadsby v. Norwalk Furniture Corp.*, 71 F.3d 1324 (7th Cir.1995).

criminatory reason for retaining the younger workers, thereby casting on the plaintiff the final burden of demonstrating the pretextual nature of that justification.[43] One defense that seems to have potency in ADEA claims more so than in actions under Title VII is that the supervisor who imposed the employment detriment (e.g. firing) on the plaintiff is the same person who had hired him. Thus it may be difficult to believe that the employer developed a certain aversion to older people only two years after hiring one.[44] In such circumstances, the plaintiff must show that this proffered justification is a pretext for age discrimination.[45]

As under Title VII, the more generalized and subjective the justification, the more vulnerable it is to a finding of "pretext." [46] The Supreme Court's recent refinement of the Title VII "pretext" concept in the *St. Mary's Honor Center* decision [47] has recently been adapted to actions under ADEA. Thus even though the employer's stated reason for its conduct is refuted by the evidence, the employer may be absolved of liability if the factfinder determines that the false explanation was not a cover for discrimination because of age.[48] Relative to cases under Title VII, ADEA plaintiffs who attempt to show pretext solely by attempting to undermine the employer's stated legitimate reason may anticipate even more exacting scrutiny under the *St. Mary's* standard, because their burden after *Hazen* is to demonstrate that age is not merely a "motivating" but rather a "determinative" factor in the employer's decision.[49] Perhaps because of this complicating consideration, the lower courts are experiencing at least as much difficulty in applying *St. Mary's*

---

43. *See King v. General Electric Co.*, 960 F.2d 617 (7th Cir.1992); *Oxman v. WLS–TV*, 846 F.2d 448 (7th Cir.1988).

44. *Brown v. CSC Logic, Inc.*, 82 F.3d 651 (5th Cir.1996); *Rand v. C.F. Industries, Inc.*, 42 F.3d 1139 (7th Cir.1994).

45. *Roper v. Peabody Coal Co.*, 47 F.3d 925 (7th Cir.1995).

46. *Compare Taggart v. Time, Inc.*, 924 F.2d 43 (2d Cir.1991) (employer's rejection of plaintiff as "overqualified" held pretextual) *with EEOC v. Insurance Co. of No. America*, 49 F.3d 1418 (9th Cir.1995) (plaintiff's rejection as overqualified not pretextual) *and Stein v. National City Bank*, 942 F.2d 1062 (6th Cir.1991) (upholding as objectively related to the goal of reducing turnover the rejection of plaintiff for a non-exempt position because he was a college graduate; employer could rationally believe that a non-graduate would less likely become bored with the work and would have fewer market alternatives). *See* Chapter 4, Section B for a discussion of "pretext."

47. *See* Chapter 4 on Title VII modes of proof for a discussion of the *St. Mary's* decision.

48. *See, e.g., Miller v. CIGNA Corp.*, 47 F.3d 586 (3d Cir.1995) (en banc); *Rea v. Martin Marietta Corp.*, 29 F.3d 1450 (10th Cir.1994); *Biggins v. Hazen Paper Co.*, ___ F.3d ___, 1993 WL 406515 (1st Cir.1993) (on remand from Supreme Court). Other ADEA cases that turn on the *St. Mary's* decision are included in a discussion in Chapter 4 of the Title VII proof requirements at issue in that opinion.

49. *See, e.g., Rhodes v. Guiberson Oil Tools*, 75 F.3d 989 (5th Cir.1996) (en banc) (holding that ADEA plaintiff's evidence of the *McDonnell Douglas* prima facie elements and of the falsity of the employer's reason must be "substantial," "not overwhelmed by contrary proof," and "adequate to enable a reasonable factfinder to infer that the intentional age-based discrimination was a determinative factor in the adverse employer action" to survive summary judgment or Rule 50 judgment as a matter of law). *See also Miller v. CIGNA Corp.*, 47 F.3d 586 (3d Cir.1995) (en banc) (referring to high hurdle facing the "indirect pretext" ADEA plaintiff after *St. Mary's* due to the requirement of showing that age was a "determinative" factor).

to ADEA cases as to actions under Title VII.[50]

Library References:

> C.J.S. Civil Rights §§ 182–185, 190, 195, 197–200.
> West's Key No. Digests, Civil Rights ⚷168.

A. "MIXED MOTIVES" IN ADEA CASES

§ 7.2 In General

Where the evidence shows lawful as well as unlawful factors for the employer's conduct, ADEA plaintiffs must show that age was a determinative factor in the challenged employment decision; the employer must then carry the burden of persuading that it would have taken the same employment action independent of the unlawful component of its aggregate complex of reasons.[1] Where there is no employer admission of unlawfulness, and the evidence does not reveal an obviously unlawful motivation, the jury should be charged that the plaintiff must prove that age played a "determinative" role in the challenged decision.[2] "Determinative" represents a middle ground that requires a showing, where the challenged decision proceeds from more than one motive, that age was a "but-for" cause of the decision, yet it does not require a showing that the unlawful factor was predominant.[3] Although the "determining factor" phrase is frequently used in the ADEA opinions of the lower federal courts, it appears nowhere in the statute and has not been squarely endorsed by the Supreme Court.[4] It is really only another attempt to wrestle with the intractable question that must be answered to resolve any claim of intentional employment discrimination, whether under ADEA or Title VII: was the adverse term or condition of employment imposed "because of" a prohibited factor. Simpler words recently recommended by the Seventh Circuit for jury instructions on this issue ask "whether age accounts for the decision—in other words, whether the same events would have transpired if the employee had been younger

---

50. *Compare Sempier v. Johnson & Higgins,* 45 F.3d 724 (3d Cir.1995), *cert. denied,* __ U.S. __, 115 S.Ct. 2611, 132 L.Ed.2d 854 (1995); *Waldron v. SL Industries,* 56 F.3d 491 (3d Cir.1995); *and E.E.O.C. v. Ethan Allen, Inc.,* 44 F.3d 116 (2d Cir.1994) (inconsistent employer explanations for action enough to send case to jury concerning ultimate issue of pretext) *with Ingels v. Thiokol Corp.,* 42 F.3d 616 (10th Cir.1994) (inconsistencies in employer explanation do not suffice to show that employer practice was a pretext for age discrimination).

§ 7.2

1. *See, e.g., Rose v. National Cash Register Corp.,* 703 F.2d 225 (6th Cir.), *cert. denied,* 464 U.S. 939, 104 S.Ct. 352, 78 L.Ed.2d 317 (1983). *See* Chapter 4, for a fuller discussion of the *Price Waterhouse* burden shifting scheme and its modification by the Civil Rights Act of 1991 for cases under Title VII.

2. *See Hazen Paper Co. v. Biggins,* 507 U.S. 604, 113 S.Ct. 1701, 123 L.Ed.2d 338 (1993); *Miller v. CIGNA Corp.,* 47 F.3d 586 (3d Cir.1995) (en banc).

3. *Miller, supra* note 2.

4. *See Gehring v. Case Corp.,* 43 F.3d 340 (7th Cir.1994), *cert. denied,* __ U.S. __, 115 S.Ct. 2612, 132 L.Ed.2d 855 (1995). Still, the ADEA "determinative influence" language of *Hazen* connotes a more stringent proof requirement than the "motivating factor" counterpart language under Title VII.

than 40 and everything else had been the same." [5]

The Supreme Court has addressed the "mixed motive" problem under Title VII. In *Price Waterhouse v. Hopkins*,[6] a plurality concluded that when an employer undertakes a challenged employment decision for more than one reason, and the conduct that is unlawful under Title VII is a "motivating" factor in the employer's decision, liability will attach unless the employer can persuade that it would have reached the same decision for one or more independent, lawful reasons. If an employer carries that persuasion burden, the plurality wrote, it should be found not to have committed an unlawful employment practice, despite the evidence of partial unlawful motive.[7]

The Civil Rights Act of 1991 substantially incorporates and even enhances the *Price Waterhouse* plurality's pro-plaintiff perspective in defining the circumstances that impose the "same decision" persuasion burden on the employer. Section 107 declares that an unlawful employment practice is established when the plaintiff demonstrates that employer reliance on protected group status was a "motivating factor" for "any" employment practice, "even though other factors also motivated the practice."[8] But the statute makes no reference to the kind of "direct" or "substantial" prima facie evidence of unlawful discrimination that the *Price Waterhouse* concurrers would have required as prerequisite to a shift of burden to the defendant.[9] Section 107 therefore apparently [10] requires the Title VII defendant employer to bear the same-decision burden regardless of the nature or strength of the plaintiff's prima facie case, so long as the plaintiff has shown in some fashion that discrimination was a motivating factor. Thus, "direct" anecdotal testimony of discriminatory motive; substantial (or less than substantial) evidence that an employer decision, practice or policy treated the plaintiff adversely on a prohibited ground; or simply the more common *McDonnell Douglas/Burdine* "inferential" evidence that the plaintiff applied, was minimally qualified, and was rejected—any of these proof modes should now serve as an adequate platform to require the *Title VII* defendant employer to demonstrate "that it would have taken the same action in the absence of the impermissible motivating factor."[11]

Section 107 also codifies the *Price Waterhouse* requirement that the required employer "demonstration," once triggered, extends to the burden of persuasion as well as production on this question.[12] And then the

---

5. *Gehring, supra* note 4. *Accord Umpleby v. Potter & Brumfield, Inc.,* 69 F.3d 209 (7th Cir.1995) (jury must determine that age was a "substantial" or "but for" cause that "tipped the balance" towards discharge).

6. 490 U.S. 228, 109 S.Ct. 1775, 104 L.Ed.2d 268 (1989).

7. *Id.* at 245 n.10, 109 S.Ct. at 1788 n.10.

8. (Adding Title VII § 703(m), 42 U.S.C.A. § 2000e–2(m)(1988)).

9. *See* Chapter 4 on Title VII modes of proof.

10. See § 4.5, *supra.*

11. Section 107(b) (amending Title VII § 706(g), 42 U.S.C.A. § 2000e–5(g) (1972)).

12. Section 104 (adding subsection 701(m) to Title VII, 42 U.S.C.A. § 2000e(m)).

legislation goes somewhat beyond the *Price Waterhouse* plurality by providing that even the defendant who makes the required "same-decision" showing has committed an unlawful employment practice and is relieved only of monetary liability. If the employer was properly required to make that showing—that is if unlawful discrimination was a "motivating" factor in the challenged employment decision—the Title VII employer does not completely escape liability but is deemed to have committed a law violation remediable by prospective relief and attorneys' fees.[13]

It is unclear whether the key modifications § 107 makes to Title VII mixed-motive cases will be definitively held to apply to ADEA actions. Although other parts of the 1991 Act refer directly to ADEA,[14] § 107 does not. If the omission is ultimately regarded as legislative oversight, the ADEA defendant, like the Title VII one, will be forced to carry the same-decision burden regardless of how the plaintiff established prima facie that age was a "determinative" factor. Moreover, the employer who carries the "same-decision" burden, because he still was found to have acted in part because of the plaintiff's age, will have violated ADEA and be liable for prospective relief and attorneys' fees. But the lower federal courts have instead been giving the 1991 Act a "plain text" reading, thereby treating the absence of any reference to ADEA in § 107 as advertent. Accordingly, they consider ADEA mixed-motive cases to be governed by the former Title VII regime of the *Price Waterhouse* plurality, as tightened up by concurring Justices White or O'Connor. Under that view the employer does not bear a "same-decision" burden unless the plaintiff's prima facie evidence of age-based motivation is "direct" (per Justice O'Connor), "substantial" (per Justice White), or both.[15] Moreover, the defendant who carries that burden will not be exposed to declaratory relief or attorneys' fees as under the amended Title VII, but will, per the assumption of all the justices participating in *Price Waterhouse,* escape liability completely.[16]

Of course if the ADEA plaintiff is really required to show prima facie that age was a "determinative" factor in the sense that "but-for" the employer's reliance on age it would not have taken the challenged action, then a "same-decision" defense could serve no sensible function in ADEA cases: the employer who carried that defense would be negating exactly what the plaintiff had by hypothesis just proved! That the lower courts continue to recognize a same-decision ADEA defense therefore suggests that a "determinative" factor, although more substantial in an

---

13. Section 107(b)(3) (adding paragraph (2)(B) to § 706(g) of Title VII, 42 U.S.C.A. § 2000e–5(g)).

14. *See, e.g.,* § 115.

15. *Miller v. CIGNA Corp.,* 47 F.3d 586 (3d Cir.1995) (en banc) (ADEA plaintiff who presents no "direct" evidence of age discrimination, relying instead on *St. Mary's*-type circumstantial evidence tending to dis-

credit the employer's asserted legitimate reasons, is not entitled to a "same-decision" burden-shifting instruction even where there is evidence of lawful as well as unlawful motivation for the employer's challenged action).

16. *Id.*

employer's calculus than a Title VII "motivating" factor, is nevertheless something less than a "but for" factor.

The individual disparate treatment evidence of age discrimination may be buttressed, as under Title VII, by statistical or anecdotal evidence or both that the employer systemically discriminates on a widespread, routine basis.[17] But courts have required refined and technically significant statistical evidence and sometimes also anecdotal testimony by multiple individuals before they will conclude that the employer is responsible for a pattern or practice of discrimination.

Although the Supreme Court has not yet decided the issue,[18] the neutral practice theory derived from the *Griggs v. Duke Power* interpretation of Title VII has until recently been widely recognized to be available to prove claims under ADEA.[19] But the continued utility of neutral practice/adverse impact proof in ADEA actions has been undermined by *Hazen,* a decision technically limited to defining age-based disparate treatment. And just as cost has proven to be a defense (albeit a limited one) in Title VII impact cases, employers have also enjoyed greater latitude in defending the adverse impact of neutral practices on older workers. For one thing, courts have not been sympathetic to showings of disparate impact measured by reference to subsets of the over–40 protected group. Rather, the plaintiff must show that the employer's practice has significant adverse impact on protected group members vis-a-vis similarly situated employees younger than 40.[20] And one court has precluded any use of the disparate impact theory to prove age discrimination resulting from across-the-board, cost-cutting measures implemented by a company in an effort to avoid bankruptcy.[21]

More generally, ADEA complainants face the defense that apparently neutral requirements or benefits limitations that have disproportionate adverse impact on the basis of age are motivated by and in fact conducive to cost reduction or productive efficiency. The problem is particularly acute where employment compensation is geared to years of service, which in turn is usually strongly correlated with age. The employer thus incurs a higher average cost in employing older than younger workers. When the employer then lays off higher-paid employees or those with greater seniority because of the greater cost reductions it thereby achieves, is it unlawfully discriminating because of age? If so, is the form of discrimination express or simply the disparate effect of a neutral practice?

17. *See EEOC v. Western Electric,* 713 F.2d 1011 (4th Cir.1983); *EEOC v. Sandia,* 639 F.2d 600 (10th Cir.1980).

18. *See Hazen Paper Co. v. Biggins,* 507 U.S. 604, 113 S.Ct. 1701, 123 L.Ed.2d 338 (1993).

19. *See, e.g., Abbott v. Federal Forge, Inc.,* 912 F.2d 867 (6th Cir.1990); *EEOC v. Borden's, Inc.,* 724 F.2d 1390 (9th Cir. 1984); *Geller v. Markham,* 635 F.2d 1027 (2d Cir.1980), *cert. denied,* 451 U.S. 945,

101 S.Ct. 2028, 68 L.Ed.2d 332 (1981). *See* Chapter 4, Section C for a discussion of the neutral practice theory under Title VII.

20. *Lowe v. Commack Union Free School Dist.,* 886 F.2d 1364 (2d Cir.1989), *cert. denied,* 494 U.S. 1026, 110 S.Ct. 1470, 108 L.Ed.2d 608 (1990).

21. *Finnegan v. Trans World Airlines, Inc.,* 967 F.2d 1161 (7th Cir.1992).

Where the covariance between compensation or seniority and age is overwhelming, most courts, until recently, treated a practice that selects employees for termination or forced early retirement on the basis of higher salary or greater service as a variety of express discrimination. Further, unless the circumstances showed the company to be teetering on the brink of bankruptcy,[22] these courts followed the EEOC's administrative interpretation,[23] and rejected the defense that cost savings is a "reasonable factor other than age" that justifies such a discrimination under § 4(f)(1) of the Act.[24] Even viewing such practices as neutral, some courts held the cost savings rationale insufficient to justify the resulting adverse impact on protected group members under the defense of business necessity.[25] Alternatively, they concluded that the defense, even if adequate on its own terms, ultimately failed because the employer bypassed available less restrictive means—for example reducing the salaries of senior workers—to effect the desired savings.[26]

The Supreme Court has now rendered much of this law obsolete by holding that discrimination on the basis of a factor merely correlated with age—for example pension status, years of service or seniority—is not unlawful disparate *treatment* under the ADEA.[27] The employer in *Hazen Paper Co. v. Biggins* allegedly fired the plaintiff to prevent his pension benefits from vesting, which the Court of Appeals found, and the Supreme Court agreed, violated ERISA. But the same conduct, standing alone, does not violate ADEA, the Court concluded, unless, for example, a particular employer is dually motivated by the employee's age as well as pension status or is shown to have treated pension status as a proxy for age. And to guide courts in determining whether the employer was motivated by the plaintiff's age, the Court described the "essence of what Congress sought to prohibit in the ADEA" as inaccurate, stigmatizing stereotyping based on beliefs that older workers are less productive or efficient.[28] It follows that if an employer fires an employee solely in order to reduce salary costs it is not intentionally discriminating on the basis of age, even if being older correlates to some degree—usually a high degree—with higher compensation.[29]

There is an instructive contrast here with Title VII's approach to disparate treatment based on factors correlated with a prohibited factor.

22. *EEOC v. Chrysler Corp.*, 733 F.2d 1183 (6th Cir.1984).

23. 29 C.F.R. § 1625.7(f)(1986).

24. 29 U.S.C.A. § 623(f). *See, e.g., Metz v. Transit Mix, Inc.*, 828 F.2d 1202 (7th Cir.1987); *Dace v. ACF Indus., Inc.*, 722 F.2d 374 (8th Cir.1983), *affirmed on rehearing*, 728 F.2d 976 (8th Cir.1984); *Geller v. Markham*, 635 F.2d 1027 (2d Cir.1980), *cert. denied*, 451 U.S. 945, 101 S.Ct. 2028, 68 L.Ed.2d 332 (1981) (regarding disparate treatment claims by individual plaintiffs). *See also Leftwich v. Harris–Stowe State College*, 702 F.2d 686 (8th Cir.1983) (similar conclusions regarding systemic treatment or disparate impact claims by plaintiff groups).

25. *Leftwich, supra* note 24; *Geller, supra* note 24.

26. *See Metz, supra* note 24.

27. *Hazen Paper Co. v. Biggins*, 507 U.S. 604, 113 S.Ct. 1701, 123 L.Ed.2d 338 (1993).

28. *Id.* at 611, 113 S.Ct. at 1707.

29. *Anderson v. Baxter Healthcare Corp.*, 13 F.3d 1120 (7th Cir.1994) (concluding that *Hazen* eroded the rationale of *Metz v. Transit Mix, Inc.*, 828 F.2d 1202 (7th Cir.1987)).

In *Los Angeles Dep't of Water & Power v. Manhart*,[30] an employer defended its requirement that female employees contribute more than their male counterparts to a pension fund on the ground that women have greater longevity and would therefore enjoy greater aggregate benefits. The Court observed that the case involved "a generalization that the parties accept as unquestionably true: Women, as a class, do live longer than men."[31] It nevertheless rejected the employer's defense that the discrimination was based not on gender but merely on a factor, longevity, that highly correlates with gender: "Even a true generalization about the class is an insufficient reason for disqualifying an individual to whom the generalization does not apply."[32] And while the Court once treated discrimination because of pregnancy as lawfully based on a neutral factor merely correlated, indeed perfectly correlated, with gender,[33] Congress replied in effect that discrimination on a ground so highly correlated with gender is indistinguishable from gender discrimination itself.[34]

The Court in *Hazen* had no occasion to decide whether employer reliance on years of service or pension status, as distinct from age as such, could violate ADEA through evidence of disparate impact, for no disparate impact claim was made there. It is now more doubtful, however, that the current Court would answer that question affirmatively. As it wrote in *Hazen*, the Court continues to view disparate treatment, as distinct from disproportionate adverse impact, "the essence of what Congress sought to prohibit...." Three justices alluded to "substantial arguments that it is improper to carry over ... impact analysis from Title VII to the ADEA."[35] The logic here seems to be that allowing the impact theory would illegitimately undermine the Court's conclusion that employer reliance on factors correlated with age is not unlawful disparate *treatment*. After all, disproportionate adverse impact results because the neutral factor on which an employer relied has had exactly that correlation.[36]

Moreover, the absence of any reference to age discrimination in the provision of the 1991 Civil Rights Act that identifies the range of permissible impact-theory claims may imply a Congressional understand-

30. 435 U.S. 702, 98 S.Ct. 1370, 55 L.Ed.2d 657 (1978).

31. *Id.* at 707, 98 S.Ct. at 1374.

32. *Id.* at 708, 98 S.Ct. at 1375.

33. *General Electric Co. v. Gilbert*, 429 U.S. 125, 97 S.Ct. 401, 50 L.Ed.2d 343 (1976).

34. *See* discussion of the Pregnancy Discrimination Act of 1978 in Chapter 3, above.

35. *Hazen, supra* note 27, at 617, 113 S.Ct. at 1710 (Kennedy, J., concurring, joined by Chief Justice Rehnquist and Justice Thomas).

36. This argument mirrors appellate court refusals to permit homosexuals to at-tack anti-homosexual practices—neutral on their face because Title VII does not prohibit sexual orientation discrimination—because they may have a disproportionate adverse impact on one or another gender. *See DeSantis v. Pacific Tel. and Telegraph*, discussed in Chapter 3. It is also reminiscent of the Seventh Circuit's conclusion that foreign employers privileged by treaty to discriminate against Americans because of their citizenship cannot be held liable when the same practice has the effect of discriminating on the basis of national origin. *See Fortino v. Quasar*, also in Chapter 3.

ing that the impact proof mode is unavailable under ADEA.[37] There is also no mention of the ADEA in the section of the 1991 Act that modifies the *Wards Cove* decision by easing to some extent the plaintiff's burden of proving a practice's disproportionate adverse impact. Even if these omissions were only oversights, the 1991 Act's tepid overturning of *Wards Cove* with respect to the plaintiff's required prima facie statistical showing that a specifically identifiable practice caused a given level of disproportionate adverse impact, the nature of the employer's defense, and the plaintiff's less discriminatory alternative rebuttal leaves federal judges ample room to manifest their skepticism about the use of impact proof in cases under ADEA.[38] A cost savings defense to an ADEA disproportionate adverse impact claim may well be treated as "job related for the position in question and consistent with business necessity," [39] or an employer may be able to avoid liability by agreeing to salary reduction as a less discriminatory alternative to termination. Alternatively, the Court may craft a more limited exclusion of disparate impact liability based on pension status or years of service. If, per *Hazen*, reliance on those grounds is not unlawful age discrimination of the disparate treatment variety, still less could it constitute unlawful discrimination through the distinctly less favored proof mode of disproportionate adverse impact.

The long shadows cast by *Hazen* have now led a circuit court to refuse to apply the neutral practice/impact theory to the ADEA claim of a rejected applicant. In *EEOC v. Francis W. Parker School*[40], the employer linked salary to work experience and also declared a salary cap on the teaching position for which plaintiff, a 63–year-old with thirty years' experience, applied. Expert testimony, not questioned by the court, showed that this policy would exclude over–40 applicants at 4.2 times the rate of younger applicants.[41] Although plaintiff would have worked for a salary within the cap, the school rejected him because, under its policy, plaintiff's experience would have yielded a salary above the cap. Relying principally on *Hazen*, the court wrote that although the school's years-of-service factor was age-correlated, its salary policy was "economically defensible and reasonable"; plaintiff therefore had the burden to "demonstrate that the reason given was a pretext for a

---

37. *Martincic v. Urban Redevelopment Authority of Pittsburgh*, 844 F.Supp. 1073 (W.D.Pa.1994) (discussing § 105 of the 1991 Act).

38. *See* Chapter VI, Section D for a discussion of how the 1991 Civil Rights Act responds to the *Wards Cove* decision.

39. *See Jones v. Unisys Corp.*, 54 F.3d 624 (10th Cir.1995) (reduction in force as attempt to halt high economic losses). It is admittedly hard to see how cost savings is related to the capability of an individual to perform a particular job. But there is some possibility that judicial interpretations of the new defense to prima facie impact proof may read that requirement out of existence, leaving only the "business necessity" prong to which costs savings manifestly does pertain. See discussion of the legislative modification of *Wards Cove Packing Co.* in Chapter 4 concerning Title VII. In any event, that approach might be justifiable under ADEA even if not under Title VII if *Wards Cove*, untouched by the 1991 Act insofar as ADEA is concerned, declared a new, modest, and sole "business justification" defense to claims under ADEA as well as Title VII.

40. 41 F.3d 1073 (7th Cir.1994), *cert. denied* ___ U.S. ___, 115 S.Ct. 2577, 132 L.Ed.2d 828 (1995).

41. *Id.* at n.1.

stereotype-based rationale." Although the court branded "the belief that older employees are less efficient or less productive" as one of the "inaccurate and stigmatizing stereotypes," it found no such belief embedded in the school's policy that linked wages to experience. It fortified its conclusion by reference to two ADEA defenses allowing differential treatment of employees "based on reasonable factors other than age" [42] and observance of "the terms of a bona fide seniority system." [43] And it observed that § 703(a)(2) of Title VII, in which the Supreme Court in *Griggs v. Duke Power* first located the neutral practice proof mode, bans employer conduct that would limit the employment opportunities of "employees or applicants," whereas ADEA's counterpart provision refers only to "employees." [44]

None of these rationales for the decision is entirely satisfactory. In *Hazen* the Supreme Court accepted that the employer's actual motivation was cost avoidance. In contrast, the Parker School's insistence on applying its salary policy linked to years of service was not calculated to reduce costs, because plaintiff would have worked for less. The court mentioned no other economic or business justification for the policy. The court's reliance on the "reasonable factors other than age" defense simply begs the question whether there was *any* factor other than age that supported application of the policy to the plaintiff. And the court mentioned no evidence from which it might be inferred that the school's policy, applied to plaintiff on an ad hoc basis (the policy normally applied only to incumbents), was part of a "bona fide seniority system." Finally, the court's suggestion, by contrast with § 703(a)(2) of Title VII, that Congress may have advertently limited use of the ADEA impact proof mode to incumbents rather than applicants ignores the fact that the

---

42. Quoting 29 U.S.C.A. § 623(f)(1). There is justification for the court's reliance on § 623(f) as revealing a defect in plaintiff's proof, even though in form § 623(f) is an affirmative defense. The Supreme Court has indicated that in ADEA, like Title VII trials it is the plaintiff's burden throughout to prove discrimination because of age; in this light the "reasonable factors other than age" provision is better viewed as merely underscoring the plaintiff's burden than as a true affirmative defense. Contrast the similar language in the Equal Pay Act that authorizes gender-based unequal pay for equal work where the differentiation is based on "any other factor other than sex," 29 U.S.C.A. § 206(d)(iv), which the Court has treated as an affirmative defense on which the employer bears all pleading and proof burdens. *Corning Glass Works v. Brennan,* 417 U.S. 188, 94 S.Ct. 2223, 41 L.Ed.2d 1 (1974).

43. Quoting 29 U.S.C.A. § 623(f)(1). This section does not permit employment practices that use age as a limiting criterion, but serves the function of declaring that an employer does not violate ADEA when it

relies on factors like health or education that correlate with age imperfectly. *See EEOC v. Johnson & Higgins, Inc.,* 91 F.3d 1529 (2d Cir.1996). The court in *Francis Parker* sensibly cited § 623(f) as revealing a defect in plaintiff's proof, even though in form § 623(f) is an affirmative defense. The Supreme Court has indicated that in ADEA, as in Title VII trials, it is the plaintiff's burden throughout to prove discrimination because of age; in this light the "reasonable factors other than age" provision is better viewed as merely underscoring the plaintiff's burden than as a true affirmative defense. Contrast the similar language in the Equal Pay Act that authorizes gender-based unequal pay for equal work where the differentiation is based on "any other factor other than sex," 29 U.S.C.A. § 206(d)(iv), which the Court has treated as an affirmative defense on which the employer bears all pleading and proof burdens. *Corning Glass Works v. Brennan,* 417 U.S. 188, 94 S.Ct. 2223, 41 L.Ed.2d 1 (1974).

44. 41 F.3d at 1077, citing 29 U.S.C.A. § 623(a).

ADEA provision was enacted in 1967 and it wasn't until four years later that the Supreme Court in *Griggs* identified § 703(a)(2) as the source of the impact proof mode under Title VII. Further, as the dissenting judge in *Parker* pointed out, even if the omission of a reference to applicants in the ADEA counterpart to § 703(a)(2) is significant, there is authority finding an alternative basis for the Title VII impact proof mode in § 703(a)(1), and therefore in ADEA's counterpart subsection 623(a)(1).[45]

In any event, if the decision rests on the contrast between ADEA's § 623(a)(2) and Title VII's § 703(a)(2), *Parker* may come to be limited to a holding that applicants cannot state a cognizable impact claim under ADEA. More recently, other circuits have launched more frontal attacks on the ADEA impact claim, relying not just on *Hazen* but on Congress' failure, when it codified the Title VII impact theory in the 1991 Civil Rights Act, to add a parallel provision to the ADEA.[46]

Section 623(d) of ADEA provides protection against retaliation in the same terms as § 704(a) of Title VII. Former employees, in particular those who have been discharged, are among the "employees" shielded by § 623(d).[47] Further, the employer need not have affected the terms or conditions of the former employment; withholding letters of recommendation or providing negative information to prospective employers may also constitute forbidden retaliation.[48] The ADEA provision, like the Title VII counterpart, has been construed to shield a wide range of on-the-job "opposition" in addition to formal participation in ADEA proceedings.[49]

The BFOQ defense declared by § 4(f)(1) was delimited stringently by the Supreme Court in *Criswell*.[50] BFOQ is now the employer's only real defense to an age-based forced retirement, since § 4(f)(2), after its amendment in 1978, no longer countenances use of benefit plans to compel retirement at any age.[51] But § 4(f)(2) also provides that an employer does not violate the Act merely by observing the terms of an age-discriminatory "bona fide seniority system or any bona fide employee benefit plan such as a retirement, pension, or insurance plan, which is not a subterfuge to evade the purposes of this chapter...." In *Betts*, the Supreme Court, rejecting the unanimous position of the courts of appeals and the EEOC, recently gave this exemption an expansive reading. First, the Court held that the exemption pertains to plans that regulate any fringe benefit (for example, disability plans) and not just to

---

45. *Id.* at 1080 n.3 (Cudahy, J., dissenting).

46. *Ellis v. United Airlines, Inc.,* 73 F.3d 999 (10th Cir.), *cert. denied,* ___ U.S. ___, 116 S.Ct. 2500, 135 L.Ed.2d 191 (1996); *Lyon v. Ohio Educ. Ass'n & Professional Staff Union,* 53 F.3d 135 (6th Cir.1995); *DiBiase v. SmithKline Beecham Corp.,* 48 F.3d 719 (3d Cir.), *cert. denied,* ___ U.S. ___, 116 S.Ct. 306, 133 L.Ed.2d 210 (1995).

47. *Passer v. American Chemical Society,* 935 F.2d 322, 330–31 (D.C.Cir.1991);

EEOC v. Cosmair, Inc., 821 F.2d 1085, 1088–89 (5th Cir.1987).

48. *Passer, supra* note 47, at 331.

49. *See, e.g., Grant v. Hazelett Strip-Casting Corp.,* 880 F.2d 1564 (2d Cir.1989).

50. *Western Air Lines, Inc. v. Criswell,* 472 U.S. 400, 105 S.Ct. 2743, 86 L.Ed.2d 321 (1985).

51. *Public Employees Retirement System of Ohio v. Betts,* 492 U.S. 158, 165 n. 2, 109 S.Ct. 2854, 2860 n. 2, 106 L.Ed.2d 134 (1989).

retirement, pension, or insurance plans. Second, as a matter of law, a plan provision adopted before an employer becomes subject to ADEA cannot be deemed a "subterfuge" to evade the Act's purposes. Third, even a plan provision adopted thereafter will not be considered a subterfuge except in the unlikely event that the plaintiff is able to prove that it was "intended to serve the purpose of discriminating in some nonfringe-benefit aspect of the employment relation," such as discrimination in hiring or compensation. As the following section explains, *Betts* has now been legislatively overruled.

Library References:

> C.J.S. Civil Rights §§ 182–185, 190, 195, 197–200.
> West's Key No. Digests, Civil Rights ☞168.

B. THE OLDER WORKERS BENEFIT PROTECTION ACT

Library References:

> C.J.S. Civil Rights §§ 182–185, 190, 195, 197–200.
> West's Key No. Digests, Civil Rights ☞168.

§ 7.3 Background

The Age Discrimination in Employment Act of 1967 ("ADEA") prohibits age discrimination against employees or job applicants in "compensation, terms, conditions or privileges of employment." Prior to the 1990 enactment of the Older Workers Benefit Protection Act ("OWBPA"), § 4(f)(2) of the ADEA exempted "a bona fide employee benefit plan such as retirement, pension, or insurance plan, which is not a subterfuge to evade the purpose of [the ADEA]."[1] The EEOC had interpreted this exemption to require an age-based, cost justification for any age discriminatory provision in an employee benefit plan. The EEOC interpretation required that any reduction in fringe benefits for older employees would be lawful only if the employer's actual cost of providing that benefit was higher for older employees than younger ones and the employer was spending the same amount for its older employees as its younger ones. Thus, an employer was permitted to reduce the health insurance coverage of an older employee only if the premiums for covering the worker were not lower than those of covering a younger employee.

§ 7.4 The Supreme Court's Betts Decision and the Enactment of OWBPA

In *Public Employees Retirement System of Ohio v. Betts*,[1] the Supreme Court rejected the EEOC's "equal cost or equal benefit" rule. The Court held that § 4(f)(2) of the ADEA broadly exempted employee

---

§ 7.3

1. 29 U.S.C.A. § 623(f)(2).

§ 7.4

1. 492 U.S. 158, 109 S.Ct. 2854, 106 L.Ed.2d 134 (1989).

benefit plans from coverage of the ADEA. The Court further held that in order to violate the ADEA the benefit plan must be truly designed as a subterfuge to disguise age discrimination in employment. Thus, if the employer reduced salaries for all employees while substantially increasing the fringe benefits for younger employees, the benefit plan might be held to be a subterfuge to evade the purposes of the ADEA.

On October 16, 1990, the OWBPA was signed into law. The Act amends the ADEA to overturn *Betts*, reinstating the EEOC interpretation, and clarifies that the ADEA prohibits age discrimination in both the design and administration of employee benefit plans.

The OWBPA applies immediately to any employee benefit established or modified on or after the date of enactment (October 16, 1990). For plans which pre-date the enactment, employers were given 180 days after enactment (until April 14, 1991) to bring their plans in compliance with the Act. Benefit payments that began prior to October 16, 1990 and continue thereafter are not affected by the passage of the OWBPA. Additionally, the legislative history of the Act indicates that the Act does not apply to current retirees' benefits or to subsequent changes in those benefits.

For plans which are part of collective bargaining agreements in effect on the date of enactment, the OWBPA amendments do not apply until the earlier of June 1, 1992 or the termination of the agreement. Finally, the OWBPA applies to States and its subdivisions. But, if the plan can be modified only through a change in applicable State or local law, the OWBPA's provisions do not apply for two years after the date of enactment.

§ 7.5   OWBPA Provisions

The OWBPA repeals the § 4(f)(2) exemption, reinstates the EEOC cost justification rule, and declares that employee benefit plans are covered by the ADEA's general prohibition against age discrimination. Specifically, the Act requires that "for each benefit or benefit package, the actual amount of payment made or cost incurred on behalf of an older worker [shall be] no less than that made or incurred on behalf of a younger work."

The OWBPA also expressly permits employers to follow the terms of a bona fide seniority system, provide for the attainment of a specified age as a condition of eligibility for a pension plan, and provide bona fide voluntary early retirement incentive plans.

C.   WAIVER OF RIGHTS OR CLAIMS UNDER THE ADEA AFTER OWBPA

Library References:

C.J.S. Release §§ 2–3, 5–8, 19.
West's Key No. Digests, Release ☞1 et seq.

§ 7.6 Background

Some employers have required employees to sign a release waiving all rights and claims, if any, under the ADEA as a condition to receiving severance benefits. Prior to the enactment of OWBPA, the ADEA did not state whether an employee could release her rights under the ADEA without supervision by the EEOC. Courts of Appeals, however, generally have upheld the validity of private releases so long as the waiver was "knowing and voluntary."

§ 7.7 OWBPA Resolution

The OWBPA resolves this question by specifically permitting unsupervised releases [1] provided that the following minimum standards are met:

(1) the waiver is in writing and written in terms likely to be understood by the average individual eligible to participate in the plan (or by the individual herself);

(2) the waiver specifically refers to the rights or claims arising under the ADEA;

(3) the individual does not waive rights or claims that may arise *after* the waiver is executed;[2]

(4) the individual waives rights or claims only in exchange for additional consideration (that is, consideration in addition to anything of value to which the individual is already entitled to receive);

(5) the individual is advised in writing to consult with an attorney prior to executing the waiver;

(6) the individual is give at least 21 days in which to consider the agreement (the individual must be given 45 days if the waiver is requested in connection with an exit incentive or group termination program);

(7) the agreement provides for a period of at least seven (7) days following execution to revoke the agreement and does not become effective until this period has expired;

(8) if the waiver is requested as part of an exit incentive or group termination program, the employer must inform the individual in writing (in understandable language), as to:

§ 7.7

1. That is, releases not supervised by the EEOC.

2. *See Adams v. Philip Morris, Inc.,* 67 F.3d 580 (6th Cir.1995) (observing in ADEA and reverse discrimination case that public policy may preclude agreements—other than possibly agreements to arbitrate, *see* section 5.5 *supra*—that resolve prospective employment discrimination claims).

(a) any class or group of individuals covered by the program and any eligibility factors and time limits for the program; and

(b) the job titles and ages of all individual eligible or selected for the program and those within the same job classification or organization unit not eligible or selected for the program.

Compliance with these minimum standards, however, does not prevent a later attack that the waiver was not "knowing and voluntary." [3] Furthermore, no waiver or settlement of an EEOC or court action is considered "knowing or voluntary" unless the above requirements have been met and the individual is given a "reasonable period" in which to consider the settlement. Finally, no waiver agreement affects the EEOC's ability to enforce the ADEA or an individual's right to file a charge or participate in an EEOC investigation or proceeding. But the circuits are in conflict as to whether a plaintiff's retention during litigation of benefits under a severance or retirement plan or agreement should be deemed a ratification of releases exacted in exchange for those benefits and hence a bar to claims that the releases were procured through fraud, misrepresentation, or other violation of OWBPA standards.[4] Resolution of this question may be affected by pre-OWBPA law which found a waiver of the right to file an ADEA charge void as against public policy.[5] The "knowing and voluntary" requirement is also implicated by employer policies that require all employees who are terminated, whatever their age, to sign a general release of all claims to be eligible for enhanced severance benefits.[6] But one court has held that such a policy does not discriminate expressly, even though it pressures only members of the over–40 protected group to waive rights under ADEA. Rather, the court concluded, that policy is facially nondiscrimi-

3. *See Griffin v. Kraft General Foods, Inc.*, 62 F.3d 368, 68 FEP 1072 (11th Cir. 1995) (waiver not "knowing and voluntary" unless employees of closed plant given information about other employees outside of that plant).

4. *Contrast Blakeney v. Lomas Information*, 65 F.3d 482 (5th Cir.1995) *and Wamsley v. Champlin Refining and Chemicals, Inc.*, 11 F.3d 534 (5th Cir.1993), *cert. denied*, ___ U.S. ___, 115 S.Ct. 1403, 131 L.Ed.2d 290 (1995) (even a release not complying with OWBPA is ratified if employees accept severance payments and refuse to tender them back) *and Blistein v. St. John's College*, 74 F.3d 1459 (4th Cir.1996) (accepting benefits under early retirement agreement that plaintiff knew did not comply with OWBPA ratified agreement and thus forfeited ADEA claim) *and O'Shea v. Commercial Credit Corp.*, 930 F.2d 358 (4th Cir.) (allowing ratification of pre-OWBPA releases) *cert. denied*, 502 U.S. 859, 112 S.Ct. 177, 116 L.Ed.2d 139 (1991) *with Smith v. World Ins. Co.*, 38 F.3d 1456 (8th Cir.1994) (plaintiff could accept early retire-

ment benefits and sue for constructive discharge, lest he be forced to remain on the job and face what he alleged were intolerable discriminatory conditions) *and Oberg v. Allied Van Lines, Inc.*, 11 F.3d 679 (7th Cir.1993) (rejecting tender-back requirement as permitting employers to circumvent OWBPA guidelines governing releases), *cert. denied*, ___ U.S. ___, 114 S.Ct. 2104, 128 L.Ed.2d 665 (1994) *and Forbus v. Sears Roebuck & Co.*, 958 F.2d 1036 (11th Cir.) (plaintiff not required to tender benefits under pre-OWBPA release in order to proceed with litigation), *cert. denied*, 506 U.S. 955, 113 S.Ct. 412, 121 L.Ed.2d 336 (1992).

5. *EEOC v. Cosmair, Inc.*, *supra* § 7.2, note 47, at 1089–90.

6. *EEOC v. Sears Roebuck & Co.*, 857 F.Supp. 1233 (N.D.Ill.1994) (suggesting that the mandatory OWBPA period for employee to consider an "agreement" may apply to a proposed severance package as a whole, not just the part in which the employee trades rights under ADEA for additional benefits).

natory because it requires all employees, as a condition of enhanced benefits, to waive whatever rights they may (or may not) have under the same group of statutes. Thus the bundle of accrued claims that an over–40 employee would have to release would not necessarily be worth more than the bundle released by any particular employee under 40. This would be true, for example, if more of the younger employees were members of minority groups or women, who as such enjoyed separate protection under other of the statutes with respect to which waiver was required.[7]

§ 7.8 Burdens of Proof

The OWBPA imposes the burden of proof upon the proponent of the release to prove that the minimum statutory requirements for ADEA release have been satisfied. The OWBPA, however, does not change the minimum requirements or burden of proof of the "knowing and voluntary" standards.

D. ADEA PROCEDURES

§ 7.9 In General

EEOC is charged with enforcement of the Act, and ADEA provides criminal penalties for intentional or willful interference with its processes. It investigates claims of age discrimination, attempts conciliation, and has the power to file civil actions. But individual actions are the major means of enforcement, and procedures and remedies are borrowed from the Fair Labor Standards Act.[1]

The standards for administrative charge filing under ADEA are even more relaxed than those under Title VII. The major superficial similarities are the twin requirements that a complainant file a charge of discrimination (1) with EEOC, within 180 days of an alleged violation, or within 300 days in a deferral state; and (2) with an appropriately empowered state agency, if one exists, which then must be deferred to for a maximum of 60 days or until it dismisses or surrenders jurisdiction. But EEOC itself is given only 60 days of deferral, in contrast to the 180 days specified by Title VII, and plaintiffs may proceed to federal court without demanding or receiving a "right to sue" letter from that agency.[2] If, however, the plaintiff awaits EEOC's right to sue notice, the action must be commenced, as under Title VII, within 90 days after the plaintiff receives it.

7. *DiBiase v. SmithKline Beecham Corp.,* 48 F.3d 719 (3d Cir.), *cert. denied,* ___ U.S. ___, 116 S.Ct. 306, 133 L.Ed.2d 210 (1995).

§ 7.9

1. *See, e.g., EEOC v. Tire Kingdom, Inc.,* 80 F.3d 449 (11th Cir.1996) (the ADEA § 7(d) timeliness requirements apply only to individual plaintiffs; therefore a timely charge by an individual is not a prerequisite to investigation and suit by EEOC).

2. *Adams v. Burlington Northern Railroad Co.,* 838 F.Supp. 1461 (D.Kan.1993).

In addition, the Supreme Court has leniently construed the ADEA's apparent requirement that a state filing precede the filing of an ADEA action in federal court. A complainant's failure to file a state agency charge before commencing a federal action is not fatal; the federal court will simply stay its proceedings until a state charge is filed and the state deferral period elapses.[3] For this reason lower courts in ADEA cases have also not followed the Supreme Court's Title VII approach of subtracting from the 300 EEOC filing deadline the 60–day state deferral period;[4] the 300 days to file with EEOC in ADEA actions remains 300, rather than 240 days.[5]

Securities industry employees who have agreed to arbitrate statutory discrimination claims have been held precluded by the Federal Arbitration Act ("FAA") from instituting judicial actions under ADEA without first exhausting the agreed upon arbitration procedures.[6] It remains unclear whether those employees will be precluded from resuming such stayed lawsuits after the issuance of an adverse arbitration award. Further, it is uncertain whether employees in other industries may be remitted to compulsory arbitration or bound by an adverse award, and if so whether the compulsion attaches where the arbitration promise is contained in a collectively bargained agreement negotiated not by the putative plaintiff but by her union. For a discussion of these issues, refer to the section on arbitration in the Title VII "Remedies" Chapter.

Until the Civil Rights Act of 1991, the plaintiff was required to initiate an ADEA action within the 2–or 3–year limitations period applicable under the Portal-to-Portal Act.[7] But an amendment made by the Civil Rights Act of 1991 eliminates the Portal-to-Portal Act limitations periods. Section 115 instead requires EEOC, when it dismisses or otherwise terminates a proceeding, to notify the charging party, who then may bring a private action against the respondent within 90 days of receipt of that notice.[8] That amendment was not made to shorten the statute of limitations on ADEA claims but rather to preserve those claims: EEOC had proven incapable of acting on many age discrimination claims before the former 2–or 3–year statutes expired.[9] Nevertheless circuit courts, regarding the new 90–day provision as "procedural,"

---

3. *Oscar Mayer & Co. v. Evans*, 441 U.S. 750, 99 S.Ct. 2066, 60 L.Ed.2d 609 (1979). *See Brodsky v. City Univ. of New York*, 56 F.3d 8 (2d Cir.1995) (ADEA complainant may file simultaneously with state agency and EEOC, because statute requires no 60-day deferral period for state on local processing).

4. *See* Chapter 5, *infra.*

5. *Thelen v. Marc's Big Boy Corp.*, 64 F.3d 264 (7th Cir.1995); *Aronson v. Gressly*, 961 F.2d 907 (10th Cir.1992).

6. *Gilmer v. Interstate/Johnson Lane Corp.*, 500 U.S. 20, 111 S.Ct. 1647, 114 L.Ed.2d 26 (1991).

7. See discussion of limitations periods under the EPA in Chapter 6, *infra.* (The complainant did not, however, have to not comply with state limitations rules. *Oscar Mayer, supra* note 3.)

8. *See Littell v. Aid Ass'n for Lutherans*, 62 F.3d 257 (8th Cir.1995); *Sperling v. Hoffmann–La Roche, Inc.*, 145 F.R.D. 357 (D.N.J.1992), *affirmed*, 24 F.3d 463 (3d Cir. 1994). For a discussion of the relationship between state agency determinations and ADEA court actions, see Chapter 13 below.

9. *Sperling, supra* note 8, at n. 14.

have applied it to bar claims filed after the effective date of the 1991 Civil Rights Act even on claims accruing before that date.[10]

ADEA may be somewhat more restrictive than Title VII in one procedural respect, although probably largely in form. No ADEA class action may be maintained under Federal Rule 23, which in appropriate circumstances permits class members to be bound without their specific consent. But multiple plaintiffs may join together under Federal Rule 20, and "representative" actions are permitted under ADEA § 7(b), which incorporates by reference, among other provisions, § 16(b) of FLSA, 29 U.S.C.A. § 216(b). The class representatives must frame their complaint so as to notify the employer that it will have to defend an opt-in representative action.[11] Section 16(b) then allows a would-be "class member" who has not filed a charge affirmatively to "opt in" the action by giving a written consent to joinder as a party plaintiff. The Supreme Court has authorized district courts to facilitate this process by ordering employers to produce the names and addresses of employees similarly situated to the representative and to issue a consent document approved in form by the court itself.[12] Further, paralleling the practice followed under Title VII in the case of true Rule 23 class actions, most circuit courts have adopted a "single-filing" rule that rather liberally permits would-be ADEA representees who have not filed timely charges with EEOC to piggyback on the timely filed charges of their co-joined individual plaintiffs or "representatives."[13]

10. *Garfield v. J.C. Nichols Real Estate,* 57 F.3d 662 (8th Cir.), *cert. denied,* __ U.S. __, 116 S.Ct. 380, 133 L.Ed.2d 303 (1995); *St. Louis v. Texas Worker's Compensation Comm'n,* 65 F.3d 43 (5th Cir.1995).

11. *Sperling v. Hoffmann–La Roche, Inc., supra* note 8. The Third Circuit has also insisted, as a prerequisite to an ADEA representative action, that the class representatives must have included a similar notice in their administrative charge filed with EEOC. *Lusardi v. Lechner,* 855 F.2d 1062, 1077–78 (3d Cir.1988).

12. *Hoffmann–La Roche, Inc. v. Sperling,* 493 U.S. 165, 110 S.Ct. 482, 107 L.Ed.2d 480 (1989). And the required degree of substantial similarity between the allegations of the putative joiner and those of the named plaintiff is less than is required for FRCP 20(a) permissive joinder. *K Mart Corp. v. Helton,* 894 S.W.2d 630 (Ky.1995), *cert. denied,* __ U.S. __, 117 S.Ct. 447, __ L.Ed.2d __ (1996). Moreover, a "class member" dismissed from such an action on the ground that he was not similarly situated enjoys tolling of the 90-day period for filing an individual lawsuit until final judgment in the class action

or even appeal from that judgment. *Armstrong v. Martin Marietta Corp.,* 93 F.3d 1505 (11th Cir.1996).

13. *See, e.g., Howlett v. Holiday Inns, Inc.,* 49 F.3d 189 (6th Cir.1995), *cert. denied,* __ U.S. __, 116 S.Ct. 379, 133 L.Ed.2d 302 (1995); *Sperling v. Hoffmann–La Roche, Inc., supra* note 8; *Tolliver v. Xerox Corp.,* 918 F.2d 1052 (2d Cir.1990), *cert. denied,* 499 U.S. 983, 111 S.Ct. 1641, 113 L.Ed.2d 736 (1991); *Anderson v. Montgomery Ward & Co., Inc.,* 852 F.2d 1008 (7th Cir.1988); *Kloos v. Carter–Day Co.,* 799 F.2d 397 (8th Cir.1986); *Naton v. Bank of California,* 649 F.2d 691 (9th Cir.1981); *Mistretta v. Sandia Corp.,* 639 F.2d 588 (10th Cir.1980). *Cf. Grayson v. K Mart Corp.,* 79 F.3d 1086 (11th Cir.1996) *cert. denied,* __ U.S. __, 117 S.Ct. 447, __ L.Ed.2d __ (1996) (permitting piggybacking into ADEA representative action by plaintiff who did not file EEOC charge but requiring her to opt into that action before applicable limitations period on her individual claim has expired). *But see Whalen v. W.R. Grace & Co.,* 56 F.3d 504 (3d Cir. 1995) (rejecting use of single-filing rule under ADEA).

Library References:

C.J.S. Civil Rights §§ 340 et seq.
West's Key No. Digests, Civil Rights ⇒331 et seq.

E. ADEA REMEDIES

§ 7.10 In General

An individual may be awarded injunctive relief, back wages, statutory "liquidated" damages equal to the amount of back wages, attorney's fees, and costs.[1] Although, as under Title VII, back pay is routinely available as a remedy for a proven ADEA violation, similar limitations on its scope apply. For example back pay will be denied for the period beginning after an employer eliminates the position from which plaintiff was terminated, provided it has not created a comparable position.[2]

With only one discovered exception,[3] the circuits approve front pay as an ADEA remedy that is almost routinely available when needed.[4] Its duration extends until the plaintiff fails to make reasonable efforts to secure substantially equivalent employment or obtains or is offered such employment.[5] At least before the Civil Rights Act of 1991, the availability of front pay under Title VII was uncertain.[6] The most common reason given for denying front pay in Title VII cases not subject to the amendments ushered in by the 1991 Civil Rights Act was that Title VII relief is equitable, whereas "frontpay resembles common law damages...."[7] But the express provision in the 1991 Act that plaintiffs who prove intentional discrimination are eligible for damages, a species

---

§ 7.10

1. 29 U.S.C.A. § 626(b) incorporates by reference the remedies authorized under the Fair Labor Standards Act, 29 U.S.C.A. §§ 216–17.

2. *Bartek v. Urban Redevelopment Authority of Pittsburgh*, 882 F.2d 739, 746–747 (3d Cir.1989).

3. The Third Circuit has ruled that front pay is not an "amount owing" within the meaning of EPA and hence of ADEA. *See Blum v. Witco*, 829 F.2d 367, 375–76 (3d Cir.1987).

4. *See, e.g., McKnight v. General Motors Corp.*, 908 F.2d 104, 117 (7th Cir.1990), *cert. denied*, 499 U.S. 919, 111 S.Ct. 1306, 113 L.Ed.2d 241 (1991). *But see Wells v. New Cherokee Corp.*, 58 F.3d 233 (6th Cir. 1995) (awarding of prompt pay when reinstatement denied is not automatic, but should be determined by trial court before jury assesses amount).

5. *See Dominic v. Consolidated Edison Co. of N.Y., Inc.*, 822 F.2d 1249 (2d Cir. 1987); *Green v. USX Corp.*, 843 F.2d 1511 (3d Cir.1988), *vacated*, 490 U.S. 1103, 109 S.Ct. 3151, 104 L.Ed.2d 1015 (1989).

6. *Compare Franks v. Bowman Transportation Co.*, 424 U.S. 747, 96 S.Ct. 1251, 47 L.Ed.2d 444 (1976) (Burger, C.J., concurring in part and dissenting in part) *and McKnight v. General Motors Corp.*, 908 F.2d 104, 117 (7th Cir.1990) (asserting, respectively, the desirability of front pay under ADEA and its doubtful availability under Title VII) *and United States v. Burke*, 504 U.S. 229, 239 n. 9, 112 S.Ct. 1867, 1873 n. 9, 119 L.Ed.2d 34 (1992) (majority notes that "some courts" have allowed Title VII front pay) *with Carter v. Sedgwick County*, 929 F.2d 1501 (10th Cir.1991) *and Weaver v. Casa Gallardo, Inc.*, 922 F.2d 1515 (11th Cir.1991) *and Edwards v. Occidental Chemical Corp.*, 892 F.2d 1442 (9th Cir.1990) *and Berndt v. Kaiser Aluminum & Chemical Sales, Inc.*, 789 F.2d 253 (3d Cir.1986) *and Shore v. Federal Express Corp.*, 777 F.2d 1155 (6th Cir.1985) (Title VII front pay available). *See* Chapter 5, Section B for discussion of Title VII remedies.

7. *Fortino v. Quasar Company*, 950 F.2d 389 (7th Cir.1991) (that decision nevertheless reserved the ADEA front pay decision for the judge rather than the jury, *id.* at 398).

of relief undeniably "legal," may lead to a unanimous judicial judgment consistent with the current weight of authority that holds front pay available to prevailing Title VII plaintiffs.

Even in jurisdictions that recognize front pay, the employer's abolition of plaintiff's former position limits the amount of front pay the plaintiff may recover.[8] Since the age 70 cap on the class protected by ADEA was removed effective January 1, 1987, it is theoretically possible for front pay to continue indefinitely, or at least for the duration of an employee's lifetime as predicted by a standard mortality table. But an employer's normal retirement age may well serve as a practical cap on the duration of what would otherwise be an astronomical total amount of front pay.[9]

Liquidated damages are available under ADEA in the same circumstances as they are available under the EPA, i.e., when the violation is "willful" within the meaning of the FLSA. This means that the double award is available only if the employer knows that its employment practice violates ADEA or recklessly disregards that its conduct will violate the Act; it is not enough that the employer knows that the Act is potentially applicable to the practice in question.[10] After *Thurston*, the Third Circuit has held that liquidated damages are available in an intentional disparate treatment case only when the plaintiff produces evidence of "outrageous" employer conduct beyond that minimally necessary to establish age discrimination.[11] Other circuits rejected this requirement that the defendant's conduct be outrageous but required as a prerequisite for liquidated damages that the underlying evidence of discrimination be "direct."[12]

A recent Supreme Court reaffirmation of the *Thurston* test, *Hazen Paper Co. v. Biggins*,[13] has specifically rejected these additional requirements. *Hazen* also made it clear that the *Thurston* definition of willfulness applies to cases concerning alleged disparate treatment against an individual employee, as well as to alleged disparate treatment resulting from the kind of formal policy at issue in *Thurston*. But the Court also reemphasized that employer conduct must be more than merely voluntary and negligent to constitute a willful violation. Indeed, the Court wrote, even an employer "who knowingly relies on age" does not

---

8. *Bartek, supra* note 2.

9. *Olitsky v. Spencer Gifts, Inc.*, 964 F.2d 1471 (5th Cir.1992), *cert. denied*, 507 U.S. 909, 113 S.Ct. 1253, 122 L.Ed.2d 652 (1993).

10. *Trans World Airlines Inc. v. Thurston*, 469 U.S. 111, 105 S.Ct. 613, 83 L.Ed.2d 523 (1985).

11. *Dreyer v. Arco Chemical Co.*, 801 F.2d 651 (3d Cir.1986), *cert. denied*, 480 U.S. 906, 107 S.Ct. 1348, 94 L.Ed.2d 519 (1987); *Anastasio v. Schering Corp.*, 838 F.2d 701 (3d Cir.1988), but was unable to develop a consistent definition of outrageous conduct. *Compare Bartek, supra*

note 2, at 744–746 (comment by superior that plaintiff might "look around for another job" if not happy at work insufficient to show outrageous conduct) *with Bruno v. W.B. Saunders Co.*, 882 F.2d 760, 771 (3d Cir.1989) (custom-tailored job description designed to fit qualifications of younger selectee rather than plaintiff sufficiently outrageous to support liquidated damages).

12. *See, e.g., Neufeld v. Searle Laboratories*, 884 F.2d 335 (8th Cir.1989).

13. 507 U.S. 604, 113 S.Ct. 1701, 123 L.Ed.2d 338 (1993).

"invariably" commit a knowing or reckless violation of the ADEA. This is because the Court's test finds willfulness only when the employer knows that or recklessly disregards whether it is violating the prohibitions of the statute, not simply when it knowingly takes age into account.[14] Specifically, the Court sought to preserve "two tiers of liability" in ADEA cases by finding liability for back pay whenever an intentional violation is established, but denying liquidated damages even for intentional violations when "an employer incorrectly but in good faith and nonrecklessly" believes that its conduct is not prohibited or is affirmatively authorized by the statute.[15] Thus although conduct constituting a constructive discharge is by its nature serious, aggravated and almost surely intentional, it does not follow that every such violation is willful.[16] Some violations, however—unlawful retaliation is an example—may inherently involve knowledge or reckless disregard of the prohibitions of the statute so that liquidated damages should follow as a matter of course from a finding of liability.[17]

Although a 1978 amendment clarifies that jury trials are available on liquidated damages claims as well as on claims for lost wages, there are unresolved legal questions about the computation of the liquidated damages award. The major issue is whether the doubling should be based on the full compensatory award, including front pay, replacement of lost pension income, and other fringe benefits or, as one circuit has held, should be limited to the amount of back pay.[18] There is also a conflict in the circuits concerning whether, when liquidated damages are

14. *Brown v. Stites Concrete, Inc.*, 994 F.3d 553, 561 (8th Cir.1993) (Loken, J., dissenting). *But see Starceski v. Westinghouse Electric*, 54 F.3d 1089 (3d Cir.1995), discussed in note 17, *infra*.

15. *Hazen Paper Co.*, 507 U.S. at 615, 113 S.Ct. at 1709. For the same reason, double damages may seldom if ever be available for ADEA violations predicated solely on disparate impact evidence, assuming, as is unclear, that ADEA liability may be predicated at all on that mode of proof. How often could a trier of fact logically conclude that an employer knowingly violated ADEA or recklessly disregarded its liability under that statute when it adopts a practice that by hypothesis does not refer to age at all? Perhaps that conclusion would have merit in the rare case where the employer's adoption of the practice followed a recent, dispositive judicial decision condemning the neutral practice in question.

16. *Peterson v. Insurance Co. of North America*, 40 F.3d 26 (2d Cir.1994).

17. *Compare Edwards v. Board of Regents*, 2 F.3d 382, 383–84 (11th Cir.1993) (declining to decide whether retaliation under ADEA necessarily entails willfulness) *with Grant v. Hazelett Strip–Casting Corp.*, 880 F.2d 1564 (2d Cir.1989) (stating that it

does). This appears to be the view relied on in *Starceski v. Westinghouse Electric*, 54 F.3d 1089 (3d Cir.1995) (upholding finding of willfulness because particular older employees were specifically targeted for layoff, so that company's decisions were not in that sense merely negligent, notwithstanding evidence that company's managers were counseled to select layoff candidates only for business reasons and that legal counsel reviewed managers' asserted justifications—in other words, despite evidence which suggested that defendant did not know it was violating ADEA).

18. *Compare Bruno, supra* note 11, at 771–772; *Graefenhain v. Pabst Brewing Co.*, 870 F.2d 1198 (7th Cir.1989) *and Cassino v. Reichhold Chemicals, Inc.*, 817 F.2d 1338 (9th Cir.1987), *cert. denied*, 484 U.S. 1047, 108 S.Ct. 785, 98 L.Ed.2d 870 (1988) (excluding front pay from the base to be doubled) *and Blum, supra* note 3, 382–383 (excluding lost pension benefits) and *Blackwell v. Sun Elec. Corp.*, 696 F.2d 1176 (6th Cir.1983) (excluding health insurance benefits from the calculation) with *Blim v. Western Electric Co.*, 731 F.2d 1473 (10th Cir.), *cert. denied*, 469 U.S. 874, 105 S.Ct. 233, 83 L.Ed.2d 161 (1984) (the liquidated amount should equal the full compensatory award including sums to replace fringe benefits).

awarded, the court may additionally award front pay [19] or prejudgment interest.[20]

Despite *Hazen's* confirmation that ADEA authorizes "legal remedies," the Civil Rights Act of 1991 gives Title VII plaintiffs alleging disparate treatment (not disproportionate adverse impact) important remedies that the circuit courts have uniformly held *unavailable* under ADEA: compensatory and punitive damages.[21] (Those damages are allowed in ADEA retaliation cases; the exception is made because both types of damages are allowed for retaliation claims under FLSA, the remedial scheme adopted by reference in the ADEA.)[22] State law claims authorizing compensatory or punitive damages may often be joined with ADEA claims, however, and care must then be taken to distinguish the respective authorizing standards.[23]

Accordingly, while it could be said categorically before the 1991 Act that an ADEA plaintiff was remedially better situated than a claimant under Title VII, that is no longer necessarily true. To be awarded more than back and, with luck, front pay, the ADEA plaintiff must prove

19. *Walther v. Lone Star Gas Co.*, 952 F.2d 119 (5th Cir.1992); *Brooks v. Hilton Casinos, Inc.*, 959 F.2d 757 (9th Cir.), *cert. denied*, 506 U.S. 906, 113 S.Ct. 300, 121 L.Ed.2d 224 (1992) (holding no); *Price v. Marshall Erdman & Associates, Inc.*, 966 F.2d 320 (7th Cir.1992); *Castle v. Sangamo Weston, Inc.*, 837 F.2d 1550 (11th Cir.1988) (holding yes).

20. Courts that, despite *Thurston*, view liquidated damages as at least partly compensatory reject prejudgment interest, holding that the plaintiff who receives both would be overcompensated. *See McCann v. Texas City Refining, Inc.*, 984 F.2d 667 (5th Cir.1993); *Fortino v. Quasar Co.*, 950 F.2d 389 (7th Cir.1991). Courts that consider liquidated damages as the ADEA's substitute for punitive damages allow prejudgment interest in addition. *Starceski v. Westinghouse Electric*, 54 F.3d 1089 (3d Cir. 1995); *Reichman v. Bonsignore, Brignati and Mazzotta*, 818 F.2d 278 (2d Cir.1987); *Lindsey v. American Cast Iron Pipe Co.*, 810 F.2d 1094 (11th Cir.1987); *Kelly v. American Standard, Inc.*, 640 F.2d 974 (9th Cir. 1981). The latter view is fortified by the Supreme Court's most recent reaffirmation that ADEA liquidated damages are designed to be punitive. *Commissioner v. Schleier*, ___ U.S. ___, 115 S.Ct. 507, 130 L.Ed.2d 415 (1994).

21. For decisions denying ADEA plaintiffs compensatory and punitive damages, including damages for pain and suffering and emotional distress, *see Moskowitz v. Trustees of Purdue University*, 5 F.3d 279 (7th Cir.1993); *Wilson v. Monarch Paper Co.*, 939 F.2d 1138, 1144 (5th Cir.1991); *Haskell v. Kaman Corp.*, 743 F.2d 113, 120–121 n. 2 (2d Cir.1984) and cases cited therein; *Pfeiffer v. Essex Wire Corp.*, 682 F.2d 684 (7th Cir.1982); *Naton v. Bank of California*, 649 F.2d 691 (9th Cir.1981); *Frith v. Eastern Air Lines, Inc.*, 611 F.2d 950 (4th Cir.1979); *Vazquez v. Eastern Air Lines, Inc.*, 579 F.2d 107 (1st Cir.1978); *Dean v. American Sec. Ins. Co.*, 559 F.2d 1036 (5th Cir.1977), *cert. denied*, 434 U.S. 1066, 98 S.Ct. 1243, 55 L.Ed.2d 767 (1978); *Rogers v. Exxon Research & Engineering Co.*, 550 F.2d 834 (3d Cir.1977), *cert. denied*, 434 U.S. 1022, 98 S.Ct. 749, 54 L.Ed.2d 770 (1978). A district court has observed that Congress' silence about ADEA in the provisions of the 1991 Act that authorized those damages for Title VII disparate treatment plaintiffs shows an intent to continue to withhold those remedies in actions under ADEA. *Capparell v. National Health Management, Inc.*, 1993 WL 516399 (E.D.Pa. 1993).

22. *Moskowitz, supra* note 21.

23. *See Sanchez v. Puerto Rico Oil Co.*, 37 F.3d 712 (1st Cir.1994) (plaintiff could recover separate awards of punitive damages under Puerto Rico law as well as under ADEA, under a punitive damages exception to the ban on multiple recoveries); *Ryther v. KARE 11*, 864 F.Supp. 1525 (D.Minn. 1994) (court finds ADEA wilfulness, and thus doubles jury's back pay award as ADEA liquidated damages, but does not find the deliberate disregard of plaintiff's rights required by state law for the award of punitive damages).

wilfulness; and even then she is likely to receive an award equal to only back pay doubled, or at best twice the amount of back and front pay combined. By contrast, the Title VII plaintiff may now recover, by showing no more than an intentional violation, significantly more than back and, probably, front pay: compensatory damages capped in amounts that vary with the size of the defendant's employee complement. Only when she seeks punitive damages must the Title VII plaintiff show something akin to ADEA wilfulness. On the other hand, the 1991 Act caps the sum of compensatory and punitive damages available under Title VII, while there is no absolute cap on the size of ADEA liquidated damages. An ADEA plaintiff who recovers a very large award of back pay, front pay or both may accordingly still find that his liquidated damages exceed the amount a Title VII counterpart could recover by way of compensatory and punitive damages.

Further, it appears that the 1991 Act denies successful ADEA plaintiffs, unlike their Title VII counterparts, any recovery for the fees of expert witnesses.[24] But in contrast to § 706(k) of Title VII, the FLSA, and therefore ADEA, authorizes attorneys' fees only to "plaintiffs," not "prevailing parties." Thus even a prevailing defendant who can make the extraordinary showing of frivolousness demanded by the *Christiansburg Garment* interpretation of § 706(k) may not be entitled to an award of attorneys' fees from the plaintiff.

In considering whether to settle an ADEA claim, counsel for both parties should also take into account the employer's potential liability for pre- and post-judgment interest;[25] compelled waiver of statutory attorney's fees either by a successful offer of judgment under Federal Rule of Civil Procedure 68 or by provision of the settlement agreement;[26] Federal Rule of Civil Procedure 54(d) "costs," defined by 28 U.S.C.A. § 1920 to include clerks' and marshals' fees, fees of court reporters for transcripts, printing and witness fees, copy costs, docket fees, and fees for court-appointed experts and interpreters; and the full taxability of plaintiffs' settlement proceeds.[27]

Library References:

C.J.S. Civil Rights §§ 426–427, 434.
West's Key No. Digests, Civil Rights ⚖406.

24. *James v. Sears, Roebuck and Co.*, 21 F.3d 989 (10th Cir.1994); *Houghton v. Sipco, Inc.*, 828 F.Supp. 631 (D.Iowa 1993), *amended*, 38 F.3d 953 (8th Cir.1994).

25. *See Gelof v. Papineau*, 829 F.2d 452 (3d Cir.1987).

26. *See* Chapter 12 on Attorneys' Fees, in particular the discussion of *Evans v. Jeff D.*, 475 U.S. 717, 106 S.Ct. 1531, 89 L.Ed.2d

747 (1986). Note, however, that FLSA, unlike Title VII, does not describe attorneys' fees as "costs." Under the logic of *Evans*, those fees might therefore still accrue even after a Rule 68 offer made by the EPA or ADEA defendant.

27. See Chapter 5, Section C above.

Chapter Eight

THE EQUAL PAY ACT OF 1963

Analysis

Library References:

C.J.S. Labor Relations § 1184.
West's Key No. Digests, Labor Relations ☞1333.

§ 8.1 Introduction

The Equal Pay Act of 1963 [1] ("EPA") requires "equal pay for equal work" within the same establishment regardless of sex. The concept of "equal work" lies at the heart of the Act. General comparisons between two jobs carrying unequal pay will not suffice to establish that work is "equal"; rather, demonstrating an EPA violation demands specific showings of equivalent skill, effort, and responsibility, as well as performance under similar working conditions. Once an inequality is found, however, it cannot be remedied by a reduction in the wages of the higher paid sex.

The EPA contains four affirmative defenses. Specifically, the EPA allows exceptions to the equal pay for equal work principle when differentials are pursuant to: (1) seniority systems; (2) merit systems; (3) systems which measure earnings by quantity or quality of production (incentive systems); or (4) factors other than sex.

After examining which employers are covered by the EPA, this chapter will discuss the elements of the plaintiff's prima facie case and the employer's defenses. Second, this chapter will address EPA's anti-retaliation provisions. Third, it will look at EPA enforcement and remedies. This chapter, next, will compare the EPA with Title VII. Finally, this chapter will examine the doctrine of comparable worth and its uncomfortable fit with either the EPA or Title VII.

A. EPA COVERAGE, THE PRIMA FACIE CASE AND AFFIRMATIVE DEFENSES

§ 8.2 Coverage

Why would a plaintiff resort to the Equal Pay Act when Title VII proscribes sex discrimination in *all* terms and conditions of employment, not just for compensation between persons of different genders holding "equal" jobs? For starters, it may be the only game in town. EPA looks

---

§ 8.1

1. 29 U.S.C.A. § 206(d). The Equal Pay Act provides:

No employer having employees subject to any provisions of this section shall discriminate, within any establishment in which such employees are employed, between employees on the basis of sex by paying wages to employees in such establishment at a rate less than the rate at which he pays wages to employees of the opposite sex in such establishment for equal work on jobs the performance of which requires equal skill, effort, and re-

sponsibility, and which are performed under similar working conditions, except where such payment is made pursuant to (i) a seniority system; (ii) a merit system; (iii) a system which measures earnings by quantity or quality of production; or (iv) a differential based on any factor other than sex. *Provided,* That an employer who is paying a wage rate differential in violation of this subsection shall not, in order to comply with the provisions of this subsection, reduce the wage rate of any employee.

Id.

primarily to the Fair Labor Standards Act [1] ("FLSA"), to which it is an amendment, for provisions on coverage, as well as enforcement. In sharp contrast to Title VII, EPA has no coverage threshold defined in terms of the employer's number of employees. Instead, it embraces in the first instance employees from employers of any size, unless the employer is in one of several specifically exempted industries.[2] These industries include certain fishing and agricultural businesses as well as small local newspapers.

An employee not in an exempted industry may assert an FLSA, and therefore an EPA claim if she has some contact with interstate commerce. This contact may be established by satisfying one of two requirements. The first concerns the nature of the work implicated by the plaintiff's claim. If the employee is "engaged in commerce" or produces "goods for commerce," the work is covered, no matter what the employer's size.

An alternative FLSA avenue protects employees who, though not themselves engaged in or producing goods for interstate commerce, work for nonexempt businesses that are. This alternative measure of FLSA coverage extends EPA's protection to persons employed by "enterprises" engaged in commerce or producing goods for commerce. Such enterprises will be deemed to meet the interstate commerce test if they (1) achieved certain sales volumes or (2) were part of certain industries specifically mentioned in FLSA, provided in each case that other employees of such enterprises were engaged in or producing goods for commerce.

A third approach, based on text unique to EPA, arguably reaches more broadly than the FLSA alternatives. It focuses on the relation between other employees' production and interstate commerce, without regard to the commerce involvement of the plaintiff or the defendant employer. The EPA prohibits employers that have "employees subject to" EPA from engaging in unequal pay discrimination against [other?] "employees." [3] Read literally, the EPA would therefore appear to protect all employees of employers that have at least two employees of different genders who are engaged in or producing goods for commerce, even if those employers are not FLSA "enterprises."

The Act defines an employer as "any person acting directly or indirectly in the interest of an employer in relation to an employee...." [4] Notwithstanding this definition, claims against supervisors or managers in their individual as distinct from official capacities are likely to be dismissed because in an individual capacity a defendant lacks control over the plaintiff's terms of employment.[5]

§ 8.2

1. 29 U.S.C.A. § 209 *et seq.*

2. 29 U.S.C.A. § 213.

3. 29 U.S.C.A. § 206(d)(1).

4. 29 U.S.C.A. § 203(d).

5. *See Welch v. Laney,* 57 F.3d 1004 (11th Cir.1995).

§ 8.3 Equal Work

The first step in the plaintiff's prima facie case is to establish that the plaintiff performed work equal to that of another of the opposite sex. *Corning Glass Works v. Brennan*[1] observes that job equivalence, as measured by skill, effort, responsibility, and working conditions, need not be precise, only substantial.[2] The circuit courts have consistently so held.[3] The Third Circuit, for example, has found that the EPA requires only that the jobs be substantially similar.[4] The court held that the disparity in rates of pay between female selector-packers and male selector-packers was discriminatory. Although the men were also available to perform physical labor, the jobs were substantially similar because other male employees who routinely performed physical labor were paid at wages close to those of the female selector-packers. There was, therefore, no appreciable economic benefit to the employer in having the male selector-packers perform these physical tasks.

The issue in *Corning Glass* was whether the employer violated the EPA by paying a higher base wage to male night shift inspectors than it paid to female day shift inspectors. Long before the advent of EPA, Corning, in order to fill the male night inspector positions, had paid the night inspectors more than the female day inspectors. After the enactment of the EPA, Corning opened both jobs to members of both genders and moved to eliminate the differential rates, but a collective-bargaining agreement perpetuated them.

In determining whether there was equal pay for equal work, the Supreme Court compared the working conditions of both the day and night inspectors.[5] Guided by legislative history, the Court defined "working conditions" by reference to its common meaning in the language of industrial relations, focusing on the job's "hazards" and "surroundings."[6] In that lexicon, "hazards" referred to the physical hazards regularly encountered by all employees and "surroundings" to constant workplace features or elements like dangerous chemicals or fumes.[7] The work performed by the Corning night and day inspectors was substantially similar, the Court found, with respect to hazards and

§ 8.3

1. 417 U.S. 188, 94 S.Ct. 2223, 41 L.Ed.2d 1 (1974).

2. *Id.* at 203 n.24, 94 S.Ct. at 2232 n.24.

3. *See, e.g., Hein v. Oregon College of Education,* 718 F.2d 910 (9th Cir.1983); *EEOC v. Kenosha Unified School Dist. No. 1,* 620 F.2d 1220 (7th Cir.1980); *Horner v. Mary Institute,* 613 F.2d 706 (8th Cir.1980); *Brennan v. South Davis Community Hosp.,* 538 F.2d 859 (10th Cir.1976); *Brennan v. Owensboro–Daviess County Hosp.,* 523 F.2d 1013 (6th Cir.1975), *cert. denied sub nom. Owensboro Daviess County Hosp., Inc. v. Usery,* 425 U.S. 973, 96 S.Ct. 2170, 48 L.Ed.2d 796 (1976); *Hodgson v. Corning Glass Works,* 474 F.2d 226 (2d Cir.1973), *affirmed on others grounds sub nom. Corn-ing Glass Works v. Brennan,* 417 U.S. 188, 94 S.Ct. 2223, 41 L.Ed.2d 1 (1974); *Hodgson v. Fairmont Supply Co.,* 454 F.2d 490 (4th Cir.1972); *Hodgson v. Brookhaven General Hosp.,* 436 F.2d 719 (5th Cir.1970); *Shultz v. Wheaton Glass Co.,* 421 F.2d 259 (3d Cir.), *cert. denied,* 398 U.S. 905, 90 S.Ct. 1696, 26 L.Ed.2d 64 (1970).

4. *Shultz v. Wheaton Glass Co., supra* note 3.

5. The EPA requires equal pay for equal work "performed under similar working conditions." 29 U.S.C.A. § 206(d)(1).

6. *Corning Glass, supra* note 1, at 202.

7. *Id.*

surroundings so defined.[8] The only substantial difference between the two jobs was time of day.[9] The Court concluded that the different time of day worked did not render unequal otherwise substantially equal working conditions.[10] Accordingly, Corning had prima facie violated the EPA by paying women less than men for equal work. Whether time of day can constitute an affirmative defense for such a prima facie claim will be discussed below.

§ 8.4 Unequal Pay

Another element of the plaintiff's prima facie case is a showing that the plaintiff was paid less than another of the opposite sex. This element involves two distinct concepts. First, the plaintiff must be paid a lesser "rate" of pay. Second, this rate must be compared with that of an individual of the opposite sex performing substantially similar work.

a. Equal "Rate" of Pay

What constitutes "equal pay" was addressed by the Sixth Circuit in *Bence v. Detroit Health Corp.*[1] Plaintiff was a female manager at a health club. The club designated certain days as women's days and other days as men's. Only staff members and managers of the sex assigned to that day's customer gender worked any one day. The managers were paid commissions on the health club memberships they sold. There were, however, more women's than men's memberships to be sold.[2] The health club thus paid a higher percentage commission, per membership sold, to its male than to its female managers, although they received approximately equal aggregate compensation.[3]

Ms. Bence challenged the practice as a violation of the EPA because she was paid a lesser "rate" (percentage commission) than a male manager.[4] The court concluded that compensation on a "per sale" basis made it clear that the female managers were being paid less than their male counterparts.[5] If total compensation had been based upon total service to the employer's clientele, the court wrote, the total equal compensation argument might have merit. But commissions worth less per sale to women than to men employees violated the EPA.[6]

---

8. *Id.* at 203.

9. The Court noted that Corning's own job evaluation plans had always treated the two positions as equal in all respects, including working conditions. *Id.* at 202–03.

10. *Id.*

§ 8.4

1. 712 F.2d 1024 (6th Cir.1983), *cert. denied*, 465 U.S. 1025, 104 S.Ct. 1282, 79 L.Ed.2d 685 (1984).

2. The ratio of women's memberships sold to men's memberships was 60:40. *Id.* at 1027.

3. The commissions paid by the employer were determined in a way that ensured equal compensation to both male and female managers. Female managers were paid 5% on the sale of memberships where male managers were paid 7½%. *Id.* at 1026. The employer argued unsuccessfully that there was no EPA violation because the men and women employees received substantially equal compensation for the equal work performed. *Id.* at 1027–28.

4. *Id.*

5. *Id.* at 1027.

6. *Id.* at 1027–28.

b. The Necessity of a "Comparator" Within a Single "Establishment"

In order to show unequal pay, there must be some comparison between the complaining individual and one of the opposite sex in a substantially similar position. The plaintiff, therefore, must demonstrate that an individual of the opposite sex received greater compensation for substantially the same job. This task is accomplished through the use of a comparator. The comparator may be one who held the job before the plaintiff,[7] who replaced the plaintiff, or who held a substantially similar position contemporaneously with the plaintiff. Finally, the comparator must also be employed in the same establishment as the plaintiff. These requirements may be subdivided into four components.

First, the comparator may not be hypothetical but rather a specific and better paid individual performing a job of substantially equal skill, effort, and responsibility.[8] Where a plaintiff identified her male comparators in general terms as "any men who got any higher salary increases than [the plaintiff] did," the plaintiff failed to carry a prima facie case.[9]

Second, the comparator must perform a substantially similar job. The court analyzes the job, not the qualification or performance characteristics of individual employees holding the job, and only the skill and qualifications actually needed to perform the job in question are considered.[10] Additionally, the examination rests on the primary, not the incidental or insubstantial job duties. Where the plaintiff performs substantially similar tasks but the comparator also has significant additional primary duties, the plaintiff has not established the plaintiff's prima facie case.[11]

Third, the comparator may be a past, present or future employee in a substantially similar position. The Eleventh Circuit recently found a valid comparison between the plaintiff, a former "Vice–President, Administration," and a current "Vice–President, Controller" because financial concerns were essential to both jobs.[12] But if the plaintiff cannot

---

7. A female employee stated EPA and Title VII claims although her male "comparators" were no longer employed or employed in equivalent positions within the applicable limitations periods. *Brinkley-Obu v. Hughes Training, Inc.*, 36 F.3d 336 (4th Cir.1994).

8. *EEOC v. Liggett & Myers, Inc.*, 690 F.2d 1072, 1076–78 (4th Cir.1982).

9. *Houck v. Virginia Polytechnic Institute and State University*, 10 F.3d 204, 206 (4th Cir.1993).

10. *Miranda v. B & B Cash Grocery Store, Inc.*, 975 F.2d 1518 (11th Cir.1992).

11. *Mulhall v. Advance Security, Inc.*, 19 F.3d 586, 593 (11th Cir.), *cert. denied*, ___ U.S. ___, 115 S.Ct. 298, 130 L.Ed.2d 212 (1994).

12. *Id.* at 593–95. Plaintiff (who held the position of Vice–President, Administra-

tion from 1981 to 1991) offered as comparator an employee holding the position of Vice–President, Controller in 1994. The plaintiff's responsibilities had included, among other things, managing costs on contracts, handling risk management, and arranging leases for the corporate headquarters. *Id.* at 594 n.17. Responsibilities of the current Vice–President, Controller included direct control of corporate accounting and financial matters. *Id.* at 594. Although the duties of the Vice–President, Controller had changed significantly since the plaintiff resigned in 1991, the Court concluded that the plaintiff had established this element of the prima facie case because the "monetary concerns permeat[ing] all aspects of the plaintiff's position" and the proposed comparator's responsibility for corporate economic well-being were substantially similar.

establish that the plaintiff's predecessor, successor, or contemporary was paid more for the same responsibilities, the plaintiff has failed to make a prima facie showing.[13]

Finally, the individual identified as the comparator must be an employee of the same "establishment" as the plaintiff. The Secretary of Labor has defined "establishment" to mean "a distinct physical place of business rather than . . . an entire business or 'enterprise' which may include several separate places of business."[14] In "unusual circumstances," however, a single establishment can include more than one physical location.[15] When there is centralized control and administration, some courts have been willing to find a single EPA establishment though there are different physical locations.[16] If there is centralized control and a working relationship between the plaintiff and the comparator, a reasonable trier of fact could infer that a single establishment existed for purposes of the EPA. For example, a plaintiff comparing herself to subordinate project managers working in separate locations satisfied the "single establishment" requirement by demonstrating "centralized control of job descriptions, salary administration and job assignments."[17] The project managers reported to the plaintiff in a central office and sought her approval on significant situations. Further, the plaintiff approved all wage and benefit levels and exercised ultimate control over operations at the separate facilities.[18]

Courts have refused to extend the definition of "establishment" beyond the bounds of single physical location when the different offices are geographically and operationally distinct—with operational distinctiveness marked principally by degree of centralized control. For example, the Eleventh Circuit restricted the consideration of salaries to employees in one physical location[19] when the local office made the ultimate hiring decision and, within a broad range set by the central office, set specific salaries.[20] Similarly, the Ninth Circuit refused to extend the "establishment" concept beyond the confines of one physical location[21] of a defense contractor that used independent management for different customers with different needs, maintained separate project

---

13. *Weiss v. Coca–Cola Bottling Co. of Chicago*, 990 F.2d 333, 337–38 (7th Cir. 1993) (plaintiff's predecessor's starting salary was the same as the plaintiff's, and her successor's was higher because he had additional duties).

14. 29 C.F.R. § 1620.9(a) (1993).

15. 29 C.F.R. § 1620.9(b) (1993) provides, "[U]nusual circumstances may call for two or more distinct physical portions of a business enterprise being treated as a single establishment."

16. *See e.g., Brennan v. Goose Creek Consolidated Indep. Sch. Dist.*, 519 F.2d 53 (5th Cir.1975).

17. *Mulhall, supra* note 11, at 591. The district court ruled that the plaintiff and the project managers, subordinates of the plaintiff, occupied positions substantially similar for EPA purposes. The court of appeals reviewed only the district court's conclusion that the project managers and the plaintiff did not work in a single establishment.

18. *Id.*

19. *Meeks v. Computer Associates International*, 15 F.3d 1013, 1017 (11th Cir. 1994).

20. *Id.* at 1017.

21. *Foster v. Arcata Associates, Inc.*, 772 F.2d 1453, 1464 (9th Cir.1985), *cert. denied*, 475 U.S. 1048, 106 S.Ct. 1267, 89 L.Ed.2d 576 (1986).

budgets, and endowed managers at separate facilities with independent authority to make personnel decisions.[22]

§ 8.5 The Employer's Defenses

Once a plaintiff has established a prima facie case, the employer bears the burden of proving—producing evidence and persuading—that the employment practice fits within one or more of EPA's affirmative defenses. The EPA provides four specific defenses. "Unequal pay" for equal work is permitted when the payment is made pursuant to (i) a seniority system, (ii) a merit system; (iii) a system which measures earnings by quantity or quality of production; or (iv) a differential based on any factor other than sex.[1]

Affirmative defenses (i)-(iii) are rarely used. These three defenses specifically require a "system." This system need not be a formalized or structured system, but employees must know about the system nonetheless. And a defendant asserting a seniority system affirmative defense must "be able to identify standards for measuring seniority which are systematically applied and observed."[2] Further, the system must be operated in good faith and not used as a way to maintain sex-based wage differences. The third defense of a system based on quality or quantity of production, however, has little independent vitality. First, if employees are paid the same "rate" for their work based on production, there is no EPA violation. Second, a quality or quantity system is so closely related to a merit system that it has no separate identity. The majority of litigation in the area of affirmative defenses, therefore, has centered around the rather ambiguous defense (iv), "any factor other than sex."

Examples of "factors other than sex" include salary retention policies, prior salary consideration, and economic benefit to the employer.[3] In determining that a salary retention policy qualified as a "factor other than sex," a district court noted that the policy was part of a company-wide business strategy.[4] Employees were permitted to retain a previous salary after transfer to a lesser paid position. The court noted that the policy recognized length of service, improved employee morale, and avoided the additional expenses of searching for new employees.

A second factor that may fall within the "any factor other than sex" exception is the use of a prior salary to set a salary with a new company.[5] The Ninth Circuit held use of a prior salary was not flatly prohibited by the EPA because the "any other factor other than sex" defense (unlike the "job relatedness" component of the Title VII "business necessity"

22. *Id.* at 1464–65.

§ 8.5

1. 29 U.S.C.A. § 206(d)(1).

2. *Irby v. Bittick,* 44 F.3d 949, 954 (11th Cir.1995) (but "defined exceptions which are known and understood by the employees" do not invalidate a system. *Id.*).

3. *See, e.g., Kouba v. Allstate Insurance, Co.,* 691 F.2d 873 (9th Cir.1982); *Hodgson v. Robert Hall Clothes, Inc.,* 473 F.2d 589 (3d Cir.), *cert. denied,* 414 U.S. 866, 94 S.Ct. 50, 38 L.Ed.2d 85 (1973).

4. *Christiana v. Metropolitan Life Insurance Co.,* 839 F.Supp. 248, 252–54 (S.D.N.Y. 1993).

5. *Kouba, supra* note 3.

defense to disparate impact) is not limited to criteria pertaining to a particular job.[6] The key questions, the court wrote, concern the genuineness and significance of the employer's business reasons for the policy. The Eleventh Circuit also allows reliance on prior salary but only when other business considerations—such as the selectee's greater amount of experience in a closely related job—reasonably explain its utilization.[7]

Another factor that has been approved as something "other than sex" is reliance on differential economic benefit to the employer of otherwise equal "male" and "female" jobs.[8] A clothier could pay its salesmen more than its saleswomen where the men produced greater benefit to the employer because the men's clothing department generated higher profit margins and revenues. Further, the employer considered sex segregation in the jobs unavoidable (deploying only male salespersons in the men's clothing department) to prevent embarrassment to customers.[9]

Some factors have been rejected by the courts as not within the "other than sex" exception. For example, compensation disparities keyed to gender-based actuarial differences unlawfully discriminated despite their link to longevity. In *City of Los Angeles, Department of Water and Power v. Manhart*,[10] female city employees were required to pay more into their pension fund than were male employees. The employer argued that the contribution differentials were based upon the statistical generalization that women live longer than men. Observing that longevity hinges on many factors other than gender that vary significantly by individual, the Supreme Court concluded that the longevity factor as applied by the defendant was itself based on gender alone and was not, therefore, a "factor other than sex."

The Court has also rejected time of day as an "other than sex" factor where time of day is the sole difference between the jobs. In *Corning Glass*, the Court determined that the time during which work is performed does not constitute the kind of difference in working conditions that renders jobs "unequal;" instead time of work should be

---

6. *Id.* at 878.

7. *Irby, supra* note 2, at 955. More experience in similar positions remains a neutral, nondiscriminatory reason even if the plaintiff has greater total service. *See EEOC v. Louisiana Office of Community Services,* 47 F.3d 1438 (5th Cir.1995) (case under ADEA). In *Irby,* for example, the male comparator employees were lawfully able to be paid at a higher rate than plaintiff based on their prior salary earned in other positions in the *same division* of the employer. The court acknowledged that prior salary *alone* cannot justify unequal pay. But it considered its holding consistent with *Kouba* because in *Irby* the facts suggested that experience played only *a* role in setting the salary at the new job. *But*

see Peters v. City of Shreveport, 818 F.2d 1148 (5th Cir.1987) (regardless of other factors, where sex is even a "but for" cause, the EPA is violated).

8. *Byrd v. Ronayne,* 61 F.3d 1026 (1st Cir.1995) (alternative holding); *Robert Hall, supra* note 3.

9. *Id.* at 597.

10. 435 U.S. 702, 98 S.Ct. 1370, 55 L.Ed.2d 657 (1978). *Manhart* involved a Title VII claim. However, the Court concluded that the Bennett Amendment to Title VII incorporated the EPA affirmative defenses into Title VII litigation. The Court therefore construed the "any factor other than sex" EPA defense and applied it to a claim under Title VII.

analyzed as a possible "factor other than sex." [11]   The Court acknowledged that a shift differential is permitted under the EPA provided that it is nondiscriminatory in origin and application.   While Corning had paid men a higher wage for night work than for day work when women were not permitted to work at night, these differentials continued even after women were admitted to night work.   Against this background, the Court found the shift differential discriminatory and not a "factor other than sex."

B.   RETALIATION

§ 8.6   In General

The FLSA anti-retaliation provision, applicable by reference to EPA, prohibits retaliation in language more cramped than § 704 of Title VII. By offering protection against reprisal only to those who have "filed any complaint" or "instituted any proceeding," it does not in terms protect those who have made an informal on-the-job protest.   But the federal judiciary views access to available avenues of protest of such importance that at least five circuit courts have nevertheless extended such protection to informal protesters.[1]   One circuit has even held that EPA authorizes compensatory and punitive damages for unlawful retaliation.[2]

C.   UNEQUAL PAY FOR EQUAL WORK: EPA AND TITLE VII COMPARED

§ 8.7   In General

Why would some plaintiffs resort to the Equal Pay Act, with its narrow proscription of one limited kind of sex-based wage discrimination, when Title VII in addition prohibits other forms of sex-based wage discrimination as well as sex discrimination affecting different terms and conditions of employment?   The answer lies in varying proof requirements and differences in enforcement and remedial schemes.

In an unequal pay for equal work situation, there are three possible ways of proving a claim under Title VII.   A plaintiff may offer "direct" evidence of gender discriminatory intent, evidence from which such

---

11. See text accompanying notes 1 through 10, *supra*, § 8.3.

§ 8.6

1. *See EEOC v. Romeo Community Schools*, 976 F.2d 985, 989 (6th Cir.1992); *EEOC v. White and Son Enterprises*, 881 F.2d 1006, 1011 (11th Cir.1989); *Brock v. Richardson*, 812 F.2d 121, 124–25 (3d Cir. 1987); *Love v. RE/Max of America, Inc.*, 738 F.2d 383, 387 (10th Cir.1984); *Brennan v. Maxey's Yamaha, Inc.*, 513 F.2d 179, 181 (8th Cir.1975).   *But see Lambert v. Genesee Hospital*, 10 F.3d 46 (2d Cir.1993) (construing language strictly to find no protection to informal protestor), *cert. denied*, __ U.S. __, 114 S.Ct. 1612, 128 L.Ed.2d 339 (1994).

2. *Travis v. Gary Community Mental Health Center, Inc.*, 921 F.2d 108, 112 (7th Cir.1990), *cert. denied*, 502 U.S. 812, 112 S.Ct. 60, 116 L.Ed.2d 36 (1991).   The court reasoned that in amending FLSA to include "legal" as well as "equitable" relief as appropriate, Congress intended to include compensatory and punitive damages for intentional torts. *Id.* at 111–12.

discriminatory intent may be inferred, or evidence that establishes an EPA violation. The federal circuit decisions are divided over which of these proof modes is permissible or indispensable. The Fifth Circuit, for example, requires direct evidence of discriminatory intent to show an "equal pay" violation of Title VII.[1] The court concluded from the Supreme Court's *County of Washington v. Gunther*[2] decision that only a transparently based sex-biased system for wage determination could state an unequal pay for equal work claim under Title VII. The Seventh Circuit has said the same.[3] For these courts, then, the *Gunther* facts represent the outer limit of Title VII liability for gender-based discrimination in compensation.

On the other hand, several circuits have decided that the *McDonnell Douglas/Burdine*[4] inferential evidence approach may be used in an unequal pay for equal work situation to prove a violation of Title VII.[5] These circuits, however, divide over whether the traditional Title VII allocation of burdens of proof, or the very different framework established by the EPA, controls. A slim majority consider Title VII and EPA claims completely independent; these courts require proof for each alleged violation that tracks the distinct elements and burden shifts of each statute.[6] Other circuits, however, hold that a violation of the EPA is *ipso facto* a violation of Title VII, so that the Title VII claim requires no additional proof of intent.[7] Regulations promulgated by the EEOC support the latter view.[8]

The difference between these approaches can make a substantial difference to outcome. The prima facie case for an EPA claim is that the employer pays different wages to employees of the opposite sex for "equal work"—work requiring equal skill, effort, and responsibility and

---

§ 8.7

1. *Plemer v. Parsons–Gilbane*, 713 F.2d 1127, 1133–34 (5th Cir.1983).

2. 452 U.S. 161, 101 S.Ct. 2242, 68 L.Ed.2d 751 (1981). See Section E below for a thorough discussion of *Gunther*.

3. *EEOC v. Sears, Roebuck & Co.*, 839 F.2d 302, 340–342 (7th Cir.1988). Only a year later, however, another panel (with, however, only one different judge) strongly suggested that a plaintiff could prevail in a gender-based compensation action under Title VII by meeting the burdens of proof specified by *McDonnell Douglas* and *Burdine*. *Fallon v. Illinois*, 882 F.2d 1206, 1213–1217 (7th Cir.1989).

4. See Chapter 4, Section B for a complete discussion of this inferential way of proving a Title VII claim.

5. *See, e.g., Miranda v. B & B Cash Grocery Store, Inc.*, 975 F.2d 1518, 1530–31 (11th Cir.1992) and cases cited *infra* notes 11–13.

6. *See Meeks v. Computer Associates International*, 15 F.3d 1013, 1021 (11th Cir. 1994); *Tidwell v. Fort Howard Corp.*, 989 F.2d 406, 410–12 (10th Cir.1993); *Fallon v. Illinois*, 882 F.2d 1206, 1213–1217 (7th Cir. 1989); *Peters v. City of Shreveport*, 818 F.2d 1148, 1154–55 (5th Cir.1987), *cert. dismissed*, 485 U.S. 930, 108 S.Ct. 1101, 99 L.Ed.2d 264 (1988); *Brewster v. Barnes*, 788 F.2d 985, 992–93 (4th Cir.1986).

7. *See Korte v. Diemer*, 909 F.2d 954, 959 (6th Cir.1990); *Floyd v. Kellogg Sales Co.*, 841 F.2d 226, 229 n. 2 (8th Cir.), *cert. denied*, 488 U.S. 970, 109 S.Ct. 501, 102 L.Ed.2d 537 (1988); *McKee v. Bi–State Dev. Agency*, 801 F.2d 1014, 1019 (8th Cir.1986); *Kouba v. Allstate Ins. Co.*, 691 F.2d 873, 875 (9th Cir.1982).

8. 29 C.F.R. § 1620.27(a) (1993). The regulation states in relevant part,"[W]here the jurisdictional prerequisites of both the EPA and [T]itle VII ... are satisfied, any violation of the [EPA] is also a violation of Title VII."

performed under similar working conditions.[9]   Once the plaintiff has made this showing, the defendant bears the burden of establishing— producing evidence and persuading by a preponderance—one of the affirmative defenses. There is no separate requirement under the EPA that the plaintiff offer evidence of intent to discriminate; in this sense the EPA has been called a "strict liability" statute.[10]

By contrast, the standard, inferential prima facie evidence required to establish a Title VII individual disparate treatment claim merely *begins* with a showing that the plaintiff occupies a job similar to that of a higher paid member of the opposite sex.[11] The defendant must then produce evidence of a legitimate nondiscriminatory reason for paying less. If the defendant does so, the plaintiff may still prevail by proving in a variety of ways that the employer intended to discriminate based on gender.[12] In sharp contrast to EPA, employer intent is critical, and it is the Title VII plaintiff who throughout the case bears the risk of nonpersuasion on the "ultimate" question of intentional disparate treatment because of sex.[13]

Until recently, different approaches in the circuits to the required elements of Title VII versus EPA proof had minimal practical importance. The remedies under EPA were more congenial to the plaintiff than the remedies under Title VII, because EPA afforded the possibility of liquidated damages while Title VII ten remitted the plaintiff to back pay. So the plaintiff with only an equal pay claim usually took the EPA route, foregoing the separate remedy under Title VII. But the passage of the Civil Rights Act of 1991 has expanded the remedies under Title VII to include compensatory as well as punitive damages for intentional or "disparate treatment" violations; and most EPA violations fit that description, even if no direct evidence of intent is required. In circuits that import the eased EPA proof standards into Title VII equal pay litigation, the plaintiff can now recover Title VII's potentially more generous remedies by carrying the lighter EPA burden. Perhaps these circuits may now reassess their conclusion that the distinction between the proof requirement under the two statutes is merely "technical."

9. *See Gunther*, 452 U.S. at 168, 101 S.Ct. at 2247.

10. *See Meeks v. Computer Associates International*, 15 F.3d 1013, 1019 (11th Cir. 1994); *Patkus v. Sangamon–Cass Consortium*, 769 F.2d 1251, 1260 n. 5 (7th Cir. 1985).

11. The Eleventh Circuit recently recognized that Title VII incorporates a more "relaxed standard" of similarity between male and female occupied jobs. The plaintiff, therefore, is not required to meet the exacting standard of substantial equality of positions set forth in the EPA. The court, however, did not elaborate on what this

"relaxed standard" was. The court explicitly stated that this "relaxed standard" applied only in "disparate treatment" cases. *Miranda v. B & B Cash Grocery Store, Inc.*, 975 F.2d 1518, 1526 & n. 11 (11th Cir. 1992).

12. *See Texas Dept. of Community Affairs v. Burdine*, 450 U.S. 248, 101 S.Ct. 1089, 67 L.Ed.2d 207 (1981); *McDonnell Douglas Corp. v. Green*, 411 U.S. 792, 93 S.Ct. 1817, 36 L.Ed.2d 668 (1973).

13. *See St. Mary's Honor Center v. Hicks* and *Burdine*, discussed at length in Chapter 4.

D. ENFORCEMENT AND REMEDIES

§ 8.8 Enforcement

Although the EEOC has enforcement responsibility and may file civil actions under the EPA, a private plaintiff need not exhaust state or federal administrative remedies before proceeding to court. Under provisions of the FLSA that EPA incorporates by reference, the action may be brought in either state or federal court against either a private or public employer.[1] A suit may be brought under the EPA by either an employee or the EEOC. The EPA grants the authority to the Secretary of Labor to initiate suit against an employer for monetary damages or injunctive relief. In 1978, President Carter, under the authority of the Reorganization Act of 1977,[2] implemented a reorganization plan that transferred EPA enforcement authority from the Secretary of Labor to EEOC. The courts have upheld the constitutionality of this transfer.[3]

While under Title VII the EEOC must try to eliminate an unlawful practice through informal methods of conciliation[4], the EPA contains no similar provision. The Court in *Gunther* noted that "the Equal Pay Act, unlike Title VII, has no requirement of filing administrative complaints and awaiting administrative conciliation efforts."[5] Accordingly, courts have found no requirement of prior administrative filing or informal conciliation.[6]

An employee may initiate suit against an employer seeking monetary damages up until the point the EEOC files a complaint against the employer. When the EEOC files against the employer, the employee's right to sue or become a party to an action brought by other employees is terminated. The EEOC's suit is deemed to commence from the date a complaint is filed that names EEOC as a party plaintiff or from the date the EEOC's name is added as a party plaintiff.

An employee may bring suit individually or on behalf of a class. As under ADEA, if the suit is brought as a class action, each class member must consent in writing to become a party and the consent must be filed with the court.[7]

§ 8.8

1. 29 U.S.C.A. § 216(b).

2. 5 U.S.C.A. §§ 901–12.

3. *See, e.g., EEOC v. Hernando Bank, Inc.,* 724 F.2d 1188 (5th Cir.1984); *Muller Optical Co. v. EEOC,* 743 F.2d 380 (6th Cir.1984) (transfer of ADEA enforcement to EEOC constitutional).

4. 42 U.S.C.A. § 2000e–5(b) requires the EEOC to "endeavor to eliminate any ... alleged unlawful employment practice by informal methods of conference, conciliation, and persuasion" before it can bring a Title VII action. See Chapter 5, Section A for discussion of the administrative prereq-

uisites and procedural requirements under Title VII.

5. 452 U.S. 161, 175 n. 14, 101 S.Ct. 2242, 2251 n. 14, 68 L.Ed.2d 751 (1981).

6. *See Hernando Bank, supra* note 3, at 1194; *Ososky v. Wick,* 704 F.2d 1264 (D.C.Cir.1983); *EEOC v. Home of Economy, Inc.,* 712 F.2d 356 (8th Cir.1983).

7. 29 U.S.C.A. § 216(b). Under either ADEA or EPA, therefore, a class action may not be pursued under Federal Rule of Civil Procedure 23, only by those who have consented in writing. See *Lachapelle v. Owens–Illinois, Inc.,* 513 F.2d 286 (5th Cir. 1975).

§ 8.9 Limitations

An EPA action is governed by the FLSA statute of limitations. The FLSA provides a two year statute of limitations for filing, three years in the case of a "willful" violation. These statutes of limitations compare favorably from the plaintiff's perspective with the 180–day or 300–day administrative filing deadlines of Title VII, now also made applicable to ADEA. (See Chapter VII, Section A for further discussion of the Title VII time limitations and see Chapter IX, Section 3 for further discussion of ADEA time limitations).

The three-year limitations period for willful violations is available, under the terms of the Portal-to-Portal Act of 1947,[1] when an employer knows that, or recklessly disregards whether, its conduct violates the statute.[2] The Court observed in *McLaughlin v. Richland Shoe Co.* that willfulness under the FLSA refers to conduct that is more than merely negligent; yet it also held that the requisite willfulness may be found not just when the employer believes its conduct violates the statute but also when the employer is shown to have been merely indifferent to whether its conduct constitutes such a violation.[3]

§ 8.10 Continuing Violations

The judicially-created "continuing violations" doctrine provides certain plaintiffs an escape from the statute of limitations. The doctrine allows a court to take jurisdiction over a cause of action, or impose liability, for a discrete EPA violation that occurred outside the limitations period. Plaintiffs have invoked the doctrine under both the Equal Pay Act and Title VII, but the courts have afforded it a wider sweep in EPA cases. This is probably because of the nature of the sole EPA violation, which is predicated on unequal compensation, a fact of workplace life that continues from paycheck to paycheck.[1]

In *Gandy v. Sullivan,*[2] the Sixth Circuit announced that "because each unequal paycheck is considered a separate violation of the Equal Pay Act, a cause of action may be brought for any or all violations occurring within the limitations period...." The plaintiff took a position at a pay rate below that of her predecessor and was paid unequally for nine years before she filed suit. The defendant argued that the statute tolled three years after the first unequal paycheck. The court concluded that an equal pay violation occurred each time the plaintiff received an "unequal" paycheck. Further, an action was not time-

§ 8.9

1. 29 U.S.C.A. §§ 251 *et seq.*

2. *See McLaughlin v. Richland Shoe Co.*, 486 U.S. 128, 133, 108 S.Ct. 1677, 1681, 100 L.Ed.2d 115 (1988).

3. *Trans World Airlines, Inc. v. Thurston,* 469 U.S. 111, 125–29, 105 S.Ct. 613, 623–26, 83 L.Ed.2d 523 (1985) (ADEA case); *Walton v. United Consumers Club, Inc.,* 786 F.2d 303, 310–11 (7th Cir.1986);

EEOC v. Madison Community Unit School District No. 12, 818 F.2d 577, 585 (7th Cir.1987).

§ 8.10

1. *Brinkley-Obu v. Hughes Training, Inc.,* 36 F.3d 336 (4th Cir.1994). For a discussion of the continuing violations doctrine in Title VII cases, *see* Section 5.3.

2. 24 F.3d 861, 865 (6th Cir.1994).

barred as long as at least one discriminatory act occurred within the limitations period.

A majority of circuits concur with *Gandy* that an actionable EPA violation occurs each time an employee receives an "unequal" paycheck; the defendant will not usually succeed by arguing that the statute began to run on the date of the first such paycheck.[3] In contrast, the Supreme Court has severely limited the scope of the continuing violation concept in Title VII actions,[4] usually by the device of defining the alleged unlawful employment practice as complete as of an early date more than 180 or 300 days before the plaintiff has filed a charge with EEOC. The circuits have followed suit.

§ 8.11 Remedies

EPA remedies are governed by two provisions of FLSA, 29 U.S.C.A. §§ 216 and 217. These sections authorize recovery not only of unlawfully withheld wages (the rough equivalent of Title VII "back pay") but also of an equal amount denominated "liquidated damages." An employee plaintiff may then recover unlawfully withheld wages, liquidated damages and attorney fees plus costs. Unlawfully withheld wages accrue from no earlier than two years prior to the filing of the complaint and continue until a court order. The accrual period begins three years prior to the filing of a complaint if the employer is found to have acted "willfully." Timeliness of filing is measured as of the date an individual plaintiff files a suit, or in a class action, from the date the plaintiff is added as a named plaintiff.

Before the Portal-to-Portal Act of 1947, the imposition of liquidated damages was mandatory. After the passage of the Act, however, liquidated damages became discretionary with the trial judge.[1] She may not award liquidated damages when the employer proves "to the satisfaction of the court" that it acted in good faith and had a reasonable belief that its conduct did not violate FLSA. The burden is on the employer to show that it acted in the sincere and reasonable belief that its conduct was lawful.

In 1974, FLSA was amended to extend the reach of EPA to state and local government employers. The constitutional validity of this extension was assured when the Supreme Court, overruling *National League*

---

3. *See, e.g., Ashley v. Boyle's Famous Corned Beef Co.,* 66 F.3d 164 (8th Cir.1995); *Gandy v. Sullivan County,* 24 F.3d 861 (6th Cir.1994); *Knight v. Columbus,* 19 F.3d 579 (11th Cir.), *cert. denied,* __ U.S. __, 115 S.Ct. 318, 130 L.Ed.2d 280 (1994); *Nealon v. Stone,* 958 F.2d 584 (4th Cir.1992); *Miller v. Beneficial Mgt. Corp.,* 977 F.2d 834 (3d Cir.1992); *Webb v. Indiana Nat'l Bank,* 931 F.2d 434 (7th Cir.1991); *Berry v. Bd. of Supervisors of La. State. Univ.,* 783 F.2d 1270 (5th Cir.), *cert. denied,* 479 U.S. 868, 107 S.Ct. 232, 93 L.Ed.2d 158 (1986); *Gibbs v. Pierce County Law Enforcement Support*

Agency, 785 F.2d 1396 (9th Cir.1986); *EEOC v. McCarthy,* 768 F.2d 1 (1st Cir. 1985).

4. *See, e.g., United Air Lines, Inc. v. Evans,* 431 U.S. 553, 97 S.Ct. 1885, 52 L.Ed.2d 571 (1977); *Delaware State College v. Ricks,* 449 U.S. 250, 101 S.Ct. 498, 66 L.Ed.2d 431 (1980); and *Lorance v. AT & T Techs.,* 490 U.S. 900, 109 S.Ct. 2261, 104 L.Ed.2d 961 (1989).

§ 8.11

1. 29 U.S.C.A. § 260.

of Cities v. Usery[2], rejected a Tenth Amendment challenge to the power of the federal government to regulate wages and hours of state and local government entities under the FLSA.[3]

E.   GENDER-BASED COMPENSATION DISCRIMI-
NATION PROHIBITED BY TITLE VII AL-
THOUGH NOT REACHED BY EPA

§ 8.12   In General

To better understand how Title VII's reach can sometimes exceed EPA's, we must start with the Supreme Court's attempt in *County of Washington v. Gunther*[1] to explain the relationship between the statutes in unequal pay situations.   *Gunther* itself dealt with a situation in which the pay discrimination alleged did not implicate EPA because it was established that the male and female comparator jobs did not involve substantially equal work.   Instead, the question raised was whether by virtue of the Bennett Amendment to Title VII[2], part of § 703(h), all gender-based compensation discrimination not prohibited by EPA is by that fact alone insulated from regulation under Title VII.   The Court's answer to that broad question was no.

The Court in *Gunther* was faced with the argument on one hand that the Bennett Amendment required that any Title VII claim for gender-based wage discrimination was prohibited unless there was unequal pay for equal work.   On the other hand, the Court heard that the Amendment merely extended the four EPA affirmative defenses to a Title VII cause of action.

The majority opinion by Justice Brennan took the latter view.   It focused on the meaning of "authorized" as used in the Amendment. The Court concluded that the only conduct affirmatively authorized by the EPA was that embraced by the affirmative defenses.   It could not imagine that the Congress that wrote EPA could have intended by silence to authorize any kind of sex-based wage discrimination other than unequal pay for equal work that the employer has justified under one of the EPA affirmative defenses; apart from those defenses, the Court observed, EPA contained only prohibitory language.   Looking to legislative history, the Court also concluded that the "technical" nature of the Bennett Amendment supported the reading that only the EPA

---

2. 426 U.S. 833, 96 S.Ct. 2465, 49 L.Ed.2d 245 (1976).

3. *Garcia v. San Antonio Metropolitan Transit Authority*, 469 U.S. 528, 105 S.Ct. 1005, 83 L.Ed.2d 1016 (1985).

§ 8.12

1. 452 U.S. 161, 101 S.Ct. 2242, 68 L.Ed.2d 751 (1981).

2. 78 Stat. 257, 42 U.S.C.A. § 2000e–2(h). The Bennett Amendment provides:

It shall not be unlawful employment practice under this title [Title VII] to differentiate upon the basis of sex in determining the amount of the wages paid or to be paid to employees of such employer if such differentiation is *authorized by* the provisions of § 6(d) of the Fair Labor Standards Act of 1938, as amended.

29 U.S.C.A. § 206(d) [i.e., EPA] (emphasis supplied).

affirmative defenses, and not the limited EPA prohibition, should be incorporated into Title VII.

Finally, the Court considered the practical ramifications of requiring gender-based wage discrimination claim to be prohibited by the EPA before it could be actionable under Title VII. This interpretation would deprive a woman who suffered intentional discrimination of any remedy for compensation discrimination when she held a unique position, i.e. one that by hypothesis is not held by any comparator. Another example, furnished by *Manhart*, is that of a woman forced to pay more into a pension fund than male employees. If no male employee in that organization holds a position "equal" to that of a particular woman plaintiff, she might have no Title VII remedy; another female employee, with a job "equal" to that of a male counterpart, would. Thus the Court concluded that at least some Title VII sex-based wage discrimination claims could lie although they are not banned by EPA.

The dissent, authored by then-Justice Rehnquist, relied principally on the legislative history of EPA to support its conclusion. The dissent found a clear congressional consensus, only a year before Title VII was enacted, against recovery in the situation of unequal pay for merely "comparable" rather than "equal" work. Interpreting Title VII to allow for recovery in that situation would dramatically expand liability that Congress had rejected when it focused on the question more particularly and extensively in the debates over EPA; the dissenters could find no warrant for such an implied repeal of EPA. Finally, the dissent attacked the Court's reliance on the public policy rationale, finding that any such determination should be made by Congress not the Court. The dissent thus concluded that all unlawful gender-based wage discrimination, whether under Title VII or EPA, must be contained within the narrow "equal work" concept of EPA.

Gunther on its facts generates a limited holding: *intentional*, indeed virtually express sex discrimination in compensation states a Title VII claim even where jobs are "unequal" within the meaning of EPA. But what if, in a non-EPA situation, the intent to discriminate can be proved only inferentially, a la *McDonnell Douglas/Burdine*? What if the employer has dual intentions, one intentionally discriminatory and another benign, as in *Price Waterhouse*, the landmark Title VII "mixed motives" decision? What of compensation practices neutral on their face that have discriminatory impact by gender? And what of comparable worth? *Gunther* provides little guidance as to the viability of these claims under Title VII.

F. THE COMPARABLE WORTH THEORY

§ 8.13 In General

Women are disproportionately concentrated in lower-wage jobs. Because the principle of equal pay for equal work is limited to comparing the wages of individual women and men who perform substantially the same work, it does not address even significant wage disparities between groups of male and female employees holding different positions. The theory of comparable worth seeks to bridge this gap. It would mandate upward adjustment in the wage rates of all those who encumber jobs traditionally held predominantly by women, even without evidence of disparate wages between particular male and female employees whose work is "equal" and without evidence of intentional discrimination based on gender. Plaintiffs would prove simply that a "woman's" job (one held mainly but not exclusively by women) was of similar "worth" to the employer as a "man's" job (one held mainly but not exclusively by men) yet commanded lesser compensation. The revised wage level is supposed to represent a court's or legislature's evaluation of the job's "worth" to the employer.

A claim of equal pay for a job of equal economic "worth" to the employer can succeed, if at all, only under Title VII. By hypothesis, a plaintiff is driven to rely on comparable worth only when there is neither "equal work" or a comparator position, so EPA affords no relief. Under the comparable worth theory, the plaintiff and the higher paid employee are performing different jobs. The similarity is not in the job or the working conditions of the job but rather in the "worth" of the respective jobs to the employer. This line, while conceptually distinct, is in practice sometimes blurred. Suppose, for example, an employer hinges salary increases on employees' contributions to their respective profit centers. Is a court that finds EPA liability because the employer fails to raise a female plaintiff's pay to a level commensurate with her profit-generating capacity implicitly resting liability on the notion of comparable worth?[1]

The difficulty with a comparable worth challenge under Title VII is that the Title VII plaintiff must prove either that a neutral practice had disproportionate adverse impact on her group or that she herself suffered disparate treatment. The impact proof mode challenges a facially neutral practice, not justified by business necessity, that has a disproportionately adverse impact upon members of a group protected by Title VII.[2] The challenge must be to a specific, clearly delineated employment practice. But most compensation systems are heavily keyed to a complex of market factors responsive to supply and demand, factors that may not amount to a single, identifiable practice of the employer. The employer does not create the disparities in the market (at least not by itself), but only builds on them. Further, even if the plaintiff succeeds in establishing the Title VII prima facie impact case, courts typically regard the employer's reliance on market factors to be justified by important, business related reasons.

The other, more common mode of Title VII challenge is disparate

---

§ 8.13

1. *See Mulhall, supra* § 8.4, note 11, at 596.

2. For a more complete discussion of the disproportionate adverse impact proof mode see Chapter 4, Section D.

treatment.[3] This claim requires proving the employer's intent to treat employees of the opposite sex differently with respect to compensation. As suggested above, the principal Title VII paradigm for proving sex-based wage discrimination is disparate treatment. The Title VII plaintiff must usually [4] prove a gender specific intent to discriminate. That intent cannot be inferred from the bare fact that the employer pays different wages to mixed-gender groups who hold jobs that have similar worth to the employer, even if one gender predominantly holds the better paying job.

Attempts to secure judicial recognition of the comparable worth theory have been conspicuously unsuccessful.[5] In *American Federation of State, County, and Municipal Employees v. Washington,*[6] for example, a class of state employees in job categories at least 70% female brought a Title VII suit alleging sex discrimination. The Ninth Circuit rejected the challenge because the plaintiffs demonstrated neither disparate impact nor disparate treatment. The court concluded that a compensation system which resulted from surveys, hearings, budget proposals, executive actions, and legislative enactments did not constitute a specific, isolatable practice that could serve as the springboard for a claim of disparate impact.[7] The compensation system was the result of complex market factors, not a single practice. The court further concluded that there was no disparate treatment where the state set salaries based upon market rates and those salaries lead to an unintended disparity for jobs deemed of comparable worth. The state did not create the market disparity and was not shown to have been motivated by impermissible sex-based considerations in using the markets to set wages for male- or female-dominated classifications.[8]

In *Spaulding v. University of Washington,*[9] nursing faculty at the University of Washington challenged their compensation under Title VII. The plaintiffs asserted that they were paid less than the faculty in other schools within the University solely because of their participation in a traditionally woman's field. The Ninth Circuit rejected their claim, refusing to infer discriminatory intent from the existence of wage differences between "unequal" jobs. Similarly, the court rejected the disparate impact claim. Reliance on competitive market prices did not constitute an actionable discrete neutral practice or policy. According to

---

3. For complete discussion of disparate treatment, see Chapter 4, Section B.

4. We have already seen the exception, in some circuits, for Title VII unequal pay claims. See text accompanying notes 7–8, *supra*, § 8.7.

5. The action on this front has been in the state legislatures; but most states, under severe budgetary pressure themselves and fearful of increasing private employers' costs in the midst of recession, continue to reject the notion that market-driven job wage rates equate to discrimination based on gender.

6. 770 F.2d 1401 (9th Cir.1985).

7. *Id.* at 1406. "[S]uch a compensation system [one responsive to supply and demand], the result of complex market forces, does not constitute a single practice that suffices to support a claim under disparate impact theory." *Id.*

8. *Id.* at 1406–07.

9. 740 F.2d 686 (9th Cir.), *cert. denied,* 469 U.S. 1036, 105 S.Ct. 511, 83 L.Ed.2d 401 (1984).

the Ninth Circuit, the court should focus on "the substance of the employer's acts and whether those neutral acts are a non-job related pretext to shield an invidious judgment." The court deemed the employer's reliance on market factors inherently job-related and thus not subject to disparate impact analysis.

The Supreme Court has not addressed the issue of comparable worth. *County of Washington v. Gunther*[10] did not present the issue. The Court made it clear that the challenge was to the employer's practice of intentionally setting the wage scale for female, but not male guards at a lower level than recommended by its survey of outside markets. The employer's survey suggested paying female guards 95% of the salary of male guards, who performed more arduous and dangerous work. Instead, male guards were paid 100% of their determined worth to the employer, while female guards were paid only 70% of the amount paid to the male guards. The failure to pay the women guards in accordance with the employer's commissioned survey was held to be the result of intentional sex discrimination. The Court specifically noted that allowing the claim did not require it to make its own subjective assessment of the value of the male and female guard jobs, or to attempt by statistics or other methods to quantify the effect of sex discrimination. Thus *Gunther* addressed the unusual situation where a wage difference was the result of a "smoking gun" intentional reduction in wages.

Faint hope for the comparable worth theory was furnished by a pair of Supreme Court decisions that suggest the viability of disproportionate adverse impact challenges to "subjective" practices. A plurality in *Watson v. Fort Worth Bank and Trust*[11] held that a discretionary promotion system could be scrutinized under disparate impact analysis even though it could reasonably be termed a "subjective" practice. The Court recognized that a plaintiff can challenge a subjective neutral factor provided she can identify a specific practice and show its causal relationship to a negative impact on her protected group. A year later in *Wards Cove Packing Co v. Atonio*,[12] a Supreme Court majority confirmed that a plaintiff could mount a disparate impact challenge to either an "objective" or "subjective" employment practice. In context, "objective" and "subjective" appear to mean something different from their dictionary definitions. "Objective" means a specific practice particular to the defendant employer. Examples include written tests or education, height and weight requirements. "Subjective," on the other hand, includes general practices, or a complex of practices, that have their origins in society in general—for example, reliance on the market to determine wages. Either type of practice is now apparently susceptible to challenge on the impact theory if the plaintiff can meet the identification and causation requirements.

10. 452 U.S. 161, 101 S.Ct. 2242, 68 L.Ed.2d 751 (1981).

11. 487 U.S. 977, 108 S.Ct. 2777, 101 L.Ed.2d 827 (1988).

12. 490 U.S. 642, 109 S.Ct. 2115, 104 L.Ed.2d 733 (1989).

But the same decisions also substantially fortified the employer's defense to the neutral practice case. Not only did the Court dilute the required link between a practice and a job or business need, it also explicitly relieved the employer of the burden of proof on the defense. The Civil Rights Act of 1991 left untouched the *Watson/Wards Cove* indication that plaintiffs may challenge not only specific, "objective" practices of the particular defendant employer but also general or "subjective" factors having more global or social origins.[13] Yet it also failed definitively to overturn the Court's permissive new formulations of the employer defense. Nominally, it is true, the Act provides, as was generally held before *Wards Cove*, that the employer bears the burden of persuasion. The Act also stiffens the content of the defense, requiring the employer to establish that the challenged practice is "job related" *and* "consistent with business necessity."[14] But the peculiar legislative history accompanying those provisions directs the courts to interpret these terms according to decisions of the Supreme Court that antedated *Wards Cove*. Included among those decisions are some that express an extremely pliable view of both quoted concepts—that effectively treat a practice as justified if it bears any plausible relation to *either* job relatedness *or* business necessity.[15]

Most comparable worth claims will therefore probably still fail. Even if the plaintiff can now establish a prima facie case of adverse impact for the "subjective" pay practice in question, the employer can assert a market-related justification still likely to be adjudged a matter of business necessity.[16] In the face of the case law that consistently rejected comparable worth claims, the silence of the Civil Rights Act of 1991 on the subject is a significant indication that Congress hews to the relatively narrow yardstick of nondiscrimination, eschewing gender-based minimum standards.[17]

13. See Chapter 4, § 4.10 *supra*.

14. 42 U.S.C.A. 2000e–2(k)(1)(A).

15. For additional discussion of the disproportionate adverse impact case and the changes brought about by the Civil Rights Act of 1991, see Chapter 4, Section D.

16. Alternatively, the practice may be justified on the theory, asserted in *Spaulding*, that a pay scale geared to the external market is "inherently" job related. The logic of this assertion is a bit elusive, however, since by definition a system that sets wages across the board is not driven by the essential requirements of any given job.

17. *See Smith v. Virginia Commonwealth Univ.*, 84 F.3d 672 (4th Cir.1996) (en banc) (female-preferential pay increases challengeable under EPA even though purportedly adopted as an informal "affirmative action program" in response to salary equity study).

Chapter Nine

PROHIBITIONS ON RACE DISCRIMINATION IN FEDERALLY FUNDED PROGRAMS AND SEX DISCRIMINATION IN FEDERALLY FUNDED EDUCATION PROGRAMS: TITLES VI AND IX

Analysis

A. INTRODUCTION

Library References:

C.J.S. Civil Rights §§ 46–50, 219–220.
West's Key No. Digests, Civil Rights ⊷126.

§ 9.1   Titles VI and IX Generally

Title VI of the Civil Rights Act of 1964 prohibits discrimination based on race, color, or national origin in federally funded programs or activities.[1] Notwithstanding this broad provision, the Title does not reach employment practices except where a primary objective of the federal assistance is to provide employment.[2] Thus, except for federally funded employment programs, Title VI is unavailable to supplement Title VII of the 1964 Civil Rights Act as a remedy for race or national origin discrimination in employment.[3]

Although in important respects Title IX of the Education Amendments of 1972 is modeled after Title VI as a ban on discrimination in federally funded programs,[4] Title IX is a prohibition only on sex discrimination and only with respect to education. In one critical respect, Title IX is broader than Title VI: it contains no counterpart to Title VI's general disclaimer of applicability to employment practices. Accordingly, Title IX redresses sex discrimination in employment, as well as in admissions and general educational activities, by federally funded education programs.[5]

Despite these differences, the statutes are mostly of similar design, and many of the issues arising under Title VI also arise under Title IX. Accordingly, in *Grove City College v. Bell*, the Supreme Court recognized the practice of looking to the substantial body of law developed under Title VI when examining Title IX questions.[6]

B. TITLE VI

Library References:

C.J.S. Civil Rights §§ 46–50, 219–220.
West's Key No. Digests, Civil Rights ⊷126.

§ 9.2   In General

The primary prohibition of Title VI provides that:

No person in the United States shall, on the ground of race, color or national origin, be excluded from participation in, be denied the

---

§ 9.1

1. Title VI of the Civil Rights Act of 1964 is codified in 42 U.S.C.A. §§ 2000d—2000d–4a.

2. 42 U.S.C.A. § 2000d–3.

3. *See* chapter on Title VII.

4. Title IX is codified at 20 U.S.C.A. §§ 1681–1688.

5. *North Haven Bd. of Educ. v. Bell*, 456 U.S. 512, 520–35, 102 S.Ct. 1912, 1917–26, 72 L.Ed.2d 299 (1982).

6.   465 U.S. 555, 566, 104 S.Ct. 1211, 1218, 79 L.Ed.2d 516 (1984), overruled in another respect by the Civil Rights Restoration Act of 1987, discussed below (interpreting Education Amendments of 1972, Title IX, 20 U.S.C.A. §§ 1681–1693).

benefits of, or be subjected to discrimination under any program or activity receiving Federal financial assistance.[1]

Programs or activities that receive federal financial support by way of grants, loans, or contracts (other than those of insurance or guaranty) are subject to Title VI sanctions.[2] The Title prohibits discrimination based on race, color or national origin, but not sex or religion.

§ 9.3   Covered Programs or Activities

The scope of the "program or activity" language in Title VI has been a source of debate. In *Grove City College*, the Supreme Court interpreted the phrase "program or activity" narrowly.[1] The Court held that Title IX, and presumably, by extension, Title VI after which Title IX was modeled, prohibited discrimination only in the *particular* program or activity receiving the federal assistance, not in all the programs and activities conducted by the institution receiving such assistance.[2]

The Civil Rights Restoration Act of 1987,[3] returned to earlier judicial interpretations by defining the programs or activities covered by Title VI to include "all" of a recipient's operations.[4] More particularly, the Restoration Act provides that where federal aid is extended to any program within a college, university or other public system of elementary, secondary or higher education, the entire institution or system is covered by the prohibitions of Title VI.[5] For state and local governments, only the department or agency that receives the aid is covered;[6] logically, however, when one entity of a state or local government receives federal aid and distributes it to another, both entities are covered. Finally, for private corporations, the entire corporation would fall under Title VI only if the aid is extended to the corporation as a whole, or if the corporation provides a public service. The entire corporation may also not be covered if the federal assistance is extended to only one geographically separate facility.[7]

The Restoration Act provides government funding agencies power to review all of an institution's programs for discrimination. This should be carefully distinguished from the scope of the allowable administrative sanction if unlawful discrimination is found. Denial or termination of funds is limited to the "particular program, or part thereof" in which the noncompliance was found.[8]

§ 9.4   Exemptions

Title VI permits no agency action with respect to "any employment practice of any employer ... except where a primary objective of the

§ 9.2

1. 42 U.S.C.A. § 2000d.

2. 42 U.S.C.A. § 2000d, d–1.

§ 9.3

1. 465 U.S. at 570, 104 S.Ct. at 1220.

2. *See* discussion under Title IX.

3. Pub.L.No. 100–259 (1988), § 7, 102 Stat. 31.

4. 42 U.S.C.A. § 2000d–4a.

5. 42 U.S.C.A. § 2000d–4a(2).

6. 42 U.S.C.A. § 2000d–4a(1).

7. 42 U.S.C.A. § 2000d–4a(3).

8. 42 U.S.C.A. § 2000d–1.

Federal financial assistance is to provide employment." Thus only federally funded employment programs are subject to Title VI penalties for the kind of race or national origin discrimination in employment prohibited by Title VII of the Civil Rights Act of 1964.

§ 9.5 The Elements of a Private Action Under Title VI

Although Title VI provides expressly only for administrative enforcement, the Supreme Court has implied a private cause of action for individuals to enforce both the statute and its implementing regulations.[1] Title VI has been held to reach claims of reverse discrimination as well.[2]

The fractionated opinions in *Guardians Associations of New York City Police Dep't, Inc. v. Civil Service Commission*[3] suggest that proof of a violation of the statute itself, as opposed to its implementing regulations, requires evidence in some form of discriminatory intent.[4] Long before *Guardians* the Court had held that Title VI would be violated by conduct that violates the Fourteenth Amendment's equal protection clause,[5] which in turn is violated only by evidence of intentional discrimination.[6] The opinions in *Guardians* have subsequently been consistently read, by the Supreme Court as well as the courts of appeals, to uphold the regulations of the administrative agencies charged with enforcing Title VI; and those regulations prohibit not just intentional race or national origin discrimination but also policies and practices that have disproportionate adverse effect or impact on those grounds. But a private plaintiff must take care to plead a distinct violation of any applicable regulatory prohibition of a funding agency in order to state an actionable disproportionate adverse impact violation under Title VI.[7]

Library References:

C.J.S. Civil Rights §§ 46–50, 219–220.
West's Key No. Digests, Civil Rights ⊗126.

§ 9.5

1. *Guardians Assoc. v. Civil Serv. Comm'n of City of New York,* 463 U.S. 582, 103 S.Ct. 3221, 77 L.Ed.2d 866 (1983).

2. *Regents of Univ. of Calif. v. Bakke,* 438 U.S. 265, 98 S.Ct. 2733, 57 L.Ed.2d 750 (1978); *Baker v. Bd. of Regents of State of Kansas,* 991 F.2d 628 (10th Cir.1993).

3. *Guardians, supra* note 1.

4. Seven justices agreed that a violation of the statute itself required discriminatory intent. *See id.* at 608, 103 S.Ct. at 3235 (Powell, J., and Burger, C.J., concurring); *id.* at 612, 103 S.Ct. at 3237 (Rehnquist, J., concurring); *id.* at 612, 103 S.Ct. at 3237 (O'Connor, J., concurring); and *id.* at 642, 103 S.Ct. at 3253 (Stevens, Brennan, and Blackmun, J.J., dissenting).

5. *Bakke, supra* note 2, at 286–287, 98 S.Ct. at 2746.

6. *See Washington v. Davis,* 426 U.S. 229, 96 S.Ct. 2040, 48 L.Ed.2d 597 (1976).

7. *Guardians,* 463 U.S. at 593, 103 S.Ct. at 3227. *See also Alexander v. Choate,* 469 U.S. 287, 293, 105 S.Ct. 712, 716, 83 L.Ed.2d 661 (1985); *Elston v. Talladega County Bd. of Educ.,* 997 F.2d 1394 (11th Cir.1993); *Latinos Unidos De Chelsea En Accion v. Secretary of Housing & Urban Dev.,* 799 F.2d 774 (1st Cir.1986); *Craft v. Bd. of Trustees of Univ. of Ill.,* 793 F.2d 140 (7th Cir.), *cert. denied,* 479 U.S. 829, 107 S.Ct. 110, 93 L.Ed.2d 59 (1986); *Castaneda v. Pickard,* 781 F.2d 456 (5th Cir.1986); *Larry P. v. Riles,* 793 F.2d 969 (9th Cir. 1984). *See also Bryan v. Koch,* 627 F.2d 612 (2d Cir.1980) (applying impact standards before *Guardians*).

§ 9.6 Damages

A year later, in *Conrail v. Darrone*, Justice Powell sought to bring coherence to the welter of *Guardians* opinions by reasoning that "[a] majority of the Court [in *Guardians*] agreed that retrospective relief is available to private plaintiffs for all discrimination, whether intentional or unintentional."[1] A unanimous Supreme Court held that backpay is an appropriate remedy for intentional violations of federally funded employment programs.[2] The Court has not, however, directly decided what types of remedies are available for unintentional violations of Title VI.[3]

The Civil Rights Remedies Equalization Amendment of 1986 permits federal courts to award retrospective relief under Title IX against a state or state agency, expressly abrogating what would otherwise be their immunity under the Eleventh Amendment. Even more recently, in *Franklin*, a Title IX case alleging intentional sex discrimination, the Court ruled that "a cognizable cause of action brought pursuant to a federal statute" is remediable by all appropriate relief, including damages, back pay and prospective relief.[4]

Yet under both statutes, substantial questions remain concerning what monetary relief is "appropriate" where the plaintiff's sole showing is of discriminatory impact. If the federal courts adhere to the Title VII analogy on the damages question, they may continue to award damages only for cases of intentional violations. The 1991 Civil Rights Act provides that in Title VII neutral-practice impact cases, backpay is the only retrospective remedy.[5]

Library References:

C.J.S. Civil Rights §§ 315–316.
West's Key No. Digests, Civil Rights �269.

C. TITLE IX

§ 9.7 In General

Title IX's primary prohibition provides that . . .

No person in the United States shall, on the basis of *sex*, be excluded from participation in, be denied the benefit of, or be subjected to

§ 9.6

1. *Consolidated Rail Corp. v. Darrone*, 465 U.S. 624, 631 n. 9, 104 S.Ct. 1248, 1253 n. 9, 79 L.Ed.2d 568 (1984).

2. *Id.*

3. It is something of a mystery how Justice Powell found five votes for the position that a plaintiff who shows only unintentional discrimination or an "impact" violation of agency regulations may receive retrospective relief. Justices White and Rehnquist approved only noncompensatory relief for victims of unintentional discrimination. *Guardians, supra* note 3, § 9.5, at

597, 103 S.Ct. at 3230. Justice Powell and the Chief Justice did not approve any remedies for private litigants. *Id.* at 609, 103 S.Ct. at 3236. And Justice O'Connor denied all relief to victims of unintentional discrimination. *Id.* at 615, 103 S.Ct. at 3239.

4. *Franklin v. Gwinnett County Pub. Sch.*, 503 U.S. 60, 112 S.Ct. 1028, 117 L.Ed.2d 208, (1992). *See infra* note 43 and accompanying text, § 9.11.

5. *See* Title VII Chapter.

discrimination under any *education* program or activity receiving Federal financial assistance.... [1]

Federal assistance includes grants, loans, or contracts other than those of insurance or guaranty.[2] The *Grove City College* holding that federal assistance funnelled directly to students constitutes "assistance" to the students' educational institutions, thus triggering Title IX regulation of programs or of the institution itself, appears undisturbed either by subsequent decisions [3] or by the 1987 Restoration Act.

§ 9.8 Covered Programs or Activities

The "program or activity" language in Title IX has followed the same interpretive evolution as the same language in Title VI. Lower courts held that discrimination in any program within an institution receiving federal assistance was a violation of Title IX even though the particular discriminatory program was not the subject of the assistance. But in *Grove City College*, the Supreme Court interpreted the phrase "program or activity" narrowly, holding that Title IX prohibited discrimination only in the *particular* educational program or activity receiving the federal assistance, not in all the educational programs and activities conducted by the institution receiving such assistance.[1] The Civil Rights Restoration Act of 1987 [2] overturned this holding by defining the "program or activity" covered by Title IX to include "all" of a recipient's operations.[3] So where federal aid is extended to any program within a college, university or other public system of elementary, secondary or higher education, the entire institution or system is covered by the prohibitions of Title IX.[4] Where a state and local government department (or agency) other than schools receives federal aid for an educational program or activity and the funds stay within that particular department, only that department is subject to Title IX sanctions; but if the aid is distributed to other departments or agencies, all entities that receive it are covered.[5] Finally, a private corporation that receives aid as a whole or that provides a public service would fall under Title VI. But

§ 9.7

1. 20 U.S.C.A. § 1681. *See also* 20 U.S.C.A. § 1684 (prohibiting discrimination because of blindness or severe visual impairment).

2. 20 U.S.C.A. § 1682. *See* 20 U.S.C.A. § 1685 (contracts of insurance or guaranty).

3. *Cf. United States Dep't of Transp. v. Paralyzed Veterans of America*, 477 U.S. 597, 106 S.Ct. 2705, 91 L.Ed.2d 494 (1986).

§ 9.8

1. *Grove City College, supra* § 9.3, note 1, at 566, 104 S.Ct. at 1218.

2. Pub.L.No. 100–259 (1988).

3. 20 U.S.C.A. § 1687.

4. 42 U.S.C.A. § 1687(2)(B). *See Yusuf v. Vassar College*, 35 F.3d 709 (2d Cir.1994) (because Vassar was an institution that receives Federal financial assistance, a claim for damages from sexual harassment could be made under Title IX).

5. 42 U.S.C.A. § 1687(1)(B).

the entire corporation may not be covered if the federal funds are extended to only a geographically separate facility.[6]

As under Title VI, a government agency that provides funding has power to review all of a recipient's programs for discrimination. But denial or termination of funds is limited to the "particular program, or part thereof" in which the noncompliance is found.[7]

Library References:

> C.J.S. Civil Rights §§ 46–50, 102–104, 107, 122, 219–220.
> West's Key No. Digests, Civil Rights ⚷126, 127.1.

§ 9.9 Exemptions

Title IX contains no counterpart to Title VI's general disclaimer on applicability to employment practices. Thus, Title IX redresses sex discrimination in employment by federally funded education institutions.[1] The Restoration Act exempts entities controlled by religious organizations from Title IX coverage if the application of Title IX's provisions would conflict with the organization's religious tenets.[2]

§ 9.10 Elements of the Private Action Under Title IX

The Supreme Court has implied a private right of action under Title IX.[1] The right of action appears to extend to claims of sex discrimination in employment.[2] The preceding statement must be qualified, however, because the Supreme Court's decision holding Title IX applicable to employment practices did not specifically consider the private right of action question.[3] Thus a lively debate is emerging in the circuit decisions over whether the existence of a detailed judicial remedy for employment discrimination under Title VII of the 1964 Civil Rights Act (amended as of 1991 to permit compensatory and punitive damages subject to statutory caps) forecloses a judicially implied remedy under Title IX (which has no cap on such relief, *see* § 11.20 c., *infra*) with respect to gender discriminatory practices by federally funded education institutions that are actionable under Title VII.[4] The circuits are also

6. 42 U.S.C.A. § 1687(3)(B).

7. 42 U.S.C.A. § 1682.

§ 9.9

1. *See North Haven Bd. of Educ., supra* § 9.1, note 5.

2. 20 U.S.C.A. § 1687(4).

§ 9.10

1. *Cannon v. Univ. of Chicago,* 441 U.S. 677, 688, 99 S.Ct. 1946, 1953, 60 L.Ed.2d 560 (1979).

2. *Preston v. Commonwealth of Va.,* 31 F.3d 203 (4th Cir.1994); *Bowers v. Baylor University,* 862 F.Supp. 142 (W.D.Tex. 1994). *Henschke v. New York Hospital–Cornell Medical Center,* 821 F.Supp. 166 (S.D.N.Y.1993).

3. *See North Haven Bd. of Educ. v. Bell,* 456 U.S. 512, 102 S.Ct. 1912, 72 L.Ed.2d 299 (1982).

4. *Compare Lakoski v. James,* 66 F.3d 751 (5th Cir.1995), *cert. denied,* ___ U.S. ___, 117 S.Ct. 357, ___ L.Ed.2d ___ (1996) (Title IX claim foreclosed) *with Lipsett v. University of Puerto Rico,* 864 F.2d 881, 896–97 (1st Cir.1988) *and O'Connor v. Peru State College,* 781 F.2d 632, 642 n. 8 (8th Cir.1986) (no foreclosure of Title IX claim) *and Mabry v. State Bd. of Community Colleges and Occupational Educ.,* 813 F.2d 311, 316–18 (10th Cir.1987) (assuming no foreclosure).

unsure, even when Title VII is not in the picture, over whether the federal education funds recipient can be liable under Title IX for gender discrimination committed by someone other than its agents—for example student on student sexual harassment.[5]

The administrative regulations promulgated under Title IX, like those under Title VI, prohibit discrimination resulting from facially neutral policies that have gender-discriminatory effect as well as intentional discrimination based on gender.[6] Lower courts have applied the impact principle to Title IX actions by incorporating the *Guardians* holding that a Title VI impact claim is actionable so long as the plaintiff distinctly pleads a violation of the applicable implementing regulations other than the terms of the statute alone.[7] Use of the impact theory is fortified by the growing judicial receptiveness to transplanting Title VII liability principles to claims under Title IX.[8]

A related uncertain question is whether individual supervisors and managers, as distinct from institutional educational federal funds recipients, are separately subject to Title IX liability. A majority of the few decisions on point hold that they are not,[9] thus reaching a result consistent with the weight of recent authority under Title VII.[10] Creative plaintiffs' counsel have attempted to skirt this obstacle by suing educational officials individually for Title IX violations under the "and laws" branch of § 1983, with mixed success.[11]

---

5. *Compare Rowinsky v. Bryan Indep. Sch. Dist.,* 80 F.3d 1006 (5th Cir.1996) (holding no) *with Davis v. Monroe County Bd. of Educ.,* 74 F.3d 1186, *vacated,* ___ F.3d ___ (11th Cir.1996) (holding yes).

6. One regulation, for example, bans "administer[ing] or operat[ing] any test or other criteria for admission which has a disproportionately adverse effect on persons on the basis of sex unless the use of such test is shown to predict validly success in the education program or activity in question and alternative tests or criteria which do not have such a disproportionate adverse effect are shown to be unavailable." 34 C.F.R. § 106.21(b)(2).

7. *See, e.g., Mabry v. State Bd. of Community Colleges & Occupational Educ.,* 813 F.2d 311, 317 n. 6 (10th Cir.), *cert. denied,* 484 U.S. 849, 108 S.Ct. 148, 98 L.Ed.2d 104 (1987); *Sharif v. New York State Educ. Dep't,* 709 F.Supp. 345, 361 (S.D.N.Y.1989).

8. *See Davis v. Monroe County Bd. of Educ.,* 74 F.3d 1186, *vacated,* 91 F.3d 1418 (11th Cir.1996); *Murray v. New York Univ. College of Dentistry,* 57 F.3d 243 (2d Cir. 1995); *Brown v. Hot, Sexy and Safer Productions, Inc.,* 68 F.3d 525 (1st Cir.1995) (applying Title VII hostile sexual environ-

ment standards to Title IX settings), *cert. denied,* ___ U.S. ___, 116 S.Ct. 1044, 134 L.Ed.2d 191 (1996).

9. *Lipsett v. University of Puerto Rico,* 864 F.2d 881, 896–97 (1st Cir.1988); *Nelson v. Temple Univ.,* 920 F.Supp. 633 (E.D.Pa. 1996); *Leija v. Canutillo Independent Sch. Dist.,* 887 F.Supp. 947 (W.D.Tex.1995); *Doe v. Petaluma City Sch. Dist.,* 830 F.Supp. 1560 (N.D.Cal.1993), *affirmed,* 54 F.3d 1447 (9th Cir.1995). *But see Mennone v. Gordon,* 889 F.Supp. 53 (D.Conn.1995) (holding individual defendant potentially liable under Title IX but according him a purported "qualified immunity" defense under that statute).

10. *See supra* § 3.3.

11. *Compare Seamons v. Snow,* 84 F.3d 1226, 1233 (10th Cir.1996); *Lillard v. Shelby County Bd. of Educ.,* 76 F.3d 716, 722–24 (6th Cir.1996); *and Doe v. Petaluma City Sch. Dist.,* 54 F.3d 1447 (9th Cir.1995) (permitting Title IX-based § 1983 "and laws" claim) *with Pfeiffer v. Marion Center Area Sch. Dist.,* 917 F.2d 779, 789 (3d Cir.1990) *and Mennone v. Gordon,* 889 F.Supp. 53 (D.Conn.1995) (rejecting use of § 1983 as vehicle for Title IX claim). *See also supra,* § 2.28.

Library References:
> C.J.S. Civil Rights §§ 46–50, 219–220.
> West's Key No. Digests, Civil Rights ⊛126.

§ 9.11   College Athletic Programs Under Title IX

The most substantial and publicized Title IX cases have resulted in settlements that stipulate funding levels sufficient to increase the participation percentages of women in college- or university-level athletics. The law in this area has developed only recently.

Title IX was enacted in 1972. Pursuant to 20 U.S.C.A. § 1682, which requires that federal funding agencies establish regulations regarding use of their funds,[1] in 1975, the Department of Health, Education and Welfare (HEW) first promulgated agency regulations concerning federal funding and athletics programs.[2] In 1979, the HEW Office for Civil Rights published a policy interpretation of the athletic provisions of the agency's regulations.[3] That same year, Congress split HEW into the Departments of Education (DOE) and Health and Human Services (HHS), and each agency adopted substantially identical agency regulations.[4] Although the policy interpretation purports to address the HHS version of the regulations, all education functions were transferred to DOE,[5] and, since then, lower courts have applied the former HEW policy interpretation to the DOE version of the regulations.[6]

When the policy interpretation was published in 1979, the "program or activity" language in Title IX was construed to reach "any" program at an institution receiving federal funds.[7] Apparently, DOE initiated many cases. But in 1984, the Supreme Court's holding in *Grove City College*, that Title IX was violated only if the "particular" program receiving federal funds was discriminatory, put an end to at least seventy such cases before any of them was decided.[8] The Civil Rights Restoration Act of 1987 reinstated the institution-wide definition of "program or activity." The legislative history suggests that one goal of the 1987 Restoration Act was to foster the development of women's athletics.[9] After the 1987 Act, college athletic programs became a focal point of Title IX litigation.[10]

§ 9.11

1. The substance of these regulations is discussed below in this section.

2. 45 C.F.R. § 86.41 (1992).

3. 45 C.F.R. Part 86: Title IX of the Education Amendments of 1972; a Policy Interpretation; Title IX and Intercollegiate Athletics, 44 Fed. Reg. 71,413 (1979).

4. *Compare* 34 C.F.R. § 106.41 (1992) (DOE regulations) *with* 45 C.F.R. § 86.41 (1992) (HHS regulations).

5. 20 U.S.C.A. § 3441(a).

6. *See, e.g., Roberts v. Colorado State,* 998 F.2d 824, 828 (10th Cir.1993), *cert. denied,* 510 U.S. 1004, 114 S.Ct. 580, 126 L.Ed.2d 478 (1993).

7. *See, e.g., Haffer v. Temple University,* 524 F.Supp. 531 (E.D.Pa.1981) (entire University subject to Title IX even though the received federal funds were not "earmarked" for athletics), *affirmed,* 688 F.2d 14 (3d Cir.1982).

8. *See Statements on Civil Rights Restoration Act,* Daily Lab. Rep. (BNA) No. 53 at D1 (Mar. 20, 1981).

9. *See* 130 Cong. Rec. S11,253 (daily ed. Sept. 17 1984) (statement of Sen. Hatch).

10. *See e.g.,* Jennifer L. Henderson, *"Gender Equity in Intercollegiate Athletics: A Commitment to Fairness,"* 5 Seton Hall J. Sports L. 133 (1995); Janet Judge *et al.,* "Perspective, *Gender Equity in the 1990s:*

a. The Regulatory Framework

The Department of Education regulations identify ten factors to be used in examining a claim that an athletic program provides unequal opportunities to members of one sex. The list includes:

1. Whether the selection of sports and levels of competition effectively accommodate the interests and abilities of members of both sexes;

2. The provision of equipment and supplies;

3. Scheduling of games and practices time;

4. Travel and per diem allowances;

5. Opportunity to receive coaching and academic tutoring;

6. Assignment and compensation of coaches and tutors;

7. Provision of locker rooms, practice and competitive facilities;

8. Provision of medical and training facilities and services;

9. Provision of housing and dining facilities and services;

10. Publicity.[11]

Even as fleshed out by DOE, these multiple unweighted factors have spawned the inevitable progeny: inconsistent, contradictory and largely ad hoc judicial decisions. Sometimes, for reasons no more compelling than convenience, a decision will turn solely on factor one. For the same reason, factors two through ten may be lumped together as solely a question of money spent. And sometimes a factor not even listed will control.

b. The Policy Interpretation

The policy interpretation separately divides Title IX coverage into three areas, including athletic scholarships, "athletic opportunity equivalence," and "effective accommodation" of the interests and abilities of athletes of both sexes.[12] Scholarships represent a new area not listed in the DOE regulations. "Athletic opportunity equivalence" represents a composite or summation of factors two through ten of the regulations. "Effective accommodation" is formed from factor one of the regulations. The courts defer substantially to the umbrella policy interpretation and evaluate claims of discrimination according to its detailed guidelines.[13]

1. Equal Opportunity in Athletic Scholarships

According to the policy interpretation, equal opportunity to receive athletic scholarships requires that proportionately equal amounts of financial assistance be available to men's and women's athletic programs

An Athletic Administrator's Survival Guide to Title IX and Gender Equity Compliance," 5 Seton Hall J. Sports L. 313 (1995).

11. 34 C.F.R. § 106.41 (1992).

12. 44 Fed.Reg. at 71,415.

13. *See. e.g., Roberts, supra* note 6; *Cohen v. Brown Univ.,* 991 F.2d 888 (1st Cir. 1993), *on remand,* 879 F.Supp. 185 (D.R.I. 1995); *Kelley v. Bd. of Trustees of the Univ. of Ill.,* 832 F.Supp. 237 (C.D.Ill.1993), *affirmed,* 35 F.3d 265 (7th Cir.1994).

as a whole.[14] The amount available for men is divided by the total number of participants in each of the men's athletic programs. A similar calculation will be made for the women's programs. If the two resulting figures are "substantially proportionate to their participation rates," the institution will be found to be in compliance with the regulations. If the figures are disparate, the institution may still be in compliance if it can offer legitimate non-discriminatory factors to explain the difference.[15]

In *Gonyo v. Drake University*,[16] members of a discontinued men's wrestling team petitioned for an injunction requiring reinstatement of the program. Drake University allotted 8.57 scholarships to the wrestling team, and the petitioners argued that the decrease in athletic scholarship awards amounted to discrimination against them. In the 1992–93 year, women were awarded 6% more scholarships than men, but there was a 17.8% disparity in participation by women. Discontinuing the wrestling program would decrease the participation disparity to 16.9%. Drake argued that the former wrestling scholarships would be used to attract more women to its athletic programs in an attempt to correct historical discrimination against them in those programs. The court denied the petition and advanced two grounds for its decision. First, the court implied that it accepted Drake's affirmative action argument as legitimate justification for discontinuing the program.[17] Second, and, perhaps in the long run, more importantly, it concluded that decreasing the participation disparity, an "effective accommodation" evaluation,[18] predominates the examination of alleged discrimination in athletic programs because Title IX was enacted to encourage athletic participation by women.[19] Thus, the district court agreed with other courts that the "effective accommodation" consideration may, in the end, be the more important factor.[20]

2. *Athletic Opportunity Equivalence*

The second area identified in the policy interpretation, athletic opportunity equivalences, involves measurements of factors two through ten listed in the regulations.[21] If comparison reveals that both sexes are treated equally, viewed from the perspective of aggregate participation in all sports, the institution will be found to be in compliance with the regulations. If the comparison reveals an inequality, the institution may still be compliance if it can show that the disparity is the result of legitimate non-discriminatory factors—the unique aspects of particular sports, an affirmative action program to overcome historical discrimination, or temporary sex-neutral factors related special circumstances, such as fluctuations in recruitment of first-year athletes.[22]

14. 44 Fed.Reg. at 71,415.

15. *Id*. at 71,415.

16. 837 F.Supp. 989 (S.D.Iowa 1993).

17. *Id*. at 995.

18. *See* item 3, *infra*.

19. 837 F.Supp. at 996.

20. *See* cases cited at note 27 *infra*.

21. 44 Fed.Reg. 71,416.

22. *Id*.

In *Favia v. Indiana University of Pennsylvania*,[23] after Indiana University of Pennsylvania (IUP) dropped two men's teams and two women's teams, members of the canceled women's gymnastics team were granted a preliminary injunction requiring reinstatement of the program based on allegations that elimination of the team created unequal athletic opportunities for women. The school sought a modification of the injunction allowing it instead to replace the fifteen-member gymnastics team with a fifty-member soccer team. IUP argued that doing so would decrease a disparity in women's participation by 4.05%. The court denied IUP's request for modification.

After first announcing that athletic opportunity equivalence may be assessed by comparing aggregate expenditures for male and female teams,[24] the court concluded that the modification would increase a funding disparity in IUP's program. Before the original spending reduction, IUP allocated more than 65% of its total athletics budget to men's programs. The proposed soccer team would cost only one-third of what the gymnastics team had cost, further increasing the gap in funding levels. But regardless of the funding issue, the court wrote, "in the absence of a continuing program expansion," a 4.05% reduction in an existing 15.6% participation disparity fell short of a school's obligation to "provide athletic opportunities in proportion to gender composition of [the] student body...."[25] Here again, a lower court indicated that the "effective accommodation" consideration may be the determinate factor.[26]

3. "Effective Accommodation" of the Interests of Both Sexes

Even if an institution provides equal athletic scholarships and athletic opportunity equivalence, it may violate Title IX if it fails effectively to accommodate the interests and abilities of athletes of both sexes.[27] Indeed, most courts say they decide Title IX claims by reference to the vague factor of "ineffective accommodation." The policy interpretation recognizes disparity in opportunities within an individual segment of the athletic program if the disparity is "substantial enough in and of [it]self to deny equality of athletic opportunity;" otherwise, the policy interpretation prescribes measuring the "institution's program as a whole."[28] In all cases to date, where a court addresses "effective accommodation," it considers the athletic program as a whole.

Three sub-factors are examined in evaluating a claim of "ineffective accommodation:" the determination of students' interests and abilities; the selection of sports offered; and the levels of competition available.[29] Just as "effective accommodation" turns out to be the most important of the three broad areas identified by the policy interpretation, the "levels

---

23. 7 F.3d 332 (3d Cir.1993).

24. *Id.* at 343.

25. *Id.* at 434–44.

26. *See* cases cited at note 27 *infra*.

27. *See, e.g., Roberts, supra* note 6; *Cohen, supra* note 13; *Favia, supra* note 23; and *Kelley, supra* note 13.

28. 44 Fed.Reg. at 71,418.

29. *Id.* at 71,417.

of competition" sub-factor is the most frequently applied measure of "effective accommodation."

(a) Determinations of Students' Interests

The first sub-factor focuses on the process an institution uses to determine its students' athletic interests and abilities. The process must reflect the increasing levels of women's interests and abilities; must not disadvantage the underrepresented sex; must consider historical team performance; and must be responsive to the expressed interests of members of the underrepresented sex who are capable of intercollegiate competition.[30]

(b) The Selection of Sports Offered

The second sub-factor focuses on equal opportunity for members of both sexes to participate in the teams an institution chooses to sponsor. This may require that the institution allow both sexes to try out for an integrated team or sponsor separate teams for each sex. If the sport is a contact sport, an institution must sponsor separate teams if: first, there is historical discrimination against the excluded sex; and, second, members of that sex possess sufficient interest and ability to maintain a viable team and a reasonable expectation of intercollegiate competition for it. If the sport is a non-contact sport, an institution must sponsor a separate team for the members of the excluded sex only if, in addition to historical exclusion and sufficient interest and ability, they possess insufficient skill to be selected for or compete actively on an integrated team.[31]

(c) The Levels of Competition Available

The final sub-factor, levels of competition, is the most important because it addresses an institution's obligation to allow both sexes equal opportunity to participate in intercollegiate competition.[32] To satisfy this measure, the institution may prove its programs provide opportunities in substantial proportion to the sexes' respective enrollments, show a history of expanding its programs for the underrepresented sex, or demonstrate that the interests and abilities of members of the underrepresented sex are fully and effectively accommodated by its program.[33]

Cases usually turn on the "substantial proportion" question.[34] The policy interpretation asks "[w]hether intercollegiate level participation

---

30. Id.

31. 44 Fed.Reg. at 71,417–8.

32. 44 Fed.Reg. at 71,418.

33. Id.

34. The United States Court of Appeals for the First Circuit identified reasons for de-emphasizing the second and third sub-factors. As far as showing a continuing expansion of programs for the underrepresented, the court noted that "in an era of fiscal austerity, few universities are prone

to expand athletic opportunities." Cohen, 991 F.2d at 989. And the full-and-effective accommodation "benchmark sets a high standard: it demands not merely some accommodation, but full and effective accommodation. If there is sufficient interest and ability among members of the statistically underrepresented gender, not slaked by existing programs, an institution necessarily fails this prong of the test." Id.

opportunities for male and female students in all sports are provided in numbers substantially proportionate to their respective enrollments." [35] The *Title IX Athletics Investigator's Manual* suggests that "[i]f the enrollment is 52% male and 48% female, then, ideally, about 52% of the participants in the athletics program should be male and 48% female." [36] There is no brightline test for acceptable levels of disparity from the norm, and the decisions illustrate the difficulty courts confront in deciding what degree of underrepresentation in participation percentages amounts to "ineffective accommodation." [37]

In *Cohen v. Brown University*,[38] the court placed on the plaintiff the burden of demonstrating both disparity and unmet interest, concluding that a Title IX plaintiff does not enjoy the shift of burden to the defendant that inures to the benefit of a Title VII plaintiff attempting to demonstrate the disproportionate adverse impact of a neutral practice. It nevertheless found that the defendant's dropping of two men's and two women's teams violated Title IX because the cut resulted in an 11.4% underrepresentation participation by women.[39] In *Roberts v. Colorado State*,[40] the court found that Colorado State University violated Title IX by eliminating a fast pitch softball team because the resulting 10.5% disparity in women's participation was excessive. In *Favia v. Indiana University of Pennsylvania*,[41] the court rejected an athletic program change that would have decreased the disparity from 15.6% to 12.6%, because even the lower figure would not have alleviated the Title IX violation.

But in *Kelley v. Board of Trustees of University of Illinois*, the court recognized that an institution can achieve substantial proportionality by decreasing participation of an overrepresented group while maintaining the level of participation of the underrepresented group.[42] Traditionally, men were overrepresented in the institution's varsity programs by about 20%. The court held that dropping the men's swimming team without dropping the women's team did not violate Title IX because apparently men would continue to be at least proportionately represented even without the swimming team.

c. *Damages*

In *Franklin v. Gwinnett County Public Schools*, the Supreme Court held that a successful Title IX plaintiff is eligible for all traditional legal and equitable relief that may be appropriate, damages as well as back

---

35. 44 Fed.Reg. at 71,418.

36. Office for Civil Rights, Dep't. of Educ., *Title IX Athletics Investigator's Manual*, at 24 (1990).

37. *Cohen v. Brown University*, 879 F.Supp. 185 (D.R.I.1995) (substantially proportionate must be stringent enough to effectuate the purposes of Title IX defined to mean that gender balance of university's intercollegiate athletic program, as a whole, must mirror the gender balance of its student enrollment).

38. 991 F.2d 888 (1st Cir.1993), on remand, 879 F.Supp. 185 (D.R.I.1995).

39. The First Circuit distinguished Title VII by asserting, among other reasons, that Title IX's goals are largely aspirational rather than mandatory. *Id.* at 902.

40. 998 F.2d 824 (10th Cir.1993).

41. 7 F.3d 332 (3d Cir.1993).

42. *Kelley, supra* note 13, at 241.

pay and prospective relief.[43]   Further, the Civil Rights Remedies Equalization Amendment of 1986 [44] permits federal courts to award retrospective relief under, among other statutes, Titles VI and IX, against a state or state agency, expressly abrogating what would otherwise be their immunity under the Eleventh Amendment.   Because *Franklin* concerned intentional discrimination, it is unclear what the effect of its broad language may be on damages in Title IX cases challenging neutral practices.

Library References:

> C.J.S. Civil Rights §§ 102–104, 107, 122.
> West's Key No. Digests, Civil Rights ⚷127.

---

43. *Franklin, supra* § 9.6, note 4 (when Title IX was passed there was a presumption in favor of all available remedies, and Congress made no effort to alter that presumption).

44. 42 U.S.C.A. § 2000d–7(b).

Chapter Ten

VOTING RIGHTS

Analysis

---

§ 10.1   Introduction

Three complementary interests fuel voting rights litigation.[1] One is individual voter's ability to *participate* in the electoral process. To safeguard this constitutional right the Supreme Court has strictly scrutinized impediments to exercising the franchise; and the Voting Rights Act of 1965[2] implements this right by requiring federal supervision of the voting process.

Voting, however, is only a means to the end of electing representatives, an end attained only by the *aggregation* of individual votes with those of other like-minded voters. In American elections this group interest has been ineluctably linked not only to politics but to race, witness the persistent phenomenon of racial bloc voting. How district lines are drawn to include or fence out affiliated voters is the chief determinant of whether the preferences of one group of voters or another are likely to be realized in the election of candidates of their choice. We will examine how the classic political and racial gerrymandering schemes have fared when tested under the Constitution and the Voting Rights Act.

Finally, even the ability of an aggregation of voters to elect their preferred representatives is itself only a means to the ultimate end of affecting *governance* after an election. Although for the most part the decisions have, absent a violation of aggregation rules, rejected claims based on this interest, the Court's recent decision in *Shaw v. Reno*[3] may implicitly further credit that interest.[4]

Voting rights litigation has centered on two features of electoral designs and practices that potentially impede the exercise or minimize the impact of the right to vote by racial, ethnic, or language minorities. The first is the "quantitative" apportionment of representatives among districts of comparable population. The Supreme Court has concluded that the Constitution requires election districts within a governmental subdivision to contain roughly the same number of constituents, so that a constituent of one district will enjoy representation comparable in force to a constituent of another.

The second broad sphere of voting rights litigation—the focus of most current activity—is the wide range of formal and ad hoc practices that dilute the electoral power of voters who belong to racial, ethnic or language minorities. These practices include apportionments drawn in a way that "qualitatively" limits or fragments the voting power these minorities would otherwise be expected to wield, as well as a host of ad

§ 10.1

1. This catalogue of interests is identified and explained by Professor Pamela Karlan in "All Over The Map: The Supreme Court's Voting Rights Trilogy," 1993 *S.Ct.Review* 245, 248–252 and "The Rights To Vote: Some Pessimism About Formalism," 71 *Texas L.Rev.* 1705, 17091–1720 (1993).

2. See especially § 2 of the Act as amended, 42 U.S.C.A. § 1973(b).

3. 509 U.S. 630, 113 S.Ct. 2816, 125 L.Ed.2d 511 (1993).

4. Karlan, "All Over the Map," *supra* note 1, at 286.

hoc devices that achieve the same effect through requirements concerning candidate qualification and voter eligibility. Such devices dilute even if an apportionment meets the minimum "quantitative" constitutional requirement of rough numerical equality.

A. REAPPORTIONMENT: ONE–PERSON, ONE–VOTE

Library References:

> C.J.S. Elections § 8.
> West's Key No. Digests, Elections ☞12(6).

§ 10.2 In General

The command of Article 1, § 2 of the Constitution that congressional representatives be chosen "by the People of the several States" was construed in *Wesberry v. Sanders*,[1] to mean that "as nearly as is practicable one man's vote in a congressional election is to be worth as much as another's."[2] Accordingly, state legislatures were forbidden to "draw the lines of congressional districts in such a way as to give some voters a greater voice in choosing a Congressman than others."[3] This principle was extended the same year to state legislative districts, which the Court held must be apportioned on a population basis to afford 14th Amendment equal protection.[4] Later, the Court applied the one-person, one-vote requirement to the drawing of districts for local government units that have "general governmental powers over the entire geographic area served by the body."[5] That requirement has consequently been imposed on elections for county governing boards (*Avery*), a citywide general elective body,[6] the election of trustees for a junior college,[7] and other county government offices.[8]

The 14th Amendment does not, however, demand that each district in a multi-district legislative body have "equal power to affect a legislative outcome." For example, if the votes of some voting members of an omnibus governing body are weighted more heavily than others, some represented districts will in effect have a greater voice than others in the governing body's own voting on particular issues. That fact alone does

---

§ 10.2

1. 376 U.S. 1, 84 S.Ct. 526, 11 L.Ed.2d 481 (1964).

2. *Id.* at 11, 84 S.Ct. at 532.

3. *Id.* at 14, 84 S.Ct. at 533.

4. *Reynolds v. Sims,* 377 U.S. 533, 84 S.Ct. 1362, 12 L.Ed.2d 506 (1964).

5. *Avery v. Midland County,* 390 U.S. 474, 484, 88 S.Ct. 1114, 1120, 20 L.Ed.2d 45 (1968).

6. *Board of Estimate v. Morris,* 489 U.S. 688, 109 S.Ct. 1433, 103 L.Ed.2d 717 (1989).

7. *Hadley v. Junior College Dist.,* 397 U.S. 50, 90 S.Ct. 791, 25 L.Ed.2d 45 (1970).

8. *Abate v. Mundt,* 403 U.S. 182, 91 S.Ct. 1904, 29 L.Ed.2d 399 (1971). *But see Pittman v. Chicago Bd. of Educ.,* 64 F.3d 1098 (7th Cir.1995) (principle not applicable to local school councils that could not tax or set budgetary limits but merely selected a principle and allocated expenditures).

not render the apportionment unconstitutional, provided it is otherwise numerically proportionate.[9]

§ 10.3　Judicial Branch Elections

Apportionment in accordance with the one-person, one-vote rule has been held inapplicable to elections for the judicial branch. The leading opinion, affirmed summarily by the Supreme Court, reasoned that judges, unlike legislative or executive branch officials, serve no representative function because they are expected to administer the law rather than espouse the cause of a particular constituency.[1]

§ 10.4　Deviation in District Size

Perhaps owing to distinct constitutional prescriptions, or to the greater number of state legislative than congressional seats within a State, "[s]omewhat more flexibility may ... be constitutionally permissible with respect to state legislative apportionment than in congressional districting."[1] In federal congressional districting the *Wesberry* "as nearly as is practicable" standard has been adhered to quite rigidly. For example, when the population of the state's largest congressional district was less than 1% greater than that of the smallest district, the Court rejected a de minimis exception to the Article 1, § 2 requirement of population equality based on census data. So long as the population differences among districts "could have been reduced or eliminated altogether by a good-faith effort to draw districts of equal population," no significant variance from absolute equality will be permitted unless "necessary to achieve some legitimate goal."[2]

By contrast, the 14th Amendment has been held to tolerate some deviation from districts of "ideal" (i.e., population-equal size) in state or local government apportionment. In a state or local case the court must compute a "maximum percentage deviation" from the "ideal population" under a formula followed since it was first applied in *Abate* in 1971. The total population of the political subdivision is divided by the number of seats to be filled to calculate a "norm" or ideal population size to be represented by one seat. This norm is then subtracted from the number of persons in each district to arrive at a positive or negative variance. That variance, in turn, is divided by the subdivision norm to yield the district's percentage variance. A negative numerical (and therefore percentage) variance means that the district has fewer people than the norm and is therefore "over-represented." The two districts with the largest positive and largest negative percentage variances are

9. *Board of Estimate v. Morris,* 489 U.S. 688, 109 S.Ct. 1433, 103 L.Ed.2d 717 (1989).

§ 10.3

1. *Wells v. Edwards,* 347 F.Supp. 453 (M.D.La.1972), *affirmed,* 409 U.S. 1095, 93 S.Ct. 904, 34 L.Ed.2d 679 (1973).

§ 10.4

1. *Reynolds v. Sims,* 377 U.S. at 578, 84 S.Ct. at 1390.

2. *Karcher v. Daggett,* 462 U.S. 725, 730–31, 103 S.Ct. 2653, 2658–59, 77 L.Ed.2d 133 (1983).

identified; these percentages are then summed to yield a "maximum" or "total" percentage deviation for the subdivision as a whole. A strong presumption of unconstitutionality attaches to total deviations of 16.5% or greater.[3] A weaker presumption of unconstitutionality attaches to total deviations of greater than 10% but less than 16.5%; these appear to be presumed unconstitutional unless "based on legitimate considerations" dictated by a "rational state policy."[4] A legislative desire to preserve existing political subdivision boundaries, to maintain natural or historical boundaries or to assure boundary compactness or contiguity are among the justifications that may overcome the presumption of unconstitutionality in this range. Total deviations of less than 10% are presumptively constitutional.[5]

Deviations from ideal district size which exceed 10% are not per se unlawful, but only create a presumption of unconstitutionality under which the defendants must justify the deviation.[6] In *Voinovich* the Court applied the Fourteenth Amendment's requirement that electoral districts be nearly equal in population. It reversed the district court's holding that a total deviation from ideal, district size which exceeds ten percent is per se unlawful. In doing so the Court reaffirmed the holdings of *Brown v. Thomson,*[7] and *Mahan v. Howell,*[8] that total deviations exceeding ten percent could be justified by a state policy of preserving the integrity of political subdivision boundaries.

B. VOTE DILUTION SCHEMES

Library References:

> C.J.S. Elections § 8.
> West's Key No. Digests, Elections ⟺12(3).

§ 10.5 Racial Gerrymandering

Even in districts fairly apportioned from the standpoint of population, the voting strength of political[1] and minority groups may be diluted

---

3. *Connor v. Finch,* 431 U.S. 407, 97 S.Ct. 1828, 52 L.Ed.2d 465 (1977). *But see Brown v. Thomson,* 462 U.S. 835, 103 S.Ct. 2690, 77 L.Ed.2d 214 (1983) (Wyoming proportionate plan with a total deviation of 89% was upheld because of a "consistent non-discriminately application of a legitimate state policy" of ensuring a seat for the state's least populous county.).

4. *See Mahan v. Howell,* 410 U.S. 315, 93 S.Ct. 979, 35 L.Ed.2d 320, *modified,* 411 U.S. 922, 93 S.Ct. 1475, 36 L.Ed.2d 316 (1973).

5. *See Gaffney v. Cummings,* 412 U.S. 735, 93 S.Ct. 2321, 37 L.Ed.2d 298 (1973); *White v. Regester,* 412 U.S. 755, 93 S.Ct. 2332, 37 L.Ed.2d 314 (1973).

6. *Voinovich v. Quilter,* 507 U.S. 146, 113 S.Ct. 1149, 122 L.Ed.2d 500 (1993).

7. 462 U.S. 835, 103 S.Ct. 2690, 77 L.Ed.2d 214 (1983).

8. 410 U.S. 315, 93 S.Ct. 979, 35 L.Ed.2d 320 (1973).

§ 10.5

1. Outside the scope of this work is a discussion of standard gerrymandering for political (as opposed to racial or ethnic) reasons. To state a claim of unconstitutional political gerrymandering is exceedingly difficult. A partisan legislative intent to affect political outcomes by manipulating district lines is virtually presumed. Karlan, "All Over The Map," *supra* § 10.1, note 1, at 250. But because political gerrymandering is treated almost as a civic virtue, see Davis v. Bandemer, 478 U.S. 109, 145, 106 S.Ct. 2797, 2817, 92 L.Ed.2d 85 (1986)

by particular apportionment techniques known generically as "gerrymandering." The term encompasses a variety of district line-drawing devices. Specific techniques include "cracking," dispersing a heavy minority voter concentration among several districts in each of which the minority lacks effective voting power; "stacking," by which a substantial minority-member population that would constitute a majority of the voters in a distinct district is poured into a multimember district with a white (or English-speaking or nonethnic) population that is large enough to control election outcomes in the combined district; and "packing," or overconcentrating minority-group member voters who span several "natural" districts, in each of which they would exercise substantial influence or control, into a smaller number of "safe" districts that they dominate overwhelmingly.

Cracking and stacking are prototypes of techniques that undermine a minority's interest in aggregation, that is, electing representatives preferred by the group. By contrast, members of a minority group who are included in a packed district suffer no deprivation of their aggregative interest; rather, packing reduces the potential number of districts in which they and their excluded members might prevail or affect a representative's behavior in office—that is, it diminishes the minority group's governance interest.[2]

The Voting Rights Act itself has become something of a partisan tool in the hands of the political parties. Cracking was originally used to prevent minority members from constituting a majority in a legislative district. In recent years, Democratic Party legislators have at times used it to disperse minority voters across district lines for a different reason. Their objective has been to create a greater number of districts in which minority group members will be influential in candidate selection and ultimately legislative governance, even if they represent only a minority (albeit a substantial one) of all voters in many or all of those districts. In this way the Democrats have sought to satisfy minority governance interests somewhat at odds with the aggregative goal of electing the maximum potential number of minority representatives.[3] And the Republicans have adopted aggregation theory as a justification for packing minorities into a small number of districts in which their

(O'Connor, J., concurring)—that intent alone fails to state a claim. In addition, the plaintiff must show that the rigging of district lines has the effect of consistently degrading a voting group's influence on the political process. *Davis*, 478 U.S. at 132, 106 S.Ct. at 2810 (plurality opinion). Professor Karlan describes *Davis* as holding that "as long as the overall distribution of power fairly reflects the political composition of the state and thereby offers fair governance, the use of aggregation rules that deliberately preclude ... subgroups of voters from directly electing their preferred candidates does not invalidate the apportionment scheme." "The Rights To Vote,"

supra § 10.1, note 1, 71 *Tex.L.Rev.* at 1723. She cites Republican Party v. Martin, 980 F.2d 943 (4th Cir.1992), *cert. denied*, 510 U.S. 828, 114 S.Ct. 93, 126 L.Ed.2d 60 (1993) as the first case since *Davis* that has upheld the legal sufficiency of a complaint alleging unconstitutional political gerrymandering. "All Over The Map," *supra* § 10.1, note 1, 1993 S.Ct. Rev. at 271 n.110.

2. Karlan, "All Over The Map," *supra* § 10.1, note 1, 1993 S.Ct. Rev. at 251–252.

3. Karlan, "The Rights To Vote," *supra* § 10.1, note 1, 71 *Tex.L.Rev.* at 1708, 1734.

interests will overwhelm the opposition, leaving most other districts largely white and, in tune with the tenor of the times, Republican.[4]

§ 10.6 "At Large" Representatives

One much litigated practice that aggravates the impact of "stacking" is the election "at large" of multiple representatives for the aggregated district. If, for example, there is substantial bloc voting by both majority and minority populations, and a jurisdiction-wide white voting majority, selecting representatives at large will tend to overwhelm even significant concentrations of black voters. A related practice with similar effect is the primary election requirement that if none of several candidates achieves an electoral majority, the two highest candidates must compete in a run-off. Assuming racial bloc voting, the group, usually white, that can summon the greatest number of persons to vote in a runoff is likely to prevail.

§ 10.7 Candidate Qualification Barriers

Candidate qualification barriers include changing the method of selecting officials from appointment to election, or vice versa, where either change would diminish the likely success of a minority candidate; extending a white incumbent's term; establishing difficult requirements for voter signature support; fixing high filing fees; or reducing the attractiveness, in responsibility or salary, of an office for which a minority candidate would likely have success; altering candidate qualification procedures while withholding critical information about the new requirements.

§ 10.8 Voter Qualification Barriers

A final set of dilution practices, hindrances placed before minority voters, run the gamut from inconvenient or burdensome registration requirements; permitting improper challenges of minority voters; changing the location of polling places with little or no public notice; affording deficient voting facilities, with consequent long lines at black polling places; scheduling elections for inconvenient times; and manipulating absentee voter rules to the disadvantage of minority candidates.

C. VOTE DILUTION CAUSES OF ACTIONS

§ 10.9 Fourteenth Amendment

District population disparities have proven remediable rather readily under the constitutional standard of one-person, one-vote. By contrast, many dilution practices (either of the apportionment variety or those that erect barriers to candidates or voters) have proven resistant to constitutional attack. True, blatant racial gerrymandering has been

---

4. *Id.* at 1708, 1733–34.

successfully attacked under the 14th and 15th Amendments.[1] And initially the Court took a relaxed approach to the kind of evidence that would suffice to condemn an at-large, multi-member district. The Court found that this election method, overlaid on cultural and economic realities and minority candidates' historical failure at the polls, had the effect of denying minority voters equal opportunity to participate in the political processes leading to nomination and election. This effect was held tantamount to the invidious intent requisite to a 14th Amendment violation.[2]

But by 1980 the Supreme Court reversed course, holding in City of *Mobile v. Bolden* that such a scheme violates the 14th Amendment only when "conceived or operated as a purposeful device to further racial discrimination."[3] The required invidious discriminatory purpose need not, however, be proved by direct evidence but may be "inferred from the totality of the relevant facts."[4] To prove purposeful racial discriminatory intent inferentially it is not enough, though, to show bloc voting, a substantial percentage of minority voters, and the fact that no member of that group has ever been elected. In addition, the plaintiff must offer evidence that current or historical discrimination has precluded effective minority participation in the political process. Evidence of specific impediments to exercising the right to register or vote, participate in political party affairs, or of discrimination in education or jury service will suffice for this purpose.[5] The district court's determinations about such intent are pure questions of fact, reviewable under the "clearly erroneous" standard of Federal Rule of Civil Procedure 52(a).[6] Finally, the *Bolden* opinion required the same showing, i.e. purposeful racial discrimination, to establish a violation of § 2 of the Voting Rights Act of 1965.

Congress responded two years later by amending the Act to substitute an effects test for the requirement of proving discriminatory intent. As amended, § 2 prohibits any voting "standard, practice, or procedure" that "results in a denial or abridgement of the right of any citizen of the United States to vote on account of race or color" or because of language minority status.[7] A new subsection clarifies that the foregoing violation is established when the "totality of circumstances" show that the political processes "are not equally open to participation" in that minority members "have less opportunity than other members of the electorate to participate in the political process and to elect representatives of their

§ 10.9

1. *Gomillion v. Lightfoot,* 364 U.S. 339, 81 S.Ct. 125, 5 L.Ed.2d 110 (1960).

2. *White v. Regester,* 412 U.S. 755, 93 S.Ct. 2332, 37 L.Ed.2d 314 (1973).

3. 446 U.S. 55, 66, 100 S.Ct. 1490, 1499, 64 L.Ed.2d 47 (1980).

4. *Rogers v. Lodge,* 458 U.S. 613, 618, 102 S.Ct. 3272, 3276, 73 L.Ed.2d 1012

(1982) (quoting *Arlington Heights v. Metropolitan Housing Dev. Corp.,* 429 U.S. 252, 266, 97 S.Ct. 555, 563, 50 L.Ed.2d 450 (1977)).

5. *Rogers v. Lodge,* 458 U.S. at 624–625, 102 S.Ct. at 3279–80.

6. *Id.* at 622–623, 102 S.Ct. at 3278–79.

7. Section 2(a), 42 U.S.C.A. § 1973(a).

choice."[8]

A new, Fourteenth Amendment cause of action declared by *Shaw v. Reno* can succeed without a showing of "effect" and without the traditional evidence of racially discriminatory intent. To succeed under *Shaw* it must be shown by direct or indirect evidence that a state has, without substantial justification, drawn district lines intentionally on the basis of race. There is no additional requirement of a showing that the lines were drawn for the purpose of disadvantaging a previously disenfranchised minority.[9]

Library References:

> C.J.S. Constitutional Law §§ 717, 720.
> West's Key No. Digests, Constitutional Law ☞215.3.

§ 10.10 Fifteenth Amendment

A race-neutral Oklahoma statute that imposed a literacy test as a condition to vote, but grandfathered in the linear descendants of all those who were entitled to vote in 1866, was found to violate the Fifteenth Amendment because it worked to bar only blacks from voting.[1] The Court later held that Congress has the power, under the enforcement clause of the Fifteenth Amendment, to prohibit the use of any discriminatory tests or devices in state or federal elections.[2] In *Mitchell* the Court upheld the 1970 amendment to the Voting Rights Act which outlawed literacy tests.

A cause of action also exists to challenge districting plans as violating the Fifteenth amendment right to vote.[3] However, no decision has explicitly held that an apportionment or reapportionment violated the Fifteenth Amendment.[4] *Voinovich*[5] reaffirmed *Beer* while overturning a three-judge court's finding that an apportionment scheme violated the Fifteenth Amendment by intentionally diluting minority voting strength for political reasons. Noting that it had never struck down an allegedly dilutive legislative apportionment as inconsistent with the Fifteenth Amendment, the Court, without deciding the reach of that Amendment, assumed its applicability. It nevertheless held that the Fifteenth Amendment was not violated in *Voinovich*, because it deemed the lower court's finding of intentional discrimination in the case at bar clearly erroneous.[6] It therefore appears that any Fifteenth Amendment restraint on apportionment, like that of the Fourteenth Amendment,[7] below, is limited to situations in which the state is found by direct or

---

8. Section 2(b), 42 U.S.C.A. § 1973(b).

9. *See Shaw* below.

§ 10.10

1. *Guinn v. United States,* 238 U.S. 347, 35 S.Ct. 926, 59 L.Ed. 1340 (1915).

2. *Oregon v. Mitchell,* 400 U.S. 112, 91 S.Ct. 260, 27 L.Ed.2d 272 (1970).

3. *Gomillion v. Lightfoot,* 364 U.S. 339, 81 S.Ct. 125, 5 L.Ed.2d 110 (1960).

4. *Beer v. United States,* 425 U.S. 130, 142, 96 S.Ct. 1357, 1364, 47 L.Ed.2d 629 (1976).

5. *See supra* § 10.4, note 6.

6. 507 U.S. at 147, 113 S.Ct. at 1152.

7. *See Shaw v. Reno,* 509 U.S. 630, 113 S.Ct. 2816, 125 L.Ed.2d 511 (1993).

powerful indirect evidence (for example, the bizarre shape of a district, as in *Shaw*) to have drawn district lines intentionally on the basis of race.

§ 10.11   Section 2 of the Voting Rights Act

Section 2, the primary basis for legal challenges to diluting practices, has been used to attack at-large voting in multi-member districts at the state, county, and city level. In addition, the Supreme Court has ruled that the statutory right to elect "representatives" specified by § 2(b), unlike the constitutional one-person, one-vote rule,[1] extends to the election of judges.[2] A contrary result, as the Court observed in *Chisom*, would have created an anomaly in jurisdictions covered by the preclearance requirement of § 5, discussed immediately below in subsection C: any changes in the election laws governing judicial elections would have been subject to § 5 increased jurisdiction preclearance, (see Section D below) but existing practices, even in these jurisdictions, would have been immune from attack under § 2.

a.   *Thornburg v. Gingles*

In *Thornburg v. Gingles*,[3] the Supreme Court not only confirmed that amended § 2 had eliminated any requirement of discriminatory intent but also greatly simplified the elements of proof. The Court held that the election of some minority candidates does not necessarily doom a § 2 challenge to at-large voting in multi-member state legislative districts, observing that "the usual predictability of the majority's success distinguishes structural dilution from the mere loss of an occasional election."[4]

In a challenge to at-large multi-member district voting, the Court wrote, the plaintiff need only demonstrate that a "politically cohesive" minority group "is sufficiently large and geographically compact to constitute a majority in a single-member district" and that the "white majority votes sufficiently as a bloc to enable it—in the absence of special circumstances ... to defeat the minority's preferred candidate."[5] Further, the Court rejected any required showing of a minimum percentage of white and minority bloc voters. Instead, polarized voting would be legally significant when "a significant number of minority group members usually vote for the same candidates" and "whites vote suffi-

---

§ 10.11

1. *See* § 10.3, *supra.*

2. *Chisom v. Roemer,* 501 U.S. 380, 111 S.Ct. 2354, 115 L.Ed.2d 348 (1991); *Houston Lawyers' Ass'n v. Attorney General,* 501 U.S. 419, 111 S.Ct. 2376, 115 L.Ed.2d 379 (1991). *Cf. Wells v. Edwards,* 347 F.Supp. 453 (M.D.La.1972), *affirmed,* 409 U.S. 1095,

93 S.Ct. 904, 34 L.Ed.2d 679 (1973) (14th Amendment inapplicable to such elections).

3. 478 U.S. 30, 106 S.Ct. 2752, 92 L.Ed.2d 25 (1986).

4. *Id.* at 51, 106 S.Ct. at 2767.

5. *Id.* at 50–51, 106 S.Ct. at 2766–67.

ciently as a bloc usually to defeat the minority's preferred candidates." [6] The *Gingles* requirement that minorities compose a "majority" in a redrawn single-member district has since been held to refer to a majority of the voting-age population.[7] The remaining factors listed by the Senate Judiciary Committee's Report accompanying the 1982 amendments—the use of specific discriminatory voting practices, discrimination in slating candidates, socioeconomic disparities by race, racial appeals in campaigning, absence of minority representation, and the lack of official responsiveness to minority needs—while "relevant" are not indispensable, and apparently serve as tipping factors when the essential question of bloc voting is in doubt.

The broad reach of amended § 2 is evident in the Court's dictum in *Gingles* that a vote dilution claim does not require a showing of historical *de jure* discrimination, thus clearing the way for the effective use of § 2 outside the deep South. In the rare case when it is easier to prove discriminatory purpose than statistical effect, it appears that the pre–1982 standard as reflected in *City of Mobile* may still be used as an alternative mode of proof.[8]

b. Growe v. Emison and Johnson v. De Grandy

Gingles set out a blueprint to facilitate § 2 vote dilution challenges to *multimember* districts. In *Growe* the Court held proof of the same elements *essential* to establish that *single*-member districts—a form far more common than multimember districts—are apportioned in violation of § 2.

The Court began by observing that multimember districts generally pose greater threats to the participation of minority voters than single-member districts. (Indeed it has since held that a vote dilution challenge to the governance of a county by a single county commissioner is not even actionable under § 2, notwithstanding evidence that the small size of the governmental authority resulted in the repeated inability of a sizable minority to elect any of its members to that post.)[9] Nevertheless, it acknowledged in *Growe* that single-member apportionment schemes that fragment or "crack" minority voters, preventing them from constituting what would otherwise be a majority in a geographically compact district, may also dilute voting strength in violation of § 2. But the Court insisted that to show such a violation, plaintiffs must show diluted impact not merely through the "totality of the circumstances" ultimately demanded by § 2. Rather, they must demonstrate that dilutive effect by showing the same three factors enumerated in *Gingles*. "It would be peculiar," the Court wrote, "to conclude that a vote-

---

6. *Id.* at 56, 106 S.Ct. at 2769.

7. *See Brewer v. Ham,* 876 F.2d 448 (5th Cir.1989); *Romero v. City of Pomona,* 883 F.2d 1418 (9th Cir.1989); *McNeil v. Springfield Park Dist.,* 851 F.2d 937 (7th Cir. 1988), *cert. denied,* 490 U.S. 1031, 109 S.Ct. 1769, 104 L.Ed.2d 204 (1989); *Valladolid v. City of National City,* 976 F.2d 1293 (9th Cir.1992); *Magnolia Bar Association v. Lee,* 994 F.2d 1143 (5th Cir.1993).

8. *See* S. Rep. No. 417, 97th Cong., 2d Sess. 27 n.108, *reprinted in* 1982 U.S. Code Cong. & Admin. News 177, 205 n.108.

9. *Holder v. Hall,* ___ U.S. ___, 114 S.Ct. 2581, 129 L.Ed.2d 687 (1994).

dilution challenge to the (more dangerous) multimember district requires a higher threshold showing than a vote-fragmentation challenge to a single-member district." [10] In other words, the factors that in *Gingles* were used to facilitate challenges to multi-member districts were in *Growe* dubbed "preconditions" to a § 2 violation in the context of a challenge to a single-member apportionment scheme.

The *Growe* plaintiffs could not make this showing because the record did not demonstrate either minority political cohesion in a compact, unfragmented district, or bloc voting by the majority. The Court stressed that these elements were items of proof incumbent on the plaintiff, and that evidence of national voting patterns could not substitute for proof of bloc voting in the specific district in question.[11] As *Gingles* distilled three primary factors from § 2's list of seven, so *Growe* makes bloc voting the single most important element of § 2 proof.

The Court in *Growe* also reiterated its insistence that federal courts defer intervening in any aspect of the state process for apportioning federal congressional or state legislative districts when either a state legislature or, as in *Growe*, a state court is still deliberating. "Absent evidence that these state branches will fail timely to perform that duty, a federal court must neither affirmatively obstruct state reapportionment nor permit federal litigation to be used to impede it." [12] Reaffirming the variety of *Pullman* deferral [13] adapted to voting reapportionment cases by *Scott v. Germano*,[14] the Court stressed the constitutional primacy of the states in reapportionment matters. The states are subject to federal judicial review that is limited to consideration of specific violations of the federal Constitution or voting rights legislation. Applying *Germano* broadly, the Court wrote that even if state court litigation challenging an apportionment scheme does not present the same legal objection as parallel federal court litigation under the Voting Rights Act, the federal court must ordinarily stay its hand if the state court challenge could afford the same reapportionment *relief*. As long as the possibility remained that a state court would, in a reasonably timely fashion, reapportion a district conformably to the Constitution and federal voting rights legislation, the federal court should defer intervening.

But while evidence of the three *Gingles* factors is indispensable to a showing that a single-member district dilutes minority voting strength in violation of § 2, such evidence does not suffice. The Court held in *Johnson v. De Grandy* [15] that the *Gingles* evidence must be accompanied by proof that minority voting strength was diluted under the "totality of the circumstances," and that such a finding based solely on an apportionment's failure to maximize the potential number of majority-minority districts is clear error. The lower court should have given greater weight to the rough proportionality between the minority group's per-

10. 507 U.S. at 39, 113 S.Ct. at 1084.

11. 507 U.S. at 41, 113 S.Ct. at 1085.

12. 507 U.S. at 33, 113 S.Ct. at 1081.

13. See Procedure Chapter above.

14. 381 U.S. 407, 85 S.Ct. 1525, 14 L.Ed.2d 477 (1965).

15. ___ U.S. ___, 114 S.Ct. 2647, 129 L.Ed.2d 775 (1994).

centage in the voting-age population and the number of "majority-minority" [16] districts in deciding whether the scheme provided that group overall equal political opportunity.

c. *Voinovich v. Quilter*

The most common § 2 challenge to a single-member district is that seen in *Growe*: district lines have been drawn so as to fragment or "crack" minority voting power by scattering among several districts members of a politically cohesive minority group that would have been large enough to constitute the majority in a single-member district. In that setting the Court held that bloc voting must be present before a federal court may correct cracking by *mandating* a district with a nonwhite majority. In *Voinovich* the § 2 objection to the single-member district concerned "packing": the concentration of minority voters into "majority-black districts in which they constitute an 'excessive majority.'" [17] The issue therefore was when could a federal court *enjoin* a principally nonwhite district. As in *Growe*, the Court's answer rested at bottom on the states' presumptive primacy in reapportionment. Together these cases "limited intervention under the Voting Rights Act to situations characterized by racial bloc voting and the ensuing process failure, thus providing a firm doctrinal basis for displacing the political process." [18]

The classic packing scheme concentrates black voters in the district where they constitute a super-majority to prevent them from constituting a *majority* in a greater number of districts. In *Voinovich*, by contrast, the plaintiffs' claim was that, had they not been packed, black voters would have constituted an influential *minority* in several "influence districts." A three-judge district court held the creation of such packed majority-minority districts violative of § 2, except as a remedy for an independent § 2 violation.

For purposes of the appeal the Supreme Court assumed without deciding that the plaintiffs' allegations stated a cognizable § 2 claim.[19] The Court nevertheless reversed, again insisting that a § 2 violation depends on the tripartite *Gingles* showing. The plaintiffs must prove that the challenged apportionment has the effect of denying the protected group an equal opportunity to elect candidates of its choice. In particular, the Court found that the *Voinovich* plaintiffs had "failed to demonstrate *Gingles'* third precondition—sufficient white majority bloc voting to frustrate the election of the minority group's candidate of choice." [20] The Court stressed that § 2 is not violated by a state's drawing of any district absent a showing that the district was drawn with the intent or *Gingles*-proven effect of diluting minority voting strength. Accordingly, the lower court had mistakenly placed on the

---

16. See text accompanying note 7, *supra*.

17. *See Thornburg v. Gingles*, 478 U.S. 30, 46 n. 11, 106 S.Ct. 2752, 2764 n. 11, 92 L.Ed.2d 25 (1986).

18. Karlan, "All Over The Map," *supra* § 10.1, note 1, 1993 S.Ct. Rev. at 247.

19. *Voinovich*, 507 U.S. at 152, 113 S.Ct. at 1155.

20. 507 U.S. at 147, 113 S.Ct. at 1152.

state authorities the burden of justifying the majority-minority districts in question.

The standard *Gingles* showing, that the apportionment diluted aggregate minority voting strength, was especially crucial in this packing context, the Court wrote, because the creation of majority-black districts could have variable affects on black-voter strength. While packing may, as claimed in *Voinovich*, diminish the influence of those voters in predominately white districts, it also enhances the influence of black voters in the newly apportioned "packed" districts by providing them a "safe" majority that virtually assures the election of their candidate of choice.[21]

The Court provided some guidance for tailoring *Gingles* to an influence dilution challenge under § 2. It recognized that the first *Gingles* precondition, a group sufficiently large to constitute a *majority* in a *single* district, would have to be "modified or eliminated" for an influence-dilution claim, because the plaintiff's argument is that packing has prevented black voters from constituting "a sufficiently large *minority*" to elect, combined with white cross-over votes, candidates of their choice in *several* districts.[22] But the Court found it unnecessary to decide on a substitute for that factor because in the case at bar there was no showing of *Gingles'* third factor, racially polarized voting by a white majority bloc.

Library References:

> C.J.S. Elections § 8.
> West's Key No. Digests, Elections ⊃12.

D. SECTION 5—PRECLEARANCE OF VOTING LAW CHANGES IN HISTORICALLY DISCRIMINATORY JURISDICTIONS

§ 10.12 Section 5 Coverage

Section 5 of the Voting Rights Act of 1965,[1] requires preclearance by the United States Department of Justice or a United States District Court of proposed voting law changes in nine states and parts of seven others that have a history of racial discrimination in voting.[2] For the covered jurisdictions, § 5 is sweeping in scope, applying to any change after the jurisdiction's coverage date (November 1, 1964, 1968, or 1972) that alters the state's voting or election law "in even a minor way."[3]

Thus, § 5 encompasses all changes in voting procedures, candidate qualifications, make-up of the electorate, and measures that might dilute

21. 507 U.S. at 154, 113 S.Ct. at 1156.

22. *Id.* at 156, 113 S.Ct. at 1157.

§ 10.12

1. 42 U.S.C.A. § 1973(c).

2. 28 CFR Part 51 App. (1993).

3. *See Allen v. State Board of Elections,* 393 U.S. 544, 89 S.Ct. 817, 22 L.Ed.2d 1 (1969); Voting Rights Act, § 4(b), 42 U.S.C.A. § 1973b(b).

minority voting power such as altering the number of officials composing an elected governmental board or unit. The Supreme Court has also held § 5 applicable to judicial elections.[4] The Court has, however, placed one boundary around the coverage of § 5. In *Presley v. Etowah County*,[5] it held § 5 preclearance not required for changes in the internal operations of an elected body, even when those changes had the effect of reducing the authority of the individual elected officials, including recently elected minorities. The Court concluded that the Voting Rights Act simply does not reach the structural allocation of the power to govern after an election, only the arrangements by which representatives are elected and the composition of electoral districts.[6]

§ 10.13 *Beer*'s Retrogression Standard

A covered state or local jurisdiction bears the burden of proving that a change does not discriminate in purpose or in effect, regardless of whether it seeks administrative preclearance by the Justice Department, or judicial preclearance by the United States District Court for the District of Columbia.[1] But the Court has limited the effectiveness of § 5 by holding that a proposed election law change does not violate the effect standard unless it would "lead to a retrogression in the position of racial minorities with respect to their effective exercise of the electoral franchise."[2] Accordingly, continued use of a practice discriminatory in effect as part of a new proposal does not violate § 5,[3] and a new reapportionment plan discriminatory in effect and only slightly "ameliorative" relative to a former plan must be approved "unless the new apportionment itself so discriminates on the basis of race ... as to violate the Constitution."[4] Since amended § 2 would be violated by a nonretrogressive plan so long as it has a discriminatory effect, it would appear, ironically, that jurisdictions covered by § 5 are subject to less stringent standards in those proceedings than they or other jurisdictions must meet under § 2. The Senate Report accompanying the 1982 amendment to § 2 suggested to the contrary, that voting law changes

---

4. *See Clark v. Roemer,* 500 U.S. 646, 111 S.Ct. 2096, 114 L.Ed.2d 691 (1991); *Haith v. Martin,* 618 F.Supp. 410 (E.D.N.C. 1985), *affirmed mem.* 477 U.S. 901, 106 S.Ct. 3268, 91 L.Ed.2d 559 (1986); *Brooks v. Georgia State Board of Elections,* 775 F.Supp. 1470 (1989) (S.D. Ga.), *affirmed mem.,* 498 U.S. 916, 111 S.Ct. 288, 112 L.Ed.2d 243 (1990).

5. 502 U.S. 491, 112 S.Ct. 820, 117 L.Ed.2d 51 (1992).

6. Karlan, "All Over The Map," *supra* § 10.1, note 1, 1993 S.Ct. Rev. at 252 and "The Rights To Vote," *supra* § 10.1, note 1, 71 Tex. L. Rev. at 1723–1725. The same unwillingness for the judicial branch to supervise post-election governance may account for the decision in *Board of Estimate*

v. Morris, 489 U.S. 688, 109 S.Ct. 1433, 103 L.Ed.2d 717 (1989) that there is no Fourteenth Amendment requirement that each district have "equal power to affect a legislative outcome."

§ 10.13

1. 28 CFR § 51.52(a) (1993).

2. *Beer v. United States,* 425 U.S. 130, 141, 96 S.Ct. 1357, 1364, 47 L.Ed.2d 629 (1976).

3. *City of Lockhart v. United States,* 460 U.S. 125, 103 S.Ct. 998, 74 L.Ed.2d 863 (1983).

4. *Beer,* 425 U.S. at 141, 96 S.Ct. at 1364.

should be denied preclearance if they violate the "results" tests of amended § 2.[5]

Lower courts have initiated rear guard action to mitigate the *Beer* retrogression standard. They have carved out exceptions for, and thus condemned, redistricting plans that are "severely malapportioned" compared with a feasible alternative single-member plan.[6] Where no legal plan is in place, a comparison of the voting changes with the options for a properly apportioned single-member district plan is considered in lieu of the nonretrogression test.[7] And in one case a district court's interim districting plan was held an *improper* benchmark for purposes of measuring retrogression in future districting plans.[8]

States must be cautious in their attempts to comply with § 5 in order to prevent conflicts with the Fourteenth Amendment. These conflicts can occur when the State, in an attempt to satisfy § 5, creates districts with such highly irregular shapes that a Court may conclude that it drew the districts along racial lines.[9]

§ 10.14   Section 5 Procedure

The Attorney General's actions under § 5 are not judicially reviewable,[1] but when administrative preclearance is denied a jurisdiction may seek a declaratory judgment.[2] On the other hand, administrative preclearance does not mean that an approved plan satisfies any other Voting Rights Act or Constitutional requirement; a reapportionment plan that satisfies § 5 may still be challenged as unconstitutional and enjoined.[3] And § 5 preclearance does not preclude a subsequent challenge to the same proposed plan under § 2.[4] So a voter can challenge a plan during or after the preclearance procedure as violating a Constitutionally guaranteed right, or as violating § 2 of the Voting Rights Act. In addition, when a plan has been submitted for preclearance, any individual or group may send the Attorney General information which they think may be relevant to the change.[5] This information will be considered along with the proposed voting plan. If this information reaches the Attorney General after there has been a decision not to object, the Attorney General may reexamine the decision within a sixty

---

5. S. Rep. No. 97–417 (1982).

6. *Wilkes County v. United States,* 450 F.Supp. 1171 (D.D.C.1978), *affirmed mem.,* 439 U.S. 999, 99 S.Ct. 606, 58 L.Ed.2d 674 (1978); proposed changes that have greater discriminatory effect than an intermediate plan adopted by a federal court, *Mississippi v. United States,* 490 F.Supp. 569 (D.D.C. 1979), *affirmed mem.,* 444 U.S. 1050, 100 S.Ct. 994, 62 L.Ed.2d 739 (1980); plans deemed nonretrogressive only by reference to a benchmark plan that itself should have been but was not precleared under § 5, *Mississippi v. Smith,* 541 F.Supp. 1329 (D.D.C.1982), *appeal dismissed,* 461 U.S. 912, 103 S.Ct. 1888, 77 L.Ed.2d 280 (1983).

7. *Edge v. Sumter County School District,* 775 F.2d 1509 (11th Cir.1985).

8. *White v. City of Belzoni, Mississippi,* 854 F.2d 75 (5th Cir.1988).

9. *See Shaw v. Reno* discussed below.

§ 10.14

1. *Morris v. Gressette,* 432 U.S. 491, 97 S.Ct. 2411, 53 L.Ed.2d 506 (1977).

2. 42 U.S.C.A. § 1973c.

3. *Allen v. State Board of Elections,* 393 U.S. 544, 89 S.Ct. 817, 22 L.Ed.2d 1 (1969).

4. *Martin v. Allain,* 658 F.Supp. 1183 (S.D.Miss.1987).

5. 28 CFR § 51.29.

day period after notifying the submitting authority of the decision not to object.[6]

Submission of a plan to the Attorney General does not foreclose the jurisdiction from bringing an action in the U.S. District Court for the District of Columbia for a declaratory judgement that the plan does not have a discriminatory purpose or effect.[7] If the Attorney General has objected to a plan, the submitting party may at any time request that the objection be reconsidered.[8]

Library References:

> C.J.S. Elections § 8.
> West's Key No. Digests, Elections ⊛12(8).

§ 10.15 Section 5 Bailout

Jurisdictions can remove themselves from coverage under § 5 through the bailout provision provided in the Voting Rights Act. If the jurisdiction succeeds in the bailout action it will no longer be subject to § 5 preclearance.[1] To initiate the action a jurisdiction must file suit in the U.S. District Court for the District of Columbia, and prove that the jurisdiction has complied with all provisions of the Voting Rights Act for the past 10 years. The Attorney General of the United States is the defendant in the suit.

The burden of proving compliance with the Voting Rights act for the preceding 10 years is on the jurisdiction seeking to bail out. In addition to full compliance with the Voting Rights Act, the jurisdiction must show three other things. First, the jurisdiction must show that no other discriminatory voting practices prohibited by law have been practiced by the jurisdiction. Second, the jurisdiction must show that it has increased minority voting access. Third, it must show that minority voter participation has increased in the jurisdiction.[2]

E. CONSTITUTIONAL LIMITS ON DILUTIVE OR SEGREGATIVE ELECTORAL DISTRICTING

Library References:

> C.J.S. Elections § 8.
> West's Key No. Digests, Elections ⊛12.

§ 10.16 Districting That Dilutes a Minority Group's Voting Strength

As seen above, one type of state voting practice subject to constitutional scrutiny concerns deprivation of an individual's right to vote,

---

6. 28 CFR § 51.43.

7. 28 CFR § 51.11; 42 U.S.C.A. § 1973c.

8. 28 CFR § 51.45.

§ 10.15

1. 42 U.S.C.A. 1973b(a).

2. *A Citizen's Guide to Understanding The Voting Rights Act,* United States Commission on Civil Rights Clearinghouse Publication 84, October 1984.

through such devices as a poll tax or literacy test.[1] Such practices impeding participation offend the Fifteenth Amendment right to vote. But a second kind of unconstitutional practice, typified by the redistricting process, is one that implicates the aggregation interest by affecting "the political strength of various groups."[2]

Racially impacting redistricting, however, differs from practices that deprive persons of the right to vote in at least two crucial ways. First, "it hardly can be doubted that legislators routinely engage in the business of making electoral predictions based on group characteristics— racial, ethnic, and the like."[3] Second, and also unlike other contexts in which the court has condemned as suspect a government's conscious use of race, in electoral districting the mere placing of an individual in one district rather than another "denies no one a right or benefit provided to others. All citizens may register, vote, and be represented."[4] But the aggregate effect of a legislature's decision to collect various types of voters in one legislative or congressional district sometimes has the consequence "that one's vote may be more or less effective depending on the interest of the other individuals who are in one's district...."[5]

Vote "dilution" accordingly implicates the effects of electoral districting decisions on the political power of a group. Indeed, in communities that are racially mixed, consideration of race in districting decisions may be not only inevitable but virtually required either to comply with § 2 of the Voting Rights Act, which forbids districting plans that have a discriminatory effect on minority groups, or to comply with § 5, requiring covered jurisdictions to demonstrate to the Attorney General that a new plan "does not have the purpose and will not have the effect" of abridging the right to vote on account of race.[6]

For these reasons, electoral districting decisions geared in some fashion to race have not traditionally been subjected to the usual brand of Fourteenth Amendment equal protection heightened scrutiny. In ordinary equal protection cases, the plaintiff's showing that a state's conscious use of race in, for example, city contracting,[7] automatically requires the state to justify its classification by showing that race was a means "narrowly tailored" and necessary to accomplish a "compelling" state interest. In redistricting cases, by contrast, the Court has generally required a showing that both a *purpose and effect* of the districting is to dilute the effectiveness of a minority group member's vote compared

---

1. *See, e.g., Oregon v. Mitchell,* 400 U.S. 112, 91 S.Ct. 260, 27 L.Ed.2d 272 (1970).

2. *Mobile v. Bolden,* 446 U.S. 55, 83, 100 S.Ct. 1490, 1508, 64 L.Ed.2d 47 (1980) (Stevens, J., concurring in judgment).

3. *Shaw v. Reno,* 61 L.W. at 4827 (White, J., dissenting); *Id.* at 4832 (Souter, J., dissenting).

4. *Id.* at 4833.

5. *Id.* at 4833.

6. 42 U.S.C.A. §§ 1973, 1973c.

7. *Richmond v. J.A. Croson Co.,* 488 U.S. 469, 109 S.Ct. 706, 102 L.Ed.2d 854 (1989) or public employment decisions, *see Wygant v. Jackson Board of Education,* 476 U.S. 267, 106 S.Ct. 1842, 90 L.Ed.2d 260 (1986).

to a plausible alternative districting decision.[8]

§ 10.17 Districting That Prima Facie Unconstitutionally Discriminates Merely Because Its Odd Shape Suggests a Racial Purpose: *Shaw v. Reno*

In *Shaw v. Reno*,[1] the Court recently considered facts strikingly similar to *UJO* in all the foregoing respects, with one key difference: the plaintiffs asserted that the majority-black districts, redrawn by North Carolina in response to the Attorney General's § 5 objections, represented an express racial classification was based on the bizarre, untraditional and uncompact shape of their contours. The five-member *Shaw* majority opinion zeroed in on this distinction: in *UJO* there was no allegation "that the plan, on its face, was so highly irregular that it rationally could be understood only as an effort to segregate voters by race." Indeed, in *UJO*, the *Shaw* majority wrote, New York had employed "sound districting principles such as compactness in population equality" and had simply taken advantage of naturally occurring "residential patterns [that] afford the opportunity" of creating majority-black districts.[2]

Why, when the shape of a district moves beyond merely irregular to become "dramatically irregular" or "bizarre," did the *Shaw* majority believe that "appearances do matter"? Because the plan, even though *prompted* by the federal government's § 5 objections, ended up bearing "an uncomfortable resemblance to political apartheid. It reinforces the perception that members of the same racial group ... think alike, share the same political interests, and will prefer the same candidates at the polls.... When a district obviously is created solely to effectuate the perceived common interest of one racial group, elected officials are more likely to believe that their primary obligation is to represent only the members of that group, rather than their constituency as a whole. This is altogether antithetical to our system of representative democracy."[3]

In effect, the Court expressed the concern that a state might seize the opportunity afforded by its obligation to comply with the Voting Rights Act as an excuse "to engage in racial gerrymandering in the name of nonretrogression."[4] Put otherwise, the majority was underlining that a reapportionment plan may satisfy § 5, or for that matter § 2 of the Voting Rights Act, and "still ... be enjoined as unconstitutional."[5] Indeed, as read by the *Shaw* majority, the Constitution may demand *retrogression* from the two majority-black districts that were produced,

---

8. *United Jewish Organizations of Williamsburgh, Inc. v. Carey,* 430 U.S. 144, 165–166, 97 S.Ct. 996, 1010, 51 L.Ed.2d 229 (1977) (plurality opinion of White, J., joined by Stevens and Rehnquist, JJ.); *id.,* at 179–180, 97 S.Ct. at 1017 (Stewart, J., joined by Powell, J., concurring in judgment).

§ 10.17

1. 509 U.S. 630, 113 S.Ct. 2816, 125 L.Ed.2d 511 (1993).

2. *Shaw v. Reno,* 509 U.S. at 650, 113 S.Ct. at 2829.

3. *Shaw,* 507 U.S. at 647, 113 S.Ct. at 2827.

4. *Id.* at 654, 113 S.Ct. at 2831.

5. *Id.*

under Justice Department prodding, by the North Carolina legislative process. The *Shaw* decision is also novel in upholding the constitutional rights of persons (white) who were denied neither the right to participate nor, in the aggregate, the right to elect their preferred candidate.[6] At the behest of white voters, the Court intervened on constitutional grounds in the state political process in a fashion strikingly similar to the federal judicial intervention it had so recently condemned in *Growe* and *Voinovich* when black voters were the suitors and "only" the Voting Rights Act was at issue.[7]

The Supreme Court has confirmed this decision on standing in *United States v. Hays.*[8] There the Court held that "[w]here a plaintiff resides in a racially gerrymandered district ..., the plaintiff has been denied equal treatment because of the legislature's reliance on racial criteria, and therefore has standing to challenge the legislature's action."[9] Justice Stevens, who dissented, questioned how a plaintiff can have standing where he has not suffered from vote dilution.[10] He contended that "[t]he majority fails to explain coherently how a state discriminates invidiously by deliberately joining members of different races in the same district; why such placement amounts to an injury to members of any race; and assuming it does, to whom."[11] The Court responded that "[v]oters in such districts *may* suffer the special representational harms racial classifications can cause in the voting context."[12] This appears to mean that nonminorities (i.e., whites) who are in the minority in specially created majority-minority districts may suffer a dilution of representation because the representative, white or black, might be expected to cater to the needs of the more numerous members of the racial minority group.

There are two striking consequences that follow from the Court's attempted distinction of *Shaw* from *UJO.* The first is a distinct easing in the prima facie proof required to show that an electoral districting violates the Equal Protection Clause. The second is that the government defendant will not necessarily be able to rely on the requirements of the Voting Rights Act as a compelling state interest that will justify a race-based drawing of district lines.

---

6. One commentator has accordingly concluded that *Shaw* in fact entertains the "meta-governance" claims of white voters, Karlan, "All Over The Map," *supra* § 10.1, note 1, 1993 Sup.Ct.Rev. at 286, even though the record did not suggest that whites were excluded from the state decisionmaking process. See Karlan, "The Rights To Vote," *supra*, 71 *Tex.L.Rev.* at 1737.

7. Karlan, "All Over The Map," *supra* § 10.1, note 1, 1993 S.Ct. Rev. at 286.

8. ___ U.S. ___, 115 S.Ct. 2431, 132 L.Ed.2d 635 (1995).

9. *Id.* at ___, 115 S.Ct. at 2436.

10. *Id.* at ___, 115 S.Ct. at 2437. *See Miller v. Johnson,* ___ U.S. ___, 115 S.Ct. 2475, 132 L.Ed.2d 762 (1995) ("if the *Shaw* injury does not flow from an increased probability that white candidates will lose, then how can the increased probability that black candidates will win cause white voters ... cognizable harm?" *Id.* at ___, 115 S.Ct. at 2498.) (Stevens, J., dissenting).

11. *Hays,* ___ U.S. at ___, 115 S.Ct. at 2439.

12. *Id.* at ___, 115 S.Ct. at 2436.

Unlike the ordinary vote-dilution variant typified by *UJO*, where the plaintiffs must show a racially discriminatory purpose *and effect*—the "fencing out" or "cancelling out" of white voting strength that *UJO* required—a suspect "racial gerrymander" can be found prima facie merely from the Court's conclusion that the redrawn district's shape is sufficiently bizarre as to suggest that it was designed solely on the basis of race. No additional showing is required that the creation of the majority-minority districts had an aggregate dilutive effect on white voting strength.

The *Shaw* majority recognized the difficulty of discerning a "bizarre" or "uncouth" shape from one that is merely "unusual" or irregular,[13] a difficulty underlined by the different results in *Gomillion v. Lightfoot*[14] and *Wright v. Rockefeller*.[15] In *Gomillion*, the Court found that a twenty-eight sided municipal boundary line having the effect of removing from an Alabama city virtually all black voters but no whites violated the Fifteenth Amendment.[16] By contrast, the Court in *Wright* concluded that the merely "unusual," but apparently not "bizarre" shape of the district had other explanations.

The Court in *Shaw* struggled painfully to draw doctrinal lines that would illuminate whether a legislature's line drawing was for an unconstitutional purpose. One Justice insisted it was not necessary to resort to Justice Stewart's definition of obscenity ("I know it when I see it") to find that "dramatically irregular shapes may have sufficient probative force to call for an explanation."[17] "In some exceptional cases, a reapportionment plan may be so highly irregular that, on its face, it rationally cannot be understood as anything other" than an effort to racially segregate.[18]

As a result, we are left with two kinds of Fourteenth Amendment challenges to electoral districting plans devised to meet the requirements of, or the Attorney General's objections under, the Voting Rights Act. Where white voters seek to establish unconstitutional vote dilution, they must meet the purpose and effect requirements of *UJO*. Where, however, they can show a districting shape so "bizarre" or "extremely irregular on its face" as to be rationally explainable only as an effort to segregate on the basis of race, no allegation of harm will be required to state a Fourteenth Amendment claim.[19]

The second critical consequence of *Shaw*'s distinction from *UJO* follows from the first. After a racial gerrymander plaintiff establishes the one-step prima facie case approved by *Shaw*, the racial factor in

---

13. *See* R. Pildes and R. Niemi, "Expressive Harms, 'Bizarre Districts,' and Voting Rights: Evaluation Election District Appearances After *Shaw v. Reno*," 92 Mich. L.Rev. 483, 575 et seq. (1993).

14. 364 U.S. 339, 81 S.Ct. 125, 5 L.Ed.2d 110 (1960).

15. 376 U.S. 52, 84 S.Ct. 603, 11 L.Ed.2d 512 (1964).

16. *Gomillion*, 364 U.S. at 341, 81 S.Ct. at 127.

17. *Shaw*, 509 U.S. at 675, 113 S.Ct. at 2843 (quoting *Karcher v. Daggett*, 462 U.S. 725, 755, 103 S.Ct. 2653, 2672, 77 L.Ed.2d 133 (1983) (Stevens, J. concurring)).

18. *Id.* (quoting *Gomillion*).

19. *See Shaw*, 61 L.W. at 4834 (Souter, J., dissenting).

electoral districting should be treated identically to any other distinction drawn on the basis of race, that is, as suspect under the Equal Protection Clause and therefore subject to the highest level of scrutiny.[20] The state will be compelled to offer a compelling justification and demonstrate that the district lines drawn (in response to a demand to conform to the requirements of the Voting Rights Act) be the means most narrowly tailored to serve a compelling end. And just as the white plaintiffs were relieved of proving discriminatory effect even though the state drew the lines in response to a demand to comply with the Voting Rights Act, so, too, when the district lines are drawn sufficiently irregularly, the need to conform to that Act will not automatically serve as a defense.

In particular, the Court wrote skeptically about North Carolina's possible justification on remand that it revised the plan in order to comply with the "nonretrogression" principle of *Beer v. United States*.[21] The *Shaw* majority responded that in *Beer* itself, while the redistricting plan was found nonretrogressive and hence did not violate § 5, the Court expressly declined to hold the plan beyond separate challenge on constitutional grounds. It warned that the "reapportionment plan would not be narrowly tailored to the goal of avoiding retrogression if the State went beyond what was reasonably necessary...."[22]

The Court expressed no opinion about North Carolina's related justification for the redistricting, that it was necessary to avoid diluting black voting strength in violation of § 2, as construed in *Gingles*. It did note the possibility that the § 2 defense might fail if the state could not show that without the district plan it would have violated the *Gingles* preconditions. In particular, it cited the white plaintiffs' argument that the state's black population could not be composed into two geographically compact majority-minority districts, and that recent evidence of white cross-over voting belied the conclusion that whites vote as a bloc. And the Court said it remained open for consideration on remand whether, if § 2 did require adoption of the bizarrely shaped district, the Voting Rights Act was to that extent unconstitutional.

Finally, the Court threw cold water on a proposed third compelling state interest, a generalized desire to eradicate the effects of past racial discrimination wholly apart from the requirements of the Voting Rights Act. The Court noted that only a minority of the justices participating in *UJO* affirmatively recognized a generalized state interest in minimizing the consequences of racial bloc voting and that even those justices found race-based districting constitutionally permissible only when preexisting residential patterns made it possible to shape majority-black districts in accordance with "sound districting principles."[23]

20. *Id.* at 4825.

21. 425 U.S. 130, 140 & n. 12, 96 S.Ct. 1357, 1363 & n. 12, 47 L.Ed.2d 629 (1976). *Beer* is discussed in § 10.13, above.

22. *Shaw*, 61 L.W. at 4825.

23. *Id.* at 4826 (quoting *UJO*, 430 U.S. at 167–168, 97 S.Ct. at 1011) (opinion of White, J.).

§ 10.18 Application of the Shaw Cause of Action

The first reported lower court opinion concerning a *Shaw* cause of action was *Hays v. Louisiana*.[1] In *Hays* the United States District Court for the Western District of Louisiana considered a Fourteenth Amendment challenge to a Louisiana redistricting plan.

The court in *Hays* first addressed the issues of finding racial gerrymandering by inferential and by direct evidence.[2] Direct evidence was found in the form of intent to district on racial grounds. This intent, the court reasoned, could be directly found because Louisiana created a new district for the purpose of electing a black representative. The court determined that the new district was not necessitated by either § 5 or § 2 of the Voting Rights Act. Because of this lack of a statutory reason to create the district, it was found that the only other purpose for the plan must have been intentionally to create a racially gerrymandered district.[3]

The court stated repeatedly that the Attorney General's Office had exceeded the bounds of its power under the Voting Rights Act by requiring this type of districting, and it seems that this excess contributed to the Court's finding of intentional racial gerrymandering.[4] Following the *Shaw* reasoning, the court next concluded that the irregular shape of the new district amounted to inferential evidence of that racial gerrymandering on the part of Louisiana.[5]

The issue of what constitutes a bizarre enough shape for purposes of *Shaw* was handled in short order by the Court in *Hays*. That the district was "highly irregular" on its face and did not comport with traditional districting principles was enough for the Court to find that it was shaped sufficiently bizarrely to fit the *Shaw* cause of action.[6] The defendant's evidence that non-racial criteria were also used in creating the district was discounted because the court reasoned that race was an important factor even if it was not the only one.[7]

This reasoning marks a slight, but significant deviation from the approach of *Shaw*. In *Shaw* the Court stated that the cause of action arose from a plan so "irrational on its face that it could be understood *only* as an effort to segregate voters by race".[8] For the *Hays* court, however, the existence of other factors underlying the districting merely creates a competing inference about segregative intent but does not bar the *Shaw* cause of action if that intent is ultimately found. Race need only constitute an "important factor." Under this analysis, if race is an important factor in a bizarrely shaped district and the district shape

---

§ 10.18

1. 839 F.Supp. 1188 (W.D.La.1993), *vacated by Louisiana v. Hays*, ___ U.S. ___, 114 S.Ct. 2731, 129 L.Ed.2d 853 (1994).

2. *Id.* at 1195.

3. *Id.* at 1195–96.

4. *Id.* at 1196.

5. *Id.* at 1198–99.

6. *Id.* at 1199.

7. *Id.* at 1202.

8. *Shaw*, 509 U.S. at 630, 113 S.Ct. at 2818 (emphasis added).

cannot be explained by traditional districting principles, a *Shaw* claim is viable.

The defendants in *Hays* contended that conforming with § 2 and § 5 of the Voting Rights Act, providing proportional representation for blacks in Louisiana, and remedying past discrimination against Louisiana blacks were interests that justified their districting plan.[9] Without deciding whether any of these interests was compelling, the court held that the plan was not narrowly tailored to meet any of them.[10] Using *Shaw* as a guide the court held that the plan could not have been narrowly tailored to satisfy § 5 of the Voting Rights Act because it went beyond what was necessary for the state to avoid a retrogression in the position of black voters.[11] The court also found that the plan was not narrowly tailored because it placed into the district a greater number of black voters than was necessary to meet any of the defendants' interests and departed from traditional districting criteria.[12]

The Supreme Court grappled with the several loosely defined variables of the *Shaw* cause of action in *Miller v. Johnson*.[13] There it struck down a Georgia congressional redistricting plan as repugnant to the Equal Protection Clause, holding that an asserted need to comply with § 5 did not on the record there furnish the Georgia General Assembly the requisite compelling need to use race as a predominant factor in drawing redistricting lines.

After the Department of Justice refused to preclear two earlier versions of the challenged plan,[14] the General Assembly drew an eleventh congressional district that stitched together at the periphery the geographically remote, dense, majority-black population centers of Atlanta, Augusta and Savannah, embracing also the lightly populated but also heavily black rural territory in between. The plan provided for three majority-minority districts as suggested by the Department's "max-black" plan. Plaintiffs, five white voters from the Eleventh District, challenged the plan as a racial gerrymander that violated the Equal Protection Clause as interpreted in *Shaw v. Reno*.[15]

The Court first decided that the plaintiffs had established a prima facie case of race-based redistricting in violation of the Equal Protection Clause. The Court expanded on *Shaw* by allowing the prima facie case to be demonstrated through direct evidence of legislative racial purpose, as an alternative to proving that purpose inferentially from unusually

---

9. 839 F.Supp. at 1205–06.

10. *Id.* at 1207.

11. *Id.* at 1207.

12. *Id.* at 1207–08.

13. __ U.S. __, 115 S.Ct. 2475, 132 L.Ed.2d 762 (1995).

14. Both the first and second plans increased the number of majority-minority congressional voting districts from one to two; and neither was found by the three-judge court below to have evidenced an

intent to discriminate against minority voters. Nevertheless, the Department of Justice continued to refuse § 5 preclearance, asserting that the state's plan still did not "recognize certain minority populations." *Id.* at 2484. In striking the two initial plans the Department relied on a "max-black" objective which called for three majority-minority districts.

15. *Id.* at __, 115 S.Ct. at 2485.

bizarre shape. Accordingly, the plaintiff's burden can now be met "either through circumstantial evidence of a district's shape and demographics [as in *Shaw*] or more direct evidence going to legislative purpose, that race was a predominant factor motivating the legislature's decision to place a significant number of voters within or without a particular district." [16] Further, a finding of presumptively unlawful racial purpose is proper even where, as in *Miller*, the legislature also took into account traditional, race-neutral districting principles (compactness, contiguity, respect for political subdivisions and for communities defined by actual shared interests) but subordinated them to considerations of race. As argued by Justice Ginsburg, dissenting, the Eleventh District's design reflected "significant consideration of traditional districting factors...." [17] Nevertheless, under the majority's "predominant" standard, states can no longer avoid judicial review simply by giving even "genuine and measurable consideration to traditional districting practices." [18] "[T]oday's decision ... opens the way for federal litigation if 'traditional ... districting principles' arguably were accorded *less weight* than race." [19] Still, one of the voters in the majority, Justice O'Connor, understood the Court's standard to be "demanding," applicable only to "extreme instances of gerrymandering." [20]

Two splintered 1996 Term decisions, *Shaw v. Hunt* ("*Shaw II*") [21] and *Bush v. Vera* [22] continue to wrestle inconclusively with the role of noncompact or even bizarre shape as necessary or sufficient to raise the presumption of unconstitutionality under *Shaw I*. Chief Justice Rehnquist's opinion for the Court in *Shaw II* repeats the *Miller* assertion that the nonminority plaintiff may erect the presumption in alternative ways: "either through 'circumstantial evidence of a district's shape and demographics' or through 'more direct evidence going to legislative purpose.'" [23] Either of these alternatives serves as a proxy for the ultimate standard of prima facie 14th Amendment transgression: a showing that race was the predominant factor underlying a legislature's decision, in drawing district lines, to include or exclude a significant number of

---

16. *Id.* at ___, 115 S.Ct. at 2488. Elsewhere the Court referred to the showing that sufficed to show a violation in *Miller* as a demonstration that race was the "dominant and controlling" or "predominant, overriding" factor in the Georgia legislature's drawing of the lines. *Id.* at ___, ___, 115 S.Ct. at 2486, 2490. Alternatively, the Court wrote that the shape of the eleventh district, although not as bizarre as that of the North Carolina district at issue in *Shaw*, constituted, "in conjunction with its racial and population densities," "quite compelling" evidence of an unlawful, i.e., racial, gerrymander. But the majority concluded that it was unnecessary to determine whether the district's shape, standing alone, was sufficiently unusual to establish a claim under *Shaw*. *Id.* at ___, 115 S.Ct.

at 2489. The Court's murky 1996 Term decisions, *Shaw II* and *Bush v. Vera*, discussed immediately below, also fail to answer that question conclusively.

17. *Id.* at ___, 115 S.Ct. at 2503.

18. *Id.* at ___, 115 S.Ct. at 2505.

19. *Id.* at ___, 115 S.Ct. at 2507 (emphasis added).

20. ___ U.S. at ___, 115 S.Ct. at 2497 (O'Connor, J., concurring).

21. ___ U.S. ___, 116 S.Ct. 1894, ___ L.Ed.2d ___ (1996).

22. ___ U.S. ___, 116 S.Ct. 1941, ___ L.Ed.2d ___ (1996).

23. *Shaw II*, at 10–11.

voters.[24] Predomination of race is the ultimate litmus, because a state that has made race a predominant factor in shaping a district may not refute a claim of racial gerrymander even where the district's shape relects a degree of adherence to traditional districting principles like compactness, contiguity, and respect for political subdivisions.[25] So "direct" evidence of predominant racial motivation serves as a clear alternative to bizarre or simply noncompact, noncontiguous shape in demonstrating a prima facie violation and thus triggering strict scrutiny.

But is the reverse true: does bizarre shape suffice to show the ultimate offense of predominant racial motivation? Perhaps not. Despite the alternative linguistic formulations quoted above, and even though the Court had branded the North Carolina district at issue in *Shaw I* as "bizarre," it found it necessary in *Shaw II* also to identify "direct evidence" of impermissible, race-based legislative purpose.[26] Indeed the *Bush* plurality wrote that a legislature's departure from traditional districting criteria, as evidenced by such factors as noncontiguity and noncompactness, "is merely necessary, not sufficient. For strict scrutiny to apply, traditional districting criteria must be subordinated to race."[27] Race, that is, must be shown to be the predominant reason why a legislature neglected or underemphasized traditional criteria.[28]

Where the Court has invoked strict scrutiny a la *Shaw*, a number of theoretically available compelling state interests have fallen short. In *Miller* the Court had identified two reasons as arguably sufficiently compelling to justify using race as a predominant factor in redistricting: "A significant state interest in eradicating the effects of past racial discrimination"[29] or "in *some* cases compliance with the Voting Rights Act...."[30] Because Georgia did not argue that it created the challenged plan's three majority-minority districts in order to remedy past discrimination, the Court focused on whether the state could justify them as essential for it to come into compliance with § 5 of the Voting Rights Act.

Without deciding that legal question, the Court found no such justification in the case at bar. First, it insisted that "compliance with federal anti-discrimination laws cannot justify race-based districting where the challenged district was not reasonably necessary under a constitutional reading and application of those laws."[31] In this connection it was important, the Court wrote, to recall that a redistricting plan violates § 5 only (a) when it is retrogressive in the limited sense defined by *Beer v. United States*[32] or (b) when "it so discriminates on the basis of race or color as to violate the constitution"—when, in other words, the

---

24. *Id.* at 11.

25. *Id.* at 15 n. 3.

26. *Shaw II* at 12.

27. *Bush*, at 7.

28. *Id.* at 7.

29. *Id.* at 2490.

30. *Id.* at 2490, 2491 (emphasis added).

31. *Id.* at 2491.

32. 425 U.S. 130, 96 S.Ct. 1357, 47 L.Ed.2d 629 (1976). *See* discussion of *Beer* at § 10.13 above.

legislature had a discriminatory purpose in designing the district.[33] Under *Beer,* all the state had to do to satisfy § 5 was maintain its existing number of majority-minority districts. Since Georgia, before the plan, had only one majority-minority district, and the two initial plans rejected by the Justice Department proposed two such districts, the state could not tenably maintain that a third district was necessary to avoid retrogression.

Furthermore, the Court accepted the state attorney general's explanation that the legislature sought to stick with two rather than three majority-minority districts not to discriminate based on race but rather to give effect to "other districting principles."[34] Section 5 would therefore not have been violated by the initial plans the Justice Department rejected; accordingly the ultimate, challenged plan could not be deemed necessary, that is narrowly tailored to effectuate even an assumed compelling interest of compliance with § 5.

The residue here is apparent tension between the Voting Rights Act and the Constitution. The Court wrote that the Voting Rights Act furnished no automatic defense just because the Department of Justice determined that race-based districting was necessary to comply with the Act, because the Court must independently review Equal Protection claims to ensure that the state's actions are narrowly tailored to meet a compelling interest.[35] And in undertaking that review the *Miller* opinion reflects some incoherence concerning the statutory and constitutional roles of race in redistricting. On one hand, the Court recognizes that political redistricting "implicates a political calculus in which various interests compete for recognition...."[36] The Court even implies that the Voting Rights Act recognizes group rights, writing that "the purpose of § 5 has always been to insure that no voting-procedure changes would be made that would lead to a retrogression in the position of racial minorities with respect to *their* effective exercise of the electoral franchise."[37] But in the end, consistent with the premise of its recent Equal Protection Decisions,[38] the Court vehemently disputes, as a constitutional matter, "that individuals of the same race share a single political interest. The argument that they do is "based on the demeaning notion

---

33. *Miller,* ___ U.S. at ___, 115 S.Ct. at 1497.

34. *Id.*

35. *Id.* at 2491.

36. *Id.* at 2487. *See Shaw,* 509 U.S. at 647, 113 S.Ct. at 2827. *See also* § 10.13 above. As Justice Ginsburg observed, "In adopting districting plans . . . states do not treat people as individuals. Apportionment schemes, by their very nature, assemble people in groups. States do not assign voters to districts based on merit or achievement. . . . Rather, legislators classify voters in groups—by economic, geographical, political, or social characteristics—and then reconcile the competing claims of [these] groups." (internal quotation marks omit-

ted). More recently, however, a Court majority has noted that the § 2 right, while undoubtedly measured by reference to dilutive effects upon a minority group, belongs to its individual members, not the group itself. *Shaw v. Hunt,* ___ U.S. ___, 116 S.Ct. 1894, 135 L.Ed.2d 207 (1996).

37. *Id.* at 2493 (emphasis added).

38. *See Adarand Constructors, Inc. v. Pena,* ___ U.S. ___, 115 S.Ct. 2097, 132 L.Ed.2d 158 (1995); *City of Richmond v. J.A. Croson Co.,* 488 U.S. 469, 109 S.Ct. 706, 102 L.Ed.2d 854 (1989); *Wygant v. Jackson Bd. of Education,* 476 U.S. 267, 106 S.Ct. 1842, 90 L.Ed.2d 260 (1986).

that members of the defined racial groups ascribe to certain "minority views" that must be different from those of other citizens.' " [39]

In *Miller* only § 5 was advanced as a justification for the presumptively unconstitutional district. As we have seen, the scant § 5 requirements for preclearance rendered it an unlikely source of justification for a legislature's predominant use of race.[40] Will states fare better if they can show that race-focused redistricting is necessary to avoid vote dilution made unlawful by § 2 of the Act? That question is not easy, because § 2 itself couples the command against dilution with a warning that its text should not be construed to guarantee proportional representation.

The Court's most recent forays in the field raise real doubt about § 2's utility as an effectively justificatory compelling state interest. In *Shaw II* the Court assumed arguendo, without deciding, that the necessity to comply with § 2 could constitute a compelling state interest. But the additional narrow tailoring requirement meant that the district actually drawn by the legislature must "substantially address" the § 2 compliance purpose by remedying an identifiable anticipated violation. In turn, the Court found that the fact of a § 2 violation (respecting the kind of compact, minority-opportunity potential district that *Gingles* stipulates as prerequisite to a § 2 violation) somewhere in North Carolina was not remedied by a largely non-coincident, noncompact majority-minority district located elsewhere in the state. That theory, wrote the Court, wrongly assumes that § 2 creates group rights for North Carolina African–Americans, as opposed to rights for individual African–Americans registered to vote in what could have been a compact *Gingles*-defined district. Because the district under challenge in *Shaw* failed to draw in many of the African–American voters who would have been included in a hypothetical *Gingles* district, it could not be considered a narrowly tailored remedy that substantially addressed a § 2 violation.[41]

39. *Miller, supra,* at p. 2487 (citations omitted).

40. The Court has persisted in refusing to decide whether an asserted need to avoid a § 5 violation could justify a *Shaw*-tainted majority-minority district. It has deemed such a decision unnecessary because it has upheld findings that the particular majority-minority districts it has reviewed sought to augment, and not merely maintain, minority voting strength. Thus those districts could not have been necessary to avoid running afoul of the minimal § 5 goals articulated in *Beer* and reaffirmed in *Miller*: to block only those new or newly drawn districts that would cause retrogression or that overtly, hostilely and purposefully discriminate on the basis of race. Presumably few if any such districts will be drawn to avoid retrogression or prevent hostile discrimination against voting minorities, and § 5 will therefore likely continue

to prove unavailing in fact, whatever its status in theory. And a majority of the Court has now cast cold water on the alternative argument that a showing of dilutive effect violative of § 2 suffices to demonstrate the discriminatory purpose requisite to a violation of § 5. *Shaw II,* at 25.

41. *Shaw II,* at 9–10. A plurality in *Bush* concluded similarly that such violations could be remedied only by "reasonably compact" districts; and it found that the noncompact, bizarrely shaped districts challenged there were drawn to include dispersed minority communities that could not have formed part of a compact, hypothetical *Gingles* district. *Bush v. Vera,* at 16 (O'Connor, J., writing for herself and Chief Justice Rehnquist and Justice Kennedy). Noncompact shape is relevant, therefore, not only as a factor tending to show that race predominated in the drawing of district lines and thus triggering strict scrutiny. It

At the same time, however, the Court noted that narrow tailoring did not require the putative remedial district "to achieve fully" its goal of avoiding a § 2 violation.[42] The *Bush* plurality elaborated that a putative § 2 remedial district "substantially addresses" a § 2 violation and accordingly is narrowly tailored if the legislature had a strong and well founded evidentiary basis "for concluding that creation of a majority-minority district is reasonably necessary to comply with § 2...."[43] It therefore bridled at the dissent's suggestion that the legislature, to survive a *Shaw* challenge, must draw the identical, compact district that a court would require after finding a § 2 violation.[44]

A third justification considered in both *Shaw II* and *Bush,* a state's generalized interest in remedying the effects of past or present race discrimination, has also proved unavailing in practice. The Court readily acknowledges that in principle a state with a strong evidentiary basis to conclude that a particular district must be drawn as a remedy to correct specifically identified discrimination by the governmental unit in question can justify race-conscious districting.[45] But the defense has failed factually, either because the only discrimination alleged to have been remedied by the creation of the district was alleged vote dilution that the Court had already determined *not* to violate § 2,[46] or because the legislature was found not to have been motivated in drawing the district as it did by a desire to ameliorate past discrimination.[47]

F. PROBLEMS PRECIPITATED BY SHAW, AND A POTENTIAL AVOIDANCE

§ 10.19 In General

Shaw and its progeny create some significant problems. First, how far a state can go past non-retrogression to compensate for past discrimination? A threshold barrier is crossed when the district takes on an unusual shape or otherwise offends the Court's conception of traditional districting criteria. Obviously, a district that is created for the sole purpose of giving strength to the minority vote will always fail the test of not having race as a predominant factor in the districting; race will also figure importantly in any districting undertaken to comply with the Voting Rights Act. Even in mixed-motive situations, the noncompact shape of a district will contribute significantly to a finding of prima facie 14th Amendment liability, even if that shape is something short of so "bizarre" as to leave no conclusion other than race-based gerrymandering. Any test of compactness and bizarreness is an easy target; it is likely to prove unworkable or at least unprincipled, centered as it is on as many subjective perceptions as there are members of a reviewing

also undermines the § 2 justification to a prima facie Equal Protection violation. *Id.* at 17.

42. *Shaw II,* at 29 n. 7.

43. *Bush v. Vera,* at 15–16.

44. *Id.*

45. *Shaw II,* at 18; *Bush* at 18.

46. *Bush,* at 18.

47. *Shaw II,* at 19.

court. Yet three justices recently contended that the *Miller* "predominant factor" test for motivation is even more unworkable.[1]

Second, what if the minorities in a state are geographically dispersed and cannot be reached, for purposes of satisfying § 5 or § 2 of the Voting Rights Act, except through an irregularly shaped district? If an irregularly shaped district is consequently compelled to avoid violations of the Voting Rights Act, the Act would then come into conflict with the Fourteenth Amendment cause of action created in *Shaw* and to that extent would be unconstitutional. The Court's current answer appears to be that the hypothesis of the question is false: § 2 does not require (and the *Shaw*-glossed Equal Protection Clause therefore does not permit) a racially adjusted *district* as a remedy for minority vote dilution manifested across a *state*.

The underlying structural problem here is winner-take-all voting systems. Academic voices argue that the current system of using racial criteria as a means to remedy racial discrimination is not in the interest of minority voters, either.

Lani Guinier has proposed a system of proportional interest representation that would address this dilemma.[2] Proportional interest representation, or cumulative voting, is a voting system in which each voter may cast as many votes as there are candidates on the ballot. For example, if North Carolina has twelve congressional representatives to elect, each voter gets twelve votes. Voters can use all their votes for one candidate, spread the votes among all 12, or use any combination in between. This system allows cohesive minorities (or other interest groups) to elect one or more candidates who enjoy little or no support from others. Cumulative voting holds the promise of avoiding race-based districting without subjecting minorities to the disadvantage of absolute exclusion that can result from at-large systems. The Fourth Circuit recently rejected a judicially ordered cumulative voting remedy for a county commissioner system that diluted the voting strength of black citizens by requiring the at-large election of all commissioners.[3]

---

§ 10.19

1. *Bush v. Vera, supra* (Souter, J., dissenting).

2. *The Triumph of Tokenism*, 89 *Mich. L. Rev.* 1077 (1991).

3. *Cane v. Worcester County,* 35 F.3d 921 (4th Cir.1994).

Chapter Eleven

DISCRIMINATION IN PROPERTY AND HOUSING

Analysis

A. INTRODUCTION

Library References:

> C.J.S. Civil Rights §§ 38, 68–74, 87.
> West's Key No. Digests, Civil Rights ☞130, 131.

§ 11.1 Discrimination Generally

There are an estimated two million occurrences of housing discrimination every year.[1] Title 42 U.S.C.A. § 1982, first enacted as part of the Civil Rights Act of 1866, and Title VIII of the 1968 Fair Housing Act,[2] as amended, both prohibit public and private housing discrimination. Title VIII covers a more comprehensive set of actionable grounds and prohibited practices, may sometimes provide the plaintiff an easier proof standard, and employs more flexible criteria for standing, but it exempts certain defendants and practices. Section 1982 covers fewer actionable grounds and prohibited practices, and employs a stricter test for standing, but offers better remedies and expresses no defendant or practice exemptions.

The two statutes operate independently. The Supreme Court has rejected the idea that Title VIII impliedly repealed or preempted § 1982.[3] By its own terms, Title VIII does not "invalidate ... any law ... of any jurisdiction ... that grants, guarantees or protects the same rights as are granted by this title." [4] So where a defendant is exempt under Title VIII, the plaintiff may proceed under the Reconstruction statute.

B. GROUNDS

Library References:

> C.J.S. Civil Rights §§ 38, 68–74, 87.
> West's Key No. Digests, Civil Rights ☞130, 131.

§ 11.1

1. *Secretary, U.S. Department of HUD v. Blackwell*, 908 F.2d 864, 868 (11th Cir. 1990).

2. Previously the Fair Housing Act, initially enacted in the Civil Rights Act of 1968 as Pub.L. No. 90–284, and currently codified, as amended by the Fair Housing Amendments Act of 1988, Pub.L. No. 100–430, at 42 U.S.C.A. § 3601 et seq.

3. *Jones v. Alfred H. Mayer Co.*, 392 U.S. 409, 426, 88 S.Ct. 2186, 2196, 20 L.Ed.2d 1189 (1968) (enactment of Title VIII had no effect on § 1982).

4. 42 U.S.C.A. § 3615.

§ 11.2 Section 1982

Section 1982, in its entirety, provides that "[a]ll citizens of the United States shall have the same right, in every State and Territory, as is enjoyed by white citizens thereof to inherit, purchase, lease, sell, hold and convey real and personal property."

The section's language protects only United States citizens, extends protection only to rights in the ownership, transfer and use [1] of real and personal property, and addresses only racial discrimination. Relying on the contemporary understanding of the enacting Reconstruction Congress, the Court has held that discrimination based on ancestry or ethnic characteristic may qualify as discrimination based on race.[2] "Ancestry" means belonging to an ethnically or physiognomically distinct group.[3] For example, persons of Jewish, Arabian and Hispanic descent have qualified as non-whites under the Reconstruction statutes.[4]

§ 11.3 Title VIII

Title VIII, by contrast, protects citizens as well as non-citizens from discrimination based not only on race and color but also on religion, national origin, sex, handicap, and familial status. Handicap and familial status are defined in §§ 3602(h) and (k), respectively.[1]

The prohibition on handicap discrimination requires that reasonable accommodation be made to enable the handicapped to enjoy equal opportunity to use a covered dwelling.[2] The Supreme Court recently held a city's single-family zoning regulation that allegedly violated this requirement ineligible for the Title VIII exemption [3] that permits reasonable restrictions on maximum dwelling occupancy because the regulation's definition of "family" included not only groups limited in number but also those related by blood, adoption or marriage.[4]

---

§ 11.2

1. Circuit courts have read the right to "hold" property free of racial interference to subsume the right of nonowner members of a synagogue to be free from violence or vandalism interfering with that property's use. *United States v. Brown,* 49 F.3d 1162 (6th Cir.1995); *United States v. Greer,* 939 F.2d 1076 (5th Cir.1991) (cases under 18 U.S.C.A. § 241 construing the same predicate right protected by § 1982).

2. *Shaare Tefila Congregation v. Cobb,* 481 U.S. 615, 107 S.Ct. 2019, 95 L.Ed.2d 594 (1987) (allowing a person of Jewish ancestry to maintain an action under the section).

3. *St. Francis College v. Al–Khazraji,* 481 U.S. 604, 107 S.Ct. 2022, 95 L.Ed.2d 582 (1987) (holding that a person of Arabian ancestry qualifies for protection under the same language in § 1981).

4. *See* cases in notes 2 and 3 *supra* and *Jaimes v. Toledo Metropolitan Housing Authority,* 758 F.2d 1086 (6th Cir.1985) (Hispanics can state a claim under § 1982).

§ 11.3

1. *See, e.g., HUD v. Downs,* 2 Fair Housing–Fair Lending (P–H) ¶ 25,011 (HUD ALJ 9/20/91), *pet. for review denied, Soules v. U.S. Dept. of HUD,* 967 F.2d 817 (2d Cir.1992) (familial status case involving discrimination based on children's noisiness).

2. 42 U.S.C.A. § 3604(f)(3)(B).

3. 42 U.S.C.A. § 3607(b)(1).

4. *City of Edmonds v. Oxford House,* ___ U.S. ___, 115 S.Ct. 1776, 131 L.Ed.2d 801 (1995).

C.　COVERED DEFENDANTS

Library References:

C.J.S. Civil Rights §§ 38, 68–74, 87.
West's Key No. Digests, Civil Rights ⚖130, 131.

§ 11.4　Section 1982

The guarantee § 1982 makes to all United States citizens may be violated by any private person.[1] Local government agencies and officials can consent to or otherwise waive Eleventh Amendment immunity to suit in general, but, if not, that immunity will shield them from liability for federal court damage awards.[2] The Amendment has been construed, however, not to relieve states or state officials from liability for prospective relief or awards of attorney's fees.[3] See the Chapter on the Civil Rights Attorney's Fees Awards Act. Federal government agencies may also be liable under § 1982.[4]

Liability may be fixed on entities through the theory of *respondeat superior*. Generally, principals are responsible for the acts of their agents,[5] and corporate officers are responsible for the acts of their employees.[6]

§ 11.5　Title VIII

Title VIII defines "respondent" as a "person," which includes private individuals and entities, municipalities, local government units, and cities,[1] as well as federal agencies.[2] Title VIII exempts certain defendants from its prohibitions, as discussed in Section V, "Exemptions."

The *respondeat superior* theory has also been applied in Title VIII actions, making principals responsible for the acts of their agents[3] and corporations responsible for the acts of corporate employees.[4]

§ 11.4

1. *Jones, supra* § 11.1 note 3, at 413.

2. *See, e.g., Freeman v. Michigan Dept. of State,* 808 F.2d 1174 (6th Cir.1987) (§ 1981 case).

3. *See, e.g., Missouri v. Jenkins,* 491 U.S. 274, 109 S.Ct. 2463, 105 L.Ed.2d 229 (1989).

4. *Selden Apartments v. HUD,* 785 F.2d 152 (6th Cir.1986).

5. *United States v. Mitchell,* 335 F.Supp. 1004 (N.D.Ga.1971), *affirmed sub nom. United States v. Bob Lawrence Realty, Inc.,* 474 F.2d 115 (5th Cir.1973), *cert. denied,* 414 U.S. 826, 94 S.Ct. 131, 38 L.Ed.2d 59 (1973).

6. *Clark v. Universal Builders, Inc.,* 501 F.2d 324 (7th Cir.), *cert. denied,* 419 U.S. 1070, 95 S.Ct. 657, 42 L.Ed.2d 666 (1974).

§ 11.5

1. *United States v. City of Parma,* 661 F.2d 562, 572 (6th Cir.1981), *cert. denied,* 456 U.S. 926, 102 S.Ct. 1972, 72 L.Ed.2d 441 (1982).

2. *Selden Apartments v. HUD,* 785 F.2d 152 (6th Cir.1986).

3. *City of Chicago v. Matchmaker Real Estate Sales Center, Inc.,* 982 F.2d 1086 (7th Cir.1992), *cert. denied sub nom. Ernst v. Leadership Council for Metro. Open Communities,* 508 U.S. 972, 113 S.Ct. 2961, 125 L.Ed.2d 662 (1993).

4. *Northside Realty Associates, Inc. v. United States,* 605 F.2d 1348 (5th Cir.1979).

D.   PROHIBITED PRACTICES

Library References:

C.J.S. Civil Rights §§ 38, 68–74, 87.
West's Key No. Digests, Civil Rights ⊱130, 131.

§ 11.6   Section 1982

In *Jones v. Alfred H. Mayer Co.,*[1] the Court held that § 1982 "bars *all* racial discrimination, private as well as public...." This decision gave § 1982 a wide sweep, and subsequent interpretations have found many of the core housing related practices specifically covered by Title VIII also within the ambit of § 1982.[2] But § 1982 does not prohibit the publishing of discriminatory notices or advertising[3] and apparently does not bar blockbusting or redlining.

§ 11.7   Title VIII

Title VIII, on the other hand, expressly encompasses the full range of practices related to housing, including sales, rentals, advertising, and financing. Title VIII's primary prohibition makes it unlawful to refuse to sell or rent to or negotiate with any person because of that person's race, color, religion, sex, familial status, handicap, or national origin.[1]

Real estate agencies and similar businesses are prohibited from discriminating in the sale, brokerage, or appraisal of a house or in the provision of services, facilities or privileges in connection with a house.[2] Accordingly, a realtor or other agent is prohibited from refusing on racial grounds to show a home; from making misleading remarks regarding the availability of a home for inspection, sale, or rental; and from steering a buyer to a particular market.[3]

Banks and financial institutions may not discriminate when financing the purchase, construction, improvement, repair, or maintenance of a house.[4] Nor can an individual be discriminated against in the purchase of a loan secured by residential real estate.[5] Title VIII also bars discrimination in the provision of brokerage services, making it unlawful

---

§ 11.6

1. 392 U.S. at 413, 88 S.Ct. at 2189. (Emphasis in original.)

2. *See Tillman v. Wheaton–Haven Recreation Ass'n, Inc.,* 410 U.S. 431, 93 S.Ct. 1090, 35 L.Ed.2d 403 (1973) (provision of facilities); *Sullivan v. Little Hunting Park, Inc.,* 396 U.S. 229, 90 S.Ct. 400, 24 L.Ed.2d 386 (1969) (refusal to rent); *Jones v. Alfred H. Mayer Co.,* 392 U.S. 409, 88 S.Ct. 2186, 20 L.Ed.2d 1189 (1968) (refusal to sell); *McDonald v. Verble,* 622 F.2d 1227 (6th Cir.1980) (racial steering); *Clark v. Universal Builders, Inc.,* 501 F.2d 324 (7th Cir.), *cert. denied,* 419 U.S. 1070, 95 S.Ct. 657, 42

L.Ed.2d 666 (1974) (discriminatory terms); *and Newbern v. Lake Lorelei, Inc.,* 24 Ohio Misc. 201, 308 F.Supp. 407 (S.D.Ohio 1968) (discriminatory refusal to negotiate).

3. *Jones, supra* § 11.1 note 3, at 413.

§ 11.7

1. 42 U.S.C.A. § 3604(a), (f).

2. 42 U.S.C.A. § 3605(b)(2).

3. 42 U.S.C.A. § 3604(d)-(f).

4. 42 U.S.C.A. § 3605(b)(1).

5. *Id.*

to deny access to any multiple listing service.[6]

Any advertising or marketing related to the sale or rental of a house—even sales exempt from Title VIII's primary prohibition—may not indicate a discriminatory preference based on the enumerated grounds of § 3604(c).[7] The selection of actors for use in advertising should also not suggest any racial preference. In addition, remarks made with regard to the sale or rental of a house that an "ordinary listener" would consider discriminatory may constitute a violation of Title VIII.[8] As in sexual harassment claims,[9] there is no brightline test for distinguishing constitutionally protected speech from prohibited discriminatory speech-in-action.

E.   EXEMPTIONS

Library References:

> C.J.S. Civil Rights §§ 38, 68–74, 87.
> West's Key No. Digests, Civil Rights ☞130, 131.

§ 11.8   Section 1982

Section 1982 contains no textual exemptions for defendants or practices within the relatively narrow range of conduct it polices.

§ 11.9   Title VIII

By contrast, Title VIII exempts several classes of otherwise covered defendants. Its ban is inapplicable to single-family homeowners if they sell or rent their homes without the use of a real estate agent or other person who is in the business of selling and renting homes and without the use of advertisements that indicate a discriminatory preference. This exemption applies only to one sale within a twenty-four month period.[1] Multi-family homeowners are exempt provided no more than four families reside in a dwelling and the owner actually resides there.[2]

A religious organization is free to limit the sale, rental, or occupancy of its dwellings to persons of the same religion, unless it discriminates in

---

6. 42 U.S.C.A. § 3606.

7. *See* 37 Fed.Reg. 6700 (1972) (Title VIII prohibition applies to all advertising). *See also United States v. Hunter*, 459 F.2d 205 (4th Cir.), *cert. denied*, 409 U.S. 934, 93 S.Ct. 235, 34 L.Ed.2d 189 (1972) (otherwise exempted single-family homeowner not exempted from ban on discriminatory advertising; statute applicable to newspaper ads); *Mayers v. Ridley*, 465 F.2d 630 (D.C.Cir.1972) (recorder of deeds cannot record racially restrictive covenants); *United States v. Gilman*, 341 F.Supp. 891 (S.D.N.Y.1972) (oral statements indicating racial preference qualify as advertising).

8. 42 U.S.C.A. § 3604(c). *See Jancik v. HUD,* 44 F.3d 553 (7th Cir.1995) (context

of facially neutral questions indicated an intent to discriminate and sustained a violation of FHA). *But compare Soules v. HUD,* 967 F.2d 817 (2d Cir.1992) (there are no legitimate reasons for discriminatory inquiries) *with United States v. Real Estate One, Inc.,* 433 F.Supp. 1140 (E.D.Mich.1977) (remarks are immaterial unless they influence a transaction).

9. See the Chapter on Title VII.

§ 11.9

1. 42 U.S.C.A. § 3603(b)(1).

2. 42 U.S.C.A. § 3603(b)(2).

membership on other grounds prohibited by Title VIII.[3] A private club is permitted to limit the rental or occupancy of its lodgings to club members.[4]

Finally, the defendant who provides housing to older persons is exempt from the familial status prohibition in three situations: where the defendant is working within a federal or state program designed to assist older persons; where housing units are intended for and solely occupied by persons 62 years of age or older; and where eighty percent of the units are occupied by at least one person 55 years of age or older.[5] A homeowners' association that failed to conduct age-verification procedures consistent with an intent to provide housing for persons 55 or older has been held ineligible for the exemption.[6]

F. STANDING

Library References:

> C.J.S. Civil Rights §§ 260, 265–266.
> West's Key No. Digests, Civil Rights ⊕199.

§ 11.10 Section 1982

In 1975, the Supreme Court announced a prudential requirement for standing under § 1982.[1] In *Warth v. Seldin*, the Supreme Court held that the plaintiff must assert "his own legal rights and interests," not the rights or interests of third parties or large classes of citizens, to have standing under the Section.[2] An allegation that the plaintiff personally could not obtain housing because of discriminatory zoning practices and an allegation that prohibited practices by private actors interfered directly with the plaintiff's attempt to obtain housing have satisfied this prudential test.[3] But the Court has flexed the standing requirement. In *Sullivan v. Little Hunting Park, Inc.*, the Court recognized standing in a plaintiff who alleged personal injury resulting not from direct discrimination against himself but from discrimination against a third party.[4]

---

3. 42 U.S.C.A. § 3607(a).

4. *Id.*

5. 42 U.S.C.A. § 3607(b).

6. *Massaro v. Mainlands Section 1 & 2 Civic Association, Inc.*, 3 F.3d 1472 (11th Cir.1993), *cert. denied*, ___ U.S. ___, 115 S.Ct. 56, 130 L.Ed.2d 15 (1994).

§ 11.10

1. For an extensive definition of prudential standing requirements, *see* 26 Federal Procedure, § 59:3.

2. *Warth v. Seldin*, 422 U.S. 490, 499, 95 S.Ct. 2197, 2205, 45 L.Ed.2d 343 (1975).

3. *See Warth v. Seldin*, 422 U.S. 490, 508, 95 S.Ct. 2197, 2210, 45 L.Ed.2d 343 (1975) (homeseekers do not have standing to challenge zoning laws in the absence of a "particularized" and personal injury); *Res-*

ident Advisory Bd. v. Rizzo, 564 F.2d 126 (3d Cir.), *cert. denied*, 435 U.S. 908, 98 S.Ct. 1457, 55 L.Ed.2d 499 (1978) (tenants in existing public housing alleged they would suffer personal injury if city delayed construction of new public housing through zoning ordinances); and *Fair Housing Council, Inc. v. Eastern Bergen County Multiple Listing Serv.*, 422 F.Supp. 1071 (D.N.J. 1976) (Title VIII and § 1982 case; complaint by individual plaintiffs alleging personal injuries from discriminatory steering survived motion to dismiss for lack of standing because the allegation satisfied the personal injury requirement of *Warth*).

4. *Sullivan v. Little Hunting Park, Inc.*, 396 U.S. 229, 237, 90 S.Ct. 400, 404, 24 L.Ed.2d 386 (1969) (a white owner seeking to sublease his house and assign his membership in a community park to blacks had

And a lower court has recognized standing in testers who allege only threatened injuries.[5] Generally, however, the plaintiff must prove a personal injury caused by the defendant's conduct to have standing under § 1982.[6]

§ 11.11 Title VIII

In contrast, the Court has announced a liberalized standing test for Title VIII cases. In *Havens Realty Corp. v. Coleman*,[1] the Court broadened the scope of constitutional standing under Title VIII to allow anyone to bring suit who can prove an actual or threatened injury, fairly traceable to the respondent's actions, and likely to be redressed by favorable court action. The test may be satisfied by aggrieved persons, testers, nonprofit fair housing associations, residential neighbors, and local governments.[2]

A more detailed discussion of current standing requirements in civil rights actions, particularly as they relate to "testers" not personally denied housing by the rejection of their applications, is found in the Procedure chapter above.

G. ELEMENTS OF PLAINTIFF'S CLAIM

Library References:

C.J.S. Civil Rights §§ 38, 68–74, 87.
West's Key No. Digests, Civil Rights ⚖130, 131.

§ 11.12 Section 1982

Under this section, the plaintiff bears the burden of persuasion in proving that he was discriminated against because of his race.[1] The Supreme Court has held that § 1981 can be violated only by "purposeful" discrimination.[2] Many lower courts accordingly limit the application of § 1982 to cases of intentional discrimination.[3] Under § 1982, the

---

standing as the "only effective adversary" to discriminatory practices by the membership approval board; quoting *Barrows v. Jackson*, 346 U.S. 249, 259, 73 S.Ct. 1031, 1036, 97 L.Ed. 1586 (1953)).

5. *Watts v. Boyd Properties, Inc.*, 758 F.2d 1482 (11th Cir.1985) (black tester had standing in a refusal to rent case).

6. For a detailed discussion of standing requirements under § 1982, *see* Daniel A. Klein, Annotation, *Standing to Sue under 42 USCS § 1982, Protecting Property Rights*, 79 A.L.R. Fed. 281 (1993).

§ 11.11

1. 455 U.S. 363, 372, 102 S.Ct. 1114, 1121, 71 L.Ed.2d 214 (1982).

2. *Havens Realty Corp.*, *supra* note 1, at 373–74, 379, 102 S.Ct. at 1121–22, 1124.

§ 11.12

1. *See, e.g., City of Memphis v. Greene*, 451 U.S. 100, 123, 101 S.Ct. 1584, 1598, 67 L.Ed.2d 769 (1981).

2. *General Building Contractors Ass'n, Inc. v. Pennsylvania*, 458 U.S. 375, 391, 102 S.Ct. 3141, 3150, 73 L.Ed.2d 835 (1982).

3. *See, e.g., Hanson v. Veterans Administration*, 800 F.2d 1381, 1386 (5th Cir. 1986); *Hamilton v. Svatik*, 779 F.2d 383, 387 (7th Cir.1985); *Vaughner v. Pulito*, 804 F.2d 873, 877 (5th Cir.1986); *Strykers Bay Neighborhood Council v. City of New York*, 695 F.Supp. 1531, 1543 (S.D.N.Y.1988); *Thomas v. First Federal Savings Bank of Indiana*, 653 F.Supp. 1330, 1342 (N.D.Ind. 1987); *and In re Malone*, 592 F.Supp. 1135, 1158–59 (E.D.Mo.1984), *affirmed without opinion*, 794 F.2d 680 (8th Cir.1986).

plaintiff may allege discrimination based solely on race or based on a mix of factors, one of which is race.

a. Proving Intentional Discrimination

Where the discrimination is based solely on race, the plaintiff may show intent directly or through the inferential prima facie case set out in *McDonnell Douglas Corp. v. Green.*[4] The prima facie case, as adapted to housing discrimination, requires the plaintiff to show that (1) he is a member of a racial minority, (2) he applied and was qualified for housing, (3) he was rejected, and (4) the housing remained available after he was rejected.[5] Once the plaintiff has made a prima facie case, the defendant has an opportunity to defeat it by articulating some legitimate business reason to justify his actions. The defendant carries only a burden of production in this matter. The plaintiff, who retains the burden of persuasion, must then prove that the proffered reason is a pretext for discrimination on one of the prohibited grounds.[6]

b. Proving Discrimination Based on Mixed Motives

Where the plaintiff alleges discrimination based on mixed motives, he must show that race was a factor in the defendant's conduct. The plaintiff may use direct or inferential evidence of a racial component in the overall complex of considerations the defendant took into account. Following the precedent set by the United States Court of Appeals for the Seventh Circuit in *Smith v. Sol D. Adler Realty Co.,*[7] many circuits have held that race need not be the primary or sole factor to establish a § 1982 violation.[8] Recent support for this "any factor" approach is found in the Civil Rights Act of 1991. Under that statute, the plaintiff establishes the existence of an unlawful employment practice by demonstrating that an employer was motivated by consideration of a prohibited classification "even though other factors also motivated the practice."[9]

In the employment discrimination context, liability potentially attaches once the plaintiff establishes a prima facie case that the defendant cannot rebut merely by producing evidence of a legitimate nondiscriminatory reason. Even if the defendant produces such evidence, the plaintiff may prevail by demonstrating that the proffered reason was not

---

4. 411 U.S. 792, 93 S.Ct. 1817, 36 L.Ed.2d 668 (1973). *See also Texas Dep't of Community Affairs v. Burdine*, 450 U.S. 248, 101 S.Ct. 1089, 67 L.Ed.2d 207 (1981). For more detail on the promises and pitfalls of inferential proof, see Chapter on Title VII Employment Discrimination.

5. *See, e.g., Asbury v. Brougham*, 866 F.2d 1276, 1279 (10th Cir.1989); *Williams v. Matthews Co.*, 499 F.2d 819, 826 (8th Cir.), *cert. denied*, 419 U.S. 1021, 95 S.Ct. 495, 42 L.Ed.2d 294 (1974).

6. *See St. Mary's Honor Center v. Hicks*, 509 U.S. 502, 113 S.Ct. 2742, 125 L.Ed.2d 407 (1993) (Title VII decision).

7. 436 F.2d 344 (7th Cir.1970).

8. *See, e.g., Hanson v. Veterans Administration*, 800 F.2d 1381, 1386 (5th Cir. 1986); *Green v. Century 21*, 740 F.2d 460, 464 (6th Cir.1984); *Robinson v. 12 Lofts Realty, Inc.*, 610 F.2d 1032, 1042 (2d Cir. 1979); *Smith v. Anchor Bldg. Corp.*, 536 F.2d 231, 233 (8th Cir.1976).

9. 42 U.S.C.A. § 2000e–2(m). For a detailed discussion of the effects of the Civil Rights Act of 1991, *see* the Title VII chapter. *See also* Harold S. Lewis, Jr., *The Civil Rights Act of 1991 and the Continued Dominance of the Disparate Treatment Conception of Equality*, 11 St. Louis U. Pub. L. Rev. 1 (1992).

the defendant's real reason and was instead a pretext for intentional discrimination on a prohibited ground.[10] The defendant may then avoid monetary liability [11] by proving that he acted for an additional reason as well and that he would have reached the same decision even in the absence of the impermissible factor.[12]

This assignment of a persuasion burden to the defendant at the end of a mixed motives employment discrimination case, originally endorsed by the Supreme Court,[13] has been expressly codified by the Civil Rights Act of 1991.[14] Accordingly, the housing discrimination defendant who relies on the mixed motives scheme may carry the ultimate burden of persuading that he would have acted similarly even if race was part of his aggregate mix of motives.

§ 11.13   Title VIII

a. *Discriminatory Intent*

The plaintiff may prevail by persuading the court that he was intentionally discriminated against because of race, color, religion, national origin, sex, handicap, or familial status. The proof modes available for proving discriminatory intent under Title VIII include all those recognized under § 1982.

b. *Discriminatory Impact or Effect*

The circuit courts are divided on whether disparate impact suffices to establish a violation.[1] While the Supreme Court has not explicitly endorsed the disparate impact test for Title VIII cases, the Court indirectly affirmed its use in invalidating the challenged zoning law in *Huntington*.[2] Nevertheless, one commentator has observed, even "[i]f plaintiffs are ultimately relieved of proving discriminatory intent to establish Title VIII violations, [recent Title VII] cases indicate that

---

10. *See* Robert S. Whitman, *Clearing the Mixed–Motive Smokescreen: An Approach to Disparate Treatment under Title VII*, 87 Mich. L. Rev. 863 (1989).

11. *See* § 107 of the Civil Rights Act of 1991, discussed in the Title VII chapter, which relieves the employer who makes this showing only of monetary liability.

12. *Price Waterhouse v. Hopkins*, 490 U.S. 228, 244, 109 S.Ct. 1775, 1787, 104 L.Ed.2d 268 (1989).

13. *Id.*

14. 42 U.S.C.A. § 2000e–5(g).

§ 11.13

1. *Compare Secretary, U.S. Department of HUD v. Blackwell*, 908 F.2d 864 (11th Cir.1990) (applying *McDonnell Douglas* analysis); *Huntington Branch, NAACP v. Town of Huntington*, 844 F.2d 926, 934 (2d Cir.1988), *affirmed*, 488 U.S. 15, 109 S.Ct. 276, 102 L.Ed.2d 180 (1988) (disparate im-

pact methodology used in Title VII cases is sufficient to establish Title VIII violation, at least with respect to public defendants); *Resident Advisory Bd. v. Rizzo*, 564 F.2d 126, 146 (3d Cir.1977), *cert. denied*, 435 U.S. 908, 98 S.Ct. 1457, 55 L.Ed.2d 499 (1978) (unrebutted proof of discriminatory effect is sufficient to establish violation of Title VIII); and *United States v. City of Black Jack*, 508 F.2d 1179, 1184–85 (8th Cir.1974), *cert. denied*, 422 U.S. 1042, 95 S.Ct. 2656, 45 L.Ed.2d 694 (1975) (no intent required, impact evidence suffices) *with Selden Apartments v. HUD*, 785 F.2d 152 (6th Cir.1986) (intentional discrimination is required). *Cf. Village of Bellwood v. Dwivedi*, 895 F.2d 1521, 1533 (7th Cir.1990) (acknowledging that while disparate impact analysis is appropriate in certain instances, intent is required for steering cases).

2. *Huntington*, *supra* note 1, at 18. *See* § 11.12, *supra*, for discussion of *McDonnell Douglas* and the elements of a prima facie inferential case.

draconian burdens will continue to be imposed upon them as they attempt to establish discriminatory effect." [3]

To make out a prima facie case based on discriminatory impact or effect, the plaintiff is required to show that the challenged policy, practice, or law has a disproportionate adverse impact or effect on the plaintiff or group.[4] For example, a zoning law that restricts the development of multi-family units to areas heavily concentrated with members of a minority group may adversely effect that group and perpetuate prior de jure segregation.[5]

As with a disparate treatment case, once the plaintiff establishes her prima facie case, the defendant has an opportunity to refute it by articulating some legitimate business interest to justify his actions. But according to the appellate court in *Huntington*,[6] the defendant, in addition to producing evidence of a justifying reason, bears the burden of persuading the court that there is no less discriminatory alternative that will protect its interest. No showing of pretext is required of the plaintiff in sharp contrast to the understanding under Title VIII.[7] But in a more recent Title VII case, *Wards Cove Packing Co. v. Atonio*,[8] the Supreme Court held that the defendant successfully refutes the prima facie case merely by producing a legitimate business justification. The Court wrote that the burden of persuasion remained with the plaintiff, who therefore had to prove that the defendant's justification was in fact a pretext for discrimination on one of the prohibited grounds. Alternatively, the plaintiff could prevail only by proving the existence of an equally efficient but less discriminatory alternative that would protect the defendant's asserted business interest as well as the challenged practice.[9]

The *Wards Cove* decision expressly overruled previous Title VII cases which, like *Huntington*, had assigned an intermediate persuasion burden to the defendant.[10] But the situation is complicated because the Civil Rights Act of 1991, responding to *Wards Cove*, altered the nature of the employer justification and reimposed on it the burden of persuasion.[11] It is greatly uncertain what exactly the employer will be required to show under Title VII in order to demonstrate a nondiscriminatory justification for a neutral employment practice that has disproportionate adverse impact.[12] In the absence of a Supreme Court decision on a Title

---

3. Richard C. Cahn, *Determining a Standard for Housing Discrimination Under Title VIII*, 7 Touro L. Rev. 193, 194 (1990). Cahn wrote before the Civil Rights Acts of 1991 eased those burdens to an as yet uncertain degree. See Title VII Chapter.

4. *Huntington, supra* note 1, at 934–35.

5. *Id*. at 926.

6. *Id*. at 939.

7. *Id*.

8. 490 U.S. 642, 109 S.Ct. 2115, 104 L.Ed.2d 733 (1989).

9. *Id*. at 660, 109 S.Ct. at 2126. See Chapter 4 for more detail on how *Wards Cove* may be modified by the Civil Rights Act of 1991.

10. *Id*. at 659, 109 S.Ct. at 2126.

11. *See* Chapter 4.

12. *Id*. It is possible that the "pretext vs. pretext-plus" controversy introduced to Title VII cases by *St. Mary's Honor Center v. Hicks*, 509 U.S. 502, 113 S.Ct. 2742, 125 L.Ed.2d 407 (1993), will bleed over into Title VIII litigation because Title VIII doctrine regarding modes of proof has paral-

VIII disparate impact case, it is unclear whether *Huntington* or the Civil Rights Act of 1991 will define the components of that defense in a case of housing discrimination.   All that does seem likely is that the housing defendant, like the employment discrimination defendant after the Civil Rights Act of 1991, will continue, per *Huntington*, to bear the burden of persuasion on that defense.

H.   DEFENSES

Library References:

> C.J.S. Civil Rights §§ 38, 68–74, 87, 235–236.
> West's Key No. Digests, Civil Rights ⊕130, 131, 210.

§ 11.14   Section 1982

Because § 1982 requires the plaintiff to prove the defendant's intent to discriminate, there are no true affirmative defenses the defendant must plead or prove to resist liability under § 1982.   The defendant will typically seek to prevent that showing of intent simply through evidence that it acted on an "honest basis unrelated to . . . race. . . ." [1]

§ 11.15   Title VIII

Under Title VIII, as we have seen, the plaintiff may base his complaint on discriminatory intent or, at least in certain circuits, discriminatory impact or effect.   Where the claim is based on discriminatory intent, there are no true affirmative defenses the defendant must plead or prove to resist liability under Title VIII.   See Federal Rule of Civil Procedure 8.

Where the claim is based on discriminatory impact or effect, the defendant should try to counter the plaintiff's showing that there was segregative adverse impact and produce evidence that the impact was justified by some legitimate and objective reason for the action.   Under the Civil Rights Act of 1991 and *Huntington*, the nondiscriminatory reason on which the defendant relies will be a true affirmative defense on which the defendant must bear the burden of persuasion as well as production.   Presumably these burdens imply a burden timely to plead the impact defense in the answer, under Federal Rule of Civil Procedure 8(c).

leled developments under Title VII.   "The Fair Housing Amendments Act of 1988: The Enforcement Report," U.S. Commission on Civil Rights, Sept.1994, p. 159.   *See* Chapter 4 for a discussion of *St. Mary's.*

§ 11.14

1. *Pughsley v. 3750 Lake Shore Drive Co–op. Bldg.,* 463 F.2d 1055 (7th Cir.1972).

I. PROCEDURES; STATUTES OF LIMITATIONS; AND AGENCY INVOLVEMENT

Library References:

> C.J.S. Civil Rights §§ 222–224, 231, 235–236.
> West's Key No. Digests, Civil Rights ⊕181, 182, 210.

§ 11.16 Section 1982

The exclusive remedy for a § 1982 claim is a private judicial action. There is no administrative agency process. Because the section contains no statute of limitations, federal as well as state courts should look to the pertinent state statute of limitations governing personal injury claims.[1] See the Procedure Chapter on limitations statutes governing Reconstruction Act claims for more detailed discussion.

§ 11.17 Title VIII

Under Title VIII, aggrieved parties may choose between private direct civil action and investigation by the Department of Housing and Urban Development ("HUD"). In addition, the Attorney General may bring suit in certain cases. An aggrieved person can prosecute claims of housing discrimination by initiating a civil suit in federal or state court within two years of the occurrence or its termination.[1] To encourage private enforcement, the Act empowers the court to appoint an attorney to financially needy persons.[2] An aggrieved person or the Secretary of HUD may file a complaint with HUD alleging housing discrimination as long as it is within one year of the discriminatory occurrence or its termination.[3]

The Attorney General is authorized to bring suit for cases involving discriminatory patterns or practices; cases of general public importance; referrals from the Secretary of HUD; and breaches of conciliatory agreements.[4]

J. DAMAGES

Library References:

> C.J.S. Civil Rights §§ 315–316.
> West's Key No. Digests, Civil Rights ⊕269.

§ 11.18 Section 1982

Actual and punitive damages, injunctive relief and attorney's fees and costs can be recovered under § 1982.[1] There are no caps on the amount of damages that can be awarded, and the amount is determined

---

§ 11.16

1. *Goodman v. Lukens Steel Co.*, 482 U.S. 656, 660, 107 S.Ct. 2617, 2620, 96 L.Ed.2d 572 (1987).

§ 11.17

1. 42 U.S.C.A. § 3613(a).

2. 42 U.S.C.A. § 3613(b).

3. 42 U.S.C.A. § 3610(a).

4. 42 U.S.C.A. § 3614(a)-(b) (actions for breach of conciliation agreements must be commenced within ninety days of alleged breach; all other actions must be commenced within 18 months of the alleged discriminatory practice).

§ 11.18

1. *Phillips v. Hunter Trails Community Ass'n*, 685 F.2d 184, 191 (7th Cir.1982).

by the principles of tort law.[2] Section 1982 cases allow attorney's fees to the prevailing party under the Civil Rights Attorney's Fees Awards Act, 42 U.S.C.A. § 1988, although the cases have construed this to mean, in all but exceptional circumstances, that only a prevailing plaintiff, not a prevailing defendant, is eligible.[3] See the chapter on the Civil Rights Attorney's Fees Awards Act.

§ 11.19   Title VIII

Where the complainant pursues a housing discrimination claim through direct suit under § 3613, the court may award actual compensatory damages (including economic damages and those caused by humiliation and embarrassment), punitive damages, and injunctive relief.[1] There is no limit on the amount of damages, and the amount is determined based on tort law principles.[2] Attorney's fees and costs may be awarded to the prevailing party other than the United States.[3] The relief authorized under § 3613 has no effect on any sale, lease, or other encumbrance completed before the granting of relief and involving a bona fide purchaser, tenant or encumbrancer without notice of the pending complaint.[4]

In administrative hearings under § 3612, the ALJ may assess against the respondent awards for actual damages and injunctive relief, but not punitive damages. The amount of damages is capped at $10,000 if the respondent has not been adjudged to have committed previous acts of any housing discrimination; $25,000 if the respondent has been adjudged to have committed another discriminatory housing practice in the five years prior to the filing of the complaint; or $50,000 if the respondent has been adjudged to have committed two or more discriminatory housing practices during the seven years prior to the filing of the complaint.[5] In addition, the ALJ may award attorney's fees and costs to the prevailing party other than the United States.[6]

In a suit brought by the Attorney General under § 3614, the court may award injunctive relief and uncapped monetary damages.[7] In addition, the court may impose a civil penalty to vindicate public interest, but the penalty may not exceed $50,000 for the first violation or $100,000 for subsequent violations.[8] Attorney's fees and costs may be awarded to the prevailing party other than the United States.[9] Another

2. *See Memphis Community School District v. Stachura,* 477 U.S. 299, 306, 106 S.Ct. 2537, 2542, 91 L.Ed.2d 249 (1986) (case indicating that damages under § 1983 should be based on tort principles).

3. *Roadway Express, Inc. v. Piper,* 447 U.S. 752, 100 S.Ct. 2455, 65 L.Ed.2d 488 (1980).

§ 11.19

1. 42 U.S.C.A. § 3613(c)(1).

2. *See Curtis v. Loether,* 415 U.S. 189, 197, 94 S.Ct. 1005, 1010, 39 L.Ed.2d 260

(1974) (suggesting tort principles should govern § 3613 damage awards).

3. 42 U.S.C.A. § 3613(c)(2).

4. 42 U.S.C.A. § 3613(d).

5. 42 U.S.C.A. § 3612(g)(3)(A), (B), (C), (p).

6. 42 U.S.C.A. § 3612(p).

7. 42 U.S.C.A. § 3614(d)(1)(A), (B).

8. 42 U.S.C.A. § 3614(d)(1)(C).

9. 42 U.S.C.A. § 3614(d)(2).

party aggrieved by the respondent's discriminatory action or a party to a breached conciliation agreement may intervene in the Attorney General initiated action under § 3614(e), and the court may award such intervening persons the same relief appropriate to a plaintiff in a private action under § 3613.

K.   CHOOSING WHICH STATUTE TO USE

Library References:

C.J.S. Civil Rights §§ 38, 68–74, 87.
West's Key No. Digests, Civil Rights ⬖130, 131.

§ 11.20   In General

Section 1982 and Title VIII differ in proscriptions, proof requirements, and remedies.   Generally, § 1982 prohibits fewer practices, and requires proof of discriminatory intent, but offers less constrained remedies.   By contrast, Title VIII prohibits a wider range of practices, allows proof through discriminatory impact, but offers more restricted remedies.   Several factors guide the choice between proceeding under § 1982 or Title VIII.

Is the defendant exempt under Title VIII?

Title VIII exempts certain single- and multi-family homeowners, religious organizations, private clubs, and persons who provide housing for older persons.

Section 1982 has no such exemptions.

Is the discrimination racial?

If it is "racial," in the restricted modern or broader nineteenth century conception, then both statutes may be available.   Otherwise, Title VIII may apply because it also addresses discrimination based on national origin, sex, religion, handicap, and familial status.

Is the discrimination in the form of a refusal to sell, lease, show or negotiate?

Both § 1982 and Title VIII proscribe these practices.   But only Title VIII reaches discriminatory advertising, redlining or blockbusting.

Did the plaintiff personally suffer injury?

Plaintiffs who personally suffer injury will have standing under both statutes.   Only Title VIII is available to plaintiffs like testers who encounter only tangible injury threatened to others.

Can the plaintiff prove discriminatory intent?

The plaintiff who can prove discriminatory intent may use either statute.   If not, Title VIII may be available, but only in some federal circuits.

Does the plaintiff want federal agency involvement?

Title VIII allows involvement by HUD and the Attorney General. Section 1982 makes no provision for federal agency involvement.

Chapter Twelve

COSTS AND FEES: FEDERAL RULE OF CIVIL PROCEDURE 54(d), THE CIVIL RIGHTS ATTORNEY'S FEES AWARDS ACT AND FEDERAL RULE 68

Analysis

A. RULE 54(d) COSTS TO PREVAILING PLAINTIFFS OR DEFENDANTS

Library References:

C.J.S. Civil Rights §§ 334–335.
West's Key No. Digests, Civil Rights ⊕291.

§ 12.1 In General

Unlike attorney's fees under Title VII or § 1988, which as we shall see are ordinarily awardable only to prevailing plaintiffs, either side that prevails is presumptively entitled to costs under Fed.R.Civ.P. 54(d). Indeed the argument has been rejected that a losing Title VII plaintiff may be assessed costs only on the same terms as she should be assessed fees—that is, when the claim was frivolous, unreasonable, or without foundation.[1]

The awarding of costs lies within the sound discretion of the district court and may be denied where the award would be inequitable.[2] Citing that discretion, a district court has recently cut in half a large award of costs to a defendant law firm that prevailed after lengthy litigation involving its alleged unlawful denial of partnership on the basis of gender. The court took into account that the case was "close"; that it presented important issues of public concern and had been pursued by the plaintiff at great financial cost; and that the plaintiff was of modest means while the defendant was a large corporate firm.[3]

The "costs" recoverable by any prevailing party are limited, however, to items specified by a separate federal statute, 28 U.S.C.A. § 1920. These include clerk and marshal fees, fees of the court reporters for transcripts "necessarily obtained for use in the case"[4]; printing disbursements and witness fees; specified docket fees; and fees for court-appointed experts and certain interpreters. Most important, "costs" as used in Rule 54(d) do *not* include the prevailing party's attorneys' fees. This is consistent with the ordinary "American rule" which, as explained by the Supreme Court, calls for each side to pay its own lawyer, win or lose, unless there is specific statutory authority for fee "shifting."[5] It is to such fee-shifting statutes that we now turn.

B.   INTRODUCTION TO THE CIVIL RIGHTS ATTORNEY'S FEES AWARDS ACT

Library References:

> C.J.S. Civil Rights §§ 319–320.
> West's Key No. Digests, Civil Rights ☞292.

§ 12.2   In General

The Civil Rights Attorney's Fees Awards Act (the "Act"), a 1976 amendment to 42 U.S.C.A. § 1988, permits a discretionary award of attorney's fees, in a "reasonable" amount, as part of the costs recoverable by prevailing parties, other than the United States, in any action or proceeding pursuant to 42 U.S.C.A. §§ 1981, 1982, 1983, 1985, and 1986,

§ 12.1

1. *Croker v. Boeing Co.,* 662 F.2d 975 (3d Cir.1981).

2. *Friedman v. Ganassi,* 853 F.2d 207 (3d Cir.1988), *cert. denied,* 488 U.S. 1042, 109 S.Ct. 867, 102 L.Ed.2d 991 (1989).

3. *Ezold v. Wolf, Block, Schorr and Solis–Cohen,* 758 F.Supp. 303 (E.D.Pa.1991).

4. Some courts have taxed at least part of the costs associated with videotaping a

deposition, *see Morrison v. Reichhold Chemicals, Inc.,* 97 F.3d 460 (11th Cir. 1996). *Barber v. Ruth,* 7 F.3d 636 (7th Cir.1993), despite the argument that those costs are not the fees of a "court reporter" for a "stenographic transcript." *Echostar Satellite Corp. v. Advanced Communications Corp.,* 902 F.Supp. 213 (D.Colo.1995).

5. *Alyeska Pipeline Serv. Co. v. Wilderness Society,* 421 U.S. 240, 95 S.Ct. 1612, 44 L.Ed.2d 141 (1975).

as well as Titles VI and IX. The purpose of the award is to enable plaintiffs to attract competent legal counsel; perhaps that is why fees have been denied for lawyers' public relations efforts on behalf of their clients.[1] The Act parallels separate statutory authority to award attorney's fees to prevailing parties in actions under the Rehabilitation Act of 1973,[2] the Age Discrimination in Employment Act,[3] the Equal Pay Act,[4] the Clean Water Act,[5] the Fair Labor Standards Act,[6] and under Title VII.[7] In fact, over a hundred separate statutes allow for court awarded attorney's fees. The principles governing eligibility for and computation of awards are largely interchangeable among these statutes.

Although a plaintiff must receive at least some relief on the merits in order to become a "prevailing party" eligible for fees, success on a "significant issue," even if it is not a "central" one, will suffice.[8] A plaintiff adjudged to be a prevailing party should ordinarily receive a fee award absent "special circumstances," such as the plaintiff's egregious misconduct.[9] These circumstances are rarely found.[10] But *pro se* plaintiffs who also happen to be attorneys have been ruled ineligible for a fee award.[11] And a plaintiff who recovers only nominal damages, although a prevailing party, is usually entitled to no fee award in view of the slight degree of success achieved in the litigation.[12]

To achieve success on a "significant issue" and thus "prevail" so as to be eligible for fees, the plaintiff need only obtain some relief, by settlement or otherwise, which changes his legal relationship with the defendant and is more than merely technical or *de minimus*. In general, if the relief plaintiff initially seeks is "of the same general type" as the relief eventually obtained, plaintiff may be considered a prevailing party.[13] An injunction requiring a company to correct a racially intimidating work atmosphere, for example, has sufficed as the predicate for a fee award to a plaintiff who lost on most of his individual claims of race

§ 12.2

1. *Halderman v. Pennhurst State School & Hospital,* 49 F.3d 939 (3d Cir.1995).

2. 29 U.S.C.A. § 794(a).

3. 29 U.S.C.A. § 626(b) (incorporating standards from the Fair Labor Standards Act, 29 U.S.C.A. § 216(b)).

4. 29 U.S.C.A. § 206(d) (incorporating standards from the Fair Labor Standards Act, 29 U.S.C.A. § 216(b)).

5. 33 U.S.C.A. § 1365.

6. 29 U.S.C.A. § 216(b).

7. 42 U.S.C.A. § 2000e–5(k).

8. *Texas State Teachers Ass'n v. Garland Independent School Dist.,* 489 U.S. 782, 109 S.Ct. 1486, 103 L.Ed.2d 866 (1989). But fee eligibility depends upon the plaintiff's having prevailed on a claim under one of the § 1988–referenced federal statutes, not, say a related claim under state law. *National Private Truck Council,*

Inc. v. Oklahoma Tax Comm'n, ___ U.S. ___, 115 S.Ct. 2351, 132 L.Ed.2d 509 (1995).

9. *See Christiansburg Garment Co. v. EEOC,* 434 U.S. 412, 98 S.Ct. 694, 54 L.Ed.2d 648 (1978). Recently, however, a state court denied fees under § 1988 to plaintiffs who successfully attacked the constitutionality of a state law enforced but not enacted by defendant municipality. *Minnesota Council of Dog Clubs v. Minneapolis,* 540 N.W.2d 903 (Minn.App.1995), *cert. denied,* ___ U.S. ___, 116 S.Ct. 2524, 135 L.Ed.2d 1048 (1996).

10. *Zimmer, Sullivan & Richards, Cases and Materials on Employment Discrimination* 663–64 (2d ed. 1988).

11. *Kay v. Ehrler,* 499 U.S. 432, 111 S.Ct. 1435, 113 L.Ed.2d 486 (1991).

12. *Farrar v. Hobby,* 506 U.S. 103, 113 S.Ct. 566, 121 L.Ed.2d 494 (1992).

13. *Lyte v. Sara Lee Corp.,* 950 F.2d 101 (2d Cir.1991).

discrimination.[14] But in applying this standard, courts have sometimes resorted to a highly subjective appraisal of plaintiff's original objective in bringing suit, denying fees where that objective was not obtained even when the suit was clearly a "catalyst" for action by the defendant that responds in part to the suit.[15]

A finding of a violation under § 1983 may lead to an award of nominal damages where the predicate constitutional violation is "absolute," that is not dependent upon the merits of the plaintiff's substantive assertions or the magnitude of injury resulting from a violation.[16] Whether such nominal damages can serve as a springboard for § 1988 attorneys' fees was until recently the subject of conflict among the circuits.[17]

In *Farrar v. Hobby*,[18] the Supreme Court resolved this conflict somewhat oddly. It formally conferred prevailing party status on plaintiffs who recover only nominal damages, but did so under standards that fix the amount of a reasonable attorneys' fee at zero when their degree of success is slight. The Court confirmed that "a plaintiff 'prevails' when actual relief on the merits of his claim materially alters the legal relationship between the parties by modifying the defendant's behavior in a way that directly benefits the plaintiff"; and it acknowledged that even a judgment for only nominal damages "modifies the defendant's behavior for the plaintiff's benefit by forcing the defendant to pay an amount of money he otherwise would not pay." But it then drained this conclusion of apparent practical significance under most circumstances by adding that when a plaintiff, having failed to prove an essential element of a claim for monetary relief, recovers only nominal damages, "the only reasonable fee is usually no fee at all." [19]

In *Carey v. Piphus*,[20] the Court had found that nominal damages must be available for deprivations of "absolute" rights like procedural due process because of "the importance to organized society that those rights be scrupulously observed...." After *Farrar*, however, it is diffi-

---

14. *Ruffin v. Great Dane Trailers*, 969 F.2d 989 (11th Cir.1992), *cert. denied*, 507 U.S. 910, 113 S.Ct. 1257, 122 L.Ed.2d 655 (1993).

15. *See, e.g., Cady v. City of Chicago*, 43 F.3d 326 (7th Cir.1994). *See also Minnesota Council of Dog Clubs v. Minneapolis*, 540 N.W.2d 903 (Minn.App.1995), *cert. denied*, ___ U.S. ___, 116 S.Ct. 2524, 135 L.Ed.2d 1048 (1996) (denying fees against city found liable for enforcing state law declared unconstitutional, where city had nondiscretionary duty to follow state law).

16. *Carey v. Piphus*, 435 U.S. 247, 98 S.Ct. 1042, 55 L.Ed.2d 252 (1978) (nominal damages available for denial of procedural due process).

17. *See, e.g., Romberg v. Nichols*, 953 F.2d 1152 (9th Cir.1992) (nominal damages award of $1 creates prevailing party status),

vacated by, 506 U.S. 1075, 113 S.Ct. 1038, 122 L.Ed.2d 348 (1993); *Ruggiero v. Krzeminski*, 928 F.2d 558 (2d Cir.1991); *Scofield v. City of Hillsborough*, 862 F.2d 759 (9th Cir.1988); *Coleman v. Turner*, 838 F.2d 1004 (8th Cir.1988); *Nephew v. City of Aurora*, 830 F.2d 1547 (10th Cir.1987) (en banc), *cert. denied*, 485 U.S. 976, 108 S.Ct. 1269, 99 L.Ed.2d 481 (1988); *Garner v. Wal–Mart Stores, Inc.*, 807 F.2d 1536 (11th Cir.1987).

18. 506 U.S. 103, 113 S.Ct. 566, 121 L.Ed.2d 494 (1992).

19. *Estate of Farrar v. Hobby, supra* note 12; *Cartwright v. Stamper*, 7 F.3d 106 (7th Cir.1993) (fees denied because $5 nominal damages award so "de minimis" that plaintiff's success on several claims would have little deterrent effect).

20. *See supra* note 16.

cult to understand how, where there is little or no actual economic or emotional injury, the Court contemplates that such rights will be enforced if attorneys' fees are only theoretically and not practically available to plaintiffs who successfully prosecute suits for their violation.[21] One possibility is that lower courts will limit *Farrar* to its facts: no jury specification of the constitutional right violated and no specific jury finding that the defendant's conduct caused the plaintiff's (nominal) damages. In one recent case, for example, a jury specifically found that a municipality's policy regarding excessive police force resulted in $1 of harm to an otherwise unsympathetic plaintiff, and the city disciplined an officer and modified its policy during the litigation. Upholding a fee award of $66,535, an appellate court has distinguished *Farrar*, concluding that the finding benefited the department and the community and might have collateral estoppel effect in subsequent litigation.[22] These distinctions, however, seem a thin evasion of *Farrar*. Plaintiffs could create them routinely by requesting special interrogatories concerning the right violated and causation, and the jury would presumably find causation whenever it awarded damages, even nominal ones. Another evasive tactic has been specifically rebuffed: if the plaintiff's lawyer first asks for nominal damages at the end of trial, when things look bleak for his client, the plaintiff who then recovers $1, while technically prevailing, will fail to recover fees by virtue of *Farrar*.[23]

Another possibility, somewhat uncertain, is that the recovery of nominal damages may permit the § 1983 plaintiff to recover punitive damages otherwise warranted by a malicious or aggravated violation of procedural due process.[24] But is there a more reliable general incentive for a lawyer to pursue a § 1983 case involving an "ordinary" constitutional or federal statutory violation in what promises to be a case of "mixed motives"—that is, where she anticipates that the defendant could carry the *Mt. Healthy City School District Bd. of Education v. Doyle*[25] burden of demonstrating that it would have subjected the plaintiff to the same loss or deprivation for a lawful reason or reasons wholly independent of a substantial federally unlawful motive? In those cases there is probably[26] no constitutional or federal statutory "viola-

21. Fees might fail in this situation either because an award of nominal damages may be trivial in relation to the relief originally sought or because no nominal damages may be recoverable. *See, e.g., Kerr-Selgas v. American Airlines, Inc.,* 69 F.3d 1205 (1st Cir.1995) (nominal damages must be timely requested before a jury retires); *cf. Walker v. Anderson Elec. Connectors,* 944 F.2d 841 (11th Cir.1991), *cert. denied,* 506 U.S. 1078, 113 S.Ct. 1043, 122 L.Ed.2d 352 (1993) (a finding of a Title VII violation does not mandate an award of nominal damages, so that if plaintiff achieves no other relief, she does not qualify for prevailing party status).

22. *Wilcox v. City of Reno,* 42 F.3d 550 (9th Cir.1994).

23. *Romberg v. Nichols,* 48 F.3d 453 (9th Cir.1995).

24. *See* discussion in Chapter 2 on remedies in § 1983 "mixed motive" cases governed by *Mt. Healthy.*

25. 429 U.S. 274, 97 S.Ct. 568, 50 L.Ed.2d 471 (1977). *Mt. Healthy* and its relation to damages is discussed in Chapter 2 on § 1983.

26. *But see* the contrary argument advanced in scholarly commentary that is discussed in Chapter 2 concerning the effect of a *Mt. Healthy* showing on plaintiff's damages.

tion," and hence no possible monetary relief on the merits or, accordingly, attorneys' fees.

On the other hand, what if the plaintiff from the outset seeks no compensatory or punitive damages, only declaratory relief or an injunction, and recovers one? Has he not then achieved substantial, indeed entire success on the merits? And what if there are multiple claims? It is clear enough that a plaintiff's recovery of compensatory damages on less than all of the claims not only makes him technically prevailing but also entitles him to attorneys' fees, although only with respect to the hours reasonably expended in pursuit of the successful claim or claims.[27] Or suppose the plaintiff prevails on several claims, obtaining only nominal damages on each? In this situation the Fifth Circuit has ruled that the plaintiff is not even a prevailing party, arguably inconsistently with even the niggardly approach of *Farrar*.[28] Recent decisions struggle to define whether a plaintiff's "primary" goal was recovery of substantial monetary damages or merely injunctive relief to vindicate constitutional rights; if the former, then a "reasonable" fee may be nothing at all where the defendant's conduct is altered but no monetary relief is obtained.[29]

Farrar leaves unresolved a related question: can one become a prevailing party without having obtained, in the Supreme Court's words, a "consent decree, enforceable judgment or settlement," but simply because the filing of a lawsuit proved to be the "catalyst" that brought about some of the lawsuit's objectives? One circuit, en banc, has rejected the catalyst theory, relying specifically on the quoted language from *Farrar*.[30] Other circuits, however, continue to embrace the theory, dismissing the quoted phrase as not pertinent to the situation *Farrar* actually addressed.[31] Still another unanswered question is when, even in fully litigated settings, an award of fees may not be "equitable and just," in the words of § 1988, even to a plaintiff who clearly prevailed on the

---

27. *See Blum v. Stenson*, 465 U.S. 886, 104 S.Ct. 1541, 79 L.Ed.2d 891 (1984). *See also Morales v. San Rafael, Calif.*, 96 F.3d 359 (9th Cir.1996) (where plaintiff suffered dismissal of § 1983 claim against municipal defendant but recovered more than $17,000 from individual police officer, *Farrar* inapplicable because those damages are not nominal, even though they were far less than plaintiff sought).

28. *Peters v. Polk County Memorial Hospital*, 7 F.3d 229 (5th Cir.1993) (unpublished opinion), *cert. denied*, ___ U.S. ___, 115 S.Ct. 53, 130 L.Ed.2d 13 (1994).

29. *Compare Cramblit v. Fikse*, 33 F.3d 633 (6th Cir.1994) (per curiam) (plaintiff deemed to have fallen short of ultimate monetary goals and hence is denied fees *with Friend v. Kolodzieczak*, 72 F.3d 1386 (9th Cir.1995) (inmate plaintiffs awarded substantial fees after settlement expanding their access to religious services and sacraments upon court's determination that their "primary" goal was an injunction), *cert. denied*, ___ U.S. ___, 116 S.Ct. 1016, 134 L.Ed.2d 96 (1996).

30. *S–1 v. State Bd. of Educ. of North Carolina*, 21 F.3d 49 (4th Cir.), *cert. denied*, ___ U.S. ___, 115 S.Ct. 205, 130 L.Ed.2d 135 (1994).

31. *Zinn by Blankenship v. Shalala*, 35 F.3d 273 (7th Cir.1994); *Baumgartner v. Harrisburg Housing Authority*, 21 F.3d 541 (3d Cir.1994). *See also Wilcox v. City of Reno*, 42 F.3d 550 (9th Cir.1994) (arrestee who was punched in the face by a police officer held entitled to attorney's fees, although he received only nominal damages, because the litigation also led to the city's disciplining of the officer and modifying its policy governing the use of force).

sole or essential issue in the case. In one recent decision, plaintiffs obtained declaratory and injunctive relief on their sole claim, a challenge to the constitutionality of a statute. The court nevertheless denied attorneys' fees because the public official defendants had never tried to enforce the statute.[32]

It has been argued that the *Farrar* limitation, while applicable to all cases under the reconstruction civil rights acts, should not apply to "mixed-motive" cases under Title VII or the ADA because Section 706(g)(2)(B), added by the 1991 Civil Rights Act, specifically authorizes an award of attorneys' fees even when the employer makes the "same-decision" showing—that is, where the plaintiff has had only partial success. But an appellate court has recently rejected that argument, observing that the decision to award and the amount of attorney's fees is discretionary under Section 706(g)(2)(B) just as under Section 1988, the provision construed in *Farrar*. And it wrote that plaintiff's rejection of a settlement offer is one factor the court may take into account in deciding the appropriate amount of a fee award.[33]

Recoverability of fees for services performed in a preliminary administrative proceeding depends in part on whether the proceeding is optional or mandatory. If the state or local administrative proceeding is mandated, as it is under Title VII, fees for legal services performed in that hearing can be recovered.[34] If the prior administrative hearing is optional, however, fees are generally not awarded because such a hearing is not considered an "action or proceeding to enforce" civil rights under the language of § 1988. For example, because a plaintiff is not required to exhaust his administrative remedies before bringing a § 1983 action,[35] services performed in administrative proceedings on § 1983 claims are not compensable under § 1988.[36] Sometimes, however, where the administrative work is "useful and of a type ordinarily necessary to advance the civil rights litigation," fees may be awarded.[37] In *Pennsylvania v. Delaware Valley Citizens' Council for Clean Air*,[38] the Court applied this exception so as to allow fees. The *Delaware I* Court found that the administrative proceedings, held to enforce a consent decree, were "crucial to the vindication of [plaintiff's] rights," and concluded that the attorneys' services performed for those proceedings were com-

---

32. *Soundgarden v. Eikenberry*, 123 Wash.2d 750, 871 P.2d 1050, *cert. denied*, ___ U.S.___, 115 S.Ct. 663, 130 L.Ed.2d 598 (1994).

33. *Sheppard v. Riverview Nursing Center*, 88 F.3d 1332 (4th Cir.1996), *cert. denied*, ___ U.S. ___, ___ S.Ct. ___, ___ L.Ed.2d ___, 1996 WL 557681.

34. *New York Gaslight Club, Inc. v. Carey*, 447 U.S. 54, 100 S.Ct. 2024, 64 L.Ed.2d 723 (1980).

35. *See Patsy v. Florida Bd. of Regents*, 457 U.S. 496, 102 S.Ct. 2557, 73 L.Ed.2d 172 (1982).

36. *Webb v. Dyer County Bd. of Education*, 471 U.S. 234, 105 S.Ct. 1923, 85 L.Ed.2d 233 (1985). *See also Duello v. University of Wisconsin Board of Regents*, No. 91–1047, 176 Wis.2d 961, 501 N.W.2d 38 (Wis.1993) (fees incurred in connection with successful internal grievance procedure not compensable under § 706(k) of Title VII).

37. *Webb, supra* note 36.

38. 478 U.S. 546, 106 S.Ct. 3088, 92

pensable.[39]

The Court in *N.C. Dept. of Transportation v. Crest Street Community Council*,[40] erects a distinct barrier to the recoverability of attorney's fees for services performed in administrative proceedings. Those fees are recoverable only if the proceedings are "a part of or followed by" a federal lawsuit on the merits. If no judicial action is ever filed, no possibility of recovery exists. At a minimum, then, a plaintiff must file a court complaint.[41] And fees may be awarded for successful Title VII or civil rights work performed in state judicial proceedings contemplated by the federal statutory scheme, even when no federal action follows.[42] A plaintiff therefore has two hurdles before recovering fees for his success at an administrative stage. First, unless, as with proceedings before state or federal antidiscrimination agencies under Title VII, resort to the particular administrative forum is mandated by the federal statute in question, the administrative work must be "useful and necessary" to advance subsequent litigation. Second, it must be "a part of or followed by" a federal lawsuit on the merits.

Fees may be awarded *pendente lite* when a plaintiff achieves some durable interim relief on the merits, for example an injunction that works some permanent change in the legal relations between the parties.[43] More generally the Supreme Court has approved the award of fees pendente lite to a party who has obtained some relief on the merits at trial or on appeal.[44] But plaintiffs did not acquire prevailing party status by virtue of obtaining an injunction pending appeal that merely preserved the status quo in a circuit that determines the propriety of such injunctions principally by balancing the equities and harms attend-

L.Ed.2d 439 (1986) ("*Delaware I*") (applying § 304(d) of the Clean Air Act).

39. In *Brooks v. Georgia State Bd. of Elections,* 997 F.2d 857 (11th Cir.1993), the court awarded a plaintiff fees with respect to his attorneys' preclearance work under § 5 of the Voting Rights Act of 1965 before the United States Justice Department, where the district court conditioned plaintiff's remedy on the results of those administrative proceedings. The court considered the preclearance work "useful and ordinarily necessary to the litigation" within the meaning of *Webb* because the judicial decision turned on the preclearance outcome. 987 F.2d at 860. It also relaxed the *Delaware I* requirement that the administrative legal work be "crucial" to the vindication of adjudicated rights "to mean not much more than that it be relevant to those rights and related to terms of the judgment." *Id.* at 864. For similar reasons, post-judgment monitoring of consent decrees is compensable under § 1988. *See Delaware I,* 478 U.S. at 559–60, 106 S.Ct. at 3095; *Miller v. Carson,* 628 F.2d 346, 348 (5th Cir.1980).

40. 479 U.S. 6, 107 S.Ct. 336, 93 L.Ed.2d 188 (1986).

41. *But c.f. Moore v. District of Columbia,* 907 F.2d 165 (D.C.Cir.1990) (en banc) (under Handicapped Children's Protection Act, 20 U.S.C.A. § 1415, fees may be recovered for administrative proceedings regardless of whether a subsequent judicial action on the merits is filed), *cert. denied,* 498 U.S. 998, 111 S.Ct. 556, 112 L.Ed.2d 563 (1990).

42. *See New York Gaslight Club, Inc. v. Carey,* 447 U.S. 54, 100 S.Ct. 2024, 64 L.Ed.2d 723 (1980).

43. *See Hanrahan v. Hampton,* 446 U.S. 754, 100 S.Ct. 1987, 64 L.Ed.2d 670 (1980); *cf. Gotro v. R & B Realty Group,* 69 F.3d 1485 (9th Cir.1995) (even contingent fee litigant who has not actually incurred the obligation to pay for his lawyer's work in obtaining remand of improperly removed case may recover those fees from the defendant as "actual expenses, including attorney fees, incurred" within the meaning of 28 U.S.C. § 1447(c)).

44. *Hewitt v. Helms,* 482 U.S. 755, 107 S.Ct. 2672, 96 L.Ed.2d 654 (1987).

ant on granting or denying relief, rather than by weighing the merits.[45] And attorney's fees for preliminary injunctive relief have been denied where the injunction is ultimately reversed on appeal, the party having obtained that injunction then being regarded as not having prevailed.[46]

Attorneys' fees may be awarded for services necessary to implement or enforce a consent decree that resulted from earlier, successful litigation.[47] And a prevailing party may also recover, to the degree of her success, fees for services rendered in an unsuccessful judicial action if she ultimately prevails in a subsequent related judicial action.[48]

To calculate the amount of a "reasonable" award of attorney's fees the court must arrive first at a "lodestar" figure that represents a reasonable hourly rate multiplied by the number of hours reasonably expended on matters on which the plaintiff prevailed.[49] Both the reasonable hours and reasonable rates questions are committed to the discretion of the district courts,[50] although elements of legal analysis integral to their decisions are reviewable de novo.[51] Fees sought by the plaintiff that are attributable to attorney time distinctly devoted to unsuccessful claims will be deducted from the overall request.[52] But where a party prevails on only one of multiple legal claims rooted in the same factual nucleus, fees should not be reduced automatically. Instead, so long as the plaintiff has obtained "excellent" relief, he should recover a fully compensatory fee encompassing all hours reasonably expended on the litigation; less than "excellent" but still "substantial" relief may warrant a fee reduction in proportion to plaintiff's overall degree of success.[53] By not reducing the fee award simply because the plaintiff fails to prevail on every contention, this approach encourages plaintiff's counsel to advance alternative grounds for relief as authorized by F.R.C.P. 8(e).

The circuit courts appear to be in accord that time spent in establishing the prevailing party's entitlement to a fee award under § 1988 is itself compensable.[54] But such requests for "fees-on-fees" are themselves subject to reduction in proportion to the degree by which the "merits fees" award was discounted, as a percentage of merits fees claimed. For example, where plaintiffs recovered 87.2% of the fees claimed for work related to the underlying merits of the action, a

45. *LaRouche v. Kezer*, 20 F.3d 68 (2d Cir.1994).

46. *N.A.A.C.P. v. Detroit Police Officers Ass'n*, 46 F.3d 528 (6th Cir.1995).

47. *Eirhart v. Libbey–Owens–Ford Co.*, 996 F.2d 846 (7th Cir.1993).

48. *Cabrales v. County of Los Angeles*, 935 F.2d 1050 (9th Cir.1991).

49. *Blum v. Stenson*, 465 U.S. 886, 897, 104 S.Ct. 1541, 1548, 79 L.Ed.2d 891 (1984); *Hensley v. Eckerhart*, 461 U.S. 424, 103 S.Ct. 1933, 76 L.Ed.2d 40 (1983).

50. *See, e.g., Zuchel v. City and County of Denver*, 997 F.2d 730, 743 (10th Cir. 1993).

51. *See, e.g., Oviatt v. Pearce*, 954 F.2d 1470, 1481 (9th Cir.1992).

52. *Daniel v. Loveridge*, 32 F.3d 1472 (10th Cir.1994).

53. *Hensley v. Eckerhart*, 461 U.S. 424, 103 S.Ct. 1933, 76 L.Ed.2d 40 (1983); *Goos v. National Ass'n of Realtors*, 74 F.3d 300, 302 (D.C.Cir.1996).

54. *See, e.g., Clark v. City of Los Angeles*, 803 F.2d 987, 992 (9th Cir.1986) (citing cases).

reduction of 12.8%, their lodestar award for the fees incurred in petitioning for those fees was also disallowed by 12.8%. The court distinguished a caution by the Supreme Court that merits fees should not be reduced simply because the trial court failed to reach or rejected alternative legal *grounds* (as opposed to *claims*) advanced by a prevailing plaintiff.[55] In fees-on-fees situations the prevailing plaintiff would have an incentive to gild the lily, and the losing defendant little incentive to challenge improper billing entries, if defendants had to pay 100% of the plaintiff's attorney's fee work in situations where one could reasonably expect only a modest trimming of the underlying merits fees.

Even with respect to claims on which the plaintiff prevailed, fees may not be awarded for hours that are "excessive, redundant, or otherwise unnecessary."[56] Where EEOC successfully prosecuted a disparate treatment claim on behalf of the plaintiff, who joined the action to assert state law claims on which she did not prevail, a circuit court ruled that she was entitled to attorneys' fees only with respect to the additional contribution, if any, by her attorney to the EEOC's successful efforts.[57] The court viewed most of the private attorneys' services as redundant or unnecessary. But where, in another case, the court halved the hours for which compensation was requested to account for duplication in services rendered by plaintiff's two counsel, it was an abuse of discretion also to cut the rate of hourly compensation on the theory that "the actual rate was the combined rates" of each counsel: that "corrected twice for a single problem."[58]

The Court in *Blum v. Stenson*[59] held that the lodestar is based on market rates in the relevant community, and therefore fees awardable to nonprofit legal services organizations may not be limited to actual costs. Similarly, fee awards may compensate for the work of law clerks and paralegals, again at market rates.[60] To say that the lodestar rate is based on rates prevailing in the relevant community masks two difficult subissues: *which lawyer's* rate in a diverse legal community where lawyers of differing experience, special skills, and reputation enjoy different degrees of market power; and *which community's* rate where a lawyer from one community performs services in another with a significantly different prevailing market average. *Blum* seems to rest on the premise that the appropriate market rate for § 1988 purposes is "the opportunity cost of that time, the income foregone by [the lawyer in] representing this plaintiff."[61] It follows that an established billing rate of the prevailing party's lawyer deserves significant weight.

55. *Thompson v. Gomez,* 45 F.3d 1365 (9th Cir.1995) (citing *Hensley v. Eckerhart,* 461 U.S. 424, 103 S.Ct. 1933, 76 L.Ed.2d 40 (1983)).

56. *Hensley v. Eckerhart,* 461 U.S. 424, 103 S.Ct. 1933, 76 L.Ed.2d 40 (1983).

57. *EEOC v. Clear Lake Dodge,* 60 F.3d 1146, 1154 (5th Cir.1995).

58. *Carter v. Sedgwick County, Kansas,* 36 F.3d 952, 956 (10th Cir.1994).

59. 465 U.S. 886, 104 S.Ct. 1541, 79 L.Ed.2d 891 (1984).

60. *Missouri v. Jenkins,* 491 U.S. 274, 109 S.Ct. 2463, 105 L.Ed.2d 229 (1989).

61. *Gusman v. Unisys Corporation,* 986 F.2d 1146 (7th Cir.1993).

But what if, as in one recent case, the rate of the prevailing party's lawyer, a member of a firm in a large urban city, is significantly greater than the rate of a hypothetical counterpart lawyer in the smaller city where the bulk of the legal services were rendered? Using the opportunity-cost premise, the Seventh Circuit held that the (in that case, higher) rate set by the market for the prevailing party's counsel is presumptively appropriate in calculating the lodestar. No burden was placed on the prevailing party to show that she could not have obtained comparable representation at the lower rates prevailing in the smaller community. Instead, the court placed the burden on the losing party to demonstrate that a lower rate would more accurately reflect the winning lawyer's opportunity cost, for example by showing that he ordinarily commands the high rate claimed in only a small percentage of the total number of hours he "sells" in a year, devoting the balance to court-fixed contingent fee litigation. In that event, the court concluded, his true "market-clearing price" may be considerably less than the hourly fee that a few of his clients were willing to pay.[62]

Another difficult task facing a court in calculating a lodestar is to identify the issues on which plaintiff prevailed and in turn the number of hours counsel reasonably expended on those issues. In this sense degree of success is a critical component of the ultimate fee award. But a lodestar-based fee award need not be proportionate to the amount of damages a plaintiff recovers with respect to a successful issue.[63]

Attorney's fees may be augmented to compensate for delay in payment (as distinct from risk of nonpayment or "contingency"—to be discussed below). Risk of delay is compensated "either by basing the award on current rates or by adjusting the fee based on historical rates to reflect its present value."[64] Nor does the Eleventh Amendment bar that adjustment in an action against a state.[65] Such fees constitute an item of "costs" under the language of § 1988 and may therefore be recovered from a state even in federal court, notwithstanding the Eleventh Amendment.[66]

Additional adjustment factors to the lodestar include the novelty and difficulty of the questions presented, the extent to which the demands of the case preclude other legal employment, the undesirability of the case, awards in similar cases, and the experience, reputation, and ability of the attorneys. These adjustment factors may refine but cannot substitute

---

62. *Id.*

63. *Riverside v. Rivera,* 477 U.S. 561, 106 S.Ct. 2686, 91 L.Ed.2d 466 (1986) (upholding attorney's fee award of $245,456 where recovery under federal civil rights statutes was only $13,300); *McKenzie v. Cooper, Levins & Pastko, Inc.,* 990 F.2d 1183, 1185 (11th Cir.1993) (after a reduction to eliminate an enhancement for contingency, appellate court approves a fee award of over $121,000 where the back pay recovery was only $8600); *Grant v. Bethle-*

hem Steel Corp., 973 F.2d 96 (2d Cir.1992) (affirming an award of over half a million dollars in attorneys' fees where plaintiffs had settled for only $60,000), *cert. denied,* 506 U.S. 1053, 113 S.Ct. 978, 122 L.Ed.2d 132 (1993).

64. *Missouri v. Jenkins, supra* note 60.

65. *Id.*

66. *Hutto v. Finney,* 437 U.S. 678, 98 S.Ct. 2565, 57 L.Ed.2d 522 (1978).

for the basic multiplication of a reasonable billing rate by the number of hours reasonably expended on successful claims.

In *Evans v. Jeff D.*,[67] the Court approved the practice of compulsory waiver of attorneys' fees by settlement. FRCP 23 requires district court approval of class action settlements. Parties are free to negotiate the terms of a settlement and may waive statutorily authorized attorney's fees. The Court in *Evans* held that § 1988 does not interfere with that freedom. The Civil Rights Act of 1991 leaves *Evans* intact.

In *Venegas v. Mitchell*,[68] the Court held § 1988 does not invalidate a contingent fee arrangement providing for payments substantially in excess of the reasonable fee recoverable from the defendant. That is, § 1988 controls only the relationship between the losing defendant and the prevailing plaintiff, not between the plaintiff and plaintiff's own attorney. *Venegas* thus reinforces a plaintiff's capacity to secure counsel of her choice by upholding the integrity of the private fee agreement. On the other hand, the plaintiff's attorney's fee award under § 1988 may not be absolutely limited by a contingent-fee arrangement that calls for a lesser sum than the lodestar.[69]

Until recently, a prevailing plaintiff was not entitled to have its expert witnesses compensated by the losing party, absent contractual or statutory authority stating otherwise.[70] In *West Virginia Univ. Hosps. v. Casey*,[71] the Court held that § 1988 does not authorize the recovery of expert witness fees. They are limited to the amount designated for all witnesses, $30 per day. Of course, the Supreme Court has already included certain related costs, e.g., those for law clerks and paralegals, as part of the attorneys' fees recoverable under § 1988.[72] The Civil Rights Act of 1991 reverses *West Virginia Univ. Hosps. v. Casey*. The Act includes expert fees as a part of an attorney's fee award under both § 1988 and Title VII.

C. LODESTAR MAY NOT BE ENHANCED FOR "CONTINGENCY," OR RISK OF LOSS

Library References:

C.J.S. Civil Rights §§ 328, 331.
West's Key No. Digests, Civil Rights ⚷302.

67. 475 U.S. 717, 106 S.Ct. 1531, 89 L.Ed.2d 747 (1986).

68. 495 U.S. 82, 110 S.Ct. 1679, 109 L.Ed.2d 74 (1990).

69. *Blanchard v. Bergeron*, 489 U.S. 87, 109 S.Ct. 939, 103 L.Ed.2d 67 (1989). *But see Time Products, Ltd. v. Toy Biz, Inc.*, 38 F.3d 660 (2d Cir.1994) (award must be reasonably related to a hypothetical fee arrangement that the prevailing party could have made with an attorney, which court set at a 33% contingency).

70. *Crawford Fitting Co. v. J.T. Gibbons*, 482 U.S. 437, 107 S.Ct. 2494, 96 L.Ed.2d 385 (1987).

71. 499 U.S. 83, 111 S.Ct. 1138, 113 L.Ed.2d 68 (1991).

72. *Missouri v. Jenkins, supra* § 12.2 note 60.

§ 12.3 In General

There is a strong presumption that the lodestar represents a reasonable fee, and any upward or downward adjustments may take into account only those factors not used in arriving at the lodestar.[1]

A decision of the Supreme Court, *Burlington v. Dague*,[2] appears to have ended a debate among the circuits in favor of flatly precluding enhancement. Although the underlying claims at issue were brought under modern environmental statutes, the Court's opinion and citations to cases, including *King v. Palmer*,[3] in which fees were sought under § 1988 or Title VII, strongly suggest that the holding will apply to fee applications under the latter statutes as well.

What if, as a result of *Dague* or otherwise, a putative plaintiff cannot attract counsel? Section 706(f)(1)(B)[4] authorizes the court, upon application and under such circumstances as it deems just, to "appoint an attorney" for a complainant and authorize commencement of the action without fees, costs, or security. And what if the court is unable, after diligent effort, to locate a lawyer willing to take the case without up-front compensation? There is authority that § 706(f)(1)(B) may be read to require the coercive appointment of counsel; this reading is partly justified by the fact that the unwilling lawyer may ultimately be compensated as the result of a statutory award of attorneys' fees if his client prevails.[5]

D. PREVAILING DEFENDANTS

Library References:

C.J.S. Civil Rights § 325.
West's Key No. Digests, Civil Rights ⊙298.

§ 12.4 In General

While a prevailing plaintiff is ordinarily to be awarded attorney's fees in all but special circumstances, the Supreme Court in *Christiansburg Garment Co. v. EEOC*[1] has interpreted § 706(k) to preclude attorney's fees to a prevailing defendant unless the plaintiff's action was "frivolous, unreasonable, or without foundation...." This appears to mean that a fee award to a prevailing defendant is unwarranted where

§ 12.3

1. *See Hensley v. Eckerhart*, 461 U.S. 424, 103 S.Ct. 1933, 76 L.Ed.2d 40 (1983); *Pennsylvania v. Delaware Valley Citizens' Council for Clean Air*, 478 U.S. 546, 106 S.Ct. 3088, 92 L.Ed.2d 439 (1986) (*"Delaware I"*).

2. 505 U.S. 557, 112 S.Ct. 2638, 120 L.Ed.2d 449 (1992).

3. *See King v. Palmer*, 950 F.2d 771 (D.C.Cir.1991) (en banc), *reversing King v. Palmer*, 906 F.2d 762 (D.C.Cir.1990) *and overruling McKenzie v. Kennickell*, 875 F.2d 330 (D.C.Cir.1989).

4. 42 U.S.C.A. § 2000e–5(f)(1)(B).

5. *See Scott v. Tyson Foods, Inc.*, 943 F.2d 17 (8th Cir.1991); *Bradshaw v. U.S. District Court*, 742 F.2d 515 (9th Cir.1984); *Bradshaw v. Zoological Soc. of San Diego*, 662 F.2d 1301 (9th Cir.1981). *Cf. Howard v. Military Department*, 5 F.3d 537 (9th Cir.1993).

§ 12.4

1. 434 U.S. 412, 98 S.Ct. 694, 54 L.Ed.2d 648 (1978).

the plaintiff's claim, although plainly flawed, is colorable.[2] The plaintiff's failure to establish a prima facie case, the unprecedented nature of a claim, the defendant's offer of a settlement, or the dismissal of an action before trial all figure in determining whether a claim is sufficiently frivolous, unreasonable, or groundless to justify taxing attorney's fees against a plaintiff. If the defendant can show that a plaintiff asserted a claim in subjective bad faith, the case for awarding the defendant his attorney's fees is stronger. But the circumstances warranting fees to a prevailing defendant must be truly exceptional, so much so that a trial court does not abuse its discretion in denying such fees even if no reason is stated for the denial.[3] And where EEOC is the plaintiff, it is not even enough for the defendant seeking attorney's fees to show that EEOC failed to present credible evidence of discrimination. In such a case the defendant has the even more difficult burden of demonstrating that EEOC should have "anticipated at the outset that none of its evidence of discriminatory conduct was credible" or that EEOC unreasonably believed that it had made adequate efforts to conciliate.[4] It is difficult to imagine a situation in which the defendant could carry that showing.

If the standard for prevailing plaintiffs announced in *Farrar* were the test of whether a defendant is a "prevailing party," the defendant might qualify for fees when the plaintiff voluntarily dismisses her suit with prejudice even before a decision on the merits by motion for summary judgment or at trial. Such a dismissal does, after all, alter the legal relationship between the parties to the benefit of the defendant. But a circuit court recently observed that the *Christiansburg* opinion reflects the Supreme Court's mandate that separate, more stringent standards govern for the fee eligibility of prevailing Title VII defendants. To show the frivolousness, unreasonableness, or groundlessness demanded by *Christiansburg*, the court concluded, the defendant must ordinarily have prevailed on a motion for summary judgment on the merits.[5] On the other hand, denial of a defendant's summary judgment motion does not necessarily prevent its recovering attorney's fees under the *Christiansburg* standard if plaintiff should have realized, from subsequent pretrial discovery, that his claim was groundless.[6] And the prevailing defendant eligible for fees under *Christiansburg* may, like the prevailing plaintiff, also recover the reasonable fees and expenses incurred in proceedings to collect the underlying fee award should plaintiff decline to pay it.[7]

2. *EEOC v. Reichhold Chemicals, Inc.,* 988 F.2d 1564, 1570–71 (11th Cir.1993). *See AFSCME v. County of Nassau,* 96 F.3d 644 (2d Cir.1996) (reversing fee award against plaintiff that prevailed on a narrow claim closely related to a broader one on which it failed).

3. *Maag v. Wessler,* 993 F.2d 718 (9th Cir.1993).

4. *EEOC v. Bruno's Restaurant,* 13 F.3d 285 (9th Cir.1993). *See EEOC v. Hendrix*

College, 53 F.3d 209 (8th Cir.1995) (upholding award where EEOC was found to have failed to investigate before filing action).

5. *Marquart v. Lodge 837, International Association of Machinists and Aerospace Workers,* 26 F.3d 842 (8th Cir.1994).

6. *Flowers v. Jefferson Hospital Ass'n,* 49 F.3d 391 (8th Cir.1995) (per curiam).

7. *Vukadinovich v. McCarthy,* 59 F.3d 58 (7th Cir.1995).

The Equal Access to Justice Act,[8] unlike § 1988 and its Title VII counterpart,[9] provides for fee awards to prevailing defendants when the plaintiff's claim is merely groundless but not frivolous, if the unsuccessful plaintiff is the U.S. government. The circuit courts are in conflict concerning whether EAJA is available in actions under statutes (like the Reconstruction Acts and Title VII) that have their own fee-shifting statutes.[10] And even where EAJA applies, a defendant employer will not be entitled to fees if the evidence presented by EEOC as plaintiff, although seriously flawed, is supported by anecdotal evidence.[11]

The *Christiansburg* test has recently been applied to govern the award of attorney's fees against unsuccessful intervenors. The Supreme Court characterized as "particularly welcome" a union's intervention challenging a proposed settlement of a sex discrimination action in order to protect "the legitimate expectations of . . . [male] employees innocent of any wrongdoing."[12] The decision encouraged intervention by holding that intervenors would be liable for plaintiffs' costs of defending a settlement only when the intervention is "frivolous, unreasonable, or without foundation. . . ."[13] In effect, then, intervention becomes *per se* a "special circumstance" that warrants denial of a fee award to a prevailing plaintiff. The Civil Rights Act of 1991 leaves this approach intact.

E. RULE 68 OFFERS OF JUDGMENT

Library References:

> C.J.S. Federal Civil Procedure § 1276.
> West's Key No. Digests, Federal Civil Procedure ⟐2725.

§ 12.5 In General

Federal Rule 68 authorizes the defendant, at least 10 days before trial, to "offer to allow judgment to be taken against [it] . . . for the money or property . . . specified in the offer, with costs then accrued." It then provides that, if the offer is not accepted and a judgment obtained by the plaintiff "is not more favorable than the offer, the offeree must pay the costs incurred after the making of the offer." On its face, then, Rule 68 merely relieves a defendant who makes such an offer that is not accepted by the plaintiff and equalled or exceeded by a final judgment from what would otherwise be its liability for the "costs" routinely taxable under Federal Rule of Civil Procedure 54(d) in favor of prevailing parties in any federal civil action. Such an offer is valid even

---

8. 28 U.S.C.A. § 2412(d).

9. 42 U.S.C.A. § 2000e–5(k).

10. *Compare Nowd v. Rubin,* 76 F.3d 25 (1st Cir.1996) (case under ADEA) *and Gavette v. Office of Personnel Management,* 808 F.2d 1456, 1463 (Fed.Cir.1986) (yes) *with Escobar Ruiz v. INS,* 787 F.2d 1294, 1296 (9th Cir.1986) (no).

11. *EEOC v. O & G Spring and Wire Forms Specialty Co.,* 38 F.3d 872 (7th Cir. 1994), *cert. denied,* ___ U.S. ___, 115 S.Ct. 1270, 131 L.Ed.2d 148 (1995).

12. *Independent Federation of Flight Attendants v. Zipes,* 491 U.S. 754, 109 S.Ct. 2732, 105 L.Ed.2d 639 (1989).

13. *Id.*

when it is conditioned upon acceptance of its terms by all plaintiffs, and a settlement agreement counts as a "judgment" that triggers the cost-shifting permitted by Rule 68.[1]

Rule 54(d) costs, however, are relatively minor, as they are universally understood not to include attorney's fees. The real bite of Rule 68 in civil rights and employment discrimination actions results from the interplay of that rule with the provisions in Title VII and § 1988 that call for an award of "a reasonable attorney's fee *as part of the costs....*"[2] Importing the underlined language into the word "costs" as it appears in Rule 68, the Supreme Court in *Marek v. Chesny*[3] held that a defendant's offer of judgment in a civil rights action governed by statutory provisions for attorney's fees can shift what would otherwise be the losing defendant's liability for the prevailing plaintiff's attorney's fees, as well as ordinary costs. Specifically, a Rule 68 offer that meets the requirements of that Rule relieves the losing defendant of liability for the plaintiff's post-offer attorney's fees as well as her ordinary costs of litigation. This holding greatly increases the defendant's incentive to make a Rule 68 offer, and the Civil Rights Act of 1991 leaves *Marek* intact. The *Marek* holding goes well beyond actions under the Reconstruction Civil Rights statutes governed by § 1988. In *Lyte v. Sara Lee Corp.*,[4] the court held that attorneys' fees are a part of the "costs" shifted by a defendant's offer of judgment under FRCP 68 in actions under any statute that allows fee awards as a part of "costs," which would include those under Title VII, EPA, ADA, and ADEA.

The defendant's offer, to avoid liability for costs and fees to the prevailing plaintiff, must, in the words of Rule 68, include the plaintiff's "costs then accrued," that is, up until the time of the offer. The "costs" that must be included in the offer—like the "costs" mentioned in the subsequent phrase of Rule 68 that shifts liability for attorney's fees if the offer is rejected—have been held to include the amount of the plaintiff's attorney's fees accrued at the time of the offer. This is because a prevailing plaintiff would, absent an offer, ordinarily be entitled by judgment to an award of attorney's fees for pre-offer work.[5] Accordingly, those fees, together with ordinary costs, must be added to the judgment to calculate the total received by judgment that the offer must equal or exceed to shift post-offer costs and fees under Rule 68. Where an offer no longer exceeded, in fact was slightly less than, the amount of plaintiff's judgment once pre-offer attorney's fees were added to the judgment, the Rule 68 requirement that the offer equal or exceed the judgement was held not met and the defendant was therefore subject

---

§ 12.5

1. *Lang v. Gates*, 36 F.3d 73 (9th Cir. 1994).

2. Section 706(k) of Title VII; 42 U.S.C.A. § 1988, final sentence.

3. 473 U.S. 1, 105 S.Ct. 3012, 87 L.Ed.2d 1 (1985).

4. 950 F.2d 101 (2d Cir.1991).

5. *See Scheeler v. Crane Co.*, 21 F.3d 791 (8th Cir.1994) (diversity case under Iowa civil rights statute).

to the usual assessment of costs and fees owed a prevailing plaintiff, including those incurred after the making of its offer.[6]

In another case, the offer promised not only "costs then accrued," as prescribed by Rule 68, but also "reasonable attorney fees as determined by the court."[7] The Ninth Circuit construed the language of the offer to authorize a district judge's award of attorney's fees for plaintiffs' counsel's preparation of a fee petition *after* they accepted the offer, even though under Rule 68 costs, and hence, under *Marek*, fees, are halted by a successful offer. The decision points up the necessity for defendant's counsel to draft tightly worded offers that not only meet Rule 68's strictures but also stay within them. Any waiver of or limitation on attorney's fees in actions under statutes providing for the recovery of fees by prevailing plaintiffs must be "clear and unambiguous." The court indicated that if the defendant had offered only to pay plaintiff's "costs then accrued," the offer would have clearly and unambiguously limited plaintiff's fees to the full extent that *Marek* and Rule 68 permit.

The inclusion of attorney's fees in the Rule 68 post-offer "costs" that the plaintiff may be precluded from recovering assumes that the underlying fee statute includes "attorney's fees" within the definition of "costs." That is the case with most fee statutes, including § 1988, its counterpart under ADEA, and the principal Title VII fee provision, Section 706(k). By contrast, since the "mixed-motive" remedies section of Title VII, Section 706(g)(2)(B), refers to "costs" and "attorney's fees" distinctly and separately, attorneys' fees will not be counted as part of the post-offer Rule 68 "costs" a plaintiff is barred from recovering where the entitlement to fees flows only from that section.[8]

Can Rule 68 be used not just to relieve the defendant of cost and fee liability to a prevailing plaintiff but as the basis for an award of costs and fees to a prevailing defendant? If so, Rule 68 could serve as the prevailing defendant's end run around the *Christiansburg Garment* test—it would become eligible for attorney's fees simply by submitting what proves to be a shrewd offer of judgment, without having to show the groundlessness, frivolousness, or subjective bad faith the Supreme Court has required. A court of appeals, citing the text of Rule 68, has rejected this argument, confirming that the provision, while a one-way street available only to defendants, helps them only if the plaintiff prevails, and then only with respect to the plaintiff's costs and fees.[9]

---

6. *Scheeler v. Crane Co., supra* note 5.

7. *Holland v. Roeser,* 37 F.3d 501 (9th Cir.1994).

8. *Sheppard v. Riverview Nursing Center,* 88 F.3d 1332 (4th Cir.), *cert. denied,* ___

U.S. ___, ___ S.Ct. ___, ___ L.Ed.2d ___, 1996 WL 557681 (1996).

9. *EEOC v. Bailey Ford, Inc.,* 26 F.3d 570 (5th Cir.1994).

Chapter Thirteen

PROCEDURAL ASPECTS OF LITIGATING CIVIL RIGHTS AND EMPLOYMENT DISCRIMINATION CLAIMS

Analysis

A. OVERVIEW—THE NEW FEDERALISM IN CIVIL RIGHTS FORUM SELECTION: STATE PRIMACY REASSERTED

§ 13.1 In General

In keeping with § 1983's historic purposes, given new voice by *Monroe v. Pape*[1], the Supreme Court has on occasion declared that the statute's provision of a federal judicial forum was an integral, purposeful element of the overall scheme envisioned by the Reconstruction Congress that enacted it. Yet concrete recognition of the desirability of preserving a federal forum for resolution of alleged federal law violations under color of state law is seldom reflected in the Court's actual holdings. Indeed, looking back over the past quarter century, only two such instances stand out.

§ 13.1

1. *See* Chapter 2.

In *Mitchum v. Foster*[2] the Court cited the availability of a federal forum as sufficiently important to create a § 1983 exception to the Anti–Injunction Act.[3] As a result there is no blanket, statutory barrier to a federal court injunction of parallel state court proceedings, preserving the federal judiciary's opportunity to render an initial decision on federal constitutional or statutory rights asserted in § 1983 litigation. As we shall see, however, the barn door had already been shut. One year earlier, in *Younger v. Harris*[4] the Court had begun to fashion its own rules restricting federal court interference, by injunction, declaratory judgment or other equitable relief, with ongoing state proceedings. *Younger,* seizing on the fact that a federal court's exercise of equity jurisdiction is discretionary, ushered in a variety of abstention doctrines that express deference not only to pending state proceedings but sometimes to state administrative or regulatory schemes.

A decade after *Mitchum* the Court again paid homage to the importance of a federal forum by deciding, in *Patsy v. Board of Regents*[5] that a § 1983 plaintiff need not exhaust state administrative remedies before commencing a judicial lawsuit. But this homage, too, has steadily dissolved into lip service. The new federalism of the Burger and Rehnquist Courts has made striking inroads into the notion that a federal judicial forum is indispensable, or even particularly important, to vindicating the federal rights actionable through the vehicle of § 1983. Without overturning, or even directly eroding *Patsy,* the Court has carved out an ever expanding domain in which would-be civil rights litigants are forced in the first instance to litigate key issues or entire claims before state administrative or judicial tribunals.

For example, the civil rights claimant who sees that she is about to be or has become entangled in state criminal or important civil litigation or even administrative proceedings and who seeks immediate relief from a federal court is usually now shunted back into the state system. For the most part the Supreme Court has accomplished this result by continually enlarging the classification of state tribunals and matters that trigger *Younger* and its progeny, which, in the name of intersystem comity, forbid federal court intervention by injunction or declaratory relief with a variety of ongoing state criminal and important civil proceedings. Indeed the policies underlying *Younger* have blossomed to such a degree that its progeny now constitute what may fairly be called the exception that swallows the *Mitchum* exception to the Anti–Injunction Act.

In addition to the pure *Younger* prescription of dismissal, the Court has developed a host of "abstention" doctrines that temporarily derail federal proceedings by means of stays pending the completion of state proceedings. Chief among these is *Railroad Comm'n of Texas v. Pull-*

2. 407 U.S. 225, 92 S.Ct. 2151, 32 L.Ed.2d 705 (1972).

3. 28 U.S.C.A. § 2283.

4. 401 U.S. 37, 91 S.Ct. 746, 27 L.Ed.2d 669 (1971).

5. 457 U.S. 496, 102 S.Ct. 2557, 73 L.Ed.2d 172 (1982).

man Co.[6], which authorizes the stay of federal actions, including those under § 1983,[7] where a particular resolution of an uncertain issue of state law may obviate the need for federal court resolution of a constitutional question. The Court has even expanded this "wait and see" approach, accomplished by a stay rather than outright abstention, to other kinds of federal court civil rights actions—those not likely to be mooted by state court resolution of uncertain issues of state law, a la *Pullman*—that seek only damages (and therefore escape dismissal under *Younger*)[8] but raise issues involved in ongoing state proceedings.[9] Similarly, the Court has now required the equivalent of federal court abstention pending the conclusion of ordinary state criminal appeals and habeas proceedings whenever the § 1983 plaintiff seeks relief even for damages.[10]

The federal courthouse door, having been shut by *Younger* or temporarily closed via a variant of abstention, is often then effectively locked by the Court's companion doctrines that accord most important state judicial and administrative determinations claim or issue preclusive effect when the civil rights claimant later resorts to federal court. The Court has found no § 1983 exception to the federal Full Faith and Credit Statute.[11] Accordingly entire "claims"—defined in broad, transactional terms—that were asserted by state court litigants may not be relitigated by them in federal court against the same adversary, at least if that state's own law of res judicata would preclude relitigation.[12] Similarly, so long as the state's law of collateral estoppel would preclude her from relitigating, a § 1983 plaintiff is ordinarily bound by adverse state court determinations on particular issues, even when the § 1983 defendant

---

6. 312 U.S. 496, 61 S.Ct. 643, 85 L.Ed. 971 (1941).

7. *See Askew v. Hargrave*, 401 U.S. 476, 91 S.Ct. 856, 28 L.Ed.2d 196 (1971).

8. The Court wrote in the case under discussion, *Deakins v. Monaghan*, 484 U.S. 193, 108 S.Ct. 523, 98 L.Ed.2d 529 (1988), that it was not deciding whether *Younger* might apply to federal court actions in which only damages are sought. But it has since held that the strong "*Younger*" medicine of outright abstention—that is, dismissal or remand—is available only where equitable or, at a minimum, discretionary relief is sought. In pure legal damages actions the defendant may be granted only the milder relief of a stay. *Quackenbush v. Allstate Ins. Co.*, ___ U.S. ___, 116 S.Ct. 1712, 135 L.Ed.2d 1 (1996).

9. *Deakins v. Monaghan*, 484 U.S. 193, 108 S.Ct. 523, 98 L.Ed.2d 529 (1988) (authorizing stay, but not dismissal, of federal court damages action under § 1983 pending completion of state grand jury proceedings). *See also Bellotti v. Baird*, 428 U.S. 132, 146, 96 S.Ct. 2857, 2865, 49 L.Ed.2d 844 (1976) (approving abstention until state law was construed by state courts if such construc-

tion "would 'at least *materially change* the nature of the problem' ..."; quoting *Harrison v. NAACP*, 360 U.S. 167, 177, 79 S.Ct. 1025, 1030, 3 L.Ed.2d 1152 (1959)) (emphasis added).

10. *Heck v. Humphrey*, 512 U.S. 477, ___ n. 8, 114 S.Ct. 2364, 2373 n. 8, 129 L.Ed.2d 383 (1994) (citing *Colorado River Water Conservation Dist. v. United States*, 424 U.S. 800, 96 S.Ct. 1236, 47 L.Ed.2d 483 (1976)). *Heck* is discussed in more detail below. Technically, however, *Heck* is based not on abstention but on an exception to the scope of § 1983 itself. The Court has since held outright abstention unavailable where no equitable or otherwise discretionary relief is sought; only a stay is available if the plaintiff seeks purely legal relief, *e.g.*, damages. *Quackenbush v. Allstate Ins. Co.*, ___ U.S. ___, 116 S.Ct. 1712, 135 L.Ed.2d 1 (1996).

11. 28 U.S.C.A. § 1738.

12. *Migra v. Warren City School District*, 465 U.S. 75, 104 S.Ct. 892, 79 L.Ed.2d 56 (1984).

was not a party to the state action.[13] Such issue preclusion will often render a practical nullity the theoretically ameliorating feature of *Pullman* abstention—the § 1983 plaintiff's ability to return to federal court after the state court action has concluded.[14]

Last, where the state proceedings were administrative rather than judicial, and the Full Faith and Credit Statute is therefore inapplicable, the Court has fashioned a federal common law of preclusion. Here, too, the Court's former preference that federal civil rights plaintiffs have access to an unencumbered federal forum has not proven sufficiently powerful to warrant an exception to the ordinary state law rules governing res judicata and collateral estoppel. The § 1983 plaintiff will be precluded (to the same degree as she would be in the state's courts) from relitigating issues determined adversely to her in state administrative proceedings that are deemed "quasi-judicial" in their formality and fairness.[15] The moral, for putative civil rights plaintiffs desirous of a fresh federal forum, is not to be unlucky. Avoid becoming the target of state criminal or important civil judicial lawsuits, or state administrative proceedings, before you have proceeded to judgment in federal court on your claims under § 1983.

It is just as dangerous to trust in state tribunals as to be trapped by them. The Supreme Court has encouraged the litigation of civil rights claims in state courts by holding that they have jurisdiction fully concurrent with that of the federal courts to entertain claims under the Reconstruction statutes [16] and Title VII.[17] In a curious decision that seemingly runs counter to the new federalism, the Court even forces state judges to relieve the § 1983 plaintiff of complying with a relatively

13. *See Allen v. McCurry*, 449 U.S. 90, 101 S.Ct. 411, 66 L.Ed.2d 308 (1980) (section 1983 plaintiff cannot relitigate issues determined against him in state criminal trial).

14. *See England v. Louisiana State Board of Medical Examiners*, 375 U.S. 411, 84 S.Ct. 461, 11 L.Ed.2d 440 (1964). Upon return of the action to federal court after *England* reservation, issue preclusion applies with respect to the state law issues litigated in state court. *Instructional Systems, Inc. v. Computer Curriculum Corp.*, 35 F.3d 813 (3d Cir.1994).

15. *University of Tennessee v. Elliott*, 478 U.S. 788, 106 S.Ct. 3220, 92 L.Ed.2d 635 (1986).

16. *Howlett v. Rose*, 496 U.S. 356, 110 S.Ct. 2430, 110 L.Ed.2d 332 (1990). The potential advantages of pursuing § 1983 claims in state court are discussed in Section F, below.

17. *Yellow Freight v. Donnelly*, 494 U.S. 820, 110 S.Ct. 1566, 108 L.Ed.2d 834 (1990). Although Title VII itself expressly confers subject matter jurisdiction on *feder-*al courts to hear "actions brought under this title," § 706(f)(3), 42 U.S.C.A. § 2000e–5(f)(3), federal question jurisdiction does not extend to suits brought to enforce Title VII settlement agreements. Such actions are based simply on state contract law, and the jurisdiction of a federal court to hear them thus depends on meeting the requirements of 28 U.S.C.A. § 1332: the happenstance presence of complete diversity of citizenship and a claim of greater than $50,000. *Morris v. Hobart, Oklahoma*, 39 F.3d 1105 (10th Cir.1994), *cert. denied*, ___ U.S. ___, 115 S.Ct. 1960, 131 L.Ed.2d 852 (1995). *See Kokkonen v. Guardian Life Insurance Co.*, 511 U.S. 375, 114 S.Ct. 1673, 128 L.Ed.2d 391 (1994) (rejecting the proposition that a federal court that failed to retain jurisdiction over a primary controversy has "ancillary" jurisdiction to hear a separate action to enforce a settlement agreement reached in the underlying action). Counsel desirous of enforcing such an agreement should therefore take care to incorporate it by reference in an order of dismissal or request the court explicitly to retain jurisdiction pending satisfaction of the agreement.

minor procedural obstacle—filing a notice of claim with a local government entity defendant before filing suit.[18] And many potential civil rights litigants, especially state employees, will find state administrative agencies able and willing to entertain related state law causes of action.

But the apparent hospitality of state tribunals can turn into a trap. Woe betide the civil rights litigant who resorts to them voluntarily in the hope of later obtaining a de novo hearing on a Reconstruction Act claim in federal court. That course is perilous even if she asserts in the state court [19] only state law causes of action with elements of proof entirely distinct from those of, say, § 1981 or § 1983. If the federal court later concludes that the federal civil rights claim stems from the same spatial and temporal circumstances as those that gave rise to the state cause of action [20]—the test in modern preclusion law for claim identity—the federal claims will likely be extinguished by the state's law of claim preclusion or "res judicata" just as that doctrine, applied by force of the Full Faith and Credit Statute, plagues the involuntary state litigant. Even if the "claims," for preclusion purposes, are viewed as different, the federal civil rights plaintiff may be bound by (or, if she prevailed in the state tribunal, take advantage of) state court findings on discrete issues.

Similar pitfalls await the civil rights plaintiff who first submits related state law claims to a "quasi-judicial" state administrative agency.[21] A loss there may jeopardize the outcome of a subsequent federal civil rights lawsuit. Depending on the potential recoveries under state law before the agency and under the federal civil rights acts before a court, it may therefore be wiser to forego the state agency forum—even if, under state law, that means abandoning the state cause of action—and proceed directly to state or federal court. In a federal court, the state cause of action could be joined to the federal claim under supplemental jurisdiction [22]; a state court, as observed above, would have concurrent jurisdiction to hear the federal claim together with the claim under state law. On the other hand, if counsel is highly confident about prevailing before such a state administrative tribunal (and also confident that the federal civil rights claim will not be precluded by res judicata), it may be tactically advantageous to pursue the state administrative remedy. In that event the agency's favorable fact findings may be accorded issue preclusive effect in the subsequent civil rights action, easing the plaintiff's burden of proof. By all means be lucky; by all means be wary as well.

But what if the particular federal statute under which the plaintiff wishes to proceed *mandates* prior resort to state administrative remedies

---

18. *Felder v. Casey*, 487 U.S. 131, 108 S.Ct. 2302, 101 L.Ed.2d 123 (1988).

19. A state administrative *agency* likely would have jurisdiction to entertain only the state, not the federal cause of action.

20. Restatement (Second) of Judgments, § 24.

21. The plaintiff in *University of Tennessee v. Elliott, supra* note 15, voluntarily initiated the state administrative proceedings that later cast a shadow on his federal court action under § 1983.

22. *See* 28 U.S.C.A. § 1367(a) and (c), discussed below.

as a prerequisite to asserting the federal law claim in (state or federal) court? Although *Patsy* relieves the Reconstruction Act plaintiff of any such requirement, the major employment discrimination statutes, Title VII and ADEA (but not EPA), require the filing of charges with state or local, as well as federal, antidiscrimination agencies in the vast majority of states that have parallel laws, procedures and remedies consistent with federal standards.[23] The Supreme Court has avoided a Catch–22 situation by holding that the employment discrimination plaintiff who resorts to a state administrative tribunal only to the extent mandated by federal law will not be claim precluded and may proceed to court for a trial de novo.[24] But even this decision had a peculiar new-federalist twist. If the plaintiff seeks review of the state antidiscrimination agency's ruling in state *court*—more resort to state process than the federal statutes demand—she runs the full risks of preclusion under the Full Faith and Credit Statute.[25]

Even the historic federal habeas writ, long a bulwark against unconstitutional state excesses, now stands, at least in relative terms, as something of an obstacle rather than an aid to the enforcement of federal constitutional rights. Current state prisoners desirous of using § 1983 to secure immediate or early release from state incarceration,[26] and current or former state prisoners seeking *any* § 1983 relief, even damages, that depends upon showing the invalidity of their underlying state convictions,[27] are now *compelled* to repair instead to federal habeas. And because the federal habeas statute mandates prior resort to state habeas remedies,[28] the upshot of these decisions is to provide state tribunals (or possibly a federal habeas court) the first and, given the likelihood of preclusion,[29] probably the only opportunity to review these federal constitutional claims.

Consider, then, the hardy, lucky or shrewd plaintiff who has threaded all these needles and gets to federal court. Even there, the litigation of her Reconstruction Act claims (but not claims of employment discrimination) will to some degree be impaired by the brooding omnipresence of state law. The Supreme Court has interpreted a remedial provision that pertains to all the Reconstruction Acts [30] to require that important quasi-substantive state rules—governing limitations periods [31], tolling circum-

---

23. *See* Chapter V, on Title VII procedures.

24. *Kremer v. Chemical Construction Corp.*, 456 U.S. 461, 102 S.Ct. 1883, 72 L.Ed.2d 262 (1982) (Title VII).

25. *Id.*

26. *Preiser v. Rodriguez*, 411 U.S. 475, 93 S.Ct. 1827, 36 L.Ed.2d 439 (1973); *Wolff v. McDonnell*, 418 U.S. 539, 94 S.Ct. 2963, 41 L.Ed.2d 935 (1974).

27. *Heck v. Humphrey*, 512 U.S. 477, 114 S.Ct. 2364, 129 L.Ed.2d 383 (1994) (holding legally insufficient a § 1983 claim analogous to malicious prosecution because

the plaintiff's proof would have to impugn his underlying criminal conviction).

28. 28 U.S.C.A. § 2254(b).

29. Why the Court's opinion in *Heck v. Humphrey* supports the conclusion in text is discussed in detail later in this chapter after introduction of the subjects of issue and claim preclusion. *See* §§ 13.20 and 13.21, especially at text accompanying note 31, § 13.21.

30. 42 U.S.C.A. § 1988.

31. *Wilson v. Garcia*, 471 U.S. 261, 105 S.Ct. 1938, 85 L.Ed.2d 254 (1985).

stances [32], and survivorship of actions [33], for example—are applicable in actions under those statutes in federal as well as state court. And will the federal judgment be accorded the same extensive preclusive effect that the Court insists federal courts accord state tribunals? The answer is not yet clear, but there are hints that it may be "No." The Court has recently raised the possibility, for example, that the diminishing class of state prisoners' claims still assertable under § 1983 rather than remitted to state and federal habeas corpus may generate judgments of doubtful potency. Federal preclusion law, the Court wrote, may take account of the policy of deference to state habeas that is embodied in the federal habeas statute, so that "preclusion [of state courts based on prior federal court findings] will not necessarily be an automatic, or even a permissible, effect." [34]

Finally, worthy of note, is an incipient development parallel to the Court's reinvigoration of federalism. Should this development ripen, it promises to oust significant additional numbers of employment discrimination and perhaps even Reconstruction Act claims from the federal (and state) courts. In recent years the Court, turning aside from an ancient judicial suspicion, has begun to countenance the arbitration of claims asserting federal statutory rights. To be sure, the extant authority is clear that an agreement to arbitrate, otherwise enforceable under the Federal Arbitration Act, cannot prevent a Reconstruction Act claimant from having her day in court. [35] But in a limited, noncollectively bargained setting where the agreement to arbitrate was not contained in the employment contract itself, the Court has stayed age discrimination litigation pending arbitration. [36] It remains to be seen if the Court will (1) extend this holding to bar statutory employment discrimination litigation under ADEA or Title VII once arbitration is completed; (2) permit arbitration agreements to delay or altogether preclude litigation when they are contained in employment contracts; and, (3) if so, adhere to precedent that holds arbitration awards ineffective to prevent de novo litigation of claims under Title VII where the agreement to arbitrate was collectively bargained. [37]

32. *Board of Regents v. Tomanio*, 446 U.S. 478, 100 S.Ct. 1790, 64 L.Ed.2d 440 (1980).

33. *Robertson v. Wegmann*, 436 U.S. 584, 98 S.Ct. 1991, 56 L.Ed.2d 554 (1978).

34. *Heck v. Humphrey, supra* note 29, at ___, 114 S.Ct. at 2373 & n. 9.

35. *McDonald v. City of West Branch*, 466 U.S. 284, 104 S.Ct. 1799, 80 L.Ed.2d 302 (1984).

36. *Gilmer v. Interstate/Johnson Lane Corp.*, 500 U.S. 20, 111 S.Ct. 1647, 114 L.Ed.2d 26 (1991).

37. *Alexander v. Gardner–Denver Co.*, 415 U.S. 36, 94 S.Ct. 1011, 39 L.Ed.2d 147 (1974). The variety of possible judicial resolutions of these questions is surveyed in Chapter 5 on Title VII procedures.

The value served here is not federalism, of course—at its broadest, deference to arbitral awards would preclude state as well as federal litigation—but easing calendar congestion at all levels of the nation's judiciary. In refusing to permit agreements to arbitrate to preclude access to judicial fora with respect to Reconstruction Act claims, the Court questioned the competence and legitimacy of arbitrators to provide authoritative resolutions of Congressionally declared rights.[38] Ironically, if arbitration should come to foreclose judicial litigation of most employment discrimination claims, but the authority denying that effect to collectively bargained arbitration agreements remains as an exception, the group of claimants arguably least in need of judicial protection—those represented by a union—would be the only ones to whom the judicial forum would remain open.

38. *McDonald v. City of West Branch,* 466 U.S. 284, 104 S.Ct. 1799, 80 L.Ed.2d 302 (1984).

When a Federal Judicial Forum for § 1983 Claims/Issues Is/Is Not So "Special" That the Plaintiff Has Access, First Access, or Unencumbered Access to It

THE FEDERAL FORUM *IS* SO SPECIAL

— that access is allowed even when defendant has acted in *violation* of *state* law and even when state courts have historically afforded a remedy for such violations: *Monroe v. Pape* (1961)

THE FEDERAL FORUM IS *NOT* SUFFICIENTLY SPECIAL

— to escape the judge-made, comity-driven *Younger* doctrine that counsels federal court dismissal of § 1983 actions seeking to enjoin or otherwise interfere with state criminal, important civil and even administrative proceedings in which the § 1983 plaintiff can conceivably raise the federal issue. *Younger* may apply whether the state proceedings were pending before or initiated after the commencement of the federal court § 1983 action, provided that the state proceeding was not instituted in manifest bad faith: *Younger v. Harris* (1971); *Hicks v. Miranda* (1975) (applying doctrine to later-filed state proceedings); *Trainor v. Hernandez* (1977) (applying doctrine to civil judicial proceedings); *Middlesex County Ethics Comm. v. Garden State Bar Ass'n* (1982) (applying doctrine to administrative proceedings); *Pennzoil Co. v. Texaco, Inc.,* 481 U.S. 1, 107 S.Ct. 1519, 95 L.Ed.2d 1 (1987) (establishing presumption that the federal issue can be raised in the state proceeding); *Samuels v. Mackell,* 401 U.S. 66, 91 S.Ct. 764, 27 L.Ed.2d 688 (1971) (extending abstention doctrine to federal actions seeking only declaratory not injunctive relief); *cf. Deakins v. Monaghan,* 484 U.S. 193, 108 S.Ct. 523, 98 L.Ed.2d 529 (1988) (approving stay of federal damages action pending conclusion of earlier commenced state grand jury proceedings).

— that § 1983 is an exception to the *categorical* ban of the Anti–Injunction Act against federal court interference with prior pending state judicial proceedings: *Mitchum v. Foster* (1972)

— to warrant an exception to collateral estoppel (*issue* preclusion) once state judicial or quasi-judicial administrative proceedings have gone to judgment or decision, in subsequent federal court actions under § 1983: *Allen v. McCurry* (1980) (estoppel under 28 U.S.C. § 1728 bars prisoner's challenge through § 1983 action to underly-

THE FEDERAL FORUM *IS* SO SPE-
CIAL

THE FEDERAL FORUM IS *NOT*
SUFFICIENTLY SPECIAL

ing conviction, even when federal
court habeas corpus not available);
University of Tennessee v. Elliott
(1986) (judge-made extension of
collateral estoppel where fact finding made in quasi-judicial state administrative proceedings)

— that § 1983 plaintiffs (excluding
some adult state prisoners) need
not exhaust available state administrative proceedings before filing
suit under § 1983: *Patsy v. Florida Bd. of Regents* (1982)

— to warrant an exception to res judicata (*claim* preclusion), if plaintiff has earlier filed a state court
civil action or counterclaim based
on federal *or* state law and arising
from the same transaction that
gives rise to the § 1983 claim: *Migra v. Warren City School District
Bd. of Education* (1984)

— that the § 1983 item may proceed
notwithstanding a prior adverse
arbitration award: *McDonald v.
City of West Branch, Mi.* (1984)

— to permit a challenge to the validity of a state criminal conviction
through a § 1983 action until and
unless that conviction is first overturned on direct review in state
court or on collateral attack by
means of federal (and accordingly
prior state) habeas corpus: *Preiser v. Rodriguez* (1973) (§ 1983 action sought release or early release
from incarceration); *Heck v. Humphrey* (1994) (§ 1983 action sought
only damages)

— that after *Pullman* abstention, the
plaintiff may return to federal
court to pursue a § 1983 claim
first commenced there: *England
v. Louisiana State Bd. of Medical
Examiners* (1964)

B.   FEDERAL SUBJECT MATTER JURISDICTION

Library References:

C.J.S. Federal Courts §§ 4(1, 2), 6.
West's Key No. Digests, Federal Courts ☞3 et seq.

§ 13.2   Original Jurisdiction

Two of the Reconstruction Act statutes, 42 U.S.C.A. §§ 1983 and 1985, create remedies only, for claims based on independently created rights; §§ 1981 and 1982 create rights; but none of these statutes confers federal court jurisdiction. Federal court jurisdiction proceeds from 28 U.S.C.A. § 1331, the federal question jurisdictional statute. Congress also added a separate statute, 28 U.S.C.A. § 1343, which provides for original jurisdiction in "any civil action" brought to "redress the deprivation, under color of State law, ... of any right ... secured by the Constitution ... or by any *Act of Congress providing for equal rights* of citizens ..." (emphasis added). The Court read this language to give jurisdiction only where the right being abridged is one granted in the Constitution or in a statute intended to secure equal rights, not simply any civil right.[1] Narrow construction of § 1343 had relevance only when § 1331 had a $10,000 amount in controversy requirement; since the elimination of that requirement for federal questions in December of 1980, civil rights plaintiffs have pleaded jurisdiction under § 1331 alone, or in combination with § 1343. There appears to be no advantage to invoking § 1343 as the basis for federal subject matter jurisdiction in civil rights claims. Contemporary employment discrimination statutes contain their own express authorizations of federal subject matter jurisdiction, although it is not clear what these add to § 1331 shorn of its amount in controversy requirement.[2]

The plaintiff should take care, however, especially when she also asserts claims under state law, to allege that her federal law claim "arises under" the predicate Reconstruction Act or employment discrimination statute. The Supreme Court has insisted that in order to invoke federal subject matter jurisdiction, the plaintiff's right to relief must be created by or at a minimum depend on federal law.[3] The allegations of a right under federal law may not be "wholly insubstantial and frivolous" (for example, negated by recent authoritative precedent) or "immaterial" (for example, a federal claim "tail" wagging a "dog" composed of multiple state law claims of greater magnitude).[4] In recent years the Court has shown reluctance to recognize federal question jurisdiction of

---

§ 13.2

1. *Chapman v. Houston Welfare Rights Organization*, 441 U.S. 600, 99 S.Ct. 1905, 60 L.Ed.2d 508 (1979); *Maine v. Thiboutot*, 448 U.S. 1, 100 S.Ct. 2502, 65 L.Ed.2d 555 (1980).

2. *See, e.g.,* Title VII § 706(f)(3), 42 U.S.C.A. § 2000e–5(f)(3).

3. *See, e.g., Louisville & Nashville R.R. v. Mottley*, 211 U.S. 149, 29 S.Ct. 42, 53 L.Ed. 126 (1908).

4. *Bell v. Hood*, 327 U.S. 678, 66 S.Ct. 773, 90 L.Ed. 939 (1946).

the district courts based on allegations that a federal statutory standard defines one of the elements of a claim existing solely by virtue of state law.[5] Similarly a defendant may not remove an action (on the basis of a federal question) where plaintiff's state law complaint refers to Title VII merely for such definitional purposes.[6]

§ 13.3   Special Situations Requiring De Facto Exhaustion of State Tribunals as Prerequisite to Asserting the Federal Claim

Unlike actions under Title VII or ADEA, there is no general requirement of exhaustion of administrative remedies before a Reconstruction Act lawsuit may be brought.[1] It is not that unusual, however, for the federal courts to conclude that the plaintiff's federal claims must exclusively, or at least initially, be presented to state *judicial* systems against the plaintiff's wishes.[2] These are now considered in detail.

The Court has in effect mandated prior resort to state judicial tribunals through at least one doctrine that in form does the very different work of narrowing the scope of a particular constitutional right sought to be vindicated under § 1983. The *Parratt* decision, discussed in the § 1983 Chapter, is a good example. It and its progeny make the availability of a federal forum to consider a procedural due process claim challenging "random and unauthorized" action by a government official turn on whether state law provides an adequate remedy. If so, and assuming no diversity of citizenship, such a plaintiff is in effect required to proceed in the state courts under state law and will have no federal law claim to pursue elsewhere.

More commonly, though, a tangle of interrelated procedural doctrines remits putative § 1983 plaintiffs to state court, leaving them free in theory—a possibility undermined in practice by estoppel doctrines and the plaintiff's sheer weariness—to pursue a federal court § 1983 claim

---

5. *See Merrell Dow Pharmaceuticals Inc. v. Thompson,* 478 U.S. 804, 106 S.Ct. 3229, 92 L.Ed.2d 650 (1986).

6. *Rains v. Criterion Systems, Inc.,* 80 F.Ed.2d 339 (9th Cir.1996).

§ 13.3

1. *Patsy v. Board of Regents,* 457 U.S. 496, 516, 102 S.Ct. 2557, 2568, 73 L.Ed.2d 172 (1982) (holding that no mandatory exhaustion of state administrative remedies is required).

2. *See, e.g., Heck v. Humphrey,* 512 U.S. 477, 114 S.Ct. 2364, 129 L.Ed.2d 383 (1994); *Preiser v. Rodriguez,* 411 U.S. 475, 93 S.Ct. 1827, 36 L.Ed.2d 439 (1973) (requiring a state prisoner who invokes § 1983 either to obtain immediate or earlier release from incarceration (*Preiser*) or any relief, including damages, that depends on neces-

sarily invalidating his state conviction (*Heck*), to pursue exclusive remedy of federal habeas corpus relief under 28 U.S.C.A. § 2254 and, hence, to resort first to state court); *Younger v. Harris,* 401 U.S. 37, 54, 91 S.Ct. 746, 755, 27 L.Ed.2d 669 (1971) (banning federal injunctive relief that would impede prior pending state criminal proceedings); *Trainor v. Hernandez,* 431 U.S. 434, 97 S.Ct. 1911, 52 L.Ed.2d 486 (1977) (banning federal declaratory relief that would impede prior pending state civil proceedings); *Railroad Comm'n of Texas v. Pullman Co.,* 312 U.S. 496, 61 S.Ct. 643, 85 L.Ed. 971 (1941) (declaring a doctrine of abstention that, theoretically at least, merely postpones the exercise of federal jurisdiction when state court clarification of uncertain state law might obviate the necessity of a federal constitutional ruling).

later. In *Preiser v. Rodriguez*,[3] for example, the Court ruled that when prisoners invoke § 1983 seeking immediate release or a shortened period of imprisonment, and not simply relief stemming from the conditions of their confinement, federal habeas corpus under 28 U.S.C.A. § 2254 is their exclusive federal remedy. Under the terms of that statute, in turn, they must first resort to state court to pursue the state's own habeas remedy. Indeed the Court so held in *Preiser* even though the conduct complained of under § 1983 related not to the underlying criminal trial but to the action of state prison officials in reducing the plaintiff's good-time credits.

In *Heck v. Humphrey*[4], the Court has recently extended *Preiser* by holding § 1983 unavailable whenever, regardless of the relief sought, the claim of a prisoner or former prisoner, in order to succeed, must necessarily invalidate an underlying state conviction. Section 1983, in other words, may only be used to challenge the validity of only those criminal convictions that have been set aside by the state's appellate courts or a state habeas tribunal or called into question on federal habeas.[5] The Court based this conclusion principally on the common law requirement prevailing when § 1983 was enacted that the tort of malicious prosecution could lie only if the underlying proceeding had terminated favorably to the plaintiff.[6] Although the court's notion is essentially one of prematurity—the § 1983 claim is not ripe unless and until the state conviction has been overturned—it took pains to describe the ground on which such an action should be dismissed as legally insufficient. Given the confusion about characterizing the nature of the *Heck* objection, it is not surprising that lower courts are split as to whether dismissal for *Heck* reasons is with or without prejudice.[7]

The potential reach of *Heck* may turn on how directly or comprehensively a § 1983 claim must call into question an unreversed, undisturbed state criminal conviction in order to be deemed legally insufficient. Even at the perceived extremes, the answers are no longer easy. A prisoner's challenge to the conditions of her confinement does not implicate the validity of the underlying conviction at all. Correlatively, prisoners' § 1983 claims predicated on unconstitutional conditions of confinement will *not* be claim precluded by a previous habeas proceeding.

---

3. 411 U.S. 475, 93 S.Ct. 1827, 36 L.Ed.2d 439 (1973).

4. 512 U.S. 477, 114 S.Ct. 2364, 129 L.Ed.2d 383 (1994).

5. Applying *Heck*, an appellate court has ordered a civil rights action remanded to permit the inmate-plaintiff to try to demonstrate that the conviction challenged in federal court had been invalidated. It was possible, the court wrote, that the subject conviction had been set aside but that the inmate had been convicted again upon retrial. *Bell v. Peters*, 33 F.3d 18 (7th Cir. 1994). *See also Davis v. Zain*, 79 F.3d 18 (5th Cir.1996) (per curiam) (pending retrial

no bar to § 1983 action where state would not re-use tainted evidence that led to plaintiff's reversed conviction).

6. 512 U.S. at ___, 114 S.Ct. at 2370.

7. *Compare Arvie v. Broussard*, 42 F.3d 249 (5th Cir.1994) (per curiam) (with prejudice) *with Williams v. Schario*, 93 F.3d 527 (8th Cir.1996) *and Fottler v. United States*, 73 F.3d 1064 (10th Cir.1996) (without prejudice). As the caption of *Fottler* would suggest, the *Heck* doctrine has been extended to "*Bivens*" claims of unconstitutional conduct against federal officers. *Williams v. Hill*, 74 F.3d 1339 (D.C.Cir.1996) (per curiam).

For claim preclusion ("res judicata") purposes, that is, a claim challenging the underlying trial or administrative handling of a prisoner's good-time credits, on the one hand, and, on the other, a claim challenging unconstitutional conditions, are distinct.[8] Of course, despite the failure of claim preclusion, issue preclusion ("collateral estoppel") remains a potential impediment to the success of the subsequent action under § 1983 if previous judicial or quasi-judicial proceedings have generated factfindings on common issues. Notwithstanding these apparently sharp lines, recent appellate decisions are in conflict about the application of *Heck* to conditions of confinement disputes that lead to prison disciplinary proceedings and consequently to prisoners' loss of good time credits, or to other determinations that effectively extend their sentences.[9]

In contrast, a successful § 1983 claim challenging the admission of particular evidence or the testimony of a police officer that was critical to a finding of guilt would squarely unsettle the foundation of a conviction, and *Heck* would thus bar the door. Suppose it is not clear, though, whether the testimony or evidence collaterally attacked by means of the action under Section 1983 was in fact necessary to the conviction? Surely the Court will recognize that possibility, which is akin to the Court's ever expanding concept of "harmless error." How, after the fact, in a subsequent state or federal court proceeding under § 1983, can the plaintiff demonstrate that the federally unlawful conduct for which she seeks damages was not instrumental to her conviction, or how can the defendant moving to dismiss under *Heck* demonstrate the contrary?

These questions are surfacing in the early appellate decisions in the wake of *Heck*. In one case claims based on allegations that police officers committed perjury and coerced witnesses to wrongfully identify the § 1983 plaintiff (as a criminal) were held barred by *Heck* absent evidence that the conviction had been invalidated; but a claim against another officer asserting cruel and unusual punishment for placing the plaintiff in a particular holding cell did not implicate the conviction's

8. *Rhodes v. Hannigan*, 12 F.3d 989 (10th Cir.1993).

9. *Compare Sheldon v. Hundley*, 83 F.3d 231 (8th Cir.1996) *and Miller v. Indiana Dep't of Corrections*, 75 F.3d 330 (7th Cir. 1996) (the "conviction" that would be undermined by the prisoner's claim includes, for *Heck* purposes, administrative rulings concerning prison discipline that have the effect of lengthening an inmate's sentence) *with Balisok v. Edwards*, 70 F.3d 1277 (9th Cir.1995) (unpublished), *cert. granted,* — U.S —, 116 S.Ct. 1564, 134 L.Ed.2d 664 (1996) *and Armento–Bey v. Harper*, 68 F.3d 215 (8th Cir.1995) *and Woods v. Smith*, 60 F.3d 1161 (5th Cir.1995), *cert. denied,* — U.S. —, 116 S.Ct. 800, 133 L.Ed.2d 747 (1996) (assuming or deciding that challenges to prison disciplinary procedures do not call into question the lawfulness of the underlying conviction and are therefore not barred by *Heck*). *Cf. Gotcher v. Wood*, 66 F.3d 1097 (9th Cir.1995) (prisoner due process challenge to procedures used in disciplinary proceedings resulting in loss of good time credits not barred by *Heck* but permissible under *Wolff v. McDonnell*, 418 U.S. 539, 94 S.Ct. 2963, 41 L.Ed.2d 935 (1974), because claim did not call into question the lawfulness of the denial of good time credits or therefore of the duration of continuing confinement). *See also Bulger v. United States Bureau of Prisons*, 65 F.3d 48 (5th Cir.1995) (losing the mere ability to accrue good-time credits automatically does not inevitably affect the duration or fundamental nature of a prisoner's sentence as required by *Sandin v. Conner*, — U.S. —, 115 S.Ct. 2293, 132 L.Ed.2d 418 (1995), and thus does not deprive prisoner of a liberty interest).

validity and hence escaped the *Heck* bar.[10] The Fifth Circuit faced a more difficult task in sorting out the claims of another § 1983 plaintiff that he had been falsely arrested (for disorderly conduct and resisting a search) in the absence of probable cause; that the arresting officers had used excessive force; and that he had been maliciously prosecuted. The court held the false arrest and malicious prosecution claims not cognizable by virtue of *Heck,* because to some degree at least both of those claims implied the invalidity of the initiation of the criminal process and in turn of the criminal conviction. By contrast, the court considered it apparent that even if the plaintiff could demonstrate that the arresting officers used excessive force, a § 1983 judgment on that ground would not demonstrate the invalidity of the criminal judgment and accordingly could proceed notwithstanding *Heck.*[11]

On at least two occasions the Fifth Circuit's opinion recites that a determination in the § 1983 action that the challenged conduct is unlawful need only "imply" the invalidity of the conviction. Yet on two other occasions the opinion recites that such a determination must "necessarily imply" the conviction's invalidity before *Heck* would stand in the way. The false arrest claim was held legally insufficient in its entirety even though the plaintiff was convicted only for resisting the search, not for disorderly conduct. The *Heck* inquiry should focus, the court reasoned, on the validity of the arrest that was challenged by the § 1983 claim, not the outcome of the charges springing from that arrest. To win his § 1983 false arrest claim, the plaintiff would have had to show no probable cause to arrest him on either charge, which in turn would have demonstrated the invalidity of his conviction for resisting search, thereby triggering *Heck.*

The most numerically important of the de facto procedural deferral situations are governed by the doctrine of *Younger v. Harris,*[12] which bans federal injunctive relief considered likely to intrude on prior pending state criminal proceedings. Purportedly to implement *Younger* and *Heck,* a recent appellate decision expands their holdings to bar § 1983 damages relief by former prisoners who bypassed the opportunity to challenge in state court the restrictions on their liberty while they were still confined.[13]

10. *Channer v. Mitchell,* 43 F.3d 786 (2d Cir.1994) (per curiam). A similar split is reflected in *Perez v. Sifel,* 57 F.3d 503 (7th Cir.1995) (claims against officer for improperly procuring plaintiff's conviction barred by *Heck;* illegal search and arrest claims required further evaluation to determine whether, if successful, they would necessarily undermine plaintiff's conviction). *See also Williams v. Schario,* 93 F.3d 527 (8th Cir.1996) (claim alleging that police officer presented false testimony during plaintiff's preliminary hearing and maliciously prosecuted plaintiff dismissed without prejudice until resulting conviction reversed, expunged, or called into question by federal habeas).

11. *Wells v. Bonner,* 45 F.3d 90 (5th Cir.1995); *cf. Johnson v. Bax,* 63 F.3d 154 (2d Cir.1995) (§ 1983 claims that violate arrested plaintiff's First Amendment rights may proceed while false imprisonment and false arrest claims may not).

12. 401 U.S. 37, 54, 91 S.Ct. 746, 755, 27 L.Ed.2d 669 (1971).

13. *Nelson v. Murphy,* 44 F.3d 497 (7th Cir.1995).

Of course, *Heck* stands as a bar to the § 1983 action only where there is an outstanding criminal judgment. There may be related bars where state criminal or important civil proceedings are pending at or after the commencement of the § 1983 action. Thus, as the following section describes, the *Younger* doctrine may compel dismissal of § 1983 claims seeking equitable or, as elaborated in *Samuels v. Mackell,* declaratory relief that would interfere with such proceedings. Moreover, even if the § 1983 plaintiff seeks only damages, her action may be stayed pending resolution of ongoing state criminal proceedings under the Court's decision in *Deakins v. Monaghan.*[14]

C. YOUNGER NONINTERVENTION

Library References:

> C.J.S. Federal Courts §§ 10(1) et seq.
> West's Key No. Digests, Federal Courts ☞48.

§ 13.4 State Proceedings

a. *Criminal*

Federal courts must dismiss constitutional challenges to pending[1] state criminal proceedings brought under 42 U.S.C.A. § 1983, unless extraordinary circumstances are shown to exist. Expressly declining to rest its decision on the Anti–Injunction Act, 28 U.S.C.A. § 2283, to which § 1983 was found to be an exception a year later in *Mitchum v. Foster,*[2] the Court in *Younger v. Harris*[3] fashioned this noninterference policy based on considerations of equity and comity that it termed "our federalism".[4] Traditional doctrines of equity, said the Court, preclude restraint of an existing criminal prosecution "when the movant has an adequate remedy at law and will not suffer irreparable injury if denied equitable relief." Moreover, principles of federalism and comity, "that is, a proper respect for state functions," prevent "undue interference with legitimate activities of the States." Drawing upon these principles, the Court established a firm bar to federal intervention in ongoing state criminal proceedings when the federal plaintiff has an opportunity to raise his constitutional challenges as a defense to the state prosecution.

The *Younger* doctrine does, however, recognize a number of exceptions. Federal interference with a pending criminal prosecution would be justified if the threat of irreparable injury is "both great and immediate" and "cannot be eliminated by his defense against a single criminal

---

14. 484 U.S. 193, 108 S.Ct. 523, 98 L.Ed.2d 529 (1988). Both *Younger* and *Deakins* principles were recently so applied in *Simpson v. Rowan,* 73 F.3d 134 (7th Cir.1995).

§ 13.4

1. For when an action is "pending," see § 13.5.

2. 407 U.S. 225, 92 S.Ct. 2151, 32 L.Ed.2d 705 (1972).

3. 401 U.S. 37, 91 S.Ct. 746, 27 L.Ed.2d 669 (1971).

4. *Id.* at 43, 91 S.Ct. at 750.

prosecution." [5] But in *Younger* itself the Supreme Court denied any categorical exception for First Amendment claims, rejecting the assertion that impeding the plaintiff's path to federal court on such claims inevitably results in irreparable injury. Instead, the Court explained, the exceptions must be truly exceptional: provable prosecutorial bad faith or harassment warrants federal interference, as do other extraordinary circumstances like challenges to state statutes that are "flagrantly and patently violative of express constitutional prohibitions in every clause, sentence, and paragraph." [6]

b. Quasi-Criminal: State a Party

The Supreme Court first extended *Younger* to the civil setting in a quasi-criminal matter to which the State was a party. In *Huffman v. Pursue, Ltd.*,[7] the Court determined that *Younger* prohibited a federal civil rights action from interfering with a state civil nuisance proceeding. The Court characterized the proceeding as "both in aid of and closely related to criminal statutes which prohibit the dissemination of obscene materials." Federal court interference might result in duplicative proceedings, could be interpreted "as reflecting negatively upon the state court's ability to enforce constitutional principles," [8] and would thus constitute "an offense to the State's interest ... likely to be every bit as great as it would be were this a criminal proceeding."

c. Civil: State a Party

In *Trainor v. Hernandez*,[9] the Court clarified that *Younger* and *Huffman* apply to all civil proceedings regardless of their nature so long as the State is a party.[10] The Court emphasized that "the State was a party to the suit in its role of administering its public-assistance programs" and was vindicating "important state policies such as safeguarding the fiscal integrity of those programs." Relying again on the *Younger* principles of federalism and comity, the Court reasoned that a federal injunction of a state civil enforcement suit would also result in duplicative proceedings, would disrupt suits by the State in its sovereign capacity, and would reflect negatively on the State's ability to adjudicate federal claims. Absent extraordinary circumstances warranting federal equitable relief, concluded the Court, "the principles of *Younger* and *Huffman* are broad enough to apply to interference by a federal court with an ongoing civil enforcement action such as this, brought by the State in its sovereign capacity."

---

5. *Id.* at 44, 91 S.Ct. at 751.

6. When the § 1983 claim is presented after the conclusion of a state court trial, however, *Younger* has been construed to bar a federal court from proceeding even when the plaintiff alleges that the underlying prosecution was undertaken in bad faith. The Fifth Circuit reasoned that the § 1983 action would then impermissibly entail review of the state court's judgment. *Musslewhite v. State Bar of Texas*, 32 F.3d 942 (5th Cir.1994).

7. 420 U.S. 592, 95 S.Ct. 1200, 43 L.Ed.2d 482 (1975).

8. *See Steffel v. Thompson*, 415 U.S. 452, 94 S.Ct. 1209, 39 L.Ed.2d 505 (1974).

9. 431 U.S. 434, 97 S.Ct. 1911, 52 L.Ed.2d 486 (1977).

10. The Court forbade lower federal courts from issuing declaratory relief that would impede prior pending state civil proceedings.

A federal appellate court has recently applied these principles in upholding the dismissal under *Younger* of an action by a mobile home park owner *against* a municipal entity. The owner challenged the city's rent control ordinance in federal court as an unconstitutional taking, after he had initiated a prior state proceeding that he asserted he was required to initiate first to meet the ripeness requirement of the Just Compensation Clause. *Younger* required dismissal, the court concluded, because of the state's substantial interest in its rent control ordinances.[11] The ruling may put a plaintiff who also has other federal claims to the choice of forfeiting either her takings claims (by bypassing state court) or, as in the case at bar, a federal forum for all her federal claims.

d. Civil: State Not a Party, but Important State Interests Involved

1. Judicial Interests

The Court has also extended *Younger* to cases in which the State is not a party, but important state interests are present. Dismissal of the federal action is required, for example, when necessary to assure the integrity of the state's judicial system. In *Juidice v. Vail* ,[12] the Court determined that the State's interest in the contempt process, though not as important as the State's interest in enforcement of its criminal laws,[13] or in the maintenance of a quasi-criminal proceeding,[14] was sufficiently important to warrant federal court nonintervention. Similarly, in *Pennzoil Co. v. Texaco Inc.*,[15] the State's interest in ensuring that its money judgments were executed was sufficiently weighty to require noninterference.

2. Administrative Interests

In *Middlesex County Ethics Comm. v. Garden State Bar Ass'n*,[16] the Court applied *Younger* to administrative proceedings as well. Refusing to allow federal court interference with a pending state bar investigation, conducted under the aegis of a state supreme court, the Court analogized bar disciplinary actions to judicial proceedings and emphasized their "special importance" in maintaining the professionalism of the State's practicing attorneys. In *Hawaii Hous. Auth. v. Midkiff*,[17] the Court refused to apply *Younger* to an administrative proceeding expressly declared by state law not to be part of the state's judicial system. But in *Ohio Civil Rights Comm'n v. Dayton Christian Schools*,[18] the Court resolved any doubt concerning the applicability of *Younger* to adminis-

---

11. *Mission Oaks Mobile Home Park v. Hollister, Calif.*, 989 F.2d 359 (9th Cir. 1993), *cert. denied*, 510 U.S. 1110, 114 S.Ct. 1052, 127 L.Ed.2d 373 (1994).

12. 430 U.S. 327, 97 S.Ct. 1211, 51 L.Ed.2d 376 (1977).

13. *See Younger*, *supra* note 3.

14. *See Huffman*, *supra* note 7.

15. 481 U.S. 1, 107 S.Ct. 1519, 95 L.Ed.2d 1 (1987).

16. 457 U.S. 423, 102 S.Ct. 2515, 73 L.Ed.2d 116 (1982). *Accord Hirsh v. Justices of Supreme Court of California*, 67 F.3d 708 (9th Cir.1995) (per curiam).

17. 467 U.S. 229, 104 S.Ct. 2321, 81 L.Ed.2d 186 (1984).

18. 477 U.S. 619, 106 S.Ct. 2718, 91 L.Ed.2d 512 (1986).

trative proceedings unconnected with the state judicial system. Federal courts must abstain from interfering with administrative proceedings "in which important state interests are vindicated, so long as in the course of those proceedings the federal plaintiff would have had a full and fair opportunity to litigate his constitutional claim." An exception has been declared where a prior *federal* administrative proceeding with facially conclusive preemptive force is pending before the state administrative proceeding commences. In that situation, it has been held that there can be no significant state interest that would be served by *Younger*-esque abstention because the state agency would be acting in excess of its lawful authority.[19]

§ 13.5 "Pendency"

a. Rationale

Younger and its progeny evince a strong federal policy against most federal court interference with pending state proceedings. Critical to the doctrine is the assumption of parity between federal and state courts in deciding constitutional issues. So long as a pending state proceeding provides the putative civil rights plaintiff an adequate forum in which to present his federal claims, a federal court should avoid reaching the claim itself by dismissing the federal action.

At least initially, the Court refused to dismiss unless it was clear not only that a state proceeding was pending but also that it provided the federal plaintiff with a forum in which his federal claims could in fact be heard. In *Trainor*, for instance, the Court remanded with a direction to address the issue of the federal plaintiffs' opportunity to litigate their constitutional claims in state court. But beginning in *Moore v. Sims*,[1] the Court in effect reversed the presumption about that opportunity, writing that *Younger* nonintervention applies "unless state law clearly bars the interposition of the constitutional claims."[2] But at least the Court there undertook an independent examination of that question, concluding that the plaintiffs had failed to present their federal issue by way of counterclaim, as state law apparently permitted.[3] By contrast in *Pennzoil Co. v. Texaco, Inc.*,[4] the Court dismissed the federal action even though it was unclear whether state procedure would permit presentation of plaintiff's constitutional claims. The Court substituted for searching inquiry the strong presumption that a federal plaintiff can

---

19. *Chaulk Servs., Inc. v. Massachusetts Comm'n Against Discrimination*, 70 F.3d 1361 (1st Cir.1995), cert. denied __ U.S. __, 116 S.Ct. 2525, 135 L.Ed.2d 1049 (1996) (distinguishing *New Orleans Public Serv., Inc. v. Council of the City of New Orleans*, 491 U.S. 350, 109 S.Ct. 2506, 105 L.Ed.2d 298 (1989), as holding that *Younger* abstention applies when plaintiff mounts a "substantial," but not "facially

conclusive," constitutional challenge to the state proceedings).

§ 13.5

1. 442 U.S. 415, 99 S.Ct. 2371, 60 L.Ed.2d 994 (1979).

2. *Id.* at 425–426, 99 S.Ct. at 2378–79.

3. *Id.* at n.9.

4. 481 U.S. 1, 107 S.Ct. 1519, 95 L.Ed.2d 1 (1987).

raise a constitutional claim in a pending state proceeding unless it "plainly appears" from "unambiguous authority to the contrary" that she cannot.[5]

b. Absence of Pending State Proceedings

When no state proceeding is pending at the time the federal complaint is filed, *Younger* is inapplicable. Federal interference cannot then result in duplicative proceedings or reflect negatively upon the competency of state courts to resolve constitutional issues. Even though as discussed in subpart "f." following, *Younger* dismissal is available even though the state prosecution was initiated after commencement of the federal action, the state prosecution must in fact be pending, not merely predictably possible.[6] Moreover, dismissal by a federal court "may place the hapless plaintiff between the Scylla of intentionally flouting state law and the Charybdis of foregoing what he believes to be constitutionally protected activity in order to avoid becoming enmeshed in a criminal proceeding."[7] But even if a federal court finds *Younger* inapplicable, relief may still be denied if the federal plaintiff fails to meet justiciability requirements by not presenting a live and continuing controversy. To determine standing to sue, the Court focuses on the nature of the threat encountered by plaintiff.

c. Actual Threats of Prosecution

Actual threats of prosecution can provide the federal plaintiff with a claim capable of surviving both justiciability and *Younger* requirements. In *Steffel*, the Court held that relief could be provided by a federal court if plaintiff had actually been threatened with prosecution, but was not then subject to a pending state proceeding. The actual threat of prosecution provided the continuing and live controversy required for standing.

d. Implied or Apparent Threats of Prosecution

Federal relief is also available, despite *Younger*, in situations involving only imminent implied or apparent threats of prosecution. In *Doran v. Salem Inn, Inc.*,[8] plaintiffs sought federal relief against a newly enacted ordinance prohibiting topless dancing. Two of the three plaintiffs complied with the ordinance while seeking federal relief, but the third violated it and was subjected to state prosecution. Relying on *Steffel*, the Court held that *Younger* did not bar a grant of federal relief to the two complying plaintiffs, against whom no state prosecution was

---

5. *Id.* at 14, 107 S.Ct. at 1527.

6. *Agriesti v. MGM Grand Hotels*, 53 F.3d 1000 (9th Cir.1995). And the state proceeding must be pending against the federal civil plaintiff. Thus, *Younger* abstention was held inapplicable where the child welfare citizens' advocacy group that sued under § 1983 was never made a party to the particular state court child custody case that generated the gag orders the group challenged as unconstitutional. *FOCUS v.*

Allegheny Court of Common Pleas, 75 F.3d 834 (3d Cir.1996). In this way, the liberal approach to standing that enabled the citizens group to challenge the gag orders on free speech grounds, see section "G," below, facilitates an end-run of the *Younger* bar.

7. *See Steffel, supra* § 13.4, note 8.

8. 422 U.S. 922, 95 S.Ct. 2561, 45 L.Ed.2d 648 (1975).

or could be pending. Furthermore, *Younger* did not require dismissal simply because the complying plaintiff's claims presented the same issue as that of the third, noncomplying plaintiff. Again, the threat of prosecution, in this case an imminent implied or apparent one, satisfied justiciability requirements.

e. *Unmatured Threats of Prosecution*

Although actual or apparent threats of prosecution can provide grounds for federal relief, claims may not be based on simply speculative threats. These claims invariably fall victim to the justiciability requirements of Article III.[9] In *Younger* itself, the Court dismissed the claims of three intervenors who alleged that the state law in question made them "feel inhibited" in advocating or teaching certain political ideologies. And in *Juidice*, the Court dismissed the claims of plaintiffs who had already been prosecuted under the challenged contempt statute, had paid their fines, and had not alleged a threat of further prosecution. The Court in both *Younger* and *Juidice* found the claims failed to present a live and continuing controversy.

f. *After-Filed Pending State Proceedings*

Even if the federal plaintiff meets justiciability requirements, a state prosecutor may still effectively abort the federal action by initiating a state prosecution thereafter.[10] In *Hicks* and *Doran*, the Court dismissed plaintiffs' federal claims when state prosecutions were initiated against plaintiffs a day after their suits were filed in federal court. Emphasizing that the initiation of state proceedings provided plaintiffs a forum in which to adjudicate their constitutional claims, the Court held that federal courts must dismiss if state proceedings are begun prior to any "proceedings of substance on the merits" on the federal claim, *Hicks*, or when "the federal litigation [is] in its embryonic stage and no contested matter [has] been decided."[11] In *Midkiff*, the Court, without deciding whether the issuance of a federal restraining order was substantial in this sense, did decide that the grant of a preliminary injunction brought the federal action past the "embryonic stage" of litigation.

g. *State Proceedings Pending on Appeal*

A state proceeding may sometimes be found still pending even after a final state judgment has been rendered against the federal plaintiff. In *Huffman*, for instance, plaintiff sought relief in federal court, rather than appeal within the state system. The Court, recognizing the finality of the state judgment, nevertheless invoked *Younger* noninterference. Intervention with the State's appellate proceedings, noted the Court, would be "even more disruptive and offensive because the State [had] already won a *nisi prius* determination that its valid policies are being violated in a fashion which justifies judicial abatement." In *Wooley v.*

---

9. *See Younger, supra* § 13.4, note 3; *Juidice, supra* § 13.4, note 12.

10. *Hicks v. Miranda,* 422 U.S. 332, 95 S.Ct. 2281, 45 L.Ed.2d 223 (1975); *Doran, supra* note 8.

11. *Doran, supra* note 8.

Maynard,[12] however, the Court found *Younger* inapplicable where the plaintiff, unlike *Huffman*, had not attempted "to annul the results of a state trial" by substituting federal action for a state appeal. Plaintiff in *Wooley* had been repeatedly prosecuted for violation of the same state statute, had acquiesced in previous convictions, and merely sought prospective relief from further prosecution.

§ 13.6   Kinds of Relief Barred

The Court has refused to except particular species of equitable relief from the *Younger* bar on the basis of their lesser intrusiveness. In *Samuels v. Mackell*,[1] for example, the Court declared that "ordinarily a declaratory judgment will result in precisely the same interference with and disruption of state proceedings that the long-standing policy limiting injunctions was designed to avoid." Moreover, in *Pennzoil* and *Doran*, the Court failed to find the grant of a preliminary injunction to be any less intrusive than the imposition of a permanent injunction. Instead, the Court has relied upon its pendency rationale to determine when federal relief is available. When a state proceeding is pending, therefore, federal courts may not grant any form of equitable relief, absent extraordinary circumstances. *Younger* applies, that is, where the federal plaintiff seeks equitable, declaratory or other discretionary relief. It is clearly out of the picture only when damages alone are at stake[2]; and even then the action may be dismissed if damages are contingent on a prior declaration that a state tax scheme is unconstitutional and may therefore no longer be enforced.[3] But if no state proceeding is pending, the federal plaintiff may be granted permanent injunctive, preliminary injunctive or declaratory relief.

D.   THE ELEVENTH AMENDMENT

Library References:

         C.J.S. Federal Courts § 49(3).
         West's Key No. Digests, Federal Courts ☞265.

§ 13.7   In General

Prior to the adoption of the Eleventh Amendment, the Supreme Court had interpreted the case and controversy language of Article III, § 2, which defined federal subject matter jurisdiction to include suits "between a State and Citizens of another state," to permit federal suits between those two parties based on pure diversity.[1] In response to that

---

12. 430 U.S. 705, 710, 97 S.Ct. 1428, 1433, 51 L.Ed.2d 752 (1977).

§ 13.6

1. 401 U.S. 66, 91 S.Ct. 764, 27 L.Ed.2d 688 (1971).

2. *Quackenbush v. Allstate Ins. Co.*, ___ U.S. ___, 116 S.Ct. 1712, 135 L.Ed.2d 1 (1996).

3. *Id.* (citing *National Private Truck Council, Inc. v. Oklahoma Tax Comm'n*, ___ U.S. ___, 115 S.Ct. 2351, 132 L.Ed.2d 509 (1995)).

§ 13.7

1. *Chisholm v. Georgia*, 2 U.S. (2 Dall.) 419, 1 L.Ed. 440 (1793).

decision, Congress promptly enacted the Eleventh Amendment ensuring state sovereign immunity in federal court.

The Eleventh Amendment provides that the "Judicial power of the United States shall not be construed to extend to any suit in law or equity, commenced or prosecuted against one of the United States by Citizens of another State, or by citizens of any foreign state." Applicable only to actions in federal court, the Eleventh Amendment bars suits against a state government by citizens of that state, other states, and foreign states.

The Supreme Court has expanded the scope of the Eleventh Amendment beyond its textual confines to apply to diversity actions involving state citizen plaintiffs, to federal questions, and to pendent claims. Coverage was extended to federal question jurisdiction in *Hans v. Louisiana.*[2] Based on the principle of sovereign immunity, the Court in *Hans* held that the Eleventh Amendment bars suits against a state government by its own citizens. Since by hypothesis original federal subject matter jurisdiction in an action against a state by one of its own citizens must be based on a federal question, one effect of *Hans* is to bar even federal question claims for damages that are asserted against a state by one of its own citizens. Further expansion occurred in *Pennhurst State School & Hosp. v. Halderman,*[3] in which the Supreme Court held that the Eleventh Amendment bars federal courts from determining pendent state law claims.

The Supreme Court has limited the Eleventh Amendment to actions against the state, units of state government, or where a money judgment will be satisfied out of state funds. It does not immunize local government units.[4] Nor does the Eleventh Amendment bar a state court from exercising jurisdiction over a state.[5] Finally, the Eleventh Amendment does not bar the United States government from suing a state in federal court.[6]

The Eleventh Amendment will sometimes not bar suit even if it otherwise applies where the relief sought is wholly prospective, or the state has consented to federal suit, or a congressional act overrides the immunity. Although the state in its own name enjoys Eleventh Amendment protection, the ability to bring suit against a state official (other than in her individual capacity) depends primarily on the type of relief

2. 134 U.S. 1, 10 S.Ct. 504, 33 L.Ed. 842 (1890).

3. 465 U.S. 89, 121, 104 S.Ct. 900, 919, 79 L.Ed.2d 67 (1984).

4. *See e.g., Lincoln Co. v. Luning,* 133 U.S. 529, 530, 10 S.Ct. 363, 363, 33 L.Ed. 766 (1890) (counties); *Workman v. Mayor, Aldermen, and Commonality of N.Y.,* 179 U.S. 552, 574, 21 S.Ct. 212, 220, 45 L.Ed. 314 (1900) (cities); *Mt. Healthy City School Dist. Bd. of Educ. v. Doyle,* 429 U.S. 274, 97 S.Ct. 568, 50 L.Ed.2d 471 (1977) (munici-

palities, school districts); *contra Florida Dept. of Health & Rehabilitative Servs. v. Florida Nursing Home Assn.,* 450 U.S. 147, 101 S.Ct. 1032, 67 L.Ed.2d 132 (1981) (state agencies protected).

5. *Nevada v. Hall,* 440 U.S. 410, 421, 99 S.Ct. 1182, 1188, 59 L.Ed.2d 416 (1979).

6. *United States v. Mississippi,* 380 U.S. 128, 140–41, 85 S.Ct. 808, 814–15, 13 L.Ed.2d 717 (1965).

sought. Under the fiction of *Ex Parte Young*,[7] the Eleventh Amendment does not act as a bar to federal suits naming a state official as defendant so long as the relief sought is characterized as prospective. Under *Edelman v. Jordan*,[8] the Eleventh Amendment permits official capacity actions against individual state agents for prospective relief, even when implementation of the judgment would adversely impact the state treasury, but bars similar actions for relief deemed retrospective.

State law, which should be borrowed as a matter of federal law so long as not inconsistent with federal policy, defines whether an official is considered an officer of the state and therefore immune from federal suit. Courts will interpret whether state law requires a state or local treasury to pay judgments rendered against its officials. In *Carr v. City of Florence, Alabama*,[9] Alabama law regarded the defendant, a county sheriff, as a state officer. The court presumed that the defendant was a state official because the plaintiff failed to present "clear evidence" that any judgment would be paid out of the local treasury rather than a state treasury. Under Florida law, however, a sheriff is considered a county official.[10] As a result, there is no presumption immunizing him. Instead, the defendant sheriff must provide evidence that the judgment would come from state funds rather than a local treasury. In some cases the characterization of the employing entity will be functionally rather than categorically defined. Thus sheriff's officials otherwise clearly county employees received Eleventh Amendment immunity from damages for actions in their official capacity when the court found that they were acting as an arm of the state judicial system in evicting tenants ancillary to a foreclosure action [11]; but sheriffs acting as county rather than state agents could be sued for damages in federal court.[12] A recent Supreme Court decision denying immunity to a bi-state entity created under the Compact Clause confirmed that the touchstone is whether, under state law, a state will bear *financial* responsibility for an adverse judgment against the entity.[13]

7. 209 U.S. 123, 159–60, 28 S.Ct. 441, 454, 52 L.Ed. 714 (1908). *Seminole Tribe of Florida v. Florida*, ___ U.S. ___, 116 S.Ct. 1114, 134 L.Ed.2d 252 (1996), generally reaffirms the vitality of *Ex Parte Young* as permitting prospective injunctive relief against state officials for federal statutory, as well as constitutional, violations. But it also renders the *Young* exception unavailable where the plaintiff complains of the violation of a federal statute that contains its own detailed, administrative remedial scheme and remedies more limited than the full powers of a federal court, including contempt, that would be brought to bear in an action pursuant to *Young*. Lower federal courts have also ousted federal court injunction suits against state officials where there was no specification of threatened enforcement action by the defendants. *See, e.g., Children's Healthcare is a Legal Duty,*

Inc. v. Deters, 1996 WL 435378 (6th Cir. 1996).

8. 415 U.S. 651, 94 S.Ct. 1347, 39 L.Ed.2d 662 (1974).

9. 916 F.2d 1521 (11th Cir.1990).

10. *Hutton v. Strickland,* 919 F.2d 1531 (11th Cir.1990).

11. *Scott v. O'Grady,* 975 F.2d 366 (7th Cir.1992), *cert. denied,* 508 U.S. 942, 113 S.Ct. 2421, 124 L.Ed.2d 643 (1993).

12. *See Ruehman v. Sheahan,* 34 F.3d 525 (7th Cir.1994) (under Illinois law).

13. *Hess v. Port Authority Trans-Hudson Corp.,* ___ U.S. ___, ___, 115 S.Ct. 394, 403–404, 130 L.Ed.2d 245 (1994). The dissent in Hess would alternatively have conferred immunity if a state exercises political or governmental control over the defendant. *Id.* at ___, 115 S.Ct. at 410–411 (O'Connor, J. dissenting).

The line between prospective and retrospective relief is delicate, sometimes appearing to be little more than semantic. For example, in *Milliken v. Bradley*,[14] the Court characterized as prospective the spending of state funds on compensatory educational programs because the funds "were a necessary consequence of compliance in the future with [the court ordered school desegregation plan]."[15] The Court recognized that compliance with the decree would entail a "direct and substantial impact on the state treasury" and that the educational components of the decree, although operating only prospectively, were designed to eliminate continuing conditions of inequality and in that sense could be considered "compensatory." But in *Edelman*'s terms, this additional spending was still only an "ancillary effect" of a plan that operated "*prospectively* to bring about the delayed benefits of a unitary school system." Similarly, a court ordered award of attorneys' fees to be paid by a state treasury was characterized as "ancillary" to prospective relief and therefore not barred by the Eleventh Amendment.[16] By contrast, the Court in *Edelman* itself characterized as retrospective, and hence barred, the payment of wrongfully withheld federal welfare benefits, treating such funds as a form of compensation for past injustices and therefore indistinguishable from an award of money damages against the state.[17] Of course those payments might also have been characterized as "part of a plan that operates *prospectively* to bring about the delayed benefits" of the statutory welfare scheme.

Even when the Eleventh Amendment otherwise applies, the action is against the state itself and the relief is characterized as retrospective, the Eleventh Amendment will not bar suit if a state is held to have consented to be sued in federal court. The Court has held that Congress intended no such consent when it enacted § 1983 in 1871, apparently because it was not until the Court's decision in *Monell* in 1978 that § 1983 was held to apply to cities or counties, let alone states.[18] In any event, the status of § 1983 under the Eleventh Amendment has been mooted by the Court's recent ruling that a state, when sued its own name rather than through one of its officials, is not a "person" suable under § 1983.[19] Accordingly, regardless of the relief sought, the state as such is simply not a proper § 1983 defendant in actions brought in either state or federal court. A recent court of appeals decision extends this principle by holding that a federal court may not remedy a civil rights violation by awarding a county contribution against its state, notwithstanding a general right to contribution under § 1983.[20]

14. 433 U.S. 267, 290, 97 S.Ct. 2749, 2762, 53 L.Ed.2d 745 (1977).

15. *Id.* at 289, 97 S.Ct. at 2762.

16. *Hutto v. Finney*, 437 U.S. 678, 692, 98 S.Ct. 2565, 2574, 57 L.Ed.2d 522 (1978).

17. *Edelman*, *supra* note 8, at 668, 94 S.Ct. at 1358.

18. *See Edelman* as explained by *Fitzpatrick v. Bitzer*, 427 U.S. 445, 456, 96 S.Ct. 2666, 2671, 49 L.Ed.2d 614 (1976); *cf. Quern v. Jordan*, 440 U.S. 332, 99 S.Ct. 1139, 59 L.Ed.2d 358 (1979), reaffirming *Edelman* on a different rationale.

19. *Will v. Michigan Dept. of State Police*, 491 U.S. 58, 109 S.Ct. 2304, 105 L.Ed.2d 45 (1989).

20. *Harris v. Angelina County, Tex.*, 31 F.3d 331 (5th Cir.1994).

In *Will v. Michigan Dept. of State Police*[21], the Supreme Court held, however, that a state official can be a defendant "person" within the meaning of § 1983, even when sued in her official capacity, to the extent that the relief sought against her is of the kind allowed under the Eleventh Amendment jurisprudence exemplified by *Ex parte Young*, *Edelman*, and *Milliken*.[22] The *Will* bifurcated definition of the statutory term "person" as applied to the individual state official is evidently driven by and devolved from the 11th Amendment, yet in turn that definition renders the 11th Amendment largely beside the point in § 1983 actions against a state.

In one unusual situation where *Will* would ordinarily bar the § 1983 action of its own force, the Eleventh Amendment may still be important. A state might neglect to raise the *Will* objection until the case is on appeal. Since *Will* in essence furnishes the basis for a defense of legal insufficiency rather than lack of subject matter jurisdiction, defendant's failure to raise that defense during trial might result in its waiver.[23] By contrast, the Eleventh Amendment objection is deemed a matter of subject matter jurisdiction and can therefore be raised for the first time, even on appeal.[24] The same characterization of the issue enables a defendant whose Eleventh Amendment dismissal motion fails to seek immediate interlocutory review.[25]

Sharply to be distinguished from § 1983 claims against a state, and from "official-capacity" actions against an individual state officer, are "personal-capacity" suits intended to establish the officer's individual liability. To the extent she is sued personally, a state official is a § 1983 "person" liable for all otherwise appropriate relief, including damages. Further, as in similar suits against city or county officials, the plaintiff need not prove that the defendant's challenged conduct was undertaken as a matter of state "policy"; it suffices to prove that, acting under color of state law, she deprived the plaintiff of a federally protected right. On the other hand, unlike the entity or entity official defendant in an "official-capacity" suit, the personal-capacity defendant may invoke the affirmative defense of qualified immunity to avoid the relief of damages.[26]

The required Congressional abrogation of the Eleventh Amendment has, by contrast, been found in other civil rights statutes. Because Congress, citing its legislative authority under section five of the Fourteenth Amendment, amended Title VII to provide expressly for the liability of state (as well as local) governments, the Court held Title VII to override the states' Eleventh Amendment immunity.[27] Damage

---

21. 491 U.S. 58, 109 S.Ct. 2304, 105 L.Ed.2d 45 (1989).

22. *Id.* at 71 n.10, 109 S.Ct. at 2312 n.10. *Will* is discussed in detail in the § 1983 Chapter above.

23. FRCP 12(h)(2).

24. *Edelman, supra* note 8, at 677–78, 94 S.Ct. at 1362–63; *see* FRCP 12(h)(3).

25. *Puerto Rico Aqueduct and Sewer Authority v. Metcalf & Eddy*, 506 U.S. 139, 113 S.Ct. 684, 121 L.Ed.2d 605 (1993).

26. *Hafer v. Melo*, 502 U.S. 21, 112 S.Ct. 358, 116 L.Ed.2d 301 (1991).

27. *Fitzpatrick, supra* note 18.

claims under ADEA against states as employers may proceed in federal court notwithstanding the Eleventh Amendment.[28]

In recent years the Court has articulated increasingly strict standards for ascertaining whether Congress has abrogated the states' immunity from retrospective relief in federal court, demanding unmistakable specificity and clarity.[29] The clear statutory statement the Court now demands as evidence of an intent to abrogate must reference "either the Eleventh Amendment or the States' sovereign immunity," rather than simply a class of defendants that expressly or by construction includes the states.[30] The Civil Rights Remedies Equalization Amendment of 1986[31] meets this test, expressly overriding what would otherwise be state immunity to permit federal courts to award retroactive relief, under, among other statutes, Titles VI and IX. Similarly, after the Court held that the original Education of the Handicapped Act failed with sufficient clarity to abrogate Eleventh Amendment immunity,[32] Congress specifically amended it in § 1403 of the Individuals with Disabilities Education Act,[33] to authorize federal courts to award retroactive relief against states and state agencies with respect to violations occurring after October 30, 1990. Moreover, no matter how specifically Congress purports to override Eleventh Amendment immunity, it lacks power to do so when it is acting only pursuant to the Commerce Clause, as distinct from the Fourteenth Amendment.[34]

Attorneys' fees, including enhancement, are wholly outside the strictures of the Eleventh Amendment. Such fees are considered compensation for "expenses incurred in litigation seeking only prospective relief," instead of "retroactive liability for prelitigation conduct."[35] Attorneys' fees against a State are available to the prevailing party based on his degree of success on any "significant" issue that "changes the legal relationship between [the plaintiff] and the defendant."[36] In addition, such an award can include prejudgment interest, or a fee enhancement, for delay in payment based on current market rates rather

28. *Hurd v. Pittsburgh State University,* 29 F.3d 564 (10th Cir.), *cert. denied,* ___ U.S. ___, 115 S.Ct. 321, 130 L.Ed.2d 282 (1994). *But cf. Blanciak v. Allegheny Ludlum Corp.,* 77 F.3d 690 (3d Cir.1996) (Eleventh Amendment bars ADEA claims against state in its capacity as employment agency, because congressional intent to abrogate immunity in that situation is not unmistakably clear).

29. *See, e.g., Atascadero State Hosp. v. Scanlon,* 473 U.S. 234, 238, 105 S.Ct. 3142, 3145, 87 L.Ed.2d 171 (1985).

30. *See, e.g., Dellmuth v. Muth,* 491 U.S. 223, 230, 109 S.Ct. 2397, 2401, 105 L.Ed.2d 181 (1989); *Welch v. Texas Dept. of Hwys. & Public Transp.,* 483 U.S. 468, 478, 107 S.Ct. 2941, 2948, 97 L.Ed.2d 389 (1987)

(explicitly overruling *Parden v. Terminal Railway of Ala. State Docks Dept.,* 377 U.S. 184, 84 S.Ct. 1207, 12 L.Ed.2d 233 (1964)).

31. 42 U.S.C.A. § 2000d–7.

32. *See Dellmuth, supra* note 30.

33. 20 U.S.C.A. §§ 1401–1485.

34. *Seminole Tribe of Florida v. Florida,* ___ U.S. ___, 116 S.Ct. 1114, 134 L.Ed.2d 252 (1996) (overruling *Pennsylvania v. Union Gas Co.,* 491 U.S. 1, 109 S.Ct. 2273, 105 L.Ed.2d 1 (1989)).

35. *Hutto v. Finney,* 437 U.S. 678, 695, 98 S.Ct. 2565, 2576, 57 L.Ed.2d 522 (1978).

36. *Texas v. Garland,* 489 U.S. 782, 792, 109 S.Ct. 1486, 1493, 103 L.Ed.2d 866 (1989).

than those rates relevant at the time the legal services were rendered.[37]

With respect to claims under § 1983, the Eleventh Amendment is of little if any significance given the Supreme Court's view that claims against the State itself, or claims against individual state officers that will be satisfied out of the state's treasury, fail to state a claim for relief under that statute.[38] But the Eleventh Amendment defense is critical in federal court actions brought against the state or state official under 42 U.S.C.A. §§ 1981, 1982, 1985, and other civil rights statutes. However, the Court has recently imported the prima facie elements of a § 1983 claim into, and thus made significantly more stringent the required elements of, § 1981 claims against local government entities.[39] Consequently, in a § 1981 action in federal court against a state entity or official, the Court might also import the § 1983 holding of *Will* that the state in its own name is not a proper defendant. In that event, a state defendant should succeed with a timely objection for failure to state a claim, and the Eleventh Amendment objection would become merely a quasi-jurisdictional backstop to the defense of legal insufficiency. Whether *Jett* removes § 1981 from the plaintiff's arsenal against state government is clouded by a provision of the Civil Rights Act of 1991 which reaffirms the availability of § 1981 in actions against government entities as well as individuals. But that provision may ultimately be construed merely to affirm that § 1981 is an available remedy against *some* government defendants, not necessarily the state. This construction is plausible not only because of the awkward wording of the provision but because its other, apparent purpose is to codify the Supreme Court's decisions that have applied § 1981 to purely private conduct.[40]

E. PENDENT JURISDICTION

Library References:

> C.J.S. Federal Courts § 11.
> West's Key No. Digests, Federal Courts ☞14.1.

§ 13.8 In General

Pendent claim jurisdiction allows a plaintiff who has a federal claim against a nondiverse defendant[1] in federal court to append a transactionally related state law claim against the same defendant. For the

37. *Missouri v. Jenkins*, 491 U.S. 274, 109 S.Ct. 2463, 105 L.Ed.2d 229 (1989).

38. *Will v. Michigan Dept. of State Police*, 491 U.S. 58, 109 S.Ct. 2304, 105 L.Ed.2d 45 (1989).

39. *Jett v. Dallas Independent School Dist.*, 491 U.S. 701, 109 S.Ct. 2702, 105 L.Ed.2d 598 (1989).

40. *See* Overview Chapter Concerning The Reconstruction Statutes, Chapter 1.

§ 13.8

1. If all the requirements of the diversity statute, 28 U.S.C.A. § 1332, are met, the federal district court is *required* to accept original jurisdiction over all claims, state as well as federal, whether or not they are related. *Cemer v. Marathon Oil Co.*, 583 F.2d 830 (6th Cir.1978).

past half-century the Court has authorized some form of pendent jurisdiction, recognizing that in its absence the plaintiff would be forced to litigate the distinct but related federal and state claims in two fora or to abandon the federal forum. The Court fully articulated the Article III criteria for pendent claim jurisdiction in *United Mine Workers v. Gibbs*.[2] For a federal court to have constitutional power to entertain the state law claim, that claim and the federal law claim on which jurisdiction is founded must arise from a "common nucleus of operative fact"; the claims must be such that the plaintiff would normally be expected to try both in one judicial proceeding; and the federal claim must be "substantial."

The *Gibbs* opinion did not allude to the settled understanding that federal subject matter jurisdiction requires not just a constitutional foundation—in this case, Article III—but also a Congressional authorization or acceptance of that jurisdiction as manifested in a federal statute. But the court did identify several factors that a federal trial court, having concluded that it has constitutional power to hear both claims, should take into account in deciding whether, in its discretion, to dismiss the state law claim. It observed that the doctrine's justification "lies in considerations of judicial economy, convenience and fairness to litigants"—a later case, *Carnegie–Mellon*[3] added "comity" to the list—and if these are absent "a federal court should hesitate to exercise jurisdiction over state claims." The *Gibbs* opinion specifically mentioned two examples of situations in which the trial judge should consider declining to exercise otherwise available pendent jurisdiction: where "the state issues substantially predominate, whether in terms of proof, of the scope of the issues raised, or of the comprehensiveness of the remedy sought"; and where there are "reasons independent of jurisdictional considerations, such as the likelihood of jury confusion in treating divergent legal theories of relief," that would warrant separate trials of the state and federal claims. *Carnegie–Mellon* read *Gibbs* as conferring substantial discretion on the trial courts to assert *or decline* jurisdiction over pendent claims, guided only by the ultimate values of judicial economy, convenience and fairness to litigants, and comity.

So the *Gibbs* authorization of pendent claim jurisdiction might have remained were it not for Congressional dissatisfaction with the Court's ultimate rejection of a parallel doctrine, pendent *party* jurisdiction. The situation arises when a plaintiff tries to append to a substantial federal question claim—for example, a claim under § 1983, Title VII, ADEA, or any of the other federal statutes prohibiting civil rights deprivations or employment discrimination—a claim under state law *against another defendant*, again where the requirements of complete diversity of citizenship are lacking. The question is whether, even assuming the state law claim bears a sufficient factual nexus to the federal law claim to meet the *Gibbs* test of constitutional power, a court should exercise jurisdiction

2. 383 U.S. 715, 86 S.Ct. 1130, 16 L.Ed.2d 218 (1966).

3. *Carnegie–Mellon Univ. v. Cohill*, 484 U.S. 343, 108 S.Ct. 614, 98 L.Ed.2d 720 (1988).

over a party "not named in any claim that is independently cognizable by the federal court." [4]

The Court first restricted pendent party jurisdiction in *Aldinger v. Howard*.[5] There a plaintiff sought to append to § 1983 claims against nondiverse individual defendants a factually related state law claim against a county. At the time, however, neither a county nor other local government entity was a suable "person" under § 1983.[6] Assuming that the *Gibbs* minimum prerequisite for Article III jurisdictional power was present—the claims arose from a common nucleus of real-life fact— and without denying the possibility of pendent party jurisdiction in principle, the Court insisted that "careful attention" also be given to the jurisdictional requirement of statutory authorization that it had ignored in *Gibbs*. It observed that 28 U.S.C.A. § 1343, the particularized statutory foundation for claims under § 1983, provides jurisdiction only over claims "authorized by law" and that § 1983 claims against a county were not so authorized. The Court in *Aldinger* therefore refused to uphold a "back door" version of pendent party jurisdiction over the county, that is to hear a state law claim that the federal jurisdictional statute on which the action against the individual defendants was founded would have barred.

Only two years later, however, the Court declared that a city or a county is a "person" suable under § 1983. Thus disappeared the specific rationale relied on in *Aldinger* for refusing to append state law claims against local government entities to § 1983 claims against individual defendants. Lower courts were then forced to decide if *Aldinger* was hinting at a more broadly based ban on pendent party jurisdiction, and they divided over this question. The Court's answer came in 1989 in *Finley*, where it interpreted *Aldinger* as indicating that "the Gibbs approach would not be extended to the pendent-party field" because "a [federal statutory] grant of jurisdiction over claims involving particular parties does not itself confer jurisdiction over additional claims by or against different parties." At the same time, the Court reaffirmed pendent claim jurisdiction as declared by *Gibbs*. The burden was on Congress, in other words, to spell out its willingness to confer subject matter jurisdiction to the full extent of its constitutional power with respect to pendent parties, though not with respect to pendent claims.

In response to *Finley*, a federal courts study committee recommended that Congress enact express statutory authority for pendent and other forms of ancillary jurisdiction. As part of the Judicial Improvements Act of 1990 [7] Congress adopted a new statute that provides for "supplemental" jurisdiction. As it relates to civil rights or employment discrimination claims based on federal law, the first sentence of § 1367(a) declares that the federal district courts "shall have" supple-

---

4. *Finley v. United States*, 490 U.S. 545, 109 S.Ct. 2003, 104 L.Ed.2d 593 (1989).

5. 427 U.S. 1, 96 S.Ct. 2413, 49 L.Ed.2d 276 (1976).

6. See Chapter 2.

7. 28 U.S.C.A. § 1367.

mental jurisdiction "over all other claims that are so related" to the foundational federal law claims "that they form part of the case or controversy under Article III of the United States Constitution." Since the *Gibbs* test for constitutional power was an interpretation of Article III, this part of the new statute provides statutory confirmation for the *Gibbs* "common nucleus" approach to pendent claim jurisdiction. The second sentence of § 1367(a) goes on to change the result of *Finley* by providing: "Such supplemental jurisdiction shall include claims that involve the joinder or intervention of additional parties." Thus there is now express statutory authorization for pendent party jurisdiction on the same relaxed "common nucleus" standard that *Gibbs* and § 1367(a)'s first sentence provide for pendent claim jurisdiction.[8]

But does this statute, the impetus for which was a desire to respond to *Finley* by providing congressional authorization for supplemental jurisdiction in pendent party situations, also, inadvertently or by design, liberalize the scope of pendent claim jurisdiction by restricting the circumstances under which federal judges may decline to exercise it? One such suggestion emerges from the first sentence of § 1367(a), which states that the district courts "shall have" supplemental jurisdiction over all state law claims that show the *Gibbs* relationship to the foundation claim based on federal law. When the Court in *Gibbs* sketched the contours of pendent jurisdiction, it carefully eschewed any such mandatory language.

A second such suggestion emerges from § 1367(c). This subdivision authorizes district courts to decline to exercise supplemental jurisdiction only in four specifically enumerated circumstances, rather than, as under *Gibbs*, for any reason not comporting with judicial economy, convenience, fairness or comity. The first three circumstances roughly track the particular examples mentioned in *Gibbs*: (1) the putative supplemental claim "raises a novel or complex issue of State law"; (2) it "substantially predominates over" the federal question claim on which federal subject matter jurisdiction is initially founded; and (3) the court has already dismissed the claims that gave it original jurisdiction—in *Gibbs* terms, the federal question claims proved insubstantial.

But the fourth appears to restrict the district judges' discretion to decline supplemental jurisdiction somewhat more than the open-ended *Gibbs* reference to generalized considerations of efficiency, fairness, and federalism: the trial court may decline pendent jurisdiction only "(4) in *exceptional* circumstances, [when] there are other *compelling* reasons...." (emphasis added). Taking their cue from the structure of the limited subdivision (c) exceptions to the supplemental jurisdiction that subdivision (a) says the district courts "shall have," lower courts have ruled that § 1367 creates a presumption in favor of supplemental

---

8. *See Ammerman v. Sween*, 54 F.3d 423 (7th Cir.1995) (upholding supplemental jurisdiction over state law assault claim

jurisdiction unless one of the specific subdivision (c) exceptions applies.[9] On this reading of the statute the range of a district judge's discretion to decline to exercise supplemental jurisdiction has been so narrowed that a decision to do so may be overturned by mandamus.[10] But the pertinent House Report seems to deny this result. It states that § 1367 merely "codifies" the *Gibbs* factors, overrules *Finley* and allows for pendent party jurisdiction.[11]

F.   STATE COURT JURISDICTION

Library References:

C.J.S. Courts § 203.
West's Key No. Digests, Courts ⊚489.

§ 13.9   In General

Under the Supremacy Clause of the U.S. Constitution, state courts have a duty to enforce federal rights unless Congress, by declaring federal court jurisdiction to be original *and exclusive*, affirmatively divests State courts of their competence to hear such claims. None of the Reconstruction Civil Rights Acts, or the modern employment discrimination statutes, asserts that the original jurisdiction of the federal courts is exclusive. Accordingly, the Supreme Court has held that state courts have full concurrent jurisdiction over federal civil rights and Title VII claims.[1] And they must exercise that jurisdiction without discrimination when it is properly invoked. The only "valid excuse" for refusing to do so is reliance on a neutral procedural policy that the state court was to apply to all kinds of claims, including those under state law—and occasionally even such a reason may be overridden if deemed inconsistent with a policy of federal law.[2]

Because of this concurrent jurisdiction, a plaintiff may choose to bring her § 1983 claim in state or federal court. The reasons for filing in state court are varied and depend on the environment of the state system under consideration.[3] For example, the assumed sympathies of a

against co-employee as sufficiently related to Title VII claim against employer).

9. *Executive Software North America, Inc. v. U.S. District Court for Central District of Calif.*, 24 F.3d 1545 (9th Cir.1994); *Growth Horizons, Inc. v. Delaware County*, 983 F.2d 1277 (3d Cir.1993).

10. *See Executive Software, supra* note 9.

11. H. Rep. No. 713, 101st Cong., 2d Sess. 29 (1990) reprinted in 1990 U.S.C.C.A.N. 6802, 6875.

§ 13.9

1. *Howlett v. Rose*, 496 U.S. 356, 110 S.Ct. 2430, 110 L.Ed.2d 332 (1990). Similarly, the Court has upheld concurrent jur-

isdiction in Title VII cases. Nothing in the legislative history indicating Congress' anticipation that most Title VII cases would be brought in federal court overcomes the presumptive jurisdiction of the state courts. Nor does the fact that a Title VII right to sue arises only after review by both state administrative agencies *and* the federal EEOC affect the question of what judicial forum should entertain the action. *Yellow Freight v. Donnelly*, 494 U.S. 820, 110 S.Ct. 1566, 108 L.Ed.2d 834 (1990).

2. *Id.*

3. For an excellent comprehensive discussion of the factors involved in choosing between state and federal court, see Steven H. Steinglass, Section 1983 Litigation in State Courts, Part B (1994).

particular state court judge or jury pool, relative to predictions about the counterpart federal judge or jury, may attract the plaintiff; an elected state judge's potentially greater susceptibility to public opinion may be particularly important here. Other factors in deciding between state and federal court fall into three categories: choice of law considerations, procedural or administrative differences, and doctrinal limitations on the federal courts.

The choice of law considerations are two-fold. First, a plaintiff who has not conclusively determined to bring suit under § 1983 may find that state law provides more rights of action more congenial from the standpoint of proof or remedies. Second, where a plaintiff is determined to pursue a § 1983 claim, she must predict whether, on each likely determinative issue not yet authoritatively construed by the Supreme Court, a state or federal judge will offer the more favorable interpretation. For instance, if the plaintiff expects to face an immunity defense, he might opt to file in state court if that court routinely answers the "clearly established right" question by reference to state rather than lower federal court decisions, provided of course that the state's law is more likely to yield a positive answer to that question. If, however, a plaintiff expects to use claim or issue preclusion offensively, he may more often prefer federal court, where offensive preclusion has received somewhat greater acceptance. For the defendant, of course, these considerations weigh in the decision whether to remove once the plaintiff opts for a state forum.

State and federal court procedural and administrative differences also figure in the calculus. For example, generally less congested state court calendars may attract the plaintiff with the prospect of an earlier trial date. And if interim relief is important, a state system may better suit since it typically supports a larger number of judges who may decide such requests more quickly than their federal court counterparts. A party who prefers less judicial pretrial intervention may opt for state court to avoid the ever increasing judicial involvement mandated by Rule 16 of the FRCP.[4] Also, a plaintiff might have better odds in state than in federal court of surviving a motion for summary judgment if the state court does not follow the Supreme Court's *Celotex Corp. v. Catrett* and *Anderson v. Liberty Lobby* decisions that ease the defendant's burden in making the motion and increase the plaintiff's burden in resisting it.

State courts also frequently offer more liberal Doe Defendant statutes.[5] State court policy may allow discovery to continue in situations

---

4. See, e.g., Richey, "Rule 16 Revised, and Related Rules: Analysis of Recent Developments for the Benefit of Bench and Bar," 157 F.R.D. 69 (1994).

5. *See, e.g., Barrow v. Wethersfield Police Dep't,* 74 F.3d 1366 (2d Cir.1996), *modifying* 66 F.3d 466 (2d Cir.1995) (no relation back of amendment substituting named officers for "John Doe" defendants permitted when plaintiff was unable or unwilling to comply with court's directive, issued within the limitations period, to name individual officer defendants; in effect, decision narrowly reads 1991 amendment to F.R.C.P. 15(c), extending relation-back period where amendment is occasioned by a plaintiff's "mistake" as to a defendant's identity, as not applicable where unnamed defendant's identity is unknown).

where federal courts would stay discovery—for example, while an immunity question is being resolved. State rules of evidence may be more favorable than the federal rules.[6] And state courts do not uniformly allow a defendant to limit his exposure to large fee awards by using offers of judgment as authorized by FRCP Rule 68.

Federal doctrinal limitations, mostly jurisdictional or quasi-jurisdictional, may also encourage filing in state court. State courts may, for example, impose looser standing requirements. Further, they may provide the only avenue for damages relief against a state in view of the Supreme Court's rather restrictive recent interpretations of the Eleventh Amendment—although the state as such may no longer be sued under § 1983 in either state or federal court.[7] A given state may authorize attorneys' fee awards to be enhanced for contingency, at least on state law claims, contrary to the view of the Supreme Court respecting claims under Title VII.[8] Federal decisionmaking may be pretermitted altogether or severely delayed by, respectively, the *Younger* and *Pullman* abstention doctrines.[9] And a plaintiff may choose state court because his action includes a colorable but tenuous pendent state law claim that a federal court might be less aggressive in interpreting because of its duty to decide in accordance with its prediction of the resolution that would be reached by the state's highest court.

---

6. Claims under the Reconstruction Acts and modern employment discrimination statutes are "federal question" claims within the meaning of 28 U.S.C. §§ 1331 & 1343; as such, federal rather than state common law governs questions of evidentiary privileges. *See* Fed.R.Evid. 501. Most federal courts have rejected the physician-patient privilege, although many states recognize it. *See Patterson v. Caterpillar, Inc.,* 70 F.3d 503 (7th Cir.1995). Similarly, F.R.C.P. 35's requirement that an order directing a physical or mental examination of a party may be made only upon "good cause shown" is more restrictive than the counterpart rules of some states. *See also O'Quinn v. New York Univ. Medical Ctr.,* 163 F.R.D. 226 (S.D.N.Y.1995) (refusing to order plaintiff to undergo a medical examination despite what the court termed her "boilerplate" allegation of "mental anguish, emotional distress, and humiliation"). *But cf. Lahr v. Fulbright & Jaworski,* 164 F.R.D. 204 (N.D.Tex.1996) (ordering plaintiff to submit to mental examination with respect to Title VII prayer for compensatory damages for emotional distress and related state law tort claim). Recently the Supreme Court has facilitated the admissibility of expert scientific testimony under Federal Rule of Evidence 702, holding that the trial judge may evaluate the validity of the reasoning and methodology underlying such testimony and admit it even if it did not enjoy widespread "general acceptance" in the relevant scientific community. *See Daubert v. Merrell Dow Pharmaceuticals Inc.,* 509 U.S. 579, 113 S.Ct. 2786, 125 L.Ed.2d 469 (1993).

On the other hand, the Supreme Court has now recognized a psychotherapist-patient privilege, one that is recognized in some form by all fifty states. *Jaffee v. Redmond,* ___ U.S. ___, 116 S.Ct. 1923, 135 L.Ed.2d 337 (1996). In finding protection of confidential psychotherapist-patient communications sufficiently important to outweigh the ordinary need for probative evidence, the Court indicated it was obeying the Rule 501 command that federal courts "continue the evolutionary development of testimonial privileges." Further, it upheld the privilege broadly beyond psychiatrists and psychologists to include communications made to all licensed social workers. It recognized only the narrowest of possible exceptions, for example, in circumstances where a therapist's disclosure would be essential to avert serious harm to the patient or others.

7. See discussion of *Will v. Michigan Department of State Police* in Chapter 2.

8. *Rendine v. Pantzer,* 141 N.J. 292, 661 A.2d 1202 (1995). *See* § 12.3, *supra,* for the Supreme Court's dim view of contingency enhancement.

9. These doctrines are discussed in Section C above.

State courts may not deny a Reconstruction Act claim in the absence of a valid excuse, i.e., one that refuses jurisdiction because of a neutral state rule of judicial administration. When a state court has entertained actions of a nature similar to the Reconstruction Act claim before it, the court may not discriminate against the federal claim. Where the defendants in the action would be subject to liability in the same action in a federal court, the state court may not grant them immunity.[10]

But the Court has in one instance gone even further to hold that a state court may not bar a § 1983 action through application of the forum's notice-of-claim statute, even though that statute would have precluded litigation against a government entity on a wide variety of state as well as federal law claims. The Court concluded that compliance with the state statute would place an undue burden on a civil rights plaintiff by forcing her to comply with a requirement she would not face in federal court. In a reverse-*Erie* twist, the Court ruled the claim statute superseded by virtue of the Supremacy Clause because it might produce different outcomes depending on whether the litigation were pursued in state or federal court.[11] Recent state appellate decisions test the limits of *Felder*. On one hand, may a state court, without discrimination against federal law claims, apply its own restrictions on obtaining orders allowing substituted service of process when those standards are more stringent than the requirements of due process and the Federal Rules of Civil Procedure?[12] On the other, may a state court refuse, consistent with its general practice, to afford a public official an immediate interlocutory appeal from the denial of that defendant's pretrial motion based on qualified immunity, even though the federal practice in such circumstances would be to treat the ruling as a "collateral order" subject to immediate appellate review?[13]

Finally, there is the substantial risk that selection of a state forum will result in an adjudication triggering claim preclusion (res judicata) or issue preclusion (collateral estoppel) that would wholly or partially pretermit the plaintiff's subsequent resort to federal court. These possibilities will be discussed in Section K, below.

G. STANDING

Library References:

C.J.S. Civil Rights §§ 260, 265–266, 364, 385.
West's Key No. Digests, Civil Rights ⚮199, 366.

10. *Howlett, supra* note 1.

11. *Felder v. Casey,* 487 U.S. 131, 108 S.Ct. 2302, 101 L.Ed.2d 123 (1988).

12. *See Britt v. Smith,* 446 Mich. 880, 522 N.W.2d 633 (1994) leave to appeal denied, *cert. denied,* ___ U.S. ___, 115 S.Ct. 1103, 130 L.Ed.2d 1070 (1995).

13. *Turner v. Giles,* 264 Ga. 812, 450 S.E.2d 421 (1994), *cert. denied,* ___ U.S. ___, 115 S.Ct. 1959, 131 L.Ed.2d 851 (1995)

(denying collateral order review). *Cf. Nelson v. County of Allegheny,* 60 F.3d 1010 (3d Cir.1995) *cert. denied,* ___ U.S. ___, 116 S.Ct. 1266, 134 L.Ed.2d 213 (1966)(observing that relevant state court practice was to permit immediate interlocutory review of order denying class certification, contrary to the federal practice dictated by *Coopers & Lybrand v. Livesay,* 437 U.S. 463, 98 S.Ct. 2454, 57 L.Ed.2d 351 (1978)).

§ 13.10 In General

Article III of the U.S. Constitution confines the federal judiciary to hearing actual "cases or controversies." The contemporary, judicially elaborated jurisprudence of standing, however, has both constitutional and "prudential," that is, judicially self-imposed, components. All these elements of standing are treated by the Court as jurisdictional, and as such a federal court will usually decide a defendant's challenge to standing at the outset of a case, often on the basis of the plaintiff's pleadings. Further, upon challenge by the defendant, the burden is on the plaintiff to prove the requisite jurisdictional facts. Standing is thus a potentially crippling roadblock to a federal court plaintiff who is unable to demonstrate the substantive requirements of standing doctrine without benefit of discovery.[1]

The constitutional dimension of standing doctrine requires that the plaintiff allege personal "injury in fact" that is "fairly traceable" to the allegedly unlawful acts of the defendant and "likely to be redressed" by the requested relief.[2] The injury in fact requirement ordinarily requires the plaintiff to allege and show personal harm that is "(a) concrete and particularized, and (b) actual or imminent, not conjectural or hypothetical."[3] An asserted right to have the government act in accordance with law is not sufficient. It has sometimes been held that even the stigmatizing injury of racial discrimination is insufficient unless plaintiffs have personally been denied equal treatment.[4] Nor will the "psychological consequence presumably produced by observation of conduct with which one disagrees" supply the requisite injury, if it is unaccompanied by more tangible or concrete harm.[5] But subjection of the plaintiff to unwelcome religious exercises may constitute adequate injury in fact even where the plaintiff is not thereby forced to assume any special burdens to avoid them.[6] It suffices that there has been an indirectly

§ 13.10

1. *Allen v. Wright*, 468 U.S. 737, 104 S.Ct. 3315, 82 L.Ed.2d 556 (1984).

2. *Id.*

3. *Lujan v. Defenders of Wildlife*, 504 U.S. 555, 559, 112 S.Ct. 2130, 2136, 119 L.Ed.2d 351 (1992) (citations, footnote, and internal quotations omitted). *See also Rizzo v. Goode*, 423 U.S. 362, 96 S.Ct. 598, 46 L.Ed.2d 561 (1976); *City of Los Angeles v. Lyons*, 461 U.S. 95, 103 S.Ct. 1660, 75 L.Ed.2d 675 (1983). Thus a lawyer who objected that his ability to practice law might be impeded by a religious sign over the entrance to a county courthouse (because he would not represent clients whose cases would be heard there) lacked standing where his practice was based elsewhere, he had never seen the courthouse in question

and had no plans to open an office in that county, and could identify no case which had required or would require his presence there. *Doe v. County of Montgomery*, 41 F.3d 1156 (7th Cir.1994). But the Supreme Court has held that on a motion to dismiss, general factual allegations of injury, in fact, may suffice. *National Organization for Women, Inc. v. Scheidler*, 510 U.S. 249, ___, 114 S.Ct. 798, 803, 127 L.Ed.2d 99 (1994) (citing *Lujan*).

4. *Allen, supra* note 1.

5. *Valley Forge Christian College v. Americans United for Separation of Church and State, Inc.*, 454 U.S. 464, 485, 102 S.Ct. 752, 765, 70 L.Ed.2d 700 (1982).

6. *Id.* at 486–487 n.22, 102 S.Ct. at 765–766 n. 22.

coerced, unwelcome exposure to a religious message that could have been avoided only by sacrificing the ordinary privileges of citizenship.[7]

Second, even where a serious personal, economic or non-economic injury is properly alleged, the injury must be "fairly traceable" to the challenged government conduct—a constitutional requirement of causation.[8] A circuit court recently upheld a property owner's standing to challenge police officers' allegedly unreasonable execution of a search warrant, in the course of which they broke or mutilated portions of the house and the owner's personal property. Even though the owner lacked a reasonable expectation of privacy regarding the house, the injury could be linked to a distinct Fourth Amendment violation arising from the defendants' significant level of interference with the owner's possessory interest in the property.[9]

Finally, even if a plaintiff properly alleges injury to herself or her class that is traceable to the defendant's conduct, she still lacks standing if the requested relief is unlikely to redress that injury.[10] Because this requirement has been applied restrictively, § 1983 plaintiffs alleging excessive use of force by police are often unable to obtain injunctive relief that would modify police disciplinary measures. If, as the evidence may often show, excessive force is used by a "small minority of officers" and plaintiffs cannot show a "real and immediate" threat that they themselves will be repeat victims of the precise practice they seek to have enjoined, the Court views the requested relief as unlikely to redress the particular injury of which they complain.[11] Indeed the plaintiff in *City of Los Angeles v. Lyons*[12] was held to lack standing to seek an injunction against the Los Angeles Police Department's procedures concerning chokeholds even though, per *Monell* and its progeny, he would have to show in support of his companion damages claim that the force allegedly used against him was pursuant to official city policy. To have standing with respect to the injunction he sought Lyons would have had to allege that the city authorized officers to apply chokeholds to suspects who offered no resistance or other provocation and "demonstrate" that he himself would again be stopped and choked by the police under those

---

7. *See, e.g., Lee v. Weisman*, 505 U.S. 577, 596–598, 112 S.Ct. 2649, 2660–2661, 120 L.Ed.2d 467, 486–487 (1992) (standing to challenge school prayer at graduation ceremony of public school where attendance was not prerequisite to receipt of diploma); *Abington School Dist. v. Schempp*, 374 U.S. 203, 224 n. 9, 83 S.Ct. 1560, 1572 n. 9, 10 L.Ed.2d 844 (1963) (standing to challenge classroom Bible reading although student could be absent or not participate). Thus citizens of a county who alleged that they were required to visit its courthouse to fulfill legal obligations or fully participate as citizens had standing to challenge a sign with a religious message that was displayed over the main and most prominent courthouse entrance. *Doe v. County of Montgomery*, 41 F.3d 1156 (7th Cir.1994).

8. *See Simon v. Eastern Ky. Welfare Rights Org.*, 426 U.S. 26, 38, 96 S.Ct. 1917, 1924, 48 L.Ed.2d 450 (1976).

9. *Bonds v. Cox*, 20 F.3d 697 (6th Cir. 1994).

10. *Allen, supra* note 1 at 752; *Goode, supra* note 3.

11. *Goode, supra* note 3; *City of Los Angeles v. Lyons*, 461 U.S. 95, 103 S.Ct. 1660, 75 L.Ed.2d 675 (1983).

12. 461 U.S. 95, 103 S.Ct. 1660, 75 L.Ed.2d 675 (1983).

circumstances.[13] The upshot is that the court will test the plaintiff's standing with respect to each claim alleged.

In *Warth v. Seldin*,[14] the injury in fact requirement was held unsatisfied when a construction firm association sought to intervene to challenge a zoning ordinance on equal protection grounds because of its alleged effect of excluding people of low and moderate income from living in the community. Critically absent, wrote the Court, was an allegation that the ordinance "delayed or thwarted any project currently proposed by the association's members."

The Court has recently distinguished *Warth* in permitting a challenge by another contractors' association to a city's 10% set-aside program challenged as a form of preferential treatment for minority-owned businesses that violated equal protection under the criteria laid down by *Richmond v. J.A. Croson Co.*[15] In *Northeastern Florida Chapter of the Associated General Contractors of America v. City of Jacksonville*,[16] the court of appeals had found the association lacked standing because it had not shown that, absent the set-aside program, any of its members would have bid successfully for one of the covered contracts. The Supreme Court reversed, summarizing its cases as holding that when "government erects a barrier that makes it more difficult for members of one group to obtain a benefit than it is for members of another group, a member of the former group seeking to challenge the barrier need not allege that he would have obtained the benefit but for the barrier...." It is enough if the plaintiff asserts that the barrier has denied him the right to be considered or compete for the benefit in question.[17] The Court observed that in *Warth*, by contrast, the claim was simply that the government would grant no variances or permits under the challenged ordinance; "there was no claim that the construction association's members could not apply for variances and building permits on the same basis as other firms...."[18] The Court's eased approach to equal protection standing in *Northeastern* has been applied to other "reverse discrimination" challenges, for example, white voters' Equal Protection challenges to male-conscious electoral redistricting and to affirmative action programs.[19]

---

13. 461 U.S. at 106 n.7, 103 S.Ct. at 1667 n.7. *Cf., Goff v. Harper*, 60 F.3d 518 (8th Cir.1995) (inability to show likelihood of recurrence of same violation fails "irreparable injury" requirement for injunction).

14. 422 U.S. 490, 516, 95 S.Ct. 2197, 2214, 45 L.Ed.2d 343 (1975).

15. 488 U.S. 469, 109 S.Ct. 706, 102 L.Ed.2d 854 (1989).

16. 508 U.S. 656, 113 S.Ct. 2297, 124 L.Ed.2d 586 (1993).

17. *Id.* at 663, 113 S.Ct. at 2302.

18. *Id.* at 665, 113 S.Ct. at 2303.

19. *See, e.g., United States v. Hays*, ___ U.S. ___, 115 S.Ct. 2431, 132 L.Ed.2d 635 (1995) (white voters have standing because they "may" be less well represented in a district drawn to enhance interests of African-Americans) and *Hopwood v. Texas*, 78 F.3d 932 (5th Cir.) *cert. denied, Texas v. Hopwood*, ___ U.S. ___, 116 S.Ct. 2581, 135 L.Ed.2d 1095 (1996) (University of Texas's law school admissions program granting preferential treatment to minorities held to violate equal protection rights of non-minority applicants).

Often the definition of a federal statutory right furnishes the requisite constitutional injury. In *Havens Realty Corp. v. Coleman*,[20] the Supreme Court upheld the standing of persons not themselves denied housing to seek relief under the Fair Housing Act.[21] That statute gives "any person" an enforceable legal right to truthful information about available housing—apart from the right to acquire or rent the housing itself[22]—and provides that this right may be enforced by civil action.[23] The Court deemed the denial of that information sufficient injury in fact to satisfy Article III.

There are also three principal "prudential" limitations on standing. Both individuals, *Schlesinger v. Reservists Comm. to Stop the War*,[24] and organizations, *Simon v. Eastern Ky. Welfare Rights Org.*[25] lack standing if they assert only generalized grievances.[26] Thus an organizational plaintiff must allege concrete injury to its activities, not merely to its abstract social interests.[27] Second, plaintiffs must show an interest within the "zone of interests protected by the law invoked."[28] Third, plaintiffs must raise their own claims; in general they may not raise the claims of third parties.[29] Although it is generally accepted that these "prudential" limitations on standing flow from Article III, a comprehensive recent analysis by a panel of the District of Columbia Circuit points out that they operate in fact as a constitutionally driven canon of statutory construction—a "set of presumptions" used to determine "whether the statutes in question confer a cause of action upon the plaintiff," rather than another.[30]

Consider, for example, an organizational plaintiff that complains that its members have been deprived of the benefits of living in an integrated community by local ordinances that exclude people of low or moderate income. Such an allegation meets the Article III requirement of an injury in fact.[31] But whether that challenge is permissible under the "prudential" standing limits depends on whether it is asserted under a *statute* that permits a litigant to raise the putative rights of third parties. Section 1981 apparently does not.[32] It affords a cause of action

20. 455 U.S. 363, 102 S.Ct. 1114, 71 L.Ed.2d 214 (1982).

21. 42 U.S.C.A. § 3604(d).

22. The Act makes it unlawful to "represent to any person because of race ...that any dwelling is not available for inspection, sale, or rental when such dwelling is in fact so available...." Section 804(d), 42 U.S.C.A. § 3604(d).

23. Section 812, 42 U.S.C.A. § 3612(a).

24. 418 U.S. 208, 217, 94 S.Ct. 2925, 2930, 41 L.Ed.2d 706 (1974).

25. 426 U.S. 26, 40, 96 S.Ct. 1917, 1925, 48 L.Ed.2d 450 (1976).

26. *See generally Warth v. Seldin, supra* note 14, at 499, 95 S.Ct. at 2205.

27. *Havens Realty Corp. v. Coleman,* 455 U.S. 363, 379, 102 S.Ct. 1114, 1124, 71 L.Ed.2d 214 (1982).

28. *Allen, supra* note 1.

29. *Sierra Club v. Morton*, 405 U.S. 727, 735, 92 S.Ct. 1361, 1366, 31 L.Ed.2d 636 (1972). *See Clay v. Fort Wayne Community Sch.*, 76 F.3d 873 (7th Cir.1996) (only African–American applicants, not parents of African–American students, had standing to complain of race discrimination in a school board's search for a superintendent).

30. *Fair Employment Council of Greater Washington, Inc. v. BMC Marketing Corporation*, 28 F.3d 1268 (D.C.Cir.1994).

31. *See Trafficante v. Metropolitan Life Ins. Co.*, 409 U.S. 205, 93 S.Ct. 364, 34 L.Ed.2d 415 (1972).

32. *Warth v. Seldin, supra* note 14, at 512–514, 95 S.Ct. at 2212–2213; *Fair Employment Council of Greater Washington, supra* note 30; *Mackey v. Nationwide In-*

to those immediately injured by a denial of the right to contract, not to "persons whose injuries derive only from the violation of others' rights."[33] The Fair Housing Act clearly does. It confers a claim "upon everyone who meets the Article III requirements—that is, anyone 'genuinely injured by conduct that violates *someone's* ...rights'...."[34]

Where does Title VII lie on this statutory continuum? Probably somewhere in between the Fair Housing Act and § 1981. The Equal Employment Opportunity Commission has decided to use "testers" to ferret out evidence of unlawful discrimination in hiring and job referrals. The chief argument against standing in such cases is that the tester—the person, usually well qualified, who on behalf of EEOC or a private organization promoting equality of opportunity in employment presents himself to the employer or employment agency—has suffered no concrete injury for lack of any bona fide interest in an advertised position. The key question is whether the Title VII right sought to be enforced in a given case describes an aggrieved person in terms sufficiently broad to embrace the particular plaintiff. How the answer may vary depending upon the identify of the plaintiff and the relief sought is nicely illustrated by the District of Columbia Circuit's panel opinion mentioned above.

The plaintiff group in *Fair Employment Council of Greater Washington* included two African–American employment testers—"equipped with fake credentials intended to be comparable" to those of the two white testers with whom they were paired—and the Fair Employment Council. The defendant employment agency had allegedly denied the African–American testers employment referrals that it gave to the white testers. An alleged "pattern" of racial discrimination against other applicants for referral assertedly made it more difficult for the plaintiff Council to carry out its goal of promoting equal opportunity in the community.

The court first rejected both the testers' and the Council's claims under § 1981. The testers, the court found, could not state a claim under that statute, which gives a cause of action only to persons deprived of what would otherwise be a legal right to make or enforce a contract. The testers could not have enforced a contract offering them employment because they had to make material misrepresentations of fact about their intentions to secure employment in order to induce the defendant employment agency to make referrals. What they really lost, was only "the opportunity to enter into a *void* contract—i.e., a contract that *neither* party can enforce...." That, the court wrote, "is not an injury cognizable under Sec. 1981, for a void contract is a legal nullity."[35] As observed above,[36] the § 1981 claim of the Council failed on

surance Companies, 724 F.2d 419 (4th Cir. 1984).

33. *Fair Employment Council of Greater Washington, supra* note 30 (relying principally on *Warth*).

34. *Id.* at 1278 (quoting *Gladstone, Realtors v. Village of Bellwood,* 441 U.S. 91, 103 n. 9, 99 S.Ct. 1601, 1609 n. 9, 60 L.Ed.2d 66 (1979)).

35. *Fair Employment Council of Greater Washington, supra* note 30. *But cf. Watts v. Boyd Properties,* 758 F.2d 1482 (11th Cir.1985) and *Meyers v. Pennypack Woods*

36. See note 36 on page 514.

prudential standing grounds. Only direct victims of an unlawful denial of the right to make or enforce a contract have standing to assert claims under that statute.[37]

The court was more equivocal about the standing of the individual testers to assert claims under Title VII. While expressly declining to decide whether testers lack standing because they have no bona fide interest in an employment position,[38] the court wrote that in general the Title VII scheme is more analogous to the Fair Housing Act provisions found to support standing in *Havens* than to the stricter requirements of § 1981. Nevertheless, the testers' claims were barred. Their claim for damages failed because only equitable relief was available under Title VII for violations that occurred before the effective date of the Civil Rights Act of 1991. Their prayer for injunctive or declaratory relief ran afoul of the *Lyons* limitations. To be eligible for prospective relief, they would have had to make "sufficient allegations that they are threatened with …future illegality." That they could do only by showing a likelihood that the defendant agency would infringe their Title VII rights again, not simply that they would continue to suffer the ill effects of its alleged past violations. And like Lyons, or indeed virtually any imaginable civil rights plaintiff, how could they make such a case on the pleadings, even before discovery? It would be sheer "speculation" for them to allege that a future violation of their rights was probable, because that would depend—as it always will—upon matters within the defendant's control and knowledge.[39]

The Council fared somewhat better. Constitutional injury in fact was satisfied by its allegations that the defendant's conduct impaired the Council's ability to assist minorities in finding jobs, thereby undermining the effectiveness of its outreach efforts. Further, Title VII's plaintiff definition, like the Fair Housing Act's, provided prudential standing "to the extent that the effects of …[the defendant's] discrimination have perceptibly impaired …[the plaintiff's] programs." The court reached this conclusion in reliance on the language of Title VII that authorizes suit by any "person claiming to be aggrieved" by an unlawful employment practice.[40] Under such a statute, a person injured by conduct that violates its own or another's rights—that is, a person who suffers Article III injury in fact—also survives the prudential restrictions on standing. If the distinctions drawn by this decision ultimately prevail, EEOC's testers may ultimately be found to have standing to sue with respect to

Home Ownership Ass'n, 559 F.2d 894 (3d Cir.1977), *overruled on other grounds by Goodman v. Lukens Steel Co.*, 777 F.2d 113 (3d Cir.1985), *affirmed*, 482 U.S. 656, 107 S.Ct. 2617, 96 L.Ed.2d 572 (1987) (according fair-housing testers standing to sue under §§ 1982 and 1981, respectively, although not squarely addressing question whether the testers had suffered legal injury within the meaning of those statutes).

36. *See* text accompanying notes 32 through 33 above.

37. *Id*. at 1280.

38. *Id*. at n.1.

39. *Id*. at 1272. *See also Goff v. Harper*, 60 F.3d 518 (8th Cir.1995) (because recurrence of alleged violation was speculative, irreparable injury requirement for injunctive relief lacking).

40. 42 U.S.C.A. § 2000e–2(b).

discriminatory job referrals, but not discriminatory refusals to hire.[41]

In any event, standing under Title VII has been liberally granted to employees who can show some personal harm resulting from their association with co-employees.[42] Unions have likewise had no difficulty gaining standing to protest discrimination against their members.[43]

H. GAP–FILLING FROM STATE LAW UNDER SECTION 1988: SURVIVORSHIP AND LIMITATIONS

Library References:

> C.J.S. Civil Rights §§ 319–320.
> West's Key No. Digests, Civil Rights ☞292.

§ 13.11   42 U.S.C.A. § 1988

42 U.S.C.A. § 1988[1] provides, in terms that at first blush appear internally contradictory, that when federal law is "deficient in the

---

41. *See also Parr v. Woodmen of the World Life Insurance Society*, 657 F.Supp. 1022 (M.D.Ga.1987) (plaintiff held ineligible to prosecute suit when court found he was not genuinely seeking employment but instead simply manufacturing the basis for a Title VII violation; the statutory provision in question, 42 U.S.C.A. § 2000e–2(a)(1), created a right to nondiscriminatory hiring, a violation the court found the plaintiff could not have suffered) and *Hailes v. United Air Lines*, 464 F.2d 1006 (5th Cir.1972) (in dictum denying possibility of suit against an employer that published an advertisement containing an unlawful discriminatory preference if the plaintiff had been a mere reader of the advertisement rather than, as was the case, a reader who actually applied for employment; the particular Title VII provision at issue, 42 U.S.C.A. § 2000e–3(b), did not specifically define the person aggrieved).

42. *See, e.g., Maynard v. City of San Jose*, 37 F.3d 1396 (9th Cir.1994) (upholding plaintiff's standing to sue for retaliation against him based on his association with members of racial minorities); *Chandler v. Fast Lane, Inc.*, 868 F.Supp. 1138 (E.D.Ark. 1994) (white plaintiff permitted to challenge discriminatory hiring and promotion practices directed only against African-American employees).

43. *See, e.g., International Woodworkers of America v. Chesapeake Bay Plywood Corp.*, 659 F.2d 1259 (4th Cir.1981); *International Woodworkers of America, Local 5 475 v. Georgia–Pacific Corp.*, 568 F.2d 64 (8th Cir.1977); *Air Line Stewards & Stewardesses Ass'n, Local 550 v. American Airlines, Inc.*, 490 F.2d 636 (7th Cir.1973), *cert. denied*, 416 U.S. 993, 94 S.Ct. 2406, 40 L.Ed.2d 773 (1974).

§ 13.11

1. 42 U.S.C.A. § 1988. Section 1988 reads in part:

> The jurisdiction in civil and criminal matters conferred on the district courts by the provisions of this Title, and of Title "CIVIL RIGHTS," and of Title "CRIMES," for the protection of all persons in the United States in their civil rights, and for their vindication, shall be exercised and enforced in conformity with the laws of the United States, so far as such laws are suitable to carry the same into effect; but in all cases where they are not adapted to the object, or are deficient in the provisions necessary to furnish suitable remedies and punish offenses against law, the common law, as modified and changed by the constitution and statutes of the State wherein the court having jurisdiction of such civil or criminal cause is held, so far as the same is not inconsistent with the Constitution and laws of the United States, shall be extended to and govern the said courts in the trial and disposition of the cause, and, if it is of a criminal nature, in the infliction of punishment on the party found guilty.

42 U.S.C.A. § 1988. A final sentence of the Section, added by the Civil Rights Attorney's Fees Awards Act of 1976, is omitted here. That Act is discussed in a separate chapter devoted to attorney's fees.

provisions necessary to furnish suitable remedies" in a civil rights action, the law of the forum state shall apply unless that law is itself inconsistent with [the nonexistent?] federal law.

Section 1988 applies to actions under 42 U.S.C.A. §§ 1981, 1982, 1983 and 1985(3). Its application involves three steps. First, the court must determine that federal law is deficient—that is, a positive provision of federal law does not address the question at issue. Second, the Court must identify the applicable state law. Third, the Court must apply that state law, but only to the extent it is "not inconsistent with the Constitution and laws of the United States." Of course, since the statute tells us to look to state law only when there is no positive federal statute on point, the federal law with which the state law must not be inconsistent must refer to the somewhat vaguer, judge-made policies that surround the federal claim. That is, on the consistency question a court must look not at "particular federal statutes and constitutional provisions"—if there were any, we wouldn't be repairing to state law in the first place—but at the policies that underlie these statutes and provisions.[2] A state statute or decision, however, cannot be considered 'inconsistent' with federal law merely because it causes the plaintiff to lose the litigation.[3]

On some issues the Court has long taken it as self-evident that federal policy dictates judge-made solutions to problems not addressed in terms by the Reconstruction Acts themselves. Two salient examples are the question of immunities for both individual and government entity defendants and the measure of damages available to a prevailing civil rights plaintiff. In these areas the Court has sometimes borrowed state common law in forging a national approach but has sometimes frankly departed from the state tradition in the name of ancient civil rights policies or federal administrative or efficiency policies invented on the spot.[4] Only rarely has the Court even formally acknowledged that § 1988 constrains the applicable rule of decision. The discussion that follows illustrates the extreme difficulty the Court has had in applying the vague "inconsistency" test of § 1988 in a principled fashion.

§ 13.12 Survivorship

Federal law is deficient in providing for rights of survivorship in actions under the Reconstruction Civil Rights Acts. Therefore, pursuant to the terms of § 1988, it is necessary to borrow the applicable state survivorship law so long as it is consistent with the underlying federal cause of action. In *Robertson v. Wegmann*[1], the Supreme Court held that Louisiana's survivorship law was not inconsistent with the federal policy underlying 42 U.S.C.A. § 1983, even though applying it caused the

---

2. *Robertson v. Wegmann*, 436 U.S. 584, 590, 98 S.Ct. 1991, 1995, 56 L.Ed.2d 554 (1978).

3. *Id.* at 593, 98 S.Ct. at 1996.

4. *See* Chapter on § 1983.

§ 13.12

1. 436 U.S. 584, 98 S.Ct. 1991, 56 L.Ed.2d 554 (1978).

§ 1983 action to abate in that case.[2] The Court stated that the "policies underlying § 1983 include compensation of persons injured by deprivation of federal rights and prevention of abuses of power by those acting under color of state law."[3] The Court concluded that because the state survivorship law was broad enough to encompass most situations of survivorship, the mere failure of this particular case to meet the state's requirements for survival of the claim was insufficient to deem the state law inconsistent with federal law.[4]

§ 13.13   Period of Limitations

Another area in which federal law is deficient is the period of limitations governing actions under the Reconstruction Civil Rights Acts.[1] Accordingly, pursuant to § 1988, state statutes of limitations will apply unless deemed inconsistent with federal law.[2] A state's period will be deemed repugnant to federal policy if there is an indication that it unfairly discriminates against the federal cause of action, as where a special statute geared specifically to actions under § 1983 is shorter than the state's limitations period applicable to personal injury actions in general.[3] Section 1988 itself gives no guidance as to which period of limitations a particular state should apply. In *Wilson v. Garcia*,[4] the Supreme Court concluded that for the purposes of "uniformity, certainty, and the minimization of unnecessary litigation," all claims under § 1983[5] should be characterized in the same manner; and it chose the state period of limitations for tortious personal injury to govern.[6]

---

2. *Id.* at 594–95, 98 S.Ct. at 1997–98.

3. *Id.* at 591, 98 S.Ct. at 1996.

4. *Id.* at 591–92, 98 S.Ct. at 1996.

§ 13.13

1. In 1990 Congress passed 28 U.S.C.A. § 1658, which reads: "Except as otherwise provided by law, a civil action arising under an Act of Congress **enacted after the date of the enactment of this section** may not be commenced later than 4 years after the cause of action accrues." 28 U.S.C.A. § 1658 (Supp. 1993). In their hornbook on civil procedure, Professors Friedenthal, Kane and Miller suggest that § 1658 is applicable to claims under the Reconstruction Civil Rights Acts—and therefore federal law is not deficient in this area. Friedenthal, Kane & Miller, *Civil Procedure* § 4.7 n. 28 (2d ed. 19___). The language of § 1658, however, unambiguously applies only to acts of Congress *enacted after* December 1, 1990, the date of enactment of § 1658. Pub. L. No. 101–650, Title III, § 313(a), 104 Stat. 5114 (enacted Dec. 1, 1990). It should therefore continue to be necessary to borrow state limitation periods in actions under the Reconstruction Civil Rights Acts.

2. *See Wilson v. Garcia*, 471 U.S. 261, 266, 105 S.Ct. 1938, 1942, 85 L.Ed.2d 254 (1985).

3. *Arnold v. Duchesne County, Utah*, 26 F.3d 982 (10th Cir.1994), *cert. denied*, ___ U.S. ___, 115 S.Ct. 721, 130 L.Ed.2d 626 (1995).

4. 471 U.S. 261, 275, 105 S.Ct. 1938, 1946, 85 L.Ed.2d 254 (1985). *But cf. Williams v. City of Oakland*, 915 F.Supp. 1074 (N.D.Cal.1996) (striking as inconsistent with § 1983 policies favoring compensation of victims a California survivorship statute that precluded recovery for pain and suffering, since statute would substantially reduce the type and amount of damages recoverable in all § 1983 actions where the victim dies before entry of judgment).

5. In fact, all the Reconstruction Acts use the applicable (although variable) state law period of limitations for tortious personal injury as announced in *Wilson*. *See Goodman v. Lukens Steel Co.*, 482 U.S. 656, 662, 107 S.Ct. 2617, 2621, 96 L.Ed.2d 572 (1987) (§ 1981 claims); *Village of Bellwood v. Dwivedi*, 895 F.2d 1521, 1528 (7th Cir. 1990) (§ 1982 claims); *Bougher v. University of Pittsburgh*, 882 F.2d 74, 79 (3d Cir. 1989) (§ 1985 claims).

6. *Id.* at 280, 105 S.Ct. at 1949.

What period applies, though when the forum state's law contains numerous limitation periods for different types of personal injury? In *Owens v. Okure*,[7] the Court acknowledged that the states have a broad range of limitations periods for intentional and unintentional injury to the person. But it also observed that each state has a general or residual statute for personal injury actions and held that period presumptively binding.[8] However, the Court also stated that each chosen residual period must be consistent with the policy underlying the federal cause of action. For example, if a court deems a residual period too short, it could hold that period inconsistent with the remedial goals of a § 1983 claim.

§ 13.14 Suspension or "Tolling" Circumstances

In *Johnson v. Railway Express Agency, Inc.*,[1] the Supreme Court held that forum state law also determines the circumstances that suspend or "toll" the running of the borrowed state statute of limitations on a claim under § 1981, so long as those tolling rules are not inconsistent with the policy of the underlying federal cause of action.[2]

> Any period of limitation ... is understood fully only in the context of the various circumstances that suspend it from running against a particular cause of action.... In borrowing a state period of limitation for application to a federal cause of action, a federal court is relying on the State's wisdom in setting a limit, and exceptions thereto....[3]

In *Johnson* the Court refused to create a federal tolling rule and held that the timely filing of a Title VII action did not suspend the running of the applicable state period of limitation on a claim under § 1981.[4]

Similarly, in *Board of Regents v. Tomanio*,[5] the Court refused to create a federal tolling rule that would suspend the running of a § 1983 limitations period pending completion of an independent action in state

7. 488 U.S. 235, 109 S.Ct. 573, 102 L.Ed.2d 594 (1989).

8. *Id.* at 236, 109 S.Ct. at 574. *See, e.g., Blake v. Dickason,* 997 F.2d 749 (10th Cir. 1993) (applying Colorado's two-year residual statute of limitations, rather than a six-year statute of limitations for sexual assault against a minor, to a § 1983 claim concerning an alleged sexual assault by a teacher against a student).

§ 13.14

1. 421 U.S. 454, 95 S.Ct. 1716, 44 L.Ed.2d 295 (1975).

2. 421 U.S. at 463, 95 S.Ct. at 1721.

3. 421 U.S. at 462–63, 95 S.Ct. at 1721–22. *See also Cervantes v. City of San Diego,* 5 F.3d 1273 (9th Cir.1993) (equitable tolling under California law during period § 1983

plaintiff pursued administrative remedies, even though federal law does not require such exhaustion before § 1983 action may be brought); *Sierra–Serpa v. Martinez,* 995 F.2d 325 (1st Cir.1993) (holding that Puerto Rico's legislature implicitly repealed statute excluding time of imprisonment from period of limitations); *Harding v. Galceran,* 889 F.2d 906 (9th Cir.1989) (state criminal proceedings tolled federal action), *cert. denied,* 498 U.S. 1082, 111 S.Ct. 951, 112 L.Ed.2d 1040 (1991); *Winters v. Lynch,* 805 F.2d 1037 (6th Cir.1986) (incarceration of plaintiff tolled federal action); *Gonzalez v. Santiago,* 550 F.2d 687 (1st Cir.1977) (state administrative proceedings did not toll federal action).

4. *Id.* at 463, 95 S.Ct. at 1722.

5. 446 U.S. 478, 100 S.Ct. 1790, 64 L.Ed.2d 440 (1980).

court.[6] In *Tomanio* the plaintiff sought relief in federal court after receiving an adverse state court judgment on an independent cause of action. The defendants moved to dismiss on the ground that the § 1983 action was time barred under the applicable state period of limitations. The district court, however, fashioned a federal rule tolling the limitations period during the pendency of the independent state court action, although state tolling provisions would not have tolled the period. The Supreme Court reversed and held that the state's failure to provide for tolling did not unduly undermine the federal policies of deterrence and compensation underlying § 1983. Federal courts have been generally unwilling to fashion their own version of a "continuing violation" theory that would have the effect of extending the limitations period where the statute has run on the defendant's primary conduct targeted by the action but some of the defendant's subsequent conduct took place or its consequences were felt within the limitations period.[7]

It is nevertheless important to keep in mind the caution in *Johnson* that federal judges may substitute their own tolling doctrine for that of a state when the state approach "would be inconsistent with the federal policy underlying the cause of action" in question.[8] In such cases of undue inconsistency, federal courts have applied either their own doctrines of equitable tolling[9] or federal-state hybrids.[10]

Some questions have been raised about the position the plaintiff's attorney is left in after the decision in *Johnson*. If the attorney chooses to seek relief under Title VII on the one hand and, on the other, § 1981 or § 1983, it is possible that both the conciliatory Title VII administrative proceeding and an adversarial judicial proceeding on the civil rights claim may run concurrently. Indeed Title VII requires the plaintiff to complete administrative agency processing before filing a judicial action under that statute.[11] The adversarial nature of the civil rights judicial proceeding could undermine the Title VII conciliation process; and absent a uniform federal tolling rule, the plaintiff will be pressured by the applicable state limitations statute to file the federal civil rights action before the related Title VII claim is administratively conciliated. In addition, a final judgment in the § 1981 or § 1983 judicial proceeding, if rendered prior to the conclusion of the Title VII administrative proceeding, may claim preclude a Title VII judicial action.[12]

---

6. 446 U.S. at 491, 100 S.Ct. at 1799.

7. *See, e.g., Russo v. Casey,* 15 F.3d 1089 (9th Cir.1993) (unpublished), *cert. denied,* ___ U.S. ___, 115 S.Ct. 65, 130 L.Ed.2d 22 (1994). See discussion on the applications of the continuing violations doctrine to claims under Title VII and EPA in Chapters 5 and 8, respectively.

8. 421 U.S. at 465, 95 S.Ct. at 1722.

9. *See, e.g., Farmers & Merchants Nat'l Bank v. Bryan,* 902 F.2d 1520, 1522 (10th Cir.1990); *Gurley v. Documation Inc.,* 674 F.2d 253, 259 (4th Cir.1982).

10. *See, e.g., Smith v. City of Chicago Heights,* 951 F.2d 834, 840 (7th Cir.1992). *But cf. Nelson v. County of Allegheny,* 60 F.3d 1010 (3d Cir.1995) (tolling in § 1983 action ends when class certification denied, because that order is not immediately appealable in federal, unlike state court, and tolling until certification question ultimately resolved would therefore extend tolling period excessively), *cert. denied,* ___ U.S. ___, 116 S.Ct. 1266, 134 L.Ed.2d 213 (1996).

11. *See* Chapter 5.

12. *See* §§ 13.20–13.22, *infra.*

In *Herrmann v. Cencom Cable Assoc., Inc.*,[13] Judge Posner suggests four methods by which the plaintiff may sidestep these pitfalls. First, the plaintiff may ask the state or federal agency to accelerate the Title VII administrative process so that it will be completed before a final Reconstruction Act judgment is entered. Second, in the hope of reaching an informal settlement in the Title VII administrative process, the employer may agree not to plead the Reconstruction Act statute of limitations. Third, the parties could agree to split the claims, so that the plaintiff avoids claim preclusion stemming from a prior judgment in the Reconstruction Act lawsuit.[14] Fourth, absent such an agreement, the employee could file suit on the Reconstruction claims, ask the court to suspend proceedings during the pendency of the Title VII administrative process, and then, if necessary, amend the complaint to include the Title VII claim after the administrative process concludes.

§ 13.15 The Limitations "Cut–Off" Event

State law, then, provides the applicable limitations period and the circumstances that suspend or "toll" the running of the statute on Reconstruction Act claims. Federal law, however, determines whether the action has been commenced in federal court within the appropriate period.[1] "[W]hen the underlying cause of action is based on federal law and the absence of an express statute of limitations makes it necessary to borrow a limitations period from another statute, the action is not barred if it has been 'commenced' in compliance with [Federal Rule of Civil Procedure] 3 within the borrowed period."[2] Rule 3 in turn provides that "[a] civil action is commenced by filing a complaint with the court."[3] This principle is now routinely applied to federal court actions under the Reconstruction Acts.[4] Accordingly, civil rights plaintiffs unable to complete service of process before the last day of the limitations period may nevertheless timely commence a federal court action simply by filing a complaint with the clerk.[5]

---

13. 999 F.2d 223, 225 (7th Cir.1993).

14. *See* Restatement Second of Judgments § 26(a).

§ 13.15

1. *West v. Conrail*, 481 U.S. 35, 107 S.Ct. 1538, 95 L.Ed.2d 32 (1987). Thus, for example, a circuit court has applied the Supreme Court's liberal "mailbox rule" to measure the timely filing of a state prisoner's pro se complaint under § 1983. *Cooper v. Brookshire,* 70 F.3d 377 (5th Cir.1995).

2. *Id.* at 39.

3. Fed.R.Civ.Pro. 3.

4. *See Lewis v. Richmond City Police Dept.*, 947 F.2d 733 (4th Cir.1991); *Gray v. Lacke*, 885 F.2d 399 (7th Cir.1989), *cert. denied*, 494 U.S. 1029, 110 S.Ct. 1476, 108 L.Ed.2d 613 (1990); *Martin v. Demma*, 831 F.2d 69 (5th Cir.1987); *Younger v. Chernovetz*, 792 F.Supp. 173 (D.Conn.1992); *Urban v. Department of Social & Rehabilitative Services*, 1989 WL 48485 (D.Kan.1989). *See also Del Raine v. Carlson*, 826 F.2d 698 (7th Cir.1987).

5. Merely filing the complaint, however, does not end the plaintiff's obligation. Rule 4(m) of the Federal Rules of Civil Procedure contains a distinct requirement of diligent prosecution of any federal civil action, whether or not timely commenced for limitations purposes:

If service of the summons and complaint is not made upon a defendant within 120 days after the filing of the complaint, the court ... shall dismiss the action without prejudice ....

When federal court jurisdiction is based on diversity of citizenship—that is, the underlying cause of action is based on state law—state law determines the events necessary to commence the action within the applicable period of limitation.[6] But pendent state law claims annexed to Title VII or Reconstruction Act claims rest not on diversity jurisdiction but on a federal court's "supplemental" jurisdiction authorized by 28 U.S.C.A. § 1367. Hence although no reported cases on the point have been discovered, federal courts appear to assume that the minimal FRCP 3 "filing" rule that governs timely commencement of federal question claims also governs timely commencement of any pendent state law claims, even though the limitations period and "tolling" rules on both claims are supplied by state law.

The end result is a patchwork of rules about limitations that pay lip service to both national civil rights policy and state prerogatives but effectively serve neither. National uniformity is defeated because the states may apply general personal injury limitations periods of varying lengths to Reconstruction Act claims, as well as their own rules on tolling. Thus where the defendant is amenable to personal jurisdiction in more than one state, the plaintiff may forum shop for a longer period of limitations. This federalism-driven deference to state choice is only slightly offset by some federal court decisions that federal law governs the determination of when a § 1983 claim accrues.[7] Yet viewed in another way the deference to state choice is little more than nominal, for the federal courts control the characterization of the Reconstruction Act claim as one involving personal injury; and what state is practically free to adjust its general personal injury limitations period based on considerations pertaining to the tiny fraction of such claims that are based on violations of federal civil rights? Further, the liberal federal rules of civil procedure on timely commencement (FRCP 3) and relation back (FRCP 15) have the potential of defeating the state policy, embedded in its chosen limitations period, of ensuring that the defendant receives notice of the action within a specified time after the claim accrues.

The Supreme Court's recent decision in *Heck v. Humphrey*[8] will force some rethinking about how state limitations periods should be applied to prisoners' civil rights claims that, if successful, would invalidate their underlying convictions. Before *Heck*, for example, it was common for federal courts to conclude that a § 1983 damages claim based on an unconstitutional search, seizure or confession accrued when the alleged unconstitutional conduct occurred,[9] not at some later time when the conviction was overturned by a state court on appeal.[10] The federal court could then stay the § 1983 action pending the conclusion of

6. *See Walker v. Armco Steel Corp.*, 446 U.S. 740, 752–53, 100 S.Ct. 1978, 1986–86, 64 L.Ed.2d 659 (1980).

7. *See, e.g., Morse v. University of Vt.*, 973 F.2d 122, 125 (2d Cir.1992).

8. 512 U.S. 477, 114 S.Ct. 2364, 129 L.Ed.2d 383 (1994).

9. *See, e.g., Day v. Morgenthau*, 909 F.2d 75, 79 (2d Cir.1990) (opinion on petition for rehearing).

10. *Woods v. Candela*, 13 F.3d 574 (2d Cir.), *vacated for further consideration in light of Heck*, ___ U.S. ___, 115 S.Ct. 44, 130 L.Ed.2d 5 (1994).

the state criminal proceedings, on the rationale that those proceedings might have outcome-determinative effect on the civil rights claim by way of issue preclusion.[11] While this approach compelled the putative civil rights plaintiff to file an action that might not be able to proceed until after state criminal proceedings were final on appeal, it protected defendants by giving them early notice of the claims they would eventually face.

Heck, however, holds that no § 1983 claim which, if successful, would necessarily undermine the state conviction of a prisoner or former prisoner even comes into being until and unless that conviction is overturned on direct appeal or state or federal habeas. Presumably, therefore, this kind of § 1983 claim accrues for limitations purposes only when the underlying conviction is reversed or set aside; if so, an earlier filing would be both premature and unnecessary.[12] But far from assisting the plaintiff, *Heck* preserves the maximum opportunity for adverse fact findings to be preclusive against him in his federal civil rights damages action, by ensuring that state courts, or perhaps a federal habeas court, will have earlier decided the questions crucial to § 1983 liability.[13] And of course the several barriers to habeas relief that the Supreme Court has raised in recent years[14] significantly reduced the possibility that the criminal conviction will ever be overturned after direct appeal, thus also barring the kinds of § 1983 claims that fall within *Heck*.

Federal and state courts have concurrent jurisdiction over claims under the Reconstruction Civil Rights Acts.[15] This raises the question whether federal civil rights claims brought in state court must comply with the timely commencement requirements of the forum state. There are three principal patterns of state commencement rules. About a third of the states follow the Rule 3 model for federal law claims by treating the filing of a complaint, without more, as commencing an action for purposes of limitations. These states require only that service be accomplished within a specified or reasonable time after filing. Roughly another third of the states require that the plaintiff not only file the complaint but also issue or deliver the summons to a designated

---

11. *See, e.g., Mack v. Varelas,* 835 F.2d 995 (2d Cir.1987). Issue preclusion in this situation could be invoked against the civil rights plaintiff based on facts necessarily found in a successful criminal prosecution, under the doctrine of *Allen v. McCurry,* discussed earlier in this chapter.

12. *Smith v. Holtz,* 87 F.3d 108 (3d Cir.), *cert. filed,* ___ U.S. ___, ___ S.Ct. ___, ___ L.Ed.2d ___, 65 U.S.L.W. 3342 (1996) (§ 1983 claim accrued only when state supreme court dismissed murder charges, not earlier when conviction reversed and new trial ordered); *Woods v. Candela,* 47 F.3d 545 (2d Cir.1995), *cert. denied,* ___ U.S. ___, 116 S.Ct. 54, 133 L.Ed.2d 18 (1995); *Triplett v. Azordegan,* 478 F.Supp. 872

(N.D.Iowa 1977) (coerced confession claim did not "ripen" until state court ordered plaintiff released from prison, seventeen years after his conviction).

13. *See, e.g., King v. Goldsmith,* 897 F.2d 885 (7th Cir.1990) (state post-conviction court's determination that police officers did not offer false testimony at plaintiff's criminal trial precludes him from relitigating that issue in action under Section 1983).

14. *See, e.g., Duncan v. Henry,* ___ U.S. ___, 115 S.Ct. 887, 130 L.Ed.2d 865 (1995) and cases cited therein.

15. § 13.9, *supra.*

officer before the limitations period runs; service may still be accomplished afterwards. The remaining states follow the strict approach, which demands that the defendant be served with process (or receive some substitute form of notice) before the limitations period expires.[16]

The question of what timely commencement rule governs in state court is sharpened by a Supreme Court decision, *Felder v. Casey*,[17] that federal civil rights plaintiffs in state court need *not* comply with state law "notice-of-claim" prerequisites to suits against municipalities and other local government entities, even though compliance would probably not derail any significant number of the federal claims. There is a residual irony of *Felder*. The Court, under the *Robertson* interpretation of § 1988,[18] respects insurmountable, quasi-*substantive* state obstacles to recovery (e.g., Louisiana's limited approach to survival of claims), in civil rights actions brought in *federal* court. At the same time, under *Felder*, it disrespects easily satisfied, nondiscriminatory state *procedural* prerequisites when civil rights actions are brought in *state* court. The former decision to some degree undermines the federal-court-access policy of § 1983, while the latter undermines the state comity/federalism shibboleth to which the Court elsewhere so frequently defers.

Despite *Felder*, it appears that the states should be free to apply their own definitions of timely commencement for limitations purposes to federal civil rights claims in their own courts. After all, the state's definition of what event "beats the clock" is as integral a component of the overall limitations calculation as the "tolling" circumstances that *Johnson* and *Tomanio* held governed by state law. And FRCP 3, like the FRCP 15(c) "relation-back" provision that can stretch a state's limitations period against misnamed defendants, is part of a body of rules designed to "govern the procedure in the United States district courts,"[19] not in state courts. Even if, under *Felder*, a plaintiff need not comply with a state law *precondition* to suit, she should be bound by ordinary provisions of state court procedure—indeed that procedure is really the only thing that she chooses when she opts for a state rather than a federal forum.

Curiously, the only reported decision even remotely dealing with this issue goes the other way. In *Pimental v. Safeway*,[20] plaintiff brought suit in state court under the National Labor Relations Act. The court held that *West v. Conrail*, and therefore the simple filing requirement of FRCP 3,[21] defined the commencement of the action even in state court. The NLRA, however, unlike the Reconstruction Acts, has its own (federal) statute of limitations, which the court may have been loathe to

---

16. Annotation, *Tolling of Statute of Limitations Where Process is Not Served Before Expiration of Limitation Period*, 27 A.L.R.2d 236 (1953 & Supps. 1970, 1978, 1981 & 1987); 54 C.J.S. *Limitations of Actions* §§ 265–68 (1948 & Supp. 1987).

17. 487 U.S. 131, 108 S.Ct. 2302, 101 L.Ed.2d 123 (1988).

18. See text accompanying notes 1–4, § 13.12, *supra*.

19. Fed.R.Civ.Pro. 1.

20. 196 Cal.App.3d 92, 241 Cal.Rptr. 568 (1987).

21. See text accompanying notes 1–4, § 13.15, *supra*.

impede by applying the stricter timely commencement rule used in the forum state's courts. The decision does not commend itself for use when the plaintiff chooses a state forum to pursue a civil rights or employment discrimination claim, where the applicable statute of limitations is supplied by state law.

I. PLEADING

Library References:

    C.J.S. Civil Rights §§ 294, 372, 389.
    West's Key No. Digests, Civil Rights ☞233, 375.

§ 13.16   In General

Rule 8(a)(2) of the Federal Rules of Civil Procedure requires "a short and plain statement of the claim." It was in a civil rights case that the Supreme Court, in the late 1950's, announced its famous relaxed standard for compliance with Rule 8(a)(2): that a complaint should not be dismissed for failure to state a claim unless it "appears beyond doubt" that a plaintiff can prove no facts in support of her claim which would entitle her to relief.[1] The Court affirmed this standard in *Haines v. Kerner*,[2] adding that a prisoner's *pro se* complaint alleging denial of due process in steps leading up to his solitary confinement would be held to "less stringent requirements than formal pleadings drafted by lawyers."

Subsequently, however, the Court's commitment to the permissive *Conley* brand of notice pleading was called into question. Most notably, and, considering the history of Rule 8(a)(2), somewhat ironically, the development has been most evident in civil rights actions. The phenomenon is illustrated by the Court's standing test articulated in *Allen v. Wright*.[3] The plaintiffs sought to enjoin the IRS from continuing to grant tax exemptions to racially discriminatory private schools across the nation. The Court acknowledged that the injury alleged—impairment of plaintiff's children's access to a desegregated education—was legally cognizable. But it wrote that injury could be fairly traceable to the IRS practice, and thus warrant standing, only if, *in their complaint*, the plaintiffs could offer evidentiary support about a number of interrelated factual propositions relating to the number of such private schools in each of their communities; the likely policy response of each such school if its tax exemption were withdrawn; and whether parents whose children attended such schools would, as a result of the schools' various responses, transfer their children to public schools in sufficient numbers to have a significant impact on the public schools' racial composition. To say the least, this kind of pleading is a far cry from *Conley*. A plaintiff purporting in the complaint to have unearthed all the informa-

---

§ 13.16

1. *Conley v. Gibson*, 355 U.S. 41, 78 S.Ct. 99, 2 L.Ed.2d 80 (1957).

2. 404 U.S. 519, 92 S.Ct. 594, 30 L.Ed.2d 652 (1972).

3. *See supra* § 13.10, note 1.

tion the Court required would in recent years at least be courting sanctions under Rule 11 for subscribing to facts not supported by a reasonable pre-filing investigation!

At the same time the federal courts of appeals considerably tightened pleading requirements not just on the jurisdictional requirement of standing but on the basic elements of claims under § 1983. Among the reasons offered for the trend were (a) to buttress Rule 11's deterrence of frivolous complaints; (b) to prevent public officials from being subjected to vexatious actions (on an analogy between vexatious suits and fraud claims which, by the express terms of Federal Rule of Civil Procedure 9(b), must be pleaded with specificity); (c) to slow the increase in the workload of federal courts, and particularly the § 1983 actions that constituted the largest single category on the federal docket; (d) to prevent the civil rights action from being misused as a device for litigating a state court claim in federal court; and (e) better to fulfill Rule 8's goal of providing the defendant fair notice.

To dam the flood of § 1983 actions after *Monell*, some courts devised "heightened pleading" requirements. The United States Court of Appeals for the Fifth Circuit began by imposing such a requirement on § 1983 suits against governmental actors in their individual capacities.[4] The Fifth Circuit's heightened pleading requirement forced the plaintiff to "alleg[e] with particularity all material facts on which he contends he will establish his right to recovery, which will include detailed facts supporting the contention that the plea of [qualified] immunity cannot be sustained."[5] In a later case, *Palmer v. City of San Antonio*,[6] the Fifth Circuit expanded the heightened pleading standard to cases involving municipal liability under § 1983.[7]

It remained to be seen if the Supreme Court would endorse the lower courts' rearguard action against *Conley* and in effect carve out a comprehensive exception to federal notice pleading for actions brought to enforce civil rights. An occasion for this decision was provided by a Fifth Circuit decision dismissing on the pleadings a *Monell/City of Canton* claim against a municipality alleging that the municipality had failed adequately to train and supervise its police officers. The Fifth Circuit had affirmed a district court ruling that the complaint failed to allege with sufficient factual detail and particularity "the requisite allegation that the municipality engaged in a policy or custom for which it can be held responsible" in conformance with the circuit's heightened pleading requirements.[8] The Supreme Court granted certiorari to resolve a conflict among the circuits as to the propriety of applying such requirements "to Section 1983 actions alleging municipal liability."

Charlene Leatherman filed suit against the Tarrant County Narcotics Intelligence and Coordination Unit (TCNICU), Tim Curry (the di-

---

4. *Elliott v. Perez*, 751 F.2d 1472, 1482 (5th Cir.1985).

5. *Id.*

6. 810 F.2d 514, 516–17 (5th Cir.1987).

7. *Id.*

8. *Leatherman v. Tarrant County Narcotics Intelligence and Coordination Unit*, 954 F.2d 1054 (5th Cir.1992).

rector of TCNICU), the cities of Lake Worth, Texas and Grapevine, Texas, and Don Carpenter (the sheriff of Tarrant County).[9] There were two searches of homes by the TCNICU. The first involved plaintiff Leatherman, who, while driving in Fort Worth, Texas, was stopped and surrounded by police officers.[10] The police informed Ms. Leatherman that her home was in the process of being searched and that the police killed her two dogs.[11] Although nothing relevant to the investigation was found in the Leatherman home, the officers remained on the Leatherman's front lawn for over an hour "apparently celebrating their unbridled power." [12]

The second incident involved plaintiff Andert.[13] Andert's home was searched by the TCNICU after receiving reports that police officers detected odors "associated with the manufacture of amphetamines" coming from Andert's home.[14] Andert and his family were mourning the death of Andert's wife when the members of the TCNICU entered the Andert home without knocking or identifying themselves.[15] Andert was beaten and injured by the TCNICU, without provocation on Andert's part.[16] After a one and one-half hour search, the police, as with the Leatherman situation, found nothing associated with drug activity.[17]

The Plaintiffs (Leatherman and Andert) then sued the TCNICU, Tim Curry, the cities of Lake Worth, Texas and Grapevine, Texas, and Don Carpenter.[18] The Plaintiffs' amended complaint centered on a theory that the municipalities had failed to "formulate and implement an adequate policy to train its officers ... on the proper manner to execute search warrants and respond when confronted by family dogs." [19] The Fifth Circuit deemed the allegations to be of the general, "boilerplate" variety.[20] Defendants TCNICU, Curry, and Carpenter moved to dismiss the complaint under Rule 12(b)(6) of the Federal Rules of Civil Procedure and alternatively for the court to enter summary judgment under Rule 56.[21]

The district court granted Defendants' motion, dismissing all Plaintiffs' claims even against defendants who failed to join in the motion.[22] The district court determined that Plaintiffs' complaint failed to meet the Fifth Circuit's heightened pleading standard, and even if it might have, the Defendants would be entitled to summary judgment as a matter of law.[23] On appeal, the Fifth Circuit noted that the Plaintiffs' complaint did state the facts surrounding the two searches in detail but

---

9. *Leatherman v. Tarrant County Narcotics Intelligence and Coordination Unit,* 755 F.Supp. 726, 727–28 (N.D.Tex.1991).

10. *Leatherman v. Tarrant County Narcotics Intelligence and Coordination Unit,* 954 F.2d 1054, 1055–56 (5th Cir.1992).

11. *Id.*

12. *Id.* at 1056.

13. *Id.*

14. *Id.*

15. *Id.*

16. *Id.*

17. *Id.*

18. *Id.*

19. *Id.*

20. *Id.*

21. *Id.*

22. *Id.* at 1057.

23. *Id.*

added that the complaint did not state "any facts with respect to the adequacy (or inadequacy) of the police training." [24] Therefore, the heightened pleading standard was not satisfied and the motion to dismiss was affirmed.[25]

In *Leatherman v. Tarrant County Narcotics Intelligence and Coordination Unit*,[26] a unanimous Court, per Chief Justice Rehnquist, reversed, repudiating special strict requirements for pleading the elements of civil rights claims against government entities. Moreover, although Justice Rehnquist's opinion specifically disclaimed any decision on the matter, the logic of the Court's opinion strongly suggests that it would reject the application of heightened pleading standards to claims against individual government officials as well.

The Court first addressed the county's assertion that *Monell*'s refusal to permit government entity liability via simple respondeat superior and its insistence instead on a showing of custom or policy [27] implied an immunity from suit that would be undermined by standard Rule 8 notice pleading. The Court replied that this argument falsely equated a mere heightened liability standard with a complete immunity from suit; it overlooked the fundamental distinction between § 1983 actions against individual governmental official defendants, who enjoy a range of absolute or qualified immunity, and actions against municipalities, which, the Court reaffirmed, enjoyed none.

Although the Court added that it therefore had "no occasion to consider whether our qualified immunity jurisprudence would require ... heightened pleading in cases involving individual government officials," the balance of its opinion suggests a negative answer to that suggestion. For the Court found it "impossible to square" the Fifth Circuit's heightened pleading standard "with the liberal system of 'notice pleading' set up by the Federal Rules." [28] In the succeeding sentence it described the *Conley* construction of Federal Rule 8(a)(2) as affirming "that the Rule meant what it said"—the "Federal Rules ... do not require a claimant to set out in detail the facts...." [29] Of course the Rules no more call for fact pleading with respect to civil rights claims against individual government officials than for claims against government entities.

The Court buttressed its conclusion by observing that in Rule 9(b) Congress imposed a pleading particularity burden in only two instances, fraud and mistake. It omitted "any reference to complaints alleging municipal liability under Section 1983. Expressio unius est exclusio alterius." Since Rule 9(b) is equally as silent about claims against individual government officials, it should follow that the Court would not

---

24. *Id.* at 1058.

25. *Id.* at 1055.

26. 507 U.S. 163, 113 S.Ct. 1160, 122 L.Ed.2d 517 (1993).

27. *See* Chapter 2.

28. 507 U.S. at 167, 113 S.Ct. at 1163.

29. *Id.* (quoting *Conley*, 355 U.S. at 47, 78 S.Ct. at 103).

subject those claims, either, to a regime of fact pleading.[30] The thorough protection those defendants already enjoy in the form of absolute and qualified immunity and related procedural accommodations [31] should reassure the Court that notice pleading alone will not cause them to be unfairly dragged through trial or saddled with liability. By extension, the Court's reasoning should also shield Title VII and other employment discrimination claims from heightened pleading requirements, because Federal Rule 9(b) does not except them either from *Conley* or the general "friendly eye" of Rule 8(f).[32]

Indeed the Fourth Circuit recently expanded the application of *Leatherman* to a claim alleging a "failure to train" or other sort of government entity inaction, excusing the plaintiff from alleging multiple instances of prior, similar violations in order to state a claim for relief.[33] So applied, *Leatherman* facilitates § 1983 damage actions against entities in precisely the respect that *City of Los Angeles v. Lyons*[34] impedes injunctive relief against them: by obviating the necessity for pre-filing discovery of "pattern" facts difficult to obtain by private investigation.

As observed above, however, Chief Justice Rehnquist, undermined the simplicity of the Court's conclusion based on Federal Rules 8 and 9 with the following statement: "We thus have no occasion to consider whether our qualified immunity jurisprudence would require a heightened pleading in cases involving individual government officials." [35] Relying on this caveat in *Leatherman*, some courts of appeals have refused to give plaintiffs the benefit of its notice pleading principle on their § 1983 claims against individual defendants. Acknowledging that "the Supreme Court's rationale would appear to apply in any case

---

30. *See Hall v. Dworkin*, 829 F.Supp. 1403, 1409 n. 5 (N.D.N.Y.1993). *See also Batiste v. Colonial Sugars, Inc.*, 1993 WL 149067 (E.D.La.1993) ("There is no logical reason to limit Leatherman's holding to claims of municipal liability, as the same Federal Rules of Civil Procedure govern all claims arising under § 1983. Imposing a heightened pleading standard for claims against individual public officials or private parties would conflict with the Federal Rules every bit as much as it would for claims against municipalities."); *Callaghan v. Congemi*, 1993 WL 114523, *5 (E.D.La. 1993) (*Callaghan* is much more blunt about the subject. "*Leatherman* ... appears to sound the death knell for *Elliott*'s requirement of heightened pleading in suits involving individual government officials."); *Timmons v. Cisneros*, 1993 WL 276863 (E.D.Pa. 1993) (Also extends *Leatherman* to "offici[al[s] employed by a municipality.").

31. See Chapter on § 1983.

32. *Garus v. Rose Acre Farms, Inc.*, 839 F.Supp. 563 (N.D.Ind.1993).

33. *Jordan v. Jackson*, 15 F.3d 333 (4th Cir.1994). *Cf. Jackson v. Marion County*,

66 F.3d 151 (7th Cir.1995) (pro se prisoner's § 1983 complaint adequately stated claim against county for conspiring to "cover up the facts" of arrests allegedly made with excessive force despite absence of factual detail).

34. *See* discussion of *Lyons* at text accompanying § 13.10, note 12.

35. *Leatherman*, 507 U.S. at 165, 113 S.Ct. at 1162. This unwillingness to extend the new rule beyond the parameters of municipal liability may trace not only to the Court's customary aversion to dictum but also to the views of Justice Kennedy. In *Siegert v. Gilley*, 500 U.S. 226, 111 S.Ct. 1789, 114 L.Ed.2d 277 (1991), his concurring opinion would have required the plaintiff to anticipate and overcome the individual government officer's affirmative defense of qualified immunity in accordance with a heightened pleading standard. 500 U.S. at 235, 111 S.Ct. at 1795. (Kennedy, J. concurring). Heightened pleading thus reinforces the qualified immunity defense the Court has devised in order to prevent discovery which would disrupt the work of the individual governmental official.

outside the fraud or mistake context," the Ninth Circuit has nevertheless joined the District of Columbia Court of Appeals in retaining the heightened pleading standard for individual defendant cases.[36] Both courts cited the Supreme Court's limitation of its decision to entity actions and its refusal to address heightened pleading requirements as applied to cases where government officials are sued in their individual capacities and are therefore entitled to raise the defense of qualified immunity. The Fifth Circuit, too, has adhered to its heightened pleading rule as applied to individual defendants asserting qualified immunity.[37]

In any event, even if heightened pleading survives in cases against individual defendants because they may assert the defense of qualified immunity, the plaintiff does not in such cases face a heightened burden of *proof* on the elements of her own claim—the ordinary preponderance-of-the-evidence standard suffices.[38] And more recently, the Fifth Circuit, sitting en banc, has recognized that the Reply, more than the Complaint, is the pleading in which plaintiff may most effectively respond to the affirmative defense of qualified immunity which, unless defendant makes a motion before serving a responsive pleading, is not even asserted until defendant serves its Answer.[39] The court stood by its insistence that the plaintiff's complaint be pled with greater than usual "factual detail and particularity," but abandoned its insistence that the plaintiff "fully anticipate the defense in his complaint at the risk of dismissal under Fed.R.Civ.P. 12."

Acknowledging that under controlling Supreme Court precedent qualified immunity is an affirmative defense, the burden of pleading which therefore rests with the defendant,[40] the Fifth Circuit effected a compromise that respects both the individual defendant's interest in a detailed recitation of the plaintiff's claim and the F.R.C.P. 7(a) and 8(a) sequence of pleading that requires defendants to assert affirmative defenses in the Answer. The plaintiff suing a public official under § 1983 must "file a short and plain statement of his complaint," but one

---

36. *Branch v. Tunnell,* 14 F.3d 449 (9th Cir.1994); *Kimberlin v. Quinlan,* 6 F.3d 789 (D.C.Cir.1993) (*Bivens* claim), *vacated,* 515 U.S. ___, 115 S.Ct. 2552, 132 L.Ed.2d 252 (1995), for consideration in light of *Johnson v. Jones,* 515 U.S. ___, 115 S.Ct. 2151, 132 L.Ed.2d 238 (1995). *See also Mendocino Environmental Center v. Mendocino County,* 14 F.3d 457 (9th Cir.1994) (heightened standard met).

37. *Cinel v. Connick,* 15 F.3d 1338 (5th Cir.), *cert. denied,* ___ U.S. ___, 115 S.Ct. 189, 130 L.Ed.2d 122 (1994). District courts have joined the chorus, relying for the most part on the Supreme Court's express refusal to apply the standard notice pleading rule to cases against individual defendants. *McDonald v. City of Freeport,* 834 F.Supp. 921, 929 n. 2 (S.D.Tex.1993);

Orange v. County of Suffolk, 830 F.Supp. 701 (E.D.N.Y.1993); *Idoux v. Lamar Univ. Sys.,* 828 F.Supp. 1252, 1256 n. 2 (E.D.Tex. 1993).

38. *See Tatro v. Kervin,* 41 F.3d 9 (1st Cir.1994) (jury instructions could not insist that § 1983 plaintiff had to prove that an arrest was "clearly" lacking probable cause or "clearly" effected with excessive force, for that would constitute a disguised, belated assertion of the qualified immunity defense that should have been determined at the outset of the action by the court as a matter of law).

39. *Schultea v. Wood,* 47 F.3d 1427 (5th Cir.1995) (en banc).

40. *Id.* (citing *Gomez v. Toledo,* 446 U.S. 635, 100 S.Ct. 1920, 64 L.Ed.2d 572 (1980)).

"that rests on more than conclusions alone." The district court may then, "in its discretion, insist that a plaintiff file a reply tailored to an answer pleading the defense of qualified immunity." If no such reply is ordered, the plaintiff need not and indeed may not reply to the allegations in the answer that assert qualified immunity.[41] Vindicating the immunity doctrine will ordinarily require such a reply, the court wrote, and the district court's discretion not to do so is narrow when greater detail might assist the defendant in maintaining the defense. The district court may ban discovery altogether at this threshold pleading stage or may limit any necessary discovery to the defense of qualified immunity.[42]

In at least one respect, plaintiffs should continue to plead with particularity. Damages under § 1983 are available against state officials only when they are sued in their individual or personal, rather than official, capacities.[43] Although a majority of the circuits give latitude to the plaintiff who fails to plead expressly the capacity in which he sues a state official, some do not.[44]

Plaintiffs may, as in other cases in federal court, plead in the alternative, as authorized by Federal Rule of Civil Procedure 8(e)(2), and in doing so they are not making binding admissions. Thus an employment discrimination plaintiff may allege both that she is not guilty of misconduct attributed to her by the employer, and that she suffered harsher discipline for that misconduct because of her race, without conceding the truth of the employer's accusations.[45]

The standard of pleading sufficiency applicable to cases that proceed in forma pauperis is governed by 28 U.S.C.A. § 1915(d), which calls for dismissal of complaints that are "factually frivolous." The Supreme Court has clarified that the quoted standard is met when the trial court deems the facts alleged to be "irrational" or "wholly incredible," even if they are not so far-fetched as to conflict with facts that are judicially noticeable. The Court also warned the federal circuits not to review § 1915(d) dismissals de novo, reminding them that the decision is confided to the discretion of the district courts and may be overturned only for an abuse of that discretion.[46]

41. Federal Rule 7(a) permits the plaintiff to reply, absent such a court order, only to the allegations of any *counterclaim* (not defense) the defendant might have asserted in its answer.

42. *Schultea, supra.*

43. *See supra* § 2.22.

44. *Biggs v. Meadows,* 66 F.3d 56 (4th Cir.1995) (applying majority view and citing cases). *But cf. Colvin v. McDougall,* 62 F.3d 1316 (11th Cir.1995) (vacating damages award against county sheriff because caption in the complaint failed to specify that he was sued in his individual rather than official capacity).

45. *Henry v. Daytop Village, Inc.,* 42 F.3d 89 (2d Cir.1994).

46. *Denton v. Hernandez,* 504 U.S. 25, 112 S.Ct. 1728, 118 L.Ed.2d 340 (1992).

J. CLASS ACTIONS

Library References:

C.J.S. Federal Civil Procedure §§ 63 et seq.
West's Key No. Digests, Federal Civil Procedure ⊸161 et seq.

§ 13.17 In General

Claims of systemic disparate treatment or of neutral practices having a disproportionate adverse impact will often be advanced through class actions. In theory, class actions should expedite the presentation of evidence on behalf of large numbers of claimants. In fact, after receiving class actions quite hospitably in the early years of the Act,[1] courts have recently erected substantial barriers to class certification through interpretations of Federal Rule 23.

The most formidable obstacle was declared by a Supreme Court decision construing the "commonality" and "typicality" requirements of Rule 23(a)(2). *General Telephone Company of the Southwest v. Falcon*[2] precludes named plaintiffs complaining of discrimination in one term and condition of employment (for example, promotion) from representing persons complaining about the same kind of discrimination with respect to other terms and conditions of employment (for example, hiring). The Court stressed that the requisite commonality and typicality must extend to defendant employer practices, not merely the general type of discrimination—race, gender, religion, or national origin—alleged.

The Court in *Falcon* did note that named plaintiffs complaining of one term or condition of employment could represent class members complaining of another where the employer used a common testing procedure or where different kinds of employees could be shown to have suffered discrimination "in the same general fashion," *e.g.*, through "entirely subjective decision making processes" or at the hands of the same employer personnel.[3] Nevertheless, many lower courts have taken a grudging approach to class action certification since *Falcon*. In any event, to apply the *Falcon* tests, district courts find it extremely challenging to obey the Supreme Court's separate admonition that they avoid considering the merits of the underlying claim when deciding class certification.[4]

Plaintiffs' counsel have tried to comply with the Court's strictures by assembling class-representative complements composed of applicants, employees and former employees complaining of varied terms and conditions of employment, with each named plaintiff offering to represent a discrete subclass. Defendants routinely reply with objections and motions asserting the existence of conflicts among the proposed subclasses and challenging plaintiffs' adequacy to represent them. When these

---

§ 13.17

1. Some of the facilitative features of Title VII class actions, and the procedural relief they afford to individual class members who would otherwise have to perfect all of that statute's preconditions to suit, are discussed in Chapter 5, above.

2. 457 U.S. 147, 102 S.Ct. 2364, 72 L.Ed.2d 740 (1982), discussed in § 5.7, *supra.*

3. *See also Bazemore v. Friday*, 478 U.S. 385, 106 S.Ct. 3000, 92 L.Ed.2d 315 (1986).

4. *Eisen v. Carlisle & Jacquelin*, 417 U.S. 156, 177, 94 S.Ct. 2140, 2152, 40 L.Ed.2d 732 (1974).

motions succeed and class certification is denied, they may doom the class action as a practical matter, since orders denying certification are not ordinarily appealable on an interlocutory basis. Instead, the named plaintiffs must incur the expense and delay of proceeding to trial on their individual claims; only later, on appeal, may they challenge the denial of certification. Even when defendants' objections are not sustained, they usually necessitate extensive discovery and briefing about the propriety of certification that can rob the class action of its intended expedition and efficiency.

The Court has also held that orders denying class action certification are not appealable before final judgment on the merits, even as it recognized that this decision would often induce a plaintiff to abandon his claim.[5] This ruling serves as another major practical impediment to broad-based civil rights or employment discrimination class actions. For example, in one case the trial judge, apparently disregarding the across-the-board approach to certifying class actions that prevailed in his circuit before *Falcon*, refused to certify a class because of dissimilarities between the allegations and employment statuses of the named plaintiffs and some of those class members whom they sought to represent. Interlocutory review of his order denying class certification not being available, class counsel sought extraordinary review by means of mandamus or prohibition, which was denied. They were then compelled to litigate on the merits the claims of the individual named plaintiffs alone. On appeal from that trial, they were permitted for the first time to challenge the trial court's ruling on class certification. But by the time that appeal could be heard, *Falcon* had intervened, effectively overruling the circuit's across-the-board approach to certification. In accordance with the doctrine that an appellate court should ordinarily apply the decisional law in effect at the time it decides, rather than contrary law in effect at the time of the decision under review,[6] the Eleventh Circuit affirmed the denial of class certification.[7]

K. CLAIM AND ISSUE PRECLUSION IN ACTIONS UNDER TITLE VII AND THE RECONSTRUCTION CIVIL RIGHTS ACTS

Library References:

C.J.S. Judgments §§ 592–593, 598 et seq.
West's Key No. Digests, Judgment ☞540 et seq.

§ 13.18 Overview

An increasingly important procedural issue is the extent, if any, to which court actions will be barred by prior agency or court determina-

---

5. *Coopers & Lybrand v. Livesay*, 437 U.S. 463, 98 S.Ct. 2454, 57 L.Ed.2d 351 (1978).

6. *See Landgraf v. USI Film Products*, 511 U.S. 244, 114 S.Ct. 1483, 128 L.Ed.2d 229 (1994).

7. *George Washington et al. v. Brown & Williamson Tobacco Corporation*, 959 F.2d 1566 (11th Cir.1992).

tions. EEOC reasonable cause determinations, as observed above, cannot prevent timely filed Title VII actions from being heard on the merits. Nor will the decisions of state or local administrative deferral agencies have preclusive effect on subsequent Title VII actions: it would make no sense to preclude a federal court when EEOC is merely required to give those decisions "substantial weight."[1] Resolving a conflict in the circuits, and reaching a result consonant with *University of Tennessee v. Elliott*,[2] the Supreme Court has recently held that the unreviewed administrative determinations of state or local agencies do not preclude private plaintiff actions under ADEA, either.[3] An ADEA lawsuit brought by EEOC, in contrast, will generally preclude private relief.

When, on the other hand, a state administrative determination is reviewed by a state court, a judgment of non-liability may bar a Title VII action in federal court by force of the Full Faith and Credit Act,[4] at least where the judicial review was sought by the employee.[5] *Kremer*, declining to create a Title VII exception to the preclusion required by the terms of § 1738, holds that a federal court presented with a Title VII claim must give the same deference to the state appellate judgment as would a court of the rendering state under the state's principles of preclusion. Consistent with *Kremer*, a state court judgment reviewing a state administrative determination will be accorded the same preclusive effect in a federal court ADEA action that it would receive in the courts of the state.[6] Preclusion under the applicable *state's* law is, however, an important precondition to *Kremer* preclusion; where the state law does not bar subsequent federal employment discrimination suits, *Kremer* will not bar federal court relitigation.[7] Nevertheless, *Kremer* stands as a warning to prospective Title VII plaintiffs that they may forego their Title VII claim by seeking state judicial review of an adverse agency determination.

Kremer has been extended by some lower courts to reach the situation where the *employer* seeks state court review of the administrative agency decision.[8] This approach is plainly questionable. Employ-

§ 13.18

1. *University of Tennessee v. Elliott*, 478 U.S. 788, 106 S.Ct. 3220, 92 L.Ed.2d 635 (1986). *But see Mitchell v. Albuquerque Bd. of Education*, 2 F.3d 1160 (10th Cir. 1993) (unpublished), *cert. denied*, 510 U.S. 1045, 114 S.Ct. 693, 126 L.Ed.2d 660 (1994).

2. 478 U.S. 788, 106 S.Ct. 3220, 92 L.Ed.2d 635 (1986). *Elliott* is discussed in Section 13.23, *infra*.

3. *Astoria Federal Sav. & Loan Ass'n v. Solimino*, 501 U.S. 104, 111 S.Ct. 2166, 115 L.Ed.2d 96 (1991).

4. 28 U.S.C.A. § 1738.

5. *Kremer v. Chemical Construction Corp.*, 456 U.S. 461, 102 S.Ct. 1883, 72 L.Ed.2d 262 (1982). (Usually, as in *Kremer* itself, relitigation is barred by issue rather than claim preclusion. This is because most state courts reviewing underlying agency decisions have appellate jurisdiction to review only claims brought under their own state anti-discrimination laws, not claims asserted under Title VII).

6. *See Hogue v. Royse City, Texas*, 939 F.2d 1249 (5th Cir.1991).

7. *Brye v. Brakebush*, 32 F.3d 1179 (7th Cir.1994); *McNasby v. Crown Cork & Seal Co.*, 888 F.2d 270 (3d Cir.1989), *cert. denied*, 494 U.S. 1066, 110 S.Ct. 1783, 108 L.Ed.2d 784 (1990).

8. *Zanders v. National Railroad Passenger Corp.*, 898 F.2d 1127 (6th Cir.1990); *Trujillo v. County of Santa Clara*, 775 F.2d 1359 (9th Cir.1985); *Hickman v. Electronic Keyboarding, Inc.*, 741 F.2d 230 (8th Cir. 1984); and *Gonsalves v. Alpine Country*

ment discrimination claimants in most states—those designated by EEOC as "deferral" jurisdictions—are required by Title VII itself to institute state administrative agency proceedings as a prerequisite to the effective filing of a charge with EEOC and therefore ultimately as a condition of prosecuting a Title VII claim in state or federal court.[9] If preclusion of the Title VII claim follows from an employer-instituted review of a state administrative proceeding that Title VII requires the potential plaintiff to commence, the employer in those states may avoid a judicial defense of Title VII claims by its own unilateral action whenever the agency finds for the claimant. The Supreme Court has repudiated a similar result under Title VII or ADEA in two decisions after *Kremer*.[10]

Against this background, *University of Tennessee v. Elliott*[11] creates an awkward dichotomy; it rejects preclusion based on judicially unreviewed state agency proceedings that underlie Title VII actions, but allows such preclusion in actions under the Reconstruction statutes. The plaintiff in *Elliott* presented both types of federal claims to the federal court, but found himself precluded only on the civil rights claim.

Federal courts have also barred Title VII claims by according preclusive effect to prior federal judgments in actions arising out of the same employment setting. In *Woods v. Dunlop Tire Corp.*,[12] for example, a Title VII claim was barred by res judicata because plaintiff had failed to raise that claim in a previous action that challenged her termination under the Labor Management Relations Act ("LMRA"). The Court invoked the broad, contemporary approach to claim preclusion, observing that it is "the identity of facts surrounding the occurrence which constitutes the cause of action" that triggers res judicata even if the legal theories advanced in the two actions are distinct. That the short statute of limitations on the labor claim ran before EEOC had finished administrative processing of plaintiff's claim did not persuade the court to relieve plaintiff of the ordinary consequences of federal common law preclusion. The court noted that plaintiff could have demanded a notice of right to sue from EEOC 180 days after filing her EEOC charge or if necessary sought a stay of the LMRA action pending completion of EEOC proceedings, and then amended the LMRA complaint to include a claim under Title VII.

In the class action employment discrimination setting, however, the Supreme Court has somewhat eased the subsequent sting of an adverse federal court judgment. Federal common law accords preclusive effect to judgments rejecting pattern-type discrimination claims in subsequent actions asserting the same theory. But adverse class action or group-

---

Club, 727 F.2d 27 (1st Cir.1984). In *Zanders* the court even precluded the Title VII claim where the *employer* instituted state court proceedings not based on employment discrimination.

9. See discussion of state and federal administrative agency proceedings under Title VII in Chapter 5, above.

10. See text accompanying notes 16–17, § 13.22, and notes 6–8, § 13.23, *infra*.

11. 478 U.S. 788, 106 S.Ct. 3220, 92 L.Ed.2d 635 (1986).

12. 972 F.2d 36 (2d Cir.1992), *cert. denied*, 506 U.S. 1053, 113 S.Ct. 977, 122 L.Ed.2d 131 (1993).

based judgments (e.g., concerning the disproportionate adverse impact of a neutral practice) do not bar the claims of individual class members alleging disparate treatment à la *McDonnell Douglas/Burdine*.[13] Moreover, when a court denies class action certification, individual class members' claims may still be timely, because the filing of a class action has been held to toll the 90–day period for filing suit until the denial of certification.[14]

§ 13.19 The Full Faith and Credit Act[1] and State–Court Proceedings: Section 1738

When an aspect of a Reconstruction Act claim, previously decided by a state court judgment, reappears in another action in a court of the same state, that state's preclusion law applies. Where the second action is in the court of another state, however, the Full Faith and Credit Clause of Article IV of the Constitution governs. Article IV, § 1 of the United States Constitution provides that "Full Faith and Credit shall be given in each State to the ... judicial Proceedings of every other State."[2] This has long been understood to require the second state's courts to give as much effect to the first state court's judgment as would the courts of the first state under its own principles of preclusion.

If the preclusion possibility is presented by the effect of a federal court judgment in another federal court, the governing rules are furnished by a federal common law of preclusion as exemplified by the Supreme Court's decisions in *Blonder–Tongue Laboratories v. University of Illinois Foundation*[3] and *Parklane Hosiery Co. v. Shore*.[4] Finally, the Supremacy Clause of the Constitution, Article VI, dictates the preclusive effect of a federal court decision, in accordance with that federal common law, in a subsequent action in state court.

But are federal courts precluded by prior *state* court judgments determining a claim of federal civil rights? Federal courts are not constrained by the requirements of the Full Faith and Credit Clause. However, shortly after the ratification of the Constitution, Congress established legislation "specifically to insure that federal courts, not included within the constitutional provision, would be bound by state judgments."[5] On May 26, 1790, Congress passed the first version of the Full Faith and Credit statute.[6] Subsequently re-enacted by Congress,[7]

---

13. *See Cooper v. Federal Reserve Bank of Richmond*, 467 U.S. 867, 104 S.Ct. 2794, 81 L.Ed.2d 718 (1984).

14. *Crown, Cork & Seal Co. v. Parker*, 462 U.S. 345, 103 S.Ct. 2392, 76 L.Ed.2d 628 (1983).

§ 13.19

1. 28 U.S.C.A. § 1738 (1988).

2. U.S. Const. Art. IV, § 1.

3. 402 U.S. 313, 91 S.Ct. 1434, 28 L.Ed.2d 788 (1971).

4. 439 U.S. 322, 99 S.Ct. 645, 58 L.Ed.2d 552 (1979).

5. *Kremer v. Chemical Construction Corp.*, 456 U.S. 461, 482 n. 24, 102 S.Ct. 1883, 1898 n. 24, 72 L.Ed.2d 262 (1982); *see also Davis v. Davis*, 305 U.S. 32, 40, 59 S.Ct. 3, 6, 83 L.Ed. 26 (1938).

6. Act of May 26, 1790, ch. 11, 1 Stat. 122.

7. Act of Mar. 27, 1804, ch. 56, 2 Stat. 298–99.

the Full Faith and Credit statute has existed in substantially the same form ever since.

Currently, this statute is located at 28 U.S.C.A. § 1738.[8] Section 1738 is divided into three parts. First, § 1738 provides for the authentication of the acts of the legislature "of any State, Territory, or Possession of the United States."[9] Second, § 1738 provides the means by which the "records and judicial proceedings of any [ ] State, Territory, or Possession ... shall be proved and admitted in other courts within the United States."[10] Third, § 1738 provides that:

> [s]uch Acts, records and judicial proceedings or copies thereof, so authenticated, shall have the same full faith and credit in every court within the United States and its Territories and Possessions as they have by law or usage in the courts of such State, Territory or Possession from which they are taken.[11]

As understood by the Supreme Court, § 1738 requires "all federal courts to give preclusive effect to state-court judgments whenever the courts of the State from which the judgments emerged would do so...."[12] Federal courts must therefore accord a state court decision the same preclusive effect as to claims ("res judicata," in the familiar earlier terminology) and issues ("collateral estoppel") that state courts would give. Of course a strong motive behind the passage of the Civil Rights Act of 1871[13] and the Civil Rights Act of 1964[14] was the "grave congressional concern that the state courts had been deficient in protecting federal rights."[15] Neither statute, however, specifically mentions § 1738, and the United States Supreme Court has had to decide whether federal court actions under the Reconstruction Civil Rights Acts and Title VII escape state court preclusion through an implied exception to § 1738.[16] We will turn to this issue shortly.

§ 13.20 Issue and Claim Preclusion

Section 1738 requires the federal courts to give state court judgments the same preclusive effect that other courts in that state would.[1] A federal court applying that statute may therefore have to consult the preclusion law of any of the fifty states. As a representative introduction to the modern law of claim and issue preclusion prevailing among

---

8. 28 U.S.C.A. § 1738 (1988).

9. 28 U.S.C.A. § 1738.

10. *Id.*

11. *Id.*

12. *Allen v. McCurry*, 449 U.S. 90, 96, 101 S.Ct. 411, 415, 66 L.Ed.2d 308 (1980).

13. 42 U.S.C.A. § 1983.

14. 42 U.S.C.A. § 2000e *et seq.*

15. *McCurry, supra* note 12, at 98, 101 S.Ct. at 417. *See also Kremer v. Chemical Construction Corp.,* 456 U.S. 461, 467, 472, 102 S.Ct. 1883, 1890, 72 L.Ed.2d 262 (1982)

(stating that although Congress intended the states to play a role in Title VII enforcement, the federal courts would be "entrusted with ultimate enforcement responsibility.").

16. *See McCurry, supra* note 12; *Kremer, supra* note 5; *Migra v. Warren City School Dist.,* 465 U.S. 75, 104 S.Ct. 892, 79 L.Ed.2d 56 (1984); and *University of Tennessee v. Elliott, supra* note 11, § 13.18.

§ 13.20

1. *See supra* note 11, § 13.19 and accompanying text.

the states, this Chapter will refer to the widely followed Second Restatement of Judgments, which is also the model for the contemporary federal common law of preclusion.

a. *Claim Preclusion*

Claim preclusion refers to the preclusive effect of prior adjudications on entire causes of action asserted in subsequent litigation. An essential prerequisite of claim preclusion is identity not only of claims but of parties in the two actions; in the subsequent litigation, the same plaintiff or someone in privity with him must be suing the same defendant or her privy. Under the Second Restatement, claim preclusion is divided into the Rule of Merger and the Rule of Bar, depending on whether the plaintiff (merger) or defendant (bar) succeeded in the initial litigation.[2] The general Rule of Merger is that

> [w]hen a valid and final[3] judgment is rendered in favor of the **plaintiff**:
>
> (1) The plaintiff cannot thereafter maintain an action on the original claim or any part thereof, although he may be able to maintain an action upon the judgment....[4]

In particular, so long as the first forum had subject matter jurisdiction to entertain the unasserted claims and provide the same remedies,[5] merger precludes the plaintiff from bringing a subsequent action based on the same real-life transaction or event, either to obtain greater or different relief from that sought originally or to assert a distinct legal theory, or to bring forth new or different evidence or arguments.[6]

The general Rule of Bar, in contrast, is triggered by a valid and final personal judgment rendered in favor of the **defendant**.... [I]t too, prevents "another action by the plaintiff on the same claim."[7] Bar precludes in fewer situations than does merger, because it is subject to an exception for judgments rendered on certain procedural grounds. The first-action outcomes that do not bar include dismissals based on lack of jurisdiction, venue, nonjoinder, misjoinder, failure to satisfy a precondition to suit, prematurity, initial voluntary dismissals, and any grounds of termination that, according to the forum state's or federal court's procedural law or rules, do not bar another action on the same

---

2. 2d Restatement of Judgments [hereinafter, "Restatement"] § 17.

3. For the purposes of both claim and issue preclusion, a judgment is final from "the date of its rendition, without regard to the date of commencement of the action in which it is rendered or the action in which it is to be given effect." *Id.* § 14. The definition includes trial court judgments on appeal, until and unless reversed.

4. 2d Restatement of Judgments § 18.

5. *Id.* § 26(1)(c) (exception to § 24 definition of "claim") (discussed *infra* at text accompanying note 13; at n. 34, § 13.21; and at text accompanying note 40, § 13.23).

Where a state habeas court lacked authority to award damages, a § 1983 claim that arose out of the same transaction and would therefore ordinarily have been claim precluded was held not barred by res judicata. The court observed, however, that fact findings reached by the habeas tribunal might have collateral estoppel effect in the judicial action under § 1983. *Burgos v. Hopkins*, 14 F.3d 787 (2d Cir.1994).

6. 2d Restatement of Judgments §§ 18, 24.

7. *Id.* § 19 (emphasis added).

claim.[8] The exception is often said to apply to judgments "not on the merits." This terminology is misleadingly overinclusive, because in contemporary practice repetitive voluntary dismissals as well as involuntary dismissals for failure to state a claim, for untimeliness, or for failure to prosecute or obey court rules or orders all trigger bar even though they plainly do not determine the factual substance of the plaintiff's claim.

A threshold prerequisite for claim preclusion is that the claim sought to be precluded in a subsequent action be the same as that asserted in a prior action. In sharp contrast to earlier, more technical and limited definitions, Restatement § 24 provides that the claim capable of extinction (by merger or bar) includes "all rights of the plaintiff to remedies against the defendant with respect to all or any part of the transaction, or series of connected transactions, out of which the action arose." [9] So long as the two actions stem from the same core of real-life events, claim preclusion is possible: the same claim is presented even if the plaintiff proceeds on different legal theories,[10] offers different supporting evidence, or seeks different or additional relief.[11] On the other hand, a prisoner's § 1983 damages claim predicated on unconstitutional conditions of confinement is spatially and temporally distinct from his habeas claim challenging an underlying criminal conviction. Accordingly, the § 1983 claim will not be claim precluded by a previous habeas determination—for res judicata purposes, these are different claims.[12]

The definition of claim identity prevents the relitigation not only of causes of action actually raised and adjudicated but of any causes that could have been raised with respect to the same real-life transaction. Thus in the lexicon of modern preclusion, claims based on state law and federal law arising from the same police arrest or employment discharge are considered part of the same transaction; if either is not raised in the original action it may be precluded in subsequent litigation, provided, as would usually be the case, the first forum had subject matter jurisdiction

---

8. See *id.* § 20 (1) and (2). For a representative list of first-action dismissal grounds that do not usually bar another action on the same claim, see FRCP 41(a)(1) and 41(b). The grounds specifically listed there include only initial voluntary dismissals and involuntary dismissals based on the dilatory defenses of jurisdiction, venue or failure to join a necessary or indispensable party. But the Federal Rule goes on to provide that an order dismissing on any other ground operates as an "adjudication upon the merits," that is, it bars, unless it "otherwise specifies." The Restatement, by including dismissals for prematurity or failure to satisfy a precondition to suit among the grounds that do not bar relitigation of the claim even where the dismissal order is silent on that point, thus bars on fewer grounds than Federal Rule

41 would suggest. A federal court using the Restatement as its guide for fashioning a federal common law of preclusion would accordingly not bar on those two grounds despite the contrary implication of the Federal Rules. Compare Restatement §§ 20(2) with 20(1)(c).

9. *Id.* § 24.

10. *See Brzostowski v. Laidlaw Waste Systems, Inc.,* 49 F.3d 337 (7th Cir.1995) (APEA claim arising from discharge claim precluded by judgment in action asserting discharge violated employment contract).

11. See the comments to Restatement 2d § 24.

12. *Rhodes v. Hannigan,* 12 F.3d 989 (10th Cir.1993).

to entertain both claims.[13]   Only if the second proceeding is significantly predicated on spatially or temporally distinct real-life events will it normally be considered a separate claim free of the preclusion defense.

These principles are easier to state than to apply.   Take, for example, *Herrmann v. Cencom Cable Assoc., Inc.*[14]   There the Seventh Circuit Court of Appeals defined "transaction" under the Restatement as follows: "[the] two claims are one for purposes of res judicata if they are based on the same, or nearly the same, factual allegations."[15]   The plaintiff, after being discharged by the defendant, filed a charge of discrimination with the EEOC.   A few months later the plaintiff also filed suit in federal court against the defendant under the continuation of benefits provision of ERISA ("COBRA").   On defendant's motion, the district court granted summary judgment in the defendant's favor.   After obtaining a right-to-sue letter from the EEOC, plaintiff then instituted a Title VII action against the defendant.   The district court held the action precluded (by merger) because the claim under ERISA and the Title VII claim should have been brought in one lawsuit.

The plaintiff appealed and the Seventh Circuit reversed.   The court of appeals, Judge Posner writing, held that although the proceedings stemmed from a common fact—the discharge of the employee—the Title VII claim concerned primarily events before, and the COBRA claim primarily events after, the discharge.   The factual overlap was therefore insufficient to constitute one claim for purposes of res judicata.[16]   On the other hand, the court hypothesized a situation in which an employee has an employment contract that protects her from being fired without cause.   After the employee is fired, the employee brings suit alleging that the termination was in violation of both the contract and Title VII.   In this situation, the "two claims would be the same for purposes of res judicata because, although they would not have identical elements, the central factual issue," whether the employee was fired for cause, would be "at the center of litigation of both claims."[17]

A subsequent appellate decision presents slightly variant facts that may fall between the categories sketched in *Hermann*.   A federal employee filed suit alleging that his nonselection for promotion violated Title VII.   The employee then filed a class action asserting that the employer had a policy of retaliating against employees who had filed discrimination complaints by denying their subsequent personnel grievances.   The Eleventh Circuit upheld a district court decision that the

---

13.   See § 26(1)(c), Restatement (Second) of Judgments. *But see Humphrey v. Tharaldson Enterprises, Inc.,* 95 F.3d 624 (7th Cir.1996)(civil rights claims barred even though state agency where plaintiff first sought relief lacked jurisdiction over those claims); *Davis v. City of Chicago,* 53 F.3d 801, 803 (7th Cir.1995) (precluding federal law claim that plaintiff failed to assert when he invoked state court review of local administrative agency determination, even though it was not clear that state

court would exercise jurisdiction over that claim); *Misischia v. Pirie,* 60 F.3d 626 (9th Cir.1995) (res judicata invoked because § 1983 plaintiff did not seek judicial review in state court of administrative agency decision).

14.   999 F.2d 223, 226 (7th Cir.1993).

15.   *Id.* at 227.

16.   *Id.* at 226.

17.   *Id.*

class action was barred by res judicata because it involved the same parties and arose from the same nucleus of operative facts as the discrimination claim.[18] Here the events at issue in the two actions both concern conduct during the term of the plaintiff's employment, in contrast to the situation in *Hermann*. But the alleged retaliation occurred subsequent to the alleged discrimination, and the two claims concern somewhat different employer conduct. Is the retaliation claim barred because it would not have arisen "but for" the underlying claim of discrimination, a measure of claim identity expressly rejected by *Hermann*? A somewhat better rationale for the result is that plaintiff would probably have been allowed to amend his federal court complaint alleging unlawful discrimination to add a claim of unlawful retaliation without being required to initiate separate administrative proceedings on the latter claim.[19]

b. Issue Preclusion

Issue preclusion prevents the relitigation not of entire claims but only of particular, actually litigated, issues that were identifiably and necessarily determined by a prior judgment. The general rule of issue preclusion is that "[w]hen an issue of fact or law is **actually litigated** and determined by a valid and final judgment, and the determination is essential to the judgment, the determination is conclusive in a subsequent action ... **whether on the same or a different claim.**"[20] Therefore, in contrast to claim preclusion, an issue must have been actually litigated to enjoy preclusive effect in subsequent litigation.

The Second Restatement of Judgments contains a number of exceptions to the general rule of issue preclusion.[21] Most of these are necessary to temper the relatively recent judicial development that permits issue preclusion, unlike claim preclusion, to be invoked "nonmutually," that is, *by* (but not against—Due Process forbids that) a nonparty to the prior proceeding.[22] The most important Restatement escape from § 1738 issue preclusion in actions under Title VII and the Reconstruction Civil Rights Acts permits relitigation if

> [t]here is a clear and convincing need for a new determination of [an] issue ... because the party sought to be precluded, as a result of the conduct of his adversary or other special circumstances, did

---

18. *Stephens v. Department of Health and Human Services*, 9 F.3d 121 (11th Cir. 1993) (unpublished), *cert. denied*, ___ U.S. ___, 114 S.Ct. 2740, 129 L.Ed.2d 860 (1994).

19. See Chapter 5 on Title VII Procedures.

20. *Id.* § 27. It may be wondered why issue rather than claim preclusion would be invoked if the issue common to the two actions were re-presented in a claim that meets the Restatement § 24's broad concept of claim identity and hence is subject to claim preclusion. The reason is that some prerequisite of claim preclusion other than claim identity might be lacking. For

example, the original judgment may not be "final" or, in the "bar" situation, a judgment may fall within a § 20 exception for procedurally-grounded judgments deemed "not on the merits."

21. *See id.* §§ 28, 29.

22. *Bills v. Aseltine*, 52 F.3d 596, 604 (6th Cir.1995) (permitting § 1983 defendants to assert collateral estoppel nonmutually based on jury's finding, through ascertainable answers to special interrogatories, against plaintiff and in favor of co-defendant).

not have an adequate opportunity or incentive to obtain a **full and fair** adjudication in the initial action.[23]

Thus, subject only to the restraints imposed by the Second Restatement's flexible exceptions, a defendant not party to a prior action may assert issue preclusion "defensively" against a plaintiff who was a party to that action,[24] or in privity with such a party.[25] Further, a plaintiff not party to the prior proceedings may assert issue preclusion "offensively" [26]—although again, because of Due Process, only against a defendant who was a party, personally or through a privy, to the earlier litigation.

§ 13.21 State Court to Federal Court Preclusion; The Civil Rights Act of 1871

In *Allen v. McCurry*,[1] the United States Supreme Court held that actions under the Civil Rights Act of 1871 are not exempt from the mandate of § 1738, at least in regard to issue preclusion.[2] Civil rights plaintiffs have no special right to relitigate an issue in a federal forum as long as the state court was "acting within its proper jurisdiction [and] has given the parties a full and fair opportunity to litigate" the issue.[3]

The decision in *McCurry* stemmed from a state court adjudication of a Fourth Amendment search and seizure issue in the context of a suppression hearing and the subsequent attempt to relitigate the issue under § 1983 in federal court. In 1977, St. Louis, Missouri undercover police officers arrested McCurry and charged him with possession of heroin and assault with intent to kill. The undercover officers had gone

---

23. Restatement § 28; *see Kremer v. Chemical Construction Corp.*, 456 U.S. 461, 480, 102 S.Ct. 1883, 1896, 72 L.Ed.2d 262 (1982). In addition, "[a] party precluded from relitigating an issue with an opposing party ... is also precluded from doing so with another person unless the fact that he lacked **full and fair opportunity** to litigate the issue in the first action or other circumstances justify affording him an opportunity to relitigate the issue." *Id.* § 29.

24. *See Blonder–Tongue Laboratories v. University of Illinois Foundation*, 402 U.S. 313, 91 S.Ct. 1434, 28 L.Ed.2d 788 (1971). In an unusual defensive preclusion context, the police officers convicted in federal court of violating Rodney King's civil rights after their state court acquittal on felony assault charges were recently denied one of the standard exceptions to issue preclusion. The city of Los Angeles was relieved of the obligation to defend the officers in King's subsequent civil suit. They were estopped from denying that they had acted with actual malice in effecting his arrest—even though that finding, based on the federal criminal conviction, was at least implicitly rejected by the prior state court verdict of acquittal. *Allen v. City of Los Angeles*, 92 F.3d 842 (9th Cir.1996).

25. *See Tyus v. Schoemehl*, 93 F.3d 449 (8th Cir.1996) (alderman challenging vote dilution allegedly violative of Voting Rights Act held issue precluded based on decision in prior action brought by voters challenging same district boundaries); *Shaw v. Hahn*, 56 F.3d 1128 (9th Cir.1995) (§ 1983 plaintiff attacking her peremptory, allegedly race-based exclusion from a civil jury in prior action held to have been in privity with plaintiffs in that action who unsuccessfully challenged her exclusion under *Batson v. Kentucky*, 476 U.S. 79, 106 S.Ct. 1712, 90 L.Ed.2d 69 (1986), on theory that she shared identity of interest with them as a matter of law; plaintiff accordingly bound by determination against prior plaintiffs on that issue), *cert. denied*, ___ U.S. ___, 116 S.Ct. 478, 133 L.Ed.2d 407 (1996).

26. *See Parklane Hosiery Co. v. Shore*, 439 U.S. 322, 99 S.Ct. 645, 58 L.Ed.2d 552 (1979).

§ 13.21

1. 449 U.S. 90, 101 S.Ct. 411, 66 L.Ed.2d 308 (1980).

2. *Id.* at 103, 101 S.Ct. at 419.

3. *Id.* at 103, 101 S.Ct. at 419.

to McCurry's home to attempt to purchase heroin from him. A gun battle ensued between McCurry and the undercover officers, and McCurry surrendered in front of his home. The officers then entered the home to conduct a "sweep" for other persons and also seized several items. At a pretrial suppression hearing McCurry contested the admission of the items, relying on the Fourth Amendment's prohibition of a search and seizure without a valid warrant. The judge excluded some of the seized items, but admitted the rest as falling within the "plain view" exception. Subsequently, McCurry was convicted on both the possession and assault counts.[4]

McCurry then filed a § 1983 action in federal court against the officers, the city of St. Louis and the police department, alleging a violation of his Fourth Amendment rights. The general requirements of issue preclusion appeared to be in place: the second action presented the same issue; that issue had been actually litigated, leading to a determination that was necessary to the criminal conviction; and preclusion was being asserted against a party who had enjoyed a full and fair opportunity in the prior proceeding to object to the constitutionality of the police conduct.

The district court granted the defendants' motion for summary judgment, holding that issue preclusion prevented McCurry from relitigating the Fourth Amendment issue in the federal courts. McCurry appealed. The court of appeals reversed and remanded.[5] It held that because *Stone v. Powell*[6] barred McCurry from seeking habeas corpus relief in federal court, issue preclusion should not prevent McCurry from litigating his constitutional claim in a federal forum under § 1983.[7] The court of appeals was careful to note that it was not creating a general exemption for § 1983 actions from the preclusive effect under 28 U.S.C.A. § 1738 of issues previously litigated in a state court.[8] However, "invoking 'the special role of the federal courts in protecting civil rights,' the court concluded that the section 1983 suit was McCurry's only route to a federal forum for his ... [fourth amendment] claim and directed the

---

4. *Id.* at 92, 101 S.Ct. at 413.

5. *Id.* at 93, 101 S.Ct. at 414.

6. 428 U.S. 465, 96 S.Ct. 3037, 49 L.Ed.2d 1067 (1976). In *Stone* the Supreme Court held that when a state prisoner has been provided a full and fair opportunity to litigate a Fourth Amendment claim, federal habeas review is not available to attack collaterally the conviction as resting on evidence obtained through an unconstitutional search and seizure. *Id.* at 474. The Court has refused numerous times to extend the holding in *Stone* to other areas of federal habeas review. *See, e.g., Withrow v. Williams*, 507 U.S. 680, 113 S.Ct. 1745, 123 L.Ed.2d 407 (1993) (refusing to extend *Stone* to claims that conviction was based on statements obtained in violation of *Mi-*

randa); *Kimmelman v. Morrison*, 477 U.S. 365, 106 S.Ct. 2574, 91 L.Ed.2d 305 (1986) (refusing to extend *Stone* to Sixth Amendment claim of ineffective assistance of counsel); *Rose v. Mitchell*, 443 U.S. 545, 99 S.Ct. 2993, 61 L.Ed.2d 739 (1979) (refusing to extend *Stone* to equal protection claim of racial discrimination in the selection of a grand jury foreman); *Jackson v. Virginia*, 443 U.S. 307, 99 S.Ct. 2781, 61 L.Ed.2d 560 (1979) (refusing to extend *Stone* to prevent federal habeas review of Fourteenth Amendment due process claim of insufficient evidence to support a state conviction).

7. *Allen, supra* note 1, 449 U.S., at 93, 101 S.Ct. at 414.

8. *Id.*

trial court to allow him to proceed to trial unencumbered by [issue preclusion]." [9]

The Supreme Court granted certiorari and reversed.[10] The Court examined the text and legislative history of §§ 1738 and 1983 and found no intent on the part of Congress to deny preclusive effect to issues of fact or law decided by a state court, so long as that court has jurisdiction to entertain the civil rights claim and gives the parties a full and fair opportunity to litigate.[11] In the absence of any express or implied repeal of § 1738, the federal court must give the conviction as much preclusive effect as under the law of Missouri,[12] but no more.[13] The Court assured itself that issue preclusion would not be unfair because the collateral

9. *Id.*

10. *Id.* at 91, 105, 101 S.Ct. at 413, 420.

11. *Id.* at 103, 101 S.Ct. at 419. The majority opinion focuses on the ability of the state-court to provide "fair procedures" for the determination of the constitutional claims. *Id.* at 98, 103, 101 S.Ct. at 417, 419. The dissent rejects the idea that Congress "was [ ] concerned solely with procedural regularity." *Id.* at 108, 101 S.Ct. at 422. The dissent argues that "[t]he availability of a federal forum was not meant to turn on whether, in an individual case, the state procedures were adequate." *Id.* at 108–09, 101 S.Ct. at 422–23. Rather, Congress was concerned with the question as to whether "substantive justice" was obtainable in the state forum. *Id.* at 108, 101 S.Ct. at 422. On the several possible Congressional purposes underlying enactment of the Civil Rights Act of 1871, see the discussion of *Monroe v. Pape* in the chapter on § 1983.

12. *Id.* at 105, 101 S.Ct. at 420.

13. *See Haring v. Prosise*, 462 U.S. 306, 103 S.Ct. 2368, 76 L.Ed.2d 595 (1983), in which the Court held that § 1738 does not preclude a § 1983 action contesting the legality of a search and seizure when the prior criminal conviction was by guilty plea. The Court reasoned that because state law would not preclude, for want of actual litigation of the issue in the criminal proceeding, there could be no preclusion under § 1738. *Id.* at 317, 103 S.Ct. at 2375. In addition, the Court rejected the petitioners' proposal that the Court fashion a federal common-law rule of preclusion to bar the § 1983 claim. *Id.* at 323, 103 S.Ct. at 2378. The Court stated that "[a]doption of petitioners' rule of preclusion would threaten important interests in preserving federal courts as an available forum for the vindication of constitutional rights." *Id.* at 322, 103 S.Ct. at 2377. *See also,* Marjorie A. Silver, *In Lieu of Preclusion: Reconciling Administrative Decisionmaking and Feder-*

al Civil Rights Claims, 65 Indiana L.J. 367, 381 n. 77 (1990).

However, just three years later in *University of Tennessee v. Elliott*, 478 U.S. 788, 106 S.Ct. 3220, 92 L.Ed.2d 635 (1986), the Supreme Court did create a federal common-law rule of preclusion for state agency factfinding in actions under 1983. *See infra* § 13.23. *Elliott* concerned factfinding in state administrative proceedings; by its own terms, therefore, § 1738 was not applicable. Even though § 1738 did not apply, the Court made it clear that nothing in the text or legislative history of the Reconstruction Civil Rights Act suggested that Congress intended to prevent the further development of preclusion law. The Court fashioned a federal common-law rule of issue preclusion for state agency factfinding in actions under the Reconstruction Civil Rights Acts. 478 U.S. at 798, 106 S.Ct. at 3226.

The *Elliott* approval of administrative preclusion of § 1983 claims appears to ignore or discount the value enunciated in *Haring* of maintaining an available federal forum for the vindication of federal constitutional rights. A distinction, however, may lie in the involuntary nature of the state proceedings in *Haring*—a criminal prosecution—and the voluntary nature of the state proceedings in *Elliott*—in which the plaintiff submitted his discrimination claims to a state administrative agency although not required to do so by § 1983. This is one of the distinctions the Court has recognized, both before and after *Elliott*, between statutory employment discrimination claims—which a plaintiff is first required to submit to the appropriate state administrative agency—and Reconstruction Act claims, which have no such prerequisite. See *Elliott* (holding that unreviewed administrative proceedings do not preclude Title VII claims) and *Astoria Federal Savings & Loan Ass'n v. Solimino*, 501 U.S. 104, 112–14, 111 S.Ct. 2166, 2172–73, 115

estoppel rules of the states, to which the Court held § 1738 demanded deference, themselves contain a built-in exception that denies preclusion whenever the party opposing it has not received a full and fair opportunity to litigate the issue in question.

The burden is on the party asserting preclusion to show that the issue as to which estoppel is claimed was actually adjudicated in a prior proceeding. Accordingly, if there is doubt whether the prior judgment was broad enough to embrace a finding on the issue subsequently presented, estoppel will be denied. It follows that where the prior judgment is based on a general verdict, estoppel will be granted only if rational jurors must have determined the common issue a discernible way.[14] These principles were applied in a recent appellate decision involving an action by a criminal suspect against the police officer who released against him a police dog named Volker, as well as the officer's superiors and the city of Los Angeles. A jury had awarded Chew, the plaintiff, (not the dog) $13,000 against Officer Bunch, and a threshold question was whether that verdict represented only compensation for the kicks that Officer Bunch administered to Chew, or also compensated, even in part, for Volker's bites. In the latter event Chew, as well as the remaining defendants, would be collaterally estopped from relitigating the issue of dog bite damages. Then, because the $13,000 judgment had been paid in full, the "one-satisfaction" rule would preclude Chew from pursuing additional damages for dog-bite injuries from the remaining defendants. Because the court could not ascertain from a general plaintiff's verdict that the prior damages were awarded solely with respect to Volker's bites, and because the burden on that issue was on the remaining defendants who asserted collateral estoppel, the court presumed that the verdict compensated Chew for Bunch's kicks alone. On such facts the plaintiff's name, Chew, now seemed peculiarly appropriate: he got a second bite at the remaining defendants. Even more remarkable—and this is a bit much to chew—the court went on to hold that Chew could seek to hold those defendants liable for the very same bites with respect to which it presumed the first jury had absolved Officer Bunch.[15]

Four years later the Supreme Court in *Migra v. Warren City School District*[16] expanded *McCurry* by permitting preclusion under § 1738 of entire civil rights claims. On April 17, 1979, the Warren City School District Board of Education offered Dr. Ethel Migra a renewal of employment for the 1979–80 school year. Dr. Migra accepted this renewal by letter to the Board. Subsequently, the Board voted to withdraw Dr. Migra's renewal and terminated her employment. Dr.

L.Ed.2d 96 (1991) (same holding re ADEA claims).

14. *Chew v. Gates,* 27 F.3d 1432, 1438 (9th Cir.1994), *cert. denied,* __ U.S. __, 115 S.Ct. 1097, 130 L.Ed.2d 1065 (1995).

15. *Id.* at 1438–1439. How the supervisory defendants and the city might be liable

for those bites, even when Officer Bunch was not, is related as part of a discussion on the distinct liability of supervisors that is contained in § 2.23, *supra.*

16. 465 U.S. 75, 104 S.Ct. 892, 79 L.Ed.2d 56 (1984).

Migra brought suit in state court against the Board and its members for breach of contract and wrongful interference by the Board members with her contract of employment. The court ruled in her favor on the issue of the contract breach and thereafter she moved for voluntary dismissal of the wrongful interference claim.

Dr. Migra then filed an action in federal court under 42 U.S.C.A. §§ 1983 and 1985 against the Board, its individual members and the superintendent of schools. The defendants moved for summary judgment on the basis that the prior state-court judgment precluded the litigation of these claims. The ordinary prerequisites of claim preclusion appeared satisfied: the federal law claims, although on different legal theories, arose from the same employment termination that gave rise to the state cause of action, and as such they met Restatement § 24's expansive definition of claim identity; the same parties were aligned in the federal action in the same positions they occupied in the prior state proceedings; the prior judgment was final; and the state court could have exercised concurrent jurisdiction over the federal civil rights claims had Dr. Migra presented them.[17] The district court granted the defendant's motion. The Court of Appeals for the Sixth Circuit affirmed and the Supreme Court granted certiorari.

In equitable terms, the argument for claim preclusion, as in *Migra*, may seem stronger than for the issue preclusion supported in *McCurry* because the plaintiff who is claim precluded chose the state forum willingly when she might first have proceeded to federal court.[18] In federalism terms, however, there is a stronger argument for issue preclusion: federal judicial relitigation of issues actually adjudicated by the state court may affront the state judiciary, while permitting federal court adjudication of a federal claim not previously asserted in state court can cause no offense and may even promote comity by encouraging state law claims to be heard in state court.[19]

The Court glossed over these competing concerns, writing woodenly that the policies underpinning § 1983 do not "justify a distinction between the issue preclusive and claim preclusive effects of state-court judgments."[20] "Having rejected in [*McCurry*] the view that state-court judgments have no issue preclusive effect in Section 1983 suits," the Court also rejected "the view that Section 1983 prevents the judgment in

17. *See* § 13.20, *supra.*

18. See Blackmun, J., dissenting in *McCurry,* 449 U.S. at 105, 101 S.Ct. at 420.

19. Shapiro, "The Application of State Claim Preclusion Rules in a Federal Civil Rights Action," 10 Ohio Northern L.Rev. 223 (1983). Despite this argument, the local federal appellate court continues to respect Ohio's claim preclusion principles, holding § 1983 claims foreclosed to the full extent of all relief that could have been obtained in earlier filed, transactionally re-lated actions in the Ohio courts. *Thomson v. Harmony,* 65 F.3d 1314 (6th Cir.1995) *cert. denied,* ___ U.S. ___, 116 S.Ct. 1321, 134 L.Ed.2d 473 (1996) (where prior action filed in Ohio Court of Claims, which could award legal but not equitable relief, § 1983 claim precluded with respect to damages, with only equitable claims for prospective relief preserved).

20. *Migra,* 465 U.S. at 83, 104 S.Ct. at 897.

[Migra's] state-court proceeding from creating a claim preclusion bar."[21] Under the standard approach to claim preclusion, this holding should mean not only that the claim of a state court plaintiff is "merged" into her judgment when she wins in state court, but that when she loses there on the "merits" of her claim[22] any subsequent federal civil rights action will be "barred" when it concerns the same transactionally defined claim. Putting *McCurry* and *Migra* together, then, § 1738 has been held to mandate that in actions under the Reconstruction Civil Rights Acts a state judgment be given the same issue and claim preclusive effect in federal court as it would have in its own courts.

Migra compounds the consequences of Supreme Court decisions that compel a Reconstruction Act plaintiff to resort first to state court. We have already seen that potential § 1983 plaintiffs initially sued or shunted into a state court proceeding—either because they were criminally prosecuted, as in *Allen v. McCurry*, or because of *Younger* nonintervention or *Pullman* abstention—may later find their day in federal court clouded by issue preclusion under the Full Faith and Credit Statute according to the rules of the state court that rendered the prior judgment. A similar fate awaits civil rights plaintiffs who have initiated or defended quasi-judicial administrative proceedings; they will be bound by agency factual determinations according to the federal common law of issue preclusion the Supreme Court began to fashion in *University of Tennessee v. Elliott.*[23]

Another possibility for issue preclusion is provided by the Court's decisions holding legally insufficient any § 1983 claims by a convicted criminal that, if successful, would lead to his immediate or speedier release[24] or, more broadly, would simply impugn the validity of his criminal conviction.[25] In *Heck v. Humphrey*[26] the Court elaborated that, in order to respect the integrity of state judicial proceedings, such § 1983 claims are not cognizable unless and until the state conviction is overturned on direct appeal or questioned by the habeas corpus decision of a state or federal court. Read as a whole, the Court's opinion in *Heck* suggests that issue preclusion of the sort approved in *Allen v. McCurry*[27] may impair the prisoner's § 1983 claim when it finally ripens if and after a judgment overturning the state criminal conviction.

21. *Id.* at 84, 104 S.Ct. at 897.

22. See discussion of the dimensions of merger and bar in § 13.20, *supra.*

23. 478 U.S. 788, 106 S.Ct. 3220, 92 L.Ed.2d 635 (1986).

24. *Preiser v. Rodriguez*, 411 U.S. 475, 93 S.Ct. 1827, 36 L.Ed.2d 439 (1973).

25. *Heck v. Humphrey*, 512 U.S. 477, 114 S.Ct. 2364, 129 L.Ed.2d 383 (1994).

26. *Id.*

27. 449 U.S. 90, 101 S.Ct. 411, 66 L.Ed.2d 308 (1980). *McCurry*, discussed in detail above, held that issues litigated and necessarily resolved by a state criminal judgment of conviction may not be relitigated by the criminal defendant in a subsequent action under § 1983. Instead, § 1983 actions are subject to the general rule of 28 U.S.C.A. § 1728, the Full Faith and Credit Statute, which directs federal courts in subsequent litigation to respect a state court judgment to the same degree as that state's courts would under their own rules of res judicata and, pertinent in *McCurry*, collateral estoppel.

Heck's criminal conviction was affirmed by the state appellate court on direct appeal while his appeal to the Seventh Circuit of the district court's dismissal of his § 1983 action was pending. (In addition, Heck's two federal habeas petitions had failed.) The Supreme Court disclaimed that it was taking a position on the application to this situation of "res judicata"—in context, a broad use of the term intended to include collateral estoppel or issue preclusion.[28] Nevertheless, citing *Migra v. Warren City School Dist. Bd. of Education*,[29] which went beyond *McCurry* to subject § 1983 actions to claim as well as issue preclusion, it wrote that the "res judicata effect of state-court decisions in § 1983 actions is a matter of state law." In this way the Court alludes to its conclusion in both *Migra* and *McCurry* that the only possible impediment to preclusion stemming from a prior criminal conviction and affirmance might be any state law limitations on the preclusive use of that judgment. This reading of *Heck* is fortified by the Court's subsequent reminder that because of its "concerns for finality and consistency," it "has generally declined to expand opportunities for collateral attack."[30]

Thus fact determinations made by a state appellate or habeas court (or, for that matter, a federal habeas court)[31] when it overturns a criminal conviction and hence gives life to the kind of § 1983 claim presented in *Heck* probably cannot be relitigated in the action under § 1983. In theory, this could help rather than hinder the § 1983 plaintiff if the prior fact findings were favorable to him, as would often be true on our hypothesis that the judgment of conviction has been

---

28. *See* 512 U.S. at ___ n. 2, 114 S.Ct. at 2368 n. 2.

29. 465 U.S. 75, 104 S.Ct. 892, 79 L.Ed.2d 56 (1984).

30. *Heck*, 512 U.S. at ___, 114 S.Ct. at 2371.

31. A federal court entertaining a § 1983 claim would not be compelled to respect federal habeas factfinding by virtue of the Full Faith and Credit Statute, 28 U.S.C.A. § 1728, which directs federal courts to respect state court judgments, but rather by virtue of a judge-made federal common law of preclusion. One can imagine thorny conflicts between efficiency and sovereignty if a federal habeas court resolves an issue contrary to the finding of the state criminal or appellate court and then the same issue is presented in litigation under § 1983. If, in the § 1983 action, the state court's resolution of the issue is binding under *Allen*, what was the purpose of federal habeas? If, on the other hand, it is not, we compound the affront to state judicial factfinding first created by the federal habeas court's contrary finding. *See* Comment, The Collateral–Estoppel Effect to be Given State–Court Judgments in Fed-

eral § 1983 Damage Suits, 128 U.Pa.L.Rev. 1471 (1980).

Perhaps the issue is solved by the standard preclusion law of the Restatement (2d) of Judgments that is used by many state civil courts and must then be applied by a federal court hearing a § 1983 claim under the terms of § 1728. Issue preclusion would usually be invoked in the civil rights action by a person who was not a party to the prior criminal proceeding. (The state will have initiated most criminal proceedings, and under the Court's decision in *Will v. Michigan Dep't of State Police*, 491 U.S. 58, 109 S.Ct. 2304, 105 L.Ed.2d 45 (1989), the state is not a "person" suable in its own name under § 1983.) When a nonparty invokes issue preclusion, § 29 of the Restatement declares it a circumstance justifying relitigation if the prior determination (e.g., federal habeas) is itself inconsistent with another determination of the same issue (e.g., the state criminal court's factfinding). Thus a federal court, in permitting relitigation rather than deferring to either the state *or* federal habeas court's determination of the fact, would be obedient to state preclusion law made applicable under § 1728.

reversed. But in practice this kind of offensive issue preclusion will seldom work. Both issue and claim preclusion, it will be recalled, may be used only against a party to the prior proceeding or someone in privity with that party. The § 1983 plaintiff would therefore usually be able to issue preclude only the state, since most criminal proceedings will have been brought by the state, rather than local government subdivisions. But the Court has held that § 1983 claims do not lie against the state sued in its own name [32]; the § 1983 plaintiff whose conviction has been overturned will be usually be suing a police or prosecutorial official rather than the state itself. In short, there will usually be no § 1983 defendant also party to the prior criminal proceeding against which the plaintiff may use issue preclusion.

Migra ups the ante past these forms of issue preclusion. It deprives the putative plaintiff of *any* day in court on a § 1983 claim if she earlier sued on the same transaction. It should also have the same preclusive effect on § 1983 plaintiffs who as state (or federal) court civil defendants in previous litigation failed to assert compulsory counterclaims.[33] So when decisions of the Court direct a plaintiff to present "first" to the state court a claim growing out of the same transaction that gives rise to a claim under § 1983, "first" may as a practical matter become "final."

An example is furnished by *Pennhurst*, which construed the Eleventh Amendment to forbid federal courts from entertaining even *state* law claims asserted against a state. Suppose the plaintiff, as in *Pennhurst* itself, also wishes to assert federal civil rights claims stemming from the same events. *Migra* would presumably prevent her from filing in federal (or state) court on those claims after the state law claim goes to judgment in state court, where *Pennhurst* requires it to be brought. To preserve a federal forum for the federal civil rights claims, the plaintiff must file there first, either foregoing the state law claim or asserting it in a separate action in state court.[34]

---

32. See *Will v. Michigan Dep't of State Police*, 491 U.S. 58, 109 S.Ct. 2304, 105 L.Ed.2d 45 (1989), discussed in detail in Chapter 2.

33. Section 22(2) of the Restatement (Second) of Judgments, which is the model for preclusion law in many states, places the defendant who fails to assert a "compulsory" counterclaim—one arising from the same transaction that underlies the plaintiff's claim—in the same position as the plaintiff who fails to assert an additional, related claim against the defendant. That is, after judgment in that action, the defendant will be precluded from asserting that claim in a new action.

34. It may be wondered why plaintiff would not encounter the claim preclusion problem in *state* court. Why, that is, should she not be precluded from bringing her state law claim there when, by hypothesis, it arises from the same transaction that gave rise to the federal civil rights claims previously asserted in state court? The reason is that, because of *Pennhurst*'s view of the Eleventh Amendment, she *could* not have asserted the state law claim in the prior, federal court action, and § 26(1)(c) of the Second Restatement excepts from the ban of res judicata claims that the first forum could not have entertained for lack of jurisdiction.

§ 13.22 Title VII

In *Kremer v. Chemical Construction Corp.*,[1] the Supreme Court held that Title VII, like § 1983, contains no express or implied exemption from the mandate of § 1738,[2] so that in Title VII actions federal courts are required to accord state court judgments full preclusive effect.

In 1975 Rubin Kremer lost his engineering job with Chemical Construction Corporation after being laid off. After several attempts to be rehired, Kremer filed a discrimination charge with the Equal Employment Opportunity Commission (EEOC) under Title VII. Pursuant to Title VII, the EEOC referred the charge to a state administrative agency for proceedings under the parallel state antidiscrimination laws. The state agency made a finding of no discrimination and this finding was upheld on administrative appeal. Kremer then sought review of the administrative decision to the state's intermediate appellate court, which affirmed.[3] Thereafter, a District Director of the EEOC made the determination that "there was no reasonable cause to believe that the charge of discrimination was true and issued a right-to-sue notice."[4] Kremer nevertheless instituted a Title VII action in federal district court. The defendants moved to have the claim dismissed on the ground that the state-court decision precluded relitigation in federal court, and the district court ultimately dismissed Kremer's complaint. The court of appeals affirmed and the Supreme Court granted certiorari.

As in *McCurry* and *Migra*, the Court in *Kremer* framed the issue as "whether Congress intended Title VII to supersede the principles of comity and repose embodied in section 1738."[5] The Court noted that although Title VII requires the EEOC to give "substantial weight" to state proceedings, including presumably state judicial proceedings, that direction is simply a floor on the level of deference required, not a ceiling as suggested by the dissent.[6] Accordingly, the Court held that in actions

<hr/>

§ 13.22

1. 456 U.S. 461, 102 S.Ct. 1883, 72 L.Ed.2d 262 (1982).

2. *Id.* at 476, 102 S.Ct. at 1895.

3. *Id.* at 463–64, 102 S.Ct. at 1888.

4. *Id.* at 465, 102 S.Ct. at 1889.

5. *Id.* at 462, 102 S.Ct. at 1887.

6. *Id.* at 470 n. 8, 488, 102 S.Ct. at 1892 n.8, 1901. The *Kremer* majority distinguished federal court review of state court proceedings, the issue there, from federal court review of state administrative agency proceedings. (The *Kremer* dissent, by contrast, viewed the state appellate court's affirmance of the agency's finding as merely a continuation of the state agency proceedings. *Id.* at 490, 102 S.Ct. at 1902 (Blackmun, J., dissenting)). The majority thus laid the foundation for one of the holdings in *University of Tennessee v. Elliott*, 478 U.S. 788, 106 S.Ct. 3220, 92 L.Ed.2d 635 (1986), discussed below, asserting in dictum that "it is clear that [judicially] *unreviewed administrative* determinations by state *agencies* ... [*under Title VII*] should not preclude [federal court] review [of federal claims under statutes that mandate prior resort to state administrative agencies] even if such a decision were to be afforded preclusive effect in a State's own courts." *Id.* at 470 n.7, 102 S.Ct. at 1891 n.7. The Court would later expand that holding from *Elliott* to permit federal court actions under the Age Discrimination in Employment Act notwithstanding a contrary state administrative determination. *Astoria Federal Savings & Loan Ass'n v. Solimino*, 501 U.S. 104, 111 S.Ct. 2166, 115 L.Ed.2d 96 (1991).

Justice Stevens, also dissenting, redefined the issue as whether the state judicial review of the agency proceedings involves a substantive review of the claims presented at the agency level—in which case the judg-

under Title VII, as under the nineteenth century civil rights acts, § 1738 requires federal courts to give as much [7] preclusive effect to court judgments as would other courts of that state.

The Court observed that prior decisions, including *McCurry*, which insisted that the person to be precluded had received a "full and fair opportunity to litigate," did not define the extent of that requirement.[8] The Court in *Kremer* did, holding that "where we are bound by the statutory directive of section 1738, state proceedings need do no more than satisfy the minimum procedural requirements of the Fourteenth Amendment's Due Process Clause in order to qualify for the full faith and credit guaranteed by federal law." [9]

The *Kremer* majority opinion apparently limits its holding by emphasizing that "[n]o provision of Title VII requires claimants to pursue

ment would be entitled to preclusive effect—or a more deferential "arbitrary and capricious" standard—in which case the judgment would have no preclusive effect. *Id.* at 507, 102 S.Ct. at 1910 (Stevens, J., dissenting). Although the majority stated that "[t]here is no requirement that judicial review must proceed de novo if it is to be preclusive," it did seem to require that the state court's holding must at least "constitute a finding 'one way or the other' on the merits of petitioner's claim." 456 U.S. at 480 n. 21, 102 S.Ct. at 1896 n.21.

In a footnote, the Court cited several cases indicating that the state-court review in *Kremer* was a review on the merits. *Id.* In *Bray v. New York Life Insurance*, 851 F.2d 60 (2d Cir.1988), the United States Court of Appeals for the Second Circuit held that a state court dismissal on statute of limitation grounds of an appeal from an administrative determination of no probable cause served to preclude a relitigation of those issues in federal court under Title VII and § 1981. *Id.* at 61. Citing *Kremer*, the court concluded that "[b]ecause New York treats a dismissal on statute of limitation grounds as a final judgment on the merits for res judicata purposes," the state court judgment served to preclude relitigation in federal court. *Id.* at 64.

7. *Id.* at 476. If state law would not accord a prior state court judgment preclusive effect in other courts of that state, neither would § 1738 give the judgment preclusive effect in a subsequent Title VII action in federal court. *See Dici v. Commonwealth of Pennsylvania*, 91 F.3d 542 (3d Cir.1996) (state court affirmance of workers compensation ruling on fact issues not issue preclusive in subsequent Title VII action because workers compensation and Title VII legal issues differed and a Pennsylvania

state court would not give preclusive effect even to fact issues under those circumstances); *McNasby v. Crown Cork and Seal Co.*, 888 F.2d 270, 271 (3d Cir.1989) (denying preclusive effect in a Title VII action to a state court judgment because the judgment would not be entitled to preclusive effect in other courts of that state), *cert. denied*, 494 U.S. 1066, 110 S.Ct. 1783, 108 L.Ed.2d 784 (1990). *See* discussion of *Haring v. Prosise*, *supra* § 13.21, note 13.

8. *Id.* at 480–82, 102 S.Ct. at 1896–98.

9. *Id.* at 482, 102 S.Ct. at 1898. In *Clark v. Clark*, 984 F.2d 272 (8th Cir.), *cert. denied*, 510 U.S. 828, 114 S.Ct. 93, 126 L.Ed.2d 60 (1993), the United States Court of Appeals for the Eighth Circuit held that the due process requirement of *Kremer* does not require a state court specifically to address each contention raised by a litigant in order for that decision to have preclusive effect. *Id.* at 273. In *Clark* the plaintiff raised several constitutional contentions in her state-court action claiming title to real property. The state court ruled against the defendant, but failed to address any of the plaintiff's constitutional arguments in its opinion. Plaintiff then brought suit under § 1983 in district court seeking an injunction. The district court dismissed the suit and the plaintiff appealed. *Id.* The court of appeals affirmed, holding that due process does not require "any particular technique of opinion-writing [and that] [c]ourts frequently reject by implication arguments urged by parties." *Id.* Although the decision in *Kremer* dealt with actions under Title VII, the Supreme Court's discussion of what constitutes a "full and fair opportunity to litigate" merely expands on the same terminology earlier used in *McCurry*. *See supra* footnote 6, § 13.21 and accompanying text.

in state court an unfavorable state administrative action...." [10]   That is, an important undercurrent to the Court's opinion appears to be the idea that the petitioner/employee in *Kremer* was precluded only because he went beyond Title VII's mandated administrative agency exhaustion by pursuing the state law employment discrimination claim to the state appellate court.   Nevertheless, some lower courts have downplayed the "voluntary" nature of the state-court review and have purported to give preclusive effect to state-court judgments even when it was the defendant employer, not the employee, who appealed the administrative finding.[11]

In one such decision, the employee, as required by Title VII, filed a state law claim with the appropriate state administrative body, which found liability.   The employer appealed to state court, which reversed. The state agency appealed that ruling and an appeals court reversed and reinstated the agency's determination of liability.   At the same time, the employee filed an action in federal court alleging violations of Title VII, § 1983 and § 1981, seeking remedies beyond those available through the state agency.   The Ninth Circuit approved a district court decision dismissing the action as precluded by the state court decisions.[12]   The court acknowledged that the *Kremer* plaintiff's resort to state court was voluntary, but it also noted the Supreme Court's statement that "the finality of state court judgments should not 'depend on which side prevailed in a given case[ ].' " [13]   The Ninth Circuit also found that the Supreme Court's 1985 decision in *Marrese v. American Academy of Orthopaedic Surgeons* (holding that the preclusive effect of a state-court judgment is determined solely by reference to applicable state law principles) [14] dictated that regardless of whether the federal plaintiff's trip to state court was voluntary, § 1738 mandated that the state-court judgment be given the same preclusive effect it would enjoy in other courts of the state.[15]

These lower court decisions seem to miss the Supreme Court's point. That *Kremer* was not concerned with which side prevailed in state court does not diminish the significance of its emphasis that the employee in *Kremer* chose the state judicial forum voluntarily, not by compulsion of federal law.   There is something manifestly unfair, and hence seemingly contrary to Due Process [16] as well as the law of preclusion, about permitting the employer to deprive the employee of a federal judicial

---

10.   *Id.* at 469, 102 S.Ct. at 1891.

11.   *See Zanders v. National Railroad Passenger Corp.*, 898 F.2d 1127 (6th Cir. 1990); *Trujillo v. County of Santa Clara*, 775 F.2d 1359 (9th Cir.1985); *Hickman v. Electronic Keyboarding, Inc.*, 741 F.2d 230 (8th Cir.1984); and *Gonsalves v. Alpine Country Club*, 727 F.2d 27 (1st Cir.1984).

12.   *Trujillo*, 775 F.2d at 1359–63, 1369.

13.   *Id.* at 1364 (quoting *Kremer, supra* note 1, at 470, 102 S.Ct. at 1891 (footnote omitted)).

14.   470 U.S. 373, 105 S.Ct. 1327, 84 L.Ed.2d 274 (1985).

15.   *Trujillo, supra* note 11, at 1363.

16.   *See Logan v. Zimmerman Brush Co.*, 455 U.S. 422, 102 S.Ct. 1148, 71 L.Ed.2d 265 (1982) (once state creates a claim and hence a contingent property right of the plaintiff, it may not adopt procedures that effectively ensure that the claim will fail).

forum on a federal claim simply by seeking judicial review of a state administrative proceeding that federal law required the employee to initiate. The Supreme Court's apparent recognition of this unfairness, and the supremacy of federal law in such situations, is implicit in two post-*Kremer* decisions that declined to preclude plaintiffs' Title VII or ADEA claims as the result of administrative proceedings that federal law obliged them to exhaust.[17]

§ 13.23 Federal Common Law Preclusion: State Agency to Federal Court

As noted above,[1] the Court squarely held in *Patsy v. Board of Regents*[2] what it had stated many times in the preceding nineteen years: that a potential plaintiff need not pursue administrative agency exhaustion as a precondition to bringing suit under § 1983.[3] In so holding the Court relied principally on the intention of the 1871 Congress that federal courts would play a paramount role in protecting federal rights and its suspicion of the ability or willingness of the "state authorities" to protect those rights or punish those who violated them. In effect it found these policies surrounding the enactment of § 1983 sufficiently weighty as to warrant an exception to the modern rule requiring exhaustion of administrative remedies before the institution of civil litigation.[4]

Interestingly, the Court could have easily reached the opposite conclusion by adopting one of the rationales it had used two years earlier in *Allen v. McCurry* to support application of collateral estoppel via 28 U.S.C.A. § 1738. There the Court expressed its assurance that § 1983 litigants would not be unfairly estopped by fact findings made in prior state criminal prosecutions because one of the standard exceptions to collateral estoppel invalidates its use where the prior litigation of the issue common to the actions was not "full and fair." Similarly, exhaustion of administrative remedies has not been required where the plaintiff

---

17. *See University of Tennessee v. Elliott,* 478 U.S. 788, 106 S.Ct. 3220, 92 L.Ed.2d 635 (1986) (Title VII plaintiffs); *Astoria Federal Savings & Loan Ass'n v. Solimino,* 501 U.S. 104, 111 S.Ct. 2166, 115 L.Ed.2d 96 (1991) (ADEA plaintiffs). *Elliott* is discussed in the text immediately following.

§ 13.23

1. See note 1, § 13.3 *supra.*

2. 457 U.S. 496, 102 S.Ct. 2557, 73 L.Ed.2d 172 (1982). The precedents the Court cited traced from *McNeese v. Board of Education,* 373 U.S. 668, 83 S.Ct. 1433, 10 L.Ed.2d 622 (1963).

3. The Court took note of a statutory exception to this proposition, the requirement of the Civil Rights of Institutionalized Persons Act that adult inmates "in any jail,

prison, or other correctional facility" must exhaust for ninety days any available administrative procedure that the U.S. Attorney General has certified as meeting minimum standards for the "plain, speedy, and effective" resolution of grievances. 42 U.S.C.A. § 1997(e). The Supreme Court has held the requirement inapplicable to a federal prisoner's claim for damages. *McCarthy v. Madigan,* 503 U.S. 140, 149, 112 S.Ct. 1081, 1088, 117 L.Ed.2d 291 (1992). Dismissal for failure to exhaust a certified grievance procedure may be with prejudice, see *Pedraza v. Ryan,* 18 F.3d 288 (5th Cir.1990) or if the prisoner tried in good faith to exhaust, may not. *See Rocky v. Vittorie,* 813 F.2d 734 (5th Cir.1987).

4. 457 U.S. at 518, 102 S.Ct. at 2568 (White, J., concurring) (citing *Myers v. Bethlehem Shipbuilding Corp.,* 303 U.S. 41, 58 S.Ct. 459, 82 L.Ed. 638 (1938)).

challenged the lawfulness of the administrative system, its practical efficacy, or the adequacy of the administrative remedy.[5] Putting *McCurry* and *Patsy* together, it might be said that § 1983's goals are not important enough to except it from ordinary rules of federal issue preclusion but are important enough to permit the plaintiff to escape the ordinary requirement of administrative exhaustion. It is unclear why the Court thinks unimpeded access to federal court is essential in the latter setting but not the former.

In *University of Tennessee v. Elliott,*[6] the Supreme Court reached divergent conclusions about the preclusive effect of unreviewed state agency factfinding on federal court actions under, respectively, Title VII and the Reconstruction Civil Rights Acts. The Court held that state agency factfinding not judicially reviewed has no preclusive effect on Title VII claims.[7] By contrast, the Court did fashion a federal common-law rule of issue preclusion for state agency factfinding in actions under the Reconstruction civil rights statutes.[8]

In 1981 the University of Tennessee informed Elliott that he was being discharged for poor work performance. He requested an administrative hearing to determine the validity of the discharge but also filed a federal action under Title VII and § 1983 alleging that the discharge was racially motivated. The administrative law judge found no racial motivation behind the discharge,[9] and Elliott did not appeal this result to state court. The university moved the federal court for summary judgment on the basis that the state administrative agency factfinding precluded any further action on the Title VII or § 1983 claims.[10]

The Supreme Court, reinstating a summary judgment granted by the trial judge, first noted that § 1738 was inapplicable. Section 1738 does not cover state administrative factfinding; by its own terms it requires prior state "judicial proceedings" like those in *McCurry, Migra,* and *Kremer.*[11] Yet federal courts have frequently devised federal common-law rules of preclusion.[12] The Court accordingly defined the issues as whether it should fashion a common law rule of preclusion "first with respect to respondent's Title VII claim, and next with respect to his claims under the ... Reconstruction civil rights statutes."[13]

---

5. *See Patsy v. Florida International University,* 634 F.2d 900 (5th Cir.1981) (en banc), *reversed Patsy v. Board of Regents,* 457 U.S. 496, 102 S.Ct. 2557, 73 L.Ed.2d 172 (1982).

6. 478 U.S. 788, 106 S.Ct. 3220, 92 L.Ed.2d 635 (1986).

7. *Id.* at 796, 106 S.Ct. at 3225. This holding was extended to federal court litigation under the Age Discrimination in Employment Act in *Astoria Federal Savings & Loan Ass'n v. Solimino,* 501 U.S. 104, 111 S.Ct. 2166, 115 L.Ed.2d 96 (1991).

8. *Elliott,* 478 U.S. at 798, 106 S.Ct. at 3226.

9. However, the administrative law judge did feel that the discharge was too harsh a response to the petitioner's poor work performance and ordered that the petitioner merely be transferred to another position with the university. *Id.* at 791, 106 S.Ct. at 3222.

10. *Id.* at 792–94, 106 S.Ct. at 3222.

11. *See supra* §§ 13.19, 13.21–13.22.

12. *Elliott,* 478 U.S. at 794, 106 S.Ct. at 3224.

13. *Id.* at 794, 106 S.Ct. at 3224.

In regard to the Title VII claim, the Court referred to the directive in 42 U.S.C.A. § 2000e–5(b) that EEOC must accord state administrative factfinding "substantial weight." [14] The Court stated that "it would make little sense for Congress to write such a provision if state agency findings were entitled to preclusive effect in Title VII actions in federal court." [15] In addition, the Court cited *Chandler v. Roudebush* as supporting the view that state administrative findings are not entitled to preclusive effect in Title VII actions.[16] *Chandler* held "that a federal employee whose discrimination claim was rejected by her employing agency after an administrative hearing was entitled to a trial de novo in federal court on her Title VII claim." [17] The Court felt that it would be inconsistent with the decision in *Chandler* to deny Elliott a trial de novo on his Title VII claim. It therefore held that in actions under Title VII, unreviewed state administrative factfinding has no preclusive effect either under § 1738 or federal common law.[18]

Several lower courts have refused to extend the *Elliott* Title VII holding, which concerned a defendant employer's attempt to invoke collateral estoppel, to give preclusive effect when the Title VII *plaintiff* invokes the doctrine offensively.[19] These courts have relied on *Elliott's* broad language, which denied preclusive effect to unreviewed state administrative determinations unfavorable to defendants, without indicating specifically that the Court also recognized the normal Title VII policy of affording claimants unimpeded access to a judicial forum; [20] or they have noted that the employer bore a heavier burden of persuasion

14. *Id.* at 795, 106 S.Ct. at 3224. *See, e.g., Heyne v. Caruso*, 69 F.3d 1475 (9th Cir.1995) (overruling trial court's exclusion from evidence of a state antidiscrimination agency's finding of probable cause). Similarly, EEOC's own probable cause determination is admissible in a subsequent judicial action under Title VII, because its probative value outweighs its potential prejudicial effect. *See Gilchrist v. Jim Slemons Imports, Inc.*, 803 F.2d 1488 (9th Cir.1986); *Plummer v. Western Int'l Hotels Co.*, 656 F.2d 502 (9th Cir.1981).

15. *Id.* at 795, 106 S.Ct. at 3225 (citing *Kremer v. Chemical Construction Corp.* 456 U.S. 461, 470, 102 S.Ct. 1883, 1891, 72 L.Ed.2d 262 (1982)).

16. *Id.* at 795, 106 S.Ct. at 3225 (citing 425 U.S. 840, 96 S.Ct. 1949, 48 L.Ed.2d 416 (1976)).

17. *Id.* at 795, 106 S.Ct. at 3225.

18. *Id.* at 796, 106 S.Ct. at 3225. The decision in *Elliott* concerned an attempt by an employer to use a favorable administrative finding to preclude a subsequent federal suit against that employer under Title VII. The United States Court of Appeals for the Third Circuit has held that the *Elliott* condemnation of Title VII administrative preclusion by defendants also serves

to prevent the offensive use of issue preclusion "in a Title VII action by an employee who has previously filed a successful [administrative] claim...." *Roth v. Koppers Industries, Inc.*, 993 F.2d 1058 (3d Cir. 1993). But given the Court's other holding in *Elliott*, that Reconstruction Act plaintiffs, unlike Title VII plaintiffs, are vulnerable to defensive issue preclusion based on prior administrative proceedings, § 1983 plaintiffs should be able to use preclusion offensively (subject to the exceptions in Restatement § 28) when they have prevailed in those proceedings. See text accompanying notes 28–32, *infra*.

19. *See, e.g., Herron v. Tennessee Board of Regents*, 42 F.3d 1388 (6th Cir.1994), *cert. denied*, ___ U.S. ___, 115 S.Ct. 2246, 132 L.Ed.2d 255 (1995); *Roth v. Koppers Industries, Inc.*, 993 F.2d 1058, 1062–63 (3d Cir.1993); *United States v. Board of Education of Piscataway*, 798 F.Supp. 1093, 1100 (D.N.J.1992); *Gallo v. John Powell Chevrolet, Inc.*, 765 F.Supp. 198, 207–08 (M.D.Pa.1991); *Johnson v. Halls Merchandising, Inc.*, 1989 WL 23201, at *2 (W.D.Mo.1989); *Caras v. Family First Credit Union*, 688 F.Supp. 586, 589 (D.Utah 1988).

20. *See Roth*, 993 F.2d at 1062.

on the common issue in the earlier proceeding, so that estoppel would be unfair.[21] But at least one court has found otherwise, in part by finding *Elliott* distinguishable because the plaintiff is more favorably situated in terms of Title VII policies.[22] Finally, it should be noted that a state (or federal) administrative agency's decision may, like that of an arbitrator,[23] be admissible in the employment discrimination lawsuit even if it is denied preclusive effect.[24]

The Court in *Elliott* next addressed the preclusive effect of state administrative findings on actions under the Reconstruction civil rights acts. Although the Court acknowledged that the decisions in *McCurry* and *Migra* were not controlling, it found them supportive of the view that Congress, in passing the Reconstruction Acts, did not intend "to create an exception to general rules of preclusion."[25] Thus, although § 1738 was not applicable, the Court found nothing in the legislative history of the Reconstruction acts to suggest that Congress intended to foreclose the further development of federal common-law rules of preclusion.

The Court then recited a number of policy reasons for giving preclusive effect in Reconstruction Act cases to "the factfinding of administrative bodies acting in a judicial capacity": to further repose as

21. *See Herron, supra* note 19. Of course an employer in an administrative proceeding under state law may often bear the burden of demonstrating some sort of "cause" or "just cause" for termination or other adverse employment action. If plaintiff proceeds to court under Title VII, and produces only inferential, *McDonnell Douglas*-type evidence of race, gender, religious or national origin discrimination, then she, rather than the employer, would bear the burden of persuasion on the ultimate issue of unlawful discrimination; and the employer would bear only a production burden with respect to a legitimate nondiscriminatory reason. *See* the *Burdine* and *St. Mary's* decisions discussed in Chapter 4. In such a case it may therefore be unfair to permit the plaintiff, based on the prior administrative proceedings, to invoke issue preclusion against the employer on the issue of "cause." If, on the other hand, the plaintiff offers "direct" evidence of unlawful discrimination, the *defendant*, per Title VII § 703(m), must persuade that it would have taken the same employment action for a reason or reasons (e.g., "just cause") independent of the unlawful one. In such a case, at least, it is not shifting any burden of persuasion to preclude the employer from relitigating the issue of cause, on which it must carry the persuasion burden in both proceedings.

22. *Driscoll v. Greene County School District and Phil Brock*, No. 94–71

(M.D.Ga.1995) (precluding defendants from relitigating state administrative agency's quasijudicial, unreviewed findings concerning facts related to Title VII defenses, and adhering to that decision on reconsideration). The author is co-counsel for plaintiff in *Driscoll*.

23. *Alexander v. Gardner–Denver Co.*, 415 U.S. 36, 94 S.Ct. 1011, 39 L.Ed.2d 147 (1974), discussed in § 5.5 above.

24. *Compare Barfield v. Orange County*, 911 F.2d 644 (11th Cir.1990) and *Baldwin v. Rice*, 144 F.R.D. 102 (E.D.Cal.1992) (admitting state unemployment compensation decisions) *with Bradshaw v. Golden Road Motor Inn, Inc.*, 885 F.Supp. 1370 (D.Nev. 1995) (denying preclusion because unemployment hearing or officer, unlike many arbitrators, will have no special competence to decide discrimination claims and for lack of issue identity). In *Walker v. Nations-Bank*, 53 F.3d 1548 (11th Cir.1995), the court observed that EEOC administrative determination letters have been held routinely admissible in bench, but not in jury trials; those determinations, the court wrote, vary significantly in their degree of detail and quality, and have the potential to create unfair prejudice in the minds of jurors.

25. *Elliott*, 478 U.S. at 797, 106 S.Ct. at 3225. In fact, the Court states that the result in *McCurry* could probably have been reached even in the absence of § 1738. *Id.*

well as facilitate "the parties' interest in avoiding the cost and vexation of repetitive litigation[,] the public's interest in conserving judicial resources ... and the value of federalism." [26] It held accordingly that in actions under the Reconstruction Civil Rights Acts, "[w]hen an administrative agency is acting in a judicial capacity and resolves disputed issues of fact properly before it which the parties have had an adequate opportunity to litigate," the federal courts must give the findings of the state agency the same preclusive effect, if any, that the findings would have in that state's courts.[27] Most but not all federal appellate courts that have considered the question have limited the scope of *Elliott's* administrative preclusion of Reconstruction Act claims to an agency's findings of fact; they have denied preclusion to an agency's conclusions of law.[28]

Justices Stevens, Brennan and Blackmun dissented from the holding that administrative fact findings were entitled to preclusive effect in actions under the Reconstruction Civil Rights Acts.[29] The dissenters were skeptical about the Court's assertion that giving preclusive effect to the findings would serve the policies of federalism and conservation of judicial resources. Justice Stevens noted that although *Elliott* may prevent federal court relitigation of issues under the Reconstruction Civil Rights Acts, it permits the trial of a companion Title VII claim.[30] He predicted that this "schizophrenic approach" would generate inconsistent findings as between the state administrative agency and the

---

26. *Id.* at 797–98, 106 S.Ct. at 3225–26. *See, e.g., JSK v. Hendry County School Bd.,* 941 F.2d 1563, 1568 (11th Cir.1991).

27. *Id.* at 797–98, 106 S.Ct. at 3226–26 (quoting *Utah Construction & Mining Co.,* 384 U.S. at 421–22, 86 S.Ct. at 1559–60). State courts apply similar issue preclusion principles with respect to determinations made in prior administrative proceedings. *See, e.g., Nummer v. Michigan Dep't of Treasury,* 448 Mich. 534, 533 N.W.2d 250, *cert. denied,* ___ U.S. ___, 116 S.Ct. 418, 133 L.Ed.2d 335 (1995).

At least one lower court has found the *Elliott* procedural prerequisites for preclusion unsatisfied. In *Yates v. Philip Morris, Inc.,* 690 F.Supp. 180, 184 (S.D.N.Y.1988), the court concluded that: (1) the state administrative proceedings did not afford the plaintiff an adequate opportunity to litigate the claim; and (2) in any event the state's own courts would refuse to give preclusive effect to the findings of the state administrative proceedings. *Id.* at 184.

28. *Edmundson v. Borough of Kennett Square,* 4 F.3d 186, 189 (3d Cir.1993); *Gjellum v. City of Birmingham,* 829 F.2d 1056, 1064–65 n. 21 (11th Cir.1987); *Peery v. Brakke,* 826 F.2d 740, 746 (8th Cir.1987). *Contra, Eilrich v. Remas,* 839 F.2d 630, 634

n. 2 (9th Cir.), *cert. denied,* 488 U.S. 819, 109 S.Ct. 60, 102 L.Ed.2d 38 (1988). *Cf. Raju v. Rhodes,* 7 F.3d 1210 (5th Cir.1993) (according collateral estoppel effect to decision by grievance committee affirmed by state court), *cert. denied* , ___ U.S. ___, 114 S.Ct. 1543, 128 L.Ed.2d 194 (1994). In according both collateral estoppel and res judicata effect to the decision of a county civil service commission in an action under § 1983, the Ninth Circuit stressed that the plaintiff had failed to pursue available state judicial review of the agency's decision. *Miller v. County of Santa Cruz,* 39 F.3d 1030 (9th Cir.1994). It has not been authoritatively decided if the availability of state judicial review is a precondition to preclusion based on prior state administrative proceedings. In *Elliott* the Supreme Court mentioned that the civil rights plaintiff had not pursued such an appeal but did not indicate whether the availability of appellate review would be essential to preclusion in another case.

29. *Id.* at 799–802, 106 S.Ct. at 3226–28.

30. *Id.* at 800, 106 S.Ct. at 3227 (Stevens, J., concurring in part, dissenting in part).

federal court, with consequent damage to federal-state comity.[31]

In a sense it was the *Patsy* decision that made it possible for the Court in *Elliott* to apply judicially crafted preclusion to actions under § 1983. Had *Patsy* required exhaustion of administrative remedies, a vast number of putative plaintiffs would find their § 1983 claims halted in their tracks by virtue of *Elliott*-type preclusion. The contrary conclusion reached in *Patsy* means that the sting of *Elliott* is principally felt only by those claimants who for tactical reasons voluntarily pursue a state administrative remedy despite the risks of preclusion. Only the § 1983 plaintiff unlucky enough to be embroiled in government-initiated administrative proceedings will—like McCurry, a § 1983 plaintiff unlucky enough to have been criminally prosecuted—suffer preclusion a la *Elliott*, involuntarily. It of course remains quite possible for the potential plaintiff to preclude himself out of a § 1983 remedy by initiating internal disciplinary proceedings first.[32]

Elliott permitted a defensive use of issue preclusion in a Reconstruction Act lawsuit—that is, the federal court defendant used state administrative findings of fact to prevent relitigation in federal court of an issue decided favorably to it by the agency. However, what happens if the state agency findings are adverse to the defendant? May the plaintiff use them offensively to prevent relitigation of the issue in a subsequent Reconstruction Act action? Apparently, there is no federal bar to the offensive use of administrative collateral estoppel in a Reconstruction Act action and the ultimate answer depends instead on the forum state's law. In *Frazier v. King*,[33] the federal court plaintiff attempted to use a state administrative finding offensively to prevent relitigation of the issue in federal court. A state agency had found that the plaintiff's employment had been terminated in violation of her right " 'to speak out....' "[34] Plaintiff then brought suit in federal court under § 1983 claiming that the defendant's actions violated her rights under the First and Fourteenth Amendments. The plaintiff contended that the state

31. *Id.* at 800 n.1, 106 S.Ct. at 3227 n.1 (quoting C. Wright, A. Miller, & E. Cooper, Federal Practice and Procedure 4471, p. 169 (Supp. 1985)). As Justice Stevens predicted, subsequent to *Elliott* several cases arose in which plaintiffs brought actions in federal court under both Title VII and one or more of the Reconstruction Civil Rights Acts only to have the Reconstruction Act claims precluded by prior administrative fact findings while the Title VII claim proceeded to a trial de novo. *See Buckhalter v. Pepsi–Cola General Bottlers, Inc.*, 820 F.2d 892 (7th Cir.1987) (1981 claim dismissed) and *DeCintio v. Westchester County Medical Center*, 821 F.2d 111 (2d Cir.) (1983 and 1981 claims dismissed), *cert. denied*, 484 U.S. 965, 108 S.Ct. 455, 98 L.Ed.2d 395 (1987).

A distinct problem is presented by prior *judicial* litigation of a Reconstruction Act claim, which would ordinarily have claim preclusive effect on a Title VII claim. Plaintiffs do have ways, however, of avoiding that kind of preclusion. *See Herrmann v. Cencom Cable Associates, Inc.*, 999 F.2d 223 (7th Cir.1993) (discussed in text accompanying notes 13–14, § 13.14, *supra*).

32. *Hunter v. City of Warner Robins*, 842 F.Supp. 1460 (M.D.Ga.1994) (precluding plaintiff based on prior administrative proceedings deemed quasi-judicial simply because of the presence of counsel, the opportunity to present evidence and cross-examine witnesses, and the tribunal's recitation of findings of fact and conclusions of law).

33. 873 F.2d 820 (5th Cir.), *cert. denied*, 493 U.S. 977, 110 S.Ct. 502, 107 L.Ed.2d 504 (1989).

34. *Id.* at 822.

findings were entitled to preclusive effect on the First Amendment issue. The district court agreed and the defendants appealed.[35] The court of appeals reversed, ruling that the administrative agency findings did not prevent relitigation of the First Amendment issue. But it reached that conclusion, it said, only because the applicable *state* law did not happen to provide for the offensive use of collateral estoppel.[36] There would have been no reason for the court to reach that issue unless it assumed that preclusion was permitted under *federal* (common) law as adumbrated by *Elliott*. And a federal district court has recently granted the plaintiff's motion in a civil rights and employment discrimination action to preclude the defendants from relitigating an administrative body's findings that rejected defendants' allegations that the plaintiff had performance deficiencies and that accordingly recommended renewal of her contract.[37]

A threshold issue in *Frazier* was whether the state agency finding had *claim* preclusive effect—that is, precluded the plaintiff from asserting in court claims not advanced before the state agency regardless of the outcome of those proceedings. The court of appeals first stated that the decision in *Elliott* did not answer whether state or federal preclusion law governed this issue.[38] The court did suggest that federal preclusion law applies[39] but reserved judgment on the question because neither federal nor state law, under the facts in *Frazier*, would have precluded the federal claim. The Second Restatement creates an exception to § 24(1)'s broad definition of "claim" if "[t]he plaintiff was unable ... to seek a certain remedy or form of relief in the first action because of the limitations on the subject matter jurisdiction of the courts...."[40] In *Frazier*, the remedies available under § 1983 were not available through the agency proceedings.

Thus because of a standard exception to preclusion under federal or state law, the plaintiff's federal claim could not be merged in the agency decision. Yet the court's discussion does appear to assume that in other

35. *Id.*

36. *Id.* at 825. *See also, Ward v. Harte,* 794 F.Supp. 109 (S.D.N.Y.1992); *Gore v. R.H. Macy & Co.,* 1989 WL 65561 (S.D.N.Y. 1989); *Farley v. North Bergen Township Bd. of Educ.,* 705 F.Supp. 223 (D.N.J.1989).

37. *Driscoll v. Greene County School District and Phil Brock,* No. 94–71 (M.D.Ga.1995). The author is co-counsel for plaintiff in the *Driscoll* litigation.

38. *Id.* at 823.

39. *Id.* (citing *Gjellum v. City of Birmingham,* 829 F.2d 1056 (11th Cir.1987)).

40. 2d Restatement of Judgments § 26(1)(c). Thus where a state habeas court lacked authority to award damages, a § 1983 claim that arose out of the same transaction and would therefore ordinarily have been claim precluded was held not barred by res judicata. The court observed, however, that fact findings reached by the habeas tribunal might have collateral estoppel effect in the judicial action under § 1983. *Burgos v. Hopkins,* 14 F.3d 787 (2d Cir.1994). Further, at least where it is arguable that the prior tribunal might exercise jurisdiction over the federal claim, the plaintiff must attempt to assert it there or face subsequent preclusion. *Davis v. City of Chicago,* 53 F.3d 801, 801–803 (7th Cir. 1995). *See also Waid v. Merrill Area Public Schools,* 91 F.3d 857 (7th Cir.1996) (Title IX claim not precluded by prior state employment discrimination proceedings where state administrative agency had jurisdiction under state law only over employment discrimination claim, not claim under Title IX, and state law claims could be pursued only in that agency).

circumstances a Reconstruction Act claim could be halted by merger based solely on prior administrative proceedings.[41] And given the Supreme Court's view in *Migra* and *McCurry* that issue and claim preclusion stand on the same footing in terms of their capacity to foreclose or limit the litigation of civil rights actions, in principle offensive preclusion based on prior administrative proceedings should also avail the plaintiff seeking to preclude a civil rights defendant on only one or more issues, rather than an entire claim. Finally, even where there is some technical barrier to both claim and issue preclusion, the administrative claimant runs the risk of having her subsequent judicial action barred by the doctrine of "judicial estoppel" if her employment discrimination or civil rights claim is predicated on an assertion—e.g., her ability to perform a job—that is undermined by a position taken in the administrative proceeding—e.g., that she was unable to work.[42]

---

41. *See also Healy v. Town of Pembroke Park*, 831 F.2d 989 (11th Cir.1987).

42. *Rissetto v. Plumbers and Steamfitters Local 343*, 94 F.3d 597 (9th Cir.1996) (estopping age discrimination plaintiff from asserting that she was performing her job adequately when she had filed a workers compensation claim based on inability to work; *McNemar v. Disney Store, Inc.*, 91 F.3d 610 (3d Cir.1996)(Americans With Disabilities Act claim barred by judicial estoppel based on plaintiffs representation to Social Security Administration and state agencies that he was totally disabled).

Appendix

RESEARCHING CIVIL RIGHTS AND EMPLOYMENT DISCRIMINATION LAW ON WESTLAW®

Analysis

Section 1. Introduction

Civil Rights and Employment Discrimination Law provides a strong base for analyzing even the most complex problem involving federal civil rights. Whether your research requires examination of case law, statutes, administrative materials or expert commentary, West books and WESTLAW are excellent sources.

WESTLAW expands your library, giving you access to decisions from federal courts and documents from the U.S. Congress, as well as to articles and treatises by well-known commentators. To help keep you up-to-date with current developments, WESTLAW provides frequently updated federal databases. With WESTLAW, you have unparalleled legal research resources at your fingertips.

Additional Resources

If you have not used WESTLAW or have questions not covered in this appendix, see the *WESTLAW Reference Manual* or call the West Reference Attorneys at 1–800–REF–ATTY (1–800–733–2889). The West Reference Attorneys are trained, licensed attorneys, available throughout the workday and on weekends to assist you with your WESTLAW or West book research questions.

Section 2. WESTLAW Federal Law Databases

Each database on WESTLAW is assigned an abbreviation called an *identifier,* which you use to access the database. You can find identifiers for all databases in the online WESTLAW Directory and in the *WEST-LAW Database List.* When you need to know more detailed information about a database, use Scope. Scope contains coverage information, related databases and valuable search tips. To use Scope from the WESTLAW Directory, type **sc** and the database or service identifier, e.g., **sc allfeds.**

The following chart lists WESTLAW databases that contain information pertaining to federal law. For a complete list of federal law databases, see the WESTLAW Directory or the *WESTLAW Database List.* Because new information is continually being added to WEST-LAW, you should also check the Welcome to WESTLAW screen and the WESTLAW Directory for new database information.

WESTLAW Federal Databases

Description	Database Identifier	Beginning Coverage (see Scope for more specific information)
Federal Case Law		
Combined Federal Cases (includes U.S. Supreme Court, courts of appeals, district courts, U.S. bankruptcy courts, U.S. Court of Federal Claims, U.S. Tax Court, former Tax Court of the United States, former U.S. Board of Tax Appeals, military courts, and other federal and territorial courts)	FCIV–CS	1789
U.S. Supreme Court	FCIV–SCT	1754
U.S. Courts of Appeals	FCIV–CTA	1891
U.S. District Courts (includes cases reported in	FCIV–DCT	1789

Description	Database Identifier	Beginning Coverage (see Scope for more specific information)
West's® Federal Rules Decisions®		
Federal Judicial Circuit Cases (includes all U.S. Supreme Court decisions, federal courts within a circuit, and decisions of the Judicial Panel on Multidistrict Litigation)	FEDX–ALL (X represents the circuit number or abbreviation)	Varies by court
U.S. Court of Federal Claims	FEDCL	1992
LRP Individuals with Disabilities Education Law Report	IDELR	1986
National Disability Law Reporter	NDLRPTR	1990
Combined Federal and State Case Law		
Federal & State Case Law	ALLCASES, ALL-CASES–OLD	1789
Individual States' State and Federal Cases	XX–CS–ALL (XX represents the state's two-letter postal abbreviation)	Varies by court
Circuits' Federal and State Cases	CTAX–ALL (X represents the circuit number or abbreviation)	Varies by court
Federal Statutes, Regulations and Court Rules		
Federal Civil Rights—United States Code Annotated®	FCIV–USCA	Current data
Americans with Disabilities Act of 1990—Legislative History	ADA–LH	
Federal Civil Rights—Federal Register	FCIV–FR	July 1980
Federal Civil Rights—Code of Federal Regulations	FCIV–CFR	Current data
Congressional Record	CR	First Session of the 99th Congress (1985)
United States Public Laws (current)	US–PL	Current data
United States Public Laws 1989–1995	US–PL–OLD	1989
Legislative History—U.S. Code, 1948 to Present	LH	1948 (securities laws since 1933)
Federal Rules	US–RULES	Current data
Federal Orders	US–ORDERS	Current data
Congressional Quarterly's Text of Congressional Bills	CQ–BILLTXT	Current data
Congressional Quarterly's Congressional Bill Tracking	CQ–BILLTRK	Current data

Description	Database Identifier	Beginning Coverage (see Scope for more specific information)
Billcast	BC	Current data
Bill Tracking—Federal (Summaries)	US–BILLTRK	Current data
Regulation Tracking—Federal (Summaries)	US–REGTRK	Current data
Federal Administrative Materials		
Americans with Disabilities Act Technical Assistance Manuals	ADA–TAM	
Information Booklets		1991
Manuals		1992
Equal Employment Opportunity Commission Decisions	FLB–EEOC	July 1969 (private sector) April 1994 (public sector)
Fair Housing Administrative Decisions	FAIRHOUS	1989
LRP Individuals with Disabilities Education Law Report	IDELR	1986
National Disability Law Reporter	NDLRPTR	1990
Office of Federal Contract Compliance Programs Decisions	OFCCP	1968
State Case Law		
Multistate Civil Rights—Cases	MCIV–CS	Varies by state
Individual State Civil Rights—Cases	XXCIV–CS (XX represents the state's two-letter postal abbreviation)	Varies by state
State Administrative Materials		
California Fair Employment and Housing Commission Decisions	CA–FEHC	1978
Illinois Human Rights Commission Decisions	ILCIV–ADMIN	1992
News and Information		
WESTLAW Bulletin—U.S. Supreme Court	WLB–SCT	Current data
WESTLAW Topical Highlights—Employment	WTH–LB	Current data
West's Legal News: Employment Law	WLN–EMP	December 1995
Texts and Periodicals		
Civil Rights Law Reviews, Texts and Bar Journals	CIV–TP	Varies by publication
American Indian Law Review	AMINDLR	Selected coverage 1983 Full coverage 1993

Description	Database Identifier	Beginning Coverage (see Scope for more specific information)
American University Journal of Gender & the Law	AMUJGL	1993
Americans with Disabilities Act Handbook	JW–ADA	Current through 1992 cumulative supplement
Asian Law Journal	ASLJ	1994
Cardozo Women's Law Journal	CDZWLJ	1995
Columbia Human Rights Law Review	CLMHRLR	Selected coverage 1984 Full coverage 1993
Duke Journal of Gender Law & Policy	DUKEJGLP	1994
George Mason University Civil Rights Law Journal	CMUCRLJ	Selected coverage 1990 Full coverage 1993
Harvard Civil Rights—Civil Liberties Law Review	HVCRCLLR	1981
Harvard Human Rights Journal	HVHRJ	1989
Harvard Women's Law Journal	HVWLJ	Selected coverage 1983 Full coverage 1994
Hastings Women's Law Journal	HSTWLJ	Selected coverage 1992 Full coverage 1993
Human Rights	HUMRT	1987
La Raza Law Journal	LARLJ	Selected coverage 1992 Full coverage 1994
Law & Inequality	LAWINEQ	Selected coverage 1985 Full coverage 1993
Law & Sexuality: A Review of Lesbian & Gay Legal Issues	LSEX	1993
Mental & Physical Disability Law Reporter	MPHYDLR	1987
National Black Law Journal	NBLJ	Selected coverage 1993 Full coverage 1994
New York Law School Journal of Human Rights	NYLSJHR	Selected coverage 1989 Full coverage 1994
Sexual Harassment: Federal Law	SEXHARASS	1995 edition
Southern California Review of Law & Women's Studies	SCARLWS	1992
Temple Political & Civil Rights Law Review	TMPPCRLR	Selected coverage 1992 Full coverage 1993
UCLA Women's Law Journal	UCLAWLJ	Selected coverage 1991 Full coverage 1994
William & Mary Journal of Women & the Law	WMMJWL	1995
Wisconsin Women's Law Journal	WIWLJ	1995
Women's Rights Law Reporter	WRLR	Selected coverage 1990 Full coverage 1993

Section 3.   Menu–Driven WESTLAW: EZ ACCESS®

EZ ACCESS is West Publishing's menu-driven research system.   It is ideal for new or infrequent WESTLAW users because it requires no experience or training on WESTLAW.

To access EZ ACCESS, type **ez.** The EZ ACCESS main menu will be displayed. Whenever you are unsure of the next step, or if the choice you want is not listed, simply type **ez**; additional choices will be displayed. Once you retrieve documents with EZ ACCESS, use standard WESTLAW commands to browse your documents. For more information on browsing documents, see the *WESTLAW Reference Manual* or the *WESTLAW User Guide.*

Section 4.   Retrieving a Document with a Citation: Find and Jump

4.1   Find

Find is a WESTLAW service that allows you to retrieve a document by entering its citation. Find allows you to retrieve documents from anywhere in WESTLAW without accessing or changing databases or losing your search result. Find is available for many documents, including case law (federal and state), the *United States Code Annotated,* the *Code of Federal Regulations,* the *Federal Register,* federal rules, federal public laws, and texts and periodicals.

To use Find, type **fi** followed by the document citation. Following is a list of examples:

To Find This Document	Type
42 U.S.C.A. § 1983	**fi 42 usca 1983**
Baskerville v. Culligan Int'l Co., 50 F.3d 428 (7th Cir.1995)	**fi 50 f3d 428**
Bates v. Runyon, 1996 WL 532210 (10th Cir.)	**fi 1996 wl 532210**
Tobias, *Civil Rights Procedural Problems,* 70 Wash.U.L.Q. 801 (1992).	**fi 70 wash u l q 801**

To display an easy-to-use, fill-in-the-blank Find template, type **fi** followed by the publication abbreviation, e.g., **fi usca.**

4.2   Jump

Use Jump to go directly from a case or law review article to a cited case, USCA® section or article; from a headnote to the corresponding text in the opinion; or from an entry in a statute index database to the full text of the statute. Press the **Tab** key until the cursor reaches the Jump marker (> or ▶) you want to select, then press **Enter.** You can also use a mouse to click or double-click the Jump marker.

Section 5.   Natural Language Searching: WIN®—WESTLAW is Natural™

Overview: With WIN, you can retrieve documents by simply describing your issue in plain English. If you are a relatively new user,

Natural Language searching makes it easier to retrieve cases on point. If you are an experienced user, Natural Language gives you a valuable alternative search method.

When you enter a Natural Language description, WESTLAW automatically identifies legal phrases, removes common words and generates variations of terms in your description. WESTLAW then searches for the concepts in your description. Concepts may include significant terms, phrases, legal citations or topic and key numbers. WESTLAW retrieves the 20 documents that most closely match your description, beginning with the document most likely to match.

5.1 Natural Language Searching

Access a database, such as Federal Civil Rights—Courts of Appeals Cases (FCIV–CTA). If your current search method is Terms and Connectors, type **nat** or select the *Natural Language* Jump marker. At the Enter Description screen, type a Natural Language description, such as the following:

continuing violations doctrine

5.2 Next Command

WESTLAW displays the 20 documents that most closely match your description, beginning with the document most likely to match. If you want to view additional documents, use the Next command. Type **next** to display the next 10 documents. To retrieve more than 10 documents, type **next** followed by the number you wish to view, such as **next25** or **next32.** You can retrieve up to 100 documents.

5.3 Browsing a Natural Language Search Result

Best Mode: To display the best portion (the portion that most closely matches your description) of each document in your search result, type **b.**

Standard Browsing Commands: You can also browse your Natural Language search result using standard WESTLAW browsing commands, such as citations list (L), Locate (loc), page mode (p) and term mode (t). When you browse your Natural Language search result in term mode (t), the five portions of each document that are most likely to match your description are displayed.

Section 6. Terms and Connectors Searching

Overview: With standard Terms and Connectors searching, you enter a query, which consists of key terms from your research issue and connectors specifying the relationship between these terms.

Terms and Connectors searching is useful when you want to retrieve a document for which you have specific information, such as the title or the citation. Terms and Connectors searching is also useful when you want to retrieve documents relating to a specific issue. To change from Natural Language searching to Terms and Connectors searching, type **tc** or select the *Terms and Connectors* Jump marker at the Enter Description screen.

6.1   Terms

Plurals and Possessives: Plurals are automatically retrieved when you enter the singular form of a term. This is true for both regular and irregular plurals (e.g., **child** retrieves *children*). If you enter the plural form of a term, you will not retrieve the singular form.

If you enter the non-possessive form of a term, WESTLAW automatically retrieves the possessive form as well. However, if you enter the possessive form, only the possessive form is retrieved.

Automatic Equivalencies: Some terms have alternative forms or equivalencies; for example, *5* and *five* are equivalent terms. WESTLAW automatically retrieves equivalent terms. The *WESTLAW Reference Manual* contains a list of equivalent terms.

Compound Words and Acronyms: When a compound word is one of your search terms, use a hyphen to retrieve all forms of the word. For example, the term **along-side** retrieves *along-side, alongside* and *along side.*

When using an acronym as a search term, place a period after each of the letters in the acronym to retrieve any of its forms. For example, the term **e.e.o.c.** retrieves *eeoc, e.e.o.c., e e o c* and *e. e. o. c.* Note: The acronym *f.t.c.* does <u>not</u> retrieve *Equal Employment Opportunity Commission,* so remember to add additional alternative terms to your query such as **"equal employment opportunity commission".**

Root Expander and Universal Character: When you use the Terms and Connectors search method, placing a root expander (!) at the end of a root term generates all other terms with that root. For example, adding the ! symbol to the root *realign*n in the query

realign!   /5   party

instructs WESTLAW to retrieve such words as *realign, realigned, realignment* and *realigning.*

The universal character (*) stands for one character and can be inserted in the middle or at the end of a term. For example, the term

s**holder**

will retrieve *shareholder* and *stockholder.* Adding three asterisks to the root *elect* in the query

elect***

instructs WESTLAW to retrieve all forms of the root with up to three additional characters. Terms like *elected* or *election* are retrieved by this query. However, terms with more than three letters following the root, such as *electronic,* are not retrieved. Plurals are always retrieved, even if more than three letters follow the root.

Phrase Searching: To search for a phrase, place it within quotation marks. For example, to search for references to bona fide occupational qualifications, type **"bona fide occupational qualification"**. When you are using the Terms and Connectors search method, you should use phrase searching only if you are certain that the phrase will not appear in any other form.

6.2 Alternative Terms

After selecting the terms for your query, consider which alternative terms are necessary. For example, if you are searching for the term *resident,* you might also want to search for the term *non-resident.* You should consider both synonyms and antonyms as alternative terms. You can also use the WESTLAW thesaurus to add alternative terms to your query.

6.3 Connectors

After selecting terms and alternative terms for your query, use connectors to specify the relationship that should exist between search terms in your retrieved documents. The connectors you can use are described below:

Use:	To retrieve documents with:	Example:
& (and)	both terms	**union & liab!**
or (space)	either term or both terms	**abstention abstain * * ***
/p	search terms in the same paragraph	**703 /p retaliat!**
/s	search terms in the same sentence	**deliberate /s indifference**
+s	one search term preceding the other within the same sentence; especially useful when searching in the title field (ti) where both parties have the same name	**ti(kurzman +s kurzman)**
/n	search terms within "n" terms of each other (where "n" is a number)	**policy /3 requirement**
+n	one search term preceding the other by "n" terms (where "n" is a number)	**hindrance +3 clause**
"..."	search terms appearing in the same order as in the quotation marks	**"bona fide occupational qualification"**
Use:	**To exclude documents with:**	**Example:**
% (but not)	search terms following the % symbol	**attorney lawyer /5 client /s privileg! % sy,di(work-product)**

6.4 Restricting Your Search by Field

Overview: Documents in each WESTLAW database consist of several segments, or fields. One field may contain the citation, another the title, another the synopsis, and so forth. Not all databases contain the same fields. Also, depending on the database, fields of the same name may contain different types of information.

To view the fields and field content for a specific database, see Scope or type **f** while in the database. Note that in some databases, not every field is available for every document.

To retrieve only those documents containing your search terms in a specific field, restrict your search to that field. To restrict your search to a specific field, type the field name or abbreviation followed by your search terms enclosed in parentheses. For example, to retrieve a case in the U.S. Court of Appeals for the Second Circuit Cases database (CTA2) entitled *Johnson v. Palma,* search for your terms in the title field:

ti(johnson & palma)

The fields discussed below are available in WESTLAW databases you might use for researching federal practice issues.

Digest and Synopsis Fields: The digest (di) and synopsis (sy) fields, added to case law databases by West Publishing's attorney-editors, summarize the main points of a case. The synopsis field contains a brief description of a case. The digest field contains the topic, headnote, court and title fields and includes the complete hierarchy of concepts used to classify the point of law, including the West digest topic name and number and the key number. Restricting your search to these fields limits your result to cases in which your terms are related to a major issue in the case.

Consider restricting your search to one or both of these fields if

- you are searching for common terms or terms with more than one meaning, and you need to narrow your search; or

- you cannot narrow your search by moving to a smaller database.

For example, to retrieve cases that discuss the disparate impact on African–American males of no-beard employment policies, access the Federal Civil Rights—U.S. Courts of Appeals Cases database (FCIV–CTA) and type

sy,di(no-beard /p disparate! /3 impact!)

Headnote Field: The headnote field (he) is a part of the digest field, but does not contain the topic number, hierarchical classification information, key number or title. The headnote field contains only the one-sentence summary of the point of law and any supporting citations given by the author of the opinion. A headnote field restriction is useful when you are searching for specific statutory sections or rule numbers. For example, to retrieve headnotes that cite 28 U.S.C.A. § 1343, type the following query:

he(28 +5 1343)

Topic Field: The topic field (to) is also a part of the digest field. It contains hierarchical classification information, including the West digest topic name and number, and the key number. You should restrict search terms to the topic field in a case law database if

- a digest field search retrieves too many documents; or

- you want to retrieve cases with digest paragraphs classified under more than one topic.

For example, the topic Civil Rights has the topic number 78. To retrieve United States district court cases that discuss disparate treatment or impact with regard to employment practices, access the Federal Civil Rights—District Courts Cases database (FCIV–DCT) and type a query like the following:

to(78) /p disparate! /p impact! treat!

/p

employment

To retrieve West headnotes classified under more than one topic and key number, search for your terms in the topic field. For example, to search for cases discussing remittitur, which may be classified to 170A, Federal Civil Procedure, or 170B, Federal Courts, among other topics, type a query like the following:

to(remittitur)

For a complete list of West digest topics and their corresponding topic numbers, access the Key Number service; type **key.**

Note: Be aware that slip opinions, cases not to be reported by West Publishing, and cases from topical services do not contain the digest, headnote or topic fields.

Prelim and Caption Fields: When searching in a database containing statutes, rules or regulations, restrict your search to the prelim (pr) and caption (ca) fields to retrieve documents in which your terms are important enough to appear in a section name or heading. For example, to retrieve federal statutes relating to civil rights applicability to foreign employment, access the Federal Civil Rights—United States Code Annotated database (FCIV–USCA) and type the following:

pr,ca(foreign /3 employ!)

6.5 Restricting Your Search by Date

You can instruct WESTLAW to retrieve documents *decided* or *issued* before, after, or on a specified date, as well as within a range of dates. The following are examples of queries that contain date restrictions:

da(aft 1992) & "qualified immunity"

da(1995) & pend*nt supplemental /3 jurisdiction

da(3/17/94) & "age discrimination in employment" a.d.e.a. /p retaliat!

You can also instruct WESTLAW to retrieve documents *added to a database* on or after a specified date, as well as within a range of dates. The following are examples of queries that contain added-date restrictions:

ad(aft 1993) & di(substantial! /3 limit! /p disab!)

ad(aft 1–1–96 & bef 4–1–96) & reasonab! /3 accommodat! /p disab!

Section 7.   Verifying Your Research with Citators

Overview: WESTLAW contains four citator services to assist you in checking the validity of cases you intend to rely on.   These citator services—Insta–Cite®, Shepard's® Citations, Shepard's PreView® and Quick*Cite*®—help you perform many valuable research tasks, saving you hours of manual research.   Sections 7.1 through 7.4 provide further information on these services.

WESTLAW also contains Shepard's Citations for federal statutes, and Shepard's citations for state statutes are being added on a state-by-state basis.

For citations not covered by the citator services, including persuasive secondary authority such as restatements and treatises, use a technique called WESTLAW as a citator to retrieve cases that cite your authority (see Section 7.5).

7.1   Insta–Cite

Insta–Cite is West Publishing's case history and citation verification service.   Use Insta–Cite to see whether your case is good law.   Insta–Cite provides the following types of information about a citation:

Direct History.   In addition to reversals and affirmances, Insta–Cite gives you the complete reported history of a litigated matter including any related cases.   Insta–Cite provides the direct history of federal cases from 1754 and state cases from 1879.   Related references (cases related to the litigation) are provided from 1983 to date.   Direct case history is available within 1–4 hours of receipt of a case at West.

Negative Indirect History.   Insta–Cite lists subsequent cases that may have a substantial negative impact on your case, including cases overruling your case or calling it into question.   Insta–Cite provides negative indirect history from 1972 to date.   To retrieve negative indirect history prior to 1972, use Shepard's Citations (see Section 7.2).

Secondary Source References.   Insta–Cite also provides references to secondary sources that cite your case.   These secondary sources include the legal encyclopedia *Corpus Juris Secundum* ®.

Parallel Citations.   Insta–Cite provides parallel citations for cases, including citations to *United States Law Week* and many topical reporters.

Citation Verification.   Insta–Cite confirms that you have the correct volume and page number for a case, as well as the correct spelling of proper names.   Citation verification information is available from 1754 for federal cases and from 1879 for state cases.

7.2   Shepard's Citations

For case law, Shepard's provides a comprehensive list of cases and other documents that have cited a particular case.   Shepard's also includes explanatory analysis to indicate how the citing cases have treated the case, e.g., "followed," "explained."

For statutes, Shepard's Citations provides a comprehensive list of cases citing a particular statute, as well as information on subsequent legislative action. The federal court rule divisions for each of the statute citators currently available on WESTLAW provide a comprehensive list of cases citing a particular federal court rule. Federal court rule divisions include:

Supreme Court Rules	Federal Rules of Criminal Procedure
Federal Rules of Evidence	Federal Rules of Civil Procedure
Bankruptcy Rules	Federal Rules of Appellate Procedure

In addition to citations from federal, state and regional citators, Shepard's on WESTLAW includes citations from specialized citators such as *Employment Law*.

7.3 Shepard's PreView

Shepard's PreView gives you a preview of citing references for case law from West's National Reporter System® that will appear in Shepard's Citations. Depending on the citation, Shepard's PreView provides citing information days, weeks or even months before the same information appears in Shepard's online. Use Shepard's PreView to update your Shepard's results.

7.4 Quick*Cite*

Quick*Cite* is a citator service that enables you to automatically retrieve the most recent citing cases on WESTLAW, including slip opinions.

There is a four- to six-week gap between a citing case's availability on WESTLAW and its listing in Shepard's PreView. This gap occurs because cases go through an editorial process at West Publishing before they are added to Shepard's PreView. To retrieve the most recent citing cases, therefore, you need to search case law databases on WESTLAW for references to your case.

Quick*Cite* formulates a query using the title, the case citation(s) and an added date restriction. Quick*Cite* then accesses the appropriate database, either ALLSTATES or ALLFEDS, and runs the query for you. Quick*Cite* also allows you to tailor the query to your specific research needs; you can choose a different date range or select another database.

Quick*Cite* is designed to retrieve documents that cite cases. To retrieve citing references to other documents, such as statutes and law review articles, use WESTLAW as a citator (see Section 7.5).

7.5 Using WESTLAW As a Citator

Using WESTLAW as a citator, you can search for documents citing a specific statute, regulation, rule, agency decision or other authority. For example, to retrieve documents citing 42 U.S.C.A. § 12113(b), access the Federal Civil Rights—Courts of Appeals Cases database (CTA) and type a query like the following:

12113(b)

7.6   Selected Citator Commands

Command: *Definition:*

ic xxx or **ic**   Retrieves an Insta–Cite result when followed by a case citation (where xxx is the citation), or when entered from a displayed case, Shepard's result or Shepard's PreView result.

sh xxx or **sh**   Retrieves a Shepard's result when followed by a case or statute citation (where xxx is the citation), or when entered from a displayed case or statute, Insta–Cite result or Shepard's PreView result.

sp xxx or **sp**   Retrieves a Shepard's PreView result when followed by a case citation (where xxx is the citation), or when entered from a displayed case, Insta–Cite result or Shepard's result.

qc xxx or **qc**   Retrieves a Quick*Cite* result when followed by a case citation (where xxx is the citation), or when entered from a displayed case, Insta–Cite result, Shepard's result or Shepard's PreView result.

sc   Retrieves the scope of coverage for Insta–Cite or Shepard's PreView when you are viewing a result from that service. From a Shepard's result, displays the scope of coverage for the publication.

sc xx   Retrieves the scope of coverage of a citator service (where xx is the citator service), e.g., **sc ic.**

sh sc xxx   Retrieves the scope of coverage for a specific publication in Shepard's, where xxx is the publication abbreviation, e.g., **sh sc f2d.**

xx pubs   Retrieves a list of publications available in the citator service and their abbreviations (where xx is the citator service abbreviation).

xx cmds   Retrieves a list of commands in the citator service (where xx is the citator service abbreviation).

sh analysis   Retrieves a list of Shepard's analysis codes, e.g., *extended, revised,* etc.

sh courts   Retrieves a list of courts and their abbreviations used in Shepard's Citations.

loc   Automatically restricts an Insta–Cite, Shepard's or Shepard's PreView result to selected categories.

loc auto   Restricts all subsequent Insta–Cite, Shepard's or Shepard's PreView results to selected categories.

xloc   Cancels a Locate request.

xloc auto   Cancels a Locate Auto request.

Section 8.   Research Examples

8.1   Retrieving Law Review Articles

Recent law review articles are often a good place to begin researching a legal issue because law review articles serve 1) as an excellent introduction to a new topic or review for a stale one, providing terminology to help in query formulation; 2) as a finding tool for pertinent primary authority, such as cases and statutes; and 3) in some instances, as persuasive secondary authority. For example, you need to gain more background information on the factors the federal courts have considered in determining what is a justiciable case or controversy.

Solution

● To retrieve recent law review articles relevant to your issue, access the Journals & Law Reviews database (JLR) by typing **db jlr;** select Natural Language searching; then enter a description like the following:

hostile work environment

● If you have a citation to an article in a specific publication, use Find to retrieve it. For more information on Find, see Section 4.1 of this appendix. For example, to retrieve the article found at 28 Boston College Law Review 146, type

fi 28 bclr 146

● If you know the title of an article, but not which journal it appeared in, access JLR and search for key terms from the title in the title field (ti). For example, to retrieve the article "Gender–Based Harassment and the Hostile Work Environment" type the following Terms and Connectors query:

ti(gender-based & hostile)

8.2 Retrieving Federal Statutes

You need to retrieve federal statutes dealing with penalties for age discrimination.

Solution

● Access the Federal Civil Rights—U.S.Code Annotated database (FCIV–USCA). Search for your terms in the prelim and caption fields using the Terms and Connectors search method:

pr,ca(age /3 discriminat! & penalt!)

● When you know the citation for a specific section of a statute, use Find to retrieve the statute. For example, to retrieve 29 U.S.C.A. § 629, type

fi 29 usca 629

● To look at surrounding statutory sections, use the Table of Contents service. Type **toc 29 usca 629.** You can also use the Documents in Sequence command. To retrieve the section preceding § 629, type **d-.** To retrieve the section immediately following § 629, type **d.**

● When you retrieve a statute on WESTLAW, it will contain an Update message if legislation amending or repealing it is available online. To display this legislation, select the Jump marker in the Update message with the **Tab** key or your mouse or type **update.**

Because slip copy versions of laws are added to WESTLAW before they contain full editorial enhancements, they are not retrieved with Update. To retrieve slip copy versions of laws, access the United States Public Laws database by typing **db us-pl,** then type **ci(slip)** and descriptive terms, e.g., **ci(slip) &** *[term].* Slip copy documents are replaced by the editorially enhanced versions within a few working days. Update also does not retrieve legislation that enacts a new statute or covers a topic that will not be incorporated into the statutes. To retrieve this legislation, access US–PL and enter a query containing terms that describe the new legislation.

8.3 Retrieving Federal Court Rules

Suppose you've misplaced your rules pamphlet and you need to check the Federal Rules of Civil Procedure.

Solution

- Access the Federal Rules database (US–RULES) and search for the rule abbreviation in the citation field (ci) and key terms in the caption field (ca):

ci(frcp) & ca(discover! & sanction)

  To determine the abbreviation for the Federal Rules of Civil Procedure, as well as the Federal Rules of Evidence, Rules of the U.S. Supreme Court, rules of the U.S. courts of appeals and other rules, use Scope; type **sc us-rules.**

  Note: Local rules of the U.S. district courts and U.S. bankruptcy courts are contained in the state court rules database (XX–RULES, where XX is the state's two-letter postal abbreviation) for the state in which the court sits. Access the appropriate database and search for the rule abbreviation in the citation field, e.g., **ci(usdct).** To determine the rule abbreviation, use Scope, e.g., **sc ia-rules.**

- When you know the rule number, use Find to retrieve the rule. For example, to retrieve Rule 11 of the Federal Rules of Civil Procedure, type

fi frcp 11

- When you retrieve a court rule on WESTLAW, it will contain an Update message if documents amending or repealing it are available online. To display these documents, select the Jump marker in the Update message with the **Tab** key or your mouse. Note: Slip copy documents, legislation enacting a new statute or rule, and legislation covering a topic that will not be incorporated into the statutes cannot be retrieved with the Update service. To retrieve these materials, run a descriptive word search in the US–PL or US–ORDERS database.

8.4 Using the Citator Services

One of the cases you retrieve in your case law research is *Price Waterhouse v. Hopkins,* 109 S.Ct. 1775 (1989). You want to see whether this case is good law and whether other cases have cited this case.

Solution

- Use Insta–Cite to retrieve the direct history and negative indirect history of *Price Waterhouse*. While viewing the case, type **ic.**

- To Shepardize ® *Price Waterhouse* from the Insta–Cite display, select the *Shepard's* Jump marker or type **sh.**

Limit your Shepard's result to decisions containing a reference to a specific headnote, such as headnote 4. Type **loc 4.**

- Check Shepard's PreView for more current cases citing *Price Water-house*. From the Shepard's display, select the *Shepard's PreView* Jump marker or type **sp.**

- Check Quick*Cite* for the most current cases citing *Price Waterhouse*. From the Shepard's PreView display, select the Quick*Cite* Jump marker or type **qc.** Then follow the on-screen instructions.

8.5 Following Recent Developments

As the employment discrimination specialist in your firm, you are expected to keep up with and summarize recent legal developments in this area of the law. How can you do this efficiently?

Solution

One of the easiest ways to stay abreast of recent developments in employment discrimination is by accessing the WESTLAW Topical Highlights—Employment database (WTH–LB). The WTH–LB database summarizes recent legal developments, including court decisions, legislation and changes in the area of employment law. Some summaries also contain suggested queries that combine the proven power of West's topic and key numbers and West's case headnotes to retrieve additional pertinent cases.

- To access the database, type **db wth–lb.** You will automatically retrieve a list of documents added to the database in the last two weeks.

- To read a summary of a document listed, type its corresponding number.

- To view the full text of a document, type **fi** while viewing the summary, or type **fi** followed by the document citation while viewing the list, e.g., **fi 92 f3d 831.**

- To search this database, type **s** to display the Enter Query screen. At the Enter Query screen, type your query. For example, to retrieve references discussing age discrimination, search for your terms in the prelim field by typing a query like the following:

pr(age /3 discriminat!)

Table of Statutes and Rules

UNITED STATES CONSTITUTION

Amend.	This Work Sec.	Note
14 (Cont'd)	10.17	
	10.18	
	13.7	
14, § 1	5.15	38
14, § 5	3.3	
	5.15	
	5.15	28
	5.15	38
15	10.9	
	10.16	

UNITED STATES CODE ANNOTATED

5 U.S.C.A.—Government Organization and Employees

Sec.	This Work Sec.	Note
901—912	8.8	2
8335	7.1	26

8 U.S.C.A.—Aliens and Nationality

Sec.	This Work Sec.	Note
1324b(a)(1)(A)	3.3	36
1324b(a)(3)	3.3	40
1324a	3.3	39
	3.3	41
1324b(a)(2)(A)	3.3	36
1324c	3.3	41

15 U.S.C.A.—Commerce and Trade

Sec.	This Work Sec.	Note
78g(a)	2.28	24
78n(a)	2.28	24

18 U.S.C.A.—Crimes and Criminal Procedure

Sec.	This Work Sec.	Note
52	2.12	37
241	1.5	17
	11.2	1
242	2.5	10
	2.12	37

20 U.S.C.A.—Education

Sec.	This Work Sec.	Note
1401	2.25	37
1401—1485	2.28	9
1415	2.28	9
	12.2	41
1415(b)(1)(C)	2.25	37
1415(b)(2)	2.25	37
1681	9.7	1
1681—1688	9.1	4

UNITED STATES CODE ANNOTATED

20 U.S.C.A.—Education

Sec.	This Work Sec.	Note
1681—1693	9.1	6
1682	9.7	2
	9.11	
1684	9.7	1
1685	9.7	2
1687	9.8	3
1687(4)	9.9	2
3441(a)	9.11	5

26 U.S.C.A.—Internal Revenue Code

Sec.	This Work Sec.	Note
104(a)	5.12	
104(a)(2)	5.12	
	5.12	1
	5.12	2
	5.12	5
104(c)	5.12	6

28 U.S.C.A.—Judiciary and Judicial Procedure

Sec.	This Work Sec.	Note
1291	2.13	
1331	13.2	
	13.9	6
1332	13.1	17
	13.8	1
1343	13.2	
	13.8	
	13.9	6
1343(3)	2.28	
1367	13.8	
	13.8	7
	13.15	
1367(a)	13.1	22
	13.8	
1367(c)	2.13	28
	13.1	22
	13.8	
1404	5.4	
1406	5.4	
1447(c)	12.2	43
1658	13.13	1
1728	13.21	27
	13.21	31
1738	13.1	11
	13.18	
	13.19	
	13.19	1
	13.19	8
	13.19	9
	13.19	10
	13.19	11
	13.20	
	13.21	
	13.21	13
	13.22	

Table of Cases

A

H

I

M

N

O

P

U

*

Index

References are to Sections

---

†

0–314–20604–3